Tanzania
with Zanzibar, Pemba & Mafia

THE BRADT TRAVEL GUIDE
Fourth Edition

Philip Briggs

Bradt Travel Guides Ltd, UK
The Globe Pequot Press Inc, USA

This fourth edition published in 2002 by Bradt Travel Guides Ltd
19 High Street, Chalfont St Peter, Bucks SL9 9QE, England
web: www.bradt-travelguides.com
Published in the USA by The Globe Pequot Press Inc, 246 Goose Lane,
PO Box 480, Guilford, Connecticut 06475-0480

First published in 1993 by Bradt Publications

ISBN 1 84162 055 6

British Library Cataloguing in Publication Data
A catalogue record for this book is available from the British Library

Library of Congress Cataloging-in-Publication Data applied for

Photographs
Cover Maasai girls at Lake Natrou (Geoffrey Roy)
Text Ariadne Van Zandbergen (AZ), Nick Garbutt (NG), Catherine Harlow (CH)

Illustrations Annabel Milne
Maps Steve Munns

Typeset from the author's disc by Wakewing
Printed and bound in Italy by Legoprint SpA, Trento

Author and Contributors

Philip Briggs is a travel writer specialising in Africa. Raised in South Africa, where he still lives, Philip first visited East Africa in 1986 and has since spent an average of six months annually exploring the highways and back roads of the continent. His first Bradt Travel Guide, to South Africa, was published in 1991, and he has subsequently written Bradt's guides to Tanzania, Uganda, Ethiopia, Malawi, Mozambique, Ghana, and East and southern Africa, and he recently co-authored the first travel guide to Rwanda. Philip has contributed sections to numerous other books about Africa, he writes a column for independent travellers for the magazine *Travel Africa*, and also contributes regular travel and wildlife features to *Travel Africa*, *Africa Geographic* and *Africa Birds & Birding*.

Ariadne Van Zandbergen, who took most of the photographs in this book and wrote the photographic tips, is a Belgian-born freelance photographer who first travelled through Africa from Morocco to South Africa in 1994–95 and is now resident in Johannesburg. She has visited more than 25 African countries and her photographs have appeared in numerous travel and wildlife guides, coffee-table books, magazines, newspapers, maps and pamphlets.

David Else is a seasoned travel writer specialising in Africa. His popular book *Zanzibar: The Bradt Travel Guide*, soon to go into a fifth edition, was the main foundation for the Zanzibar chapter in earlier editions of this guide.

Heather Tyrrell, who updated the Zanzibar and Pemba sections for this edition, first travelled to Africa on an expedition to the Kalahari in 1989. She has since researched and travelled extensively in Namibia, Zimbabwe, Botswana, Zambia, South Africa and Mozambique. She now runs the East African programme for Sunvil Africa – the specialist tour operator. She has spent much of 2001 and 2002 concentrating on southern Tanzania, Zanzibar and Mafia and is also co-authoring *Zanzibar: The Bradt Travel Guide*.

Christine Osborne, who wrote the chapter on Mafia Island, is no stranger to Africa or the Indian Ocean islands. Born in Australia, she wrote her first travel article – on Djibouti – in 1965 and has subsequently visited more than 17 countries on the African continent.

Contents

LIST OF MAPS

Acknowledgements

My greatest debt, as ever, is to my wife, travel companion and photographic collaborator Ariadne Van Zandbergen, whose support and dedication kept me going over the four months we spent travelling in Tanzania to research this fourth edition, and a similar period writing at home.

We received an enormous amount of assistance and support during the course of researching this fourth edition, and (in no particular order) we would like to express our gratitude to the following for various services rendered: John and Debbie Addison of Wild Frontiers in South Africa; Mr L Melamari, Director of TANAPA; Ally Ibriham of Akaro Tours in Moshi; Susan D'Costa of Roy Safaris; Barbara and Victor of Safari Makers; Mehul Jotangia, Mustafa Panju and Leodigard Sumawe of Bushbuck Safaris; Dean Yeadon and Carolyn Johnson of Halcyon; George Crossland and Charlie Bailey; Mike and Claire at Maasai Camp; Peter Lindstrom of Hoopoe Adventure Tours; Jean and Meggan at Serena Active; Nicky FitzGerald, Debra Fox and Duncan Butchart of CCA; Mohammed Khatau of Business Rent-A-Car; Marian Jost of Flycatcher Safaris; Rodney D'Mello of Kearsley Ltd; David Guthrie and David Barker of the Safari Scene; Roland and Zoe Purcell; Chris McIntyre and Heather Tyrrell of Sunvil Africa; Peter Byrne; Nigel Crofton; Andrew Douglas-Jones; Elias Moshi of Precision Air; Fatema and Nicola at Coastal Travel; Paul Chizi of Air Tanzania; and Tony Pascoe of Serengeti Balloon Safaris.

For hospitality and respite from guesthouse tedium, many thanks to the management and staff of the Oyster Bay Hotel (Dar es Salaam); the Old Boma in Mikindani; Lazy Lagoon (Bagamoyo); Migration Camp and Grumeti Camp (Serengeti); Saadani Tented Camp; Tarangire Treetops; Tarangire Safari Lodge; Ndutu Lodge (Serengeti); the Tarangire, Ngorongoro and Serengeti Sopa Lodges; the Ngorongoro and Manyara Serena Lodges; Impala Hotel (Arusha); Rubondo Island Camp; Rufiji River Camp, Beho Beho and Sable Mountain Lodge (Selous); Vuma Hills and Kikoboga Lodge (Mikumi); Mwagusi Lodge (Ruaha); Kigoma Hilltop Hotel; Nkungwe Tented Camp (Mahale); Katavi Camp and Kinasi Lodge (Mafia).

Tamim Amijee supplied much useful information about Tanga and surrounds, as did Steven Fischer in Lushoto. The ornithologist Dr Terry Oatley provided text for the Minziro Forest Reserve, while Neil and Liz Baker of the Tanzanian Bird Atlas Project forwarded valuable current information about Tanzania's birds. Tony Pike and Greg Vogl provided all the update material for Bukoba, and Maggie Mlengeya of Serengeti Stop Over passed on useful details of tourist attractions in the Musoma area. Brian Doench of the Peace Corps supplied a mass of information about the Katesh and Hanang area, pointed us towards several nearby attractions we might otherwise have missed, and later read over and corrected the relevant chapter. Jaos Kahembe in Babati introduced us to the Barabaig, and Frank Malisa of Akaro Tours encouraged us to visit the Hadza, Lake Jipe and much else. Brian Currie, Ian

Smith, George Barrett, Matt Maddocks and Shaibu of the Old Boma in Mikindani all supplied information about various parts of the southern coast. Tim Davenport prepped me on the Kitulo Plateau and checked over the Southern Highlands chapter. An extended essay by Kevin Pretorius of CCA was the basis of the section on Manyara's lions. David Moyer provided invaluable information about Udzungwa, and Roy of Tembowengi about Kilombero. Imtiaz Lalji of the Kigoma Hilltop Hotel provided all sorts of back up in the Lake Tanganyika region and later checked over that chapter. Roland and Zoe Purcell and Goodluck Philip Nnko and Alfred Nkoma Kabisi of Katavi Camp gave us the safari of a lifetime in the incomparable Katavi National Park. Chris Walley and Dudley Iles allowed me to reproduce quotes from their excellent Chole Booklet. I am indebted to them all.

Thanks also to the readers of the third edition who wrote in with update information: Michael Boller, Evylyn Brakopp, Robert Budd, Gerhard Buttner, Florence Capone, Nicola Cornforth, Roger Davidson, Claudia Gaemperle, Arthur Gerfers, Daniel Gorman, Josephine Harden, Michael Kroll, Jakob Lederer, Robert H Lindley, Udo and Renate Mahahrens, Christine McNeal, Graham Mitchell-Innes, Roos Molendijk, Denis Montgomery, Rainer Neumann, Steve Newton-Howes, Paul Norrish, Suzanne Pegg, David Poole, Paul Reed, Annalinda and Tobin Robinson, Matt Ross, Annie Rutter, Barbara Sherrington, Christian Steer, JBK and CJK Turtle, John Tuson, and Arie van Oosterwyk.

Finally, my ongoing gratitude goes to those whose efforts were acknowledged in earlier editions of this guide, and my apologies to anybody whose name was inadvertently omitted from the lists above.

PHOTOGRAPHING THE MAASAI

There are two ways of photographing the Maasai:

- Visiting bomas (family enclosures) that operate as tourist 'cultural villages' in the vicinity of Tarangire, Lake Manyara and Ngorongoro. Your driver can arrange it, and you will usually agree a price for the whole group.
- Snapping one of the individual Maasai that hang around spots along the northern safari circuit selling their beadwork and deriving income from tourist traffic. Payment will rightly be demanded.

Many tourists conclude that the Maasai are 'too commercialised' – a reflection of Western misconceptions rather than any aspect of modern Maasai culture. It is easy to perceive an absolute cultural division between those Tanzanians who are outwardly modern and those who are outwardly traditional in their appearance. Yet the Maasai are living in the 21st century, and while theirs is a conservative society, it does not exist in a social or economic vacuum.

But, make no mistake: wander into a Maasai boma that doesn't routinely deal with tourists and the inhabitants will refuse to be photographed, no matter the monetary incentive. Indeed, you might find a spear dangling from the end of your lens if you don't respect their wishes!

There is a strong irony in a group of well-off tourists accusing a resilient and non-materialistic culture of being 'too commercialised'. We create the demand, the Maasai satisfy it. If you don't like it, leave the camera behind. You'll probably get a lot more from being around these charismatic people if you do so.

Introduction

It would be easy to reduce an introduction to Tanzania to a list of facts and figures. This vast East African country really is a statistician's dream: within its borders lie Africa's highest and fifth-highest mountains, the world's largest intact volcanic caldera, Africa's most famous national park and the world's largest game reserve, as well as portions of the three most expansive lakes on the continent, one of which is the second-largest freshwater body in the world, another the second-deepest.

When it comes to wildlife, Tanzania is practically without peer. An unprecedented 25% of the country is protected in national parks and other conservation areas. Together, these conservation areas support an estimated 20% of Africa's large mammal population, and one of them plays host to the singular spectacle of an annual migration of some two million wildebeest, zebra and gazelle. Furthermore, Tanzania is poised to overtake Kenya as boasting Africa's second-longest bird checklist (after the Democratic Republic of the Congo), with significantly more than 1,000 bird species recorded, and new endemics being discovered all the time. And as if that were not enough, the three great lakes that lie along Tanzania's borders vie with each other for the honour of harbouring the world's greatest diversity of fish species.

The map of Tanzania may have statisticians salivating, but it will also touch the heart of any poet. It is a virtual litany of Africa's most evocative place names – Zanzibar, Kilimanjaro, Serengeti, Selous, Ngorongoro Crater, Olduvai Gorge, Gombe Stream, Dar es Salaam, Kilwa, Lake Victoria, Lake Tanganyika, Lake Malawi, the Rift Valley, the Maasai Steppe… In short, Tanzania is the Africa you have always dreamed about: vast plains teeming with wild animals; rainforests alive with cackling birds and monkeys; Kilimanjaro's snow-capped peak rising dramatically above the flat scrubland; colourful Maasai herding their cattle alongside herds of grazing wildebeest; perfect palm-lined beaches lapped by the clear warm waters of the Indian Ocean stretching as far as the eye can see.

You might expect a country that can be described in such superlative terms to be crawling with tourists. Yet, oddly enough, until recently Tanzania attracted a fraction of the tourism of countries such as Kenya, South Africa and Zimbabwe. When I first visited the country in 1986, it appeared to be in irreversible economic decline, and tourist arrivals were practically restricted to those backpackers who were crossing between Kenya and southern Africa and had no option but to pass through Tanzania. This dearth of tourism had several causes: an underfunded and underdeveloped tourist infrastructure, a reputation for corruption and bureaucracy, persistent food and fuel shortages, poor roads and grossly inefficient and uncomfortable public transport. Critically, too, Tanzania lacked international exposure – not because people hadn't heard of places such as Ngorongoro, Serengeti and Kilimanjaro, but because they tended to associate these archetypal East African reserves with Kenya.

Today, all this has changed. Modern Tanzania has an excellent tourist infrastructure, and the public transport along the main roads compares favourably with that of most African countries. What started off in the late 1980s as a trickle of tourism, lured across the Kenyan border to visit such big name attractions as the Serengeti, Ngorongoro Crater and Zanzibar, is threatening to become a veritable flood. However, practically all visitors to Tanzania follow the same well-defined tourist circuit, which combines some of Africa's finest game viewing with the historical old town and superb beaches of Zanzibar Island, and those who have two weeks or less in the country rarely stray much beyond it. This is not a criticism – I've visited most corners of Tanzania over the six-plus months I've spent travelling there between 1986 and 1998, and I have to confess that were my time in the country limited to a couple of weeks, then my first priorities would undoubtedly be the Serengeti, Ngorongoro and Zanzibar. They are very special places.

The important implication of this is that the parts of Tanzania most frequently visited by tourists are also the most atypical in terms of tourist development. It is not improbable that the number of tourists who descend daily into the Ngorongoro Crater would be greater than the combined monthly total of visitors to all the reserves of southern and western Tanzania; just as probable that there are restaurants on Zanzibar whose average daily custom exceeds the number of tourists who make it to the splendid medieval ruins on Kilwa Kisiwani in any given year. In other words, while a few select spots in Tanzania are heavily touristed and well equipped to cater for this, Tanzania as a whole remains a surprisingly low-key tourist destination.

This is of interest to two classes of visitor, ironically lying at the extreme ends of the spectrum. For those seeking exclusivity at a price, the southern and western tourist circuit, which includes Mafia Island, Selous Game Reserve, and Udzungwa, Ruaha, Mikumi, Mahale, Gombe Stream, Katavi and Rubondo Island National Parks, has generally retained a real wilderness atmosphere, offering quality lodge accommodation and (mostly) fly-in safari packages at a price comparable to an upmarket lodge safari on the more popular northern safari circuit. And make no mistake, these are wonderful reserves, forming a safari circuit that many African countries would kill for. Their relative obscurity is largely due to the fact that they lie in the same country as the renowned Serengeti ecosystem.

With the exception of Udzungwa National Park, the southern and western reserves are rather inaccessible to those on a tight budget, but adventurous travellers who are willing to learn a smattering of Swahili and prepared to put up with basic accommodation and slow transport will find Tanzania to be one of the most challenging, rewarding and fascinating countries in Africa. Virtually anywhere south of the Dar es Salaam–Mwanza railway line (the part of the country covered in *Chapter 14* onwards) is miles from any beaten tourist track, and even in the more 'touristy' northeast there are plenty of attractive spots that see little tourism (check out *Chapters 9* and *10*).

Travel isn't simply about ticking off the sights. When you spend a long time in a country, your feelings towards it are determined more than anything by the mood created by its inhabitants. I have no hesitation in saying that, on this level, my affection for Tanzania is greater than for any other African country I have visited. It is an oasis of peace and egalitarian values in a continent stoked up with political and tribal tensions, and its social mood embodies all that I respect in African culture. As a generalisation, I've always found Tanzanians to be polite and courteous, yet also warm and sincere, both amongst themselves and in their dealings with foreigners.

The one thing I can say with near certainty is that you will enjoy Tanzania. Whether you decide to stick to the conventional tourist circuit, opt to carry a dusty backpack around the Southern Highlands, or charter a plane to go chimp tracking in the rainforests of Mahale, Tanzania is a wonderful country.

Part One

General Information

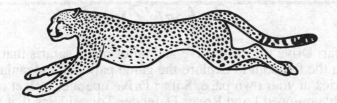

Background and History

FACTS AND FIGURES
Location
The United Republic of Tanzania came into being in 1964 when Tanganyika on the African mainland united with the offshore state of Zanzibar, the latter comprised of the Indian Ocean islands of Unguja (Zanzibar) and Pemba. It lies on the East African coast between 1° and 11°45' south, and 29°20' and 40°35' east, and is bordered by Kenya and Uganda to the north, Rwanda, Burundi and the Democratic Republic of the Congo to the west, and Zambia, Malawi and Mozambique to the south.

Size
Tanzania covers an area of 945,166km² (364,929 square miles). It is one of the largest countries in sub-Saharan Africa, covering a greater area than Kenya and Uganda combined. To place its size in a European context, Tanzania is more than four times the size of Britain, while in an American context, it's about 1.5 times the size of Texas.

Capital
Dodoma was earmarked as the future capital of Tanzania in 1973. It has subsequently displaced Dar es Salaam as the official national capital, and is also where all parliamentary sessions are held. Most government departments, however, are still based in Dar es Salaam, which remains the most important and largest city in the country, and is the site of the main international airport, most diplomatic missions to Tanzania, and most large businesses.

TANZANIA AT A GLANCE
Size 945,166km²
Climate Tropical
Population 35–40 million
Languages Over 100 regional variations. Official languages are KiSwahili and English
Time GMT + 3 hours
Money Tanzanian shilling (Tsh)
Capital Dodoma
Largest city Dar es Salaam
Major exports Coffee, cotton, cashew nuts, sisal, tobacco, tea, diamonds, gold
Ruling party Chama Cha Mapinduzi (CCM)
President Benjamin Mkapa
Flag Blue and green, with diagonal black and yellow stripe

Population

The total population of Tanzania is estimated at between 35 and 40 million. The most densely populated rural areas tend to be the highlands, especially those around Lake Nyasa and Kilimanjaro, and the coast. The country's largest city is Dar es Salaam, whose population, estimated at 2.5 million in 2002, exceeds that of the country's next 10 largest towns combined. Other towns with a population estimated to exceed 100,000, in descending order of size, are Mwanza, Zanzibar Town, Morogoro, Mbeya, Tanga, Moshi, Dodoma, Arusha, Tabora, Iringa, Geita, Musoma, Songea, Kigoma, Shinyanga and Korogwe.

There are roughly 120 tribes in Tanzania, each speaking their own language, and none of which exceeds 10% of the country's total population. The most numerically significant tribes are the Sukuma of Lake Victoria, Haya of northwest Tanzania, Chagga of Kilimanjaro, Nyamwezi of Tabora, Makonde of the Mozambique border area, Hehe of Iringa and Gogo of Dodoma.

Administrative regions

Tanzania is divided into 21 administrative divisions, each with a local administrative capital. These are listed below in descending order of population density.

Region	Capital	Population (millions)	Area	People per km^2
Dar es Salaam	Dar es Salaam	2.6	1,393km^2	1,870
Zanzibar & Pemba	Zanzibar	1.0	2,460km^2	406
Mwanza	Mwanza	3.0	19,592km^2	153
Kilimanjaro	Moshi	1.8	13,309km^2	135
Mtwara	Mtwara	1.4	16,707km^2	83
Mara	Musoma	1.5	19,566km^2	76
Tanga	Tanga	2.0	26,808km^2	75
Kagera	Bukoba	2.1	28,388km^2	74
Shinyanga	Shinyanga	2.8	50,781km^2	55
Dodoma	Dodoma	2.0	41,311km^2	48
Mbeya	Mbeya	2.4	60,350km^2	40
Kigoma	Kigoma	1.4	37,037km^2	38
Iringa	Iringa	1.9	56,864km^2	33
Pwani	Bagamoyo	1.0	32,407km^2	31
Morogoro	Morogoro	1.9	70,799km^2	29
Arusha	Arusha	2.1	82,306km^2	25
Singida	Singida	1.2	49,341km^2	24
Tabora	Tabora	1.7	76,151km^2	22
Ruvuma	Songea	1.2	63,498km^2	18
Rukwa	Sumbawanga	1.1	68,635km^2	16
Lindi	Lindi	1.0	66,046km^2	15

Government

The ruling party of Tanzania since independence has been Chama Cha Mapinduzi (CCM). Up until 1995, Tanzania was a one-party state, under the presidency of Julius Nyerere and, after his retirement in 1985, Ali Hassan Mwinyi. Tanzania held its first multi-party election in late 1995, when the CCM was returned to power with an overwhelming majority under President Benjamin Mkapa, the country's present leader.

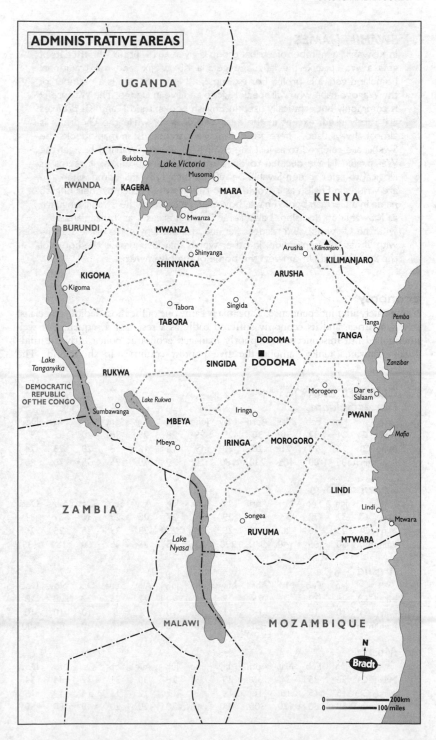

ADMINISTRATIVE AREAS

SWAHILI NAMES

In KiSwahili, a member of a tribal group is given an M- prefix, the tribe itself gets a Wa- prefix, the language gets a Ki- prefix, and the traditional homeland gets a U-prefix. For example, a Mgogo person is a member of the Wagogo tribe who will speak Kigogo and live in Ugogo. The Wa- prefix is commonly but erratically used in English books; the M- and Ki- prefixes are rarely used, except in the case of KiSwahili, while the U- prefix is almost always used. There are no apparent standards; in many books the Swahili are referred to as just the Swahili while non-Swahili tribes get the Wa- prefix. I have decided to drop most of these prefixes: it seems as illogical to refer to non-Swahili people by their KiSwahili name when you are writing in English as it would be to refer to the French by their English name in a German book. I have, however, referred to the Swahili language as KiSwahili on occasion. I also refer to tribal areas – as Tanzanians do – with the U- prefix, and readers can assume that any place name starting with U has this implication, in other words that Usukuma is the home of the Sukuma and Unyamwezi the home of the Nyamwezi.

Economy

Immediately after independence, Tanzania became one of the most dedicated socialist states in Africa, and its economy suffered badly as a result of a sequence of well intentioned but misconceived or poorly managed economic policies. By the mid-1980s, Tanzania ranked among the five poorest countries in the world. The

CLIMATE CHARTS
Dar es Salaam

	Jan	Feb	Mar	April	May	June	July	Aug	Sept	Oct	Nov	Dec
Max (°C)	31	32	30	30	29	29	28	29	30	30	31	31
Min (°C)	24	23	21	20	20	19	18	18	18	20	23	24
Rain (mm)	85	80	105	230	180	22	20	20	25	55	70	80

Zanzibar Town

	Jan	Feb	Mar	April	May	June	July	Aug	Sept	Oct	Nov	Dec
Max (°C)	32	32	33	30	29	28	27	28	29	30	31	31
Min (°C)	25	25	26	26	25	24	23	23	23	25	25	26
Rain (mm)	50	65	140	310	290	45	25	25	35	60	180	135

Arusha

	Jan	Feb	Mar	April	May	June	July	Aug	Sept	Oct	Nov	Dec
Max (°C)	29	29	28	25	22	21	20	22	25	27	28	28
Min (°C)	10	12	12	14	11	10	10	9	9	10	10	10
Rain (mm)	50	85	180	350	205	20	10	15	15	20	105	100

Moshi

	Jan	Feb	Mar	April	May	June	July	Aug	Sept	Oct	Nov	Dec
Max (°C)	36	35	34	30	29	29	28	30	31	32	34	34
Min (°C)	15	15	15	16	14	13	12	12	13	14	14	15
Rain (mm)	50	60	120	300	180	50	20	20	20	40	60	50

subsequent swing towards a free market economy, making the country more attractive to investors, has resulted in dramatic improvement, and Tanzania today – while hardly wealthy – has managed to ascend out of the list of the world's 20 poorest countries. The mainstay of the economy is agriculture, and most rural Tanzanians are subsistence farmers who might also grow a few crops for sale. The country's major exports are traditionally coffee, cotton, cashew nuts, sisal, tobacco, tea and diamonds, but gold – Tanzania is now the third largest gold producer in Africa after South Africa and Ghana – and a unique gem called Tanzanite are of increasing importance to the export economy. Zanzibar and Pemba are important clove producers. The tourist industry that practically collapsed in the mid-1980s has grown steadily over the last decade. Over the past few years, more than 500,000 visitors annually have generated up to US$750 million annually in foreign revenue, a fivefold increase since 1990.

Languages

More than 100 different languages are spoken across Tanzania, but the official languages are KiSwahili and English. Until recently, very little English was spoken outside of the larger towns, but this is changing rapidly, and visitors can be confident that almost anybody involved in the tourist industry will speak passable English. KiSwahili, indigenous to the coast, spread through the region along the 19th-century caravan routes, and is today spoken as a second language by the vast majority of Tanzanians.

Currency

The unit of currency is the Tanzanian shilling (pronounced *shillingi*), which is in theory divided into 100 cents. The rate of exchange has deteriorated against all hard

Dodoma

	Jan	Feb	Mar	April	May	June	July	Aug	Sept	Oct	Nov	Dec
Max (°C)	29	28	29	28	28	29	27	27	28	30	31	30
Min (°C)	18	18	18	17	15	13	12	13	14	17	18	18
Rain (mm)	150	100	135	50	–	–	–	–	5	15	25	100

Mbeya

	Jan	Feb	Mar	April	May	June	July	Aug	Sept	Oct	Nov	Dec
Max (°C)	23	24	23	22	21	21	20	22	24	26	26	23
Min (°C)	14	14	14	13	11	9	8	10	11	12	12	13
Rain (mm)	195	160	160	110	15	–	–	–	10	15	50	135

Kigoma

	Jan	Feb	Mar	April	May	June	July	Aug	Sept	Oct	Nov	Dec
Max (°C)	26	27	27	27	28	28	29	29	29	28	26	25
Min (°C)	20	19	19	20	20	18	17	18	20	20	19	19
Rain (mm)	110	115	130	120	45	10	5	10	25	50	130	120

Mwanza

	Jan	Feb	Mar	April	May	June	July	Aug	Sept	Oct	Nov	Dec
Max (°C)	33	34	33	31	31	30	29	29	30	32	32	31
Min (°C)	15	16	16	16	14	13	12	13	15	16	15	15
Rain (mm)	105	110	165	160	100	20	15	25	30	45	105	120

currencies over the last two decades. Between the publication of the third edition of this guide in 1999 and the fourth edition in 2002, the exchange rate against the US dollar slid from Tsh 670 to around Tsh 900, a drop of around 10% annually. It is reasonable to expect a similar trend will persist during the lifespan of this edition.

Climate

Tanzania on the whole has a pleasant tropical climate, but there are large regional climatic variations across the country, influenced by several factors, most significantly altitude. The hottest and most humid part of the country is the coast, where daytime temperatures typically hit around 30°C on most days, and are often higher. The high level of humidity exaggerates the heat on the coast, and there is little natural relief at night except from sea breezes – for which reason town centres often feel a lot hotter than nearby beaches.

Low-lying areas such as the Rift Valley floor, in particular the Lake Nyasa and Tanganyika areas, are also hot, but far less humid, and thus more comfortable. At altitudes of 1,000m or higher, daytime temperatures are warm to hot, and above 2,000m moderate to warm. Most parts of the interior cool down significantly at night, and montane areas such as the rim of the Ngorongoro Crater or Marangu on the foothills of Kilimanjaro can be downright chilly after dark. Alpine conditions and sub-zero night-time temperatures are characteristic of the higher slopes of Mount Meru and especially Kilimanjaro.

Tanzania is too near the Equator to experience the sort of dramatic contrast between summer and winter experienced in much of Europe or North America. The months between October and April are marginally hotter than May to September. In Dar es Salaam, for instance, the hottest month is February (average maximum 32°C; average minimum 23°C), and the coolest month is July (28°C; 18°C). Insignificant as this difference might look on paper, the coast is far more pleasant in the cooler months, while highland towns are far chillier.

Virtually all of Tanzania's rain falls between November and May. The rainy season is generally spilt into the short rains or *mvuli*, over November and December, and the long rains or *masika* from late February to early May. This pattern of two rainy seasons is strongest in coastal areas and in the extreme north around Arusha, where there is relatively little rainfall in January and February. Even then, there are years when the rain falls more continuously from November to May than is indicated by average rainfall figures. In many other parts of the country, figures suggest that rain falls fairly consistently between mid-November and mid-April.

Geography

The bulk of East Africa is made up of a vast, flat plateau rising from a narrow coastal belt to an average height of about 1,500m. This plateau is broken dramatically by the 20-million-year-old Great Rift Valley, which cuts a trough up to 2,000m deep through the African continent from the Dead Sea to Mozambique. The main branch of the Rift Valley bisects Tanzania. A western branch of the Rift Valley forms the Tanzania–Congo border. Lakes Natron, Manyara, Eyasi and Nyasa/Malawi are all in the main rift, Lake Tanganyika lies in the western branch, and Lake Victoria lies on an elevated plateau between them.

East Africa's highest mountains (with the exception of the Ruwenzori Mountains in Uganda) are volcanic in origin, created by the same forces that caused the Rift Valley. Kilimanjaro is the most recent of these: it started to form about one million years ago, and was still growing as recently as 100,000 years ago. Mount Meru is older. Ngorongoro Crater is the collapsed caldera of a volcano that

TRADITIONAL MUSICAL INSTRUMENTS

Tanzania's tribal diversity has meant that a vast array of very different – and, for that matter, very similar – traditional musical instruments are employed around the country under a bemusing number of local names. Broadly speaking, however, all but a handful of these variants can be placed in one of five distinct categorles that conform to the classes of musical instrument used in Europe and the rest of the world.

The traditional music of many Tanzanian cultures is given its melodic drive by a **marimba** (also called a *mbira*), a type of instrument that is unique to Africa but could be regarded as a more percussive variant on the familiar keyboard instruments. The basic design of all marimbas consists of a number of metal or wooden keys whose sound is amplified by a hollow resonating box. Marimbas vary greatly in size from one region to the next. Popular with several pastoralist tribes of the Rift Valley and environs are small hand-held boxes with 6–10 metal keys that are plucked by the musician. In other areas, organ-sized instruments with 50 or more keys are placed on the ground and beaten with sticks like drums. The Gogo of the Dodoma region are famed for their marimba orchestras consisting of several instruments that beat out a complex interweave of melodies and rhythms.

The most purely melodic of Tanzanian instruments is the **zeze**, the local equivalent to the guitar or fiddle, used throughout the country under a variety of different names. The basic zeze design consists of between one and five strings running along a wooden neck that terminates in an open resonating gourd. The musician rubs a bow fiddle-like across the strings, while manipulating their tone with the fingers of his other hand, generally without any other instrumental accompaniment, but sometimes as part of an orchestra. Less widespread stringed instruments include the zither-like *enanga* of the Lake Tanganyika region and similar *bango* and *kinubi* of the coast, all of which are plucked like harps rather than stroked with a bow, to produce more defined melodic lines than the zeze.

The most important percussive instrument in African music is the **drum**, of which numerous local variations are found. Almost identical in structure and role to their European equivalent, most African drums are made by tightly stretching a membrane of animal hide across a section of hollowed tree trunk. A common and widespread type of drum, which is known in most areas as a *msondo* and is often reserved for important rituals, can be up to 1m tall and is held between the drummer's legs.

Percussive backing is also often provided by a variety of instruments known technically as **idiophones**. Traditionally, these might include the maraca-like *manyanga*, a shaker made by filling a gourd with dry seeds, as well as metal bells and bamboo scrapers. A modern variant on the above is the *chupa*: a glass cold drink bottle scraped with a piece of tin or a stick. Finally, in certain areas, horned instruments are also used, often to supply a fanfare at ceremonial occasions. These generally consist of a modified animal horn with a blowing hole cut into its side, through which the musician manipulates the pitch uising different mouth movements.

Readers with an interest in traditional music are pointed towards an excellent but difficult-to-locate booklet *The Traditional Musical Instruments of Tanzania*, written by Lewis and Makala (Music Conservatoire of Tanzania, 1990), and the primary source of this box.

would once have been as high as Kilimanjaro is today. The only active volcano in Tanzania, Ol Doinyo Lengai, lies a short way north of Ngorongoro.

HISTORY

Tanzania has a rich and fascinating history, but much of the detail is highly elusive. Specialist works often contradict each other to such an extent that it is difficult to tell where fact ends and speculation begins, while broader or more popular accounts are commonly riddled with obvious inaccuracies. This is partly because there are huge gaps in the known facts; partly because much of the available information is scattered in out-of-print or difficult-to-find books; partly because once an inaccuracy gets into print it tends to spread like a virus through other written works. For whatever reason, there is not, so far as I am aware, one concise, comprehensive and reliable book about Tanzanian history in print.

The following account attempts to provide a reasonably comprehensive and readable overview of the country's history. It is, to the best of my knowledge, as accurate as the known facts will allow, but at times I have had to decide for myself the most probable truth amongst a mass of contradictions, and I have speculated freely where speculation seems to be the order of the day. My goals are to stimulate the visitor's interest in Tanzanian history, and to give easy access to information that would have enhanced my first trip to Tanzania greatly. Many of the subjects touched on in this general history are given more elaborate treatment elsewhere in the book, under regional history sections or tint boxes.

Pre-history of the interior

The part of the Rift Valley passing through Ethiopia, Kenya and northern Tanzania is almost certainly where modern human beings and their hominid ancestors evolved. Hominids are generally divided into two genera, called *Australopithecus* and *Homo*, the former extinct for at least a million years, and the latter now represented by only one species – *Homo sapiens* (modern man). The paucity of hominid fossils collected before the 1960s meant that for many years it was assumed the most common australopithecine fossil, *A. africanus*, had evolved directly into the genus *Homo* and was thus man's oldest identifiable ancestor.

This neat linear theory of human evolution became blurred when Richard and Mary Leakey, who were excavating Olduvai Gorge in northern Tanzania, discovered that at least two australopithecine species had existed. Carbon dating and the skeletal structure of the two species indicated that the older *A. robustus* had less in common with modern man than its more lightly built ancestor *A. africanus*, implying that the *Australopithecus* line was not ancestral to the *Homo* line at all. This hypothesis was confirmed in 1972 with the discovery of a two-million-year-old skull of a previously undescribed species *Homo habilis* at Lake Turkana in Kenya, providing conclusive evidence that *Australopithecus* and *Homo* species had lived alongside each other for at least one million years. As more fossils have come to light, including older examples of *Homo erectus* (the direct ancestor of modern humans), it has become clear that several different hominid species existed alongside each other in the Rift Valley until perhaps half a million years ago.

In 1974, Donald Johansen discovered an almost complete hominid skeleton in the Danakil region of northern Ethiopia. Named Lucy (the song *Lucy in the Sky with Diamonds* was playing in camp shortly after the discovery), this turned out to be the fossil of a 3.5-million-year-old australopithecine of an entirely new species dubbed *A. afarensis*. Lucy's anatomy demonstrated that bipedal hominids (or rather semi-bipedal, since the length of Lucy's arms suggest she would have been as comfortable swinging through the trees as she would have been on a morning jog) had evolved much earlier than previously assumed.

In the 1960s it was widely thought that humans and apes diverged around 20 million years ago. Recent DNA evidence has shown, however, that modern man and chimpanzees are far more closely related than previously assumed – to the extent that less biased observers might place us in the same genus. It is now thought that the hominid and chimpanzee evolutionary lines diverged from a common ancestor between four and six million years ago. In 2001, it was announced that the candidate for the so-called 'missing link' between humans and chimps had been discovered in northern Ethiopia: the fossilised remains of a 5.8-million-year-old hominid that has been assigned to a new genus *Arpipithecus*, with clear affiliations with both chimpanzees and humans.

The immediate ancestor of modern man is *Homo erectus*, which appeared about 1.5 million years ago. *Homo erectus* was the first hominid to surmount the barrier of the Sahara and spread into Europe and Asia, and is credited with the discovery of fire and the first use of stone tools and recognisable speech. Although modern man, *Homo sapiens*, has been around for at least half a million years, only in the last 10,000 years have the African races recognised today more or less taken their modern form. Up until about 1000BC, East Africa was exclusively populated by hunter-gatherers, similar in physiology, culture and language to the Khoisan (or bushmen) of southern Africa. Rock art accredited to these hunter-gatherers is found throughout East Africa, most notably in the Kondoa-Irangi region of central Tanzania.

The pastoralist and agricultural lifestyles that were pioneered in the Nile Delta in about 5000BC spread to parts of sub-Saharan Africa by 2000BC, most notably to the Cushitic-speaking people of the Ethiopian Highlands and the Bantu-speakers of West Africa. Cushitic-speakers first drifted into Tanzania in about 1000BC, closely followed by Bantu-speakers. Familiar with iron-age technology, these migrants would have soon dominated the local hunter-gatherers. By AD1000, most of Tanzania was populated by Bantu-speakers, with Cushitic-speaking pockets in areas such as the Ngorongoro Highlands.

There is no detailed information about the Tanzanian interior prior to 1500, and even after that details are sketchy. Except for the Lake Victoria region, which supported large authoritarian kingdoms similar to those in Uganda, much of the Tanzanian interior is too dry to support large concentrations of people. In most of Tanzania, an informal system of *ntemi* chiefs emerged. The *ntemi* system, though structured, seems to have been flexible and benevolent. The chiefs were served by a council and performed a role that was as much advisory as it was authoritarian. By the 19th century there are estimated to have been more than 200 *ntemi* chiefs in western and central Tanzania, each with about 1,000 subjects.

The *ntemi* system was shattered when southern Tanzania was invaded by Ngoni exiles from what is now South Africa, refugees from the rampantly militaristic Zulu Kingdom moulded by Shaka in the early 19th century. The Ngoni entered southern Tanzania in about 1840, bringing with them the revolutionary Zulu military tactics based on horseshoe formations and a short-stabbing spear. The new arrivals attacked the resident tribes, destroying communities and leaving survivors no option but to turn to banditry. Their tactics were observed and adopted by the more astute *ntemi* chiefs, who needed to protect themselves, but had to forge larger kingdoms to do so. The situation was exacerbated by the growing presence of Arab slave traders. Tribes controlling the areas that caravan routes went through were able to extract taxes from the slavers and to find work with them as porters or organising slave raids. This situation was exploited by several chiefs, most notably

VOICES OF THE EXPLORERS

In many instances, the best or indeed only surviving accounts of places and cultures in their 19th-century incarnation is to be found in the original writings of the Victorian explorers. One of the pleasures of researching this fourth edition has been wading through a few of these obscure or out-of-print works for contemporary descriptions. What I discovered was not the stuffy, self aggrandising, judgemental twaddle one might expect, but some remarkably vivid and fresh passages, of their time, for sure, but far more riveting and instructive than many of the blatantly masturbatory exercises that pass for modern travelogue writing.

Extended quotes from these and other works are scattered throughout this guide, with the intent of fleshing out the dry bones of corresponding factual historical accounts. In many instances, space restrictions have necessitated some vigorous editing, and I make no apology for having omitted irrelevant chunks of text, or even having re-ordered scattered but associated sections from a long notebook to create a greater sense of cohesion. Because this is not an academic work, I have taken the liberty of changing obsolete place spellings in line with the contemporary ones used elsewhere in this guide (for instance, Quiloa to Kilwa). I've also converted imperial measurements to their rough metric equivalent, and all written numbers to digits (for example, five thousand to 5,000). All quotes are otherwise exactly as their author wrote them – and I hope you enjoy them as much as I have!

Mirambo of Unyamwezi and Mkwawa of the Uhehe, charismatic leaders who dominated the interior in the late 19th century.

The coast to 1800

There have been links between the Tanzanian coast and the rest of the world for millennia, but only the barest sketch is possible of events before AD1000. The ancient Egyptians believed their ancestors came from a southerly land called Punt. In about 2500BC an explorer called Sahare sailed off in search of this mysterious land. Sahere returned laden with ivory, ebony and myrrh, a booty that suggests he had landed somewhere on the East African coast. There is no suggestion that Egypt traded regularly with Punt, but they did visit it again. Interestingly, an engraving of the Queen of Punt, made after an expedition in 1493BC, shows her to have distinctly Khoisan features. The Phoenicians first explored the coast in about 600BC. According to the 1st-century *Periplus of the Ancient Sea* they traded with a town called Rhapta, which is thought to have lain upriver of a major estuary, possibly the Pangani or the Rufiji Delta.

Bantu-speakers arrived at the coast about 2,000 years ago. It seems likely they had trade links with the Roman Empire: Rhapta gets a name check in Ptolemy's 4th-century *Geography*, and a few 4th-century Roman coins have been found at the coast. The fact that the Romans knew of Kilimanjaro, and of the great lakes of the interior, raises some interesting questions. One suggestion is that the coastal Bantu-speakers were running trade routes into the interior and that these collapsed at the same time as the Roman Empire, presumably as a result of the sudden dearth of trade partners. This notion is attractive and not implausible, but the evidence seems rather flimsy. The Romans could simply have gleaned the information from Bantu-speakers who had arrived at the coast recently enough to have some knowledge of the interior.

Historians have a clearer picture of events on the coast from about AD1000, by which time trade between the coast and the Persian Gulf was well established. The earliest known Islamic buildings on the coast, which stand on Manda Island off Kenya, have been dated to the 9th century AD. Items sold to Arab ships at this time included ivory, ebony and spices, while a variety of Oriental and Arabic goods were imported for the use of wealthy traders. The dominant item of export, however, was gold, mined in the Great Zimbabwe region, transported to the coast at Sofala (in modern-day Mozambique) via the Zambezi Valley, then shipped by local traders to Mogadishu, where it was sold to the Arab boats. The common assumption that Swahili language and culture was a direct result of Arab traders mixing with local Bantu-speakers is probably inaccurate. KiSwahili is a Bantu language, and although it did spread along the coast in the 11th century, most of the Arabic words that have entered the language did so at a later date. The driving force behind a common coastal language and culture was almost certainly not the direct trade with Arabs, but rather the internal trade between Sofala and Mogadishu.

More than 30 Swahili city-states sprung up along the East Africa coast between the 13th and 15th centuries, a large number of which were in modern-day Tanzania. This period is known as the Shirazi era after the sultans who ruled these city-states, most of whom claimed descent from the Shiraz region of Persia. Each city-state had its own sultan; they rarely interfered in each other's business. The Islamic faith was widespread during this period, and many Arabic influences crept into coastal architecture. Cities were centred on a great mosque, normally constructed in rock and coral. It has long been assumed that the many Arabs who settled on the coast before and during the Shirazi era controlled the trade locally, but this notion has been questioned in recent years. Contemporary descriptions of the city-states suggest that Africans formed the bulk of the population. It is possible that some African traders claimed Shirazi descent in order to boost their standing both locally and with Shirazi ships.

In the mid-13th century, probably due to improvements in Arab navigation and ship construction, the centre of the gold trade moved southward from Mogadishu to the small island of Kilwa. Kilwa represented the peak of the Shirazi period. It had a population of 10,000 and operated its own mint, the first in sub-equatorial Saharan Africa. The multi-domed mosque on Kilwa was the largest and most splendid anywhere on the coast, while another building, now known as Husuni Kubwa, was a gargantuan palace, complete with audience courts, several ornate balconies, and even a swimming pool.

Although Mombasa had possibly superseded Kilwa in importance by the end of the 15th century, coastal trade was still booming. It came to an abrupt halt in 1505, however, when the Portuguese captured Mombasa, and several other coastal towns, Kilwa included, were razed. Under Portuguese control the gold trade collapsed and the coastal economy stagnated. It was dealt a further blow in the late 16th century when a mysterious tribe of cannibals called the Zimba swept up the coast to ransack several cities and eat their inhabitants before being defeated by a mixed Portuguese and local army near Malindi in modern-day Kenya.

In 1698, an Arabic naval force under the Sultan of Oman captured Fort Jesus, the Portuguese stronghold in Mombasa, paving the way for the eventual Omani take-over of the coast north of modern-day Mtwara. Rivalries between the new Omani and the old Shirazi dynasties soon surfaced, and in 1728 a group of Shirazi sultans went so far as to conspire with their old oppressors, the Portuguese, to overthrow Fort Jesus. The Omani re-captured the fort a year later. For the next 100 years an uneasy peace gripped the coast, which was

TRIBES

The word 'tribe' has fallen out of vogue in recent years, and I must confess that for several years I rigorously avoided the use of it in my writing. It has, I feel, rather colonial connotations, something to which I'm perhaps overly sensitive having lived most of my life in South Africa. Some African intellectuals have argued that it is derogatory, too, insofar as it is typically applied in a belittling sense to non-European cultures, where words such as 'nation' might be applied to their European equivalent.

All well and good to dispense with the word tribe, at least until you set about looking for a meaningful substitute. 'Nation', for instance, seems appropriate when applied in a historical sense to a large and cohesive centralised entity such as the Zulu or Hehe, but rather less so when you're talking about smaller and more loosely affiliated tribes. Furthermore, in any modern sense, Tanzania itself is a nation (and proud if it), just as are Britain or Germany, so that describing, for instance, the modern Chagga as a nation would feel as inaccurate and contrived as referring to, say, the Liverpudlian or Berliner nation.

It would be inaccurate, too, to refer to most African tribes in purely ethnic or cultural or linguistic terms. Any or all of these factors might come into play in shaping a tribal identity, without in any sense defining it. All modern tribes contain individuals with a diverse ethnic stock, simply through intermarriage. Most modern Ngoni, for instance, belong to that tribe through their ancestors having been assimilated into it, not because all or even any of their ancestors were necessarily members of the Ngoni band who migrated up from South Africa in the 19th century. And, for sure, when the original Bantu-speaking people moved into present-day Tanzania thousands of years ago, local people with an entirely different ethnic background would have been assimilated into the newly established communities. Likewise, the linguistic and cultural differences between two neighbouring tribes are often very slight, and may be no more significant than dialectal or other regional differences within either tribe. The Maasai and Samburu, for instance, share a long common history, are

nominally under Omani rule, but dominated in economic terms by the Shirazi Sultan of Mombasa.

Slavery and exploration in the 19th century

The 19th century was a period of rapid change in Tanzania, with stronger links established between the coast and the interior as well as between East Africa and Europe. Over the first half of the 19th century, the most important figure locally was Sultan Seyyid Said of Oman, who ruled from 1804 to 1854. Prior to 1804, Britain had signed a treaty with Oman, and relations between the two powers intensified in the wake of the Napoleonic Wars, since the British did not want to see the coast fall into French hands. In 1827, Said's small but efficient navy captured Mombasa and overthrew its Shirazi sultan, to assert unambiguous control over the whole coast, with strong British support.

Having captured Mombasa, Sultan Said chose Zanzibar as his East African base, partly because of its proximity to Bagamoyo (the terminus of a caravan route to Lake Tanganyika since 1823) and partly because it was more secure against attacks from the sea or the interior than any mainland port. Said's commercial involvement with Zanzibar began in 1827 when he set up a number of clove

of essentially the same ethnic stock, speak the same language, and are culturally almost indistinguishable. Yet they perceive themselves to be distinct tribes, and are perceived as such by outsiders.

A few years ago, in mild desperation, I settled on the suitably nebulous term ethno-linguistic group as a substitute for tribe. Clumsy, ugly, and verging on the meaningless it might be, but it does sound impressively authoritative, without pinning itself exclusively on ethnicity, language or culture as a defining element, and it positively oozes political correctness. It's also, well, a little bit silly! Just how silly dawned on me during the four months I spent back in Tanzania researching this fourth edition. Just as Tanzanians are unselfconscious about referring to themselves as black and to *wazungu* as white, so too do they talk about their tribe without batting an eyelid. For goodness sake, at every other local hotel in Tanzania, visitors are required to fill in the 'Tribe' column in the standard-issue guesthouse visitors' book! And if it's good enough for Tanzanians, well, who am I to get precious about it?

More than that, it strikes me that even in an African nation as united as Tanzania certainly is, the role of tribe in shaping the identity of an individual has no real equivalent in most Western societies. We may love – or indeed loathe – our home town, we might fight to the death for our loved ones, we might shed tears when our football team loses or our favourite pop group disbands, but we have no equivalent to the African notion of tribe. True enough, tribalism is often cited as the scourge of modern Africa, and when taken to fanatical extremes that's a fair assessment, yet to damn it entirely would be rather like damning English football, or its supporters, because of the actions of a fanatical extreme. Tribalism is an integral part of African society, and pussyfooting around it through an overdeveloped sense of political correctness strikes me as more belittling than being open about it.

So, in case you hadn't gathered, Tanzania's 120 ethno-lingual-cultural groupings are tribes for this edition of the guide, a decision that will hold at least for so long as I'm expected to fill in my tribe – whatever that might be – every time I check into a Tanzanian guesthouse!

plantations there, with scant regard for the land claims of local inhabitants. Said and his fellow Arabs had come to totally dominate all aspects of commerce on the island by 1840, the year in which the Sultan permanently relocated his personal capital from Oman to Zanzibar.

The extent of the East African slave trade prior to 1827 is unclear. It certainly existed, but was never as important as the gold or ivory trade. In part, this was because the traditional centre of slave trading had always been West Africa, which was far closer than the Indian Ocean to the main markets of the Americas. In the early 19th century, however, the British curbed the slave trade out of West Africa, leaving the way open for Said and his cronies. By 1839, over 40,000 slaves were being sold from Zanzibar annually. These came from two sources: the central caravan route between Bagamoyo and the Lake Tanganyika region, and a southern route between Kilwa Kivinje and Lake Nyasa.

The effects of the slave trade on the interior were numerous. The Nyamwezi of the Tabora region and the Yua of Nyasa became very powerful by serving as porters along the caravan routes and organising slave raids and ivory hunts. Weaker tribes were devastated. Villages were ransacked; the able-bodied men and women were taken away while the young and old were left to die. Hundreds of thousands of slaves were sold in the mid-19th century. Nobody knows how many more died of disease or exhaustion between being captured and reaching the coast. Another long-term effect of the slave trade was that it formed the driving force behind the second great expansion of KiSwahili, which became the *lingua franca* along caravan routes.

Europeans knew little about the African interior in 1850. The first Europeans to see Kilimanjaro (Rebmann in 1848) and Mount Kenya (Krapf in 1849) were ridiculed for their reports of snow on the Equator. The Arab traders must have had an intimate knowledge of many parts of the interior that intrigued Europeans, but, oddly, at least in hindsight, nobody seems to have thought to ask them. In 1855, a German missionary, James Erhardt, produced a map of Africa, based on third-hand Arab accounts, which showed a large slug-shaped lake in the heart of the continent. Known as the Slug Map, it was wildly inaccurate, yet it did serve to fan interest in a mystery that had tickled geographers since Roman times: the source of the Nile.

The men most responsible for opening up the East African interior to Europeans were David Livingstone, Richard Burton, John Speke and, later, Henry Stanley. Livingstone, who came from a poor Scots background and left school at the age of ten, educated himself to become a doctor and a missionary. He arrived in the Cape in 1841 to work in the Kuruman Mission, but, overcome by the enormity of the task of converting Africa to Christianity, he decided he would be of greater service opening up the continent so that other missionaries could follow. Livingstone was the first European to cross the Kalahari Desert, the first to cross Africa from west to east and the first to see Victoria Falls. In 1858, Livingstone stumbled across Africa's third largest lake, Nyasa. Later in the same year, on a quest for the source of the Nile funded by the Royal Geographical Society, Burton and Speke were the first Europeans to see Lake Tanganyika, and Speke continued north to Lake Victoria. Speke returned to the northern shore of Lake Victoria in 1863 and concluded – correctly, though it would be many years before the theory gained wide acceptance – that Ripon Falls in modern-day Uganda formed the source of the Nile.

Livingstone had ample opportunity during his wanderings to witness the slave caravans at first hand. Sickened by what he saw – the human bondage, the destruction of entire villages, and the corpses abandoned by the traders – he became an outspoken critic of the trade. He believed the only way to curb it was to open up Africa to the three Cs: Christianity, Commerce and Civilisation. Though not an imperialist by nature, Livingstone had seen enough of the famine and misery caused by the slavers and the Ngoni in the Nyasa area to believe the only solution was for Britain to colonise eastern Africa.

In 1867, Livingstone set off from Mikindani to spend the last six years of his life wandering between the great lakes, making notes on the slave trade and trying to settle the Nile debate. He believed the source of the Nile to be Lake Bangweulu (in northern Zambia), from which the mighty Lualaba River flowed. In 1872, while recovering from illness at Ujiji, Livingstone was met by Henry Stanley and became the recipient of perhaps the most famous words ever spoken in Africa: 'Dr Livingstone, I presume'. Livingstone died near Lake Bangweulu in 1873. His heart was removed and buried by his porters, who then carried his cured body over 1,500km via Tabora to Bagamoyo, a voyage as remarkable as any undertaken by the European Explorers.

Livingstone's quest to end the slave trade met with little success during his lifetime, but his death and highly emotional funeral at Westminster Abbey seem to have acted as a catalyst. Missions were built in his name all over the Nyasa region, while industrialists such as William Mackinnon and the Muir brothers invested in schemes to open Africa to commerce (which Livingstone had always believed was the key to putting the slavers out of business).

In the year Livingstone died, John Kirk was made the British Consul in Zanzibar. Kirk had travelled with Livingstone on his 1856–62 trip to Nyasa. Deeply affected by what he saw, he had since spent years on Zanzibar hoping to find a way to end the slave trade. In 1873, the British navy blockaded the island and Kirk offered Sultan Barghash full protection against foreign powers if he banned the slave trade. Barghash agreed. The slave market was closed and an Anglican Church built over it. Within ten years of Livingstone's death, the volume of slaves was a fraction of what it had been in the 1860s. Caravans reverted to ivory as their principal trade, while many of the coastal traders started up rubber and sugar plantations, which turned out to be just as lucrative as their former trade. Nevertheless, a clandestine slave trade continued on the mainland for some years – 12,000 slaves were sold at Kilwa in 1875 – and even into the 20th century, only to be fully eradicated in 1918, when Britain took control of Tanganyika

The partitioning of East Africa

The so-called scramble for Africa was entered into with mixed motives, erratic enthusiasm and an almost total lack of premeditation by the powers involved. Britain, the major beneficiary of the scramble, already enjoyed a degree of influence on Zanzibar, one that arguably approached informal colonisation, and it was quite happy to maintain this mutually agreeable relationship unaltered. Furthermore, the British government at the time, led by Lord Salisbury, was broadly opposed to the taking of African colonies. The scramble was initiated by two events. The first, the decision of King Leopold of Belgium to colonise the Congo Basin, had little direct bearing on events in Tanzania. The partitioning of East Africa was a direct result of an about-face by the German premier, Bismarck, who had previously shown no enthusiasm for acquiring colonies and probably developed an interest in Africa in the hope of acquiring pawns to use in negotiations with Britain and France.

In 1884, a young German metaphysician called Carl Peters arrived inauspiciously in Zanzibar, then made his way to the mainland to sign a series of treaties with local chiefs. The authenticity of these treaties is questionable, but when Bismarck announced claims to a large area between the Pangani and Rufiji Rivers, it was enough to set the British government into a mild panic. Britain had plans to expand the Sultanate of Zanzibar, its informal colony, to include the fertile lands around Kilimanjaro. Worse, large parts of the area claimed by Germany were already part of the Sultanate. Not only was Britain morally bound to protect these, it also did not want to surrender control of Zanzibar's annual import/export turnover of two million pounds.

Despite pressure put on the British government by John Kirk, angry that his promises to Barghash would not be honoured, there was little option but to negotiate with Germany. A partition was agreed in 1886, identical to the modern border between Kenya and Tanzania. (You may read that Kilimanjaro was part of the British territory before Queen Victoria gave it to her cousin, the Kaiser, as a birthday present. This amusing story, possibly dreamed up by a Victorian satirist to reflect the arbitrariness of the scramble, is complete fabrication.) In April 1888, the Sultan of Zanzibar unwillingly agreed to lease Germany the coastal strip south of the Umba River. Germany mandated this area to Carl Peters' German East Africa Company (GEAC), which placed agencies at most of the coastal settlements north of Dar es Salaam. These agents demanded heavy taxes from traders and were encouraged to behave high-handedly in their dealings with locals.

The GEAC's honeymoon was short. Emil Zalewski, the Pangani agent, ordered the Sultan's representative, the Wali, to report to him. When the Wali refused,

Zalewski had him arrested and sent away on a German war boat. In September 1888, a sugar plantation owner called Abushiri Ibn Salim led an uprising against the GEAC. Except for Dar es Salaam and Bagamoyo, both protected by German war boats, the GEAC agents were either killed or driven away. A horde of 20,000 men gathered on the coast, including 6,000 Shambaa who refused to relinquish their right to claim tax from caravans passing the Usambara. In November, the mission at Dar es Salaam was attacked. Three priests were killed and the rest captured. The coast was in chaos until April 1889 when the Kaiser's troops invaded Abushiri's camp and forced him to surrender. The German government hanged Abushiri in Pangani; they withdrew the GEAC's mandate and banned Peters from ever setting foot in the area.

The 1886 agreement only created the single line of partition north of Kilimanjaro. By 1890, Germany had claimed an area north of Witu, including Lamu, and there was concern in Britain that they might try to claim the rich agricultural land around Lake Victoria, thereby surrounding Britain's territory. Undeterred by the débâcle at Pangani (and with a nod and a wink from Bismarck), Carl Peters decided to force the issue. He slipped through Lamu and in May 1890, after a murderous jaunt across British territory, he signed a treaty with the King of Buganda entitling Germany to most of what is now southern Uganda. This time, however, Peters' plans were frustrated. Bismarck had resigned in March of the same year and his replacement, Von Kaprivi, wanted to maintain good relations with Salisbury's government. In any case, Henry Stanley had signed a similar treaty with the Buganda when he passed through the area in 1888 on his way from rescuing the Emin Pasha in Equatoria.

Germany had its eye on Heligoland, a small but strategic North Sea island that had been seized by Britain from Denmark in 1807. To some extent, German interest in Africa had always been related to the bargaining power it would give them in Europe. In 1890, Salisbury and Von Kaprivi knocked out the agreement that created the modern borders of mainland Tanzania (with the exception of modern-day Burundi and Rwanda, German territory until after World War I). In exchange for an island of less than 1km² in extent, Salisbury was guaranteed protectorateship over Zanzibar and handed the German block north of Witu, and Germany relinquished any claims it might have had to what are today Uganda and Malawi.

German East Africa

The period of German rule was not a happy one. In 1891, Carl Peters was appointed governor. Peters had already proved himself an unsavoury and unsympathetic character: he boasted freely of enjoying killing Africans and, under the guise of the GEAC, his lack of diplomacy had already instigated one uprising. Furthermore, the 1890s were plagued by a series of natural disasters: a rinderpest epidemic at the start of the decade, followed by an outbreak of smallpox, and a destructive plague of locusts. A series of droughts brought famine and disease in their wake. Many previously settled areas reverted to bush, causing the spread of tsetse fly and sleeping sickness. The population of Tanganyika is thought to have decreased significantly between 1890 and 1914.

It took Peters a decade to gain full control of the colony. The main area of conflict was in the vast central plateau where, led by Mkwawa, the Hehe had become the dominant tribe. In 1891, the Hehe ambushed a German battalion led by Emil Zalewski. They killed or wounded more than half Zalewski's men, and made off with his armoury. Mkwawa fortified his capital near Iringa, but the Germans razed it in 1894. Mkwawa was forced to resort to guerrilla tactics, which

THE MAJI-MAJI REBELLION

The people of what is now the southeast of Tanzania suffered throughout the 19th century. They had been terrorised by the notoriously cruel Kilwa slavers and suffered regular raids by the Ngoni, and a misguided German cotton scheme, which created backbreaking work for little financial return, was the final straw. In 1905, a prophet called Kinjikitile discovered a spring that spouted out magic water. He claimed that bullets fired at anyone who had been sprinkled with this water would have no effect. His messengers carried the water to people throughout the region; by August 1905 the entire southeast was ready to rise against the Germans.

The Maji-Maji (water-water) Rebellion began in Kinjikitile's village in the Mutumbi Hills near Kilwa. The house of the German agent in Kibatu was burnt down, as was a nearby Asian trading centre. Troops from the regional headquarters at Kilwa captured and hanged Kinjikitile, but the news of his magic water had already spread. A group of missionaries led by the bishop of Dar es Salaam was speared to death when they passed through the region, several trading posts were burnt along with their occupants, and the entire staff of the Ifakara garrison was killed.

The first setback came when several thousand warriors attacked the Mahenge garrison. The commander had been warned of the attack and a bank of machine guns awaited its arrival. Although many warriors were killed, the garrison was pinned down until troops from Iringa forced the rest to retreat. The Iringa troops then continued to the Ngoni capital of Songea, which was brewing up for its own rebellion. The Ngoni were extremely dubious about the water's power, so when a few Ngoni were shot, the rest of them fled.

News of the water's ineffectiveness spread; the rebellion had lost much of its momentum by mid-October when Count Gotzen and 200 German troops arrived in the area. Gotzen decided the only way to flush out the ringleaders was to create a famine. Crops were burnt indiscriminately. Within months most of the leaders had been hanged. The ensuing famine virtually depopulated the area: over 250,000 people died of disease or starvation and the densely populated Mutumbi and Ungindo hills were reclaimed by *miombo* woodland and wild animals. They now form part of the Selous Game Reserve.

The Maji-Maji rebellion was the most important and tragic event during German rule, but it did leave some good effects in its wake. It was the first time a group of disparate tribes had dropped their own disputes and united against European invaders. Many Tanzanians feel the rebellion paved the way for the non-tribal attitude of modern Tanzania and it certainly affected the strategies used against colonial powers throughout Africa. More immediately, the public outcry it caused forced Germany to rethink its approach to its colonies.

he used with some success until 1898, when he shot himself rather than face capture by the Germans.

Germany was determined to make the colony self-sufficient. Sugar and rubber were well established on parts of the coast; coffee was planted in the Kilimanjaro region, a major base for settlers; and cotton grew well around Lake Victoria. The colony's leading crop export, sisal, was grown throughout the rest of the country.

In 1902, Peters decided that the southeast should be given over to cotton plantations. This was an ill-considered move: the soils were not right for the crop and the scheme was bound to cause great hardship. It also led to the infamous and ultimately rather tragic Maji-Maji rebellion, which proved to be perhaps the most decisive event in the colony during German rule (see box page 19).

Carl Peters was fired from the colonial service in 1906. He believed his African mistress had slept with his manservant, so he flogged her close to death then hanged them both. His successor introduced a series of laws protecting Africans from mistreatment. To the disgust of the settler community, he created an incentive-based scheme for African farmers. This made it worth their while to grow cash crops and allowed the colony's exports to triple in the period leading up to World War I.

When war broke out in Europe, East Africa also became involved. In the early stages of the war, German troops entered southern Kenya to cut off the Uganda Railway. Britain responded with an abortive attempt to capture Tanga. The balance of power was roughly even until Jan Smuts led the Allied forces into German territory in 1916. By January 1918, the Allies had captured most of German East Africa and the German commander, Von Lettow, retreated into Mozambique. The war disrupted food production, and a serious famine ensued. This was particularly devastating in the Dodoma region. The country was taken over by the League of Nations. The Ruanda-Urundi District, now the states of Rwanda and Burundi, was mandated to Belgium. The rest of the country was re-named Tanganyika and mandated to Britain.

Tanganyika

The period of British rule between the wars was largely uneventful. Tanganyika was never heavily settled by Europeans so the indigenous populace had more opportunity for self-reliance than it did in many colonies. Nevertheless, settlers were favoured in the agricultural field, as were Asians in commerce. The Land Ordinance Act of 1923 secured some land rights for Africans; otherwise they were repeatedly forced into grand but misconceived agricultural schemes. The most notorious of these, the Groundnut Scheme of 1947, was an attempt to convert the southeast of the country into a large-scale mechanised groundnut producer. The scheme failed through a complete lack of understanding of local conditions; it caused a great deal of hardship locally and cost British taxpayers millions of pounds. On a political level, a system of indirect rule based around local government encouraged African leaders to focus on local rivalries rather than national issues between the wars. A low-key national movement called the TAA was formed in 1929, but it was as much a cultural as a political organisation.

Although it was not directly involved in World War II, Tanganyika was profoundly affected by it. The country benefited economically. It saw no combat so food production continued as normal, while international food prices rocketed. Tanganyika's trade revenue increased sixfold between 1939 and 1949. World War II was a major force in the rise of African nationalism. Almost 100,000 Tanganyikans fought for the Allies. The exposure to other countries and cultures made it difficult for them to return home as second-class citizens. They had fought for non-racism and democracy in Europe, yet were victims of racist and non-democratic policies in their own country.

The dominant figure in the post-war politics of Tanganyika/Tanzania was Julius Nyerere. Schooled at a mission near Lake Victoria, he went on to university in Uganda and gained a master's degree in Edinburgh. After returning to Tanzania in 1952, Nyerere became involved in the TAA. This evolved into the more political and nationalist TANU in 1954. Nyerere became the President of TANU at the age of 32. By supporting rural Africans on grass roots issues and advocating self-government as the answer to their grievances, TANU gained a strong national following. By the mid-1950s, Britain and the UN were looking at a way of moving Tanganyika towards greater self-government, though over a far longer time-scale than TANU envisaged. The British governor, Sir Edward Twining, favoured a multi-racial system that would give equal representation to whites, blacks and Asians. TANU agreed to an election along these lines, albeit with major reservations. Twining created his own 'African party', the UTC.

In the 1958 election, there were three seats per constituency, one for each racial group. Electors could vote for all three seats, so in addition to putting forward candidates for the black seats, TANU indicated their preferred candidates in the white and Asian seats. Candidates backed by TANU won 67% of the vote; the UTC did not win a single seat. Twining's successor, Sir Richard Turnball, rewarded TANU by scrapping the multi-racial system in favour of open elections. In the democratic election of 1960, TANU won all but one seat. In May 1961, Tanganyika attained self-government and Nyerere was made Prime Minister. Tanganyika attained full independence on December 9 1961. Not one life had been taken in the process. Britain granted Zanzibar full independence in December 1963. A month later the Arab government was toppled and in April 1964 the two countries combined to form Tanzania.

Tanzania

At the very core of Tanzania's post-independence achievements and failures lies the figure of Julius Nyerere, who ruled Tanzania until his retirement in 1985. In his own country, where he remains highly respected, Nyerere is called *Mwalimu* – the teacher. In the West, he is a controversial figure, often portrayed as a dangerous socialist who irreparably damaged his country. This image of Nyerere doesn't bear scrutiny. He made mistakes and was intolerant of criticism – at one point Tanzania had more political prisoners than South Africa – but he is also one of the few genuine statesmen to have emerged from Africa, a force for positive change both in his own country and in a wider African context.

In 1962, TANU came into power with little policy other than their attained goal of independence. Tanganyika was the poorest and least economically developed country in East Africa, and one of the poorest in the world. Nyerere's first concerns were to better the lot of rural Africans and to prevent the creation of a money-grabbing elite. The country was made a one-party state, but had an election system which, by African standards, was relatively democratic. Tanzania pursued a policy of non-alignment, but the government's socialist policies and Nyerere's outspoken views alienated most Western leaders. Close bonds were formed with socialist powers, most significantly China, who built the Tanzam Railway (completed in 1975).

Relations with Britain soured in 1965. Nyerere condemned the British government's tacit acceptance of the Unilateral Declaration of Independence (UDI) in Rhodesia. In return, Britain cut off all aid to Tanzania. Nyerere also gave considerable vocal support to disenfranchised Africans in South Africa, Mozambique and Angola. The ANC and Frelimo both operated from Tanzania in the 1960s.

Nyerere's international concerns were not confined to white-supremacism. In 1975, Tanzania pulled out of an Organisation of African Unity (OAU) conference in Idi Amin's Uganda saying: 'The refusal to protest against African crimes against Africans is bad enough...but...by meeting in Kampala...the OAU are giving respectability to one of the most murderous regimes in Africa.' Tanzania gave refuge to several Ugandans, including the former president Milton Obote and the current president Yoweri Museveni. Amin occupied part of northwest Tanzania in October 1978, and bombed Bukoba and Musoma. In 1979, Tanzania retaliated by invading Uganda and toppling Amin. Other African leaders condemned Tanzania for this action, despite Amin having been the initial aggressor. Ousting Amin drained Tanzania's financial resources, but it never received any financial compensation, either from the West, or from any other African country.

At the time of independence, most rural Tanzanians lived in scattered communities. This made it difficult for the government to provide such amenities as clinics and schools and to organise a productive agricultural scheme. In 1967, Nyerere embarked on a policy he called villagisation. Rural people were encouraged to form *Ujamaa* (familyhood) villages and collective farms. The scheme met with some small-scale success in the mid-1970s, so in 1975 Nyerere decided to forcibly re-settle people who had not yet formed villages. By the end of the year 65% of rural Tanzanians lived in *Ujamaa* villages. In many areas, however, water supplies were inadequate to support a village. The resultant mess, exacerbated by one of Tanzania's regular droughts, ended further villagisation. *Ujamaa* is often considered to have been an unmitigated disaster. It did not achieve what it was meant to, but it did help the government improve education and health care. Most reliable sources claim it did little long-term damage to agricultural productivity.

By the late 1970s Tanzania's economy was a mess. There were several contributory factors: drought, *Ujamaa*, rising fuel prices, the border closure with Kenya, lack of foreign aid, bureaucracy and corruption in state-run institutions, and the cost of the Uganda episode. After his re-election in 1980 Nyerere announced he would retire at the end of that five-year term. In 1985, Ali Hassan Mwinyi succeeded Nyerere as Prime Minster. Nyerere remained Chairman of the CCM, the party formed when TANU merged with the Zanzibari ASP in 1975, until 1990.

Under President Mwinyi, Tanzania moved away from socialism. In June 1986, in alliance with the IMF, a three-year Economic Recovery Plan was implemented. This included freeing up the exchange rate and encouraging private enterprise. Since then Tanzania has achieved an annual growth rate of around 4% (in real terms). Many locals complain the only result they have seen is greater inflation. In 1990 attempts were made to rout corruption from the civil service, with surprisingly positive results. The first multi-party election took place in October 1995. The CCM was returned to power with a majority of around 75% under the leadership of Benjamin Mpaka, who remains the President today. As with independence, this transition caused no bloodshed.

Into its fourth decade of independence, most of Africa still suffers from the tribal problems it had at the outset. Nyerere's great achievement is the tremendous sense of national unity he created by making KiSwahili the national language, by banning tribal leaders, by forcing government officials to work away from the area in which they grew up, and by his own example. Things look better for Tanzania now than they have at any time since independence. It remains one of the world's least developed countries, but most sources agree that the economic situation of the average Tanzanian has improved greatly since independence, as have adult literacy rates and health care. Tanzania's remarkable political stability and its increasingly pragmatic economic policies form a positive basis for future growth.

Natural History

There are plenty of good reasons to visit Tanzania – the beautiful coastline, fascinating history and magnificent scenery – but for most people one attraction overwhelms all others, and that is the wildlife. Tanzania is Africa's prime game-viewing country, best known for the deservedly well publicised Serengeti and Ngorongoro Crater, highlights in a mosaic of national parks and other conservation areas that cover almost 25% of the country and protect an estimated 20% of Africa's large mammals.

MAIN CONSERVATION AREAS

There are currently 12 national parks in Tanzania, with two more likely to be gazetted in the immediate future, and numerous other conservation areas gazetted, ranging from the vast Selous Game Reserve and Ngorongoro Conservation Area to several smaller forest reserves and even a couple of marine parks. All the national parks receive detailed coverage in the main part of the guide, as do other conservation areas that are reasonably accessible, and several that are not. The following potted descriptions are intended to provide an introductory overview to the country's most significant and accessible conservation areas, not to replicate the more extended descriptions in the main body of the guide. The listings start with the Serengeti in the north of the country and run roughly clockwise from there.

Serengeti National Park This world-famous national park, notable for its million-strong migratory herds of wildebeest and zebra, is the lynchpin of the popular northern safari circuit. It also harbours large numbers of predators; it is not unusual to see lion, leopard, cheetah, spotted hyena, bat-eared fox and a couple of jackal and mongoose species in the same day. The Serengeti is so vast that any sense of over-crowding in this popular park is restricted to the Seronera area in the southeast. The northern and western Serengeti have more of a wilderness feel, with surprisingly little tourist traffic around, except when the migration passes through them. Numerous lodges and campsites are dotted around the park.

Ngorongoro Conservation Area This dual-use conservation area – inhabited by the Maasai and their cattle as well as wildlife – protects a large part of the Ngorongoro Highlands, including the magnificent Ngorongoro Crater, the largest intact caldera in the world. Ngorongoro Crater supports the world's densest population of lions and spotted hyena. It is the last place in Tanzania where black rhinoceros are reasonably easy to see, and is also notable for its magnificent old tuskers, a rare sight today elsewhere in Tanzania. The Ngorongoro Crater is heavily touristed, which does detract from many people's visit. A number of other remote natural landmarks in the Ngorongoro Highlands can be visited by vehicle or on foot. Numerous lodges and campsites are found on the crater rim.

AFRICAN CONSERVATION

The plight of the mountain gorilla, rhinoceros and elephant has made African conservation a household concern in the West. Despite this, few Westerners have any grasp of the issues. What follows is certainly opinionated, and probably simplistic, but does attempt to clarify the root problem as I see it. You may well disagree...

We all romanticise Africa. An incredible amount of drivel was written about it during the colonial era, and this dominates our perception of the continent. The macho blustering of Hemingway and exaggerated accounts of the Great White Hunters vie in our heads with the nostalgic meandering of *Out of Africa*. For the West, Africa represents wildness and space, vast horizons and shimmering red sunsets; powerful images we do not want shattered by the realities of the 21st century.

It was, of course, European settlers who destroyed the Africa they mythologised. The vast herds that had existed alongside people for millennia were decimated during the colonial era. By the early 1960s, when most of Africa became independent, these herds were by and large restricted to conservation areas that had been set aside by the colonial governments to preserve something of the Africa they loved. Their vision of unspoilt Africa did not include people: when an area was declared a national park, the people who lived there were moved to the fringes. Local people had both hunted and conserved the animals for centuries; now hunting was forbidden and they needed new sources of food.

Areas suitable for national parks are not normally densely populated, since they tend to be relatively infertile. Even if someone succeeded in growing crops on the fringe of an unfenced park, one hungry or angry elephant could wipe out their efforts in the space of minutes. This created a circle of poverty around many game reserves, a scenario that ultimately worked in the interests of ivory and rhino horn traders. People living on the verges of reserves would happily kill an elephant or rhinoceros for what was a fraction of the market price, but a fortune in local terms.

As you are no doubt aware, rhinoceros are close to extinction in most African countries. In Tanzania, there are 20 left in the Ngorongoro Conservation Area and at best a couple of hundred in the Selous. Africa's elephant population is now thought to number about half a million. Tanzania is home to a significant number of these. There are an estimated 60,000 animals in the Selous alone, and probably a similar number scattered across other reserves.

In the late 1980s the elephant situation seemed hopeless. In some reserves, herds had been poached to within 20% of their size ten years previously. In the

Lake Manyara National Park The most low-key of the triad of reserves situated between Lake Victoria and the main Arusha–Dodoma Road, Lake Manyara has a fabulous situation at the base of the Rift Valley and is a worthy addition to any itinerary taking in the Serengeti and Ngorongoro. The small park's once famous elephant population suffered badly at the hands of poachers in the 1980s, but it is well on the way to recovery today, and the elephants are perhaps the least jittery anywhere in Tanzania. Manyara is also renowned for its tree-climbing lions, and the large flocks of flamingo that sometimes congregate on the lake. A recent development at Manyara is a number of adventure activities – canoeing, mountain biking, walking and absailing – run out of the Serena Hotel. There is one lodge in

Selous, up to 20,000 were killed in a two-year period. Most African governments lacked the finance to arrest this process; in some cases they also lacked the will, with strong rumours of corruption and the involvement of government officials. Anti-poaching units armed with old-fashioned rifles were fighting bands of poachers armed with AK47s, and losing. In 1988, I was driven through a part of Kenya's Tsavo East National Park, one of the worst-hit reserves, where less than a quarter of its 1972 population of 17,000 animals were left. I saw more elephant corpses than I did live animals; those elephants I did see ran off in terror at the approach of a vehicle.

A moratorium on the world ivory trade was implemented in 1989. There is a wide consensus that this ban has worked in East Africa: elephant numbers increased and, without a market, poaching virtually stopped. Southern African countries want this moratorium to be lifted. Herds in South Africa, Botswana and Zimbabwe are stable and growing, and since elephants are extremely destructive when overpopulated, excess animals were until recently culled. This issue was greatly misrepresented in Britain at least, where emotive and irresponsible newspaper columns and television programmes equated culling with murder. Obviously culling is not the ideal solution, but it is difficult to see a practical alternative when populations become unnaturally high, an almost inevitable reality in the fenced reserves of southern Africa. (The suggestion most often put forward is that the animals could be moved. To the Cotswolds? Or somewhere else where African crops can be trampled?)

It has become evident to many conservationists that a complete change of approach is the only chance for the long-term survival of Africa's large animals. Local people must be included in the process. If they benefit from the reserves, they will side with conservationists; if they do not they will side with the poachers. Attempts must be made to ensure that locals benefit from money raised by the reserves, that they are given meat from culled animals, and that, wherever possible, work is found for them within the reserve. In an increasingly densely populated continent, reserves can only justify their existence if they create local wealth.

Africa does not belong to the West. I see no reason why Africans should conserve their wildlife for the sake of Western aesthetics, unless they perceive it to be in their interest to do so. If some gun-happy soul with a Hemingway fixation is idiot enough to pay enough money to support a village for a year in order that he can hunt an elephant, good. If the meat from an elephant can feed a village for a week, and the money from the sale of the ivory be put back into conservation, good. If we Westerners can drop the idealism and allow Africans to both conserve their wildlife and feed their bellies, only then is there a chance

the park, a lovely campsite at the gate, and accommodation to suit all budgets within 5km of the gate.

Tarangire National Park Lying to the east of Lake Manyara, this excellent national park is included on many northern circuit itineraries. It preserves a classic piece of dry African woodland studded with plentiful baobabs and transected by the perennial Tarangire River. Best known for the prodigious elephant herds that congregate along the river in the dry season, Tarangire also harbours a rich birdlife and such localised antelope species as fringe-eared oryx and gerenuk. Several lodges are to be found in and around the park.

Arusha National Park This underrated but eminently accessible park lies an hour's drive from Arusha town, the northern 'safari capital', and is best known perhaps for protecting Mount Meru, Africa's fifth tallest peak. Other attractive features include the Momella Lakes, which host large concentrations of waterbirds including flamingos, and Ngurdoto Crater, a smaller version of Ngorongoro, whose jungle-clad slopes harbour a variety of monkeys and forest birds. The park can be visited as a day trip from Arusha, but there is a remote lodge on the northern border and a budget campsite on the southern one.

Kilimanjaro National Park Encompassing the two peaks and higher slopes of Africa's highest mountain, Kilimanjaro is of all the country's national parks the least oriented towards game viewing. Thousands of tourists climb it every year, however, to stand on the snow-capped pinnacle of Africa, and to experience the haunting and somewhat otherworldly Afro-montane moorland habitat of the upper slopes. Accommodation within the park is limited to simple mountain huts and campsites, but several lodges lie outside the boundary.

Mkomazi Game Reserve The most obscure of Tanzania's northeastern conservation areas, Mkomazi is essentially a southern extension of Kenya's vast Tsavo East and West National Parks. Wildlife is relatively skittish, and tourist development practically non-existent, but it's a definite possibility for travellers seeking to get away from the beaten track. Basic accommodation and campsites are available.

Amani Nature Reserve This reserve in the Eastern Usambara Mountains, inland of Tanga, protects some of the most important montane forest in Tanzania and a wealth of rare and endemic birds, mammals, butterflies and other creatures. Comfortable and inexpensive accommodation is available within the nature reserve, and a good range of walking trails will keep hikers and birdwatchers busy for days. It's easily accessible on public transport, too.

Saadani National Park This proposed national park (likely to be gazetted very soon) is the only savannah reserve in East Africa to be lapped by the shores of the Indian Ocean. As things stand, it is more accurately characterised as a beach retreat with some wildlife around than as a full-blown safari destination. Boat and walking safaris are a bonus, peace and quiet a given, and the beach really is lovely. One excellent lodge lies on the beach.

Jozani Forest Reserve The main stronghold for the rare Kirk's red colobus, endemic to Zanzibar Island, this small forested reserve is well worth the slight effort required to reach it from Zanzibar Stone Town or the beach resorts of the island's east coast.

Mafia Marine Reserve Protecting the extensive reefs that surround the Mafia archipelago, Tanzania's first marine park offers superlative snorkelling, diving and game fishing – as do the several upmarket lodges on Mafia Island.

Selous Game Reserve This is the largest game reserve in Africa, and the lynchpin of Tanzania's under-utilised but utterly compelling southern safari circuit. Main attractions include the wetland scenery associated with the Rufiji River, the largest remaining population of the endangered African wild dog, large numbers of lion, elephant, hippo, buffalo, giraffe, and the other usual safari suspects. Several low-key upmarket lodges offer game walks, river trips, and fly-camps, as well as the standard game drives.

Mikumi National Park Transected by the main surfaced road through southern Tanzania, Mikumi is an underrated savannah reserve that forms a westerly extension of the much larger Selous. Game viewing can be excellent on the plains to the north of the main road, with substantial elephant and lion populations present, along with large herds of grazers. The lodges in this park are among the cheapest in Tanzania.

Udzungwa Mountains National Park Gazetted in 1992, this seldom-visited national park protects part of the Udzungwa Mountain chain, home to a host of endangered endemics including three primate and two bird species as well as numerous plants and invertebrates. Several hiking opportunities, easy access on public transport, and affordable accommodation at the entrance gate add up to a good destination for backpackers.

Kilombero Valley This extensive floodplain ecosystem immediately west of the Selous Game Reserve is one of the most important wetlands in Africa, home to 70% of the continent's puku antelope, large herds of elephant, a high density of lions, and three endemic bird species. Tourist development is minimal, but a recently established eco-tourism project offers organised trips to the area, and backpackers have limited access from the Ifakara ferry.

Ruaha National Park Tanzania's second-largest national park protects a variety of woodland, grassland and riverine habitats, as well as the full gamut of large predators (including African wild dog), huge elephant herds and localised antelope such as sable, roan and greater and lesser kudu. Game viewing is almost secondary to the untrammelled wilderness atmosphere that envelops this park, serviced by only two (top-notch) lodges.

Kitulo Plateau National Park Another proposed national park, likely to be gazetted over the next year or two, Kitulo is the least conventional of Tanzania's main conservation areas. Little wildlife is to be seen in the area, but it's a hiker's and botanist's paradise, especially during the rainy season when the prodigious wildflowers are in bloom.

Katavi National Park The wildest and most underrated savannah reserve in East Africa, Katavi offers mind-boggling game viewing during the dry season, and you can explore the area for days without encountering another vehicle. If you're after an exclusive wilderness experience – and hang the expense – look no further. One very exclusive tented camp operates seasonally.

Mahale Mountains National Park This large and scenic park runs from the lovely shores of Lake Tanganyika to forested peaks almost 2,000m above the lakeshore. It harbours the greatest variety of primates of any Tanzanian national park, including 700–1,000 chimps, as well as several West African species that occur nowhere else in Tanzania. The main attraction is chimp tracking, which is normally excellent. Two upmarket tented camps lie on the lake shore, and inexpensive *bandas* are available too.

Gombe Stream National Park Also situated on the shores of Lake Tanganyika, Gombe Stream is where Jane Goodall undertook her famous research into chimp behaviour in the 1960s. Although smaller than Mahale Mountain, and less scenically majestic, Gombe also offers great chimp tracking, and it is very accessible on public transport. It can also be visited (at a cost) as a day trip from the main lake port of Kigoma. Inexpensive *banda* accommodation is available.

Rubondo Island National Park This immensely peaceful national park protects a forested island in Lake Victoria, and is well suited for those who want to explore

DANGEROUS ANIMALS

The dangers associated with Africa's wild animals have frequently been overstated since the days of the so-called Great White Hunters – who, after all, rather intensified the risk by shooting at animals that are most likely to turn nasty when wounded – and others trying to glamorise their chosen way of life. Contrary to the fanciful notions conjured up by images of rampaging elephants, man-eating lions and psychotic snakes, most wild animals fear us more than we fear them, and their normal response to human contact is to flee. That said, many travel guides have responded to the exaggerated ideas of the dangers associated with wild animals by being overly reassuring. The likelihood of a tourist being attacked by an animal is indeed very low, but it can happen, and there have been a number of fatalities caused by such incidents in recent years, particularly in southern Africa.

The need for caution is greatest near water, particularly around dusk and dawn, when hippos are out grazing. Hippos are responsible for more human fatalities than any other large mammal, not because they are aggressive but because they tend to panic when something comes between them and the safety of the water. If you happen to be that something, then you're unlikely to live to tell the tale. Never consciously walk between a hippo and water, and never walk along riverbanks or through reed beds, especially in overcast weather or at dusk or dawn, unless you are certain that no hippos are present. Watch out, too, for crocodiles. Only a very large crocodile is likely to attack a person, and then only in the water or right on the shore. Near towns and other settlements, you can be fairly sure that any such crocodile will have been consigned to its maker by its potential human prey, so the risk is greatest away from human habitation. It is also near water that you are most likely to unwittingly corner a normally placid terrestrial animal – the waterbuck. The population on Crescent Island in Kenya's Lake Naivasha has acquired a nasty reputation for attacking on close approach, and the riverine-forest-dwelling bushbuck has a reputation as the most dangerous African antelope when cornered.

There are areas where hikers might still stumble across an elephant or a buffalo, the most dangerous of Africa's terrestrial herbivores. Elephants almost invariably mock charge and indulge in some hair-raising trumpeting before they attack in earnest. Provided that you back off at the first sign of unease, they are most unlikely to take further notice of you. If you see them before they see you, give them a wide berth, bearing in mind they are most likely to attack if surprised at close proximity. If an animal charges you, the safest course of action is to head for the nearest tree and climb it. Black rhinos are prone to charging without apparent provocation, but they're too rare in Tanzania to be a cause for concern. Elephants are the only animals to pose a potential danger in a vehicle, and much the same advice applies – if an elephant evidently doesn't want you to pass, then back off and wait until it has crossed the road or moved further away before you try again. In general, it's a good idea to leave your

on foot or by boat. The indigenous fauna includes the sitatunga antelope and spotted-necked otter – both surprisingly easily observed – and introduced elephant, giraffe and chimps can also be seen. The island offers good birdwatching and game fishing. An upmarket lodge and national park *bandas* are found on the island.

engine running when you are close to an elephant, and you should avoid letting yourself be boxed in between an elephant and another vehicle.

There are campsites in Tanzania where vervet monkeys and baboons have become pests. Feeding these animals is highly irresponsible, since it encourages them to scavenge and may eventually lead to them being shot. Vervet monkeys are too small to progress much beyond being a nuisance, but baboons are very dangerous and have often killed children and maimed adults with their vicious teeth. Do not tease or underestimate them. If primates are hanging around a campsite, and you wander off leaving fruit in your tent, don't expect the tent to be standing when you return. Chimpanzees are also potentially dangerous, but unlikely to be encountered except on a guided forest walk, when there is little risk provided that you obey your guide's instructions at all times.

The dangers associated with large predators are often exaggerated. Most predators stay clear of humans and are only likely to kill accidentally or in self-defence. Lions are arguably the exception, but it is unusual for a lion to attack a human without cause. Should you encounter one on foot, the important thing is not to run, since this is likely to trigger the instinct to give chase. Of the other cats, cheetahs represent no threat and leopards generally attack only when they are cornered. Hyenas are often associated with human settlements, and are potentially very dangerous, but in practise they aren't aggressive towards people and are most likely to slink off into the shadows when disturbed. A slight but real danger when sleeping in the bush without a tent is that a passing hyena or lion might investigate a hairy object sticking out of a sleeping bag, and you might be decapitated through predatorial curiosity. In areas where large predators are still reasonably common, sleeping in a sealed tent practically guarantees your safety – but don't sleep with your head sticking out and don't at any point put meat in the tent.

All manner of venomous snakes occur in Tanzania, but they are unlikely to be encountered since they generally slither away when they sense the seismic vibrations made by a walking person. You should be most alert to snakes on rocky slopes and cliffs, particularly where you risk putting your hand on a ledge that you can't see. Rocky areas are the favoured habitat of the puff adder, which is not an especially venomous snake, but is potentially lethal and unusual in that it won't always move off in response to human foot treads. Wearing good boots when walking in the bush will protect against the 50% of snake bites that occur below the ankle, and long trousers will help deflect bites higher up on the leg, reducing the quantity of venom injected. Lethal snake bites are a rarity (in South Africa, which boasts almost as many venomous snakes as Tanzania, more people are killed by lightning than by snake bites) but some discussion of treatment is included in the chapter on health, page 105.

When all is said and done, the most dangerous animal in Africa, exponentially a greater threat than everything mentioned above, is the anopheles mosquito, which carries the malaria parasite. Humans – particularly when behind a steering wheel – run them a close second!

HABITATS AND VEGETATION

The bulk of Tanzania is covered in open grassland, savannah (lightly wooded grassland) and woodland. The Serengeti Plains are an archetypal African savannah: grassland interspersed with trees of the acacia family – which are typically quite short, lightly foliated, and thorny. Many have a flat-topped appearance. An atypical acacia, the yellow fever tree, is one of Africa's most striking trees. It is relatively large, has yellow bark, and is often associated with water. Combretum is another family of trees typical of many savannah habitats. The dry savannah of central Tanzania can be so barren during the dry season that it resembles semi-desert.

Woodland differs from forest in lacking an interlocking canopy. The most extensive woodland in Tanzania is in the *miombo* belt, which stretches from southern and western Tanzania to Zimbabwe. *Miombo* woodland typically grows on infertile soil, and is dominated by broad-leafed *brachystegia* trees. You may come across the term mixed woodland: this refers to woodland with a mix of *brachystegia*, acacia and other species. Many woodland habitats are characterised by an abundance of baobab trees.

True forests cover less than 1% of Tanzania's surface area, but are the most diverse habitat ecologically. The forests of the Usambara, for instance, contain more than 2,000 plant species. Most of the forest in Tanzania is montane. Montane forest is characteristic of a group of mountain ranges known as the Eastern Arc mountains. These form a broken line from north to south, between 50km and 200km inland, and include the Pare, Usambara, Uluguru, Udzungwa and Poroto ranges. The forests of the Eastern Arc mountains, characterised by a high level of endemics (species found nowhere else), form one of Tanzania's most ecologically precious habitats. The most accessible montane forests are on the slopes of Kilimanjaro, Meru, the Udzungwa and the Usambara.

The lowland forests found in the extreme west of the country have strong affinities with the rainforests of Congo. Three national parks contain extensive lowland forests: Gombe Stream, Rubondo Island and Mahale Mountains.

Other interesting but localised vegetation types are mangrove swamps (common along the coast, particularly around Kilwa) and the heath and moorland found on the higher slopes of Kilimanjaro and Meru.

ANIMALS
Mammals
Over 80 large mammal species live in Tanzania. On an organised safari your guide will normally be able to identify all the mammals you see. For serious identification purposes (or a better understanding of an animal's lifestyle and habits) it is worth investing in a decent field guide or a book on animal behaviour. Such books are too generalised to give much detail on distribution in any one country, so that the section that follows is best seen as a Tanzania-specific supplement to a field guide. A number of field guides are available (see *Further Reading*) and are best bought before you get to Tanzania.

In the listings below, an animal's scientific name is given in parenthesis after its English name, followed by the Swahili (Sw) name. The Swahili for animal is *mnyama* (plural *wanyama*); to find out what animal you are seeing, ask '*mnyama gani?*'

Cats, dogs and hyenas
Lion (*Panthera leo*) Sw: *simba*. Shoulder height: 100–120cm; weight: 150–220kg. Africa's largest predator, the lion is the one animal that everybody hopes to see on safari. It is a sociable creature, living in prides of five to ten animals and defending a territory of between 20 and 200km². Lions hunt at night, and their favoured prey is large or medium antelope such as wildebeest and impala. Most of the hunting is done by females, but dominant males normally feed first after a kill. Rivalry between males is intense, and battles to take over a pride are frequently fought to the death, for which reason two or more males often form a coalition. Young males are forced out of their home pride at three years of age, and male cubs are usually

killed after a successful takeover. When not feeding or fighting, lions are remarkably indolent – they spend up to 23 hours of any given day at rest – so the anticipation of a lion sighting is often more exciting than the real thing. Lions naturally occur in any habitat but desert and rainforest, and once ranged across much of the Old World, but these days they are all but restricted to the larger conservation areas in sub-Saharan Africa (one remnant population exists in India). They are reasonably common in most savannah and woodland reserves in Tanzania, notably Selous, Katavi and Ruaha. The Serengeti and Ngorongoro Crater are arguably the best places in Africa for regular lion sightings.

Leopard (*Panthera pardus*) Sw: *chui*. Shoulder height: 70cm; weight: 60–80kg. The powerful leopard is the most solitary and secretive of Africa's large cat species. It hunts using stealth and power, often getting to within 5m of its intended prey before pouncing, and it habitually stores its kill in a tree to keep it from hyenas and lions. The leopard can be distinguished from the superficially similar cheetah by its rosette-like spots, lack of black 'tear marks' and more compact, powerful build. Leopards occur in all habitats, favouring areas with plenty of cover such as riverine woodland and rocky slopes. There are many records of individuals living in close proximity to humans for years without being detected. The leopard is the most common of Africa's large felines, found throughout Tanzania, yet a good sighting must be considered a stroke of extreme fortune. Relatively reliable spots for leopard sightings are the Seronera Valley in the Serengeti and the riverine bush in Ruaha National Park. An endemic race of leopard occurs on Zanzibar, though recent research suggests that it is probably extinct on the island, and that the handful of local reports of leopard sighting were probably the result of confusion with the African civet and introduced Java civet.

Cheetah (*Acynonix jubatus*) Sw: *duma*. Shoulder height: 70–80cm; weight: 50–60kg. This remarkable spotted cat has a greyhound-like build, and is capable of running at 70km/h in bursts, making it the world's fastest land animal. It is often seen pacing the plains restlessly, either on its own or in a small family group comprised of a mother and her offspring. A diurnal hunter, favouring the cooler hours of the day, the cheetah's habits have been adversely affected in areas where there are high tourist concentrations and off-road driving is permitted. Males are territorial, and generally solitary, though in the Serengeti they commonly defend their territory in pairs or trios. Despite superficial similarities, you can easily tell a cheetah from a leopard by its simple spots, disproportionately small head, streamlined build, diagnostic black tear marks, and preference for relatively open habitats. Widespread, but thinly distributed and

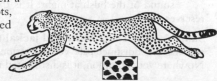

increasingly rare outside of conservation areas, the cheetah is most likely to be seen in savannah and arid habitats such as the Serengeti Plains (where sightings are regular on the road to Seronera) and the floor of the Ngorongoro Crater.

Similar species The **serval** (*Felis serval*) is smaller than a cheetah (shoulder height: 55cm) but has a similar build and black-on-gold spots giving way to streaking near the head. Seldom seen, it is widespread and quite common in moist grassland, reed beds and riverine habitats.

Caracal (*Felis caracal*) Sw: *simbamangu*. Shoulder height: 40cm; weight: 15–20kg. The caracal resembles the European lynx with its uniform tan coat and tufted ears. It is a solitary hunter, feeding on birds, small antelope and livestock, and ranges throughout the country favouring relatively arid savannah habitats. It is nocturnal and rarely seen.

Similar species The smaller **African wild cat** (*Felis sylvestris*) ranges from the Mediterranean to the Cape of Good Hope, and is similar in appearance to the domestic tabby cat. Like the caracal, it is common, but nocturnal, and infrequently seen.

African wild dog (*Lycaon pictus*) Sw: *mbwa mwitu*. Shoulder height: 70cm; weight: 25kg. Also known as the African hunting dog or painted dog, the wild dog is distinguished from other African canids by its large size and cryptic black, brown and cream coat. Highly sociable, living in packs of up to 20 animals, the hunting dog is a ferocious hunter that literally tears apart its prey on the run. Threatened with extinction as a result of its susceptibility to diseases spread by domestic dogs, it is extinct in several areas where it was formerly abundant, for instance in the Serengeti and most other reserves in northern Tanzania. The global population of around 4,000 wild dogs is spread across much of eastern and southern Africa, but the Selous Game Reserve is the most important stronghold (estimated population 1,300) and Ruaha National Park also hosts a viable population. The only place in northern Tanzania where hunting dogs can reliably be observed is the Mkomazi Game Reserve, where a recently re-introduced population is reportedly thriving. A few recent scattered sightings in Tarangire and Lake Manyara National Parks provide some hope that this endangered creature might yet re-colonise this area.

Black-backed jackal (*Canis mesomelas*) Sw: *mbweha*. Shoulder height: 35–45cm; weight: 8–12kg. The black-backed (or silver-backed) jackal is an opportunistic feeder capable of adapting to most habitats. Most often seen singly or in pairs at dusk or dawn, it is ochre in colour with a prominent black saddle flecked by a varying amount of white or gold. It is probably the most frequently observed small predator in Africa south of the Zambezi, and its eerie call is a characteristic sound of the bush at night. It is the commonest jackal in most Tanzanian reserves.

Similar species The **side-striped jackal** (*Canis adustus*) is more cryptic in colour, and has an indistinct pale vertical stripe on each flank and a white-tipped tail. Nowhere very common, it is distributed throughout Tanzania, and most likely to be seen in the southern reserves. The **common jackal** (*Canis aureus*), also known as the Eurasian or golden jackal, is a cryptically coloured North African jackal, relatively pale and with a black tail tip. Its range extends as far south as the Serengeti and Ngorongoro Crater, and it is probably more readily seen than the black-backed jackal on the crater floor, since it is more diurnal in its habits.

Bat-eared fox (*Otocyon megalotis*) Shoulder height: 30–35cm; weight: 35kg. This small, silver-grey insectivore, unmistakable with its huge ears and black eye-mask, is most often seen in pairs or small family groups during the cooler hours of the day. Associated with dry open country, the bat-eared fox is quite common in the Serengeti and likely to be encountered at least once in the course of a few days' safari, particularly during the denning season (November and December).

Spotted hyena (*Crocuta crocuta*) Sw: *fisi*. Shoulder height: 85cm; weight: 70kg. Hyenas are characterised by their bulky build, sloping back, brownish coat, powerful jaws and dog-like expression. Despite looking superficially canine, they are more closely related to mongooses and bears than to cats or dogs. Contrary to popular myth, hyenas are not exclusively scavengers: the spotted hyena in particular is an adept hunter capable of killing an animal as large as a wildebeest. Nor are they hermaphroditic, an ancient belief that stems from the false scrotum and penis covering the female hyena's vagina. Sociable animals, and fascinating to observe, hyenas live in loosely structured clans of about ten animals, led by females who are stronger and larger than males. The spotted hyena is the largest hyena, distinguished by its blotchily spotted coat, and it is probably the most common large predator in eastern and southern Africa. It is most frequently seen at dusk and dawn in the vicinity of game reserve lodges, campsites and refuse dumps, and is likely to be encountered on a daily basis in the Serengeti and Ngorongoro Crater.

Similar species The North African **striped hyena** (*Hyaena hyaena*) is pale brown with several dark vertical streaks and an off-black mane. It occurs alongside the spotted hyena in dry parts of Tanzania, but is scarce and secretive. The equally secretive **aardwolf** (*Proteles cristatus*) is an insectivorous striped hyena, not much bigger than a jackal, occurring in low numbers in northern Tanzania.

African civet (*Civettictus civetta*) Sw: *fungo*. Shoulder height: 40cm; weight: 10–15kg. This bulky, longhaired, rather feline creature of the African night is primarily carnivorous, feeding on small animals and carrion, but will also eat fruit. It has a similarly coloured coat to a leopard or cheetah, and this is densely blotched with large black spots becoming stripes towards the head. Civets are widespread and common in many habitats, but very rarely seen.

Similar species The smaller, more slender **tree civet** (*Nandinia binotata*) is an arboreal forest animal with a dark-brown coat marked with black spots. The **small-spotted genet** (*Genetta genetta*) and **large-spotted genet** (*Genetta tigrina*) are the most widespread members of a group of similar small predators, all of which are very slender and rather feline in appearance, with a grey to golden brown coat marked with black spots and an exceptionally long ringed tail. Most likely to be seen on nocturnal game drives or scavenging around game reserve lodges, the large-spotted genet is golden brown with very large spots and a black-tipped tail, whereas the small-spotted genet is greyer with rather small spots and a pale tip to the tail.

Banded mongoose (*Mungos mungo*) Shoulder height: 20cm; weight: around 1kg. The banded mongoose is probably the most commonly observed member of a group of small, slender, terrestrial carnivores. Uniform dark brown except for a dozen black stripes across its back, it is a diurnal mongoose occurring in family groups in most wooded habitats and savannah.

Similar species Several other mongoose species occur in Tanzania, though several are too scarce and nocturnal to be seen by casual visitors. The **marsh mongoose** (*Atilax paludinosus*) is large, normally solitary and has a very scruffy brown coat. It's widespread in the eastern side of Africa where it is often seen in the vicinity of water. The **white-tailed ichneumon** (*Ichneumia albicauda*) is another widespread, solitary, large brown mongoose, easily identified by its bushy white tail. The **slender mongoose** (*Galerella sanguinea*) is as widespread and also solitary, but it is very much smaller (shoulder height: 10cm) and has a uniform brown coat and black tail tip. The **dwarf mongoose** (*Helogate parvula*) is a diminutive (shoulder height: 7cm) and highly sociable light brown mongoose often seen in the vicinity of termite mounds, particularly in Tarangire National Park.

Ratel (*Mellivora capensis*) Sw: *nyegere*. Shoulder height: 30cm; weight: 12kg. Also known as the honey badger, the ratel is black with a puppyish face and grey-to-white back. It is an opportunistic feeder best known for its symbiotic relationship with a bird called the honeyguide which leads it to a bee hive, waits for it to tear the nest open, then feeds on the scraps. The ratel is among the most widespread of African carnivores, but it is thinly distributed and rarely seen.

Similar species Several other mustelids occur in the region, including the **striped polecat** (*Ictonyx striatus*), a common but rarely seen nocturnal creature with black underparts and bushy white back, and the similar but much more scarce **striped weasel** (*Poecilogale albincha*). The **Cape clawless otter** (Aonyx capensis) is a brown freshwater mustelid with a white collar, while the smaller **spotted-necked otter** (*Lutra maculicollis*) is darker with white spots on its throat.

Primates

Chimpanzee (*Pan troglodytes*) Sw: *sokwe-mtu*. Standing height: 100cm; weight: up to 55kg. This distinctive black-coated ape, along with the bonobo (*Pan paniscus*) of the southern Congo, is more closely related to man than to any other living creature. The chimpanzee lives in large troops based around a core of related males dominated by an alpha male. Females aren't firmly bonded to their core group, so emigration between communities is normal. Primarily frugivorous (fruit-eating), chimpanzees eat meat on occasion, and though most kills are opportunistic, stalking of prey is not unusual. The first

GALAGO DIVERSITY IN TANZANIA

The Prosimian galago family is the modern representative of the most ancient of Africa's extant primate lineages, more closely related to the lemurs of Madagascar than to any other mainland monkeys or apes. With their wide round eyes and agile bodies, they are also – as their alternative name of bushbaby suggests – uniquely endearing creatures, bound to warm the heart of even the least anthropomorphic of observers. And no natural history lover could fail to feel some excitement at the revolution in the taxonomy of the galago family that has taken place over recent years, largely due to research undertaken in the forests of Tanzania by the Nocturnal Primate Research Group of Oxford Brookes University.

In 1975, only six species of galago were recognised by specialists. By 1998, that number had risen to 18, of which 10 are confirmed or likely to occur in Tanzania, including three probable endemic species and two with a core range within Tanzania. The reasons behind this explosion of knowledge probably lies in their nocturnal habits, which makes casual identification tricky, particularly in relatively inaccessible forested habitats. Previously biologists based their definition of galago species largely on superficial visual similarities. It has recently been recognised, however, that the distinctive vocal repertoires of different populations, as well as differences in the penile structure, provide a more accurate indicator of whether two populations would or indeed could interbreed given the opportunity – in other words, whether they should be regarded as discrete species.

By comparing the calls, penile structures and DNA of dwarf galago populations around Tanzania, the Nocturnal Primate Research Group has discovered four previously undescribed species since the early 1990s. These are the Mozambique galago *Galagoides granti* (coastal woodland south of the Rufiji River), Matundu galago *Galagoides udzungwensis* (Udzungwa Mountains), Mountain galago *Galagoides orinus* (Uluguru and Usambara Mountains) and Rondo galago *Galagoides rondoensis*. The last of these species, initially thought to be confined to the Rondo Plateau inland of Lindi, has recently been discovered living in the Pugu Hills, right outside the country's largest city! It is not so much possible as certain that further galago species await discovery: in East Africa alone populations that require further study are found in southeast Tanzania, in the isolated forests of Mount Marsabit in northern Kenya, and in the mountains along the northern shores of Lake Nyasa-Malawi.

Simon Bearder of the Nocturnal Primate Research Group argues convincingly that the implications of these fresh discoveries in galago taxonomy might extend to other 'difficult' groups of closely related animals. He points out that our most important sense is vision, which makes it easiest for us to separate species that rely primarily on vision to recognise or attract partners. It becomes more difficult for us to separate animals that attract their mates primarily by sound and scent, more so still if they use senses we do not possess such as ultrasound or electric impulses. 'Such "cryptic" species,' Bearder writes, 'are no less valid than any other, but we are easily misled into thinking of them as being much more similar than would be the case if we had their kind of sensitivity. The easiest way for us to distinguish between free-living species is to concentrate on those aspects of the communication system that the animals themselves use to attract partners.'

recorded instance of a chimp using a tool was at Gombe Stream in Tanzania, where modified sticks were used to 'fish' in termite mounds. In West Africa, chimps have been observed cracking open nuts with a stone and anvil. In the USA, captive chimps have successfully been taught Sign Language and have created compound words such as 'rock-berry' to describe a nut. A widespread and common rainforest resident, the chimpanzee is thought to number 200,000 in the wild. In East Africa, chimps occur in western Uganda and on the Tanzanian shore of Lake Tanganyika, where they can be seen at the research centre founded by primatologist Jane Goodall in Tanzania's Gombe Stream, as well as at Mahale Mountains and on Rubondo Island.

Common baboon (*Papio cynocaphalus*) Sw: *nyani*. Shoulder height: 50–75cm; weight: 25–45kg. This powerful terrestrial primate, distinguished from any other monkey by its much larger size, inverted U-shaped tail and distinctive doglike head, is fascinating to watch from a behavioural perspective. It lives in large troops that boast a complex, rigid social structure characterised by matriarchal lineages and plenty of inter-troop movement by males seeking social dominance.

Omnivorous and at home in almost any habitat, the baboon is the most widespread primate in Africa, frequently seen in most Tanzanian game reserves. There are several races of baboon in Africa, regarded by some authorities to be full species. In Tanzania, the yellow baboon (*P. c. cynocephalus*) is the light yellow-brown race occurring in the south and east of the country, while the olive or anubis baboon (*P. c. anubis*) is the darker and hairier green-brown baboon found in the northern reserves.

Vervet monkey (*Cercopithecus aethiops*) Sw: *tumbili*. Length (excluding tail): 40–55cm; weight: 4–6kg. Also known as the green or grivet monkey, the vervet is probably the world's most numerous monkey and certainly the most common and widespread representative of the *Cercopithecus* guenons, a taxonomically controversial genus associated with African forests. An atypical guenon in that it inhabits savannah and woodland rather than true forest, the vervet spends a high proportion of its time on the ground and in most of its range could be confused only with the much larger and heavier baboon. However, the vervet's light-grey coat, black face and white forehead band should be diagnostic – as should the male's garish blue genitals. The vervet is abundant in Tanzania, and might be seen just about anywhere, not only in reserves.

Similar species The terrestrial **patas monkey** (*Erythrocebus patas*), larger and more spindly than the vervet, has an orange-tinged coat and black forehead stripe. Essentially a monkey of the dry northwestern savannah, the patas occurs in low numbers in the northern Serengeti.

Blue monkey (*Cercopithecus mitis*) Sw: *kima*. Length (excluding tail): 50–60cm; weight: 5–8kg. This most variable of African monkeys is also known as the samango, golden, silver and Syke's monkey, or the diademed or white-throated guenon. Several dozen races are recognised, divided by some authorities into more than one species. Taxonomic confusion notwithstanding, *C. mitis* is the most common forest guenon in eastern Africa, with one or other race occurring in just about any suitable habitat. Unlikely to be confused with another species in Tanzania, the blue monkey has a uniformly dark blue-grey coat broken by a white throat which in some races extends all down the chest and in others around the collar. It lives in troops of up to ten animals and associates with other primates where their ranges overlap. It is common in Arusha and Lake Manyara National Parks and in many forest reserves.

Similar species The **red-tailed monkey** (*Cercopithecus ascanius*) is a small brown guenon with white whiskers, a red tail and distinctive white heart on its nose. In Tanzania, it is restricted to forested parts of the Lake Tanganyika shore, such as Mahale Mountains and Gombe Stream. The **crested mangabey** (*Cercocebus galeritus*) is a yellowish West African monkey, two isolated populations of which occur in East Africa, one in Tanzania's Udzungwa Mountains and another along Kenya's Tana River. Both are classified as full species by most authorities.

Black-and-white colobus (*Colobus guereza*) Sw: *mbega mweupe*. Length (excluding tail): 65cm; weight: 12kg. This beautiful jet-black monkey has bold white facial markings, a long white tail and in some races white sides and shoulders. Almost exclusively arboreal, it is capable of jumping up to 30m, a spectacular sight with white tail streaming behind. Several races have been described, and most authorities recognise more than one species. The black-and-white colobus is a common resident of forests in Tanzania, often seen in the forest zone of Kilimanjaro and in Arusha National Park.

Similar species The **Angola colobus** (*Colobus angolensis*) is very similar in appearance to the black-and-white colobus, and both species are subdivided further into a number of races. Some controversy surrounds the breakdown of the various races and species, but three Tanzanian races, those of the Eastern Arc, Southern Highlands, and Lake Tanganyika forests, are now generally assigned to *C. Angolensis*.

Red colobus (*Procolobus badius*) Length (excluding tail): 60cm; weight: 10kg. The status of this variable monkey is again controversial, with between one and ten species recognised by different authorities. Most populations have black on the upper back, red on the lower back, a pale tufted crown and a long-limbed appearance unlike that of any guenon or mangabey. Four populations are known in East Africa, of which two live in isolated pockets in Tanzania, and are regarded by some authorities to be full species. The first of these is Kirk's red colobus *P. kirkii*, which is restricted to Zanzibar Island. Only 1,500 of these animals remain in the wild, but they are easily seen in the Jozani Forest on eastern Zanzibar. The Uhehe red colobus *P. gordonorum* is a fairly common and conspicuous resident of the Udzungwa Mountains in southern Tanzania.

Lesser bushbaby (*Galago senegalensis*) Sw: *komba*. Length (without tail): 17cm; weight: 150g. The lesser bushbaby is the most widespread and common member of a group of small and generally indistinguishable nocturnal primates, distantly related to the lemurs of Madagascar. More often heard than seen, the lesser bushbaby can sometimes be picked out by tracing a cry to a tree and shining a torch into its eyes.

Similar species The most easily identified bushbaby due to its size, the **greater bushbaby** (*Galago crassicaudatus*) occurs throughout the eastern side of Africa as far south as East London. It produces a terrifying scream, which you'd think was emitted by a chimpanzee or gorilla. Recent studies in Tanzania have determined that the smaller bushbabies are far more specifically diverse than was previously realised; see *Galago diversity in Tanzania*, page 35).

Large antelope

Roan antelope (*Hippotragus equinus*) Sw: *korongo*. Shoulder height: 120–150cm; weight: 250–300kg. This handsome equine antelope is uniform fawn-grey with a pale belly, short de-curved horns and a light mane. It could be mistaken for the female sable antelope, but this has a well-defined white belly, and lacks the roan's distinctive black-and-white facial markings. The roan is widespread but thinly distributed in most reserves in southern Tanzania, and it is very rare in the Serengeti.

Sable antelope (*Hippotragus niger*) Sw: *pala hala*. Shoulder height: 135cm; weight: 230kg. The striking male sable is jet black with a distinct white face, underbelly and rump, and long de-curved horns. The female is chestnut brown and has shorter horns. The main stronghold for Africa's sable population is the *miombo* woodland of southern Tanzania, where a population of 30,000 is concentrated in Ruaha National Park and Selous Game Reserve. The sable is absent from most reserves in northern Tanzania.

Oryx (*Oryx gazella*) Sw: *choroa*. Shoulder height: 120cm; weight: 230kg. This regal, dry-country antelope is unmistakable with its ash-grey coat, bold black facial marks and flank strip, and unique long, straight horns. The fringe-eared oryx is the only race found in Tanzania, where it is most common in Tarangire National Park, though present in small numbers in the northern Serengeti and Mkomazi Game Reserve.

Waterbuck (*Kobus ellipsiprymnus*) Sw: *kuro*. Shoulder height: 130cm; weight: 250–270kg. The waterbuck is easily recognised by its shaggy brown coat and the male's large lyre-shaped horns. The Defassa race of the Rift Valley and areas further west has a full white rump, while the eastern race has a white U on its rump. The waterbuck is frequently seen in small family groups grazing near water in all but the most arid of game reserves in Tanzania.

Blue wildebeest (*Connochaetes taurinus*) Sw: *nyumbu*. Shoulder height: 130–150cm; weight: 180–250kg. This rather ungainly antelope, also called the brindled gnu, is easily recognised by its dark coat and bovine appearance. The superficially similar buffalo is far more heavily built. Immense herds of blue wildebeest occur on the Serengeti Plains, where the annual migration of more than a million heading into Kenya's Maasai Mara forms one of Africa's great natural spectacles. There are also significant wildebeest populations in the Ngorongoro Crater, Tarangire and in most reserves in southern Tanzania.

Hartebeest (*Alcelaphus buselaphus*) Shoulder height: 125cm; weight: 120–150kg. Hartebeests are ungainly antelopes, readily identified by the combination of large shoulders, a sloping back, red-brown or yellow-brown coat and smallish horns in both sexes. Numerous races are recognised, all of which are generally seen in small family groups in reasonably open country. The race found in northern Tanzania, Coke's hartebeest or kongoni, is common in open parts of the Serengeti and Ngorongoro. In southern Tanzania, it is replaced by Lichtenstein's hartebeest, which is regarded by some authorities to be a full species.

Similar species The **topi** or **tsessebe** (*Damaliscus lunatus*) is basically a darker version of the hartebeest with striking yellow lower legs. Widespread but thinly and patchily distributed, the topi occurs alongside the much paler kongoni in the Serengeti National Park, where it is common.

Common eland (*Taurotragus oryx*) Sw: *pofu*. Shoulder height: 150–175cm; weight: 450–900kg. Africa's largest antelope, the common eland is light brown in colour, sometimes with a few faint white vertical stripes. It has a somewhat bovine appearance, accentuated by the relatively short horns and large dewlap. It is widely distributed in East and southern Africa, and small herds may be seen almost anywhere in grassland or light woodland. The eland is fairly common in the Serengeti and Mikumi National Parks, but difficult to approach closely

Greater kudu (*Tragelaphus strepsericos*) Sw: *tandala*. Shoulder height: 140–155cm; weight: 180–250kg. In many parts of Africa, the greater kudu is the most readily observed member of the genus *tragelaphus*, a group of medium to large antelopes characterised by the male's large spiralling horns and a dark coat generally marked with several vertical white stripes. The greater kudu is very large, with a grey-brown coat and up to ten stripes on each side, and the male has magnificent double-spiralled horns. A widespread animal occurring in most wooded habitats except for true forest, the greater kudu is rare in northern Tanzania, but more common in the southern reserves, where it is most often seen in mixed- or single-sex herds of up to ten animals.

Similar species The thinly distributed and skittish **lesser kudu** (*Tragelaphus imberbis*) is an East African species largely restricted to arid woodland. In Tanzania, it often occurs alongside the greater kudu, from which it can be distinguished by its smaller size (shoulder height: 100cm), two white throat patches and greater number of stripes (at least 11). Nowhere common, it is most likely to be encountered in Tarangire and Ruaha National Parks. The semi-aquatic **sitatunga** (*Tragelaphus spekei*) is a widespread but infrequently observed inhabitant of west and central African swamps from the Okovango in Botswana to the Sudd in Sudan. Tanzania's Rubondo Island is one of the few places where it is readily observed. The male, with a shoulder height of up to 125cm and a shaggy fawn coat, is unmistakable in its habitat. The smaller female might be mistaken for a bushbuck (see below) but is much drabber.

Medium and small antelope
Bushbuck (*Tragelaphus scriptus*) Sw: *pongo*. Shoulder height: 70–80cm; weight: 30–45kg. This attractive antelope, a member of the same genus as the kudu and sitatunga, shows great regional variation in colouring. The male is dark brown, chestnut or in parts of Ethiopia black, while the much smaller female is generally pale red-brown. The male has relatively small, straight horns for a *tragelaphus* antelope. Both sexes have similar throat patches to the lesser kudu, and are marked with white spots and sometimes stripes. One of the most widespread antelope species in Africa, the bushbuck occurs in forest and riverine woodland throughout Tanzania, where it is normally seen singly or in pairs. It tends to be secretive and skittish except where it is used to people, so it is not as easily seen as you might expect of a common antelope.

Thomson's gazelle (*Gazella thomsoni*) Shoulder height: 60cm; weight: 20–25kg. Gazelles are graceful, relatively small antelopes that generally occur in large herds in open country, and have fawn-brown upper parts and a white belly. Thomson's gazelle is characteristic of the East African plains, where it is the only gazelle to have a black horizontal stripe. It is common to abundant in the Serengeti and surrounds.

Similar species Occurring alongside Thomson's gazelle in many parts of East Africa, the larger **Grant's gazelle** (*Gazella granti*) lacks a black side stripe and has comparatively large horns. An uncharacteristic gazelle, the **gerenuk** (*Litocranius walleri*) is a solitary, arid country species of Ethiopia, Kenya and northern Tanzania, similar in general colour to an impala but readily identified by its very long neck and singular habit of feeding from trees standing on its hind legs. Good places to see it include Mkomazi, Tarangire and the Loliondo area.

Impala (*Aepeceros melampus*) Sw: *swala pala*. Shoulder height: 90cm; weight: 45kg. This slender, handsome antelope is superficially similar to some gazelles, but in fact belongs to a separate family. Chestnut in colour, the impala has diagnostic black and white stripes running down its rump and tail, and the male has large lyre-shaped horns. One of the most widespread antelope species in sub-equatorial Africa, the impala is normally seen in large herds in wooded savannah habitats, and it is one of the most common antelope in many Tanzanian reserves.

Reedbucks (*Redunca spp*) Sw: *tohe*. Shoulder height: 65–90cm; weight: 30–65kg. The three species of reedbuck are all rather nondescript fawn-grey antelopes generally seen in open grassland near water. The mountain reedbuck (*Redunca fulvorufula*) is the smallest and most distinctive, with a clear white belly, tiny horns, and an overall grey appearance. It has a broken distribution, occurring in mountainous parts of eastern South Africa, northern Tanzania, Kenya and southern Ethiopia. The Bohor reedbuck is found in northern Tanzania, whereas the southern reedbuck occurs in southern Tanzania.

Similar species The golden brown **puku** (*Kobus vardoni*), similar in appearance to the kob of Uganda, lives in marsh and moist grassland from Lake Rukwa in Tanzania to the Okovango in Botswana. Its main stronghold is the Kilombero Valley in southeast Tanzania.

Klipspringer (*Oreotragus oreotragus*) Sw: *mbuze mawe*. Shoulder height: 60cm; weight: 13kg. The klipspringer is a goat-like antelope, normally seen in pairs, and easily identified by its dark, bristly grey-yellow coat, slightly speckled appearance and unique habitat preference. Klipspringer means 'rockjumper' in Afrikaans, an apt name for an antelope that occurs exclusively in mountainous areas and rocky outcrops. It is found throughout Tanzania, and is often seen around the Lobo Hills in the Serengeti and the Maji Moto area in Lake Manyara.

Steenbok (*Raphicerus cempestris*) Sw: *tondoro*. Shoulder height: 50cm; weight: 11kg. This rather nondescript small antelope has red-brown upper parts and clear white underparts, and the male has short straight horns. It is probably the most commonly observed small antelope in Africa, though it has a broken range, and is absent from southern Tanzania despite being common in the north of the country and in areas further south. Like most other antelopes of its size, the steenbok is normally encountered singly or in pairs and tends to 'freeze' when disturbed.

Similar species The **oribi** (*Ourebia ourebi*) is a widespread but uncommon grassland antelope which looks much like a steenbok but stands about 10cm higher at the shoulder and has an altogether more upright bearing. **Kirk's dik-dik** (*Madoqua kirki*), smaller than the steenbok and easily identified by its large white eye circle, is restricted primarily to Tanzania and Kenya, and it is particularly common in Arusha National Park.

Red duiker (*Cephalophus natalensis*) Sw: *pofu*. Shoulder height: 45cm; weight: 14kg. This is the most likely of Africa's 12 to 20 'forest duikers' to be seen by tourists. It is deep chestnut in colour with a white tail and, in the case of the East African race *C. n. harveyi* (sometimes considered to be a separate species), a black face. The red duiker occurs in most substantial forest patches along the eastern side of Africa, though it is less often seen than it is heard crashing through the undergrowth.

Similar species The **blue duiker** (*Cephalophus monticola*) is widespread in Africa and the only other forest duiker to occur in countries south of Tanzania, and it can easily be told from the red duiker by its greyer colouring and much smaller size (it is the smallest forest duiker, about the same size as a suni). **Abbott's duiker** (*Cephalophus spadix*) is a large duiker, as tall as a klipspringer, restricted to a handful of montane forests in Tanzania, including those on Kilimanjaro and the Usambara, Udzungwa and Poroto Mountains. The endangered **Ader's duiker** (*Cephalophus adersi*) is presumably restricted to forested habitats on Zanzibar Island, where as few as 1,000 animals may survive, most of them in the Jozani Forest. Recent reports suggest that this duiker is extinct in the only other locality where it has been recorded, the Sokoke Forest in Kenya.

Common duiker (*Sylvicapra grimmia*) Sw: *nysa*. Shoulder height: 50cm; weight: 20kg. This anomalous duiker holds itself more like a steenbok and is the only member of its family to occur outside of forests. Generally grey in colour, the common duiker can most easily be separated from other small antelopes by the black tuft of hair that sticks up between its horns. It occurs throughout Tanzania, and tolerates most habitats except for true forest and very open country.

Other large herbivores

African elephant (*Loxodonta africana*) Sw: *tembe*. Shoulder height: 2.3–3.4m; weight: up to 6,000kg. The world's largest land animal, the African elephant is intelligent, social and often very entertaining to watch. Female elephants live in close knit clans in which the eldest female plays matriarch over her sisters, daughters and granddaughters. Mother-daughter bonds are strong and may last for up to 50 years. Males generally leave the family group at around 12 years to roam singly or form bachelor herds. Under normal circumstances, elephants will range widely in search of food and water, but when concentrated populations are forced to live in conservation areas, their habit of uprooting trees can cause serious environmental damage. Elephants are widespread and common in habitats ranging from desert to rainforest and, despite heavy poaching, they are likely to be seen on a daily basis in most of the country's larger national parks, the exception being the Serengeti where they are common only in the Lobo region.

Black rhinoceros (*Diceros bicornis*) Sw: *faru*. Shoulder height: 160cm; weight: 1,000kg. This is the more widespread of Africa's two rhino species, an imposing, sometimes rather aggressive creature that has been poached to extinction in most of its former range. It occurs in many southern African reserves, but is now very localised in East Africa, where it is most likely to be seen in Tanzania's Ngorongoro Crater. The most substantial Tanzanian population is in the Selous Game Reserve, but sightings here are infrequent.

Hippopotamus (*Hippopotamus amphibius*) Sw: *kiboko*. Shoulder height: 150cm; weight: 2,000kg. Characteristic of Africa's large rivers and lakes, this large, lumbering animal spends most of the day submerged, but emerges at night to graze. Strongly territorial, herds of ten or more animals are presided over by a dominant male who will readily defend his patriarchy to the death. Hippos are abundant in most protected rivers and water bodies, and they are still quite common outside of reserves, where they kill more people than any other African mammal.

African buffalo (*Syncerus caffer*) Sw: *nyati*. Shoulder height: 140cm; weight: 700kg. Frequently and erroneously referred to as a water buffalo (an Asian species), the African buffalo is a distinctive ox-like animal that lives in large herds on the savannah and occurs in smaller herds in forested areas. Common and widespread in sub-Saharan Africa, herds of buffalo are likely to be encountered in most Tanzanian reserves and national parks. The best place to see large buffalo herds is on the Ngorongoro Crater floor or in Katavi National Park.

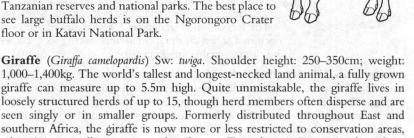

Giraffe (*Giraffa camelopardis*) Sw: *twiga*. Shoulder height: 250–350cm; weight: 1,000–1,400kg. The world's tallest and longest-necked land animal, a fully grown giraffe can measure up to 5.5m high. Quite unmistakable, the giraffe lives in loosely structured herds of up to 15, though herd members often disperse and are seen singly or in smaller groups. Formerly distributed throughout East and southern Africa, the giraffe is now more or less restricted to conservation areas, where it is generally common and easily seen. Two places in Tanzania where there are no giraffe are the part of the Selous south of the Rufiji and the Ngorongoro Crater floor.

Common zebra (*Equus burchelli*) Sw. *punda milia*. Shoulder height: 130cm: weight: 300–340kg. This attractive striped horse is common and widespread throughout most of East and southern Africa, where it is often seen in large herds alongside wildebeest. The common zebra is the only wild equine to occur in Tanzania, and is common in most conservation areas, especially the Serengeti.

Warthog (*Phacochoreus africanus*) Sw: *ngiri*. Shoulder height: 60–70cm; weight: up to 100kg. This widespread and often conspicuously abundant resident of the African savannah is grey in colour with a thin covering of hairs, wartlike bumps on its face, and rather large upward curving tusks. Africa's only diurnal swine, the warthog is often seen in family groups, trotting off briskly with its tail raised stiffly (a diagnostic trait) and a determinedly nonchalant air.

Similar species Bulkier, hairier and browner, the **bushpig** (*Potomochoerus larvatus*) is as widespread as the warthog, but infrequently seen due to its nocturnal habits and preference for dense vegetation. Larger still, weighing up to 250kg, the **giant forest hog** (*Hylochoerus meinertzhageni*) is primarily a species of the West African rainforest. It does occur in certain highland forests in northern Tanzania, but the chance of a sighting is practically non-existent.

Small mammals

Aardvark (*Orycteropus afer*) Shoulder height: 60cm; weight: up to 70kg. This singularly bizarre nocturnal insectivore is unmistakable with its long snout and huge ears. It occurs practically throughout the region, but sightings are extremely rare.

Similar species Not so much similar to an aardvark as equally dissimilar to anything else, **pangolins** are rare nocturnal insectivores with distinctive armour plating and a tendency to roll up in a ball when disturbed. Most likely to be seen in Tanzania is Temminck's pangolin (*Manis temmincki*). Also nocturnal, but spiky rather than armoured, several **hedgehog** and **porcupine** species occur in the region, the former generally no larger than a guinea pig, the latter generally 60–100cm long.

Rock hyrax (*Procavia capensis*) Sw: *pimbi*. Shoulder height: 35–30cm; weight: 4kg. Rodent-like in appearance, hyraxes are more closely related to elephants. The rock hyrax and similar bush hyrax (*Heterohyrax brucei*) are often seen sunning in rocky habitats and become tame when used to people, for instance at Seronera and Lobo lodges in the Serengeti. The less common tree hyrax (*Dendrohyrax arboreus*) is a nocturnal forest creature, often announcing its presence with an unforgettable shrieking call.

Similar species The **elephant shrews** (Sw: *sange*) are rodents that look like miniature kangaroos with absurdly elongated noses. A number of species are recognised, but they are mostly secretive and nocturnal, so rarely seen. The smaller species are generally associated with savannah habitats, but the much larger chequered elephant shrew is a resident of Eastern Arc forests – I've only ever seen it in Amani and Udzungwa.

Scrub hare (*Lepus saxatilis*) This is the largest and commonest African hare or rabbit. In some areas a short walk at dusk or after nightfall might reveal three or four scrub hares. They tend to freeze when disturbed.

Unstriped ground squirrel (*Xerus rutilus*) An endearing terrestrial animal of arid savannah, the unstriped ground squirrel is grey to grey-brown with a prominent white eye ring and silvery black tail. It spends much time on its hind legs, and has the characteristic squirrel mannerism of holding food in its forepaws. In Tanzania, it is most likely to be seen in the Serengeti.

Bush squirrel (*Paraxerus cepapi*) This is the typical squirrel of the eastern and southern savannah, rusty brown in colour with a silvery black back and white eye rings. A great many other arboreal or semi-arboreal squirrels occur in the region, but most are difficult to tell apart in the field.

Birds

Tanzania is a birdwatcher's dream, and it is impossible to do justice to its rich avifauna in the confines of a short introduction. Casual visitors will be stunned at the abundance of birdlife: the brilliantly coloured lilac-breasted rollers and superb starlings, the numerous birds of prey, the giant ostrich, the faintly comic hornbills, the magnificent crowned crane – the list could go on forever. For more dedicated birdwatchers, Tanzania, following an explosion in ornithological knowledge of the country over the past two decades, must now surely rank with the top handful of birding destinations in Africa.

The national checklist, which stood at below 1,000 species in 1980, has risen to 1,112 in 2002, according to a new working checklist compiled by Neil and Liz Baker of the Tanzania Bird Atlas Project. This astonishing gain (more than 10% over two decades) is exaggerated by the Bakers' admitted bias towards splitting controversial species, but it also reflects an unparalleled accumulation of genuine new records. In 1987, the Minziro Forest on the Uganda border yielded 17 additions to the national checklist, and at least 60 new species have been recorded since then. Even if one discounts the controversial splits on the working checklist, Tanzania is poised to overtake Kenya (1,080 species) as the African country with the second most varied avifauna.

Virtually anywhere in Tanzania offers good birding, and species of special interest are noted under the relevant site throughout the main body of this guide. In many areas a reasonably competent novice to East African birds could hope to see between 50 and 100 species in a day. Any of the northern reserves are recommended: Arusha and Lake Manyara National Parks are both good for forest and water birds; the Serengeti and Tarangire are good for raptors and acacia and grassland species. *Miombo*-associated species can be seen in the southern reserves: the Selous, with the advantage of the many birds that live along the Rufiji River, is particularly recommended. Western reserves such as Gombe Stream and Rubondo Island offer a combination of water and forest habitats, with the possibility of glimpsing one or two West African specials..

Recent new discoveries now place Tanzania second to South Africa for its wealth of endemic birds – species that are unique to the country. At present, 33 endemic species are recognised, including a couple of controversial splits, three species discovered and described in the 1990s, and four that still await formal description. Five of the national endemics are readily observed on the northern safari circuit, but a greater number are restricted to the Eastern Arc mountains, together with about 20 eastern forest and woodland species whose core range lies within Tanzania. The forests of the Eastern Arc mountains must therefore rank as the country's most important bird habitat, with the Amani Nature Reserve and Udzungwa National Park the most accessible sites for seeing some of the Eastern Arc specials.

Field guides are discussed under *Further Reading*. A comprehensive and regularly updated checklist of Tanzania's birds, together with atlas maps for a growing number of species, is posted on the Tanzania Bird Atlas Project website: www.home.no.net/stencil1/TZbirdatlas/tzatlas.htm. Experienced birders who wish to fill in species cards for the atlas project based on their observations are also welcome to contact them through the website.

Brief details of the confirmed and probable endemics, compiled with reference to the atlas checklist, follow:

Grey-breasted spurfowl *Francolinus rufopictus* Game bird with distinctive combination of a red mask under which is a white stripe. Confined to the Serengeti and immediate vicinity, where it is common in scattered woodland in the Seronera area.

Udzungwa forest partridge *Xenoperdix udzungwensis* First discovered in 1991, this unique bird, placed in its own genus, is restricted to forest interiors in the Udzungwa Range.

Pemba green pigeon *Treron pembaensis* Large green pigeon confined to Pemba Island, greyer underneath than the mainland equivalent, but unmistakable in its limited range.

Fischer's lovebird *Agapornis fischeri* Stunning and colourful parrot-like bird with bright red head and white eye, most often first noticed when a flock passes overhead squawking and screeching. Its natural range is centred on the Serengeti, where it is common. A popular caged bird in Europe, a feral population of this lovebird occurs in Naivasha (Kenya) where it regularly interbreeds with the next species.

CHAMELEONS

Common and widespread in Tanzania, but not easily seen unless they are actively searched for, chameleons are arguably the most intriguing of African reptiles. True chameleons of the family Chamaeleontidae are confined to the Old World, with the most important centre of speciation being the island of Madagascar, to which about half of the world's 120 recognised species are endemic. Aside from two species of chameleon apiece in Asia and Europe, the remainder is distributed across mainland Africa.

Chameleons are best known for their capacity to change colour, a trait that has often been exaggerated in popular literature, and which is generally influenced by mood more than the colour of the background. Some chameleons are more adept at changing colour than others, with the most variable being the common chameleon *Chamaeleo chamaeleon* of the Mediterranean region, with more than 100 colour and pattern variations recorded. Many African chameleons are typically green in colour but will gradually take on a browner hue when they descend from the foliage in more exposed terrain, for instance while crossing a road. Several change colour and pattern far more dramatically when they feel threatened or are confronted by a rival of the same species. Different chameleon species also vary greatly in size, with the largest being Oustalet's chameleon of Madagascar, known to reach a length of almost 80cm.

A remarkable physiological feature common to all true chameleons are their protuberant round eyes, which offer a potential 180° degree vision on both sides and are able to swivel around independently of each other. Only when one of them isolates a suitably juicy-looking insect will the two eyes focus in the same direction as the chameleon stalks slowly forward until it is close enough to use the other unique weapon in its armoury. This is its sticky-tipped tongue, which is typically about the same length as its body and remains coiled up within its mouth most of the time, to be unleashed in a sudden, blink-and-you'll-miss-it lunge to zap a selected item of prey. In addition to their unique eyes and tongues, many chameleons are adorned with an array of facial casques, flaps,

Yellow-collared lovebird *Agapornis personatus* Another endemic lovebird – with black rather than red head – that has gone feral in Naivasha, Kenya. Naturally confined to the Maasai Steppes and other semi-arid parts of central Tanzania, the yellow-collared lovebird is common in Tarangire National Park.

Pemba scops owl *Otus pembae* Small and very rare owl confined to Pemba Island, where it could not be mistaken for another species.

Nduk eagle owl *Bubo vosseleri* Large owl associated with the forests of the Eastern Arc. It occurs on several different mountain ranges, including the Usambara, Uluguru and Udzungwa. Heard more often than it is seen, it's unlikely to be located without expert local guidance.

Usambara nightjar *Caprimulgus guttifer* Recently split from the more widespread mountain nightjar *C. poliocephalus*, this nocturnal bird is found in the Usambara Mountains and possibly some of the other Eastern Arc ranges.

Spike-heeled lark *Chersomanes albofasciata* The Tanzanian population of this widespread lark is thought by some authorities to be a full species, endemic to the country.

horns and crests that enhance their already somewhat fearsome prehistoric appearance.

In Tanzania, you're most likely to come across a chameleon by chance when it is crossing a road, in which case it should be easy to take a closer look at it, since most chameleons move painfully slowly and deliberately. Chameleons are also often seen on night game drives, when their ghostly nocturnal colouring shows up clearly under a spotlight – as well as making it pretty clear why these strange creatures are regarded with both fear and awe in many local African cultures. More actively, you could ask your guide if they know where to find a chameleon – a few individuals will be resident in most lodge grounds.

The flap-necked chameleon *Chamaeleo delepis* is probably the most regularly observed species of savannah and woodland habitats in East Africa. Often observed crossing roads, the flap-necked chameleon is generally around 15cm long and bright green in colour with few distinctive markings, but individuals might be up to 30cm in length and will turn tan or brown under the right conditions. Another closely related and widespread savannah and woodland species is the similarly sized graceful chameleon *Chamaeleo gracilis*, which is generally yellow-green in colour and often has a white horizontal stripe along its flanks.

Characteristic of East African montane forests, three-horned chameleons form a closely allied species cluster of some taxonomic uncertainty. Typically darker than the savannah chameleons and around 20cm in length, the males of all taxa within this cluster are distinguished by a trio of long nasal horns that project forward from their face. The most widespread three-horned chameleon in Tanzania is *Chamaeleo johnstoni*, while the most localised is the Ngosi three-horned chameleon *Chamaeleo fuelleborni*, confined to the forested slopes of Ngosi Volcano in the Poroto Mountains. Perhaps the most alluring of East Africa's chameleons is the giant chameleon *Chamaeleo melleri*, a bulky dark green creature with yellow stripes and a small solitary horn, mainly associated with the Eastern Arc forests, where it feeds on small reptiles (including snakes) as well as insects.

Neumann's greenbul *Andropadus neumanni* Recently split from *A. tephrolaemus* and confined to the forests of the Uluguru Mountains.

Usambara akalat *Sheppardia montana* Small, drab robin-like ground-bird confined to forest interiors in the Western Usambara, most easily observed in the Magambo Forest near Lushoto.

Iringa akalat *Sheppardia lowei* Small robin-like ground-bird with reddish flanks and white eye-stripe known from several ranges in the southern Eastern Arc, most common on the Udzungwa Mountains.

Rubeho akalat *Sheppardia sp* Recently discovered in the forests of the Rubeho Mountains by J Feldsa, this species still awaits formal description.

Mrs Moreau's warbler *Bathmocercus winifredae* Small but pretty red-headed warbler of dense forest undergrowth known from Udzungwa, Rubeho, Uluguru and a couple of other Eastern Arc ranges.

Usambara hyliota *Hyliota usambarae* East Usambara endemic recently split from *H. australis*.

MARINE TURTLES
Tricia Hayne

Turtles live largely in water, coming ashore only to nest, and unlike their landlubber cousins they are unable to retract either their heads or their flippers into their shell for protection. The world's eight species of marine turtle are all protected under the Convention on International Trade in Endangered Species (CITES), and five have been recorded off the waters of Tanzania. The most common is the green turtle *Chelonia mydas*, so-called because its fat is a greenish colour. Also indigenous to these waters is the hawksbill turtle *Eretmochelys imbricata*, whose exquisite shell is the source of traditional 'tortoiseshell', long coveted for ornamental purposes, and an important trade item along the coast since Ancient Egyptian times, but now outlawed under the CITES agreement. The loggerhead turtle *Caretta caretta*, named for its unusually large head, and the leatherback, *Dermchelys coriacea*, which can reach a length of greater than 2m, are both present off the shores of Tanzania but do not nest on its beaches. The olive ridley turtle *Lepidochelys olivacea* was first recorded breeding off the coast of Tanzania in 1974.

Turtles do not nest until they are at least 25 years old, when they lay their eggs deep in the sand. The eggs take around 60 days to hatch, at which time the hatchlings make their way towards the sea, attracted by the play of moonlight on the waves. The green turtle, the most likely of the five species to be seen by visitors, lays between 300 and 540 eggs per season in the wild, nesting every three or four years, with the eggs hatching from May to September. In captivity, these figures increase, with up to 1,700 eggs in total laid over several batches in a season. In their first year, the hatchlings grow up to 2.7kg, and they can be expected to weigh up to 24kg by the time they are three or four. Green turtles may live to be centuries old, and can weigh in excess of 200kg. Turtles are cold-blooded animals, requiring warm water to survive. In fact, water temperature affects the sex of the hatchlings – at 28°C a balance between male and female is to be expected; cooler than that and males will dominate; hotter and there will be a predominance of females.

Kilombero cisticola *Cisticola sp* One of two recently discovered and as yet undescribed cisticolas from the Kilombero Valley.

White-tailed cisticola *Cisticola sp* One of two recently discovered and as yet undescribed cisticolas from the Kilombero Valley.

Reichenow's batis *Batis reichenowi* An Eastern Arc batis of the forest canopy, similar to and sometimes considered conspecific with *B. mixta*.

Banded green sunbird *Anthreptes rubritorques* Small green-backed sunbird, male with thin red collar, associated with forest fringe canopies in the Udzungwa, Nguru, Uluguru and East and West Usambara.

Rufous-winged sunbird *Nectarinia rufipennis* Discovered in 1981, this pretty medium-sized sunbird has a violet back and head, rufous wing coverts and white belly, and is endemic to forest undergrowth in the Udzungwa Mountains.

Rubeho sunbird *Nectarinia sp* Recently discovered in the forests of the Rubeho Mountains by J Feldsa, this species still awaits formal description.

Moreau's sunbird *Nectarinia moreaui* Small green-backed, red-breasted forest sunbird confined to the East Usambara, Udzungwa and several other ranges in the Eastern Arc.

Loveridge's sunbird *Nectarinia loveridgei* Similar to above but with orange breast, known only from the forests of the Uluguru Mountains.

Pemba sunbird *Nectarinia pembae* The commonest of the Pemba endemics, the male is darker than most sunbirds, with a glossy green head and purplish throat band.

South Pare white-eye *Zosterops winifredae* A controversial species endemic to the South Pare Mountains, this typical white-eye, bright yellow in colour, is unmistakable within its highly limited range.

Pemba white-eye *Zosterops vaughani* Endemic to the Pemba Island, this is another typical white-eye that's unmistakable within its limited range.

Uhehe fiscal *Lanius marwitzi* Similar to the common fiscal, with which some authorities regard it to be conspecific, this pied shrike is distinguished by its white eyebrow, and it replaces the common fiscal in highland areas around Iringa, where it is regularly seen perching on branches and fences.

Uluguru bush shrike *Malaconotus alius* This characteristically pretty bush shrike, distinguished from all allied species by its black cap, is confined to forest canopies in the Uluguru Mountains.

Ashy starling *Cosmopsarus unicolor* A drab but nevertheless distinctive member of this normally colourful group of birds, the ashy starling is associated with semi-arid parts of central Tanzania. It's common in Tarangire National Park, and can be seen at the southern end of its range in Ruaha National Park.

Rufous-tailed weaver *Histurgops ruficauda* Large, sturdily built weaver of the central savannah, whose scaly feathering, pale eyes and habit of bouncing around boisterously in small flocks could lead to it being mistaken for a type of babbler, albeit one with an unusually large bill. It is a common and visible resident of the Serengeti, Ngorongoro and Tarangire National Parks.

Kilombero weaver *Ploceus burnieri* Recently described 'masked' weaver confined to wetlands of the Kilombero Valley.

Usambara weaver *Ploceus nicolli* Striking weaver with olive-brown upper parts, yellow belly and red bib, localised and rare resident of forests in the East Usambara, Uluguru and Udzungwa Mountains.

Kipengere seedeater *Serinus melanochrous* Dull, streaked seedeater with strikingly heavy bill, confined to grassland habitats in the Southern Highlands.

Reptiles

The world's largest reptile, the Nile crocodile (Sw: *mamba*), is common in most large rivers and lakes, except where it has been hunted out. On the Rufiji River, in Selous Game Reserve, we saw some of the largest crocodiles we have seen anywhere in Africa. Crocodile feed on a variety of fish and mammals; the latter they drag into the water, submerge till drowned, then store underwater for a period of time until suitably decomposed.

Hundreds of different snakes and lizards are found in Tanzania. Perhaps fortunately, snakes are generally shy and are very seldom seen. You can expect to see lizards everywhere, even in hotel rooms. Saa Nane Island near Mwanza is a prime spot for reptile enthusiasts, with colourful rock agama in abundance, a healthy population of water monitor (Africa's largest lizard which grows up to about 2m long), and a chance of seeing crocodile. Several species of chameleon are found in Tanzania, but though they are common, even in towns, they are difficult to find unless you know where to look (see box *Chameleons,* pages 46–7).

HIKING

In the 1980s, the only recognised hiking areas in Tanzania were Mount Kilimanjaro and more recently Mount Meru. Travellers who attempted to hike off the beaten track frequently met with suspicion, and if they did not have a permit they risked being arrested. This is no longer the case, and while few travellers explore the hiking possibilities in Tanzania, there are few obstacles preventing them from doing so.

When you hike through remote villages, it would be polite to exchange greetings with the village chairman. You are also less likely to arouse suspicion if you do this. Be discreet with your camera. Never photograph villagers without asking first and don't photograph anything in the vicinity of bridges, railway lines, radio masts or any other government property. It is forbidden to hike in national parks without a ranger or without paying the entrance fee. If you do the latter you could be arrested.

New hiking areas

It is not only Kilimanjaro and Arusha National Park (Mount Meru) that allow walking. In the west of the country, Rubondo Island and Mahale Mountains can only be explored by foot, while the newer and more accessible Udzungwa Mountains National Park boasts a number of good hiking trails. It is possible to hike in the Ngorongoro Conservation Area with the permission of the Conservation Authority in Arusha. Hiking in national parks is relatively expensive as an entrance fee of US$15–25 per 24 hours is charged along with a camping fee of US$20 per night. You may only hike accompanied by an armed ranger, which costs US$10 per day. Outside of the national parks, the most accessible areas for hiking are the Usambara and Pare Mountains in the northeast, Mount Hanang near Babati, the Uluguru Mountains near Morogoro, and the Mbeya Range and Poroto Mountains in the far south.

Maps and equipment

In the national parks you may only walk when accompanied by a guide, so maps are probably not necessary. In the Poroto, Usambara and Mbeya Mountains there are day hiking possibilities that would not require you to have detailed maps or specialist equipment. If you plan to undertake other hikes in these areas or to explore elsewhere, you will need good maps and equipment, and should ideally have some previous experience of wilderness hiking.

Essential equipment includes a compass, a tent, a sleeping bag and mat, warm clothing for areas at altitudes above about 1,500m, a stove and food, water bottles and, if you are hiking in the wet season, waterproof clothing. Unless you have a fair grip on the language already, a KiSwahili dictionary or phrase book will be more than useful.

You should be able to buy 1:50,000 survey maps of the area you plan to visit from the Department of Lands and Surveys in Dar es Salaam. This is a straightforward procedure and maps cost no more than US$2 apiece. You must decide where you want to hike before you leave Dar es Salaam. You will not be able to get hold of maps elsewhere in the country.

Planning Your Trip

TOURIST INFORMATION

The Tanzania Tourist Board (TTB) has improved greatly over recent years, and its offices in London, New York, Stockholm, Milan and Frankfurt may be able to supply you with an information pack and leaflets about the country.

Head office PO Box 2485, Dar es Salaam; tel: 051 111244; fax: 051 116420; email: md@ttb.ud.or.tz

UK Tanzania Tourist Office, 80 Borough High St, London SE1 1LL; tel: 020 7407 0566

US Tanzania Tourist Office, 210 E 42 St, New York, NY 10017; tel: 212 986 7124

WHEN TO VISIT

You can visit Tanzania at any time of year. Each season has different advantages, and unless you have strong reasons to travel in a certain season, I would tend to let the timing of your visit be dictated by your schedule at home rather than seasons in Tanzania. For those with the option, there is much to be said for trying to avoid peak tourist seasons, as the parks and other main tourist attractions will be less crowded, and you can often negotiate camping safaris at prices that wouldn't be offered in season. Broadly speaking, tourism arrivals are highest during the northern hemisphere winter, while the low season runs from the end of the Easter weekend until the end of September, though this is distorted by a surge of tourism over June and July, when the wildebeest migration is on in the Serengeti.

The rainy season between November and April is a good time to visit the Serengeti; it is when the countryside is greenest, and it offers the best birdwatching, with resident species supplemented by a number of Palaearctic and intra-African migrants. The rainy season is hotter than the period May to October, but in most parts of the country this will only be by a matter of a couple of degrees. The seasonal difference in temperature is most noticeable along the humid coast, which can be rather uncomfortable in the hotter months. The wettest months are March and April, when parts of the country may experience storms virtually on a daily basis.

The dry season, in particular March and September, offers the best trekking conditions on Mount Kilimanjaro and Meru. The dry season is the best time for hiking generally, and for travelling in parts of the country with poor roads. Temperatures at the coast tend to be more bearable during the dry season, which is also considerably safer than the wet season in terms of malaria and other mosquito-borne diseases.

RED TAPE

Check well in advance that you have a valid **passport** and that it won't expire within six months of the date on which you intend to *leave* Tanzania. Should your passport be lost or stolen, it will generally be easier to get a replacement if you have a photocopy of the important pages.

If there is any possibility you'll want to drive or hire a vehicle while you're in the country, do organise an **international driving licence**, which you may be asked to produce together with your original license. Any AA office in a country in which you're licensed to drive will do this for a nominal fee. You may sometimes be asked at the border or international airport for an **international health certificate** showing you've had a yellow fever shot.

For security reasons, it's advisable to detail all your important information on one sheet of paper, photocopy it, and distribute a few copies in your luggage, your money-belt, and amongst relatives or friends at home. The sort of things you want to include are your travellers' cheque numbers and refund information, travel insurance policy details and 24-hour emergency contact number, passport number, details of relatives or friends to be contacted in an emergency, bank and credit card details, camera and lens serial numbers, etc.

For up-to-the-minute advice on travel in Tanzania, also check www.fco.gov.uk/knowbeforeyougo.

Visas

Visas are required by most visitors to Tanzania, and will cost between US$30 and US$60, depending on your nationality. At the time of writing, nationals of some Commonwealth countries are exempt from visa requirements, as are nationals of the Scandinavian countries and the Republic of Ireland, but such rulings can change, and it would be advisable for all visitors to check the current situation in advance. Since early 1996, British nationals require a visa to enter Tanzania, at a cost of £39 (US$60). It used to be mandatory to buy your visa in advance at a Tanzanian Embassy or High Commission abroad. It is now possible, however, to obtain a visa on arrival at the airport, and all major international borders. This is a very straightforward procedure, and no photographs or other documentation is required. On the last couple of occasions that we've landed in Dar es Salaam we actually got through the queue for people requiring a visa faster than we would have got through the queue for those who do not require a visa (or who had bought one in advance). The visa is normally valid for three months after arriving in the country, and it evidently allows for multiple entry to Tanzania from neighbouring countries (ie: you can cross to any neighbouring country and back within the three-month period on your original visa).

Embassies abroad

There are Tanzanian embassies or high commissions in Angola, Belgium, Britain, Burundi, Canada, China, CIS, Congo, Egypt, Ethiopia, France, Germany, Guinea, India, Japan, Kenya, Mozambique, Namibia, Netherlands, Nigeria, Rwanda, Sudan, Sweden, Uganda, USA, Zambia and Zimbabwe. Below are addresses of those you are most likely to need.

Belgium 363 Av Louise, 1050 Brussels; tel: 640 6500

Canada 50 Range Rd, Ottawa, Ontario KIN 8JA; tel: 232 1500; fax: 232 5184

Germany Theaterplatz 26, 5300 Bonn; tel: 353219; fax: 358226

Netherlands Prinsessegracht 32, 2514 AP The Hague; tel: 070 365 3800-1; direct line: 070 364 6981; fax: 070 310 6686

Uganda 6 Kagera Rd, PO Box 5750, Kampala; tel: 257357

UK High Commission, 43 Hertford St, London W1Y 8DB; tel: 020 7499 8951; fax: 020 7491 9321

US 2139 R St NW, Washington DC 20008; tel: 202 884 1080/939 6125; fax: 202 797 7408

Zimbabwe Ujamaa House, 23 Baines Av, Harare; tel: 721870; direct line: 251 511063; fax: 724172

Immigration and customs

Once stringently enforced, the official requirements for entering Tanzania are an onward ticket (a ticket out of Tanzania) and sufficient funds (common wisdom is that this is around US$1,000). These days, however, immigration officials seem a lot more relaxed than a few years back; in practice you are most unlikely to be asked about funds provided that you arrive with a return air ticket. Neither ruling is likely to be raised at an overland border. Nevertheless, if you will be arriving with less than US$1,000 on your person, it might be worth carrying a credit card, which will normally be considered to be as good as cash or travellers' cheques.

Assuming that your papers are in order, the only situation in which you are likely to hit problems upon entering Tanzania is with a one-way ticket (though a ticket home from another African country will normally be as good as a return ticket). You obviously won't have an onward ticket if you fly into Tanzania to start extended African travels and only plan to buy a ticket home at a later stage. The smarter you are in appearance, and the more money you have, the less likely it is you'll be refused entry. A credit card will help you to get through, while a visa or visitor's pass for a neighbouring country will back up your claim that you plan to become that country's problem rather than Tanzania's within a reasonable time span. I have met plenty of travellers who flew into Tanzania without an onward ticket, and none had a problem. At the very worst, you may have to buy an air ticket home at the airport before you are allowed to enter the country, in which case you ought to get a ticket for a day as far in advance as the airline and immigration officials will accept, and to check with the airline whether the ticket will be refundable.

GETTING TO TANZANIA
By air

The following airlines fly to Tanzania from Europe or the United Kingdom: Air Tanzania, British Airways, Gulf Air, KLM, Lufthansa and Swissair. African airlines which fly to Tanzania from elsewhere in Africa include Air Botswana, Air Tanzania, Air Zimbabwe, EgyptAir, Ethiopian Airlines, Kenya Airways, Royal Swazi, South African Airways and Zambia Airways.

There are two international airports on the Tanzanian mainland. Dar es Salaam airport is the normal point of entry for international airlines, which is generally convenient for business travellers, but for tourists Dar es Salaam is usually no more than a point of entry, and many people transfer directly on to flights to elsewhere in the country. Kilimanjaro International Airport, which lies midway between Moshi and Arusha, is the more useful point of entry for tourists, and following recent privatisation this airport is likely to catch on with more international airlines. For the meantime, however, the only prominent airlines that run direct flights to Kilimanjaro from outside of Africa are the national carrier Air Tanzania and KLM, which flies there daily from Europe. Quite a number of international flights land at Zanzibar, and many tourists fly into East Africa at Nairobi and transfer from there to Arusha by road or local flight. Once in Tanzania, a good network of domestic flights connects Kilimanjaro, Dar es Salaam and Zanzibar, as well as other less visited towns. You will generally get a better price (and will definitely save yourself a lot of hassle) by booking all your international and domestic flights as a package from home.

Budget travellers looking for flights to East Africa may well find it cheapest to use an airline that takes an indirect route. London is the best place to pick up a cheap ticket; many continental travellers buy their tickets there. It is generally cheaper to fly to Nairobi than to Dar es Salaam, and getting from Nairobi to

Arusha by shuttle bus is cheap, simple and quick. Be warned, however, that a high proportion of travellers are robbed in Nairobi, so it isn't the greatest introduction to the continent. Nairobi is the best place to pick up cheap tickets out of East Africa. For short stays in East Africa, some of the best deals are charter flights to Mombasa (Kenya), a few hours' bus ride from Tanga, or an overnight train ride from Nairobi.

When you fly out of Tanzania, a US$20 airport tax must be paid in hard currency. Many airlines now incorporate this tax into the ticket price, but if you need to pay it directly, do be aware that travellers' cheques are *not* accepted.

Getting a flight that lets you feel as if you've got a good deal is becoming more daunting as local flight specialists fight with global flight consolidators. Put everybody on the internet, and the competition just gets hotter. Below is a list of operators who give good service at a reasonable price. Getting the cheapest price will require several calls and may result in some rather complicated re-routing of the plan.

From the UK

Bridge the World targets the independent traveller. Their offices are at 47 Chalk Farm Rd, Camden Town, London NW1 8AJ; tel: 020 7911 0900; fax: 020 7813 3350; email: sales@bridgetheworld.com; web: www.bridgetheworld.com

Flight Centre is an independent flight provider with over 450 outlets worldwide. In the UK, contact 13 The Broadway, Wimbledon SW19 1PS; tel: 020 8296 8181; fax: 020 8296 0808. They also have offices in Australia, New Zealand, South Africa and Canada.

Quest Travel 4–10 Richmond Rd, Kingston-upon-Thames, Surrey KT2 5HL; tel: 020 8481 4000; fax: 0870 442 3545. An independent agent that has been in operation for a decade offering competitive prices specialising in long-haul flights.

STA Travel 6 Wrights Lane, London W8 6TA; tel: 020 7361 6262l fax: 0207 937 9570; email: enquiries@statravel.co.uk; web: www.statravel.co.uk. STA has 12 branches in London and 25 or so around the country and at different university sites. STA also has several branches and associate organisations around the world.

Trailfinders has several offices in the UK. The main office is at 194 Kensington High St, London W8 7RG; tel: 020 7938 3939; fax: 020 7938 3305; web: www.trailfinders.com. With origins in the discount flight market, Trailfinders now provides a one-stop travel service including visa and passport service, travel clinic and foreign exchange.

Travel Bag provides tailor-made flight schedules and holidays for destinations throughout the world. Its main office is at 12 High St, Alton, Hampshire GU34 1BN; tel: 01420 541441. The London office is at 52 Regent St, London W1R; tel: 0207 287 5535; fax: 0207 287 4522; web: www.travelbag.co.uk

Travel Mood provides flights and tailor-made holidays. 214 Edgware Rd, London W2 1DH; tel: 020 7258 0280; fax: 020 7258 0180; email: sales@travelmood.com; web: www.travelmood.com

WEXAS is more of a club than a travel agent. Membership is around £40 a year, but for frequent fliers the benefits are many. 45–49 Brompton Road, Knightsbridge, London SW3 1DE; tel: 020 7589 3315; fax: 020 7589 8418; email: mship@wexas.com; web: www.wexas.com

From the USA

Airtech Tel: 212 219 7000; email: fly@airtech.com; web: www.airtech.com. Standby seat broker that also deals in consolidator fares, courier flights and a host of other travel-related services.

Around the World Travel provides fares for destinations throughout the world. Email: travel@netfare.net; web: www.netfare.net

Council on International Educational Exchange Email: info@ciee.org; web: www.ciee.org. Although the Council focuses on work exchange trips, it also has a large travel department.

Council Travel sells cheap tickets at over 60 offices around the US. Tel: 1 800 226 8624; web: www.counciltravel.com

STA Travel has several branches around the country. Freephone: 1 800 781 4040; email: go@statravel.com; web: www.sta-travel.com

Worldtek Travel operates a network of rapidly growing travel agencies. Email: info@worldtek.com; web: www.worldtek.com

From Canada

Flight Centre Freephone: 1 888 9675 331; web: www.flightcentre.ca

Travel CUTS is a Canadian student-based travel organisation with 60 offices throughout Canada. Call toll free on 1 866 246 9762 or visit the website at www.travelcuts.com

From Australia

AusTravel Web: www.austravel.com. There are several offices in Europe and the US, as well as Australia.

Flight Centre Freephone: 133 133; web: www.flightcentre.com.au

STA Travel Tel: 1300 733 035; web: www.statravel.com.au

From New Zealand

Flight Centre Tel: 0800 2435 44; web: www.flightcentre.co.nz. A good starting point for cheap air fares.

From South Africa

Flight Centre Shop L3, Eastgate Centre, Bradford Road, Bedfordview, Johannesburg 2008; tel: 11 622 5634; fax: 11 622 5642.

Student Travel Centre is linked to the STA network. The Arcade, 62 Mutual Gardens, Corner of Oxford Road & Tyrwhitt Avenue, Rosebank, Johannesburg 2196; tel: 11 447 5551; fax: 11 447 5775.

Wild Frontiers This excellent Johannesburg-based tour operator has years of experience arranging general and ornithological safaris to East Africa, as well as reasonably priced air tickets. Tel: 11 702 2035; fax: 11 468 1955; email: wildfront@icon.co.za; web: www.wildfrontiers.com

Tour operators
UK

Aardvark Safaris RBL House, Ordnance Rd, Tidworth, Hants SP9 7QD; tel: 01980 849160; fax: 01980 849161; email: mail@aardvarksafaris.com; web: www.aardvarksafaris.com. Tailored trips to southern and northern Tanzania, including walking safaris.

Abercrombie and Kent Sloane Square House, Holbein Place, London SW1W 8NS; tel: 0845 0700610; fax: 0845 0700607; web: www.abercrombiekent.co.uk. Tailored safaris.

Africa-in-Focus (UK) Northay, Blagdon Hill, Taunton, Somerset TA3 7SF; tel: 01823 421303; fax: 01823 421756; email: africainfocus@yahoo.co.uk; web: www.africa-in-focus.com. Comfortable mobile camping safaris targeting wildlife enthusiasts, photographers and families.

Africa Select Earsdon Hill, Morpeth, Northumberland NE61 3ES; tel: 01670 787646; fax: 01670 787719; email: pg@africaselect.com; web: www.africaselect.com. Tailor-made itineraries, including tours to safari and mountain destinations.

Africa Travel Centre 21 Leigh St, London WC1H 9EW; tel: 020 7387 1211; fax: 020 7383 7512.

Alpha Travel 98 Bessborough Rd, Harrow, Middx HA1 3DT; tel: 020 8423 0220; fax: 020 8423 0201; web: www.arpsafaris.com. Arranges tours with Ranger Safaris in Tanzania.

BAOBAB – Alternative Roots to Travel Old Fallings Hall, Old Fallings Lane, Wolverhampton WV6 0AE; tel: 01902 558316; fax: 01902 558317; email: info@baobabtravel.com; web: www.baobabtravel.com. An ethical tour operator specialising in eco-tourism in Africa.

Cazenove and Loyd Safaris 9 Imperial Studios, 3–11 Imperial Rd, London SW6 2AG; tel: 020 7384 2332; fax: 020 7384 2399; email: safaris@caz-loyd.com; web: www.caz-loyd.com

Crusader Travel 57 Church St, Twickenham, Middx TW1 3NR; tel: 020 8892 7606; fax: 020 8744 0574; email: info@crusader-travel.com

Explore Worldwide 1 Frederick St, Aldershot, Hants GU11 1LQ; tel: 01252 760000; fax: 01252 760001; email: info@exploreworldwide.com; web: www.exploreworldwide.com

Footloose 3 Springs Pavement, Ilkley, West Yorks LS29 8HD; tel: 01943 604030; fax: 01943 604070; email: info@footlooseadventure.co.uk; web: www.footlooseadventures.co.uk. Tailor-made tours, safaris and treks throughout Tanzania, and including Zanzibar.

Gane and Marshall 98 Crescent Rd, New Barnet, Herts EN4 9RJ; tel: 020 8441 9592; fax: 020 8441 7376; email: holidays@ganeandmarshall.co.uk; web: www.ganeandmarshall.co.uk

Hartley's Safaris The Old Chapel, Chapel Lane, Hackthorn, Lincolnshire LN2 3PN; tel: 01673 861600; fax: 01673 861666; email: info@hartleys-safaris.co.uk; web: www.hartleys-safaris.co.uk. Safaris to East and southern Africa, as well as diving and island holidays in the region.

High Places Globe Centre, Penistone Rd, Sheffield S6 3AE; tel: 0114 275 7500; fax: 0114 275 3870; email: treks@highplaces.co.uk; web: www.highplaces.co.uk

Journeys by Design 17 Sussex Sq, Brighton BN2 5AA; tel: 01273 623 790; web: www.journeysbydesign.co.uk

Okavango Tours and Safaris Marlborough House, 298 Regents Park Rd, London N3 2TJ; tel: 020 8343 3283; fax: 020 8343 3287; email: info@okavango.com; web: www.okavango.com. Individually tailored holidays to East and southern Africa.

Phoenix Expeditions College Farm, Far St, Wyneswold, Leicester LE12 6TZ; tel: 01509 881818; fax: 01509 881822; email: info@phoenixexpeditions.co.uk; web: www.phoenixexpeditions.co.uk

Rainbow Tours 64 Essex Rd, London N1 8LR; tel: 020 7226 1004; email: info@rainbowtours.co.uk; web: www.rainbowtours.co.uk

Safari Drive Wessex House, 127 High St, Hungerford, Berks RG17 0DL; tel: 01488 681611; fax: 01488 685055; email: Safari_Drive@compuserve.com; web: www.safaridrive.com. Self-drive and tailor-made safaris.

Sherpa Expeditions 131A Heston Rd, Hounslow, Middx TW5 0RF; tel: 020 8577 2717; email: sales@sherpaexpeditions.com; web: www.sherpaexpeditions.com

Steppes Africa 51 Castle St, Cirencester, Glos GL7 1QD; tel: 01285 650011; fax: 01285 885888; email: safaris@steppesafrica.co.uk; web: www.steppesafrica.co.uk

Sunvil Africa Sunvil House, Upper Sq, Isleworth, Middx TW7 7BJ; tel: 020 8232 9777; email: africa@sunvil.co.uk; web: www.sunvil.co.uk

Tanzania Odyssey 2nd Floor, Eden House, 59 Fulham High St, London SW6 3JJ; tel: 020 7471 8780; email: worldarc@compuserve.com; web: www.tanzaniaodyssey.com. Tailor-made tours throughout Tanzania.

Tribes Travel 12 The Business Centre, Earl Soham, Woodbridge, Suffolk IP13 7SA; tel: 01728 685971; email: bradtanz@tribes.co.uk; web: www.tribes.co.uk

Tropical Trekking PO Box 278, Watford, Herts WD19 4WH; tel: 01923 255462; email: tropicaltrekking@aol.com

Wildlife Worldwide Chameleon House, 162 Selsdon Rd, South Croydon, Surrey CR2 6PJ; tel: 020 8667 9158; email: sales@wildlifeworldwide.com; web: www.wildlifeworldwide.com

World Odyssey 1A St Martin's House, St Martin's Gate, Worcester WR1 2DT; tel: 01905 731373; fax: 01905 726872; email: info@world-odyssey.com; web: www.world-odyssey.com. Tailor-made safaris.

US

Abercrombie and Kent Tel: 800 323 7308; web: www.abercrombiekent.com. A leader in luxury adventure travel.

Adventure Center Tel: 800 228 8747. Provides safaris, treks, expeditions and active vacations worldwide, with a focus on value. Represents Explore Worldwide (see opposite).

Baobab Safari Company Tel: 1 800 835 3692; web: www.baobabsafaris.com

Big Five Tours and Expeditions Tel: 800 244 3483; web: www.bigfive.com. Family-owned safari company.

Eco-resorts Tel: 1 866 326 7376; web: www.eco-resorts.com. Offers a variety of safaris. A percentage of the booking fee is used to support local communities and the environment.

Ker and Downey USA Tel: 800 423 4236; web: www.kerdowney.com.

Micato Safaris Tel: 800 642 2861; web: www.micato.com. Family company, based in Nairobi but with an office in New York.

Naipenda Safaris PO Box 587, Hunt, Texas TX 78024-0587; tel: 1 830 238 4066; email: jo@naipendasafaris; web: www.naipendasafaris.com

Next Adventure Tel: 1 800 562 7298; web: www.nextadventure.com. California-based company with strong ties to Tanzania.

Park East Tel: 800 223 6078; web: www.parkeast.com.

Thomson Safaris Tel: 800 235 0289; web: www.thomsonsafaris.com. Specialising in Tanzania for 20 years, Thomson operates innovative safaris throughout the country, including walking tours and adventure camps.

Remote River Expeditions 5075 West Montcrieff Pl, Denver, CO 80212; tel: 1 800 558 1083; email: gary@remoterivers.com; web: www.remoterivers.com

United Touring Company Tel: 1 800 223 6486. One of the oldest safari companies in Africa.

Safari specialists in Tanzania are found under their different regions in *Part Two, The Guide*.

Overland

All of the established overland routes between Europe and East Africa are difficult at present, though depending on the current political situation (and right now the Eritrea–Ethiopia border area is a problem), it may be possible to get to East Africa via Egypt, northern Sudan, Eritrea and Ethiopia. I've probably met four or five people who've used this route in the last three years, but it's not easy to predict the local political situation in advance, and many people get stuck in the Sudan and either have to turn back or else fly from Khartoum to Ethiopia or Kenya, an expensive option. As for the so-called 'Nile Route', a variant on the above passing through southern Sudan to Uganda, the south of Sudan has been closed to tourists for nigh on a decade.

A final route via the Sahara and West Africa used to be favoured by several overland truck companies. Unfortunately, it has been impassable since the mid-1990s, at first due to banditry, then after a major bridge collapsed in what was then Zaire, and at the time of writing due to the civil war in what is currently the Democratic Republic of the Congo. This route has always been tough going for independent travellers, whether or not they have a vehicle, and in the present climate of instability I would advise anybody who is considering travelling this way to think seriously about going with an overland truck company. However you plan to travel, it would be advisable to contact a couple of overland truck companies for current advice about safety.

With the end of apartheid, the Cape to Nairobi route has become the backpackers' standard in Africa. Some people start this trip in East Africa, others start in South Africa – there's not a lot in it. The advantage of starting in the south is that you can adapt to African conditions in the more organised environment of South Africa and Zimbabwe before you hit the relative chaos of East Africa. The disadvantage is that you will have to put up with the most trying travel conditions of the trip towards the end, after the novelty of being in Africa has worn off. These days Johannesburg is almost as good as Nairobi for cheap air tickets, so that is not a factor. Either way, my regional guide *East and Southern Africa: The Backpackers Manual*, also published by Bradt, is the only book to cover the full range of backpacking possibilities between Ethiopia and South Africa in one dedicated volume.

There is a proliferation of overland truck companies which run regular trips between southern Africa (normally Johannesburg or Harare) and East Africa. A few of these are:

Acacia Expeditions Ltd, Lower Ground Floor, 23A Craven Terrace, London W2 3QH; tel: 020 7706 4700; fax: 020 7706 4686

Dragoman Camp Green, Kenton Rd, Debenham, Suffolk IP14 6LA; tel: 01728 861133; fax: 01728 861127

Exodus 9 Weir Rd, London SW12 0LT; tel: 020 8675 5550; fax: 020 8673 0779

Kumuku 40 Earls Court Rd, Kensington, London S8 6EJ; tel: 020 7937 8855; fax: 020 7937 6664; web: www.kumuku.com

Tana Travel 2 Ely St, Stratford-upon-Avon, Warwicks CV37 6LW; tel: 01789 414200; fax: 01789 414420

The advantages of travelling on an overland truck are that it will visit remote areas that you would be unlikely to reach otherwise, and that you will see far more than you would by travelling independently for the same period of time. The disadvantages are that you will be in the company of the same 10 to 20 other people for the duration of the trip, and that the truck will cut you off from everyday African life. Most of the people I've spoken to say that their main reason for travelling on a truck is that it seems to be safer than travelling alone. It's worth noting, therefore, that this is by-and-large a safe and well-travelled region (something that cannot be said for the overland truck route between Europe and Nairobi via West Africa) and that you will meet plenty of other single travellers. If you feel you would prefer to travel independently, don't let fear swing you in the opposite direction.

Border crossings

Tanzania borders eight countries. A brief outline of frequently used border crossings follows:

To/from Kenya

The most popular crossing is between Nairobi and Arusha via the Namanga border post, and several shuttle bus services run along this route daily in both directions. Reliable options include the Riverside, Devanu and Pallson's Shuttles, which connect Nairobi to Arusha and Moshi, departing in either direction at around 07.30 and 13.30 daily. The trip from Nairobi to Arusha lasts about four hours, and you will be dropped at the hotel of your choice on arrival. A ticket costs around US$25 one-way for non-residents and Tsh10,000 for residents. In practice, you should be allowed to pay the resident rate if you ask – we've used this service on several occasions recently and never had a problem. You can book on to the shuttle at most tour operators in any of these towns, or ring 057 4311 in Arusha or 02 222002 in Nairobi.

You can also do the trip between Nairobi and Arusha in stages, by catching a minibus between Nairobi and Namanga (these leave Nairobi from Ronald Ngala Road), crossing the border on foot, and then catching a shared taxi to Arusha. Expect this to take around six hours and cost US$7 total in fares.

Provided your papers are in order, Namanga is a very straightforward border crossing. There is a bank where you can change money during normal banking hours. At other times, you'll have to change money with private individuals – don't change more than you need, as there are several con artists about.

An increasingly popular route between Kenya and Tanzania is from Mombasa to Tanga (three to four hours following recent improvements on the road) or Dar es Salaam. Again, this is straightforward enough, and a couple of buses do the run every day. If you arrive at Tanga after about 13.00, you are strongly advised against taking the bus all the way to Dar es Salaam, as it arrives after dark and you run a high risk of being mugged.

Another route is between Kisumu and Mwanza on Lake Victoria. There are several buses daily along this route, leaving in the early morning and taking around 12 hours.

Several airlines run daily flights between Nairobi and Kilimanjaro International Airport.

To/from Uganda

The best way to cross from Uganda to Tanzania depends on which part of Tanzania you want to visit. The weekly ferry service between Port Bell and Mwanza was suspended after the MV *Bukoba* sank in 1996, but it resumed in early 1999 (see page 405). If that doesn't fit in with your timing, the alternative is to travel by road from Masaka to Bukoba, by ferry from Bukoba to Mwanza and then by train to Dar es Salaam on the coast or Kigoma on Lake Tanganyika. If you are in Uganda and want to get to Arusha or Moshi, it will be quicker, cheaper and more comfortable to travel via Kenya.

The direct route between Masaka and Bukoba passes through the Mutukula border post. If all goes well, you can get from Masaka to Mutukula in a couple of hours. Regular minibuses go as far as Kyotera, where you won't have to wait long to find a pick-up truck going through to Mutukula. If you arrive at Mutukula in the late afternoon and don't think you are going to get as far as Bukoba, you may want to stay at the basic guesthouse on the Ugandan side of the border and cross into Tanzania the following morning. The road between Mutukula and Bukoba is fairly rough, but a couple of 4WD vehicles travel up and down it every day with the express purpose of transporting passengers. These take ages to fill up, so it's also worth seeing if you can get a lift with a truck. If you can get a lift as far as Kyaka, there's more transport to Bukoba from there. For details of ferries between Bukoba and Mwanza, see page 405.

Travellers who are heading between Uganda and Arusha via Kenya can travel between Kampala and Nairobi in a day, using any of a number of bus companies. The Akamba bus is recommended, as is the Lafiq bus. The latter connects with the same company's service from Nairobi to Dar es Salaam via Arusha and Moshi. If you are just passing through Nairobi, remember that it is East Africa's crime capital, and that wandering around with all of your luggage on your back is practically asking to be mugged.

To/from Rwanda
The only route between Kigali and Mwanza is by road, through the Rusumu border post. Plenty of minibuses zoom along the road between Kigali, the capital of Rwanda, and the border. From there, you'll need to catch a bus to Mwanza over a few days. For further details see the section *To Rwanda* on pages 419–20.

To/from Burundi
The straightforward option is the Lake Tanganyika ferry (see pages 462–3). The trip can also be done in steps. Minibuses go from Bujumbura to the immigration office at Nyanza Lac and on to the border. At Kagunga, a 20-minute walk past the border, lake-taxis run to Gombe Stream and Kalalangabo, 3km from Kigoma. Burundi is another country with a troubled recent history, and if the Lake Tanganyika ferry isn't running there – as has been the case for the past few years – I would tend to assume it's for a good reason.

To/from the Congo
Cargo boats between Kigoma and Kalemie might sometimes carry passengers, but don't rely on this. Most people used to go via Burundi, but this whole part of central Africa is too dangerous for travel to be recommended.

To/from Zambia
Zambia, the main gateway between East and southern Africa, can be reached by boat, rail or road. Tazara trains run twice weekly from Dar es Salaam to Kapiri Mposhi, and are met by a bus to Lusaka (see box *The Tazara Railway* page 484). From western Tanzania, the easiest way to get to Zambia is on the Lake Tanganyika ferry (see box *The Lake Tanganyika Ferry* pages 462–3).

To/from Malawi
The turn-off to the Malawi border at Songo is 5km from Kyela, on the Mbeya road. At the time of writing all buses between Mbeya and Kyela divert to the border to avoid road works. Once they resume their normal route, you will have to take a bicycle taxi to the border or wait for a lift. In Malawi, a bus to Karonga arrives at the border at 19.00 and leaves at 06.00, but provided that you arrive at the border before late afternoon, you should have no difficulty picking up a ride on a pick-up truck to Karonga. There is now a very good guesthouse on the Tanzanian side of the border if you arrive there late in the day.

To/from Mozambique
The only viable border crossing from Tanzania to Mozambique is at Kilamba, which lies on the Rovuma River between Mtwara and Palma. This used to be a difficult route, but there is now a regular motorboat across the river at high tide, and a fair amount of transport on to Palma. For further details see the box *The Rovuma Ferry and Northern Mozambique* on pages 596–7.

To travel between the countries by dhow, take a bus from Mtwara to the nearby fishing village of Msimbati, where you can complete immigration formalities and, depending on the tides and weather, negotiate for space on a dhow heading south (expect to pay around US$6–7 per person). The trip shouldn't take more than ten hours, depending on the weather and exactly where the boat is headed. If you're lucky, you'll be dropped right at Palma or Mocimboa do Praia, but you may also be dropped on a beach somewhere and have to walk to Palma. If you are heading in the opposite direction, things are much simpler, since you can pick up a dhow at either Palma or Mocimboa do Praia and you'll almost certainly be dropped at Msimbati.

PACKING

There are two simple rules to bear in mind when you decide what to take with you to Tanzania, particularly for those using public transport. Rule one is to bring with you *everything* that you could possibly need and that mightn't be readily available when you need it. Rule two is to carry as little as possible. Somewhat contradictory rules, you might think, and you'd be right – so the key is finding the right balance, something that probably depends on personal experience as much as anything. Worth stressing is that most genuine necessities are surprisingly easy to get hold of in the main centres in Tanzania, and that most of the ingenious gadgets you can buy in camping shops are unlikely to amount to much more than deadweight on the road. If it came to it, you could easily travel in Tanzania with little more than a change of clothes, a few basic toiletries and a medical kit.

Carrying your luggage

Visitors who are unlikely to be carrying their luggage for any significant distance will probably want to pack most of it in a conventional suitcase. Make sure it is tough and durable, and that it seals well, so that its contents will survive bumpy drives to the game reserves. A lock is a good idea, not only for flights, but for when you leave your case in a hotel room – in our experience, any theft from upmarket hotels in Africa is likely to be casual, and a locked suitcase is unlikely to be tampered with. A daypack will be useful when on safari, and you should be able to pack your luggage in such a manner than any breakable goods can be carried separately in the body of the vehicle and on your lap when necessary – anything like a Walkman or camera will suffer heavily from vibrations on rutted roads.

If you are likely to use public transport, then a backpack is the most practical way to carry your luggage. An internal frame is more flexible than an external one. Once again, ensure your pack is durable, that the seams and zips are properly sewn, and that it has several pockets. If you intend doing a lot of hiking, you definitely want a backpack designed for this purpose. On the other hand, if you'll be staying at places where it might be a good idea to shake off the sometimes negative image attached to backpackers, then there would be obvious advantages in using a suitcase that converts into a backpack.

Before I started travelling with my wife Ariadne and her heavy camera equipment, my preference over either of the above was for a robust 35l daypack. The advantages of keeping luggage as light and compact as possible are manifold. For starters, you can rest it on your lap on bus trips, avoiding complications such as extra charges for luggage, arguments about where your bag should be stored, and the slight but real risk of theft if your luggage ends up on the roof. A compact bag also makes for greater mobility, whether you're hiking or looking for a hotel in town. The sacrifice? Leave behind camping equipment and a sleeping bag. Do this, and it's quite possible to fit everything you truly need into a 35l daypack, and possibly even a few luxuries – I refuse to travel without binoculars, a bird field guide and at least five novels, and am still able to keep my weight down to around 8kg. Frankly, it puzzles me what the many backpackers who wander around with an enormous pack and absolutely no camping equipment actually carry around with them!

If your luggage won't squeeze into a daypack, a sensible compromise is to carry a large daypack in your rucksack. That way, you can carry a tent and other camping equipment when you need it, but at other times reduce your luggage to fit into a daypack and leave what you're not using in storage.

Travellers carrying a lot of valuable items should look for a pack that can easily be padlocked. A locked bag can, of course, be slashed open, but in Tanzania you are still most likely to encounter casual theft of the sort to which a lock would be real deterrent.

Camping equipment

If you go on a budget safari or do an organised Kilimanjaro climb, camping equipment will be provided by the company you travel with. Taken together with the limited opportunities for camping outside of the safari circuit, this means that for most travellers a tent and sleeping bag will be dead weight in Tanzania. Nevertheless, it is advisable to carry a tent if you plan to travel or hike in remote areas.

If you decide to carry camping equipment, the key is to look for the lightest available gear. It is now possible to buy a lightweight tent weighing little more than 2kg, but make sure that the one you buy is mosquito-proof. Other essentials for camping include a sleeping bag and a roll-mat, which will serve as both insulation and padding. You might want to carry a stove for occasions when no firewood is available, as is the case in many montane national parks where the collection of firewood is forbidden, or for cooking in a tropical storm. If you do carry a stove, it's worth knowing that Camping Gaz cylinders are not readily available in Tanzania. A box of firelighter blocks will get a fire going in the most unpromising conditions. It would also be advisable to carry a pot, plate, cup and cutlery.

Clothes

Assuming that you have the space, you ought to carry at least one change of shirt and underwear for every day you will spend on safari. Organising laundry along the way is a pain in the neck, and the dusty conditions will practically enforce a daily change of clothes. It's a good idea to keep separate one or two shirts for evening use only.

Otherwise, and especially if you are travelling with everything on your back, try to keep your clothes to a minimum, bearing in mind that you can easily and cheaply replace worn items in markets. In my opinion, the minimum you need is one or possibly two pairs of trousers and/or skirts, one pair of shorts, three shirts or T-shirts, one light sweater, maybe a light waterproof wind-breaker during the rainy season, enough socks and underwear to last five to seven days, one solid pair of shoes or boots for walking, and one pair of sandals, thongs or other light shoes.

When you select your clothes, remember that jeans are heavy to carry, hot to wear, and slow to dry. Far better to bring light cotton trousers and, if you intend spending a while in montane regions, tracksuit bottoms, which will provide extra cover on chilly nights. Skirts are best made of a light natural fabric such as cotton. T-shirts are lighter and less bulky than proper shirts, though the top pocket of a shirt (particularly if it buttons up) is a good place to carry spending money in markets and bus stations, since it's easier to keep an eye on than trouser pockets. One sweater or sweatshirt will be adequate in most parts of the country, though you will need serious Alpine gear for Kilimanjaro and to a lesser degree Mount Meru.

Socks and underwear *must* be made from natural fabrics. Bear in mind that re-using sweaty undergarments will encourage fungal infections such as athlete's foot, as well as prickly heat in the groin region. Socks and underpants are light and compact enough that it's worth bringing a week's supply. As for footwear, genuine hiking boots are worth considering only if you're a serious off-road hiker, since they are very heavy whether on your feet or in your pack. A good pair of walking shoes, preferably made of leather and with good ankle support, is a good compromise. It's also useful to carry sandals, thongs or other light shoes.

Another factor in deciding what clothes to bring are the sensibilities of Tanzania's large Muslim population, which finds it offensive for a woman to expose her knees or shoulders. It is difficult to make hard and fast rules about what to wear, but some generalisations may help. Shorts are fine at most beach resorts, in game reserves, and possibly in Dar es Salaam, Zanzibar Town or Arusha where people are used to tourists. Elsewhere, I wouldn't wear shorts. For women, trousers are frowned upon in some quarters but my impression is that they are viewed to be unconventional rather than offensive. The ideal thing to wear is a skirt that covers your knees. A shoulderless T-shirt that exposes your bra – or worse – is unlikely to go down well (you laugh: I met someone dressed like this who couldn't figure out why she was hissed at wherever she went in Tanzania).

Men, too, should be conscious of what they wear. Shorts seem to be acceptable, but few Tanzanian men wear them and it is considered more respectable to wear trousers. Walking around in a public place without a shirt is totally unacceptable.

Many Tanzanians think it is insulting for Westerners to wear scruffy or dirty clothes. Quite accurately, they feel you wouldn't dress like that at home. It is difficult to explain that at home you also wouldn't spend three successive days in crowded buses on dusty roads with a limited amount of clothing crumpled up in a backpack. If you are travelling rough, you are bound to look a mess at times, but it is worth trying to look as spruce as possible.

Other useful items

Most backpackers, even those with no intention of camping, carry a **sleeping bag**. A lightweight sleeping bag will be more than adequate in most parts of Tanzania, better still in this climate would be to carry a sheet sleeping bag, something you can easily make yourself. The one time when you will definitely need an all-weather sleeping bag is on Mount Meru or Kilimanjaro. You might meet travellers who, when they stay in local lodgings, habitually place their own sleeping bag on top of the bedding provided. Nutters, in my opinion, and I'd imagine that a sleeping bag placed on a flea-ridden bed would be unlikely to provide significant protection, rather more likely to become flea-infested itself.

I wouldn't leave home without **binoculars**, which some might say makes *me* the nutter. Seriously though, if you're interested in natural history, it's difficult to imagine anything that will give you such value-for-weight entertainment as a pair of light compact binoculars, which these days needn't be much heavier or bulkier than a pack of cards. Binoculars are essential if you want to get a good look at birds (Africa boasts a remarkably colourful avifauna even if you've no desire to put a name to everything that flaps) or to watch distant mammals in game reserves. For most purposes, 7x21 compact binoculars will be fine, though some might prefer 7x35 traditional binoculars for their larger field of vision. Serious birdwatchers will find a 10x magnification more useful.

Some travellers like to carry their own **padlock**. This would be useful if you have a pack that is lockable, and in remote parts of the country it might be necessary for rooms where no lock is provided. If you are uneasy about security in a particular guesthouse, you may like to use your own lock instead of or in addition to the one provided. Although combination locks are reputedly easier to pick than

PHOTOGRAPHIC TIPS
Ariadne Van Zandbergen
Equipment

Although with some thought and an eye for composition you can take reasonable photos with a 'point and shoot' camera, you need an SLR camera with one or more lenses if you are at all serious about photography. If you carry only one lens in Tanzania, a 28–70mm or similar zoom should be ideal for anything but wildlife photography, whereas a 80–200mm or 70–300mm or similar will be better for candid shots and wildlife. Carrying both will allow you to play more with composition. If you're serious about wildlife photography a higher magnification than 300 is useful but expensive and bulky. For a small loss of quality, tele-converters are a cheap and compact way to increase magnification: a 300 lens with a 1.4x converter becomes 420mm, and with a 2x it becomes 600mm. Note that tele-converters reduce the speed of your lens by 1.4 and 2 stops respectively. For wildlife photography from a safari vehicle, a solid beanbag, which you can make yourself very cheaply, will be necessary to avoid blurred images and is more useful than a tripod.

Film

Print film is the preference of most casual photographers, slide film of professionals and some dedicated amateurs. Slide film is more expensive than print film, but this is broadly compensated for by cheaper development costs. Most photographers working outdoors in Africa favour Fujichrome slide film, in particular Sensia 100, Provia 100 (the professional equivalent to Sensia) or Velvia 50. Slow films (ie: those with a low ASA [ISO] rating) produce less grainy and sharper images than fast films, but can be tricky without a tripod or beanbag in low light. Velvia 50 is extremely fine-grained and shows stunning colour saturation; it is the film I normally use in soft, even light or overcast weather. Sensia or Provia may be preferable in low light, since 100 ASA allows you to work at a faster shutter speed than 50 ASA. Because 100 ASA is more tolerant of contrast, it is also preferable in harsh light. For extreme situations it is always good to carry some faster films. Provia 400 ASA is a relatively fine-grained fast film.

For print photography, a combination of 100 or 200 ASA film should be ideal. For the best results it is advisable to stick to recognised brands. Fujicolor produces excellent print films, with the Superia 100 and 200 recommended.

Some basics

The automatic programmes provided with many cameras are limited in the sense that the camera cannot think, but only make calculations. A better investment than any amount of electronic wizardry would be to read a photographic manual for beginners and get to grips with such basics as the relationship between aperture and shutter speed.

Beginners should also note photographs taken at a low shutter speed are often affected by camera shake, resulting in a fuzzy image. For hand-held photographs of static subjects using a low magnification lens such as 28–70mm, select a shutter speed of at least 1/60th of a second. When hand-holding lenses of higher magnification, the rule of thumb is that the shutter speed should be at least the inverse of the highest magnification of the lens (for instance, a speed of 1/300 or faster on a 70–300mm lens). You can use far lower shutter speeds with a tripod or beanbag.

Most modern cameras include a built-in light meter, and allow a choice of three different types of metering, ie: matrix, centre-weighted, or spot metering. You will need to understand how these different systems work to make proper use of them. Built-in light meters are reliable in most circumstances, but in uneven light, or where there is a lot of sky, you may want to take your metering selectively, for instance by taking a spot reading on the main subject. The meter will tend to under- or overexpose when pointed at an almost white or black subject. This can be countered by taking a reading against an 18% grey card, or a substitute such as grass or light grey rocks – basically anything that isn't almost black, almost white or highly reflective.

Dust and heat
Dust and heat are often a problem in Africa. Keep your equipment in a sealed bag, stow films in an airtight container (such as a small cooler bag), leave used films in your hotel room, and avoid changing film in dusty conditions. On rough roads, I always carry my camera equipment on my lap to protect against vibration and bumps. Never stow camera equipment or film in a car boot (it will bake), or let it stand in direct sunlight.

Light
The light in Africa is much harsher than in Europe or North America, for which reason the most striking outdoor photographs are often taken during the hour or two of 'golden light' after dawn and before sunset. Shooting in low light may enforce the use of very low shutter speeds, in which case a beanbag (from a vehicle) or tripod (on foot) or monopod (lighter but less steady than a tripod) will be required to avoid camera shake. Be alert to the long shadows cast by a low sun; these show up more on photographs than to the naked eye.

With careful handling, side lighting and back lighting can produce stunning effects, especially in soft light and at sunrise or sunset. Generally, however, it is best to shoot with the sun behind you. Because of this, most buildings and landscapes are essentially a 'morning shot' or 'afternoon shot', depending on the direction in which they face. When you spend a couple of nights in one place, you'll improve your results by planning the best time to take pictures of static subjects (a compass can come in handy).

When photographing people or animals in the harsh midday sun, images taken in light but even shade are likely to look nicer than those taken in direct sunlight or patchy shade, since the latter conditions create too much contrast. Fill-in flash is almost essential if you want to capture facial detail of dark-skinned people in harsh or contrasting light.

Protocol
Except in general street or market scenes, it is unacceptable to photograph people without permission. Expect some people to refuse or to ask for a donation. Don't try to sneak photographs as you might get yourself into trouble, especially where the Maasai are concerned. Even the most willing subject will often pose stiffly when a camera is pointed at them; relax them by making a joke, and take a few shots in quick succession to improve the odds of capturing a natural pose.

conventional padlocks, I think you'd be safer with a combination lock in Tanzania, because potential thieves will have far more experience of breaking past locks with keys.

Your **toilet bag** should at the very minimum include soap (secured in a plastic bag or soap holder unless you enjoy a soapy toothbrush!), shampoo, toothbrush and toothpaste. This sort of stuff is easy to replace as you go along, so there's no need to bring family-sized packs. Boys will probably want a **razor**. Girls should carry at least enough **tampons** and/or **sanitary pads** to see them through at least one heavy period, since these items may not always be immediately available. Nobody should forget to bring a **towel**, or to keep handy a roll of **loo paper** which, although widely available at shops and kiosks, cannot always be relied upon to be present where it's most urgently needed.

Other essentials include a **torch**, a **penknife** and a compact **alarm clock** for those early morning starts. If you're interested in what's happening in the world, you might also think about carrying a **short-wave radio**. Some travellers carry **games** – most commonly a pack of cards, less often chess or draughts or travel scrabble. A light plastic **orange-squeezing device** gives you fresh orange juice as an alternative to fizzy drinks and water.

You should carry a small **medical kit**, the contents of which are discussed in the chapter on health, as are **mosquito nets**. If you wear **contact lenses**, bring all the fluids you need, since they are not available in Tanzania. You might also want to bring a pair of glasses to wear on long bus rides, and on safari – many lens wearers suffer badly in dusty conditions. In general, since many people find the intense sun and dry climate irritates their eyes, you might consider reverting to glasses. For those who wear **glasses**, it's worth bringing a spare pair, though in an emergency a new pair can be made up cheaply (around US$10) and quickly in most Tanzanian towns, provided that you have your prescription available.

MONEY
Organising your finances
There are three ways of carrying money: hard currency cash, travellers' cheques, or a credit card. My advice is to bring at least as much as you think you'll need in the combination of cash and travellers' cheques, but if possible to also carry a credit card to draw on in an emergency. I would strongly urge any but the most denominationally chauvinistic of backpackers to bring their cash and travellers' cheques in the form of US dollars, and to learn to think and budget in this currency.

From the point of view of security, it's advisable to bring the bulk of your money in the form of travellers' cheques, which can be refunded if they are lost or stolen. Best to use a widely recognised type of travellers' cheque such as American Express or Thomas Cook, and to keep your proof of purchase discrete from the cheques, as well as noting which cheques you have used, in order to facilitate a swift refund should you require one. Buy your travellers' cheques in a healthy mix of denominations, since you may sometimes need to change a small sum only, for instance when you're about to cross into another country. On the other hand, you don't want an impossibly thick wad of cheques. For a trip to one country, I'd take five US$20 cheques and the remainder of my money in US$100 cheques. Whatever your bank at home might say, currency regulations and other complications make it practically impossible to break down a large denomination travellers' cheque into smaller ones in most African countries, so don't bring travellers' cheques in denominations larger than US$100.

In addition to travellers' cheques, you should definitely bring a proportion of your money in hard currency cash, say around US$200 to US$300, since you are bound to hit situations where travellers' cheques won't be accepted, and cash gets a better exchange rate than travellers' cheques, especially large denomination bills. This would not be much consolation were all your money to be stolen, so I'd strongly advise against bringing cash only, but would suggest that you save what cash you do bring for situations where it will buy you a real advantage. Note that US dollar bills printed before 1992, particularly larger denominations such as US$100 and US$50, may be refused by banks and foreign exchange (forex) bureaux.

Carry your hard currency and travellers' cheques as well as your passport and other important documentation in a money belt – one that can be hidden beneath your clothing rather than the sort of fashionable externally worn codpiece which in some circumstances will serve as a beacon rather than protection. Your money belt should be made of cotton or another natural fabric, and everything inside the belt should be wrapped in plastic to protect it against sweat.

Credit cards are widely accepted in at upmarket tourist-oriented shops and facilities in Arusha, Dar es Salaam and Zanzibar, as well as most game lodges and upper range hotels. They can also be used to draw cash directly from an ATM in Dar es Salaam, Arusha and Mwanza. Otherwise, they are of limited use. I've often bumped into panicked travellers who strayed too far from the beaten track with only a credit card to support them. I would tend to carry a credit card as a fallback more than anything, and to be conservative in my assumptions about where I'll be able to draw money against it. No matter how long you are travelling, do make sure that you are set up in such a way that you won't need to have money transferred or drafted across to Tanzania.

Budget planning

Any budget for a holiday in a country such as Tanzania will depend so greatly on how and where you travel that is almost impossible to give sensible advice in a general travel guide. At one end of the spectrum, a fly-around safari staying at the very best lodges might set you back US$500 per person per day, while at the other end a budget traveller could probably get by on US$10 per day in some parts of southern Tanzania.

As a rule, readers who are travelling at the middle to upper end of the price range will have pre-booked most of their trip, which means that they will have a good idea of what the holiday will cost them before they set foot in Tanzania. Pre-booked packages do vary in terms of what is included in the price, and you are advised to check the exact conditions in advance. Generally, however, the price quoted will cover everything but drinks, tips and perhaps some meals (safari lodge accommodation is normally on a full-board basis, but city hotels are typically bed and breakfast only, though some packages may include other meals). Another variable, assuming that you are visiting Zanzibar, is whether the package does or doesn't include the cost of a spice tour and other day trips. To give some idea of what 'extras' might entail on a typical package tour, a meal in a top-notch restaurant will cost around US$10–15, a beer in a lodge or upmarket hotel around US$3, a bottle of wine US$15–20, and a soda US$1. Tips are at the discretion of the individual traveller, but you should be looking at around US$10 per day for your safari driver.

For budget travellers, Tanzania can be very cheap, though day-to-day costs are now higher than in countries such as Malawi and Ethiopia, and most recognised tourist activities are relatively expensive. Day-to-day costs vary regionally, and are highest in major tourist centres such as Arusha, Moshi, Dar es Salaam and

Zanzibar. Throughout the country, a soft drink will cost you around US$0.50 and a beer slightly over US$1 in a local bar, but twice that in a hotel or restaurant that caters primarily to Westerners. A meal in a local restaurant will costs US$2–3, while a meal in a proper restaurant might cost US$5–10. Basic local guesthouses typically cost around US$3–4, though you can expect to pay double this amount in towns which see a lot of tourist traffic. Self-contained rooms in moderate hotels start at around US$10, while you might pay anything up from US$200–650 for a double room in a game lodge. Public transport costs will vary on how far and how regularly you travel, but buses aren't expensive. Taking the above figures into account, I think that budget travellers could get by in most parts of Tanzania on around US$15 per day for one person or US$20 per day for two. Double this amount, and within reason you can eat and stay where you like.

The above calculations don't allow for more expensive one-off activities, such as climbing Mount Kilimanjaro, going on safari, or catching the ferry between Dar and Zanzibar. If you want to keep to a particular budget and plan on undertaking such activities, you would be well advised to treat your day-to-day budget separately from what you are likely to spend on safari. I would set aside at least US$120 for each day you plan to spend on safari (bearing in mind additional costs such as tips and drinks) and perhaps US$180 for each day you plan to spend on Kilimanjaro, again allowing for tips.

ITINERARY PLANNING

Tanzania has a well-defined tourist circuit. It would be no exaggeration to say that as many as 90% of visitors probably divide their time in the country between the two main tourist attractions, which are the game reserves of the northern safari circuit and the island of Zanzibar. If this is what you plan on doing, then any tour operator or safari company in Arusha will be able to put together a package to meet your requirements. A 10–14-day trip is ideal for the Zanzibar-safari combination. You might want to read the section on organising a safari before making contact with a tour operator. With Zanzibar, the main decision you need to make in advance is whether you want to be based at a hotel in the old Stone Town, or out on one of the beaches, or a combination of the two. For a short trip to Tanzania, it is advisable to fly between Arusha (the springboard for safaris in northern Tanzania) and Zanzibar. If you are really tight for time, you'll get more out of your safari by flying between lodges. A fly-in safari will also be less tiring than the more normal drive-in safari.

For those with budgetary restrictions, it will probably work out cheaper to make your travel arrangements once you are in Tanzania. It is easier to get a cheap camping safari in Arusha on the spot, and you will be able to stay at cheaper guesthouses and hotels than those favoured by tour operators. The disadvantage of doing this is that you will lose time making arrangements once you are in the country, and will probably need two days to travel overland and by sea from Arusha to Zanzibar. If you plan on arranging things as you go along, I would advise against trying to squeeze a safari and a visit to Zanzibar into a trip of less than 14 days.

After the northern safari circuit and Zanzibar, Tanzania's main tourist attraction is Kilimanjaro, which can be climbed over five or six days. A Kilimanjaro climb is one of those things that you either do or don't want to undertake: for a significant minority of travellers, climbing Kilimanjaro is the main reason for visiting Tanzania, but for the majority it is of little interest. If you want to do a Kili climb, it can be organised in advance through any number of tour operators and safari companies, and there is a lot to be said for arranging the climb through the same operator who organises your safari. As with safaris, it is generally possible to get cheaper prices on the spot. To combine a Kili climb with a few days on safari and a visit to Zanzibar, you would need an absolute minimum of two weeks in the country on an organised package, and even that would be very tight, allowing for no more than two nights on Zanzibar. Bank on at least three weeks in the country if you are travelling independently.

Beyond the above, it is difficult to recommend any particular itinerary. The southern circuit of game reserves is slowly catching on with tourists, normally combined with a visit to Mafia or Zanzibar Island, but it is not a cheap option. Few would claim that the southern reserves offer a game-viewing spectacle to compare with the Serengeti or Ngorongoro in northern Tanzania, but they are fine reserves by any standard, and the relative exclusivity of tourist facilities in the south means that the reserves have retained more of a wilderness character. Other reserves that are of great interest to fly-in tourists are Gombe Stream, Mahale Mountains and Rubondo Island National Parks, all of which support substantial patches of rainforest habitats and offer the opportunity to see chimpanzees in the wild. Accessibility is a problem with all of the 'chimp reserves' at the time of writing, and short of chartering a direct flight you would need to set aside the best part of a week to visit any of them.

For budget travellers with sufficient time, a visit to the Usambara or Pare Mountains, or to the historical seaports of Tanga, Bagamoyo and Pangani, can easily be appended to the overland trip between Arusha and Zanzibar. With yet more time, and a sense of adventure, the southern and western parts of Tanzania are rich in off-the-beaten-track possibilities, ranging from the Shirazi ruins on Kilwa Kisiwani to the fantastic hiking country around Tukuyu and the memorable steamer ride down Lake Tanganyika. The most sensible advice that I can give to adventurous travellers is to allocate their time generously, or they are likely to spend a disproportionate amount of time on public transport.

To give some idea, if you wanted to visit Rubondo Island overland, you would be looking at a 10–14-day round trip from Dar es Salaam, and even Gombe Stream would be a week's round trip. The south coast could be explored comfortably over seven to ten days, the Udzungwa Mountains would be a good four-to-five-day trip, the Southern Highlands and Lake Nyasa would be good for anything over a week, and the Selous is normally visited on a four-to-five-day safari.

Independent travellers who have a longer period of time could do one of a few loops. You could, for instance, catch a train to Mbeya, spend a few days exploring around Tukuyu, cross to Mtwara via Lake Nyasa and Songea and then work your way up the south coast, a trip that will open your eyes to just how 'untouristy' even a popular tourist destination such as Tanzania can be. Another possibility from Mbeya is to work your way up to Mwanza via Lake Tanganyika taking in some of the western national parks on the way, then catch a bus across the Serengeti to Arusha and return to Dar es Salaam from there. For either of these trips, you would need at least a month.

72

Travelling in Tanzania

TOURIST INFORMATION AND SERVICES

There are Tanzania Tourist Board (TTB) offices in Dar es Salaam and in Arusha. Both are reasonably helpful and well-informed when it comes to tourist-class hotels and major tourist attractions, but neither is generally able to offer much help when it comes to more remote destinations. The TTB office in Arusha is a good source of information about the various cultural tourism programmes that have been established in northern Tanzania over the past few years. Its list of registered and blacklisted safari companies is a useful resource for travellers working through cheap safari companies.

PUBLIC HOLIDAYS

Tourists visiting Tanzania should take note of public holidays, since all banks, forex bureaux and government offices will be closed on these days. In addition to Good Friday, Easter Monday, Idd-ul-Fitr, Islamic New Year and the Prophet's Birthday, which fall on different dates every year, the following public holidays are taken in Tanzania:

January 1	New Year's Day
January 12	Zanzibar Revolution Day
February 5	CCM Day
April 26	Union Day (anniversary of union between Tanganyika and Zanzibar)
May 1	International Workers' Day
July 7	Saba Saba (Peasants') Day
August 8	Nane Nane (Farmers') Day
December 9	Independence Day
December 25	Christmas Day
December 26	Boxing Day

MONEY

The unit of currency is the Tanzanian shilling, divided into 100 cents. At the time of writing the exchange rate of roughly US$1 = Tsh900 is reasonably stable, but like most African currencies the Tanzanian shilling has steadily devalued against most hard currencies in recent years. This devaluation was most dramatic in the late 1980s, following a period when the exchange rate had been kept artificially high, resulting in a huge black market economy. In 1986, the exchange rate stood at around US$1 = Tsh20 and the black market rate at about ten times that. The rate dropped to something like US$1 = Tsh400 in the early 1990s. By contrast, the Tanzanian shilling has devalued by a relatively modest figure of 125% since the first edition of this guide was researched in 1992.

Most upmarket hotels and safari companies quote rates in US dollars. Some will also demand payment in this or another prominent hard currency, though increasingly many hotels and lodges actually prefer payment in local currency. National park fees and port and airport taxes must be paid in hard currency, and if you don't have the exact amount in US dollar bills or travellers' cheques, you risk being given change in local currency at a rather poor exchange rate. In practice, most tourists won't need to pay their park fees directly, since it will be included in the safari or lodge price.

The above exceptions noted, most things in Tanzania are best paid for in local currency, including restaurant bills, goods bought at a market or shop, mid-range and budget accommodation, public transport and most other casual purchases. Indeed, most service providers geared towards the local economy or to the backpacker market will have no facilities for accepting any currency other than Tanzanian shillings. Tanzanian shillings come in Tsh10,000, 5,000, 1,000, 500 and 200 denomination bills. It is often very difficult to find change for larger denomination bills, so try always to have a fair spread of notes available. Bulky small denomination coins are floating around, but they are worth considerably less than their weight in whatever leaden metal is used to mint them!

Throughout this guide, prices are quoted in the same currency as they are quoted in locally. In most cases, this is the Tanzanian shilling, but where a hotel or another service provider quotes its rates in US dollars, then I have followed suit. As a broad rule, safari companies, upmarket hotels and government institutions quote tourist rates in US dollars, while cheaper hotels, buses, restaurants and local eco-tourism concerns stick to local currencies. There are

CHANGING MONEY AT OVERLAND BORDERS

At most overland borders into or out of Tanzania, there will be nowhere to change money legally. Almost certainly, however, you will need some local currency to pay for a bus ride on to the next town and a room when you get there. If you expect to arrive after the banks have closed or over a weekend, you will also need enough local currency to see you through until the next banking day. This means that most border crossings are spiced up with the added adventure of trying to locate some local cash. You will have to do this by changing money with the individuals who hang around the borders for this purpose. This is technically illegal, but where there is no alternative it is usually handled fairly openly and there is no real risk of running into trouble with the authorities assuming you are reasonably discreet. The exchange rate is generally poor at borders – the guys who exchange currencies back and forth need to make a cut on the deal both ways – so there is no point in changing more money than you will need to see you through until you can get to a bank. If you are offered an exceptionally good rate, you're being set up!

You should be aware that con artists tend to thrive in border situations, so there is always a substantial risk of being tricked. One way around this, assuming that the opportunity presents itself, is to get hold of some Tanzanian money in advance, for instance by asking travellers coming from Tanzania if they have some left over to swap. Otherwise, rather than exchange hard currency at overland borders, I prefer to carry a small surplus of the currency of the country I am leaving (the equivalent of about US$10) to change into the currency of the country I am entering. I also try to ascertain the rough exchange rate in advance, and to calculate ahead of reaching the border more-or-less what I should be offered for the amount I want to exchange. Personally, I'm not too worried about being offered a slightly lower rate than I might have

some instances where a few hotels in the same price bracket in the same town quote rates in US dollars while others quote in Tanzanian shillings. To compare rates, simply lop three zeros off the end of the shilling price – US$25 and Tsh25,000, for instance, are close enough in real terms for all working purposes. Having to move between dollars and shillings might be doubly confusing for readers used to thinking in terms of euro, pound sterling or whatever, but the reality is that the US dollar is the main international currency used in Africa. People travelling between African countries soon start to think in US dollars, and those who are visiting Tanzania in isolation will find life much more straightforward if they bring their cash (and ideally travellers' cheques) in US dollars. For European visitors, the US dollar to Tanzanian shilling ratio of 1:1,000 is adequate when mentally converting to the euro.

African currencies are notoriously prone to sudden devaluation, and when this happens it is normal for local prices to adjust accordingly. Should it be, for instance, that the Tanzanian shilling devalues by 30% during the lifespan of this edition, and local guesthouse and bus prices increase by about the same amount in shilling terms, prices in this guide might start to look dated. They will, however, be pretty much unchanged in hard currency terms. This might seem obvious, but in my experience many travellers struggle with this concept. The bottom line is that in 2004, say, a hotel room quoted in this guide as costing Tsh5,000 in 2002 will in all probability charge a rate somewhere between Tsh5,000 and whatever the current Tanzanian shilling equivalent of US$5 happens to be at the time.

expected, but I am wary of allowing a quick talking money changer in a chaotic environment to exploit the decimal shifts involved in many African currency transactions.

Whether you intend to exchange local or hard currency at a border, it is strongly advised that you carry whatever bill(s) you intend to change in a pocket or elsewhere discrete from your main stash of foreign currency. Should you be surrounded by a mob of yelling money changers, pick any one of them and tell him that you will only discuss rates when his pals back off. Having agreed a rate, insist on taking the money and counting it before you hand over, or expose the location of, your own money. Should the amount that the money changer hands you be incorrect, it is almost certainly not a mistake, but phase one of an elaborate con trick, so safest to hand the wad of cash back to the guy and refuse to have anything further to do with him. Alternatively, if you do decide to continue, then recount the money after he hands it back to you and keep doing so until you have the correct amount counted in your hand. The reason for this is that some crooked money changers have such sleight of hand that they can seemingly add notes to a wad while actually removing a far greater number of notes than they add, all right in front of your eyes. Only when you are sure you have the right amount should you hand over your money.

Finally, it's long been the case that 'passengers' or 'staff' on public transport between Nairobi and the Namanga border will try to persuade travellers that if they arrive at the border without local currency they will be in trouble. Having sowed the seed of doubt, concerned of Nairobi will then offer to change money with the distressed traveller at a laughable exchange rate, or pull some other fast one. The bottom line is that you can safely assume *anybody*, no matter how persuasive, who approaches you with this sort of story on public transport heading towards any border is a con artist – ignore them!

Foreign exchange

Foreign currencies can be changed into Tanzanian shillings at any bank or bureau de change (known locally as forex bureaux). All banks are open from 08.30 to 12.30 on weekdays and in many larger towns they stay open until 15.00. They open from 08.30 to 11.30 on Saturdays. Most private forex bureaux stay open until 16.00 or later. You can normally change money at any time of day at Dar es Salaam's international airport. Most private forex bureaux deal in cash only (sometimes US dollars only), for which reason you'll probably be forced to change your travellers' cheques at a bank. The rate for this is often slightly lower than the cash rate and a small commission is also charged.

Generally, private forex bureaux offer a better rate of exchange than banks, though this is not so much the case as it was a few years ago, and some forex bureaux actually give notably lower rates than the banks. It's worth shopping around before a major transaction. The private bureaux are almost always far quicker for cash transactions than the banks, which might be a more important consideration than a minor discrepancy in the rate they offer. Before you change a large amount of money, check the bank or forex bureau has enough high denomination banknotes, or you'll need a briefcase to carry your local currency.

The opening of private forex bureaux has killed the black market that previously thrived in Tanzania. Private individuals may give you a slightly better rate than the banks, but the official rate is so favourable it seems unfair to exploit this. In Dar es Salaam or Arusha you will be offered exceptionally good rates on the street, but if you are stupid or greedy enough to accept these, you can expect to be ripped off. There are plenty of forged US$100 bills floating around Tanzania, and you can assume that anyone who suggests a deal involving a US$100 bill is trying to unload a forgery.

Credit cards

Only a few years ago, credit cards were practically useless in Tanzania. Today, however, most major international credit cards (Visa, Master and American Express, as well as Visa debit cards) are widely accepted by the better safari operators and in upmarket hotels and, to a lesser extent, in smarter restaurants in Dar es Salaam, Arusha, Moshi and Zanzibar Town. They are also accepted in many but certainly not all game lodges and upmarket beach resorts, and in a handful of city hotels elsewhere in the country. Increasingly, carrying a credit card is a viable alternative to cash or travellers' cheques, since it can be used to draw up to Tsh200,000 daily (about US$210) at 24-hour ATMs (autotellers) outside selected banks in Dar es Salaam, Arusha and Mwanza.

Having said that, ATM facilities are not available in other towns as yet, there are still many lodges and beach resorts that only accept payments in cash or travellers' cheques, and you are not permitted to pay park fees and the like with a card. Budget travellers can safely assume that hotels and other facilities within their reach cannot process credit card payments. Although things are changing, and surprisingly rapidly, I would still tend to carry most of the money you're likely to need in cash or travellers' cheques, and carry a credit card primarily as a backup for emergencies. Tourists on pre-booked holidays will not of course need to carry a vast amount of cash, and can check with their tour operator whether the lodges they are booked into will accept credit card payments for extras.

GETTING AROUND
Air

There has been a tremendous improvement in the network of domestic flights within Tanzania over recent years, especially between major tourist centres. In addition to the national carrier, Air Tanzania, several private airlines now run scheduled flights around Tanzania, most prominently Precision Air, Coastal Travel and Eagle Air. Between them, these carriers offer reliable scheduled flights to most parts of the country. Scheduled flights operate to Dar es Salaam; Zanzibar, Pemba and Mafia Islands; Kilimanjaro International Airport (for Moshi and Arusha); Serengeti (Grumeti and Seronera), Ngorongoro and Lake Manyara; Mwanza, Rubondo Island, Bukoba and Musoma; Tabora and Kigoma; Selous Game Reserve, Ruaha National Park and Mbeya; and Kilwa, Lindi and Mtwara. There are also regular flights between Arusha and Mombasa and Nairobi in Kenya.

For visitors with limited time and sufficient funds, flying is the best way to get around this large country, and any safari operator or tour company will be able to set up flights as required. It should be noted, however, that domestic flights are generally prohibitively expensive to travellers with stringent budgetary restrictions. To give some idea, a flight from Arusha to Zanzibar costs US$155 one-way, from Arusha to Mwanza US$145 one-way, and Dar es Salaam to Mbeya US$165 one-way. One flight that is relatively cheap, especially when you consider that the only alternative is a ferry costing around US$30, is from Dar es Salaam to Zanzibar at US$55.

Air Tanzania Tel: 022 211 0245; fax: 022 211 3114; email: commercial@airtanzania.com; web: www.airtanzania.com. Has a head office on Ohio St in Dar es Salaam and branch offices all around the country.

Precision Air Tel: 027 250 6903/2818/7319; fax: 027 250 8204; email: information@precisionairtz.com; web: www.precisionairtz.com. Has offices in Arusha, Dar es Salaam, Mwanza and Zanzibar. The head office is in the Arusha International Conference Centre's Ngorongoro Wing.

Coastal Travel Tel: 022 211 7959/60; fax: 022 211 8647/7895; email: safari@coastal.cc; web: www.coastal.cc.is. Based in Dar es Salaam. The head office is on Ohio St close to the Royal Palm Hotel.

Rail

There are three main railway lines in Tanzania, though passenger trains along the northern line, which connects Dar es Salaam, Tanga and Moshi, were discontinued a few years ago due to the improvements in the corresponding road route, and there is no reason to suppose that they will be resumed.

The most important railway to travellers is the central line, which connects Dar es Salaam to Tabora, Kigoma, Mwanza and Mpanda. Aside from flying, the regular passenger trains along the central line are the most reliable and comfortable way of getting between the coast and the west of the country. As a rule, the trains along this route are reasonably punctual, but there has been little maintenance in the last decade and the compartments are very rundown. For further details, see the box *The Central Railway* on pages 374–5.

The Tazara line connects Dar es Salaam to Ifakara, Mbeya, and Kapiri Mposhi in Zambia. It remains the best way of travelling directly between Tanzania and Zambia, and it would certainly be my preference over the buses were I travelling directly from Dar es Salaam to Mbeya. Passenger trains on the Tazara are normally fairly reliable, though when things do go wrong, you could be set for a delay measured in days rather than hours. For further details, see the box *The Tazara Railway* on page 484.

Boat

There are several useful ferry services on Tanzania's oceans and lakes. The most important to travellers are the several boats daily that connect Dar es Salaam to

Zanzibar Island, some of which continue on to Pemba. For further details, see the *Getting there and away* section for Zanzibar (pages 315–17). The ferry services run by the Tanzania Railway Corporation on all three of Tanzania's great lakes are covered in the chapters about Lake Victoria, Lake Tanganyika and Lake Nyasa.

Road

Buses are the main mode of road transport for independent travellers. Tanzania's buses used to be among the worst in Africa, old and poorly maintained vehicles that trundled lethargically along dramatically pot-holed roads through a country where spares were practically non-existent. Since the mid-1980s, however, there has been a gradual improvement in Tanzania's major roads and also in the standard of vehicles. Bus and coach services along major routes through Tanzania are now reasonably efficient. Good express coach services, typically covering in excess of 60km per hour, connect Arusha, Moshi, Lushoto, Tanga and Dar es Salaam. Bus services along the Tanzam Highway running south from Dar es Salaam to Morogoro, Iringa and Mbeya are now also reasonably quick and reliable, as are services between Mbeya and Kyela, and Dar es Salaam and Dodoma.

For long trips on major routes, ensure that you use an 'express bus', which should travel directly between towns stopping only at a few prescribed places, rather than stopping wherever and whenever a potential passenger is sighted or an existing passenger wants to disembark. Be warned that so far as most touts are concerned, any bus that will give them commission is an express bus, so you are likely to be pressured into getting in the bus they want you to get in. The best way to counter this is to go to the bus station on the day before you want to travel, and make your enquiries and bookings in advance, when you will be put under less pressure and won't have to worry about keeping an eye on your luggage. The new and reliable Scandinavia Coach company is highly recommended, approaching if not quite attaining Greyhound-type standards, and with at least one daily service on the country's two most important routes, ie: Dar es Salaam to Arusha and Dar es Salaam to Mbeya.

For the nostalgic and masochistic, it is still perfectly possible to capture the flavour of Tanzanian public transport in the 1980s by bussing through more remote areas, where as a generalisation buses are only worth considering where no rail or lake transport exists. Most non-trunk roads in Tanzania are in very poor shape, the vehicles are old and usually very crowded, and they tend to stop every couple of kilometres to pick up more passengers. A travelling time of around 20km per hour is not unusual, which means that a 250km trip can take up to 12 hours. In the southern coastal region, you're pretty much stuck with bus transport, but in the west, you are strongly advised to use trains and ferries. Routes that have a bad reputation for long delays, particularly during the dry season, are those between Arusha and Dodoma, and Arusha and Mwanza via Babati and Singida. The latter route can take anything from 36 hours to three days in one stretch, but is not quite so daunting if broken up with stops at Babati, Katesh et al.

The alternative to buses on most routes, and the only means of transport on more obscure routes, are *dalla-dallas* – a generic name that seems to encompass practically any public transport vehicle other than a bus. This can be a minibus, a covered 4WD, or a pick-up truck. On the whole, *dalla-dallas* are overcrowded by comparison to buses, more likely to try to overcharge tourists, and are driven by maniacs, resulting in regular fatal accidents. True, many bus drivers are also rather reckless, but were I to be involved in an accident on one of the flat roads characteristic of Tanzania, I'd fancy my chances in a bus over a pick-up truck or minibus any day.

SOME BUS JOURNEYS IN TANZANIA

The information included in this guideline table of routes, timings and fares has been accumulated over several trips to Tanzania, so it may not always be precise and is quoted in dollars rather than local currency. In dollar terms, bus fares – which are determined largely by imported petrol costs – have stayed pretty consistent over the last decade on journeys that I've undertaken several times. For trips not mentioned below, expect the fare to work out at around US$2 per 100km, more on some short hauls or on very bad roads that exaggerate the duration of the journey.

Journey	Vehicle	Km	Duration (hrs)	Approx fare (US$)
Arusha/Dar es Salaam	bus	647	12–15	10
Arusha/Dar es Salaam	express bus	647	10	15
Arusha/Moshi	bus	85	1.5	1.5
Tanga/Lushoto	minibus	154	3	3
Mwanza/Arusha	bus via Serengeti	692	12–18	85 *
Mwanza/Arusha	bus via Singida	855	36+	12
Tanga/Dar es Salaam	express bus	354	4–6	7
Mtwara/Dar es Salaam	bus	555	15–25	8
Dar es Salaam/Morogoro	minibus	196	2–3	3
Dar es Salaam/Iringa	bus	501	12–15	5
Morogoro/Iringa	minibus	305	7	3
Dar es Salaam/Mbeya	express coach	851	12	15
Dodoma/Iringa	bus	251	10	3
Dodoma/Arusha	bus	687	20	8
Mbeya/Kyela	bus	141	3	2.5
Mbamba Bay/Mbinga	pick-up truck	61	3+	3
Mbinga/Songea	bus	103	3	1.5
Songea/Njombe	bus	237	5	2.5
Mbeya/Sumbawanga	bus	322	8	3.5
Sumbawanga/Mpanda	bus	235	6–8	4
Mpanda/Ikola	lift with truck	126	4+	4
Rusumu/Mwanza	lift with truck	400	18+	10

* includes US$60 in national park fees

On busy routes and relatively short hauls, say up to 200km, buses tend not to operate to any fixed schedule, but instead simply set off when they are full. There is no need to book for such bus services, but be warned that long waits for a bus to fill up are commonplace. On long hauls and quieter routes, buses more normally leave at a fixed time, so it is advisable to book a seat a day in advance. Locally, I have often been given wildly inaccurate information about bus schedules, so I would recommend that you ask a few people and don't take the word of the first person you speak to. In the main part of the guide I have given the current situation regarding frequency of buses and indicated where booking is necessary. Things change, however, so you should make your own enquiries.

When you check out bus times, be very conscious of the difference between Western time and Swahili time. Many Tanzanians will translate the Swahili time to English without making the six-hour conversion – in other words, you might be told that a bus leaves at 11.00 when it actually leaves at 05.00. This fools a high proportion of travellers over their first few days in Tanzania. The best way to get around this area of potential misunderstanding is to confirm the time you are quoted in Swahili – for instance ask '*saa moja?*' if you are told a bus leaves at 13.00. See *Appendix 1* for more details.

Buses and minibuses are generally very inexpensive. To give some idea, the 647km journey between Dar and Arusha costs around US$12 by express bus, and even less on a standard 'stopping' bus. Overcharging is unusual on short routes and in parts of the country that carry a low volume of tourists. By contrast, tourists are routinely overcharged on long-haul buses along the main routes in northeast Tanzania. Before bussing out of Arusha, Moshi, Tanga or Dar es Salaam, you should try to establish the correct fare in advance. If you don't, I would query the fare as a matter of course (see box *Some bus journeys in Tanzania*, page 79).

Hitching

There is little scope for hitching in Tanzania. On routes where there is no public transport you may have to hitch, but generally this will be on the back of a truck and you will have to pay. Hitching is an option on the Arusha–Dar es Salaam–Mbeya road.

Car hire

Self-drive car hire isn't a popular or particularly attractive option in Tanzania, as it is generally more straightforward to visit game reserves on an organised safari.

ACCOMMODATION

The volume of hotels in Tanzania's towns, and particularly in major tourist centres such as Arusha and Dar es Salaam, is quite remarkable. So, too, is the variety in standard and price, which embraces hundreds of simple local guesthouses charging a couple of US dollars a night, as well as fantastic exclusive beach resorts and lodges charging upwards of US$300 per person – and everything in between.

In order to help readers of this fourth edition wade through the lengthy accommodation listings, all entries have been placed in one of six categories: exclusive, upmarket, moderate, budget, shoestring and camping. The purpose of this categorisation is twofold: to break up long hotel listings that span a wide price range, and to help readers isolate the range of hotels that will best suit their budget and taste. The application of categories is not rigid. Aside from an inevitable element of subjectivity, I have categorised hotels on their feel as much as their rates (the prices are quoted anyway), and this might be influenced by what other accommodation is available in any given town. It should also be noted that assessments relating to the value for money represented by any given hotel are to be read in the context of the individual town and the stated category. In other words, a hotel that seems to be good value in one town might not be such a bargain were it situated in another town where rates are generally cheaper. Likewise, a hotel that I regard to be good value in the upmarket category will almost certainly seem to be madly expensive to a traveller using budget hotels.

Before going into more detail about the different accommodation categories, it's worth noting a few potentially misleading quirks in local hotel-speak. In Swahili, the word *hoteli* refers to a restaurant while what we call a hotel is generally called a lodging, guesthouse or *gesti* – so if you ask a Tanzanian to show you a hotel you might well be taken to an eatery (see *Appendix 1*). Another local quirk is that most Tanzanian hotels in all ranges refer to a room with an en-suite shower and toilet as being self-contained, a term that is generally used widely in this guide. Finally, at most hotels in the moderate category or below, a single room will as often as not be one with a three-quarter or double bed, while a double room will be what we call a twin, with two single or double beds. 'HB' refers to half board, 'FB' to full board.

Exclusive

This category does not generally embrace conventional international-style hotels, but rather small and atmospheric beach resorts and game lodges catering to the most exclusive end of the market. Lodges in this category typically consist of no more than ten double accommodation units built and decorated in a style that complements the surrounding environment. The management will generally place a high priority on personalised service and quality food and wine, with the main idea being that guests are exposed to a holistic 24-hour bush or beach experience, rather than just a hotel room and restaurant in a bush/beach location. In several instances, lodges that fall into the exclusive category might be less conventionally luxurious, in terms of air conditioning and the like, than their competitors in the upmarket category. It is the bush experience more than any facilities that lends lodges in this category a quality of exclusivity. Rates are typically in the range US$250–500 per person all-inclusive. This is the category to look at if you want authentic, atmospheric bush or beach accommodation and have few financial restrictions.

Upmarket

This category includes most hotels, lodges and resorts that cater almost entirely to the international tourist or business travel market. Hotels in this range would typically be accorded a two- to four-star ranking internationally, and they offer smart accommodation with en-suite facilities, mosquito netting, air conditioning or fans depending on the local climate, and satellite television in cities and some beach resorts. Hotels in this bracket might charge anything from under US$100 to upwards of US$300 for a double room, dependent on quality and location. As a rule, upmarket hotels in areas that see few foreign visitors are far cheaper than equivalent hotels in or around urban tourist centres such as Dar es Salaam or Arusha, which are in turn cheaper than beach hotels and particularly lodges in national parks and game reserves. Room rates for city and beach hotels invariably include breakfast, while at game lodges they will also normally include lunch and dinner. Most package tours and privately booked safaris use accommodation in this range.

Moderate

In Tanzania, as in many African countries, there is often a wide gap in price and standard between the cheapest hotels geared primarily towards tourists and the best hotels geared primarily towards local travellers and budget travellers. For this reason, the moderate bracket is rather more nebulous than other accommodation categories, essentially consisting of hotels which, for one or other reason, couldn't really be classified as upmarket, but equally are too expensive or of too high quality to be considered budget lodgings. Many places listed in this range are superior local hotels that will suffice in lieu of any genuinely upmarket accommodation in a town that sees relatively few tourists. The category also embraces decent lodges or hotels in recognised tourist areas that charge considerably lower rates than their upmarket competitors, but are clearly a notch or two above the budget category. Hotels in this range normally offer comfortable accommodation in self-contained rooms with hot water, fan and possibly satellite television, and they will have decent restaurants and employ a high proportion of English-speaking staff. Prices for moderate city and beach hotels are generally in the US$20–50 range, more in some game reserves. This is the category to look at if you are travelling privately on a limited or low budget and expect a reasonably high but not luxurious standard of accommodation.

Budget

Hotels in this category are aimed largely at the local market and definitely don't approach international standards, but are still reasonably clean and comfortable, and a definite cut above the basic guesthouses that proliferate in most towns. Hotels in this bracket will more often than not have a decent restaurant attached, English-speaking staff, and comfortable rooms with en-suite facilities, running cold or possibly hot water, fans (but not air conditioning) and good mosquito netting. Hotels in this category typically charge around Tsh7,000–10,000 (around US$10) for a self-contained double room, but they may charge as little as Tsh5,000 in relatively out-of-the-way places and closer to US$20 in major tourist centres. This is the category to look at if you are on a limited budget, but want to avoid total squalor!

Shoestring

This category is aimed at travellers who want the cheapest possible accommodation irrespective of quality. In most Tanzanian towns, this will amount to a choice of dozens of small private guesthouses, which are almost exclusively used by locals, are remarkably uniform in design, and generally charge from Tsh1,500 to Tsh3,500 (US$2–4) for an uncluttered room. The typical guesthouse consists of around ten cell-like rooms forming three walls around a central courtyard, with a reception area or restaurant at the front. Toilets are more often than not long-drops. Washing facilities often amount to nothing more than a lockable room and a bucket of water, though an increasing number of guesthouses do have proper showers, and a few have hot water. Tanzanian guesthouses may be basic, and in many cases they double as brothels, but the majority are reasonably clean and pleasant, and are good value when compared to similar establishments in some neighbouring countries. I have found that guesthouses run by women or with a strong female presence are generally cleaner and more hospitable than those run by men. There is a strong town-to-town variation in guesthouse quality and price: in some towns a clean, freshly painted room with mosquito nets and a fan is standard; in others – Iringa and Bukoba leap to mind – three-quarters of the places we looked at were total dumps. In most medium-sized towns there are a couple of dozen guesthouses, usually clustered around the bus station and often with little to choose between them. In such cases I have avoided making individual recommendations. There are several cheap church-run guesthouses and hostels in Tanzania, and these are normally also included under the shoestring listings.

Camping

There are surprisingly few campsites in Tanzania, and those that do exist tend to be in national parks, where camping costs US$20 per person. Along the coast north of Dar es Salaam and in Moshi and Arusha, several recently opened private sites cater to backpackers and overland trucks. If you ask at moderate hotels in out of the way places, you may sometimes be allowed to camp in their grounds for a small fee.

If you are hiking in areas off the beaten track, a tent will be a distinct asset. You should, however, be discreet; either set up well away from villages or else ask permission from the village headman before you pitch a tent. I've not met many people who have camped rough in Tanzania, but it's hard to imagine there would be a significant risk attached to camping in rural areas, provided you didn't flaunt your presence or leave your tent unguarded for a lengthy period.

EATING AND DRINKING
Eating
If you are not too fussy and don't mind a lack of variety, you can eat well and cheaply almost anywhere in Tanzania. In most towns numerous local restaurants, called *hotelis*, serve unimaginative but filling meals for around US$2. *Hotelis* vary greatly in quality: I have had some very tasty meals in them, but as often as not gristle and sludge would be an appropriate description of what you are served.

Most *hoteli* food is based around a stew eaten with one of four staples: rice, *chapati*, *ugali* or *batoke*. *Ugali* is a stiff maize porridge eaten throughout sub-Saharan Africa. *Batoke* or *matoke* is cooked plantain, served boiled or in a mushy heap. In the Lake Victoria region, *batoke* replaces *ugali* as the staple food. The most common stews are chicken, beef, goat and beans. In coastal towns and around the great lakes, whole fried fish is a welcome change.

Mandaazi, the local equivalent of doughnuts, are tasty when freshly cooked. They are served at *hotelis* and sold at markets. You can eat cheaply at stalls around markets and bus stations. Goat kebabs, fried chicken, grilled groundnuts and potato chips are often freshly cooked and sold in these places.

Cheap it may be, but for most travellers *hoteli*-fare soon palls. In most larger towns, there are what could be termed proper restaurants. These are normally within the reach of any budget, and would typically serve a variety of meat, steak and chicken dishes with potato chips or rice, and cost around US$5 for a main course. There is considerably more culinary variety in Dar es Salaam and Arusha, where for around US$8–10 you can eat very well.

At one time, walking around a Tanzanian market you would see little but onions and bananas. This has improved, and in most towns a reasonable variety of fruits, vegetables and pulses can be bought, depending on the season. The most common fruits are mangoes, oranges, bananas, pineapples, papayas and coconuts. Fresh fruit is dirt cheap in Tanzania.

Note: KiSwahili names for various foods are given in *Appendix 1*.

Drinks
The most widely drunk beverage is *chai*, a sweet tea where all ingredients are boiled together in a pot. Along the coast *chai* is often flavoured with spices such as ginger. In some places *chai* is served *ya rangi* or black; in others *maziwa* or milky. Sodas such as Coke, Pepsi, Sprite and Fanta are widely available, and normally cost less than US$0.50. In large towns you can often get fresh fruit juice. On the coast and in some parts of the interior, the most refreshing, healthy and inexpensive drink is coconut milk, sold by street vendors, who will decapitate the young coconut of your choice to create a natural cup, from which the juice can be sipped.

Tap water in Tanzania is often dodgy, and most travellers try to stick to mineral water, which is available in most tourist centres, coming in 1.5l bottles that cost around US$1. We've been told that in some countries it is common practice to fill mineral water bottles with tap water, but I've not heard of this happening in Tanzania, and wouldn't be concerned about it provided that the bottle is sealed.

The two main alcoholic drinks are beer and *konyagi*. *Konyagi* is a spirit made from sugar cane. It tastes a bit strange on its own, but it mixes well and is very cheap. The local Safari lager used to be appalling, but since the national brewery was taken over by South African Breweries a few years ago, there has been a dramatic improvement not only in the quality of Safari, but also in the selection of other brands available. Around ten different lager beers are now available, of which Castle, Kilimanjaro and Serengeti seem to be the most popular. All beers come in 500ml bottles and cost anything from US$1 at a local bar to US$5 at the most upmarket hotels.

A variety of imported spirits is available in larger towns. South African wines are widely available at lodges and hotels, and they are generally of a high standard and reasonably priced by international standards. I must say that as a South African I do find it hard to bring myself to pay more than US$20 for a bottle of plonk that I know would cost US$2 at home.

SHOPPING

Until a few years ago it was difficult to buy anything much in Tanzania. One of my most vivid memories of Dar es Salaam in 1986 was walking into a general store where a lone shelf of teaspoons was the only stock. Things have improved greatly since then. In Dar es Salaam and most other large towns a fair range of imported goods is available, though prices are often inflated. If you have any very specific needs – unusual medications or slide film for instance – bring them with you.

Toilet roll, soap, toothpaste, pens, batteries and locally produced food are widely available. *Duka*s, the stalls you see around markets or lining roads, are cheaper than proper shops and are open seven days a week. Even in Dar es Salaam, we were rarely overcharged because we were tourists.

Shopping hours are normally between 08.30 and 16.30, with a lunch break between 13.00 and 14.00.

Curios

A variety of items specifically aimed at tourists is available: Makonde carvings, Tingatinga paintings (see box, page 299), batiks, musical instruments, wooden spoons, and various soapstone and malachite knick-knacks. The curio shops near the Clock Tower in Arusha are the best places to shop for curios. Prices are competitive and the quality is good. Prices in shops are fixed, but you may be able to negotiate a discount. At curio stalls, haggling is necessary. Unless you are good at this, expect to pay more than you would in a shop.

If you have an interest in African music, a good range of tapes is available at stalls in Dar es Salaam city centre. Most are of Congolese groups popular in East Africa: Loketa, Kanda Bongoman, Bossi Bossiana and the like.

The colourful *vitenge* (the singular of this is *kitenge*) worn by most Tanzanian women can be picked up cheaply at any market in the country. I've been told Mwanza is a particularly good place to shop for these and other clothes.

MEDIA AND COMMUNICATIONS
Newspapers

The English language *Daily News* and *Daily Guardian* are available in Dar es Salaam and other major towns. They don't carry much international news, but the local news can make interesting reading and the international coverage seems to be steadily improving. The Kenyan *Daily Nation*, available in Dar es Salaam, Arusha and Mwanza, is slightly better. The excellent *East African* is a weekly newspaper published in Kenya but distributed throughout the three countries to which it dedicates roughly equal coverage, ie: Kenya, Tanzania and Uganda. Stalls in Uhuru Avenue, Dar es Salaam sell *Time* and *Newsweek*, as well as a variety of European, British and American papers. You can sometimes buy the same from vendors around the Clock Tower in Arusha.

Post

Post from Tanzania is cheap and reasonably reliable. Incoming post arrives surprisingly quickly. The poste restante service in Dar es Salaam used to be among the best in Africa, though these days, with internet access being so straightforward and cheap, it is used by very few travellers. There is a nominal charge for collecting letters. Mail should be addressed as follows:

Philip Briggs
Poste Restante
Main GPO
Dar es Salaam
Tanzania

Suggest when people write to you that they underline your surname, so that the letter doesn't get misfiled. It is advisable to check under both names when you visit the post office.

Phone calls

If you want to make an international phone call or send a fax, there is a TCC Extelcomms centre in most large towns. The staff at the centres are normally helpful and calls are cheap by international standards. Some Extelcomms centres will receive as well as send faxes. Phone calls and faxes to Europe cost around US$16 per minute or page.

Internet and email

The spread of internet use in Africa has been remarkable over the last year or so, and the existence of email represents a real communications revolution on a continent where international lines tend to be unreliable and expensive. Internet and email have caught on particularly quickly in Tanzania, where internet cafés are more prolific and affordable than in any other African country I've visited recently. Numerous internet cafés are dotted around major urban tourist centres such as Dar es Salaam, Arusha, Mwanza and Moshi, while the likes of Mbeya, Tanga, Dodoma, Iringa and Morogoro all have at least one decent internet café. The standard rate countrywide is around Tsh500 for 30 minutes' browsing, and the servers in the main centres are generally pretty fast, at least by comparison to most other African countries. Towns that don't as yet have good internet access include Musoma, Kigoma and Tabora, but this is bound to change eventually. Worth noting that internet access is not available in most game reserves and national parks, and the few game lodges that do offer internet browsing or email services tend to charge very high rates.

INTERACTING WITH TANZANIANS

Tanzania has perhaps the most egalitarian and tolerant mood of any African country that I've visited. As a generalisation, Tanzanians tend to treat visitors with a dignified reserve, something that many Westerners mistake for a stand-offish attitude, but in my opinion is more indicative of a respect both for our culture and their own. Granted, dignified probably won't be the adjective that leaps to mind if your first interaction with Tanzanians comes from the pestilence of touts that hangs around bus stations in Arusha or Moshi, or somewhere similar. But then in most poor countries, you'll find that people who make a living on the fringe of the tourist industry tend be pushy and occasionally confrontational in their dealings – from their perspective, they probably have to be in order to make a living. But I do think that anybody who spends time travelling in Tanzania will recognise the behaviour of touts to be wholly unrepresentative of what is essentially a conservative, unhurried and undemonstrative society.

On the whole, you would have to do something pretty outrageous to commit a serious *faux pas* in Tanzania. But, like any country, Tanzania does have its rules of etiquette, and while allowances will always made for tourists, there is some value in ensuring that they are not made too frequently!

General conduct

Perhaps the most important single point of etiquette to be grasped by visitors to Tanzania is the social importance of formal greetings. Tanzanians tend to greet each other elaborately, and if you want to make a good impression on somebody who speaks English, whether they be a waiter or a shop assistant (and especially if they work in a government department), you would do well to follow suit. When you need to ask somebody directions, it is rude to blunder straight into interrogative mode without first exchanging greetings. With Tanzanians who don't speak English, the greeting 'Jambo' delivered with a smile and a nod of the head will be adequate.

Whenever I visit Tanzania after travelling elsewhere in Africa, I am struck afresh by how readily people greet passing strangers, particularly in rural areas. In Tanzania, this greeting doesn't normally take the form of a shrieked *mzungu* (or whatever local term is used for a white person), or a 'give me money', something that you become accustomed to in some African countries. On the contrary, in Tanzania adults will normally greet tourists with a cheerful *Jambo*, and children with a subdued *Shikamu* (a greeting reserved for elders). I find this to be a very charming quality in Tanzanian society, one that is worth reinforcing by learning a few simple Swahili greetings.

Among Tanzanians, it is considered poor taste to display certain emotions publicly. Affection is one such emotion: it is frowned upon for members of the opposite sex to hold hands publicly, and kissing or embracing would be seriously offensive. Oddly, it is quite normal for friends of the same sex to walk around hand-in-hand. Male travellers who get into a long discussion with a male Tanzanian shouldn't be surprised if that person clasps them by the hand and retains a firm grip on their hand for several minutes. This is a warm gesture, one particularly appropriate when the person wants to make a point with which you might disagree. On the subject of intra-gender relations, homosexuality is as good as taboo in Tanzania, to the extent that it would require some pretty overt behaviour for it to occur to anybody to take offence.

It is also considered bad form to show anger publicly. It is difficult to know where to draw the line here, because many touts positively invite an aggressive response, and I doubt that many people who travel independently in Tanzania will get by without the occasional display of impatience. Frankly, I doubt that many bystanders would take umbrage if you responded to a pushy tout with a display of anger, if only because the tout's behaviour itself goes against the grain of Tanzanian society. By contrast, losing your temper will almost certainly be counterproductive when dealing with obtuse officials, dopey waiters and hotel employees, or uncooperative safari drivers.

Muslim customs

Visitors should be aware of the strong Muslim element in Tanzania, particularly along the coast. In Muslim society, it is insulting to use your left hand to pass or receive something or when shaking hands. If you eat with your fingers, it is also customary to use the right hand only. Even those of us who are naturally right-handed will occasionally need to remind ourselves of this (it may happen, for instance, that you are carrying something in your right hand and so hand money to a shopkeeper with your left). For left-handed travellers, it will require a constant effort. In traditional Muslim societies it is offensive for women to expose their

Previous page Male lions may spend as much as 23 hours a day sleeping (AZ)

Above Lion, *Panthera leo*, cub in Serengeti National Park (AZ)

Right The cheetah, *Acynonix jubatus*, is the world's fastest land animal, a common predator in open plains such as those of the Serengeti (AZ)

Below A lioness with its zebra kill. Females of the pride do most of the hunting (AZ)

knees or shoulders, a custom that ought to be taken on board by female travellers, especially on parts of the coast where tourists remain a relative novelty.

Tipping and guides

The question of when and when not to tip can be difficult in a foreign country. In Tanzania, it is customary to tip your guide at the end of a safari and/or a Kilimanjaro climb, as well as any cook and porter that accompanies you. A figure of roughly US$5–10 per day is accepted as the benchmark, though it is advisable to check this with your safari company in advance. I see no reason why you shouldn't give a bigger or smaller tip based on the quality of service. Bear in mind, however, that most guides, cooks and porters receive nominal salaries, which means that they are largely dependent on tips for their income. It would be mean not to leave a reasonable tip in any but the most exceptional of circumstances.

In some African countries, it is difficult to travel anywhere without being latched on to by a self-appointed guide, who will often expect a tip over and above any agreed fee. This sort of thing is comparatively unusual in Tanzania, but if you do take on a freelance guide, then it is advisable to clarify in advance that whatever price you agree is final and inclusive of a tip. By contrast, any guide who is given to you by a company should most definitely be tipped, as tips will probably be their main source of income. In Zanzibar and Arusha, a freelance guide may insist upon helping you find a hotel room, in which case they will be given a commission by the hotel, so there is no reason for you to provide an additional tip. In any case, from the guide's point of view, finding you a room is merely the first step in trying to hook you for a safari or a spice tour, or something else that will earn a larger commission.

It is not customary to tip for service in local bars and *hotelis*, though you may sometimes *want* to leave a tip (in fact, given the difficulty of finding change in Tanzania, you may practically be forced into doing this in some circumstances). A tip of 5% would be very acceptable and 10% generous. Generally any restaurant that caters primarily to tourists and to wealthy Tanzania residents will automatically add a service charge to the bill. Since the government claims the lion's share of any formal service charge, it would still be reasonable to reward good service with a genuine tip.

Bargaining

Tourists to Tanzania will sometimes need to bargain over prices, but generally this need exists only in reasonably predictable circumstances, for instance when chartering a private taxi, organising a guide, agreeing a price for a safari or mountain trek, or buying curios and to a lesser extent other market produce. Prices in hotels, restaurants and shops are generally fixed, and overcharging in such places is too unusual for it to be worth challenging a price unless it is blatantly ridiculous. You may well be overcharged at some point in Tanzania, but it is important to keep this in perspective. After a couple of bad experiences, some travellers start to haggle with everybody from hotel owners to old women selling fruit by the side of the road, often accompanying their negotiations with aggressive accusations of dishonesty. Unfortunately, it is sometimes necessary to fall back on aggressive posturing in order to determine a fair price, but such behaviour is also very unfair on those people who are forthright and honest in their dealings with tourists. It's a question of finding the right balance, or better still looking for other ways of dealing with the problem.

The main instance where bargaining is essential is when buying curios. What should be understood, however, is that the fact a curio seller is open to negotiation does not mean that you were initially being overcharged or ripped off. Curio sellers will generally quote a price knowing full well that you are going to bargain it down (they'd probably be startled if you didn't) and it is not necessary to respond aggressively or in an accusatory manner. It is impossible to say by how much you should bargain the initial price down. Some people say that you should offer half the asking price and be prepared to settle at around two-thirds, but my experience is that curio sellers are far more whimsical than such advice allows for. The sensible approach, if you want to get a feel for prices, is to ask the price of similar items at a few different stalls before you actually contemplate buying anything.

In fruit and vegetable markets and stalls, bargaining is the norm, even between locals, and the most healthy approach to this sort of haggling is to view it as an enjoyable part of the African experience. There will normally be an accepted price band for any particular commodity. To find out what it is, listen to what other people pay and try a few stalls. A ludicrously inflated price will always drop the moment you walk away. When buying fruit and vegetables, a good way to feel out the situation is to ask for a bulk discount or a few extra items thrown in. And bear in mind that when somebody is reluctant to bargain, it may be because they asked a fair price in the first place.

It appears that the conductors on bus services connecting Arusha, Moshi, Tanga and Dar es Salaam (but not elsewhere in the country) routinely overcharge tourists. One reader who spent three months in northern Tanzania and travelled regularly between towns reckons that overcharging *wazungu* is almost customary on long-haul bus rides in this part of the country, but not on shorter trips. This concurs with our experience: we have never been quoted the wrong fare on minibuses within Arusha, or when travelling between Arusha and Moshi, yet we've had to argue to get the correct fare on the last three occasions when we travelled between Moshi and Tanga. The best way to avoid being overcharged is to check the correct ticket price in advance with an impartial party, and to book your ticket a day in advance of when you want to travel. Failing that, you will have to judge for yourself whether the price is right, and if you have reason to think it isn't, then question the conductor. In such circumstances, it can be difficult to find the right balance between standing up for your rights and becoming overtly obnoxious. On a recent trip, we disembarked from a bus in Tanga when the conductor refused to budge on a fare we *knew* to be about double what it should have been, and even that made no difference to his position! Fortunately, we found another bus heading in the direction we wanted.

A final point to consider on the subject of overcharging and bargaining is that it is the fact of being overcharged that annoys; the amount itself is generally of little consequence in the wider context of a trip to Tanzania. Without for a moment wanting to suggest that travellers should routinely allow themselves to be overcharged, I do feel there are occasions when we should pause to look at the bigger picture. Backpackers in particular tend to forget that, no matter how tight for cash they are, it is their choice to travel on a minimal budget, and most Tanzanians are much poorer than they will ever be. If you find yourself quibbling over a pittance with an old lady selling a few piles of fruit by the roadside, you might perhaps bear in mind that the notion of a fixed price is a very Western one. When somebody is desperate enough for money, or afraid that their perishable goods might not last another day, it may well be possible to push them down to a lower price than they would normally accept. In such circumstances, I see nothing wrong with erring on the side of generosity.

Women travellers

Women travellers in Tanzania have little to fear on a gender-specific level. Over the years, I've met several women travelling alone in Tanzania, and none had any serious problems in their interactions with locals, aside from the hostility that can be generated by dressing skimpily. Otherwise, an element of flirtation is about the sum of it, perhaps the odd direct proposition, but nothing that cannot be defused by a firm 'no'. And nothing, for that matter, that you wouldn't expect in any Western country, or – probably with a far greater degree of persistence – from many male travellers.

It would be prudent to pay some attention to how you dress in Tanzania, particularly in the more conservative parts of the Swahili coast. In areas where people are used to tourists, they are unlikely to be deeply offended by women travellers wearing shorts or other outfits that might be seen to be provocative. Nevertheless, it still pays to allow for local sensibilities, and under certain circumstances revealing clothes may be perceived to make a statement that's not intended from your side.

More mundanely, tampons are not readily available in smaller towns, though you can easily locate them in Dar es Salaam and Arusha, and in game lodge and hotel gift shops. When travelling in out-of-the-way places, carry enough tampons to see you through to the next time you'll be in a large city, bearing in mind that travelling in the tropics can sometimes cause heavier or more regular periods than normal. Sanitary pads are available in most towns of any size.

Bribery

Bribery is not much of an issue. There is said to be plenty of corruption in Tanzanian business circles, but it is unlikely to affect tourists. I have never been in a situation where I felt a bribe was being hinted at, nor have I heard of one from another traveller.

Bureaucracy

In the 1980s you often heard stories about travellers clashing with Tanzanian officials. Most incidents were camera-related: it was illegal to take photographs outside tourist areas, largely because of the number of ANC training centres in Tanzania at that time. It may have been paranoid to suspect every backpacker with a camera of being a spy, but as South Africa had used European passport holders disguised as backpackers to bomb an alleged ANC office in Zimbabwe, it was understandable. Things have relaxed greatly since South Africa unbanned the ANC in 1990, and on several trips through Tanzania since then I've experienced nothing more sinister than mild abruptness. In general, Tanzanian officials will go out of their way to accommodate foreigners.

Some travellers behave as if they expect to be allowed to do what they like in African countries, as if they are above the law because they have a white skin and a foreign passport. This attitude is on the decline, but it still persists amongst some budget travellers. So, for the sake of clarity: if, for instance, you climb Kilimanjaro via an illegal route to avoid paying park entrance fees and are arrested, the person who arrests you is not being officious or bureaucratic, he is merely doing his job.

In remote parts of the country, you may from time to time be approached by an immigration or police officer who wants to look at your passport. This happened to us a few times and in every instance it was handled in a relaxed, friendly manner. If it happens to you, expect to be asked where you have come from, where you are going, what you are doing in Tanzania, etc. Don't read too much into this; it is the typical stuff of KiSwahili small talk. The officer concerned is as likely to be

THEF ON BUSES

Tanzanian buses have a bad reputation for theft, though my experience and that of travellers I've met would suggest that this is probably not so much a general problem as one specific to a few particular routes. Bear the following in mind when you travel by bus:

* The roof is the most risky place to put your luggage, especially on a bus that will travel into the night. Some conductors insist on putting it there (there is often no real option) but if possible try to get it into the body of the bus. If it does not fit on the racks, put it up near the driver.
* Avoid overnight buses. Almost all the theft stories I have heard relate to overnight buses between Arusha and Dodoma or on the Dar es Salaam and Mbeya routes.
* Be wary of strangers who offer you food. Instances of travellers being given drugged food and having their possessions taken while they are asleep seem to be on the increase, with long-haul routes the main area of risk. First-hand accounts would suggest that the most likely offenders in this regard are smooth-talking, well-dressed fellow passengers who know how to guilt-trip *wazungu* (Europeans) into acting against their better instincts.
* Be vigilant when the bus is stationary. The snatch-and-grab experts who hang around most bus stations are not above grabbing something through the window. If anyone is hanging around, catch their eye so that they know you are aware of them.
* Don't leave valuables on your lap. It sounds obvious; I once met someone whose money belt was snatched from his lap while he was fiddling in his daypack.

savouring an opportunity to practise his English as he is to have any professional interest in the trivia of your holiday. If you are in a rush, it can be a bit irritating to be cornered like this, but there is no point in letting your irritation show. Smile, keep your answers simple, and you will soon be on your way.

CRIME AND SECURITY

Crime exists in Tanzania as it does practically everywhere in the world. There has been a marked increase in crime in Tanzania over recent years, and tourists are inevitably at risk, because they are far richer than most locals, and are conspicuous in their dress, behaviour and (with obvious exceptions) skin colour. For all that, Tanzania remains a lower crime risk than many countries, and the social taboo on theft is such that even a petty criminal is likely to be beaten to death should they be caught in the act. With a bit of care, you would have to be unlucky to suffer from more serious crime while you are in Tanzania.

Mugging

There is nowhere in Tanzania where mugging is as commonplace as it is in, say, Nairobi or Johannesburg, but there are certainly several parts of the country where walking around alone at night would place you at high risk of being mugged. Mugging is generally an urban problem, with the main areas of risk being Dar es Salaam, Arusha, Tanga and Zanzibar Town, as well as the beach at Pangani, and anywhere in the vicinity of Bagamoyo or Kanduchi Beach. Even in these places, the risk is often localised. In Dar es Salaam, for instance, I have always felt perfectly safe in the area immediately around Maktaba Street, but I would probably catch a taxi if I were crossing from, say, the New Africa Hotel to the Jumbo Inn after dark. The best thing is to ask local advice at your hotel, since the staff there will generally know of any recent incidents in the immediate vicinity.

The best way to ensure that any potential mugging remains an unpleasant incident rather than a complete disaster is to carry as little as you need on your person. If you are mugged in Tanzania, the personal threat is minimal provided that you promptly hand over what is asked for.

Casual theft

The bulk of crime in Tanzania consists of casual theft such as bag-snatching or pickpocketing. This sort of thing is not particularly aimed at tourists (and as a consequence it is not limited to tourist areas), but tourists will be considered fair game. The key to not being pickpocketed is not having anything of value in your pockets; the key to avoiding having things snatched is to avoid having valuables in a place where they could easily be snatched. Most of the following points will be obvious to experienced travellers, but they are worth making:

- Many casual thieves operate in bus stations and markets. Keep a close watch on your belongings in these places, and avoid having loose valuables in your pocket or daypack.
- Keep all your valuables – passport, travellers' cheques, etc – in a money belt. One you can hide under your clothes has obvious advantages over one of the currently fashionable codpieces that are worn externally.
- Never carry spending money in your money belt. A normal wallet is fine provided it only contains a moderate sum of money. Better still is a wallet you can hang around your neck. If I plan to visit a risky area such as a busy market, I sometimes wear shorts under my trousers and keep my cash in the pockets of the shorts. In my opinion, it is difficult for somebody to stick a hand in the front pocket of a shirt unobserved, for which reason this is normally my favourite pocket for keeping ready cash.
- Distribute your money throughout your luggage. I always keep the bulk of my foreign currency in my money belt, but I like to keep some cash and travellers' cheques hidden in various parts of my pack and daypack.
- Many people prefer to carry their money belt on their person at all times. I think it is far safer to leave it hidden in your hotel room. I'm not saying that it's impossible for a locked hotel room to be broken into, but I've not heard of it happening in Tanzania, whereas I have met countless people who have been pickpocketed, mugged, or had possessions snatched from them. Circumstances do play a part here: in a large city, I would be far happier with my valuables locked away somewhere, whereas in a game lodge the risk of theft from a room has to be greater than that of theft from your person. One factor to consider is that some travellers' cheque companies won't issue refunds on cheques stolen from a hotel room.
- If you have jewellery that is of high personal or financial value, leave it at home.
- If you can afford it, catch a taxi to your hotel when you first arrive in a large town. If you arrive after dark, catch a taxi to your hotel even if you can't afford it.
- Avoid overnight buses. They have a bad reputation for theft. On Zanzibar and on overnight buses I have heard of people being given drugged food and then robbed (see box *Theft on buses*, opposite).

- If you are robbed, think twice before you chase the thief, especially if the stolen items are of no great value. An identified thief is likely to be descended on by a mob and quite possibly beaten to death. I have met a few travellers who found themselves in the bizarre position of having to save someone who had just ripped them off.

Con tricks

Dar es Salaam is not Nairobi as far as con artists are concerned. A few dodgy characters hang around the New Africa Hotel trying to change money, but they are pretty transparent. You may encounter similar characters in Arusha, but you would have to be very gullible to get involved with them. The main type of con relates to budget safaris out of Arusha, a subject covered in greater detail in the Northern Safari Circuit chapter.

Documentation

The best insurance against complete disaster is to keep things well documented. If you carry a photocopy of the main page of your passport, you will be issued a new one more promptly. In addition, keep details of your bank, credit card (if you have one), travel insurance policy and camera equipment (including serial numbers).

Keep copies of your travellers' cheque numbers and a record of which ones you have cashed, as well as the international refund assistance telephone number and local agent. If all this information fits on one piece of paper, you can keep photocopies on you and with a friend at home.

You will have to report to the police the theft of any item against which you wish to claim insurance.

Security

Tanzania is a very secure country, with a proud record of internal stability since independence. The bombing of the US Embassies in Dar es Salaam and Nairobi resulted in large-scale cancellations of US tours to Tanzania in late 1998, despite a mass of evidence that would provide any rational human with greater cause to give a wide birth to US embassies than to cancel a holiday in East Africa. Aside from this, the only part of Tanzania where there is currently a security problem is in the remote tract of Maasailand lying between Lake Natron and the Serengeti. The security situation here is the direct result of the recent incursion of a group of armed Somalis from Kenya, and while it has resulted in several deaths locally, the only effect on tourists to date has been an isolated incident in which a safari vehicle was held up along the road west of Natron. The indications are that this is a short-term problem, and it is unlikely that any responsible safari company would risk taking tourists into this area until it is resolved.

Tanzania shares a western border with the troubled countries of the Congo, Rwanda and Burundi, an area that sees very little tourism. So far as I am aware, the recent civil war in the Congo has had little direct effect on Tanzania, probably because Lake Tanganyika divides the two countries. The Rwanda and Burundi border areas have been overrun with refugees at several points over the last few years, a situation that is of some concern to locals, officials and international aid workers, but has had no effect on parts of Tanzania likely to be visited by tourists.

Health

with Dr Jane Wilson-Howarth and Dr Felicity Nicholson

PREPARATIONS

Preparations to ensure a healthy trip to Tanzania require checks on your immunisation status: it is wise to be up to date on tetanus (ten-yearly), polio (ten-yearly), diphtheria (ten-yearly), and for many parts of Africa immunisations against yellow fever, meningococcus, rabies and hepatitis A are also needed.

Hepatitis A vaccine (Havrix Monodose or Avaxim) is comprised of two injections given about a year apart. The course costs about £100, but protects for ten years. It is now felt that the vaccine can be used even close to the time of departure and has replaced the old-fashioned gamma globulin. The newer typhoid vaccines (eg: Typhim Vi) last for three years and are about 85% effective. They should be encouraged unless the traveller is leaving within a few days for a trip of a week or less when the vaccine would not be effective in time. Meningitis vaccine (containing strains ACW and Y) is also recommended, especially for trips of more than four weeks (see Meningitis). Immunisation against cholera is no longer required for Tanzania. Vaccinations for rabies are advised for travellers visiting more remote areas (see Rabies). Hepatitis B vaccination should be considered for longer trips (two months or more) or for those working with children or in situations where contact with blood is likely. Three injections are needed for the best protection and can be given over a four-week period if time is short. Longer schedules give more sustained protection and are therefore preferred if time allows. A BCG vaccination against tuberculosis (TB) is also advised for trips of two months or more.

Ideally you should visit your own doctor or a specialist travel clinic (see page 96) to discuss your requirements about eight weeks before you plan to travel.

Protection from the sun

Give some thought to packing suncream. The incidence of skin cancer is rocketing as Caucasians are travelling more and spending more time exposing themselves to the sun. Keep out of the sun during the middle of the day and, if you must be exposed to the sun, build up gradually from 20 minutes per day. Be especially careful of sun reflected off water and wear a T-shirt and lots of waterproof SPF15 suncream when swimming; snorkelling often leads to scorched backs of the thighs so wear bermuda shorts. Sun exposure ages the skin and makes people prematurely wrinkly; cover up with long, loose clothes and wear a hat when you can. The glare and the dust can be hard on the eyes, too, so bring UV-protecting sunglasses and, perhaps, a soothing eyebath.

Malaria prevention

There is no vaccine against malaria, but there are other ways to avoid it; since most of Africa is very high risk for malaria, travellers must plan their malaria protection properly. Seek current advice on the best antimalarials to take. If mefloquine (Lariam)

LONG-HAUL FLIGHTS

There is growing evidence, albeit circumstantial, that long-haul air travel increases the risk of developing deep vein thrombosis. This condition is potentially life threatening, but it should be stressed that the danger to the average traveller is slight.

Certain risk factors specific to air travel have been identified. These include immobility, compression of the veins at the back of the knee by the edge of the seat, the decreased air pressure and slightly reduced oxygen in the cabin, and dehydration. Consuming alcohol may exacerbate the situation by increasing fluid loss and encouraging immobility.

In theory everyone is at risk, but those at highest risk are shown below:

* Passengers on journeys of longer than eight hours duration
* People over 40
* People with heart disease
* People with cancer
* People with clotting disorders
* People who have had recent surgery, especially on the legs
* Women on the pill or other oestrogen therapy
* Pregnancy
* People who are very tall (over 6ft/1.8m) or short (under 5ft/1.5m)

A deep vein thrombosis (DVT) is a clot of blood that forms in the leg veins. Symptoms include swelling and pain in the calf or thigh. The skin may feel hot

is suggested, start this two-and-a-half weeks (three doses) before departure to check that it suits you; stop it immediately if it seems to cause depression or anxiety, visual or hearing disturbances, severe headaches, fits or changes in heart rhythm. Side effects such as nightmares or dizziness are not medical reasons for stopping unless they are sufficiently debilitating or annoying. Anyone who is pregnant, who has suffered fits in the past, has been treated for depression or psychiatric problems, has diabetes controlled by oral therapy or who is epileptic (or who has suffered fits in the past) or has a close blood relative who is epileptic, should avoid mefloquine.

Malarone (proguanil and atovaquone) is a new drug that is almost as effective as mefloquine. It has the advantage of having few side effects and need only be continued for one week after returning. However, it is expensive and because of this tends to be reserved for shorter trips. Malarone may not be suitable for everybody (it has yet to receive a licence for children under 40kg in the UK) so advice should be taken from a doctor.

The antibiotic doxycycline (100mg daily) is a viable alternative when either mefloquine or Malarone are not considered suitable for whatever reason. Like Malarone it can be started one day before arrival. Unlike mefloquine, it may also be used in travellers with epilepsy, although certain anti-epileptic medication may make it less effective. Users must be warned about the possibility of allergic skin reactions developing in sunlight which can occur in about 3% of people. The drug should be stopped if this happens. Women using the oral contraceptive should use an additional method of protection for the first four weeks when using doxycycline. It is also unsuitable in pregnancy or for children under 12 years.

Chloroquine and proguanil are no longer considered to be very effective for Tanzania. However, they may still be recommended if no other regime is suitable.

All prophylactic agents should be taken with or after the evening meal, washed

to touch and becomes discoloured (light blue-red). A DVT is not dangerous in itself, but if a clot breaks down then it may travel to the lungs (pulmonary embolus). Symptoms of a pulmonary embolus (PE) include chest pain, shortness of breath and coughing up small amounts of blood.

Symptoms of a DVT rarely occur during the flight, and typically occur within three days of arrival, although symptoms of a DVT or PE have been reported up to two weeks later.

Anyone who suspects that they have these symptoms should see a doctor immediately as anticoagulation (blood thinning) treatment can be given.

Prevention of DVT
General measures to reduce the risk of thrombosis are shown below. This advice also applies to long train or bus journeys.

* Whilst waiting to board the plane, try to walk around rather than sit.
* During the flight drink plenty of water (at least two small glasses every hour).
* Avoid excessive tea, coffee and alcohol.
* Perform leg-stretching exercises, such as pointing the toes up and down.
* Move around the cabin when practicable.

If you fit into the high-risk category (see above) ask your doctor if it is safe to travel. Additional protective measures such as graded compression stockings, aspirin or low molecular weight heparin can be given. No matter how tall you are, where possible request a seat with extra legroom.

down with plenty of fluid and with the exception of Malarone (see above) continued for four weeks after leaving.

Travellers to remote parts would probably be wise to carry a course of treatment to cure malaria. Experts differ on the costs and benefits of self-treatment, but agree that it leads to over-treatment and to many people taking drugs they do not need; yet treatment may save your life. Discuss your trip with a specialist to determine your particular needs and risks, and be sure you understand when and how to take the cure. If you are somewhere remote in a malarial region you probably have to assume that any high fever (over 38°C) for more than a few hours is due to malaria (regardless of any other symptoms) and should seek treatment. Diagnosing malaria is not easy, which is why consulting a doctor is sensible: there are other dangerous causes of fever in Africa, which require different treatments. Presently quinine and doxycycline, or quinine and fansidar, are the favoured regimes, but check for up-to-date advice on the current recommended treatment. And remember malaria may occur anything from seven days into the trip to up to one year after leaving Africa.

The risk of malaria above 1,800m above sea level is low. It is unwise to travel in malarial parts of Africa whilst pregnant or with children: the risk of malaria in many parts is considerable and these travellers are likely to succumb rapidly to the disease.

In addition to antimalarial medicines, it is important to avoid mosquito bites between dusk and dawn. Pack a DEET-based insect repellent, such as Repel (roll-ons or stick are the least messy preparations for travelling). You also need either a permethrin-impregnated bednet or a permethrin spray so that you can 'treat' bednets in hotels. Permethrin treatment makes even very tatty nets protective and prevents mosquitoes from biting through the impregnated net when you roll against it; it also deters other biters. Putting on long clothes at dusk means you can reduce the amount of repellent you need to put on your skin, but be aware tha

MALARIA IN TANZANIA
Philip Briggs

Along with road accidents, malaria poses the single biggest serious threat to the health of travellers in most parts of tropical Africa, Tanzania included. The Anopheles mosquito which transmits the parasite is most abundant near marshes and still water, where it breeds, and the parasite is most prolific at low altitudes. Parts of Tanzania lying at an altitude of 2,000m or higher (a category that includes the Ngorongoro Crater rim, Mount Kilimanjaro and Meru, and parts of the Eastern Arc mountains) are regarded to be free of malaria. In mid-altitude locations, malaria is largely but not entirely seasonal, with the highest risk of transmission occurring during the rainy season. Moist and low-lying areas such as the Indian Ocean coast and the hinterland of Lakes Tanganyika, Victoria and Nyasa are high risk throughout the year, but the danger is greatest during the rainy season. This localised breakdown might influence what foreigners working in Tanzania do about malaria prevention, but all travellers to Tanzania must assume that they will be exposed to malaria and should take precautions throughout their trip (see page 101 for advice on prophylactic drugs and avoiding mosquito bites).

Even those who take their malaria tablets meticulously and do everything possible to avoid mosquito bites may contract a strain of malaria that is resistant to prophylactic drugs. Untreated malaria is likely to be fatal, but even strains resistant to prophylaxis respond well to prompt treatment. Because of this, your immediate priority upon displaying possible malaria symptoms – which might include any combination of a headache, flu-like aches and pains, a rapid rise in temperature, a general sense of disorientation, and possibly even nausea and diarrhoea – is to establish whether you have malaria.

The blood test for malaria takes ten minutes to produce a result and costs about US$1 in Tanzania. A positive result means that you have malaria. A negative result suggests that you don't have malaria, but bear in mind that the parasite doesn't always show up on a test, particularly when the level of infection is mild or is 'cloaked' by partially effective prophylactics. For this reason, even if you test negative, it would be wise to stay within reach of a laboratory until the symptoms clear up, and to test again after a day or two if they don't. It's worth noting that if you have a fever and the malaria test is negative, you may have typhoid, which should also receive immediate treatment. Where typhoid-testing is unavailable, a routine blood test can give a strong indication of this disease.

malaria mosquitoes hunt at ankle level and will bite through socks, so apply repellent under socks too. Travel clinics usually sell a good range of nets, treatment kits and repellents.

Travel clinics and health information

A full list of current travel clinic websites worldwide is available on www.istm.org/. For other journey preparation information, consult ftp://ftp.shoreland.com/pub/shorecg.rtf or www.tripprep.com.

UK

British Airways Travel Clinic and Immunisation Service There are now only three BA clinics, all in London: 156 Regent St, W1B 5LB (no appointments); 101 Cheapside, EC1V6DT (tel: 020 7606 2977); 115 Buckingham Palace Rd, SW1W 9SJ (Victoria Station;

It is preferable not to attempt self-diagnosis or to start treatment for malaria before you have tested. There are, however, many places in Tanzania where you will be unable to test for malaria, for instance in the game reserves and in most of the popular hiking areas. With malaria, it is normal enough to go from feeling healthy to having a high fever in the space of a few hours (and it is possible to die from falciparum malaria within 24 hours of the first symptoms). In such circumstances, assume that you have malaria and act accordingly – whatever risks are attached to taking an unnecessary cure are outweighed by the dangers of untreated malaria.

It is imperative to treat malaria promptly. The sooner you take a cure, the less likely you are to become critically ill, and the more ill you become the greater the chance you'll have difficulty holding down the tablets. There is some division about the best treatment for malaria, but the quinine/doxycycline regime is safe and very effective. Alternatively quinine and fansidar can be used if doxycycline is unavailable. And if there is no quinine either then fansidar alone can be used. The latter is widely available in Tanzania. One cure that you should avoid is Halfan, which is dangerous, particularly if you are using Lariam as a prophylactic.

In severe cases of malaria, the victim will be unable to hold down medication, at which point they are likely to die unless they are hospitalised immediately and put on a drip. If you or a travelling companion start vomiting after taking your malaria medication, get to a hospital or clinic quickly, ideally a private one. Whatever concerns you might have about African hospitals, they are used to dealing with malaria, and the alternative to hospitalisation is far worse.

Malaria typically takes around two weeks to incubate (minimum time seven days), but it can take much longer, so you should always complete the prophylaxis as recommended after returning home. If you display possible malaria symptoms up to a year later, then get to a doctor immediately and ensure that they are aware you have been exposed to malaria.

Every so often I run into travellers who prefer to acquire resistance to malaria rather than take preventative tablets, or who witter on about homoeopathic cures for this killer disease. That's their prerogative, but they have no place expounding their ill-informed views to others. Travellers to Africa cannot acquire any effective resistance to malaria, and those who don't make use of prophylactic drugs risk their life in a manner that is both foolish and unnecessary.

tel: 020 7233 6661); see also www.britishairways.com/travelclinics. Also sell a variety of health-related goods.

Fleet Street Travel Clinic 29 Fleet St, London EC4Y 1AA; tel: 020 7353 5678

Hospital for Tropical Diseases Travel Clinic Capper St (off Tottenham Ct Rd), London WC1; tel: 020 7388 9600; web: www.thhtd.org. Offers consultations and advice, and is able to provide all necessary drugs and vaccines for travellers. Runs a healthline (09061 337733) for country-specific information and health hazards. Also stocks nets, water purification equipment and personal protection measures.

MASTA (Medical Advisory Service for Travellers Abroad) Keppel St, London WC1 7HT; tel: 09068 224100. This is a premium-line number, charged at 50p per minute.

NHS travel website, www.fitfortravel.scot.nhs.uk, provides country-by-country advice on immunisation and malaria, plus details of recent developments, and a list of relevant health organisations.

Nomad Travel Pharmacy and Vaccination Centre 364 Wellington Terrace, Turnpike Lane, London N8 0PX; tel: 020 8889 7014; email: sales@nomadtravel.co.uk; web: www.nomadtravel.co.uk. As well as dispensing health advice, Nomad stocks mosquito nets and other anti-bug devices, and an excellent range of adventure travel gear.
Thames Medical 157 Waterloo Rd, London SE1 8US; tel: 020 7902 9000. Competitively priced, one-stop travel health service. All profits go to their affiliated company, InterHealth, which provides health care for overseas workers on Christian projects.
Trailfinders Immunisation Centre 194 Kensington High St, London W8 7RG; tel: 020 7938 3999.
Travelpharm The Travelpharm website, www.travelpharm.com, offers up-to-date guidance on travel-related health and has a range of medications available through their online mini-pharmacy.

Irish Republic
Tropical Medical Bureau Grafton Street Medical Centre, Grafton Buildings, 34 Grafton St, Dublin 2; tel: 1 671 9200. Has a useful website specific to tropical destinations: www.tmb.ie

USA
Centers for Disease Control 1600 Clifton Rd, Atlanta, GA 30333; tel: 877 FYI TRIP; 800 311 3435; web: www.cdc.gov/travel. The central source of travel information in the USA. Each summer they publish the invaluable Health Information for International Travel, available from the Division of Quarantine at the above address.
Connaught Laboratories PO Box 187, Swiftwater, PA 18370; tel: 800 822 2463. They will send a free list of specialist tropical-medicine physicians in your state.
IAMAT (International Association for Medical Assistance to Travelers) 736 Center St, Lewiston, NY 14092; tel: 716 754 4883. A non-profit organisation that provides lists of English-speaking doctors abroad.

Canada
IAMAT (International Association for Medical Assistance to Travellers) Suite 1, 1287 St Clair Av W, Toronto, Ontario M6E 1B8; tel: 416 652 0137; web: www.sentex.net/~iamat
TMVC (Travel Doctors Group) Sulphur Springs Rd, Ancaster, Ontario; tel: 905 648 1112; web: www.tmvc.com.au

Australia, New Zealand, Thailand
TMVC Tel: 1300 65 88 44; web: www.tmvc.com.au. 20 clinics in Australia, New Zealand and Thailand, including:
Auckland Canterbury Arcade, 170 Queen Street, Auckland City; tel: 373 3531
Brisbane Dr Deborah Mills, 6th floor, Qantas Domestic Building, 247 Adelaide St, Brisbane, QLD 4000; tel: 7 3221 9066; fax: 7 3321 7076
Melbourne Dr Sonny Lau, 2nd floor, 393 Little Bourke St, Melbourne, VIC 3000; tel: 3 9602 5788; fax: 3 9670 8394
Sydney Dr Mandy Hu, 7th Floor, Dymocks Building, 428 George St, Sydney, NSW2000; tel: 2 221 7133; fax: 2 221 8401

South Africa
SAA-Netcare Travel Clinics PO Box 786692, Sandton 2146; fax: 011 883 6152; web: www.travelclinic.co.za or www.malaria.co.za. Clinics throughout South Africa.
TMVC (Travel Doctor Group) 113 DF Malan Drive, Roosevelt Park, Johannesburg; tel: 011 888 7488; web: www.tmvc.com.au. Consult the website for details of clinics in South Africa.

MEDICAL FACILITIES IN TANZANIA
Philip Briggs

Private clinics, hospitals and pharmacies can be found in most large towns, and doctors generally speak fair to fluent English. Consultation fees and laboratory tests are remarkably inexpensive when compared to most Western countries, so if you do fall sick it would be absurd to let financial considerations dissuade you from seeking medical help. Commonly required medicines such as broad-spectrum antibiotics are widely available and cheap throughout the region, as are malaria cures and prophylactics. Quinine and doxycycline, or quinine and fansidar, are best bought in advance – in fact it's advisable to carry all malaria-related tablets on you, and only rely on their availability locally if you need to restock your supplies.

If you are on any medication prior to departure, or you have specific needs relating to a known medical condition (for instance if you are allergic to bee stings or you are prone to attacks of asthma), then you are strongly advised to bring any related drugs and devices with you.

Switzerland
IAMAT (International Association for Medical Assistance to Travellers) 57 Voirets, 1212 Grand Lancy, Geneva; web: www.sentex.net/~iamat

Personal first-aid kit
The more I travel, the less I take. My minimal kit contains:

- A good drying antiseptic, eg: iodine or potassium permanganate (don't take antiseptic cream)
- A few small dressings (Band-Aids)
- Suncream
- Insect repellent; malaria tablets; impregnated bednet
- Aspirin or paracetamol
- Antifungal cream (eg: Canesten)
- Ciprofloxacin antibiotic, 500mg x 2 (or norfloxacin) for severe diarrhoea
- Tinidazole (500mg x 8) for giardia or amoebic dysentery (see below for regime)
- Antibiotic eye drops, for sore, 'gritty', stuck-together eyes (conjunctivitis)
- A pair of fine pointed tweezers (to remove hairy caterpillar hairs, thorns, splinters, coral, etc)
- Condoms or femidoms
- Maybe a malaria treatment kit and thermometer

MAJOR HAZARDS
People new to exotic travel often worry about tropical diseases, but it is accidents that are most likely to carry you off. Road accidents are very common in many parts of Tanzania, so be aware and do what you can to reduce risks: try to travel during daylight hours and refuse to be driven by a drunk. Listen to local advice about areas where violent crime is rife, too.

COMMON MEDICAL PROBLEMS
Travellers' diarrhoea
Travelling in Tanzania carries a fairly high risk of getting a dose of travellers' diarrhoea; perhaps half of all visitors will suffer and the newer you are to exotic

TREATING TRAVELLERS' DIARRHOEA

It is dehydration which makes you feel awful during a bout of diarrhoea and the most important part of treatment is drinking lots of clear fluids. Sachets of oral rehydration salts give the perfect biochemical mix to replace all that is pouring out of your bottom but other recipes taste nicer. Any dilute mixture of sugar and salt in water will do you good: try Coke or orange squash with a three-finger pinch of salt added to each glass (if you are salt-depleted you won't taste the salt). Otherwise make a solution of a four-finger scoop of sugar with a three-finger pinch of salt in a glass of water. Or add eight level teaspoons of sugar (18g) and one level teaspoon of salt (3g) to one litre (five cups) of safe water. A squeeze of lemon or orange juice improves the taste and adds potassium, which is also lost in diarrhoea. Drink two large glasses after every bowel action, and more if you are thirsty. These solutions are still absorbed well if you are vomiting, but you will need to take sips at a time. If you are not eating you need to drink three litres a day plus whatever is pouring into the toilet. If you feel like eating, take a bland, high carbohydrate diet. Heavy greasy foods will probably give you cramps.

If the diarrhoea is bad, or you are passing blood or slime, or you have a fever, you will probably need antibiotics in addition to fluid replacement. A single dose of ciprofloxacin (500mg) repeated after 12 hours may be appropriate. If the diarrhoea is greasy and bulky and is accompanied by sulphurous (eggy) burps, the likely cause is giardia. This is best treated with tinidazole (four x 500mg in one dose, repeated seven days later if symptoms persist).

travel, the more likely you will be to suffer. By taking precautions against travellers' diarrhoea you will also avoid typhoid, cholera, hepatitis, dysentery, worms, etc. Travellers' diarrhoea and the other faecal-oral diseases come from getting other peoples' faeces in your mouth. This most often happens from cooks not washing their hands after a trip to the toilet, but even if the restaurant cook does not understand basic hygiene you will be safe if your food has been properly cooked and arrives piping hot. The maxim to remind you what you can safely eat is:

PEEL IT, BOIL IT, COOK IT OR FORGET IT.

This means that fruit you have washed and peeled yourself, and hot foods, should be safe but raw foods, cold cooked foods, salads, fruit salads which have been prepared by others, ice-cream and ice are all risky. And foods kept lukewarm in hotel buffets are often dangerous. If you are struck, see box below for treatment.

Water sterilisation

It is much rarer to get sick from drinking contaminated water but it happens, so try to drink from safe sources.

Water should have been brought to the boil (even at altitude it only needs to be brought to the boil), or passed through a good bacteriological filter or purified with iodine; chlorine tablets (eg: Puritabs) are also adequate although theoretically less effective and they taste nastier. Mineral water has been found to be contaminated in Tanzania but should be safer than contaminated tap water.

Malaria

Whether or not you are taking malaria tablets, it is important to protect yourself from mosquito bites (see box, *Malaria in Tanzania*, on pages 96–7 and *Malaria prevention*, above), so keep your repellent stick or roll-on to hand at all times. Be aware that no prophylactic is 100% protective but those on prophylactics who are unlucky enough to catch malaria are less likely to get rapidly into serious trouble. It is easy and inexpensive to arrange a malaria blood test.

Dengue fever

This mosquito-borne disease may mimic malaria but there is no prophylactic medication available to deal with it. The mosquitoes that carry this virus bite during the daytime, so it is worth applying repellent if you see any mosquitoes around. Symptoms include strong headaches, rashes, excruciating joint and muscle pains, and high fever. Dengue fever lasts only for a week or so and is not usually fatal. Complete rest and paracetamol are the usual treatment; plenty of fluids also help. Some patients are given an intravenous drip to prevent dehydration. It is especially important to protect yourself if you have had dengue fever before, since a second infection with a different strain can result in the potentially fatal dengue haemorrhagic fever.

Insect bites

It is crucial to avoid mosquito bites between dusk and dawn; as the sun is going down, don long clothes and apply repellent on any exposed flesh. This will protect you from malaria, elephantiasis and a range of nasty insect-borne viruses. Otherwise retire to an air-conditioned room or burn mosquito coils (which are widely available and cheap in Tanzania) or sleep under a fan. Coils and fans reduce rather than eliminate bites. During the day it is wise to wear long, loose (preferably 100% cotton) clothes if you are pushing through scrubby country; this will keep ticks off and also tsetse and day-biting Aedes mosquitoes which may spread dengue and yellow fever. Tsetse flies hurt when they bite and are attracted to the colour blue; locals will advise on where they are a problem and where they transmit sleeping sickness.

Minute pestilential biting blackflies spread river blindness in some parts of Africa between 190°N and 170°S; the disease is caught close to fast-flowing rivers since flies breed there and the larvae live in rapids. The flies bite during the day but long trousers tucked into socks will help keep them off. Citronella-based natural repellents do not work against them.

QUICK TICK REMOVAL

African ticks are not the prolific disease transmitters they are in the Americas, but they may spread Lyme disease, tick-bite fever and a few rarities. Tick-bite fever is a non-serious, flu-like illness, but still worth avoiding. If you get the tick off whole and promptly the chances of disease transmission are reduced to a minimum. Manoeuvre your finger and thumb so that you can pinch the tick's mouthparts, as close to your skin as possible, and slowly and steadily pull away at right angles to your skin. This often hurts. Jerking or twisting will increase the chances of damaging the tick, which in turn increases the chances of disease transmission, as well as leaving the mouthparts behind. Once the tick is off, dowse the little wound with alcohol (local spirit, whisky or similar are excellent) or iodine. An area of spreading redness around the bite site, or a rash or fever coming on a few days or more after the bite, should stimulate a trip to a doctor.

Mosquitoes and many other insects are attracted to light. If you are camping, never put a lamp near the opening of your tent, or you will have a swarm of biters waiting to join you when you retire. In hotel rooms, be aware that the longer your light is on, the greater the number of insects will be sharing your accommodation. Tumbu flies or putsi are a problem where the climate is hot and humid. The adult fly lays her eggs on the soil or on drying laundry and when the eggs come in contact with human flesh (when you put on clothes or lie on a bed) they hatch and bury themselves under the skin. Here they form a crop of 'boils' which each hatches a grub after about eight days, when the inflammation will settle down. In putsi areas either dry your clothes and sheets within a screened house, or dry them in direct sunshine until they are crisp, or iron them.

Jiggers or sandfleas are another flesh-feaster. They latch on if you walk barefoot in contaminated places, and set up home under the skin of the foot, usually at the side of a toenail where they cause a painful, boil-like swelling. They need picking out by a local expert; if the distended flea bursts during eviction the wound should be dowsed in spirit, alcohol or kerosene, otherwise more jiggers will infest you.

Bilharzia or schistosomiasis
with thanks to Dr Vaughan Southgate of the Natural History Museum, London
Bilharzia or schistosomiasis is a disease that commonly afflicts the rural poor of the tropics who repeatedly acquire more and more of these nasty little worm-lodgers. Infected travellers and expatriates generally suffer fewer problems because symptoms will encourage them to seek prompt treatment and they are also exposed to fewer parasites. However, it is still an unpleasant problem that is worth avoiding.

The parasites digest their way through your skin when you wade, bathe or even shower in infested fresh water. Unfortunately, many African lakes, rivers and irrigation canals carry a risk of bilharzia.

The most risky shores will be close to places where infected people use water, wash clothes, etc. Winds disperse the cercariae, though, so they can be blown some distance, perhaps up to 200m from where they entered the water. Scuba-diving off a boat into deep offshore water, then, should be a low-risk activity, but showering in lake water or paddling along a reedy lake shore near a village is risky.

Although absence of early symptoms does not necessarily mean there is no infection, infected people usually notice symptoms two or more weeks after parasite-penetration. Travellers and expatriates will probably experience a fever and often a wheezy cough; local residents do not usually have symptoms. There is now a very good blood test which, if done six weeks or more after likely exposure, will determine whether you need treatment. Since bilharzia can be a nasty illness, avoidance is better than waiting to be cured and it is wise to avoid bathing in high risk areas.

Avoiding bilharzia
- If you are bathing, swimming, paddling or wading in fresh water which you think may carry a bilharzia risk, try get out of the water within ten minutes.
- Dry off thoroughly with a towel; rub vigorously.
- Avoid bathing or paddling on shores within 200m of villages or places where people use the water a great deal, especially reedy shores or where there is lots of water weed.
- If your bathing water comes from a risky source try to ensure that the water is taken from the lake in the early morning and stored snail-free, otherwise it should be filtered or Dettol or Cresol added.
- Bathing early in the morning is safer than bathing in the last half of the day.
- Covering yourself with DEET insect repellent before swimming will protect you.

MARINE DANGERS

Most established tourist beaches in Tanzania can be assumed to be safe for swimming. Elsewhere along the coast, it would be wise to ask local advice before plunging in the water, and to err on the side of caution if no sensible advice is forthcoming, since there is always a possibility of being swept away by strong currents or undertows that cannot be detected until you are actually in the water.

Snorkellers and divers should wear something on their feet to avoid treading on coral reefs, and should never touch the reefs with their bare hands – coral itself can give nasty cuts, and there is a danger of touching a venomous creature camouflaged against the reef. On beaches, never walk barefoot on exposed coral. Even on sandy beaches, people who walk barefoot risk getting coral or urchin spines in their soles or venomous fish spines in their feet.

If you do tread on a venomous fish, soak the foot in hot (but not scalding) water until some time after the pain subsides; this may be for 20–30 minutes in all. Take the foot out of the water to top up; otherwise you may scald it. If the pain returns, re-immerse the foot. Once the venom has been heat-inactivated, get a doctor to check and remove any bits of fish spine in the wound.

- If you think that you have been exposed to bilharzia parasites, arrange a screening blood test (your GP can do this) MORE than six weeks after your last possible contact with suspect water.

Skin infections

Any mosquito bite or small nick in the skin gives an opportunity for bacteria to foil the body's usually excellent defences; it will surprise many travellers how quickly skin infections start in warm humid climates and it is essential to clean and cover even the slightest wound. Creams are not as effective as a good drying antiseptic such as dilute iodine, potassium permanganate (a few crystals in half a cup of water), or crystal (or gentian) violet. One of these should be available in most towns. If the wound starts to throb, or becomes red and the redness starts to spread, or the wound oozes, and especially if you develop a fever, antibiotics will probably be needed: flucloxacillin (250mg four times a day) or cloxacillin (500mg four times a day). For those allergic to penicillin, erythromycin (500mg twice a day) for five days should help. See a doctor if the symptoms do not start to improve in 48 hours.

Fungal infections also get a hold easily in hot moist climates so wear 100% cotton socks and underwear and shower frequently. An itchy rash in the groin or flaking between the toes is likely to be a fungal infection. This needs treatment with an antifungal cream such as Canesten (clotrimazole); if this is not available try Whitfield's ointment (compound benzoic acid ointment) or crystal violet (although this will turn you purple!).

Eye problems

Bacterial conjunctivitis (pink eye) is a common infection in Africa; people who wear contact lenses are most open to this irritating problem. The eyes feel sore and gritty and they will often be stuck together in the mornings. They will need treatment with antibiotic drops or ointment. Lesser eye irritation should settle with bathing in salt water and keeping the eyes shaded. If an insect flies into your eye,

Baby Powder!

extract it with great care, ensuring you do not crush or damage it otherwise you may get a nastily inflamed eye from toxins secreted by the creature.

Prickly heat

A fine pimply rash on the trunk is likely to be heat rash; cool showers, dabbing dry, and talc will help. Treat the problem by slowing down to a relaxed schedule, wearing only loose, baggy, 100% cotton clothes and sleeping naked under a fan; if it's bad you may need to check into an air-conditioned hotel room for a while.

Meningitis

This is a particularly nasty disease as it can kill within hours of the first symptoms appearing. The telltale symptoms are a combination of a blinding headache (light sensitivity), a blotchy rash and a high fever. Immunisation protects against the most serious bacterial form of meningitis and the tetravalent vaccine ACWY is recommended for Tanzania. Other forms of meningitis exist (usually viral) but there are no vaccines for these. Local papers normally report localised outbreaks. A severe headache and fever should make you run to a doctor immediately. There are also other causes of headache and fever; one of which is typhoid, which occurs in travellers to Tanzania. Seek medical help if you are ill for more than a few days.

Safe sex

Travel is a time when we may enjoy sexual adventures, especially when alcohol reduces inhibitions. Remember that the risks of sexually transmitted infection are high, whether you sleep with fellow travellers or locals. About 40% of HIV infections in British heterosexuals are acquired abroad. Use condoms or femidoms; spermicide pessaries help reduce the risk of transmission. If you notice any genital ulcers or discharge, get treatment promptly since these increase the risk of acquiring HIV.

Rabies

Rabies is carried by all mammals (beware the village dogs and small monkeys that are used to being fed in the parks) and is passed on to man through a bite, scratch or a lick of an open wound. You must always assume any animal is rabid (unless personally known to you) and seek medical help as soon as possible. In the interim, scrub the wound with soap and bottled/boiled water, then pour on a strong iodine or alcohol solution. This helps stop the rabies virus entering the body and will guard against wound infections, including tetanus.

If you intend to have contact with animals and/or are likely to be more than 24 hours away from medical help, then pre-exposure vaccination is advised. Ideally three doses should be taken over four weeks. Contrary to popular belief these vaccinations are relatively painless!

If you are exposed as described, treatment should be given as soon as possible, but it is never too late to seek help as the incubation period for rabies can be very long. Those who have not been immunised will need a full course of injections together with rabies immunoglobulin (RIG), but this product is expensive (around US$800) and may be hard to come by. Another reason why pre-exposure vaccination should be encouraged in travellers who are planning to visit more remote areas!

Tell the doctor if you have had pre-exposure vaccine, as this will change the treatment you receive. And remember that, if you do contract rabies, mortality is 100% and death from rabies is probably one of the worst ways to go!

Snakes

Snakes rarely attack unless provoked, and bites in travellers are unusual. You are less likely to get bitten if you wear stout shoes and long trousers when in the bush. Most snakes are harmless and even venomous species will dispense venom in only about half of their bites. If bitten, then, you are unlikely to have received venom; keeping this fact in mind may help you to stay calm. Many so-called first-aid techniques do more harm than good: cutting into the wound is harmful; tourniquets are dangerous; suction and electrical inactivation devices do not work. The only treatment is antivenom. In case of a bite which you fear may have been from a venomous snake:

- Try to keep calm – it is likely that no venom has been dispensed.
- Prevent movement of the bitten limb by applying a splint.
- Keep the bitten limb BELOW heart height to slow the spread of any venom.
- If you have a crepe bandage, bind up as much of the bitten limb as you can, but release the bandage every half hour.
- Evacuate to a hospital which has antivenom.

And remember:

NEVER give aspirin; you may offer paracetamol, which is safe.
NEVER cut or suck the wound.
DO NOT apply ice packs.
DO NOT apply potassium permanganate.

If the offending snake can be captured without risk of someone else being bitten, take this to show the doctor – but beware since even a decapitated head is able to bite.

the ET effect

Europe

North America

Asia

Addis Ababa

Africa

Fifty five years ago, we were barely a ripple. But, like any self respecting ripple, we had bigger ideas. Initially the effects were only felt closer to home, as we went about building Africa's most extensive network. More recently we have been broadening our horizons. Today, we have almost 50 international destinations, spread across 4 continents. Ripples are a thing of the past, **these days we're making waves.**

GOING TO GREAT LENGTHS TO PLEASE **ETHIOPIAN** **AIRLINES**

Visit us on-line at www.ethiopianairlines.com
Ethiopian Airlines. London Office Tel: (44 - 20) 8987 7000. Fax: (44 - 20) 8747 9339.

Services to Abidjan, Accra, Addis Ababa, Athens, Bamako, Bangkok, Beijing, Beirut, Bujumbura, Cairo, Copenhagen, Dar-es-Salaam, Djibouti, Dubai, Entebbe, Frankfurt, Harare, Hargeisa, Jeddah, Johannesburg, Kano, Karachi, Khartoum, Kigali, Kilimanjaro, Kinshasa, Lagos, Lilongwe, Lome, London, Luanda, Lusaka, Maputo, Mumbai, Nairobi, N'Djamena, New Delhi, New York, Riyadh, Rome, Sanaa, Tel Aviv, Washington, D.C. & Zanzibar.

Spaulding & Co.

Part Two

The Guide

Arusha

Arusha is Tanzania's so-called 'safari capital', the base from which most travellers visit the country's most renowned game reserves, and the busiest tourist centre anywhere on the Tanzanian mainland. Arusha is also an increasingly important gateway into Tanzania, the first town visited by travellers coming from Nairobi in Kenya, and the entry point for an ever-increasing number of fly-in tourists, a trend that is likely to gather further momentum with the recent privatisation of the nearby Kilimanjaro International Airport.

In all probability, your first impression of Arusha will be that practically *everything* revolves around the safari industry. Prolonged exposure to Arusha is unlikely to change your mind on that score. True, this moderately sized town does lie at the heart of the fertile agricultural lands surrounding Mount Meru, but ultimately its economy is ruled by the tourist dollar. Every second vehicle you see in Arusha is a 4WD sporting a safari company logo. And many of the *dalla-dallas* that weave through the streets of Arusha are former safari vehicles. There is something comically incongruous about the sight of your standard crowded Tanzanian *dalla-dalla* with a bunch of heads sticking out of the open-topped roof as if waiting for an elephant to emerge from the nearest bush.

We've always found Arusha to be a pleasantly relaxed place to hang out, but there is no doubt that it can be a daunting prospect on first contact, especially for those who arrive by bus. Competition between the various safari companies is fierce, particularly at the bottom end of the price range, and the 'flycatchers' – the street touts who solicit custom for many budget safari companies – know that their best tactic is to catch backpackers as early as possible. As a consequence, your first few minutes in Arusha bus station are likely to be spent dodging the attention of a dozen yelling touts, all of whom can offer you the cheapest safari and best room in town. Fortunately, once you've run the bus station gauntlet, things do calm down – you can expect to be approached by the occasional flycatcher, but you need only tell them that you've already been on safari and they'll be on their way. I've probably spent some 20 days in Arusha over the years, and can't ever recall hitting a situation that so much as threatened to become unpleasant.

Despite the booming safari industry, Arusha is in appearance something of an African everytown, where low-rise buildings dating to the colonial era stand alongside a small but gradually increasing number of more modern structures. In some respects, Arusha encapsulates the conflicting images that greet the modern Africa traveller; the safari industry may have generated immense wealth, but this also serves to accentuate the vast differences that separate the haves from the have-nots. Here, too, you'll encounter that spectrum of cultural influences which tends

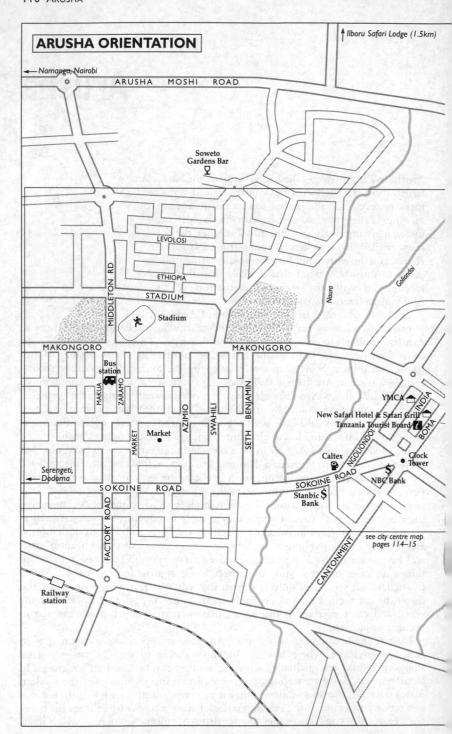

ARUSHA ORIENTATION

↑ Ilboru Safari Lodge (1.5km)

← Namanga, Nairobi

ARUSHA MOSHI ROAD

Soweto
Gardens Bar

LEVOLOSI

ETHIOPIA

STADIUM

MIDDLETON RD

Stadium

MAKONGORO

MAKONGORO

Naura

Goliondoi

Bus
station

MAKUA

ZARAMO

AZIMIO

SWAHILI

SETH BENJAMIN

YMCA

INDIA

New Safari Hotel & Safari Grill
Tanzania Tourist Board

BOMA

MARKET

Market

Caltex

NGOLIONDOI

Clock
Tower

Serengeti,
← Dodoma

SOKOINE ROAD

SOKOINE ROAD

NBC Bank

FACTORY ROAD

Stanbic
Bank

CANTONMENT

see city centre map
pages 114–15

Railway
station

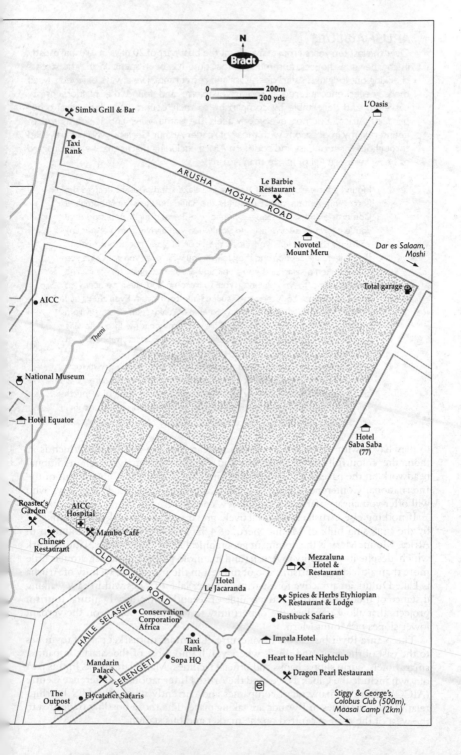

ARUSHA BLUES

Over the last ten years I must have spent the best part of 20 days in Arusha, mostly in cheaper guesthouses, and much of that time has been spent pacing the streets checking out lodgings, safari operators and restaurants. I've always enjoyed myself there, never encountered a serious problem, and found the hustlers pretty easygoing and deflectable by comparison to their counterparts in several other parts of Africa. But not everybody feels the same way, and it seems worth countering my impressions with those of reader Arthur Gerfers, who has travelled throughout most of East and southern Africa, including places that I would regard as being far more full of hassle than Arusha:

> I found your description of Arusha as 'relaxed and pleasant despite the fierce competition that surrounds the safari business' unfathomable. Con artists and safari stooges hound you day and night non-stop until you leave. They swarm around you when you arrive, they accompany you until the moment you close the door of your guesthouse room, they linger at reception and they follow you wherever you go. Once you have booked a safari and you think you are in the clear, forget it. The urchins come to you wanting you to recommend their company to some other poor sods they have sucked into their orbit. Even after I had returned from safari and sat trying to enjoy breakfast an operator from my safari company swooped in and tried to browbeat me into following him to some other guesthouse where undecided tourists supposedly sat awaiting my blessing!
>
> A lone woman we met had five days in which to find a group for a four-day safari. She was herded to an office where she was assured that three Australians had already signed up and were in need of a fourth person. She paid up and waited at the appointed time outside her

to play havoc with the minds of visitors in search of the real Africa. Which is it, then: the colourfully dressed Maasai and Arusha women who sell traditional beadwork on the pavement, the suited businessmen who scurry in and out of the International Conference Centre, or the swaggering, sunglassed wide-boys who will offer you cheap safaris, change money, cocaine...?

If nothing else, Arusha is an attractively green town, with a skyline dominated by the imposing hulk of Mount Meru, at 4,556m the fifth-highest mountain in Africa. Mount Meru is the dominant geographical feature in Arusha National Park which, despite its proximity to Arusha and manifold points of interest, attracts little more than a trickle of tourism. Also of interest in the immediate vicinity of Arusha is Lake Duluti, an attractive forest-fringed crater lake that lies within easy walking distance of the Moshi Road, and a couple of recently introduced cultural tourism projects that allow travellers the opportunity to visit local villages on the verdant lower slopes of Mount Meru.

The Naura River bisects the town centre. The more upmarket part of town lies to the east of the river, and this is where you'll find most of the safari companies, smart hotels, curio shops, banks and official facilities. Major landmarks in this part of town include the Clock Tower and the Arusha International Conference Centre (AICC), home to many safari companies and currently where the UN hearings relating to war crimes in Rwanda are taking place. The more bustling trade area to the west of the river is centred on the market and bus station.

guesthouse the next morning. One of the company's urchins came around later to tell her that the Australians had taken ill and the safari would have to be postponed. Despite the fact that these Australians did not exist, the woman was now left with only three days for the safari. She was unable to find anyone in time and ended up leaving Arusha disappointed.

We booked a safari where we were also promised two Australians to fill out the requisite four needed to meet the agreed price. We waited at the appointed hour outside of our guesthouse only to hear that our Australians had disappeared. A similar situation befell another couple on the same day, only their safari companions were Kiwis. By the time the Kiwis failed to materialise, we had decided to go on safari together. The couple demanded their money back from their company, claiming breach of contract, and the argument that ensued was nothing short of disgusting. Imagine yourself surrounded by a dozen leering touts, one of them in a Mobutu leopard hat and glasses claiming to be from the Tourist Board and foaming at the mouth about imaginary laws and regulations prohibiting refunds. In the end, our friends got their money back minus a US$100 refund fee.

My advice is to arrive in Arusha with plenty of time to spare, since the flycatchers can smell if you are in a rush and will screw you accordingly. Although it is draining, check out several safari companies, with a group already intact where possible. And talk to other tourists coming back from safari about their impressions of the different companies, without urchins present.

I should add that Arthur stayed at the Mashele Guesthouse, a long-standing flycatcher haunt and the one lodge in Arusha that I would avoid at all costs.

Arusha used to be notorious for having an erratic electricity and water supply, but we experienced no cuts over the several days we spent in Arusha in 1998 or 2001, so it seems that things have improved. The same cannot be said for the pot-holed roads, one of the few reminders of the economic doldrums that Arusha found itself in during the tourist industry crisis of the 1980s.

GETTING THERE AND AWAY

As tourism to Tanzania increases, so does Arusha play an increasingly pivotal role as the main transport hub for visitors to the country, whether they travel by air or by road.

By air

Kilimanjaro International Airport (KIA) lies roughly halfway along the 80km road that connects Arusha to Moshi. The privatisation of KIA in late 1998 has greatly improved facilities, with one result being that KLM now flies there directly from Europe on a daily basis, eliminating the need to travel to Arusha via Nairobi or Dar es Salaam – it's to be hoped other airlines will follow suit. In addition to flights to Dar es Salaam and Nairobi, scheduled flights connect KIA to Mwanza, Bukoba, Zanzibar, Pemba, Mafia and Mbeya. Travellers arriving at or leaving from KIA with Air Tanzania should note that they offer a free shuttle service between the airport and Arusha connecting with all flights and dropping you at the hotel of

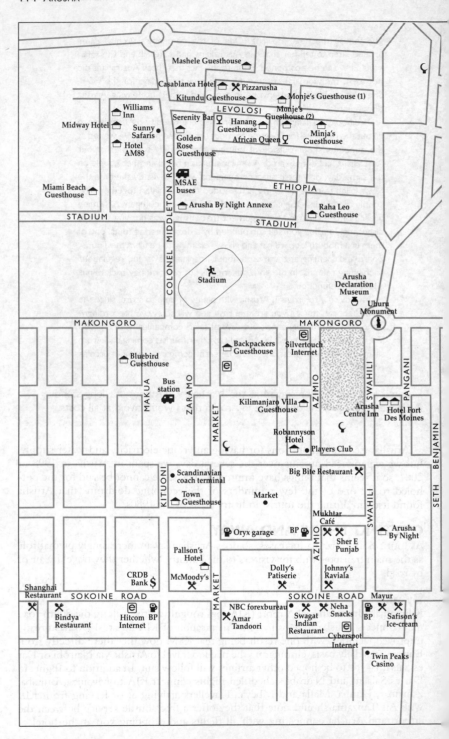

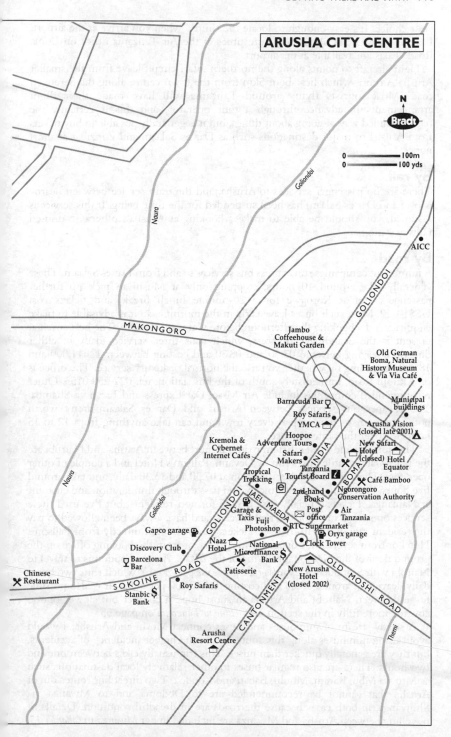

ARUSHA CITY CENTRE

Bradt

N

0 ——— 100m
0 ——— 100 yds

Naura

Goliondoi

AICC

MAKONGORO

GOLIONDOI

Jambo
Coffeehouse &
Makuti Garden

Old German
Boma, Natural
History Museum
& Vía Vía Café

Municipal
buildings

Barracuda Bar

Roy Safaris
YMCA

Arusha Vision
(closed late 2001)

Hoopoe
Adventure Tours

Kremola &
Cybernet
Internet Cafés

Safari
Makers

New Safari
Hotel
(closed)

Hotel
Equator

INDIA

BOMA

Tropical
Trekking

Tanzania
Tourist Board

Café Bamboo

Naura

Goliondoi

2nd-hand
Books

Ngorongoro
Conservation Authority

GOLIONDOI

JAEL MAEDA

Garage &
Taxis

Post
office

Air
Tanzania

Fuji
Photoshop

RTC Supermarket

Gapco garage

Oryx garage

Discovery Club

Naaz
Hotel

National
Microfinance
Bank

Clock Tower

Barcelona
Bar

SOKOINE

ROAD

Patisserie

New Arusha
Hotel
(closed 2002)

OLD MOSHI ROAD

Chinese
Restaurant

Roy Safaris

CANTONMENT

Themi

Stanbic
Bank

Arusha
Resort Centre

your choice. It's easy enough to locate the shuttle when you arrive at the airport. Leaving Arusha, ask about departure times at the Air Tanzania office on Boma Road. Taxis are available at the airport.

Light aircraft to points along the northern safari circuit leave from the smaller Arusha Airport, which lies about 5km from the town centre along the Serengeti road. Most tourists flying around Tanzania will have made their flight arrangements in advance through a tour operator, and this is certainly the recommended way of going about things, but it is generally possible to buy tickets from Arusha to major destinations such as Dar es Salaam and Zanzibar at short notice.

By rail

There are no passenger services to Arusha, and the train service between nearby Moshi and Dar es Salaam has been suspended for the time being. If this service is resumed, you should be able to make a booking at Arusha's otherwise unused railway station.

By road

A number of companies run express bus services to and from Dar es Salaam. These generally take around 10 hours, stopping only at Moshi to pick up further passengers and at Korogwe for a 20-minute lunch break, and tickets cost US$10–12. Most such buses leave early in the morning, so it is advisable to make enquiries and a booking the afternoon before you want to leave. The best coach at present is the Scandinavia Express, which runs three services daily in either direction, leaving between 07.30 and 08.30 and costing between Tsh11,000 and 18,000 depending on whether you use the normal or luxury service. The office is on Kituoni Road, immediately south of the bus station; tel: 027 250 0153. Other recommended companies include Air Msae, Dar Express and Fresh ya Shamba. The cheaper bus services between Arusha and Dar es Salaam aren't worth bothering with, as they stop at every town and can take anything from 12 to 15 hours to cover the same distance.

The quickest and most efficient road transport between Arusha and Nairobi are the twice-daily shuttle buses run by Devanu, Pallson's Hotel and a couple of other operators. These leave in either direction at 07.30 and 13.30 daily, and take around five hours, depending on how quickly you pass through immigration and customs at Namanga. Tickets officially cost US$25 for non-residents, but I've used these services on several occasions in recent years, and have always been allowed to pay the resident rate of Tsh10–12,000. Tickets can be bought directly from Pallson's Hotel or from several tour operators in Arusha, or from the booking office on the ground floor of the Ngorongoro Wing of the AICC. Another option is to travel to Nairobi with Scandinavia Express (see previous paragraph), which runs two buses daily, leaving at around 15.00 and costing Tsh10,000 per ticket. It is also possible to get between Nairobi and Arusha in short hops, a cheaper but slower option covered more fully in the section on *Getting to Tanzania* on page 55.

A steady stream of minibuses and buses connect Moshi and Arusha. I would avoid using minibuses along this route due to the higher incidence of accidents, but they are generally quicker than buses. This trip usually takes between one and two hours. There are also regular buses to other relatively local destinations such as Mto wa Mbu, Karatu, Mbulu, Babati and Kondoa. Two direct bus routes out of Arusha that cannot be recommended are to Dodoma and to Mwanza via Shinyanga, in both cases because the roads are in dreadful condition. Details of travelling between Arusha and Mwanza are included under *Mwanza* in *Chapter 15*.

WHERE TO STAY

This section covers accommodation located in central Arusha or within a roughly 5km radius of the town centre. Do note, however, that a number of popular lodges, particularly in the upmarket and moderate brackets, are located further out of town, close to Lake Duluti or Usa River on the main Moshi road, or in the immediate vicinity of Arusha National Park. While these hotels are covered under the appropriate headings later in the chapter, they all lie within an hour's drive of Arusha and are in several instances far more aesthetically pleasing than the more central hotels.

Exclusive

Arusha Coffee Lodge Tel: 027 254 4521; fax: 027 254 4574; email: res@halcyontz.com; web: www.arushacoffeelodge.com. Arusha Coffee Lodge opened after the research for the fourth edition of this guide was completed, but since it is constructed and managed by Halcyon – also responsible for the outstanding Tarangire Treetops Lodge – there's every reason to accept its claim to be the 'first truly five-star hotel in Arusha'. The lodge lies a few kilometres out of town along the Serengeti road, on a coffee estate with a good view of Mount Meru. Accommodation is in smart private chalets featuring multi-level living areas, huge balconies and stunning fireplaces. Each chalet also has its own private coffee in-room percolator, to get the true aroma of the coffee estate. Rates are US$175/250 B&B or US$195/300 HB, increasing slightly over the peak season.

Upmarket

Karama Lodge Tel: 027 250 0359; mobile: 0744 745 188; fax: 27 254 8299; email: karama@tropicaltrails.com; web: www.karama-lodge.com. This fabulous new eco-lodge, constructed by Tropical Trails, has a genuine bush atmosphere, despite being situated only 3km from central Arusha along the Old Moshi Road. Perched on the small but densely wooded Suye Hill, the lodge consists of 12 stilted wood-and-makuti units with Zanzibar-style beds draped in netting, en-suite shower and toilet, and private balcony facing Kilimanjaro. The *brachystegia* woodland in the lodge grounds and adjacent forest reserve harbours a wide range of birds – the localised brown-throated barbet prominent among them – as well as small nocturnal mammals such as bushbaby, genet and civet. Highly recommended as a refreshing alternative to the bland city hotels that otherwise characterise Arusha and environs. Accommodation costs US$90/110 single/double B&B.

Impala Hotel Tel: 027 250 2398/3453/7394; fax: 027 250 8680/8220; email: impala@cybernet.co.tz or impala@habari.co.tz; web: www.impalahotel.com. The recently expanded and renovated Impala Hotel, situated about 10 minutes' walk from the town centre, is justifiably rated by many tour operators as the best hotel in its range in the immediate vicinity of Arusha. Facilities include four restaurants variously specialising in Indian, Italian, Chinese and Continental cuisine, an internet café, a foreign exchange bureau offering good rates, a swimming pool, a gift shop and an in-house safari operator. The rooms are comfortable and attractively decorated, and have satellite television, hot showers and a fridge. The only criticism that could be levelled at this reliable, well-run and very reasonably priced hotel is that it is somewhat lacking in character. Accommodation costs US$65/75 single/double B&B, while HB and FB rates work out at an additional US$10 per person per meal. Double executive rooms and suites are available at US$90 and US$190 B&B respectively.

Moivaro Coffee Plantation Lodge Tel: 027 255 3242; fax: 027 255 3243; email: moivaro@habari.co.tz; web: www.moivaro.com. This elegantly rustic lodge, set on a 40-acre coffee estate 7km from central Arusha and 1.5km from the Moshi road, has received consistently good reports from travellers and tour operators since it opened a couple of years ago. The self-contained bungalows, set in a circular arrangement around a clean swimming pool and flowering lawns, cost US$65/90 single/double B&B or US$93/146 FB.

The main dining and reception building has a large patio facing Mount Meru. Facilities include walking and jogging paths, internet facilities and a massage room.
Klub Afriko Hotel Tel: 027 250 9205; mobile: 0744 369475; email: dino@klubafriko.com; web: www.klubafriko.com. The intimate and stylish Klub Afriko is a newly opened lodge set in compact, neat grounds on the Moshi Road about 3km out of Arusha. The six self-contained chalets have a traditional African appearance with a bright and airy interior, while the spacious dining area is decorated in a more classical style. Accommodation costs US$40 per person B&B, and three-course set lunches and dinners cost Tsh7,000 and 8,000 respectively.
Ilboru Safari Lodge Tel: 027 250 9658/7834; email: ilboru-lodge@habari.co.tz; web: www.habari.co.tz\ilborulodge. Highly regarded by several tour operators, Ilboru Safari Lodge lies about 2km from the town centre in neat and leafy suburban grounds below Mount Meru. It's a pleasant and peaceful if unremarkable retreat, and reasonably priced at US$65/75/125 single/double/triple.
L'Oasis Lodge Tel: 027 250 7089; mobile: 0744 286731; fax: 027 250 7089; email: loasis@africaonline.co.tz; web: www.loasislodge.com. Set in large green grounds off the Moshi Road, about 500m along a side road signposted opposite the Mount Meru Novotel, this pleasant and popular lodge is notable for its excellent restaurant. Accommodation rates are US$65/90/115 single/double/triple.
Mount Meru Novotel Tel: 027 250 2711/2; fax: 027 250 8503/8221; email: mtmeruho@africaonline.co.tz or sales-novotel@cybernet.co.tz.; web: www.novotel.com. Government owned but managed by the French Novotel chain, the Mount Meru Hotel was at one time the only truly international standard option situated within walking distance of the town centre. Set in landscaped gardens overlooking the golf course, it remains an attractive set-up, and popular with international business travellers for its good facilities, including a large outdoor swimming pool, two restaurants and an efficient business centre. Large rooms with en-suite bathrooms, private balconies and satellite television seem relatively overpriced for what they are at US$135/155 single/double B&B or US$300 for a suite, with a 30% discount for Tanzanian residents.

Moderate

Mezzaluna Hotel Tel: 027 4381; email: mezzalunahotel@yahoo.com. This homely and sensibly priced Italian-owned hotel lies in green grounds close to the Impala Hotel and is attached to the excellent Mezzaluna Restaurant. It charges US$35/45 single/double B&B for clean, comfortable self-contained rooms.

NEW ARUSHA HOTEL
A sign of Arusha's growing significance in the 1920s was the construction of the New Arusha Hotel, the small town's first hostelry, which was closed in 2001 for long overdue renovations. A 1929 government brochure eulogises this newly opened establishment as having 'hot and cold water in all bedrooms, modern sanitation, teak dancing floor, electric light and really excellent food, as well as golf, tennis, big game and bird shooting'. Less complimentary the description included in Evelyn Waugh's amusingly acerbic travelogue *A Tourist in Africa* in 1960: it 'seeks to attract by the claim to be exactly midway between Cape Town and Cairo... I did not see any African or Indian customers. Dogs howled and scuffled under the window at night. Can I say anything pleasant about this hotel? Yes, it stands in a cool place in a well-kept garden and it stocks some potable South African wines in good conditions'.

Hotel Equator Tel: 027 250 8409/3727/3127; email: nah@tz2000.com. This recently refurbished former government hotel on Boma Road, though somewhat bland and nondescript, currently offers the most comfortable accommodation in the town centre. Decent value at US$55/65 single/double. The equally central New Safari and New Arusha Hotels are both former government hotels that were looking somewhat tired before they were privatised and closed for renovations in 2001.

Arusha Resort Centre Tel: 027 250 8333; email: philpht@africaonline.co.tz. This comfortable hotel is conveniently located on Fire Road about 200m from the Clock Tower. Although popular with (and recommended to) Tanzanian residents requiring a temporary home in Arusha, it does seem overpriced for tourists and other non-residents. Well-screened double rooms with hot showers cost Tsh18,000 for residents or US$40 for non-residents B&B, while double apartments with en-suite kitchens cost Tsh42,000 for residents or US$80 for non-residents B&B, with a 10% discount for weekly occupation. There is a bar and restaurant attached.

Hotel Le Jacaranda Tel: 027 254 4624/6529; email: jacaranda@cybernet.com.tz. Situated in the garden suburbs immediately east of the town centre, this converted residential property doesn't lack for character, and it is set in pretty, slightly overgrown grounds. Unfortunately, the rates of US$40/25 for a single/double using common showers or US$50/55 for an en-suite room seem slightly optimistic.

Hotel Saba Saba Tel: 027 254 8054; fax: 027 254 8407; email: hotel77@tz2000.com. The Saba Saba claims to be the largest tourist village in East or Central Africa, a title that is not so much meaningless as downright misleading. The hotel consists of several cheerless concrete quadrangles, reminiscent of a prison more than any village I've encountered. The rooms are adequate and sensibly priced at US$30/40, but I do pity the tourist who spends their first night in Africa in such an austere and institutional environment.

Budget

Pallson's Hotel Tel/fax: 027 254 8123; email: pallsonshotel@yahoo.com. This well-established multi-storey hotel has a central location, a short walk south of the bus station on the corner of Market and Sokoine Roads. The self-contained double rooms, with satellite television, fan and hot shower, would be adequate value at the official non-resident rate of US$25/30 single/double B&B. At the resident rate of Tsh12,000, which walk-in clients are evidently allowed to pay irrespective of their residence status, Pallson's is probably the best budget deal in Arusha.

Midway Hotel and **Williams Inn** Situated alongside each other near to the stadium, these hotels both charge US$10 for an ordinary double with nets and fans or US$15 for a self-contained double with nets, fans and a balcony. Both of these places are reasonable value without being anything special.

The Outpost Tel: 027 250 8405; email: info@outposttanzania.com or outpost@ark.eoltz.com; web: www.outposttanzania.com. This welcoming and homely Australian-owned lodge, set in a suburban Arusha garden at 37A Serengeti Street between the town centre and the Impala Hotel, has proved to be consistently popular with travellers seeking comfortable accommodation at the upper end of the budget range. A bed in a dormitory costs US$15 per person B&B, while private rooms cost US$28/36 single/double self-contained or US$25/32 using common shower. Cheap lunches and dinners are available. To get here from the Clock Tower, follow Uhuru Avenue east out of town for about 1km, then take the signposted right turn about 500m further, and the house is about 300m down the road to your left.

Naaz Hotel Tel: 027 250 2087. Situated on Sokoine Road close to the Clock Tower, the clean, convenient and secure Naaz Hotel has been popular with budget travellers for as long as I can remember. These days, however, is seems to be attracting custom primarily on its long-standing but inflated reputation. Self-contained doubles in the new wing with nets and fans are just about reasonable value at US$25. Not so the doubles in the old wing, which cost a hefty US$20 despite being cramped, rundown, and using communal showers. There is a good, inexpensive restaurant on the ground floor.

YMCA Hostel Tel: 027 250 6907. Centrally located on India Street and formerly quite popular with travellers, the YMCA now seems pretty poor value at US$13/15/23 single/double/triple for a scruffy room using common cold showers.

Hotel Fort Des Moines Tel: 0741 511156. The pretentious name of this clean and reasonably smart new hotel near the market and bus station is reflected in the optimistic non-resident rates of US$25/30 for a self-contained single/double.

Shoestring

Arusha By Night Annexe Tel: 027 250 6894. Situated close to the stadium and not far from the bus station, this slightly rundown but perfectly adequate hotel seems excellent value following a recent drop in price to Tsh6,000/8,000 for a self-contained single/double with hot shower.

Backpackers Guesthouse Tel: 0741 652158; email: backpackersguesthouse@hotmail.com. This new Indian owned lodge also stands close to the market and bus station, and seems pretty good value at Tsh6,000 for a large clean double room with netting. The common showers have hot water, and an internet café is attached.

Kilimanjaro Villa Tel: 027 250 8109. A long-standing backpacker standby situated close to the market and bus station, the Kilimanjaro Villa is nothing special, but it's adequately friendly and clean at Tsh3,500/5,000 single/double using common showers.

Robannyson Hotel Under renovation for some years, this multi-storey hotel opposite the market is pretty good value at around Tsh6,000/8,000 for a self-contained single/double.

Monje's Guesthouse The pick of a cluster of popular cheap guesthouses in the back roads north of the stadium, Monje's is a quiet, family-run affair which actually consists of three guesthouses on opposite sides of the same road. All three places have clean rooms, friendly staff, hot showers and a vigorously enforced anti-flycatcher policy! Rooms are around Tsh3,000/4,000 single/double. The nearby and similarly priced **Kitundu Guesthouse** (also known as 'K' Guesthouse) and **Minja's Guesthouse** are also recommended.

Mashele Guesthouse The apparent popularity of this guesthouse in the back roads north of the stadium is largely due to it being the lodge to which most flycatchers first point travellers. The reason why the flycatchers do this is because it is one of the few guesthouses in the area that allows them to hang out on the premises. And if having to make friends with half the flycatchers in Arusha isn't reason enough to put you off staying there, then a recent spate of theft from the rooms and bar-room brawls between rival flycatchers should be.

Camping

Maasai Camp Tel: 027 250 0359; mobile: 0744 745 188; fax: 27 254 8299; email: info@tropicaltrails.com; web: www.tropicaltrails.com. Situated about 2km out of town along the Old Moshi Road, Maasai Camp is one of the most popular campsites in Tanzania, used mostly by overland trucks but large enough that there's plenty of space for independent travellers. Facilities include an ablution block with hot water, a pool table, volleyball and a lively 24-hour bar. The restaurant is well known for its pizzas, which cost around Tsh4,000. If you're without transport, you can get a taxi here for around Tsh2,000, and there are plans to introduce a lift service from the town centre. Camping costs US$3 per person. Tents can be hired for US$3 per night. Self-contained double *banda*s (huts) are under construction at the time of writing, and should be available by the time you read this at around US$25. A safari company called Tropical Trails is based at Maasai Camp.

The only central campsite, **Arusha Vision Camp** next to the Equator Hotel, was closed in late 2001, with no indication as to whether it will re-open. Out of town camping options at Lake Duluti, Usa River and on the edge of Arusha National Park – are covered under the respective headings later in the chapter.

WHERE TO EAT

Any number of good restaurants are dotted around Arusha, with a wide number of international cuisines represented and most budgets catered for by a number of places. The following is an alphabetical selection of some long standing favourites and interesting recent additions, but new places open and close frequently, so don't be afraid to try restaurants that aren't listed.

Amar Tandoori Restaurant Good and long-standing Indian restaurant on Sokoine Street, serving meat and vegetarian dishes in the Tsh3,000–5,000 range.

Café Bamboo Restaurant This homely restaurant on Boma Road serves decent filter coffee, good fruit juices, as well as a huge range of sandwiches, pancakes and other snacks. The home-cooked lunch of the day is a real bargain for Tsh2,000. It's justifiably packed at lunchtime, but closed in the evenings.

Everest Chinese Restaurant Situated a short distance from the Clock Tower along the Old Moshi Road, the Everest is widely regarded to be the best place of its sort in town, and isn't too expensive.

Ice Cream Parlour Situated on Sokoine Road, close to Neha Snacks, this bright parlour serves cheap sundaes and cones, as well as other gooey snacks.

Jambo Coffee House & Makuti Garden The coffee house serves arguably the best coffee in town (not a lot of competition) as well as good cooked breakfasts and light snacks. The adjacent Makuti Garden, set in a green courtyard, is one of the best places in the town centre for evening meals – curries and grills in the Tsh3,000–4,500 range.

Johnny's Raviala Restaurant Tasty snacks and fruit juices in a rather seedy atmosphere.

Le Barbie Restaurant Situated on the Moshi Road close to the Mount Meru Novotel, this vast and very pleasant *makuti* construction, affiliated to L'Oasis Hotel, serves a good variety of grills and seafood dishes, mostly in the Tsh4,000–5,000 range.

McMoody's This Macdonald's clone on Sokoine Street serves reasonable hamburgers and cheeseburgers for around Tsh2,000 – the plastic décor, like the food, is designed to make fast food junkies feel at home.

Mezzaluna Restaurant Situated close to the Impala Hotel, the Mezzaluna is generally regarded to serve the best Italian food in Arusha. Pizzas are something of a speciality here, and they cost around Tsh4,000–5,000. There is an indoor dining room, but weather permitting it's much more pleasant to eat in the spacious thatched garden area.

Mukhtar Café aka Khan's Barbecue. Situated in Mosque Street to the north of the market, this singular and popular place has become something of an Arusha institution, functioning as a spare motor parts shop by day and a street barbecue in the evening. It serves fabulous kebabs of beef, chicken and lamb, with a huge selection of salads, naan bread and the like. It's not particularly cheap given its unromantic setting, but the food is great and you can pick and choose what you like. No alcohol allowed.

Neha Snacks Indian vegetarian snacks and light meals on Sokoine Road close to Pallson's Hotel.

Patisserie Centrally located, on Sokoine Road close to the Clock Tower, this popular backpackers' and volunteers' hangout is pretty much unique in Tanzania – a huge range of freshly baked loaves, rolls and pastries, great light meals, fruit juice and filter coffee. The coffee is frequently disappointing, but everything else is excellent. Great for a light (and inexpensive) breakfast or lunchtime snack! Closed in the evenings. Good internet café attached.

SOME HISTORY

Little is known about the Arusha area prior to the 17th century, when the Bantu-speaking Meru people, migrants from the west with strong linguistic and cultural affinities to the Chagga of Kilimanjaro – settled and farmed the fertile and well-watered northern foothills of Mount Meru. In 1830 or thereabouts, the southern slopes of the mountain verging on the Maasai Steppes were settled by the Arusha, a Maasai subgroup who lost their cattle and territory in one of the internecine battles characteristic of this turbulent period in Maasailand. The Arusha people speak the same Maa language as the plains Maasai and share a similar social structure based around initiated age-sets, but when they settled in the Mount Meru area they forsook their pastoralist roots, turning instead to agriculture as a primary source of subsistence.

The Arusha economy was boosted by the trade in agricultural produce – in particular tobacco – with the closely affiliated Maasai of the plains. The Arusha also became known as reliable providers of food and other provisions for the Arab slave caravans that headed inland from the Pangani and Tanga area towards modern-day Kenya and Lake Victoria. Boosted by this regular trade, the Arusha had, by 1880, cleared the forested slopes of Mount Meru to an altitude of around 1,600m to make way for cultivation. As their territory expanded, however, the Arusha people increasingly came into contact with their northern neighbours, the Meru, resulting in several territorial skirmishes and frequent cattle raids between the two tribes.

In 1881, prompted by the need to defend their combined territories against the Maasai and other potential attackers, the incumbent warrior age-sets of the Arusha and Meru united to form a formidable military force. Since they were settled on the well-watered slopes of Mount Meru, and their subsistence was not primarily dependent on livestock, the Arusha and Meru people were less affected than the plains pastoralists by the devastating series of droughts and rinderpest epidemics of the 1880s and early 1890s. As a result, the combined army, known as the Talala – the Expansionists – was able to exert considerable influence over neighbouring Maasai and Chagga territories.

The Talala staunchly resisted German attempts to settle in their territory, killing the first missionaries to arrive there and repelling an initial punitive attack by the colonial army. In October 1896, however, the Arusha and Meru were soundly defeated by a military expedition out of Moshi led by Karl Johannes and consisting of 100 German troopers and supported by some 5,000 Chagga warriors. In the aftermath of this defeat, the Germans drove home the point by razing hundreds of Arusha and Meru smallholdings, killing the men, confiscating the cattle, and repatriating women of Chagga origin to the Kilimanjaro area.

In 1889, the Germans established a permanent settlement – modern day Arusha town – on the border of Arusha and Maasai territories, and used forced Arusha and Maasai labour to construct the Boma that can still be seen on the north end of Boma Road. Relations between the colonisers and their unwilling subjects remained tense, to say the least. During the construction of the fort, a

Pizzarusha Restaurant Most backpackers who stay in the guesthouses north of the stadium will find themselves eating at this excellent budget eatery opposite the Mashele Guesthouse. Huge tasty meals, ranging from pizzas to curries to steaks, are great value at around Tsh2,500. The atmosphere is great, too – the building is constructed from traditional

minor dispute led to at least 300 labourers being massacred while marching peacefully along present-day Boma Road, and several local chiefs from outlying areas were arbitrarily arrested and taken to Moshi to be hanged in the street.

Following the construction of the Boma, Arusha quickly developed into a significant trading and administrative centre, with about two dozen Indian and Arab shops clustered along what is today Boma Road. John Boyes, who visited Arusha in 1903, somewhat fancifully compared the Boma to 'an Aladdin's Palace transported from some fairyland and dropped down in the heart of the tropics'. The town, he wrote, was 'a real oasis in the wilderness' and 'spotlessly clean', while 'the streets [were] laid out with fine sidewalks, separated by the road from a stream of clear water flowing down a cemented gully'.

At the outbreak of World War I, the small German garrison town was of some significance as a local agricultural and trade centre, but it remained something of a backwater by comparison to Moshi, which lay a week's ox-wagon trek distant at the railhead of the Tanga line. Much of the area around Arusha was, however, settled by German farmers, who had forcibly displaced the original Arusha and Meru smallholders. In 1916, British troops captured Arusha and expelled the German farmers, resulting in some resettlement by indigenous farmers, but the German farmland was eventually re-allocated to British and Greek settlers. The British also set aside large tracts of land around Arusha for sisal plantations, which meant that by 1920, less than 20% of the land around Mount Meru was available to local farmers, most of it on dry foothills unsuited to cultivating the local staple of bananas.

Arusha grew steadily between the wars. The settler economy was boosted by the introduction of coffee, sisal and other export crops, and trade links were improved with the construction of road links to Moshi and Nairobi and the opening of the railway line to Moshi and the coast in 1929. Yet the land issues continued to simmer, eventually coming to a head after World War II, with the eviction of thousands of Meru farmers from north of Mount Meru to make way for a peanut production project overseen by 13 white farmers. The peanut project, aside from being a dismal and costly failure, resulted in the pivotal Meru Land Case, which not only caused great embarrassment to the UN Trusteeship Council, but also proved to be an important catalyst to the politicisation of the anti-colonial movement in Tanganyika.

Prior to independence, Arusha remained a relatively small town whose primary role was to service the surrounding agricultural lands. The official census of 1952 placed the urban population at fewer than 8,000 people, of which more than half were of Asian or European stock. The town has, however, grown markedly since independence, attracting large numbers of domestic migrants from surrounding rural areas and beyond. This can be attributed to a number of factors: the town's short-lived but prestigious role as capital of the East African community in the 1960s, the tanzanite mining boom, and perhaps most of all its strategic location as the springboard for the northern safari circuit. The population of Arusha is currently estimated at around 160,000, with up to 250,000 tourists passing through annually!

materials, and the candle-lit tables look into the kitchen, so you can be sure your food is freshly prepared. An internet café is attached. Easily the best value restaurant in Arusha!
Roaster's Garden Situated on the Old Moshi Road, a short distance from the Clock Tower, this garden bar is one of the most pleasant in Arusha. In addition to an endless

supply of cold beer, it serves a variety of cheap meals as well as good *nyama choma* (grilled meat).

Shamiara Restaurant Excellent Indian eatery on the second floor of Pallson's Hotel on the corner of Sokoine and Market Streets. The service is notoriously slow, but the food is worth waiting for – huge and very tasty portions for around Tsh5,000.

Spices & Herbs Restaurant The only Ethiopian restaurant in Arusha is situated about 1km out of town between the Impala Hotel and Mezzaluna Restaurant. If you're already a fan of sub-Saharan Africa's most distinctive cuisine (a spicy meat or vegetarian stew called *kai wat* served with a flat round sour bread called *injera*) you won't need me to persuade you to give this place a try. Vegetarian dishes cost around Tsh2,500 and meat dishes around Tsh4,000.

Stiggy's Thai Restaurant Situated on the Old Moshi Road less than 500m past the Impala Hotel, this enjoyably unpretentious restaurant is owned and managed by an Australian-Thai couple whose relaxed informality is matched by their golden touch behind the stove. The Thai and Continental cuisine isn't cheap (around Tsh7,000 or more for a main course), but the quality and presentation are up to international standards. Even if you don't want to eat here, the bar has a pool table and is a pleasant place to hang out and meet people. The area is one you'd only want to visit by night in a taxi.

Via Via Restaurant Belgian-owned garden restaurant tucked away behind the Old Boma on the north end of Boma Road. Despite the central location, it has a relaxing suburban atmosphere, and probably the best (or at least the most eclectic) selection of music in Arusha. The food's good too – filled baguettes at Tsh1,500 and meals at Tsh2,500.

BARS AND NIGHTSPOTS

There has been a notable increase in nightspots around Arusha in recent years. The liveliest at the time of writing is the recently relocated **Colobus Club**, which lies on the Old Moshi Road opposite Stiggy's Thai Restaurant, and doubles as disco, snack bar, boozer and pool hall – it keeps going all night over weekends. A good outdoor bar is **Roaster's Garden**, perhaps 200m from the Clock Tower along the Old Moshi Road. Roughly 1km further along this road, **Stiggy's Thai Restaurant** is a popular drinking spot with expatriates. There are several decent bars in the same area as the cluster of guesthouses behind the Golden Rose Hotel. The best place to drink in this part of town is **Soweto Gardens**, a relaxed but atmospheric garden bar which normally hosts live bands over the weekends.

In the town centre, the **Barracuda Bar** serves cold beer and inexpensive *mishkaki* kebabs and chips in a lively, earthy atmosphere, as does the bar attached to the **Chinese Restaurant**, which also sometimes hosts live music. Near to the market, the **Cavern Bar** was pretty quiet when we popped in, but it's about the only place in the town centre with pool tables. The **Twin Peaks Casino** south of Sokoine Road has its devotees

OTHER INFORMATION
Tourist information

The **Tanzania Tourist Board** (TTB) office on Boma Road is refreshingly helpful and well informed. It stocks a useful colour road map of Tanzania, which is given free of charge to tourists, though this doesn't stop the booksellers on the streets of Arusha from trying to sell it at silly prices. The TTB has been actively involved in the development of several cultural tourism programmes in northern Tanzania; the Arusha office stocks informative pamphlets about these programmes, and can help out with information on prices and access. If you want to check out a safari company, the TTB office keeps a regularly updated list of all registered safari and trekking companies, as well as those that are blacklisted.

The **Netherlands Development Agency** (SNV) has been working with the TTB to help establish the cultural tourism programmes in Ng'iresi, Mulala, Mkuru, Longido, Mto wa Mbu, Usambara, North Pare and South Pare, as well as several projects further afield. Although the TTB office can provide pamphlets and information adequate to the needs of most tourists, those with specialised interests are invited to contact SNV directly. The SNV office is in room 643 of the Serengeti Wing of the AICC. Email: tourinfo@habari.co.tz.

The head office of **Tanzania National Parks** (TANAPA) recently moved to the new Mwalimu J K Nyerere Conservation Centre about 3km out of town along the Serengeti Road, roughly opposite the Cultural Heritage Centre. Contact details are PO Box 3134, Arusha; tel: 027 250 1930/4; fax: 027 250 8216; email: tanapa@habari.co.tz.

The **Ngorongoro Conservation Authority** has recently opened an information office on Boma Road close to the Tourist Board office. In addition to some worthwhile displays on the conservation area, it sells a good range of books and booklets about the northern circuit.

The **Immigration Office** on Simeon Road can normally extend visas on the spot.

Safety

The central market vicinity has long been a haven for pickpockets and for bag-slashers – avoid visiting it with valuables or large sums of money on your person. Muggings are on the increase, mostly at night, so you are advised against walking along quiet roads after dark, and to charter a taxi when in doubt. Con artists generally take the form of fake money changers or dodgy agents for safari companies who approach travellers on the street. Don't let guys like these engage you in a conversation – a polite 'no thanks' will normally deflect an annoying tout, but if that doesn't work, then just ignore him.

Swimming

The swimming pools at the Mount Meru Novotel and Impala Hotel are open to non-hotel residents for a fee of Tsh2,000 daily.

Foreign exchange

Bureaux de change are dotted all around Arusha, and it is worth shopping around to find the best rate for US dollars cash. Many bureaux de change won't accept less widely used international currencies or travellers' cheques, but the National Bank of Commerce on Sokoine Road will, as will the bureau de change at the Impala Hotel. Whatever else you do, don't change money on the streets of Arusha, as you are sure to be ripped off. If you are desperate for local currency at an inconvenient hour, it is better to ask a shop owner or a safari company or hotel to help you out with a small transaction.

Taxis

There are plenty of taxis in Arusha. Good places to pick them up include the market and bus station, the filling station on the junction of Goliondoi Road and the Old Moshi Road, and the open area at the north end of Boma and India Roads. A taxi ride within the town centre should cost roughly Tsh1,000–1,500, though tourists are normally asked a slightly higher price. A taxi ride to somewhere outside the town centre will cost more.

ARUSHA'S MUSEUMS

Two museums are to be found in central Arusha, neither of which could be described as wholly inspirational. The **Natural History Museum**, housed in the old German Boma on the north end of Boma Road, might more accurately be renamed the Archaeological or Palaeontological Museum. The limited displays – you can walk around the museum in one minute – include a selection of animal and hominid fossils unearthed at Olduvai and Laetoli in the Ngorongoro Conservation Area, as well as life-size models of *Australopithecus* hunter-gatherers at play. Although the museum recently closed for quite some time for renovations, evidence of any such activity was thin on the ground in 2001 when we visited. The museum is open from 09.00 to 17.00 daily and a nominal entrance fee is charged.

The **Arusha Declaration Museum**, by contrast, is dedicated primarily to Tanzania in the 20th century, with some interesting displays on the colonial period and particular focus on the post-independence Nyerere era. It also contains a few decent ethnographic displays. Diverting rather than essential sightseeing, this museum is located on the northwest side of the Uhuru Monument Circle. Opening hours are 08.30 to 17.30 and entrance costs Tsh1,000.

Books, maps and newspapers

The bookshop next to Café Bamboo on Boma Road probably has the largest selection of publications that are likely to be of interest to tourists, for instance travel guides, field guides, maps, current paperback novels, national park booklets and coffee-table books about East Africa. A few vendors usually hang around the Clock Tower selling the maps and national park booklets at highly inflated prices. To buy or exchange second-hand novels, there are a couple of stalls dotted around town, the best of which is the stall on the alley connecting Boma and India Roads. A selection of local newspapers is available on the day of publication, as is the , which is generally stronger on international news. You won't need to look for these newspapers, because the vendors who sell them will find you quickly enough. The excellent *East African*, a weekly newspaper, is available at several newspaper kiosks. The British *Weekly Telegraph* and *International Express* can sometimes be bought at the newspaper stands near the Clock Tower, but do check the price on the cover or you'll probably be overcharged. The American weeklies *Time* and *Newsweek* are widely available in Arusha.

The 64-page booklet *Arusha*, published in 2001 for Tanzania National Parks by the Africa Publishing Group, includes plenty of information about Arusha town and the national park, and is widely available at bookstalls and curio shops for US$8–10.

Curio shops

Arusha is one of the best places in East Africa to buy Makonde carvings, batiks, Maasai jewellery and other souvenirs. The curio shops are far cheaper than those in Dar es Salaam and their quality and variety is excellent. Most of the curio shops are clustered between the Clock Tower and India Road, though be warned that the outdoor stalls can be full of hassle. One reader has warmly recommended The Craft Shop on Goliondoi Road, which has great items at very reasonable prices, will arrange shipment home if required, and you can look around at leisure without any harassment. The Cultural Heritage Centre, about 3km out of town on the Serengeti road, stocks one of the best selections of curios you'll come across anywhere in Tanzania - it can be visited on the way back from a safari, or as a short taxi trip from Arusha.

Post and telephone

The main post office is on Boma Road facing the Clock Tower. The telecommunications centre further along Boma Road is a good place to make international phone calls and faxes.

Internet and email

There are numerous internet cafés dotted all over Arusha, charging a fairly uniform Tsh500 per 30 minutes for internet access. One of the most reliable and central places is the Kremola Internet Café on India Road, but we used several on our most recent visit and they were all pretty fast and efficient. In the town centre, try the Cybernet Centre on India Road, Cyberspot Internet Café off Sokoine Road, or the internet café in the Patisserie, also on Sokoine Road. If you're staying in the market or stadium area, the Silver Touch Internet Café on Makongoro Road can be recommended.

SAFARI OPERATORS

The list below is by no means definitive, but it provides a good cross-section of the sort of services that are on offer, and except where otherwise noted, it sticks to companies that have maintained high standards over several years. There are, of course, many other good operators in Arusha, but with so many fly-by-night companies around, I prefer to stick to a few select companies in which I have total confidence. This policy may be unfair to other good companies, but my first responsibility is to readers, and it is vindicated by the simple fact that I've only ever received one letter of complaint from a reader who used one of the safari operators recommended in previous editions of this guide. The companies listed below generally specialise in safaris on the northern circuit, but most can also set up Kilimanjaro and Meru climbs, fly-in safaris on the southern safari circuit, and excursions to Zanzibar.

Bushbuck Safaris Tel: 027 250 7779/254 4186/254 8924; fax: 027 254 8293/2954; email: bushbuck@yako.habari.co.tz; web: www.bushbuckltd.com. This reliable and rapidly expanding company specialises almost exclusively in lodge safaris and its burgeoning reputation is such that it was selected for Hilary Clinton's Tanzanian safari a few years ago. Prices and service are relatively upmarket, but not extortionate. It has a large fleet of new and competently maintained 4WD vehicles, and employs a high standard of articulate drivers and guides. The office is about ten minutes' walk from the town centre next to the Impala Hotel.

Conservation Corporation Africa Tel: 027 254 8549/8038 or (South Africa) 11 809 4447; email: res@ccafrica.co.tz or reservations@ccafrica.com; web: www.ccafrica.com. This South African organisation, lauded throughout southern Africa for its superlative lodges and commitment to genuine eco-tourism, recently expanded into East Africa. CCA owns excellent upmarket lodges or tented camps in Ngorongoro, Serengeti and Lake Manyara, as well as on Zanzibar, and it arranges fly-in, drive-in (or mixed) safaris throughout northern Tanzania. The CCA makes no bones about its commitment to high cost, low impact tourism, and its Tanzanian properties are notable for their fine attention to detail, informal and personalised service, well-trained guides and rangers, and general air of exclusivity. If quality is higher on your priorities list than cost, then the CCA is probably the company to contact.

Hoopoe Adventure Tours Tel: 027 250 7011 or (UK) 1923 255462; fax: 027 254 8226 or (UK) 1923 255452; email: hoopoeUK@aol.com or hoopoesafari@africaonline.co.tz; web: www.hoopoe.com. Hoopoe is one of the most highly regarded companies in Arusha, specialising in personalised luxury camping and lodge safaris. I've been on safari with them on three occasions since 1992, and can recommend them without reservation to anybody looking for high quality service, reliability, flexibility and reasonable (but not cheap) prices. Their prices for lodge-based safaris are very competitive, and they regularly arrange safaris using the special campsites in the various parks. Hoopoe owns tented camps outside of Lake Manyara and Tarangire National Parks, as well as a superb private lodge on a Maasai concession at Loliondo to the east of the Serengeti. Following a recent merger with Tropical Tours, Hoopoe is one of the best companies to contact with regard to trekking and walking safaris in Natron, the Ngorongoro Highlands, and the game-rich Maasai plains to the east of the Serengeti. Their office is on India Street.

East African Safari and Touring Company Tel: 0744 470447; email: eastafricansafaris@habari.co.tz. Affiliated to the established and highly regarded Let's Go Travel in Nairobi, this reputable safari operator specialises in customised itineraries for those wishing to avoid the mainstream lodges. Prices and services are comparable with Hoopoe. The office is in the Adventure Centre on Goliondoi Road.

Roy Safaris Tel: 027 250 8010/2115; fax: 027 254 8892; email: roysafaris@intafrica.com; web: www.roysafaris.com. Founded in the late 1980s, this dynamic and remarkably efficient company has established itself as a leading operator when it comes to high quality but reasonably priced budget camping safaris, and it is used by several overland truck companies (who cannot afford to take their foreign registered vehicles into the parks). Their vehicles are always in excellent condition and the drivers are competent and knowledgeable. Roy would be my first recommendation when it comes to budget camping safaris, and they also offer very reasonably priced semi-luxury camping safaris and lodge safaris. Out of season, they sometimes offer specials on lodge safaris that cost little more than the equivalent budget camping safari. The office is along an alley off Sokoine Road opposite the junction with Goliondoi Road.

Safari Makers Tel: 0744 300817/318520; email: safarimakers@habari.co.tz; web: www.safarimakers.com. This relatively new company, based on India Road, has established itself as one of the few registered companies that is prepared to slug it out with the flycatchers and pirate companies for the backpacker trade. Particularly out of season, they can offer rates that few other companies will match, but they also own their vehicles (where most shoestring operators simply hire the cheapest vehicle and driver they can find) and will provide a refund or send out a replacement in the event of breakdown. Safari Makers now also offer very competitively priced lodge safaris, and it is one of the few companies in Arusha committed to promoting the various cultural programmes established by the SNV – all in all, a good first contact at the budget and shoestring level.

Swala Safaris Tel: 057 270 6424; mobile: 0744 300806; fax: 027 270 8424; email: sengo@habari.co.tz or swala@habari.co.tz. Highly praised by several readers, this flexible company provides the standard safari options but also organises a number of hikes in northern Tanzania and is a good contact for any itinerary incorporating Lake Natron. Special hiking packages include a three-day trip to Ol Doinyo Lengai and Natron, three days at Empakaai Crater, a four-day Rift Valley hike, and a six-day hike through the Ngorongoro Highlands to Empakaai. Swala also owns three very reasonably priced rustic camps on the northern circuit: Migunga at Lake Manyara, Ikoma in the western Serengeti, and Lake Natron Camp near the lake of the same name.

Sunny Safaris Tel: 027 250 7145; fax: 027 250 8035; email: info@sunnysafaris.com or sunny@arusha.com; web: www.sunnysafaris.com. This established company has long offered the cheapest reliable camping safaris in Arusha, though rates vary depending on season and group size. Their cheapest safaris won't involve camping in national parks, and you might find your driver inflexible about doing any excursion that puts extra kilometres on the clock, but otherwise you will get a thoroughly reliable service, with good vehicles and drivers. They also organise more upmarket camping safaris and lodge-based safaris at reasonable rates. The office is opposite the Golden Rose Hotel.

Thomson Safaris Tel/fax: 027 250 8551 or (USA) 617 923 0246 or 800 235 0289; email: info@thomsonsafaris.com. Catering primarily to the US market, this company offers good lodge-based safaris and, based on the number of their vehicles we saw while we were last on safari, it must be one of the most popular in Arusha – a good contact for Americans who plan on visiting Tanzania.

Tropical Trekking Email: tropicaltrekking@aol.com; web: www.tropicaltrekking.com. Other contact details as for Hoopoe Adventure Tours. This excellent company, now affiliated to Hoopoe Adventure Tours, specialises in walking and mixed walking/driving tours in remote parts of northern Tanzania. Most trips are run in collaboration with local communities. Areas visited include the Monduli Mountains (35km hike over three days through mountain forest and acacia woodland, where there is a good chance of seeing elephants, buffaloes, and various antelope and monkey species); the Longido Mountains (20km hike over three days through pristine montane forest where elephants and buffaloes are still common); northern Maasailand; Mount Meru; and Kilimanjaro (using the less popular routes). They also do attractive semi-safari packages that combine walking and motorised transport in and around the Ngorongoro Crater, Lengai Volcano, and the game-rich plains immediately east of the Lobo part of the Serengeti. If you're looking for something different, this company is highly recommended, and the people who run it are very flexible, knowledgeable and enthusiastic without being pushy.

Tropical Trails Tel: 027 250 0358; fax: 027 254 8299; email: info@tropicaltrails.com; web: www.tropicaltrails.com. Based at Maasai Camp, this is a genuinely eco-friendly company which arranges standard lodge-based and camping safaris for all budgets, as well as walking excursions on the fringes of the main national parks, and Kili climbs along the Machame and Shira routes. Tropical Trails is especially worth contacting if you have unusual requirements, or you want to get really off the beaten track. They also have some experience in arranging special one-off charity or group events.

Wildersun Safaris Tel: 057 250 3880; fax: 057 250 7834. This is a well-established and highly regarded company, concentrating almost exclusively on upmarket lodge-based safaris. The office is on the corner of Goliondoi and Jael Maeda Roads opposite a filling station.

CULTURAL TOURS AROUND ARUSHA

A number of widely praised and increasingly popular cultural tourism programmes have been implemented around Arusha in recent years with the assistance of the Dutch agency SNV. Any one of these programmes makes for an excellent half- or full-day trip out of Arusha, offering tourists the opportunity to experience something of rural Africa away from the slick lodges and main safari circuit. You can ask your safari company to tag a visit to one of the cultural programmes on to your main safari, or can arrange a stand-alone day trip once you arrive in Arusha. Several of the programmes also offer the opportunity to spend a night locally, though it should be stressed that accommodation is not up to accepted tourist class standards. Of the various programmes, the one at Longido can easily be visited on public transport, but the rest are only realistically visited in a private vehicle. Details of recommended safari operators are included above. The TTB office on Boma Road stocks useful pamphlets about all the cultural programmes, and can advise you about current costs and accessibility.

ALL THAT GLISTERS...

In 1962, local legend goes, a Maasai cattle herder called Ali Juyawatu was walking through the Mererani Hills after a bush fire, and noticed some unusual blue crystals lying on the ground. Ali picked up the beautiful stones, and took them to the nearby town of Arusha, from where they somehow made their way to the New York gemstone dealer Tiffany & Co, which had never seen anything like them before. In 1967, Tiffany launched the newly discovered gem on the market, naming it tanzanite in honour of its country of origin.

Tanzanite is by any standards a remarkable stone. A copper brown variety of zoisite, it is rather dull in its natural condition, but responds to gentle heating, transforming into a richly saturated dark blue gem, with purple and violet undertones that have been compared among other things to the, um, eyes of Elizabeth Taylor! The stone is known only from Tanzania's Mererani Hills – rumours of a second deposit in Usangi, 75km from Arusha, have yet to be confirmed – and it is in the order of being a thousand times rarer than diamonds. Despite its upstart status in the jewellery world, tanzanite has rocketed in popularity since its discovery. By 1997, 30 years after its launch, it had become the second most popular gemstone in the North American market, second to sapphires and ahead of rubies and emeralds, generating a annual trade worth US$300 million in the USA alone.

Remarkable, too, is the degree of controversy that the tanzanite trade has attracted in recent years. In the late 1990s, the Tanzanian government, comparing international tanzanite trade figures against their documented exports, realised that as much as 90% of the tanzanite sold in the USA was being smuggled out of Tanzania, resulting in a huge loss of potential government revenue in taxes and royalties. The ease with which the stones were being smuggled was clearly linked to the unregulated nature of the workings at Mererani, which consisted of more than 300 small claims operating in what has been described by more than one observer as a Wild West atmosphere. For the small claim holders, rather than distributing the stones they collected through legitimate sources, it was more profitable – and considerably more straightforward – to sell them for cash to illicit cross-border traders.

The lack of regulations at Mererani, or at least the lack of a body to enforce what regulations do exist, is also largely to blame for a recent series of tragedies that has dogged the workings in recent years. The greatest single catastrophe occurred during the El Niño rains of 1998, when one of the shafts at Block D flooded and at least 100 miners drowned. But it has been estimated that a similar number of miners died underground subsequent to this mass tragedy, as a result either of suffocation, or of inept dynamite blasting, or of periodic outbreaks of violent fighting over disputed claims. Aside from such accidents, it has long been rumoured that miners who are down on their luck will kidnap

Ng'iresi Village

Set on the slopes of Mount Meru some 7km from Arusha town, this cultural tourism programme based in the traditional Wa-Arusha village of Ng'iresi offers many insights into the local culture and agricultural practices. There are also some lovely walks in the surrounding Mount Meru foothills, an area characterised by fast-flowing streams, waterfalls and remnant forest patches. From Ng'iresi, it is

and sacrifice children from neighbouring villages, in the hope it will bring them good fortune and prosperity.

In 1999, the Tanzanian government put out to tender a lease on Block C, the largest of the four mining blocks, accounting for about 75% of the known tanzanite deposit. The rights were acquired by a South Africa company – with a 25% Tanzanian stake – called African Gem Resources (AFGEM), which reputedly pumped US$20 million into establishing the mine with the intention of going online in early 2000. This goal proved to be highly optimistic, as local miners and stakeholders, understandably hostile to the corporate intrusion on their turf, not to mention the threat it posed to the illicit tanzanite trade, attempted to disrupt the new project and persuade AFGEM to withdraw.

The long simmering tensions erupted in April 2001, when a bomb was set off in the new mining plant, killing nobody, but causing large scale material damage nonetheless. Later in the same month, AFGEM security guards opened fire on a group of 300 irate miners that had invaded the plant, killing one trespasser and causing serious injury to nine. When the Minister for Energy and Minerals visited the scene a few days later, the trespassers claimed to have been protesting against AFGEM's alleged complicity in the alleged death of 20 miners who were buried alive. AFGEM refuted the claims as pure fabrication, part of a smear campaign designed to discredit them and protect the illicit tanzanite trade. The result of the official investigation into the incident has yet to be released.

The tanzanite plot took a new and wholly unexpected twist in late December 2001, when press reports linked four of the men convicted on charges relating to the 1998 US Embassy bombings in Nairobi and Dar es Salaam with the illicit tanzanite trade. Amid wild speculation that the underground tanzanite trade was funding Osama bin Laden and his Al-Qaeda organisation, three major US jewellery dealers announced a total boycott on the purchase or sale of the gem. Among them, ironically, was the retailer that had first placed it in the spotlight back in 1967. Tiffany & Co publicly conceded a lack of hard evidence supporting the bin Laden link, but announced that it 'troubled' them regardless. By the end of January 2002, the price of tanzanite had fallen from around US$300 per gram to below US$100.

The Tanzanian government elected to suspend operations at Mererani until the claims were fully investigated. At a Tucson trade fair in February 2002, the American Gem Trade Association and Tanzanian Minister of Energy and Minerals signed a protocol that placed several significant new controls on local access to the Tanzanite mines. After the protocol was signed, Mike O'Keefe of the US State Department made the following declaration: 'Tanzania, I assure you, has done everything in its power to assist us in the war against terrorism.' The same office also announced that: 'We have seen no evidence that Al-Qaeda or any other terrorist group is currently using tanzanite sales to finance its efforts or launder money.'

possible to walk to Lekimana Hill, from where there are good views over the Maasai Steppe and on a clear day to Kilimanjaro. Another walk takes you to Kivesi Hill, an extinct volcano whose forested slopes support a variety of birds and small mammals.

Three different 'modules' are available at Ng'iresi. The half-day module costs US$16, the full-day module US$21, and the overnight module US$27. All prices include meals prepared by the Juhudu Women's Group and guided activities, while the overnight module also covers the fee for camping in the garden of Mzee Loti. For all modules, a sum of US$4 goes directly towards the improvement of the local primary school. There is no public transport to Ng'iresi, so you must either set up a visit through a safari company or make arrangements with a private vehicle.

Mulala Village

This is another cultural tourism programme situated in a village on the footslopes of Mount Meru. Mulala lies at an altitude of 1,450m, some 30km from Arusha, in a fertile agricultural area, which produces coffee, bananas and other fruit and vegetables. Several short walks can be undertaken in the surrounding hills, including one to the forested Marisha River, home to a variety of birds and primates, and to Mazungu Lake, where it is said that a *mazungu* was once lured to his death by a demon. Another local place of interest is Mama Anna's dairy, which supplies cheese to several upmarket hotels in Arusha. The tourist programme here is run in conjunction with the Agape Women's Group, which provides most of the guides as well as snacks and camping facilities.

All visitors must pay a village development fee of US$3, while a daily guide fee of US$4.50 is charged per group. Camping costs US$1.50 per person per night, and meals cost around US$4 each.

Mkuru Camel Safari

This cultural tourism programme is based at Mkuru, at the northern base of Mount Meru near a pyramid shaped mountain known as Ol Doinyo Landaree. The main attraction here is organised camelback trips, which range in duration from a short half-day excursion to a week-long camel safari through the surrounding dry plains, which are rich in birds and still support small numbers of game animals. Other options include a bird walk on the plain, or a hike to the top of Ol Doinyo Landaree.

Camel trips cost roughly US$25 per person per night all-inclusive. Visitors must provide their own tent. If you only visit the camel camp, this costs US$5 per person. For walks and hikes, you will pay a village development fee of US$2.50 per person as well as a guide fee of US$6 per group. A cottage is available to tourists at a charge of US$15/18 single/double.

TANZANIA'S GREAT TREK

Among Germany's more improbable – and less successful – attempts to populate the Arusha area with Europeans was the sponsored settlement of 100 Boer families, mostly of German descent, in the aftermath of South Africa's divisive Anglo–Boer War. In 1904, the Germans arranged for the Boers to be taken by boat to Tanga, from where they travelled to Arusha by ox-wagon. When the oxen all succumbed to tsetse-borne disease, the Germans provided the Boers with teams of local Africans as a substitute. The families were granted large ranches, mainly around Ol Doinyo Sambu on the northern slopes of Mount Meru, but most of them fell out with their benefactors and eventually packed up their ox-wagons to head across the border into Kenya, where several settled in the Eldoret area. A neatly whitewashed stone monument to this latter-day Great Trek still stands in a field near Ol Doinyo Sambu.

Longido

The cultural tourism project run out of Longido is one of the most accessible in the region for independent travellers, and it is an excellent place to visit for those who want to spend time among the Maasai. The programme co-ordinator is a local Maasai who studied abroad as a sociologist before he was paralysed in a serious accident, and he can tell you anything you want to know about Maasai culture. Three different walking modules are on offer to tourists. The first is a half-day bird walk through the Maasai plains, which also includes a visit to a rural Maasai *boma* (homestead), and a meal cooked by the local women's group. Then there is a full-day tour which follows the same route as the bird walk does, before climbing to the top of Longido mountain, an ascent of roughly 400m, offering views to Mount Meru and Kilimanjaro on a clear day, as well as over the Maasai plains to Kenya. The two-day module follows the same route as the one-day walk, but involves camping out overnight in the green Kimokouwa Valley, before visiting a dense rainforest that still harbours a number of buffaloes as well as the usual birds and monkeys. On all modules, you can expect to see a variety of birds (including several colourful finches and barbets), and there is a fair amount of large game left in the area, notably gerenuk, lesser kudu, giraffe, Thomson's gazelle and black-backed jackal. It is worth trying to be in Longido on Wednesday, when there is a busy cattle market.

Longido straddles the main Namanga road roughly 100km from Arusha, so any vehicle heading between Arusha and Namanga can drop you there. There are a couple of guesthouses in the small town, or you can arrange to pitch a tent for US$3 per person. All visitors are charged a daily development fee of US$7.50 per day, which will go towards the construction of a much-needed cattle dip. In addition to this, visitors must pay a co-ordination fee of US$7.50 per group per visit, a daily guide fee of US$6 per group, and a 'present' of around US$3–6 to any *boma* that you visit. Meals are available from the local women's group at US$4 (lunch or dinner) or US$2.50 (breakfast).

LAKE DULUTI

The small but attractive lake Duluti, about 70ha in extent, 15m deep and fed by subterranean springs, is nestled within an extinct volcanic crater, roughly 10km east of Arusha and only 2km from the Moshi Road. Although much of the surrounding area is cultivated and settled, the steep walls of the crater support a fringing gallery of riparian forest, while the lake itself is lined with beds of papyrus. The lake and its environs are of particular interest to birdwatchers. Forest birds that are resident or regular visitors include Hartlaub's touraco, crowned and silvery-cheeked hornbills, Narina trogon, brown-breasted and white-eared barbets, Africa broadbill, little greenbul, black-throated wattle-eye, paradise flycatcher, white-starred robin and black-breasted apalis. The lake supports numerous diving and shorebirds, as well as seven kingfisher species and breeding colonies of various weavers. An added attraction are the good views of Mount Meru and Kilimanjaro from the lakeshore on clear days.

Getting there and away

Lake Duluti lies about 2km south of the Arusha–Moshi road, and the side roads to Mountain Village Lodge and the Duluti Club, both on the lakeshore, are signposted. On public transport, any vehicle heading from Arusha towards Moshi can drop you at the junction – hop off when you see a large carved wooden giraffe to your left coming from Arusha. The turn-off to Duluti Club is signposted to the right opposite this statue, and the turn-off to Mountain Village Lodge is another 200m or so towards Moshi. It's about 20 minutes' walk from the main road to the campsite.

Where to stay
Upmarket
Serena Mountain Village Lodge Tel: 027 255 3313/4/5; fax: 027 255 3316; email: mtvillage@serena.co.tz. With expansive green lawns verging on the northern shore of the gorgeous Lake Duluti, and fabulous views across to Mount Meru and Kilimanjaro, Mountain Village Lodge is easily one of the most attractive upmarket lodges in the greater Arusha area. The main building is a converted thatched farmhouse dating to the colonial era, and accommodation is in comfortable self-contained chalets. Subsequent to the lodge being taken over by the excellent Serena chain a couple of years ago, the quality of service, meals and décor have all been upgraded to match the atmospheric setting. Non-resident rates are US$115/150 single/double B&B or US$145/210 FB. Resident rates are about 25% cheaper.

Camping
Duluti Club The lovely and surprisingly little-used campsite at the Duluti Club is slightly rundown, but the lakeshore setting more than compensates. Facilities include an ablution block and a cafeteria serving basic meals and cold drinks. Camping costs Tsh2,000 per person.

USA RIVER
The small and rather amorphous settlement of Usa River straddles the Moshi road about 20km east of Arusha, close to the turn-off to Arusha National Park. It is of interest to tourists primarily for a cluster of upmarket and mid-range hotels, most of which form a more attractive overnight base than their counterparts in Arusha town, as well as being conveniently located for day safaris into the national park.

Where to stay
Upmarket
Mount Meru Game Sanctuary Tel: 057 250 8106; fax: 057 250 8273. This lodge has something of an *Out of Africa* ambience, consisting of a main stone building and a few semi-detached wooden cabins surrounded by bougainvillaea-draped gardens. The sanctuary includes a large open enclosure in front of the rooms, stocked with a variety of antelope, and also the site of a large papyrus heronry where hundreds of cattle egrets roost at dusk. Behind the main building, a small zoo is home to a few ill or orphaned animals, and there is potentially good birding in the stretch of forest that fringes the Usa River. Despite the artificiality of the surrounds, the sanctuary sets the tone nicely for a safari, particularly rooms one and two where the animals are practically on your doorstep and the evening air reverberates with the incessant squawking from the heronry. Rooms cost US$75/95 single/double B&B. The food is excellent: lunch costs US$12 and three-course dinner US$15.

Dik Dik Hotel Tel/fax: 027 250 8110; email: dikdik@ATGE.automail.com. This smart Swiss-owned lodge is set in green grounds with a swimming pool. The restaurant is rated by some as the best in the Arusha area, and the rooms are certainly among the most comfortable in Tanzania. Rates are US$141/212 single/double B&B or US$160/250 FB.

Ngere Sero Lodge Tel: 057 250 3629; fax: 057 250 8690; email: ngere-sero-lodge@habari.co.tz. This small, exclusive retreat is set in an old colonial residence on the footslopes of Mount Meru, with views to Kilimanjaro on a clear day. The grounds are noted for their prolific birdlife, and enclose a waterfall and a small lake stocked with trout. Accommodation costs US$150 per person FB.

Moderate and camping
Tanzanite Hotel Tel: 027 255 3867; email: zapata_35@hotmail.com. Recently taken over by Serengeti Tours, the Tanzanite is a serviceable and reasonably priced hotel set in green grounds and charging US$50/60/70 for a comfortable single/double/triple room. Camping

Above left The topi, *Damaliscus lunatus*, is one of the more commonly seen large antelope in the Serengeti National Park (AZ)

Above right Kirk's dikdik, *Madoqua kirki*, easily distinguished from other small antelope by its white eye-circle, Arusha National Park (AZ)

Below Elephant, *Loxodonta africana*, Ngorongoro Crater (AZ)

Above Lilac-breasted roller, *Coracius cordata*, one of the most eye-catching birds of the Serengeti and other lightly wooded habitats (NG)

Above right Superb starling, *Spreo superbus*, often become very tame at game lodges in northern Tanzania (AZ)

Right Hooded vulture, *Necrosyrestes monachus*, waiting at a lion kill, Serengeti National Park (AZ)

Below Lesser flamingoes, *Phoenicopterus minor*, in flight at Lake Magadi in the Ngorongoro Crater (AZ)

costs US$5 per person. Meals cost around US$7. Facilities include a large swimming pool, which can be used at no charge by hotel residents and campers.

ARUSHA NATIONAL PARK

This 137km² national park not only protects Africa's fifth-highest mountain, but it also boasts clear views to the continent's highest peak.Kilimanjaro, and several lovely landmarks including a group of attractive lakes and a spectacular volcanic crater. The habitat diversity encompasses everything from montane rainforest to lush savannah to Alpine moorland, and a wide variety of large mammals and birds is present. Situated less than one hour's drive from one of Africa's major safari capitals, you might reasonably expect Arusha National Park to be crawling with tourists. In reality, however, it is, aside from Rubondo Island, easily the least frequently visited of northern Tanzania's six national parks, making it a wonderful and rewarding off-the-beaten-track excursion for those with an interest in natural history that extends beyond ticking-off the so-called Big Five.

Arusha National Park's most-publicised draw is Mount Meru, the eastern slopes and 4,566m peak of which lie within the park boundaries. Mount Meru is the product of the same volcanic activity that formed the Great Rift Valley 15 to 20 million years ago, and it attained a height similar to that of Kilimanjaro until a massive eruption tore out its eastern wall 250,000 years ago. Meru is regarded as a dormant volcano, since lava flowed from it as recently as 100 years ago, but visitors will be pleased to know that there is no reason to suppose it will do anything dramatic in the foreseeable future. Though low-key by comparison to nearby Kilimanjaro, Mount Meru is regarded by many as perhaps the most rewarding mountain to climb in East Africa, a hike that can be done over three days at half the cost of a Kilimanjaro climb. Details of the hike are given in the box *Climbing Mount Meru* on pages 136–7.

Arusha National Park has much to offer non-hikers. The Ngurdoto Crater is in itself worth the entrance fee, a fully intact 3km-wide, 400m-deep volcanic caldera that has often been described as a mini-Ngorongoro. Tourists are not permitted to descend into the crater, but the viewpoints on the forest-fringed rim over the lush crater floor are fantastic. A large herd of buffalo is resident on the crater floor, and with binoculars it is normally possible to pick up other mammals, such as warthog, baboon and various antelope. Look out, too, for augur buzzard, black eagle and other cliff-associated raptors soaring above the crater. The forests around the crater rim harbour many troops of black-and-white colobus and blue monkey, as well as a good variety of birds including several types of hornbill and the gorgeous Hartlaub's touraco and cinnamon-chested bee-eater.

Another area worth exploring is Momella Lakes to the north of Ngurdoto. Underground streams feed this group of shallow alkaline lakes, and each has a different mineral content and is slightly different in colour. In the late evening and early morning, it is often possible to stand at one of the viewpoints over the lakes and see Kilimanjaro on the eastern horizon and Mount Meru to the west. The lake area is one of the best places to see water birds in Tanzania: flamingo, pelican, little grebe and a variety of herons, ducks and waders are common. Among the more common mammals around the lakes are hippo, waterbuck and buffalo. You should also come across a few pairs of Kirk's dik-dik, an attractively marked small antelope that seems to be far less skittish here than it is elsewhere in the country.

Other large mammals likely to be seen in Arusha National Park include giraffe, zebra and vervet monkey. Elephants are present according to the official checklist, but several people we spoke to say that they haven't been seen in years, though it is possible a few survive in the forest zone of Mount Meru. The only large predators found in the park are leopard and spotted hyena; we were lucky enough

CLIMBING MOUNT MERU

The Arusha and Meru people deify Mount Meru as a rain god, but it is unlikely that any local person actually climbed to the 4,556m peak prior to Fritz Jaeger's pioneering ascent in 1904. Often overlooked by tourists today because it is 'only' the fifth highest mountain in Africa, Meru is admittedly no substitute for Kilimanjaro for achievement-orientated travellers. On the other hand, those who climb both mountains invariably enjoy Meru more. Also going in its favour, Meru is less crowded than Kilimanjaro, considerably less expensive to climb, and – although steeper and almost as cold - less likely to engender the health problems associated with Kilimanjaro's greater altitude. Meru is just as interesting as Kilimanjaro from a biological point of view and, because comparatively few people climb it, you are more likely to see forest animals. A lot of big game can be seen on the lower slopes.

Meru can technically be climbed in two days, but three days is normal, allowing time to explore Meru Crater and to look at wildlife and plants. Most people arrange a climb through a safari company in Arusha. The going rate for a three-day hike is around US$250 per person. You can make direct arrangements with park officials at the gate, but won't save much money by doing this. The compulsory armed ranger/guide costs US$20 per day (US$10 park fee and US$10 salary), hut fees are US$20 per night, and there is the usual park entrance fee of US$30 per day. A rescue fee of US$20 per person covers the entire climb. The minimum cost for a three-day climb is therefore US$150 per person, plus an additional US$60 divided between the number of people in the party. Food and transport must be added to this, and porters cost an additional US$5 per day each.

Meru is very cold at night, and you will need to bring clothing adequate for Alpine conditions. In the rainy season, mountain boots are necessary. At other times, good walking shoes will probably be adequate. The best months to climb are between October and February.

to see both driving between Momella Lodge and the campsite shortly after nightfall. Bird life is varied, with almost 400 species recorded.

From a vehicle, most of the park can be seen in a day. You can walk in the part of the park that lies to the west of the main road accompanied by an armed ranger, whose services cost US$10 per outing. Mount Meru can be climbed in two or three days (see box). The 52-page booklet *Arusha National Park*, available from the National Parks office in Arusha for US$5, contains detailed information on every aspect of the park's ecology and wildlife. An excellent map of Arusha National Park, with a detailed map of the ascent of Mount Meru on the flip, was published in 1997 by Giovanni Tombazzi in collaboration with Hoopoe Adventure Tours. The standard park entrance fee of US$25 per 24-hour period is charged.

The MBT Snake Park at the entrance to Arusha National Park has been recommended for the good collection of reptiles and intelligent guided tour.

Getting there and away

To reach Arusha National Park from Arusha, you must first follow the surfaced Moshi Road for about 20km until you arrive at a signposted turn-off to the left near Usa River. This dirt road enters the park boundary after about 8km, and runs through it for another 15km or so to Momella Lodge, immediately outside the northern boundary of the national park. This road is in fair condition and can sometimes be driven in an ordinary saloon car, though a 4WD would be essential

If you arrange your own climb, check hut availability at the National Park Office in Arusha before you head off to the gate. At present the huts are rarely full, but Meru is growing in popularity, and this could change.

Day one The trail starts at Momella Gate (1,500m). From there it is a relatively gentle three-hour ascent to Miriakamba Hut (2,600m). On the way you pass through well-developed woodland where there is a good chance of seeing large animals such as giraffe. At an altitude of about 2,000m you enter the forest zone. If you leave Momella early, there will be ample time to explore Meru Crater in the afternoon. The 1,500m cliff rising to Meru Peak overlooks the crater. The 3,667m-high ash cone in the crater is an hour from Miriakamba Hut, and can be climbed.

Day two It is three hours to Saddle Hut (3,600m), a bit steeper than the previous day's walk. You initially pass through forest, where there is a good chance of seeing black-and-white colobus, then at about 3,000m you will enter a moorland zone similar to that on Kilimanjaro. It is not unusual to see Kilimanjaro peeking above the clouds from Saddle Hut. If you feel energetic, you can climb Little Meru (3,820m) in the afternoon. It takes about an hour each way from Saddle Hut.

Day three You will need to rise very early to ascend the 4,566m peak, probably at around 02.00. This ascent takes four to five hours. It is then an eight to nine hour walk back down the mountain to Momella Gate.

Note Some people prefer to climb from Miriakamba Hut to Saddle Hut and do the round trip from Saddle Hut to Meru Peak on the second day (eleven hours altogether), leaving only a five-hour walk to Momella on the third. Others climb all the way up to Saddle Hut on the first day (six hours), do the round trip to the peak on the second (eight hours), and return to Momella from the Saddle Hut on the third (five hours).

after rain. Although it runs through the national park, it is a public road and no entrance fee is charged for driving along it. There are two entrance gates to the national park. Momella Gate lies along the public road through the park a short distance south of Momella Lodge. Ngurdoto Gate lies in the forested southern part of the park, along a side road branching east from the public road about 2km after you enter the actual national park.

The park is normally visited as an easy day trip or overnight trip out of Arusha. Any safari company can organise this. Most companies can also organise a three-day climb up Meru. If you want to organise your own climb or spend some time exploring the park on foot, you will have to find your own way there. You could hire a taxi in Arusha, but it is cheaper to catch a bus or *dalla-dalla* along the Moshi Road as far as the turn-off, from where 4WD vehicles serve as *dalla-dallas* to the village of Ngare Nanyuki about 3km past the northern boundary of the park, passing the Momella Gate on the way.

Where to stay
Upmarket
Momela Lodge Tel: 057 255 3743/5; fax: 057 250 8264; email: lions-safari@safaristal.com; web: www.safaristal.com. Set in the shadow of Mount Meru about 3km past Momella Gate, this cosy, low key and under-utilised lodge seems a world away from its slick, crowded counterparts elsewhere in the northern circuit. It is possessed of a rather time-

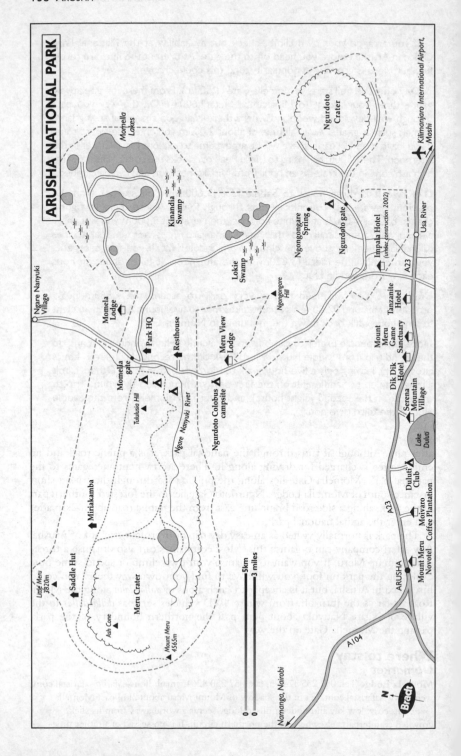

warped Alpine atmosphere, enhanced by the log fires in the bar and lounge and black-and-white movie posters that decorate the walls of the dining area and bar. The story behind the posters is that the actor Hardy Kruger built the lodge after falling in love with the area when it was used as the location for the 1961 film *Hatari*, which also starred John Wayne. A video copy of the film is tucked away somewhere, and can be shown to interested visitors. Accommodation in chalets costs US$56/74 self-contained single/double B&B or US$80/122 FB for non-residents, while residents pay Tsh19,750/23,700 B&B or Tsh27,650/39,500 FB. Facilities include a large swimming pool and satellite television.

Impala Hotel Tel: 027 250 2398/3453/7394; fax: 027 250 8680/8220; email: impala@cybernet.co.tz or impala@habari.co.tz or impala@africaonline.co.tz; web: www.impalahotel.com. This popular hotel in Arusha is currently constructing a new satellite lodge on a coffee estate along the road between Usa River and Arusha National Park.

Moderate
Meru View Lodge Tel 027 255 3876; email: meru.view.lodge@habari.co.tz. This small German-owned lodge lies on the eastern side of the road from Usa River, about 1km south of where the road enters the national park. It consists of seven comfortable self-contained rooms dotted around flowering gardens and a large swimming pool, and is superb value at US$50 double B&B, with other meals an additional US$10 per person.

National Park Resthouse Situated 2km from Momella Gate, this self-catering resthouse sleeps up to five people and costs US$20 per person per night. You can book it in advance through the National Parks office outside Arusha.

Budget and camping
Ngurdoto Colobus Restaurant and Campsite Tel: 027 255 3632. Clearly signposted and only 200m from the public road between Usa River and Ngare Nanyuki, this new development lies in the shadow of Mount Meru immediately outside the southern boundary of the park. Camping on the large, green lawn costs US$5 per person, and rooms – scheduled to open in 2002 – are likely to cost around double that. The centrepiece of the site is an open-sided bar and restaurant with a tall *makuti* roof, serving sensibly priced Western and local dishes.

National Park campsites Three sites lie at the foot of Tululusia Hill, 2km from Momella Gate, and one is situated in the forest near Ngurdoto Gate. All are scenically located close to a stream, have drop toilets and firewood, and cost US$20 per person. Note, however, that you may not walk between the campsites and the entrance gates without an armed ranger.

Shoestring
An anonymous and unsignposted guesthouse in Ngare Nanyuki, the village 3km past Momela Lodge, charges Tsh3,000 for a basic room.

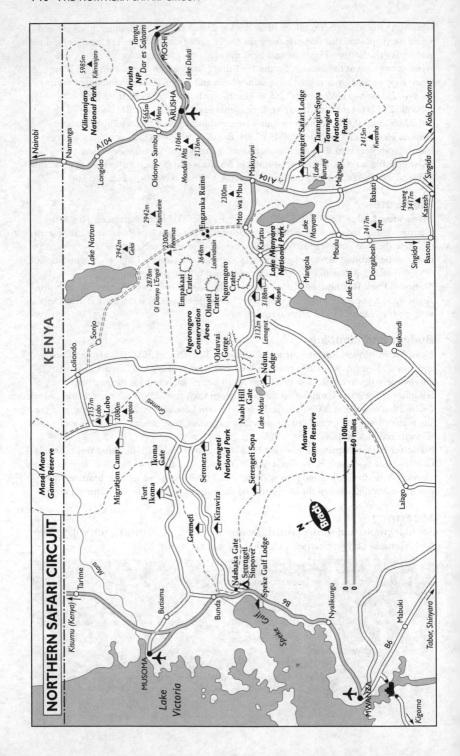

NORTHERN SAFARI CIRCUIT

The Northern Safari
Circuit

The cluster of national parks, game reserves and other
conservation areas that runs southwest from Arusha town
through to the eastern shore of Lake Victoria forms one
of the most extensive safari circuits in Africa, and
arguably the finest. The Serengeti National Park and
adjacent Ngorongoro Conservation Area, the latter
dominated by the Ngorongoro Crater, are possibly the
most publicised game reserves in the world. And justifiably
so: the Serengeti Plains host Africa's greatest wildlife spectacle,
the annual migration of more than a million wildebeest and zebra,
while also supporting remarkably dense populations of predators
such as lion, cheetah, leopard and spotted hyena. The floor of the spectacular
Ngorongoro Crater is if anything even more densely packed with large mammals,
and the best place in East Africa to see the endangered black rhino. Less celebrated
components of this safari circuit include Lake Manyara and Tarangire National
Parks, the former protecting a shallow but expansive lake on the Rift Valley floor,
the latter a tract of dry acacia woodland notable for its innumerable ancient baobabs
and dense elephant population.

The main reserves in northern Tanzania are covered fully in this chapter, as
is the process of organising a safari to them. Although Arusha National Park
(covered in the previous chapter) can be appended to the northern safari circuit,
it lies in a different direction from Arusha, and is most often visited as a self-
contained trip out of Arusha. Those travellers who want to climb Mount Meru
(in Arusha National Park) or Kilimanjaro (100km east of Arusha) will almost
certainly treat this climb separately from their safari, and might well want to
deal directly with a company that specialises in trekking rather than a standard
safari company.

CLIMATE
The northern safari circuit as a whole is far cooler than many visitors expect. Lying
at an elevation of roughly 2,300m, the Ngorongoro Crater rim in particular tends
to be chilly at night and misty in the morning, and it also receives a sufficiently
high annual rainfall to support a belt of montane rainforest. The crater floor and
Serengeti Plains are warmer but, since they lie above the Rift Valley escarpment at
elevations of well over 1,000m, they are far from being oppressively hot. Tarangire
and Lake Manyara National Parks lie at lower elevations and are considerably
warmer, with Tarangire in particular sometimes becoming seriously hot in the
afternoon. Both areas cool down after dusk, however, and most visitors to Manyara
will sleep at one of the lodges on the cool, breezy escarpment.

The main rainy seasons fall over November and December and from March to
May, though this can often vary considerably from one year to the next. Game

viewing in the Ngorongoro Crater and Lake Manyara is not strongly affected by season, and tends to be good at any time of year. The southern Serengeti, the part of the park visited by most tourists, hosts the greatest concentrations of animals between December and March, while the northern and western Serengeti are normally best over May to July and late October to November, when the migration passes through. That said, game viewing in the Serengeti is pretty good at any time of year, and the more remote northern and western areas have the big advantage of being practically bereft of tourists outside of the migration periods. Tarangire National Park has the most seasonal game viewing on the northern circuit, with animal concentrations generally peaking between July and the start of the rains in November or early December.

GETTING AROUND
Access to the Serengeti, Ngorongoro and Manyara is via the B142, the road which runs northwest from the junction village of Makuyuni on the main Dodoma Road about 80km southwest of Arusha. The Dodoma Road as far as Makuyuni is surfaced and in good condition, and it can easily be covered in one hour from Arusha. The B142 northwest of Makuyuni bypasses Lake Manyara at Mto wa Mbu village after 37km, then ascends the rift escarpment before passing through cultivated highlands for about 25km to reach the busy market town of Karatu, about 15km before the main eastern entrance gate to the Ngorongoro Conservation Area. From the crater, the B142 descends to the Serengeti Plains, passing through the park headquarters in the Seronera valley before reaching Bunda on the main Musoma–Mwanza road. Seronera lies about halfway along the 300km stretch of road between the crater and Bunda. Unlike the other northern reserves, Tarangire National Park lies to the east of the Dodoma road, about 30km south of the junction with the B142.

Some stretches of the 80km road between Makuyuni and the Ngorongoro entrance gate are legendarily poor and rutted, and the road has closed down completely at least once in recent years through flooding. This entire 80km stretch was in the process of being surfaced in 2002, and road works are scheduled for completion during the lifespan of this edition. The improved road will cut the driving time from Arusha to the Ngorongoro Crater from a long three hours to perhaps two hours, meaning that it will just about lie within realistic day-tripping distance of Arusha, which could place further environmental strain on this already over-touristed reserve. On the plus side, it will cut down the proportion of unproductive driving time associated with northern safaris – not to mention the wear on safari vehicles and their passengers' spines – though some argue that arriving at Ngorongoro on a pristine surfaced road will dilute the romance of the safari experience!

The most viable ways of exploring this area are in a private 4WD or on an organised safari out of Arusha, Moshi or other major town (see *Organising a safari* below). People driving themselves through the region should note that the higher entrance fees charged to all foreign registered vehicles mean that it may actually work out more cheaply to join an organised safari. The options for backpackers with limited financial resources are laid out in the box *The Northern Safari Circuit on Public Transport* on pages 146–7.

FURTHER INFORMATION
About ten years ago, Jeanette Hanby and David Bygott wrote a series of excellent booklets covering Serengeti National Park, Tarangire National Park and Lake Manyara National Park. These were published by TANAPA and can still be

bought for US$5 at many bookshops in Arusha, and possibly at some safari lodges. The same authors have written an equally informative and widely available self-published booklet covering the Ngorongoro Conservation Area. These older guides have been formally superseded by a series of booklets, one covering each of the four major reserves, published by the African Publishing House in association with TANAPA. These newer booklets are more up-to-date and colourful than the older ones, but they are also twice the price, and are not substantially more informative.

Giovanni Tombazzi's lively, colourful and accurate maps covering (among other places) the Serengeti, Lake Manyara, Tarangire and the Ngorongoro Conservation Area are probably the most user-friendly maps I've seen anywhere in East Africa. Each of these maps shows details of the appropriate conservation area in both the dry and wet seasons, and is liberally dotted with illustrations of common trees and other points of interest. Giovanni has also produced a map covering the whole northern safari circuit, useful to those who don't want to splash out on the whole series of more detailed maps. The maps are produced in collaboration with Hoopoe Adventure Tours (see *Safari operators*, page 128, for contact details) who also distribute them in northern Tanzania. As with the booklets mentioned above, these maps are widely available in Arusha and at the national park lodges, but vary in price depending on where you buy them.

ORGANISING A SAFARI

There are two basic approaches to organising a safari. The first is to pre-book a package before you leave for Tanzania; the second is to make your arrangements after you arrive in Tanzania. The first approach is the one taken by most fly-in tourists, and its advantages are self-evident. Pre-booking saves you time once you are in the country, and it ensures that you get the itinerary and lodge bookings you want. Many budget travellers, by contrast, prefer the second approach, since they often cannot predict in advance exactly when they will be in Arusha, and cheaper rates are generally offered to walk-in clients.

Arusha is the most popular and convenient base from which to organise a safari to Tanzania's northern reserves, though a small proportion of tourists do organise safaris out of Moshi, Dar es Salaam and even Mwanza. With literally hundreds of safari companies operating out of Arusha, competition for custom is fierce, particularly at the bottom end of the price scale where there are several unscrupulous and incompetent companies willing to cut any corner and promise anything in order to keep down costs and attract budget travellers. Given that you are likely to face an onslaught of safari touts from the moment that you arrive in Arusha, with the most dubious companies generally being the most pushy, it is important that you give some advance thought to exactly what you want from a safari. The following advice is aimed primarily at people who organise safaris after arrival in Tanzania, since it is they who are most likely to be taken in by con artists. The individual company recommendations and general comments regarding itineraries and group sizes do apply equally to those organising a safari in advance.

The issue for travellers on a limited budget boils down to one simple thing: to what degree should you compromise in order to cut costs? There are several ways you can reduce the cost of a safari – by going as part of a group, by using a cheap but possibly unreliable operator, by camping in private campsites rather than in reserves – but every compromise has the potential to spoil your safari. My own view is that if you've gone to the expense of flying to Africa, and the safari is a once-in-a-lifetime experience, it seems a bit short-sighted to cut corners unless it's absolutely unavoidable. But, as a high number of visitors to Tanzania make economically driven decisions which they later regret, it does seem worth laying out in detail the sort of options that exist.

Safari 'types'

There are, in essence, four types of safari package on offer: budget camping safaris, standard lodge-based safaris, upmarket camping safaris, and fly-in safaris. Budget camping safaris are generally designed to keep costs to a minimum, so they will make use of the cheapest camping options, often outside the national parks, and clients are normally expected to set up their own tents. Most backpackers and volunteers working in Tanzania go on budget camping safaris, though even with these there is a gap between the real shoestring operators, who'll skimp on everything, and those operators who offer a sensible compromise between affordability and adequate service.

Most fly-in tourists go on a standard lodge-based safari, which will generally cost around double the price of a similar budget camping safari. For the extra outlay, you get a roof over your head at night, restaurant food, and a far higher degree of luxury and comfort. If you decide to go on a lodge safari, the probability is that the operator will decide which lodges you stay at. If you have the choice, however, it's worth noting that the TAHI (Tanzania Hotel Investments Ltd) lodges, part of a government chain managed by the French Novotel Group, generally have the best natural settings, but the rooms are relatively basic. The Sopa Lodges are far more luxurious and slightly more expensive, but only the Ngorongoro Sopa Lodge has a setting to compare with its TAHI equivalent. The lodges in the Serena chain are generally the best of the mainstream chain lodges, with modern facilities, good locations and attractive décor.

The above chain lodges are all of the institutionalised 'hotel in the bush' variety, but there are also a number of smaller lodges scattered around the circuit offering accommodation in standing tents and a more intimate bush atmosphere. Many of these, though absolutely superlative, are considerably more expensive than the larger chain lodges – well worth it if you can afford it, but not within everybody's means. Into this most exclusive category fall the four CCA lodges (Lake Manyara Tree Lodge, Ngorongoro Crater Lodge, Grumeti River Camp and Klein's Camp) and the two Halcyon Lodges (Tarangire Treetops and Migration Camp) and a few other private lodges. Fortunately, there are also a number of tented camps offering a bush atmosphere at rates comparable to the chain lodges – Tarangire Safari Lodge, Kirurumu Tented Camp and Ndutu Lodge stand out – and these are highly recommended to those seeking a bush experience at a package price.

Camping isn't necessarily a cost-reducing device. Sleeping under canvas and eating under the stars will unquestionably make you feel more integrated into the bush environment than staying in a lodge, and this is where upmarket camping safaris come into play. At the top end of the range, you can organise safaris using private or so-called 'special' campsites, as well as tented lodges, and these will be as luxurious as any lodge safari, with top-quality food, a full team of staff, large tents, portable showers and the like. The cost of a safari like this will depend on your exact requirements, but it will probably cost at least as much as a similar lodge safari. What you are paying for is exclusivity and a real bush experience.

Regular scheduled flights connect all the main reserves in northern Tanzania, and an increasingly high proportion of safari-goers choose to fly around rather than bump along the long, dusty roads that separate the parks. Flying around will be particularly attractive to those who have bad backs or who tire easily, but it is more expensive and does dilute the sense of magic attached to driving through the vast spaces that characterise this region. Fly-in safaris allow you to see far more wildlife in a shorter space of time, because you don't lose hours on the road.

In all categories of safari, the price you are quoted should include the vehicle and driver/guide, fuel, accommodation or camping equipment and fees, meals and park entrance fees. You are expected to tip the driver and cook. Around US$5 per day per party seems to be par, but you should check this with the company. Drivers and cooks are poorly paid; if they have done a good job, be generous.

Group safaris and private safaris

A factor that all visitors should consider is the size of the group doing the safari. It is almost invariably cheaper to go on safari as part of a group, as the operator can divide most transport costs between a greater number of people. Typically, a group of four people will pay about 30% less per head than a group of two people. This is a considerable saving, but it does have many disadvantages, and I would advise anybody who can afford it to arrange a private safari.

The first problem with forming an impromptu group, or going on an organised group safari, is compatibility. My own experience of going on safari as part of a group has generally been good, but I've also had one horrendous experience with a mother and daughter who did nothing but bicker, moan and ask moronic questions ('Is that an African or Indian elephant? How can you tell...?'). Had this been a once-in-a-lifetime experience, they would have ruined it.

A group safari will be highly frustrating to those who have a special interest such as birding or serious photography. And, frankly, I think it is unfair to impose this sort of interest on other passengers, who will have little interest in identifying every raptor you drive past, or in waiting for two hours at a lion kill to get the perfect shot. On a private safari, you will almost certainly find the driver to be responsive to your specific needs and interests, and you can use his local knowledge to plan each day to your requirements. For instance, any photographer's top priority will be to be photographing during the first and last two hours of light, not to waste these precious hours on breakfast or sleeping in. On a group safari, the driver simply cannot pander to this sort of individual requirement, nor is it fair to expect him to.

Another consideration regarding group size is that most Land Rovers feel rather cramped with four people in the back, especially when the luggage is in the vehicle, and jostling for head room out of the roof can be a nightmare when four cameras are vying for the best position. If you do decide to go as part of a group, more than four people will get seriously cramped, and will mean some members can't sit next to a window. Some companies are willing to take five or even six people in a Land Rover, but the minuscule saving attached to having more than four people on board really isn't worth it, no matter how tight you are for cash.

A small proportion of companies – generally the large package tour operators – use minibuses as opposed to conventional 4WDs. In my opinion, minibuses have several disadvantages, notably that the larger group size (typically around eight people) creates more of a package tour atmosphere, and that it is difficult for a large group to take proper advantage of the pop-up roofs which are usually found on safari vehicles. In any event, bouncing around rutted roads in a Land Rover is an integral part of the safari experience – it just wouldn't be the same in a minibus.

Finally, there is the question of aesthetics. Without wishing to wax too lyrical, the thrill of being on safari doesn't derive merely from the animals you see. There is an altogether more elusive and arguably spiritual quality attached to simply being in a place as wild and vast and wonderful as the Serengeti, one that is most easily

THE NORTHERN SAFARI CIRCUIT ON PUBLIC TRANSPORT

The combination of steep national park entrance and camping fees, and the expense of running 4WD vehicles in northern Tanzania, places the northern safari circuit pretty much out of bounds for travellers on a very tight budget. It is possible, however, to see parts of the circuit relatively cheaply by using public transport and/or hiring vehicles locally.

The most affordable way of traversing the Serengeti National Park is on one of the buses and Land Rovers that run daily along the B142 between Arusha and Mwanza. This route passes through conservation areas for a total of about 250km, firstly the Serengeti's Western Corridor and Seronera Plains, then the plains of the western Ngorongoro Conservation Area and over the Ngorongoro Crater Rim. You'd get a good feel of the scenery and landscapes from a bus window, and between November and July you should see plenty of game, including large predators, but of course the vehicle cannot be expected to stop for special sightings. The trip will entail paying US$60 in park entrance fees, over and above the bus fare. In theory, it is possible to make advance arrangements for one of these buses to drop you off at Seronera, and to pick you up at a later stage, but it's difficult to see any reason why anybody would want to do this

A more satisfying option for travellers who specifically want to see the Serengeti, have time on their hands, and cannot afford a safari of several days' duration, is to approach the park from the western side. This cuts out the long drive and overnight stops coming from Arusha, allowing you to get within 1km of the entrance gate on public transport and to visit the park as a day or overnight trip rather than as part of a longer safari. The best place to set something like this up would be Safari Stopover, a private campsite situated right next to the entrance gate to the Serengeti's Western Corridor and alongside the main road between the Lake Victoria ports of Mwanza and Musoma. The Western Corridor itself generally offers good game viewing, particularly when the migration passes through between May and July, and the

absorbed in silence, whether you travel on your own or with somebody with whom you feel totally relaxed. It isn't the same when one has to make small talk to new acquaintances, crack the rote jokes about who should be put out of the vehicle to make the lion move, decide democratically when to move on, listen to the driver's educational monotones, and observe social niceties that seem at odds with the surrounding wilderness.

Itinerary

Your itinerary will depend on how much time and money you have, and also the time of year. There are endless options, and most safari companies will put together the package you ask for. They know the ground well and can advise you on what is possible, but may tend to assume you will want to cover as many reserves as possible. This is not always the best approach.

A typical five- or six-day safari takes in Ngorongoro, Serengeti, Manyara and Tarangire. A typical three-day trip takes in all these reserves except for the Serengeti. In the dry season (July to October) there is little game in the Serengeti; most safari companies will suggest you spend more time in Tarangire.

The distances between these reserves are considerable and the roads are poor; you will have a more relaxed trip if you visit fewer reserves. On a five-day safari, I

game-rich Seronera Plains and Campsite are only about two hours drive from the western entrance gate. Safari Stopover charges US$130 per day for a vehicle that can carry up to five people into the park, which means that a day trip would work out at around US$100 per person for two people including park fees, and about US$70 per person for four people. For further details, see *Between Mwanza and the Kenyan Border* on page 410.

On the eastern side of the northern safari circuit, affordable local buses run daily from Arusha to Karatu, stopping at the village of Mto wa Mbu near the entrance of Lake Manyara National Park. The Ngorongoro Safari Resort in Karatu rents out 4WD vehicles seating up to four people, or five at a push, for US$110/120 for a half/full day visit to Lake Manyara National Park or the Ngorongoro Crater. Once again, this would work out to be reasonably affordable, at US$90–100 per person for two people, or around US$65 per person for four people, for a day trip to either of these reserves. Should you want to make advance arrangements, the resort's contact details are included under the accommodation listings for Karatu. Worth noting, too, that safari vehicles are found in abundance in Mto wa Mbu and Karatu, so there's every chance you could make cheaper private arrangements to hire a vehicle for a day. Were you to do something like this, you should be very clear about what the deal covers and how long you will spend in the game reserve – ambiguities at the negotiating stage often result in frayed tempers later in the day.

Hitching into most of the reserves covered in this chapter is pretty much out of the question. Relatively few private vehicles pass this way, and most safari companies forbid their drivers to pick up hitchhikers. In any case, people who have paid for a safari, or who are in a private vehicle loaded with supplies, are unlikely to want to carry freeloaders. Even if you were to catch a lift, you may well get stuck in the Serengeti or Ngorongoro and although you will see little game from a campsite or lodge, you will still have to pay park fees.

would drop either the Serengeti or Tarangire. To visit all four reserves, six days is just about adequate, seven or more days would be better.

Three days isn't long enough to get a good feel for Tarangire, Manyara and Ngorongoro; four days would be better. The combination of Ngorongoro and Tarangire would make an unhurried three-day safari. If you are limited to two days, you could either visit Tarangire on its own or do a combined trip to Manyara and Ngorongoro. If your budget is really limited, Tarangire can be visited as a day trip from Arusha; it is less than two hours' drive each way.

At the other end of the time scale, there is enough to see and do in the area to warrant a safari of two weeks in duration, or even longer. You could easily spend a few days exploring the Serengeti alone. In a two-week package, you could also visit Lake Natron, the Kondoa-Irangi rock art and/or the northern part of the Ngorongoro Conservation Area.

Safari companies

I cannot overstate the need for caution in your dealings with safari companies, especially if you are shopping around for a cheap price. Any number of reputable companies are there to be to chosen from, but putting together a reliable safari costs money, and at the bottom end of the price scale reputable companies are overwhelmingly outnumbered by the incompetent and the unethical. To give some idea, less than half the companies currently operating out of Arusha are legally registered, a status which on its own gives the authorities the right to refuse their vehicles entry to any national park.

Before you panic, I should stress that in Arusha you will generally get what you pay for. If you organise your safari with a registered safari operator asking middle- to upper-range prices, there is no cause for concern, as the problem is pretty much confined to the bottom end of the price scale. It is also the case that the attitude of many budget travellers is largely responsible for allowing this problem to develop. If a significant proportion of travellers will take the cheapest price offered, it is only to be expected that some companies will cut corners in order to undercut their rivals' prices. Likewise, if, after having been warned, you still choose to go on a cheap safari with an unknown quantity, you have little legitimate cause for complaint if the vehicle and service aren't up to scratch. You could even argue that these rogue companies offer a legitimate service – high risk, low cost safaris – and that the only question is whether you want to make use of it.

On a budget camping safari, you will get a better price if you opt to camp at sites outside of the national parks. Tarangire, Manyara and Ngorongoro Crater can all be visited from private campsites, and doing this as opposed to camping within the national parks will cut around US$15 per night from the cost of a safari. The disadvantage of doing it this way is that camping outside the parks will inevitably dilute the safari experience – arguably a false economy unless you're on a very tight budget. You can assume that any very cheap safari company will use campsites outside of national parks where possible, so the onus is on you to specify that this isn't what you want – and to offer to pay the extra cost to camp in the parks.

At the time of writing, the lowest price you'll pay for a camping safari is around US$90 per person per day for four people. Superficially, this price may seem extortionate, but when you consider that it covers park entrance fees, camping fees, petrol and car maintenance, food, and the services of a cook and driver, it is difficult to see how a company could charge any less and still make a reasonable profit. For some years I have regarded Sunny Safaris and Roy Safaris (see pages 128–9) to be reliable benchmarks for the lowest price offered by a reputable company. If you are offered a safari for a lower price, you can be certain the company will be cutting corners, most commonly by providing a sub-standard vehicle or by keeping petrol costs to a minimum with game drives that last for only one or two hours. In some cases, they may also dodge paying park fees – and if you think that this isn't your problem, then be warned that several regular offenders have recently been turned back from the park gates. End of safari, no refund offered.

There is little point in naming individual offenders – most companies will change their name if they get any negative press. I've met several people who booked with a 'new' company and, after they had paid, found themselves on safari with a company they knew to be disreputable. Likewise, I've met many people who asked to look at the vehicle before they paid, and were shown a different vehicle to the one that was used. Once you've paid, any thoughts of a refund belong in the realms of fantasy. To give some idea of the extent of deceit to which some companies will go to attract custom, one blacklisted company recently changed its name to that of another company which gets a rave recommendation in another guide book, duping many travellers into thinking they were using a recommended company. The long and short of it is that you should not take anything at face value.

The situation in Arusha creates a slight dilemma for me. I would ideally like to be able to provide a list of every reputable safari company in Arusha, but there is no practical way of checking them all out myself. Nor is it possible to rely on the experiences of other travellers – even the worst company will get it right some of the time. In the 1990s, I met at least four victims of the most high profile and unscrupulous cheap company that was operating at the time, yet I also met a good number of travellers that praised the same company's services.

The best advice I can give is to allow yourself a full day or longer to shop around and feel out the situation before you rush into a decision, and to check on any unknown operator with the TTB Office on Boma Road in Arusha. The TTB keeps a regularly updated list of registered companies, as well as a short list of blacklisted companies, and any company that doesn't appear on the former list is best avoided. Despite the fact that so many travellers get caught out by dodgy operators, sorting the wheat from the chaff is primarily a question of common sense.

A full list of Arusha-based safari companies is provided in the Arusha chapter on pages 128–9. Most of the operators recommended in the listings in Moshi and Dar es Salaam offer reliable northern circuit safaris.

Miscellaneous warnings

Malaria is present in most parts of the region, with the notable exception of the Ngorongoro Crater rim, and the normal precautions should be taken. Aside from malaria, there are no serious health risks attached to visiting this area. Tsetse flies are seasonally abundant in well-wooded areas such as Tarangire and the Western Corridor of the Serengeti. Sleeping sickness is not cause for serious concern, but the flies are sufficiently aggravating that it is worth applying insect repellent to your arms and legs before game drives (though this doesn't always deter tsetse flies) and avoiding the dark clothing that tends to attract them.

Tarangire can be reached via a good tar road, and so too will Lake Manyara and the Ngorongoro Crater rim in the near future. The roads between the Ngorongoro Crater and Serengeti are very rough, for which reason safari-goers with serious back problems or a low tolerance for bumping around in the back of a vehicle might want to consider flying between the reserves. If one member of a safari party has a particular need to avoid being bumped around, they will be best off in the front passenger seat or the central row of seats – the seats above the rear axle tend to soak up the most punishment.

The combination of dust and glare may create problems for those with sensitive eyes. Sunglasses afford some protection against glare and dust, and if you anticipate problems of this sort, then don't forget to pack eye drops. Many people who wear contact lenses suffer in these dusty conditions, so it is a good idea to wear glasses on long drives, assuming that you have a pair. Dust and heat can damage sensitive camera equipment and film, so read over the precautions mentioned in the box about photography on pages 66–7.

As is standard practice in many countries, safari drivers earn a commission when their clients buy something from one of the many curio stalls in Mto wa Mbu and elsewhere in the region. There's nothing inherently wrong with this arrangement, but you might find that your safari driver is very keen to stop at a few stalls along the way. If this isn't what you want, then the onus is on you to make this clear the first time it happens – there's no need to be rude or confrontational, just explain gently that this isn't why you're on safari. Even if you do want to buy curios, don't fall into the obvious trap of assuming that you'll get a better deal buying locally. Many of the curios you see in places like Mto wa Mbu probably found their way there from outside, and they will generally be cheaper in Arusha than they will be at roadside stalls dealing exclusively with tourists.

Travellers on a budget camping safari who want to keep down their extra costs should be aware that drinks, although available at all game lodges, are very expensive. A beer at a lodge will typically cost around US$3, as opposed to US$1 in a shop or local bar, and prices of sodas are similarly inflated. It is definitely worth stocking up on mineral water in Arusha (at least one 1.5l bottle per person per day), since this will be a lot more expensive on the road. Once in the game reserves, some travellers might feel that it's worth spending the extra money to enjoy the occasional chilled beer or soda at a lodge. Those travellers who don't should ask their driver where to buy drinks to bring back to the campsite – there are bars aimed at drivers near to all the budget safaris' campsites, and the prices are only slightly higher than in Arusha.

Finally, and at risk of stating the obvious, it is both illegal and foolhardy to get out of your safari vehicle in the presence of any wild animal, and especially buffalo, elephant, hippo and lion.

LAKE MANYARA NATIONAL PARK

Lake Manyara is a shallow, alkaline lake at the base of a sheer stretch of the western Rift Valley escarpment. The northwest of the lake and the land around it are protected in a scenic 330km² national park which, despite its surface area being comprised of two-thirds water, contains a remarkably wide diversity of terrestrial habitats. These include the open grassy floodplain that follows the lakeshore, the rocky base of the escarpment, the belt of thick acacia woodland that divides them, as well as a lush and extensive patch of groundwater forest around the northern entrance gate. The park's habitat diversity is mirrored by its varied fauna, with some of the more common and visible large mammal species being elephant, buffalo, wildebeest, giraffe and lion. I've read elsewhere that Lake Manyara is frequently a disappointment to visitors. It's difficult to see why, since Manyara is a valuable addition to a safari of several days' duration, offering the opportunity to see several species that are less common or shyer elsewhere on the northern circuit. Those on shorter safaris, however, might reasonably elect to forsake Manyara and its biodiversity for an additional day on the predator-rich plains of the Serengeti.

Lake Manyara National Park and its well-defined game-viewing circuit kick off a high proportion of safaris through northern Tanzania. For logistical reasons, most safari operators visit this national park in the afternoon, but if you have any say in things, I would strongly recommend a morning game drive, starting as soon as possible after the entrance gate opens at 06.30. The park is wonderfully and unexpectedly peaceful in the morning, and you'll probably see fewer other vehicles over two or three hours than you would in five minutes in the late afternoon. Less certainly, by being the first car through the gate, we have twice disturbed one of the park's profuse but skittish leopards before it vanished into the thickets for the day.

At whatever time of day you enter the park, your game drive will start at the northern entrance gate, which lies near the village of Mto wa Mbu. From the entrance gate, the main road winds for several kilometres through a cool, lush, mature groundwater forest dominated by large ficus trees and a tangle of green epiphytes. With appropriate jungle noises supplied by outsized silvery-cheeked hornbills, this is the one part of the northern safari circuit that might conjure up images of Tarzan swinging into view. But, unless you're hoping for a rare glimpse of a leopard, the forest isn't really big game territory. The most notable resident of the forest is the olive baboon – the park supports a remarkable density of 2,500 baboons in 100km² of land – which are normally plonked down alongside the road, sometimes in the company of the smaller and more beautiful blue monkey. The

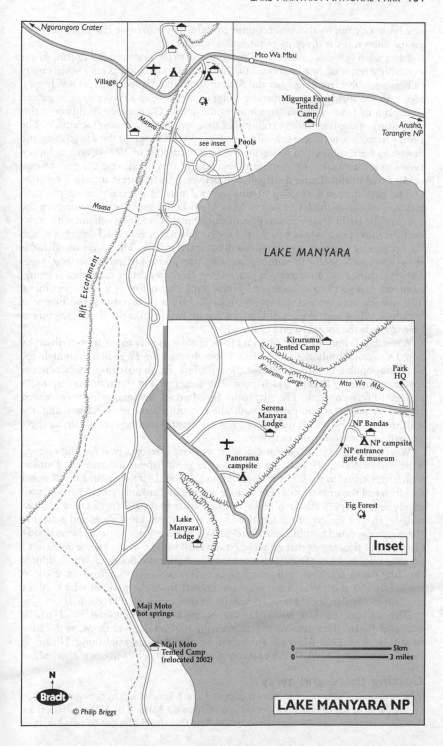

Ngorongoro Crater

Mto Wa Mbu

Village

Migunga Forest
Tented Camp

Marera

Arusha,
Tarangire NP

see inset

Pools

Msasa

LAKE MANYARA

Rift Escarpment

Kirurumu
Tented Camp

Park
HQ

Kirurumu Gorge

Mto Wa Mbu

Serena
Manyara
Lodge

NP Bandas

NP campsite

Panorama campsite

NP entrance
gate & museum

Fig Forest

Lake
Manyara
Lodge

Inset

Maji Moto
hot springs

Maji Moto
Tented Camp
(relocated 2002)

0   5km
0   3 miles

N

Bradt

© Philip Briggs

LAKE MANYARA NP

shy bushbuck might also be encountered here, but otherwise the main point of faunal interest is the diversity of birds and butterflies.

Most safari vehicles emerge from the forest on to the northern floodplain, where currently a series of small pools on the Mto wa Mbu river supports a wide variety of birds, notably giant kingfisher and African and painted snipe. This is a lovely spot, too, with the Rift Valley escarpment rising to the west, and the sparsely vegetated floodplain of Lake Manyara stretching to the south. Giraffes are common in this area, many of them so dark in colour that they appear to be almost melanistic. The nearby hippo pools (where several dozen hippos used to spend the day soaking and yawning) were submerged following the El Niño floods of 1997/8, and its hippos now live in the main lake. A more visible relic of this flooding is the ghost forest of dead tree stumps lining the floodplain between the fig forest and the lakeshore.

The best mammal viewing in this national park is generally along the road running inland of the lake towards Maji Moto Lodge and the hot springs in the south of the park. En route, you pass through tangled acacia woodland with views over the flood plain, where you should see large herds of zebra and wildebeest, and the occasional warthog, impala, Kirk's dik-dik and giraffe. The acacia woodland is the place to look out for the famous tree-climbing lions of Manyara (see box, pages 154–5) – though on an afternoon game drive, the safari driver grapevine is bound to ensure that you know about any arboreal lions long before you encounter them. The marshy area around the springs reliably harbours waterbuck and plenty of buffaloes, while several pairs of klipspringer are resident on the rocky escarpment base towards the southern end of the park.

A notable feature of Lake Manyara is its prolific elephants, as immortalised by Iain Douglas-Hamilton in his 1970s book *Amongst the Elephants*. Although the elephant population suffered a subsequent decline due to poaching, this was not as severe as in many larger parks in southern Tanzania and the numbers are today almost fully recovered. The elephants in Manyara are generally very relaxed around vehicles by comparison with their counterparts in Tarangire and the southern reserves, which makes for great elephant watching – especially as there are still some serious tuskers around.

Worth noting is that Manyara, despite its small size, is a *great* birding reserve, with almost 400 species recorded due to the great habitat diversity. As Duncan Butchart, writing in the CCA ecological journal, noted, 'If a first-time birdwatcher to Africa had the time to visit only a single reserve in Tanzania, then Manyara must surely be it.' It's perfectly feasible for a casual birder to see 100 species here in a day, ranging from a variety of colourful bee-eaters, barbets, kingfishers and rollers to the gigantic ground hornbill and white-backed pelican. Prior to the El Niño floods, the flocks of flamingoes that gathered on the shallow lake rivalled those on Kenya's famous Lake Nakuru. The flamingoes vanished after the flooding, which diluted the lake's alkaline level, but small flocks were starting to return in 2001. A remarkable 51 diurnal raptor species are known from the park, of which 28 are resident or regular. In addition, six species of owl are regularly recorded.

The 44-page booklet *Lake Manyara National Park*, published by Tanzania National Parks, gives detailed coverage of the park's flora and fauna, as does the newer booklet *Lake Manyara* published by the African Publishing House in association with TANAPA. An entrance fee of US$30 per 24 hours is charged.

Getting there and away

The main – indeed only – entrance gate to Lake Manyara lies at the northern end of the park on the outskirts of the village of Mto wa Mbu. The 120km drive from Arusha currently takes two to three hours, but this should be cut to two hours or

ACTIVITIES AROUND LAKE MANYARA

An exciting new development at Lake Manyara is the introduction of several mild adventure activities that allow safari-goers tired of bouncing around dusty roads within the confines of a vehicle the opportunity to stretch their legs or arms in natural surrounds. The activities are operated exclusively by Serena Active, which is based out of the Manyara Serena Lodge, but takes on guests staying at other lodges in the area. No experience is required for any of the activities, and all equipment is supplied at no extra cost. On the spot enquiries are welcomed, but bookings can be made through any safari operator or directly through Serena Active; tel: 027 253 9160/1/2; fax: 027 253 9163; email: serenaactive@serena.co.tz.

The most popular of these activities are leisurely two-hour canoe trips along the shallow western shore of the lake, which offer a hippo's-eye perspective of this magnificent part of the Rift Valley and the animals that come to the water to drink. There is plenty of game to be seen from the canoes – we encountered two herds of elephant, as well as zebra, giraffe, wildebeest and various antelope – and a profusion of waterbirds can be taken for granted, as can (comfortably distant) encounters with a hippo or three. Above all, perhaps, there is the simple delight of experiencing the Tanzanian bush without a car engine within earshot. The canoe trips cost US$100 per person and include a game drive en route from the gate to the lakeshore and sundowner drinks at the end of the trip.

Another popular activity is mountain biking down the Rift Valley escarpment, with different itineraries ranging in price from US$30 to US$35 per person. Also offered are an afternoon walk through the groundwater forest in the Kirurumu Gorge outside the national park entrance for US$35 per person, and a village walk with a local guide through agricultural areas around Mto wa Mbu. For more hardcore adventurers, there is the option of abseiling down the rift escarpment above the lake with a qualified instructor, which costs US$55 per person.

less following the completion of the new surfaced road from Makayuni. Most tourists visit Manyara as part of an organised safari, but it would be possible to bus to Mto wa Mbu and arrange a day trip from there.

Where to stay and eat

There is only one lodge sited within the park boundaries, the new Lake Manyara Tree Lodge. There is, however, plenty of accommodation bordering the park. Most of the tourist-class lodges are situated on the Rift Valley escarpment overlooking Lake Manyara, while the budget accommodation and campsites are dotted around the small village of Mto wa Mbu outside the main entrance gate.

Exclusive

Lake Manyara Tree Lodge (formerly Maji Moto Lodge) Tel: 027 254 8549/8038 or (South Africa) 11 809-4447; email: res@ccafrica.co.tz or reservations@ccafrica.com; web: www.ccafrica.com. Scheduled to open in December 2002 as a replacement for their defunct Maji Moto Lodge, Lake Manyara Tree Camp is a small and luxurious CCA tented camp set deep in the forest about 20 minutes' drive south of the hot springs at Maji Moto. Like other CCA lodges, Lake Manyara Tree Lodge will offer the ultimate in exclusive bush

THE TREE-CLIMBING LIONS OF MANYARA

Edited from 'Notes on Tree-climbing Lions of Manyara' by Kevin Pretorius, a former manager of Maji Moto Lodge, as originally published the CCA Ecological Journal volume 2:79–81 (2000). The CCA Journal can be ordered online at www.wildwatch.com.

Lake Manyara National Park is famous for its tree-climbing lions, which, unlike conventional lions, habitually rest up in the branches for most of the day, to the excitement of those lucky tourists who chance upon them. But while the tree-climbing phenomenon is well documented, the explanation behind it remains largely a matter of conjecture.

In the 1960s, Stephen Makacha undertook research into lion behaviour at Manyara to compare with similar studies being conducted by George Schaller in the Serengeti. In Schaller's book, *The Serengeti Lion: a study of predator–prey relations*, he noted that:

> The lions in the Lake Manyara National Park climbed trees far more often than those in the Serengeti. They were resting in trees on two-thirds of the occasions on which we encountered them during the day... The reason why Manyara lions rest in trees so often is unknown. Fosbrooke noted that lions in the Ngorongoro Crater ascended trees during an epidemic of biting flies, but this is an unusual situation... and the vegetation in the various parks is in many respects so similar that no correlation between it and tree climbing is evident. The Manyara lions sometimes escaped from buffalo and elephant by climbing trees, but there would seem to be no reason for lions to remain in them all day because of the remote chance that they might have to climb one. I think that the behaviour represents a habit, one that may have been initiated by for example, a prolonged fly epidemic, and has since been transmitted culturally.

Schaller's suggestion that the lions were climbing trees to avoid flies made the most sense to me, but I had also heard that the lions climbed to enjoy the cool breezes that came off the lake, and to keep a lookout for prey and threats. So I decided to make notes whenever I saw the lions in order to explore these theories. For every sighting I noted whether flies were present on the ground or in the trees; the temperature and breeze conditions; whether buffalo or

luxury, consisting of ten standing tents with en-suite bathrooms overlooking the lake. Exciting walking routes are planned from the lodge to the lakeshore through the forest. The FB rates of US$350 per person in the low season and US$445 in the high season are inclusive of all meals, drinks, game drives and game walks, and a reduction is offered for stays of more than three nights.

Upmarket

Lake Manyara Serena Lodge Tel: 027 250 4058; fax: 027 250 8282; email: reservations@serena.co.tz. This smart and popular upmarket lodge is situated on the edge of the escarpment overlooking the lake and its environs. Like other lodges in the Serena chain, it is a very appealing set-up, run through by a small wooded stream that attracts a wide range of birds including chattering flocks of breeding weavers. Canoe trips on Lake Manyara, as well as other adventure activities such as abseiling and mountain biking, are

elephant were in the vicinity; how high up the tree the lions were and the view it afforded; and the species of tree.

In the 1960s, Iain Douglas-Hamilton noted that on 80% of the occasions when tree-climbing lions were observed, they were in one of just 17 individual trees. These favoured trees were so well known to park guides at the time that they were given particular names and – to protect them from debarking and destruction by elephants – wrapped in coils of wire mesh. My observations indicated a similar pattern. Lions were found to be resting in trees on about half of the times they were sighted, and although six different tree species were used, three – *Acacia tortilis*, *Kigelia africana* and *Balanites aegyptiaca* – accounted for 90% of sightings. Specific trees were usually favoured, and the lions often moved a considerable distance to reach them.

In most cases the lions were seen to be resting during the heat of the day, and they would usually come down at dusk. Only 5% of sightings coincided with hot weather and breezy conditions, and at most sightings there was no significant breeze, so it seems unlikely that the lions climb to escape the heat. Although buffalo have been documented killing lions at Manyara, there was never any sign of the lions taking to trees to avoid harassment. Most of the time the lions were found to be resting approximately 5–6m above the ground, which afforded them a better view of their surroundings, but since the trees were normally in densely vegetated areas, it would have been difficult for them to observe any potential prey or threat.

My conclusions were similar to those of Makacha and Schaller. Although lions that I found resting on the ground were apparently not greatly concerned by biting flies, lions observed in trees were surrounded by flies in only 10% of cases, when flies were present on the ground below them about 60% of the time. Because the lions generally rested above 5m and flies were seldom encountered at this height, it seems likely that the behaviour was originally initiated during a fly epidemic, and it has since been passed on culturally. I observed the cubs of the Maji pride begin their attempts to climb up to the adults when they were about seven or eight months old. It seemed definitely to be a case of 'lion see lion do', as there was no apparent reason as to why they should have climbed. Once they had mastered climbing, they too spent a lot of time playing and climbing up and down the trees. More thorough research would be required to fully understand the reasons for this unusual and fascinating behaviour.

offered by Serena Active, a company based in the lodge. Accommodation is in attractively furnished ethnic-looking rondavels with private balconies. The buffet food is generally very good. Rooms cost US$230/350 single/double FB.

Lake Manyara Lodge Tel: 027 250 2711/2; fax: 027 250 8221; email: tahifin@habari.yako.co.tz. This government property, though barely recognisable from its rundown state of a few years ago, remains somewhat Spartanly decorated and architecturally confrontational, though the rooms do have mosquito nets and en-suite bathrooms with running hot water. A definite attraction of the lodge is a large swimming pool, but its single best feature remains its peerless position right on the edge of the escarpment. The grounds offer a panoramic view over the forest and lake, with the Rift Valley hills fading to the horizon. With binoculars, you should be able to pick out elephants, giraffes and buffaloes on the Rift Valley floor; closer to home, there is good birding within the lodge grounds. US$140/196/280 single/double/triple FB.

MTO WA MBU

This village, which lies close to the Lake Manyara entrance gate, sees a large volume of tourist traffic and is said locally to be the only place in Tanzania where representatives of 120 Tanzanian tribes are resident. Mto wa Mbu is the normal base for budget safaris visiting Lake Manyara, and even if you aren't staying in the village or visiting Lake Manyara, your safari driver will probably stop at the huge curio market in the hope of picking up a commission. Mto wa Mbu (pronounced as one word *mtowambu*) means River of Mosquitoes, and if you do spend the night here, then you'll be in no doubt about how it got its name. By day, the curio dealers who will swarm around you the moment you leave your vehicle might draw an obvious analogy.

Mto wa Mbu is a realistic target for backpackers who can't afford a proper safari. Buses connecting Arusha to Karatu all stop at Mto wa Mbu, and there is no shortage of affordable accommodation in the village (see *Where to stay* at Lake Manyara). The nearby Lake Manyara National Park is reasonably accessible to non-motorised travellers, since practically all tourists enter it as a day trip, which means there is no danger of being stranded there overnight. It would also be possible to do any of the activities listed in the box *Activities around Lake Manyara* out of Mto wa Mbu.

Another reason to bus to Mto wa Mbu is the clutch of walking tours that have been set up as part of a cultural tourism programme with the assistance of SNV. One of the most interesting of these walks is the papyrus lake tour, which takes you to the Miwaleni waterfall, as well as to a papyrus lake where Rangi people collect basket- and mat-weaving material, and to the homesteads of Sandawe hunter-gatherers. Other tours take you to Balaa Hill, which boasts excellent views over the village and lake, and to Chagga farms and Maasai *bomas*. The tourism programme is run out of the Red Banana Restaurant in the centre of the village, where you must pay your fees, arrange a guide and (if you like) rent a bicycle. The guide fee works out at US$7.50 per group per day, in addition to which you must pay a village development fee of US$1.50 per person. Bicycle hire costs US$2 per day.

Kirurumu Luxury Tented Lodge Tel: (UK) 1923 255462; fax: 1923 255452; email: hoopoeUK@aol.com; web: www.kirurumu.com. Owned and managed by Hoopoe Adventure Tours, this popular tented lodge is perched on the rift escarpment to the north of the Serena, from where it offers a grand view across the plains of the Rift Valley to the north of Lake Manyara. The unpretentious rustic bush atmosphere that characterises Kirurumu contrasts strongly with that of the other more built-up lodges on the Rift escarpment, and it will be far more attractive to people who want to feel like they are sleeping in the bush rather than in a large hotel. The food is good and the service friendly and efficient. Accommodation is in 20 luxury double tents, each of which has a private veranda, and a shower and toilet. Rates are US$150/225 single/double FB.

Moderate

Migunga Forest Tented Camp Tel: 057 270 6424; mobile: 0744 300806; fax: 027 270 8424; email: sengo@habari.co.tz or swala@habari.co.tz. This well-established but little-known tented camp shares many of Kirurumu's assets, and although it is considerably more downmarket in feel, the rates are correspondingly much lower. Migunga has a winning location in a tall patch of yellow fever acacia forest near the northeast shore of the lake about 5km by road from Mto wa Mbu, and a walking trail leads down to the nearby lakeshore. Reedbuck, bushbuck and buffalo sometimes pass through, while the lesser bushbaby is often seen at night and roughly 70 acacia-associated bird species have been recorded within the camp. Accommodation is in comfortable double standing tents with en-suite hot showers. At US$50 per person FB, it's an excellent compromise between the smarter but more expensive lodges and the relatively utilitarian accommodation in Mto wa Mbu.

Budget and camping
National Park Bandas & Campsite Situated in a lovely forest glade immediately outside the national park entrance gate, this is easily the most inherently attractive place to stay in this price category, though unfortunately it feels a bit overpriced for what you get. Clean self-contained brick bandas with hot water but no net – the latter a serious omission in Mto wa Mbu – cost US$20 per person for non-residents or Tsh5,000 for residents. Camping costs the same. Facilities include a kitchen and dining area, and an elevated tree house looking into the forest canopy.
Panorama Campsite Tel: 027 253 9286/7. Boasting a prime location on the escarpment overlooking the lake, this promising new campsite lies only 500m from the main road and forms an attractive alternative to the cheapies in town. Accommodation in a large standing tent with beds costs US$30 single or double, while a small standing tent with a mattress and no bed costs US$5 per person, and camping in your own tent costs Tsh3,000 per person. There's a clean shower and toilet block, and a bar, restaurant and swimming pool were under construction in early 2002.
Twiga Campsite and Lodge Tel: 025 253 9101; mobile: 0811 510937; email: twigacampsite@hotmail.com. Justifiably the most popular of the locally run lodges in Mto wa Mbu, Twiga charges US$10 per person to pitch a tent in the spacious, neatly cropped campsite. It also has a block of large self-contained double rooms with hot water and nets for US$25 double B&B. A three-course meal at the restaurant costs US$6, while most dishes on the à la carte menu work out at around US$4. There are 'wild video shows' in the lounge every evening.
Holiday Fig Camp Tel: 025 253 9102. Also situated in Mto wa Mbu, this is another popular site with budget camping safari operators, pleasant enough but marred by the somewhat cramped grounds. Camping costs US$5 per person. More attractive at US$15 per person are the self-contained double rooms with fan, net and hot water. Facilities include a restaurant and bar, as well as a swimming pool which I've yet to see in a functioning state.
Jambo Campsite Tel: 025 253 9170. A bit of a dump by comparison with the above, this site in Mto wa Mbu charges Tsh3,000 per person to camp, Tsh5,000/7,500 for an adequate single/double with nets, or Tsh10,000 for a self-contained double.

Shoestring
Camp Vision Lodge Catering primarily to safari drivers, this bright little lodge welcomes travellers and charges Tsh1,500 per person for a room using a common shower or Tsh5,000 for a self-contained double. The rooms are clean and have nets, and there is hot running water.
Mashanga Guesthouse This is similar in standard and identical in price to Camp Vision Lodge.
Sayari Lodge Another decent local lodge aimed firstly at safari drivers, this has self-contained doubles with nets and hot water for Tsh4,000 and similar rooms using common showers for Tsh3,000.

KARATU

This small, dusty town straddling the main road between Manyara and Ngorongoro may not look like much when you pass through coming from Arusha, but it is probably the most populous settlement anywhere along the 400km length of the B142. Most tourists who are on a lodge-based safari will pass through Karatu in the blink of an eye. Quite a number of camping safaris stay in the small town – nicknamed 'safari junction' – and use it as a base for day trips to the nearby Ngorongoro Crater, since camping is a lot cheaper than in the conservation area. A worthwhile day trip out of Karatu is to Lake Eyasi and one of the Hadzabe settlements in the surrounding area (see box *The last hunter-gatherers*, pages 160–1). The National Bank of Commerce next to Ngorongoro Safari Lodge is the one place on the safari circuit where foreign travellers' cheques and cash can be exchanged at normal rates.

Getting there and away

Regular buses connect Karatu to Arusha via Mto wa Mbu. There are also a few buses daily running south from Karatu to Mbulu, described in the chapter *Dodoma and the Central Rift Valley*. The Ngorongoro Safari Resort in Karatu rents 4WD vehicles for day safaris to Ngorongoro and Manyara at US$120 per day.

Where to stay
Upmarket

Gibb's Farm Tel: 027 250 8930; fax: 027 250 8310; email: ndutugibbs@habari.co.tz; web: www.gibbsfarm.net. This small and appealingly idiosyncratic hotel lies 4km from the main road near Karatu, on an active coffee farm bordering a patch of indigenous forest on the footslopes of Ngorongoro. Extensively renovated over recent years, Gibb's Farm consists of only 20 double rooms and its rustic colonial ambience is far removed from the relative uniformity that characterises many of the more upmarket lodges in northern Tanzania. Many safari-goers rate it among their favourite hotels in Tanzania, and the home-style cooking made with organic produce grown on the farm is excellent. It's a popular base for day trips into the Ngorongoro Crater, though it does have the disadvantage of lying away from the spectacular crater rim. Other activities include bird walks with the resident naturalist and a two-hour hike to a waterfall and cave made by elephants on the forested slopes of the crater. Accommodation in self-contained bungalows costs US$128/156 single/double B&B or US$172/245 FB for non-residents, while residents pay US$63/88 B&B or US$107/176 FB. Significant low season discounts are offered.

Plantation Lodge Tel: 027 253 4364/5; email: plantation@les-raisting.de. This new German-owned lodge is set in flowering grounds only 2km from the Ngorongoro road a few kilometres out of Karatu. It has a classic whitewash and thatch exterior, complemented by the stylish décor of the spacious self-contained rooms. As with Gibb's Farm, Plantation Lodge stands in refreshingly individualistic contrast to the chain lodges that characterise the northern circuit, while also forming a good base for day trips to Ngorongoro Crater. Rates are US$107/147 single/double HB or US$122/179 FB.

Moderate and camping

Ngorongoro Safari Lodge Tel: 025 253 4287; fax: 025 253 4288; email: safariresort@yahoo.com. This smart new complex in Karatu offers accommodation in clean, comfortable self-contained rooms for US$65/80 single/double, as well as camping in a neat well-maintained site for US$5 per person. The attached supermarket, though not cheap, is the best in Karatu, and the restaurant serves a good range of tasty Indian and Continental dishes at around Tsh5,000. Other facilities include an internet café, a filling station, a large bar with satellite television, and 4WD rental.

Kudu Lodge & Campsite Tel: 025 253 4055; fax: 025 453 4268. Currently about the best of a few campsites in the Karatu area catering primarily to budget camping safaris, Kudu Lodge lies just outside town in the direction of Ngorongoro. Camping on the neat lawn costs US$7 per person, and rooms are available in the US$25–60 range.

Shoestring
Empakaai Guesthouse This is probably the pick of several central guesthouses catering mainly towards safari drivers. Clean double rooms with a net cost Tsh2,500 and there's a piping-hot common shower. A couple of nearby guesthouses are similar in standard but, since they charge highly inflated rates to non-residents, they are poor value for money.

LAKE EYASI AND SURROUNDS
The vast Lake Eyasi verges on the remote southern border of the Ngorongoro Conservation Area, and lies at the base of the 800m Eyasi Escarpment, part of the western Rift Valley wall. In years of plentiful rain, this shallow soda lake can extend for 80km from north to south, but in drier periods it sometimes dries out altogether to form an expansive white crust. Most of the time, it falls somewhere between the two extremes: an eerily bleak and windswept body of water surrounded by a white muddy crust and tangled dry acacia scrub. When we visited in the middle of the day, the lake had a rather desolate appearance, but I imagine that it might be very beautiful in the early morning or late afternoon. There is little resident wildlife in the area, aside from dik-dik and baboons, but depending on the water level, the lake is an important source of fish for Arusha and it often supports hundreds of thousands of flamingoes as well as a variety of other waterbirds.

Lake Eyasi is primarily of interest to tourists as the home of the Hadza (see box *The last hunter-gatherers,* pages 160–1), and it is now reasonably straightforward to visit a Hadza encampment and go hunting with its male inhabitants. These visits must be arranged through one of three appointed guides based in the largest village in the region, which is called Mangola but sometimes referred to as Lake Eyasi (misleadingly, since it actually lies about 10km from the lakeshore). In addition to the entrance fee of Tsh2,000 per person charged by the council of Mangola, fees of Tsh10,000 and Tsh15,000 per party must be paid respectively to the guide and to the Hadza encampment visited.

We felt our visit to a Hadza encampment highly worthwhile. The people struck us as being very warm and unaffected, and going on an actual hunt was a primal and exciting experience – even if the waiting wives were mildly disappointed when their men returned to camp with only two mice and one bird to show for their efforts. Other travellers we've spoken to were luckier, though do be warned that a temporary conversion to vegetarianism might be in order should you come back from the hunt with a baboon or another large mammal – as a guest, you'll be offered the greatest delicacy, which is the raw liver. It could be argued that regular exposure to tourists might erode the traditional lifestyle of certain Hadza bands, but I saw no sign of this, and it should be borne in mind that the Hadza have chosen their nomadic lifestyle despite repeated attempts to settle them by successive governments. So far as I can ascertain, the guides ensure that no one band is visited more than once or twice a week, and the fee paid to the community is used to buy metal for spears and beads for decoration, but not food. And, incidentally, if you're the sort of daft bugger who wanders around African villages armed with piles of sweets or pens or whatever to hand out, then either don't visit the Hadza, or if you do, please leave the bag of goodies in Karatu.

Mangola lies about one hour's drive from Karatu, and can be reached by following the Ngorongoro road out of town for about 5km, then taking a left turn

THE LAST HUNTER-GATHERERS

The Hadza (or Hadzabe) of the Lake Eyasi hinterland, which lies to the east of Karatu, represent a unique – and increasingly fragile – link between modern East Africa and the most ancient of the region's human lifestyles and languages. Numbering at most 2,000 individuals, the Hadza are Tanzania's only remaining tribe of true hunter-gatherers, and their Hadzame language is one of only two in the country to be classified in the Khoisan family, a group of click-based tongues that also includes the San (Bushmen) of southern Africa.

The Hadza live in nomadic family bands, typically numbering about 20 adults and a coterie of children. Their rudimentary encampments of light grass shelters are erected in the space of a couple of hours, and might be used as a base for anything from ten days to one month before the inhabitants move on. These movements, though often rather whimsical, might be influenced by changes in the weather or local game distribution, and a band will also often relocate close to a fresh kill that is sufficiently large to sustain them for several days. The Hadza are fairly indiscriminate about what meat they eat – anything from mice to giraffe are fair game, and we once saw a family roasting a feral cat, fur and all, on their campfire – but baboons are regarded to be the ultimate delicacy and reptiles are generally avoided. Hunting with poisoned arrows and honey gathering are generally male activities, while women and children collect roots, seeds, tubers and fruit – vegetarian fodder actually accounts for about 80% of the food intake.

The Hadza have a reputation for living for the present and they care little for conserving food resources, probably because their lifestyle inherently places very little stress on the environment. This philosophy is epitomised in a popular game of chance, which Hadza men will often play – and gamble valuable possessions on – to while away a quiet afternoon. A large master disc is made from baobab bark, and each participant makes a smaller personal disc, with all discs possessing distinct rough and smooth faces. The discs are stacked and thrown in the air, an action that is repeated until only one of the small discs lands with the same face up as the large disc, deciding the winner.

Many Hadza people still dress in the traditional attire of animal skins – women favour impala hide, men the furry coat of a small predator or baboon – which are often decorated with shells and beads. Hadza social groupings are neither permanent nor strongly hierarchical: individuals and couples are free to move between bands, and there is no concept of territorial possession. In order to be eligible for marriage, a Hadza man must kill five baboons to prove his worth. Once married, a couple might stay together for several decades or a lifetime, but there is no taboo against separation and either partner can terminate the union at any time by physically abandoning the other partner.

towards the lake. Once at Mangola, it's easy enough to locate the guides and arrange a visit to a Hadza encampment. The full excursion can be completed as a half-day trip out of Karatu with private transport, and can easily be appended to a standard northern circuit safari. Using public transport, regular minibuses run between Karatu and Mangola, but you should be prepared to walk anything from 5–10km from there to get to the nearest encampment. There is no accommodation in Mangola. The council does, however, operate a lovely but unfacilitated campsite, which is set in a glade of acacias surrounding a hot spring about 4km from the town on the road towards the lake.

The Hadza might reasonably be regarded as a sociological and anthropological equivalent of a living fossil, since they are one of the very few remaining adherents to the hunter-gatherer lifestyle that sustained the entire human population of the planet for 98% of its history. In both the colonial and post-independence eras, the Hadza have resolutely refused to allow the government to coerce them into following a more settled agricultural or pastoral way of life. The last concerted attempt to modernise Hadza society took place in the 1960s, under the Nyerere government, when a settlement of brick houses with piped water, schools and a clinic was constructed for them alongside an agricultural scheme. Within ten years, the model settlement had been all but abandoned as the Hadza returned to their preferred lifestyle of hunting and gathering. The government, admirably, has since tacitly accepted the right of the Hadza to lead the life of their choice; a large tract of communal land fringing Lake Eyasi has been set aside for their use and they remain the only people in Tanzania automatically exempt from taxes!

The Khoisan language spoken by the Hadza is also something of a relic, belonging to a linguistic family that would almost certainly have dominated eastern and southern Africa until perhaps 3,000 years ago. As Bantu-speaking agriculturists and pastoralists swept into the region from the northwest, however, the Khoisan-speaking hunter-gatherer communities were either killed, or assimilated into Bantu-speaking communities, or forced to retreat into arid and montane territories ill-suited to herding and cultivation. This process of marginalisation has continued into historical times: it has been estimated that of around 100 documented Khoisan languages only 30 are still in use today, and that the total Khoisan-speaking population of Africa now stands at less than 200,000.

That most Khoisan languages, if not already extinct, are headed that way, takes on an added poignancy if, as a minority of linguists have suggested throughout the 20th century, the unique click sounds are a preserved element of the very earliest human language. In order to investigate this possibility, the anthropological geneticists Alec Knight and Joanna Mountain recently analysed the chromosome content of samples taken from the geographically diverse San and Hadza, and concluded that they 'are as genetically distant from one another as two populations could be'. Discounting the somewhat improbable scenario that the clicking noises of the Hadza and San languages arose independently, this wide genetic gulf would imply a very ancient common linguistic root indeed. Knight and Mountain's conclusions are disputed by several linguists, but if they are correct, then Hadzame, along with Africa's other dying Khoisan languages, might represent one last fading echo of the first human voices to have carried across the African savannah.

NGORONGORO CONSERVATION AREA

The 8,300km² Ngorongoro Conservation Area is named after its central feature, the Ngorongoro Crater, the world's largest intact volcanic caldera, and arguably its most spectacular natural arena. Ngorongoro Crater has often been described as one of the wonders of the world, not only because of its inherent geological magnificence, but also because it serves as a quite extraordinary natural sanctuary for some of Africa's densest populations of large mammals.

The approach road from Karatu to the crater rim is sensational, winding through the densely forested outer slopes to Heroes Point, where most visitors will catch their first breathtaking view over the 260km² crater floor lying 600m below. Even at this distance, it is possible to pick out ant-like formations – thousand-strong herds of wildebeest and buffalo – chomping their way across the crater floor, and with binoculars you might even see a few of the elephants that haunt the fringes of Lerai Forest. The drive along the crater rim to your lodge will be equally riveting: patches of forest interspersed with sweeping views back across to the Rift Valley, and the possibility of encountering buffalo, zebra, bushbuck, elephant and even the occasional leopard.

The Ngorongoro Crater is the main focal point of tourist activity in the crater, and is covered in more detail later in this section. Those who have the time can explore any number of less publicised natural features further afield. Olduvai Gorge, for instance, is the site of some of Africa's most important hominid fossil finds, and can easily be visited en route from the crater rim to the Serengeti. An excellent 84-page booklet, *Ngorongoro Conservation Area*, similar in style to the national park booklets, is readily available in Arusha and has good information on the crater and Olduvai Gorge. It is especially worth buying if you plan to visit some of the off-the-beaten-track parts of the conservation area.

The Ngorongoro Conservation Authority charges an entrance fee of US$30 per person per 24 hours. This must be paid even if you just pass through the conservation area between Arusha and the Serengeti. An additional crater service fee of US$30 per vehicle is charged upon descending to the crater floor.

The crater rim gets very cold at night, and is often blanketed in mist in the early morning. You will need a jumper or two, and possibly a windbreaker if you are camping.

Geology and history

The mountains in the Ngorongoro region date from two periods. The Gol Mountains, to your left as you descend from Ngorongoro to the Serengeti, are exposed granite blocks over 500 million years old. Ngorongoro and the other free-standing mountains are volcanic in origin, formed during the fracturing process that created the Rift Valley 15 to 20 million years ago. When Ngorongoro peaked in size two to three million years ago, it was a similar height to Kilimanjaro today. There are two other volcanic craters in the area: Olmoti and Empakaai. A volcano lying immediately north of the conservation area, Ol Dionyo L'Engai – a Maasai phrase that means 'Mountain of God' – last erupted in 1983.

Evidence found at Olduvai Gorge and Laetoli (discussed more fully later in the chapter) shows hominids have occupied the area for at least three million years. It was occupied by hunter-gatherers until a few thousand years ago, when pastoralists moved in. The only hunter-gatherers now living in the area are the Hadza of the Lake Eyasi Basin to the south of Ngorongoro (see *Lake Eyasi* on page 159). The fate of the early pastoralists is not known, because a succession of immigrants replaced them. The ancestors of the Cushitic-speaking Mbulu arrived 2,000 years ago. The Nilotic-speaking Datoga arrived 300 years ago. A century later the Maasai drove both groups out in a violent conflict, the Datoga to the Eyasi Basin and the Mbulu to the highlands near Manyara. Most place names in the area are Maasai. I have heard several explanations of the name Ngorongoro; the most believable, told to me by a Maasai, is that it is named after a type of Maasai bowl that it resembles.

Europeans settled in the area around the turn of the 20th century. Two German brothers farmed on the crater floor until the outbreak of World War I. One of their old farmhouses is still used by researchers working in the crater, and a few sisal plants dating to this time can be seen in the northeast of the crater. Tourism began in the 1930s when the Ngorongoro Crater Lodge was built on the crater rim. Ngorongorc

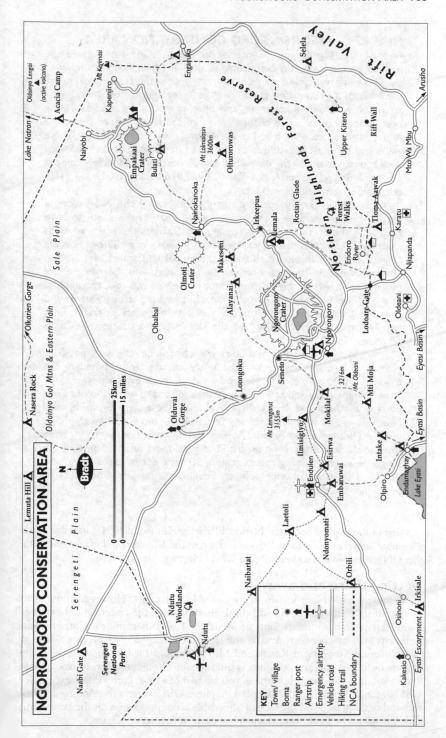

NGORONGORO CONSERVATION AREA

N

Bradt

25km
15 miles

0
0

KEY

- Town/village
- Boma
- Ranger post
- Airstrip
- Emergency airstrip
- Vehicle road
- Hiking trail
- NCA boundary

Rift Valley

Northern Highlands Forest Reserve

Serengeti Plain

Sale Plain

Oldoinyo Gol Mtns & Eastern Plain

Serengeti National Park

Eyasi Basin

Eyasi Escarpment

Lake Eyasi

Selela

Engaruka

Arusha

Mto Wa Mbu

Rift Wall

Upper Kitete

Karatu

Njiapanda

Oldeani

Tloma-Aawak

Forest Walks

Endoro River

Lodoare Gate

Ngorongoro

Seneto

Ngorongoro Crater

Rotian Glade

Irkeepus

Nemala

Nainokanoka

Makeseni

Olmoti Crater

Olbalbal

Loongoku

Alayanai

Mt Lolmalasin 3600m

Olturorowas

Empakaai Crater

Bulati

Kapenjiro

Naiyobi

Mt Kerimasi

Acacia Camp

Oldoinyo Lengai (active volcano)

Lake Natron

Olkarien Gorge

Nasera Rock

Lemuta Hill

Naabi Gate

Olduvai Gorge

Ndutu Woodlands

Ndutu

Kakesio

Osinoni

Irkisale

Orbili

Ndonyomati

Laetoli

Naibartat

Olpiro

Intake

Endamaghay

Embaruwai

Endulen

Esirwa

Ilmisiglyo

Mt Lemagarut 3155m

Mokilal

Mti Moja

Mt Oldeani

3216m

3155m

HIKING IN NGORONGORO CONSERVATION AREA

Because the Ngorongoro Conservation Area (NCA) lies outside the national park system, it is permissible to walk and hike along a number of trails covering most main points of interest (but not the crater floor) in the company of an authorised guide. For those seeking a short morning or afternoon walk on the crater rim appended to a standard road safari, the best option is to take one of three short guided hikes offered by Serena Active, a new company based in the Ngorongoro Serena Lodge. These walks can be pre-booked, but it's also fine just to pitch at their booking desk spontaneously on the day, whether you're staying at the Serena or at another lodge on the crater rim. Tel: 027 253 9160/1/2; fax: 027 253 9163; email: serenaactive@serena.co.tz.

You could in theory spend a fortnight exploring the NCA along a network of longer trails that connects Lake Eyasi in the south to Lake Natron in the north, as well as running west across the plains towards Laetoli and Lake Ndutu and northwest to Olduvai Gorge. Other possible targets for hikers include the Olmoti and Empakaai Craters, the 3,600m Mount Lolmalasin (the third highest in Tanzania), and the remote Gol Mountains. In theory, any safari operator can advise you about routes and arrange hikes with the NCA authorities, but I would strongly advise the traveller thinking of doing this to work through an operator with specialist trekking experience (see the *Safari Operators* listings in Arusha on pages 128–9).

It would also be possible to set up a trekking trip directly with the NCA, bussing to the crater rim from Arusha. Were you to attempt something like this, you would have to organise food yourself, to clarify arrangements for a tent, sleeping bag and other equipment, and to take warm clothes since parts of the NCA are very chilly at night. The best place to make initial enquiries and arrangements for any DIY trekking trip would be the NCA office on Boma Road in Arusha. At least five different one-day hiking trails from the crater rim can be arranged at very short notice. Some of the longer hikes and trekking routes require 30 days' notice to set up, so you will need to make advance contact. Email: ncaa_hq@cybernet.co.za or ncaa_hq@habari.co.tz.

was part of the original Serengeti National Park proclaimed in 1951, but it was made a separate conservation area in 1956 in order that the Maasai could graze their cattle there. Ngorongoro Crater was made a World Heritage Site in 1978.

Getting there and away

Most tourists visit Ngorongoro as part of a longer safari. However, those who cannot afford to do this could still think about visiting the crater on a short one-night self-contained safari out of Arusha. The Ngorongoro Conservation Authority staff bus between Arusha and the park headquarters runs twice daily in each direction, stopping at Karatu and Mto wa Mbu. Bear in mind that the value of arriving at Ngorongoro on a bus is questionable. You could hire a park vehicle to take you into the crater, but unless you are part of a large group this is expensive: US$140 for a full day, plus US$1 per km, plus a US$30 crater fee. Adding on park fees and bearing in mind the lack of affordable accommodation on the crater rim, and you would be better off organising a safari in Arusha or Karatu.

Where to stay and eat

There are no accommodation or camping facilities within the crater, and with the exception of Ndutu Lodge on the Serengeti border, all the lodges and the main campsite lie perched on the crater rim.

Exclusive

Ngorongoro Crater Lodge Tel: 027 254 8549/8038 or (South Africa) 11 809 4447; email: res@ccafrica.co.tz or reservations@ccafrica.com; web: www.ccafrica.com. This top-of-the-range lodge was originally built in 1934 as a private hunting lodge with a commanding view over the crater, and was converted to a hotel shortly after independence in 1961. The property was bought by CCA in 1995 and rebuilt from scratch with the stated aim of creating 'the finest safari lodge in Africa'. Architecturally, the lodge is literally fantastic. Each individual suite consists of two adjoining round structures, similar to African huts but distorted in an almost Dadaist style. The large interiors boast a décor as ostentatious as it is eclectic, combining elements of baroque, classical, African, colonial and much more besides in a manner the management describes as 'Maasai meets Versailles'. The entire lodge has been designed in such a way that the crater is almost constantly in sight (even the baths and the toilets have a view!), and the food, service and ambience are all world class. Whether or not the CCA has succeeded in creating Africa's finest safari lodge is a matter of taste and opinion – certainly, the decidedly non-'bush' atmosphere might offend some purists – but it is difficult to fault in terms of ambition and originality. The fact that it was commended in *Conde Nast Traveller*'s prestigious 1998 end-of-year listings says enough. The FB rates of US$400 per person in the low season and US$525 in the high season are inclusive of all meals, drinks and game drives, and a reduction is offered for stays of more than three nights.

Upmarket

Ngorongoro Serena Lodge Tel: 027 250 4058; fax: 027 250 8282; email: reservations@serena.co.tz. Meeting the usual high Serena standards, this is arguably the pick of the more conventional lodges on the crater rim, receiving consistent praise from tourists and from within the safari industry. It lies on the western crater rim along the road towards Seronera, several kilometres past the park headquarters and Crater Lodge. It is the closest of the lodges to the main descent road into the crater, a decided advantage for those who want to get to the crater floor as early as possible. The setting is a secluded wooded valley rustling with birdlife and offering a good view over the crater. Serena Active, which operates out of the lodge, offers a good range of afternoon and full-day walks ranging from a gentle stroll through the grassy highlands to a rather more challenging ascent of Olmoti Crater. The facilities, food and service are all of a high standard. Rooms cost US$230/340 single/double FB.

Ngorongoro Sopa Lodge Tel: 057 250 6886; fax: 057 250 8245; email: info@sopalodges.com; web: www.sopalodges.com. Situated on the forested eastern edge of the crater rim some 20km distant from the headquarters and main cluster of lodges, this attractive modern hotel is similar in standard to the Serena and arguably nudges ahead of it on the basis of location. Accommodation is in vast semi-detached suites, each with two double beds, a heater, a large bathroom, a fridge, and a wide bay window facing the crater and Ol Mokarot Mountain. There is a swimming pool in front of the bar, and the food and service are excellent. One thing that stands out about this lodge is the large, forested grounds, a good place to look for characteristic montane forest birds, with sunbirds (tacazze, golden-winged and eastern double-collared) well represented and a variety of weavers, seedeaters and robins present. Another is that it lies close to what, in effect, is a private road that can be used both to ascend from and descend into the crater, which greatly reduces the driving time either side of game drives – particularly useful for an early

NORTH OF NGORONGORO CRATER

Few tourists venture into the northern part of the Ngorongoro Conservation Area, since it doesn't fit comfortably into the standard three- to five-day safari. There are, however, a few places which would be attractive additions to your itinerary if you had time or wanted to head to less touristed spots. Most experienced safari operators can arrange trips up here, generally taking Lake Natron as their focal point, though many will also try to discourage visiting the area as it is rough on vehicles. The roads in the region are poor and may be impassable after rain. If you plan to explore the area, allocate time generously. If you visit this area in your own vehicle, treat it as you would any wilderness trip: carry adequate supplies of food, water and fuel. You should also have essential spares for your vehicle. If you go with a safari company, avoid those at the lower end of the price scale. Two operators specialising in the area are Swala Safaris and Hoopoe Adventure Tours, which respectively operate a moderately priced tented camp at Lake Natron and a more exclusive and pricier upmarket tented camp in Loliondo (contact details are included under the appropriate heading below).

Note that the scenic 194km, eight-hour drive between Natron and Serengeti suffered a spate of unrest in 1998–99 instigated by Somali exiles from Kenya. The insurgents killed at least one police officer and several local Maasai, and a tourist vehicle was attacked in this area, fortunately without any fatalities. The situation seems fine at the time of writing, but you are advised to confirm this with a specialised Natron operator.

Olmoti Crater This sunken caldera lies near to the village of Nainokanoka. A track leads from the village to a ranger's post west of it. The crater can only be reached on foot, so at the ranger's post you will have to organise an armed ranger to guide you. From the ranger's post it is a half-hour walk through montane forest to the rim. This is a shallow crater, covered in grass, and it offers good grazing for Maasai cattle and a variety of antelope. From the rim you can walk to a pretty waterfall where the Munge River leaves the crater.

Empakaai Crater Almost half the floor of this 6km-wide, 300m-high crater is taken up by a deep soda lake. A road circles the forested rim and another leads to the crater floor. Bushbuck, buffalo and blue monkey are likely to be seen on the rim, which also boasts good views across to L'Engai Volcano and, on clear days, Kilimanjaro and Lake Natron. The crater floor is home to a variety of antelope and water birds. With permission from park headquarters, you may camp wild on the crater rim or sleep in a cabin on the southern shore of the lake.

Engaruka Ruins The ruins of a terraced stone city and complex irrigation system, estimated to be more than 500 years old, lies just outside the Ngorongoro Conservation Area on the eastern foothills of Mount Empakaai. Nobody knows who built the city – there is no tradition of stone building in this part of Africa – but it was almost certainly occupied by the Mbulu people immediately before the Maasai came into the area. The main road north from Mto wa Mbu towards Lake Natron leads past Engaruka, and there is a basic community-run campsite near the ruins. .

morning start. Full board accommodation costs US$175/280 single/double in peak season, dropping to US$70/140 in low season.
Ngorongoro Wildlife Lodge Tel: 027 250 2711/2; fax: 027 250 8221; email: tahifin@habari.yako.co.tz. Like Ngorongoro Crater Lodge, roughly 2km away, this is a

Ol Doinyo L'Engai The challenging ascent to the crater of the Maasai's Mountain of God, the only active carbonate volcano in the world, passes through some magnificently arid scenery, and offers spectacular views of the Rift Valley. L'Engai last erupted in 1966, but the crater has been filling with lava since 1996, though it has not as yet spilt over the edge. The ascent requires a fair degree of fitness, as the track to the top is very steep, climbing in altitude from around 800m to over 3,000m. The ascent normally takes around five hours along slopes practically bereft of shade, for which reason many safari operators recommend leaving at midnight to avoid the intense heat and reach the crater rim in time for sunrise. If you ascend by day, a 05.00 start is advised, and precautions should be taken against dehydration and sunstroke. Either way, the descent takes about two hours. The mountain lies outside any conservation area, so no park fees are charged.

Lake Natron This spectacular soda lake, to the north of Ol Doinyo L'Engai, lies at an altitude of 610m in the harsh Kenyan border area below the Rift Valley escarpment. The scenery here has an almost primeval quality, and the concentration of sodium carbonate dissolved in the lake is so high that it is often viscous to the touch. As well as being highly scenic, the lake offers good game viewing and birding. Among the 'specials' of the region are such dry country antelope as gerenuk, lesser kudu and oryx. Natron is the only known breeding ground for East Africa's millions of lesser flamingos, which usually congregate there to breed between August and October. The only place to stay in the Natron area is Natron Lake Camp, which consists of nine standing tents and a swimming pool in a spectacular setting next to a stream below the Rift Valley escarpment 4km from the southern lake shore. Accommodation costs US$60 per person full board or US$120 per person inclusive of all meals and activities. The camp can organise guided climbs of nearby Ol Dionyo L'Engai for US$35 for the first climber plus US$20 per additional climber. Although any safari operator can arrange to include Lake Natron in your itinerary, the camp is owned and managed by Swala Safaris; tel: 057 270 6424; mobile: 0744 300806; fax: 027 270 8424; email: sengo@habari.co.tz or swala@habari.co.tz.

Loliondo Bounded by the Serengeti National Park to the west, Lake Natron to the east, and the Ngorongoro Conservation Area to the south, the vast Loliondo Game Controlled Area has been developed over recent years as an award-winning eco-tourism project run by Hoopoe Adventure Tours in collaboration with local Maasai communities. A good base for visits to Lake Natron and ascents of Ol Doinyo L'Engai, Loliondo also supports a similar range of species to the neighbouring national park, with the advantage that game viewing can be undertaken on foot – with a local Maasai guide – as well as by vehicle. Access to this vast untrammelled area is exclusive to people staying at the small and upmarket Loliondo Tented Camp. For rates and further details, contact Hoopoe Adventure Tours; tel: 027 250 7011 or (UK) 1923 255462; fax: 027 254 8226 or 1923 255452; email: hoopoeUK@aol.com or hoopoesafari@africaonline.co.tz; web: www.hoopoe.com.

relatively old lodge, managed by TAHI and showing its antiquity both in the architecture and the fittings. The once appalling service and food have improved greatly in the last few years, and the location – on the crater rim directly above the forest of yellow fever acacias – defies superlatives. The rooms are functionally comfortable, with piping-hot baths (welcome at this chilly altitude) and windows facing the crater. You can pick out animals on the crater floor using a telescope fixed on the patio. The grounds support a fair range of forest birds. Solid value for money at US$140/196/280 single/double/triple FB.

Moderate

Rhino Lodge Owned by the Ngorongoro Conservation Authority, this low-key lodge near the conservation headquarters was of interest primarily for its relatively cheap rates prior to closing a couple of years ago. The property is currently up for sale and seems likely to re-open under private management within the next few years. What price range it will fall into then is anybody's guess, but no amount of renovation will disguise its greatest inherent flaw, which is that it is set back from the crater rim and has no view worth talking about.

Budget and camping

The only place where you can pitch a tent on the crater rim is at **Simba Campsite**, about 2km from the park headquarters. This site is hardly great value at US$20 per person (facilities are limited to a cold shower and rubbish pit) but the wonderful view still makes it a preferable option to camping in Karatu, in my opinion at least. The only cheap rooms on the crater rim are at the driver's lodge in the village, but tourists are not normally allowed to stay there. Your best bet for a cheap room is in Karatu. The village near the headquarters has a few basic bars and shops, and there is nothing preventing you from dropping into nearby Wildlife Lodge for a drink or snack.

Around Ngorongoro Conservation Area
Ngorongoro Crater Floor

The opportunity of spending a day on the crater floor is simply not to be missed. There are few places where you can so reliably see such large concentrations of wildlife all year round, and your game viewing (and photography) will only be enhanced by the striking backdrop of the 600m-high crater wall. The crater is also excellent Big Five territory: lion, elephant and buffalo are all but guaranteed, rhino are regularly seen, and a leopard is chanced upon from time to time. The official road down to the crater descends from Malanja Depression to the western shore of Lake Magadi, while the official road up starts near Lerai Forest and reaches the rim on the stretch of road between Wildlife and Crater Lodges. There is a third road into the crater, which starts near the Sopa Lodge, and this can be used either to ascend or to descend.

There are several notable physical features within the crater. Lerai Forest consists almost entirely of yellow fever trees, large acacias noted for their jaundiced bark (it was once thought that this tree, which is often associated with marsh and lake fringes, the breeding ground for mosquitoes, was the cause of yellow fever and malaria). To the north of this forest, Lake Magadi is a shallow soda lake that varies greatly in extent depending on the season. To the south and east of this, the Gorigor Swamp also varies in extent seasonally, but it generally supports some water. There is a permanent hippo pool at the Ngoitokitok Springs at the western end of the swamp. The northern half of the crater is generally drier, though it is bisected by the Munge River, which is lined by thickets and forms a seasonally substantial area of swamp to the immediate north of Lake Magadi.

The open grassland that covers most of the crater floor supports large concentrations of wildebeest and zebra (the population of these species is estimated at 10,000 and 5,000 respectively), and smaller numbers of buffalo, tsessebe, and Thomson's and Grant's gazelle. The vicinity of Lerai Forest is the best area in which to see waterbuck, bushbuck and eland. The forest and adjoining Gorigor Swamp a the main haunt of the crater's elephant population, which typically stands at around 70. All the elephants resident in the crater are old males (though females and families sometimes pass through the area), and you stand a good chance of seeing big tuskers of the sort that have been poached away elsewhere in East Africa. Two curious absentees from the crater floor are impala and giraffe, both of which are common in the surrounding plains, Some researchers attribute the absence of giraffe to a lack of suitable browsing fodder, others to their presumed inability to descend the steep crater walls. Quite why there are no impala in the crater is a mystery.

The crater floor reputedly supports the densest concentration of predators in Africa. The resident lion population has fluctuated greatly ever since records were maintained, partly as a result of migration in and out of the crater, but primarily because of the vulnerability of the concentrated and rather closed population to epidemics. Over the course of 1962, the lion population dropped from an estimated 90 to about 15 due to an outbreak of disease spread by biting flies, but it had recovered to about 70 within a decade. In recent years, the pattern of fluctuation saw the population estimated at 80 in 1995, 35 in 1998, and 55 divided into four main prides and a few nomadic males in 2000. The crater's lions might be encountered just about anywhere, and are generally very relaxed around vehicles.

The most populous large predator is the spotted hyena, the population of which is estimated at around 400. You won't spend long in the crater without seeing a hyena: they often rest up on the eastern shore of Lake Magadi during the day, sometimes trying – and mostly failing – to sneak up on the flamingoes in the hope of a quick snack. Until recently, no cheetahs were resident within the crater, which might seem surprising given that the open grassland is textbook cheetah habitat, but is probably due to the high rate of competition from other predators. At least two female cheetahs recently colonised the crater floor – one of which had four cubs in late 2001 – and sightings are now fairly regular. Leopards are resident, particularly in swampy areas, but they are not often seen. Other common predators are the golden and black-backed jackals, with the former being more frequently encountered due to its relatively diurnal habits.

The crater floor offers some great birding. Lake Magadi normally harbours large flocks of flamingo, giving its edges a pinkish tinge when seen from a distance. The pools at the Mandusi Swamp can be excellent for waterbirds, with all manner of waders, storks, ducks and herons present. The grassland is a good place to see a number of striking ground birds. One very common resident is the kori bustard, reputedly the world's heaviest flying bird, and spectacular if you catch it during a mating dance. Ostrich are also common, along with the gorgeously garish crowned crane, and (in the rainy season) huge flocks of migrant storks. Less prominent, but common, and of great interest to more dedicated birders, is the lovely rosy-throated longclaw. Two of the most striking and visible birds of prey are the augur buzzard, sometimes seen here in its unusual melanistic form, and the foppish long crested eagle. The localised Egyptian vulture – whose ability to crack open ostrich eggs by holding a stone in its beak makes it the only bird that arguably uses tools – is sometimes seen in the vicinity of Mungu Stream.

There are a few hippo pools in the crater, but the one most often visited is Ngoitokitok Springs, a popular picnic spot where lunch is enlivened by a flock of black kites which have become adept at swooping down on tourists and snatching the food from their hands.

The authorities rigidly forbid tourists from entering the crater before 07.00, and they must be out of the crater before 18.00. This is a frustrating ruling for photographers, since it means that you miss out on the best light of the day, and it has encouraged a situation where most safari drivers suggest that their clients take

NOT A BLOODY ZOO

A regular criticism of the Ngorongoro Crater, one that in my opinion is desperately misguided, is that it is 'like a zoo'. Aside from being yawningly unoriginal – I must have heard this phrase two dozen times in the course of researching this fourth edition – this allegation is as facile as it is nonsensical. The wildlife in the crater is not caged, nor is it artificially fed, surely the defining qualities of a zoo, but is instead free to come and go as it pleases. Yes, the crater's animals are generally very relaxed around vehicles, but that doesn't make them tame, merely habituated – no different, really, to the mountain gorillas of Rwanda or the chimps at Mahale.

The point that many visitors to Ngorongoro miss is that, for all the elitism attached to Africa's more remote game reserves, it is only in places where the wildlife is almost totally habituated that casual visitors can watch the animals behave much as they would were no human observers present. And, trust me, this is an infinitely more satisfying experience than travelling through a reserve where the wildlife is so skittish that most sightings amount to little more than a rump disappearing into the bush.

I suspect that the notion of Ngorongoro as a glorified zoo stems from something else entirely. This is the high volume of tourist traffic, which admittedly robs the crater floor of some of its atmosphere, and has some potential to cause environmental degradation, but is of questionable impact on the animals. On the contrary, the wildlife of Ngorongoro is apparently far less affected by the presence of vehicles than, say, the elephants and giraffes in the Selous, which regularly display clear signs of distress at the approach of a vehicle.

The problem, basically, is that the high volume of other tourists in the relatively small and open confines of the crater jars against our sense of aesthetics – especially when game spotting entails looking for a group of vehicles clustered together in the distance rather than looking for an actual animal! Personally, I feel that the scenery and abundance of animals more than makes up for the mild congestion, but if crowds put you off, then there are other places to visit in Tanzania. Instead of adding to the tourist traffic, then moaning about it, why not give the crater a miss? Or, better still, as suggested in the main body of the text, make the effort to be in the crater first thing in the morning, when, for a brief hour or two before the post-breakfast crowds descend, it really does live up to every expectation of untrammelled beauty.

breakfast before going on a game drive, and carry a picnic lunch. This programme is difficult to avoid if you are on a group safari, but for those on a private safari, it is well worth getting down to the crater as early as permitted. Photography aside, this is the one time in the day when you might have the crater to yourself, the one time, in other words, when you can really experience the Ngorongoro Crater of television documentary land. Note that it is forbidden to descend to the base of the crater after 16.00.

Olduvai Gorge

Difficult to believe today perhaps, but for much of the past two million years the seasonally parched plains around Olduvai – or more correctly *oldupai*, the Maasai word for sisal – were submerged beneath a lake that formed an important watering

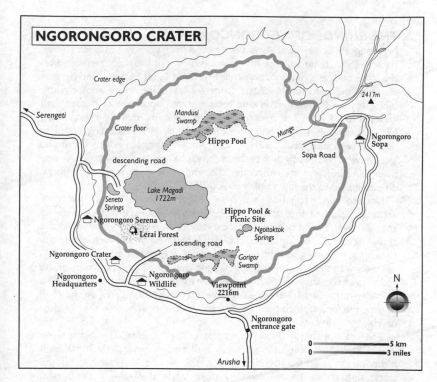

hole for local animals and our hominid ancestors. This was a fluctuating body of water, at times expansive, at other times drying up altogether, creating a high level of stratification accentuated by sporadic deposits of fine ash from the volcanoes that surrounded it. Then, tens of thousands of years ago, volcanic activity associated with the rifting process caused the land to tilt, and a new lake formed to the east. The river that flowed out of this new lake gradually incised a gorge through the former lakebed, exposing layers of stratification up to 100m deep. Olduvai Gorge thus cuts through a chronological sequence of rock beds preserving a practically continuous archaeological and fossil record of life on the plains over the past two million years.

The significance of Olduvai Gorge was first recognised by the German entomologist Professor Katwinkle, who stumbled across it in 1911 while searching for insect specimens. Two years later, Katwinkle led an archaeological expedition to the gorge, and unearthed a number of animal fossils before the excavations were abandoned at the outbreak of World War I. In 1931, the palaeontologist Louis Leakey visited the long-abandoned diggings and realised that the site provided ideal conditions for following the hominid fossil record back to its beginnings. Leakey found ample evidence demonstrating that ancient hominids had occupied the site, but lacking for financial backing, his investigations went slowly and frustratingly refused to yield any truly ancient fossilised hominid remains.

The payoff for the long years of searching came in 1959 when Mary Leakey – Richards's wife, and a more than accomplished archaeologist in her own right – discovered a heavy fossilised jawbone that displayed unambiguous human affinities but was also clearly unlike any other hominid fossil documented at the time. Christened 'Nutcracker man' by the Leakeys in reference to its bulk, this jawbone proved to be that of an Australopithecine (now designated as

THE RHINOS OF NGORONGORO

Ngorongoro Crater has always been noted for its density of black rhinos. Back in 1892, Baumann, the first European to visit the area, remarked on the large numbers of rhino, particularly around Lerai Forest – and he shot seven of the unfortunate beasts to prove his point. More recently, the biologist John Goddard estimated the resident population at greater than 100 in 1964. By 1992, thanks to poachers, no more than 10 rhinos were left, although this number had increased to 18 by 1998, including a mother and calf relocated from South Africa's Addo National Park to boost the local genetic pool. Sadly, five of these rhinos have died since late 2000, one taken by a lion and the remainder thought to be victims of a tick-borne disease linked to the low rainfall of 2000/1.

Despite the decline in numbers, Ngorongoro is today the only accessible part of the northern safari circuit where these endangered animals haven't been poached to local extinction. For many visitors to the crater, therefore, seeing rhino is a very high priority, and fortunately the chances are pretty good. In the wet season, the rhinos are often seen in the vicinity of the Ngoitokitok Springs and the Sopa Road. For most of the year, however, they range between the Lerai Forest by night and Lake Magadi by day. Early risers are very likely to encounter a pair on the road fringing the forest, since they tend to move towards the lake shortly after dawn.

The crater's rhinos display a couple of local quirks. The black rhino (unlike its 'white' cousin) is normally a diurnal browser, which makes it rather odd to see them spending most of the day in open grassland, but the story is that they mostly feed by night while they are in the forest. Baumann noted that the crater's rhinos were unusually pale in colour, a phenomenon that is still observed today, due to their predilection for bathing and rolling in the saline lake and fringing salt flats.

Australopithecus boisei) that had lived and died on the ancient lakeshore some 1.75 million years ago. Subsequently superseded by more ancient fossils unearthed elsewhere in East Africa, this was nevertheless a critical landmark in the history of palaeontology: the first conclusive evidence that hominid evolution stretched back over more than a million years and had been enacted on the plains of East Africa.

This important breakthrough shot the Leakeys' work to international prominence, and with proper funding at their disposal, a series of exciting new discoveries followed, including the first fossilised remains of *Homo habilis*, a direct ancestor of modern man that would have dwelt on the lakeshore contemporaneously with *Australopithecus boisei*. After Richard's death in 1972, Mary Leakey continued working in the area until she retired in 1984. In 1976, at the nearby site of Laetoli, she discovered footprints created more than three million years ago by a party of early hominids which had walked through a bed of freshly deposited volcanic ash – still the most ancient hominid footprints ever found.

Olduvai Gorge lies within the conservation area about 3km north of the main road between Ngorongoro Crater and the Serengeti, and is a popular and worthwhile place to stop for a picnic lunch. The actual diggings may only be explored with a guide, and – since all fossils are immediately removed – they are probably of greater immediate interest for the geology than for the archaeology. Not so the excellent site museum, which displays replicas of some of the mor interesting hominid fossils unearthed at the site as well as the Laetoli footprints. Also on display are genuine fossils of some of the extinct animals that used to roam the plains: pygmy and short-necked giraffes, giant swine, river elephant, various equines, and a bizarre antelope with long de-curved horns. Outside the museum, evolutionary diversity is represented by the variety of colourful – and very alive – dry-country birds that hop around the picnic area: red-and-yellow barbet, slaty-coloured boubou, rufous chatterer, speckle-fronted weaver and purple grenadier are practically guaranteed.

Lake Ndutu
This alkaline lake lies south of the B142 on the Ngorongoro–Serengeti border. When it is full, Maasai use it to water their cattle. In the rainy season it supports large numbers of animals, so Ndutu Lodge (see *Where to stay* above) is a good base for game drives. The acacia woodland around the lake supports different birds to those in surrounding areas. The campsite on the lakeshore costs US$40 per person.

SERENGETI NATIONAL PARK
There is little I can say about the Serengeti that hasn't been said already. This is Africa's most famous game reserve, renowned for its dense predator population and annual wildebeest migration, the sort of place that's been hyped so heavily you might reasonably brace yourself for disappointment when you actually get to visit it. But the Serengeti is all it is cracked up to be. The sense of space attached to exploring the vast Serengeti Plains is overwhelming, as are the sheer numbers of animals these plains support. The Serengeti is the best game reserve I have visited anywhere in Africa – no competition!

Serengeti National Park covers an area of almost 15,000km², but the Serengeti ecosystem – which includes a number of game reserves bordering the national park as well as Kenya's Maasai Mara Game Reserve – is more than double that size. Most of the national park is open and grassy, broken by isolated granite *koppies* and patches of acacia woodland. There is little permanent water, so animal migration in the area is strongly linked to rainfall patterns.

The Maasai occupied the Serengeti Plains in the 17th century, displacing the Datoga pastoralists who had previously lived there. The name Serengeti derives from a Maasai word *Serengit*, meaning Endless Plain. The Maasai are no longer allowed to graze their cattle within the national park, but evidence of their previous occupation of the area can be seen at Moru Koppies, where there are well-preserved Maasai rock paintings. Partly because it lay within Maasailand, the Serengeti area was little known to Europeans until after World War I, when hunters moved in. The national park was created in 1951 and became famous through the work of Professor Bernard Grzimek (pronounced *Jimek*) and his son Michael. At the age of 24, Michael died in an aeroplane crash over the Serengeti. He is buried at Heroes Point on the Ngorongoro Crater rim. Published in the late 1950s, Grzimek's book *Serengeti Shall Not Die* remains worthwhile reading.

Using figures from the 1984/5 census, the Serengeti's most common antelope species are wildebeest (1,300,000), Thomson's gazelle (250,000), impala (70,000), topi (50,000), Grant's gazelle (30,000), kongoni (15,000) and eland (10,000). Other antelope species include Kirk's dik-dik, klipspringer (often seen on *koppies*) and small numbers of roan, oryx, oribi and waterbuck. After wildebeest, the most populous large mammal is zebra (200,000), and the two are often seen in mixed herds. There are significant numbers of buffalo, giraffe and warthog. Elephant are relatively scarce on the open plains, but more common in the north and west, and the few remaining black rhinoceros are restricted to an inaccessible part of the park.

SERENGETI BALLOON SAFARIS

Serengeti Balloon Safaris is – no prizes for guessing – the name of the company that runs balloon safaris from a launch site close to Seronera Lodge at 06.00 every morning. Although not cheap, a balloon safari is definitely worth the expense if you can afford it. Gliding serenely above the trees as the sun rises allows you to see the expansive plains from a new and quite thrilling angle. It also offers the chance to see secretive species such as bushbuck and reedbuck, and, because you leave so early in the morning, you are likely to spot a few nocturnal predators (we saw hyenas in abundance, civet twice and had a rare glimpse of an African wild cat). That said, any images you have of sweeping above innumerable wildebeest and zebra may prove a little removed from reality; you can only be confident of seeing large herds of ungulates if you're fortunate enough to be around during the exact week or two when animals concentrate immediately around Seronera.

The safari culminates with a champagne breakfast in the bush, set up at a different site every day, depending on which way the balloons are blown. The meal is presented with some flourish: the immaculately uniformed waiters in particular conjure up images of the safaris of old. Our particular mad-hatters' breakfast party was enlivened by the arrival of three male lions, who strolled less than 100m from the table apparently oblivious to the unusual apparition of 24 people eating scrambled eggs and sausages at a starched tablecloth in the bush. Presumably, this sort of thing doesn't happen every day, whether you're a lion or a human!

The package, which costs US$399 per person, includes the transfer to the balloon site, a balloon trip of roughly one hour's duration, and the champagne breakfast. There is a booking desk at the Seronera Wildlife Lodge, as well as at the Serengeti Sopa and Serena Lodges. The other Serengeti lodges are too far from the launching site to get there in time (as things stand the transfer from Seronera leaves at 05.30 and from the other lodges at around 04.30!). If you want to be certain of a place, however, it is advisable to book in advance, particularly during high season. Reservations can be made through your safari company, directly through Serengeti Balloon Safaris' Arusha office (tel: 027 250 8578 or 254 8967; email: balloons@habari.co.tz) or through the UK office (tel: 01225 873756; email: tpsafari@globalnet.co.uk).

The olive baboon and vervet monkey are the most common and widespread primates, but an isolated and seldom seen population of patas monkey is resident in the north, and black-and-white colobus haunt the riparian woodland along the Grumeti River through the Western Corridor.

Ultimately, the success of any safari lies in the number and quality of encounters with big cats. There is something infinitely compelling about these animals, a fascination that seems to affect even the most jaded of safari drivers – many of whom are leopard obsessive, content to drive up and down the Seronera Valley all day in the search for a telltale tail dangling from a tree. And when it comes to big cats, the Serengeti rarely disappoints. Lions are a practical certainty: some 250 to 300 of these animals stalk the plains around Seronera, with the main concentration around Simba Hills north of the Ngorongoro road. It's normal to see two or three prides in the course of one game drive. Sociable, languid and

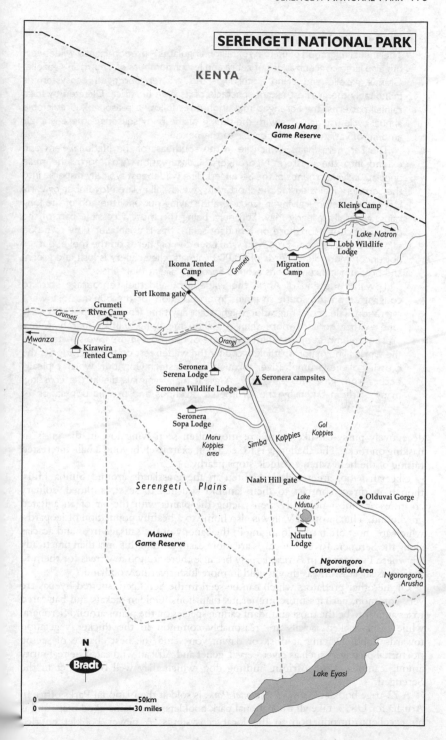

SERENGETI NATIONAL PARK

KENYA

Masai Mara
Game Reserve

Kleins Camp

Lake Natron

Lobo Wildlife
Lodge

Ikoma Tented
Camp

Grumeti

Migration
Camp

Fort Ikoma gate

Grumeti
River Camp

Grumeti

Mwanza

Orangi

Kirawira
Tented Camp

Seronera
Serena Lodge

Seronera campsites

Seronera Wildlife Lodge

Seronera
Sopa Lodge

Moru
Koppies
area

Simba Koppies

Gol
Koppies

Serengeti Plains

Naabi Hill gate

Lake
Ndutu

Olduvai Gorge

Maswa
Game Reserve

Ndutu
Lodge

Ngorongoro
Conservation Area

Ngorongoro,
Arusha

N

Bradt

0   50km
0   30 miles

Lake Eyasi

THE GREAT MIGRATION

The annual migration of up to two million ungulates – predominantly wildebeest but also large concentrations of zebra and lesser numbers of Thomson's gazelle, Grant's gazelle and eland – through the greater Serengeti ecosystem is indubitably the greatest extant spectacle of its type in Africa. Dictated by local rainfall patterns, the Serengeti migration does follow a reasonably predictable annual cycle, though – as with the timing of the rainy seasons – there is a fair amount of variation from one year to the next.

The Seronera Plains, which lie in the southeast of the National Park and extend into the western Ngorongoro Conservation Area, form the main ungulate calving grounds of the Serengeti. The wildebeest typically disperse into the Seronera Plains during the short rains, which fall in late November or early December, before calving in January, and staying put until the end of the long rains, generally in early May. Seronera being the most accessible part of the park, particularly for those on a budget safari, this is a fantastic time to be on safari in the Serengeti. True, you won't see the big herds on the move, but it's not uncommon to see herds of 10,000 animals, the scenery is lush and green, and predator concentrations around Seronera are at their peak.

Towards the end of April, the wildebeest and their entourage start to congregate on the southern plains in preparation for the 800km northward migration. The actual migration might start any time from late April into early June, with a herd of more than a million migrating animals marching in a braying column of up to 40km long, one of the most impressive spectacles in the world. The major obstacle faced by the wildebeest on this migration is the crossing of the Grumeti River through the Western Corridor, which typically occurs from June into early July. A great many animals die in the crossing, many of them taken by the Grumeti's ravenous and prolific population of

deceptively pussy-cat-like, lions are most often seen lying low in the grass or basking on rocks. The challenge is to see a lion exert itself beyond a half-interested raising of the head when a vehicle stops nearby.

Cheetahs, too, are regularly sighted in the grasslands around Simba Hills, though in direct contrast to their languid cousins, these streamlined, solitary creatures are most normally seen pacing the plains with the air of an agitated greyhound. The Seronera Valley is also home to a healthy population of leopards, which are most often seen lounging in the canopy of the sausage trees and acacias along the Seronera River. Leopards are more easily seen in this area than practically anywhere I've visited in Africa, largely because there are too few trees for them to hide in as successfully as they would in more lush riverine woodland.

Of the other predators which can be seen in the Serengeti, spotted hyenas are very common, perhaps more numerous than lions. Golden jackals and bat-eared foxes appear to be the most abundant canine species on the plains around Seronera, while black-backed jackals are reasonably common in the thicker vegetation towards Lobo. Driving at dusk or dawn, you stand the best chance of seeing nocturnal predators such as civet, serval, genet and African wild cat. The real rarity among canines is the African hunting dog, which may well be extinct in the Serengeti.

A 72-page booklet, *Serengeti National Park*, is sold at the National Parks office in Arusha for US$5. Like all the national park booklets, it contains good maps and is an excellent introduction to the local ecosystems. A newer booklet entitled

outsized crocodiles, and the first herds to cross are generally at the greatest risk. For this reason, it can take up to two weeks from when the first wildebeest arrive at the southern bank of the river for the actual crossing to begin, by which time thousands upon thousands of wildebeest are congregated in the Western Corridor.

From July to October, the ungulates disperse again, with about half of them crossing the Mara River into Kenya's Maasai Mara Game Reserve, and the remainder spreading out through the northern and western Serengeti. The best base at this time of year is the Lobo area (not really practical for a camping safari) in the northern Serengeti. By late October, the animals have generally started to plod back southward to the Seronera Plains, to arrive there in late November, when the cycle starts all over again.

Whether is it worth planning your safari dates around the migration is a matter of choice. With the best will in the world, it would be practically impossible to ensure that a few days in the Serengeti will coincide with the exact and unpredictable date of the spectacular river crossing. On the other hand, if you choose the right part of the Serengeti, large herds of grazers should be easy to locate at any time of year bar July to November. Furthermore, bearing mind that most species other than zebra and wildebeest, and predators especially, are strongly territorial and do not stray far from their core territory over the course of any given year, there is a lot to be said for avoiding the migration. Most of the lodges charge considerably lower rates between April and June, with a knock-on effect on the rates offered by safari companies that suddenly become hungry for business. Furthermore, the safari circuit as a whole is far less crowded outside of peak seasons, and in our experience the Serengeti, irrespective of season, will still offer game viewing to equal that of any game reserve in Africa,

Serengeti, similar in content but glossier in appearance, is published by African Publishing House in association with TANAPA. An entrance fee of US$30 per 24 hours is charged.

The Seronera Plains and surrounds

The Seronera area is the most accessible part of the Serengeti for those coming from the direction of Arusha, and it is the site of the main park headquarters as well as a small staff village, most of the larger lodges and the main pubic camping site. The Seronera Plains, which stretch east from the park headquarters as far as the Ngorongoro foothills, are the 'classic' Serengeti: a vast open expanse studded with rocky *koppies* and teeming with wild animals, especially between December and May when the wildebeest and zebra are concentrated in the southern Serengeti. Seronera is probably the best base in the park for seeing lion, leopard and cheetah which, combined with its relative proximity to Arusha, means that it also carries the heaviest tourist traffic. It is normally the only part of the park explored by those with limited time.

Where to stay
Upmarket
Seronera Wildlife Lodge Tel: 027 250 2711/2; fax: 027 250 8221; email: ahifin@habari.co.tz. The most central and popular lodge in the Serengeti, Seronera lies only a couple of kilometres from the synonymous park headquarters. The lodge was built

between 1970 and 1974, and it is a fine example of a lodge utilising natural features to create an individual and unmistakably African character. The lodge is built around a granite *koppie*: the bar, frequented by bats and rock hyraxes, is reached through a narrow corridor between two boulders, while the restaurant is sited in a cavernous space, its natural rock walls decorated with traditional paintings. For some years, the service and facilities at Seronera were significantly inferior to the architecture, and to this day many of the fittings create a slightly tacky 1970s feel. Since being taken over by TAHI, however, there has been a great improvement in service and catering, though it still doesn't match the Sopa or Serena lodges on these scores. Rooms are small but comfortable, with en-suite bathrooms and large windows facing the surrounding bush. The best reason to select this lodge, aside from relative affordability, is simply its brilliant location for game drives, right on the fringe of the wonderful Seronera circuit. Rooms cost US$140/196/280 single/double/triple FB.

Seronera Serena Lodge Tel: 027 250 4058; fax: 027 250 8282; email: reservations@serena.co.tz. Situated on a hilltop roughly 20km west of Seronera, this recently opened lodge is probably the most comfortable of the lodges in this part of the Serengeti. Accommodation is in a village-like cluster of Maasai-style double-storey rondavels, built with slate, wood and thatch to create a pleasing organic feel. The spacious self-contained rooms each have one single and one king-size bed, nets and fans, and hot showers. There is a swimming pool, and the buffet meals are far superior to those in most East African safari lodges. The one negative is that game viewing in the thick scrub around the lodge is poor except for when the migration passes through, and it's a good half-hour drive before you reach the main game-viewing circuit east of Seronera Lodge. Full board accommodation costs US$230/340 single/double.

Serengeti Sopa Lodge Tel: 057 250 6886; fax: 057 250 8245; email: info@sopalodges.com; web: www.sopalodges.com. This large and rather ostentatious lodge lies about 30 minutes' drive south of Seronera, on the side of a hill near the Moru Koppies. The rooms here are practically suites: each has two double beds, a small sitting room, a large bathroom complete with bidet, a private balcony and a large window giving a grandstand view over the plains below, perfectly appointed to catch the sunset. The building itself is an idiosyncratic, faintly preposterous construction, with the appearance of an unfinished Greek villa, presumably meant to blend into the rocks. The food is good and facilities include a swimming pool. Game viewing in the surrounding area is generally very good, and there's much less traffic in the immediate vicinity than there is closer to Seronera. Full board accommodation costs US$175/280 single/double in peak season, dropping to US$70/140 in low season.

Ndutu Safari Lodge Tel: 027 250 8930/6702; fax: 027 250 8310; email: ndutugibbs@habari.co.tz; web: www.ndutu.com. Although it is actually situated just within the Ngorongoro Conservation Area on the southeast border with the Serengeti, Ndutu is most logically bracketed with the Seronera lodges, since the western plains of the conservation area essentially belong to the same seasonal ecosystem. A low-key and underrated retreat, Ndutu Lodge is set in thick acacia woodland overlooking the seasonal Lake Ndutu, and it has a distinct 'bush' atmosphere lacking from other comparably priced lodges in the Serengeti ecosystem. The rooms are in small, unfussy stone chalets and have netting and hot water. The bar and restaurant are open-sided stone and thatch structures frequented by a legion of genets by night. This is an excellent place to stay if you want to avoid the crowds, and the surrounding plains offer good general game viewing, particularly during the wet season when they are teeming with wildebeest. Despite lying within the NCA, Ndutu isn't well positioned for visiting Ngorongoro Crater. It should also be noted that crossing into the Serengeti while staying at Ndutu would attract a separate national park entrance fee. Accommodation in self-contained bungalows costs US$114/138 B&B single/double in the high season, or US$62/82 in the low season. Residents of eastern and southern Africa pay US$61/85 and US$44/65 in high and low season respectively. Lunch costs US$19 per person and dinner US$26.

Budget and camping

There is a simple resthouse at the Seronera park headquarters charging US$30 per person per night B&B, as well as a hostel with bunk accommodation at US$20 per person per night B&B. A cluster of seven campsites lies about 5km from Seronera Lodge. Camping costs the usual US$20 per person. Facilities are limited to long-drop toilets and a rubbish pit. You may be able to organise a shower and fill up water containers for a small fee at the lodge. There is a good chance of seeing nocturnal scavengers such as hyena and genet pass through the campsites after dark.

Lobo and surrounds

The wildly beautiful northern Serengeti is characterised by green rolling hills and large granite outcrops covered in lushly foliated trees. The area is particularly worth visiting in September and October, when the wildebeest migration passes through. At other times of the year, game is generally less prolific than in the Seronera area, though Lobo does support the park's main concentrations of elephants, and it is also noted for large prides of lions. Outside of the migration season, the relatively low volume of game is compensated for by the vast scenery, abundant birds and untrammelled wilderness feel – we've often gone for an entire game drive without seeing another vehicle in this part of the Serengeti.

Where to stay
Exclusive

Migration Camp Tel: 027 254 4521; fax: 027 254 4574; email: res@halcyontz.com; web: www.serengetimigrationcamp.com. Set in the Ndassiata Hills not far from Lobo, this formerly rather rundown tented camp has been totally renovated since being acquired by the Halcyon Group in 1998 and it now ranks as one of the most exclusive lodges within in the Serengeti National Park. It consists of about 20 spacious standing tents, all with en-suite facilities, built on a *koppie* overlooking the perennial Grumeti River. The lushly wooded grounds are rustling with birds and lizards, and there is a hippo pool on the river, with larger mammals often passing through camp. The surrounding area supports resident populations of lion, leopard, elephant and buffalo, and is fantastic when the migration passes through. Facilities include a swimming pool, Jacuzzi, cocktail bar, library and lounge. An unusual feature of the camp is that short, guided game walks can be undertaken along several trails leading out from it. Drive-in rates range from US$185/290 single/double FB in the low season to US$290/450 in peak season, while fly-in packages inclusive of game drives and walks range from US$320/480 in the low season and US$500/770 in the peak season.

Klein's Camp Tel: 027 254 8549/8038 or (South Africa) 11 809 4447; email: res@ccafrica.co.tz or reservations@ccafrica.com; web: www.ccafrica.com. This excellent CCA lodge lies just outside the eastern border of the national park, on a private conservancy leased from the local Maasai, and it effectively functions as an exclusive private game reserve, since camp residents have sole use of the concession. Because Klein's Camp lies outside the national park, there are no restrictions prohibiting night drives and guided game walks, both of which add an extra dimension to a safari. The camp has a stunning location on the side of a hill offering panoramic views in all directions, and game viewing in the region is generally good, particularly along the Grumeti River, with a similar range of species as found in the Lobo area. The camp consists of eight self-contained *bandas*, all with

SERENGETI BIRDS

Adapted from an article by the author that originally appeared in the April/May 2002 issue of 'Africa Birds & Birding'.

The Serengeti National Park, though popularly associated with grassland and open savannah, is in fact a reasonably ecologically varied entity. The western part of the national park consists of broken savannah, interspersed with impenetrable stands of whistling thorns and other acacias, and run through by the perennial Grumeti River and an attendant ribbon of riparian forest. The north, abutting Kenya's Maasai Mara Game Reserve, is unexpectedly hilly, particularly around Lobo, and it supports a variety of more-or-less wooded savannah habitats. So, while the actual Serengeti Plains in the southeast of the park do support the relatively limited avifauna one tends to associate with open grassland, the national park ranks with the best of them in terms of avian variety. The working Serengeti checklist compiled by Schmidt tallied 505 species, and a further 30 species have been added since 1990.

The Serengeti-Mara ecosystem is one of Africa's Endemic Bird Areas, hosting six bird species found nowhere else, half of which are confined to the Tanzanian portion of the ecosystem. These 'Serengeti specials' are easy to locate and identify within their restricted range. The grey-throated spurfowl, a common roadside bird around the park headquarters at Seronera, is easily distinguished from the similar red-throated spurfowl by the white stripe below its red mask. In areas of woodland, parties of exquisite Fischer's lovebird draw attention to themselves by their incessant screeching and squawking as they flap energetically between trees. If the endemic spurfowl and lovebird are essentially local variations on a more widespread generic type, not so the rufous-tailed weaver, a fascinating bird placed in its own genus, but with nesting habits that indicate an affiliation to the sparrow-weavers. The rufous-tailed weaver is significantly larger and more sturdily built than most African ploceids, and its scaly feathering, pale eyes and habit of bouncing around boisterously in

hot shower, nets, and a private balcony with a view. The FB rates of US$350 per person in the low season and US$445 in the high season are inclusive of all meals, drinks, game drives, game walks and a visit to a Maasai *boma*, and a reduction is offered for stays of more than three nights.

Upmarket

Lobo Wildlife Lodge Tel: 027 250 2711/2; fax: 027 250 8221; email: tahifin@habari.co.tz. The government-owned hotel, now managed by TAHI, was built between 1968 and 1970, at which time the majority of tourism to the Serengeti came directly from Kenya. Lobo has dropped in popularity now that visitors to the Serengeti come through Arusha, which is a shame, because it is an amazing construction. Like Seronera, it's built around a *koppie*, but the design is even more impressive and imaginative than that of the more southerly lodge, spanning four floors and with a fantastic view over the surrounding plains. Once again, however, the tacky 1970s fittings let the architecture down, and the rooms and food are perfectly acceptable without inviting any superlatives. The surrounding hills can offer some wonderful game viewing (a pride of 20 lions is resident in the immediate vicinity of the lodge), and the grounds are crawling with hyraxes and colourful agama lizards. Lobo is relatively good value at US$140/196/280 single/double/triple FB.

small flocks could lead to it being mistaken for a type of babbler – albeit one with an unusually large bill!

Of the three other Serengeti-Mara EBA endemics, the most visible and widespread is the Usambiro barbet, a close relative of the slightly smaller D'Arnaud's barbet, with which it is sometimes considered conspecific. The sooty chat, a plain black bird with a white shoulder patch, is apparently absent from the southern Serengeti, but it is easily observed around the Lobo Hills. Altogether more elusive is the grey-crested helmetshrike, which strongly resembles the white helmetshrike but is larger, has a more upright grey crest, and lacks an eye wattle. Although this striking bird indulges in typically conspicuous helmetshrike behaviour, with small parties streaming noisily from one tree to the next, it is absent from the southern Serengeti, and thinly distributed in the north, where it is often associated with stands of whistling thorns.

Endemic chasing will be a priority of any serious birding visit to the Serengeti, but the mixed woodland and grassland of the north and west produce consistently good birdwatching including many species that will delight non-birders. The massive ostrich is common, as are other primarily terrestrial giants such as the kori bustard, secretary bird and southern ground hornbill. Perhaps the most distinctive of the smaller birds is the lilac-breasted roller, an exquisitely coloured gem often seen perched on trees alongside the road. Highlights are inevitably subjective, but recent memorable sightings included a breeding colony of Jackson's golden-backed weaver at Grumeti River Camp, a magnificent black eagle soaring above the cliffs at Lobo, and six different vulture species squabbling over a kill in the Western Corridor. And there is always the chance of an exciting 'first'. Recent additions to the Tanzanian bird list from Serengeti include turtle dove (1997), short-eared owl (1998) and long-tailed nightjar, black-backed cisticola and swallow-tailed kite (2000). In 2001, close to Grumeti River Camp, we were fortunate enough to see (and photograph) the first golden pipit ever recorded in the national park.

Camping

The campsite immediately outside of the Lobo Wildlife Lodge is little used by comparison with those at Seronera. It also costs US$20 per person. Facilities are limited to a toilet and rubbish pit. You can pop into the neighbouring lodge for a drink or meal if you like.

The Western Corridor

The part of the Serengeti which stretches west from Seronera towards Lake Victoria is characterised by dense stands of ghostly grey 'whistling thorn' *acacia drepanolobrium* interspersed with park-like broken woodland. The dominant physical feature of the region is the Grumeti River, its course marked by a thin string of riparian woodland. The crossing of the Grumeti, which usually takes place between May and July, is one of the most dramatic sequences in the annual wildebeest migration, and a positive bonanza for the river's large crocodile population. Tourist traffic in this part of the park is very low: few camping safaris ever come this way, and accommodation is limited to a few small tented camps. The game viewing is superlative between May and July, when the migration passes through, and it is pretty good throughout the year. The broken plains to the south of the Grumeti River between Grumeti River Camp and Kirawira Tented Camp support substantial resident populations of lion, giraffe, wildebeest, zebra and most other typical plains animals, while the riverine forest harbours a few troops of the exquisite black-and-white colobus monkey.

Where to stay
Exclusive
Grumeti River Camp Tel: 027 254 8549/8038 or (South Africa) 11 809 4447; email: res@ccafrica.co.tz or reservations@ccafrica.com; web: www.ccafrica.com. Overlooking a small pool near the Grumeti River, this archetypal bush camp easily ranks as our favourite lodge anywhere in the Serengeti. The mood here is pure in-your-face Africa: the pool in front of the bar supports a resident pod of hippos and attracts a steady stream of other large mammals coming to drink, while birdlife is prolific both at the water's edge and in the surrounding thickets. At night, the place comes alive with a steady chorus of insects and frogs, and hippos and buffaloes grazing noisily around the tents. This place isn't for the faint-hearted, and you shouldn't even think about walking around at night without an armed escort, as the buffaloes have been known to charge. Facilities include an outdoor *boma*, where evening meals are served (except when it rains), and a small circular swimming pool from where you can watch hippos bathing while you do the same thing. Accommodation consists of ten stylish tents, each of which has a netted king-size bed and en-suite toilet and showers. The atmosphere is very informal, and the service is excellent without ever becoming impersonal. The FB rates of US$350 per person in the low season and US$445 in the high season are inclusive of all meals, drinks and game drives, and a reduction is offered for stays of more than three nights.

Kirawira Tented Camp Tel: 027 250 4058; fax: 027 250 8282; email: reservations@serena.co.tz. Part of the Serena chain, this is another very upmarket tented camp, set on a small acacia-covered hill offering sweeping views over the western corridor. The Edwardian décor of the communal areas creates something of an *Out of Africa* feel, and while the atmosphere is neither as intimate nor as 'bush' as at Grumeti, Kirawira does have a definite charm – and it will probably appeal more to safari-goers who don't find the thought of having hippo and buffalo chomping around their tent a major draw. Accommodation consists of 25 standing tents, each of which is set on its own raised platform, and is comfortably decorated with a netted king-size bed and en-suite shower and toilet. There is a large swimming pool, the service is immaculate, and the food is probably the best in the Serengeti. Accommodation costs US$395/630 single/double inclusive of all meals, drinks and game drives and walks.

Moderate
Ikoma Bush Camp Tel: 057 270 6424; mobile: 0744 300806; fax: 027 270 8424; email: sengo@habari.co.tz or swala@habari.co.tz. Situated outside of the national park, roughly 1km from the Ikoma Gate and 40km from Seronera, Ikoma Bush Camp offers accommodation in simple but comfortable standing tents at a cost of US$75/130 single/double FB. Because it lies outside the park boundaries, guided game walks are permitted.

Kijireshi Tented Camp Tel: 028 2500517/617; fax: 018 2500141; email: tilapia@mwanza.com. Under the same ownership as the Tilapia Hotel in Mwanza, this little-known camp lies close to Bunda on the western border of the Serengeti. It offers comfortable accommodation in furnished tents for US$75 self-contained double, and has a bar and restaurant.

Budget and camping
Affordable *bandas* and camping are offered by **Serengeti Stop Over**, which lies immediately outside the park entrance gate alongside the main road between the

Lake Victoria ports of Mwanza and Musoma. For further details see the Lake Victoria chapter, page 412.

TARANGIRE NATIONAL PARK

Tarangire may be less well known than the other main national parks of northern Tanzania, but it is no less rewarding. Like the Serengeti, Tarangire is part of a wider ecosystem within which there is a great deal of migratory movement. During the wet season, most of its animals disperse to the Maasai Steppe, while the wildebeest and zebra move northwest to the Rift Valley floor between Lakes Natron and Manyara. In direct contrast to the Serengeti, Tarangire comes into its own during the dry season between July and November, when the large herds of game attracted to the permanent waters of the Tarangire River make this reserve every bit as alluring as the Serengeti. In general, Tarangire is more densely vegetated than the Serengeti, covered primarily in acacia and mixed woodland. Near the Tarangire River, however, there is a cover of dense elephant grass broken by the occasional palm tree, and baobab trees are abundant throughout.

Tarangire supports a similar range of large mammals to the Serengeti. The full range of large predators is harboured within the park, but the dense vegetation can make it difficult to pick up the likes of lion and leopard, even though they are common on the main tourist road circuit. Tarangire is justifiably famous for the prolific elephant herds that congregate along the river during the dry season. It is no exaggeration to say that you might see 500 elephants over the course of a day in the park – though they are generally more skittish than their counterparts in Manyara and Ngorongoro. Two localised antelope found in Tarangire are the fringe-eared oryx and gerenuk. According to the 1980 census, the greater Tarangire ecosystem supported 25,000 wildebeest, 30,000 zebra, 6,000 buffalo, 3,000 elephant, 2,700 giraffe, 5,500 eland, 30,000 impala and 2,000 warthog. Of the smaller mammals, the colonial dwarf mongoose is characteristic of the park, and often seen on the termite hills where it breeds.

Tarangire's reputation as the best of the northern reserves for birds is, in my experience, slightly overstated, since Lake Manyara has a far greater habitat and avian diversity. All the same, with around 500 species recorded in the park, you should see a good variety of birds over the course of a day. A wide variety of resident raptors includes bateleur eagle, fish eagle and palmnut vulture, while the river supports saddle-billed and yellow-billed storks and several other waterbirds. Characteristic acacia birds are yellow-necked spurfowl, orange-bellied parrot, barefaced go-away bird, red-fronted barbet, and silverbird. A personal favourite is the red-and-yellow barbet, with its quaintly comical clockwork duet, typically performed on termite mounds. Tarangire's location means it lies at the western limit of the normal range of several species associated with drier parts of the Somali-Maasai biome, for instance vulturine guineafowl, Donaldson-Smith's nightjar, pink-breasted lark, northern pied babbler and mouse-coloured penduline tit. It is also the easiest place to observe a pair of birds endemic to the dry heartland of central Tanzania, the lovely yellow-collared lovebird and rather drab ashy starling.

Most people spend only one day in Tarangire and thus concentrate on the roads of the well-developed northern circuit, which follows the river between the two main lodges within the park boundaries. For those who have more time, Lake Burungi circuit offers the best chance of seeing bushbuck and lesser kudu and the Kitibong Hill area is home to large herds of buffalo, while Lamarkau Swamp supports hippo and numerous water birds during the wet season, and cheetahs favour the southern plains. The Mkungero Pools is the place to look for waterbuck and gerenuk.

THE MAASAI

The northern safari circuit passes through the homeland of the Nilotic-speaking Maasai, whose reputation as fearsome warriors ensured that the 19th-century slave caravans studiously avoided their territory, which was also one of the last parts of East Africa ventured into by Europeans. The Maasai today remain the most familiar of African people to outsiders, even if their modern reputation rests as much on their continued adherence to a traditional lifestyle as on any of their past exploits. Instantly identifiable, Maasai men drape themselves in toga-like red blankets, carry long wooden poles, and often dye their hair with red ochre and style it in a manner that has been compared to a Roman helmet. And while the women dress similarly to many other Tanzanian women, their extensive use of beaded jewellery is highly distinctive too.

Although the Maasai are often regarded to be the archetypal East African pastoralists, they are in fact relatively recent arrivals to the area. Their language, called Maa (Maasai literally means 'Maa-speakers'), is closely affiliated to those spoken by the Nuer of southwest Ethiopia and the Bari of southern Sudan, and oral traditions suggest that the proto-Maasai would have started to migrate southward from the lower Nile area in the 15th century. They arrived in their present territory in the 17th or 18th century, where they forcefully displaced earlier inhabitants such as the Datoga and Chagga, who respectively migrated south to the Hanang area and east to the Kilimanjaro foothills. The Maasai territory reached its greatest extent – covering virtually the entire Rift Valley and several neighbouring areas from Mount Marsabit in the north to Dodoma in the south – in the mid-19th century. Over the 1880/90s, the Maasai were hit by a series of disasters linked to the arrival of Europeans – rinderpest and smallpox epidemics exacerbated by a severe drought and a bloody secession dispute – and much of their former territory was re-colonised by tribes who they had displaced a century earlier. During the colonial area, a further 50% of their land was lost to game reserves and settler farms. These territorial incursions notwithstanding, the area occupied by the Maasai today is among the most extensive of any Tanzanian tribe, ranging across the vast Maasai Steppes of the northeast to large parts of the Ngorongoro Highlands and Serengeti Plains.

The Maasai are monotheists whose belief in a single deity with a dualistic nature – the benevolent Engai Narok (Black God) and vengeful Engai Nanyokie (Red God) – has some overtones of the Judaic faiths. They believe that Engai, who resides in the volcano Ol Doinyo L'Engai, made them the rightful owners of all the cattle in the world, a view that has occasionally made life difficult for neighbouring herders. Traditionally, this arrogance does not merely extend to cattle: agriculturist and fish-eating peoples are scorned, while Europeans' uptight style of clothing earned them the Maasai name *Iloredaa Enjekat* – Fart Smotherers! Today, the Maasai co-exist peacefully with their non-Maasai compatriots, but while their tolerance for their neighbours' idiosyncrasies has increased in recent decades, they show little interest in changing their own lifestyle.

The Maasai measure a man's wealth in terms of cattle and children rather than money – a herd of about 50 cattle is respectable, the more children the better, and a man who has plenty of one but not the other is regarded to be

A 56-page booklet, *Tarangire National Park*, is available from the National Parks headquarters in Arusha. A park entrance fee of US$25 per 24-hour period is charged.

poor. Traditionally, the Maasai will not hunt or eat vegetable matter or fish, but feed almost exclusively off their cattle. The main diet is a blend of cow's milk and blood, the latter drained – it is said painlessly – from a strategic nick in the animal's jugular vein. Because the cows are more valuable to them alive than dead, they are generally only slaughtered on special occasions. Meat and milk are never eaten on the same day, because it is insulting to the cattle to feed off the living and the dead at the same time. Despite the apparent hardship of their chosen lifestyle, many Maasai are wealthy by any standards. On one safari, our driver pointed out a not unusually large herd of cattle that would fetch the market equivalent of three new Land Rovers!

The central unit of Maasai society is the age-set. Every 15 years or so, a new and individually named generation of warriors or *Ilmoran* will be initiated, consisting of all the young men who have reached puberty and are not part of a previous age-set – most boys aged between 12 and 25. Every boy must undergo the *Emorata* (circumcision ceremony) before he is accepted as a warrior. If he cries out during the five minute operation, which is performed without any anaesthetic, the post-circumcision ceremony will be cancelled, the parents are spat on for raising a coward, and the initiate will be taunted by his peers for several years before he is forgiven. When a new generation of warriors is initiated, the existing *Ilmoran* will graduate to become junior elders, who are responsible for all political and legislative decisions until they in turn graduate to become senior elders. All political decisions are made democratically, and the role of the chief elder or *Laibon* is essentially that of a spiritual and moral leader.

Maasai girls are permitted to marry as soon as they have been initiated, but warriors must wait until their age-set has graduated to elder status, which will be 15 years later, when a fresh warrior age-set has been initiated. This arrangement ties in with the polygamous nature of Maasai society: in days past, most elders would typically have acquired between three and ten wives by the time they reached old age. Marriages are generally arranged, sometimes even before the female party is born, as a man may 'book' the next daughter produced by a friend to be his son's wife. Marriage is evidently viewed as a straightforward child-producing business arrangement: it is normal for married men and women to have sleeping partners other than their spouse, provided that those partners are of an appropriate age-set. Should a woman become pregnant by another lover, the prestige attached to having many children outweighs any minor concerns about infidelity, and the husband will still bring up the child as his own. By contrast, although sex before marriage is condoned, a girl who falls pregnant before she has been circumcised is regarded as having brought disgrace on her family, and in former times she would have been fed to the hyenas.

It is impossible to do full justice to the complexities of Maasai society and beliefs in this short space, and interested readers are urged to get hold of a copy of the coffee-table book *Maasai*, published by Harry N Abrams in New York in 1980 and reprinted in 1993. This visually sumptuous book is initially most impressive for the photography of Carol Beckwith, but the detailed and insightful text, written by the Maasai historian Tepelit Ole Saitoti, is exemplary – highly recommended!

For notes on photographing the Maasai, see page VIII.

Getting there and away

Tarangire lies about 7km off the main Arusha–Dodoma road. Coming from Arusha, this road is tarred as far as the Tarangire turn-off about 100km south of

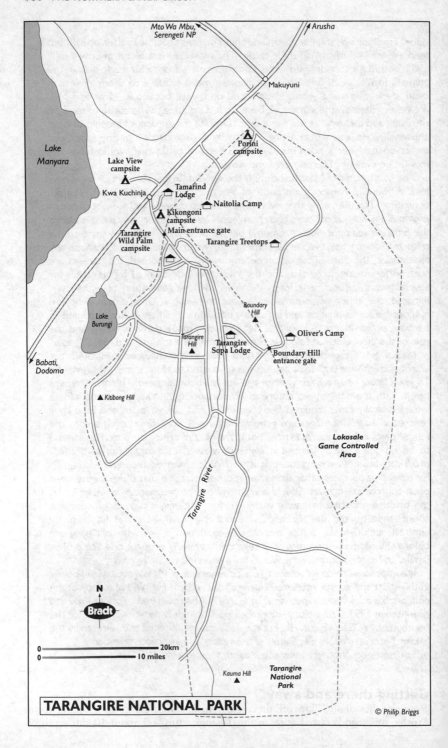

Mto Wa Mbu, Serengeti NP

Arusha

Makuyuni

Lake Manyara

Porini campsite

Lake View campsite

Kwa Kuchinja

Tamarind Lodge

Naitolia Camp

Kikongoni campsite

Main entrance gate

Tarangire Treetops

Tarangire Wild Palm campsite

Lake Burungi

Tarangire Hill

Boundary Hill

Tarangire Sopa Lodge

Oliver's Camp

Boundary Hill entrance gate

Babati, Dodoma

Kitibong Hill

Lokosale Game Controlled Area

Tarangire River

N

Bradt

0   20km
0   10 miles

Kauma Hill

Tarangire National Park

TARANGIRE NATIONAL PARK

© Philip Briggs

Arusha and 20km past Makayuni junction. Most people tag a visit on to the end of a longer safari, but if your time or money is limited, a one- or two-day safari to Tarangire is a viable option. It would be easy enough to reach Kikongoni Camp outside the park by using public transport, then walking from the junction, but also rather pointless as no vehicles are available for hire outside the park.

Where to stay
Exclusive

Tarangire Treetops Lodge Tel: 027 254 4521; fax: 027 254 4574; email: res@halcyontz.com; web: www.tarangiretreetops.com. The newest and most architecturally innovative of the lodges around the national park is the utterly wonderful Tarangire Treetops, which consists of 20 spacious and luxurious en-suite tree houses set high in the branches of a stand of massive baobab trees. The only criticism you could make of these suites is that they are so atmospheric and comfortable it almost seems a shame to leave them to go on a game drive! Tarangire Treetops lies in an exclusive Maasai concession on the northeast border of the national park, and a portion of the proceeds are used to fund community projects such as the construction of schools and bore holes. Because the lodge lies on private land, activities such as game walks, birding walks along a nearby watercourse, night drives and mountain biking excursions supplement the usual diurnal game drives. The quality of game viewing in the immediate vicinity of the lodge varies seasonally, but it's only 45 minutes by road to Boundary Hill Gate, the main road circuit in northern Tarangire. Ideal for honeymooners, this lodge is also a wonderful place to recover from jetlag at the start of a safari, or to stretch your legs at the end of one. Many safari drivers are not aware that park entrance fees cannot be paid at Boundary Hill, so that unless you have paid your park fees in advance, entering the national park from Tarangire Treetops entails a two-hour drive back to the Arusha–Dodoma road and the main entrance gate. The best way around this is to drive to the lodge through the national park, which allows you to pay entrance fees upfront at the main entrance gate. Drive-in rates range from US$185/290 single/double FB in the low season to US$290/450 in peak season, while fly-in packages inclusive of game drives and walks range from US$320/480 in the low season to US$500/770 in the peak season.

Oliver's Camp Tel: 027 250 8548; fax: 027 250 4116; email: olivers@habari.co.tz. This excellent owner-managed bush camp consists of only six furnished tents set in a marshy basin below the Kikoti *koppies* 3km outside the Boundary Hill entrance gate to Tarangire. Oliver's Camp will cater for one- or two-night stays incorporated into more wide-ranging safaris. The speciality, however, is extended stays of five to seven nights' duration during which visitors explore the area on foot and by vehicle, spend a few nights at a mobile fly-camp, and also go on night drives to seek out nocturnal predators. The lodge itself is unpretentious and comfortable rather than opulently luxurious, the guides are unusually personable and knowledgeable, and the emphasis on substance over style is underscored by a superb library of natural history books – the most extensive I've seen anywhere in Africa. Strongly recommended to anybody seeking a genuine and holistic bush experience, Oliver's Camp is built on a Maasai concession and a portion of the proceeds is used to fund community projects. Full board rates and details of fly-in packages are available on application.

Upmarket

Tarangire Safari Lodge Tel: 027 254 4222; mobile: 0742 401199; tel/fax: 027 7182; email: tarsaf@habari.co.tz or sss@habari.co.tz. This owner-managed lodge is the oldest in the park, with a sublime location on a tall bluff overlooking the Tarangire River. Game viewing from the veranda can be excellent, with large herds of hippo, giraffe and other animals coming down to the river to drink. The grounds are also highly attractive to birders, not only for the remarkably habituated hornbills, buffalo weavers and starlings that parade around the common areas, but also for the host of smaller birds that are resident in the acacia scrub. Facilities include a swimming pool. This comfortable, unpretentious and well-managed lodge ranks as one of my favourites anywhere on the northern circuit. The accommodation in standing tents with en-suite toilets is outstanding value at US$52/65 single/double B&B, and the bungalows are equally sensibly priced at US$60/75/95 single/double/triple, with a 50% reduction offered in the low season. Lunch costs US$12, dinner US$15, and a limited selection of snacks is available at around US$4 each.

Tarangire Sopa Lodge Tel: 057 250 6886; fax: 057 250 8245; email: info@sopalodges.com; web: www.sopalodges.com. Set in the heart of the national park, the Tarangire Sopa is the largest and most conventionally luxurious – and least 'bush' – of the lodges around Tarangire. The facilities and accommodation match the customary high standards of this chain, with smart self-contained suites and excellent food. My one, rather large, reservation is the indifferent location, alongside a small and normally dry watercourse below a baobab-studded slope – surely a more scenic site could have been chosen? Full board accommodation costs US$175/280 single/double in peak season, dropping to US$70/140 in low season.

Naitolia Camp Tel: 0744 470447; email: eastafricansafaris@habari.co.tz. This excellent new bush camp is set in 11,000 acres of Maasailand on the northern border of the park. The main camp consists of three attractively furnished canvas, stone and thatch huts, each of which has a king-size bed with walk-in netting and a private balcony, shower and a toilet with a view. Because the camp lies on communal land, guided game walks can be undertaken, with a good chance of spotting giraffe, elephant, zebra and a variety of antelope and birds, and it is possible to be taken to Maasai *bomas* that don't normally receive tourists. Accommodation costs US$225/350 single/double FB, inclusive of all activities. They also do overnight walking safaris within the community area, using fly-camps, at a cost of US$365/570 single/double per night. There is a separate campsite close to the main camp where campers can pitch their own tents. The lodge management pays a fee of US$20 per client per night to local Maasai communities.

Tamarind Camp Tel: (UK) 1923 255462; fax: 1923 255452; email: hoopoeUK@aol.com; web: www.kirurumu.com. Owned by Hoopoe Adventure Tours, Tamarind Camp is a similar set-up to Naitola, situated in a private Maasai concession and conveniently located less than 30 minutes' drive from the main park entrance. Consisting of only ten standing tents, the exclusive, personalised atmosphere is underscored by a variety of optional activities including night drives, game walks and village visits. Accommodation costs a reasonable US$130/200 FB.

Budget and camping

Kikongoni Campsite This small private camp, which lies a few kilometres outside the park entrance gate, is firmly aimed at budget travellers and used by most budget camping safaris to Tarangire. Camping costs US$3 per person, and rooms are available at US$10 per person. To get to Kikongoni, turn off from the main Arusha–Dodoma road as if heading towards the entrance gate to Tarangire. After about 2km, you'll see the campsite immediately to your left. There is also a small local guesthouse in the village on the junction of the Arusha–Dodoma road and the turn-off to Tarangire. There is no reason why you couldn't catch a Dodoma-bound bus to the turn-off and walk to the camp from there; hitching into the park might not be easy, but at least you don't stand to lose anything in terms of paying park fees while you wait.

For those on camping safaris, there are a couple of campsites within Tarangire. These are strong on bush atmosphere, but short on facilities, and rather costly at the customary US$20 per person.

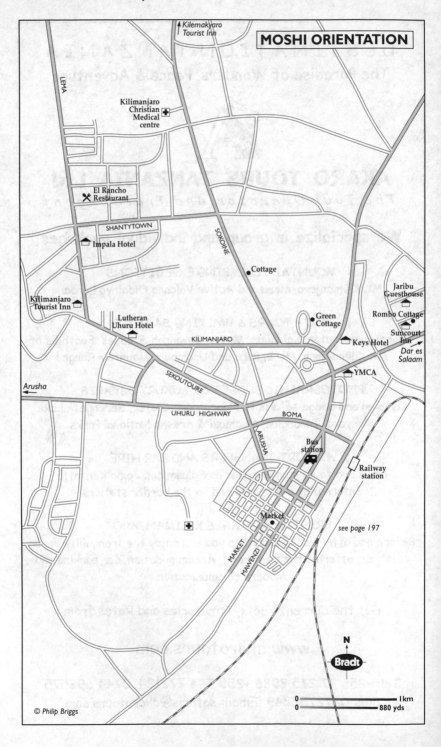

MOSHI ORIENTATION

Kilemakyaro Tourist Inn

LEMA

Kilimanjaro Christian Medical centre

El Rancho Restaurant

SHANTYTOWN

Impala Hotel

SOKOINE

Cottage

Jaribu Guesthouse

Rombo Cottage

Kilimanjaro Tourist Inn

Lutheran Uhuru Hotel

Green Cottage

Suncourt Inn

KILIMANJARO

Keys Hotel

Dar es Salaam

SEKOUTOURE

Arusha

YMCA

UHURU HIGHWAY

BOMA

ARUSHA

Bus station

Railway station

Market

see page 197

MARKET

MAWENZI

N

Bradt

0   1 km
0   880 yds

© Philip Briggs

Moshi and Kilimanjaro

Kilimanjaro is Africa's highest mountain, and one of the most instantly recognisable landmarks on the continent. It is also the highest mountain anywhere that can be climbed by an ordinary tourist, and thousands of visitors to Tanzania attempt to reach its peak every year. Kilimanjaro straddles the border with Kenya, but because the peaks all lie within Tanzanian territory they can be climbed only from within Tanzania. There are several places on the lower slopes from where the mountain can be ascended, but most people use the Marangu or 'tourist' route (which begins at the village of Marangu), largely because it is the cheapest option and has the best facilities. The less heavily trampled Machame route, starting from the village of the same name, has grown in popularity in recent years. A number of more obscure routes can be used, though they are generally only available through specialist trekking companies. Prospective climbers can arrange their ascent of 'Kili' – as it is popularly called – at one of the hotels in Marangu, or in Arusha town, but the main cluster of trekking companies is to be found in the town of Moshi on the plains to the south of the mountain.

CLIMATE

The higher slopes of Kilimanjaro are cold at all times. Moshi is relatively low-lying and has a climate typical of this part of the African interior, hot by day and cool by night, though it is often more humid than you might expect. Kilimanjaro can be climbed at any time of year, but the hike is more difficult in the rainy months, especially between March and May.

GETTING AROUND

Moshi is an important public transport hub, connected by surfaced roads and regular express buses to Dar es Salaam, Tanga and Arusha. If you want to arrange your hike in Marangu, plenty of public transport runs there from Moshi. Most travellers prefer to make all arrangements for the climb in Moshi, and this includes transport to and from the trailhead.

MOSHI

Situated at the heart of a major coffee-growing region, Moshi is an attractive, if intrinsically unremarkable, small town of 150,000 people, salvaged from anonymity by one of the most imposing backdrops imaginable. Moshi lies at the base of Kilimanjaro; at dusk or dawn, when the peaks most often emerge from their customary blanket of cloud, they form a sight as stirring and memorable as any in Africa. Despite the teasing proximity of snow-capped Kilimanjaro, Moshi is not the cool highland settlement you might expect. Instead, lying at an altitude of 810m, it has a surprisingly humid, sticky climate, reminiscent of the coast.

Prior to the arrival of the Germans, Moshi was the capital of the area ruled by Rindi, who came into power in about 1860 and, largely through his diplomatic skills, became one of the most important chiefs in the area. By allying with the Maasai, Rindi extracted large taxes from passing caravans. He made a favourable impression on John Kirk, the British Consul in Zanzibar, and signed a treaty with Carl Peters in 1885. When the first German colonial forces arrived at Kilimanjaro in 1891, Rindi assured them he ruled the whole area. At his insistence, they quelled his major rival, Sina of Kibosha.

Moshi means smoke in Swahili, but the origin of this name is something of a mystery. Some sources suggest that the town was called Moshi because it was the terminus for the steam railway line from Tanga, but my understanding is that the name Moshi predates the arrival of the railway in 1911 by many years. Equally improbable is the suggestion that the reference to smoke is due to the town lying at the base of a volcano – after all, Kilimanjaro hadn't been active for thousands of years when its present Bantu-speaking inhabitants arrived there.

Getting there and away
Air
Moshi is served by Kilimanjaro International Airport (KIA), which lies about 45km from the town centre off the Arusha Road. The national carrier Air Tanzania flies directly to KIA from some (but not all) international destinations, and KLM now operates a direct flight from Europe to KIA daily. Most other international flights to Tanzania land at Dar es Salaam International Airport. For domestic flights, Air Tanzania and several private airlines fly daily between KIA and Dar es Salaam or Zanzibar, while regular Air Tanzania flights also connect KIA to Mwanza and other major urban centres. A potential source of confusion to travellers booking their own flights is that the light aircraft services to parks on the northern safari circuit don't leave from KIA, but from Arusha Airport on the outskirts of Arusha town.

If you fly to KIA with Air Tanzania, note that all their flights tie in with a free shuttle service to Moshi, easily located at the airport. When you leave Moshi for the airport, the correct shuttle departure time can be checked in advance at the Air Tanzania office near the Clock Tower. For flights operated by other airlines, you'll need to charter a taxi (around Tsh10–15,000) or to arrange to be met by a safari company

Road
Moshi lies off the main surfaced road to Dar es Salaam some 80km east of Arusha. The driving time from Arusha in a private vehicle is about 90 minutes, and from Dar es Salaam at least seven hours. It is possible to drive from Nairobi (Kenya) to Moshi via Namanga and Arusha in about five hours.

Express coaches between Dar es Salaam and Moshi take roughly seven hours, with a 20-minute lunch break in Korogwe or Mombo. A recommended coach service is Freshi Ya Shamba, which leaves Moshi daily at 10.00 from a private terminal at the Caltex Garage on Market Street. Tickets, best booked a day in advance, cost Tsh9,500. Also recommended, but slightly more expensive, are Royal Coach (tel: 027 275 0940) and Scandinavia Coach (tel: 0744 295245). Numerous cheaper bus services leave from the main bus station, mostly in the morning. There are also plenty of direct buses between Moshi and Tanga, which can drop you off at Same, Mombo, Muheza and other junction towns mentioned in the chapter *The Pare and Usambara Mountains*.

A steady flow of buses and *dalla-dallas* runs between Arusha and Moshi, taking up to two hours, and to a lesser extent between Moshi and Marangu. There is no need to book ahead for these routes, as vehicles will leave when they fill up. Most shuttle bus services between Nairobi and Arusha continue on to Moshi, or start there. The Devanu Shuttle (tel: 027 275 3416), based in Kahawa House near the Clock Tower circle, runs two services daily, as does the Riverside Shuttle (tel: 027 275 0093) in the THB building on Boma Road. These coaches generally leave at 08.00 and 14.00 daily in either direction, but timings may change to fit in with departure and arrival times for Arusha.

Rail
Passenger services between Moshi, Tanga and Dar es Salaam were suspended indefinitely several years ago, and are unlikely to be resumed.

Where to stay
Upmarket
Kilemakyaro Mountain Lodge Tel: 027 275 1224; mobile: 0744 264845/288745; email: kyaro@habari.co.tz. Wonderfully sited, on a hilltop 5km north of the town centre, this smart new hotel was formerly part of the Kifumbu Tea Estate, and the gracious reception and dining areas are housed in the restored 1920s' homestead of the estate owner. The attractive landscaped gardens offer wonderful views over the forested slopes and peak of Kilimanjaro. The accommodation, in newly built self-contained chalets with satellite television, is nothing special for US$65/85 single/double B&B, but this hotel is probably first choice in Moshi for overall atmosphere and location.
Impala Hotel Tel: 027 275 3443/4; fax: 027 275 3440; email: impala@cybernet.co.tz or impala@africaonline.co.tz. Related to the synonymous hotel in Arusha, but smaller and plusher, the recently opened Impala Hotel lies in the leafy suburbia of Lema Road about 2km from the town centre. The large wood-panelled rooms with fan, hot bath and satellite television are good value at US$90 B&B double (US$65 for residents), while vast suites with video cost US$135 double. Although the Impala Hotel lacks the fine location of the Kilemakyaro, the rooms are better and there are more facilities, notably a swimming pool, internet café and foreign exchange bureau, and a good restaurant specialising in Indian dishes.
Keys Hotel Tel: 027 275 2250/1870; fax: 027 275 0073; email: keys-hotel@africaonline.co.tz; web: www.keys-hotels.com. Situated in attractive suburban grounds about 1km from the Clock Tower, the Keys Hotel has offered good value for several years, and it remains, with justification, the most popular hotel within its price range. The self-contained rooms cost US$50 double with fan or US$60 double with AC, discounted by roughly 50% for Tanzanian residents. Keys is also one of the more reliable places to organise climbs of Kilimanjaro, and while rates are a little higher than at some other places, they do include one night's HB accommodation at the hotel on either side of the climb. Camping in the grounds costs US$5 per person.

Moderate
Kilimanjaro Crane Hotel Tel: 027 275 1114/53037; fax: 027 275 4876; email: kilicrane@eoltz.com; web: www.geocities.com/TheTropicself-containedove/7585. This new high-rise hotel, the smartest place in the town centre, is probably the best compromise between quality and cost in the upmarket or moderate listings for Moshi. The self-contained rooms with large beds, satellite television, private balcony, netting, fan and hot bath are exceptional value at US$30/40 single/double B&B. The garden is compact but green, there's a welcome swimming pool, and the rooftop bar is a great spot for sundowners facing Kilimanjaro. A good restaurant serves pizzas for around Tsh2,500 and

other meals – mostly Chinese and Indian – for around Tsh3,500–4,000. The ground floor souvenir shop stocks probably the most comprehensive selection of books in Moshi.

Bristol Cottages Kilimanjaro Tel: 027 275 5083/3745; fax: 027 275 2833; email: bristol@daiichicorp.com or bristol@kilinet.co.tz; web: www.bristolkilimanjaro.com. Located behind the Standard Chartered Bank close to the bus station, this commendable lodge consists of 20 newly constructed self-contained cottages with AC and hot shower set in peaceful manicured gardens. Facilities include secure parking, internet, email, fax and secretarial services. Rates are US$40/50 single/double B&B.

Mountain Inn Tel: 027 275 5622; fax: 027 275 2998; email: kilimanjaro@eoltz.com. Owned and managed by Shah Tours, Mountain Inn lies in wooded grounds 6km out of town along the Dar es Salaam road. Comfortable self-contained rooms cost US$35/45 single/double, while deluxe doubles cost US$65. A decent restaurant and well-stocked climbing and souvenir shop are attached, and substantial discounts are offered to clients who climb or go on safari with Shah Tours.

Philip Hotel Tel: 027 275 4746/7/8; fax: 027 275 0456; email: philipht@africaonline.co.tz. Fab name aside, this central hotel lacks for any ambience, and the rooms seem relatively poor value at US$30/40 for a self-contained single/double B&B with net, fan and balcony.

Leopard Hotel Tel: 027 275 0884; fax: 027 275 1261; email: leopardhotel@eoltz.com. For some years the most commodious option in the town centre, the Leopard Hotel is clean, comfortable and thoroughly adequate without approaching the Kilimanjaro Crane Hotel in terms of quality or amenities. Indifferent value at US$30/40 single/double B&B with fan, netting and hot shower. For residents, a 50% discount makes this considerably more attractive.

New Kilimanjaro Hotel Tel/fax: 027 275 5212. Formerly the government-owned Moshi Hotel, the New Kilimanjaro couldn't have a more central location – right opposite the Clock Tower – and the drop in prices since it was privatised makes it a more realistic prospect that it was a few years back. The staff seemed as dopey as ever when we dropped by in 2001, and the rather scruffy, institutional rooms still aren't worth the non-resident asking price of US$10/15 for a single/double using common shower or US$25 for a self-contained double. More recent reports suggest it has ceased operating.

Kilimanjaro Tourist Inn Tel: 027 2733252; fax: 027 275 2748; email: kkkmarealle@yahoo.com. This converted colonial house set in a large suburban garden has a friendly, homely atmosphere that will appeal to travellers who avoid more institutionalised hotels. The resident rate of Tsh12,000 for a self-contained twin or double with large beds, net, fan and shower is good value, but not so the non-resident rate of US$30.

Lutheran Uhuru Hostel Tel: 027 275 4084; fax: 027 275 3518; email: uhuruh@africaonline.co.tz or uhuruh@eoltz.com. Set in vast and pretty suburban gardens 1.5km from the town centre, this hostel used to be popular with tourists, but the recent boom in hotel construction in and around Moshi seems to have reduced its custom. It consists of 60 self-contained rooms, all with running hot water and private balconies, and ranging in price from US$30–45 for a single to US$45–50 for a double (about 30% cheaper for residents). The attached Bamboo Restaurant serves decent meals, but smoking and drinking are strictly prohibited. The hostel is about 3km out of town on Sekou Toure Road.

Budget

New Kindoroko Hotel Tel: 027 275 4054; fax: 027 275 4062; email: kindoroko@eoltz.com; web: www.africaonline.co.tz/kindorokohotel. Currently the most popular of several good budget hotels situated on and around Mawenzi Road, a couple of blocks south of the bus station, the four-storey New Kindoroko has maintained high standards and reasonable prices over several years. Small but very clean rooms cost Tsh6,000/12,000 single/double B&B, and come with hot shower, fan, netting and satellite television. Facilities include a lively courtyard bar, popular with travellers and locals alike, a

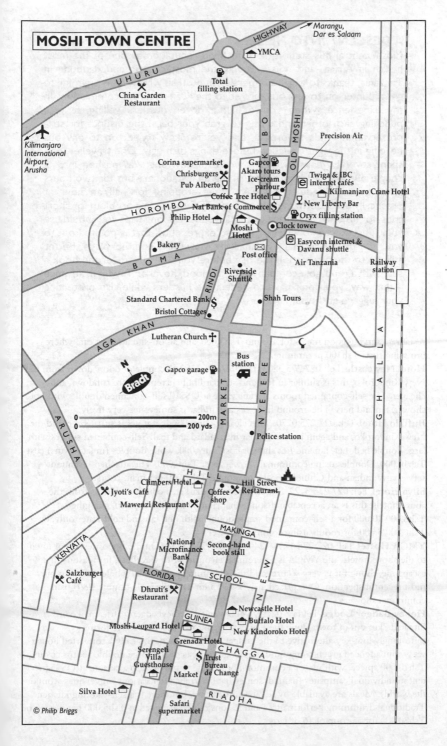

MOSHI TOWN CENTRE

YMCA

Total filling station

China Garden Restaurant

Kilimanjaro International Airport, Arusha

UHURU

HIGHWAY

Marangu, Dar es Salaam

KIBO

OLD MOSHI

Precision Air

Corina supermarket
Chrisburgers
Pub Alberto
Coffee Tree Hotel
Nat Bank of Commerce
Philip Hotel

Gapco
Akaro tours
Ice-cream parlour

Twiga & IBC internet cafés
Kilimanjaro Crane Hotel
New Liberty Bar
Oryx filling station

HOROMBO

Moshi Hotel

Clock tower

BOMA

Bakery

Post office

Easycom internet & Davanu shuttle

Air Tanzania

Railway station

Riverside Shuttle

RINDI

Standard Chartered Bank
Bristol Cottages

Shah Tours

AGA KHAN

Lutheran Church

Gapco garage

Bus station

GHALLA

Bradt

N

0   200m
0   200yds

ARUSHA

MARKET

NYERERE

Police station

HILL

Climbers Hotel
Jyoti's Café
Mawenzi Restaurant

Coffee shop

Hill Street Restaurant

MAKINGA

National Microfinance Bank

Second-hand book stall

NEW

KENYATTA

Salzburger Café

FLORIDA

SCHOOL

Dhruti's Restaurant

GUINEA

Newcastle Hotel
Buffalo Hotel
New Kindoroko Hotel

Moshi Leopard Hotel

Grenada Hotel

CHAGGA

Serengeti Villa Guesthouse

Trust Bureau de Change

Market

Silva Hotel

RIADHA

Safari supermarket

© Philip Briggs

A DESCENT INTO HELL...

Moshi central bus station has a justified reputation as one of the most hellish in Africa, and it is certainly the most chaotic and daunting in Tanzania, thanks to gaggles of persistent hustlers who will say anything to get a punter on to any bus, provided they can secure a commission. In my experience, when you've half a dozen hustlers yelling at you, punching each other and trying to grab your bags, the instinct for self-preservation tends to prevail, and you're likely to get on to any bus heading in the right direction before things turn ugly. One traveller who spent several weeks in Moshi wrote of how she was pushed into 'a couple of nightmarish journeys, sitting on a stationary bus for two hours after it was scheduled to leave, then stopping for half an hour at practically every settlement it passed'. This isn't such a problem for short trips, for instance to Arusha or Marangu, but for long trips you should use your judgement in boarding the first 'express bus' that is pointed out to you, and be aware that overcharging *wazungu* is commonplace. Better still, go to the bus station the day before you want to travel and book a seat with a reputable company such as Hood, Royal or Tawfiq in advance – that way, you don't have to deflect the hustlers while also protecting your luggage at the same time.

restaurant serving good meals for around Tsh3,000, and an on-site internet café where browsing costs Tsh100 per minute.

Hotel Newcastle Tel: 027 275 3203; fax: 027 275 1382. A couple of doors down from the New Kindoroko, this is similar in feel and standard but currently more rundown and cheaper. The self-contained rooms are fair value at US$10 self-contained double with hot shower, fan and nets. The ground floor restaurant/bar is sometimes very lively.

Buffalo Hotel Tel: 027 275 0270. This clean, popular budget hotel is situated behind the New Kindoroko, and again is very similar in standard and feel. Self-contained singles with large double bed, net, fan and hot shower cost Tsh7,000, while doubles (in fact twins) cost Tsh10,000. Doubles using communal showers cost Tsh6,000. The attached restaurant serves tasty Indian and Chinese meals for around Tsh2,000 per main course.

Silva Hotel Tel: 027 275 3122. Situated near the market, a couple of blocks from the above hotels, this is an acceptable if somewhat rundown budget option, charging Tsh8,000/10,000 for a self-contained single/double with net, fan and cold water only, or Tsh6,000/8,000 for rooms using common showers.

YMCA Hostel Tel: 027 275 1754/4240; fax: 027 275 1734. On the opposite side of town to the above hotels, the YMCA is a perennial favourite with travellers, for reasons that escape me, though it is very secure, and the swimming pool actually held water on our most recent inspection. Overpriced at US$13/15 for a small single/double B&B using communal showers.

Honey Badger Lodge Tel/fax: 027 275 4608; email: honeybadger@africamail.com. Situated 7km out of town along the Dar es Salaam road, this new lodge forms a refreshingly low-key alternative to the budget hotels in town. Basically a converted house set within a fenced green compound, the lodge consists of five large double rooms costing Tsh10,000 apiece, with use of a common hot bath. Camping is also available at US$5 per tent in individual campsites (named, somewhat bizarrely, after various universities around the world). Meals are available by advance order only, but there is a self-catering kitchen. Traditional drumming performances and lessons can be arranged at Tsh5,000 per person or Tsh80,000 for a group of 16 or larger.

Green Hostel Tel: 027 275 2229. This formerly popular backpackers haunt is now wildly overpriced at US$20 for an acceptable self-contained double with hot water and nets. The resident rate of Tsh8,000 is a more realistic reflection of what the accommodation is worth.

Rombo Cottage Inn Another former favourite, one that has suffered through no fault of its own, but rather due to the recent mushrooming of good budget hotels in the town centre. The clean self-contained double rooms are good value at US$8, and a fair restaurant is attached.

Shoestring
Coffee Tree Hotel Tel: 027 275 5040. This long-standing cheapie really couldn't be more centrally located, and the spacious rooms, though admittedly a bit rundown, are very good value at Tsh3,500 single using common shower or Tsh4,000/6,000 self-contained single/double with net, fan and cold water. The restaurant isn't up to much, but if affords good views towards Kilimanjaro.

Climbers Hotel Tel 027 8025. Another decent cheapie, situated a short distance from the bus station, the Climbers Hotel charges Tsh3,000 for a small but clean double using common shower, and Tsh4,000 for a similar self-contained room.

Suncourt Inn Right next to Rombo Cottage, this has rooms of a similar quality, and is really good value at Tsh4,000 for a self-contained double with hot water.

Jaribu Guesthouse Basic but clean singles close to the Suncourt Inn for Tsh2,000.

Serengeti Villa Guesthouse About the best of several local dives clustered behind the market. You'd still have to be pretty desperate to want to stay here for Tsh3,000 double.

Camping
The best place to camp close to Moshi is in the grounds of the **Golden Shower Restaurant**, which lies 1km from the town centre along the Marangu road and charges US$3 per person. Camping is also available at US$5 per person at the **Keys Hotel**. Further out of town, the campsite at the **Honey Badger Lodge** is nicer than either of the above, and better value for couples or groups at US$5 per tent.

Where to eat
Many of the places listed under *Where to Stay* have restaurants. Of the costlier places, the one most likely to attract passing custom to its restaurant is the **Kilimanjaro Crane Hotel**, which has a central location, good Indian food at around Tsh4,000, pizzas for Tsh2,500, and a great view of Kilimanjaro from the rooftop bar. The restaurant at the **New Kindoroko Hotel** is popular with budget travellers, and there's a lively bar attached.

El Rancho Top-notch Indian restaurant and bar in a converted old house and green garden close to the Impala Hotel. A broad selection of vegetarian meals is available at around Tsh3,000, while meat dishes are slightly more expensive. Highly recommended, though the distance from the town centre will enforce travellers starting more centrally to walk back (probably not a clever idea after dark) or to arrange to be collected by taxi. Closed Mondays.

Golden Shower Restaurant Long-serving and highly regarded Continental restaurant 1km out of town along the Dar es Salaam road. The menu includes everything from steaks and fried fish to curry, with most main dishes costing less than Tsh5,000. Walking out here at night would be dodgy, so arrange for a taxi to collect you.

Salzburger Café Owned by a Tanzanian formerly resident in Austria, this new restaurant is an unexpected gem, decorated with mementos of the old European city to create an atmosphere of full-on kitsch. If the décor doesn't do it for you, then the food certainly should – Tsh1,500–2,200 for a variety of very good steak, chicken and spaghetti dishes, with the unusual (for Tanzania) accompaniment of mashed potato and salads in addition to the conventional chips and rice.

China Garden Excellent and well-established Chinese restaurant situated in the CCM building on the Arusha–Dar Highway a few hundred metres from the YMCA. A main course with rice or noodles will set you back around Tsh6,000.

The Coffee Shop Tucked away on Hill St between the bus station and market, this is the place to head for when you're craving a fix of real coffee, and it also serves a selection of cakes, pies, snacks and light lunches at very reasonable prices. Irresistible!

Dhruti's Restaurant Situated on Market St opposite the Leopard Hotel, this low-key local restaurant is best known for its Tandoori chicken (Tsh1,500). Open late, but no alcohol served.

Chrisburgers Cheap daytime snacks such as hamburgers, samosas and excellent fruit juice, opposite the Clock Tower. Open daily except Sunday from 08.00 to 15.00.

Pub Alberto Not much food on offer at this brightly decorated nightclub next to Chrisburgers, but – open from 18.00 to 06.00 – it's a good place for an early morning last round. Closed Mondays.

General information

Tourist information There's no tourist information office as such in Moshi, but if you are spending some time there it's worth getting hold of the *Moshi Guide*, compiled and sold by the people who run the Coffee Shop on Hill Street. Most of the tour operators in town can provide – not necessarily impartial – local travel information.

Books A good second-hand bookstall can be found on Mawenzi Street, between the bus station and the Newcastle Hotel. For new books, particularly material relating specifically to Tanzania, the bookshop on the ground floor of the Kilimanjaro Crane Hotel is the best-stocked in town.

Foreign exchange The National Bank of Commerce opposite the Clock Tower changes cash and travellers' cheques at the usual rate and commission. Several forex bureaux are dotted around town, but while exchange rates are fairly good, you will generally get better in Arusha or Dar es Salaam. One exception is the Trust Bureau de Change, diagonally opposite the New Kindoroko Hotel, which offers good rates on US dollar travellers' cheques or cash, charges no commission, and is open from 09.00 to 18.00 from Monday to Saturday and 09.00 to 14.00 on Sundays. There is an ATM at the Standard Chartered Bank, where up to Tsh200,000 in local currency can be drawn against a Visa or Master card.

Internet and email Numerous internet cafés are dotted around town, with a standard rate of Tsh500 per 15 minutes. We regularly used IBC Internet and Twiga Communications, which are set alongside each other near the Coffee Tree Hotel, and found the service speedy and helpful. The Kilimanjaro Computer Centre in the THB Building on Boma Road, and Kilimanjaro Information Technology on Ghalla Street, have also been recommended. Although some hotels have internet cafés, they are generally a lot pricier than average.

Supermarkets and shops Aleem's Supermarket on Boma Road (behind the post office) stocks a good range of imported goods and foods. The Carina Supermarket next to Chrisburgers is also very well stocked. Opposite Aleem's, the Hot Bread Shop sells freshly baked bread as well as a selection of cakes and pies.

Swimming pool Use of the swimming pool at the YMCA is free to hostel residents, but visitors must pay a daily entrance fee of Tsh3,000 per person. The Keys Hotel charges a similar price to casual swimmers, but the pool is smaller and

LAKE CHALA

Straddling the Kenyan border some 30km east of Moshi as the crow flies, this roughly circular crater lake, a full 3km wide yet invisible until you virtually topple over the rim, is one of northern Tanzania's true off-the-beaten-track scenic gems. The brilliant turquoise water, hemmed in by sheer cliffs draped in tropical greenery, is an arresting sight at any time, and utterly fantastic when Kilimanjaro emerges from the clouds to the immediate west. Abundant birds aside, wildlife is in short supply, though local fishermen claim that crocodiles – presumably the exotic (and harmless) pygmy species introduced 80 years ago by the eccentric colonial Ewart Grogan – leer from the water on occasion. In common with other African crater lakes, or Loch Ness for that matter, Chala also reputedly harbours its due quota of dubious home-grown beasties. Not for the faint-hearted, a very steep footpath leads from the rim to the edge of the lake, its translucent waters plunging near-vertically to an undetermined depth from the rocky shore.

Previous attempts to attract tourism to Chala, notably a tourist lodge on the Kenyan rim (which, when we dropped in a couple of years ago, was most memorable for the bat colonies in the toilets) could hardly be deemed an unqualified success. It remains to be seen whether the opening of the Kilimanjaro Chala Lodge and Campsite on the Tanzanian side will change that. The lodge, still under construction in early 2002, has a marvellous location on the rim, and looks like it could be pretty special when it finally opens – expect prices to be in the US$100-plus league. The large, grassy campsite, already functioning in late 2001, has a large ablution block with running water and charges US$5 per person. For the time being, the only practical way to reach Chala is as an organised day or overnight trip out of Moshi, or in a private 4WD vehicle. If you're driving, follow the Dar es Salaam road out of Moshi for 25km until you reach the junction at Himo, where a left turn leads to the Kenyan border at Taveta. About 7km along the Taveta Road, turn left on to the rough road signposted for Kilimanjaro Mountain Lodge, which you must follow for about 40 minutes to reach the lake.

it is further out of town. You could also try the pool at the Kilimanjaro Crane Hotel.

Telephone Phone cards can be bought and used at the Tanzania Telecommunications Centre next to the post office near the Clock Tower. This is also the best place to make international phone calls, and to send and receive faxes.

Short excursions There are many possibilities for day or overnight excursions out of Moshi, whether one travels independently or arranges things through a local tour operator. All the sites covered under the heading *Between Moshi and Mombo* in *Chapter 9* make for feasible overnight excursions, while Marangu, covered below, is the obvious rural base for travellers who don't climb Kilimanjaro to wander the foothills in hope of that elusive view. See also *Lake Chala* (above) and *Cultural Tours around Moshi and Kilimanjaro* (pages 200–1).

MARANGU

The village of Marangu, which lies about 5km south of the main gate to Kilimanjaro National Park, has something of an Alpine feel, surrounded by lush vegetation and bisected by a babbling mountain stream. Once the most popular base for organising Kilimanjaro climbs, Marangu remains a good place to set up climbs with top-quality operators (charging top-of-the-range prices), but these days Moshi is a more popular centre from which to arrange a budget climb. Most people who organise climbs in Moshi will do little more than pass through Marangu, as they will be provided with transport as far as the park entrance gate. For those who cannot afford to climb the mountain, Marangu would be a pleasant place to spend a few days taking walks on the foothills of Kilimanjaro, were it not for a lack of genuine budget accommodation in the area.

The only prescribed tourist attraction in Marangu is the Marangu or Kinukamori – 'Little Moon' – Waterfall. About 20 minutes' walk and signposted from the town centre, this approximately 15m-high waterfall lies in a small park maintained by the district council (Tsh1,000 entrance) as an eco-tourism project in collaboration with two nearby villages. It's pretty enough without being an essential side-trip, though the wooded banks of the Unna River above the waterfall harbour a variety of forest birds, and regularly attract troops of black-and-white colobus in the rainy season. A legend associated with Kinukamori relates to an unmarried girl called Makinuka, who discovered she was pregnant, a crime punishable by death in strict Chagga

CULTURAL TOURS AROUND MOSHI AND KILIMANJARO
The cultural tourism projects developed by the SNV in association with local communities around Arusha and the Pare and Usambara Mountains have more recently spread to the Kilimanjaro foothills. Two such projects have been implemented in the area, one near Macheme, about 15km from Moshi, and the other at the popular trekking base of Marangu. In addition to offering insights into Chagga culture and the opportunity to limber up the limbs before a full-on ascent of Kilimanjaro, these cultural tours allow non-climbers to get a good look at the scenic Kilimanjaro foothills, with a chance of catching a glimpse of the snow-capped peak itself. In addition to the local telephone contacts given below, full details of the programmes can be obtained through the central website www. tourismtanzania.org or by emailing info@tourismtanzania.org. One operator in Moshi that specialises in setting up budget-friendly day trips to the cultural programmes, as well as running its own day hike in the Kilimanjaro foothills, is Akaro Tours (see *Recommended tour operators*, pages 212–13, for contact details).

Machame Cultural Tourism Programme.
This programme is based at the village of Kyalia, close to the Machame Gate of Kilimanjaro National Park. A good day tour for those with a strong interest in scenery is the five-hour Sieny-Ngira Trail, which passes through the lush montane forest to a group of large sacred caves, a natural rock bridge over the Marire and Namwi Rivers, and a nearby waterfall. For those with a greater interest in culture, the five-hour Nronga Tour, which visits a milk purification and processing co-operative run by women, is best done on Monday, market day in Kalali village. Of similar duration, the Nkuu Tour focuses instead on agriculture, in particular coffee production. Longer excursions include the two-day Ng'uni Hike and three-day Lyamungo Tour. In a private vehicle, Kyalia can be reached by following the Arusha road out of Moshi for 12km, then following the turn-off signposted for Machame Gate and driving for another 14km. The road to Kyalia is surfaced in its entirety, and regular minibuses run to Kyalia from the junction on the Moshi–Arusha road. Tel: 027 275 7033; fax: 027 275 1113.

society, and decided to take her own life by jumping over the waterfall. When Makinuka arrived at the waterfall and looked over the edge, she changed her mind and turned to go home to plead for mercy. As she did so, however, she came face to face with a leopard and ran back screaming in fear, forgetting about the gorge behind her, to plunge to an accidental death. A statue of Makinuka and her nemesis stands above the waterfall. The waterfall can be visited independently, or by arrangement with your hotel as part of a longer sightseeing tour (see box *Cultural Tours around Moshi and Kilimanjaro*, below).

Getting there and away

Buses between Moshi and Marangu leave in either direction when they are full. Normally, this will be every hour or so, and the trip shouldn't take more than 45 minutes.

Where to stay and eat
Upmarket

Marangu Hotel Tel: 027 275 6591; fax: 027 275 6594; email: marangu@africaonline.co.ke; web: www.maranguhotel.com. The comfortable, family-run

Marangu Cultural Tourism Programme

Geared primarily towards travellers staying in Marangu prior to a Kilimanjaro climb, this programme offers a variety of half-day trips taking in various natural and cultural sites in the surrounding slopes. Popular goals include any of three waterfalls, as well as the first coffee tree planted in Tanzania more than a century ago, and a traditional conical Chagga homestead. Few prospective climbers will be unmoved by the grave of the legendary Yohanu Lauwo, who guided Hans Meyer to the summit of Kilimanjaro back in 1889, continued working as a guide into his seventies, and lived to the remarkable age of 124! Other walks lead to nearby Mamba and Makundi, known for their traditional Chagga blacksmiths and woodcarvers, and for the Laka Caves, where women and children were hidden during the frequent 19th-century clashes with the Maasai of the surrounding plains. Guided tours can be arranged through any of the hotels in and around Marangu.

Materuni and Kuringe Waterfall Tour

Operated exclusively by Akaro Tours, whose owner grew up in a nearby *shamba*, this rewarding half- or full-day tour starts at the village of Materuni on the foothills of Kilimanjaro some 14km from Moshi. The walk follows sloping roads and footpaths through the surrounding mountainside to the Kuringe Waterfall, a 70m-high 'bridal veil' fall set at the head of a steep wooded gorge. One of the loveliest waterfalls I've seen anywhere in Africa, Kuringe is genuinely worth making an effort to visit, something I don't say lightly after having regularly hiked for miles in the line of duty to check out what, it transpired, was yet another unmemorable small cataract. On the full-day, you continue from the waterfall, climbing steep cultivated slopes, to a Chagga homestead, where lunch and home-grown coffee are provided. From here, you can continue on to the Rua Forest, which harbours black-and-white colobus monkeys as well as most of the montane forest birds associated with Kilimanjaro. The full-day version can also incorporate a visit to a typical Chagga coffee and banana subsistence farm.

hotel, situated 5km from Marangu along the Moshi road, has an unpretentiously rustic feel, all ivy-draped walls and neat hedges that might have been transported straight from the English countryside. It also has a long-standing reputation for organising reliable Kilimanjaro climbs, whether you're looking at the standard all-inclusive package or the 'hard way' package aimed at budget travellers. Accommodation in self-contained rooms costs US$70/100 single/double B&B. The large green campsite behind the main hotel buildings has a hot shower and charges US$3 per person, probably the best value for campers in the Marangu area.

Capricorn Hotel Tel: 027 275 1309; fax: 027 275 2442; email: capricorn@africaonline.co.tz; web: www.africaonline.co.tz/capricornhotel. Straggling over a steep hillside some 2km from Marangu along the road towards Kilimanjaro National Park's Marangu entrance gate, this relatively new hotel charges US$60 B&B per person for accommodation in spacious, colourfully decorated and carpeted self-contained rooms. The hotel is situated within the forest zone, and the lushly wooded grounds are teeming with birds. The restaurant has an excellent reputation, as do Kilimanjaro climbs arranged through the hotel.

Nakara Hotel Tel: 027 275 6571; fax: 027 275 6599; email: mail@nakaratz.com or nakaratz@hotmail.com; web: www.nakaratz.com. This smart new hotel lies about 1km past the Capricorn and 2km before the park entrance gate. Nothing wrong with the compact but comfortable self-contained twin rooms, though they hardly qualify as outstanding value at US$70/100 single/double B&B, and the rather cramped grounds lack the greenery and character of other options in this price range.

Moderate

Kibo Hotel Tel/fax: 027 275 1308; email: kibohotel@yahoo.com; web: www.kibohotel.com. The venerable Kibo Hotel stands in attractive flowering gardens roughly 1km from the village centre towards the park entrance gate. Formerly on a par with the Marangu Hotel, the Kibo has emphatically seen better days – incredibly, lest it escape your attention, former US President Jimmy Carter stayed here several years ago – but it has retained a winning air of faded dignity epitomised by the liberal wood-panelling and creaky old verandas. If nothing else, following a recent change of management and sensible cut in rates, the large, self-contained rooms are decent value by any standards and exceptional by those of Marangu at US$25/40 single/double B&B.

Babylon Lodge Tel/fax: 027 275 1315; email: babylon@africaonline.co.tz. Situated 500m from Marangu Post Office along the Mwika Road, this once vastly overpriced budget hotel has undergone a recent facelift that nudges it into the moderate category. The immaculately clean but rather cramped self-contained rooms seem overpriced at US$25/40 single/double B&B, and the grounds – flat grass quadrangles enclosed by white walls – deserve to be patented as a superlative-repellent. To my taste, not a patch on the identically priced Kibo Hotel, but I could see that some travellers might feel the opposite way – the proactive, helpful management and staff certainly count it in the Babylon's favour.

Ashanti Lodge Email: ashantilodge@habari.co.tz. This low-key lodge lies about 2km out of town along the Mwika road, next door – appropriately – to the Ghana Bar. The grounds are very pretty, and the accommodation in small circular self-contained chalets with banana-leaf roofing costs US$25/40 single/double B&B. It was very quiet and overhung with a gentle air of neglect when we last looked in, but the lodge lacks not for ambience, and it seems pretty decent value in its price range.

Budget and camping

Coffee Tree Campsite Tel: 027 275 4818; email: alpinetrekking@eoltz.com. Situated along the road to the park entrance gate, alongside the Nakara Hotel, this neatly laid out site is also a good place to arrange budget Kilimanjaro climbs. Accommodation in double chalets costs US$12 per person, while a bed in a rondavel cost US$10 per person – not exactly great value, but you won't find cheaper in Marangu. The camping seems a bit dear at US$8 per person, and even allowing for the above average facilities – fridge, bar, barbecue, sauna and hot shower – the campsite at the Marangu Hotel (see *Upmarket* above) seems infinitely better value. Tents and gas stoves are available for hire, various cultural tours can be arranged, and there are on-site email and internet facilities. If you don't fancy self-catering, you could eat at the nearby Nakara Hotel.

Bismarck Hotel Tel: Marangu 192. Situated on the road to the entrance gate, between the Kibo and Nakara Hotels, this budget hotel has pleasant enough grounds, but the rundown rooms are lousy value at US$10 per person excluding breakfast. Camping costs US$5 per tent.

MOUNT KILIMANJARO NATIONAL PARK

Reaching an altitude of 5,895m (19,340ft), Kilimanjaro is the highest mountain in Africa, and on the rare occasions when it is not veiled in clouds, the mountain's distinctive silhouette and snow-capped peaks are one of the most breathtaking sights on the continent. There are, of course, higher peaks on other continents, but Kilimanjaro is effectively the world's largest single mountain, a free-standing entity rising an incredible 5km above the surrounding plains. It is also the highest mountain anywhere that can be ascended by somebody without specialised mountaineering experience or equipment.

In geological terms, Kilimanjaro is a relatively young mountain. Like most other large mountains near the Rift Valley, it was formed by volcanic activity, first erupting about one million years ago. The 3,962m-high Shira Peak collapsed around half a million years ago, but the 5,895m-high Uhuru Peak on Mount Kibo and 5,149m-high Mawenzi Peak continued to grow until more recently. Shira plateau formed 360,000 years ago, when the caldera was filled by lava from Kibo after a particularly violent eruption. Kibo is now dormant, and nobody knows when it last displayed any serious volcanic activity. The Kilimanjaro National Park, gazetted in 1977, protects the entire Tanzanian part of the mountain above the 2,700m contour, an area of 756km².

Vegetation and biology

There are five vegetation zones on Kilimanjaro: the cultivated lower slopes, the forest, heath and moorland, alpine, and the barren summit zone. Vegetation is sparse higher up due to lower temperatures and rainfall.

The **lower slopes** of the mountain were probably once forested, but are now mainly covered in cultivation. The volcanic soils make them highly fertile and they support a dense human population. The most biologically interesting aspect of the lower slopes is the abundance of wild flowers, seen between Marangu and the park entrance gate.

The **montane forest zone** of the southern slopes lies between the altitudes of 1,800m and 3,000m. Receiving up to 2,000mm of rainfall annually, this zone displays a high biological diversity, and still supports a fair amount of wildlife. The most frequently seen mammals are the black-and-white colobus and blue monkey, while typical forest antelope include three duiker species and the beautifully marked bushbuck. Leopard, bushpig and porcupine are fairly common but seldom encountered by hikers, while eland, buffalo and elephant are present in small numbers. The forest is home to many varieties of butterfly, including four endemic species. The forests of Kilimanjaro are less rich in birds (particularly endemics) than the more ancient forests of the Eastern Arc mountains, but some 40 species peculiar to Afro-montane forest have been recorded. Most forest birds are quite difficult to observe, but trekkers should at least hear the raucous silvery-cheeked hornbill and beautiful Hartlaub's touraco.

ABBOTT'S DUIKER

An antelope occasionally encountered by hikers on Kilimanjaro is Abbott's duiker *Cephalophus spadix*, a montane forest species that was formerly quite widespread in suitable East African habitats, but is today endemic to eastern Tanzania due to environmental loss and poaching elsewhere in its natural range. After Ader's duiker, a lowland species of East African coastal belt, Abbott's is the most threatened of African duikers, categorised as Vulnerable in the IUCN red data list for 2000, but based on present trends likely to decline to a status of Critically Endangered in the foreseeable future. Abbott's duiker is today confined to five forested montane 'islands' in eastern Tanzania, namely Kilimanjaro, Usambara, Udzungwa, Uluguru and Rungwe. The total population is unknown – a 1998 estimate of 2,500 based on limited data is not implausible – but Udzungwa probably harbours the most substantial and secure single population, followed by Kilimanjaro. Should you be lucky enough to stumble across this rare antelope, it has a glossy, unmarked off-black torso, a paler head, and a distinctive red forehead tuft. Its size alone should, however, be diagnostic: the shoulder height of up to 75cm is the third largest of any duiker species, and far exceeds that of other more diminutive duikers that occur in Tanzania.

The semi-Alpine **moorland zone**, which lies between 3,000m and 4,000m, is characterised by heath-like vegetation and abundant wild flowers. As you climb into the moorland, two distinctive plants become common. These are *Lobelia deckenii*, which grows to 3m high, and the groundsel *Senecio kilimanjarin*, which grows up to 5m high and can be distinguished by a spike of yellow flowers. The moorland zone supports a low density of mammals, but pairs of klipspringer are quite common on rocky outcrops and several other species are recorded from time to time. Hill chat and scarlet-tufted malachite sunbird are two birds whose range is restricted to the moorlands of large East African mountains. Other localised birds are lammergeier and Alpine swift. Because it is so open, the views from the moorland are stunning.

The **Alpine zone** between 4,000 and 5,000m is classified as a semi-desert because it receives an annual rainfall of less than 250mm. The ground often freezes at night, but ground temperatures may soar to above 30°C by day. Few plants survive in these conditions; only 55 species are present, many of them lichens and grasses. Six species of moss are endemic to the higher reaches of Kilimanjaro. Large mammals have been recorded at this altitude, most commonly eland, but none is resident.

Approaching the summit, the **arctic zone** starts at an altitude of around 5,000m. This area receives virtually no rainfall, and supports little permanent life other than the odd lichen. Two remarkable records concern a frozen leopard discovered here in 1926, and a family of hunting dogs seen in 1962. The most notable natural features at the summit are the inner and outer craters of Kibo, a 120m-deep ash pit, and the Great Northern Glacier, which has retreated markedly since it was first seen by Hans Meyer in 1889.

Climbing Kilimanjaro

As Africa's highest peak and most identifiable landmark, Kilimanjaro offers an irresistible challenge to many tourists. Dozens of visitors to Tanzania set off for Uhuru Peak every day, ranging from teenagers to pensioners (a seven-year-old boy recently became the youngest person to the summit), and those who make it generally regard the achievement to be the highlight of their time in the country. A major part of Kilimanjaro's attraction is that any reasonably fit person stands a fair chance of reaching the top. The ascent requires no special climbing skills or experience; on the contrary, it basically amounts to a long uphill slog over four days, followed by a more rapid descent.

The relative ease of climbing Kilimanjaro should not lull travellers into thinking of the ascent as some sort of prolonged Sunday stroll. It is a seriously tough hike, with potentially fatal penalties for those who are inadequately prepared or who belittle the health risks attached to being at an altitude of above 4,000m. It should also be recognised that there is no such thing as a cheap Kilimanjaro climb. Most reliable operators now charge well in excess of US$500 per person for a five-day climb along the Marangu Route; those who cannot afford this sort of sum would be wiser forgetting about the climb than trying to work through a dodgy operator.

Marangu Route

Starting at the Marangu Gate some 5km from the village of the same name, the so-called 'tourist route' is the most popular way to the top of Kilimanjaro, largely because it is less arduous than most of the alternatives, as well as having better facilities and being cheaper to climb. Marangu is also probably the safest route, due to the volume of other climbers and good rescue facilities relative to more obscure routes, and it offers a better chance of seeing some wildlife. It is the only route where you can sleep in proper huts throughout, with bathing water and bottled drinks normally available too. The main drawback of the Marangu route is that it is heavily trampled by comparison to other routes, for which reason many people complain that it can feel overcrowded.

Day one: Marangu to Mandara Hut (12km, 4 hours) On an organised climb you will be dropped at the park entrance gate a few kilometres past Marangu. There is a high chance of rain in the afternoon, so it is wise to set off on this four-hour hike as early in the day as you can. Foot traffic is heavy along this stretch, which means that although you pass through thick forest, the shy animals that inhabit the forest are not likely to be seen. If your guide will go that way, use the parallel trail which meets the main trail halfway between the gate and the hut. Mandara Hut (2,700m) is an attractive collection of buildings with room for 200 people.

Day two: Mandara Hut to Horombo Hut (15km, 6 hours) You continue through forest for a short time before reaching the heather and moorland zone, from where there are good views of the peaks and Moshi. The walk takes up to six hours. Horombo Hut (3,720m) sleeps up to 120 people. It is in a valley and surrounded by giant lobelia and groundsel. If you do a six-day hike, you will spend a day at Horombo to acclimatise.

Day three: Horombo Hut to Kibo Hut (15km, 6–7 hours) The vegetation thins out as you enter the desert-like Alpine zone, and when you cross the saddle Kibo Peak comes into view. This six- to seven-hour walk should be done slowly: many people start to feel the effects of altitude. Kibo Hut (4,703m) is a stone construction which sleeps up to 120 people. Water must be carried there from a stream above Horombo. You may find it difficult to sleep at this altitude, and as you will have to rise at around 01.00 the next morning, many people feel it is better not to bother trying.

Days four and five: Kibo Hut to the summit to Marangu The best time to climb is during the night, as it is marginally easier to climb the scree slope to

Gillman's Point on the crater rim when it is frozen. This 5km ascent typically takes about six hours, so you need to get going between midnight and 01.00 to stand a chance of reaching the summit in time to catch the sunrise. From Gillman's Point it is a further two-hour round trip along the crater's edge to Uhuru Peak, the highest point in Africa. From the summit, it's a roughly seven-hour descent with a break at Kibo Hut to Horombo Hut, where you will spend your last night on the mountain. The final day's descent from Horombo to Marangu generally takes 7–8 hours, so you should arrive in Marangu in the mid-afternoon.

Other routes

Although the vast majority of trekkers stick to the Marangu Route, some prefer to ascend Kilimanjaro using one of five relatively off-the-beaten-track alternatives. While the merits and demerits of avoiding the Marangu Route are hotly debated, there is no doubt about two things: firstly that you'll see few other tourists on the more obscure routes, and secondly that you'll pay considerably more for this privilege. Aesthetic and financial considerations aside, two unambiguous logistical disadvantages of the less-used routes are that they are generally tougher going (though only the Umbwe is markedly so), and that the huts – where they exist – are virtually derelict, which enforces camping.

Machame Route

In recent years, the Machame Route has grown greatly in popularity. It is widely regarded to be the most scenic viable ascent route, with great views across to Mount Meru, and as a whole it is relatively gradual, requiring at least six days for the full ascent and descent. Short sections are steeper and slightly more difficult than any part of the Marangu Route, but this is compensated for by the longer period for acclimatisation.

The route is named after the village of Machame, from where it is a two-hour walk to the park gate (1,950m). Most companies will provide transport as far as the gate (at least when the road is passable), from where it's a six- to eight-hour trek through thick forest to Machame Hut, which lies on the edge of the moorland zone at 2,890m. The Machame Hut is now a ruin, so camping is necessary, but water is available. The second day of this trail consists of a 9km, four- to six-hour hike through the moorland zone of Shira Plateau to Shira Hut (3,840m), which is near a stream. Once again, this hut has fallen into disuse, so the options are camping or sleeping in a nearby cave.

From Shira, a number of options exist: you could spend your third night at Lava Tower Hut (4,630m), four hours from Shira, but the ascent to the summit from there is tricky and only advisable if you are experienced and have good equipment. A less arduous option is to spend your third night at Barranco Campsite (3,950m), a tough 12km, six-hour hike from Shira, then to go on to Barafu Hut (4,600m) on the fourth day, a walk of approximately seven hours. From Barafu, it is normal to begin the steep seven- to eight-hour clamber to Stella Point (5,735m) at midnight, so that you arrive at sunrise, with the option of continuing on to Uhuru Peak, a two-hour round trip, before hiking back down to Mweka Hut via Barafu in the afternoon. This day can involve up to 16 hours of walking altogether. After spending your fifth night at Mweka Hut (3,800m), you will descend the mountain on the sixth day via the Mweka Route, a four- to six-hour walk.

Although the huts along this route are practically unusable, you still get to pay the US$40 'hut fee'. Any reliable operator will provide you with camping equipment and employ enough porters to carry the camp and set it up.

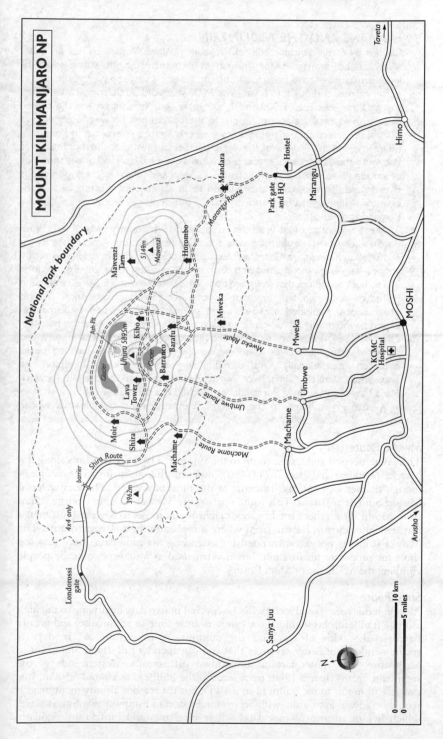

MOUNT KILIMANJARO NP

National Park boundary

Taveta

Himo

Hostel

Mandara

Marangu Route

Park gate and HQ

Marangu

Mawenzi Tarn

Mawenzi 5149m

Horombo

Ash Pit

Kibo

Glacier

Uhuru 5895m

Lava Tower

Glacier

Barranco

Barafu

Mweka

Mweka Route

Mweka

MOSHI

KCMC Hospital

Umbwe

Umbwe Route

Machame

Machame Route

Machame

Moir

Shira

Shira Route

3962m

barrier

4x4 only

Londorossi gate

Sanya Juu

Arusha

N

0   5 miles

0   10 km

HUMANS AND THE MOUNTAIN

Blessed by fertile volcanic soil and reliable rainfall, Kilimanjaro has probably always been a magnet for human settlement. Ancient stone tools of indeterminate age have been found on the lower slopes, as have the remains of pottery artefacts thought to be at least 2,000 years old. Archaeological evidence suggests that, between 1,000 and 1,500 years ago, Kilimanjaro was the centre of an Iron Age culture spreading out to the coastal belt between Pangani and Mombasa. Before that, it's anybody's guess really, but references in Ptolemy's *Geography* and the *Periplus of the Aerythrian Sea* suggest that the mountain was known to the early coastal traders, and might even have served as the terminus of a trade route starting at modern-day Pangani and following the synonymous river inland. Kilimanjaro is also alluded to in an account written by a 12th-century Chinese trader, and by the 16th-century Spanish geographer, Fernandes de Encisco.

These ancient allusions fired the curiosity of 19th-century geographers, who outdid each other in publishing wild speculations about the African interior. In 1848, Johan Rebmann, a German missionary working in the Taita Hills, was told about a very large mountain called Kilimanjaro, reputed to be covered in silver and to host evil spirits that froze anybody who tried to climb it. When Rebmann visited the mountain, he immediately recognised the silver to be snow. Yet his observations, published in 1849, were greeted with derision by European experts, who thought it ludicrous to claim there was snow so near the Equator. Only in 1861, when an experienced geologist Von der Decken saw and surveyed Kilimanjaro, was its existence and that of its snow-capped peaks accepted internationally. Oral tradition suggests that no local person had successfully climbed Kilimanjaro – or at least returned to tell the tale – before Hans Meyer and Ludwig Purstscheller reached the summit in 1889.

Kilimanjaro is home to the Chagga, Bantu-speaking agriculturists whose

Mweka Route

This is the steepest and fastest route to the summit. There are two huts along it – Mweka (3,100m) and Barafu (4,600m), uniports that sleep up to 16 people – though neither is reputedly habitable at the time of writing. There is water at Mweka but not at Barafu. This route starts at the Mweka Wildlife College, 12km from Moshi. From there it takes about eight hours to get to Mweka Hut, then a further eight hours to Barafu, from where it replicates the Machame Route. The Mweka Route is not recommended for ascending the mountain, since it is too short for proper acclimatisation, but is often used as a descent route by people climbing the Machame or Shira Routes.

Shira Route

Although this route could technically be covered in five days by driving to the high altitude trailhead, this would allow one very little time to acclimatise, and greatly decrease the odds of reaching the summit. A minimum of six days is recommended, but better seven so that you can spend a full day at Shira Hut to acclimatise. The route starts at Londorossi gate on the western side of the mountain, from where a 19km track leads to the trailhead at around 3,500m. It is possible to motor to the trailhead in a 4WD, but for reasons already mentioned it would be advisable to walk, with an overnight stop to camp outside Simba Cave, which lies in an area of moorland where elephants and buffalo are regularly

ancestors are said to have arrived in the area in the 15th century. This dating is apparently contradicted by an intriguing local legend relating to an eruption of Kilimanjaro, which doesn't tally with the geological evidence for the past 500 years, but it's probable the story was handed down by earlier inhabitants. The Chagga have no tradition of central leadership. As many as 100 small chieftaincies existed in the region in the mid-19th century. They are efficient and industrious farmers, and the lower slopes of Kilimanjaro are covered in their disused dams and irrigation furrows. Because they have always produced a food surplus, the Chagga have long traded with the Maasai and other local groups, and later with Arab caravans.

Today, the Chagga remain self-sufficient for basic foodstuffs, and the mountain is scattered with family smallholdings of traditional conical huts that produce a variety of subsistence crops. The major cash crop is coffee, which, although it was introduced to the region during the colonial era, has always been grown by small-scale farmers to be marketed through a co-operative rather than by the large settler-owned plantations found elsewhere in Africa. Today, the Chagga have a reputation for industriousness, and are generally relatively well-educated, for which reason you'll find that a high proportion of salaried workers and safari guides come from Kilimanjaro region.

Oddly, nobody is certain of the source of the name Kilimanjaro, or even whether it is Swahili, Maasai or Chagga in origin. That the term *Kilima* is Swahili for little mountain (a joke?) is not in doubt. But *njaro* could derive from the Chagga word for caravan (the mountain was an important landmark on the northern caravan route), the Maasai word for water (it is the source of most of the region's rivers), or the name of a Swahili demon of cold. Another version of the origin of the name is that it has been bastardised from Kilemakyaro, meaning 'hard climb'.

encountered. From the trailhead, it's a straightforward 4km to the campsite at the disused Shira Hut. If you opt to spend two nights at Shira in order to acclimatise, there are some worthwhile day walks in the vicinity. From Shira Hut, the route is identical to the Machame Route, and it is normal to return along the Mweka Route.

Rongai Route

The only route ascending Kilimanjaro from the northeast, the recently re-opened Rongai Route starts close to the Kenyan border and was closed for several years due to border sensitivity. In terms of gradients, it is probably less physically demanding than the Marangu Route, and the scenery, with views over the Tsavo plains, is regarded by many to be as beautiful. The Rongai Route can be covered over five days, with equally good if not better conditions for acclimatisation than the Marangu Route, though as with Marangu the odds of reaching the summit improve if you opt for an additional day.

The route starts at the village of Nale Moru (2,000m) near the Kenyan border, from where a footpath leads through cultivated fields and plantation forest before entering the montane forest zone, where black-and-white colobus monkeys are frequently encountered. The first campsite is reached after between three and five hours, and lies at about 2,700m on the frontier of the forest and moorland zone. On the five-day hike, the second day involves a gentle five- to six-hour ascent,

MOUNTAIN HEALTH

Do not attempt to climb Kilimanjaro unless you are reasonably fit, nor if you have heart or lung problems (although asthma sufferers should be all right). Bear in mind, however, that very fit people are more prone to altitude sickness because they ascend too fast.

Above 3,000m you may not feel hungry, but you should try to eat. Carbohydrates and fruit are recommended, whereas rich or fatty foods are harder to digest. You should drink plenty of liquids, at least three litres of water daily, and will need enough water bottles to carry this. Dehydration is one of the most common reasons for failing to complete the climb. If you dress in layers, you can take off clothes before you sweat too much, thereby reducing water loss.

Few people climb Kilimanjaro without feeling some of the symptoms of altitude sickness: headaches, nausea, fatigue, breathlessness, sleeplessness and swelling of the hands and feet. You can reduce these by allowing yourself time to acclimatise by taking an extra day over the ascent, eating and drinking properly, and trying not to push yourself. If you walk slowly and steadily, you will tire less quickly than if you try to rush each day's walk. Acetazolamide (Diamox) helps speed acclimatisation and many people find it useful; take 250mg twice a day for five days, starting two or three days before reaching 3,500m. However, the side effects from this drug may resemble altitude sickness and therefore it is advisable to try the medication for a couple of days about two weeks before the trip to see if it suits you.

through an area of moorland where elephants are sometimes seen, to Third Cave campsite (3,500m). On the third day, it's a four- to five-hour walk to School Campsite (4,750m) at the base of Kibo, with the option of camping here or else continuing to the nearby Kibo Hut, which is more crowded but more commodious. The ascent from here is identical to the Marangu Route. A six-day variation on the above route involves spending the second night at Kikelewa Caves (3,600m, six- to seven-hour walk), a night at Mawenzi Tarn near the synonymous peak (4,330m, four-hour walk), then crossing the saddle between Mawenzi and Kibo to rejoin the five-day route at School Campsite.

Umbwe Route

This short, steep route, possibly the most scenic of the lot, is not recommended as an ascent route as it is very steep in parts and involves one short stretch of genuine rock climbing. It is occasionally used as a descent route, and can be tied in with almost any of the ascent routes, though many operators understandably prefer not to take the risk or charge a premium for using it. Umbwe Route descends from Barranco Hut, and comes out at the village of Umbwe. It is possible to sleep in two caves on the lower slopes along this route.

Arranging a climb

The *only* sensible way to go about climbing Kilimanjaro is through a reliable operator that specialises in Kili climbs. Readers who pre-book a climb through a known tour operator in their own country can be confident that they will be going with a reputable ground operator in Tanzania. Readers who want to make their arrangements after they arrive in Tanzania will find several such companies operating out of Moshi, Arusha and Marangu, and will generally be able to negotiate a better price than if they had pre-booked. A list of respected operators is included in

Should symptoms become severe, and especially if they are clearly getting worse, then descend immediately. Even going down 500m is enough to start recovery. Sleeping high with significant symptoms is dangerous; if in doubt descend to sleep low.

Pulmonary and cerebral oedema are altitude-related problems that can be rapidly fatal if you do not descend. Symptoms of the former include shortness of breath when at rest, coughing up frothy spit or even blood, and undue breathlessness compared to accompanying friends. Symptoms of high altitude cerebral oedema are headaches, poor co-ordination, staggering like a drunk, disorientation, poor judgement and even hallucinations. The danger is that the sufferer usually doesn't realise how sick he/she is and may argue against descending. The only treatment for altitude sickness is descent.

Hypothermia is a lowering of body temperature usually caused by a combination of cold and wet. Mild cases usually manifest themselves as uncontrollable shivering. Put on dry, warm clothes and get into a sleeping bag; this will normally raise your body temperature sufficiently. Severe hypothermia is potentially fatal: symptoms include disorientation, lethargy, mental confusion (including an inappropriate feeling of well-being and warmth!) and coma. In severe cases the rescue team should be summoned.

A US$20 rescue fee is paid by all climbers upon entering the national park. The rescue team ordinarily covers the Marangu route only; if you use another route their services must be organised in advance.

the box overleaf, and while such a list can never be comprehensive, it is reasonable to assume that anybody who can offer you a significantly cheaper package than the more budget-friendly companies on this list is probably not to be trusted.

In 2001, you could safely assume that a five-day Marangu climb with any reliable operator would start at an all-inclusive price of around US$600–700 per head for two people, and this is certain to increase when park fees are raised by 20% in July 2002. You may be able to negotiate the starting price down slightly, especially for a larger group, but when you are paying this sort of money, it strikes me as sensible to shop around for the best quality of service rather than a fractional saving. A reputable operator will provide good food, experienced guides and porters, and reliable equipment – all of which go a long way to ensuring not only that you reach the top, but also that you come back down alive. You can assume that the cost of any package with a reputable operator will include a registered guide, two porters per person, park fees, food, and transport to and from the gate. It is, however, advisable to check exactly what you are paying for, and (especially for larger parties) to ensure that one porter is also registered as a guide, so that if somebody has to turn back, the rest of the group can still continue their climb. It might also be worth pointing out the potential risk attached to forming an impromptu group with strangers merely to cut 5% or so off the price. If you hike on your own or with people you know well, you can dictate your own pace and there is less danger of personality clashes developing mid-climb.

The standard duration of a climb on the Marangu Route is five days. Many people with repeated experience of Kilimanjaro recommend adding a sixth day to acclimatise at Horombo Hut. It is often said that this will improve the odds of reaching the summit by as much as 20%. Others feel that the extra day makes little difference except that it adds a similar figure to the cost of the climb. One person

KILIMANJARO: RECOMMENDED TOUR OPERATORS

The most popular base for organising a Kilimanjaro climb on the spot is Moshi, but most of the hotels at Marangu arrange reliable climbs, and many tourists who pre-book a climb prefer to work through a company based in Arusha. The following companies are all recommended.

Moshi

Shah Tours Tel: 027 275 2370; fax: 027 275 1449; email: kilimanjaro@eoltz.com. Situated on Mawenzi Road, between the bus station and Clock Tower, this long-standing operator has been arranging mid- to upper-range Kili climbs for as long as I can remember.

Keys Hotel Tel: 027 275 2250/1870; fax: 027 275 0073; email: keys-hotel@africaonline.co.tz; web: www.keys-hotels.com. Excellent and experienced operator based out of one of the town's best hotels, and very reasonably priced.

Zara International Tel: 027 275 4240; fax: 027 275 3105; email: zara@form-net.com. Probably the biggest safari operator in Moshi, this is another long-standing company with an excellent reputation for mid-range Kili climbs and other activities in northern Tanzania.

Akaro Tours Tel: 027 275 2986; mobile: 0744 272124; fax: 027 275 2249; email: safaris@akarotours.com; web: www.akarotours.com. This relatively new company is owned and managed by a dynamic former Kilimanjaro guide with vast hands-on experience of the mountain. Good prices for Kili climbs, as well as a great range of cultural day tours out of Moshi.

Marangu

The family-run Marangu Hotel has been taking people up Kilimanjaro for decades, and they have an impeccable reputation. The standard packages aren't

who owns a climbing company in Arusha kept records for three years and noted only a slightly increased success rate in people who take the extra day, and which he attributes to their extra determination to reach the top after having paid more money. Anecdotally, I've definitely noticed that most travellers who spent six days on the mountain, whether or not they reached the peak, enjoyed the climb far more than those who spent five days. The choice is yours.

Of the less popular routes up Kilimanjaro, the one most frequently used by tourists is the Machame Route, which requires a minimum of six days. Most operators will charge at least 25% more for this route, because it requires far more outlay on their part. The huts along the Machame Route are in such poor condition that tents and camping equipment must be provided, along with a coterie of porters to carry and set up the makeshift camp. The same problem exists on all routes except Marangu, so that any off-the-beaten-track climb will be considerably more costly than the standard one. Should you decide to use a route other than Marangu, it is critical that you work through an operator with experience of that route.

The alternative to using a reputable company is to take your chances with a small operator or private individual who approaches you in the street. These guys will offer climbs for around US$100 cheaper than an established operator, but the risks are greater and because they generally have no office, there is little accountability on their side. Many of these guides *are* genuine and reliable, but it's difficult to be certain who you're dealing with unless you have a recommendation from somebody who has used the same person. A crucial point when comparing this situation to the similar one that surrounds arranging a

the cheapest available, but the standard of service and equipment is very high. The 'hard-way' climbs organised by the Marangu Hotel are probably the cheapest reliable deals you'll find, assuming that you are prepared to self-cater. Also regarded to be reliable are the Capricorn and Kibo Hotels and Babylon Lodge. Contact details for these hotels are found under *Where to stay* in Marangu.

Arusha

Most safari companies in Arusha arrange Kilimanjaro climbs, but will generally work through a ground operator in Moshi or Marangu, which means that they have to charge slightly higher rates. Any of the Arusha-based safari companies listed in that section can be recommended, and short-stay visitors who are already going on safari with one of these companies will probably find that the ease and efficiency of arranging a Kilimanjaro climb through that company outweighs the minor additional expenditure.

There are a few companies that arrange their own Kili climbs out of Arusha. Tropical Tours has a long track record of organising climbs along the lesser-known routes, and is well worth contacting should you want to do that sort of thing. So is the highly specialised Africa Walking Company, which offers eight different trekking itineraries, ranging from five to eight days in duration, for the various routes up Kilimanjaro. Tropical Trails, based at Maasai Camp on the outskirts of Arusha, also has an excellent reputation for Kili climbs. Roy Safaris also arranges its own trekking and climbing on Kilimanjaro, Mount Meru and elsewhere. Contact details of all these companies are on pages 127–9.

safari out of Arusha is that you're not merely talking about losing a day through breakdown or something like that. With Kilimanjaro, you could literally die on the mountain. I've heard several stories of climbers being supplied with inadequate equipment and food, even of travellers being abandoned by their guide mid-climb. The very least you can do, if you make arrangements of this sort, is to verify that your guide is registered; he should have a small wallet-like document to prove this.

The reason why climbing Kilimanjaro is so expensive boils down to the high park fees. In 2001, these were a daily entrance fee of US$25 per person, plus a rescue fee of US$20 per person per climb, plus a hut fee of US$40 per person per night. In addition to this, a daily entrance fee of US$10 is charged for the guide, along with a rescue fee of US$20. In other words, the fixed costs attached to a five-day Marangu climb work out at more than US$300 per person, to which must be added the cost of transport, food and cooking fuel, and the guide's and porters' salaries. It isn't difficult to figure out why any company offering you a deal significantly below US$550 must be cutting corners somewhere.

Hikers are expected to tip their guides and porters. The company you go with can give you an idea of the going rate, but around US$5 per day per guide/porter per climbing party is fair.

Other preparations

Two climatic factors must be considered when preparing to climb Kilimanjaro. The obvious one is the cold. Bring plenty of warm clothes, a windproof jacket, a pair of gloves, a balaclava, a warm sleeping bag and an insulation mat. During the rainy season, a waterproof jacket and trousers will come in useful. A less obvious factor is the sun, which is fierce at high altitudes. Bring sunglasses and sunscreen.

Other essentials are water bottles, solid shoes or preferably boots. Most of these items can be hired in Moshi or at the park gate, or from the company you arrange to climb with. I've heard varying reports about the condition of locally hired items, but standards seem to be far higher than they were only a few years back.

A good medical kit is essential, especially if you are climbing with a cheap company. You'll go through plenty of plasters if you acquire a few blisters (assume that you will), and can also expect to want headache tablets.

You might want to buy biscuits, chocolate, sweets, glucose powder and other energy-rich snacks to take with you up the mountain. No companies supply this sort of thing, and although they are sometimes available at the huts, you'll pay through your nose for them.

Maps and further reading

Trekkers are not permitted on the mountain without a registered guide, and all sensible trekkers will make arrangements through a reliable operator, which means that there is no real need for detailed route descriptions once you're on the mountain. Nevertheless, many trekkers will benefit from the detailed practical advice and overview of route possibilities provided in the highly regarded *Kilimanjaro and Mount Kenya Climbing and Trekking Guide* by Cameron Burns, published in 1998 by The Mountaineers, Seattle. This book is essential reading for anybody planning to do serious rock climbing or to hike away from the main routes.

More concerned with the overall geology and natural history of Kilimanjaro, making it a more useful companion to trekkers on organised hikes, *Kilimanjaro: Africa's Beacon* is one of a series of glossy and informative pocket-sized guides published by the Zimbabwe-based African Publishing Group in association with TANAPA. It is widely available in Arusha and Moshi for around US$8. Its predecessor, the 60-page national park handbook *Kilimanjaro National Park*, is arguably more informative but less attractively put together, and is still widely available in Arusha and Moshi for around US$5.

The Walker's Guide and Map to Kilimanjaro by Mark Savage (African Mountain Guides, 32 Sea Mill Crescent, Worthing, UK) is a popular and reliable map, with useful practical information printed on the back. It is difficult to locate in Arusha, and has to some extent been superseded by Giovanni Tombazzi's more current *New Map of Kilimanjaro National Park*, published in 1998 in conjunction with Hoopoe Adventure Tours and available all over Arusha and Moshi. Current climbing tips are printed on the back of this map, along with a close-scale map of the final ascent to Kibo, and day-by-day contour 'graphs' for the Macheme and Marangu Routes.

Before you leave home – or as a memento when you get back – try to get hold of *Kilimanjaro* by John Reader (Elm Tree Books, London, 1982). Although it is superficially a coffee-table book, it offers a well-written and absorbing overview of the mountain's history and various ecosystems. The photographs are good too.

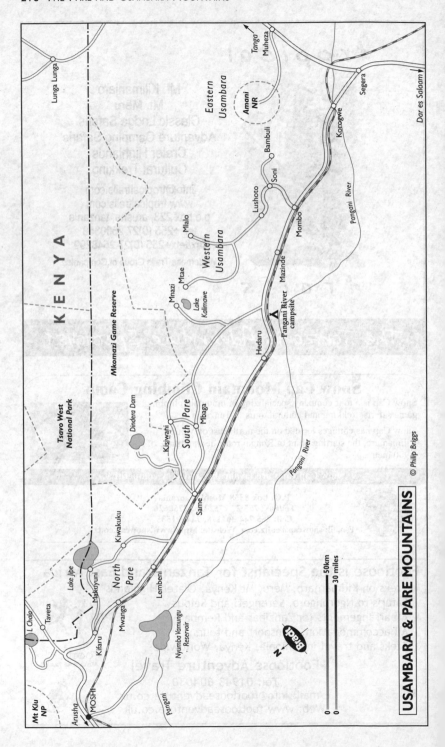

© Philip Briggs

USAMBARA & PARE MOUNTAINS

The Pare and Usambara Mountains

The series of forested mountain ranges running to the east of the B1 between Moshi and Tanga offers some of the best and most accessible hiking, rambling and birdwatching in northern Tanzania. The main ranges, running from north to south, are the North Pare, South Pare, Western Usambara and Eastern Usambara. The two parts of the Usambara effectively form one geological entity, divided into eastern and western components by a deep, difficult to traverse valley cut by the river Lwengera. By contrast, the North and South Pare are discrete ranges, which lie to the north and south of the town of Same and are named after the Pare inhabitants of the region. All four ranges form part of the Eastern Arc formation (see box *An African Galápagos?* pages 222–3).

Pare and Usambara, situated a short distance from the main north–south road connecting Arusha and Moshi to Dar es Salaam, make a logical extension to Tanzania's busy northern circuit. Until recently, however, the only places in the area that were to any extent developed for tourism were the town of Lushoto in the Western Usambara and Amani in the Eastern Usambara. This is gradually changing, following the implementation of several small-scale eco-tourism ventures by the Tanzania Tourist Board (TTB) in collaboration with a Dutch development organisation called SNV. The well-organised and diverse cultural tourism programme at Lushoto remains the most prominent of these, but similar programmes operate in both Pare ranges. These tourist projects are all reasonably accessible to independent travellers, and a number of safari operators in Arusha and particularly Moshi now routinely arrange day or overnight trips there for interested clients.

The Usambara and Pare Mountains will be attractive to budget-conscious travellers not least because they allow for a few relatively inexpensive days' break between the wallet-draining tourist centres of Arusha and Zanzibar. Characterised by lush vegetation, some stunning viewpoints, and a refreshingly breezy high-altitude climate, the mountains also offer a great opportunity to limber up your limbs after a few days spent confined in a safari vehicle or sweating it out in the paralysing humidity of the coast. If you have the time, a few days rambling in the Usambara or Pare would serve as good preparation for the infinitely more demanding hike up Kilimanjaro.

It nevertheless remains the case that only a tiny fraction of tourists to Tanzania come anywhere near the mountains, and that few visitors find time to squeeze in more than one of the four ranges. By far the most popular is the Western Usambara, where Lushoto, the established regional focal point for backpackers, forms an excellent base for a number of day or overnight trips deeper into the range. The Pare Mountains, by contrast, are newly developed, low-key and seldom visited, and will hold more appeal to travellers who want to get right away from the established tourist beat. Ecologically, however, the region's undisputed highlight – indeed one of the most underrated destinations anywhere in East Africa – is Amani Nature Reserve in the Eastern Usambara. Although all four ranges are part of the Eastern Arc formation, Eastern Usambara is the only one where substantial tracts of indigenous forest persist, and it's probably the best and most accessible place to see a fair range of species endemic to, or primarily associated with, this unique habitat.

CLIMATE

The mountains of northeast Tanzania have a similar rainfall pattern to most parts of Tanzania, with the short rains falling in November and December and the long rains coming between March and May. Most places of interest in these mountains lie at an elevation of between 1,500m and 2,000m, so they have a relatively moist and temperate climate, and can be quite chilly at night. By contrast, the lower-lying access towns along the B1 (for instance Korogwe and Same) tend to be hot, dusty and relatively dry.

GETTING AROUND

Regular buses run along the surfaced roads connecting Moshi to Tanga and Dar es Salaam. Express buses covering these routes are generally quite fast, typically covering around 80km per hour with stops. Other buses can be very slow, not least because they stop at every town or village.

Regular minibuses connect Lushoto in the Western Usambara to Tanga via Mombo, Korogwe and Muheza. These are a very quick and efficient means of getting around, and they stop to pick up passengers at all the main towns, but they are generally driven with far greater abandon than buses – if you use these minibuses, don't underestimate the risk of being involved in a fatal accident.

There is public transport of sorts connecting the B1 to all the main centres in the various mountain ranges covered in this chapter. Details of individual routes are given under the appropriate heading later in the chapter.

FURTHER INFORMATION

Most of the places of interest covered in this chapter have been developed for tourism under the TTB and SNV, one result of which is a greater level of organisation than you'll find in other relatively remote parts of Tanzania. There are good tourist information centres in Lushoto, Same, Mbaga and Usangi. Useful pamphlets about the various projects in this area, as well as up-to-date travel information, can be obtained in advance from the helpful TTB office in Arusha. Those with detailed questions or specialised interests can contact the SNV in room 643 of the Serengeti Wing in the Arusha International Cultural Centre; email: tourinfo@habari.co.tz. For further background information, useful websites include www.usambara.com and www.easternarc.com.

BETWEEN MOSHI AND MOMBO

Several worthwhile sites can be visited from the roughly 230km section of the B1 connecting Moshi to Mombo, the junction town for Lushoto in the Western Usambara. In addition to the two Pare ranges, places of interest that are accessible from this road include the little-known Lake Jipe and the remote Mkomazi Game Reserve on the Kenyan border. Basic accommodation is available at most of the small towns en route, but the only vaguely upmarket accommodation in the area is at Same. For overlanders and dedicated campers, the Pangani River Campsite 47km north of Mombo is an excellent place to break up the trip.

Lake Jipe

Shallow, narrow and enclosed by dense beds of tall papyrus, Lake Jipe runs for 10km along a natural sump on the Kenyan border between Kilimanjaro, the main source of its water, and the Mkomazi Game Reserve. It's an atmospheric body of water, with a fabulous setting: the Pare Mountains to the south, Chala crater rising from the flat plain to the east, and – when the clouds clear – Kilimanjaro hulking over the northeast skyline. Lake Jipe is seldom visited, and almost never from the Tanzanian side, but it is reasonably accessible, and there's quite a bit of wildlife around, since part of the northern shore is protected within Kenya's unfenced Tsavo National Park. Gazelle and other antelope are likely to be seen in the arid country approaching the lake, and cheetah and lion are occasionally observed darting across the road. The lake itself is teeming with hippopotami and crocodiles, and the papyrus beds harbour several localised birds, such as lesser jacana, African water rail, pygmy goose and black egret. Elephants regularly come to drink and bathe along the northern shore, especially during the dry season. Look out, too, for the lovely impala lily – this shrub-sized succulent, known for its bright pink and white flowers, is common in the dry acacia plains approaching the lake.

The junction town for Lake Jipe, called Kifaru, straddles the B1 some 40km south of Moshi. At Kifaru, turn to the east along a reasonable dirt road towards Kiwakuku. After about 15km, turn on to a track running to the left, distinguished by a blue signpost reading 'Jipe' and, up ahead, a hill with a prominent bald boulder on top. Follow this track for about 2km, and you'll be in Makayuni on the

A RETREATING LAKE?

Although the papyrus that encloses Lake Jipe gives the lake much of its character, the rapid expansion of the plant over some 50% of the water in the last few decades is possibly symptomatic of a dying lake. Certainly, local fishermen, who now have to reach the open water along shallow canals cut through the crocodile-infested reeds, claim that the fish yield decreases every year along with the amount of open water. The probable explanation for the recent proliferation of papyrus – which can only grow at depths where it can take root in soil – is that the lake has gradually become shallower, due to increased silt levels in the water that flows down from Kilimanjaro. In a chain of cause and effect, the infestation of papyrus on Jipe would thus appear to be a result of the extensive deforestation and a corresponding increase in erosion on Kilimanjaro's lower slopes over the last 50 years.

Whether or not this process will result in the lake drying up entirely is a matter of conjecture, but researchers have expressed serious concerns for its future. The loss of Jipe would be immense, not only to the thousands of villagers for whom the lake has traditionally formed a source of fresh water and protein, but also to the wildlife that is drawn to its water during the dry season. Measures that would contribute to the lake's future – and which are in any case ecologically sound – include an extensive reforestation programme on the Kilimanjaro footslopes, and an attempt to modernise traditional farming methods that tend to cause soil erosion as land pressure intensifies and the earth is worked harder.

lakeshore. In a private vehicle, the drive from Kifaru takes 30–45 minutes, depending on the condition of the road, so it would be feasible to visit Jipe as a day trip from Moshi. The only public transport from Kifaru is the daily bus to Kiwakuku. This generally leaves Kiwakuku at 04.00, passes the Makayuni junction at around 06.30 and arrives in Kifaru at 09.00 to start the return trip at around 14.00. One Moshi-based safari company that regularly arranges day or overnight trips to Lake Jipe is Akaro Tours.

Once at Makayuni, it's straightforward enough to arrange to be poled on to the lake in a local dugout canoe, whether you want to fish, watch birds, or just enjoy the lovely scenery and hope for glimpses of big game on the nearby Kenyan shore. Expect to pay around Tsh3,000 for a short excursion or Tsh10,000 for a full day on the lake. The best time to head on to the lake is in the early morning or late afternoon, when it's not too hot, game is more active, and Kilimanjaro is most likely to be visible. Getting out on to the open water first involves a long pole through shallow papyrus marsh, with brightly coloured kingfishers darting in front of the boat and hippos grunting invisibly in the nearby reeds. This stretch can be quite difficult with two passengers weighing down the dugout, so it's best to take one per person. There is no accommodation near Lake Jipe (along the Tanzanian shore, anyway) but it is permitted to pitch a tent in Makayuni for about Tsh1,000 per head. Aside from fish, no food is available locally, and you'll need to bring all drinking water with you too. Mosquitoes (and occasionally lake flies) are prolific on the shore, so do cover up at dusk. Away from the lake, a few basic guesthouses can be found in Kifaru.

Usangi and the North Pare
In tourist terms, the North Pare is the least developed of the mountain ranges covered in this chapter, despite lying a mere 35km southeast of Kilimanjaro. The high plateau of the range is extensively settled and ecologically degraded: only seven tracts of indigenous forest remain, isolated from each other by cultivated fields and *shambas*. The main base for exploring South Pare, the attractive small town of Usangi is ringed by 11 peaks and particularly lively on the market days of Monday and Thursday. At the cultural tourism office in the secondary school you can organise a number of excursions to nearby points of interest. A good half-day walk is the Mangatu tour, which takes you through the Mbale Forest to a viewpoint facing nearby Kilimanjaro and Lake Jipe on the Kenyan border. The half-day Goma tour visits a set of caves that were dug by the Pare people in the 19th century as a hiding place from slave raiders. This tour can be extended to be a full-day walk to the upper slopes of Mount Kindoroko, which supports the largest relic forest patch in the range – around 900ha – and harbours a variety of monkeys and birds. Notable among these is Abbot's starling, a localised East African highland forest endemic at the most southern extension of its very limited range. Several other day walks are available to visitors, and it is possible to organise overnight hiking trails. All hikes cost around Tsh6,000 per group per day, with an additional village development and administration fee of Tsh3,000 per person per day.

Usangi lies roughly 25km east of the junction town of Mwanga on the B1. It is reached via a good dirt road, covered by a few buses daily. Should you need to overnight in Mwanga, basic and inexpensive rooms are available at the **Izungu and Mountain Guesthouses**. In Usangi, there is no formal accommodation, but you should be able to stay in the three-bedroom resthouse at **Lomwe Secondary School** for Tsh3,000 per person. If the resthouse is full, then the teachers are happy to put up visitors for a similar fee (the headmaster of the school is the co-ordinator of the tourism project). Inexpensive local meals are available by request.

Same

This dusty small town straddling the B1, 105km south of Moshi, is the gateway to Mbaga in the South Pare Mountains, as well as to the Mkomazi Game Reserve on the Kenyan border. The most notable feature of Same, aside from the mountainous backdrop, is a strong Maasai presence – otherwise it's not a terribly interesting place. You're only likely to stop here if you plan on visiting Mbaga or Mkomazi, in which case there is a fairly good chance you'll have to spend the night. The tourist centre at the Sasa Kazi Hotel is the best place to ask for current advice about lifts to Mbaga, or about anything else.

The drive from Moshi to Same, along a good surfaced road, shouldn't take longer than 90 minutes in a private vehicle. Any public transport heading from Moshi to places further south can drop you off at Same. The smartest accommodation is at the **Elephant Motel**, which lies about 1km from the town centre along the B1 towards Dar es Salaam, and offers adequate self-contained rooms with netting and hot running water for Tsh7,000 (single with large double bed) or Tsh10,000 double. In the town centre, 100m from the bus station, the **Kambeni Guesthouse** is an excellent local lodging, with standard rooms for Tsh2,000/2,500 and self-contained doubles for Tsh4,000. Also recommended in this range are the **Tumaine Guesthouse** and **Amani Lutheran Centre**. The **Sasa Kazi Hotel** doesn't have rooms but it serves reasonable local meals.

Mbaga and the South Pare

The extensive mountains of the South Pare, separated from the Western Usambara by the 20km Mkomazi River Valley, offer a rich combination of cultural sites and natural attractions, most of which have only recently opened up to visitors following the implementation of a cultural tourism programme in 1998. This project operates out of the Hilltop Tona Lodge in the small town of **Mbaga**, an attractively wooded semi-urban sprawl that follows the main road along the northern slopes of the range. The set-up here is rather low-key by comparison to the Usambara, with a greater emphasis on cultural sightseeing, and we would recommend it to travellers who want to get right away from the beaten tourist track.

Getting there and away

One bus and a couple of *matatus* daily run along the 35km road connecting Same to Mbaga. Normally, all transport out of Mbaga leaves before 07.00, and begins the return trip from Same at around 11.00. Depending on demand, one of these

---

THE LEGACY OF JAKOB DANNHOLZ

In 1902, Mbaga became the site of one of the earliest Lutheran missions in the interior of what was then German East Africa, founded by Jakob Dannholz. The original church built by Dannholz is still in use, an oddly Bavarian apparition in these remote African hills, as is the stone house in which he lived. A more enduring legacy of the man's work, however, is his seminal and sympathetic treatise documenting Pare oral traditions that might otherwise have been forgotten. Written between 1912 and 1918, Dannholz's work was finally translated into English and published in 1989 under the name *Lute: The Curse and the Blessing*. It provides much insight into the cultural sites around Mbaga and can be bought cheaply at most bookshops in Same or Moshi.

AN AFRICAN GALÁPAGOS?

The phrase Eastern Arc, though in wide circulation today, was first coined in the mid-1980s, when Dr Jon Lovett sought a term to encompass a string of 13 ancient East African mountain ranges which, despite being physically isolated from each other, share a very similar geomorphology and ecology. Aside from the Taita Hills in southern Kenya, the crystalline ranges of the Eastern Arc all lie within eastern Tanzania, where – as their name implies – they form a rough crescent running from the Pare Mountains in the north to the Udzungwa and Mahenge ranges in the south. The oldest mountains in East Africa, the Eastern Arc ranges formed at least 100 million years ago, along a fault in the earth's crust which lay to the east of the far more geologically recent Rift Valley and associated modern landmarks such as Mounts Kilimanjaro, Meru and Kenya.

The ecological significance of the Eastern Arc mountains lies in their extensive rainforests, which stretch back more than 30 million years to a time when Africa was part of a much larger landmass known as Gondwanaland. During the drier and colder climatic conditions that have periodically characterised the globe, causing most African rainforests to retreat, the forests of the Eastern Arc have flourished thanks to a continuous westerly wind that blows in moisture from the Indian Ocean. It was during one such phase, about ten million years ago, that the Eastern Arc forests became isolated from the lowland rainforests of western and central Africa. More recently, probably, each of the individual forested ranges of the Eastern Arc became a discrete geographical entity, transforming the Eastern Arc into an archipelago of forested islands jutting out from an ocean of low-lying savannah. Following a pattern characteristic of true islands, the isolated, ancient forests of the Eastern Arc became a veritable evolutionary hotspot.

The Eastern Arc mountains host an assemblage of endemic taxa – unique races, species and genera – that has few peers in Africa or anywhere on the planet. A few statistics are perhaps required to convey something of the biodiversity of these mountains. In the two Usambara ranges alone, more than 2,850 plant species have been identified, a list that includes 680 types of tree, a greater tally than that of North America and Europe combined. At least 16 plant genera and 75 vertebrate species – including ten birds and ten mammals – are endemic to the forests of the Eastern Arc. The wealth of invertebrate life, and degree of diversity between the different ranges, can be gauged by the fact that 265 described invertebrate species are thus far known from just one of the 13 different ranges – an average of 20 endemics per range. Little wonder, then, that the Eastern Arc mountains have recently been classified as one of the world's 20 most important biodiversity hotspots, and is frequently referred to as the 'Galápagos of Africa'.

The Eastern Arc endemics fall into two broad and not always distinguishable categories: old endemics that often show little divergence from relict evolutionary lineages, and new endemics representing recently evolved lineages. A clear example of a 'living fossil' falling into the former category is the giant elephant shrew of the suborder Rhynchocyonidae, represented by three similar species almost identical in structure to more widespread 20-million-year-old fossils of their ancestors. In many cases, these older, more stable endemics are affiliated to extant West African species from which they have become isolated – among the larger mammals, Abbot's duiker and the two endemic monkeys of Udzungwa are cases in point. The origins of new endemics are more variable. Some, such as the African violets, probably evolved from an ancestral stock blown across the ocean from Madagascar in a freak cyclone. Others, including many of the birds and flying insects, are essentially locally adapted variants on similar species found in neighbouring savannahs or in other forests in East Africa. The origin of several other Eastern Arc endemics is open to conjecture: four of the endemic birds show sufficient affiliations to Asian species to suggest they may have arrived there at a time when moister coastal vegetation formed a passage around the Arabian peninsula.

The forests of the Eastern Arc mountains vary greatly in their extent and biodiversity, and in the degree to which they have been studied and accorded official protection. W D Newmark's recent assessment of the forests (*Journal of East African Natural History*, 1998) indicates that the vast Udzungwa range retains almost 2,000km² of natural forest, of which 20% has a closed canopy. The forest cover on Kenya's Taita Hills, by contrast, has been reduced to a mere 6km². Newmark's tentative figures suggest that, after Udzungwa, the most heavily forested ranges are as follows: Nguru (647km² of natural forest), Uluguru (528km²), Rubeho (499km²), East Usambara (413km²), South Pare (333km²) and Western Usambara (328km²). The most significant forests in terms of biodiversity – bearing in mind that such things are difficult to quantify – are generally regarded to be the Udzungwa, East Usambara and Uluguru. And, while the forests of Usambara have been studied since early colonial times, and the Udzungwa has yielded several previously undescribed bird species and two new monkey taxa in recent years, other ranges such as the Nguru and Rubeho remain relatively unexplored in scientific terms.

The Eastern Arc forests are of great interest to birdwatchers as the core of the so-called Tanzania-Malawi Mountains Endemic Bird Area (EBA). Although this EBA includes roughly 30 forest pockets scattered across Malawi, Mozambique and Kenya, these outlying forests cover a combined area of about 500 km², as compared to 7,200km² of qualifying forest in Tanzania. So it is that of 37 described range-restricted bird species endemic to this EBA, all but five occur in Tanzania, and roughly half are confined to the country. In terms of avian diversity, the Udzungwa Mountains are by far the most significant range in the EBA, with 23 regional endemics present, including several species found nowhere else or shared only with the inaccessible Rubeho Mountains. For first time visitors, however, Amani Nature Reserve in the Eastern Usambara probably has the edge over Udzungwa in terms of ease of access to prime birding areas and affordable facilities.

The individual distribution patterns of several range-restricted bird species of the Tanzania-Malawi Mountains EBA provide clear evidence of the mountains' pseudo-island ecology, with several species widespread on one particular range but absent from other apparently suitable ones. The Usambara akalat, for instance, is confined to the Western Usambara, while Loveridge's sunbird and the Uluguru bush-shrike are unique to the Uluguru Mountains. The most remarkable distribution pattern, however, is that of the long-billed tailorbird or apalis, a poorly known forest fringe species confined to two ranges situated an incredible 2,000km apart – the Eastern Usambara in northern Tanzania and Mount Namuli in central Mozambique. Stranger still is the case of the Udzungwa partridge: this evolutionary relict, discovered as recently as 1991 and known only from the Udzungwa and Rubeho Mountains, evidently has stronger genetic affiliations to the Asian hill partridges than to any other African

continued overleaf

AN AFRICAN GALÁPAGOS? continued

bird! It would appear, too, that the Eastern Arc mountains have yet to yield up all their ornithological secrets: a recent expedition to the relatively poorly known Rubeho Mountains discovered a sunbird and an akalat that await formal description, but are presumably new to science and endemic to this one range.

The Eastern Arc mountains have suffered extensive forest loss and fragmentation in the past century, primarily due to unprecedented land-use pressure – the population of the Western Usambara, for instance, has increased twenty-fold over the last hundred years. Of the 12 Eastern Arc ranges within Tanzania, Newmark estimates that just one – the inaccessible Rubeho massif – has retained more than half of its original forest cover, while five have lost between 75% and 90% of their forest in the last two centuries. Fortunately, none of Tanzania's Eastern Arc forests has yet approached the crisis point reached in Kenya's Taita Hills, where a mere 2% of the original forest remains.

All the same, given that many Eastern Arc species are highly localised, and that animal movement between forest patches is inhibited by increased fragmentation, some researchers claim that 30% of species indigenous to the mountains have either become extinct in the last century, or else face some threat of extinction. True, the salvation of a few rare earthworm taxa might be dismissed as bunny-hugging esoterica, but the ecological preservation of every one of the Eastern Arc mountains – and their forests – as a crucial water catchment area is an issue of direct humanistic concern. Most of the extant Eastern Arc forests are now protected as forest reserves. The proclamation of a large part of the Udzungwa Mountains as a national park in 1992 is a further step in the right direction. Even more encouraging is the more recent creation of Amani Nature Reserve as part of a broader effort to introduce sustainable conservation and eco-tourism with the involvement of local communities in the Eastern Usambara (details of this project are available online at www.usambara.com).

A useful resource for readers interested in the mountains and their conservation is the website www.easternarc.com. Anybody wishing to come to grips with the fascinating phenomenon of 'island' ecology in the Eastern Arc mountains (and elsewhere on the African mainland) is pointed to Jonathon Kingdon's superb and erudite book entitled *Island Africa*.

vehicles may do a second run backwards and forwards in the afternoon, but this is the exception rather than the rule. There isn't much private transport between Same and Mbaga, so trying to hitch is probably a waste of time. The owner of the Sasa Kazi Hotel in Same doubles as the tourist information officer and he will be able to tell you if he knows of any other vehicles heading up to Mbaga. Realistically, you will probably have to spend the night in Same if you arrive there after 11.00.

With private transport, the direct drive to Mbaga is reasonably straightforward, depending on the current condition of the road. It is also possible to reach Mbaga via a road that skirts the boundary of Mkomazi Game Reserve before passing through the small town of Kisiwani, an old slave trading centre which has retained a distinctly coastal feel, and then ascending the mountains via a spectacular forest-fringed pass. It used to be possible to see a bit of game along this road, but local sources say that they haven't seen much in the last couple of years. The route via Kisiwani covers roughly the same distance as the main road to Mbaga, but it is generally in poorer condition and currently requires a good 4WD.

An obscure onward option from Mbaga takes you to Gonja, which lies about 15km further along the road and is the terminal for buses coming from Same. The Bombo Hospital in Gonja is the largest in the area, and cheap rooms are available at the Vuje Guesthouse.

Where to stay and eat
Hilltop Tona Lodge Tel: 022 260 0158. This hotel, which opened in 1998 as part of the South Pare Tourism Programme, consists of several self-contained cottages straddling the main road through the town, in a wonderful jungle setting with great views over the Mkomazi Plains. There is a natural swimming pool in the river below the lodge. Furnished accommodation starts at around Tsh3,000 per person depending on the size and quality of the room, or you can camp for around Tsh1,000. The restaurant serves meals in the Tsh1,000–3,000 bracket. Beer, sodas and mineral water are available.

In addition, cleared campsites are to be found in several places in the hills, with the site near Ranzi Dam particularly recommended. Camping costs Tsh1,000; further details can be obtained through the Hilltop Tona Lodge.

What to see and do
A number of activities can be arranged out of Mbaga. One interesting half-day excursion is the walk along the main road towards **Gonja** to the house of a highly respected traditional healer (who also happens to be a Seventh Day Adventist, so don't bother visiting on Saturdays). Another takes you to the **Mghimbi Caves**, where the Pare hid from slave raiders in the 1860s, and then to **Malameni Rock**, where thousands of children were sacrificed to appease evil spirits until the practice was outlawed in the 1930s. For natural history enthusiasts, the day walk to **Ronzi Dam** through patches of rainforest and montane moorland is recommended, as is the walk to the legendary '**Red Reservoir**'.

Longer hikes include a three-day trip through the 150km² **Chome Forest Reserve** on the upper slopes of Mount Shengena, at 2,462m the highest point in the range. Chome, the largest and most properly studied of a dozen existing or proposed forest reserves in South Pare, harbours several types of monkey and a wide range of forest birds. The South Pare white-eye *zosterops winifridae*, a grey-bellied form regarded by some authorities as a full species and listed as vulnerable by the IUCN, is endemic to Chome and other forests on South Pare. Hikers must pay a guide fee of Tsh4,000 per group (full day) or Tsh2,500 per group (half day) as well as a village development fee of Tsh3,000 per person per walk. It is possible to explore the roads around the village without a guide, in which case no fees are payable.

Another option is a performance of traditional dancing in the evening, which costs around Tsh6,000 per group.

Mkomazi Game Reserve
Mkomazi Game Reserve is the southern extension of Kenya's vast Tsavo National Park, covering an area of 3,701km² to the east of Kilimanjaro and immediately north of the Pare Mountains. The reserve is practically undeveloped for tourism, and it has been subject to considerable pressure over the last 20 years as the human population around its peripheries has grown in number. Together with Tsavo,

Mkomazi forms part of one of East Africa's most important savannah ecosystems, characterised by the semi-arid climatic conditions of the Sahel arc.

In 1992, the Tanzanian government invited the Royal Geographical Society to undertake a detailed ecological study of Mkomazi. Although mammal populations are low, it was determined that most large mammal species present in Tsavo are either resident in Mkomazi or regularly migrate there from Kenya, including lion, cheetah, elephant, giraffe, buffalo, zebra, impala and Tanzania's most significant gerenuk population. African hunting dogs were recently re-introduced into Mkomazi, as was a herd of black rhinos from South Africa. The reserve is listed as an Important Bird Area, with more than 400 species recorded, several of which are northern dry-country endemics newly added to the Tanzania list by the RGS – for instance three-streaked tchagra, Shelley's starling, Somali long-billed crombec, yellow-vented eremomela and the extremely localised Friedmann's lark.

Mkomazi doesn't offer game viewing to compare with other reserves in northern Tanzania, and it is certainly not a conventional safari destination. However, this is compensated for by the wild scenery and near certainty of not seeing another tourist. So far as facilities go, there is a two-bedroom *banda* available at Ibaya Camp on a first-come, first-served basis. Otherwise, there is a basic campsite (little more than cleared areas) about 2km from Zange Gate and another about 20km from Zange overlooking Dindera Dam, a good place to see large mammals. The reserve is best avoided in the rainy season, due to the poor roads, and all visitors should be self-sufficient in water, food and fuel.

Because Mkomazi is not a national park, walking is permitted. The northeast of the reserve, near Zange Gate, is very hilly (tough walking but great scenery) and there is a very real chance of encountering large game animals such as lions and buffaloes on foot. The best way to go about organising a walking trip into Mkomazi would be to walk or hitch the 5km from Same to Zange Gate, where you can make arrangements with the warden to hire an armed ranger/guide. To stand a chance of seeing a fair range of large mammals, you would need to spend a couple of days walking in the reserve, so you'd need camping gear and adequate provisions. The owner of the Sasa Kazi Hotel in Same can organise car hire into the reserve.

Entrance to Mkomazi costs US$20 per person per 24-hour period.

Pangani River Campsite

This attractive new South African-owned campsite lies in the shadow of the South Pare Mountains, on the east bank of a pretty palm-lined stretch of the Pangani River. Blue and vervet monkeys are frequently to be seen in the palms, while hippos and crocs are resident in the river, and the area supports an interesting variety of birds. Facilities include a kitchen and hot showers, and beers and soft drinks are served. The bar and restaurant should be up and running by late 2002, and lightweight canoes should also be available by that time. The campsite lies 1.3km from the main road; the turn-off is clearly signposted 18km south of Hedaru and 47km north of Mombo. Ring the owner on 0744 483761 for further details.

Mombo

The scruffy little town of Mombo on the Moshi–Dar es Salaam road is the springboard for trips into the Western Usambara. It's an unremarkable place: one traveller comments that 'the best thing about Mombo is the potato samosas you can buy from the street vendors – they really are delicious' (frankly, the samosas we ate here recently were almost inedible for grease!). Fortunately, you're unlikely to need to linger in Mombo. Any bus heading along the B1 can drop you at the main junction, from where a steady stream of minibuses runs up to Lushoto via Soni. If you do need to overnight, the **Midway Inn** and adjacent **Sandali Inn** both have reasonable doubles with net and fan for around Tsh2,500. The **Midway Express Restaurant**, next to the Midway Inn on the junction of the Lushoto Road, serves acceptable meals for a similar price.

LUSHOTO AND THE WESTERN USAMBARA

Lushoto is the principal town and administration centre of the Western Usambara, the largest, most densely populated and most cultivated of the mountain ranges in northeast Tanzania. Although lacking the ecological wealth of its eastern counterpart, the mountains around Lushoto form superb walking country, riddled with small footpaths and winding roads, and open to gentle exploration as well as longer overnight hikes. The area is scenically varied, with steep-sided valleys covered in euphorbia, exotic plantations, relic patches of indigenous forest, and cultivated Shambaa homesteads. Most memorable, perhaps, are the stirring views from several points at the edge of Usambara escarpment to the low-lying plains below.

Situated at an elevation of approximately 1,400m, Lushoto was a town of some note in the German colonial era, and a slightly anachronistic aura still hangs over it today. Many buildings on the main street date to the early part of the 20th century, when Lushoto – known as Wilhelmstal at the time – provided weekend relief for German settlers farming the dry, dusty Maasai Steppe below, and was earmarked as the centre of a failed coffee scheme. And yet where the main street through Lushoto recalls an Alpine village, the side roads lined with mud-and-thatch homesteads are unambiguously African in architecture and spirit. So, too, is the vibrant market – busiest on the main market days of Sunday and Thursday – where colourfully dressed Shambaa women sell fresh fruit grown in the surrounding mountains and other agricultural ware. The vegetation around Lushoto reflects these contradictions: papaya trees subvert neat rows of exotic pines and eucalyptus, which in turn are interspersed by patches of lush indigenous forest alive with the raucous squawking of silvery-cheeked hornbill.

In recent years, Lushoto has developed into a popular and rewarding base for travellers with limited time and a desire to see something of Africa outside of the beach resorts and safari circuits. Its convenient location, less than an hour's drive from the main drag between Moshi and Dar es Salaam along a good surfaced road, is undoubtedly a factor in its popularity. Another is the efforts of the well-organised Usambara Mountains Tourism Project (UMTP), which runs the tourist office and arranges a good variety of walks and cultural excursions (described later in this section), and the allied Friends of the Usambara Society, responsible for publishing an excellent glossy annual booklet *Usambara View*. If you can fit Lushoto into your itinerary, it's well worth the minor diversion from the B1.

Getting there and away

Lushoto is connected to Mombo on the B1 by a surfaced 33km road that offers splendid views in all directions. In a private vehicle, the drive from Moshi normally takes about three hours and that from Tanga about two hours, with the actual ascent from Mombo taking 45 minutes or so. Coming from Tanga on public transport, the best way to get to Lushoto is to hop on one of the regular minibuses that connect the two towns via Muheza, Korogwe and Mombo, a three-hour trip. Coming from Arusha, Moshi or Dar es Salaam, it's better to take a bus heading through Mombo and asked to be dropped there to pick up one of the regular minibuses through to Lushoto.

Where to stay
Moderate
Lawns Hotel Tel: 027 264 0005; fax: 027 264 2311; email: lawns@habari.co.tz. The
venerable Lawns Hotel possesses a certain faded charm (emphasis on the 'faded') and
although it doesn't compare in quality to the better lodges at Migambo and Soni, it's a
pleasant and atmospheric set-up, situated in large gardens on a low hill overlooking the
town centre. Comfortable self-contained rooms cost Tsh20,000/25,000 single/double while
rooms using communal shower cost Tsh12,000/16,000. Camping is permitted at Tsh3,000
per person. The restaurant, by default the smartest in town, serves decent three-course
meals for Tsh5,500. Mountain bike hire and horseback excursions can be arranged through
reception, and other facilities include a satellite television, table tennis and a library.
Saint Eugene Montessori Training Centre Tel: 027 264 0055; fax: 027 264 0267. Situated
about 2km from Lushoto town centre at Ubiri, on the road towards Soni, this modern
training centre is run by the Usambara Sisters and is known locally for the excellent jam,
cheese and banana wine it produces. Within the landscaped grounds stands a comfortable and
well-maintained hostel with 14 self-contained double rooms and a good restaurant.
Accommodation costs Tsh16,000/24,000 single/double B&B, and other meals cost Tsh2,500.

Superior accommodation is available in the Migambo Forest and near Soni, both
of which lie 30 minutes or so by road from Lushoto and are described under the
heading *Around the Western Usambara*.

Budget
Usambara Lodge This new lodge, set on the first floor of an old building opposite the
park, is exceptional value at Tsh5,000 for a clean, airy self-contained double. Facilities
include a common lounge and balcony overlooking central Lushoto. The absence of a bar or
restaurant means it's very quiet. Only four rooms are available, and there's no telephone or
other contact at the time of writing, but definitely my first choice in this range if it's not full.
White House Annex Tel: 027 264 0177; email: whitehouse@raha.com. Also highly
recommended is this well-run and friendly local hotel, situated less than 5 minutes' walk
from the bus station. The slightly cramped self-contained double rooms aren't anything
special at Tsh5,000, but the more spacious rooms using the common hot shower are good
value at Tsh3,000/4,000 single/double. Best of all are the meals – a heaped plate of meat,
roast potatoes and vegetables for Tsh1,000 per head. Internet access costs Tsh1,500 per
hour.
Green Valley Annex This is another reasonably priced and clean budget hotel, situated a
short walk from the bus station on the same road as the White House Annex. Clean rooms
with a large double bed and netting cost Tsh3,000 (common hot shower) or Tsh5,000 self-
contained with hot shower.
Lushoto Sun Hotel Tel: 027 264 0083. This is an established travellers' favourite, with a
usefully central location and welcoming atmosphere. The large self-contained double
rooms with hot showers at Tsh10,000 feel seriously overpriced when you look at the
competition. Decent local food is available at around Tsh1,500 per portion.
New Friend's Corner Hotel A few doors down from the Usambara Lodge, this
established budget hotel is looking decidedly past its prime nowadays. Small tatty singles
using a common shower cost Tsh3,000, while larger but equally scruffy self-contained
doubles with hot shower cost Tsh6,000. You could do worse if all the other options listed
are full, but otherwise difficult to recommend.

Shoestring
Kilimani Guesthouse This formerly popular backpackers' haunt has suffered the fate of
many a budget hotel garlanded by ubiquitous guidebook praises – standards drop, prices

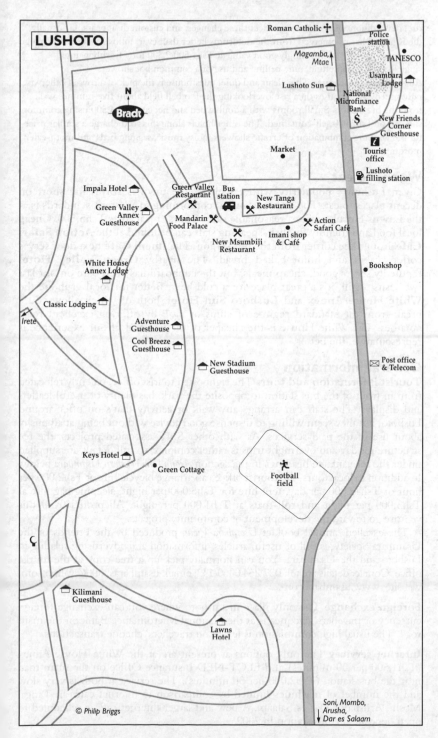

LUSHOTO

Roman Catholic ✝

Police station

Magamba,
Mtae ↑

TANESCO

Lushoto Sun

Usambara Lodge

National Microfinance Bank $

New Friends Corner Guesthouse

Bradt

N

Market

Tourist office

Lushoto filling station

Impala Hotel

Green Valley Restaurant

Bus station

New Tanga Restaurant

Green Valley Annex Guesthouse

Mandarin Food Palace

Action Safari Café

New Msumbiji Restaurant

Imani shop & Café

White Horse Annex Lodge

Bookshop

Classic Lodging

Irete

Adventure Guesthouse

Cool Breeze Guesthouse

New Stadium Guesthouse

Post office & Telecom

Keys Hotel

Green Cottage

Football field

Kilimani Guesthouse

Lawns Hotel

© Philip Briggs

Soni, Mombo,
Arusha,
↓ *Dar es Salaam*

rise, new editions of guidebooks reflect these changes, and custom disappears. Unusually, the Kilimani has re-emerged from the doldrums better than ever, following a recent change of ownership – it's outstandingly good value at Tsh1,500/2,500 for a freshly painted single/double with netting, pine ceiling and use of a common hot shower.

Adventure Guesthouse This clean and quiet guesthouse is the pick of a row of otherwise rather seedy guesthouses on a rise overlooking the football field about five minutes walk from the bus station. Small rooms with a double bed and net cost Tsh1,500 using common shower, or Tsh2,000 self-contained. The other hotels along this road charge a similar price for the winning combination of erratic showers, noisy music, sagging beds and moth-eaten mosquito nets.

Where to eat
Given Lushoto's popularity with travellers, the town is surprising short on decent places to eat. The only restaurant conforming to Western standards is at the **Lawns Hotel**, where a reasonable three-course meal costs Tsh5,500. Cheap local food and friendly English-speaking staff can be found at the **Action Safari Café** around the corner from the bus station. The **Imani Café** next door serves coffee, cakes and home-baked bread. The nearby **Green Valley Hotel** reputedly serves good, cheap meals, but the cupboard has been bare on our last two visits – still, it's a great place for a cold beer. Better for local grub are the **White House Annex** and **Lushoto Sun Hotel**, both of which allow you a break from the standard regime of chips or *ugali* by offering excellent roast potatoes. The White House is the cheaper of the two and, if our experience is representative, the better.

General information
Tourist information and tours The signposted tourist office, recently relocated from in front of the bus station to opposite the park, has plenty of useful leaflets and displays. The staff can arrange any walk or activity that's on offer around Lushoto, but they seem willing to dispense good advice without being at all pushy about use of the paid services. As with other SNV-associated projects, the fee structure for day and overnight trips is rather complex, so full details are supplied under the relevant site headings in the section *Around the Western Usambara* below. In addition to local tours, the tourist office can arrange bicycle hire at Tsh2,000 per hour or Tsh12,000 per day, tent hire for Tsh5,000 per night, sleeping bag hire at Tsh3,000 per night and roll-mats at Tsh1,000 per night. All profits from this venture go toward the development of community projects.

The excellent annual booklet *Usambara View*, produced by the Friends of the Usambara Society, is full of useful articles, information and advertising relating to Lushoto and the Usambara. You can normally pick up a free copy at the tourist office. Contact details are tel: 027 264 0060/132; email: usambaras2000@yahoo.com; website: www.usambara.com.

Foreign exchange The only place in Lushoto where you can exchange foreign currency or travellers' cheques is at the National Microfinance Bank on the main road. The usual high commission is levied on travellers' cheque transactions.

Internet services The only options at present are at the White House Annex (Tsh1,500 per 30 minutes) and ELCT-NED Insurance Office on the main road near the bus station (Tsh2,000 per 30 minutes). The service at both is very slow and the number of machines limited by comparison to internet cafés in Tanga, Moshi, Arusha or Dar es Salaam. A new and larger internet café is scheduled to open opposite the bus station in 2002.

Around the Western Usambara

A number of different day and overnight trips can be undertaken using Lushoto as a base. Popular goals within day tripping distance by foot or public transport include the Soni Falls on the Mombo Road, the spectacular Irente Viewpoint and the indigenous Migambo Forest. Worthwhile destinations further afield include the small towns of Bambuli, Mtae and Mlalo. All these places can be visited independently or with a guide provided by the tourist office in Lushoto.

Irente and Yoghoi Viewpoints

The Irente Viewpoint, which lies about 7km from Lushoto by road, is probably the most popular goal for day trips in the Usambara. The viewpoint lies at the edge of the Usambara massif, and offers a fantastic, vast view across the B1 and small lowland town of Mazinde across the Maasai Steppe 1,000m below. Look out, too, for the Egyptian vultures that apparently nest on the cliffs below the viewpoint. A second viewpoint at Yoghoi, about 1km further south, offers a very similar view encompassing the viewpoint at Irente. Either of the two viewpoints can be visited as a round trip from Lushoto, or you can loop between the two on foot.

The road to Irente and Yoghoi leads eastward out of Lushoto. You can join it in a few places, but most convenient is probably the road forking east from between the White House Annex and New Milimani Guesthouse. Once you're on this road, there's no serious likelihood of getting lost, provided you keep asking directions (ask for Irente farm), and the scenery is lovely. About 3km out of Lushoto, you pass through the village of Yoghoi and a large junction. Here, you need to keep going straight if you are headed to Irente, but must turn left along a signposted side road to reach Yoghoi Viewpoint. By road, it's 4km from this junction to either of the viewpoints. You cannot drive between the two viewpoints directly, but you can walk between them along a footpath.

Although it's perfectly possible to do this walk alone, most travellers arrange an official guide through the tourist office, which works out at Tsh6,000 per party plus Tsh2,000 per person. You're advised against taking an unofficial guide, as we've heard of people who did this being robbed on the way. Expect the round trip to take around three hours.

If you want to stay at Irente overnight, the recently opened **Irente View Campsite** is an excellent set-up, perched right on the cliff and run by a friendly Tanzanian. Camping costs Tsh2,500 per person (if you don't have camping gear, you can use one of the fixed tents or *bandas*). Facilities include a hot shower and a bar serving beers and sodas. Meals and drinks are available and cheap, and all food is made from produce bought from local farmers. The helpful caretaker offers guided walks to the different sights and mountains, as well as tours with mountain bikes. There is also a campsite – unguarded, lacking any facilities, and presumably free – marked out at Yoghoi Viewpoint. The shop at Irente farm sells fresh farm produce.

Soni Falls

Straddling the surfaced road that connects Mombo to Lushoto, the small town of Soni is of interest primarily for the attractive but less than spectacular Soni Falls. This waterfall is visible from the main road to Lushoto, but to see it properly you need to stop in the town, from where a short, steep path leads to the rocky base. The drive between Lushoto and Soni takes no more than 30 minutes in either direction, using one of the regular minibuses that run back and forth to Mombo. If you visit Soni as a day trip, there is no reason to take a guide along. The tourist office in Lushoto organises a half day tour out of Soni, taking in Kwa Mongo peak, known for its colourful butterflies, as well as the 300-year-old grave of the

THE LION KING OF SHAMBAAI

The Shambaa people of West Usambara are Bantu-speaking agriculturalists whose modern population totals around 200,000. The origin of the Shambaa is difficult to ascertain. Some clans claim that they have always lived in the mountains, others that they moved there during times of drought, or in response to the 18th-century Maasai invasion of the plains. Quite possibly, these divergent accounts are an accurate reflection of divergent clan histories, since the ancestral Shambaa had a reputation for welcoming refugees, and the loosely structured political system that characterised the region until about 300 years ago would have made it relatively easy for newcomers to be assimilated peacefully. The notion that Shambaa identity was initially forged by physical proximity rather than cultural affiliations or centralised leadership is reinforced when one realises the root of their name is Shambaai ('where the banana trees thrive'), a geographical term describing the moister reaches of the mountains above an altitude of 1,000m.

Prior to the 18th century, the social structure of Shambaai was similar to the *ntemi* chieftaincies of western Tanzania. Each clan lived in a clearly defined territory, and established its own community and petty leadership of elders. A regional council of elders had the authority to settle disputes between different clans, and to approve marriages that would help cement inter-clan unity. According to tradition, the move towards centralised power – probably a response to the threat posed by the Maasai – was led by an outsider called Mbegha, the first *Simba Mwene* (Lion King) of Shambaai. That Mbegha is a genuine historical figure is not in doubt, and the oral traditions of neighbouring tribes support the local tradition that he moved to the mountains from the plains below and became king after resolving a major crisis in Shambaai. Quite how Mbegha achieved his leonine coup is open to question. An implausible local tradition has it that, as a hunter of renown, Mbegha was called upon by a delegation of elders to rid the mountains of the bushpigs that were destroying all their crops, and was so effective in his campaign that he was appointed ruler of all Shambaai.

Mbegha forged regional unity by taking a wife from each major clan and placing their firstborn son in charge of that clan. The Shambaa invested Mbegha and the dynasty of Lion Kings that succeeded him with supernatural powers, believing among other things that they were able to control the elements. The dynasty consolidated its power under the rule of Mbegha's grandson Kinyashi, who adopted a militaristic policy with the aim of forging the most important state between the coast and the great lake region. This ambition was realised by Kinyashi's son and successor, Kimweri, routinely cited as the greatest Kilindi leader. Towards the end of his reign, Kimweri was held in sufficient esteem outside his kingdom that, in 1857, Richard Burton decided to undertake the trek inland from Pangani specifically to visit the Shambaa capital of Fuga (close to the modern settlement of Bambuli, and now more often called Vuga). Burton's account of the visit, published in Volume 83 of Blackwell's *Edinburgh Magazine* in 1858, is probably the most revealing description of pre-colonial Shambaai ever printed. Some edited extracts follow:

'Kimweri half rose from his cot as we entered, and motioned us to sit upon dwarf stools before him. He was an old, old man, emaciated by sickness. His head was shaved, his face beardless, and wrinkled like grandam's; his eyes were red, his jaws disfurnished, and his hands and feet were stained with leprous spots. The royal dress was a Surat cap, much the worse for wear, and a loinwrap as tattered. He was covered with a double cotton cloth, and he rested upon a Persian rug, apparently coeval with himself. The hut appeared that of a simple cultivator, but it was redolent of dignitaries, some fanning the Sultan, others chatting, and all holding long-stemmed pipes with small ebony bowls.

'Kimweri, I was told, is the fourth of a dynasty... originally from Nguru, a hilly region south of the river... Kimweri, in youth a warrior of fame, ranked in the triumvirate of mountain kings above Bana Rongua of Chagga, and Bana Kizunga of the Wakuafy. In age he has lost ground [and] asserts kinghood but in one point: he has 300 wives, each surrounded by slaves, and portioned with a hut and a plantation. His little family amounts to between 80 and 90 sons, some of whom have Islamised, whilst their sire remains a 'pragmatical pagan'. The Lion [King]'s person is sacred; even a runaway slave saves life by touching royalty. Presently [Kimweri] will die, be wrapped up in matting, and placed sitting-wise under his deserted hut, a stick denoting the spot. Dogs will be slaughtered for the funeral-feast, and [Kimweri's son] Muigni Khatib will rule in his stead, and put to death all who dare, during the two months of mourning, to travel upon the king's highway.

'Kimweri rules ... by selling his subjects – men, women, and children, young and old, gentle and simple, individually, or, when need lays down the law, by families and by villages.... Confiscation and sale are indigenous and frequent. None hold property without this despot's permission... In a land where beads are small change, and sheeting and 'domestics' form the higher specie, revenue is thus collected. Cattle-breeders offer the first fruits of flocks and herds; elephant-hunters every second tusk; and traders a portion of their merchandise. Cultivators are rated annually at ten measures of grain... The lion's share is reserved for the royal family; the crumbs are distributed to the councillors and [royal bodyguards].

'Fuga, a heap of some 3,000 souls, [is] defenceless, and composed of ... circular abodes [made with] frameworks of concentric wattles, wrapped with plantain-leaves ... fastened to little uprights, and plastered internally with mud ... The [people] ... file their teeth to points, and brand a circular beauty-spot in the mid-forehead; their heads are shaven, their feet bare, and, except talismans round the neck, wrists, and ankles, their only wear is a sheet over the shoulders, and a rag or hide round the loins. A knife is stuck in the waist-cord, and men walk abroad with pipe, bow, and quiverless arrows. The women are adorned with charm-bags; and collars of white beads-now in fashion throughout this region, from three to four pounds weight, encumber the shoulders of a 'distinguished person'. Their body-dress is the African sheet bound tightly under the arms, and falling to the ankles...'

Kimweri's death, a few years after Burton's visit, was the catalyst for the first major rift in Shambaai. Vuga was too deep in the mountains to have attracted regular contact with the Kilimanjaro-bound caravans. Not so the Shambaa town of Mazinde, on what is now the main Moshi–Dar es Salaam road, whose chief Semboja exerted considerable influence over passing traders and was able to stockpile sufficient arms to overthrow Kimweri's successor at Vuga. This event split the Shambaai into several splinter groups, and although Semboja retained nominal leadership of Shambaai, he controlled a far smaller area than Kimweri had. Shambaa unity was further divided under German rule. Although the people of the Usambara played a leading role in the Abushiri Uprising of 1888/9, their resistance crumbled after Semboja's son and successor Mputa was hanged by the Germans in 1898. The Kilindi dynasty has, however, retained a strong symbolic role in modern Shambaa culture. Mputa's grandson Magogo, who took the throne in 1947, was one of the most respected leaders in Tanzania prior to his death in 2000.

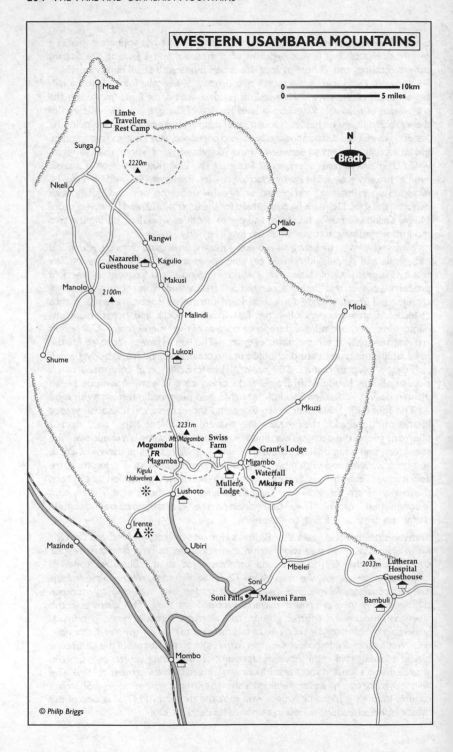

WESTERN USAMBARA MOUNTAINS

0 ——————— 10km
0 ——————— 5 miles

N

Bradt

Mtae

Limbe Travellers Rest Camp

Sunga

Nkeli

2220m

Rangwi

Mlalo

Nazareth Guesthouse

Kagulio

Makusi

Manolo

2100m

Malindi

Mlola

Lukozi

Shume

Mkuzi

2231m

Mt Magamba

Swiss Farm

Magamba FR

Magamba

Grant's Lodge

Kigulu Hakwelwa

Migambo

Waterfall

Muller's Lodge

Mkusu FR

Lushoto

Irente

Mazinde

Ubiri

2033m

Lutheran Hospital Guesthouse

Mbelei

Soni

Soni Falls

Maweni Farm

Bambuli

Mombo

© Philip Briggs

Shambaa King Mbegha and the so-called 'Growing Rock' at Magila. This excursion costs Tsh8,000 per party plus Tsh2,000 per person.

Where to stay
Moderate
Maweni Farm Tel: 027 264 0426; email: maweni@meneno.net; web: www.maneno.net. This newly opened and commendable moderate to upmarket retreat is set on a farm 2km from Soni, from where it is reached along a side road signposted to the right of the Mombo–Lushoto road near the junction with the Bambuli road. Set in pretty gardens below a tall granite cliff, the lodge consists of five rooms in the main house and eight rooms in chalets, and can take up to 30 guests at one time. Buffet meals are made almost entirely from local organic produce. Full-board accommodation costs US$45 per person in self-contained rooms, or US$35 in rooms using common showers, inclusive of a free minibus transfer from Mombo if required. Maweni also arranges four-day cultural and natural history walking tours, with two nights spent at Maweni and one each in a local guesthouse and at a forest lodge in the Mazumbai Forest Reserve, for US$160 per person.

Budget
Soni Falls Hotel This small hotel was built in the 1930s overlooking the waterfall, and has recently been renovated without losing anything of its rustic period feel. Clean comfortable self-contained rooms with netting cost Tsh5,000/7,000 single/double B&B. There's only cold running water in the shower, but hot water is provided in buckets by request.

Shoestring
Kimalube Hotel This is a friendly, family-run place on the Mombo road about 1km from the centre of Soni. Double rooms cost Tsh4,000 without breakfast or Tsh6,000 with breakfast, and evening meals are available for around Tsh2,000. As with the Soni Falls Hotel, the cold running water will be supplemented with buckets of hot water on request.

Bumbuli
The small town of Bumbuli, best known today for its old Lutheran mission and associated hospital, lies 23km from Soni amid the hills of the eastern edge of the Western Usambara. Oral tradition has it that Bumbuli is where King Mbegha entered the Usambaras about 300 years ago. The town lies in the shadow of Mazumbai Peak, the upper slopes of which are covered in high montane forest, owned by a tea estate, and regarded to be one of the most important sanctuaries in the Western Usambara for indigenous plants and rare birds. A small waterfall lies on the outskirts of the town, close to the Soni road. The Saturday market at Bambuli is very colourful, and there are many walking opportunities in the surrounding hills. Although Bambuli can easily be visited independently, the tourist office in Lushoto offers overnight hikes to the town and Mazumbai Forest for Tsh25,000 per person per day, inclusive of guide, public transport and accommodation but exclusive of meals and the Tsh4,000 forest entry permit.

Getting there
The 23km road between Soni and Bumbuli takes about 45 minutes to cover in a private vehicle, passing through the small villages of Mbelai, Kiboani and Kwahangara on the way. Using public transport, several buses daily connect Bambuli directly to Korogwe, Mombo and Lushoto. All these buses pass through Soni, so if no direct bus is about to leave, you could always catch one of the more frequent minibuses along the Mombo–Lushoto road, and hop off at Soni to board the next Bumbuli-bound vehicle.

Where to stay

The most attractive accommodation option in Bumbuli is the unexpectedly good **Lutheran Hospital Guesthouse** in the mission grounds about 10 minutes' walk uphill from the town centre. This atmospheric restored colonial building consists of eight guestrooms, costing Tsh2,500/4,000 single/double (ground floor) or Tsh3,700/6,800 single/double (first floor). There is a lounge, a common shower and bath with hot and cold water, and a self-catering kitchen. Meals cost around Tsh1,200. Of the cheaper places in town, the pick is the friendly **New Gulf Guesthouse** along the Soni road, which asks Tsh2,000 for a self-contained single or Tsh2,500 for a double using the common shower.

Magamba Forest Reserve

Situated about 15km from Lushoto, this is the most accessible patch of rainforest in the Western Usambara, covering the slopes of Mount Magamba, which at 2,230m is the highest peak in the range. It is of great interest to birdwatchers, with the track to the old sawmill in particular offering a good chance of seeing a wide selection of forest birds, including such localised species as the Usambara weaver, Usambara akalat and red-capped forest warbler. The elusive ground-dwelling Usambara akalat is of particular interest to dedicated birders, since it is endemic to the Western Usambara, but it is only likely to be seen in the deep forest interior. The Western Usambara is the main stronghold for the Usambara weaver, one of Africa's rarest birds, but relatively conspicuous due to its habit of chattering noisily in the canopy. A variety of mammals also live in this forest, though only black-and-white colobus and blue monkey are likely to be encountered by the casual visitor. Guided day walks to the forest can be arranged through the tourist office in Lushoto at a cost of Tsh8,000 per party plus Tsh6,000 per person (inclusive of a forest entry permit).

It is equally possible to visit Magamba under your own steam, ideally staying at one of the three moderate to upmarket lodges in the area or camping in the forest (see *Where to stay* below). Details of various self-guided trails can be supplied by any of the lodges in the area. To visit the forest as a day trip from Lushoto, any vehicle that's heading north to Mtae, Mlalo and Mlola can drop you at the Magamba junction, 7km from Lushoto. The road heading to the right at this junction leads through the heart of the forest, roughly following the course of the lushly vegetated Mkusu River, before emerging at Migambo village after 7km. You could walk the length of this road in about 90 minutes in either direction, with the possibility of catching a lift in a private vehicle. The daily bus between Lushoto and Mlola covers the Magamba–Migambo road in its entirety.

The most popular goal for day walks in the Magamba Forest is a small but pretty waterfall on the forest-fringed Mkuzu River about 2km from Migambo village. To reach this waterfall, take the right fork immediately as you enter Migambo on the Magamba road. Follow this road downhill for about 20 minutes, passing a group of rocks in the river where local people wash their clothes, until you reach a bridge across the river. To your right, immediately after crossing the river, you'll see the signpost for Dr Kwangua's residence. You need to turn to the left – opposite the signpost – to follow a rough track along the riverbank for about 10 minutes to the waterfall.

Where to stay
Moderate

Mullers Mountain Lodge Tel: 027 264 0204; fax: 027 264 0205; email: mullersmountainlodge@yahoo.com. Consisting of a 1930s' farm cottage set in flowering gardens within the Magamba Forest, this low-key, family-run lodge is arguably the most attractive place to stay anywhere in the Western Usambara, and an excellent base for birdwatchers. Accommodation in the main cottage costs Tsh18,000/32,000 single/double B&B using common shower, or Tsh20,000/36,000 for a self-contained single/double. More basic accommodation is available in traditional huts at Tsh10,000/18,000 single/double, while camping costs Tsh3,500 per person. Home cooked meals are available in the small restaurant or the gardens. Several day trails lead from the lodge, and useful maps and directions can be supplied on request. To reach it by private transport, follow the Mtae road out of Lushoto for 7km to Magamba junction, then turn right along the Migambo road. After another 5–6km, you'll see the lodge signposted to your left. Backpackers heading to Mullers could pop into the central garage in Lushoto to check whether the owner is making a trip in or out of town later that day.

Grant's Lodge Tel/fax: 027 264 2491; email: tanga4@tanga.net; web: www.grantslodge.com. This is another colonial era farmhouse set in an attractive garden on the outskirts of Migambo village. The house contains four large bedrooms and a library with a collection of old books and magazines. Good food is available, and numerous day walks lead from the lodge grounds. Full-board accommodation costs US$44 per person (East Africa residents) and US$49 pert person (non-residents). Bed and breakfast rates are US$12 cheaper. Transfers from Mombo or Lushoto can be arranged at US$19 per party.

Swiss Cottage Farm Tel: Lushoto 171 (or through Mullers Mountain Lodge). This new lodge is yet another peaceful retreat set on a working farm in the Magambo Forest area. Two double guestrooms are available at US$20 per person B&B, while home-cooked lunch and dinner, using organic farm produce, cost US$7 apiece. Coming from Magamba junction, the 1.5km turn-off to Swiss Farm Cottage lies to the left about 5km along the Migambo road, and 500m before the turn-off to Mullers.

Sawmill Campsite The campsite at the old sawmill lies in the heart of the forest, in an area known for its excellent birding. Facilities include a toilet and running water. Camping costs Tsh2,000 per person per night, in addition to which a daily forest permit costs Tsh4,000. The best way to get to the campsite is to hire a car in Lushoto; this won't be prohibitively expensive and can be organised through the tourist office.

The Mtae road

The small but sprawling town of Mtae, which lies 63km north of Lushoto by road, has perhaps the most spectacular location of any town in the Western Usambara. The town runs for about 2km along what is in effect a dry peninsula, jutting out to the north of the range, and with a drop of several hundred metres on either side. Mtae offers panoramic views across Lake Kalimawe and Mkomazi Game Reserve, and on a clear morning Mount Kilimanjaro, 250km distant, is often visible. The nearby Shagayu Mountain can be visited as a day-hike, preferably with a guide, and its forested slopes support a rich birdlife as well as many species of colourful butterfly.

The name Mtae translates as 'Place of Counting', a reference to its strategic importance to the Shambaa people during the 19th-century Maasai wars, when it was the site of several battles won by the Shambaa, who were able to see and count any raiding Maasai war party from afar. The striking Lutheran Church that stands in the middle of the town was built in the late 19th century on a site where, formerly, the most powerful ancestral spirits were believed to reside. The story is that the local chief showed this site to the missionaries, expecting them to flee in fear. Instead, the missionaries were unmoved, and the chief – concluding that they must be in touch with more powerful spirits – granted them permission to build a church there.

Getting there

About six buses run directly from Lushoto to Mtae daily, with the Fasaha bus originating in Arusha, the Commando bus in Dar es Salaam, and the Jackie and Sharif bus in Tanga. These buses all pass through Lushoto in the early afternoon – between 13.00 and 15.00 – and arrive in Mtae about three hours later. The buses usually start the return trip out of Mtae at around 05.00, and if you miss them, then you'll quite likely be stuck in Mtae for another 24 hours. It is also possible to do the trip between Lushoto and Mtae in hops, stopping at settlements such as Lukozi, Kagulio and Rangwi on the way.

Where to stay

There are **three lodgings within Mtae**, of which the Mwivano is about the best, with a friendly owner-manager and clean but small rooms at Tsh1,500/2,500 single/double using a common cold shower. Similar in standard and price is the Kuna Menaeno Guesthouse. En route from Lushoto, the substantial market town of **Lukozi**, 24km along the Mtae road, has a few basic lodgings, of which the Al-Ahli Guesthouse is about the best. In **Kagulio**, 43km from Lushoto, the Nazareth Guesthouse – rather bizarrely adorned with a model aeroplane on the roof – charges Tsh1,500 for a single room. At **Rangwi**, 3km further towards Mtae, there are a couple of basic guesthouses, and more comfortable accommodation is available at the Catholic Mission Resthouse.

More attractive than any of the above is the new **Limbe Travellers Rest Camp**, which lies on a smallholding 6km before Mtae and 3km after the village of Sunga, and is owned by the vice chairman of the Friends of the Usambara Society. The camp consists of four comfortable self-contained rooms (no running water but hot and cold buckets provided) for Tsh3,000 double. Camping is also permitted. Beers and sodas are sold on site, and simple meals can be prepared at Tsh1,000 per person. The owner-manager speaks good English and is an excellent source of local travel advice. The camp is affiliated with the tourist office in Lushoto, and can arrange guided day walks to Shagayu Forest, 30 minutes' walk away, and other local sites of interest at Tsh6,000 per party plus Tsh2,000 per person. A good sunset viewpoint lies about 15 minutes' walk from the camp. All buses between Lushoto and Mtae pass the entrance to Limbe.

Mlalo

This bizarre town sprawls over a large valley situated some 50km from Lushoto along a road that forks from the Mtae road at Malindi, 30km from Lushoto. Mlalo has an insular, almost otherworldly feel, one that made me feel like Indiana Jones entering a misplaced Mediterranean montane kingdom when I visited it a few years ago. Initially, I was struck by the unusual style of many of the buildings: two-storey mud houses with intricately carved wooden balconies which seem to show both German and Arab influences. The town apparently sprawls for miles, yet even in its nominal centre rural homesteads cling precipitously to steep-sided hillocks. There is no electricity. At night, the lamps that light the surrounding hills bob up and down and flicker like fireflies.

Getting there

Three buses run daily between Lushoto and Mlalo, leaving Lushoto in the early afternoon and Mlalo at around 07.00. The trip takes around two hours.

Where to stay

Near the bus stop, there are a few guesthouses in the Tsh1,500–2,000 range, of which the **Sambamba Annex** is recommended. The slightly smarter **Silver**

Dollar Guesthouse charges Tsh3,000/4,000 for a single/double using common showers.

Overnight hikes
The UMTP office in Lushoto can organise a number of guided overnight hikes into the surrounding mountains. The three-day hike through Musambae Forest reputedly offers better birding even than Magamba, and also takes in a visit to an old German mission. Another possibility is to hike to Mtae, a three- to six-day trip depending on the route you choose. Both hikes cost around Tsh17,000 per person per day inclusive of public transport to the trailhead, accommodation and a guide, but exclusive of meals and drinks, and the Tsh4,000 forest entry permit.

KOROGWE
Probably the largest town along the stretch of the B1 covered in this chapter, Korogwe is an important route focus and the favoured lunch stop of most buses travelling between Dar es Salaam and Moshi or Arusha. Otherwise, it is a less than remarkable place, with only an appealing Usambara backdrop to raise it above dusty small-town anonymity. The improvements in public transport in this part of Tanzania over the last few years make it unlikely that any traveller would end up spending a night in Korogwe these days, but those who explore the Usambara area might well find themselves swapping vehicles here at some point.

Getting there and away
Any bus heading between Moshi and Tanga or Dar es Salaam will be able to drop you in Korogwe, while the regular minibuses that connect Lushoto to Tanga via Mombo and Muheza generally pick up passengers at the bus station that lies just off the main road.

Most express buses between Dar es Salaam and Arusha or Moshi stop at the Korogwe Transit Hotel for a 20-minute lunch break.

Where to stay
The **Korogwe Traveller's Inn**, which lies on the B1 practically opposite the bus station, has adequate self-contained doubles for Tsh6,000, as well as a bar and restaurant. The newer **Korogwe Transit Hotel** is marginally smarter, and reasonable value at Tsh10,000 for a self-contained double, but it is also rather noisy as most of the buses stop here for meals. There are several cheaper lodgings dotted around town, including the **New Savari Guesthouse** and **Miami Guesthouse**, which lie 100m from the bus station and offer clean double rooms with mosquito nets for around US$3. Campers might take note that the alluring sounding **Mountain View Resort**, situated 1km from the town centre and prominently signposted from the road towards Dar es Salaam, is basically just a small, scruffy garden with few facilities and less atmosphere.

AMANI AND THE EASTERN USAMBARA
The Eastern Usambara is one of the smallest of the Eastern Arc ranges, as well as being one of the lowest, barely exceeding an altitude of 1,500m. It is, however, one of the most important ecologically, receiving an annual rainfall of up to 2,000mm, and covered in some of the most extensive and least degraded montane rainforest extant in Tanzania. In some places the indigenous vegetation has been replaced by tea plantations, while in others there has been more recent encroachment by subsistence farmers, but at least 400km² of natural forest is estimated to remain,

THE GENUS SAINTPAULIA

Without doubt the most familiar of the thousands of taxa that are endemic to the Eastern Arc mountains is a small flowering plant first collected in the Eastern Usambara in 1892 by the District Commissioner of Tanga, Baron Walter von Saint Paul Illaire. Subsequently described as *Saintpaulia ionantha* in honour of its discoverer, the African violet (as it is more commonly known) was made commercially available in 1927, when ten different blue-flowered strains were put on the market. It is today one of the world's most popular perennial potplants, with thousands of cultivated strains generating a global trade worth tens of millions of US dollars, and yet few enthusiasts realise that the wild flower is regarded to be endangered within its natural range.

Although they vary greatly in shape and colour, most cultivated strains of African violet are hybrids of the original seeds collected by Baron Saint Paul, which – although it was only recognised years after cultivation began – actually belonged to two discrete but unusually malleable species *Saintpaulia ionantha* and *Saintpaulia confusa*. The specific taxonomy of the genus *Saintpaulia* remains subject to further study, but it is currently thought that some 20 species occur in the wild. The genus is unique to the Eastern Arc mountains, and its main stronghold is the Eastern Usambara, which harbours 12 species, all but four of which are unknown from any other site.

Not affiliated to the true violets, *Saintpaulia* is thought to be a relatively recently evolved genus which radiated outwards from the Eastern Usambara. It is probable that the light seeds of the ancestral stock were blown across to the mainland in a cyclone coming from Madagascar (a flowering plant in the genus *Streptocarcus* has been cited as the probable ancestor). The wild *Saintpaulia* has probably never enjoyed a wide distribution or a high level of habitat tolerance. In the wild, as in the home, most *Saintpaulia* species require continuous shade and humidity in order to flourish. Because it depends on surface rather than underground moisture, *Saintpaulia* has an unusually shallow root system. It typically grows in moist cracks in porous rocks close to streams running through closed canopy forest – though some specimens do lead an epiphytic existence on cycad trunks or the shady branches of palms.

The main threat to the wild *Saintpaulia* is the logging of tall trees, which creates breaks in the closed canopy. Researchers in the Eastern Usambara have come across dead or dying plants at several established *Saintpaulia* sites where the canopy has been broken due to logging. One of the many positive effects of the gazetting of Amani Nature Reserve in 1997 is that it should help secure the future of the *Saintpaulia* genus – or at least those species that are resident within the reserve. The local guides will be able to show you the wild flower on several of the established walking and driving trails.

roughly half of it with a closed canopy. In common with the other montane forests of eastern Tanzania, the Eastern Usambara is cited as a biodiversity hotspot, characterised by a high level of endemism (see box *An African Galápagos?*, pages 222–3). It is also a vital catchment area, providing fresh water to some 200,000 people. The East Usambara Catchment Management Project (EUCAMP), established in 1991 and funded by FINNIDA, has been charged with implementing a community-based conservation plan to protect the forests of the area.

The centrepiece of this project is the Amani Nature Reserve, which formally opened in 1997 and protects almost 10,000ha of relatively undisturbed forest. Amani must rank close to being the most underrated reserve anywhere in northern Tanzania, offering the combination of excellent walking, beautiful forest scenery and a wealth of animal life. Although the nature reserve is a recent creation, Amani was settled by Germany as an agricultural research station in 1902, at which time the surrounding area was set aside to form what is reputedly still the second-largest botanical garden in the world. Lying at an altitude of roughly 900m, Amani remains a biological research station of some note, as well as an important centre for medical research. Most of the buildings date to the German and British colonial eras, giving it the genteel appearance of an English country village transplanted to the African jungle.

The development of Amani for eco-tourism, with the emphasis on walking and hiking, has been a high priority over the last few years. Nine trails have been demarcated at Amani, ranging in length from 3–12km, and leaflets with trail descriptions are available to visitors. The directions in the leaflets are reportedly not 100% accurate, so it might be worth hiking with a trained guide, who will also help you to spot birds and monkeys. In December 2000, the rehabilitated German stationmaster's house at Sigi (aka Kisiwani), some 7km from Amani on the Muheza road, opened as an entrance gate and information centre, with an adjoining resthouse offering visitors a second, lower-altitude site from which to explore the forest.

It is worth consulting with the reserve's guides about the trail most suited to your specific interest. The 10km Konkoro Trail, which can be covered on foot or in a vehicle, is good for African violets, and it cuts through several different forest types, as well as passing a viewpoint and terminating in an overnight campsite in the heart of the forest. The shorter Turaco and Mbamole Hill trails are recommended first options for birdwatchers. In addition to the prescribed walking trails, there is much to be seen along the roads and paths that lie within the research centre and botanical garden. Wandering around the forest-fringed village, you are likely to encounter a wide variety of birds, as well as black-and-white colobus and blue monkey – and you might even catch a glimpse of the bizarre and outsized Zanj elephant shrew.

Entrance to Amani Nature Reserve costs Tsh4,000 per person, which – unlike national park fees – is a one-off payment no matter how long you spend in the reserve. If you want to take pictures, an additional photography fee of Tsh2,500 per photographer daily is levied. The daily guide fee is Tsh8,000 per person, and visitors with a private vehicle must pay a one-off parking fee of Tsh1,000 per vehicle. Twenty percent of all fees paid will go toward the development of local communities.

Getting there and away

The springboard for visits to Amani is the small town of Muheza, which lies about 40km west of Tanga on the main surfaced road to Moshi and Dar es Salaam. All buses between Moshi or Dar es Salaam and Tanga can drop you at Muheza, as can the minibuses that ply back and forth between Tanga and Lushoto. One reader describes Muheza as a 'charming town', for reasons that are lost on me, but it does boast a good half-dozen small guesthouses should you need to spend a night, and Uncle J's Bar is a good place to eat and drink. Muheza is most lively on Thursday and Sunday, the local market days.

From Muheza, the road to Amani is clearly signposted, and the drive should take about 90 minutes in a private 4WD vehicle, passing through the 'entrance

BIRDING IN AMANI

Although the Eastern Usambara probably takes second place to the Udzungwa range as inherently the most important avian site in the Eastern Arc mountains, it is without question one of the most significant and alluring birdwatching sites anywhere in East Africa. Amani in particular has several logistical advantages over the best birdwatching sites in the Udzungwa, namely relative ease of access, proximity to the established tourist circuit of northern Tanzania, and a superior tourist infrastructure and quality of guides. The Eastern Usambara's avifauna has received far more scientific attention than that of the other Eastern Arc ranges, dating from 1926–48 when Amani was the home of the doyen of Tanzania ornithology, Reginald Moreau, credited with discovering and describing several new species including the long-billed tailorbird. This extensive study is reflected in a checklist of 340 bird species, including 12 that are globally threatened and 19 that are either endemic to the Eastern Arc mountains or to the East African coastal biome.

The temptation on first arriving at Amani might be to rush off along one of the trails into the forest interior. In fact some of the most productive general birdwatching is to be had in the gardens and forest fringe around Amani village, slow exploration of which is likely to yield up to 50 forest associated species including half a dozen genuine rarities. One of the more conspicuous and vocal residents around the resthouse is the green-headed oriole, a colourful bird that is restricted to a handful of montane forests between Tanzania and Mozambique. The flowering gardens are a good site for three of the four range-restricted sunbirds associated with the Eastern Usambara, ie: Amani, banded green and Uluguru violet-backed sunbird. The rare long-billed tailorbird has recently been discovered breeding at two sites within Amani village.

Having explored the resthouse area, the guided Turaco and Mbamole Hill trails are recommended for sighting further montane forest specials. Noteworthy birds resident in the forest around Amani include the Usambara eagle owl, southern banded snake eagle, silvery-cheeked hornbill, half-collared kingfisher, African green ibis, Fischer's touraco, African broadbill, East Coast akalat, white-chested alethe, Kenrick's and Waller's starlings, and several forest flycatchers. It is also worth noting that several of the more interesting Usambara specials are lowland forest species, more likely to be seen in and around Sigi than at Amani. Among the birds to look out for on the trails around Sigi are eastern green tinkerbird, African cuckoo-hawk, square-tailed drongo, bar-tailed trogon and chestnut-fronted helmetshrike.

A regularly updated checklist of birds recorded in the Eastern Usambara can be accessed online at www.usambara.com.

gate' at Sigi after about an hour. Driving times will depend on the condition of the road, in particular the spectacular but steep 7km stretch between Sigi and Amani. Three buses daily run between Muheza and Sigi, leaving Muheza at around 12.30 to arrive in Sigi about two hours later. Only one of these buses continues along the steep road up to Amani, arriving there about an hour after that. The bus from Amani to Muheza leaves at 06.30 and passes through Sigi at about 07.00.

Where to stay
Moderate
Malaria Medical Research Centre Resthouse Situated in Amani village, this is a similar but smarter set-up to the two resthouses below, and although it is aimed primarily at researchers, tourists are welcome when rooms are available. Full-board accommodation costs US$30 for non-residents and Tsh10,000 for residents.

Budget
Amani Club Resthouse Tel: 053 264 6907; email: usambara@twiga.com. The official resthouse at Amani is a well-maintained and comfortable stone building set in the middle of the research village and dating to the colonial era. The cosy lounge, heated by a log fire in the evenings, houses an improbable collection of yellowing books. Accommodation costs Tsh5,000 per person, while meals can be provided at Tsh1,000 for breakfast or Tsh2,000 for lunch or dinner. Camping at the resthouse costs Tsh2,500 per person.
Sigi Resthouse Tel: 053 264 6907; email: usambara@twiga.com. The new resthouse at Sigi is similar in standard to the one at Amani, albeit with a rather more modern feel. Accommodation costs Tsh5,000 per person, while meals can be provided at Tsh1,000 for breakfast or Tsh2,000 for lunch or dinner. Camping at the resthouse costs Tsh2,500 per person.

Camping
Kamkoro Campsite This little-utilised campsite lies in a stand of forest some 10km from Amani along the Komkoro Vehicle Trail. Camping costs Tsh2,500 per person.

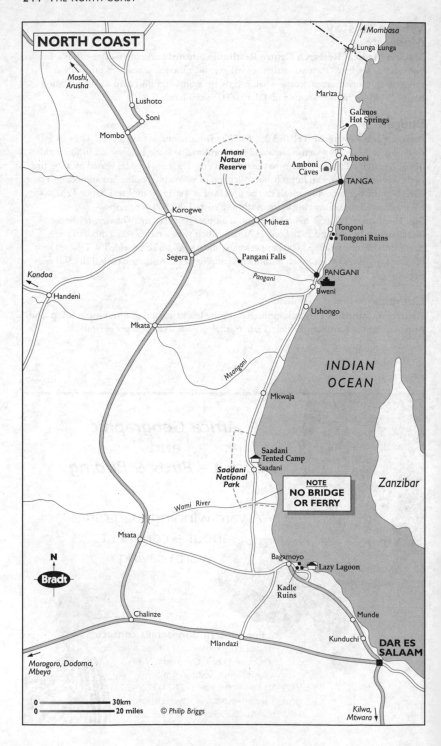

NORTH COAST

Moshi,
Arusha

Lushoto
Soni
Mombo

Amani
Nature
Reserve

Korogwe

Muheza

Segera

Pangani Falls

Pangani

Kondoa

Handeni

Mkata

Msangani

Mombasa
Lunga Lunga

Mariza

Galanos
Hot Springs

Amboni
Amboni
Caves

TANGA

Tongoni
Tongoni Ruins

PANGANI
Bweni

Ushongo

INDIAN
OCEAN

Mkwaja

Saadani
Tented Camp
Saadani

*Saadani
National
Park*

Zanzibar

Wami River

NOTE
NO BRIDGE
OR FERRY

Msata

Bagamoyo
Lazy Lagoon

Kadle
Ruins

N

Bradt

Chalinze

Munde

Kunduchi

DAR ES
SALAAM

Mlandazi

Morogoro, Dodoma,
Mbeya

0   30km
0   20 miles

© Philip Briggs

Kilwa,
Mtwara

The North Coast

10

The stretch of coast between the Kenyan border and Dar es Salaam is not as underdeveloped as the south coast, but it remains surprisingly little-visited by tourists, presumably as a result of having to compete with Zanzibar as the country's main coastal resort area. Like the mountain ranges covered in the previous chapter, the north coast offers little that cannot be seen elsewhere in East Africa, and it can easily be bypassed by those who want to bus directly between Moshi or Arusha and Dar es Salaam. Nevertheless, the area is rich in off-the-beaten-track travel possibilities, and it will be highly rewarding to those with the time and initiative to explore them.

The principal town along the north coast is Tanga, a somewhat time-warped port that briefly served as the capital of German East Africa before this role was usurped by Dar es Salaam. Also of interest are the ancient Swahili trading centres of Bagamoyo and Pangani, which lie between Dar es Salaam and Tanga, separated by the remote Saadani Game Reserve.

CLIMATE

This part of Tanzania has a typical coastal climate, hot and humid throughout the year. The short rains fall in November and December and the long rains between March and May. The hottest and most humid period falls between the rains, from mid-December to March. At this time of year, the north coast can be rather oppressive, with daytime temperatures well in excess of 30°C and night-time temperatures rarely falling much below 25°C. By contrast, the period from June to September is much cooler, with temperatures generally dropping below 20°C at night.

GETTING AROUND

The surfaced side road to Tanga branches from the B1 between Dar es Salaam and Moshi at Segera. Tanga is connected to both Moshi and Dar es Salaam by regular express buses. There is no longer a passenger train service to Tanga.

The unsurfaced coastal road between Tanga and Dar es Salaam is in poor condition. The stretch between Saadani and Bagamoyo has been impassable for some years due to a collapsed bridge, and most other stretches can be navigated in a 4WD vehicle only. Note that although this chapter works along the coast from south to north, there is no public transport between Bagamoyo and Pangani, so that Bagamoyo is most easily visited as a round trip from Dar es Salaam, and Pangani as a round trip from Tanga.

TANGA

Characterised by quiet, pot-holed avenues lined with time-worn pastel-shaded German and Asian buildings, Tanga's compact city centre has a somnambulant aura belying its status as Tanzania's third largest town (estimated population 140,000) and second busiest port. Perhaps because it is bypassed by the main northern highway, the city has never attracted a great volume of travellers, and it seems to have dropped even further off the East African travel map since passenger train services to Moshi and Dar es Salaam were suspended in the 1990s. This, I feel, is a shame! True, Tanga itself boasts few specific sites of interest, but it certainly doesn't lack for atmosphere, and makes for a pleasant, relaxed base to explore a number of alluring sites, notably the vast limestone caverns of Amboni and the extensive medieval ruins at Tongoni.

The air of sleepy semi-abandonment that hovers over the city centre, reminiscent of much of Tanzania during its mid-1980s' economic nadir, does reflect a real demise in Tanga's commercial fortune in recent decades. Vast improvements in the national road infrastructure, and the corresponding decline in the importance of rail transport, has meant the once bustling harbour is increasingly peripheral to Dar es Salaam. The local economy also suffered as a result of the collapse of the post-independence sisal boom, and the widespread closure of local industries in Tanzania's darkest economic days. As a barometer of Tanga's gradual descent into backwater status, it is the only Tanzanian town where fewer hotel rooms are available in the city centre today than when the first edition of this guide was researched – every last central hotel recommended in that edition has subsequently closed.

The other factor in the town centre's unusually sedate atmosphere is that it is no longer the real hub of Tanga's commercial activity. For an altogether different picture, wander through the grid of streets that surround the bus station and market – colourful, crowded, and bustling with low-key entrepreneurial activity. Different again is the well-preserved residential area, complete with upmarket(ish) hotels and swimming beach, that sprawls attractively along the Raskazone Peninsula to the northeast of the town centre. For students of colonial architecture, the main waterfront houses several buildings of note, including the German-era Regional Headquarters and Cliff Block, the century-old Clock Tower, and the whitewashed public library (see box *Historical Tanga*, pages 248–9).

Getting there and away

A well-maintained surfaced road connects Tanga to Segera, the junction town on the main road between Moshi and Dar es Salaam. The total driving distance to Tanga from Moshi is 360km, from Lushoto about 200km, and from Dar es Salaam 460km. In a private vehicle, expect to cover a distance of around 80km/h on any of these routes. It is not possible to drive directly between Tanga and Dar es Salaam via the coast. With a 4WD vehicle, one could follow the coast south as far as Saadani, returning to the main Dar es Salaam road via Miono (see *Saadani National Park*, pages 267–70 for further details).

Regular minibuses run between Tanga and the above three towns, charging Tsh2,500 for the three-hour trip to Lushoto, Tsh4,000 for the five-hour trip to Moshi, and Tsh5,000 for the six-hour trip to Dar es Salaam. Buses cover the same routes, but the journey is about 50% longer than by minibus, and often also entails a long wait for the bus to fill up. Inexpensive local minibuses also connect Tanga to Muheza (for Amani) and Korogwe. For details of transport to Pangani, see the *Pangani* section (pages 257–67). The main bus station in Tanga lies about 500m out of town past the railway station; if you arrive heavily laden or after dark, you might want to catch a taxi to your hotel.

There are no scheduled flights to Tanga. Passenger trains between Moshi, Dar es Salaam and Tanga were suspended a few years ago, following the improvement to the trunk roads through the region, and the service is unlikely to be resumed. Intermittent ferry or motorboat services have connected Tanga to the islands of Pemba and Zanzibar in the past, but none has lasted for very long and nothing appears to be running at the time of writing. It may be possible to catch a fishing dhow between Tanga and Pemba, but this is a dangerous and uncomfortable way of travelling long distances – and it also seems to be illegal for tourists to use dhows.

Where to stay
Upmarket
Mkonge Hotel Tel/fax: 053 264 3440. The long-serving Mkonge Hotel is the smartest option in Tanga, with a superb beachfront location overlooking the harbour and Toten Island. Less inspiring is the monolithic architecture and lethargic, rundown atmosphere. Facilities include a good bar and restaurant, and (take heed!) a popular disco over weekends. Air-conditioned double rooms cost US$40 for non-residents and Tsh21,000 for residents, inclusive of a full English breakfast. There's nothing wrong with the Mkonge, but unless you have a compelling reason to overnight in Tanga, the comparably priced resorts towards and around Pangani are far more attractive.

Moderate
Hotel Raskazone Tel/fax: 053 264 3897; mobile: 0741 670790. Set on a back road about five minutes' walk from the Mkonge Hotel, this is regarded as the best deal in town by many expatriates. All rooms are self-contained doubles with a fridge, telephone, hot shower and nets; those with a fan cost Tsh10,000 while those with AC cost Tsh16,000, inclusive of a full breakfast. A 20% discount is offered for stays of three nights or longer. Camping costs US$4 per person.
Motel Panori Tel: 053 264 4806; fax: 053 264 7425. Close to the Raskazone and similar in standard, the Motel Panori offers air-conditioned accommodation in two types of room. Those in the old wing are rather rundown and seem poor value at Tsh17,640 self-contained double, but the rooms in the new wing are very comfortable and seem much better value at Tsh22,680 self-contained double. The *makuti*-style restaurant, widely regarded to be the best place to eat in Tanga, has a varied menu with most dishes in the Tsh4,000–6,000 range.
Hotel Kola Prieto Tel: 053 264 4206; fax: 053 264 2648; email: kolaprieto@tanga.net. The newest and most central of Tanga's classier hotels, this neat multi-storey block is situated on India Road a few minutes' walk from the waterfront and market square. The smart self-contained rooms all have hot running water and cost between Tsh15,000 and Tsh21,000 depending on whether occupancy is single or double, and whether the room is air-conditioned or fan only. The good ground floor restaurant specialises in Indian dishes and seafood, with most items falling into the Tsh2,000–3,000 range.

Budget
Ocean Breeze Hotel Tel: 053 264 3441. The best budget lodging in the town centre is this relatively new multi-storey block facing the main market square. Large clean doubles with mosquito net, fan, firm double bed, hot shower and a balcony are great value at Tsh6,000. An attached restaurant and beer garden serves reasonable Indian food for around Tsh2,000–3,000, as well as reliably cold beers and sodas.
Inn by the Sea Tel: 053 264 4613. Situated alongside the Mkonge Hotel, the Inn by the Sea has long been the only option offering cheap seafront accommodation away from the town centre. It could do with a bit of a facelift, but the self-contained double rooms are more than adequate at Tsh7,000 with a fan or Tsh10,000 with AC. No alcohol is served,

HISTORICAL TANGA

Tanga, despite its aura of faded prosperity, would appear to lack the historical pedigree of smaller ports such as Pangani or Bagamoyo. The ruined mosques on Toten Island in Tanga Harbour indicate the presence of a small trading centre in the Omani and Shirazi eras, as do similar ruins at several other sites within a 20km radius of the modern city. But, while it seems reasonable to assume that some sort of fishing settlement has existed on the harbour's mainland for millennia, there is no written or archaeological evidence of a more substantial settlement prior to the early 19th century. The city's name – which means 'sail' in Swahili – is most probably derived from Mtangani, the contemporary name for the nearby Tongoni Ruins. It could well be that the foundation of modern Tanga was linked to the decline and eventual abandonment of Mtangani.

By the mid-19th century, Tanga was an established and substantial centre of the ivory trade, neither as renowned as Pangani, nor as architecturally distinguished, but nevertheless sufficiently profitable to be governed by an agent of the Sultan of Zanzibar. Richard Burton, who spent several days in the fledgling city in 1857, wrote that:

> Tanga... is a patch of thatched pent-shaped huts, built upon a bank overlooking the sea, in a straggling grove of coconuts and calabash. The population numbers between 4,000 and 5,000...The citizens are a homely-looking race, chiefly occupied with commerce, and they send twice a-year, in June and November, after the great and little rains, trading parties to the Chagga and the Maasai countries. The imports are chiefly cotton-stuffs, brass and iron wires, and beads... The returns consist of camels and asses, a few slaves, and ivory, of which I was told 70,000lb passes through Tanga. The citizens also trade with the coast savages, and manufacture hardware from imported metal.... Of late years Tanga has been spared the mortification of the Maasai, who have hunted and harried in this vicinity many a heard. It is now, comparatively speaking, thickly inhabited.

When the Sultan of Zanzibar leased the coastal strip to Germany in 1887, few would have predicted that Tanga would rise to its modern prominence. Yet only two years after establishing their first headquarters at Bagamoyo, Germany recognised the limitations of the town's shallow harbour, and relocated their administration to the deep and well-protected natural harbour at Tanga. Thus did Tanga become Germany's *ipso facto* East African capital, and although it relinquished this status to Dar es Salaam in 1891, its excellent harbour ensured that it would be earmarked for future colonial development. The first school in German East Africa was built at Tanga in 1893, and several other impressive buildings on the modern waterfront – notably the Regional Headquarters and Cliff Block – date to the German era. A more significant German legacy was the introduction of sisal, eventually to become Tanzania's most important

and the food looks rather bland, so you might well find yourself gravitating towards the adjoining Mkonge Hotel or Raskazone Swimming Club at meal times.

New Era Hotel Tel: 053 264 3466. Ten minutes' walk from the town centre, the New Era has been converted from a private house in a pretty suburban area. Many travellers love the

agricultural export, and still the most visible crop in Tanga region. In 1911, the completion of a railway line to Moshi and the fertile foothills of Kilimanjaro sealed Tanga's future as the country's second busiest port.

In late 1914, German Tanga was the setting of a tragically farcical British naval raid. Suffering from seasickness after a long voyage from India, 8,000 Asian recruits were instructed to leap ashore at Tanga, only to become bogged down in the mangroves, then stumble into a swarm of ferocious bees, and finally trigger-off German trip-wires. The raid was eventually aborted, but not before 800 British troops lay dead, and a further 500 were wounded. In the confusion, 455 rifles, 16 machine guns and 600,000 rounds of ammunition were left on the shore – a major boon to the Germans. This battle forms a pivotal scene in William Boyd's excellent novel *An Ice-cream War*. The Germans were eventually forced out of Tanga in 1916, when the British, better prepared this time, launched a land offensive from Moshi on the weakened German outpost. There are two important World War I cemeteries in Tanga: the German Sakarani Cemetery on Swahili Street, at the east end of Market Street, and the Commonwealth War Cemetery on Bombo Road. A British War Memorial in Usagara, near the Mkonge Hotel, consists of a plaque with illustrations and a brief history of the war.

Along the tree-lined avenues of Tanga's modern town centre lies a wealth of colonial era buildings. Characteristic of the old town are numerous early 20th-century two-storey residences, many of which were built for Indian and Arabic merchants and would originally have doubled as shops. Notable for their intricately carved wooden balconies, thick pillars, large raised verandas, carved hardwood doors, small grilled windows and wooden shutters, these old residences are generally in a poor state of repair, but the Tanga Heritage Centre intends to restore some of them in the near future. Another central landmark is the Tanga School opposite the stadium on Eckenford Avenue, the oldest school in the country, built in 1895 and currently used as a medical college. The current railway station on Ring Road was built by the British, but the older German station, dating to 1896, can be found by following the railway line towards the port. The Usambara Courthouse on Usambara Street is a beautiful two-story building that has recently been fully restored and renovated by the Tanga Heritage Centre.

The main concentration of official German buildings lies between Independence Avenue and the waterfront. The old German Boma, complete with underground bunkers and passages to the sea, is now the police station, and stands close to the gracious whitewashed library built during the British colonial era. Also along Independence Avenue you'll find the original Clock Tower, dating to 1901, and the courthouse, built during the German era as a provisional regional headquarters. Further from the town centre, along Hospital Road, the rundown and partially disused Cliff Block was the first hospital in the country, built by the Germans in the 1890s. Good examples of British architecture include the Katani Building and Lead Memorial Hall on Hospital Road, both dating to the early 1950s.

place for the friendly, homely atmosphere generated by the Anglo-Asian couple that owns and manages it. Unfortunately, the rooms, which look like something out of a 'how-not-to' DIY manual, are nothing to shout about at Tsh3,500/6,000 for a self-contained single/double with fan. Camping costs Tsh2,500 per person.

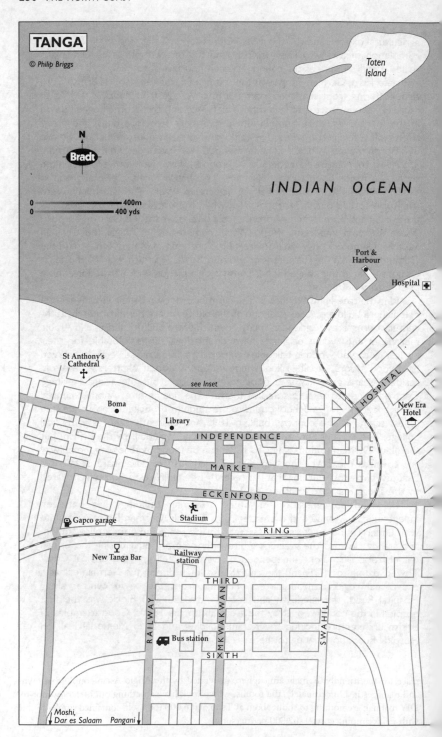

TANGA

© Philip Briggs

N

Bradt

0 ———————— 400m
0 ———————— 400 yds

Toten
Island

INDIAN OCEAN

Port &
Harbour

Hospital

St Anthony's
Cathedral

see Inset

Boma

Library

INDEPENDENCE

MARKET

ECKENFORD

Gapco garage

Stadium

RING

New Tanga Bar

Railway
station

HOSPITAL

New Era
Hotel

THIRD

RAILWAY

M K V A K W A N

Bus station

SIXTH

S W A H I L I

Moshi,
Dar es Salaam   Pangani

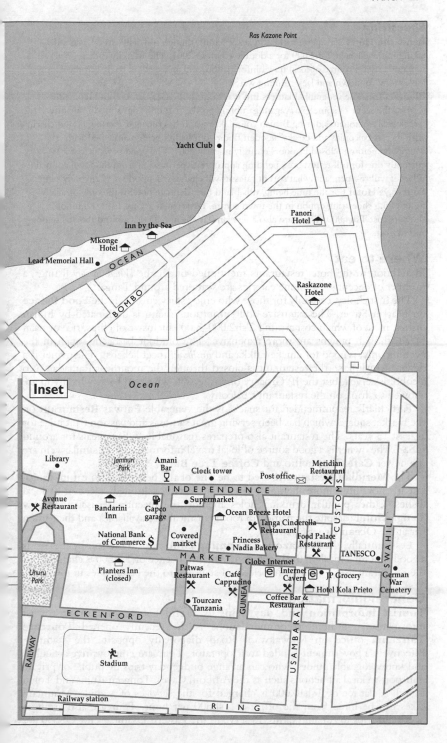

Ras Kazone Point

Yacht Club ●

Panori
Hotel 🏨

Inn by the Sea ●

Mkonge
Hotel 🏨

Lead Memorial Hall ●

OCEAN

BOMBO

Raskazone
Hotel 🏨

Inset

Ocean

Library ●

Jamhuri
Park

Amani
Bar 🍷

Clock tower ●

Post office ✉

Meridian
Restaurant ✕

Avenue
Restaurant ✕

INDEPENDENCE

Bandarini
Inn 🏨

Gapco
garage ⛽

● Supermarket

National Bank
of Commerce 💲

Covered
market ●

Ocean Breeze Hotel 🏨

✕ Tanga Cinderella
Restaurant

Princess
● Nadia Bakery

Food Palace
Restaurant ✕

TANESCO ●

CUSTOMS

SWAHILI

Uhuru
Park

Planters Inn
(closed) 🏨

MARKET

Patwas
Restaurant ✕

Café
Cappucino ✕

Globe Internet

Internet
Cavern 🇪

🇪 ● JP Grocery

Hotel Kola Prieto 🏨

German
War
Cemetery

GUINEA

Coffee Bar &
Restaurant

USAMBARA

● Tourcare
Tanzania

ECKENFORD

Stadium 🏃

Railway station

RAILWAY

RING

Shoestring

Bandarini Hotel This perennial backpacker haunt, though officially closed, was still taking in travellers at Tsh4,000 for a double room in 2001. The friendly Indian owner remains a useful source of local travel information, and an excellent cook, but the rooms look pretty rundown and lack running water.

Planters Inn The venerable Planters Inn was built in the German era, and reputedly formed the scene of some extravagant gambling on the part of Tanga's predominantly Greek sisal millionaires during British colonial times. It has retained a strong period charm with its vast balconies and creaky wooden floors, but hadn't been maintained with any conviction before it closed its doors entirely in early 2001. The good news is that it is currently due for full renovation, pending appropriate permission from the town council. When it will re-open, and what sort of rates it will charge when it does, is anybody's guess.

Fourways Hotel For the time being, this bland but adequate hotel is the only officially functioning shoestring option in the town centre. Basic single rooms using common showers cost Tsh4,000. There are also a few similar cheap lodgings around the bus station and market.

Where to eat

In addition to the hotel restaurants mentioned under the *Where to stay* listings, a number of decent stand-alone eateries are scattered around Tanga.

The first choice, certainly for those who enjoy spicy cuisine, is the **Food Palace** on Market Street. The extensive and sumptuous menu is dominated by Indian dishes, most of which cost around Tsh2,000–3,000 inclusive of chips, rice or naan bread, though prawns are more expensive. The outdoor barbecue, open in the evening only, is good for chicken tikka and *mishkaki* (beef kebabs). The owner is a devout Muslim, so the restaurant is closed through the month of Ramadan. No alcohol is served, but the JP Grocery opposite sells wine and beer, which you are allowed to drink on the restaurant's balcony.

Particularly recommended for snacks is the venerable **Patwas Restaurant** on the market square, which has been serving great samosas and passion fruit juice for at least 15 years. The restaurant also prepares reasonable Indian meals for around US$3. The owner is a good source of local travel information. In a similar vein are the newer **Café Cappucino** and **Coffee Tree Bar**.

The **Meridian Restaurant** used to be one of the best places to eat in Tanga, but it's now little more than a glorified bar serving a limited selection of local dishes. Other popular drinking holes include the recently resuscitated **New Tanga Hotel** (despite the name, no rooms or meals are available) and the garden bar at the **Ocean Breeze Hotel**.

Less centrally, the **Raskazone Swimming Club** next to the Inn by the Sea is a good spot for a meal on the beachfront. An entrance fee of Tsh500 is charged, but the restaurant itself is similar in price and standard to the better ones in town.

General information

Tourist information and day trips A useful source of current tourist information and hotel recommendations is the recently opened **Tourcare Tanzania** office on Mkwakwani Road diagonally opposite the stadium. Effectively a government-funded tour operator, Tourcare employs five articulate and knowledgeable guides, who can arrange budget day trips by public or private transport to local attractions such as the Amboni Caves, Tongoni Ruins and Toten Island. A flat fee of Tsh10,000 is charged for the services of a guide. Mountain bikes can be hired from the office at Tsh500 per hour. Tourcare also arranges overnight trips to Amani Nature Reserve in the Eastern Usambara for US$50 per person per night (minimum two people) inclusive of transport, guides, accommodation, food and entrance fees. To contact the office in advance, ring 0741 417512, or email samashavri2002@yahoo.com.

The **Tanga Heritage Centre** is a local organisation committed to the development and publicising of a variety of cultural projects and historical sites in and around Tanga. *Urithi*, the centre's quarterly newsletter, is well worth a look. The centre, which can be contacted at 0744 264 6582 or urithitanga@yahoo.com, intends to open an information office in mid-2002, situated on the corner of Independence Avenue and Usambara Street, diagonally opposite the main post office.

Foreign exchange The **National Bank of Commerce** on Market Street offers full foreign exchange facilities for cash and travellers' cheques during normal banking hours. There is no private forex bureau in Tanga, which means that travellers who come from Kenya and expect to arrive in Tanga in the late afternoon or over the weekend ought to change sufficient cash into local currency at the border.

Internet The best internet café in Tanga is **Globe Online Internet** on Market Street. Browsing costs Tsh500 for 15 minutes or Tsh1500 for a full hour. Other options include the **Internet Cavern**, also on Market Street, and a new internet café in the **Hotel Kola Prieta**.

Swimming There's no public swimming pool in Tanga. If you fancy a dip in the ocean, the most convenient spot is the small, sandy beach at the **Raskazone Swimming Club** (next to the Inn by the Sea), where entrance costs Tsh500. Popular with expatriates, and with slightly better facilities, the **Tanga Yacht Club** also has a swimming beach, and charges a daily entry fee of Tsh2,000 per person. Both places have a shower, bar and restaurant. There's also a swimming beach on Toten Island.

Football matches Tanga's home matches are played at the central Mkwakwani Stadium. Match days are mostly Wednesday and Saturday from March to August, with kick-off normally at 16.30. Tickets cost from Tsh500–2,000.

Day trips from Tanga
Toten Island
Protected within Tanga Harbour, the tiny Toten Island is uninhabited today, but it bears several somewhat overgrown relics of earlier Islamic settlements. Most significant among these, situated on the west of the island, is the ruin of a large mosque, probably established in the 14th or 15th century and extensively renovated during the late 18th century. Notable features of this mosque include a large east-facing balcony, a staircase leading to the roof, a well-preserved ornamental mihrab, and a nearby cemetery with inscribed Islamic tombs. A smaller and more ruinous mosque stands on the southern shore, and a variety of ceramic artefacts and household objects dating from between the 15th and 18th centuries have been unearthed around the island. No trace has been found of a third mosque depicted on a German era map, or of the large rectangular fort described by Richard Burton, who visited the island in 1857, some 30 years before the last inhabitants deserted it for the mainland. There is also a German war cemetery on the island, and a small swimming beach. The northern shore is the site of a recently implemented mangrove conservation project.

Toten Island can be reached by boat as a three- to four-hour round excursion from Tanga. The most straightforward way to visit is with Tourcare, which charges Tsh10,000 per group for a guide, and Tsh22,000 for the use of a motorised boat. Alternatively, you can negotiate with local boatmen at the harbour for a cheaper price using a traditional dhow. It is advisable to visit during low tide, when it is easier to walk on the beaches and some parts of the island.

Amboni Caves

The labyrinth of subterranean passages that runs through the 250km² limestone bed to the east of Tanga is probably the most extensive cave system in East Africa, and certainly the most accessible and impressive. Caves 3a and 3b, known less prosaically as the Amboni Caves (despite lying far closer to the village of Kiomoni than to Amboni), have been open to the public for years, and offer a combined 750m of accessible passages. Another two caves, 7 and 8, were opened in October 2000. The total network of caves is often said to be more than 200km long, and a persistent rumour has it that one passage runs all the way to Fort Jesus in Mombasa. Countering such claims, the most comprehensive survey of the caves to date, undertaken by a German-Turkish expedition in 1994, found the largest of the ten caves studied to be less than 1km long.

Whatever their true extent, there's no doubt that the Amboni Caves make for an excellent day trip out of Tanga. Sadly, their initial impact is diminished by the liberal graffiti around the entrance – the handiwork of past visitors who couldn't resist the urge to paint their names for posterity. This unsightly roll call of buffoons doesn't extend far into the main cave, which after 50m or so opens out into a magnificent 15m-high chamber overhung with large rippled stalactites. From this first chamber, the route leads through a succession of narrow passages and larger caverns, and passes several impressive natural sculptures including the so-called Madonna and Statue of Liberty. The caves support thousands upon thousands of bats, which can be seen streaming out of

LEGENDS AND LOST DOG STORIES

The main Amboni Cave has long held a strong spiritual significance to the local Digo people, who refer to it as Mabavu. According to the caretaker, this translates as 'sacrifice', though most written sources suggest Mabavu is the name of a deity who lives within the cave. The chamber associated with this deity is called Mzimuni (Place of Spirits) and it contains a sacrificial altar that is normally scattered with bones, food and other gifts, left by pilgrims from all around East Africa. The cave's resident deity can reputedly alleviate all forms of illness and misfortune, but his speciality is making barren women fertile. The perceived powers of Amboni remain as strong today as ever – Tanga's football team reputedly slaughters a cow or goat at the altar before pivotal matches.

Amboni has attracted its fair share of modern legends. During the time of Kenya's Mau-Mau rebellion, the main cave formed a hideout for the brave freedom fighter (or heinous bandit, depending on who's telling the tale) Osale Otango and his Tanzanian sidekick Paul Hamiso, at least until Otango was shot dead by the authorities in 1958. It is difficult to know what to make of another popular legend relating to two retired army officers who undertook a survey expedition of Amboni shortly after World War II. The men reputedly vanished without trace, but the dog that accompanied them into the caves turned up four months later at the entrance to another cave – on the lower slopes of distant Kilimanjaro!

the entrance at dusk, and whose droppings feed a variety of cockroaches and weird invertebrates.

The entrance to the main cave lies on the north bank of the Mkulimuzi River, a beautiful clear stream that rises in the Usambara Mountains and is also fed locally by freshwater springs. The river is fringed by palms, and runs through one of the largest extant patches of coastal forest in northern Tanzania. A variety of localised birds inhabit the forest near the caves, as does a resident and regularly observed troop of black-and-white colobus monkeys. This is also a good place to look for the African violet in a wild state, but note that it is forbidden to pick or damage this protected flower.

To reach the Amboni Caves from Tanga, follow the Mombasa road for 5km, then turn left on to a dirt road signposted for 'Mohamed Enterprises'. About 100m along this dirt road turn left again, then continue more-or-less straight along a rough road through the *shambas* of Kiomoni village for 1.5km to the signposted entrance to the caves. There is no public transport to the caves, but *dalla-dallas* between Tanga and Amboni village, which lies 2km further along the Mombasa road, will drop passengers at the first junction, from where it's a 20–30-minute walk. It is also possible to charter a taxi from Tanga, or to cycle there – mountain bikes can be rented from the Tourcare office, and local bikes are available to rent on the main market square. The caves are open from 08.00 to 17.00 daily, and the entrance fee of Tsh2,000 includes the services of the English-speaking caretaker/guide and use of a good torch. Entering the caves without a guide would be extremely foolhardy, and there is a real danger of getting lost or being injured. No accommodation or camping facilities are available at the caves.

Galanos Hot Springs

Named after the Greek sisal plantation owner who built a bathing house fed by their pumped water in the 1950s, the Galanos Hot Springs lie about 8km from the Amboni Caves, and the two are often visited in conjunction. The clear, green water, which forms a large pool before flowing into a stream caked with lime deposits, is reputed to cure rheumatism, arthritis and various skin ailments. It's possible to bathe in the pool – plenty of locals do – though the strong sulphuric odour doesn't make this an overwhelmingly attractive prospect. An entrance fee of Tsh1,000 is reputedly charged to visit the springs, though as often as not there's nobody around to collect it. The bath built by Galanos, located on a cliff-top across the Zigi River from the Amboni workshops, is not currently operational.

To reach the springs from Amboni, return to the main Tanga–Mombasa road, and follow it in the direction of Mombasa. After 2km, the road passes through the small settlement of Amboni, immediately before crossing a bridge over a stretch of the Sigi River where crocodiles are occasionally observed. About 1km past the bridge, turn right at an unsignposted junction on to a dirt track (there was a Coca-Cola billboard opposite this junction in 2001). After following this track for another 1km, you'll come to a fork in front of a school building. The 2km track to the springs lies along the left fork. If you need to ask directions, the Swahili for 'hot springs' is *maji moto*.

Tongoni Ruins

Tongoni means 'Place of Ruins', and the village of that name, situated alongside the Pangani road 20km south of Tanga, stands adjacent to the remains of an abandoned Swahili town known contemporaneously as Mtangata. Little is known about the early history of this settlement, but archaeological evidence indicates it was in existence by the late 14th century, and one unverifiable local tradition relates that it was founded at the same time, and by the same family, as Kilwa. Although never as important as Kilwa – nor Mombasa and Malindi for that matter – Mtangata was a prosperous trade centre, and the most significant for 100km in either direction during its 15th-century commercial peak.

Mtangata was one of the first places in East Africa to be visited by Europeans, when one of the three ships under the command of the Portuguese explorer Vasco da Gama ran aground there in 1498. A year later, da Gama spent two weeks at Mtangata, where he abandoned and set fire to one of his ships due to a shortage of hands, and named a distant mountain range – the Usambara – in honour of Sao Raphael. Traditionally hostile to the Sultan of Mombasa, the rulers of Mtangata maintained a good relationship with the Portuguese, and the town evidently remained reasonably prosperous throughout the Portuguese occupation. After 1698, when the Portuguese were evicted from Mombasa, Mtangata slid rapidly into obscurity, to be abandoned in about 1730. It evidently enjoyed a minor revival in the late 18th century, when it was re-named Sitahabu (*Better Here Than There*) by refugees from Kilwa who settled there. The new settlers appear not to have renovated the larger structures, but archaeological evidence suggests that they did leave offerings in the mihrab of the abandoned mosque, and they also appropriated the old cemetery.

Mtangata was long deserted in 1857, when Richard Burton stopped by en route between Tanga and Pangani. Burton, clearly affected by the ruinous apparition, wrote that:

> Moonlight would have tempered the view; it was a grisly spectacle in the gay and glowing shine of the sun. Shattered walls, the remnants of homesteads in times gone by, rose, choked with the luxuriant growth of decay, and sheltering in their desert shade the bat and the nightjar... I was shown the grave of a *wali* or saint – his very name had perished – covered with a cadjan roof, floored with stamped earth, cleanly swept, and garnished with a red and white flag. Near a spacious mosque, well built with columns of cut coralline, and adorned with an elaborate prayer-niche, are several tall mausoleums of elegant construction, their dates denoting an antiquity of about two hundred years. Beyond the legend of the bay, none could give me information concerning the people that have passed away... [One particular engraved tile] was regarded with a superstitious reverence by the Swahili, who declared that Sultan Kimweri of Usambara had sent a party of bold men to bear it away; nineteen died mysterious deaths, and the tile was thereupon restored to its place.

Today, the ruins at Tongoni consist of one large mosque, several disused wells and walls, and a cemetery containing some 40 tombs. The ruined mosque, with a ground plan of 150m^2, is the only vaguely habitable structure that remains, and aside from the ornate niche referred to by Burton, even it is rather poorly preserved. The main point of interest is the tombs, roughly half of which are of the medieval pillar type, the largest such concentration on the East African coast. Most of the pillar tombs have decorated borders and white plaster panels, and all except one have toppled over. The other, less distinguished tombs date to the 18th and 19th centuries. Much of old Mtangata has been submerged through erosion, and it is feared that without adequate protection the cemetery may also eventually crumble into the ocean. In nearby Tongoni village stand the discrete ruins of a more recent mosque, dating from the Omani era. Tongoni village also gives interesting insight into the present coastal Swahili-Islamic culture and lifestyle; the main economic activity is subsistence fishing and the surrounding area forms one of the successful mangrove conservation areas on the Tanga coast.

To reach the ruins from Tanga, follow the Pangani road south for 18km to Tongoni village, then turn left at the signposted junction and follow this motorable track for 1km. Any bus heading to Pangani can drop you at the junction, from where it is a ten-minute walk to the ruins. If you are dependent on buses, try to get to Tongoni early in the day, since there isn't much transport later in the day, and there is nowhere to stay nearby. If you want to charter a taxi to Tongoni, expect to pay around Tsh20,000 for the round trip from Tanga. The caretaker, who also acts as a guide, will collect the entrance fee of Tsh1,500.

PANGANI AND USHONGO

Pangani, in common with Bagamoyo further south, is a pivotal 19th-century trade centre that has been largely bypassed by 20th-century developments. Endowed with a number of crumbling old buildings, dating from the earliest years of its existence through to the colonial era, Pangani retains the most traditional Swahili character of any of port on the north coast. It also has a superb location, on the north bank of the mouth of the forest-fringed Pangani River, from where a gorgeous beach stretches northward as far as the eye can see.

Pangani enjoyed a passing popularity with travellers a few years ago, but like nearby Tanga it has subsequently fallen off the backpackers' circuit. I'm not sure why that should be. True, if it is prescribed entertainment you are after, then it *is* difficult to think of any compelling reason to visit Pangani. On the other hand, for those travellers to whom travel means something more than careering from one established backpackers' hangout to the next, it is enough perhaps that this strangely time-warped Swahili settlement – like the peaks that captivate mountaineers – should simply be there.

The coast within a 15km radius of Pangani has witnessed an extraordinary (and on the basis of existing custom wholly unfathomable) mushrooming of reasonably priced beach resorts in recent years. For budget travellers, the most accessible and affordable resorts lie to the north of Pangani along the road back towards Tanga. Costlier, but far more attractive, is the cluster of newly established resorts at Ushongo, an attractive coastal village set among coconut plantations some 12km south of Pangani. With its fabulous and practically deserted beach, Ushongo ranks as one of the best-kept secrets on the Tanzanian coast, and forms a highly recommended and affordable but otherwise equivalent alternative to other, better publicised beach nirvanas.

Once settled into Pangani, there's plenty to keep yourself busy with. The old town itself warrants a couple of hours' exploration, whether on a self-guided walking tour, or with a guide from the recently established tourist office on the waterfront. There's a good beach in front of the Pangadeco Beach Hotel, but you're advised against taking valuables there, or straying too far north from the

---

PILLAR OF STONE

In the early days of Pangani, there was an important annual celebration day on which it was forbidden to swim in the ocean. One wealthy Arab woman decided to ignore this taboo, and went in the ocean with her slave to wash her hair. When God saw this, he was so incensed that he punished both women by turning them into a stone which stands in the water outside town to this day.

hotel, as several mugging incidents have been reported. Other activities, easily arranged through the tourist office or through any of the beach resorts, include a boat trip up the forested Pangani River, a snorkelling excursion to Maziwe Island, and an agricultural walking tour of the hinterland. For more details, see *Activities and excursions from Pangani* on pages 265–7). Pangani also makes a suitable base for a day trip to the Tongoni Ruins (see pages 255–7).

Getting there and away

Pangani is situated 53km south of Tanga. The direct dirt road following the coast between the two ports is generally in reasonable condition, and can be covered in about 1.5 hours in a private vehicle. The beach resorts between Tanga and Pangani all lie within 1–2km of this road. The five buses that run daily in either direction between Tanga and Pangani charge Tsh1,500 per person and take less than three hours. There are no minibuses along this route. An alternative 45km route connects Pangani to Muheza on the Tanga–Segera road. The Muheza road did serve briefly as the main access road to Pangani after the El Niño floods of 1997–98, but generally it is in poor condition by comparison to the direct road to Tanga, and there is little public transport along it.

Ushongo and the Protea Hotel Pangani River lie to the south of the Pangani River. There is no bridge over the Pangani mouth, but a motor ferry is permanently in place to carry vehicles and passengers across on demand. The crossing takes five to ten minutes, and costs Tsh4,000 per vehicle and Tsh100 per person. Small local boats can take passengers without a vehicle for the same price.

From the south bank of the river, an erratic dirt road leads to Saadani village in the synonymous game reserve, an 80km drive that should take about two hours in dry conditions but might be impossible after heavy rain. The short, steep turn-off to the Protea Hotel Pangani River lies about 1km past the ferry along this road. The 5km turn-off to Ushongo, accessible in any weather, is signposted 10km along the Saadani road. The largest settlement before Saadani, about 40km south of Pangani, is Mkwaja, also the site of some minor Shirazi ruins. The daily bus that leaves Mkwaja for Pangani every morning, and starts the return trip in the early afternoon, is of limited use to travellers due to the lack of accommodation in Mkwaja, and absence of onward options using public transport. There is also no public transport along the 5km road between the junction and Ushongo.

Aside from the river ferry, no formal boat service runs out of Pangani. A private boatman associated with the New River View Lodge will, however, charter his motorised boat to Nungwi on the north of Zanzibar Island, a trip of roughly three hours. The starting price is Tsh60,000 for a private charter, but it's much cheaper if the boat is already going to Zanzibar for another reason.

There are no scheduled flights to Pangani, but Coastal Travel does offer a scheduled flight to Ushongo from Dar es Salaam, Zanzibar and Pemba. Coming from Arusha or elsewhere on the northern safari circuit, you'll need to charter a flight to Ushongo airstrip.

Where to stay and eat
Exclusive
Protea Hotel Pangani River Tel: 0811 324422; fax: 0811 410099; email: proteapangani@africaonline.co.tz; web: www.proteahotels.com. Unexpectedly plush – indeed, one of the smartest establishments anywhere on the coast of Tanzania – this 40-room clifftop hotel on the south bank of the Pangani River has had a brief but tumultuous history. Lavishly constructed in the mid-1990s to cater to a mega-wealthy game fishing market that never existed on the scale for which it was designed, the hotel went into

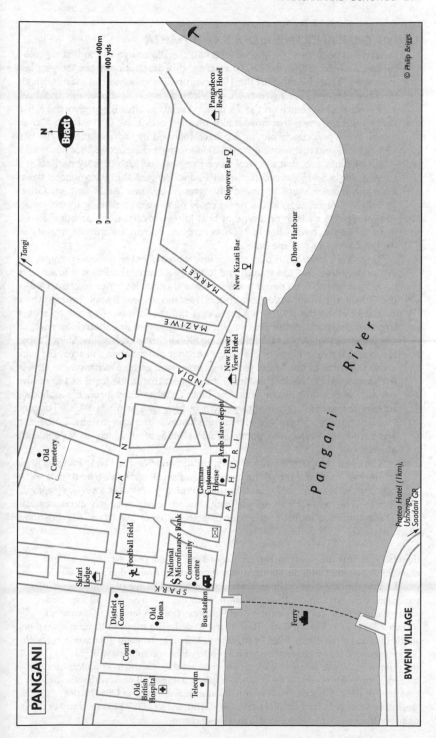

PANGANI

N

Bradt

400m
400 yds

© Philip Briggs

Tangi

Old
Cemetery

MAIN

Safari
Lodge

Football field

District
Council

Old
Boma

Court

Old
British Hospital

Telecom

National
Microfinance Bank

Community
centre

Bus station

SPARK

German
Customs
House

Arab slave depot

JAMHURI

INDIA

MAZIWE

MARKET

New River
View Hotel

New Kizati Bar

Stopover Bar

Dhow Harbour

Pangadeco
Beach Hotel

Pangani River

Ferry

Protea Hotel (1km),
Ushongo,
Saadani GR

BWENI VILLAGE

PANGANI AND THE RIDDLE OF RHAPTA

Pangani has been cited by one historian as 'the Bagamoyo of the first eighteen centuries of the Christian era'. In a sense, this description is probably rather misleading. True, for much of the 19th century, Pangani was the main terminus for slave caravans heading to the Lake Victoria region, and probably the most important trading centre on the Tanzanian mainland after Bagamoyo and Kilwa Kivinje. But the town that now stands on the north bank of the Pangani river mouth is not particularly old, having been founded by Omani Arabs in the late 18th century and totally rebuilt in 1810 following a destructive flood.

It is possible, too, that the very name Pangani is of 19th-century derivation – *panga* being a Swahili word for arrange, and Pangani the place where slaves from the interior were arranged into groups by their Arab captors. Other sources, however, suggest the name could be far older, alluding to the locally common *panga* shellfish or a type of boat known locally as *mtepe* but referred to by an English naval offer in 1608 as *pangaia*. Burton, meanwhile, translated Pangani as meaning 'in the hole'.

Pangani is a relatively modern settlement, possibly even a modern name, but it is equally true that the mouth and lower reaches of the Pangani River have played a major role in coastal trade for several centuries. Prior to the arrival of the Omani, the main settlement on the river mouth was Bweni, situated then, as it is now, on the southern bank facing the modern town. Prior to that, a larger trading post, Muhembo, was situated on Pangani Bay about 2km north of the present town. A local tradition dating Muhembo to the earliest Shirazi times is supported by the name of the oldest coconut plantation in the area, El Harth – also the name of the Arabic founding family who arrived at Pangani in AD900. Archaeological excavations at Muhembo suggest that, aside from its impressive ruined mosque, the town was less built up than, and probably politically subservient to, the contemporary town of Mtangata at modern-day Tongoni. Muhembo suffered heavily in 1588 at the hands of the cannibalistic Zimba, and was razed in a Portuguese punitive raid in 1635, after which it was evidently abandoned.

The most intriguing historical question surrounding the lower Pangani River is whether it was the site of the ancient trade settlement referred to in the 1st-century *Periplus of the Ancient Sea* and Ptolemy's 4th-century *Geography* as Rhapta. The case for Pangani as Rhapta is compelling, if largely circumstantial. The anonymous author of the *Periplus* places Rhapta 'two days' sail' beyond a

liquidation shortly after opening, was repossessed and closed, only to re-open under a management contract with the South African Protea chain. Follies don't come much grander than this: the immaculate grounds, centred around a large swimming pool, offer a panoramic view over Pangani River and town, while the stylish rooms – all imported material and fittings – could grace any world-class city hotel. A long list of excursions includes day visits to Saadani Game Reserve and Amani, river trips and Pangani town tours, snorkelling and game fishing – and beach trips to Ushongo, wherein lies the one big catch. This, essentially, is a beach resort without a beach, which – combined with its unfashionable, off-the-beaten-track location – ensures that it is the most underpatronised hotel of comparable quality in the country, regularly going a full week without a single customer. If these things don't worry you, it's also fantastic value at US$129/180 single/double with AC and satellite television, discounted to US$99/130 for a stay of three nights or longer – all highly negotiable to walk-in clients.

'flat and wooded' island he calls Menouthesias, which itself lay 'slightly south of southwest after a voyage of two days and nights' from 'the Pyralaae Islands and the island called Diorux [the Channel]'. These vague directions lack any name that has survived into the modern era, and are open to interpretation, but they do seem to point to Menouthesias as either Pemba or Mafia Island, respectively making Pangani or the Rufiji Delta the most likely location of Rhapta.

Ptolemy's *Geography*, based on the first- and second-hand observations of three different sailors, talks of Rhapta as 'the metropolis of Barbaria, set back a little from the sea' on the river Rhapton, but – contradicting the *Periplus* – it places Menouthias Island (presumably the same as Menouthesias) as lying considerably further south. More intriguingly, based on information gathered by a Greek merchant called Diogenes, Ptolemy talks of two snow-capped peaks and two large lakes lying 25 days' trek up the river Rhapton. The Pangani River has its source near Moshi, at the base of snow-capped Kilimanjaro.

No trace of an appropriately ancient settlement has ever been found near Pangani, which would not be entirely surprising had Rhapta been situated upriver and lacked the permanent stone structures of later medieval ports. Several other possible locations for Rhapta have been suggested, including Ras Kimbiji near Dar es Salaam and more plausibly the Rufiji Delta, the latter so vast and labyrinthine that the remains of a 2,000-year-old settlement would be difficult to locate and might well be submerged. To further complicate the picture, many historians regard it to be unlikely that Rhapta was the local name for a port, since it appears to derive from *ploiaria rhapta*, the Greek name for a type of boat which, coincidentally, was later referred to by an English navigator as *Pangaia*. Furthermore, given that these two ancient documents were written centuries apart, and appear to contradict each other on several details, there's every chance that the Rhapta of the *Periplus* is a totally different port to the Rhapta described by Ptolemy's sources.

Whatever the truth of the matter, it does seem certain that the Pangani River has long formed an important route for exploration of the interior, largely because it provides a reliable source of fresh water as far inland as Moshi. It almost certainly served as an important inland trade corridor for Mtangata and Muhembo in the Shirazi era, and could as easily have done so 2,000 years ago. Ptolemy's information about the Rhapton River and the African interior, flawed and confusing as it may have been, seems too close to the truth to be dismissed as mere coincidence.

Upmarket

Emayani Beach Lodge Tel/fax: 027 250 1741; mobile: 0742 401199; email: emayani@habari.co.tz or sss@habari.co.tz; web: www.emayanilodge.com. This intimate beachfront resort, constructed by the owners of Tarangire Safari Lodge, consists of 12 airy chalets made entirely from organic material and spaced out along a long, deserted stretch of sandy beach at Ushongo. It's a great place just to chill out with a beach towel and novel, but there's also plenty on offer for more active visitors. The beach is good for swimming at high tide, while the exposed reefs and mudflats in front of the lodge offer decent snorkelling at low tide. Snorkelling and game fishing excursions further afield can also be arranged, as can trips along the Pangani River and to a nearby private nature reserve. Sea kayaks can be used to explore a mangrove-lined creek about 1km north of the lodge – a good place to see the localised mangrove kingfisher, beautiful malachite kingfisher and a host of waders and marine birds. Also available are wind-surfers and a catamaran.

A FORGOTTEN REVOLUTIONARY

Pangani was the birthplace and home of Abushiri ibn Salim al-Harthi, the half-caste African-Arabic trader who masterminded the first and most successful indigenous uprising against German rule. On September 20 1888, Abushiri's hastily assembled troops evicted the German East Africa Company from Pangani and several other minor German stations along the coast. On September 22, Abushiri personally led a force of 8,000 men in an assault on Bagamoyo, at that time the German capital, and days of intense fighting resulted in the destruction of much of the town before a German Marine detachment of 260 men deflected Abushiri's army. Nevertheless, by the end of the month, only Bagamoyo and Dar es Salaam remained fully under German control, while Kilwa Kivinje was under permanent siege.

In the face of this onslaught, the trading company appealed to its government for support. A ragbag army of 21 German officers, 40 NCOs and 1,000 African mercenaries assembled by the German commander Hermann von Wissmann recaptured a number of the ports following naval bombardments that drove the occupying forces away, but the spirit of revolt remained high. The naval force was able to further secure the coast by setting up a blockade preventing arms and equipment from reaching the rebels. In May 1889, the Germans attacked Abushiri's fort at Jahazi (also called Nzole), between Pangani and Bagamoyo. Using artillery fire, Wissmann drove the defenders back from the 2m-high fortifications then led a charge in which more than 100 Arabs were killed and Jahazi was captured. Abushiri escaped, to launch a new series of mostly unsuccessful assaults assisted by Yao and Shambaa recruits.

Von Wissmann, realising he would not be able to wrest control of the hinterland while the revolution's leader remained at large, put a price of 10,000 rupees on Abushiri's head. This rich bounty persuaded a local chief who had been harbouring Abushiri to hand him over to the German commander. On December 15 1889, Abushiri was taken to his hometown of Pangani, paraded through the streets clad in a skimpy loincloth, and hanged later the same day. The town bears no trace of the revolutionary's existence today.

Accommodation is very good value at US$60/75 single/double for non-residents or US$45/55 for residents, to which must be added US$5 per person for breakfast and US$12 for lunch or dinner.

The Tides Tel/fax: 0741 325812; email: thetides@habari.co.tz. Also in Ushongo, this German-owned beachfront lodge, popular with Tanzanian residents, is of a similar standard to Emayani, but very different in character. Accommodation is in brightly painted chalets with an airy, classical interior of stone floors and whitewashed walls. Facilities and activities are similar to – and often run in conjunction with – Emayani. Half-board accommodation costs US$55 per person for residents and US$45 per person for non-residents – once again, top value by comparison with rates charged elsewhere in Tanzania.

Moderate

Coco Beach Resort Tel/fax: 0741 333449. The cheapest of the Ushongo resorts, Coco Beach is a comfortable, functional set-up with a great beachfront location, but the buildings lack the atmosphere and aesthetics that distinguish its two neighbours. Accommodation in clean self-contained chalets is good value at US$42 double, while chalets using communal showers cost US$18/36 single/double. The camping rate of US$6 per person is unlikely to win many takers. The open-air restaurant serves decent grills and seafood in the Tsh3,500–7,000 range.

Peponi Holiday Resort Tel: 0741 540139; email: peponi@twiga.com; web: www.peponiresort.com. Owned and managed by long-term East Africa residents Denys and Gilly Roberts, this popular and friendly beachfront resort lies a short distance off the Pangani road and is clearly signposted 33km south of Tanga. Accommodation in atmospheric *makuti bandas* costs US$35 single or double B&B high season, and US$22/35 single/double low season, with a special rate of US$12 per person B&B for backpackers and students. Camping under shelters costs US$4 per person. Facilities include clean ablution blocks, laundry service, and an attractive bar and restaurant serving good Western meals. Dependent on tides, the beach in front of the resort is good for swimming and offers reasonable snorkelling. Local boats can be arranged for snorkelling or fishing excursions to the outer reefs or Maziwe Island. The owners are a reliable source of information about local tourist attractions. Overall, it's a very chilled spot, and good value!

Argovia Tented Camp & Campsite Tel: 055 53531; fax: 055 51186; email: frey@eoltz.com. This recently opened German-owned tented camp is set in large, landscaped grounds that sprawl down to a swimming pool on a low cliff overlooking the deserted beach at Mkoma Bay. It lies 1km off the main road, along a side road signposted 49km from Tanga and 5km before Pangani. Accommodation in comfortable, attractive self-contained standing tents, with fan and netting, costs US$30/50 single/double B&B or US$48/75 HB. There are also a few clean *bandas* using communal showers at US$15/25 single/double B&B, and a campsite where you can pitch a tent for US$5 per person. The restaurant serves good Continental meals and seafood.

Tingatinga Resort Tel: Pangani 22. The large, green grounds and attractive beachfront location of this resort, signposted 500m past the Argovia Beach Resort in the direction of Pangani, doesn't quite compensate for its aura of having seen better days. The large, functional self-contained rooms with net and hot shower aren't bad value at Tsh22,000 double B&B, but there's a musty, boarding house feel to them that contrasts sharply with the bright, clean aesthetics of Peponi or Argovia. Camping costs Tsh3,000 per person. The restaurant serves meals in the Tsh4,000–5,000 range.

Budget

Pangani Beach Resort Tel: 053 269031/3 ext 88. Signposted 500m past the Tinga Tinga Resort, the Pangani Beach Resort is similar in feel and standard, exuding a faintly depressing aura of mildewed neglect. As with its northerly neighbour, however, the beach is all you could ask for. Further in its favour, the rates, YMCA excluded, are at Tsh15,000 for a spacious self-contained double by far the cheapest on this stretch of coast. Camping costs Tsh3,000 per tent. Inexpensive meals are available.

Safari Lodge The only accommodation in Pangani town to nudge above the shoestring category, this new lodge is situated on the same road as, but a block back from, the ferry jetty. The cramped self-contained rooms cannot be described as good value at Tsh7,500/8,000 double/twin, but they do at least have running water and a fan. It's difficult to believe a Tanzanian would pay this rate, so some negotiation might be in order. The Safari Lodge's restaurant looks to be the best in Pangani, which isn't saying a lot.

Shoestring

Pangani YMCA Youth Hostel Situated some 500m from the main road along a signposted track 5m south of the road to Argovia, the YMCA is by far the cheapest beachfront option in the Pangani area. Accommodation in basic and rather rundown self-contained chalets is pretty good value at Tsh5,000 double, even if there's only running water in the morning. Camping costs Tsh2,500 per person. The restaurant and bar are not

PANGANI IN 1857

The following edited extracts from Richard Burton's *Zanzibar and Two Months in East Africa*, originally published in 1858 in Blackwell's *Edinburgh Magazine* volume 83, provide a vivid impression of Pangani in the mid-19th century, as well as its relationship with the kingdoms of the immediate interior:

'Pangani... and its smaller neighbour Kumba, hug the left bank of the river, upon a strip of shore bounded by the sea, and a hill range 10 or 11 miles distant. Opposite are Bweni and Mzimo Pia, villages built under yellow sandstone bluffs, impenetrably covered with wild trees... Pangani boasts of 19 or 20 stone houses. The remainder is a mass of *cadjan* huts, each with its wide mat-encircled yard, wherein all the business of life is transacted... Pangani, with the three other villages, may contain a total of 4,000 – Arabs, Moslem Swahili, and heathens. Of these, female slaves form a large proportion.

Pangani, I am told, exports annually 35,000lb of ivory, 1750lb of black rhinoceros horn, and 16lb of hippopotamus' teeth... Twenty Banyans manage the lucrative ivory trade... These merchants complain loudly of their *pagazi*, or porters, who receive 10 dollars for the journey, half paid down, the remainder upon return; and the proprietor congratulates himself if, after payment, only 15% run away. The Hindus' profits, however, must be enormous. I saw one man to whom 26,000 dollars were owed by the people. What part must interest and compound interest have played in making up such a sum...? Their only drawback is the inveterate beggary of the people. Here the very princes are mendicants; and the Banyan dare not refuse the seventy or eighty savages who every evening besiege his door with cries for grain, butter, or a little oil...

Coconuts... and plantains grow about the town. Around are gardens of paw-paws, betel, and jamlis; and somewhat further, lie extensive plantations of... maize... and other grains. The clove

madly inviting, it must be said, but you could always head over to the Argovia for a chilled drink and a meal. If the facilities are indifferent, the setting is everything you could hope for, on a low cliff overlooking Mkoma Bay's lovely beach.

New River View Lodge The better of two cheap guesthouses in Pangani town, the New River View lies on the main waterfront road about 300m from where the buses stop. It is a very clean little place with running water and electricity. Rooms with nets cost Tsh2,000/4,000 single/double using communal showers. A good variety of street foods are available along the nearby waterfront in the evening.

Pangadeco Beach Hotel The relatively rundown state of the Pangadeco is arguably compensated for by its excellent beachfront location. It lies 5–10 minutes' walk from the bus stop. Rooms with nets cost Tsh2,000/2,500 single/double. No food is available but the bar has a fridge.

Camping

Several of the resorts listed in the moderate and budget category allow camping. Full details are supplied under the above listings, but the most attractive campsite is unquestionably the one at Peponi, the cheapest for one person the YMCA, the cheapest for two people sharing a tent the Pangani Beach Resort.

flourishes, and as elsewhere upon the coast a little cotton is cultivated for domestic use. Beasts are rare. Cows die after eating the grass; goats give no milk; and sheep are hardly procurable. But fish abounds. Poultry thrives, as it does all over Africa; and before the late feuds, clarified cow-butter, that 'one sauce' of the outer East, was cheap and well-flavoured... The wells produce heavy and brackish drink; but who, as the people say, will take the trouble to fetch sweeter? The climate is said to be healthy in the dry season, but the long and severe rains are rich in fatal bilious remittents.

The settlement is surrounded by a thorny jungle, which at times harbours a host of leopards. One of these beasts lately scaled the high terrace of our house, and seized upon a slave girl. Her master... who was sleeping by her side, gallantly caught up his sword, ran into the house, and bolted the door, heedless of the miserable cry, 'Bwana, help me!' The wretch was carried to the jungle and devoured. The river is equally full of alligators [crocodiles], and whilst we were at Pangani a boy disappeared. When asked by strangers why they do not shoot their alligators, and burn their wood, the people reply that the former bring good-luck, and the latter is a fort to which they can fly in need.

Pangani and Bweni, like all settlements upon this coast, belong, by a right of succession, to the [Sultan] of Zanzibar, who confirms and invests the governors and diwans. At Pangani, however, these officials are *par conge d'elire* selected by Kimweri [the king of Usambara], whose ancestors received tribute and allegiance from Pare to the seaboard. On the other hand, Bweni is in the territory of the Wazegura, a violent and turbulent heathen race, inveterate slave-dealers, and thoughtlessly allowed by the Arabs to lay up goodly stores of muskets, powder, and ball. Of course the two tribes [Usambara and Wazegura] are deadly foes. Moreover, about a year ago, a violent internecine feud broke out amongst the Wazegura, who, at the time of our visit, were burning and murdering, kidnapping and slave-selling in all directions.

General information

A waterfront **tourist information office** was recently opened by the Pangani Coast Cultural Tourism Program (tel: Pangani 11), an eco-tourism project developed in association with the Dutch SNV agency. Independent travellers can arrange most of the activities listed at the tourist office, which levies a development and administration fee of Tsh3,000 per person, and a guide fee of Tsh3,000 per group for all activities. **Bicycles** can be hired at Tsh100 per hour or Tsh1,000 for a full day. Travellers staying at the smarter beach lodges to the north and south of town should be able to arrange the same activities through their hotel.

Foreign exchange and **internet** facilities are not available in Pangani. The closest place where they exist is in Tanga.

Activities and excursions from Pangani
Pangani town tour
Strongly Swahili in mood, Pangani has seen little development in recent decades, and several buildings date to the 19th and early 20th centuries. Guided tours of the old town can be arranged through the tourist office, but it is equally possible to explore the town independently, following the walking tour described below.

COCONUT PALMS

Industry and associated opportunities for formal employment are thin on the ground in Pangani, but the surrounding district is self-sufficient in food, thanks to its fertile soil and the rich bounty of the ocean. Cashew and sisal – the latter introduced by a German botanist in 1892 – form the region's main export crops, but Pangani is also known for its extensive coconut palm plantations. The coconut plantations around Pangani are significant employers (monthly salaries are equivalent to US$40), and also provide an estimated 50% of Tanzania's coconut yield!

Even on a casual stroll around Pangani, the ubiquity of coconuts is striking. Vendors selling young nuts provide travellers with a refreshing and nutritious alternative to bottled soft drinks. Near the harbour, you'll see large piles of drying husks, the debris of nuts shipped to other parts of the country. Women wander home from the market carrying their goods in palm fronds converted with a few deft strokes into disposable shopping baskets.

No part of the coconut palm goes unused. The flesh of the mature nut, harvested twice annually, is not only a popular snack, but also an important ingredient in Swahili cuisine, and a source of cooking oil. The fibrous husks surrounding the nut are twined to make rope and matting, or dried for fire fuel. Palm fronds form the basis of the *makuti* roofs characteristic of the Swahili coast, and are also used as brooms. The sap and flower are brewed to make a popular local wine, and the timber is used for furniture. A multi-faceted resource indeed!

The obvious place to start is the ferry jetty at the raised waterfront, where an Omani trader erected a coral rag wall in 1810 after the town was destroyed by flooding. From the ferry jetty, walk a few metres up Spark Street, and to your left, surrounded by an open park-like area, stands the **Old Boma**. This rectangular two-storey building, the oldest in Pangani, was constructed in 1810 as the residence of the same wealthy Omani trader who was responsible for the waterfront wall. Legend has it that several slaves were buried alive under the pillars of the Old Boma, which was supposed to ensure it strong foundations. The carved Zanzibar-style doors are thought to be the originals. The fortified roof is a later addition, dating to the early German era, when the building was appropriated to serve as an administrative centre (*boma*). The Old Boma has been maintained well: it was used as the District Commissioner's Office in colonial times, and today houses Pangani's immigration office.

About 100m further west, behind the new Telecommunications Office, the **Former British Hospital** was built in 1918 as a 'native hospital' and subsequently served as a gaol. A double-storey building with a creaky old balcony, the building shows some Arabic influences in its architecture. It is currently used as a government office, but there is some talk of restoring it and converting it to a resthouse. About 500m west of the hospital behind a football field, stands a cemetery of what appear to be 17th-century **Portuguese graves** and another of 19th-century **German graves**. Both are quite difficult to locate in the dense bush.

Two significant buildings stand adjacent to each other on the waterfront east of the ferry jetty. The older of the two, probably built in the 1850s, is the castellated double-storey **Slave Depot**. It is said that the building led into a subterranean tunnel through which slaves were taken to Bweni on the south bank of the river.

The building is derelict today, but the façade remains intact, and there is talk of restoring it as a tourist information centre and/or museum. The **German Customs House**, constructed in the Hanseatic style with an impressive castellated front, is reminiscent of a fort or cathedral, though it has served as the customs house since its construction in 1910 up to the modern day. Inland of these buildings, **India Street**, the main shopping drag through Pangani, is lined with old Indian residences. Dating to the late 19th century, these are typically double-storey buildings with ornate iron balconies, and the ground floors are used as shops.

Some travellers may also elect to catch a boat across to **Bweni**, on the south side of the Pangani River, which predates the modern town by perhaps two centuries, though no significant relics of this occupation can be seen today. About 1km east of the ferry crossing at Bweni, however, stands the shell of a **German Fort** built in 1916 to repel British naval invasions. A further 1.5km along this stretch of coast, stands a tall **commemorative pillar** dedicated to Christian Luutherborn, a Danish sisal estate director whose death in 1907 was probably linked to the Maji-Maji rebellion. Of greater antiquity is the Shirazi mosque at **Muhembo**, some 2km north of Pangani and accessible from the Tanga road. This mosque was larger than its counterpart in Mtangani, but is more poorly preserved possibly as a result of damage perpetrated in the Portuguese raid of 1635.

Pangani river trip

Boat trips up the forested Pangani River are of interest primarily for the scenery and birds, though some large mammals still occur in the area, most visibly vervet monkeys. In the wet season, it is possible to go upriver all the way to the base of the Pangani Falls. A hydro-electric plant has swallowed the actual waterfall, but the pools are a reliable place to see crocodiles and hippos. Boat trips can be arranged through the Protea Hotel Pangani River, which has its own boat, or with any of the beach resorts at Ushongo. The tourist office in Pangani charges Tsh20,000 to arrange the boat, plus the guide and development fees. Boats can be chartered through the New River View Lodge at a similar price, but without the additional fees.

Maziwe and Fungu islands

These two small islands off the coast south of Pangani form the centrepieces of a recently proclaimed marine park. Maziwe was once regarded as the most important nesting site on the Tanzanian coast for sea turtles, but it has been abandoned since the 1980s due to erosion, which submerges the beach at high tide. Today, the main attraction is the snorkelling on the offshore reefs, where the usual host of colourful reef fish can be observed. It is important to time a visit so you arrive at low tide, when the snorkelling is best. Boat trips to the islands can be arranged through the resorts at Ushongo, which charge Tsh30,000 to charter a large local dhow. The tourist office in Pangani arranges trips for Tsh40,000 inclusive of gear but excluding the development fees of Tsh3,000 per person. The New River View Hotel in Pangani charges Tsh30,000 for up to six people inclusive of snorkelling equipment. A park entrance fee of Tsh1,000 is levied.

SAADANI NATIONAL PARK

Protected as a game reserve since 1969, Saadani – due to be gazetted as a national park before the end of 2002 – is the only wildlife sanctuary in East Africa with an Indian Ocean beachfront. The original 200km^2 game reserve, centred on the small but ancient fishing village of Saadani, was expanded to cover 500km^2 in 1996, and it is likely to redouble in area with the proposed incorporation of a tract of former ranchland when the national park is gazetted. As recently as ten years ago, Saadani

– despite its proximity to Dar es Salaam – was among the most obscure and inaccessible conservation areas in East Africa, lacking for tourist facilities in any form. Inadequate protection and resultant poaching also meant that game had been severely depleted, to the extent that Saadani's status as a game reserve seemed all but nominal. In recent years, however, Saadani has received renewed attention from conservationists and tourists alike. One factor in this has been the establishment of a top-notch private tented camp and improved access. Another has been the concerted clampdown on poaching and attempt to integrate adjacent villages into the conservation effort that was initiated by the Department of Wildlife with assistance from Germany's GTZ agency in 1998. Viewed purely as a wildlife destination, Saadani cannot yet bear comparison to Tanzania's finest – though if present trends continue, it may well be up with them ten years hence. But even as things stand, Saadani is a thoroughly worthwhile and enjoyable retreat, allowing visitors to combine the hedonistic pleasures of a perfect sandy beach with guided bush walks, game drives, and boat trips up the Wami River. It is also the closest national park to Zanzibar – 15 minutes away by air, with scheduled flights likely to be introduced in the near future.

Inland of its 20km coastline, Saadani supports a park-like cover of open grassland interspersed with stands of acacia trees and knotted coastal thicket. Along the coast, palm-lined beaches are separated by extensive mangrove stands, while the major watercourses are fringed by lush riparian woodland. The park supports a wide range of ungulates, with game densities generally highest in January and February, and from June to August, when the plains near the lodge hold more water. At all times of year, however, you can be reasonably confident of encountering giraffe, buffalo, warthog, common waterbuck, reedbuck, hartebeest and wildebeest, along with troops of yellow baboon and vervet monkey. Something of a Saadani special, likely to be seen a few times on any game drive, is the red duiker, a diminutive, beautiful and normally very shy antelope of coastal scrub and forest. Quite common, but less easily seen, are greater kudu and eland. Saadani also harbours a small population of Roosevelt's sable, an endangered race elsewhere found in the Selous Game Reserve and Kenya's Shimba Hills. The elephant population, though small, is on the increase, and herds of up to 30 head are sighted with increasing frequency. Lion are also making something of a comeback, with at least three different prides observed during 2001, one of which actually came to drink at the lodge waterhole! Leopard, spotted hyena and black-backed jackal are also around, along with the usual small nocturnal predators. In addition to game drives, guided walks offer a good chance of seeing various antelope and representatives of Saadani's rich variety of woodland birds. Hippos and crocodiles are normally encountered on river trips, along with a good selection of marine and riverine birds. The beaches in and around Saadani form one of the last major breeding sites for green turtles on mainland Tanzania.

The settlement of Saadani, which lies within the reserve about 1km from the tented lodge, is today little more than a fishing village, with a population estimated at less than 1,000. In the 19th century, however, it was an important trade centre, briefly rivalling Bagamoyo in stature. The town's growth was inhibited by a defensive wall, built to protect against the warring Wadoe and Wazigua clans, whose ongoing fighting also dissuaded caravans from passing through the Saadani hinterland. Saadani was briefly considered as a site for the London Missionary Society's first East African mission, but it was passed over in favour of Bagamoyo. Few relics of the trade era remain, but the crumbling old German Customs House and a clutch of late 19th-century German and British graves serve as a reminder that Saadani was still a significant settlement in the early colonial era.

Entrance to the game reserve costs US$20 per person per 24 hours. Whether this will increase once the national park is gazetted remains to be seen. The lodge – and effectively the park – is often forced to close over April and May when the black cotton soil roads tend to become waterlogged.

Getting there and away

No scheduled flight currently lands at Saadani airstrip, though negotiations are underway for a scheduled service to be introduced from Zanzibar. Otherwise, air charters can be arranged through the Original Saadani Experience, the company that runs Saadani Safari Lodge. The lodge also operates a thrice-weekly road shuttle, leaving Dar es Salaam at 09.00 on Wednesday, Friday and Sunday, and arriving at Saadani at around 13.00. The shuttle starts the return trip to Dar es Salaam on the same days at 14.00, arriving there about four hours later. The shuttle is for the exclusive use of lodge clients.

Coming from Dar es Salaam using a private vehicle or public transport, the shortest route on paper is the coastal road via Bagamoyo, but this has in fact been impassable for a decade, ever since the government ferry over the Wami River sank. There is some talk of a new ferry being installed, but until such time as that happens, the only viable route from the south is through Chalinze and Miono. This route, a drive of roughly four hours, entails following the main surfaced road towards Morogoro west out of Dar es Salaam for 105km to the junction town of Chalinze, then turning right along the Moshi road. After 50km, the Moshi road crosses a bridge over the Wami River, and 1.5km further a signpost to your right reads 'Tent With a View Safaris Saadani Game Reserve 58km'. Follow this road through Mandera, Miono (10km) and Mkange (27km), ignoring the signpost to your right for the WWF Forestry Centre (48km) and crossing a railway track (53km) until you reach the reserve entrance gate (58km). From the entrance gate, it's an 8km drive to Saadani village and a further 1km or so to the lodge. Parts of this road are *very* rough, and can only be attempted in a good 4WD. The road is sometimes impassable during April and May, so you are advised to ask about the current condition when you book. One very beat-up bus runs between Dar es Salaam and Saadani daily. It would probably be a lot quicker to catch a fast bus heading in the direction of Moshi as far as the Miono junction, where you could hop on the Saadani bus or one of the occasional pick-up trucks that ply the route.

Coming from the north, the coastal road from Tanga through Pangani and Mkwaja is normally viable in a 4WD vehicle, though it may become impassable after heavy rain. The drive from Pangani to Saadani generally takes about two hours. A daily bus connects Pangani and Mkwaja, leaving Mkwaja in the early morning and Pangani in the early afternoon, but there is no public transport at all between Mkwaja and Saadani.

Where to stay
Upmarket
Saadani Safari Camp Tel/fax: 022 215 1106; email: tentview@intafrica.com; web: www.saadani.com. This small and intimate tented camp runs attractively along a palm-fringed beach about 1km north of Saadani village. Accommodation is in comfortable framed canvas tents with a *makuti* roof, en-suite facilities, solar electricity and twin or double bed. The open wooden bar and dining area is very peaceful, while a tree house overlooks a waterhole regularly visited by waterbuck, bushbuck, buffalo and various waterbirds – and very occasionally by lion and elephant. Activities include game drives at US$30 per person, guided walks with a ranger at US$15 per person, and boat trips on the

river for US$35 per person. Full board rates are US$75 per person (residents) or US$95 per person (non-residents).

Budget and camping

At present, no budget accommodation is available at Saadani. The former government resthouse, having spent several decades quietly attempting to biodegrade, was recently refurbished for the exclusive use of the GTZ people working with the Department of Game. Word is that GTZ will not stay on in Saadani after the national park is gazetted, in which case it's not inconceivable that the resthouse will re-open to the public. There is also some talk of a campsite being opened next to the old German Customs House, either by the owners of Saadani Safari Camp or by the local community. For the time being, I heard from people who camped wild here in late 2001 without any problem.

BAGAMOYO

Situated on a superb white beach some 70km north of Dar es Salaam, Bagamoyo must rank as one of the most historically compelling towns in East Africa. Although the modern town was probably founded as recently as the late 18th century, Bagamoyo Bay has long been an important centre of maritime trade. During the Shirazi era, the main centre of activity, situated some 5km south of the modern town, was Kaole. Founded in the 12th century, Kaole enjoyed strong trade links with Kilwa, and prospered for the three centuries prior to the Portuguese occupation before it fell into economic decline, eventually to be abandoned. The ruins of Kaole can still be visited outside Bagamoyo.

Bagamoyo flourished in the mid-19th century, when – as the closest mainland port to Zanzibar – it formed the coastal terminus for slave caravans from the Lake Tanganyika area. At the peak of the slave trade, approximately 50,000 captives arrived in Bagamoyo annually, chained neck-to-neck and hoarded in dingy dungeons before being shipped to Zanzibar. Ironically, Bagamoyo's trade links to the interior ensured that it became the springboard for the European exploration of the African interior, which in turn played a major role in ending the slave trade. Such Victorian luminaries as Burton, Speke, Grant, Stanley and Livingstone all passed through Bagamoyo at some point. Livingstone's graphic descriptions and outright condemnation of the trade he described as 'the open sore of the world' led to the Holy Ghost Fathers establishing Bagamoyo Mission in 1868. The newly founded mission ransomed as many slaves as it could afford to, and settled its purchases in a Christian Freedom Village on the outskirts of Bagamoyo. Fittingly, when Livingstone died in 1873, his preserved body was carried 1,600km by his porters to Bagamoyo Mission, before being shipped to Zanzibar (on the improbably named HMS *Vulture*) and eventually to England.

Between 1868 and 1873, the slave-based society of Bagamoyo town co-existed in uneasy proximity to the free society of the adjacent Catholic compound. This period was marked by a pair of disasters: first, the cholera epidemic of 1869, which claimed 25–30% of the townspeople's lives, then in 1872 a destructive hurricane that razed large parts of the town. In 1873, Bagamoyo suffered a third blow, when the Sultan of Zanzibar, reacting to British pressure, abolished the slave trade. Bagamoyo's main source of revenue was curtailed – or at least forced underground – and the already battered town entered a period of economic transition and physical reconstruction. Nevertheless, its established trade infrastructure and proximity to Zanzibar made Bagamoyo the obvious site for the first German headquarters in East Africa, established in 1888. Stanley, who returned to

Bagamoyo in 1889 after three years' absence, was struck by how much the port town had grown in its first year of German occupation.

By 1890, Germany had realised Bagamoyo harbour was too shallow for long-term use, and it opted to relocate the administration first to Tanga and then to Dar es Salaam. Bagamoyo remained an important regional centre for some years after this (the impressive State House was built in 1897) but its steady decline since 1900 is testified to by the near absence of large buildings in the town centre post-dating Omani and German times. In the 1890s, Bagamoyo's population was estimated at more than 10,000. By 1925, it had dropped below 5,000, and Bagamoyo had been reduced to little more than a glorified fishing village, with one of the highest unemployment rates in the country.

Bagamoyo's fortunes have looked up somewhat over the last decade, with a minor tourist boom precipitating a flurry of beachfront hotel construction – as recently as ten years ago the only such accommodation was the (then very rundown) Badeco Beach Hotel. Trade opportunities can only be enhanced by the current rehabilitation of the once appalling road south to Dar es Salaam, which will also improve tourist access, and may well see Bagamoyo gaining popularity as an alternative pre-safari stopover to the big city. Assuming that the mooted installation of a ferry on the Wami River goes ahead, this would open up the coastal route north, ending Bagamoyo's current end-of-the-road status, with obvious advantages for locals and tourists alike. For the time being, however – although it probably offers little consolation to residents of the once prosperous town – the museum-like quality that makes Bagamoyo so absorbing is difficult to disentangle from the pervasive air of economic stagnation and physical disintegration.

Getting there and away

The 70km road between Dar es Salaam and Bagamoyo was in an advanced state of rehabilitation at the time of writing, with only the last 10km remaining unsurfaced. It is scheduled for completion before the end of 2002, after which the drive should take no longer than one hour. Regular buses run between Dar es Salaam and Bagamoyo. At present, no public transport or passable road of interest to tourists runs north from Bagamoyo.

Where to stay and eat
Exclusive
Lazy Lagoon Tel: 023 244 0194; mobile: 0741 237422; fax: 0741 327706; email: fox@twiga.com; web: www.ruahariverlodge.com. This excellent new resort, under the same ownership as Ruaha River Lodge, is set on the tip of a long spit on the Mbegani Lagoon about 7km south of Bagamoyo. The beautiful, isolated setting – it is to all intents and purposes an island – is complemented by the uncluttered accommodation, which consists of 10 en-suite *makuti* beach chalets cut off from each other by the thick coastal scrub. The seafood is excellent, too, with a speciality being beach dinners below a sparkling night sky, and the lights of Bagamoyo twinkling in the distance. The emphasis is very much on chilling out at the beach or next to the swimming pool, but there's decent snorkelling in the coral shore close to the lodge and good walking along the spit. Day trips to Bagamoyo, Kaole and elsewhere can also be arranged. Coming from Dar es Salaam, the turn-off to Lazy Lagoon lies about 7km before Bagamoyo and is signposted for the Kasika Marine Camp. Follow the turn-off for about 2km to the fenced Mbegani Fisheries compound, where you need to enter the gate and continue along the road for another 500m to the landing jetty. The boat transfer to the lodge takes about 20 minutes and should be arranged in advance. A more direct 7km road between the landing strip and Bagamoyo runs close to the coast, passing through Kaole en route.

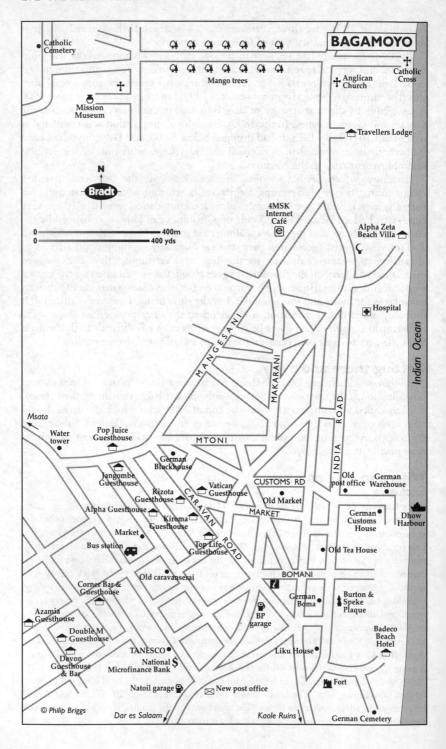

Catholic
Cemetery

Mission
Museum

Mango trees

BAGAMOYO

Anglican
Church

Catholic
Cross

Travellers Lodge

N

Bradt

0   400m
0   400 yds

4MSK
Internet
Café

Alpha Zeta
Beach Villa

Hospital

Indian Ocean

MANGESANI

MAKARANI

Msata

Water
tower

Pop Juice
Guesthouse

MTONI

German
Blockhouse

Jangombe
Guesthouse

Kizota
Guesthouse

Vatican
Guesthouse

CUSTOMS RD

INDIA ROAD

Old
post office

German
Warehouse

CARAVAN ROAD

Old Market

MARKET

German
Customs
House

Dhow
Harbour

Alpha Guesthouse

Kiroma
Guesthouse

Market

Bus station

Top Life
Guesthouse

Old caravanserai

Old Tea House

BOMANI

Corner Bar &
Guesthouse

German
Boma

Burton &
Speke
Plaque

Azamia
Guesthouse

Double M
Guesthouse

BP
garage

Badeco
Beach
Hotel

Devon
Guesthouse
& Bar

TANESCO

National
Microfinance Bank

Liku House

Natoil garage

New post office

Fort

© Philip Briggs

Dar es Salaam

Kaole Ruins

German Cemetery

Livingstone Club Tel: 023 244 0059/80; fax: 023 244 0104; email: info@livingstone-club.com; web: www.livingstone-club.com. Distinguished by the imaginative and impressive use of traditional Swahili elements in the architecture and decor, the Livingstone Club is a top quality beach hotel situated 600m north of the town centre, past the turn-off to the old mission. Centred around a great swimming pool area overlooking the beach, the hotel has all the facilities you would expect as well as an internet café and Italian-style coffee bar. A good range of activities, also on offer to visitors not resident at the hotel, and generally with a minimum group size of four, includes snorkelling excursions (US$20pp), boat trips to the Ruvu Delta (US$25pp), as well as guided town walks and mountain bike excursions. Accommodation in spacious semi-suites costs US$75/95 single/double B&B or US$98/140 FB.

Upmarket

Paradise Holiday Resort Tel: 023 244 0136/40; fax: 023 244 0142; email: paradise@raha.com; web: www.paradiseresortraha.com. Situated on the beach some 400m past the junction to the old mission, the blandly plush Paradise Holiday Resort is comprised of 32 rooms divided between eight thatched, whitewashed blocks. It has a great beach and swimming pool area, a good seafood restaurant, and offers a wide range of activities from table tennis and beach volleyball to scuba diving and game fishing. Internet facilities are available at Tsh3,000 per hour. The standard rooms, with large double bed, netting, satellite television, AC and private balcony, cost US$40/60 single/double B&B, while superior rooms (same facilities but more spacious) cost US$50/70. Characterless as its name would suggest, this lodge is good value and difficult to knock, without being anything to get excited about.

Kasiki Marine Camp Tel: 0744 278590; email: kasiki@africaonline.co.tz; web: www.bagamoyo.org. This comfortable and attractive small out-of-town lodge, which consists of about ten cottages set on a low rise above the mangrove-lined western shore of the Mbegani Lagoon, is compromised only by the absence of a good swimming beach. Otherwise, it's a peaceful and scenic spot, far more low-key and serene than the lodges closer to town, with a variety of boat and land excursions on offer. The authentic Italian cuisine is highly regarded. Self-contained cottages cost US$28 per person B&B, US$41 HB or US$54 FB. Directions are the same as for Lazy Lagoon above, except that when you reach the marine compound, instead of entering the compound gate you need to follow a signposted 2km road to the right.

Moderate

Travellers Lodge Tel: 023 244 0077; fax: 023 244 0154; email: travellerslodge@bagol.com. Probably the pick in this range, the German-owned Travellers Lodge is set in large green grounds that sprawl down to an attractive beach on the edge of the town centre. Accommodation in spacious, simply decorated cottages with large beds, netting, and a private balcony costs Tsh28,000/32,000 single/double B&B (self-contained with AC), or Tsh18,000/22,000 (self-contained with fan only) or Tsh10,000/12,000 (common showers, fan only). Camping is permitted for Tsh1,500 per person. A good restaurant and bar are attached.

Palm Tree Village Tel: 023 244 0245/6. Situated out of town about 200m past the Livingstone Club, Palm Tree Village is perhaps too new to have acquired any discernible character – the grounds in particular look very bare – but otherwise it's a decent, sensibly priced set-up with the usual good beach and alluring swimming pool. Accommodation is in whitewashed chalets in which two self-contained rooms with AC share a common entrance hall and balcony, making it especially suitable for families. Good value at Tsh26,000/32,000 single/double.

Bagamoyo Beach Resort Tel: 023 244 0083; fax: 023 244 0154; email: bbr@ud.co.tz or bbr@bagol.com. This unpretentious, slightly scruffy but perennially popular resort charges

THE BURDEN OF BAGAMOYO

In a pattern repeated all along the East African coast, the modern town of Bagamoyo is essentially a 19th-century entity, constructed by Omani slave traders close to the ruins of a medieval Shirazi town (in this case Kaole) that fell into disuse during the Portuguese era. The name Bagamoyo, too, dates to the 19th century, but while it is clearly linked to the town's role in the iniquitous slave trade, its precise meaning is open to interpretation. One Victorian explorer claimed that Bagamoyo referred to the port's role as the gateway to the African interior. Today, it is more widely accepted to be a corruption of the phrase *bwaga moyo*, at least a dozen translations of which have been published, falling into two broad categories.

The first set of interpretations, variations on 'lose heart' or 'lay down my heart', would have the phrase as the refrain of a slave lament: although the captives were to be shipped from the African mainland, their hearts would be left behind, in Bagamoyo. The second is that the phrase translates as 'lay down the burden of your heart' or similar, and was coined by caravan porters for whom Bagamoyo afforded an opportunity to lay down their burden at the end of the arduous trek from the Lake Tanganyika hinterland. The traditional Swahili porter's song, displayed in the Catholic Museum and loosely translated below, would certainly back up the second theory:

> Be happy, my soul, release all cares, for we soon reach the place
> you yearn for
> The town of palms, Bagamoyo!
> When you were far away, how my heart ached when I thought of
> you, you pearl
> You place of happiness, Bagamoyo!
> The women wear their hair parted; you can drink palm wine all
> year through
> In the gardens of love of Bagamoyo!
> The dhows arrive with streaming sails to take aboard the treasures
> of Europe
> In the harbour of Bagamoyo!
> Oh, such delight to hear the drums and the lovely girls swaying in
> dance
> All night through in Bagamoyo!
> Be quiet, my heart, all cares are gone. Let the drumbeats rejoice:
> We are reaching Bagamoyo!

Tsh24,000/28,000 B&B for a single/double with en-suite facilities and AC, or Tsh16,000/20,000 for a similar room with fan only. Budget rooms are available at Tsh10,000 single or double. It is situated on an attractive beach between the junction for the old mission and the Paradise Holiday Resort. The menu, with most items at around Tsh5,000, reflects the nationality of its French owners. A variety of watersport activities and other excursions are on offer.

Badeco Beach Hotel Tel: 023 244 0018; fax: 023 244 0154. Once – incredibly – the closest thing in Bagamoyo to upmarket accommodation, the venerable Badeco Beach Hotel has improved to near unrecognisability over the intervening years, while always remaining within reach of most budget travellers. The grounds are dominated by an open-sided *makuti* bar and restaurant overlooking a fine beach, while the double rooms, with Zanzibar-style beds draped in netting and a fan, are fair value at Tsh24,000 self-contained or Tsh12,000 double using common shower.

Budget

None of the resorts in Bagamoyo caters specifically to budget travellers, while none of the guesthouses could realistically be placed above the shoestring category. Of the four lodges listed in the *Moderate* category above, however, all but Palm Tree Village offers non-self-contained accommodation in the Tsh10–12,000 range, aimed squarely at backpackers.

Shoestring

Double M Guesthouse Tel: 0744 311058. By far the best of a dozen or more generally squalid guesthouses scattered around Bagamoyo, the Double M lies about 500m from the bus station and charges a very reasonable Tsh3,500 for a self-contained room with net, fan and three-quarter bed. The Devon Bar 50m away is a good spot for a mellow drink below a *makuti* roof.

Azania Guesthouse This clean and quiet (no bar) guesthouse also stands out from the pack, charging Tsh1,500 for a single room using common showers.

Camping

The best place to camp is **Travellers Lodge**, (see under the *Moderate* heading), which charges Tsh1,500 per person.

General information

Tourist information and day trips No official tourist office exists in Bagamoyo and vague plans to restore the old Caravanserai for this purpose are unlikely to come into fruition in the foreseeable future. All the beach resorts can offer good advice, however, as well as set up walking tours, trips to Kaole and other activities discussed below. Travellers staying at local guesthouses can set up activities and guides through the beach resort, or through the private tourist information centre on Caravan Road opposite the BP filling station.

Foreign exchange Aside from the beach hotels, which will only change money for hotel residents, and then generally at poor rates, the only foreign exchange service is at the **National Microfinance Bank** on the Dar es Salaam road opposite the new post office.

Internet The internet cafés at the **Paradise Holiday Resort** and **Livingstone Club** are open to all comers, but the rates (Tsh3,000 per hour) are high by local standards. Far cheaper is the **MSK Internet Café** near the junction of Mangosani and India streets. If patterns elsewhere in Tanzania offer any indication, this recently opened internet café in Bagamoyo is likely to be the first of many.

Swimming The entire waterfront of Bagamoyo amounts to one long swimming beach, though wandering around public parts of the beach in swimming trunks or bikini probably wouldn't be massively appreciated. Better to swim from one of the resorts: the Badeco is the most convenient for travellers staying in town, and the most likely to be amenable to casual visitors, though it would be courteous to buy a drink or meal if you use their beach.

Activities and excursions

Town walking tour

The old town of Bagamoyo holds sufficient sites of interest that you ought to dedicate a good half-day to exploration. Local guides can be arranged at any of the

SECURITY IN BAGAMOYO

An unfortunate truism of travel in the developing world is that once a particular place has acquired a reputation for crime, no matter how flimsy or dated the basis, it tends to be stuck with the tag. Travel guides are instrumental in propagating such reputations, since it is part of their function to alert readers to known trouble spots. Often there's no ambiguity about the warnings issued by travel guides – you won't, for instance, spend long in Kenya without hearing first- or second-hand reports of muggings in Nairobi. In other cases, a writer might be conscious of a place's reputation, without having any real evidence to support it, and will feel duty bound to make the right noises – quite possibly reinforcing an obsolete or baseless legend in the process.

Bagamoyo is a case in point. The town has never shaken off a reputation for armed muggings it acquired in the late 1980s, but this particular writer has heard of no specific incident in the last decade to substantiate the legend. When the first edition of this guide was researched, ten years ago, some local sources claimed that Bagamoyo's reputation stemmed from one isolated incident, the violent rape of a traveller, which has little or no bearing on safety in Bagamoyo today. Others – admittedly local guides, who had a vested interest in propagating the legend – reckoned that walking without a guide along the avenue to the old mission or the road to Kaole was tantamount to inviting an attack. So, is Bagamoyo any more or less crime-ridden than Tanga or Pangani? The honest answer: I have no idea!

Personally, I've always erred on the side of caution in Bagamoyo, and taken local guides to walk me along the suspect roads. I would advise readers to do the same. Should you disregard this advice, however, then do at least ensure you leave all valuables, cameras and money – except for whatever cash you need for the excursion – locked up safely at your hotel. Finally, whatever risks might be attached to wandering out of town, I've never heard anything to suggest a security problem in central Bagamoyo.

beach hotels, or you can wander around independently – though do first read the box *Security in Bagamoyo*, above.

Even if you are staying in the town centre, a recommended first port of call is the **Holy Ghost Mission** which lies on the outskirts of town, and is reached via a straight avenue overhung by mango trees planted by the missionaries in 1871. Situated within the mission grounds, the superb **Catholic Museum**, which re-opened in September 2001 after having been expanded and relocated to the old Sisters' House, provides a good overview of the history of Bagamoyo and Kaole, as well as housing several more general exhibits. The museum, open from 10.00 to 17.00 daily, charges an entrance fee of Tsh1,000, and sells an extensive selection of books and booklets about Bagamoyo past and present.

Built in 1876, the double-storey Sisters' House, which houses the museum, is one of several interesting buildings within the mission grounds. Foremost among these is the **original Holy Ghost Church**, built in 1872 and reputedly the oldest church on the East African mainland. Opposite the church and of a similar vintage, the wide-balconied three-storey **Old Fathers' House** is a fine, though somewhat deteriorated, example of a style of pre-colonial mission architecture more normally associated with West Africa. In front of this building stands the **New Holy Ghost Church**, which was constructed shortly before World War I, and is more imposing than its predecessor. A few hundred metres past the main mission buildings is the **cemetery** where the early missionaries are buried, and a **grotto** built in 1876 by the emancipated slaves living in the mission grounds. Several of the exotic trees in the wooded grounds were the first of their type to be planted in Tanzania. Returning to town from the mission, follow the mango-lined avenue to the junction with Ocean Road. The unimposing tin-roofed **Anglican Church** on the right side of the intersection is where, in 1874, Livingstone's sun-dried body, after an initial night in the Holy Ghost Mission, was interred before it was shipped to Zanzibar. On the seafront, about 200m behind this church, a green marble monument and cross, erected in the 1870s and replanted in 1993, marks the spot where Father Horner landed in 1868 to establish the Holy Ghost Mission.

From the Anglican church, you can follow Ocean Road southwards until it becomes India Street, the main thoroughfare through **Dunda**, the old stone town of Bagamoyo. Dunda, which houses most of the town's old buildings and administrative offices, has changed little in shape since the late 19th century. It also retains a singularly Swahili atmosphere, and a tangible sense of community exists among its estimated 1,000 human residents. At the junction of India Street and Customs Road stands the **old post office**, the first to be established on the Tanzanian mainland, in active use until as recently as 1995. Opposite the old post office is one of the oldest and most ornate of several carved **Zanzibar doors** that decorate the façades of India Street.

From the intersection with India Street, Customs Road leads down to the main port, still dominated by the **German Customs House** built in 1895, opposite which stand the remains of a **German Storehouse** built in 1888. The old beachfront **slave market** is today a fish market; the white sands in front of it are lined with picturesque fishing dhows and scuttled across by legions of ghostly white crabs at dusk.

Continuing south for a few hundred metres, India Street runs past a trio of noteworthy buildings. First up is the **Former Bagamoyo Tea House**, one of the town's oldest buildings – possibly predating the German occupation – and notable for its authentic carved Zanzibar door. Next to this, the dilapidated **German Boma**, built in 1897 as the regional headquarters, is an impressive two-storey building with a fortified roof, but it does seem in urgent need of restoration work. Opposite the Boma, in front of an abandoned bandstand, stands the **Uhuru Monument** celebrating Tanzania's independence in 1961, together with a plaque commemorating Burton and Speke's departure from Bagamoyo on their famous expedition to lakes Tanganyika and Victoria. The third building of note, **Luku House**, is a pre-colonial two-storey construction that was appropriated by the Germans to serve as their first East Africa headquarters from 1888 to 1891 (see box *The Emin Pasha's Fall*, page 278).

A short distance south of this, at the junction for the Badeco Beach Hotel, stands the **Old Fort**, the structure of which incorporates the oldest extant house in Bagamoyo. The fort was built by an Arab trader in 1860 as a slave prison – a subterranean passage leads to a landing point where slaves were herded to dhows on the shore – and fortified by the Sultan of Zanzibar circa 1880. The building served as a fortified garrison in German times, and later as a police post. Today, it houses the Department of Antiquities.

In the grounds of the nearby Badeco Beach Hotel, marked by a plaque, stands the **hanging tree** used by the Germans to dispatch any Africans considered insufficiently sympathetic to their rule. Immediately south of the Old Fort and Badeco Beach Hotel, the Muslim **Mwana Mahuka Cemetery** houses the oldest tomb in Bagamoyo, dating to 1793, while the **German Cemetery** is the last

THE EMIN PASHA'S FALL

In 1889, the renowned explorer Henry Stanley marched into Bagamoyo at the end of a three-year trek across Africa that had seen his original party of 700 reduced to fewer than 200. With him was the Emin Pasha, the German-born governor of Equatoria Province (then nominally part of Egypt, now part of southern Sudan), who against all odds had managed to defend his isolated territory against the Mahdist onslaught for three years following the fall of Khartoum in 1885. The German garrison at Bagamoyo, then at the height of the Abushiri Rebellion, must have embraced any excuse for a bit of festivity. Stanley and the Emin Pasha were welcomed with open arms – and a stockpile of open bottles – culminating in a wild party at the headquarters in present-day Luku House. The festivities ended in tragedy, as the Emin Pasha – presumably drunk at the time, and certainly as short-sighted as the best of them – celebrated his safe return from the trials of Equatoria and a trans-Africa march with a fall from the balcony of Luku House to the street below. Scheduled to sail to Zanzibar with Stanley the next day, the Governor of Equatoria instead spent the next six weeks in the Holy Ghost Mission hospital recuperating from head injuries. The offending balcony, still present in 1992, appears to have been removed during the subsequent restoration of Luku House.

resting place for 20 German soldiers who died in the late 19th century. Further south, perhaps 100m along the Kaole Road, the **Bagamoyo Art College** or **Chuo Cha Sanaa** is a striking example of modern architecture constructed entirely from traditional materials. At weekends, the students often stage local plays or put on a show of traditional music, dancing and mime.

Walk northwest from the Old Fort along Caravan Road and you soon arrive in **Magomeni**, a relatively modern settlement, home to more than 95% of Bagamoyo's population. The bustling market and bus station are situated alongside each other in this part of town, as are most of the local guesthouses, but the only historical buildings are the **Caravanserai** and **German Blockhouse**. The Caravanserai, situated close to the modern bus station, is where caravan parties assembled and stocked up before trekking into the interior. In its prime, the Caravanserai consisted of a open central courtyard surrounded by low-rise market stalls and shops – not dissimilar, in fact, to many modern bus terminals in Tanzania – but it has fallen into disuse and only the coral rag outer walls remain. Far better preserved is the German Blockhouse (also known as Dunda Tower), a circular coral rag structure with a ladder leading to the fortified roof, built in 1889 by von Wissmann to protect Bagamoyo against the Abushiri rebellion.

Kaole Ruins

On the outskirts of Kaole village, 5km south of Bagamoyo, stand the brooding ruins of the urban precursor to modern Bagamoyo, a relatively minor but wealthy trading settlement that would have peaked in prosperity at the about same time as Kilwa Kisiwani and Mtangata (Tongoni). The main ruins consist of one large mosque with a well preserved outer staircase and ornate engraved mihrab, surrounded by a cemetery of 22 graves including four tall pillar tombs, the largest of which stands about 7m high. Close to the mosque stand a footbath and well, the latter still containing water. Some 300m away, a second mosque and a building of unknown purpose stand in total isolation from the main ruins.

Previous page Maasai boy after his initiation ceremony (AZ)

Above Mount Kilimanjaro, the highest free-standing mountain in the world (CH)

Below A small mosque on the outskirts of Arusha (AZ)

Opposite A balloon safari offers a completely different perspective of the vast plains of the Serengeti (AZ)

Surprisingly little is known about the history of the medieval settlement at Kaole. No reference to it is found in the surviving chronicles of the Shirazi or early Portuguese era, and all that can be said about the town's name is that it is highly unlikely it would have been called Kaole – or Bagamoyo, for that matter – in its commercial heyday. Even the dating of the ruins is controversial. One reliable source regards the main mosque to display features consistent with a 7th-century construction date (which would make it the oldest surviving mosque on the East African mainland), but a 12th- or 13th-century foundation seems far more probable. It has been suggested, too, based on the humpback topography of the site and the absence of secular buildings, that it may not actually have been a settlement, but would have rather served as a religious retreat, set on a holy offshore island.

In common with many other Shirazi trading centres, Kaole was abandoned in the 16th century, presumably due to the intervention of the Portuguese or the appetite of the Zimba. The port is known to have enjoyed a revival as a military and administrative centre for the Sultan of Zanzibar in the late 18th century, though the actual ruins bear little trace of this resettlement other than a few Omani period graves. By the early 19th century, the main centre of trade had relocated to Bagamoyo, for reasons that remain unclear. The most probable explanation, given the explosion of the slave trade at this time, is that Bagamoyo's larger harbour could hold a greater volume of ships, while Kaole's had become increasingly clogged by mangrove swamps.

While the major buildings at Kaole don't stand comparison to the splendid architecture of Kilwa – or even the Gedi Ruins in Kenya – the decorated tombs are perhaps the best preserved on the Swahili coast. A better reason to visit, perhaps, is the aura of mystery that surrounds the ruins: crumbling relics of an undocumented centre of international trade, one that must have flourished for three centuries or longer – a powerful physical reminder of Africa's forgotten past.

Getting there and away

With a private vehicle, Kaole can easily be reached by following the south coastal road out of Bagamoyo, past the Art College, for 5km. In Kaole village, a signposted 600m turn-off leads to the ruins. Unfortunately, no *dalla-dallas* head out this way, so the options are walking (about an hour each way), cycling (ask your hotel to

---

A SNAPSHOT OF BAGAMOYO CIRCA 1890

Caravan trade in Bagamoyo was of little importance. The old caravanserai below the station has been evacuated; it will no longer be used, for hygienic reasons. A new location has been chosen to lodge the caravans, further above the station, within the palms. While slave trade in general can be regarded as suppressed, in singular cases, men deep-rooted in the slave trade try to catch free men and ship them from smaller coastal places in the vicinity of Bagamoyo. A certain Ibrahim, who has been arrested for slave trade last year, but who had succeeded in escaping from the prison, was again brought in by natives a few weeks ago, as, with a few aides, he had ambushed free men, killed some, captured the others and sold them as slaves. As his crimes were proven by numerous witness reports, he was hung on September 23rd.

Extracted from a report by the Deputy Commissioner of German East Africa, September 1890

arrange a bike) or hanging around the junction to wait for a lift with one of the very occasional pick-up trucks that run along this road. If you're walking or cycling, it would probably – given Bagamoyo's reputation for muggings – be advisable to leave all valuables and extra cash behind. If you want a receipt, the entrance of Tsh1,500 must be paid at the Department of Antiquities office in Bagamoyo. Otherwise, you can pay on site.

Dar es Salaam

The country's largest city and most important port, Dar es Salaam is the commercial and social capital of Tanzania in all but name; a lively, bustling Indian Ocean port which in modern East Africa is rivalled in maritime significance only by Mombasa in Kenya. Often simply referred to as 'Dar', Tanzania's premier city supports a population estimated at 2.5 million in 2002, but it is not a tourist centre of great note. On the contrary, the increasing ease with which one can fly between Tanzania's main tourist centres means an increasingly small proportion of fly-in tourists ever set foot in Dar.

Whether or not this is a good thing is a matter of opinion. Dar es Salaam is one of those cities that draws extreme reactions from travellers, a real 'love it or hate it' kind of place, and its many detractors would probably regard any Dar-free itinerary through Tanzania to be a highly desirable state of affairs. Personally, however, I enjoy Dar es Salaam more perhaps than any other major East African city, since it boasts all the hustle and bustle of somewhere such as Nairobi, yet has none of that city's underlying aggression or bland architectural modernity.

If nothing else, Dar is imbued with a distinctive sense of place, one derived from the cultural mix of its people and buildings, not to say a torpid coastal humidity that permeates every aspect of day-to-day life. Architecturally, the city boasts elements of German, British, Asian and Arab influences, but it is fundamentally a Swahili city, and beneath the superficial air of hustle, a laid-back and friendly place. People are willing to pass away the time with idle chat and will readily help out strangers, yet tourists are rarely hassled, except in the vicinity of the New Africa Hotel, where a resident brigade of hissing money changers froths into action every time a *mzungu* walks past.

Part of my personal attachment to Dar es Salaam comes from having watched the city undergo a quite remarkable economic renaissance since I first visited Tanzania in 1986. Back then, Dar es Salaam looked decidedly down-at-heel. The streets were acneous with pot-holes and the pavements lifeless; shops had long given up the pretence of having anything to sell; water ran for about an hour on a good day; and 'tourist traffic' was limited to the occasional overland traveller crossing between eastern and southern Africa. In 1988, when I next passed through Dar, things were still pretty torpid, but there were definite signs of recovery. Four years later, when I researched the first edition of this travel guide, Dar had been transformed into a relatively lively bustling city, comparable in many ways to Nairobi. With each subsequent visit it has become more difficult to recapture the ghost of the weary urban tip I passed through in 1986. True, many of Dar es Salaam's buildings could do with a scrub and a whitewash, while poverty remains as rife as it does in any large African city. But the overall impression on visiting Dar

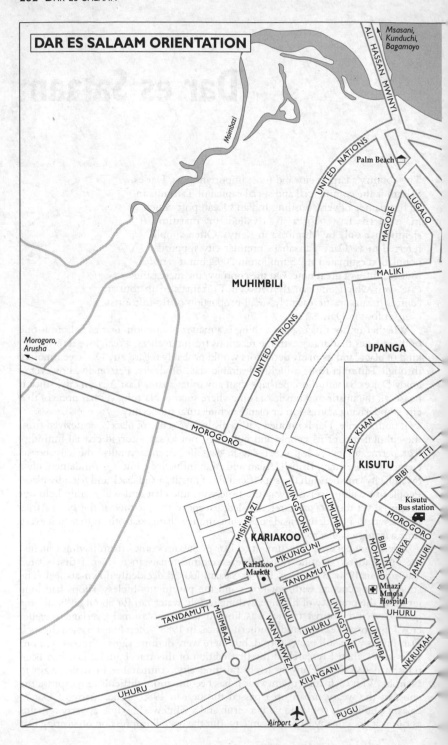

DAR ES SALAAM ORIENTATION

Msasani,
Kunduchi,
Bagamoyo

ALI HASSAN MWINYI

Msimbazi

UNITED NATIONS

Palm Beach

MAGORE

LUGALO

MALIKI

MUHIMBILI

UNITED NATIONS

UPANGA

Morogoro,
Arusha

ALY KHAN

MOROGORO

KISUTU

BIBI

TITI

Kisutu
Bus station

MOROGORO

LIVINGSTONE

LUMUMBA

BIBI TITI
MOHAMED

LIBYA

JAMHURI

MSIMBAZI

KARIAKOO

MKUNGUNI

Mnazi
Mmoja
Hospital

UHURU

Kariakoo
Market

TANDAMUTI

SIKIKUU

LIVINGSTONE

LUMUMBA

NKRUMAH

TANDAMUTI

MSIMBAZI

WANYAMWEZI

UHURU

KIUNGANI

UHURU

PUGU

Airport

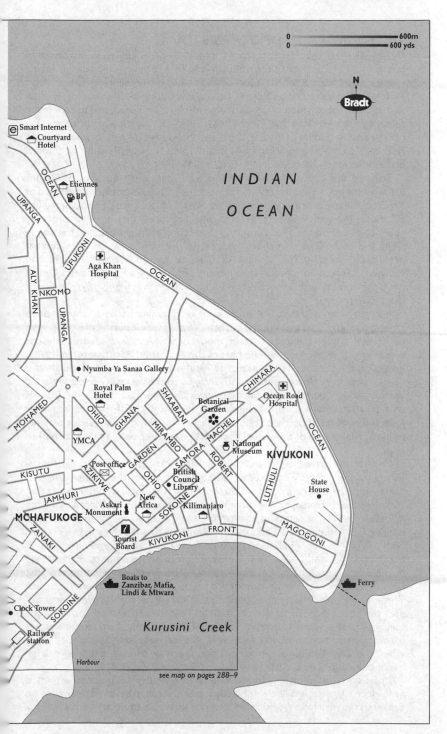

INDIAN

OCEAN

N

Bradt

Smart Internet
Courtyard Hotel

OCEAN

Etiennes
BP

UPANGA

ALY KHAN

NKOMO

UFUKONI

UPANGA

Aga Khan Hospital

OCEAN

Nyumba Ya Sanaa Gallery

Royal Palm Hotel

CHIMARA

Ocean Road Hospital

Botanical Garden

MOHAMED

OHIO

GHANA

SHAABANI

MIRAMBO

SAMORA

MACHEL

National Museum

KIVUKONI

OCEAN

YMCA

GARDEN

ROBERT

LUTHULI

State House

KISUTU

AZIKIWE

Post office

OHIO

British Council Library

JAMHURI

New Africa

SOKOINE

Kilimanjaro

MCHAFUKOGE

Askari Monument

Tourist Board

FRONT

MAGOGONI

ZANAKI

KIVUKONI

Boats to Zanzibar, Mafia, Lindi & Mtwara

Ferry

SOKOINE

Clock Tower

Kurusini Creek

Railway station

Harbour

see map on pages 288–9

THE FOUNDATION OF DAR ES SALAAM

Dar es Salaam is, by coastal standards, a modern city, founded as the capital of Sultan Majid of Zanzibar in the 1860s, close to a relatively insignificant fishing village called Mzizima (which stood on the site of the present-day Ocean Road Hospital). The name Dar es Salaam, first coined during Majid's tenancy, is often said to be an abbreviation of Bandari Salaam (Haven of Peace) and to reflect the sultan's great love of the site. More likely, however, that it is a minor corruption of Dari Salaam (House of Peace), the name Majid gave his palace with probable reference to the nearby village of Mzizima, which means healthy or tranquil place in the local dialect.

Prior to the 1860s, the only evidence of maritime trade out of Dar es Salaam's harbour is a quantity of 13th-century Chinese pottery unearthed at Kivukoni, near the present-day ferry terminal. An absence of structural ruins or more modern artefacts at this site indicates that it was probably abandoned before the 14th century, when stone buildings became the vogue along the coast. This one short-lived settlement aside, the most important pre-1860s' ports in the vicinity of Dar es Salaam were Kunduchi and Mbwamaji, which both house the remains of Shirazi era mosques and Omani era pillar tombs, and respectively lie about 30km north and 15km south of the modern city,

It might seem odd that Dar es Salaam, with its fine harbour, stands alone among modern Tanzanian ports in that it was ignored during the great eras of coastal trade – indeed, some modern writers have treated this as something of an oversight on the part of the Arabs and Portuguese. In reality, however, the harbour's main assets to modern ships – its depth and shelter – would not have been significant advantages to the relatively small seafaring vessels used in earlier eras. Furthermore, the approach to the harbour is unusually hazardous to small ships, as noted by the 19th-century explorer Joseph Thomson, who described it as 'a narrow, zigzag dangerous channel [where] a false turn of the wheel or a mistaken order would bring [a ship] to grief'.

Prior to the arrival of Sultan Majid in 1862, Mzizima was a typical coastal fishing village, ruled by small-time self-styled sultans of the Shomvi and Pazi clans with a peripheral interest in the coastal trade. Local tradition has it that Majid visited Mzizima at the prompting of one of its residents, Said bin Abdullah, the illegitimate son of a prominent Zanzibari merchant and a high ranking Pazi woman. Said had sailed to Zanzibar to seek the sultan's counsel with regard to the unpunished murder of a wealthy merchant's son at Mzizima. Impressed by his guest's description of his home port, Sultan Majid decided to sail back with him, and was so enamoured with what he saw that he immediately made arrangements to lease land from the Shomvi leaders. Three years later, Majid returned with a small garrison and several artisans, and set about building a palace, a hotel, a fort and several other stone buildings along what is today Sokoine Drive, about 1km southwest of Mzizima. Majid's customised capital was officially opened in September 1867, when the English, French, American and German consuls attended a large banquet held in the new palace.

Majid's motives in moving to Mzizima were probably not quite so whimsical as folklore suggests. It is likely, for a start, that the sultan believed relocating his capital to the mainland would make him less vulnerable to the internal political intrigues that characterised his rule, as well as removing him from the influence of the various European consuls sited on Zanzibar. Furthermore, Majid evidently intended his new capital to replace Bagamoyo as the main centre of trade on the mainland opposite Zanzibar. A letter written in November 1866 by Dr Seward of the British Consulate on Zanzibar notes that Majid 'hopes to form the nucleus of a trading port, whence caravan routes shall radiate into the interior, and which bye and bye roads along the coast may connect with Kilwa and Lamu'. One factor in this decision might have been that Dar es Salaam's harbour was more suitable to large European ships than Bagamoyo. Seward noted that 'the capacity of this new port for shipping is of the best' and that although 'the narrowness of the leading channel is a drawback which only a steam tug can countervail... this want has been anticipated and a powerful tug has been ordered from Hamburg'.

We shall never know whether Majid would in time have realised his grand plans for Dar es Salaam. In 1870, the sultan slipped in his new palace, broke several bones, one of which punctured a lung, and although he was hastily shipped across to Zanzibar for medical treatment, it came too late and he died a few days later. Majid was succeeded by his brother Barghash, who had never enjoyed the best of relationships with his sibling, and was quite content to maintain his capital on Zanzibar and the existing trade network through the mainland ports of Bagamoyo and Kilwa Kivinje. Barghash did retain an agent at Dar es Salaam, and his abode – a two-storey building that still stands on Sokoine Road – was well maintained, but the palace and other buildings were abandoned. By 1873, Majid's capital had become something approaching a ghost town.

In 1877 the anti-slaver Sir William Mackinnon proposed Dar es Salaam as the starting point for the construction of 'Mackinnon's Road', intended to encourage legitimate trade between the coast and Lake Nyasa, but eventually abandoned after 112km had been completed. In 1887, a GEAC station was established at Dar es Salaam under Leue, who penned a brief but vivid description of his posting: 'a town of ruins [that] had sunk as quickly as it had risen under Majid... Streets were overgrown with grass and bush [and] teeming with snakes, scorpions, centipedes and other pests... In the halls of the Sultan's palace lived bats... part of the palace was used as a gaol and... where once the harem ladies' tender feet had trodden, now clanked the prisoners' chains'.

Ironically, it would be the German colonists who revived and realised Majid's grand plans for Dar es Salaam. Four years after Leue first set foot there, the 'town of ruins' replaced Tanga as the capital of German East Africa. Between 1893 and 1899 several departments of the colonial government were established there and in 1898 a Roman Catholic cathedral was built. The construction of the central railway consolidated Dar es Salaam's position; by 1914, when the line was completed, Dar was the country's most significant harbour and trading centre. Dar es Salaam was captured by a British ship soon after the outbreak of World War I. When German East Africa became Tanganyika, Dar es Salaam remained the capital, and its importance has never been challenged, although the capital is now Dodoma. Dar es Salaam remains the country's economic hub, with a population that increased from about 1,000 people in 1867 to 20,000 in 1900, 270,000 in 1967 and around 2.5 million in 2002.

today is that of a modern, vibrant city: smoothly surfaced streets, pavements spilling over with pedlars and colourful informal markets, well-stocked shops, an increasing number of smart high-rise buildings, and water and electricity supplies as reliable as you could hope for.

GETTING THERE AND AWAY

Dar es Salaam has good local and international transport links. Details of transport to other parts of the country are given throughout this guide, under the relevant town or area, but a brief overview follows.

By air

There are air links between Dar es Salaam and many African and European cities, and domestic flights to most large Tanzanian towns. For further details see the sections on *Getting to Tanzania: By air* in *Chapter 3* and *Getting around: By air* in *Chapter 4*. International and domestic airlines represented in Dar es Salaam are listed under *Airlines* below.

The Dar es Salaam International Airport lies 13km from the city centre, a 20-minute taxi ride that costs Tsh8,000–15,000 dependent on how hard you bargain. You can get to the airport on a number 67 bus, though I would be hesitant to risk exposing all my valuables in this way, as city buses in Dar es Salaam have something of a reputation for thieves and pickpockets.

By boat

Several boats run between Dar es Salaam and Zanzibar every day, with the more reliable services generally taking around two hours. There are also regular services to Pemba Island, and the MV *Safari* normally travels once weekly to Mtwara on the south coast. All the commercial boat operators have kiosks near the harbour on Sokoine Drive, so it's easy enough to shop around for prices to Zanzibar and to check departure dates for other destinations.

By rail

Trains on the central railway to Dodoma, Tabora, Mwanza and Kigoma leave from the railway station on Sokoine Drive in the city centre. Bookings to these

AIRLINES

Air India opp Peugeot House, cnr Ali Hassan Mwinyi and Bibi Titi; tel: 022 215 2642-4

Air Tanzania ATC Building, Ohio St; tel: 022 211 0245-8

Air Zimbabwe Avalon House, Zanaki St; tel: 022 212 3526/1747

British Airways Sheraton Hotel, Ohio St; tel: 022 211 3820-2

Egypt Air Matasalamat Building, Samora Ave; tel: 022 211 3333

Emirates Air Haidery Plaza, Ali Hassan Mwinyi Rd; tel: 022 211 6100-3

Ethiopian Airlines TDFL Building, cnr Ohio and Ali Hassan Mwinyi; tel: 022 211 7063-5

Gulf Air Raha Towers, cnr Bibi Titi and Maktaba; tel: 022 213 7851-2

Kenya Airways Peugeot House, cnr Ali Hassan Mwinyi and Bibi Titi; tel: 022 211 9376-7

KLM Peugeot House, cnr Ali Hassan Mwinyi and Bibi Titi; tel: 022 211 3336-7

South Africa Airways Raha Towers, Maktaba St; tel: 022 211 7044-8

Swissair Luther House, Sokoine Drive; tel: 022 211 8870-2

destinations should also be made at this station. For details of departure times, see box *The Central Railway* on pages 374–5. Trains to southern destinations such as Ifakara and Mbeya leave from the separate Tazara Station, 5km from the city centre. The booking office for southbound trains is at Tazara Station. Regular buses run between the central Post Office (*Posta*) on Maktaba Road in the city centre and the Tazara Railway Station. Details of Tazara train services are under the heading *By rail* in Chapter 4.

By bus

Until recently, long-haul buses from Dar es Salaam left from a confusing number of different terminals scattered in and around the city centre. This has changed, however, with the recent opening of the large Ubungu Bus Station out of town along the Morogoro road. Practically all long-haul buses to destinations around the country now leave from this terminus, which simplifies matters greatly, though it does more-or-less enforce a special trip out of town to book tickets a day ahead of departure (strongly advised for most destinations). A taxi from the city centre to Ubungu will cost Tsh3,000–6,000, depending on how receptive the driver is to negotiation.

A notable exception to the above is the excellent Scandinavia Express, a relatively luxurious but reasonably affordable coach service whose vehicles leave from a private terminus at the junction of Nyerere and Msimbazi Streets on the airport road. These services connect Dar es Salaam to Arusha (thrice daily), Nairobi (once daily), Mwanza (once daily), Dodoma (once daily), Iringa (five times daily), Mbeya (three times daily), Songea (once daily) and Kyela (once daily). Tel: 022 218 4833/4 or 285 0847/9; mobile: 0811 336625 or 0741 325474; fax: 022 285 0224; email: scandinavia@raha.com.

WHERE TO STAY

There are plenty of hotels in and around the city centre to suit all budgets, and new places seem to open at an ever-increasing pace. The section below covers all accommodation that lies within the confines of the city centre and as well as in greater Dar es Salaam north towards the Msasani Peninsula. The (mostly more attractive) accommodation along the stretches of coast immediately north and south of the city are covered later in the chapter under the headings *Beaches north of Dar* and *Beaches south of Dar*.

It used to be the case that most budget hotels in central Dar would fill up early in the day, but this is no longer the case. Nevertheless, budget travellers who arrive in Dar late in the afternoon may find it easier to settle for something more expensive and to look for a cheap room on the subsequent morning. Travellers who arrive in Dar after dark stand a high risk of being mugged. Ideally, you should avoid catching a bus that will pull into Dar in the evening, but where there is no choice you are strongly advised to look for a room using a taxi. Although things have improved greatly in recent years, water and electricity cuts are still a real possibility at budget hotels in Dar es Salaam. If there's running water when you check into your room, it's not a bad idea to shower while the going is good!

Exclusive

Sea Cliff Hotel Tel. 022 260 0380-7; fax: 022 260 0476; email: information@hotelseacliff.com; web: www.hotelseacliff.com. Arguably the top hotel within Dar's greater city limits, the Sea Cliff boasts a fabulous seafront location on the Msasani Peninsula, at the north end of Toure Drive, yet is only 15 minutes by taxi from the city centre. It is particularly recommended to business travellers who want to spend their

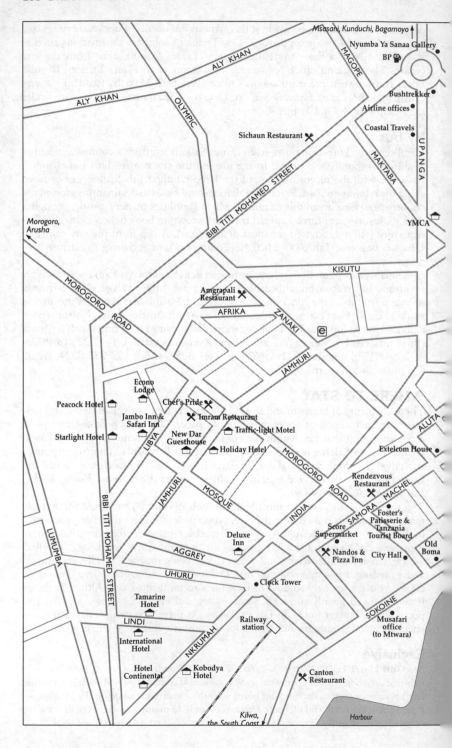

Msasani, Kunduchi, Bagamoyo
Nyumba Ya Sanaa Gallery
BP
MAGOPE
ALY KHAN
ALY KHAN
ALY KHAN
OLYMPIC
Bushtrekker
Airline offices
Coastal Travels
UPANGA
MAKTABA
Sichaun Restaurant
BIBI TITI MOHAMED STREET
Morogoro, Arusha
YMCA
KISUTU
Amgrapali Restaurant
AFRIKA
ZANAKI
JAMHURI
MOROGORO ROAD
Econo Lodge
Peacock Hotel
Chef's Pride
Imram Restaurant
Jambo Inn & Safari Inn
Traffic-light Motel
Starlight Hotel
LIBYA
New Dar Guesthouse
Holiday Hotel
MOROGORO ROAD
ALUTA
Extelcom House
Rendezvous Restaurant
MACHEL
JAMHURI
MOSQUE
INDIA
SAMORA
Foster's Patisserie & Tanzania Tourist Board
BIBI TITI MOHAMED STREET
LUMUMBA
Deluxe Inn
Score Supermarket
Old Boma
Nandos & Pizza Inn
City Hall
AGGREY
UHURU
Clock Tower
SOKOINE
Tamarine Hotel
Musafari office (to Mtwara)
LINDI
NKRUMAH
Railway station
International Hotel
Hotel Continental
Kobodya Hotel
Canton Restaurant
Kilwa, the South Coast
Harbour

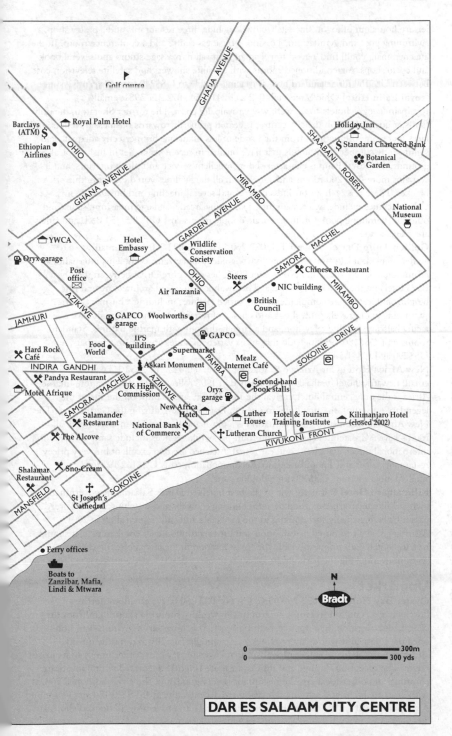

Golf course

Barclays (ATM) $
Ethiopian Airlines

Royal Palm Hotel

Holiday Inn
Standard Chartered Bank $
Botanical Garden

National Museum

GHANA AVENUE
GHAJA AVENUE
OHIO
SHAABANI ROBERT
MIRAMBO
GARDEN AVENUE
SAMORA MACHEL

YWCA
Oryx garage

Hotel Embassy
Wildlife Conservation Society

Chinese Restaurant

Post office
Air Tanzania
OHIO
Steers
NIC building

British Council

AZIKIWE
JAMHURI

GAPCO garage
Woolworths
GAPCO
MIRAMBO
SOKOINE DRIVE

Hard Rock Café
Food World
IPS building
Supermarket
Mealz Internet Café

INDIRA GANDHI

Pandya Restaurant
Askari Monument
PAMBA
Second-hand book stalls

Motel Afrique
SAMORA MACHEL
UK High Commission
AZIKIWE
Oryx garage

Salamander Restaurant
New Africa Hotel
Luther House
Hotel & Tourism Training Institute
Kilimanjaro Hotel (closed 2002)

The Alcove
National Bank of Commerce $
Lutheran Church
KIVUKONI FRONT

Shalamar Restaurant
Sno-Cream
SOKOINE

MANSFIELD
St Joseph's Cathedral

Ferry offices

Boats to Zanzibar, Mafia, Lindi & Mtwara

N

Bradt

0   300m
0   300 yds

DAR ES SALAAM CITY CENTRE

leisure hours out of town, since its facilities include three restaurants and a pastry shop, a swimming pool and gymnasium, a casino, a business centre and a conference room. In the attached mall, you'll find a good travel agent, hair salon, massage studio and several book and curio shops. Air-conditioned rooms with en-suite showers and satellite television cost between US$160 for a standard non-sea-facing double to US$240 for an executive suite.

Royal Palm Hotel Ohio Street; tel: 022 211 2416; fax: 022 211 3981; email: royalpalm@legacyhotels.co.za; web: www.royalpalm.co.za. The former Sheraton, the only five-star quality hotel in the city centre, is geared primarily towards business travellers, and faces increasing competition from the horde of less luxurious but perfectly adequate and significantly cheaper chain hotels that have opened in recent years. Set in lush tropical grounds, this Royal Palm is characterised by excellent service and plush interiors, and it contains more than 200 rooms and suites with all the facilities you'd expect in this price bracket. There is a 24-hour business centre, and several meeting and business rooms. Other facilities include two restaurants, a shopping arcade, and a gymnasium, sauna and outdoor swimming pool. Ordinary single/double rooms cost US$225/250 B&B and suites are available too.

Golden Tulip Dar es Salaam Tel: 022 260 1442; fax: 022 260 1443; email: goldentuliptanzania@afsat.com; web: www.goldentuliptanzania.com. This international chain hotel, which opened in November 2001, lies on Toure Drive between the Oyster Bay Hotel and the Msasani Peninsula. The Swahili-influenced architecture and fine beachfront location are complemented by varied facilities including a business centre, swimming pool, travel agent, shops and choice of restaurants. The rooms all have a sea-facing balcony, satellite television, and a large bathroom with marble fixtures. Standard rooms cost US$180/195 single/double and a variety of suites are available for between US$290 and US$1,500.

New Africa Hotel Cnr Azikiwe & Sokoine Drive; tel: 022 211 7050/1; fax: 022 211 6731; email: newafricahotel@raha.com. Re-opened in 1998 following total renovation, the New Africa is the only central hotel to rival the Royal Palm, and is built on the site of the legendary Kaiserhof, the first hotel to open in Dar es Salaam, during the German era. The New Africa in its most recent incarnation is a plush and thoroughly modern hotel: all rooms have AC, satellite television and mini-bar, while services include same-day laundry, international direct-dial phone and car rental. Attached are two excellent but very pricey restaurants, a bar and a popular casino. Accommodation costs US$162/192 for a single/double room or US$300 for a double suite.

Kilimanjaro Hotel Formerly one of the best hotels in Dar es Salaam, the government-owned Kilimanjaro spent a good decade counting cobwebs and watching the new breed pass it by before finally succumbing to the inevitable and shutting up shop in 2001. Assuming that a rumoured privatisation and total renovation ever come to pass, it should be a top hotel, with unquestionably the finest location in the city centre, on the main seafront overlooking the harbour.

Upmarket

Oyster Bay Hotel Tel: 022 260 0352/3/4; fax: 022 260 0347; email: oysterbay-hotel@twiga.com. Set in rambling grounds in wealthy suburbia about 6km from the city centre, and overlooking a popular bathing beach, this long-serving family-run hotel, once the finest in town, today provides a refreshingly friendly and mildly quirky alternative to the bland internationalism that characterises most other hotels in its price range. The reception, lounge and dining areas are brightly decorated with Tingatinga paintings and other local art, the restaurant is very good, and the air-conditioned rooms with en-suite baths and satellite television are decent value at US$120/150 single/double. A shopping mall with a coffee shop, an internet café and several well-stocked shops is attached.

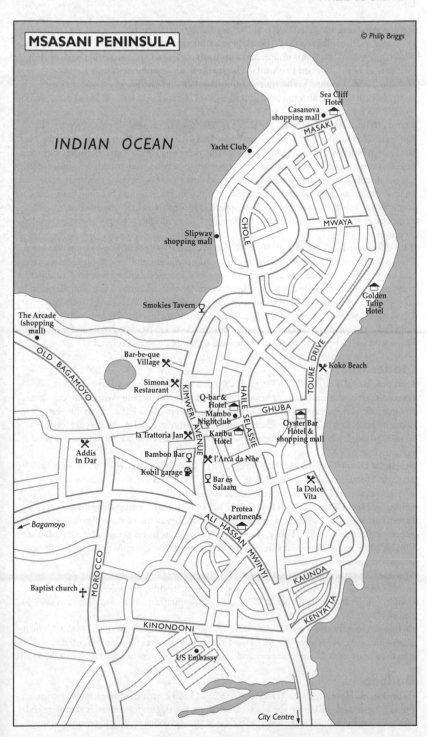

MSASANI PENINSULA

© Philip Briggs

INDIAN OCEAN

Sea Cliff Hotel

Casanova shopping mall

MASAKI

Yacht Club

CHOLE

MWAYA

Slipway shopping mall

Golden Tulip Hotel

The Arcade (shopping mall)

Smokies Tavern

TOURE DRIVE

Koko Beach

OLD BAGAMOYO

Bar-be-que Village

KIMWERI AVENUE

Simona Restaurant

Q-bar & Hotel

Mambo Nightclub

HAILE SELASSIE

GHUBA

Oyster Bar Hotel & shopping mall

la Trattoria Jan

Karibu Hotel

Bamboo Bar

l'Arca da Noe

Addis in Dar

Kobil garage

Bar es Salaam

la Dolce Vita

Bagamoyo

Protea Apartments

ALI HASSAN MWINYI

MOROCCO

KAUNDA

Baptist church

KENYATTA

KINONDONI

US Embassy

City Centre

Protea Apartments Tel: 022 266 6665; fax: 022 266 7760; email: proteadar@africaonline.co.tz. Particularly recommended to business travellers spending a while in Dar es Salaam, this unique modern complex lies about 2km from the city centre on the road to the Msasani Peninsula. The spacious, air-conditioned units are self-contained with a lounge, well-equipped mini-kitchen and satellite television, and the complex contains a swimming pool and restaurant. Units range from US$145 for a studio to US$185 for a suite.

Dar es Salaam Holiday Inn Tel: 022 213 7575; fax: 022 213 9070; web: www.holiday-inn.com. This spanking new and centrally located international chain hotel is situated on the eastern end of Garden Avenue, and contains more than 150 rooms. Facilities include a business centre, two good restaurants, 16-hour room service, non-smoking rooms, facilities for the disabled, an on-site travel centre, a good curio and bookshop, a swimming pool, a fitness centre, and local day tours by arrangement. Idiosyncratic and bristling with character it is not, but any hotel that receives widespread criticism from more established competitors for its cut-throat rates – US$116/131 single/double – has to be recommended to punters!

The Courtyard Tel: 022 213 0130/0560; fax: 022 213 0100; email: courtyard@raha.com. This is another newly opened international chain hotel, centrally located on Ocean Drive, and very reasonably priced by comparison to several more established hotels of a similar standard. Facilities include a good business centre, several restaurants, satellite television in all rooms, a swimming pool, a conference centre, and a library. Accommodation costs US$119/139 single/double B&B. Self-catering apartments in a discrete block 500m away (and linked to the main hotel by a regular shuttle) costs US$90/160/220 daily for one/two/three bedroom units, with substantial monthly discounts offered.

Moderate

Peacock Hotel Tel: 022 211 4071; fax: 022 211 7962; email: mlangila@twiga.com or reservation@peacockhotel.co.tz. Arguably the best value in its range within the city centre, the Peacock Hotel on Bibi Titi Mohammed Street offers bland but comfortable self-contained rooms with AC, hot water, satellite television and fridge at a very reasonable US$60/70 single/double, with a small discount for Tanzanian residents. There is a good restaurant attached.

Starlight Hotel Tel: 022 213 9387; fax: 022 211 9391; email: starlight@cats-net.com. The Starlight Hotel is situated alongside the Peacock, and is very similar in standard. It's also very good value at US$40/50 self-contained single/double.

Embassy Hotel Tel: 022 211 1181; fax: 022 211 2634; email: embassy@raha.com. Incredibly, this rather stuffy and musty concrete block was one of the top hotels in Dar es Salaam a mere decade ago. Today, it seems very rundown and is barely adequate value at US$60/70 for a self-contained single/double (US$40/60 for Tanzania residents) with hot water and satellite television.

Smokies Tavern Tel: 0742 760567/780567; fax: 022 260 1077; email: smokies@twiga.com. Attached to this popular expatriate drinking hole is a pleasant and homely guesthouse that charges US$70/90 for self-contained single/double rooms with AC and nets.

Q-Bar & Guesthouse Tel: 022 260 2150; mobile: 0744 261918; fax: 022 211 2667; email: qbar@hotmail.com. Rather like Smokies Tavern, this is a smart but unpretentious guesthouse attached to a popular bar and restaurant. Rooms cost in the range of US$50–70.

Budget

Palm Beach Hotel Tel: 022 212 2931; fax: 022 211 9272; email: palmbeach@cctz.com. About 20 minutes' walk from the town centre along the Bagamoyo road, this rambling and rather atmospheric hotel is possessed of a time-warped colonial charm that elevates it way above most of the other options in this range. The rooms are a touch rundown, but in a manner that is endearing rather than off-putting, and they seem pretty good value at Tsh17,000/22,000 for a single/double with fan, using a common shower, or Tsh25,000/34,000 with AC and en-suite hot bath or shower. The popular garden bar is a pleasant place to hang out, too, and serves decent meals and snacks in the Tsh1,500–4,000 range.

Econo Lodge Tel: 022 211 6048/9; fax: 022 211 6053; email: econolodge@raha.com; web: www.econolodge.co.tz. This smart new hotel has a convenient central location off Libya Street, and is outstandingly good value in its range. Self-contained rooms with fans cost US$13/18/22 single/double/triple, while air-conditioned doubles cost US$28.

Hotel Continental This high-rise hotel close to the Clock Tower must once have been quite a smart place, but today it wears an air of neglect which some travellers might conceivably regard as charming, but most will find simply depressing. Still, it isn't bad value at around Tsh12,000/18,000 B&B for a self-contained single/double with fan and netting, or Tsh25,000 for an air-conditioned double with television and fridge. The chances of this place ever being full are slim, and it's where I'd catch a taxi to were I to arrive in Dar after dark and simply want to find *any* room that isn't ridiculously expensive.

Kobodya Hotel Tel: 022 213 1312. One of the best compromises between quality and price in Dar, the Kobodya Hotel charges Tsh15,000 for clean self-contained doubles with hot water, fan and netting. It is often full, but it's certainly worth checking on before you head to any of the other hotels in this area.

Shoestring

Salvation Army Mgulani Hostel Tel: 022 285 1467; email: david-burrows@tnz.salvationarmy.org. The pick in this range is this excellent hostel, which lies about 5km out of town on the Kilwa road, and has a swimming pool and a good restaurant, as well as 50 clean self-contained rooms with fans and nets for Tsh6,000/9,000/12,000 single/double/triple including breakfast.

Jambo Inn Tel: 022 211 4293; fax: 022 211 3149. This secure and sensibly priced lodge in Libya Street has been deservedly popular with budget travellers for as long as I can remember, and it remains our favoured standby in the city centre. Self-contained rooms with a reliable hot water supply and fans cost around Tsh7,000/10,000 single/double, while doubles with AC cost Tsh16,000. The ground-floor restaurant serves some of the tastiest and most reasonably priced Indian food you'll find in Tanzania, and a 10% discount on meals is offered to hotel residents.

Safari Hotel Tel: 022 211 9104; fax: 022 211 6550. Situated at the end of a cul-de-sac off Libya Street, this is another long-serving and popular budget lodge, and similarly priced to the Jambo Inn around the corner.

YWCA Tel: 022 212 2439; mobile: 0741 622707. Centrally located on Maktaba Street, the YWCA has long been a favourite with couples and single women travelling on the cheap, but single men are not accommodated. Clean rooms with fans and mosquito netting cost Tsh4,000 single, Tsh6,000 double (for two women sharing), Tsh5,000 compartmentalised double (for couples) or Tsh10,000 for a self-contained flat. The canteen serves inexpensive if unexciting meals.

YMCA Tel: 022 211 0833. The YMCA, situated in the city centre around the corner from the superior and more affordable YWCA, charges Tsh8,000/8,500 for a clean single/double with a net but no fan.

Etienne's Hotel That this quaintly sleepy and timeworn colonial hotel on Ocean Drive has survived into the modern era is remarkable, but whether you'll be willing to pay Tsh12,000 for one of the rather mildewed self-contained doubles is open to question. Some might argue that the architectural integrity and rambling gardens compensate for such minor inconveniences as maddeningly dopey staff and a faint but pervasive smell of urine, but not me!

Luther House Tel: 022 212 0734. This perennially popular hostel has a useful central location, tucked away in a building behind the main Lutheran Church on the waterfront. It used to be practically impossible to get a room here without booking days in advance, but these days there are normally plenty of vacancies – in large part because it's not the bargain it used to be. Tired-looking single/double using common showers cost Tsh13,000/15,000.

Tamarine Hotel Tel: 022 212 0233. Although rather rundown, this is one of the better cheapies in central Dar es Salaam, and very reasonably priced at Tsh3,500/4,500 for a single/double using common showers or Tsh7,000 for a self-contained double.

Traffic Light and **Holiday Hotels** These very rundown and basic lodgings close to the disused Morogoro Road bus terminal charge around Tsh5,000 for a squalid room.

WHERE TO EAT

Dar es Salaam has a good range of restaurants to suit all tastes and budgets, and the number of options seems to have grown exponentially every time we visit the city. Typically, restaurants open for lunch between 12.00 and 15.00 and for dinner between 19.00 and 22.00. Generally food is of a high standard and good value for money. It would be impossible to list every restaurant and *hoteli* in Dar es Salaam, so you might well want to venture beyond the following recommendations.

City centre

The Alcove Long-standing and central restaurant serving top-notch Indian and Chinese food at around Tsh8,000–10,000 for a main course and condiments.

Chef's Pride Popular central café serving a good selection of inexpensive snacks and light meals, as well as tasty fruit juice. Closed in the evenings.

Chinese Restaurant Established in the 1970s, the Chinese Restaurant in NIC Investment House on Samora Avenue serves a wide selection of Chinese, African and Continental dishes for Tsh5,000 or less.

Food World Inexpensive burgers, sandwiches, doughnuts, ice-cream and other fast foods.

Foster's A central patisserie and bakery, serving coffee, ice-cream and snacks.

Hard Rock Café With an ambience that will be familiar to anybody that has visited one of its namesakes elsewhere in the world, the Hard Rock Café serves predominantly Western food, and is nothing too special. It is, however, a good place for a few beers in air-conditioned surrounds (chilled draught is available), the music is varied, and there are pool tables and slot machines upstairs.

Jambo Inn The reliable ground floor restaurant here boasts an extensive menu concentrating on Indian dishes, but also with some Chinese and Western selections. Portions are generous, the food is really tasty, and it's excellent value at around Tsh3,000–4,000 for a main course with rice or naan bread. Meals are served throughout the day, and there's also a Tandoori barbecue in the evening. No alcohol, but great fresh fruit juice.

Nando's Excellent and inexpensive South African sit-down or take-away franchise specialising in spicy peri-peri chicken.

Salamander Café This popular and central eatery has a deserved reputation for serving the best cheap lunches in town, with dishes such as fish and chips or spaghetti Bolognese for around Tsh2,500. It is closed in the evenings

Saswadee Restaurant Situated on the ninth floor of the New Africa Hotel, with a grandstand view over the harbour, this superb Thai restaurant is one of the best places to eat anywhere in Dar, but it's also relatively expensive – expect a bill of at least US$15 per head.

Serengeti Restaurant Situated on the ground floor of the Royal Palm Hotel, the Serengeti Restaurant prepares sumptuous buffets with a different theme every night. These are Mediterranean on Monday, Italian on Tuesday, Oriental on Wednesday, Seafood on Thursday, Fondue on Friday, Mexican on Saturday and Indian on Sunday. The food has been described as 'the ultimate culinary experience in Dar' – and so it should be at around US$30 per head.

Sichuan Restaurant This fabulous Chinese restaurant, tucked away in a parking lot on Bibi Titi Mohamed Street, is one of the best value eateries in Dar es Salaam, with a wide range of Chinese dishes mostly coming in at around Tsh4,000–5,000. Unreservedly recommended.

Sno-Cream Parlour This Dar institution dates back to the days when the city's other ice-cream parlours served nothing but orange juice spiced with flies. The extravagant interior and marvellous sundaes don't have quite the air of surrealism they did back then, but the sundaes are still the best in town

Steers Deprived fast food junkies should make a beeline for this South African franchise, which serves good burgers, steak rolls and the like.

Subway This American franchise, popular at lunchtime, serves good baguettes with a wide selection of tasty hot and cold fillings for Tsh2,000 upwards.

Suburban

Addis in Dar Spicy Ethiopian dishes in the Oyster Bay area near the new US Embassy.

Azuma Japanese Restaurant Situated in the Slipway shopping mall, the Azuma is known for its excellent Japanese and Indian cuisine. Main courses are in the Tsh4,000–6,000 range.

Bar-Be-Que Village Restaurant This relaxed and reasonably priced Indian-owned restaurant has rooftop and garden dining areas. Seafood dishes go for around Tsh4,500–6,000 and Indian and Chinese dishes (good vegetarian choice) for Tsh2,500–4,000. Open 18.30–23.00 daily except for Mondays.

Dhow Restaurant Situated in the Hotel Sea Cliff, this seafood restaurant has been described as 'Dar es Salaam's finest eating out experience' – expect a bill of around US$15 per head.

Europub Situated 7km out of town in Kawe (off the Old Bagamoyo Road) this popular beach restaurant serves top-quality seafood and Mexican dishes for around Tsh8,000 and it also has a very lively bar. If you are driving yourself, ring 0741 222463 for directions. Any taxi driver will know where to drop you, but it would be wise to arrange to be collected at a specified time.

La Dolce Vita This recently re-opened Italian restaurant, in an open-sided building with a tall *makuti* roof, has a great waterfront location. The three-course set menu is good value at around Tsh6,000. À la carte pizzas, grills and seafood in the Tsh4,000–6,000 range.

La Trattoria Jan Also known as Jan's Pizzeria, this busy restaurant in the Namanga area serves the best pizzas in town for Tsh3,000–4,000, as well as other Italian dishes and grills.

L'Arca di Noe Situated in the Namanga area, this is widely regarded to be the best Italian restaurant in Dar, with most dishes falling into the Tsh5,000–6,000 range.

Mashua Waterfront Good, moderately priced pizzeria and grill overlooking the Indian Ocean in the Slipway shopping mall.

The Pub This English-style pub has a decidedly non-English tropical beach setting in the Slipway shopping mall. Indoor and courtyard seating is available, along with draught beer, bar meals and a Sunday lunchtime roast.

Q-Bar This popular drinking hole in the Oyster Bay area serves good bar grub and does an evening barbecue with *mishkaki* and chicken tikka. Most meals cost less than Tsh5,000. There's live music on Friday nights.

Serengeti Spaghetti Situated in the Casanova shopping mall alongside the Sea Cliff Hotel, this Italian restaurant serves pasta dishes at around Tsh3,500, and grills and seafood dishes in the Tsh5,000–6,000 range.

Simona Restaurant This continental restaurant in the Namanga area serves decent grills and seafood for around Tsh5,000.

Smokies Tavern This beachfront bar, popular with expatriates, prepares an excellent rooftop buffet barbecue (meat and seafood) for Tsh9,600 per head. Bar snacks – smoked fish and filled pitta bread – cost around Tsh2,500. There is live music every Thursday night and on the first Saturday of the month.

NIGHTLIFE

There is something of a dearth of decent bars in the centre of Dar, presumably due to the strong Muslim presence, and many hotels and restaurants don't serve alcohol. The **Hard Rock Café** is one of the few genuine drinking holes in the city centre, and the beers aren't as expensive as you might fear. On Kivukoni Front close to the Lutheran Cathedral, the somewhat uninvitingly named **Hotel and Tourism Training Institute** is actually about the earthiest drinking hole in the city centre. More of a disco than a bar, **Club Bilicanas** is only worth visiting if you intend to settle in for the night, on account of the entrance charge of around US$3 per person.

Not far from the city centre, the **Las Vegas Casino** complex includes **Ryan's Pub**, a decent mock-Irish boozer, and the popular **California Dreamer Nightclub**. Further out of town, among the better places for a drink are **Smokies Tavern**, **Q-Bar**, **Europub** and **The Slipway**, all of which are mentioned in the restaurant listings and can only be reached by taxi or with private transport. The **Coco Beach Bar** at Oyster Bay is a good place to while away a day sipping cold beers and eating *mishkaki* kebabs.

GENERAL INFORMATION
Tourist information

The tourist information office of the **Tanzania Tourist Corporation** (TTC) has recently relocated from opposite the New Africa Hotel to a new office on the

---

EMBASSIES AND DIPLOMATIC MISSIONS

Major embassies and high commissions in Dar es Salaam are listed below. Most are open mornings only and not at all at weekends. Typical hours are 09.00 to 12.30, but this varies considerably.

Algeria 34 Ali Hassan Mwinyi Rd; tel: 022 211 7619; fax: 022 211 7620
Angola 78 Lugalo Rd, Upanga; tel: 022 211 7674
Belgium 5 Ocean Rd, Upanga; tel: 022 211 2688/3466; fax: 022 211 7621
Burundi Plot 1007 Lugalo Road, Upanga; tel: 0812 341777; fax: 022 212 1499
Canada 38 Mirambo Close; tel: 022 211 2831/5; fax: 022 211 6897
China 2 Kajifcheni Close; tel: 022 266 7586/694; fax: 022 266 6353
Denmark Ghana Ave; tel: 022 211 3887/8; fax: 022 211 6433
Egypt 24 Ghana Ave; tel: 022 211 3591; fax: 022 211 2543
Finland cnr Mirambo St and Garden Ave; tel: 022 211 9170; fax: 022 211 9173
France Ali Hassan Mwinyi Rd; tel: 022 266 6021-3; fax: 022 266 8435
Germany 10th floor, NIC House, Samora Ave; tel: 022 211 7409/15; fax: 022 211 2944
Great Britain Social Security House, Samora Ave; tel: 022 211 7659/94; fax: 022 211 2951
Greece 64 Upanga Rd; tel: 022 211 5895; fax: 022 260 0151
Hungary 204 Chake Chake Rd, Oyster Bay; tel: 022 266 8573; fax: 022 266 7214
India 11th Floor, NIC House, Samora Ave; tel: 022 211 7175/6; fax: 022 211 8761
Indonesia 299 Ali Hassan Mwinyi Rd; tel: 022 211 9119; fax: 022 211 5849

ground floor of the Matasalamat Building on Samora Avenue. The office is open on weekdays and on Saturday mornings. We found the staff very helpful, but not that knowledgeable when it came to off-the-beaten-track destinations. The address is PO Box 2485, Dar es Salaam; tel: 022 213 1555/212 0373; fax: 022 211 6420; email: md@ttb.ud.or.tz.

Two excellent sources of current information about the city are the bi-monthly booklet *Dar es Salaam Guide*, published by East African Movies Ltd (email: eam@raha.com), and the monthly *What's Happening in Dar es Salaam* published by Hakuna Matata Travels (email: kakunamatata@raha.com). Both booklets can be obtained at no charge from the foyers or gift shops in most upmarket hotels, embassies and other diplomatic missions, and A Novel Idea bookshop in the Slipway shopping mall. They should also be stocked at most Tanzanian embassies abroad.

Books

Most bookshops in Dar es Salaam (and in Tanzania for that matter) only stock textbooks, but there are several stalls around the Motel Agip and along Samora Avenue selling second-hand novels and much else besides at very negotiable prices. There are shops or kiosks selling books in the foyers of most tourist class hotels, though the one in the Sheraton tends to be very overpriced. **A Novel Idea** (tel: 022 266 6068) in the Slipway, a shopping mall in the suburb of Msasani, is easily the best bookshop in town, stocking a good selection of novels, field and travel guides, and other books with local interest.

The **government bookshop** on Samora Avenue (close to the Askari Monument) mostly stocks textbooks, but it's the best place to buy Swahili dictionaries and phrase books, and will be much cheaper than the street stalls.

The **British Council library** and reading room has plenty of up-to-date British newspapers and magazines. Membership costs US$2.50 per month. You

Ireland Msasani Rd; tel: 022 266 0614/2355; fax: 022 266 7852
Italy 316 Lugalo Rd; tel: 022 211 5935/6; fax: 022 211 5938
Japan 1081 Ali Hassan Mwinyi Rd; tel: 022 211 5827; fax: 022 211 5830
Kenya 14th Floor, NIC House, Samora Ave; tel: 022 211 2955/7; fax: 022 211 3098
Malawi 6th Floor, NIC House, Sokoine Dr; tel: 022 211 3240; fax: 022 211 3360
Mozambique 25 Garden Ave; tel: 022 211 6502; fax: 022 211 6502
Netherlands 2nd Floor, ATC Building, Ohio Rd; tel: 022 211 8566/8; fax: 022 211 2828
Norway Cnr Mirambo St and Garden Ave; tel: 022 211 3366/3610; fax: 022 211 8564
Pakistan 149 Malik Rd; tel: 022 211 7630; fax: 022 211 3205
Poland 63 Ali Kahn Rd; tel: 022 211 5271; fax: 022 211 5812
Romania 11 Ocean Rd, Upanga; tel: 022 211 5899; fax: 022 211 3866
Russia 73 Ali Hassan Mwinyi Rd; tel: 022 266 6005/6; fax: 022 266 6818
Rwanda 32 Ali Hassan Mwinyi Rd; tel: 022 213 0119; fax: 022 211 5888
South Africa Mwaya Rd, Msasani; tel: 022 260 1800; fax: 022 260 1684
Spain 99B Kinondoni Rd; tel: 022 266 6936/6018; fax: 022 266 6938
Sudan 64 Ali Mwinyi Rd; tel: 022 211 7641; fax: 022 211 5811
Sweden Cnr Mirambo St and Garden Ave; tel: 022 211 1235; fax: 022 211 3420
Switzerland Kinondoni Rd; tel: 022 266 6008/9; fax: 022 266 6736
Uganda 25 Msasani Rd; tel: 022 266 7391; fax: 022 266 7224
USA 140 Msese Rd, Kinondoni; tel: 022 266 6010-5; fax: 022 266 6701
Zambia Cnr Ohio Rd and Sokoine Drive; tel: 022 211 8481/2; fax: 022 211 2977
Zimbabwe NIC House, Sokoine Drive; tel: 022 211 6789; fax: 022 211 2913

can sometimes buy recent European and American newspapers at the stalls on Samora Avenue near the Salamander Café.

Car rental

Most safari operators in Dar es Salaam can arrange car rental. A recommended specialist is **Business Rent A Car**, which owns a fleet of modern air-conditioned minibuses, 4WDs and saloon cars suitable both for safaris further afield, and for travel in and around the city centre. Self-drive and chauffeur services are available. City tours and airport transfers can also be arranged. The office is in the city centre on Kisutu Street; tel 022 212 2852; mobile: 0744 614958; email: business@raha.com.

Cinema and theatre

There are six cinemas in Dar es Salaam, and you'll be in your element if you are a fan of Indian and kung fu films, or gung-ho American war films. The only theatre in Dar es Salaam is the **Little Theatre** near Oyster Bay. The British Council holds weekly film screenings – the programme is posted outside its library.

Communications

The central **post office** on Azikiwe Street is the place to collect your poste restante, and to buy stamps. There are several kiosks outside the post office selling postcards, envelopes and writing paper.

For **international phone calls and faxes**, the telecommunications centre is close to the post office, on Simu Street. This is also where you can buy phone cards, which are now more useful than coins when it comes to finding a phone box to use. There are also a few private shops dotted around the city centre offering more efficient international phone and fax facilities at slightly inflated prices. If you're staying in the part of town, there's a good one on Libya Street roughly opposite the Kisutu bus terminal.

Internet cafés are dotted all over the city centre, generally charging a very reasonable Tsh500 per 30 minutes' internet access. We regularly used, and can thoroughly recommend, Mealz Internet on the corner of Pamba Road and Sokoine Drive, which has plenty of computers, comparatively fast access, and is open from 08.00 to 21.00 Monday to Saturday and 09.00 to 14.00 Sundays. There is, however, plenty of choice (better internet cafés are marked on the map), but most places are closed on Sundays.

Hairdressers

There are unisex salons in most of the upmarket hotels, and in the YMCA building.

Maps

The Department of Lands and Surveys building is on Kivukoni Front, about 100m past the Kilimanjaro Hotel. Their map office is not in this building but in a small office tucked away behind a building on the block before it. It stocks 1:50,000 maps covering practically the whole country, particularly useful should you plan to hike off the beaten track in areas such as the Pare, Poroto, Usambara or Udzungwa mountains. The staff are helpful, and although the stock of maps for sale is depleted by comparison to a few years ago, they will make a black and white copy of the original for maps that are out of stock. The price either way is Tsh4,000 per sheet. Allow two hours for copying, if not a request to come back the next day – get to the office early to be safe!

TINGATINGA PAINTINGS

Visitors to the coast of Tanzania are bound to notice the brightly coloured paintings of fabulous creatures that line the streets of the country's main tourist centres. These are Tingatinga paintings, unique to Tanzania, and named after their originator Edward Tingatinga. The style arose in Dar es Salaam in the early 1960s, when Tingatinga fused the vibrant and popular work of Congolese immigrants with art traditions indigenous to his Makua homeland in the Mozambique border area (a region well known to aficionados of African art as the home of Makonde carving). When Tingatinga died in 1972, the accidental victim of a police shoot-out, his commercial success had already spawned a host of imitators, and shortly after that a formal Tingatinga art co-operative was formed with government backing.

In the early days, Tingatinga and his followers produced fairly simple paintings featuring a large, bold and often rather surreal two-dimensional image of one or other African creature on a monotone background. But as the paintings took off commercially, a greater variety of colours came into play, and a trend developed towards the more complex canvases you see today. Modern Tingatinga paintings typically depict a menagerie of stylised and imaginary birds, fish and mammals against a backdrop of a natural feature such as Kilimanjaro or an abstract panel of dots and whorls. An offshoot style, reputedly initiated by Tingatinga himself, can be seen in the larger, even more detailed canvases that depict a sequence of village or city scenes so busy you could look at them for a hour and still see something fresh.

Tingatinga painters have no pretensions to producing high art. On the contrary, the style has been commercially driven since its inception: even the largest canvases are produced over a matter of days and most painters work limited variations around favourite subjects. It would be missing the point altogether to talk of Tingatinga as traditional African art. With its bold, bright images – tending towards the anthropomorphic, often subtly humorous, always accessible and evocative – Tingatinga might more appropriately be tagged Africa's answer to pop art.

Labels aside, souvenir hunters will find Tingatinga paintings to be a lively, original and surprisingly affordable alternative to the identikit wooden animal carvings that are sold throughout East Africa (and, one suspects, left to gather dust in cupboards all over Europe). Take home a Tingatinga panel, and you'll have a quirky but enduring memento of your African trip, something to hang on your wall and derive pleasure from for years to come.

Based on a short article which first appeared in the December 1998 issue of the magazine Discover Africa

The kiosk in the foyer of the New Africa Hotel usually stocks maps of Dar es Salaam and Tanzania; if they don't have what you want, try the TTC office or the bookshop in the Kilimanjaro Hotel.

The recently published *Dar es Salaam City Map and Guide* is accurate, and readily available at most tourist class hotels in the city centre.

Money

Most people change money at one of the numerous forex bureaux that sprang up after the exchange rate was floated a few years ago. Forex bureaux give better rates than banks and are open for longer hours. Rates vary considerably, so shop around before you change large sums. I cannot recommend individual bureaux: the one giving the best rate in town when we first visited Dar es Salaam had dropped almost as low as the bank rate three months later. There are plenty of forex bureaux on Samora Avenue and Zanaki Street.

If you need to change money after the bureaux have closed, you can do so at the airport. It's also possible to do this at any hotel that accepts payment in dollars, providing you have a room at that hotel. Under no circumstance should you exchange money with street dealers – there is no black market worth talking about in Dar es Salaam, but there are plenty of con artists.

Rickshaw Travel is the Tanzanian representative of American Express, and can provide financial services such as emergency cashing of cheques and foreign exchange. Their offices on Ali Hassan Mwinyi Road and in the lobby of the Sheraton Hotel are open from 08.00 to 17.00 on Monday to Saturday. Contact details are PO Box 1889, Dar es Salaam; tel: 022 211 5110 or 211 4094; fax: 022 211 3227; email: amex@twiga.com or rickaccts@twiga.com. You can get cash with a credit card at Coastal Travel (see *Tour operators*), though the exchange rate isn't brilliant.

Visa, Mastercard and most other internationally recognised credit or debit cards can be used to draw up to Tsh200,000 of local currency daily at any of several ATMs (auto-tellers) in central Dar es Salaam. Some of the more convenient ATMs are at the Barclays Banks in the TDFL Building opposite the Royal Palm Hotel, and in the Slipway shopping mall, and at the Standard Chartered Bank on Garden Avenue next to the new Holiday Inn. Unless the ATM is temporarily closed, money can be drawn 24 hours, seven days a week.

Public transport

The main mode of transport is *dalla-dallas*, which are generally privately owned minibuses, and cover almost every conceivable route through the city. The most important *dalla-dalla* station is the one outside the new post office on Azikiwe Street, but other important stops can be found at the old post office on Sokoine Drive and outside the railway station near the Clock Tower. The route system is confusing for new arrivals which, coupled with the high incidence of theft on both buses and *dalla-dallas*, probably makes it rather pointless to try to get to grips with public transport on a short visit to the city. The one exception is if you want to buy a ticket for the Tazara Railway to Zambia, in which case you can hop into a vehicle marked *Vigunguti* at the main post office.

Under no circumstances would I attempt using public transport when I was loaded down with luggage – aside from the crowding, petty theft is a real risk. When you first arrive in town (or at any other time when you are carrying luggage or valuables), use a taxi.

Taxis

There are taxis all over the place. A good place to find a taxi is in front of the New Africa Hotel, though you are more likely to be overcharged there than elsewhere. The standard price for a ride within the city centre is about Tsh1,500-2,000, though you'll probably be asked slightly more at first, and should expect to pay more for trips further afield.

Shopping

Although it has improved greatly in recent years, Dar es Salaam is some way short of being a shopper's paradise. Locally produced goods are cheapest at stalls such as those lining Maktaba Street. The supermarket on Samora Avenue (see map) is one of many so-called luxury shops, selling a variety of imported foodstuffs and toiletries at inflated prices. There is a branch of Woolworths on Samora Road. Several clothes shops and fruit stalls line Zanaki Street, but the most colourful place to buy this sort of thing is Kariakoo Market (described under *What to Do*). Curio stalls in Dar es Salaam are very expensive when compared to those in Arusha. The last few years have seen a proliferation of shopping malls constructed in suburban Dar es Salaam. The best mall is probably the Slipway on the Msasani Peninsula, which has four restaurants, an excellent bookshop, a South African chain supermarket, and a bank with an ATM. Also good are the Oyster Bay shopping centre, and the Arcade and Shoppers Paradise on the Old Bagamoyo Road.

Swahili courses
Swahili Language Trainers, located in the Oyster Bay shopping mall behind the synonymous hotel, offers a variety of beginners and advanced courses, as well as cultural familiarisation courses, and translation and other linguistic services. Tel: 0741 272296.

Swimming pool
The Mission to Seamen, on Bandari Road near the intersection with Kilwa Road, charges US$3.50 for use of their swimming pool. Good food is available here too.

Tour operators
Most tour operators in Dar es Salaam specialise in visits to the southern reserves. It is more normal to organise northern safaris in Arusha. It is also cheaper, as most tour operators in Dar es Salaam are in the middle to upper range. Some tour companies can do day trips to Bagamoyo. Safaris can usually be arranged through the owners of various camps in the Selous; see *Chapter 17* for details of these. Because few budget safaris run out of Dar es Salaam, there is no pirate safari industry similar to the one in Arusha, which means that you can be reasonably confident in your dealings with any tour company. The following companies are recommended:

Coastal Travel Tel: 022 211 7959/60; fax: 022 211 8647/7895; email: safari@coastal.cc; web: www.coastal.cc. A long-standing and highly regarded company that serves as the main booking agent for numerous lodges and hotels and can arrange personalised safaris throughout Tanzania. They also run scheduled flights to several destinations not serviced by Air Tanzania, for instance Pemba Island, the reserves of the northern safari circuit, Rubondo Island, Selous and Ruaha.
Hippo Tours & Safaris Tel: 022 277 5164/1610; mobile: 0811 320849; fax: 022 277 5165; email: hippo@twiga.com or info@hippotours.com. Another long-standing operator specialising in good-value fly-in Selous safaris, based out of its own excellent Rufiji River Camp, as well as other southern circuit safaris and the islands.
Kearsley Travel Tel: 022 211 5026-30; fax: 022 211 5585; email: kearsley@raha.com; web: www.kearsley.net. Based on Indira Gandhi St, this is another well-established safari company, known for its dynamic management, and with years of experience arranging safaris throughout Tanzania, but particularly the southern circuit.
Safari Scene Tel/fax: 022 270 1497; mobile 0741 323318; email: safariscene@intafrica.com; web: www.safariscene.com. Based next to the Shoppers Plaza on the Old Bagamoyo Road, this new agency acts as a booking agency for several leading safari lodges and beach resorts in southern and western Tanzania.

Wildlife Conservation Society

The Wildlife Conservation Society of Tanzania holds monthly talks at its headquarters on Garden Avenue. Tel: 022 211 2518; fax: 022 212 4572; email: wcst@africaonline.co.tz.

WHAT TO DO

Dar es Salaam is an interesting city, but not one that offers much in the way of conventional sightseeing. It is worth strolling around the harbour area and through the back streets between Maktaba Road and the station. There are several old German buildings in the older part of town near the national museum and botanical gardens. If you have a couple of days to kill in Dar es Salaam, you might want to spend them at the beaches north or south of the city centre (covered later in this chapter) or Bagamoyo (see *Chapter 10*). The beaches immediately north or south of Dar also form realistic goals for a day trip from the city centre.

Historical buildings

You can spend a worthwhile couple of hours exploring the several relics of Dar es Salaam's early days that are dotted around the city centre. The oldest surviving building is the **Old Boma** on the corner of Morogoro Road and Sokoine Drive. A plain, rather austere whitewashed monolith, built using coral rubble in the traditional coastal style, the Old Boma is easily recognised by its inscribed Zanzibari door. It was built in 1867 as a hotel to house visitors to the court of Sultan Majid, whose palace stood alongside it. Between 1870 and 1887, the building was the residence of the Sultan of Zanzibar's local agent, and it subsequently served as the GEAC's first administrative headquarters in Dar es Salaam, and the police charge office.

Several late-19th-century German buildings have survived into modern times. The **Ocean Road Hospital,** which lies east of the city centre at the end of Samora Avenue, was built in 1897, and is notable for its twin domed towers. The nearby **State House** also dates to a similar time, though it was heavily damaged in World War I, and the modern building, restored in 1922, bears little resemblance to photographs of the original.

The **Lutheran Church** on the corner of Sokoine Drive and Maktaba Road was built in 1898 in a Bavarian style. Following the recent restoration of its exterior, this is a very striking and attractive church, best viewed from the park on Sokoine Drive. A few blocks down on Sokoine Drive, the Gothically influenced **St Joseph's Cathedral** was built between 1897 and 1902. Other buildings dating from the German era include the **City Hall** (on Sokoine Road opposite the Old Boma), several ex-civil servants' residences around the botanical garden, and the buildings housing the Department of Lands and Surveys and Magistrate's Court on Kivukoni Front.

Kariakoo Market

A huge variety of clothes, foodstuffs, spices and traditional medicines can be bought at this lively and colourful covered market which extends on to the surrounding streets in the form of a chaotic miscellany of stalls. The name *Kariakoo* derives from the British Carrier Corps, which was stationed in the area during World War II.

Tanzania National Museum

This is one of the better museums I have visited in Africa. The section on early hominid development contains some of the world's most important fossils. The history displays upstairs have a good selection of exhibits dating back to the era of

European exploration and German occupation. If you plan to visit Kilwa Kisiwani, don't miss the display of coins, pottery and other artefacts found during excavations there. Entrance costs Tsh2,400 and photography an additional Tsh3,600.

The area around the museum is notable for its pre-1914 German buildings, recognisable by their red-tiled roofs. The botanical garden, established in 1906, and now pretty rundown, is worth a look, as is the State House, built by the British in 1922. From the State House, if you walk back to town along Kivukoni Front, you will be rewarded by good views of the city and harbour. You will also pass the 19th-century Lutheran Church, the oldest building in the city.

Nyumba ya Sanaa

This well-known gallery was founded by a nun, and is now housed in an unusually designed building, erected in 1983 with the help of Norwegian funding. It exhibits arts and crafts made by handicapped people. A variety of carvings, batiks and pottery items can be bought. The standard of craftsmanship is generally regarded to be high. There is a café in the complex.

Oyster Bay

This is the closest swimming beach to the city centre. It is a reasonably attractive spot and very popular at weekends. The Oyster Bay Hotel, which overlooks the beach, is a pleasant place to have a drink or meal, as is the nearby La Dolce Vita. No public transport goes directly to Oyster Bay, but if you take any *dalla-dalla* out of the city centre towards Msasani Peninsula, it can drop you at a junction near Q-Bar about 500m from the beach. A taxi from the city centre will cost around Tsh5, US$2.50.

Village Museum and Mwenge Market

The Village Museum consists of 16 life-size replicas of huts built in architectural styles from all over Tanzania. It is open daily from 09.30 to 18.00, but the best time to visit is between 14.00 and 16.00 on weekends and public holidays, when a traditional dance performance is held. The entrance fee is Tsh2,400, and an additional Tsh2,400 is charged for photography. Tel: 022 270 0437; mobile: 0744 695443; email: village@rwiga.com. The nearby Mwenge market is a traditional Makonde carving community, and one of the best places to buy these unique sculptures – prices are negotiable.

Both places are along the Bagamoyo road, 10km and 13km from the city centre respectively. If you want to get there on public transport, pick up a *dalla-dalla* from the post office to Makumbusha bus stand, which lies around the corner from the Village Museum.

Bongoyo Island

This small island lies within a marine reserve, and has a pretty beach where – unusually for Tanzania – swimming is possible at any time of day due to the absence of an offshore reef. A dhow service runs between the island and the Slipway shopping mall four times daily, leaving Dar at 09.30, 11.30, 13.30 and 15.30, and leaving Bongoyo at 10.30, 12.30, 14.30 and 16.30. The return trip costs Tsh5,000.

Pugu Hills Forest Reserve

The main water catchment for Dar es Salaam is the forested Pugu Hills, which lie about 25km southwest of the city centre, and receive a significantly higher rainfall, due to their greater elevation. In 1954, a roughly 20km^2 tract of evergreen forest in the hills was set aside as a forest reserve, much of which has subsequently been destroyed or severely degraded due to a combination of commercial logging, planting of exotic eucalyptus trees, and local subsistence exploitation for charcoal, firewood and timber. Today, less than 5km² of pristine forest remains, supporting a surprisingly varied fauna. The reserve is crossed with trails and roads, making it one of the most accessible coastal forests in Tanzania.

Large mammals resident in the hills include vervet and blue monkey, bushpig, suni antelope, the striking chequered elephant shrew, and the recently described and very localised Rondo galago, while lion, spotted hyena and elephant are reputedly observed from time to time. The bird checklist of more than 100 species includes several localised forest dwellers, including Sokoke pipit, spotted ground thrush, east coast akalat and Angola pipit, as well as crowned eagle and southern banded snake eagle. A wealth of butterflies can be seen, as with luck can chameleons. A site of particular interest is a large artificial cave in a disused limestone quarry that is estimated to harbour around 100,000 bats of two species – the whole flock streams out of the cave entrance at dusk, a quite spectacular phenomenon.

The base for visiting Pugu Hills is the small town of Kisarawe, which lies about 25km from Dar es Salaam by road, and is connected to it by regular *dalla-dallas*. To reach Kisarawe in a private vehicle, you need to follow Nyerere Road out of Dar es Salaam, passing the airport, until about 20km from the city centre you reach a fork in the road opposite a filling station. Here, you need to head straight along a dirt road (as opposed to forking left along a surfaced road). After about 1km, this dirt road passes through a corner of the forest reserve and perhaps 2km further it enters Kisarawe. At the second traffic circle in Kisarawe, a road to the left leads into the forest, and is also the starting point for the 3km Mpugu Pugu walking trail. There is a forestry checkpoint at the junction where you must pay the entrance fee of Tsh5,000. The poor road into the forest is suitable for 4WD vehicles only, and parts may be washed away during the rains. The bat cave lies about 3km from Kisarawe, on the right side of the road no more than 20m after it passes through a small tunnel.

THE COAST NORTH OF DAR ES SALAAM

Two major resort clusters lie along the coast immediately north of Dar es Salaam, the more established of which is Kunduchi Beach, about 35km from the city centre off the Bagamoyo road. Immediately south of Kunduchi, and divided from it by a large lagoon, Mbezi Beach has seen major tourist development over the last decade, and is now fringed by a compact string of upmarket and moderate resort hotels, generally of a higher quality than the older hotels at Kunduchi. While neither beach is as scenic as Tanzania's finest, both are likely to be a more attractive prospect to the average holidaymaker than staying in or around the city centre.

Both beaches are sandy and quite attractive, and good for swimming at high tide, though Kunduchi Beach is detracted from scenically by the series of concrete piles that were constructed along the waterfront to control erosion. At both beaches, tied to one or other hotel, there are diving, snorkelling, watersport and angling facilities, as well as motorboats for hire to visit one of the many small offshore islands dotted along the coastline. In all honesty, however, nothing along this stretch of coast matches Bagamoyo – only 50km further north and in the process of being linked to Dar by a zippy surfaced road – for scenery or for atmosphere.

A short walk from the Kunduchi Beach Hotel, the Kunduchi Ruins are well worth a visit. Little is known about their history, but at least one ruined building, a mosque, dates to the 16th century. The main point of interest, however, is an

18th-century graveyard set amongst a grove of baobab trees. The pillar tombs at Kunduchi, the most extensive such assemblage on the East Africa coast, are decorated with porcelain plates, and are inscribed in a manner that is unique among Swahili graveyards of this period. Pottery collected at the site suggests the town was wealthy and had trade links with China and Britain.

Getting there and away

If you are driving, head out of Dar es Salaam along the Bagamoyo road until after about 35km you see the Karibu Art Gallery to your right. A short distance after this, the turn-off for Mbezi Beach and associated hotels – several of which are signposted – lies to the right. The beach and hotels are no more than 3km from the main road. For Kunduchi Beach, bypass this junction and continue towards Bagamoyo for about 2km, then turn right along the side road signposted for the various Kunduchi Beach resorts.

For day trippers, especially those on a budget, Kids Transport Service runs a shuttle bus between central Dar and the hotels on Kunduchi Beach. The bus leaves Dar from in front of the New Africa Hotel at 09.00, 14.00 and 17.00 daily, and it leaves from the beaches at around 10.00, 15.00 and 18.00. It stops first at the Kunduchi Beach Hotel, followed by Silversands and the Bahari Beach Hotel. It then returns directly to the city centre. The trip out takes about an hour. Timings for the return trip are vague. If, for instance, you want to return to Dar es Salaam on the bus that leaves the New Africa at 09.00, it could pass your hotel any time between 09.45 and 10.15.

There are ordinary buses to Kunduchi and Mbezi village, from where you could walk to one of the hotels. This is not recommended if you are weighed down with luggage or carrying valuables, as thefts and muggings have been reported, but if you're just out for the day with a bit of cash, the risk of a problem is lessened.

Where to stay
Upmarket
Jangwani Seabreeze Lodge Tel: 022 264 7215/7067; fax: 022 264 7069; email: info@jangwani.com; web: www.jangwani.com. This smart and tastefully decorated German-owned hotel straddles the main road along Mbezi Beach, dividing the accommodation, restaurant and reception area from the beach bar, swimming pool and diving centre. The restaurant has a good reputation for its German cuisine and seafood, and the long palm-lined beach in front of the hotel is one of the most attractive around Dar es Salaam. The on-site diving centre offers PADI dives and courses, as well as boat trips to the

---

WET, WILD AND FUN...

A particularly attractive feature of Kunduchi Beach for families – and children of all ages – is the new Kunduchi Wet & Wild Water World complex, which is situated alongside the recently renovated Kunduchi Beach Hotel. Consisting of 22 water slides, the longest of which is 200m, as well as seven swimming pools, the complex also offers go-kart racing and watersports, and has a good selection of shops, video games and restaurants, as well as an internet café. A diving centre is planned, too. A day pass costs Tsh3,600. It is open daily, but only women are allowed in on Tuesday, a move geared towards the sensibilities of the local Muslim community. A similar but less elaborate water slide park called Waterworld can be found on Mbezi Beach, right next to the Beachcomber Hotel.

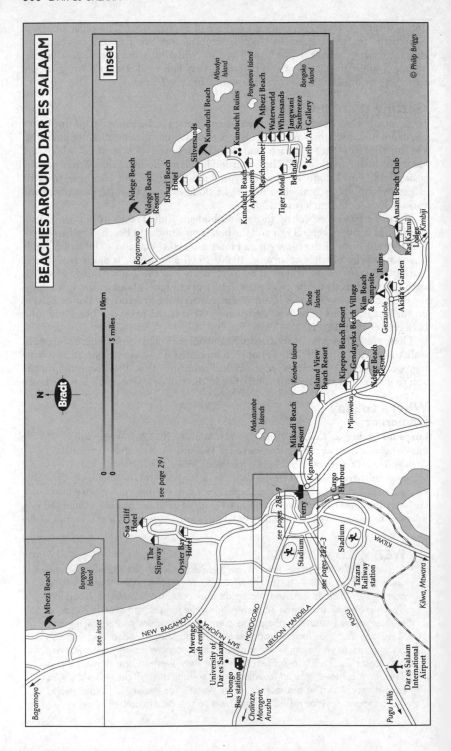

BEACHES AROUND DAR ES SALAAM

© Philip Briggs

islands, water-skiing and paragliding from a motorboat. Large and comfortable rooms with AC, fan, hot water, fridge, safe and satellite television cost US$110/134 single/double B&B, while slightly smaller rooms with similar facilities cost US$106/130.

White Sands Hotel Tel: 022 264 7621/2; fax: 022 211 8483; email: whitesandshotel@raha.com; web: www.hotelwhitesands.com. The largest hotel on Mbezi Beach, White Sands feels a bit like a city hotel transplanted to the beach, though the monolithic structure is redeemed by the attractive location and smart whitewashed exterior. It's pretty good value at US$88/98 B&B for a large self-contained single/double with AC and satellite television, and the weekender special of US$90 double FB is a real bargain. The attached Blue Chip Diving School offers diving courses, dives and various other water sports.

The Beachcomber Tel: 022 264 7772/3/4; fax: 022 264 7050; email: beachcomber@afsat.com; web: www.beachcomber.co.tz. This modern hotel at the north end of Mbezi Beach is marred slightly, in my opinion, by the overuse of concrete and the garish blue and pink décor, but otherwise it's a very attractive set-up with a great beachfront swimming pool area facing Mbupi Island. Facilities include diving, a health club, and free airport transfers. The seafood restaurant comes highly recommended. Self-contained rooms with AC, satellite television, fridge and private balcony cost US$104/122 single/double B&B, while suites cost US$134/158.

Bahari Beach Hotel Tel: 022 265 052; fax: 022 2650351; email: bbhbuz@intafrica.com. This former government hotel, constructed from coral rock and thatch in the traditional Swahili style, lies in large naturally vegetated grounds running down to arguably the finest stretch of beach on the north coast. The self-contained chalets are very comfortable, if somewhat Spartan in the furnishing, and have satellite television, AC, and private sea-facing balconies. Other facilities include a restaurant, a swimming pool and watersport equipment. Rates are US$90/110 double/triple B&B. Day visitors are charged a nominal entrance fee. Unlike the other upmarket hotels on this stretch of coast, credit cards are not accepted.

Moderate, budget and camping

Silversands Hotel, Campsite & Conference Centre Tel: 022 265 0567; fax: 022 265 0428; email: silversands@africaonline.co.tz. Silversands has for years provided an alternative to the main upmarket hotels for budget–conscious travellers wishing to spend time on the north coast beaches, and it remains the best place to head for in several price categories. Slightly rundown but nevertheless pleasantly laidback, it has a good beachfront location, as well as a decent restaurant and bar, and a range of marine activities on offer including snorkel hire and diving courses. Self-contained 'deluxe' rooms with AC cost US$50/65 single/twin inclusive of a full English breakfast, while standard rooms with a fan cost US$30/45 inclusive of a Continental breakfast. Dormitory accommodation is available at US$7 per person, while camping costs US$3 per person plus US$2 per vehicle.

Belinda Ocean Resort Tel: 022 264 7551; fax: 022 264 7552; email: belinda@africaonline.co.tz. Situated on a back road about 500m from the beach at Mbezi, this new lodge seems too pricey to be a viable mid-range alternative to the smarter beachfront hotels, and too tacky and too far from the beach to offer them much competition on the aesthetic front. Ugly grounds and lack of direct beach access aside, the rooms are fair value at Tsh45,000/65,000 B&B for a single/double with AC, satellite television and private balcony, and there's a pleasant swimming pool area.

Tiger Motel Situated on the main Bagamoyo Road about halfway between the junctions to Mbezi and Kunduchi Beaches, this low-key and rather rundown local hotel feels overpriced at Tsh20,000 for a double with AC, and is miles from any beach.

Ndege Beach Resort It is difficult to know what to make of this isolated beach resort, which lies about 2km from the Bagamoyo Road along a turn-off signposted some 10km north of the Kunduchi turn-off. No quibbles about the setting, a wide, sandy palm-lined

DHOWS OF THE SWAHILI COAST

The word dhow, commonly applied by Europeans to any traditional seafaring vessel used off the coast of East Africa, is generally assumed to be Arabic in origin. There is, however, no historical evidence to back up this notion, nor does it appear to be an established Swahili name for any specific type of boat. Caroline Sassoon, writing in *Tanganyika Notes & Records* in 1970, suggests that the word dhow is a corruption of não, used by the first Portuguese navigators in the Indian Ocean to refer to any small local seafaring vessel, or of the Swahili *kidau*, a specific type of small boat described below.

The largest traditional sailing vessel in wide use off the coast of East Africa is the *jahazi*, which measures up to 20m long and whose large billowing sails are a characteristic sight off Zanzibar and other traditional ports. With a capacity of about 100 passengers, the *jahazi* is mainly used for transporting cargo and passengers over relatively long distances or in open water, for instance between Dar es Salaam and Zanzibar. Minor modifications in the Portuguese and Omani eras notwithstanding, the design of the modern *jahazi* is pretty much identical to that of similar seafaring vessels used in medieval times and before. The name *jahazi* is generally applied to boats with cutaway bows and square sterns built on Zanzibar and nearby parts of the mainland. Similar boats built in Lamu and nearby ports in Kenya are called *jalbut* (possibly derived from the English 'jolly boat' or Indian 'gallevat') and have a vertical bow and wineglass-shaped stern. Smaller but essentially similar in design, the *mashua* measures up to 10m long, has a capacity of about 25

beach many miles from any other resort development, but not so the faintly depressing aura of neglect that hangs over the resort itself. The self-contained rooms with netting and running water are reasonable value at Tsh6,000 double, assuming you can live with the absence of a fan in this muggy climate, while larger but equally scruffy rooms with AC seem madly overpriced at Tsh28,000–40,000. Camping is permitted at a negotiable rate, and snacks and chilled drinks are served. Emphatically not for those expecting slick luxury – or slick anything for that matter – but equally many budget travellers might love the place for its fabulous setting and affordable rates. If you're using public transport, any bus heading to Bagamoyo can drop you at the junction.

Visiwa Guesthouse This bog standard local guesthouse in Kunduchi charges Tsh3,000 for a simple double using common showers.

BEACH RESORTS SOUTH OF DAR

Separated from central Dar es Salaam by the main harbour entrance – not bridged, but crossed by a regular motor ferry – the coast immediately south of Dar es Salaam seems worlds rather than a kilometre or two from the city centre. The suburban belt south of the harbour consists of the village of Kigamboni, a small cluster of shops and houses that sprawl for about 500m past the ferry terminal. Once past that, the road south passes through rustic fields barely touched by urban development, and overlooking a series of idyllic beaches pockmarked with large mushroom-shaped coral outcrops. A few years ago, these southern beaches were also practically bereft of tourist resorts. Today, however, the area is studded with a varied selection of resorts and lodges that – possibly because they are relatively new – seem to be far more geared towards the requirements of modern travellers of all budgets than are the generally somewhat outmoded monolithic hotels that characterise the northern beaches.

passengers, and is mostly used for fishing close to the shore or as local transport.

The most rudimentary and smallest type of boat used on the Swahili Coast is the *mtumbwi*, which is basically a dugout canoe made by hollowing out the trunk of a large tree – the mango tree is favoured today – and used for fishing in mangrove creeks and other still water environments. The *mtumbwi* is certainly the oldest type of boat used in East Africa, and its simple design probably replicates that of the very first boats crafted by humans. A more elaborate and distinctive variation on the *mtumbwi* is the *ngalawa*, a 5–6m long dugout supported by a narrow outrigger on each side, making it sufficiently stable to be propelled by a sail. The *ngalawa* is generally used for fishing close to shore as well as for transporting passengers across protected channels such as the one between Mafia and Chole Islands in the Mafia Archipelago.

The largest traditional boats of the Indian Ocean, the ocean-going dhows that were once used to transport cargo between East Africa, Asia and Arabia, have become increasingly scarce in recent decades due to the advent of foreign ships and other, faster modes of intercontinental transport. Several distinct types of ocean-going dhow are recognised, ranging from the 60-ton *sambuk* from Persia to 250-ton boats originating from India. Oddly, one of the largest of these vessels, the Indian *dengiya*, is thought to be the root of the English word dinghy. Although a few large dhows still ply the old maritime trade routes of the Indian Ocean, they are now powered almost exclusively with motors rather than by sails.

The best known accommodation on the southern beaches are the exclusive Ras Kutani Beach Resort and Protea Amani Beach Hotel, which abut each other about 35km past the ferry, and vie with each other for the accolade of the best tourist lodge serving Dar es Salaam. For budget travellers, an increasingly popular goal is Kipepeo Beach Campsite, which lies about 7km south of the ferry at Mjimwema, and is the closest thing to a conventional backpacker hostel in the Dar es Salaam area. Another 5km south of this, the village of Gezaulole is the site of a new cultural tourist project and a low-key, low-budget locally run lodge and campsite aimed at backpackers.

Getting there and away

The Kivukoni Ferry leaves Dar es Salaam from the southeast of the city centre, where Kivukoni Front meets Ocean Road, every 15 minutes or so. The crossing takes about five minutes and costs Tsh1,000 per vehicle plus Tsh100 per person.

In a private vehicle, you can drive straight off the ferry and through Kigamboni on a good surfaced road for about 7km until you reach the Y-junction at Mjimwema. Kipepeo Lodge and other resorts around Mjimwema are signposted along a road leading east just before this Y-junction. To reach any coastal resort that lies south of Mjimwema, you need to turn along a dirt road that forms the left fork of the Y junction. The surfaced right fork leads further southwest to the coastal villages of Kongowe and Mbajura, which are of little interest to travellers unless they happen to be trying to catch a dhow to Mafia Island.

Those using public transport will find plenty of *dalla-dallas* lined up at Kigamboni to take ferry passengers to various villages further south. If you are heading to Kipepeo Lodge at Mjimwema, you shouldn't have to wait for more than a few minutes, since all vehicles heading south must pass through the village.

GEZAULOLE

The village of Gezaulole, which lies on a fabulous sandy bay about 13km south of the Kivukoni ferry and Dar es Salaam, reputedly received its name many hundreds of years ago, when it was settled by a group of Zaramo fishermen. In the 16th century, Gezaulole became an Arabic trading post, and for reasons that sadly go unrecorded it was renamed Mbwamaji (literally 'Dog Water' or possibly a derivation of Mbu Maji, ie: 'Mosquito Water'!) The name Mbwamaji remained in use until the 1970s, when the village became one of the first Ujamaa villages established under the Nyerere administration, and the old Zaramo name – which means 'try and see' in the local dialect – took on a fresh resonance.

The people of Gezaulole have recently established a low-key cultural eco-tourism project which, based on our short visit, deserves greater support, and will be very rewarding to those travellers who do support it. This project is centred out of Akida's Garden near the beach – Akida being the name of the project co-ordinator – and the Kali Mata Ki Ji women's project office on the main road. Guided walking tours introduce visitors to a wide range of local crafts – batik dying, basketwork and woodcarving – as well as local agricultural practices. The guides can also show visitors to the remains of the 16th-century mosque at Mbwamaji, and several nearby 18th-century pillar tombs, all located close to the small local fishing harbour. Snorkelling excursions to the uninhabited Sinda Island in a local dhow are also offered.

It is possible to visit the cultural project as a day trip from Dar es Salaam – or any other beach resort south of the city – either in a private vehicle or by boarding a Kimbiji-bound *dalla-dalla* at the Kivukoni Ferry Terminal and asking to be dropped at Gezaulole. More realistic, however, would be to spend the night – Akida's Garden and Kali Mata Ki Ji both offer simple local accommodation (with mosquito nets) and meals.

Dalla-dallas leave more erratically for Gezaulole, but several vehicles pass through the village daily en route to Gomvu or Kimbiji.

Where to stay
Exclusive
Ras Kutani Tel: 022 213 4802; fax: 022 211 2794; email: selous@twiga.com. Closer in spirit and feel to a bush retreat than a typical beach resort, Ras Kutani is a wonderful small lodge – 12 sleeping units only – situated on a wild and isolated stretch of coast some 35km south of Dar es Salaam. The *bandas*, constructed almost entirely with organic materials such as wood, bamboo and *makuti* leaf, are set well apart in a thick patch of coastal woodland overlooking a small lagoon lined with mangroves and a wide sandy beach. The lovely setting, organic building materials and ethnic décor combine to create a very soothing and relaxed atmosphere, with vervet and blue monkeys and prolific birdlife in the woodland complemented by good snorkelling and fishing in the nearby reefs. A good selection of non-motorised watersports is on offer, and there is a swimming pool, but diving facilities are not available. Full board accommodation costs US$200 per person for non-residents in season and US$147 in low season. Resident rates, also FB, are US$88 per person Monday to Thursday, rising to US$99 per person over the weekend.

Protea Amani Beach Hotel Tel: 0811 410033/321257; email: abc@twiga.com or proteadar@cats-net.com. No less exclusive than Ras Kutani, but with a more cultivated, perhaps even mildly pretentious feel, the Amani Beach Hotel consists of several whitewashed chalets, with a traditional Swahili architectural influence, whose vast interior is dominated by a four-poster Swahili bed. To my taste, the cropped flowering lawns, crossed by neat footpaths, seem rather tepid compared to the wilder bush atmosphere of Ras Kutani. Facilities for fishing and other watersports are available, and there is a lovely beachfront swimming pool and a tennis court in the grounds. Full-board accommodation costs US$200/300 single/double for non-residents or US$149/238 for residents.

Budget, shoestring and camping
Note that the listings below start closest to the ferry terminal and continue south from there.

Mikadi Beach Resort Situated perhaps 2km south of the ferry terminal, this resort caters more to locals than to tourists, and the simple beach *bandas* are poor value at Tsh15,000 double. It also gets rowdy at weekends, making it perhaps of interest less as a place to stay than as somewhere for a few drinks away from the established expatriate hangouts.

Island View Beach Resort Tel: 022 280 0086. This is a new and evidently very friendly locally owned lodge set on a beach facing a small island about 5km south of the ferry terminal. The rooms are clean, have netting and in most cases fans (the rooms at the front are supposedly kept cool by the sea breeze), and seem adequate value at Tsh15,000 double/twin. A seafood restaurant is attached. The grounds are rather barren but will hopefully gain some character with time.

Kipepeo Beach Campsite Tel: 022 212 2931; mobile: 0744 276168; fax: 022 211 9272; email: info@kipepeocamp.com; web: www.kipepeocamp.com. This relatively new camp is the closest thing around Dar es Salaam to a backpacker hostel, and it seems destined to become very popular with travellers once it is better known. It is set on a lovely beach at Mjimwema, less than 1km along a side road signposted from the main surfaced road 7km south of the ferry terminal. In addition to camping at Tsh2,000 per person, it offers dormitory accommodation (nets and fans) in the main house for Tsh5,000 per person, as well as simple double beach *bandas* (no fan but a reliable sea breeze) for Tsh8,000 per person. Facilities include beach volleyball and a pool table. The food is good – snacks such as chicken in pitta bread cost Tsh1,500, and full meals cost around Tsh3,500. The camp has become a quite popular weekend hangout for young expatriates working in Dar, for which reason an entrance fee of Tsh3,000 is charged over weekends, refundable against drinks and food bought at the bar.

Gendayeka Beach Village This quiet and pleasant new lodge, which lies on the beach at Mjimwema about 50m past Kipepeo, is – depending on how you look at these – more peaceful or less atmospheric than its popular neighbour. Accommodation in breezy *bandas* with a net but no fan costs US$10 per person, while camping costs Tsh3,000 per person. A bar and restaurant are attached.

South Beach Campsite Also on Mjimwema Beach, about 200m past the above resorts, this is a very basic campsite consisting of a row of makeshift *makuti* beach shelters that are offered for day use or overnight camping at Tsh2,000 per unit per day. The campsite is very exposed, but a security guard is posted 24 hours a day, though even then I'd personally be uncomfortable about leaving anything of value lying around. Meals and drinks are not available on site, but can be bought at one of the neighbouring resorts.

Akida's Garden This is a rustic set-up in Gezaulole village, owned by the welcoming family of the local cultural tourism co-ordinator, and apparently ideally suited to travellers seeking unaffected exposure to the local coastal culture. Accommodation currently consists of just one traditional local hut, with a double bed and netting, for Tsh3,000 per night, but more huts are likely to be constructed in the near future. Camping costs Tsh1,500. Basic meals can be provided, as can beers and sodas, and there is excellent swimming at the nearby Kim Beach (see below) and the Islamic Club, both of which are open to visitors staying at Akida's Garden. Dhow trips to Sinda Island can be arranged at Tsh15,000 per boat for the day. See also the box *Gezaulole* on page 310.

Kim Beach Campsite Also in Gezaulole, five minutes walk from Akida's Garden, this is a very basic campsite situated on a quite superb sandy beach, with the tankers in Dar es Salaam harbour visible in the distance and two large coral islands closer by in the bay. Facilities are limited to a long-drop toilet and bucket shower, food is not available (though drinks can be arranged) and there's little in the way of watersport facilities – but if these things don't worry you, this is a real stunner. Camping costs Tsh2,000 per person.

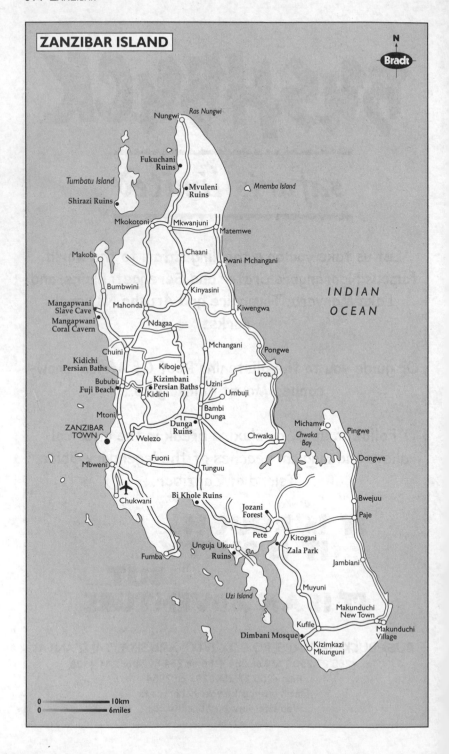

ZANZIBAR ISLAND

N
Bradt

Nungwi
Ras Nungwi
Fukuchani Ruins
Tumbatu Island
Mvuleni Ruins
Shirazi Ruins
Mnemba Island
Mkokotoni
Mkwanjuni
Matemwe
Makoba
Chaani
Pwani Mchangani
Bumbwini
Kinyasini
INDIAN OCEAN
Mangapwani Slave Cave
Mahonda
Kiwengwa
Mangapwani Coral Cavern
Ndagaa
Chuini
Mchangani
Pongwe
Kidichi Persian Baths
Kiboje
Uroa
Bububu
Kizimbani Persian Baths
Uzini
Fuji Beach
Kidichi
Umbuji
Mtoni
Bambi Dunga
Michamvi
Pingwe
ZANZIBAR TOWN
Dunga Ruins
Chwaka Bay
Welezo
Chwaka
Dongwe
Mbweni
Fuoni
Tunguu
Chukwani
Bi Khole Ruins
Bwejuu
Jozani Forest
Paje
Pete
Kitogani
Fumba
Unguja Ukuu Ruins
Zala Park
Jambiani
Muyuni
Uzi Island
Makunduchi New Town
Kufile
Makunduchi Village
Dimbani Mosque
Kizimkazi Mkunguni

0 ———— 10km
0 ———— 6miles

Zanzibar

By Philip Briggs and David Else,
updated for this edition by Heather Tyrrell

Zanzibar is one of those magical travel names, richly evocative even to the many Westerners who would have no idea where to start looking for it on a global map. Steeped in history, and blessed with a sultry tropical climate and a multitude of idyllic beaches, Zanzibar is also that rare travel destination which genuinely does live up to every expectation. Whether it's a quick cultural fix you're after, or scintillating diving, or just a palm-lined beach where you can laze away the day, a few days on Zanzibar is the perfect way to round off a dusty safari on the Tanzanian mainland.

A separate state within Tanzania, Zanzibar consists of two large islands, Unguja (Zanzibar Island) and Pemba, plus several smaller islets. Zanzibar Island is about 85km long and between 20km and 30km wide; Pemba is about 75km long and between 15km and 20km wide. Both are flat and low lying, surrounded by coasts of rocky inlets or sandy beaches, with lagoons and mangrove swamps, and coral reefs beyond the shoreline. Farming and fishing are the main occupations, and most people live in small villages. Cloves are a major export, along with coconut products and other spices. The capital, and by far the largest settlement, is Zanzibar Town on the west coast.

Zanzibar used to be hard to reach, with a reputation for being expensive and unfriendly. Not any more! The island now positively welcomes tourists, and it offers facilities suitable to all tastes and budgets. For many, the highlight of a stay on Zanzibar is the old Stone Town, with its traditional Swahili atmosphere and wealth of fascinating buildings. For others, it is the sea and the coral reefs, which offer diving, snorkelling and game fishing to compare with anywhere in East Africa. And then there are the clove and coconut plantations that cover the interior of the 'Spice Island'; the dolphins of Kizimkazi; the colobus monkeys of Jozani; and the giant sea turtles of Nungwi. . . and above all, some will say, those seemingly endless tropical beaches.

CLIMATE

Zanzibar has a typical coastal climate, warm to hot all year round and often very humid. It receives more rainfall and is windier than the mainland.

GETTING THERE AND AWAY
By air

An ever-increasing number of airlines offer direct flights between Zanzibar and Dar es Salaam, a 30-minute trip that costs around US$50–60. There are also regular flights to Zanzibar from Kilimanjaro International Airport (between Moshi and Arusha), some of which are direct, taking roughly one hour, while others require a change of

A BRIEF HISTORY

Zanzibar has been trading with ships from Persia, Arabia and India for about 2,000 years. From about the 10th century AD, groups of immigrants from Shiraz (Persia) settled in Zanzibar and mingled with the local Swahili. The Portuguese established a trading station on the site of Zanzibar Town in the early 16th century. At the end of the 17th century, the Sultan of Oman's navy ousted the Portuguese from the island.

In 1840, Sultan Said of Oman relocated his capital in Muscat to Zanzibar. Many Omani Arabs settled on Zanzibar as rulers and landowners, forming an elite group, while Indian settlers formed a merchant class. The island became an Arab state, an important centre of regional politics, and the focus of a booming slave trade. Britain had interests in Zanzibar throughout the 19th century; explorers such as Livingstone, Speke and Burton began their expeditions into the African interior from there. In 1890 Zanzibar became a British protectorate.

Zanzibar gained independence from Britain in December 1963. In 1964, the Sultan was overthrown in a revolution, and nearly all Arabs and Indians were expelled. Later the same year, Zanzibar and Tanganyika combined to form the United Republic of Tanzania.

Today, the distinctions between Shirazi and Swahili are often blurred. The islanders fall into three groups: the Hadimu of southern and central Zanzibar, the Tumbatu of Tumbatu Island and northern Zanzibar, and the Pemba of Pemba Island. Many people of mainland origin live on Zanzibar, some the descendants of freed slaves, others more recent immigrants. Many of the Arab, Asian and Goan people expelled in 1964 have since returned.

plane at Dar and might take three to four hours depending on your connection. The main established airlines covering these routes are Air Tanzania, Precision Air, Zanair and Coastal Aviation, all of which offer a range of other domestic flights (as well as flights to Kenya), so the best choice will depend largely on your other travel plans. Any reliable tour operator will be able to advise you about this.

By boat

A number of hydrofoils and catamarans run between Dar es Salaam and Zanzibar daily and the booking kiosks for all these boats are clustered together at the ports on Zanzibar and in Dar. New companies seem to come and go with remarkable speed, so there's a lot to be said for asking around before you make any firm arrangements, or for using a tour operator to make your booking (this won't cost much more and saves a lot of hassle). Do be wary of the hustlers who hang around both ports – many are con artists and some are thieves. Tickets must be paid for in hard currency, as must the port tax of US$5.

An efficient boat that's been around for a while is the *Sea Express*, which crosses between Dar and Zanzibar once daily, leaving Zanzibar at 16.00 and Dar es Salaam at 17.30 and taking around 70 minutes in either direction. Tickets cost US$35 inclusive of port tax, though you may be able to knock that price down to around US$25 at short notice. Other reliable ferries – all much the same price – are *Sea Star* (departs Zanzibar 07.00 and Dar es Salaam 10.30, two hours each way) and *Seabus* (departs Zanzibar 13.10 and Dar es Salaam 16.00, two hours each way).

Flying Horse is a slower catamaran that runs once in either direction daily, charging US$20 inclusive of port tax, and taking about three hours in either direction. The boat leaves Dar es Salaam at 12.30 and Zanzibar at 22.00. If you cross by night from Zanzibar to Dar, you must sleep on the boat, as customs don't open until 06.00 (mattresses are provided – a pain in the butt or a free night's accommodation, depending on how you look at it).

It is both unsafe and illegal to travel between Zanzibar and the mainland by fishing dhow.

Organised tours
Although a number of local tour operators are listed later in this chapter, it's worth noting that most international companies offering safaris to Tanzania can append a flight to Zanzibar (or a full travel package on the island) to your safari arrangements. Likewise, most safari companies based in Arusha are able to set up excursions to Zanzibar. If you are booking a safari in advance, there is probably a lot to be said for making all your travel arrangements in Tanzania through one company.

Arrival and departure
As Zanzibar is a separate state from mainland Tanzania, all visitors are required to complete an immigration card and show their passport and visa upon arrival. Otherwise, entrance formalities are minimal, and you're unlikely to spend longer than a minute being processed. Travellers flying into Zanzibar from outside of Tanzania can now buy a visa on arrival at the airport. The airport tax of US$20 for international flights out of Zanzibar *must* be paid in US dollars cash – if you don't have cash, you'll be forced to change travellers' cheques at a poor rate. Flights within Tanzania attract a US$3–5 airport tax, payable in local currency.

If you lose your passport while on Zanzibar, you will need to have an Emergency Travel Document issued at the Ministry of the Interior. This will allow you to travel back to the mainland (where nationals of most countries will find diplomatic representation in Dar es Salaam) or directly to your home country.

GETTING AROUND
Car hire
To hire a car (in reality, probably a Suzuki jeep) or scooter, contact one of the island's tour operators (see pages 329–30). A jeep for a day will cost around US$45–60, and is unlikely to have much fuel in the tank when you hire it. Insurance cover is in theory comprehensive, but it may be as well to have your own personal cover as well.

Taxis
Taxis are fairly widely available. A short hop within the town generally costs Tsh1,500 while the trip to Mtoni costs around Tsh4,000. The going rate for airport transfers is US$10 and to Jozani or the east coast US$20–25.

Bicycle hire
Most of the tour operators in Zanzibar town can arrange bicycle hire. The going rate for a heavy Chinese bike is US$10 per day, while mountain bikes go for around US$15.

ZANZIBAR TOWN
Zanzibar's old quarter, usually called the Stone Town, is a fascinating maze of narrow streets and alleyways which lead the visitor past numerous old houses and mosques, ornate palaces, and shops and bazaars. Many buildings in the Stone Town date from the 19th-century slave boom. Houses reflect their builder's wealth: Arab houses have plain outer walls and large front doors leading to an inner

courtyard; Indian houses have a more open façade and large balconies decorated with railings and balustrades. Most are still occupied.

A striking feature of many houses is the brass-studded doors with their elaborately carved frames. The size of a door and intricacy of its design was an indication of the owner's wealth and status. The use of studs probably originated in Persia or India, where they helped prevent doors being knocked down by war-elephants. In Zanzibar, studs were purely decorative.

The area outside the Stone Town used to be called Ng'ambo (The Other Side), and is now called Michenzani (New City). Attempts have been made to modernise it: at the centre of Michenzani are some ugly apartment blocks, built by East German engineers as part of an international aid scheme.

Walking is the easiest way to get around Zanzibar Town. Buses, pick-up vans (called *dalla-dallas*) and taxis are available. You can also hire bikes and motor scooters.

Where to stay

It isn't that long ago that even the most robust of budget travellers had difficulty finding acceptable accommodation on Zanzibar, but you'd hardly believe it today. Recent years have seen a positive mushrooming of new hotels in Zanzibar Town, as well as around the island, and there are now numerous options at every level, from basic guesthouses to smart upmarket hotels. As a rule, room rates on Zanzibar are quoted in US dollars, and at the top end of the range the management will probably insist that you pay in hard currency. Our experience was that hotels at the lower end of the price bracket generally accept local currency at an exchange rate similar to those given at forex bureaux.

Most prices include breakfast, though at budget hotels this may amount to little more than a slice of stale bread and a banana. The rates quoted in this guide are high season only; most upmarket hotels will offer a discount out of season. At the lower end of the price range, rates may be negotiable depending on how busy the hotel is and the intended duration of your stay. It is advisable to make an advance reservation for any upmarket or mid-range hotel, particularly during peak seasons, but this shouldn't be necessary for cheaper lodgings.

Travellers who arrive on Zanzibar by boat can expect to be met by a group of hotel touts. Some are quite aggressive and likely to take you to whichever hotel gives them the largest commission, while others are friendly and will find you a suitable hotel if you tell them what you want. Either way, the service shouldn't cost you anything, since the tout will get a commission from the hotel, and it may save a lot of walking in the confusing alleys of the Stone Town. Given the difficulty of getting past the touts and the general aura of chaos around the ferry port, there is probably a lot to be said for taking the path of least resistance when you first arrive. Should you not like the place to which you are first directed, you can always look around yourself once your bags are securely locked away, and change hotel the next day.

However you arrive, many of the hotels in the Stone Town cannot be reached by taxi. You are liable to get lost if you strike out on foot without a guide, though we found that people were always very helpful when it came to being pointed in the right direction (bearing in mind that the right direction may change every few paces). Most taxi drivers will be prepared to walk you to the hotel of your choice, but they will expect a decent tip.

Upmarket

Zanzibar Serena Inn Tel: 024 223 3587; fax: 024 223 3019; email: zserena@zanzibar.com or serena@yako.habari.co.tz. Part of the Serena chain, which also owns lodges in most of the northern game reserves. This hotel, which opened in 1997, is the smartest in the Stone Town, combining international-class accommodation and service with atmospheric Zanzıbarı décor. The hotel spans two restored buildings on the beachfront, the early-20th-century Extelcommunications House and the 19th-century 'Chinese Doctor's residence', the latter where Livingstone slept on one of his many visits to Zanzibar, and later the home of the British consul. In addition to a fine beachfront position, the hotel boasts a swimming pool, bar, restaurant, coffee shop, curio shop and business centre. Standard air-conditioned rooms with a sea-facing balcony, mosquito nets, TV, and en-suite bathroom cost US$190/240 single/double B&B. Cheaper rates are available from April to June, and may sometimes be offered midweek at other times of the year through travel agents.

Emerson's & Green Tel: 024 223 0171; fax: 024 223 1038; email: emegre@zanzibar.org; web: www.zanzibar.org/emegre. At one time the second-tallest building in the Stone Town, this fabulous hotel consists of two adjoining buildings, one of which dates to the early 1800s and the other to the 1870s, when it was the residence of Tharia Topan, the principal financial advisor to Sultan Barghash. It was in imminent danger of collapse when Emerson Skeens (of the sadly defunct Emerson's House, listed by the British *Sunday Times* as 'one of the great little hotels of the world') and Tom Green bought it in 1994. Faithfully restored and lavishly decorated in period style, it opened as a hotel in 1997. The atmosphere is much like that of the original Emerson's House, though the rooms are larger and more elaborately furnished, with high ceilings, fans, good ventilation through traditional shutters, amazing en-suite bathrooms and netted Arabic four-poster beds. The rooftop restaurant offers excellent views over some of the major landmarks in the Stone Town and down to the harbour, as well as serving some of the best food in town. Double rooms cost US$150.

Protea Hotel Mbweni Ruins Tel: 024 223 1832; fax: 024 223 0536; email: hotel@mbweni.com; web: www.proteahotels.com. Situated a few kilometres south of town, off the airport road, this exclusive hotel lies in the grounds of the Mbweni Ruins, the remains of a mission school built in the 1870s for freed slaves, and close to St John's Anglican Church, built in 1882. It is set in attractive, well-maintained grounds overlooking the sea, and the nearby mangroves will be alluring to birders. Facilities include a private beach, swimming pool, nature trail, botanical garden, natural heath centre, airport and town shuttle service, top-class restaurant, and boat trips to the nearby islands. Accommodation in air-conditioned rooms with en-suite bathroom costs US$95/175 single/double B&B.

Zanzibar Beach Resort Tel: 024 223 0208; fax: 024 223 0556; email: znzbeachresort@zanlink.com; web: www.zanzibarbeachresort.co.tz. Formerly the Fisherman's Resort (and before that the Zanzibar Reef Hotel), this large resort-like hotel lies about 7km from the Stone Town and 3km from the airport. The landscaped gardens overlook the sea, and facilities include a restaurant, bar, disco, squash court, sauna, gym, swimming pool, and fishing and watersport equipment. Double rooms with AC and en-suite bathroom cost US$100/130 or US$120/160 single/double, depending on whether they have a sea view.

Moderate
Mtoni Marine Centre Tel: 024 225 0140; fax: 024 225 0496; email: mtoni@zanzibar.cc; web: www.coastal.cc. Situated in Mtoni, 4km north of the port, this well-run and attractive resort is attached to a marine centre offering a good variety of day trips including snorkelling and city tours. Comfortable self-contained accommodation includes standard rooms at US$30 per person, rooms in the palm garden for US$60/80 single/double, and two- or three-bed bungalows at US$50 per person. The restaurant is excellent, and there's a swimming pool.

Coconut Beach Inn Tel: 025 223 5897. This pretty Finnish-owned hotel lies about 9km south of town on a beach facing Chumbe Island. Unfussy but comfortable self-contained

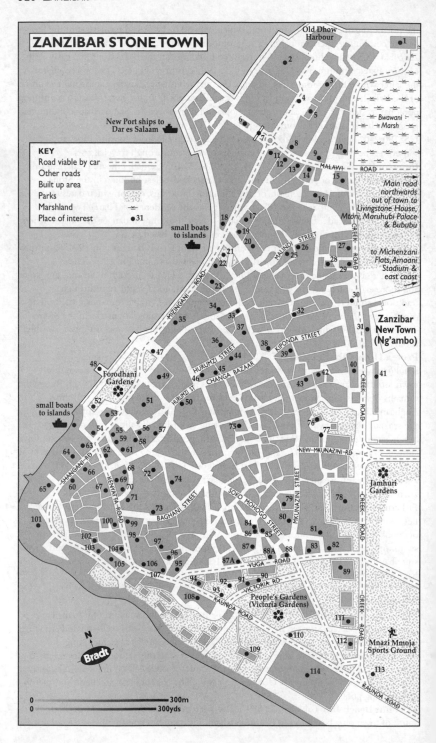

ZANZIBAR STONE TOWN

Old Dhow Harbour

New Port ships to Dar es Salaam

KEY
- Road viable by car
- Other roads
- Built up area
- Parks
- Marshland
- Place of interest ● 31

small boats to islands

Bwawani Marsh

MALAWI ROAD

Main road northwards out of town to Livingstone House, Mtoni, Maruhubi Palace & Bububu

to Michenzani Flats, Amaani Stadium & east coast

CREEK ROAD

MALINDI STREET

MIZINGANI ROAD

Forodhani Gardens

small boats to islands

Zanzibar New Town (Ng'ambo)

KIPONDA STREET

HURUMZI STREET

CHANGA BAZAAR

HURUMZI ST

SHANGANI RD

KENYATTA ROAD

NEW-MKUNAZINI-RD

BAGHANI STREET

SOKO MOHOGO STREET

MKUNAZINI STREET

Jamhuri Gardens

VUGA ROAD

VICTORIA RD

KAUNDA ROAD

People's Gardens (Victoria Gardens)

Mnazi Mmoja Sports Ground

KAUNDA ROAD

N

Bradt

0   300m
0   300yds

Numerical key to Zanzibar Stone Town map opposite

1	Bwawani Hotel	59	Karibu Inn
2	Clove Distillery	60	Stone Town Inn, Garage Club
3	Malindi Guesthouse	61	Coco de l'Ier Hotel
4	Fish market	62	Zanzibar Gallery
5	Warere Guesthouse	63	Old British Consulate
6	Shipping company ticket offices	64	Tembo Hotel
7	Port gates	65	Starehe Club
8	Ciné Afrique	66	Fisherman Restaurant, Bashasha Bar
9	Mzuri Guesthouse	67	Shangani Hotel
10	Petrol station	68	Namaste Indian Restaurant
11	Hotel Marine	69	Post office
12	Malindi Bureau de Change	70	Blue Ocean Hotel
13	Zan Air	71	Dolphin Restaurant
14	Passing Show Restaurant	72	St Joseph's Catholic Cathedral
15	Police station (main)	73	Chavda Hotel
16	Zan Tours	74	Chit-Chat Restaurant
17	Old Dispensary (Stone Town Cultural	75	Hamamni Baths
	Centre)	76	Anglican Cathedral
18	Mercury's Restaurant	77	St Monica's Hostel
19	Gulf Air	78	Haile Selassie School
20	Ijumaa Mosque	79	Jambo Guesthouse
21	The Big Tree	80	Flamingo Guesthouse
22	Sea View Indian Restaurant	81	Zanzibar Medical & Diagnostic Centre
23	Old Customs House	82	Kiswahili Language Institute
25	Pyramid Hotel	83	Air Tanzania
26	Narrow Street Hotel	84	Manch Lodge (guesthouse)
27	Zanzibar Tourism Corporation	85	Nyambani Restaurant
28	Kokoni Hotel	86	Haven Hotel
29	BP petrol station	87	Florida Guesthouse
30	Taxi rank	87A	Kenya Airways
31	Container shops	88	Fisherman Tours, Fernandes Tours
32	Narrow Street Annexe Hotel	88A	Maha Travel & Tours
33	Palace Restaurant	89	Ben Bella School
34	Hotel Kiponda	90	Victoria House (guesthouse)
35	Palace Museum	91	Zi-Bar & Restaurant
36	Hindu Temple	92	Two Tables Restaurant
37	Aga Khan Mosque	93	Garden Lodge
38	Spice Inn	95	Dr Mehta's Hospital
39	Hotel International, Bureau de Change	96	Afya Medical Hospital
40	Market	97	Zanzibar Hotel
41	Bus & dala-dala station	98	Dhow Palace Hotel, Baghani House
42	Masumo Bookshop		Hotel
43	Shamshuddin Cash & Carry Supermarket	99	Sunrise Restaurant & Pub
44	Emerson & Green Hotel	100	Mazsons Hotel
45	Bottoms Up Guesthouse	101	Serena Inn
46	Clove Hotel	102	Tippu Tip's House
47	Taxi rank	103	Jasfa Tours
48	Blues (restaurant)	104	Pagoda Chinese Restaurant
49	House of Wonders	105	Africa House Hotel
50	Sama Tours	106	Camlur's Restaurant
51	Arab Fort	107	Maharaja Restaurant
52	Suna	108	High Court
53	Orphanage	109	State House
54	Zanzibar Dive Centre	110	Zanzibar Milestone
55	Radha Food House	111	Museum Annexe
56	People's Bank of Zanzibar	112	Peace Memorial Museum
57	The Gallery	113	Old Cricket Pavilion
58	People's Bank of Zanzibar (Foreign	114	Mnazi Moja Hospital
	Exchange)		

rooms centred on a swimming pool cost US$30 per person. A good restaurant specialises in seafood dishes. Recommended.

Shangani House Tel: 024 223 0171; fax: 024 223 1038; email: emegre@zanzibar.org; web: www.zanzibar.org/emegre. This atmospheric old four-bedroom house stands on the western side of the Stone Town, draped in vines and surrounded by an overgrown garden that create a 'lost city' feel. Managed by Emerson's & Green, the whole house can be rented at US$250 per night, making it great value for groups of 5–8 people.

Tembo Hotel Tel: 024 223 3005; fax: 024 223 3777; email: tembo@zitec.org; web: www.tembohotel.com. Around the corner from the Serena, this atmospheric and reasonably smart hotel has been extended from a restored Omani residence, and it combines an excellent beachfront position with ready access to the Stone Town. Facilities include a good restaurant and swimming pool. Air-conditioned doubles with en-suite bathrooms cost from US$80/90 single/double to US$175 for a presidential suite.

Chavda Hotel Tel: 024 223 2115; fax: 024 223 1931; email: chavda@zanzinet.com. This well-run hotel in the heart of the Stone Town has a traditional feel undermined slightly by the inauthentic period furniture and rather small, gloomy rooms. It's fair value at US$90 double, though overall a less compelling option than other similarly priced hotels listed in this range. The rooftop restaurant, however, is great and open to all comers, with curries at around Tsh3,000–4,000 and seafood dishes for Tsh5,000.

Mazson's Hotel Tel: 024 223 3694; fax: 024 223 3695; email: mazsons@zanjcom.net. Constructed on what is now Kenyatta Rd in the early 1800s by Said bin Dhahin, one of the first Omani Arabs to settle on Zanzibar, Mazson's first served as a hotel in the early 20th century before becoming a private residence. Now fully restored, the communal areas are decorated in period style, though the air-conditioned self-contained rooms are rather florid and soulless. Facilities include satellite TV and a business centre. Accommodation costs US$60/80 single/double B&B, dropping to US$48/64 in the low season.

Dhow Palace Hotel Tel: 024 223 3012; fax: 024 223 3008; email: dhowpalace@zanjcom.net; web: www.zanzibar.net/dhow. Another hotel set in the heart of the Stone Town in a renovated old house, enclosing a cool central courtyard, the Dhow Palace is very atmospheric and tastefully decorated in period style. The rooms come complete with Persian baths, and lack only for sea views. The rooftop restaurant comes highly recommended. Accommodation costs US$55/85 single/double B&B.

Baghani House Hotel Tel: 024 223 5654; fax: 024 223 3030; email: baghani@zanzinet.com. Clean, friendly, attractively decorated in period style, and meticulously maintained, Baghani House lies close to Mazson's Hotel, along an alley leading off the opposite side of Kenyatta Rd. The self-contained, air-conditioned rooms are excellent value, too, at US$45/55 single/double.

Shangani Hotel Tel: 024 223 6363; fax: 024 223 3688; email: shanganihotel@hotmail.com. Situated on Kenyatta Rd, close to the old post office, the Shangani Hotel is another reasonably priced, traditionally decorated hotel with a useful location in the Stone Town. Comfortable air-conditioned double rooms with en-suite bathroom cost US$65. Good facilities include a restaurant and coffee bar, and satellite TV in all rooms.

Hotel International Tel: 024 223 3182; fax: 024 223 6248; email: hotelinter@zanzibar.net; web: www.zanzibar.net/hotelinternational. Situated in the alleys close to Emerson's & Green, this is yet another restored Omani residence. An air of dilapidation hangs over the large rooms, and the relatively modern furnishing isn't particularly inspiring. It's adequate, but a touch overpriced at US$50/70 for a self-contained single/double with satellite TV and AC.

Hotel Malindi Tel: 024 223 2088; fax: 023 223 0822; email: hotelmarine@africaonline.co.tz. This large hotel has a friendly atmosphere and a convenient though potentially noisy location opposite Malindi Port, and it doesn't lack for character.

The rooms are a little confined and rundown to justify the asking price of US$50/55 single/double on the ground floor to US$65/70 on the second floor with balcony. **Africa House Hotel** Tel: 024 223 0708. This potentially lovely waterfront hotel – it served as the English Club from 1888 until the end of the colonial era – has been under restoration for some years now. Based on the current state of play, it seems likely to remain so for some time after the scheduled re-opening date of October 2002. On the plus side, the sea-facing balcony bar (once again functional) is a wonderful place for a sundowner, though traditionally also a noted hangout for annoying touts.

Budget

Even the cheapest lodgings in Zanzibar are rather pricy, for which reason all hotels charging US$50 or below for a double room are listed in the budget category and the cut-off price for the shoestring category is around US$20 per double. There is not one hotel listed in either category that wouldn't be laughably overpriced were it situated anywhere on the Tanzanian mainland.

Hotel Kiponda Tel: 024 223 3052; fax: 024 223 3020; email: hotelkiponda@email.com. This small quiet hotel, formerly a sultan's harem and renovated in period style, has proved to be consistently popular with travellers over the years: one correspondent described it as a 'budget Emerson's'. The Kiponda has plenty of character, a welcoming atmosphere, and a convenient location in the Stone Town close to the seafront. There's a decent restaurant attached, and facilities include an international phone and fax service. Rooms using common showers cost US$18/35/45 single/double/triple, while self-contained doubles cost US$45 and triples US$55.

Stone Town Inn Tel: 024 223 3101. With an excellent location roughly opposite the Tembo Hotel, the Stone Town Inn is definitely one of the better options in this range. Clean rooms using communal showers cost US$15 per person, while self-contained doubles cost US$50.

Karibu Inn Tel: 024 223 3058; email: karibuinn@zanzinet.com. This friendly and conveniently located but rather institutional guesthouse charges US$20/25 for a single/double room using common showers, and US$30 for a self-contained double. All rooms have nets and fans, and some have AC – which costs an extra US$10 if used. Four-, six- and seven-bed dormitories are available to appropriately sized groups at US$10 per person. Basic, but still one of the better places in this category.

Pyramid Hotel Tel: 024 223 3000; fax: 024 223 0045; email: pyramidhotel@yahoo.com. This long-serving hotel, situated behind the Ijumaa mosque near the seafront, is justifiably popular with budget travellers. It charges US$10 per person for a room using common showers, or US$15/25/35 for a self-contained single/double/triple. Rooms are highly variable in standard, so ask to look at a few – if you can secure a good one, it's very good value!

Island View Hotel Tel: 054 223 4605; email: islandview@africamail.com. This family-run out-of-town hotel – on the road to the airport – charges a very reasonable US$20/30/40 for clean and spacious self-contained single/double/triple rooms with fan and netting. Air conditioning costs an extra Tsh3,000 per room. There is no restaurant but the owners are helpful about lifts into town during the day and in the evening. It's exceptional value, and would be a useful option should you arrive in Zanzibar late in the day and not want to muck about looking for a room in the alleys of the Stone Town after dark.

Coco de Mer Hotel Tel: 024 223 0852; email: cocodemer_znz@yahoo.com. Clean and airy, the Coco de Mer charges US$35/50 for a small self-contained single/double. The ground-floor rooms aren't as nice as those upstairs.

Spice Inn Tel: 0747 415048; fax: 024 223 2174. With its authentic façade and location in the heart of the Stone Town, this long-serving budget hotel has plenty of character. The reasonably spacious but somewhat rundown rooms represent indifferent value at US$20/25 single/double using common showers, or US$25/30 self-contained. A decent café is attached, as is the Curry Pot Restaurant – the latter, despite its name, serving breakfast only.

Narrow Street Hotel Tel: 024 223 2263; email: narrow22@yahoo.com. A clean, functional hotel charging US$30/40 for a self-contained single/double with AC, this is one of the better options in this price range.

Blue Ocean Hotel Tel: 024 223 3566. Located just off Kenyatta Rd, this acceptable if unremarkable small hotel charges US$20/38 per person for functional self-contained single/double rooms.

Clove Inn Tel: 024 223 6724. Dusty no-frills hotel on Harumzi St charging US$18/25 for a self-contained single/double with fans but no nets.

Narrow Street Hotel Annex II Tel: 024 223 3006. Fairly popular with travellers, but the large rooms are starting to look very shabby and none too clean – indifferent value at US$25/35 for a self-contained single/double with netting, AC and Zanzibari-style beds.

Hotel Kokoni Tel: 0747 421515. This rather dilapidated hotel seems poor value at US$20/35 for a cramped and gloomy self-contained single/double.

Mzuri Guesthouse Tel: 024 223 0463. Situated on Malawi Rd near the cinema, this basic guesthouse charges US$15 per person for small self-contained rooms with hot water, fan and noisy AC battling for aural dominance with the passing traffic.

Annex Kid's Play Hotel Tel: 024 223 6315. Distinguished only by its imponderable name (a reference to the age of the staff, perhaps?), this really is pathetic value at US$35/50 for a cramped single/double or US$15 for a bed in the dormitory. To be considered as a last resort only – assuming that the sound system hasn't yet blown the roof off.

Shoestring

Malindi Guesthouse Tel: 024 223 2359; fax: 024 223 3030. Consistently popular with travellers for years, the Malindi Guesthouse, next to the Ciné Afrique, remains the clear pick of the shoestring options clustered in the Malindi area near the port. Clean whitewashed rooms with AC cost US$10 per person. Communal showers only.

Jambo Guesthouse Tel: 024 223 3779; email: jamboguest@hotmail.com. Another good cheapie, located in a quiet part of the Stone Town near St Monica Church, the Jambo Guesthouse charges US$15/20 for a single/double room with AC or fan (inclusive of a full English breakfast). Internet and laundry facilities are available, as is a free pick-up from the airport or ferry harbour, with advance notice.

Haven Hotel Tel: 024 223 5677; fax: 024 223 8426; email: havenhouse@hotmail.com. The rooms at this friendly and popular guesthouse are nothing special at US$10 per person using a common shower, but it's very clean, with extras such as free tea and coffee, hot water, a generator for power cuts, a travel information board and a self-catering kitchen. Also recommended.

St Monica's Hostel Tel: 024 223 5348; fax: 024 223 6772; email: cathedral@zanzinet.com. A bit pricier than the other options in this range, this atmospheric and very secure hostel, set in an old building attached to the Anglican Cathedral, is worth the extra couple of dollars. Spotless, cool rooms with nets and a balcony cost US$12 per person using common showers, or US$28/32 single/double self-contained.

Garden Lodge Tel: 024 223 3298. Situated on Kaunda St near the hospital, this clean double-storey hotel charges US$15/20 single/double for ground-floor rooms and US$25/40 for first-floor rooms. All rooms are self-contained and fairly spacious, but the first-floor rooms are airier and brighter.

Flamingo Guesthouse Tel: 024 223 2850; fax: 024 223 3144; email: flamingoguesthouse@hotmail.com. This basic but pleasant hotel has a rather noisy location on Mkunazani St, but it's clean enough, and reasonably good value at US$8 per person for a room using common showers, or US$10 per person for a self-contained room. Facilities include satellite TV and a book exchange service.

Florida Guesthouse Tel/fax: 024 223 3136. Another adequate guesthouse with a rather noisy location, in this case off Vuga Rd, the Florida charges US$10 per person for a clean room (the ones upstairs are brighter) using common showers. One four-bed self-contained room with AC and satellite TV is available at US$40 – pretty good value for small groups.

Manch Hotel Tel: 024 223 1918; fax: 024 223 0670; email: moddybest@yahoo.com. Just around the corner from the Haven Hotel, and under renovation in early 2002, this adequate hotel charges US$10 per person for a spacious self-contained room.

Pearl Guesthouse Tel: 024 333 7661. Shabby hotel on Kiponda St charging a fair US$8 per person for basic rooms using common showers, and a steep US$15 per person for equally basic self-contained rooms.

Bottoms Up Guesthouse Seedy, and difficult to find in the alleys between the Spice Inn and the House of Wonders, the once popular Bottoms Up Hotel can no longer be recommended at an asking price of US$10 per person for a basic room using communal showers.

Riverman Hotel Tel: 024 223 3188; email: rivermanhotel@hotmail.com. Simple and reasonably pleasant – but increasingly rundown – guesthouse behind the Anglican Cathedral charging US$10 per person for rooms using a communal shower.

Victoria Guesthouse Tel: 024 223 2861. Situated on Victoria Rd opposite the People's Gardens, this acceptable guesthouse charges US$10 per person for a spacious and clean, but rather timeworn, room.

New Happy Lodge Tel: 024 223 9326. Around the corner from the synonymous bar, in the rather pleasant Shangani area, the only thing this exceptionally basic hotel has going for it is the very shoestring-friendly rate of Tsh5,000 for a room.

Where to eat and drink

There are now dozens of restaurants catering specifically to tourists, and the following serves as an introduction only.

At the top end of the range, the rooftop restaurant at **Emerson's & Green** is generally regarded to live up to its billing as the 'best on the island'. The fixed-menu dinner is a languid affair stretched over the whole evening, and the emphasis is on seafood. Dinner normally costs US$25 per person, though the price rises to US$30 on weekends when the meal is accompanied by traditional dancing. Space is limited and booking is essential – though the spill over is now catered for in their adjacent and equally good **Kidude Restaurant**. Another exceptional – and costly – restaurant is **The Dhow**, literally a moored dhow in the main harbour that serves great seafood-dominated set menus accompanied by live Swahili music for around US$25 per person. A more affordable experience is offered at the **Old Arab Fort** on the seafront, which puts on displays of traditional dancing at least three times a week, more often in peak season, accompanied by a reasonable buffet barbecue. Entrance costs US$10 per person, assuming that you want to eat, or US$5 per person to see the dancing only.

There are a few good places to eat on the Stone Town seafront. The trendiest spot in this area is **Blues**, sister to the synonymous restaurant in Cape Town, which serves seafood, pizzas and grills starting at around US$8–10 for a main course. The food at this floating restaurant is as good as any we've had in Tanzania, with the option of eating inside or on the wooden balcony, but the atmosphere lacks for anything that might be called distinctively Zanzibari. Further north along the seafront is **Mercury's Bar & Restaurant**, dedicated to (exploiting the?) memory of Zanzibar-born Queen vocalist Freddie Mercury, who has evidently managed to communicate his food preferences to the proprietor from the great opera house in the sky – 'Freddie's Favourite salad' et al. Still, a great spot for a sundowner (anybody for a 'Freddie Mercury Deep Blue'?), and it serves the best fruit juice in the Stone Town, as well as good pizzas and seafood in the US$4-6 range. The nearby **Sea View Indian Restaurant** serves a range of cheap snacks and good fruit juice, as well as a selection of top curries in the US$7-10 range.

Other recommended restaurants and hotels serving main courses in the US$5-10 range include the **Hotel Kiponda** (Zanzibari dishes and seafood), **Serena Zanzibar Inn** (Continental and seafood), the **Fisherman Restaurant** on Shangani Road (seafood and grills), **Chit-Chat Restaurant** on Kenyatta Street (Zanzibari and Goan dishes), **Pagoda Chinese Restaurant** at the north end of the Stone Town (authentic Chinese food), **Luna Mare Restaurant** on Gizenga Street (European, Indian and Chinese), **Barracuda Restaurant** on Kenyatta Road (sandwiches, crayfish and other seafood), **Sweet Easy Restaurant** on the beachfront (Thai, Japanese and – soon to come – dishes from all over Africa) and **La Fenice** near the Zanzibar Serena Inn (top-notch Continental and seafood). There are plenty more to choose from, and the level of competition for custom means that standards are generally reflected by prices.

The cheapest place to eat in the Stone Town is at **Forodhani Gardens**, opposite the fort, where dozens of vendors serve freshly grilled meat, chicken, fish, calamari and prawns with salad and chips or naan bread. This is far and away the best street food we've come across anywhere in Africa, and you'd have to be seriously hungry or prawn-obsessed not to come back with change from US$3. The stalls in the gardens cater primarily to locals, but plenty of travellers eat here, and many return night after night.

You can eat cheaply in the evening in the Malindi area, near the Ciné Afrique, where stalls sell cakes, chapatis, samosas and mandazi. In the nearby streets several simple and inexpensive eating houses cater mainly for locals, including the **Malindi Restaurant**, **Malkiya Restaurant**, **Al Jabry Restaurant** and the **Passing Show Hotel**. An excellent budget Indian restaurant, near the Karibu Inn, is the **Radha Food House**, where a buffet-like Thali set menu costs around US$4.

About the cheapest place for a sit-down meal in the southern end of the Stone Town is the **Dolphin Restaurant** on Kenyatta Road, which serves a wide range of curries and grills for up to US$3 per portion. The food here is remarkably good at the price, and the service is friendly. **Fanny's Green Restaurant** next door serves seafood dishes and pizzas at a similar price.

Most tourist restaurants serve beer and many of the larger hotels have separate bars. The rooftop bar at the **Africa House Hotel** is popular at sunset, as is the seafront bar at **Mercury's Restaurant**. The **Livingstone Bar** in the Baghani House Hotel and **Le Pêcheur Bar** next to the Fisherman Restaurant are about the nearest things in Zanzibar to a pub. Both are popular with expatriates, though the latter attracts a fair number of prostitutes and can get dauntingly lively later in the evening. Cheaper beer is available at the seafront **Cave Disco** (near the Tembo Hotel) and the **New Happy Bar** (a few doors down from the Africa House Hotel), since both cater to a predominantly local clientele. The **Garage Club** near the Tembo Hotel is the newest and busiest disco in the Stone Town.

General information

The Zanzibar Tourist Corporation head office in Livingstone House, about 1km from the town centre along the Bububu Road, is the best place to make bookings for the ZTC bungalows on the east coast. For general information, the ZTC office on Creek Road will probably be more clued up and helpful.

Top Ruined slave chamber, Zanzibar Island (AZ)

Above Kirk's red colobus, *Procolbus kirkii*, Jozani Forest, Zanzibar (AZ)

Right Woman by a traditional door, Zanzibar Stone Town (AZ)

Airlines
The Air Tanzania office is on Vuga Road, near its junction with Creek Road. The Kenya Airways office is at the northern end of Creek Road. Coastal Travel and Precision Air, both of which fly daily between Dar es Salaam and Zanzibar, have offices respectively at Zanzibar Airport (tel: 024 223 3112) and next to Mazson's Hotel (tel: 024 223 4521).

Books and newspapers
The best bookshop is the Zanzibar Gallery on Gizenga Street, a new branch of which has recently opened on Kenyatta Road. Newspapers from the mainland and Kenya can be bought at Masumo Bookshop behind the market, along with a limited selection of international magazines and paperback novels. Most of the upmarket hotels have curio shops selling guidebooks, field guides and glossier publications about Zanzibar and East Africa, as does the gallery on Gizenga Street.

Communications
The main **post office**, which lies outside the Stone Town towards the stadium, is the place to collect poste restante mail addressed to Zanzibar. Other postal transactions can be conducted more conveniently at the old post office on Kenyatta Road. The old post office is also a good place from which to make international phone calls and send faxes, though the private services offered by Zanzibar Global Communications (near the Flamingo Guesthouse) and Next Step Services on Gizenga Street aren't a great deal more expensive and are generally more efficient.

Numerous **internet cafés** have sprung up in Zanzibar Town over the past few years, charging a fairly uniform Tsh500 per 30 minutes. These include Stone Town Memories (Gizenga Road), Sanjay Internet Café (off Gizenga Road near the House of Wonders), Zanzibar Cyber Café (Changa Bazaar Road), New Net Services (Harumzi Road), Chei Chei E-services (Shangani Road), ISP Internet Café (Kenyatta Road), Shangani Internet Café (Kenyatta Road) and Too Short Internet Café (Shangani Street).

Foreign exchange
A number of banks and forex bureaux are dotted around the Stone Town, offering similar exchange rates to those on the mainland. Forex bureaux generally give marginally higher rates than banks, and they tend to be more efficient, but they may not accept travellers' cheques or relatively obscure currencies. The forex bureau in the International Hotel is efficient and offers good rates, and so far as I'm aware it is the only place in Zanzibar where anybody can change money over the weekend. Avoid changing money at the Commercial Bank of Zanzibar, as it offers very poor rates. It is rumoured that a Barclays Bank with an ATM (where local currency can be drawn against major credit cards) will soon open in the Stone Town. Until that happens, the only place where you can draw money against a Visa card is the forex bureau attached to Jojoba Tours & Safaris on Shangani Road.

Although most upmarket hotels will accept the major **credit cards**, drawing money against a credit card is either impossible or expensive. The one exception is Mtoni Marine Centre (see page 319), the official agent for Visa International, which will allow you to draw funds against a visa card with a minimum of fuss and expense.

Maps
The most accurate and attractive map of the Stone Town is Giovanni Tombazzi's Map of Zanzibar Stone Town, which also has a good map of the island on the flip side. Giovanni has lived in the Stone Town for several years, and he spent days

pacing the alleys taking distance measurements with a bicycle milometer to ensure the map is more accurate than any of its predecessors. You can buy this map for around US$5 at most upmarket hotels and curio shops.

Survey maps of the island are sold for around US$2 each at the map office in the Commission of Land and Surveys in the Ministry of Environment building near the old fort and People's Bank of Zanzibar.

Medical facilities
The Zanzibar Medical and Diagnostic Centre (tel: 024 223 3313; after hours: 024 233 3113 or 0747 413714), which lies off Vuga Road near the Majestic Cinema, is regarded to have the best doctors on the island, and is run to Western standards. For cheap malaria tests, the Fahaud Health Centre near St Joseph's Cathedral has been recommended, and it normally sells various malarial cures.

The main public hospital on Zanzibar Island is at Mnazi Moja, on the south side of the Stone Town. Other private medical centres include Island Private Hospital on Soko Muhogo Street (tel: 024 233 1837), Afya Medical Hospital near the Zanzibar Hotel (tel: 024 233 1228) and Mkunazini Hospital near the market (tel: 024 233 0076).

Swahili lessons
The Taasisi KiSwahili Institute on Vuga Road offers week-long courses for US$80.

Swimming pool
The pool at the Tembo Hotel charges Tsh3,000 to non-residents.

Spice tours and other excursions
The one organised trip that practically all visitors to Zanzibar undertake is a 'spice tour', something that would be logistically difficult to set up independently, and which relies heavily on the local knowledge of a guide. In addition to visiting a few spice plantations, most spice tours include a walk around a cultivated rural homestead, as well as a visit to one of the island's ruins. A traditional Swahili lunch is normally included in the price, which can range from US$10 to US$35 per person.

Several other short excursions can be undertaken out of Zanzibar Town, and while most visitors seem to prefer to do their exploring in the form of an organised day tour, most places of interest on the island can be visited independently. Popular excursions from the Stone Town include a boat trip to one or more of the nearby islands, a visit to the dolphins at Kizimkazi, and a trip to Jozani Forest to see the endemic Kirk's red colobus. Also easily explored from Zanzibar is the 10km of coastline stretching northwards to the small seaside settlement of Bububu, which boasts a number of interesting ruins, while Fuji Beach at Bububu is the closest public swimming beach to the Stone Town. In fact, the only parts of Zanzibar which are more often visited for a few nights than as a day trip are Nungwi and Mnemba Island in the north, and the several beach resorts that line the east coast of the island.

A number of tour companies operate out of Zanzibar Town, offering the tours mentioned above as well as transfers to the east coast and Nungwi. The better companies can set up bespoke trips to anywhere on the island, as well as make hotel reservations and other travel arrangements. For straightforward day trips and transfers, there is no real need to make bookings before you arrive in Zanzibar, as they can easily be set up at the last minute. If, however, you want to have all your travel arrangements fixed in advance through one company, or you have severe time restrictions, then it would be sensible to make advance contact with one of the companies with good international connections.

While prices vary greatly depending on standard of service, season and group size, the typical cost per person for the most popular outings are US$20 for a Stone Town tour, US$15 for a Prison Island tour, US$35 for a spice tour, US$35 for a trip to Jozani Forest and US$45 for a Kizimkazi dolphin tour. Prices are negotiable, particularly out of season when a group of ten people might be able to fix up a spice tour with a reputable company for as little as US$10 per head, but do be wary of unregistered companies offering substandard trips at very low rates.

It's possible to arrange many of the standard tours more cheaply through taxi drivers or independent guides (nicknamed *papaasi* after a type of insect). With spice tours, this may often turn out to be a false economy, in that the guide will lack botanical knowledge and may cut the excursion short, rendering the whole exercise somewhat pointless. One taxi driver who has been consistently recommended by travellers over many years is Mr Mitu (tel: 024 223 4636). His spice tours leave every morning from in front of the Ciné Afrique, though these days they are so popular that you might find yourself joining a fleet of minibuses rather than hopping into Mr Mitu's own vehicle! It makes little difference if you use *papaasi* to set up trips to the islands, because specialist knowledge isn't required, and you can agree in advance how long you want to spend on any given island.

You can assume that any tour operator working through one of the upmarket hotels will be reliable and accountable, bearing in mind that they will deal primarily with a captive, big-spending clientele, though their costs may be somewhat inflated. A list of a few recommended and well-established tour companies follows. Most of them offer a pretty similar selection of trips at reasonably uniform prices, and can also make flight, ferry and hotel bookings, so I have only made additional comments where necessary.

Centre Island Tours & Travel Tel: 024 223 3845; email: ctours@zenjcom.net. Efficient multi-lingual set-up catering to small groups and individuals of several nationalities.
Eco & Culture Tours Tel: 024 223 6808; email: ecoculture@gmx.net; web: www.ecoculture-zanzibar.org. Non-profit operator with office opposite Emerson's & Green Hotel offering slightly more expensive day trips catering to those who want to avoid the more established circuits.
Easy Travel & Tours Tel: 024 223 5372; email: easytravel@zitec.org. Clued-up operator affiliated to a major Arusha-based safari company; runs a good variety of tours.
Fisherman Tours Tel: 024 223 3060; email: fisherman@costech.gn.apc.org. Office on Vuga Rd near Air Tanzania. In addition to the normal services, can arrange safari excursions to mainland Tanzania.
Madeira Tours Tel: 024 233 0406; email: madeira@zenjcom.com. Efficient office arranging the usual tours and transfers.
Mreh Tours & Safaris Tel: 024 223 3476; email: mrehtours@zanzinet.com. Specialises in bicycle tours around the island, aimed at reasonably fit travellers.
Sama Tours Tel/fax: 054 223 3543; email: next@zanzinet.com. UK agent Footloose Adventure Travel; tel: 1943 604030; fax: 1943 604070. Office on Gizenga St behind House of Wonders. Spice tours guided by a knowledgeable local naturalist, who knows plant names in several languages. Offer all-inclusive tailormade tours around the island with guides speaking English, French, German or Italian.
Suna Tours Tel: 024 223 7344; email: habdallazooz@hotmail.com. Based in Forodhani Gardens, Suna is the agent for several east coast hotels and runs good general tours.

Sun 'n' Fun Tours Tel: 024 223 7381; email: zanzibarsun@hotmail.com. Office in Sea View Indian Restaurant. Good range of trips (including Kizimkazi dolphins) at very reasonable prices. Can arrange car and bicycle hire.
Tropical Tours & Safaris Tel: 0747 413454; email: tropicalts@hotmail.com. Small, efficient operator on Kenyatta Rd, opposite Mazson's Hotel, offering the usual tours, hotel and transport bookings and transfers, as well as Suzuki jeeps at US$45 per day, motorbikes at US$35 per day, and mountain-bike hire.
Zan Tours Tel: 024 223 3116; fax: 024 223 3042; email: zantours@zitec.com; web: www.zantours.com. Large, professional organisation catering to international market, and able to arrange anything from accommodation (all budgets) and flights to day tours for walk-in clients. Recommended.

Stone Town walking tour
You can spend many idle hours getting lost in the fascinating labyrinth of narrow streets and alleys of the old Stone Town, and will almost inevitably hit most of the main landmarks within a couple of days of arriving. However, the following roughly circular walking tour through the Stone Town will allow those with limited time to do their sightseeing in a reasonably organised manner (though they are still bound to get lost), and should help those with more time to orientate themselves before they head out to explore the Stone Town without a map or guidebook in hand.

The obvious starting point for any exploration of Zanzibar Town is **Forodhani Gardens**, a small patch of greenery lying between Mizingani Road and the main sea wall. Laid out in 1936 to mark the silver jubilee of Sultan Khalifa, the gardens are a popular eating and meeting point in the evening, and the staircase rising from the gardens to the arched bridge to the south offers a good view over the old town.

Three of the most significant buildings in the Stone Town lie alongside each other overlooking the seafront behind the Forodhani Gardens. The **Palace Museum** (entrance US$3 per person, open 09.00–18.00 weekdays, 09.00–15.00 weekends) is the most northerly of these, a large white building with castellated battlements dating from the late 1890s. The palace was the official residence of the Sultan of Zanzibar from 1911 until the 1964 revolution, after which it was renamed the People's Palace. For many years after this, it served as a government office and was closed to the public. Since 1994, however, it has housed an excellent museum, with a variety of displays relating to the early days of the sultanate, including a room devoted to artefacts belonging to Princess Salme. The graves of all the early sultans of Zanzibar are in the palace garden.

Next to the Palace Museum, the **House of Wonders** is a square, multi-storey building surrounded by tiers of impressive balconies and topped by a clocktower. It was built as a ceremonial palace in 1883, and was the first building on Zanzibar to have electric lights. Local people called it Beit el Ajaib, meaning the House of Wonders. Until recently it was the CCM party headquarters, and it has recently opened to tourists (entrance US$2) and in 2002 it was in the process of being turned into a Museum of History and Culture, which will house eight permanent exhibitions dedicated to the history of the Swahili Coast, and Zanzibar in particular.

Directly facing Forodhani Gardens, the **Old Arab Fort** is probably the oldest extant building in the Stone Town, built by Omani Arabs between 1698 and 1701 over the site of a Portuguese church constructed a century before that, remnants of which can still be seen in the inner wall. A large, squarish, brown building with castellated battlements, the fort ceased to serve any meaningful military role in the

19th century, since when it has served variously as prison, railway depot and women's tennis club. The interior of the fort is open to visitors, who can climb to the top of the battlements and enter some of the towers. There is a restaurant in the fort, serving cold drinks, and traditional dancing shows take place there at least three evenings every week.

Heading southwest from the fort, under an arched bridge, the fork to your right is Shangani Road, the site of notable important buildings. Just before following this fork, to your left, the **Upimaji Building** was the home of the German merchant Heinrich Ruete (later the husband of Princess Salme) in the 1860s. To the left of the fork is a block of government offices which served as the **British Consulate** from 1841 until 1874, and next to that the **Tembo Hotel**, a restored 19th-century building. As you follow Shangani Road around a curve, you'll come out to a leafy green square, where the **Zanzibar Shipping Corporation Building**, dating to around 1850, stands to your left and the **Zanzibar Serena Inn**, formerly Extelcomms House, to your right.

Perhaps 100m past the Serena Inn, to your left, you'll see the rear of **Tippu Tip's House**, a tall brown building which once served as the residence of Tippu Tip, the influential 19th-century slave trader who helped explorers such as Livingstone and Stanley with supplies and route planning. The building is privately owned and is closed to visitors, but if you follow the alley around the rear of the house, you can see its huge carved front door from the street, and the residents will sometimes show visitors around. From here, wander up another 50m past the New Happy Bar, and you'll pass the **Africa House Hotel**, which served as the English Club from 1888 onwards, and is a good place to punctuate your walk with a cold drink on the attractively positioned balcony.

From the Africa House Hotel a small alley leads to Kenyatta Road, an important thoroughfare dotted with hotels, shops and restaurants, as well as a number of old buildings with traditional Zanzibari doors. Follow Kenyatta Avenue eastwards for about 300m, passing the somewhat unkempt **People's Gardens**, originally laid out under Sultan Barghash for the use of his harem, until you reach the **Zanzibar Milestone**. This octagonal marble pillar shows the distance from Zanzibar Town to various settlements on the island and further afield.

Cross the gardens in front of the milestone to the distinctive **Beit el Amani (House of Peace) Memorial Museum**, which houses interesting (though rather poorly organised and labelled) displays relating to the island's archaeology, the slave era, and various palaces, sultans, explorers, missionaries, traditional crafts and coins. In the annexe on the opposite side of the road there is a library and a natural history collection where dodo bones are exhibited. The Zanzibari door at the back of the building is reputedly the oldest in existence. The museum is open from 08.30 to 19.00 Monday to Friday and 08.30 to 15.00 Saturday and Sunday. There is a small entrance charge.

From the museum, follow Creek Road northwards for about 400m, and to your left you'll easily pick out the imposing **Anglican Cathedral** built by the Universities' Mission in Central Africa (UMCA) over the former slave market between 1873 and 1880. Tradition has it that the altar stands on the site of the market's whipping block, and the cellar of the nearby St Monica's Guesthouse is reputed to be the remains of a pit where slaves were kept before being sold. Sultan Barghash, who closed the slave market, is reputed to have asked Bishop Steere, leader of the mission, not to build the cathedral tower higher than the House of Wonders. When the bishop agreed, the sultan presented the cathedral with its clock. The foundation of the UMCA was inspired by Livingstone: a window is dedicated to his memory, and the church's crucifix is made from the tree under

PRINCESS SALME

Tricia Hayne

Princess Salme was born at Bet il Mtoni, a palace on the coast about five miles outside Zanzibar Town. The daughter of Seyyid Said, Sultan of Oman and Zanzibar, she had around 36 brothers and sisters, almost all of different mothers, and some of whom were old enough to be her grandparents. Her own mother, one of around 75 'wives' or *sarari*, owned by the sultan, was a Circassian by birth, but had been abducted by bandits as a child from her home near the Black Sea.

It was at Bet il Mtoni that Salme spent her early years, playing with her brothers and sisters, floating toy boats on the river. Hers was an idyllic childhood, surrounded by love and attention, and wanting for nothing. Much of the palace social life was centred on the numerous bathing houses, where people would spend several hours each day, praying, working, reading or even taking their meals. In spite of the restrictions of traditional 19th-century Muslim society, members of the household had considerable freedom and Salme and her sisters were encouraged to be active. Twice a day, children over five years of age were given riding lessons. While the boys rode on horseback, the girls were given much-valued white donkeys. Unusually for a woman, Salme was also taught to read and write.

Salme's father had several properties on the island, many by the sea, some in the city and others on his 45 plantations. At the age of seven, Salme and her

which his heart was buried in present-day Zambia. Several other missionaries are remembered on plaques around the cathedral wall, as are sailors killed fighting the slave trade and servicemen who died in action in East Africa during World War I. The cathedral is open to visitors for a nominal fee, which also covers entrance to the dungeon below the guesthouse.

A short distance further along Creek Road lies the **covered market**, built at around the turn of the 20th century, and worth a visit even if you don't want to buy anything. It's a vibrant place where you can buy anything from fish and bread to sewing machines and second-hand car spares. Once you've taken a look around the market, follow Creek Road back southwards for 100m or so, passing the cathedral, then turn into the first wide road to your right. This is New Mkunazini Road, and if you follow it until its end, then turn right into Kajificheni Street and right again into Hammani Street, you'll come out at the **Hammani Baths**. This is one of the most elaborate Persian baths on Zanzibar, built for Sultan Barghash, and the caretaker will show you around for a small fee.

Barely 200m from the baths, on Cathedral Street, **St Joseph's Catholic Cathedral** is notable for its prominent twin spires, and was built between 1896 and 1898 by French missionaries and local converts. There are now few Catholics on Zanzibar, and the cathedral is infrequently used, but visitors are welcome when the doors are open. The best way to get here from the baths is to retrace your steps along Kajificheni Street, then turn right into the first alley (which boasts several good examples of traditional Zanzibari carved doors) until you reach an open area where several roads and alleys meet – Cathedral Street among them.

From the cathedral, continue northwards along Cathedral Street for perhaps 50m, then turn right into Gizenga Street, a good place to check out the work of local Tingatinga artists. Gizenga Street boasts a cluster of curio shops, of which **The Gallery** is widely regarded to be the best, and also stocks a good selection of

mother reluctantly moved with an older brother into the town at Bet il Watoro. As her brothers Barghash and Majid grew older, petty jealousies surfaced, and at around the time of her father's death, when she was nine, such jealousies turned to intrigue and feuds. Three years later, after a cholera epidemic carried off Salme's mother, the princess became entangled in a web of conspiracy as Barghash, supported by Salme, sought to overthrow his brother. Although Majid defeated the rebellion, Salme claims that he continued to maintain a good relationship with his younger sister.

It was shortly after this that Salme found herself living next door to a young German who worked for a Hamburg mercantile firm. Although their friendship was known to Salme's family, the prospect of a Christian marriage would not have been acceptable, and the two planned their escape so that they could marry in a Christian church. With the help of the British Vice-consul, Salme boarded a British man-of-war, the *Highflier*, and headed north to Aden. Here she was baptised, taking the name Emily, and shortly after this the two were married. They spent just three years together in Germany before Emily was widowed, left alone in a strange country with three young children. Nevertheless, she made her home in Germany, and later in London; it was 19 years before she was to set foot once again on Zanzibar soil.

Emily Ruete's 'Memoirs of an Arabian Princess from Zanzibar' is published by Markus Wiener.

books and maps about Zanzibar. If you follow Gizenga Street until you see the old Arab Fort to your left, you can conclude your walk by wandering back out to Forodhani Gardens. Alternatively, if you want to keep going, turn right opposite the fort into Harumzi Street and, after continuing straight for about 300m, you'll come to the open square in front of the **Spice Inn**, which is one of the oldest hotels in the Stone Town (and a good place to take a break for a cake or samosa and a fruit juice). A left turn as you enter this square takes you past the Jamat Khan Mosque and on to Jamatini Road, which after about 200m will bring you out at the seafront opposite the **Big Tree**. Known locally as Mtini, this well-known landmark was planted in 1911 by Sultan Khalifa and now provides shade for traditional dhow builders.

On Mizingani Road, next to the Big Tree, the **Old Customs House**, a large, relatively plain building dating to the late 19th century, is where Sultan Hamoud was proclaimed sultan in 1896. Next to this is another large old building, formerly **Le Grand Hotel**, which is currently being renovated, is likely to re-open under its original name in the next couple of years.

From the open area next to the Big Tree, a left turn along Mizingani Road will take you back to the Arab Fort, passing the above-mentioned buildings. Turn right into Mizingani Road, however, and after about 100m you'll pass the **Old Dispensary**, an ornate three-storey building built in the 1890s. Restored to its former glory by the Aga Khan, the dispensary now also contains a small exhibition hall of old monochrome photographs of the Stone Town. You can continue for a few hundred metres further, past the port gates, to the **traditional dhow harbour**, though based on our experience you are unlikely to be allowed inside.

If the above directions seem too complicated, or you want further insight into the historical buildings of the Stone Town, most tour operators can arrange a guided city tour for around US$20 (see pages 329–30 for tour operator listings).

ISLANDS CLOSE TO ZANZIBAR TOWN

Several small islands lie between 2km and 6km offshore of Zanzibar, many of them within view of Zanzibar Town and easily visited from there as a day trip. Boat transport to Chumbe arranged with an independent guide will cost around US$20, but you will pay more to go on an organised tour (see pages 329–30 for tour operators). To cut the individual cost, it is worth getting a group together.

Changuu (Prison) Island

Changuu was originally owned by a wealthy Arab, who used it as a detention centre for disobedient slaves. A prison was built there in 1893, but never used. A path circles the island (about an hour's easy stroll). There is a small beach and a restaurant, and masks and flippers can be hired for snorkelling. The island is home to several giant tortoises, probably brought from the Seychelles in the 18th century, which spend much of their time mating, a long and noisy process which is apparently successful as the tortoise population is said to be growing. An entrance fee of US$5 per person must be paid in hard currency.

The **Changuu Island Guesthouse** (tel: 024 223630/0747 410341; email: prisonisland@hotmail.com) consists of a group of wooden bungalows set back from the beach. Accommodation costs US$30/35 single/double, and should be booked in advance through one of the ZTC offices. Camping is permitted, and meals are available at the restaurant.

Chapwani (Grave) Island

This long, narrow and very pretty island has been the site of a Christian cemetery since 1879, and it also has a small swimming beach – good at low and high tide – and faces Snake Island, where thousands of egrets roost overnight. Most of the graves on the island belong to British sailors who were killed fighting Arab slave ships, while others date from World War I, when the British ship *Pegasus* was sunk in Zanzibar harbour. The indigenous forest supports about a hundred duikers, large numbers of fruit bats, and various coastal scrub birds, while the giant coconut crab is often seen along the shore. A lovely low-key lodge called **Chapwani Island Camp** (tel: 024 223 3360; email: chapwani@houseofwonders.com) has recently opened on the island, and charges from US$80–110 per person per day, half-board, depending on the season.

BUBUBU AND SURROUNDS

The small town of Bububu served as the terminus for a 10km stretch of 36-inch gauge track to connect the north coast to the Arab fort, constructed in 1904 and used until 1928. The springs outside Bububu supply most of Zanzibar Town's fresh water, and the name of the town presumably derives from the bubbling sound that they make. For most tourists, Bububu's main attraction will be **Fuji Beach**, the closest swimming beach to town, no more than 500m to your left when you disembark from a 'Route B' *dalla-dalla* at the main crossroads at Bububu.

Of interest in Bububu is a small, centuries-old **mosque** about 200m from the main crossroads, along the road back towards Zanzibar Town. There is a little-known but large **double-storey ruin** on the beachfront about 500m north from where you arrive at the Fuji Beach. Complete with Arabic frescos, this house must date to the early 19th century, and it could well have been the Bububu residence of Princess Salme in the 1850s, as described in her autobiography.

Between Zanzibar Town and Bububu lie the ruined palaces of Maharubi and Mtoni, and Bububu is the closest substantial settlement to the Persian baths at Kidichi and Kizimbani.

CHUMBE ISLAND CORAL PARK

The coral island of Chumbe, in near pristine condition because it served as a military base for many years and visitors were not permitted, has been gazetted as a nature reserve along with several surrounding reefs. Snorkelling here is as good as anywhere around Zanzibar, with more than 350 reef fishes recorded, as well as dolphins and turtles. A walking trail circumnavigates the island, passing rock pools haunted by starfish, and beaches marched upon by legions of hermit crabs. Look out, too, for the giant coconut crab, a rare nocturnal creature that weights up to 4kg. Some 60 species of bird have been recorded on the island, including breeding pairs of the rare roseate tern. There are plans to re-introduce the localised Ader's duiker, which was hunted out in the 1950s. Of historical interest are an ancient Swahili mosque and a British lighthouse built in 1904. Day trips to the island cost US$70 per person, inclusive of transfers, guides, snorkelling equipment and lunch, and can only be arranged through reputable tour operators or from the Mbweni Ruins Hotel.

Overnight stays are encouraged at a small and regularly praised eco-lodge, all profits from which are pumped into conservation and education. The seven self-contained bungalows are very rustic and attractive – it's lovely to watch the moon and stars over the sea at night – and have solar electricity, compost toilets, and funnelled roofs designed to collect rainwater. An ingenious main *boma* houses the dining room (good seafood), education centre, snorkelling equipment room and lounge/bar.

Chumbe makes no pretension to be a chill-out beach resort – the emphasis is very much on ecology and wildlife – but it is highly recommended to those with a strong interest in conservation. Full board accommodation costs US$200 per person. For further information and reservations, contact Chumbe Island Coral Park. Tel/fax: 024 223 1040; mobile: 0747 413582; email: chumbe@zitec.org; web: www.chumbeisland.com.

Getting around

Although some of the places mentioned below might be included in your spice tour, it is easy to visit most of them independently, using the combination of 'Route B' *dalla-dallas* (which run to Bububu every few minutes from the bus station on Creek Road) and your legs. Another possibility is to hire a motor scooter or bicycle from Sun 'n' Fun Tours, Maharouky Bicycle Hire (between the market and petrol station) or Nasor Aly Mussa's Scooter Service (near the UMCA cathedral).

Where to stay and eat

Most people visit the places listed below as a day-trip out of Zanzibar Town, but it is perfectly possible to explore the area using Bububu as a base. For upmarket authenticity in Bububu (and perhaps anywhere on Zanzibar), you can't beat **Salme's Garden** (contact the agent in Italy on tel: +39 051 234 974; fax: +39 051 239 086; email: info@houseofwonders.com; web: www.houseofwonders.com), a restored 19th-century house, it is set above Fuji Beach and decorated in masterly period style by Emerson of Emerson's House. Set in beautiful grounds, and with a private mosque attached, this house is another candidate for Princess Salme's Bububu residence. It can be rented as a unit or by the room through Nicole (the chef at Emerson's & Green), or through the owners in Italy. Double rooms cost between US$120 and US$150.

The recently upgraded **Bububu Beach Guesthouse** (tel: 024 225 0110) provides good value accommodation one minute's walk from Fuji Beach. Standard rooms cost US$25/35 single/double, while smarter bungalows cost US$60/80. There is another **anonymous guesthouse** around the corner next to the Cave Bar. The **Cave Bar** serves ice-cold beer in pleasant gardens, while the **Fuji Beach Restaurant** serves OK meals in the US$4–5 range. If you are mobile or don't mind using *dalla-dallas* by night, the somewhat misleadingly named **Milan Restaurant** about 4km back towards town serves superb Indian food in the US$5–6 range.

Excursions

Maharubi Palace

This is probably the most impressive ruin on this part of the coast, built in 1882 for the concubines of Sultan Barghash. At one time he kept around a hundred women here. The palace was destroyed by fire in 1899, and all that remains are the great pillars which supported the upper storey, and the Persian-style bathhouse. You can also see the separate bathrooms for the women, the large bath used by the sultan, and the original water tanks, now overgrown with lilies. The palace lies about 200m from the Bububu road, roughly 3km from the Stone Town, and it is signposted. A nominal entrance fee of around US$0.30 is charged, and the ticket also allows entrance to most of the other sites in this area. Traditional dhow builders can be seen at work on the beach in front of the palace.

Mtoni Slave Chambers

The ruins of a large slave chamber overlook the beach about 500m north of Maharubi, in the grounds of a Tourism Training College. It is physically possible to walk to the ruins along the beach, though the security people at Maharubi discourage this due to a spate of mugging, so it can only be recommended if you have no valuables on you or are in the company of a trustworthy local. The other option is to go back to the main road and follow this for about 500m until you reach the entrance to the training college.

Mtoni Palace

The ruins of Mtoni Palace lie a short way north of Maharubi, and can be reached along the beach. Mtoni is the oldest palace on Zanzibar, built for Sultan Said in the 1840s. A book written by his daughter Salme describes the palace in the 1850s. At one end of the house was a large bathhouse, at the other the quarters where Said lived with his principal wife. Gazelles and peacocks wandered around the large courtyard. Mtoni was abandoned before 1885, and only the main walls and roof now remain. It was used as a warehouse in World War I; evidence of this alteration can still be seen. In October 1998, we were told at Maharubi that this palace was closed to tourists, but when we walked there from the main road we were allowed in by the caretaker. Presumably, we were being warned off walking along the beach, so once again you are advised against taking a seaside short cut!

Kidichi and Kizimbani Persian Baths

The Kidichi baths were built in 1850 for Said's wife, Binte Irich Mirza, the granddaughter of the Shah of Persia, and are decorated with Persian-style stucco. You can enter the bathhouse and see the bathing pool and toilets, but there is mould growing on much of the stucco. The baths lie about 3km east of Bububu; from the main crossroads follow the road heading inland (ie: turn right coming from Zanzibar Town) and you'll see the baths to your right after a walk of around 30 minutes.

The Kizimbani baths are less attractive and less accessible on foot, lying a further 3km or so inland. The surrounding Kizimbani clove plantation, which is visited by many spice tours, was founded in the early 19th century by Saleh bin Haramil, the Arab trader who imported the first cloves to Zanzibar.

Mangapwani Slave Cave
Near the synonymous village, 10km north of Bububu and 20km north of Zanzibar Town, this large natural cavern and manmade slave cave can easily be visited using a no 2 *dalla-dalla*. The natural coral cavern has a narrow entrance and a pool of fresh water at its lowest point. The Slave Cave, a square cell cut into the coral, was used to hold slaves after the trade was abolished in 1873. The natural cavern may also have been used to hide slaves, but this is not certain. Coming by *dalla-dalla*, you'll have to disembark at Mangapwani, where a road forks left towards the coast. About 2km past the village this road ends and a small track branches off to the right. Follow this for 1km to reach the Slave Cave. About halfway between Mangapwani and the track to the Slave Cave, a narrow track to the left leads to the natural cavern.

NUNGWI AND THE FAR NORTH
The large fishing village of Nungwi, situated on the northern end of the island, is the centre of Zanzibar's traditional dhow-building industry. It has also emerged over the last decade as probably the most popular tourist retreat on Zanzibar, thanks to a lovely beach lined with palm and casuarina trees, and the good snorkelling and diving in the surrounding waters. A few reasonably isolated upmarket hotels stand on the north end of the beach, while the southern end hosts a dense cluster of low-key and rather overpriced guesthouses and restaurants, creating a party atmosphere reminiscent of such established backpacker hangouts as Cape Maclear in Malawi. Conservative local villagers evidently view this influx of travellers with understandable ambivalence, and many travellers find that the bustling atmosphere that characterises Nungwi is not to their taste.

A short walk along the beach east of Nungwi brings you to the headland of Ras Nungwi, where there is an old lighthouse (photography forbidden). Next to this, the Mnarani Turtle Sanctuary (entrance US$1) consists of a fenced-off saline natural pool, in which lives a community of perhaps 15 greenback and hawksbill turtles. Further afield, the Fukuchani Ruins lie about 200m off the main road to Zanzibar Town, about 10km south of Nungwi. Also known as the Portuguese House, this well-preserved ruin dates from the 16th century and, while it may have been occupied and even extended by Portuguese settlers, it was probably built in the Shirazi era.

Getting there and away
An erratic handful of *dalla-dalla*s daily connect Zanzibar Town to Nungwi, but the vast majority of travellers prefer to be transferred by private minibus, which can cost up to US$10 per person depending on group size and your negotiating skills. The ideal is to get a group together in Zanzibar when you want to head out to Nungwi, then organise a transfer through a *papaasi*, a taxi driver or a tour company. Unless you have very rigid timings, there is no need to organise your transfer back to Zanzibar Town in advance, since several vehicles can be found waiting around for passengers in Nungwi, especially in the mid-morning.

Where to stay and eat
Upmarket
Ras Nungwi Beach Hotel Tel: 024 223 3767; fax: 024 223 3098; email: rasnungwi@zanzibar.net; web: www.zanzibar.net/nungwi. This widely praised hotel, built

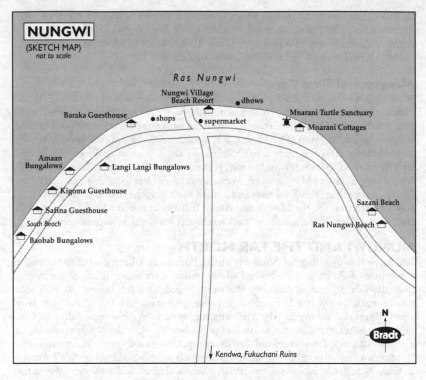

almost entirely with local materials such as fossilised coral limestone, has an organic feel, a lovely beach setting, and an atmosphere that is far less 'packaged' than at most equivalently priced places on the east coast. The emphasis is very much on diving, snorkelling, game fishing and non-motorised watersports, although many visitors are content merely to laze on the idyllic beach. Day trips to most points of interest around the island can be arranged. The PADI dive centre runs single dives from US$40 per person, as well as discounted packages for those wanting to do several dives, and full five-day courses for US$330. A good selection of watersport and snorkelling equipment can be hired. The superb restaurant, affiliated to Blues in Zanzibar Town, specialises in seafood and Swahili dishes. All accommodation is en-suite with a ceiling fan, private balcony and netted four-poster bed in the traditional Swahili style. Full-board rates range from US$110/160 single/double in an ordinary room to US$140/220 in a sea-facing chalet, with a substantial low season discount.

Moderate

Mnarani Beach Cottages Tel: 024 224 0494; email: mnarani@cctz.com; web: www.lighthousezanzibar.com. Situated between the village and the lighthouse on Ras Nungwi, this small cluster of cottages, built in local style, is one of the more peaceful and attractively located retreats in the Nungwi area. The self-contained rooms are good value, too, at US$60/84 single/double B&B.

Sazani Beach Hotel Tel: 024 224 0014; email: divemaxx@zanlink.com or sazanibeach@aol.com; web: www.sazanibeach.com. Set in pretty grounds close to the Ras Nungwi Hotel – and some distance from the main cluster of cheaper guesthouses – this lodge consists of ten simple but comfortable double beach rondavels at US$40–60, depending on whether they have a sea view or not. Good diving and snorkelling facilities are offered on site. Meals cost Tsh4,500.

Baobab Beach Bungalows Tel: 0747 416964; email: baobabnungwi@zanzinet.com; web: baobabbeachbungalows.com. This excellent new complex with 39 guestrooms is situated at the far end of the south beach, away from the main cluster of cheap guesthouses. Accommodation in fairly large self-contained bungalows with hot water and nets costs US$34/44 single/double, while smaller but smarter sea-facing rooms with television, fan and nets cost US$40/60 single/double. There's a great beachfront restaurant in the complex. **Langi Langi Beach Bungalows** Tel: 024 224 0470; fax: 024 224 0471; email: langi_langi@hotmail.com. This small new resort, with a limited beachfront next to Dive Zanzibar, charges US$55/70 single/double for comfortable but fairly basic self-contained bungalows with hot water. Nets are available on request only. The best feature of the lodge is its rooftop restaurant, which serves toasted sandwiches for around Tsh2,500 and seafood meals in the Tsh4,500–7,000 range.

Budget
Amaan Bungalows Tel: 024 224 0026; email: amaanbungalow@yahoo.com; web: www.amaanbungalow.com. One of the oldest budget lodges in Nungwi, Amaan Bungalows is now also the largest, a sprawling complex of 35 self-contained bungalows with nets costing US$25 double B&B, with a few larger and pricier rooms also available. With good diving facilities on site, and a busy beach, it's a justifiably popular spot with sociable budget travellers, but emphatically not the place to head for if you're seeking a peaceful beach retreat. A decent restaurant serves pasta, pizzas and burgers in the Tsh2,500–3,500 range, and seafood dishes for around Tsh5,000–6,000.
Baraka Guesthouse Tel: 024 224 0412. This friendly, owner-managed local guesthouse, which charges US$15/35 for a basic self-contained single/double, is probably the most likeable place in the budget range.
Safina Guesthouse Tel: 0747 415726. Similar in standard to the above, this small lodge close to Amaan Bungalows charges US$25 for a self-contained double with nets and cold shower and US$50 for a double room with a hot shower.
Kigoma Guesthouse Tel: 0747 415421. Next door to the Safina, this is similar in standard, and charges US$30 for a double with nets and cold water only.

General information
Several of the hotels in Nungwi have attached dive centres, and there are also a few stand-alone dive centres along the beach. These generally charge around US$30 per person for single dives, while multiple dives go for US$25 per person and full five-day courses for US$300 per person. Snorkelling and watersport equipment can easily be rented, too. An internet café near Amaan Bungalows charges Tsh100 per minute for a minimum of five minutes online.

Kendwa
Situated on the west coast of Zanzibar 3km south of Nungwi, this lovely sandy beach has also seen plenty of tourist development since the mid-1990s, when it was the site of a solitary backpacker lodge and campsite. There are now several moderately priced lodges along the beach, as well as a few restaurants and an excellent dive centre, but the atmosphere at Kendwa remains – for the time being – distinctly more relaxed than at Nungwi.

Where to stay
Kendwa Rocks Tel: 0747 415475/527; email: kendwarocks@hotmail.com. The original backpacker lodge has smartened up considerably in recent years, though a few palm leaf *bandas* are still available at US$8–10 per person. More comfortable self-contained double bungalows cost US$40–45.

Whitesands Tel: 0747 415720; email: whitesandsken60@hotmail.com. This pleasant beach lodge charges US$7–10 per person for basic *bandas* and US$20–35 per unit for small bungalows.

Sunset Bungalows Tel: 0747 413818; email: sunsetbungalow@hotmail.com. The smartest lodge on Kendwa Beach, Sunset Bungalows charges US$30 for a comfortable and attractively decorated double bungalow. A decent restaurant and a dive centre are attached.

Palm Leaf Hotel Tel: 0747 416548. This new and very attractive small lodge lies at the end of the beach, and charges US$10 per person for rooms in palm leaf *bandas* or US$25 per person for more comfortable double *bandas*.

JOZANI FOREST AND SURROUNDS

The Jozani Forest Reserve protects the last substantial remnant of the indigenous forest that once covered much of central Zanzibar, and it is the most important mammal sanctuary on the island. The main tourist attraction is Kirk's red colobus, a beautiful and cryptically coloured monkey with an outrageous pale tufted crown. Unique to Zanzibar, Kirk's red colobus is regarded by most authorities to be a distinct species, though it is closely related to the common red colobus of West Africa. A few years ago, the island's colobus population had fallen to 1,000–1,500 individuals, but recent estimates place it at around 2,300. A good network of forest trails runs through the forest, and the habituated colobus troops are easily seen by tourists – and great fun to watch because they more or less ignore human observers.

Jozani used to be the main haunt of the Zanzibar leopard, a race that is found nowhere else, but which recent research suggests may well be extinct. The forest is also home to Ader's duiker, a small antelope that effectively may now be a Zanzibar endemic, as it is probably extinct and certainly very rare in Kenya's Sokoke Forest, which is the only other place where it has ever been recorded. Several other mammal species live in Jozani, and the forest is one of the best birding sites on the island, hosting a good range of coastal forest birds, including an endemic race of the lovely Fischer's turaco.

The entrance and reception at Jozani Forest lie a short distance from the main road connecting Zanzibar Town to the east coast. Most tour operators can organise day trips to the forest, though it is perfectly possible to visit independently using a number 9 or 10 bus or *dalla-dalla*. Also of interest in the Jozani area are Zala Park, a small private zoo lying about 3km past the forest and about 1km off the main east coast road, and the Bi Khole Ruins, the remains of a mid-19th-century homestead lying 6km south of the village of Tunguu to the west of the main east coast road. A new development in the area, based in the village of Pete 1km from the entrance to the forest, is a mangrove boardwalk, allowing visitors a rare view into the unique mangrove habitat.

THE EAST COAST

The east coast of Zanzibar is where you will find the idyllic tropical beaches you dreamed about during those interminable bus rides on the mainland: clean white sand lined with palms, and lapped by the warm blue water of the Indian Ocean. Some travellers come here for a couple of days, just to relax after seeing the sights of Zanzibar Town, and end up staying for a couple of weeks. Visitors on tighter time restrictions always wish they could stay for longer...

The east coast is divided into two discrete stretches by Chwaka Bay, which lies at the same latitude as Zanzibar Town on the west coast. Traditionally, the most popular stretch of coast is to the south of this bay, between Bwejuu and Makunduchi, but recent years have seen an increasing number of developments further north, between Matemwe and Chwaka. Most hotels have restaurants, and

MNEMBA ISLAND LODGE

Private Bag X27, Benmore, South Africa; tel: 024 223 3110; fax: 024 223 3117; email: ccafricazanzibar@zanzinet.com

If you've ever fancied owning your own private tropical island, then a stay at the Mnemba Island Lodge may be the closest you ever get to realising that dream, if only for a few days. The tiny island of Mnemba, which lies a kilometre or so off the northeastern shore of Zanzibar, forms part of the much larger submerged Mnemba Atoll. The island itself boasts wide beaches of white coral sand, fine and cool underfoot, backed by patches of tangled coastal bush and a small forest of casuarina trees. The small reefs immediately offshore offer a great introduction to the fishes of the reef for snorkellers, while diving excursions further afield allow you to explore the 40m-deep coral cliffs, a good place to see larger fish including the whale shark, the world's largest fish. The bird checklist for the island, though short, includes several unusual waders and other marine birds.

Accommodation consists of ten large, airy, beach chalets, constructed using organic materials. The chalets are very private, separated from the beach and other chalets by thick bush, and each one has a private balcony as well as netting, a fan and an en-suite bathroom. The food is good, and (weather permitting) evening meals are taken at a table on the beach. Accommodation costs US$500 per person per night, inclusive of all meals and drinks, transfers from Zanzibar Town, use of watersport and snorkelling equipment, and dives (including diving courses) with the resident diving instructor.

you can usually buy fish and vegetables in the villages, but supplies are limited. If you are self-catering, stock up in Zanzibar Town.

Getting there and away

The east coast can easily be reached by bus or *dalla-dalla* from Zanzibar Town. North of Chwaka Bay, no 6 buses go to Chwaka (directly east of Zanzibar Town), no 14 to Uroa via Chwaka, no 17 to Kiwengwa and no 18 to Matemwe. South of the bay, no 9 goes to Paje (sometimes continuing to Bwejuu or Jambiani) and no 10 to Makunduchi. Chwaka Bay can be crossed by lake-taxis between Chwaka and Michamvi.

Most travellers prefer to use private transport to the east coast: several tour companies and some independent guides arrange minibuses which cost between US$3 and US$5 per person each way. Unless you specify where you want to stay, minibus drivers prefer to take you to a hotel that gives them commission.

Where to stay

The listings below run from north to south, and the stretches of coastline to the north and the south of Chwaka Bay are split under separate headings. The listings are not comprehensive, particularly with regard to upmarket hotels that cater almost exclusively to Italian fly-in beach packages.

North of Chwaka Bay

The roughly 40km of coastline north of Chwaka Bay is lined with numerous lovely beaches and punctuated by a number of small traditional fishing villages, the most important of which – running from north to south – are Matemwe, Pwani Mchangani, Kiwengwa, Uroa and Chwaka. Hotels along this stretch of coast mostly fall into the mid-range to upmarket bracket, though good budget accommodation is available at Kiwengwa.

Upmarket

Protea Zanzibar Beach Resort Tel: 0747 417782/3/4; fax: 0747 417785; email: enquiries@zanzibarbeachresort.com; web: www.proteahotels.com. This large beach resort, run by the South African Protea chain, caters to package tours as well as individuals. It offers an excellent range of diving and snorkelling excursions in the Mnemba Atoll as well as most other watersports. Rates are in the US$100 per person range.

Matemwe Bungalows Tel: 024 223 6535; fax: 024 223 6536; email: matemwe-znz@twiga.com; web: www.matemwe.com. This small, simple but comfortable hotel facing Mnemba Island lies near the pretty Matemwe village, on a low coral cliff above a palm-lined beach. It is a good base for diving and snorkelling, and is close to the exceptional Mnemba Atoll. The attached diving school charges US$35 for a single dive and US$350 for a full diving course. Accommodation in en-suite chalets costs US$85 per person.

Shooting Star Inn Tel: 024 223 2926; email: star@zanzibar.org; web: www.zanzibar.org/star. Situated on Kiwenga Beach, about 8km south of Matemwe, this small, friendly hotel is regarded to have one of the best restaurants on the island, and is visited by many people for the food alone, which costs from US$10 upwards. Accommodation in luxurious en-suite bungalows costs US$110 double B&B. More basic *bandas* using common showers go for US$15 per person.

Blue Bay Beach Resort Tel: 024 224 0240/1/2; email: mail@bluebayzanzibar.com; web: www.bluebayzanzibar.com. This is a huge but pleasantly low-key beach hotel geared primarily to the package market, though individual guests are also catered for. The self-contained rooms, which all have two double beds, AC, satellite TV and a sea view, cost US$135/220 single/double B&B with an extra US$18 per person charged for FB. The dive school, which offers single dives and courses in the excellent Mnemba Atoll, is open to non-residents of the hotel.

Zanzibar Safari Resort Tel: 024 233 8553; email: zanzibar.safari.club@africaonline.co.tz; web: www.zanzibarsafariresort.co.tz. This attractive and relatively small package hotel on Uroa Beach consists of 40 bungalows centred on a swimming pool area, and charges US$85/150 for a self-contained single/double with AC. A good restaurant, dive school and watersport centre are attached.

Moderate

Matemwe Beach Village Tel: 024 223 8374; email: matemwebeachvillage@zitec.org; web: www.zanzibaroneocean.com. This comfortable small lodge is situated about 1km

UFUFUMA FOREST HABITAT

Ufufuma is an underpublicised eco-tourism development based out of the village of Jidele, which straddles the main road from Zanzibar Town about 5km before Chwaka. The project is centred on a 1km² relic patch of forest that harbours small populations of Ader's duiker and Kirk's red colobus and other monkeys, as well as a fair variety of coastal forest birds. A guided tour also incorporates a visit to a trio of caves that are still used as sacrificial sites to the Shetani (spirits) by traditional healers. Guides can easily be located in Jidele, and a one- to two-hour walk costs Tsh4,000. It is also possible to arrange to see a Shetani ceremony for US$50 per party.

from Matemwe Bungalows, and charges US$40 per person B&B for a very spacious and attractively decorated double room with a fan, netting and hot showers. There's a good dive centre on site.

Uzioni Beach Bungalows Tel: 0747 417701; email: uzioni@hotmail.com. This is a new and very pleasant locally owned guesthouse situated near Pwani Mchangani, 6km south of Matemwe. Accommodation in neat thatched bungalows with nets, fans, running hot water and a sea view starts at US$40/50 single/double B&B. A good open-air restaurant is attached.

Tamarind Beach Hotel Tel: 0747 413709; email: tamarind@zanzinet.com. One of the older lodges on this part of the coast, the Tamarind Beach Resort on Uroa Beach consists of several self-contained villas overlooking the palm-lined seashore. Although starting to look a bit rundown, it's decent value at US$30/40 for a self-contained single/double B&B.

Budget
Reef View Tel: 0747 413294; email: reefviewinzanzibar@hotmail.com; web: www.reefview.com. The pick of the limited selection of budget options on the coast north of Chwaka Bay, Reef View is situated on a beach 1km south of Kiwengwa and run by a mixed Zanzibari-English couple. It charges US$10 per person for simple *banda* accommodation, serves pretty good meals for Tsh5,000–6,000, and has a good stock of paperbacks for exchange.

South of Chwaka Bay
The coastline south of Chwaka Bay caters better to budget travellers than the coast further north, though a few relatively upmarket hotels are also found in the area. Until a few years ago, the southeast stretch of coast had the most crowded beaches on Zanzibar, but these days the area is quieter than Nungwi on the north coast. Coming from Zanzibar Town along the main road through the Jozani Forest, the first coastal settlement you'll hit is Paje, a small fishing village situated at a junction, from where minor roads run north and south along the coast. The most important settlement north of Paje and south of Chwaka Bay is Bwejuu, a fishing village whose livelihood is linked to the gathering and production of seaweed. Several resorts catering to all budgets lie within a few kilometres' radius of Bwejuu. South of Paje, Jambiani is a substantial town that runs for several kilometres along the beach, while the more southerly town of Makunduchi – not accessible by public transport – lacks for any real tourist development.

Upmarket
Breezes Beach Club Tel: 0741 326595; email: breezes@africaonline.co.tz. The most northerly hotel on this stretch of coast is the Breezes Beach Club, which despite its name and large size is a relatively unpackaged family-run set-up sprawling around a well-maintained sea-facing garden. Accommodation costs around US$100 for a self-contained double, and a dive school is attached. Recommended.

Sunrise Hotel Tel: 024 224 0170; email: sunrise@zanlink.com; web: www.sunrise-zanzibar.com. This established small hotel, which lies about 3km north of Bwejuu village, is routinely recommended by travellers, and it seems excellent value at US$65/75 for a single/double bungalow with en-suite bathroom. The restaurant is also very good, and there's a new swimming pool.

Sun & Sea View Hotel Tel: 0747 420774; email: ssvresort@zanjcom.com. This new resort lies in a spacious beach plot about halfway along the 5km road between Bwejuu and Paje. It has a lovely stilted *makuti* dining area and serves good food. Accommodation consists of ten smart self-contained bungalows and costs US$50/75 single/double B&B.

Sau Inn Hotel Tel: 024 224 0169/0205; email: sauinn@zanlink.com. Formerly one of the most highly rated hotels on the southeast coast, the Sau Inn in Jambiani is due for some maintenance work, but it remains a pleasant enough retreat. The lodge consists of a number of comfortable and spacious en-suite rooms and cottages set in pleasant gardens, and costs US$60/70 single/double B&B, with lunch and dinner each costing an additional US$10 per head. Snorkelling and diving excursions can be arranged from the hotel, and the internet facilities are open to non-residents.

Moderate
Andy's Bungalows Tel: 0742 740037; email: makupenda@bluemail.ch. This small, attractive and reasonably priced owner-managed lodge lies 1km north of the Sunrise Hotel and charges US$35/40 for a lovingly decorated single/double bungalow. A good restaurant serves Swahili, Hungarian and Italian dishes.
Robinson's Place Tel: 0747 413479; email: robinsonsplace@hotmail.com. Owned by a mixed Swiss-Zanzibari couple, this rustic and individualistic lodge charges US$20 per person for B&B accommodation. It's a very laidback and friendly set-up, and good Zanzibari food is available – warmly recommended!
Palm Beach Inn Tel/fax: 024 224 0221; email: mahfudh@hotmail.com. Situated in well-tended gardens on an attractive beach at Bwejuu, a village whose economy is based on seaweed farming, the relaxed and pretty Palm Beach Inn charges US$30/50 single/double for a self-contained room with fan and nets (rooms with AC cost US$10 more). The airy restaurant serves excellent seafood for around Tsh5,000.
Paradise Beach Bungalows Tel: 024 223 1387; fax: 024 223 0891; email: saori@hotmail.com. Situated 1km north of Paje, Paradise Beach is a rustic but likeable small lodge charging US$25/35 for spacious single/double rooms. The restaurant specialises in Japanese cuisine.
Paje By Night Bizarre Hotel Email: hotelpbn@yahoo.com; web: www.pajebynight.com. This popular, funky and individualistic lodge, owned and managed by a young German couple, is set on the beach at the village of Paje. Standard self-contained rooms with cold showers cost US$25/40 single/double, while double rooms with a hot shower cost US$50. The restaurant is well known for its pizzas, which cost from Tsh2,500 to Tsh4,500.
East Coast Visitors Inn Tel: 024 224 0150; email: visitorsinn@zitec.org. This clean and popular lodge in Jambiani is rather bland but very friendly and comfortable. The rates of US$13 per person for a room using common showers or US$40 for a self-contained double span the budget and moderate ranges. Decent meals are available, and a bureau de change is attached.
Blue Oyster Hotel Tel: 024 224 0163; email: blueoysterhotel@gmx.de. Also situated in Jambiani, the Blue Oyster is a new and attractively laid out German-owned lodge with an open-air feel and a good restaurant. Bright, comfortable rooms with nets and fans cost US$25/30 single/double using common showers, or US$30/40 self-contained. The management offers several excursions.

Budget
Bellevue Bungalows Tel: 0747 328361; email: bellevue01@hotmail.com. Situated on a hill overlooking the beach a few kilometres north of Bwejuu, this simple lodge charges US$15/25 single/double for a room with nets but no fans or electricity. The restaurant serves good seafood and coffee. A good range of water activities can be arranged through the lodge.
Kilimani Bungalows Email: drabien@kilimani.de. Situated just outside Bwejuu, this small lodge was built by a Dutch volunteer in collaboration with local villagers, and all profits are channelled into community projects. Accommodation in four whitewashed self-contained bungalows with nets but no fans costs US$15 per person.

Dere Beach Guesthouse Tel: 024 224 0197. This popular and constantly expanding lodge in Bwejuu charges from US$10 per person for rather rundown and gloomy rooms. The restaurant serves good value meals, and snorkelling equipment and bicycles can be hired at very reasonable rates.

Seven Seas Guesthouse Situated about halfway along the 5km road between Bwejuu and Paje, Seven Seas is a simple but very pleasant small budget lodge. Accommodation in seven sea-facing self-contained bungalows with nets and fans costs US$15/25 single/double, and a good beachfront bar and restaurant are attached.

Kitete Guesthouse Tel: 024 224 0226; email: kitete@hotmail.com; web: www.kitete.com. This small and homely Swedish-owned guesthouse lies in the village of Paje, facing the beach and next to a recently opened diving centre. Self-contained rooms cost US$20/30 single/double B&B and an attached restaurant serves good snacks and meals in the Tsh2,000–5,000 range.

Horizontal Inn This small and friendly family-run guesthouse, located at the north end of Jambiani, charges US$7 per person for basic accommodation.

Oyster Hotel Tel: 0741 333125. Also in Jambiani, this popular double-storey hotel charges US$20 for a clean double using common showers and US$30 for a self-contained double. An atmospheric rooftop bar and restaurant serves pizzas and seafood in the US$4,000–5,000 range.

Oasis Beach Hotel Tel: 024 224 0259. Another clean budget guesthouse in Jambiani, Oasis Beach charges US$25 for a self-contained double bungalow and US$16 for a double room using common showers. Inexpensive snorkelling trips and decent food are available.

Jambiani Beach Hotel Tel: 024 224 0155. This established budget hotel in Jambiani is starting to show its age, and lacks for a beachfront position, but it's adequate value at US$20/30 for a self-contained single/double.

Shehe Bungalows Tel: 024 224 0149; email: shehebungalows@hotmail.com. The long-serving Shehe in Jambiani, though looking a bit rundown of late, remains decent value at US$10 per person for a bungalow using common showers and US$25-45 for a self-contained double bungalow. The restaurant has an extensive menu, with most dishes in the Tsh5,000-6,000 range.

Shiaba Guesthouse This simple local guesthouse at the south end of Jambiani charges US$8 per person for adequate self-contained rooms.

Gomiani Guesthouse Tel: 024 224 0153/4. Set on a low cliff immediately south of Jambiani, the Gomiani Guesthouse charges US$30 for a spacious, clean, self-contained double with great sea views.

Red Monkey Bungalows Tel: 024 224 0207; email: standard@zitec.org. Above the beach at the south end of Jambiani, Red Monkey Bungalows is an atmospheric new set-up, charging US$25 for a small but comfortable self-contained double. The restaurant serves inexpensive seafood and the endemic red colobus monkey is sometimes seen in the nearby bush.

KIZIMKAZI

The small town of Kizimkazi lies on the southwestern end of the island, and is best known to tourists as *the* place to see humpback and bottlenose dolphins, both of which are resident in the area. Most tourists visit Kizimkazi on an organised day tour out of Zanzibar Town (see pages 329–30), which costs between US$25 and US$100 all-inclusive per person, depending on group size, season and quality. Sightings cannot be guaranteed, but the chances of seeing dolphins here are very good. It may also be possible sometimes to swim with the dolphins, though you should never encourage your pilot to chase them or try to approach them too closely yourself. With up to a hundred people visiting Kizimkazi daily in the high season, there is genuine cause to fear that tourism may be detrimental to the animals. If you do get close enough and you want to try your luck swimming with the dolphins, slip (rather than dive) into the water next to the boat, and try to excite the dolphins' interest by diving frequently and holding your arms along your body to imitate their streamlined shape!

If you stay overnight at Kizimkazi, it's worth heading out to the Kizimkazi Mosque at the nearby settlement of Dimbani. Kizimkazi is one of the oldest known mosques in East Africa, dated by Kufic inscriptions to AD1107, when it was part of a large walled city. The Kufic inscriptions, on the niche at the eastern end of the mosque, are in a decorative floriated style similar to some old inscriptions found in Persia. The silver pillars on either side of the niche are decorated with pounded shells from Mafia Island. Two clocks, which show Swahili time, were presented by local dignitaries. To see inside the mosque, now protected by a corrugated iron roof, you must find the caretaker who lives nearby. It is respectful to cover any bare limbs and take off your shoes when you enter.

Getting there and away
Although most people visit Kizimkazi on an organised day trip, it can be reached independently in a hired car, or with a no 3 bus or *dalla-dalla* from Zanzibar Town.

Where to stay and eat
Kizimkazi Beach Villa Tel: 0741 352685. This rather basic bungalow charges US$10 per person for rooms using common showers, and US$15 per person for self-contained accommodation. Meals are available if ordered in advance. To see the dolphins, you can arrange to hire a boat from the hotel at around Tsh30,000 per group, or join a group that has come for the day from Zanzibar Town.

Dolphin Shadow Guesthouse This small lodge consists of only two double bungalows rented out at US$20 per night.

Dolphin View Village Tel: 024 223 6577; email: rukiandame@hotmail.com. About 1km south of the small town centre, this friendly lodge consists of three spacious bungalows, also rented out at US$20 per night.

Cabs Restaurant Tel: 0747 415544; email: cabsrestaurant@yahoo.com. The popular restaurant serves a variety of seafood and other dishes in the Tsh3,000–4,000 range. It is also the best place in Kizimkazi to arrange dolphin trips, charging a negotiable Tsh30,000 per party or Tsh2,500 per person for a two-hour excursion in one of its six boats.

Kizidi Bungalows Tel: 0747 417053; email: kizidi@hotmail.com. Popular with tour groups for its excellent restaurant, Kizidi also offers accommodation in three comfortable bungalows at US$40 double. It has its own boats and arranges dolphin trips at roughly the same rates as Cabs Restaurant.

PEMBA ISLAND
Lying to the northeast of the larger island of Zanzibar, directly east of the mainland port of Tanga, Pemba is visited by few travellers. While tourist facilities on Zanzibar have mushroomed in recent years, Pemba has changed little over the last decade, making it a particularly attractive destination for those who are prepared to put up with relatively basic conditions in order to 'get away from it all'.

Pemba has a more undulating landscape than Zanzibar, and is more densely vegetated with both natural forest and plantation. The main agricultural product is cloves, which Pemba now produces in greater abundance than Zanzibar. There is nothing on the island to compare with Zanzibar's Stone Town, but it does boast a number of attractive beaches, as well as some absorbing ruins dating to the Shirazi era. During holidays, traditional bullfights are sometimes held on Pemba, presumably introduced during the years of Portuguese occupation. Pemba is also a centre for traditional medicine and witchcraft. People seeking cures for spiritual or physical afflictions come from Zanzibar Island and the

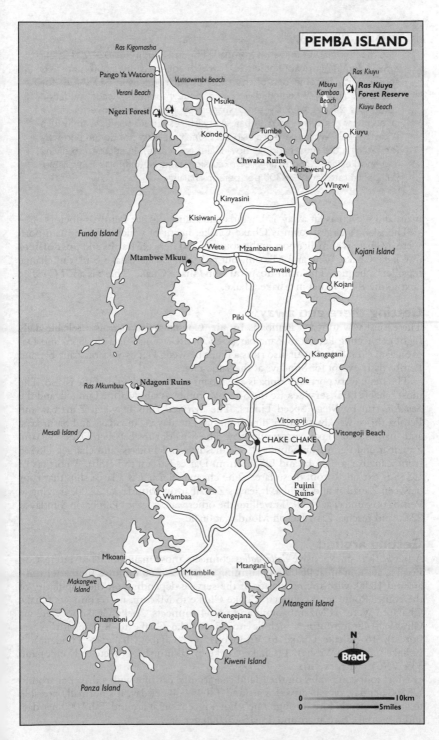

PEMBA ISLAND

FUNDU LAGOON

The most upmarket lodge on Pemba is Fundu Lagoon (tel: 024 223 2926; email: fundu@africaonline.co.za), which opened in 2000 and has subsequently become one of the most popular lodges in East Africa for dedicated and well-heeled divers and honeymooners. Accommodation comprises 20 large luxury tents shaded by *makuti* roofs overlooking a lagoon near the village of Wambaa. A stylish restaurant serves wonderful à la carte meals, while there are two bars, one on a jetty positioned perfectly for catching the sunset (drinks now included in rate). In addition to diving and snorkelling, a good range of excursions and watersports is available. Full board rates are US$300 per person sharing.

mainland – even as far away as Uganda and Zaire – to see Pemba's doctors.

The island's largest town is Chake Chake, north of which lies the main port, Wete. Mkoani is a smaller port in the southwest. There are **banks** and **post offices** in Chake Chake, Wete and Mkoani, but only the Chake Chake bank can change travellers' cheques. The main **hospital** is in Chake Chake. There is a **ZTC** office next to the ZTC Hotel in Chake Chake.

Getting there and away

The easiest way to reach Pemba is **by air**. Coastal Aviation runs a reliable daily flight connecting Pemba to Zanzibar (US$70 one-way), Tanga (US$55) and Dar es Salaam (US$85). ZanAir also runs a flight between Dar es Salaam, Zanzibar and Pemba daily except for Sundays at the same rate.

The main ferry port on Pemba is at Mkoani on the south end of the island. The most reliable **boat services** are the *Serengeti*, run by Azam Marine Limited, and the *Sepideh*, run by Mega Speed Liners. The *Serengeti* runs between Zanzibar and Pemba thrice weekly in either direction, on Tuesdays, Thursdays and Saturdays, and charges US$25 per person one-way. The *Sepideh* runs between Dar es Salaam, Zanzibar and Pemba on Mondays, Wednesdays and Fridays, and charges US$35 from Zanzibar to Pemba and US$55 from Dar es Salaam to Pemba. A port tax of US$5 is excluded from these fares. The cheaper *Aziza 1* is a large ship that runs between Zanzibar and Pemba. It leaves Zanzibar on Saturday at 22.00, arriving at Pemba on Sunday at 06.00. Travelling the other way, it leaves Pemba on Sunday at 22.00 and reaches Zanzibar on Monday at 06.00.

Getting around

A network of inexpensive *dalla-dallas* connects most main points of interest on Pemba, starting up at 06.00 and running every 15 to 60 minutes thereafter until around 16.00, with the regularity of the service depending on the popularity of the route. Route no 3 connects Chake Chake to Mkoani, no 6 connects Chake Chake to Wete via Mzambaorani and no 34 connects Cheke Chake to Wete via Chwale. Minor routings include no 35 (Chake Chake to Konde, for Ngezi Forest), 16 (Chake Chake to Vitongoji), 17 (Chake Chake to Tundaua), 5 (Chake Chake to Wesha), 4 (Chake Chake to Ukutini), 24 (Wete to Konde) and 33 (Wete to Micheveni).

Most tour companies on the island can arrange car hire with a driver at around US$60 per day, or self-drive for around Tsh45,000 per day. It's normally possible to arrange bicycle hire through one's hotel reception at around Tsh2,000 per day, and motorbike hire at around Tsh15–20,000 per day.

Chake Chake

This is the largest town on Pemba, and several centuries old, but it has never achieved a degree of importance comparable to Zanzibar Town. The busy market area and old port are pleasant to walk around, and seem very relaxed and untouristy after Zanzibar, but sightseeing is pretty much limited to the remains of an Omani Fort near the modern hospital.

The best place to stay in Chake Chake is **The Old Mission Lodge** (tel: 024 245 2786, email: swahilidivers@intafrica.com), a very relaxed and unpretentious set-up on the northern edge of the town centre. Self-contained double rooms here cost US$50, while dormitory accommodation costs US$15 per person inside and US$7 outside. A good terrace café and bar are attached, serving snacks, cakes, full meals and excellent coffee, and snorkelling, diving and several other excursions are offered.

Also recommended is the **Hotel La Taverne** (tel: 024 245 2660), where clean rooms with nets and towels cost US$15 per person. The nearby **Chake Chake Hotel**, owned by the ZTC, is a somewhat rundown angular concrete building with no running water, and charges US$10 per person. The restaurant is nothing to shout about, but the bar is one of the few in Chake Chake to serve chilled beers. Two private guesthouses lie about 4km from town, and can be reached by taking a no 34 *dalla-dalla* towards Wete. The **Venus Lodge** (tel: 0744 312484) is the first of these, a friendly and spotless lodge where self-contained doubles cost US$25. A few hundred metres further, opposite Gombani Stadium, the **Star Inn** (tel: 024 245 2190) has a selection of different rooms ranging in price from US$10 for a basic single to US$30 for a self-contained double. The staff are friendly and the food good.

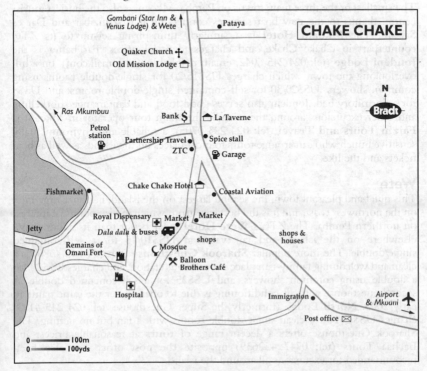

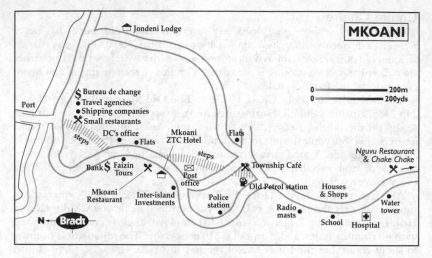

For tours, transport bookings and most other travel services, **Partnership Travel** (tel: 024 245 2278) is by far the most switched-on agency in Pemba. The newer **Jimmy Travel & Tours** next door (tel: 024 245 4193) has also been recommended, and is generally a bit cheaper. Diving and snorkelling trips can be arranged through **Swahili Divers** in the Old Mission Lodge.

Mkoani

The smallest of the three main towns on Pemba, Mkoani is also the busiest tourist centre, thanks to the new boat services connecting it to Zanzibar and Dar es Salaam. The **Mkoani Hotel** is a similarly uninspiring set-up to its ZTC counterpart in Chake Chake, and charges identical prices. Far better is the **Jondeni Lodge** (tel: 024 245 6042, email: pembablue@hotmail.com), on a hill overlooking the town, which charges US$15/20 for single/double rooms using common showers, US$20/30 for self-contained single/double rooms, and US$8 for a dormitory bed. Jondeni also serves good food and can arrange snorkelling and other excursions around the island. The main tour operator in Mkoani is **Faizin Tours and Travel** (tel: 024 223 0705), a reliable and environmentally sensitive bunch who can arrange tours to most places on the island, as well as boat tickets and the like.

Wete

This quiet and pleasant town, the second largest on the island, lies on a large inlet on the northwest coast, and it is the best base from which to visit points of interest on northern Pemba. The ZTC's **Wete Hotel** is far better than its counterparts elsewhere on the island, and fair value at US$10/15 for a self-contained single/double. The more popular **Sharook Guesthouse** (tel: 024 245 4386) is a clean and welcoming family-run place near the bus station, and charges US$20 for a double using common showers, and US$25 for a self-contained double. A second guesthouse with air conditioning is due to open under the same name in early 2003. **North Lodge** (formerly the Super Guesthouse, tel: 024 245 4193) charges US$10/25 for clean single/double rooms with a fan but no netting. The Sharook Guesthouse offers a decent range of **tours** at reasonable prices, and Bachaa Tours (tel: 0747 422639) opposite the post office has also been recommended for excursions all around the island.

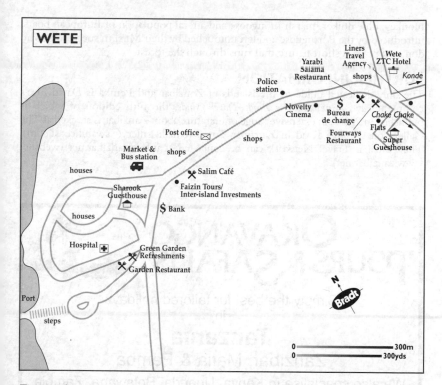

WETE

Liners Travel Agency
Wete ZTC Hotel
Yarabi Salama Restaurant
shops
Konde
Police station
Novelty Cinema
Bureau de change
Chake Chake
Fourways Restaurant
Flats
Post office
shops
Super Guesthouse
Market & Bus station
shops
houses
Salim Café
Sharook Guesthouse
Faizin Tours/ Inter-island Investments
Bank
houses
Hospital
Green Garden Refreshments
Garden Restaurant
Port
steps

N

0 ———— 300m
0 ———— 300yds

Excursions

Ras Mkumbuu Ruins These 11th century ruins on the end of the peninsula west of Chake Chake include the remains of a mosque and several pillar-tombs. The most enjoyable way to reach Ras Mkumbuu is by boat, combined with a visit to Mesali Island.

Mesali Island This small island west of Chake Chake is surrounded by a coral reef. Its idyllic beach is good for swimming, whether at high or low tide, and it's worth bringing a mask and snorkel for the excellent reef fish. The notorious pirate Captain Kidd is reputed to have had a hideout here in the 17th century. The forested interior of the island, criss-crossed by a network of clear walking trails, harbours a rich variety of birds including the endemic Pemba white-eye and sunbird.

Pujini Ruins This is about 10km southeast of Chake Chake. You can walk there and back in a day, but it is easier to travel by hired bike or car. The ruins are the remains of a 13th-century Swahili town, known locally as Mkame Ndume ('milker of men'), after a despotic king who forced the inhabitants to carry large stones for the town walls while shuffling on their buttocks. The overgrown remains of the walls and ditches can be seen, as can a walkway which joined the town to the shore, some wide stairways that presumably allowed access to the defensive ramparts, and the site of the town's well.

Ngezi Forest Reserve This small reserve on the north of the island supports an interesting range of vegetation, including the most substantial patch of moist forest on Pemba. It is a good place for birders, who can seek out the Pemba white-eye, green pigeon, scops owl and sunbird, all of which are endemic to the island. Mammals include the endemic Pemba flying fox, Kirk's red colobus, vervet monkey, blue duiker, marsh mongoose and a feral population of European boars, introduced by the Portuguese and left untouched by their Muslim successors, who don't eat pork. A short nature trail runs through the forest.

FURTHER INFORMATION

The only dedicated guide to the islands of Zanzibar and Pemba is David Else's comprehensive *Zanzibar: The Bradt Travel Guide*, the fifth edition of which is published in 2002. An extensive range of literature about Zanzibar is stocked at The Gallery on Gizenga Road in Zanzibar Town (email: gallery@swahilicoast.com). The Zanzibar Travel Network can be contacted at info@zanzibar.net (website: www.zanzibar.net).

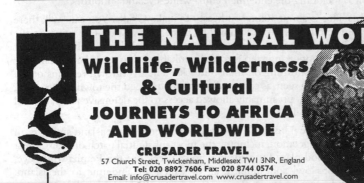

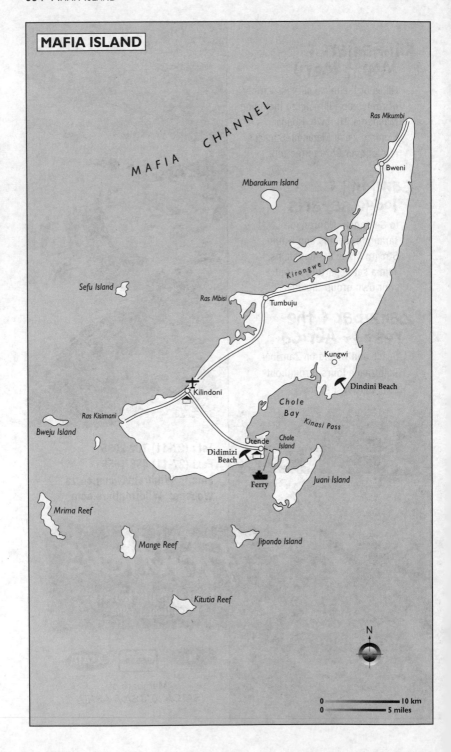

MAFIA ISLAND

Mafia Island

by Christine Osborne, updated and expanded for this edition by Philip Briggs

While Zanzibar is entrenched as probably the most popular ocean resort in East Africa, the island of Mafia 160km to its south remains virtually unknown. Poor communications with the mainland and a rather unfortunate name have not served Mafia well, but a growing trickle of visitors over recent years have been unanimous in singing the island's praises. A few interesting Swahili ruins notwithstanding, Mafia lacks for an equivalent to Zanzibar's atmospheric Stone Town, so that it cannot be recommended as an alternative destination for those whose primary interest in Tanzania's islands is cultural or historical. By contrast, the combination of a clutch of fabulous upmarket lodges, offshore diving and snorkelling that ranks with the very best in the Indian Ocean, and a conspicuous absence of hustle and crime, make it the ideal destination for those seeking an exclusive but low-key Indian Ocean retreat. Paradoxically, perhaps, Mafia also has considerable potential for budget travellers seeking a truly off-the-beaten-track and adventurous experience.

The Mafia Archipelago, which lies in the Indian Ocean some 20km east of the Rufiji River Delta in central Tanzania, probably became isolated from the mainland some 20,000 years ago. It is comprised of about 15 sandstone and coral islands and numerous smaller atolls and sandbars, none of which reaches an elevation of greater than 80m, and all but two of which are little more than 1km² in extent. The central island, known today as Mafia (though it seems that this name applied to the archipelago rather than any specific island prior to the 20th century), is by far the largest, approximately 50km long by 15km across. The second largest island is Juani, about 8km long and up to 4km wide, which lies to the southeast of the main island and was the centre of local political activity in medieval times. Sandwiched between these two larger islands, the tiny Chole Island superseded Juani as the local centre of trade in the Omani era.

The archipelago's estimated population of around 40,000 lives in rustic fishing communities and farming villages dotted all over Mafia and the smaller islands. The largest town and port on Mafia Island is Kilindoni in the southeast, the site of the airstrip, and the main landing point for dhows from the mainland. Although several local guesthouses can be found in Kilindoni, the centre of upmarket tourist development is Chole Bay on the western side of the island. The three established tourist lodges lie within 1km of each other near the village of Utende, roughly 10km from Kilindoni by road, while a newer lodge is situated on Chole Island within the bay.

The majority of the islanders are Muslim, but there are also many Christians. Voodoo manifests itself in ritual dances linked to the lunar cycle. While traditionally reserved, the islanders are tolerant of visitors provided they dress

MAFIA IN THE PAST

Little is known about the early history of the Mafia Archipelago, but presumably it has been settled for millennia, and it may well have participated in the ancient coastal trade with Arabia. The eminent archaeologist Neville Chittick regarded Mafia to be a strong candidate for the 'low and wooded' island of Menouthesias, described in the 1st-century *Periplus of the Erythrian Sea* as being two days' sail or 300 stadia (roughly 50km) from the river port of Rhapta (which, according to this theory, was situated in the Rufiji Delta). Although the anonymous writer of the *Periplus* also mentions the sewn boats and hollowed-out tree canoes that are still used widely on Mafia today (as they are elsewhere on the coast), several other aspects of the description count against Mafia. Two days rather exaggerates the sailing distance from the island to the Rufiji Delta; furthermore, the *Periplus* was either mistaken in its assertion that there are 'no wild beasts except crocodiles' on Menouthesias, or the crocs have subsequently vanished and the island's few hippos are a later arrival. For more details, see the box *Pangani and the riddle of Rhapta* on pages 260–1.

The earliest known settlement on the archipelago, Kisimani Mafia, was situated at Ras Kisimani in the far southwest of the main island. Archaeological evidence suggests that this town, which covered about three acres, was founded in the 11th century, possibly by a favoured son of the Sultan of Kilwa. Several coins minted at Kilwa have been unearthed at the site, as have coins from China, Mongolia, India and Arabia, all minted prior to 1340. A second important town, Kua, was probably founded in the 13th century, again as a dependency of Kilwa, and it must surely have usurped Kisimani as the islands' political and economic hub soon after that. In its prime, Kua was probably the second-largest city along what is now the southern coast of Tanzania, boasting seven mosques as well as a double-storey palace and numerous stone homesteads spread over an area of more than 30 acres.

Following the Portuguese occupation of the coast, Kua was chosen as the site of a Portuguese trade agency in 1515, when a fortified blockhouse was built at the town. The name Mafia (more accurately *Morfiyeh*) was well established by this time, and the islands are marked as such on the earliest Portuguese naval charts. Several explanations have been put forward for the origin of this name, the simplest and most likely being that *morfiyeh* is Arabic for archipelago. Because the archipelago lies 20km offshore, Mafia attracted a large influx of refugees from the mainland during the cannibalistic Zimba raids that dealt the final deathblow to so many coastal settlements during the late 16th century. Control of Mafia changed hands frequently in the 17th century

discreetly and behave in a manner becoming of local customs. Mafia women wear the colourful patterned *kanga* of the Swahili coast, and on weekends and religious holidays men exchange Western dress for the long, white *kanzu*. Older folk who remember the British can speak some English, as can staff working at the tourist lodges, but it can help to know a little Swahili when talking to other islanders.

Natural vegetation on Mafia ranges from tidal mangrove thickets and scrubby coastal moorlands to palm-wooded grassland and lowland rainforest. Baobabs are prominent along with the native *Albinza*. A patch of coastal high forest, the Chunguruma Forest is a dense tree canopy interlaced with lianas and having an abundant floor covering of ferns. A large reed-lined lake in central Mafia,

as Portugal's fortunes declined. An Omani naval raid in 1670 effectively terminated the Portuguese presence on the Mafia Islands, and by 1598 the entire East African coast north of modern-day Mozambique was under Omani control. Little is known about events on the islands over the next two centuries. In about 1829, however, the archipelago was attacked by the cannibalistic Sakalafa of Madagascar, who succeeded in wreaking havoc at Kua, one of the few coastal towns left untouched by their Zomba forbears 250 years earlier. Kisimani, though also attacked by the Malagasy, stumbled on into the 1870s, when a devastating cyclone dealt it a final deathblow, but Kua was abandoned to go to ruin.

One reason why Kua was not resettled after 1820 is that a new seat of the Sultanate of Zanzibar had been founded on the north end of Chole Island barely 10 years earlier. Known as Chole Mjini (Chole Town), this settlement was also attacked by the Sakalafa, but it was soon rebuilt to emerge as the most important town on the islands. Chole became the established home of a number of wealthy Omani traders and slave owners, while the main island of Mafia, known at the time as Chole Shamba (Chole Farm), was occupied by newly established coconut plantations and the slaves who worked on them. Although Chole was not so directly involved in the slave trade as Pangani, Bagamoyo or Kilwa Kivinje, it was an important stopover for slave ships heading between Kilwa and Zanzibar, and the ruined mansions that survive today indicate that it was a very wealthy settlement indeed.

Mafia was part of the Zanzibar Sultanate throughout the Omani era, and it should have remained a part of Zanzibar in the colonial era, according to a treaty that placed it under British protectorateship along with Zanzibar and Pemba Islands. However, in the complex Anglo-German treaty of 1890 Mafia was ceded to Germany in exchange for a part of what is now Malawi, and it has been administered as part of mainland Tanzania ever since. In 1892, Germany sent a local administrator to Chole, who constructed the two-storey customs house that can still be seen on the beach today. In 1913, Germany relocated its administration from Chole to the deeper harbour at Kilindoni on the main island. Two years later, Mafia was the first part of German East Africa to be captured by British forces. The island was subsequently used as the base for a series of aerial assaults on the German cruiser *Konigsberg* which, having evaded capture in the Rufiji Delta, was finally sunk on August 11 1915. A 6c German *Tanganyika Territory* stamp overprinted *Mafia* by the British and listed at £9,000 in *Stanley Gibbons* catalogue makes philatelists one of the few groups of people aware of the existence of the islands.

probably a relic lagoon dating from when the island was joined to the mainland, harbours half a dozen hippo that were washed out to sea during flooding in the Rufiji River system. Other island fauna includes a colony of flying foxes, a type of pygmy shrew, at least one bushbaby species, the monitor lizard (known locally as *kenge*) and five endemic butterflies. Monkeys and squirrels were introduced for the pot by the Portuguese. An official bird list kept by Kinasi Lodge records more than 120 different species, including five different types of sunbird, living in and around the hotel gardens. The island is of particular interest to birders for its concentrations of resident and migrant shorebirds, which include ringed plover, crab plover, grey plover, Mongolian plover, great sandplover, curlew, whimbrel and turnstone.

Of far greater ecological importance than any of Mafia's terrestrial habitats is the immensely rich marine life associated with the barrier reef that surrounds the island. Coral reefs are the most biodiverse of marine habitats, supporting innumerable small organisms that are fed upon by a dazzling variety of reef fish. Because they are associated with warm shallow water, however, coral reefs generally lie close to the mainland or to habitable islands, and are thus highly vulnerable to human exploitation, pollution and other destructive practices. The reefs off Mafia, in common with many others in East Africa, had suffered as a result of coral mining, dynamite fishing and various other human activities prior to 1995, when Tanzania's first marine park was gazetted off Mafia, with support from the Worldwide Fund for Nature. The 820km² marine park embraces most of the southern and eastern shore of Mafia, including Chole Bay and associated reefs, and a number of isolated atolls to the south of the main island, and the reefs enclosing Juani, Jipondo and Bwejuu Islands. Some 400 fish and five turtle species have been recorded in the zone around Chole Bay alone, along with 50 genera of coral, and the marine park as a whole is among the finest snorkelling and diving sites in the Indian Ocean.

CLIMATE

The Mafia Archipelago experiences a tropical climate tempered by ocean breezes. Rainfall averaging 2,000mm a year occurs mainly between April and May, although November can also be wet. February and March are hot and humid, while a strong southerly wind, the *kusi,* blows during July. The best holiday period is from June until mid-October, when the islands enjoy blue skies with temperatures kept pleasant by light coastal breezes.

GETTING THERE AND AWAY

Getting to Mafia used to be a difficult exercise without a confirmed reservation at Kinasi Lodge on Mafia Island, which has an aircraft to transfer guests. In late 1998, however, the domestic airline Precision Air began operating a thrice-weekly service to Mafia from Dar es Salaam via Zanzibar for US$100 return. Kinasi Lodge transfers clients from Dar es Salaam and the Selous Game Park (for US$70 per person one-way) and from Zanzibar (US$100 per person one-way). The flight by Cessna takes about 45 minutes from Dar es Salaam – add an hour if you come via the Selous on a spectacular flight tracing the Rufiji River Delta. Zanzibar to Mafia is one hour's flight. Mafia's small airport is situated on the edge of the main town of Kilindoni, a 15km drive from Utende, where the tourist lodges are located. The airport has a comfortable waiting room and basic toilets but there are no other facilities. Visitors holding a hotel reservation will be met at the airport. Individual travellers should ask for a Land Rover taxi which costs US$15 to Utende. There is a US$3 airport departure tax.

The options for budget travellers who wish to visit Mafia are limited to local dhows connecting Kilindoni to the mainland. These dhows are generally uncomfortable and crowded, the trip can take anything from 10 to 24 hours, and the safety record is none too inspiring. Even if these factors don't put you off, foreigners are technically forbidden from boarding local dhows, and many captains will be unwilling to transgress this ruling. If you want to give it a go, the closest possibility to Dar es Salaam is from Kimbiji, easily reached by catching the motor ferry from the city centre to Kigomboni (boats leaving every 10 minutes or so and take five minutes) then a *dalla-dalla* direct to Kimbiji (about one hour). Another possibility is from Kisiju, the closest mainland port to Mafia, situated 45km southeast of Mkuranga on the Kilwa road. There are also dhows connecting Mafia to Kilwa Kivinje. The fare should work out at around Tsh5,000, but this is negotiable, and foreigners may be asked a higher rate on account of the illegality of boarding a dhow.

GETTING AROUND
The island infrastructure is basic. Hardly any villages are connected to mains water or electricity and at the time of writing there are no tarmac roads. The road to Utende is rough in places, but the main road along the west coast between Kilindoni to Bweni has been re-graded. Elsewhere roads are sandy tracks or paths. At present there is no public transport on Mafia, with fewer than 50 vehicles, mainly Land Rover pick-ups and 4WDs belonging to the hotels, UNICEF and the Hellas fish processing factory. Hitchhiking is an accepted means of getting about, but it usually entails a long wait. Islanders also use *jahazis*, widely referred to in English as dhows, to commute between Kilindoni and outlying villages on Mafia, and for inter-island travel. Bicycles can be rented by arrangement with the Hotel Lizu in Kilindoni.

FURTHER INFORMATION
The lodges listed below can provide full information about activities on the island. Kinasi Lodge has an impressive library of books and documents covering the history and natural history of Mafia and the rest of the coast. The Mafia Island Marine Park can be contacted at tel: 023 240 2690; fax: 023 240 2526; email mimpmafia@raha.com.

WHERE TO STAY
Upmarket
Kinasi Lodge Email: kinasi@intafrica.com; web: www.mafiaisland.com. This ultimate Indian Ocean hideaway, owned by an agricultural economist born in the western Pacific, is named for the indigo pass through the outer reef that frames Mafia. The large landscaped grounds, studded with coconut palms, have an idyllic quality, sloping down to a swimming pool area and small sandy beach. Accommodation consists of 14 self-contained bungalows with *makuti* roofs, Zanzibar-style double beds enveloped in vast mosquito nets, and a wooden veranda complete with armchairs and addictive hammocks. The large, open-sided bar area contains a top-notch reference library as well as a book swap service, while the adjacent dining area serves excellent seafood. An on-site dive centre arranges dives to several sites in and around Chole Bay, as well as snorkelling trips, windsurfing and game fishing. The lodge has constructed a two-hour nature walk for birdwatching along the coastal flats, which are rich in waders, and through patches of coastal scrub that harbour sunbirds, tinker-birds and bee-eaters. Mountain bikes are available for exploring local villages. Closed during the wet season April–May. Full board rates are US$150 per person inclusive of airport transfers, laundry, lasers, windsurfing, kayaks and bicycles.
Pole Pole Bungalow Resort Tel: 022 260 1530; fax: 022 260 0140; email: contact@polepole.com; web: www.polepole.com. This small, comfortable Italian-managed lodge lies five minutes' walk from Kinasi along the same beach, and consists of nine bungalows built of basic natural materials. The large bungalows, made almost entirely from organic materials, have en-suite bathrooms, a roof fan and a large patio, and cost US$260/400 single/double FB. The beachfront *bandas* are more basic, using common showers, but do have a fan, and cost US$169/260 single/double FB. There is no swimming pool, but snorkelling (US$3 per mask and snorkel), diving (US$35 per person plus US$12 for eqipment), game fishing and other boat excursions are offered.
Chole Mjini Lodge Email: 2chole@bushmail.net; web: www.intotanzania.com. This fabulous new Treetops-style lodge, situated on Chole Island opposite the Utende lodge,

consists of six large accommodation units perched high in the baobabs amongst the crumbling 19th-century ruins of Chole Mjini. The owners, who live on site, stress that they are emphatically not catering for people seeking Sheraton-style luxury or a conventional beach retreat – there is no electricity, for starters, and the waterfront in front of the lodge is overgrown with mangroves. Nevertheless, this must rank as one of the most original and aesthetically pleasing lodges on the East African coast, and it makes an atmospheric base for diving, snorkelling and exploring Chole Island. In keeping with the eco-friendly ethos, a community fee is included in the rates, and all construction has been undertaken using local artisans and materials. Full board accommodation is in the US$110–200 per person bracket.

Moderate

Mafia Island Lodge PO Box 2, Mafia; tel: Mafia 76. This package-type hotel, built by the government in 1971, is situated on an open palm-lined beach, about 10 minutes' walk from Kinasi Lodge, directly opposite the ruins of Chole Mjini on Chole Island. It consists of 40 small but comfortable double rooms with French windows facing the sea, AC, Zanzibar beds and en-suite bathrooms. Despite the large size of this hotel, it sees very little custom, and it's easy to chuckle at the institutional architecture and dated décor, the featureless lawn running down to the beach, the gloomy bar and restaurant, and overall atmosphere of torpor that extends to the (understandably) bored staff. On the other hand, this is reflected in the very reasonable rate of US$48/96 single/double FB, with substantial discounts in April and May.

Budget

Lizu Hotel Bookings c/o Post Office, Mafia; tel: 96. This is the most comfortable of three local lodges in Kilindoni. It has basic double rooms with fan and shared washing facilities for US$10.50, and one room with en-suite bathroom. A simple bar-restaurant at the rear of the hotel sells beer, sodas and simple rice and seafood meals. Used by local traders, the hotel is a minute's walk from the market, close to the airport, and ten minutes from the dhow landing jetty.

AROUND MAFIA ISLAND
Kilindoni

All arrivals on Mafia pass through Kilindoni, the main town as well as the island's airport and sea port. New by East African standards, it was established by the Germans in 1913 on discovering that Chole Island lacked a deep-water anchorage. While Kilindoni has none of the Arab architecture of the Stone Town on Zanzibar, its coral and lime mortar shop-houses with quaint signs and rusting corrugated iron roofs exude an ambience of old Indian Ocean days.

Peaceful rather than bustling, the **market** is the centre of local life. Tomatoes, chillies, potatoes, onions, limes, dried prawns, bananas, cassava and whatever the trader can get his hands on are arranged in little piles. Stalls sell fish, spices, pottery, *kangas* and second-hand clothes. A **café** at the back is the only place in Kilindoni where a starving tourist might conceivably eat a plate of sardines and maize meal soup. There are more stores on the road descending to the dhow landing. The **Market General Supply Store** and the **Peace and Love** sell soft drinks. Off the **main square**, Utende Road has a rather gross monument presented by the fish factory. On the left is a grey weather-beaten **mosque** and further along the Roman Catholic church. Beyond a final shop-house selling dried fish are rice fields and finally coconut plantations near Utende.

A **bank** and a **post office** are located on the airport road. The National Microfinance Bank is open 08.30–15.00 Monday to Friday and 08.30–12.30 on

Saturdays. Stamps are sold at the post office, but your letter may take months to leave Mafia. Kinasi Lodge will mail your post in Dar es Salaam. The **dhow landing** in Kilindoni usually has 15–20 *jahazis* moored on the beach. Whether unloading fish or mending their nets, the fishermen object strongly to being photographed, as do the people frying cassava chips and cooking octopus on small stoves under the trees. A café next to the fish factory sells soft drinks.

North of Kilindoni

Bweni village is approximately 47km north of Kilindoni, and the drive there, following the west coast of Mafia, takes about two hours direct, or all day if you want to include swimming and a picnic. Bring everything you are likely to need from your hotel.

About 8km from Kilindoni is a picturesque swamp covered in mauve lotus. Small tilapia and catfish dart among the reeds. Further on, the old agricultural village of **Kirongwe** counts a score of houses, three stores and a market selling the usual dried octopus, bananas and coconuts. Beyond here the countryside is intensively cultivated with beans, pigeon pea and cassava. Syke's and vervet monkeys raiding the crops flee at the sound of any vehicle.

The north of Mafia is markedly different to the wetter southern part of the island, which is dominated by vast coconut plantations. After **Jimbo**, the landscape suddenly becomes open grassland with outcrops of *mia'a* or palm, and baobabs similar to the mainland coastal plain. Birdlife is plentiful with bee-eaters and lilac-crested rollers flashing amongst the trees and large flocks of guinea fowl scuttling off the road. While only about 30m above sea level, it is noticeably cooler than on the coast.

Bweni village, built behind a glistening white sand beach, seems a likely spot for future tourism development. Its traditional Swahili-style houses of coral and lime plaster are dotted among slender coconut palms. Someone will slash the top off a young coconut for you to try *madafu,* its sweet, fresh juice. Bweni women are experts at weaving striped prayer mats from the palms on the plateau.

The lighthouse at **Ras Mkumbi** is a 3km drive on a good stretch of road from Bweni. Built on coral rag on the northern tip of Mafia, the red and white structure is kept locked but the key is obtainable from a keeper in the village. It is worth climbing the 15m up to the top for a spectacular view of the Mafia Channel lying between the archipelago and the mainland. The stretch of deep blue water is reputed to offer some of the best big game fishing in East Africa.

Kisimani Mafia

Kisimani (KiSwahili for 'the place of the well') lies on Ras Kisimani, at the south end of the island 30-minutes' drive from Kilindoni. The town was an important centre during the Shirazi domination of Kilwa between the 12th and 14th centuries (see box *Mafia in the past,* pages 356–7). Legend has it that the hands of the sultan's chief mason were cut off after he built the palace, so that he could never repeat the task. The story goes on to claim that this was why a few months later Kisimani was inundated by the sea. There is little left of the submerged medieval settlement, but you can see the well for which it is named on the beach. Wandering about, you might find a few coins and pottery shards. The shady coconut palms are a nice spot for a picnic, but bring everything you want to eat or drink. A fare to Kisimani can be negotiated with one of the Land Rover pick-ups near the market place.

Utende

The three lodges on Mafia Island all lie along the beach below this small village at the end of the 15km road west from Kilindoni. Many of Utende's inhabitants are

Makonde people from the mainland, who keep their fishing boats in Chole Bay. One or two shop-houses sell strings of dried octopus and fish. Like everywhere else on Mafia, the village is quite safe to explore, being only ten minutes' walk from any of the hotels. The beach in front of Utende (close to Mafia Island Lodge) is where local dhows leave for Chole Island every 30 minutes or so, or on demand at a small extra fee.

Other places of interest

Most other villages on Mafia are inaccessible by road and, like the offshore islands, may only be visited by boat. Given advance warning, Kinasi Lodge can arrange an excursion with overnight camping.

The village of **Mchangani** is the goal for an interesting excursion winding for nearly 3km up a creek on the north side of Chole Bay. Syke's monkeys can be seen in the mangrove forests and fish eagles are commonly observed. The village of Mchangani lies on the east bank of the creek. Depart only on a high tide.

Dindini Beach is likewise only accessible at high tide. It faces the ocean from Mafia Island just north of Chole Bay. Behind the beach is a large sea-fed rock pool, which contains a variety of marine life. There are also low sand dunes and interesting vegetation on the coral rag.

Didimizi Beach is the lovely beach seen from Chole Bay, around 4km from Kinasi Lodge. You could arrange for a vehicle going to Kilindoni to drop you at the turn-off and walk back. Take refreshments.

Baracuni Island, lying 12km northwest of Mafia, can be visited by arrangement. Uninhabited and said to be very beautiful, it is used by fishing dhows.

CHOLE ISLAND

Chole is the lush, tropical island lying to the west of Kinasi Pass. With the adjacent islands of Juani and Jipondo, it forms a barrier between Mafia and the open ocean. The shallow reef in front is rich in soft corals, sea anemones and sponges, and sloping to 15m, it is a good spot to practice drift diving. The bay itself is ideal for sailing and windsurfing. The town of Chole Mjini was the main urban centre on the archipelago for much of the 19th century, the home of wealthy merchants whose plantations lay on the main island of Mafia (see boxes *Mafia in the past*, pages 356–7 and *Recollections of Chole*, opposite). Ruins dating from this era include a reasonably preserved German Customs House on the waterfront, and several more ruinous mansions dating to the Omani era. Behind the landing site are several huge pink frangipani trees that were probably planted by the Germans. A path behind the new market leading to the village brings you to a prison, whose broken cells are invaded by tangled tree roots. Farther along and also in ruins is a Hindu temple.

Hanging upside down in a nearby baobab is a colony of fruit bats of the same family as the Comoros Islands' lesser flying fox (*Pteropus seychellenis comorensis*). Each evening the bats fly across Chole Bay to feed on the cashew nut and mango trees of Mafia. Like the Comoros bats they dip over the surface of the water – an action which scientists believe may be an attempt to rid themselves of parasites. A more enchanting local explanation claims 'they are washing before evening prayers'.

Chole's population was estimated at 5,000 during the early years of German rule, but today it is no more than 1,000. The islanders cultivate smallholdings of cassava, beans, mangoes, paw-paw, citrus and passion fruit. Encouraged by Kinasi Lodge, the latter has flourished and is now exported to Mafia. Most of the menfolk fish. Winding past traditional houses, the path brings you to a beach where

RECOLLECTIONS OF CHOLE

Factual histories of the East African coast tend to focus on the activities of the ruling classes – whether indigenous, Arabic or European – largely because such accounts are drawn from historical sources written by the powerful, and archaeological excavations of their mosques and palaces. The following quotes provide a rather different perspective, though it should be borne in mind that they are not first-hand accounts, but traditions passed from one generation to the next. The woman quoted is the late Bi Hadija Mahommedi Bacha of Chole Island, and her stories are reproduced from the *Chole Handbook* with the kind permission of its editors Chris Walley and Dudley Iles. The *Chole Handbook* is available from any of the lodge gift shops on Mafia.

> The wife of an Arab slave owner said, 'I don't understand how a child lies in the womb', so [her husband] cut open a pregnant slave woman to show his wife how the foetus lay inside. That young woman was cut open like a piece of dried fish so they could see how the child lay inside the womb of its mother... Next the wife asks the slave master, 'When a monkey is shot what happens?'. So a person is found to climb up a tree, like that baobab over there. He sends a gun over there, he shoots, Pow! Down falls a human being. That slave master was called Masinda; he was the owner of Kaziwa... He was harsh! If you did anything at all, you would be made to climb a tree and shot – boom! – with a gun. You would fall down like an animal. You would already be dead and then you would be thrown away.
>
> [Under the Germans,] if someone did something wrong, that person would be hanged at the Boma there on the beach, near the Casuarina tree at the spot along the beach where people today like to sit. It was an open spot and a box would be placed below and the person's neck would be placed in a rope. It was the Germans who arranged to use the place in this manner, and indeed they were the ones who did the hanging.

fishermen can be seen mending nets, or making sails and coconut coir ropes. Chole's school and small hospital were built on foreign aid. A young Zanzibari woman is training local women how to market their weaving while her husband is teaching some of the younger men *Tingatinga* art.

Kinasi Lodge and the Pole Pole Bungalow Resort on Mafia Island operate boat-trips to Chole, or you can visit it independently from Mafia. A dhow dubbed the 'Chole taxi' leaves the beach in front of Mafia Island Lodge throughout the day – last sailing at 16.00 – a crossing of 10–15 minutes depending on the wind and tide, for a cost of Tsh200 one-way. It is also possible to charter a local boat across for a higher (but still not particularly daunting) negotiable fee. If you plan to stay more than a few hours on the island it is advisable to bring a picnic and refreshments from your hotel. There is no transport on the island. Aside from the new Chole Mjini Lodge (see *Where to stay*, pages 359–60), which isn't set up to cater to passing custom, there is also nothing that passes as a restaurant. Nor is there a budget hotel, though it's difficult to imagine anybody would object to a tent being pitched in the village for a small fee.

JUANI ISLAND

The boat trip from Mafia to Juani, site of the ruined city of Kua, takes about ten minutes longer than the one to Chole, but the island can only be approached at high tide. The landing, in a small bay sheltered by dense mangroves, is covered in thousands of opened oyster-shells. Seafood is the staple diet on Juani, but unlike Chole, Juani has no well water, and locals practice rain-dependent cultivation. Beneath three big baobabs near the landing, your shoes crunch on a buried civilisation. Bits of blue and white pottery from Shirazi suggesting trade links with China are embedded in the dirt. In the past, people from the mainland came to Juani to bathe in a seawater cave reputed to have curative properties for rheumatism. It is a long, difficult walk across to the ocean side, where there are also said to be three turtle-nesting beaches. The Kua Channel slices a tiny chunk off Juani as it opens into Chole Bay. It makes a superb picnic excursion with birdwatching and swimming. A friendly grouper lives in one of the rock pools at the southern end.

The ruined city of **Kua** (see box *Mafia in the past*, pages 356–7), spread across 15 acres on the west coast of Juani, was the Shirazi capital of Mafia. It was one of the few East African ports to be continuously inhabited from medieval times into the early 19th century, when it was sacked by raiders from Madagascar. A trail hacked out of the undergrowth leads up to a large building shedding masonry: the former palace, still revered locally as a 'spirit place' where offerings such as bits of glass are left. The path passes other ruined edifices, including two 14th-century mosques and a series of tombs. The caretaker expects and deserves a small gratuity; ask him to show you the foundations of the house referred to in the box *Kua's Revenge* below. There is a guide and map of the ruins, as well as the report on its archaeology, in the library at Kinasi Lodge.

KUA'S REVENGE

The political relationship between Kisimani and Kua is unclear, but an intriguing if unverifiable oral tradition recounted by T M Revington in an essay in *Tanganyika Notes and Records*, suggests that it was not always amicable:

> The people of Ras Kisimani constructed a ship, and when it was finished and still on the stocks, they made a feast to which they invited the people of Kua. From amongst the guests they took by force several children, laid them on the sand, and launched the ship over their bodies. When the Kua people heard what had been done at Ras Kisimani, they were infuriated and thought out a scheme of revenge. Seven or eight years later, when they thought that the incident had been forgotten, an invitation was sent to the inhabitants of Ras Kisimani to attend a wedding at Kua. When the guests arrived in the evening they were ushered to a room that had been especially prepared beneath a house; the hosts one by one left their guests on the excuse of inquiring into the food, until only an old man remained to entertain them. This he did so well that the doors were bricked up without the guests perceiving it. The bodies are there to this day.

So, too, is the sealed off basement in which the bodies lie, according to the site's caretaker, who claims that it is situated below the ruins in front of his hut!

JIPONDO ISLAND

Jipondo is a long, low-lying island another 20 minutes' sail from Juani. It too has little fresh water, so the inhabitants perform their ablutions in the sea. Coming ashore, a white mosque is one of the first things you see. The big *jahazi* dhow at the entrance was built 15 years ago, but it has never been launched and is subsequently something of a museum piece. Jipondo people are well known as shipmasons, and use only traditional tools. Even the nails are hand-made and the holes are plugged with local kapok and shark fat. Local women play a prominent role in trading as well as fishing. They also sail boats, which is unusual in African society, and are more affable and confident than women elsewhere.

Another unusual aspect of Jipondo is that cultivation is carried out at one end of the island while the people live in an urban community at the other. The village, which consists of traditional Swahili-style houses with *makuti* roofs, is laid out in a grid pattern. As on Chole and Juani, there is no transport other than boats which shelter on the western side of the narrow neck of the island. On holidays Jipondo children hold sailing races in toy *ngalawas* with sails made out of plastic bags. The island has one school but no other social services, and only a basic shop. Local cattle are given water each evening from one or two private wells. Otherwise the island depends on rain which is trapped in a primitive concrete catchment area.

DIVING OFF MAFIA

Underwater Mafia is a paradise for divers and snorkellers, with a staggering variety of hard and soft corals and an immense variety of tropical fish. All of the lodges on Mafia offer diving excursions as well as full PADI courses. Kinasi Lodge specialises in diving holidays and offers every conceivable type of dive site

SNORKELLING FROM MAFIA

The snorkelling possibilities off Mafia are among the finest in East Africa, whether for beginners or the experienced. Many of the reefs lie in very shallow water, and the constant tidal movements and clear water create great light conditions, showing off the wonderful colours of the corals and the fish that feed around them.

A good starting site – one of the finest around the islands – is the area around the two larger coral islets in Kinasi Pass, which has good protected anchorage. The lionfish and titan triggerfish are very common here, while a pool hidden in the centre of the largest islet harbours small groups of nocturnal cardinal fish. The bommie adjacent to the largest islet falls away to about 15m and houses a fascinating complex of corals and fish.

Another good site is the so-called Coral Garden on the shallow reef backing the Chole and Kinasi Walls. This site reaches a maximum depth of 8m (though the snorkeller is more usually in 3–6m-deep water (and supports a high diversity of reef fish concentrated around several bommies, as well as stands of fire coral (*Millepora spp*). Also close to the lodges is the Chole Channel, where a shallow reef with many soft corals and seagrasses slopes to a depth of 15m. A high diversity of bottom-living filter feeders can be found in this area, while numerous small coral bommies support their own individual communities.

Several other good snorkelling sites lie further afield around Mafia and the smaller islands. The dive centres at Kinasi or Pole Pole Lodges will be able to offer travellers further details.

POPULAR DIVES

Kinasi Wall This sheltered bank reef sloping from 8–21m and extending for approximately 800m is a great place to see many species of corals and a variety of shoaling and reef fish, including wrasse and large groupers. There are also turtles, the hawksbill being the most commonly encountered.

Chole Wall Joining Kinasi Wall is another long bank of coral sloping to 15m, which offers good visibility and a rich tapestry of corals with clouds of brilliant fish. It forms an excellent introduction for beginners as well as a great night dive.

The Pinnacle A 12m spire of ancient coral rock pokes out of the water inside of Kinasi Pass. There is a thrilling dive down to the base 24m deep, with a variety of large local residents including a huge cod, a moray eel and giant batfish

Kinasi Pass After descending the pinnacle, divers usually head out into the pass for an awesome drift-dive among shoals of juvenile and adult reef fish, parrotfish, groupers, tunny, barracuda and big pelagics including sharks, which come in with the current. Dutch tourists who had dived in many exotic locations described it as 'fantastic'.

Dindini North Wall and Forbes Bay Part of the barrier reef on the southeast coast of Mafia, these are two of many thrilling dives outside the bay. Grouper, sharks, guitarfish and enormous tuna are seen off the Dindini Wall, which lies close to the drop-off where the edge of the continental shelf plunges to more than 300m. Forbes Bay presents a spectacular coral wall frequented by a great diversity of fish, including many large rays. The boat trip to the site, 10km north of Kinasi Pass, is a thrilling excursion past jagged cliffs, with the chance of taking giant trevally and other game fish on a trolling rig.

– reefs and bommies, channels, walls, caves, drift, ocean and night dives. All these are accessible in a day, while diving safaris catering for 12 people can be arranged to destinations further afield such as Ras Mkumbi, Forbes Bay southeast of Mafia, and the spectacular reef complex around the Songo Songo Islands. This island group lies about 80km south of Mafia and about 50km north of Kilwa.

Almost all Mafia's best diving is in depths of less than 30m. The Marine Park off Chole Bay has most examples of coral including giant table corals, delicate seafans, whip corals and huge stands of blue and pink-tipped staghorn coral. As well as the spectacular variety of reef fish there are turtles and large predatory fish such as grouper, napoleon and barracuda. Manta rays and several species of shark are encountered in Kinasi Pass. See also the box *Popular Dives* above.

The lodges on Mafia also offer night dives, which allow one to encounter a variety of reef creatures that are active at night in order to avoid daytime predators. As the light fades and the rich 'soup' of plankton rises from deeper water, the daytime, rock-like appearance of corals is transformed into a brilliance of colour as the polyps emerge from their stony cups to feed on the plankton. Many sheltering, daytime fish will be seen resting amongst the corals and in crevices, while octopus, sea cucumbers and crayfish forage on the reef. Night diving focuses the attention on the many small, delicate reef species usually missed during the day. A spectacular occurrence is the spawning behaviour of corals. Chole Wall and the Coral Gardens are an excellent night dive.

FISHING OFF MAFIA

Mafia is one of the world's great fishing grounds. I had heard this since my childhood, but although mad about fishing, it was many years before I found myself fighting a giant trevally in the Kinasi Pass.

That there are big fish around Mafia is certain. There are even huge fish off Mafia, but at the time of writing there are few facilities for catching the legendary pelagics (fish of the open ocean). You will catch kingfish, barracuda, dorado and trevally, and the reef fishing is second to none, but marlin, sailfish and wahoo – prey of most serious international fishermen – are a rare sight when the boat returns.

Of the local fishing grounds, Mafia itself, the deep channel off Ras Mkumbi and the inshore waters of the Rufiji Delta offer some of the best opportunities in East Africa. In 1950, the author Sir Arthur Conan Doyle set an all-Africa record for a dorado of 34.2kg, which still stands, and judging from the size of the fish you see while blue-water diving, Mafia has the potential to break many other world records. A dog-toothed tuna landed when I was there weighed 55kg.

The main game-fishing season extends from August to March, but reef and channel fishing on both light and heavy tackle as well as fly-fishing in the saltwater creeks is good at any time. July to November is the main season for dog-toothed and yellowfin tuna, bonito, kingfish, wahoo, trevally, cobia and rainbow runners following the bait fish. December to March is the billfish run.

Other species such as the five-fingered jack and the horse mackerels *karambisi* and *kolikoli* are caught at all times using fish bait or spoons. The wahoo found on the seaward side of most reefs, will strip off 50–60m in the first burst while kingfish can take 90m or more in the initial run. Six-inch feathered jigs, spoons and the *Rapala magnum* are popular lures, while a fresh bonito – if you can land one – makes excellent bait for the bigger pelagics.

A member of the International Game Fishing Association, Kinasi Lodge has basic weighing facilities. Their boat takes four rods with tackle supplied, but keen fishermen might prefer to bring their own equipment. It is also possible to rent a traditional outrigger for inshore casting. A very limited number of fishing lines, hooks and sinkers are sold in Kilindoni Market.

There is an annual Mafia Island fishing competition staged in February by Kinasi Lodge.

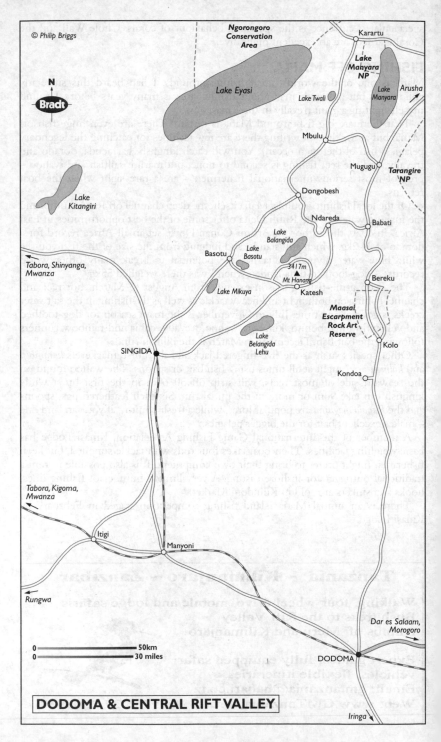

© Philip Briggs

DODOMA & CENTRAL RIFT VALLEY

Dodoma and the Central Rift Valley

This chapter covers Dodoma, the official capital of Tanzania, as well as a number of relatively obscure sites in the central Rift Valley that are reasonably accessible from the rough road that leads northward from Dodoma to Tarangire National Park and Arusha. Dodoma itself – political status notwithstanding – is of little interest to travellers except as a place to crash for the night, and the same can reasonably be said for the vast and predominantly flat badlands that lie to its east. Not so the central Rift Valley, which sees very few tourists, but nevertheless boasts a string of worthwhile attractions likely to be highly alluring to travellers with a yen for getting right off the beaten track. Highlights of this little-known region range from the renowned rock paintings around Kolo to the scenic and eminently climbable Mount Hanang; from numerous shallow natural lakes studded with all manner of birds to the opportunity to interact with traditional pastoralists such as the Barabaig and Bulu.

CLIMATE

Dodoma and the Rift Valley to its north have a climate typical of semi-arid parts of Africa. During sunlight hours, temperatures are high to very high, but the heat is less noticeable than on the coast because humidity levels tend to be relatively low. At night, the heat swiftly dissipates, and temperatures are generally pleasantly cool to slightly chilly. Rainfall patterns are typical of Tanzania, though the actual amount of precipitation in this drought-prone region is rather low, so that travel is generally as straightforward during the rainy season as at drier times of year. Mount Hanang supports its own microclimate, moister than elsewhere in the region, and often quite cold on the upper slopes. Mbulu, which lies in the highlands immediately west of the Rift Valley, is also far cooler than other places described in this chapter.

GETTING AROUND

Dodoma is a major route focus and it forms the southern gateway to the region described in this chapter. It is connected to Dar es Salaam and Morogoro by a good surfaced road and reliable bus services, to Arusha and Iringa by rougher gravel roads, and to Tabora, Mwanza and Kigoma by rail (see box *The Central Railway*, pages 374–5). Most of the sites covered in this chapter can be reached in a private 4WD, or any other vehicle with good clearance, but many roads are too rough to be a realistic prospect in an ordinary saloon car. Public road transport can be used to reach practically all sites covered in this chapter, bearing in mind that the combination of poor roads and rundown buses means you're unlikely to get anywhere in a rush.

DODOMA

The city of Dodoma, set at an altitude of 1,135m on the arid, windswept plains that characterise the central Tanzanian plateau, is the mildly improbable designated capital of Tanzania. The notion of Dodoma becoming the post-colonial capital of Tanzania was raised by parliament as early as 1959, during the transitional period leading up to independence, on the equitable basis that it is the country's most centrally located large town. President Nyerere formally earmarked Dodoma for this role in 1974, and it was originally expected to function as full capital before 1990. Lack of funding, an absence of decent roads in three directions – and quite possibly the sense of contrivance attached to the entire project – have conspired to ensure that this deadline has been set back repeatedly over the past 25 years. The national parliament finally moved across to Dodoma in February 1996, but most

THE GOGO OF DODOMA

Dodoma is the principal town of the Gogo (referred to in Swahili as Wagogo) people, and its name – probably in use before any major settlement existed at the site – is derived from the local word *Idodomya*, which means 'Place of Sinking'. The most widely accepted explanation for this name is that it was coined by a group of villagers who came down to a stream to collect water, to find an elephant stuck irretrievably in the muddy bank. Another version of events is that a local clan stole some cattle from a neighbouring settlement, slaughtered and ate the stolen beasts, then placed their dismembered tails in a patch of swamp. When a search party arrived, the thieves claimed that the lost animals had sunk in the mud (whether or not anybody actually believed this unlikely story goes unrecorded!).

One of the most populous of Tanzania's ethno-linguistic groups, the Gogo people are semi-pastoral Bantu-speakers, noted within Tanzania for their exceptional musicianship and basketwork. Their homeland around Dodoma is characterised by a low annual rainfall figure, and historically it has proved to be unusually prone to drought and crop failure. Gogo oral tradition recalls more than half a dozen serious famines in the 19th century. The first of these, and according to tradition the most severe, is remembered by the name *Mpingama* ('Hindrance'). The famine of 1870, referred to in the writings of Henry Stanley, is remembered as *Mamudemu* ('Burst Intestine'). A famine in 1881 is known as *Kubwa-Kidogo* (Big-Small), presumably because it was initiated by a plague of quelea – a sparrow-sized bird that sometimes flock in their tens of thousands to descend locust-like on grain fields.

The threat of famine has played a significant role in moulding the lifestyle and society of the Gogo, who traditionally live in small permanent villages of wood-and-clay huts, around which they practise low-yield subsistence agriculture. Herders would, however, move long distances to find grazing and water for their cattle, relying – particularly in years of low rainfall – on a co-operative social structure that allowed for the communal use of water sources and grazing within extended clans. The construction of several large dams within a 100km radius of Dodoma region notwithstanding, recurrent drought remains a feature of the region to this day. One of the most severe famines in living memory occurred in the early 1960s, when an at least 600,000 people received emergency food rations.

government departments and embassies are still based out of the former capital of Dar es Salaam, a situation that seems unlikely to change in the immediate future.

Dodoma developed as an important stopover on the 19th-century caravan route to Lake Tanganyika, and was made a regional administration centre after Germany built a railway station there in 1910. In 1915, Germany gave serious consideration to having Dodoma replace Dar es Salaam as the colonial capital. This plan might well have been realised after World War I, had Tanganyika not been mandated to Britain, which regarded Dodoma as having few advantages over Dar es Salaam other than a central location. The British administration must have been further dissuaded by the series of famines that affected the region between 1916 and 1920, cruelly capped by an influenza epidemic that claimed at least 30,000 lives. Nevertheless, Dodoma grew steadily between the wars, in large part due to its strategic location at the junction of the central railway and the trans-Tanzania road, which made it one of the country's most important internal crossroads. The town's national importance declined after a much better north–south road was constructed between Iringa and Morogoro, but it retained its role as the market centre for a vast but low-yielding agricultural region producing maize, beans, peanuts, grains and wine – as well as boasting several large cattle ranches.

Since becoming designated capital, Dodoma has experienced a high influx of people from surrounding rural areas and other parts of the country. The city's population has risen from 45,000 in 1978, when it was the 13th-largest urban centre in the country, to an estimated 170,000, placing it eighth on that list in 2002. But whatever its past and future claims to importance (and we *are* talking about a town that served as a staging post on the renowned Cape-to-Cairo flights of the 1930s), Dodoma remains unremittingly 'small town' in atmosphere and of limited interest to tourists. True, there must be some travellers out there who collect capital cities as others collect passport stamps, in which case a foray into Dodoma might well be the highlight of a visit to Tanzania. Wine enthusiasts, too, might be tempted to visit Dodoma to taste the product of Tanzania's viniculture industry, founded by a priest in 1957, at source. The local wine and port can be tasted at the Tanganyika Vineyard Company on the outskirts of town, but it's really nothing special, and is just as readily available in Arusha and other tourist centres. Otherwise, you'd be unlikely to visit Dodoma from choice, and if for some reason you do wash adrift there, then it probably won't be long before you think about moving on.

Getting there and away

Most travellers who pass through Dodoma are on one of the trains crossing between Dar es Salaam and Kigoma or Mwanza. Coming from the west, should you want to take a proper look at Dodoma, there's nothing stopping you from buying a ticket as far as Dodoma and spending a night there before bussing on to Dar es Salaam the next day. Coming in the opposite direction, it's possible to buy a ticket out of Dodoma from the railway station in Dar es Salaam. Westbound trains pass through Dodoma between 08.00 and 10.00 the morning after they leave Dar es Salaam. For further details, see the box *The Central Railway*, pages 374–5.

The 450km road between Dar es Salaam and Dodoma is surfaced in its entirety and shouldn't take longer than five or six hours to cover in a private vehicle. A fairly steady stream of buses runs between the past and designated capitals, generally leaving before midday and taking around seven hours. You can pick up these buses at Morogoro.

Dodoma is strategically positioned in the centre of Tanzania. As a consequence, many travellers are tempted to cut between other parts of the country through

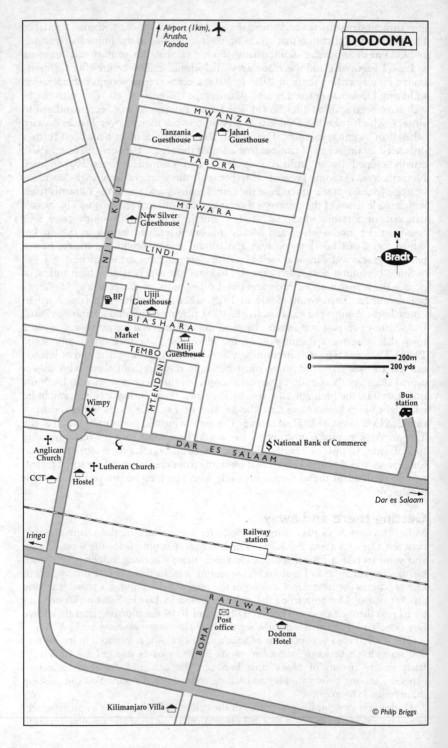

DODOMA

Airport (1km),
Arusha,
Kondoa

Bradt

N

MWANZA

Tanzania
Guesthouse

Jahari
Guesthouse

TABORA

MTWARA

New Silver
Guesthouse

LINDI

NJIA KUU

BP

Ujiji
Guesthouse

BIASHARA

Market

Mliji
Guesthouse

TEMBO

MTENDENI

0   200m
0   200 yds

Wimpy

Bus
station

Anglican
Church

Lutheran Church

DAR ES SALAAM

National Bank of Commerce

CCT

Hostel

Dar es Salaam

Iringa

Railway
station

RAILWAY

BOMA

Post
office

Dodoma
Hotel

Kilimanjaro Villa

© Philip Briggs

Dodoma, based solely on the impressions of distance gained from a map. It's emphatically worth stressing that most plans which hang on bussing through Dodoma as a 'short cut' should be nipped firmly in the bud, certainly if they involve using the direct road south to Iringa, north to Arusha or west to – well anywhere in the west really. Should you use one of these routes, buses generally leave in either direction in the early morning – you're advised to book a seat an afternoon in advance and to check the exact time of departure (bearing in mind you'll almost certainly be quoted Swahili time).

Note that while it would be an act of masochism to bus along the 440km road between Dodoma and Arusha for the pleasure of it, there are a couple of spots along this road that really *are* worth making an effort to visit, as covered later in this chapter. A few days exploration of the region between Dodoma and Arusha would allow you to break the unsurfaced 330km south of the Tarangire National Park junction into three discrete chunks, an altogether more manageable prospect than covering the road in one go.

Where to stay
Moderate
Dodoma Hotel Tel: 026 232 2991; fax: 026 232 4911. Formerly run by the TRC but now in private hands, this attractively designed building is directly opposite the railway station. The rooms are excellent value at Tsh10,000/12,000 self-contained single/double for Tanzania residents. Non-residents must technically pay US$25/30, but we were asked the resident rates when we last stayed here, and so probably will you, unless you draw attention to your non-resident status – tourists aren't exactly something the receptionist encounters on a daily basis. This is also the best place to eat in Dodoma, at least for those whose taste stretches much beyond *ugali* or rice and slop. The restaurant serves good, sensibly priced meals, for instance steak and chips for Tsh3,000, as well as a three-course set menu for Tsh6,000. There is live music in the bar on some nights.

Budget
The **Kilimanjaro Villa** is probably the most attractive of the cheaper options, in a leafy suburban property about 500m from the railway station. Large self-contained rooms cost US$5/7 and rooms using communal facilities cost US$4/5. Also worth a look is the **CCT Hostel**, a church-run place about 300m from the railway station next to a large domed church, offering a variety of rooms from between US$5 and US$7. This used to be a very clean and reasonably pleasant place to stay, but a recent report suggests it has gone downhill over the last couple of years. Food is available, though alcoholic drinks are banned from the premises.

Shoestring
There are at least ten basic resthouses clustered around the market and bus station. It's difficult to make any specific recommendations – for starters, half of them are likely to be full on any given day – but you should have no problem finding a room for around Tsh2,000. Most places have nets and communal showers, so I'd tend to pass over a room that doesn't.

Where to eat
The **Dodoma Hotel** opposite the railway station is a reliable and central bet for decent if unmemorable Western-style dishes. The **ice-cream parlour** opposite the Wimpy has been recommended by a reader who visited most major towns in Tanzania as possibly the best in the country. The same reader rates the **NK Disco** as the most kicking spot in the town centre, while another recommends the

THE CENTRAL RAILWAY

Between 1905 and 1914, Germany constructed a 1,238km railway line from Dar es Salaam to Kigoma, following the centuries-old caravan route, through Dodoma and Tabora to Ujiji, that had been used by Burton and Speke on their quest for the Nile, and by Stanley in his search for Livingstone. Almost a century later, the so-called Central Railway Line remains the best way for budget-conscious travellers to get between the coast and the west of Tanzania, if only because it is cheaper than flying and more comfortable than bussing.

Expanded since German times, the central line now consists of two main lines, running from Dar es Salaam to Mwanza on Lake Victoria and Kigoma on Lake Tanganyika, and stopping en route at Morogoro, Dodoma and Tabora. The train splits at Tabora, with one half going on to Mwanza and the other to Kigoma. A branch line running from Tabora to Mpanda is run as a separate service. Opened in 1999, another branch line, also run as a self-standing service, connects Dodoma to Singida via Manyoni.

Westbound trains leave Dar es Salaam on Tuesday, Wednesday, Friday and Sunday at 17.00, while trains out of Kigoma and Mwanza leave on Tuesday, Thursday, Friday and Sunday, usually at around 16.00. The full trip on either line is scheduled to take 40 hours, and often it does just that, but delays are increasingly frequent and it's not unusual to pitch up 10 hours late. On the Mpanda sideline, trains leave from Tabora on Monday, Wednesday and Friday at 21.00 and from Mpanda on Tuesday, Thursday and Saturday at 13.00, with the trip taking anything from 10 to 15 hours. Trains for Singida leave Dodoma on Wednesday, Friday and Sunday at 08.00, while trains for Dodoma leave Singida on Monday, Thursday and Saturday at the same time – the trip takes about 19 hours.

There are three classes on all trains except those heading between Dodoma and Singida. First class consists of two-berth compartments and second class consists of six-berth compartments. Men and women may not share a first- or second-class compartment unless they book it as a whole. One-way tickets between Dar es Salaam and Kigoma or Mwanza work out at around US$45/35/25 for first/second/third class. Tickets between Mpanda and Tabora work out at US$16/11/6 for first/second/third class. The Dodoma–Singida line is third class only and works out at around US$6.

Tickets on the main central line can only be booked in advance at Dar es Salaam, Kigoma, Tabora and Mwanza, and it's generally advisable to book as far in advance as possible (though odds of getting a ticket on the day aren't bad). Elsewhere you will have to get on the train and hope for the best. It is

Climax Club on the outskirts of town as a good place to meet expatriates, down a cold beer, eat, or swim in the pool.

KONDOA

Kondoa, the principal town of the Irangi people, lies on the north bank of the small but perennial Kondoa River, roughly 160km north of Dodoma and some 4km west of the so-called Great North Road to Arusha. Comprised of a dust-blown grid of roads lined with low-rise shops and houses, Kondoa exudes something of a Wild West character, and it's a more than adequate place to break up the journey north from Dodoma. Nevertheless, a decided deficit of distinguishing features means that Kondoa would scarcely warrant a mention in a travel guide, were it not the

difficult to buy tickets for the Tabora–Mpanda trains except at the terminal towns, but since first and second class are seldom fully booked, you should be all right on the night! There is no direct service between Kigoma and Mwanza. You will have to take a train to Tabora, where you can make an onward booking. Extra carriages are added at Tabora, so most people have no problem getting through.

As for eating and drinking, the dining cars on the lines to Kigoma and Mwanza serve acceptable and reasonably priced meat, fish and chicken meals, with beers and sodas also available. If you travel first class and do not want to leave your cabin empty, the steward can bring meals to you. In second class I would have no hesitation about going to the dining car provided other passengers remain in the compartment. No meals are currently available on the lines to Mpanda and Singida. On all lines, vendors sell snacks, meals, sodas and bottled water through the window at most large and many small stations. Still, many travellers will want to stock up on a few packaged foods and drinks before they travel.

Historical the central line may be, convenient too, but whether it would rank among the world's greatest rail journeys is debatable. Scenically, the trip is less than spectacular, with the stretch between Dodoma and Tabora passing through what is perhaps the most barren and monotonous part of Tanzania, a seemingly endless plain of baked red sand and sparse *brachystegia* woodland. The scenery is lusher closer to Kigoma, with patches of indigenous forest, swamp and dense *miombo* woodland along the line, while the stretch between Shinyanga and Mwanza on Lake Victoria is memorable for the strange granite formations that break the monotony.

Nor would it do to eulogise about the amenities. First and second class compartments may have a light, fan and running water, but you can count yourself lucky if all three are operating. The train also seems to get dirtier every time I use it; on several recent trips a scourge of cockroaches inhabited our compartment, spiced with a pervasive smell of sweat and urine. As for third class – seated carriages with more passengers than seats – well, it's only worth thinking about if you value neither your comfort nor your possessions. The trains are better than the buses, but don't expect much more than that!

Finally, do take note that theft from train windows at night is not unusual. You should close the windows securely when you turn the light off, using the block of wood provided for this purpose. Don't leave loose objects lying around the compartment; keep your luggage under the bunks. If you leave the compartment take all valuables with you.

most convenient base from which to explore the proposed Maasai Escarpment Rock Art Reserve, covered later in the chapter.

Getting there and away

The 160km road to Dodoma isn't in the greatest condition at the best of times, and it occasionally becomes impassable after heavy rain. The trip will take the best part of four hours in a private vehicle, and longer in one of the regular buses that run between the two towns.

The road northwards to Arusha is no better, at least not until the Tarangire National Park junction, which lies about 170km north of Kondoa. The 110km road between this junction and Arusha is surfaced and in good condition. In a private vehicle, the drive from Arusha should take up to six hours. Direct buses can take as long as 12 hours, for which reason it's advisable to break the trip up with a night at Babati or similar. Regular public transport runs between Kondoa and Kolo (20km) and on to Babati (70km).

Infrequently used by tourists, a reasonable unsurfaced road leads eastward from Kondoa to Korogwe on the Moshi–Tanga road, running across the southern Maasai Steppe and passing through the small town of Kibaya and more substantial settlement of Handeni. At least one bus daily covers the road from Kondoa to Handeni, from where there is regular transport on to Korogwe, Tanga and Moshi. Should you need to spend the night in Handeni, there are several inexpensive lodgings, including the Home Best and Tulivu Guesthouses.

Where to stay
Budget
New Planet Hotel Tel: Kondoa 180. This pleasant and well-managed small hotel lies about 200m from the bus station and charges Tsh5,000 for a self-contained double with net, fan and running water.

Sunset Beach Hotel Tel: Kondoa 152. This is another clean and pleasant set-up, though less convenient than the above for travellers dependent on public transport, since it lies at least 1km from the bus station. Self-contained doubles with fan and net cost Tsh4,000.

Shoestring
Savannah Inn Guesthouse A clean and friendly local guesthouse, only 300m from the bus station, and charging Tsh2,000 for a single using common shower, or Tsh3,500 for a self-contained double.

New Splendid Guesthouse Similar to the above, with rooms using common shower at Tsh2,000/3,000 single/double.

Where to eat
The restaurant at the **New Planet Hotel** is the best in town, serving tasty meals such as chicken and chips or steak and rice in the Tsh1,000–1,500 range. A pleasant spot for a drink is the **Just Imagine Bar**, a green outdoor drinking hole right opposite the New Splendid Guesthouse

MAASAI ESCARPMENT ROCK ART RESERVE
The prodigious rock art of the Kondoa region is among the most ancient and stylistically varied on the African continent, but although it makes for a reasonably straightforward addition to a standard northern circuit safari, it has thus far received greater attention from academics and archaeologists than from tourists. Some 200 rock art sites have been documented in the region, with new ones still being discovered from time to time. The greatest concentration of sites lies in the vicinity of Kolo, a small village straddling the Great North Road some 20km north of Kondoa, and the centre of the proposed Maasai Escarpment Rock Art Reserve, the first in East Africa to be dedicated to prehistoric art. This roughly 600km² sanctuary, bounded by the Bubu River to the west and Maasai Escarpment to the east, will protect at least 50 rock art panels, most of which lie along the eastern escarpment or stand on the hills overlooking the Bubu River.

The concentration of rock art sites around Kolo and Kondoa is the largest in Africa north of the Zambezi and south of the Sahel. To some extent, this is simply due to the lay of the land. Like the equally rich South African Drakensberg and Zimbabwean Plateau, Kondoa is endowed with numerous granite outcrops suitable for painting, though it is notable that many equally suitable regions – the Lake Victoria Basin and Masasi leap to mind in Tanzania – lack for a significant concentration of paintings. The major rock art sites in Kondoa District are generally situated within small caves or beneath solid overhangs aligned to an east–west axis, a propensity that might reflect the preferences of the artists, or might simply have provided conditions favourable to preservation from the elements. The paintings of Kondoa and Kolo are tentatively placed at between 200 and 4,000 years old, and the identity and intent of the artists is a matter of speculation (see box *But what does it mean?*, pages 382–3).

The pigments for the paintings were made with leaf extracts (yellow and green), powdered ochre and manganese (red and black), and possibly bird excrement (white), and were bound together by animal fat. The subjects and styles vary greatly. Most common are various animals, with giraffe and eland probably the most widely depicted creatures. It has been suggested that these animals might have held a mystical significance to the artists, but it is equally possible they were simply favoured as prey – while almost every common herbivore is reasonably well represented across the various sites, paintings of predators are conspicuous in their scarcity. A large number of panels also contain human figures, generally highly stylised and often apparently engaged in ritual dances or ceremonies. At some sites, particularly those of the relatively recent and unformed 'late white' style, readily identifiable subjects are vastly outnumbered by abstract or geometric figures, the significance of which can only be guessed at. A common feature of the more elaborate panels is the jumbled superimposition of images, which is now widely regarded to be a deliberate ploy to associate two or more significant images with each other.

The recent proposal to enshrine the Kondoa rock art as a UNESCO World Heritage Site states that 'in terms of conservation, most of the sites are stable and relatively well preserved although there are a variety of problems including salt encrustation, erosion, water damage, and fading caused by sunlight'. Exposure to the elements notwithstanding, the rock art has been left undisturbed by locals in the past because it is regarded as sacred or taboo. In 1931, a government employee AT Culwick documented an example of one such taboo, so deeply ingrained that its source had evidently been forgotten. When Culwick needed to climb Ilongero Hill near Singida on official business, the chief of the village at the base warned him off, saying that the hill was inhabited by a demon. Culwick eventually persuaded the reluctant chief and entourage to accompany him on the ascent, where he discovered a large shelter covered with ancient rock art. The fear displayed by the villagers before climbing, combined with their startled reaction to the rock panel, left Culwick in no doubt that they had genuinely never suspected the existence of the paintings.

The erosion of traditional beliefs in recent years places the art at greater threat of local interference. A few sites have already been partially defaced by graffiti or scratching. Tourist volumes may be low, but unofficial guides have been recorded splashing the paintings with water to bring out the colours for snap-happy visitors, and many tourists photograph the paintings using a flash, which can cause great damage to sensitive organic pigments over repeated exposure. More bizarrely, a local legend that the Germans buried a hoard of gold near one of the rock art sites during World War I has resulted in fortune-seekers manually excavating and dynamiting close to several rock sites. Under such circumstances, the formal proclamation of the proposed reserve – hopefully to be followed by its addition to the UNESCO World Heritage Site list – will be a welcome move indeed.

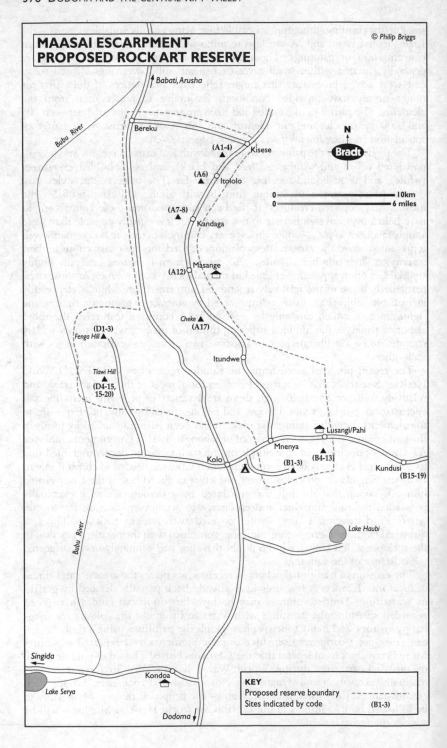

MAASAI ESCARPMENT
PROPOSED ROCK ART RESERVE

© Philip Briggs

↑ Babati, Arusha

Bubu River

Bereku

(A1-4)

Kisese

(A6)

Itololo

N

Bradt

(A7-8)

0   10km
0   6 miles

Kandaga

(A12)

Masange

Cheke ▲
(A17)

(D1-3)
Fenga Hill ▲

Itundwe

Tlawi Hill
(D4-15,
15-20)

Lusangi/Pahi

Mnenya

(B4-13)

(D1-3)

Kolo

(B1-3)

Kundusi
(B15-19)

Bubu River

Lake Haubi

Singida

Kondoa

KEY
Proposed reserve boundary   - - - - - -
Sites indicated by code   (B1-3)

Lake Serya

Dodoma ↓

Getting there and away

It is forbidden to explore the rock art within the proposed reserve without an official guide, and even if this were not the case, most of the sites would be difficult to locate independently. For this reason, all prospective visitors must first report to the Department of Antiquities office on the main junction in Kolo, where they will pay the entrance fee of Tsh2,000 and collect a guide. Kolo lies about 20km north of Kondoa and 50km south of Babati on the Great North Road, and any public transport heading between these two towns can drop you alongside the Department of Antiquities office.

Further details of reaching the individual sites are provided under the heading *Major rock art sites* below, but it is worth noting that, while distances between various sites are relatively short, the roads are very rough (4WD only) and visiting most sites will entail some walking, often on steep slopes. For this reason, even motorised travellers will find it unrealistic to visit more than one cluster of sites in the space of one morning or afternoon, and a full three days would be required to explore the lot.

Travellers without private transport will find exploring the area more tricky. It is possible to undertake the round trip from Kolo to the famous Mungomi wa Kolo site on foot, but this would take the best part of a day, and you'd be expected to pay the guide a reasonable fee for walking out, which way exceeds the bounds of duty. More accessible are Lusangi and Pahi, which are connected to Kolo by a few *dalla-dallas* daily (Pahi also has a guesthouse) passing through Mnenya. A few *dalla-dallas* run daily between Kolo and Kisese via Mnenya. In both cases, however, you'd still need to cover the costs of a guide, and offer him a fair fee for his efforts. Another option would be to hire a vehicle for the day in Kondoa – since the distances involved would be relatively short, no more than 100km in all, this shouldn't be too costly.

Although few people do so, it is perfectly feasible to tag a trip to the proposed reserve on to a standard northern circuit safari. Some safari companies will visit the rock art sites as a day trip from Tarangire National Park, a slightly pressured but by no means impossible foray. Equally, you could spend a night in the region, either camping at the Department of Antiquities site outside Kolo or sleeping in one of Kondoa's guesthouses. The advantage of a day trip for travellers for whom comfort is a high priority is that it will allow you to make use of one of the commodious lodges in Tarangire rather than roughing it at Kolo or Kondoa. For more adventurous or budget-conscious travellers, a night in the area will save on wasted national park entrance fees as well as allowing you to see a greater variety of sites.

Where to stay

Accommodation options in the immediate vicinity of Kolo are somewhat restricted, for which reason travellers using private transport are advised to overnight in Kondoa, which boasts a fair selection of budget lodgings (see *Kondoa* above). Otherwise, the Department of Antiquities in Kolo runs an attractive campsite on the banks of the seasonal Kolo River about 3km east of town, along the road towards Mungomi wa Kolo site and Mnenya. Water and toilet facilities are available at the campsite, which costs Tsh2,500 per person, but food and other drinks must be brought from Kolo. There is no accommodation in Kolo, but basic local guesthouses can be found in Pahi and Masange, both of which lie below the Maasai Escarpment within walking distance of several good sites.

A recent report suggests that the disused Chungai Rest Camp near Mnenya, formerly the base camp of the Leakeys and subsequent researchers, has been privatised with a view to establishing a tented camp or hotel on the site, and possibly a museum.

Major rock art sites
Mungomi wa Kolo
Most visitors with limited time are taken to the region's recognised showpiece, the cluster of three sites that are scattered across the craggy upper slopes of Ichoi Hill about 10km from Kolo by road. Prosaically labelled B1–3, more evocatively known as Mungomi wa Kolo (*The Dancers of Kolo*), this cluster of panels provides a good overview of the region's rock art, and – aside from the last, very steep, foot ascent to the actual panels – it is easily reached in a 4WD vehicle. To get there from Kolo, you need to follow the Mnenya Road west for about 4km, crossing the normally dry Kolo River on the way, before turning right on to a rough 4WD track that reaches the base of the hill after about 6km.

Probably the most intriguing of the panels is B1, which lies in a tall overhang right at the top of the hill. This panel includes several fine, but very faded, paintings of animals (giraffe, leopard, zebra and rhino), as well as some abstract designs, as well as numerous humanoid forms. Richard Leakey regarded this site to represent a particularly wide variety of superimposed styles and periods, and it must surely have been worked over hundreds if not thousands of years. One striking scene, which Mary Leakey dubbed *The Abduction*, depicts five rather ant-like humanoid forms with stick bodies, spindly limbs and distended heads. The two figures on the right have elongated heads, while the two on the left have round heads, as does the central figure, which also appears to have breasts and whose arms are being held by the flanking figures. Leakey interpreted the painting as a depiction of an attempted abduction, with the central female figure being tugged at by two masked people on the right, while friends or family try to hold on to her from the left. Of course, a scene such as this is open to numerous interpretations, and it could as easily depict a ritual dance or similar as an abduction. And why stop there? I recently stumbled across a web page that makes an oddly compelling case for this haunting scene, and others paintings in Kondoa, providing evidence of extraterrestrial visits to Kondoa region in the distant past. If this sort of speculation tickles you, the long-snouted figures to the right, according to this interpretation, are alien abductors, while a separate scene to the right shows another alien standing in a hot air balloon!

Panel B2, also in an overhang, is even larger and more elaborate, though most of the paintings have been partially obliterated by termite activity. Prominent among several animal portraits are those of elephants and various antelope. The most striking scene consists of three reposed humanoid figures with what appear to be wild, frizzy hairstyles (some form of headdress?) and hands clutching a vertical bar. A small cave in front of the panel is used for ceremonial purposes by local rainmakers, and sacrifices are still sometimes left outside the shelter. Note that while I've followed most written sources in the use of the tags B1 and B2, our guide reversed this usage. Furthermore, while no written source mentions a third panel at this site (and maps place site B3 as being several kilometres distant), our guide showed us a much smaller third panel near the base of the slope and referred to it as B3. It is this panel of animated humanoids that our guide – with some justification – referred to as *The Dancers of Kolo*, though most literature refers to B1 by this name.

Pahi-Lusangi and Kinyasi
Panels B4–13 all lie close to the base of the escarpment near the twin villages of Lusangi and Pahi about 12km from Kolo. To reach them from Kolo, follow the same road you would to get to Mungomi wa Kolo, but instead of turning right after crossing the river, keep straight on the main road, passing through Mnenya, until you reach Lusangi. This site is normally accessible in any vehicle, though 4WD

may be useful after rain. Lusangi can be reached by *dalla-dalla* from Kolo, and there is a guesthouse about 1km away in Pahi. A 1km piste leads from the main road to the base of the escarpment, from where a flat 100m footpath leads to three shelters about 20m apart.

The art at Lusangi is not as impressive as that at Mungomi wa Kolo, but it is probably a more suitable goal for those unwilling or unable to climb steep footpaths. Several figures do stand out however, the most notable being a 70cm-high outlined giraffe superimposed on a very old painting of a rhino. Below this, a red and yellow figure of an eland-like antelope with a disproportionately small head is regarded by archaeologists to be one of the very oldest paintings known in Kondoa region. Only a couple of clear humanoid figures are found across these sites, and several of the panels are dominated by bold, childlike patterns in the 'late white' style, often superimposed over older and more finely executed portraits.

From Pahi it is possible to drive another 12km to Kinyasi, where sites B14–19 are situated in a valley below the 1,000m-high Kome Mountain. The most interesting of these sites is a one-square-metre panel of small, finely executed antelopes, which also includes one of the few known examples of a painting depicting a homestead.

Mnenya to Kisese

Sites A1–18 all lie along the stretch of the Maasai Escarpment that runs immediately east of the reasonable dirt road connecting Mnenya to Kisese. This road itself runs roughly parallel and about 10km east of the Great North Road, and is connected to it by a roughly 8km road between Kolo and Mnenya in the south and a roughly 15km road between Bereku and Kisese in the north. In theory, travellers driving southwards from Babati or Arusha along the Great North Road would ideally explore sites A1–18 by turning on to the Kisese road at Bereku, then following the Mnenya road south and returning to the Great North Road at Kolo. Unfortunately, however, it is mandatory to pass through Kolo first to pay fees and collect a guide, which will enforce quite a bit of backtracking for southbound travellers (but makes no real difference to travellers driving north from Kondoa). There isn't much public transport on the Mnenya–Kisese road, but a few *dalla-dallas* run along it daily, and there is basic accommodation in Masange.

Running northwards from Mnenya, the direction in which regulations practically enforce one to travel, the first major site is A17 or Cheke III, which lies about 5km along the Kisese road. This extensive, intricate panel is rich in superimposition, and studded with various animals as well as surreal humanoids with circular heads and pincer legs and a couple of unusually robust human figures seemingly draped in robes. The shelter is dominated by the so-called *Dance of the Elephant*, a red painting of a solitary elephant surrounded by perhaps a dozen people – who might as easily be worshipping or hunting the elephant as dancing around it. Getting to Cheke III involves following a 2km motorable track west of the main road, followed by a short but steep ascent to the actual panel.

About 5km further along the road, you arrive at Masange village, from where a roughly 1km-long side road leads to the base of the escarpment, and another 5–10 minutes' climb brings you to sites A12–14. The most compelling panel in this cluster is A13, another elaborately decorated overhang with numerous superimposed paintings, but A14 is of interest for its solitary painting of ten faded human figures in a row. Most of the sites between Masange and Kisese lie some distance from the main road, but site A9 or Kandaga III, 6km past Masange, is particularly recommended to serious enthusiasts, consisting of a series of geometric representations in the 'late white' style first described in 1931 by Julian

BUT WHAT DOES IT MEAN?

There is a strangely eerie sensation attached to emerging from a remote and nondescript tract of bush to be confronted by an isolated panel of primitive paintings executed by an artist or artists unknown, hundreds or maybe thousands of years before the time of Christ. Faded as many of the panels are, and lacking the perspective to which modern eyes are accustomed, one can still hardly fail to be impressed by the fine detail of many of the animal portraits, or to wonder at the surrealistic distortion of form that characterises the human figures. And, almost invariably, first exposure to these charismatic works of ancient art prompts three questions: how old are they, who were the artists, and what was their intent?

When, who and why? The simple answers are that nobody really knows. The broadest time frame, induced from the absence of any representations of extinct species in the rock galleries of Kondoa, places the paintings at less than 20,000 years old. The absence of a plausible tradition of attribution among the existing inhabitants of the area – a Gogo claim that the paintings were the work of the Portuguese can safely be discounted – makes it unlikely that even the most modern paintings are less than 200 years old. Furthermore, experts have noted a clear progression from the simplest early styles to more complex, expressive works of art, and a subsequent regression to the clumsy graffiti like finger painting of the 'late white' phase, indicating that the paintings were created over a substantial period of time.

Early attempts at dating the Kondoa rock art concentrated on categorising it chronologically based on the sequence of superimposition of different styles on busy panels. The results were inconclusive, even contradictory, probably because the superimposition of images was an integral part of the art, so that a foreground image might be roughly contemporaneous with an image underneath it. It is also difficult to know the extent to which regional style, or even individual style, might be of greater significance than chronological variation. The most useful clue to the age of the paintings is the stratified organic debris deposited alongside red ochre 'pencils' at several sites. Carbon dating of a handful of sites where such deposits have been found suggests that the artists were most active about 3,000 years ago, though many individual paintings are undoubtedly much older. The crude 'late white' paintings, on the other hand, are widely agreed to be hundreds rather than thousands of years old, and there is evidence to suggest that some underwent ritual restoration by local people who held them sacred into historical times.

The identity of the artists is another imponderable. In the first half of the 20th century, the rock art of southern Africa was solely attributed to 'bushmen' hunter-gatherers, a people whose click-based Khoisan tongue is unrelated to Bantu and who are of vastly different ethnic stock to any Bantu speakers. True, the bushmen are the only people who practised the craft in historical times, but much of the rock art of southern Africa (like that of eastern Africa) dates back thousands of years. Coincidentally, two of East Africa's few remaining click-tongued hunter-gatherers, the Sandawe and the Hadzabe, both live in close proximity to the main concentration of Tanzanian rock art, but neither has a tradition relating to the paintings.

Given that the archaeological record indicates east-southern Africa was populated entirely by hunter-gatherers when the paintings were probably executed, furthermore that a succession of human migrations have subsequently passed through the region, postulating an ancestral link between the artists of

Kondoa and modern hunter-gatherers would be tenuous in the extreme. If anything, the probable chronology of the rock art points in the opposite direction. Assuming that creative activity peaked some 3,000 years ago, it preceded the single most important known migration into East Africa, the mass invasion of the Bantu-speakers who today comprise the vast majority of Tanzania's population. Most probable, then, that a Bantu- or perhaps Nilotic-speaking group, or another group forced to migrate locally as a ripple effect of the Bantu invasion, moved into the Kondoa region and conquered or assimilated the culture responsible for the rock art, resulting in the gradual stylistic regression noted by archaeologists. All that can be said about the artists with reasonable certainty is they were hunter-gatherers whose culture would have vanished without trace, were it not for the painted testament left behind on the granite faces of Kondoa.

The most haunting of the questions surrounding the rock art of Kondoa is the intent of their creators. In determining the answer to this, one obstacle is that nobody knows just how representative the surviving legacy might be. Most extant rock art in Kondoa is located in caves or overhangs, but the small number of faded paintings that survive on more open sites must be a random subset of similarly exposed panels that have been wiped clean by the elements. We have no record, either, of whether the artists dabbled on canvases less durable than rock, but unless one assumes that posterity was a conscious goal, it seems wholly presumptuous to think otherwise. The long and short of it, then, is that the extant galleries might indeed represent a sufficiently complete record to form a reliable basis for any hypothesis, but they might just as easily represent a fraction of a percentage of the art executed at the time. Furthermore, there is no way of telling whether rocks were only painted in specific circumstances – it is conceivable that the rock art would maker greater sense viewed in conjunction with other types of painting that have not survived.

Two broad schools of thought surround the interpretation of Africa's ancient rock art. The first has it that the paintings were essentially recreational, documentary, and/or expressive in intent – art for art's sake if you like – while the second regards them to be mystical works of ritual significance. It is quite possible that the truth of the matter lies between these poles of opinion. A striking feature of the rock art of Kondoa is the almost uniform discrepancy in the styles used to depict human and non-human subjects. Animals are sometimes painted in stencil form, sometimes filled with bold white or red paint, but – allowing for varying degrees of artistic competence – the presentation is always naturalistic. The people, by contrast, are almost invariably heavily stylised in form, with elongated stick-like bodies and disproportionately round heads topped by a forest of unkempt hair. Some such paintings are so downright bizarre that they might more reasonably described as humanoid than human (a phenomenon that has not gone unnoticed by UFO theorists searching for prehistoric evidence of extraterrestrial visits).

The discrepancy between the naturalistic style favoured for animals and highly stylised presentation of humans has attracted numerous theoretical explanations. Most crumble under detailed examination of the evidence, but all incline towards supporting the mystical or ritualistic school of interpretation. Ultimately, however, for every tentative answer we can provide, these enigmatic ancient works pose a dozen more questions. It is an integral part of their charisma that we can speculate to our heart's content, but will never know the whole truth!

BACKGROUND TO THE ROCK ART OF KONDOA DISTRICT

Outside attention was first drawn to the rock art of Kondoa District in the 1920s, though it would be several decades before the full extent of its riches was grasped. In 1923, District Commissioner Bagshawe visited and described the two main shelters at Mungomi wa Kolo, and six years later several of the sites on and around Twali Hill were visited by Dr T Nash. In the early 1930s, the eminent archaeologists Louis and Mary Leakey explored a handful of new sites, notably Cheke III, on which was based Louis Leakey's formative attempt at stylistic categorisation and relative chronology, published in his 1936 book *Stone Age Africa*.

By the late 1940s, enthusiasts and archaeologists had located 75 sites in the Kondoa region, and their discoveries led to the publication in 1950 of a unique special edition of *Tanganyika Notes and Records* dedicated solely to the rock art. The first intensive survey of the region was undertaken in 1951 by Mary Leakey, who boosted the tally of known panels for A sector alone from 17 to 186, of which one-third were sufficiently well preserved to be studied. Leakey traced and redrew 1,600 figures and scenes, an undertaking that formed the basis of her 1983 book *Africa's Vanishing Art: The Rock Paintings of Tanzania*. Leakey said of her time in the Kondoa region that: 'No amounts of stone and bone could yield the kinds of information that the paintings gave so freely... here were scenes of life, of men and women hunting, dancing, singing and playing music'.

The two works mentioned above are out of print and difficult to locate. Worth the small asking price, however, is the National Museums of Tanzania's Occasional Paper no 5 *The Rock Art of Kondoa and Singada*, written by Fidelis Masao and available at the National Museum in Dar es Salaam. A newer book with detailed coverage of the Kondoa rock art, placed within a broader African context, is *African Rock Art: Paintings and Engravings on Stone* by David Coulson and Alec Campbell, published by Harry N Abrams in 2001.

Huxley. The excellent and well preserved site dubbed Kisese II or A4 lies another 8km past Kandaga on a tall rock no more than 10 minutes' walk from the road.

Bubu River sites

Unlike the other rock art sites within the proposed reserve, this cluster lies to the west of the Great North Road, overlooking the Bubu River about 12km from Kolo. Short of walking there and back from Kolo, this is the one cluster that cannot easily be reached without private transport, ideally a 4WD. It is, nevertheless, perhaps the best cluster of them all, with several panels in close proximity and in a particularly good state of preservation.

Of the three panels D1–3 situated on Fenga Hill, the most worthwhile is D3, sometimes referred to as the *Trapped Elephants*. Covered in a jumble of superimposed red features, including several slim humanoid figures with distended heads and headdresses, this panel is named for the central painting of two elephants surrounded by a stencilled oblong line. Some experts believe that this depicts an elephant trap, a theory supported by three fronds below the elephants that might well represent branches used to camouflage a pit. Others believe that it might have a more mystical purpose, placing the elephants in a kind of magic circle. A trickle of circles dripping from the left base of the picture could be blood, or the elephants' spoor.

About 3km south of Fenga Hill, the immediate vicinity around Tlawi Hill hosts at least ten panels, numbered D4–5 and D15–22. A dedicated enthusiast could easily devote half a day to this cluster of very different sites. Panel D19 is notable for an almost life-size and unusually naturalistic attempt to paint a human figure in a crouched or seated position, and it also contains some finely executed paintings of animals, including a buffalo head and a giraffe leaning forward. Directly opposite this panel, site D20 depicts several seated human figures, while 500m further away site D22 is also known as the *Red Lion* for the striking painting of a lion, with a stencilled black outline and red fill, that dominates the shelter.

Five minutes' walk along the same ridge towards the Bubu River brings you to a pair of shelters called D17 or *The Hunter*, for a rare action painting of a hunter killing a large antelope – presumably an eland – with his bow and arrow. Several other interesting human figures are found on these twin shelters. Another 10–20 minutes' walk downhill towards the river stand two large rock faces, D4 and D5, respectively known as *The Rhino* and *The Prancing Giraffe*. The former is named for a 60cm-long portrait of a rhino, with rather narrow head, and it also depicts what appears to be a herd of antelope fleeing from human pursuers. The nominate painting at site D5 is a strikingly life-like depiction of a giraffe with its front legs raised as if cantering or rearing, but no less interesting is a tall pair of very detailed, shaggy headed human figures sometimes referred to as *The Dancers*.

BABATI

The small but bustling market town of Babati lies on the Great North Road at the junction with the road west to Katesh and Singida, some 70km north of Kondoa. Babati itself is nothing out of the ordinary, but a useful place to break up the bus journeys, and the best springboard for travel west to the Mount Hanang region. Further justification for stopping over in Babati comes in the form of the synonymous lake on the town's outskirts, easily reached by walking along the Kondoa road for about 10 minutes. The papyrus-fringed stretch of shore alongside the road supports a good selection of waterbirds – egrets, waders and storks – while flotillas of pelican sail pompously across the open water. Several pods of hippo are resident in the lake, too, and it's straightforward enough to negotiate a sensible rate with a local fisherman to take you out in search of them. The Babati and Hanang Cultural Tourism Project, based in Babati, is a useful contact for arranging local excursions and Hanang climbs (see box, page 386).

Getting there and away

Babati lies 172km south of Arusha. The road is surfaced for the first 110km out of Arusha, after which it deteriorates rather abruptly, but it shouldn't take longer than three hours to cover the full distance in a private vehicle. Buses between Arusha and Babati leave throughout the day, starting in either direction at 07.30, and taking three to four hours in either direction. There are also several buses daily to Katesh and Singida in the west, as well as to Kondoa via Kolo in the south. The driving distance from Babati to Kondoa in a private vehicle is about 90 minutes (an hour to Kolo) in a private vehicle. The drive to Katesh is similar in duration.

Where to stay
Budget

Motel Paapaa Tel: 057 253 1111. This decent if slightly rundown hotel is about the smartest in town, and conveniently situated next to the bus stop. Self-contained doubles

BABATI AND HANANG CULTURAL TOURISM PROGRAMME

Based in Babati, this highly commendable set-up, which started life in the mid-1990s as a private eco-tourism concern called Kahembe's Enterprises, has recently been formalised into an official cultural tourist project in collaboration with the SNV. It remains under the management of Jaos Kahembe, and is an excellent contact for travellers who want to explore a little-known part of Tanzania in an organised manner, but without paying through the nose.

Kahembe's arranges a variety of local tours, of which the most popular are the three-day and two-day Hanang climbs out of Babati, respectively using the Gendabi and Jorodom routes. Mr Kahembe also offers a wide selection of other local trips, ranging from a three-day Barabaig walking safari, to a couple of seven- and eight-day walking itineraries that visit several local *bomas* as well as incorporating walks on the game-rich verges of Lake Manyara and Tarangire National Parks. The 16-day 'African rural life adventure' includes overnight stays with a number of different ethnic groups, as well as an ascent of Mount Hanang, and game walks around Lake Burungi (on the edge on Tarangire National Park) and on the eastern shores of Lake Manyara. Day trips on Lake Babati and to local villages can also be arranged, and special requests and interests can be catered to with advance notice.

These overnight trips are not luxurious by any standard, but they are well organised and informative, and offer interested travellers an unforgettable glimpse into an ancient way of life that has vanished in most other parts of Africa. They are also very reasonably priced, at a uniform US$40 per person per day for one or two people, or US$30 per person per day for larger groups, inclusive of travel on local transport, accommodation and meals in local guesthouses or villages, and local guide and village fees. I personally feel that it's great to see somebody offering trips like this to the increasingly significant proportion of travellers who want to see more of Tanzania than the Big Five and the beaches. It is not mandatory to make advance bookings, but it would be advisable if you're operating to a tight time frame. You can do this through the contact details below, or through the TTB information centre in Arusha.

Tel: 027 253 1088; email: tourinfo@habari.co.tz;
web: www.infojep.com/culturaltours

with cold running water cost Tsh3,800 while rooms using a common shower cost Tsh2,500. The restaurant serves large portions of reasonable food at around Tsh1,500 per plate.

Dodoma Transport Guesthouse This clean hotel has decent self-contained doubles at Tsh3,500.

Shoestring

Kahembe's Guesthouse Tel: 027 253 1088. This pleasant guesthouse is owned by the manager of the Babati and Hanang Cultural Tourism Programme, and is situated right next door to its office less than 500m from the bus station. Rooms cost Tsh1,100/1,600 single/double.

Where to eat
Aside from the good restaurant at the **Paapaa Hotel**, the **Paradise** and **Wagon Restaurants** are decent and affordable local eateries.

MOUNT HANANG AND KATESH
Mount Hanang is Tanzania's fourth-highest mountain after Kilimanjaro, Meru and Lolomalasin in the Ngorongoro Conservation Area. Like the other peaks in this list, it is volcanic in origin, a product of the same geological process that sculpted the Rift Valley, though it is the only one of these mountains to actually stand within the Great Valley. Hanang's extinct caldera, which towers to an altitude of 3,418m above the low-lying plains of the Barabaig people, is visible from hundreds of kilometres away on a clear day. Not surprisingly, this imposing free standing mountain is held in high reverence by the Barabaig pastoralists who inhabit its lower slopes, and features prominently in their myths. Hanang supports its own distinct microclimate and forms an important local watershed. Most of the rain falls on the northern and eastern slopes, where extensive forests still support elusive populations of bushbuck, duiker and various monkeys, as well as a wide range of forest birds.

Seldom visited by tourists, Hanang is nevertheless eminently climbable, and – because it lies outside the national park system – it forms a very affordable prospect by comparison with Kilimanjaro or Meru. The slopes support the usual range of montane forest and grassland habitats, and offer excellent views over a stretch of the Rift Valley studded with smaller volcanic cones and shallow lakes. The normal springboard for climbing Hanang is the dusty and rather amorphous small town of Katesh, which straddles the Singida road 75km west of Babati at the southern base of the mountain. Further details of routes and costs are provided under the heading *Climbing Hanang*, but travellers broadly have one of two options, which are placing themselves in the experienced hands of the cultural tourism programme in Babati, or making their own arrangements out of Katesh.

The attractions of the Hanang area are not restricted to the mountain. Several substantial lakes also lie in the vicinity of Katesh, including the shallow and highly saline Lake Balangida, which is set at the base of the Rift Valley scarp immediately north of Mount Hanang. Katesh also forms the starting point for an obscure but not unrewarding back route to Karatu and the Ngorongoro Crater Highlands via Basotu, Dongobesh and Mbulu, covered later in this chapter.

One could scarcely spend time in the Hanang area without being conscious of the Barabaig, colourful traditional pastoralists who have consciously retained their traditional way of life. Anybody in Katesh will be able to tell you about market days in nearby villages, where you're most likely to see traditionally dressed people assembled. For a deeper insight into Barabaig culture and customs, the cultural tourism programme in Babati (see box, opposite) arranges day trips to the traditional Barabaig homestead of Mzee Gavachu in Dirima village. They can also set up three-day round hikes from Katesh culminating with two nights and a full day in the same village. This is one of the most rewarding cultural programmes we've been exposed to anywhere in Africa – the family are fabulous hosts, and the visit offers a genuine opportunity to explore the customs of Africa's shrinking population of traditional pastoralists, as well as the modern realities they face. (See the box *The Barabaig*, pages 390–1.)

Getting there and away
Katesh lies 250km from Arusha, some 75km west of the junction town of Babati on the Great North Road. In a private vehicle, the drive from Arusha – surfaced for the first 110km – will take less than five hours, and the drive from Babati about

90 minutes. For those travellers dependent on public transport, buses run between Babati and Singida via Katesh throughout the day, taking 2–3 hours in either direction between Babati and Katesh. Several buses travel between Arusha and Singida via Katesh; the thrice-daily service operated by Mtei Express Coaches is recommended, and takes about six hours.

Travellers who opt to explore Mount Hanang and surrounds through the cultural tourist programme in Babati need only get themselves to Babati (regular buses from Arusha), and the tourism programme will take over from there.

Where to stay and eat

Until recently the smartest lodging in Katesh, the excellent **Colt Guesthouse** lies close to the main market and charges Tsh5,000 for a clean and spacious self-contained double with hot running water. Better, however, is the **Mtei Guesthouse**, which opened near the bus station in early 2002, and charges between Tsh5,000 and Tsh10,000 for self-contained accommodation. The pick of several cheaper options is the **Hanang View Guesthouse**, a decent, clean set-up charging Tsh1,000 for a small room with three-quarter bed, using a common shower. If it's full, the nearby **Matunda Guesthouse** is similar in standard.

Katesh, at the time of writing, has some fair guesthouses and the usual collection of seedy bars, but it is practically bereft of attractive restaurants. It would definitely be worth checking whether the **Mtei Guesthouse** is now serving any food. Otherwise, all things being relative, the best place to eat is **Mama Kaborge's Restaurant**, a cramped but homely *hoteli* serving cheap, unremarkable local food. Unsignposted, it lies only a couple of blocks from the Colt Guesthouse – anybody will be able to point you in the right direction.

Excursions from Katesh
Climbing Mount Hanang

Although several routes can be used to ascend Hanang, only two are recommended to first-time hikers. These are the Jorodom or Giting routes, which start from the villages of the same name, the former situated on the southern slopes of the

BARABAIG WINE
Brian Doench

The Barabaig are enthusiastic beekeepers, and their unique wine Gesuda is made from honey, together with a rare local root that is gathered on the upper slopes of Mount Hanang and said to lend the drink a medicinal property. Gesuda is fermented in huge gourds, the size of a half keg, and it takes a week to reach perfection, during which period entry to the room in which it is being made is restricted to the brewers. Reserved for special occasions, the drinking of Gesuda is governed by a complex and rigid set of rules and procedures. The wine is traditionally drunk from hollowed cow horns, and since the drinking rules revolve around age and rank, the most important people are served in the biggest horns. The man who supplied the honey for any given batch of Gesuda will monitor the drinking, and one needs his invitation – or to be a member of his family – to join a drinking party. A close friend or brother of the host will be designated the wine pourer, in charge of keeping the guests' horns filled, and of refusing to refill the horn of any man who is obnoxious or drinking irresponsibly. Any outsider who is offered the drink should regard it to be a great honour.

mountain some 2km from Katesh and the latter on the eastern slopes about 10km out of town. The Jorodom Route – also sometimes referred to as the Katesh Route – is marginally the easier of the two, and the more accessible, making it a clear first choice for travellers making their own arrangements out of Katesh. The Giting Route ascends on the side of the mountain that receives more rain, which means it is far more densely forested, but also that it is likely to be more slippery underfoot during the rainy season.

The most straightforward way of arranging a climb is through the cultural tourism programme in Babati, which charges a pretty reasonable US$40 per person per day for one or two people, or US$30 per person per day for a larger group. The obvious advantages of working through the cultural tourism programme are that they have plenty of experience on the mountain, will provide an English-speaking guide and food, and will make sure that you carry enough water and whatever else is necessary. For more details, see the box *Babati and Hanang Cultural Tourism Programme*, page 386. You should cut at least 50% off the cost were you to arrange your own climb, but should bear in mind that this will involve arranging your own food and water, and working with guides and porters who may not speak a word of English between them.

In theory, Hanang can be climbed as a full-day round trip out of Katesh, but this will reduce the hike to something of an endurance test, with little opportunity to enjoy the scenery. What's more, while a very fit hiker could complete the full ascent and descent in a tight 12 hours, less fit hikers may struggle to do it all within one day. It is therefore recommended that you overnight on the mountain: there are several good places to pitch a tent, or you can sleep in the caves on the Giting route (checking in advance that your guide knows their location). Either way, the upper slopes of Hanang get very chilly at night, so you'll need a good sleeping bag or thick blanket, and enough warm clothes.

Climbers intending to use the Jorodom Route will need to walk the 2km from Katesh to Jorodom village, where they must check in at the village office (*Ofisi ya Kijiji*). Here, you can arrange for a guide (Tsh5,000 per party) and porters (Tsh2,000 per porter). It is recommended that you take two porters per climber, one to carry the luggage and the other the water. From Jorodom, the hike to a good campsite on the lower ridge takes about six hours. The upper ridge looks deceptively close to this point, but is in fact at least four hours distant. It is thus advisable to camp at the top of the lower ridge, then to tackle the final ascent and full descent the next day.

To climb via the Giting Route, you must first follow the Babati road out of Katesh for 5km to Nangwa. Here, turn left on to a side road and continue for another 4km to the village of Giting. The main office of the Hanang Forestry Department, where you can arrange a guide and porters at the same rate charged in Jorodom, is situated on the outskirts of Giting. There is no accommodation in Giting, but you can camp in the grounds of the Forestry Department Office.

Please note that there is no permanent standing or running water on the mountain. Climbers must bring all the drinking water they will require with them. Bottled mineral water is available in Katesh, but not in Giting or Jorodom. An *absolute* minimum of 4l per climber per day (more during the hot, dry season) is essential, and better to overestimate your requirements than run out of water en route.

Mount Hanang road loop

A loop of rough roads out of Katesh circles around the north side of Mount Hanang, making for an interesting half-day drive for motorised travellers, or a worthwhile hike for backpackers who don't particularly want to climb the

THE BARABAIG

The Barabaig are the most populous of a dozen closely related tribes, the Datoga or Tatoga. At around 100,000, the Datoga are one of Tanzania's smaller ethno-linguistic groupings, but their territory, centred on Mount Hanang, extends into large semi-arid tracts within Arusha, Dodoma and Singida.

Superficially similar to, and frequently confused with, their Maasai neighbours by outsiders, the Barabaig are dedicated cattle-herders, speaking a Nilotic tongue, who have steadfastly resisted external pressure to forsake their semi-nomadic pastoralist ways. Unlike the Maasai, however, the Barabaig are representatives of the earliest known Nilotic migration into East Africa from southwest Ethiopia. Their forebears probably settled in western Kenya during the middle of the first millennium AD, splitting into two groups. One – the Kalenjin – stayed put. The other, the proto-Datoga, migrated south of Lake Natron 500 to 1,000 years ago to the highlands of Ngorongoro and Mbulu, and Rift Valley plains south towards Dodoma.

Datoga territory was greatest before 1600, thereafter being eroded by migrations of various Bantu-speaking peoples into northern and central Tanzania. The most significant incursion came in the early 19th century, with the arrival of the Maasai. Oral traditions indicate that several fierce territorial battles were fought between the two pastoralist groups, resulting in the Maasai taking over the Crater Highlands and Serengeti Plains, and the Datoga retreating to their modern homeland near Mount Hanang. The Lerai Forest in Ngorongoro Crater is said to mark the grave of a Datoga leader who fell in battle in about 1840, and the site is still visited by Datoga elders from the Lake Eyasi area. The Maasai call the Barabaig the 'Mangati' (feared enemies), and the Barabaig territory around Mount Hanang is sometimes referred to as the Mangati Plains.

The Barabaig used to move around the plains according to the feeding and watering requirements of their herds. They tend a variety of livestock, including goats, donkeys and chickens, but their culture and economy revolves around cattle, which are perceived to be a measure of wealth and prestige, and every part and product of the animal, including the dung, is ingested, or worn, or used in rituals. In recent years, agriculture has played an increasingly significant support role in the subsistence of the Barabaig, which together with increased population pressures has more-or-less put paid to the nomadic lifestyle.

Barabaig territory receives an average annual rainfall of less than 500mm, which means that water is often is short supply. Although the area is dotted with numerous lakes, most are brackish and unsuitable to drink. Barabaig women often walk miles every day to collect gourds of drinking water, much of which comes from boreholes dug with foreign aid. The cattle cannot drink from the lakes directly when water levels are low and salinity is high, but the Barabaig get around this by digging wells on the lakes' edges and allowing the water to filter through the soil. Even so, the herders won't let their cattle drink from these wells on successive days for fear that it will make them ill.

Barabaig social structure is not dissimilar to that of the Maasai, although it lacks the rigid division into hierarchical age-sets pivotal to Maasai and other East African pastoralist societies. The Barabaig do not recognise one centralised leader, but are divided into several hereditary clans, each answering to a chosen elder who sits on a tribal council. The central unit of society is the family homestead or *gheida*, dwelt in by one man, his wives, and their unwed offspring.

This consists of a tall outer protective wall, built of thorny acacia branches and shaped like a figure eight, with one outer gate entered through a narrow passage. Within this wall stand several small rectangular houses – low, thick-roofed constructions of wooden poles plastered with mud – and the all important cattle stockade. Different huts are reserved for young men, young women, wives and elders. A number of *gheida* may be grouped together to create an informal community, and decisions are made communally rather than by a chief.

Patrilineal polygamy is actively encouraged. Elders accumulate four or more wives, up to three of which might share one hut, but marriage within any given clan is regarded to be incestuous. The concept of divorce is not recognised, but a woman may separate from her husband and return to her parent's home under some circumstances. The Barabaig openly regard extramarital sex to be normal, even desirable, although a great many taboos and conventions dictate just who may have intercourse with whom, and where they can perform the act. Traditionally, should a married woman bear a child whose biological father is other than her husband, the child remains the property of the husband – even when husband and wife are separated.

The appearance of the Barabaig is striking. The women wear heavy ochre-dyed goatskin or cowhide dresses, tasselled below the waist, and decorated with colourful yellow and orange beads. They adorn themselves with brass bracelets and neck-coils, tattoo circular patterns around their eyes, and some practice facial scarification. Men are less ornate, with a dyed cotton cloth draped over the shoulders and another around the waist. Traditionally, young men would prove themselves by killing a person (other than a Datoga) or an elephant, lion or buffalo, which might be used as the base of a ceremonial headdress along with the pelts of other animals they had killed.

The Barabaig are monotheists who believe in a universal creator whom they call Aseeta. The sun – which they give the same name – is the all-seeing eye of Aseeta, who lives far away and has little involvement in their lives. Barabaig legend has it that they are descend from Aseeta's brother Salohog, whose eldest son Gumbandaing was the first true Datoga. Traditionally, most Barabaig elders can trace their lineage back over tens of generations to this founding father, and ancestral worship plays a greater role in their spiritual life than direct worship of God. Oddly, given the arid nature of their homeland, the Barabaig have a reputation as powerful rainmakers. It is said that only one percent of the Barabaig have abandoned their traditional beliefs in favour of exotic religions – a scenario which, judging by the number of internet sites devoted to the state of the Barabaig's souls, has spun quite a few evangelical types into a giddy froth.

The above statistic is indicative of the Barabaig's stubborn adherence to a traditional way of life. In the colonial era, the Barabaig refused to be co-opted into the migrant labour system, on the not unreasonable basis that they could sell one good bullock for more than the typical labourer would earn in a year. Other Tanzanians tend to view the Barabaig as a embarrassingly primitive and ignorant – when the Nyerere government outlawed the wearing of traditional togas in favour of Westernised clothing, the Barabaig resolutely ignored them. Even today, few have much formal education or speak a word of English – it would, for that matter, be pretty unusual to meet a Barabaig who could hold a sustained conversation in Swahili.

mountain or who want to explore the area without guides. The scenery along this road is lovely, passing through cultivated montane meadows and lower-lying acacia scrub, with the mountain looming to the south and Lake Balangida and the Rift Valley escarpment about 5km to the north. A diversion to the lake and its hinterland offers good birding and the opportunity to seek out some little-known rock paintings, as well as exposure to rustic Barabaig and Iraqw villages.

Leave Katesh along the Babati Road, and after 5km you'll reach Nangwa, a small settlement noted locally for its Catholic Church with impressive stained glass windows. A left turn at Nangwa leads you on to the loop road and, after about 4km, the semi-urban sprawl of Giting, also the trailhead for the Hanang ascent route of that name. From Giting, you'll probably need to ask somebody to point you in the right direction for Barjomet, which lies another 5–6km along the loop. The cultivated highlands between Giting and Barjomet buffer the forest zone of Hanang, and once you reach Barjomet, a small crater, clearly visible from the road, hosts a seasonal lake where local villagers bring cattle and sheep to drink. Moving on from Barjomet, the road deteriorates to become little more than a rough track as it descends into a hot valley, densely covered in acacia woodland. After about 5km and 10km respectively, it passes through the small traditional villages of Gendabi and Dawar, with fine views of Lake Balangida to the north. About 2km past Dawar, the loop road emerges on the main road between Katesh (to the left) and Basotu (to the right).

A worthwhile excursion from this loop, best undertaken in the company of a local guide, and about 5km long in either direction, leads from Giting to Gidawira on the shore of Lake Balangida. This shallow body of water, far too saline to drink, is set in the sweltering depression that divides Hanang from the Rift Valley scarp, and it often harbours substantial concentrations of flamingoes. In recent years, Balangida has often been reduced to a puddle, or dried up entirely, during the dry season. When this happens, the extensive white flats are exposed, and the local Barabaig can be seen extracting coarse salt by the bucket load. Also of interest are some faded rock paintings, depicting both animals and people, which can be reached by scrambling up a rock face close to Gidawira. This is a hot walk, with no potable water to be had along the way, so do bring some bottled water with you.

Exploring this loop is straightforward enough in a private 4WD vehicle, and should take no longer than half a day allowing for stops and diversions. As for public transport, you'll have no problem finding transport along the Babati road as far as Nangwa, and may be able to pick something up from here to Giting. But, barring a lucky hitch, you'll probably have to cover the roughly 20km from Giting to the Basuto road on foot. With time, and the right frame of mind, this is a far from unattractive prospect, though covering the loop in its entirety in one day would be pretty tough going. Assuming you have a tent, it's permitted to camp at the Forestry Department office at Giting, and local PCVs reckon you'd be unlikely to hit any obstacles to camping elsewhere in the area, provided you ask permission from the local chief first. Even if you don't fancy covering the whole loop, you could consider camping at the Forestry Department in Giting and from there arranging a guide for a day trip to Lake Balangida.

Lake Basotu

The little-known but very accessible Lake Basotu lies about 40km northwest of Katesh, and is reached via a scenic road that ascends the Rift Valley scarp north of Mount Hanang and Lake Balangida before passing through grassy highlands populated by Barabaig and Bulu pastoralists. Lake Basotu is a lovely, atmospheric spot, fringed by stands of papyrus and tall yellow fever trees, with Hanang towering on the eastern horizon. Large numbers of hippo are resident in the shallows, and troops of vervet monkey commandeer the wooded shore. The birdlife is fabulous, too, particularly on the far eastern shore, where a ghostly forest of waterlogged trunks supports a seasonal breeding colony of reed cormorant, pink-backed pelican and black-headed, grey and squacco herons.

The aforementioned heronry can be explored on foot at the point where the road from Katesh first skirts the eastern shore of the lake. This is also a favourite watering spot for traditionally attired Barabaig, Bulu and Maasai, who march their cattle here from miles around. Directly opposite this stretch of shore, only 50m from the road, but invisible until you stand on the wooded rim, is a small green crater lake with waters too saline to support any fish. The cattle herders who congregate here don't see many tourists and, based on our experience, are likely to be more than willing to show you the lake – ask for it by the Barabaig name of Gida Monyot (Salt Lake). Assuming you have a fair grasp of Swahili, you might also want to enquire about the folklore surrounding the lake. It is said that the local Barabaig used to throw their dead into it, because it is so deep, and also that when a woman had sexual intercourse outside of marriage, she would undress and wade into the lake up to her shoulders to cleanse her of wrongdoing.

After reaching the eastern part of Lake Basotu, the road from Katesh continues roughly parallel to the shore for about 3km before reaching the town of Basotu, which sprawls across a pretty peninsula on the southern shore of the lake. Today a sleepy and unexpectedly traditionalist small fishing town, though somewhat more bustling on Monday, the main market day, Basotu was the scene of the decisive battle in the German campaign to coerce the resistant Barabaig into their colony before World War I. The German garrisons at Singida and Mbulu marched into Barabaig territory, converging on Basotu, where after a short battle, they hanged 12 leading elders and the most revered of the Barabaig medicine men, leaving the bodies dangling from the scaffold to discourage future resistance.

Whether in a private vehicle or on public transport, it is perfectly feasible to visit Basotu as a self-standing day trip out of Katesh. The drive takes about 60–90 minutes, following the Singida road for a few kilometres out of Katesh, then turning right at the first major intersection. A bus service runs between Katesh and Haidom (about 50km past Basotu) daily except for Sundays. This leaves from Katesh in the early morning, passes through Basotu two or three hours later, then passes through again in the early- to mid-afternoon on the return trip, allowing you a good four or five hours to explore the area. Details of approaching the lake from the north – or leaving it in that direction – are included under the next heading, *Katesh to Karatu via Mbulu*.

Should you choose to overnight in Basotu, the basic but adequate **Saria Guesthouse**, charging Tsh2,000 for a double room using common bucket showers, is about the sum of your options. A couple of local restaurants serve fresh fish from the lake and other local staples.

KATESH TO KARATU VIA MBULU

A series of back roads leads northward from Katesh to the so-called 'safari junction' of Karatu, a small town situated in the crater highlands along the main road connecting Lake Manyara National Park to the Ngorongoro Conservation Area. This route could, at a push, be driven in about five hours, or more comfortably over a full day allowing for a few stops. Using public transport, it would probably take two or three days to cover comfortably. Aside from its logistical significance in connecting the Hanang area to the northern safari circuit, this route passes through a varied and often very scenic landscape, ranging from the Rift Valley floor and escarpment, to several pretty lakes, to the wooded highlands around Mbulu. Roads in the Mbulu area are pretty good in the dry season, but they can become quite waterlogged during the rains when even 4WD vehicles might fail to get through.

Two alternative routes can be used. The **shorter route** involves heading northeast along the Babati road for about 50km to Ndareda, where a left turn leads directly via Dongobesh and Mbulu to Karatu. The second and **more interesting option**, which involves heading northwest to Lake Basuto, then continuing on to Dongobesh to connect with the road to Mbulu and Karatu, is recommended. Using the second route, it should be noted that there is little or no direct public transport between Basuto and Mbulu, so you may need to board the daily Katesh–Basotu–Haidom bus service, then overnight at a guesthouse in Haidom before continuing towards Mbulu. At least one bus daily travels between Haidom and Arusha via Dongobesh, Mbulu and Karatu, and there is also some local transport along the Haidom–Dongobesh, Katesh–Dongobesh and Dongobesh–Mbulu stretches.

The two routes converge at **Dongobesh**, or rather about 2km north of Dongobesh, where the road from Basuto joins the road from Ndareda to Mbulu. A ramshackle but quite traditional settlement set on the bank of a small seasonal river, Dongobesh is scarcely worth a conscious diversion, but it is of some interest to backpackers as a local public transport hub. A couple of cheap local lodges are dotted around town, of which the **Gerawin Guesthouse** looks about the best bet.

Less than 500m west of the road between Dongobesh and Mbulu, next to the village of Kwanzali, lies the moderately sized, kidney-shaped **Lake Tlawi**. The reedy verges of this pretty lake support large numbers of birds, most visibly squacco heron and red-knobbed coot, while the locally uncommon maccoa duck and great crested grebe are sometimes seen on the open water. The lake also harbours a resident pod of hippo, which can often be seen by walking to the stretch of shore closest to the road.

Far more substantial and attractive than Dongobesh, **Mbulu** is set in a moist wooded valley encircled by the tall mountains of the Mbulu Highlands, essentially a southern extension of the so-called Crater Highlands around Ngorongoro. The tallest of these mountains can be climbed as a day excursion from the town, offering great views across Lake Manyara and the Rift Valley, and passing through patches of montane forest rattling with birds. The town itself, an agricultural sprawl over leafy slopes emanating from a muddy central grid of roads, doesn't quite match its lovely setting, but it does possess a rustic small-town charm. The old German Boma, built in 1905, is still in use as an administrative office, and several other buildings appear to date to the British colonial era.

Public transport runs from Mbulu to Karatu throughout the day, but if you want to spend the night, there's no shortage of undistinguished cheap guesthouses in and around the bus station to keep you amused. More appealing than any of these – or quieter, anyway – is the **Mbulu Gardens Guesthouse**, which charges Tsh1,500 for acceptable doubles with nets, and lies opposite the football pitch on the Katesh side of the town centre. A notch or three up, the **DRDP Resthouse** charges Tsh7,500/9,000 single/double for semi-detached self-contained suites with running water, netting and a sofa. Situated in wooded grounds about 1km out of town along the Katesh Road, the resthouse is poorly signposted but easy enough to find, since it lies 100m past the prominently marked police station, though on the opposite side of the road. If you stay at the DRDP Resthouse, there's an equipped self-catering kitchen, where you can cook up some of this fertile area's fresh produce. Otherwise, the **Riverside 2000 Bar & Restaurant**, about 200m downhill from the bus station and market area, serves adequate but greasy chicken and chips washed down with lukewarm beers.

SINGIDA

The modestly sized town of Singida (population 60,000), administrative centre of the synonymous district, is situated at an altitude of 1,500m on a slightly elevated plateau within the Rift Valley about 80km west of Katesh. An important regional transport hub, Singida is most likely to be visited by travellers who are bussing or driving from the central Rift Valley through to the Lake Victoria region via Shinyanga. It makes a good stopover along this tough route, with a small regional museum in the town centre and a pair of Rift Valley lakes on its outskirts to keep you occupied. Curio hunters might also want to seek out the neat Singida baskets for which the region is known.

Lake Singida, which lies 10–20 minutes' walk northeast of the town centre, is a shallow and highly saline body of water, surrounded by striking granite outcrops, and characterised by wide fluctuations in water level – it has been known to dry up entirely in years of drought. Together with the smaller and less saline Lake Kindai to its south, Lake Singida is listed as an Important Bird Area, with white-backed duck, great white pelican, black-tailed godwit and gull-billed tern among the more noteworthy species that regularly occur in significant number. For casual visitors, the greatest attraction of Lake Singida will be the tens of thousands of lesser flamingo that congregate on the lake when the water level is suitable. In the dry season, you can generally walk around Lake Singida over a couple of hours, but you'd need a full day to do this during the rains.

Getting there and away

Coming from the east, Singida lies 350km from Arusha, a drive that could be covered in a day assuming you had no interest in stopping along the way. Several buses travel daily between Arusha and Singida via Katesh; the thrice-daily service operated by Mtei Express Coaches is recommended, and takes about nine hours. Plenty of buses connect Singida to more nearby towns along the Arusha road, such as Katesh and Babati

Although a rough road links Singida to Dodoma, a more attractive public transport option is the recently completed rail extension from Manyoni on the Central Railway line west of Dodoma. Overnight trains now connect Dodoma and Singida via Manyoni three times a week, offering third-class seating only, and taking about ten hours.

The 500km road northeast to Mwanza on Lake Victoria is pretty rough going, and it would be something of a test of character to drive – or bus – along it in one go, for which reason it is advisable to break up the journey at Shinyanga, the largest town en route. Plenty of buses cover this road, but many are in poor condition, so try to pre-book a ticket with a relatively reliable company such as Mtei Express Coaches. See also the box *Along the Singida–Shinyanga road* on page 396.

Where to stay and eat

The popular **Legho Singida Motel** (tel: 026 250 2426) lies in a pretty garden about 500m from the bus station in the same direction as Lake Singida, and charges Tsh7,000/10,000 for a self-contained single/double including a full breakfast. Also recommended, the more central but similarly priced **Hotel Stanley** has the best restaurant in town. Cheaper options include the **Sinai Hotel** (tel: 026 250 2459)

ALONG THE SINGIDA–SHINYANGA ROAD

Of particular interest to birdwatchers, two of Tanzania's wetland Important Bird Areas, both part of the Wembere River System draining into the southwest end of Lake Eyasi, are accessible from the road between Singida and Shinyanga. The less intriguing of the two is **Lake Kitangiri**, which lies about 20km north of the main road close to the village of Sekenke. A typically shallow and moderately saline Rift Valley lake, Kintangiri lies at the western base of the Mbulu Highlands below a 500m high scarp, and it extends over more than 100km² when full. Although the reed-lined shore and mudflats harbour a wide variety of waders and waterfowl, the main attraction of this lake are sporadic concentrations of up to 500,000 lesser and greater flamingo.

A few kilometres west of the turn-off to Lake Kitangiri, the Singida-Shinyanga road crosses the **Wembere Steppe**, which is one of the largest seasonal wetlands in Tanzania, extending over 1,000km² and more than 30km wide in parts. The avifauna of the Wembere Steppe has not been properly studied as yet, but the limited information that is available indicates that it is one of Tanzania's most important breeding grounds for waterbirds, including reed cormorant, yellow-billed stork and glossy ibis. The site is particularly rich in herons and relatives, including relatively scarce and elusive species such as the black egret, white-backed and black-capped night herons, purple and Goliath herons, and dwarf and little bitterns. The patches of acacia woodland also support a diversity of birds, including three confirmed and one unconfirmed restricted range species endemic to the Serengeti biome, ie: Fischer's lovebird, rufous-tailed weaver, Karamoja apalis and possibly grey-throated spurfowl.

Little information is available regarding Wembere's mammalian fauna, but Captain Hichins' 1937 report on African Mystery beasts (see box *The Killer Cat of Lindi*, page 588) does refer to an **elusive human-like creature** that haunts the forest on its western fringe. Hitchins recalls: 'Some years ago… I saw two small, brown furry creatures come from the dense forest… like little men, about four feet high, walking upright, but clad in russet hair. The native hunter with me gaped in mingled fear and amazement. They were, he said, agogwe, the little furry men whom one does not see once in a lifetime… They may have been monkeys, but if so, they were no ordinary monkeys… The local [villagers] told me strange tales of them; how, if one put out a gourd of *ntulu*-beer and a bowl of food in the grain-gardens, these little folk would take the food and do some hoeing and weeding at night, as thanks. That, I can well believe, is myth; but my little brown men were real enough.' Happy hunting!

Should the birding – or little furry men – detain you on your way to Shinyanga, it might be worth knowing that the junction town of **Nzega**, 90km south of Shinyanga, is a pretty substantial place with the usual motley assortment of places to bed down for the night. Among the more appealing lodgings are the **Fourways Annex Hotel** (tel: 026 269 2535) and **Shani Hotel** (tel: 026 269 2190).

and **Lutheran Guesthouse** (tel: 026 250 2013) which offer accommodation in the Tsh2,500–4,000 range. The central **Shana Resort** is recommended for above average local food at Tsh1,000 per heaped plate.

SHINYANGA

Set on the open plains that slope towards the Lake Victoria Basin, the synonymous administrative centre of Shinyanga District supports a predominantly Sukuma population of greater than 100,000. Shinyanga town flourished in the post-World War II era, on the back of the local gold and diamond mining industry, and was supplemented by a major cotton boom. Unfortunately, however, the mineral wealth has all but dried up in recent decades, and the rundown colonial buildings that line the town centre serve today as an anachronistic memento of headier days. Shinyanga remains a bustling market centre for the surrounding agricultural land, which, with its fabulous granite outcrops, is very scenic in places. All the same, it is of interest to travellers primarily as a local public transport hub, and a convenient place to break up the 600km road trip from Singida to Mwanza. Should you want to take a day off between bus trips, you might think about catching local transport to the settlement of old Shinyanga, 20km to the north, where Lake Ningwa often hosts concentrations of waterfowl, as well as being the site of a mildly diverting zoo.

Getting there and away

Shinyanga lies about 170km south of Mwanza by road, and roughly 320km northwest of Singida. The roads in this part of Tanzania are not the greatest, and it would be unrealistic to expect to average much more than 50km per hour in the dry season, less during the rains. Plenty of buses run back and forth between Mwanza and Shinyanga throughout the day, taking four to five hours one way. Buses between Singida and Shinyanga take the best part of a day.

Shinyanga lies on the central railway line between Dar es Salaam and Mwanza. There are no scheduled flights to the airstrip on the edge of town, but charter flights arrive quite regularly and it is sometimes possible to get a seat on them.

Where to stay and eat

The smartest option is the **Mwoleka Hotel** (tel: 028 276 2249/3004), which has comfortable self-contained rooms with fan and net. The **Shinyanga Motel** (tel: 028 276 2458), **Safari Hotel** (028 276 2406) and **New Butiama Hotel** (tel: 028 276 2793) have also been recommended as reasonably comfortable. There are numerous cheaper lodgings scattered around the railway and bus stations. The smarter hotels all prepare Western or Indian dishes, and **Mama Shitta's** in the town serves decent local food.

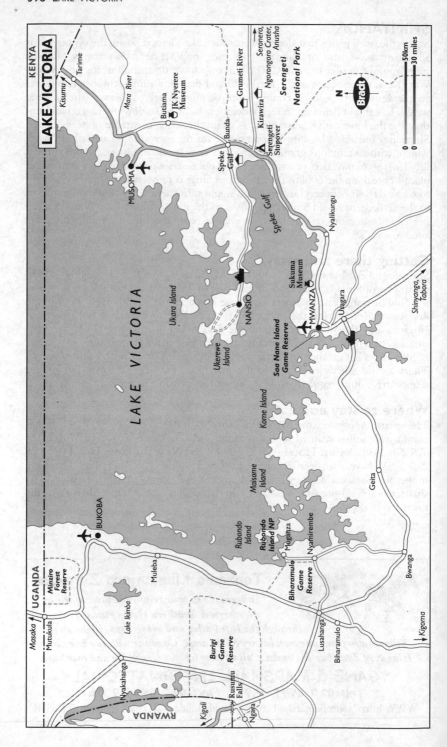

Lake Victoria

Straddling the borders with Kenya and Uganda in the northwest of Tanzania, Lake Victoria extends over almost 70,000km² – an area comparable to Ireland – making it the second largest freshwater body in the world after North America's Lake Superior. Some 51% of the lake's surface area falls within Tanzania, and the largest ports on the Tanzanian part of the lake are Mwanza, Musoma and Bukoba. Other important ports include Kisumu in Kenya, and Port Bell, Entebbe and Jinja in Uganda. It has been estimated that 30 million people across the three countries are dependent on Lake Victoria as a primary source of water and/or food.

Lake Victoria fills an elevated depression situated between the two major forks of the Great Rift Valley. It is nowhere more than 75m deep, making it very shallow by comparison to Lakes Tanganyika and Nyasa, both of which are more than 1,000m deep and hold a far greater volume of water. Much of the shoreline is shallow and marshy, and the lake contains numerous islands, of which four – including Ukerewe and Rubondo in Tanzania – are among the 20 largest freshwater islands in the world. The water level of Lake Victoria has remained more-or-less unchanged in historical times, but recent studies suggest that it dried up entirely as recently as 10–15,000 years ago. The lake's major affluent is the Kagera River, whose sources in the highlands of Burundi and Rwanda are also the most remote sources of the Nile River, which flows out of Lake Victoria near Jinja in Uganda.

Lake Victoria, though it practically borders the western Serengeti, has never featured prominently on Tanzania's tourist circuit. The one nascent upmarket tourist attraction in the region is the pedestrian-friendly Rubondo Island National Park, the popularity of which is likely to be boosted by the recent opening of an excellent new lodge and introduction of scheduled daily flights. This national park aside, Lake Victoria generally lacks the scenic qualities that make Tanzania's other large lakes such worthwhile off-the-beaten-track excursions, and the area is mostly of interest to people travelling overland between Tanzania and Uganda. Mwanza, the largest port on the lake, is the main regional route focus and public transport hub, but other significant ports are Musoma, Bukoba and Muleba. Away from these towns, most of the people who live around Lake Victoria are fishermen, whose livelihood is increasingly threatened by the recent proliferation of introduced Nile perch and other ecological threats touched on in greater detail in the box *A Dying Lake* on pages 416–17.

GETTING AROUND

Roads in this part of the country tend to be in poor condition, for which reason most travellers arrive in Mwanza by air, ferry (see box *Lake Victoria Ferries*, page

405) or rail (see box *The Central Railway*, pages 374–5). There are also scheduled flights to Mwanza from Dar es Salaam and Arusha, but these are relatively expensive. The only reasonable road in the region is the one connecting Mwanza to Musoma, and this is the only stretch for which buses can be recommended. Further details of transport are provided under the appropriate town headings.

CLIMATE

Lying at an altitude of 1,133m, Lake Victoria is not quite as hot as the coast or Lakes Tanganyika and Nyasa, but it shares with these areas a sticky tropical climate, with high humidity levels and daytime temperatures generally hovering at around 30°C. The wettest months are November, December, March and April, but average monthly rainfall figures of 100mm or greater are recorded through the period November to May.

MWANZA

Mwanza is comfortably the second-largest city in Tanzania – depending on which estimates you believe, the population currently stands at between 300,000 and 450,000 – but it is still pretty small by comparison to the tenfold more populous Dar es Salaam. The city sprawls across the undulating and rocky southwest shore of Lake Victoria, below the small hill where Speke reputedly first arrived at the lake back in 1858. The name Mwanza is widely regarded to be a European bastardisation of the Sukuma word *nyanza*, which simply means lake, and there is no reason to suppose that a settlement of any significance existed on the site of the modern town during Speke's time. Mwanza was founded as a German administrative outpost in 1890, and the surrounding area was simultaneously developed for cotton production, but few relics of this era remain today.

Captured by the British in July 1916, Mwanza received two important economic boosts in the 1920s. The first was the discovery of significant gold deposits in Mwanza district and the adjacent Musoma district. The second was the completion of the northern extension of the Central Railway line from Tabora to Mwanza via Shinyanga in 1928, which terminated a long-standing dependence on Kisumu, on the Kenyan shore of Lake Victoria, as a rail link to the coast. By the late 1930s, gold – most of it mined in the Lake Victoria region and channelled through Mwanza – had become Tanganyika's second most profitable export after sisal. Production dried up in the post-independence era – a mere 84 ounces of gold was sold in 1975 – largely due to the established mines being depleted. The Mwanza area remains rich in minerals, however, and several new veins of gold discovered in the 1990s are currently being mined, most notably at Geita. In addition to the local mines, the cotton and textile industries remain important economic mainstays for Mwanza region.

Mwanza's main significance to travellers today is as a transport hub, it being the most important air, rail, road and lake terminal in northwest Tanzania. The city centre, lined with the usual mildly decaying colonial era buildings, is nothing very special, but it does have a likeable and quite lively atmosphere – and travellers arriving from the sticks will doubtless enjoy the proliferation of reasonably priced lodgings, restaurants, bars and internet facilities. The best-known local landmark is Bismarck Rock, a precariously balanced granite formation that lies within the main harbour, but several similarly impressive outcrops can be seen by wandering along Station Road on the peninsula to the south of the city centre. For a good view over the lake from the city centre, clamber up the rocky green hill immediately behind the Pamba Hostel – the rocks are crawling with colourful agama lizards, and surprisingly, given the urban location, the trees still harbour a small troop of vervet monkeys. Further afield, worthwhile day or overnight trips from Mwanza include the Sukuma Museum at Bajoro, the 'game reserve' on the tiny Saa Nane Island, and the much larger Ukerewe Island in the heart of the lake.

Getting there and away

Mwanza is the main transport hub on Lake Victoria, and likely to be passed through at some point by any traveller exploring the northwest of Tanzania, or travelling between Tanzania and Uganda or Rwanda.

The most normal way to get between Lake Victoria and the coast is by train. The railway station lies on the southern end of the town centre; details of the four-times-weekly services to and from Dar es Salaam via Tabora are included in the box *The Central Railway* on pages 374–5. Note that no direct train service runs between Mwanza and Kigoma (on Lake Tanganyika), so travellers covering this route will need to change trains at Tabora – a relatively minor inconvenience when the only affordable alternative is bussing along some truly appalling roads!

A weekly ferry service connects Mwanza to Port Bell in Uganda, and several ferries leave every week between Mwanza and Bukoba, the main Tanzania port on the western side of the lake. At least one ferry daily connects Mwanza to Ukerewe Island, and there is a weekly service to Kome and Maisome Islands. No ferries run along the eastern part of the lake to Musoma and Kisumu. All ferries leave from the harbour on the western side of the city centre. Timetables change frequently, dependent to some extent on which boats happen to be in service and which are in for repair, but current details are included in the box *Lake Victoria Ferries* on page 405.

Mwanza airport is situated on the lakeshore about 12km north of the city centre. Air Tanzania runs daily flights to Mwanza from Dar es Salaam, and on most days these stop en route at Kilimanjaro International Airport (for Arusha). Smaller airlines such as Eagle Air and Regional Air fly regularly to Bukoba and Musoma, and a number of small charter companies operate out of Mwanza airport, with most of their business linked to the gold mines. Coastal Aviation flies three times weekly between Grumeti in the western Serengeti, Mwanza, Geita and Rubondo Island National Park. The taxis that hang around in the airport parking lot generally ask around Tsh5,000 for a ride to the town centre, but regular minibuses to town leave from along the main road about 500m from the airport. The best central source of current information about flights out of Mwanza, and a good place to book tickets, is the **Fourways Travel Service** around the corner from the Pamba Hostel. For specific charter requirements, contact Coastal Travel in Dar es Salaam (see page 30), which operates a fleet of light aircraft from Mwanza and Geita.

Roads out of Mwanza are generally in poor condition. The most obvious exception to this (if one excludes the first 30km or so out of Mwanza, which is horrific but reputedly scheduled for imminent resurfacing) is the surfaced road running east of the lake, via the turn-off to Serengeti National Park, to Musoma and the Kenyan port of Kisumu. The drive from Mwanza to Musoma should take about three hours in a private vehicle and four to five hours by bus. Note that buses to Musoma and other easterly destinations no longer leave from the central bus station near the market, but from the new Buzuruga terminal about 5km – a Tsh2,000–3,000 taxi ride – from the town centre. Regular minibuses run between the two bus stations.

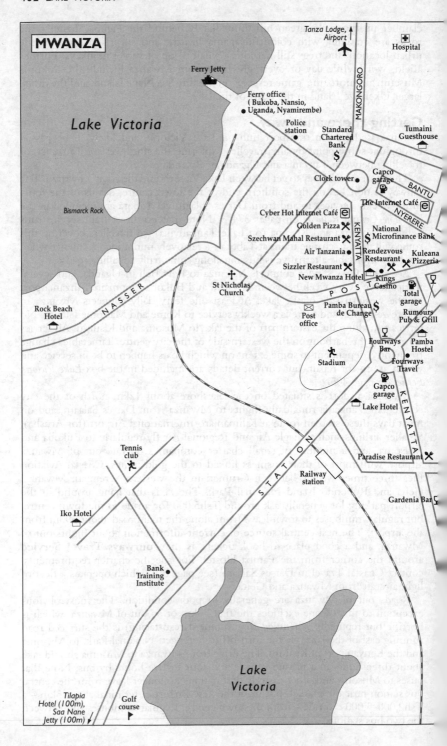

MWANZA

Tanza Lodge,
Airport

Hospital

Ferry Jetty

Ferry office
(Bukoba, Nansio,
Uganda, Nyamirembe)

Lake Victoria

Police
station

Standard
Chartered
Bank

MAKONGORO

Tumaini
Guesthouse

Clock tower

Gapco
garage

BANTU

Bismarck Rock

Cyber Hot Internet Café

The Internet Café

NYERERE

Golden Pizza

Szechwan Mahal Restaurant

National
Microfinance Bank

Air Tanzania

Rendezvous
Restaurant

Kuleana
Pizzeria

KENYATTA

Sizzler Restaurant

New Mwanza Hotel

Kings
Casino

POST

Total
garage

NASSER

St Nicholas
Church

Pamba Bureau
de Change

Rumours
Pub & Grill

Rock Beach
Hotel

Post
office

Pamba
Hostel

Fourways
Bar

Stadium

Fourways
Travel

Gapco
garage

Lake Hotel

Tennis
club

Paradise Restaurant

STATION

Railway
station

Iko Hotel

Gardenia Bar

KENYATTA

Bank
Training
Institute

*Lake
Victoria*

Tilapia
Hotel (100m),
Saa Nane
Jetty (100m)

Golf
course

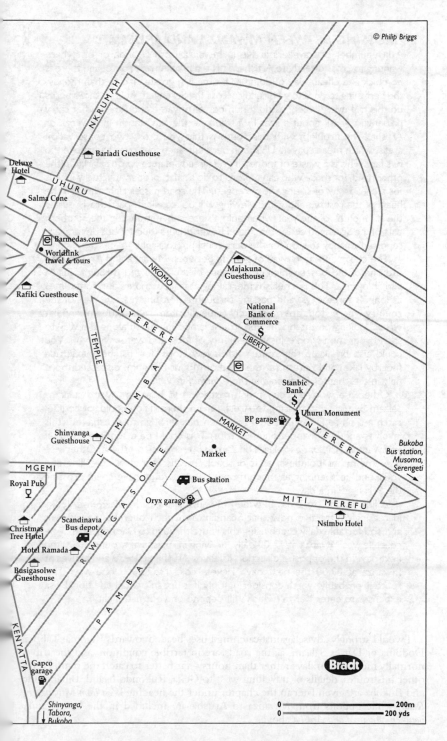

© Philip Briggs

Bariadi Guesthouse

Deluxe
Hotel

NKRUMAH

UHURU

Salma Cone

Barmedas.com

Worldlink
travel & tours

NKOMO

Majakuna
Guesthouse

Rafiki Guesthouse

National
Bank of
Commerce

NYERERE

TEMPLE

LIBERTY

e

Stanbic
Bank

Uhuru Monument

BP garage

Shinyanga
Guesthouse

LUMUMBA

MARKET

Market

NYERERE

Bukoba
Bus station,
Musoma,
Serengeti

MGEMI

Royal Pub

Bus station

RWEGASORE

Oryx garage

Christmas
Tree Hotel

Scandinavia
Bus depot

MITI   MEREFU

Nsimbu Hotel

Hotel Ramada

Busigasolwe
Guesthouse

PAMBA

KENYATTA

Gapco
garage

Shinyanga,
Tabora,
Bukoba

0 ————————— 200m
0 ————————— 200 yds

Bradt

CROSSING BETWEEN MWANZA AND ARUSHA

A fair number of travellers arrive in Mwanza from Uganda or elsewhere wanting to cross directly to Arusha. This is a problematic route, and there is no quick and cheap way of doing it. If time is a greater factor than money, the best thing to do is to go directly across the Serengeti. At least three buses do this trip every week, as do a number of private Land Rovers that carry passengers – ask about a seat in advance at the bus station in Mwanza or Arusha. The problem with this route is that you cross two conservation areas, which means paying US$60 in park entrance fees over and above the bus fare. This is a waste of money if you already plan to go on safari. On the other hand, for those who can't afford to do a safari proper, it actually makes for a cheap way of seeing the Serengeti. The road passes right through the heart of the reserve and game viewing will be excellent, particularly during the six months of the year when animals are concentrated in the southern part of the Serengeti ecosystem. Land Rover drivers (but not bus drivers) are reportedly happy to stop for the occasional photograph!

The cheap and nasty way of getting between Mwanza and Arusha is to use one of the buses which cross south of the Serengeti through Singida and Shinyanga. This is a hellish ride, taking at least 36 hours and sometimes as long as three days, and passing through a dry, unattractive part of the country where stops are most likely to be dictated by breakdowns and flat tyres. Looking on the bright side, there is nothing much along the way to spend your money on – just take plenty of food and water with you. You could also break up this route with a few stops, for instance at Singida (nearby lake) and Katesh (at the base of Mount Hanang), discussed more fully in the chapter *Dodoma and the Central Rift Valley*.

Otherwise, you're pretty much restricted to heading towards Dar es Salaam by train and bussing to Arusha from there. (You could, of course, catch a train as far as Dodoma and then bus through to Arusha, but this involves another unappetising bus trip.) This could be a sensible option if you want to visit Dar es Salaam or Zanzibar en route to Arusha. Otherwise it seems rather pointless, as it probably means four days travelling and you'll end up spending as much money as you would have spent crossing the Serengeti in a day.

A final option, to cross between Mwanza and Arusha via Kenya, looks increasingly attractive now that Scandinavia Coach operates an efficient and comfortable daily coach using this route through to Dar es Salaam. The coach leaves Mwanza at 12.00 daily, arriving in Arusha at around 06.00 the next day. In the opposite direction it leaves Arusha at 15.30 and arrives at Mwanza at 09.00 the next day. Tickets cost Tsh20,000 one-way. This route is probably worth considering only if it doesn't entail additional visa expenses to enter Kenya (which will depend on your nationality).

I would strongly advise against catching buses headed towards Kigoma, Tabora, Dodoma or Dar es Salaam, as the roads are in terrible condition, and the trip is normally measured in days rather than hours – far better to catch the train! As for other bus routes, details of travelling west to Geita, Rubondo Island, Biharamulo and Bukoba are given later in the chapter under the heading *West from Mwanza by Road*, while options from Mwanza to Arusha are included in the box *Crossing between Mwanza and Arusha* above.

LAKE VICTORIA FERRIES

The Tanzania Railway Corporation (TRC) runs a network of ferries out of Mwanza, including an international service to Port Bell in Uganda and domestic services to Bukoba, Nyamirembe, Kome and Ukerewe Island. Most of the ferries are in unexpectedly good condition, with first- and second-class cabins offering a level of comfort matched in East Africa only by the train between Nairobi and Mombasa in Kenya. The restaurants serve good, inexpensive meals and chilled beers and sodas. First or second class is definitely preferable if you can afford it, because third class tends to be overcrowded and there is a real risk of theft.

Timetables for individual routings change regularly, since one or other boat is almost always in dry dock, but the current schedules are listed below together with fares. In addition to these fares, a port tax of US$5 must be paid in hard currency upon leaving any Tanzanian port. On international services, you may be required to show a vaccination certificate and, if required, a visa for the country you intend to enter.

Mwanza to Port Bell (Uganda) This international service was suspended after the MV *Bukoba* sank in 1996, a tragedy that resulted in hundreds of fatalities, but it was resumed in early 1999. The MV *Victoria* now runs in either direction once weekly, leaving from Mwanza on Sunday afternoon and Port Bell on Monday afternoon. The trip takes 18 hours. Fares are US$55 (own room), US$35 (first class), US$30 (second class sleeping), US$20 (second class sitting) and US$20 (third class). You can take a vehicle on board for US$80.

Mwanza to Bukoba There is one overnight ferry in each direction on three days a week, with duties split between MV *Serengeti* and the larger MV *Victoria*. Ferries leave Mwanza at 22.00 on Tuesday, Thursday and Sunday, and they leave Bukoba at 21.30 on Monday, Wednesday and Friday. The trip takes around 12 hours one-way. Single one-way fares are Tsh12,500 for first class cabins, Tsh10,200 for second class cabins, Tsh7,600 for second class sitting and Tsh7,100 for third class.

Mwanza to Nyamirembe via Kome, Kahunda and Maisome Island MV *Butiama* leaves Mwanza at 09.00 on Wednesday and arrives in Nyamirembe at 0.900 on Thursday. The return trip leaves Nyamirembe at 16.00 on Thursday and arrives in Mwanza at 07.00 on Friday. The fare (third class only) is Tsh3,000 one-way.

Mwanza to Nansio (Ukerewe Island) There is at least one ferry service daily in each direction, with two services running on most days. The trip takes about three hours and costs Tsh2,400 second class sitting or Tsh2,000 third class. One boat normally leaves Mwanza between 08.00 and 09.00 and Nansio at around 13.30, but the schedule does vary slightly from day to day, so check it out in advance.

Where to stay
Upmarket

Hotel Tilapia Tel: 028 250 0517/617; fax: 018 250 0141; email: tilapia@mwanza.com. This comfortable hotel, situated about 1km from the town centre along Station Road, has an attractive lakeshore position adjacent to the jetty for Saa Nane Island. Large double chalets with satellite television cost US$70 with fan or US$80 with AC, or Tsh55,000 and Tsh42,000 for residents (all inclusive of breakfast). Facilities include a swimming pool, car hire, business centre, Thai and Indian restaurants, and an attractive wooden bar and patio overlooking the lake.

New Mwanza Hotel Tel: 028 250 1070/1; fax: 028 250 3202; email: nmh@raha.com or nmh@mwanza-online.com. Recently privatised and renovated, this former government hotel on Post Road is now similar in standard to the Hotel Tilapia, with the advantages of a more central location and cheaper rates for non-residents, and disadvantages of a blander atmosphere and the absence of a lake view. A business centre, coffee shop, restaurant, casino and shopping arcade are all located within the hotel building. Standard doubles with AC and satellite television cost Tsh55,000 B&B, while suites cost Tsh85,000 and the ostentatious presidential suite comes in at a hefty Tsh250,000.

Tunza Lodge Tel: 028 256 2215; email: renair@africaonline.co.tz; web: www.renair.com. The closest thing to a genuine beach resort anywhere on the Tanzanian portion of Lake Victoria is the recently opened Tunza Lodge, which lies in the village of Hemela only 3km from the airport. Accommodation in clean, simply furnished self-contained chalets costs US$45/55/70/90 single/twin/double/triple B&B. The green gardens verge on a small private swimming beach, with windsurfers available for the use of hotel residents. Fishing trips with rod, tackle and boat supplied can be arranged at US$100 for one or two people, or US$50 per person for larger groups. A good open-sided thatch bar and restaurant serves a variety of grills and fish meals for around Tsh5,000. The lodge lies about 2km from the main airport road along an unsignposted junction about 1km south of the airport and 10km north of town.

Moderate

Iko Hotel Tel: 028 40900. A pleasant and friendly lodge on a rocky hill overlooking the lake behind the golf course and Hotel Tilapia. The rooms show some signs of wear, but they are fair value at Tsh16,000 for a comfortable self-contained double or Tsh30,000 for a suite. The restaurant serves meals for around Tsh3,000, and the surrounding suburban lanes make for attractive rambling and birding.

Budget

Christmas Tree Hotel Tel: 028 250 2001. This excellent (if rather daftly named) new high-rise hotel lies a short distance from the bus station, yet also within five minutes' walk of the better restaurants and shops in the town centre. Clean self-contained rooms come with a large double bed, net, fan, satellite television and running hot water, making them top value at Tsh10,000 single or double, inclusive of a full breakfast for one.

Lake Hotel Tel: 028 254 2030. The long-serving Lake Hotel is conveniently situated off Kenyatta Road between the railway station and town centre, and despite looking a bit rundown of late it remains a reliable fallback in the budget range. Large self-contained rooms with hot water, nets and fan cost Tsh7,000/8,400 single/double, inclusive of a derisory breakfast. Aside from slicing up stale bread in the morning, the restaurant has been closed for some years, but the outdoor bar remains one of the better drinking holes in Mwanza.

Hotel Ramada Tel 028 250 1691. This smart new multi-storey budget hotel on Rwegasore Road is conveniently located close to the bus station and immediately next to the Scandinavia Coach depot. The clean self-contained rooms, with fan and hot water, aren't bad value at Tsh7,800/9,600 for a single/double, but unfortunately they are very cramped and – a serious omission in this neck of Tanzania – they lack mosquito nets.

Deluxe Hotel Tel: 028 40644. Like the costlier Lake Hotel, the Deluxe on Uhuru Road has been justifiably popular with travellers for years, and it remains a good compromise between comfort and price. The clean but rather worn self-contained rooms have nets and running water, and are very good value at Tsh4,000/5,000 single/double. A good restaurant and two bars are on the ground floor, along with a disco – over weekends, the latter can generate a level of noise that may be annoying should you not intend joining in.

Nsimbo Hotel Tel: 028 40948. Situated on Miti Meferu Road a stone's throw away from the bus station, the Nsimbo Hotel is looking a bit rundown these days, but it's difficult to take issue with a rate of Tsh3,600 for a large and reasonably clean self-contained double with fan, net and running water.

Pamba Hostel Tel: 028 255 3396. This rather basic but very central multi-storey hostel on Station Road is managed by the Tema Hotels Group, which also organises all the catering on trains and ferries in Tanzania. The rooms, a definite notch above the similarly priced guesthouses scattered around the bus station, cost Tsh2,500/3,000 single/double with net and use of common shower. There's a restaurant on the ground floor (if you've already eaten on a train or ferry, you know what to expect) and a rooftop bar serving cold beers and sodas.

Where to eat and drink

Deluxe Hotel The ground floor restaurant at this hotel looks rather seedy, but the food is pretty good – mostly Asian and African dishes – and very reasonably priced at around Tsh2,000 for a heaped plate!

Fourways Bar Pleasant garden bar on the main circle towards the railway station, with cheap chilled beer all day long and *mishkaki* in the evenings.

Golden Pizza A good spot for light lunches and snacks, the Golden Pizza serves a variety of inexpensive sandwiches, juices, shakes and ice-creams, as well as pizzas in the Tsh2,200–4,000 range.

Kuleana Pizzeria Run by a charity for street children, the popular Kuleana Pizzeria, open from 09.00 to 17.00, is best known for its good pizzas, but it also serves a selection of other snacks and sandwiches. Prices are in the Tsh2,000–4,000 range. Fresh brown bread is usually available to take away.

Open House Café Attached to the New Mwanza Hotel, this airy café is a good place for fresh coffee and cakes, but it also serves pizzas, pasta dishes, Indian food and light grills in the Tsh4,000–7,000 range.

Rock Beach Garden Hotel About five minutes' walk from the town centre, this slick new outdoor bar and restaurant is pretty much unique for Mwanza in that it actually has a view over the lake and Bismarck Rock. It's primarily a drinking hole – great sundowners spot! – but the restaurant serves decent Italian food and grills for around Tsh4,000. The rooms, which had been under construction for several years in late 2001, are scheduled to open in 2003, but I for one won't be holding my breath.

Royal Pub Lively outdoor bar around the corner from the Christmas Tree Hotel.

Rumours Pub & Grill This 'sports bar' type set-up, opposite the New Mwanza Hotel, serves (pricey) draught beer, a good range of cocktails and bar grub. A debatable attraction is the loud MTV and stereo – particularly debatable when the barman opts to have both blaring at the same time!

Salma Cone Great ice-cream sundaes and fresh popcorn at reasonable prices.

Sizzler Restaurant A couple of doors down from the Szechwan Mahal (see below), and not quite in the same class, the Sizzler is nevertheless a very Indian restaurant, and meals are about half the price. In the evenings, an outdoor barbecue does *mishkaki*, chicken tikka and fresh chapatis and roti bread. It used to close Thursdays but is now open daily for lunch and dinner.

Szechwan Mahal Restaurant This world-class restaurant, situated roughly opposite the New Mwanza Hotel, serves a huge variety of Indian and Chinese dishes for around Tsh4,000–5,000 with rice or naan bread. You won't find a better Indian restaurant anywhere in Tanzania, and it's definitely the first choice in Mwanza if price isn't an issue.

General information

Tourist information There is no tourist information office in Mwanza. A website devoted to the town, www.mwanza.com, is currently under construction.

Foreign exchange All the main banks are represented, and have foreign exchange facilities. The banks are mostly clustered close to the roundabout at the junction of Makongoro and Nyerere Roads, or in the vicinity of the Clock Tower at the other end of Nyerere Road. The only private foreign exchange facilities are at the Pamba bureau de change on Kenyatta Road.

Internet There's no shortage of internet cafés dotted around Mwanza city centre (see map). One of the best and most central is the Cyber Hot Café next to Golden Pizza on Kenyatta Road.

Swimming I'm not aware of a public swimming pool in Mwanza. Swimming in the lake around town is emphatically not recommended due to the high risk of contracting bilharzia.

Tour operators The best is generally regarded to be **Fourways Travel** (tel: 028 250 2273 or 250 2630; email: fourways.mza@raha.com) on the main roundabout on Station Road. For budget travellers, a day or overnight safari to the Serengeti National Park from the Mwanza side will be far cheaper than a full northern circuit safari out of Arusha. A good contact for affordable Serengeti excursions is **Serengeti Stopover** near the national park's Ndaraka Entrance Gate (see *Between Mwanza and the Kenyan Border*, pages 410–11). You could also try a new company in Mwanza called **Masumin Tours and Safaris**, which deals with car hire and Serengeti safaris (tel: 028 241391 or 241628; fax: 028 250 0192; email: masumins@mbio.net).

Excursions from Mwanza
Saa Nane Island
This small, rocky island in Lake Victoria makes for a worthwhile, affordable and straightforward day trip out of Mwanza, despite its glaring failure to live up to its nominal billing as a game sanctuary. Saa Nane is essentially a glorified zoo, and has been since the 1960s, when it served as the interim home to a variety of captive large mammals prior to their release on to Rubondo Island. Game sanctuary or zoo, Saa Nane is on either account something of a washout. The only free-ranging animals are a herd of re-introduced antelope, which wander around grazing on the grassy shore. Higher up on the island, a cluster of small cages confine a moribund trio of hyenas as well as a listless lion and leopard – quite how this lot ended up permanently stalled on Saa Nane is anybody's guess, since none of these species was ever introduced to Rubondo. This motley collection is completed by a decidedly pissed-off chimpanzee, caged in solitary confinement, a fate as cruel to any sociable primate as it would be to a human.

Depressing as they might be, the caged animals cannot detract from the island's more persuasive attractions, which are the small animals that inhabit it naturally. Gaudily coloured agama lizards bask on the rocks, while water monitors (the largest African lizard) crash gracelessly through the undergrowth. Birdlife is profuse, with fish eagle, pied kingfisher and white-bellied cormorant common near the shore, and more localised species such as swamp flycatcher, yellow-throated leaflove, grey kestrel and slender-billed weaver present in the forest. The rock hyrax is the most visible naturally occurring mammal.

Saa Nane lies about five minutes from the mainland using the motorboat service that leaves from the jetty next to the Tilapia Hotel, ten minutes' walk from Mwanza town centre along Station Road. The boat departs for the island every two hours between 11.00 and 17.00 and does the return trip every two hours from 12.00 to 18.00. The daily entrance fee of Tsh1,000 is inclusive of the boat ride. You can spend as long as you like on the island provided that you take the last boat back to town.

Bujora Sukuma Museum

The excellent Sukuma Museum, situated within the Bujora parish grounds about 20km east of Mwanza, is dedicated to the culture and history of the Sukuma, Tanzania's most populous tribe (see box *The Dancers of Usukuma*, pages 410–11). The museum was established in the 1950s by Father David Clement (whose local nickname *Fumbuka* translates as 'Unexpected'), and designed in collaboration with a Sukuma committee with the primary intent of preserving this culture for local visitors.

The museum consists of five discrete pavilions or buildings, each of which is devoted to a particular aspect of Sukuma culture. First up is the Sukuma homestead, which contains traditional household effects such as cooking utensils, religious objects and agricultural tools. The blacksmith's house is a low circular thatched hut containing cowhide bellows and other implements used to forge metal, as well as metal tools and spearheads made by the blacksmith. The concrete house of the *Iduku* (traditional healer) contains medicinal calabashes, divination tools, various charms and other traditional medical paraphernalia. The Dance Society Pavilion concentrates on the history and costumes of the Bagika and Bagalu, the competing dance societies of the Sukuma. Most impressive of all is the Royal Pavilion, a two-storey building designed in the shape of a royal throne. This section houses a vast collection of royal Sukuma thrones and crowns, while a wall display delineates the area and name of each of the 52 Sukuma chiefdoms, as well as lineages for the more important ones. The second storey of the pavilion houses royal drums donated by some local chiefs. The colourful Bujora Church, on a hilltop overlooking the museum, is also worth a look around, since it incorporates large elements of Sukuma royal symbolism into its design, for instance an altar shaped like a traditional throne.

The Sukuma Museum lies a short walk from Kissesa on the Mwanza–Musoma road. Any bus to Musoma can drop you off there at the junction. The best day to visit is Saturday, when the Sukuma Snake Dance is sometimes performed with a live python. Entrance costs Tsh1,000 per person. An inexpensive campsite and a few rooms are available for travellers who want to stay the night, though recent reports suggest they have become very rundown.

Ukerewe Island

The 530km² Ukerewe Island is the largest island in Lake Victoria – actually, trivia lovers, the sixth largest lake-bound landmass in the world! It is also the most accessible substantial island on the Tanzanian part of the lake. The principal town and port, Nansio, takes two to three hours to reach using the daily ferry service from Mwanza (see *Lake Victoria Ferries* box, page 405, for details), and it is also connected to Bunda on the main Mwanza–Musoma road by a causeway and occasional *dalla-dalla*s. The ferry trip to Nansio is a good way to see some of Africa's largest lake, and if Nansio itself is a rather scruffy little place, the island is very pretty, boasting some attractive sandy (and reputedly bilharzia-free) beaches and plenty of possibilities for casual rambling.

If you visit the island as a day trip out of Mwanza, you'll only have an hour or so to explore, so it's worth dedicating a night to the visit. The best place to stay is the **Gullu Beach Hotel**, which lies on the lakeshore about 500m from Nansio Port and has self-contained rooms with nets for Tsh10,000 double, as well as cheaper rooms using a common shower. Camping costs Tsh2,000 per person and

THE DANCERS OF USUKUMA

Usukuma – literally 'Northern Land' – lies to the immediate south and east of Lake Victoria, and is home to the Bantu-speaking Sukuma, the largest tribe in Tanzania, comprising approximately 13% of the national population. The Sukuma are thought to have migrated into their present homeland prior to the 17th century, possibly from elsewhere in the Lake Victoria hinterland. Pre-colonial Usukuma differed from the centralised states that characterised areas to the north and west of the lake in that it was comprised of about 50 affiliated but autonomous local chieftaincies. Historically, culturally and linguistically, the Sukuma are strongly affiliated to the Nyamwezi of the Tabora area. It may well be that no marked division between the local chieftaincies of the two groups existed until the latter half of the 19th century, when the militant aspirations of Mirambo, who forged the more centralised Nyamwezi state, would have enforced a greater degree of political unity among the Sukuma.

The traditional political structure of Usukuma is typical of the *ntemi* chieftaincies of central Tanzania. Chiefs are part of a royal line, and are invested with mystical and religious properties as well as political power. However, any autocratic tendencies are curbed by the necessity for a chief to be elected by a committee of princes and elders, which also has the ability to remove any chief whose actions are unpopular or inappropriate. The chief is thought to be mystically linked to the supreme being, who is regarded by the Sukuma as having many of the attributes of the sun. Ancestor worship plays as important a role in Sukuma religion as direct worship of the creator, since the spirits of the dead are seen to occupy a realm close to God. Although most Sukuma today are practising Christians or Muslims, many adhere concurrently to the traditional religion, and particularly in rural areas it is normal to leave offerings to the ancestors in the hope this will bring rain, health and prosperity.

The Sukuma have the reputation within Tanzania of being snake charmers, and are also known for their varied and spectacular traditional dances, disciplines which combine in a ritual dance called the Bugobogobo. The dancers coil a live python around their body, then writhe to a frenetic drumbeat, alternately pretending to embrace the gigantic snake and to fight with it. The dance becomes more frenzied as the drumbeat speeds up and the snake becomes increasingly excited or agitated, often causing the audience to scatter

a restaurant and bar are attached. If this place is too expensive, there are several local guesthouses in Nansio, of which the **Panda Hostel** and **Island Inn** are about the best.

BETWEEN MWANZA AND THE KENYAN BORDER

The 240km road between Mwanza and the Kenyan border is of interest primarily as a through route to Kenya and because it skirts the western edge of the Serengeti National Park. Except for the first 30km out of Mwanza, the road is in good condition, and plenty of public transport runs along it. The roadside scenery is quite attractive, too, as you pass through dry, flat country dotted with small granite outcrops and rustic Sukuma homesteads, with regular glimpses of Lake Victoria to the west. Before reaching Bunda, herds of zebra and wildebeest are likely to be seen along the eastern side of the road.

in all directions. Bugobogobo dances are sometimes held at the Bujora Sukuma Museum (see page 409) on Saturday afternoons.

Traditionally, most Sukuma people under the age of 30 will belong to one of several dance societies, of which the largest and oldest are the Bagika and Bagalu. According to oral tradition, the two societies were respectively founded about 150 years ago by Ngika and Gumha, rival dancers and traditional healers who held regular competitions to determine which had the most potent medicine. The two would dance alongside each other, using magic charms to attract spectators and induce errors in their rival's routine, and the winner was the one who eventually attracted the largest crowd.

A similar format is followed in modern dance competitions held by the rival societies, with the two troupes dancing concurrently and attempting to outdo each other in order to attract the greater number of spectators. The dancers mostly base their performance around traditional routines, but innovative and outrageous stunts are encouraged – masks, props, costumes or fresh steps – and may well be decisive in attracting the crowd required in order to win the competition

Until recent times, the dancing societies of Sukuma were important spiritual entities with somewhat Masonic overtones. Members of any given society would wear a distinctive tattoo. The Bagika favour a diagonal double incision running from one of their shoulders to the opposite side of their waist, and sometimes a series of arrow-shaped incisions on one cheek. The Bagalu used circular rather than linear incisions, sometimes around the left eye or breast, sometimes around the torso. Today, the dance competitions are held mainly as entertainment, but a large element of mysticism is still attached to the societies. The leader of a troupe will consult traditional spiritual leaders prior to the competition, and cover his body in a paste made from a powdered dance medicine called *samba* when dancing. Some dancers even build ancestral shrines on the dance ground!

Dance competitions take place throughout Usukuma after the end of the harvest season, starting in June and running through to August, with particularly impressive festivals likely to be held on the public holidays of July 7 and August 8. If you're in the area at the time, ask around about where competitions are being held. For more information about the Sukuma dancers and other aspects of Sukuma culture, take a look at the excellent website www.wasukuma.com, which links to a number of other good websites covering most aspects of Sukuma culture and history.

The largest town in this part of Tanzania is Musoma, a substantial port and regional administrative centre situated on the lakeshore 18km west of the main road to the border and 180km from Mwanza, and covered under a separate heading below. Other significant towns, both situated along the main road, are Bunda, which lies close to the Serengeti about 70km south of Musoma, and Tarime, 20km south of the border. The smaller town of Butiama, which lies about 30km east of the main road, is of note as birth and burial place of former President Nyerere, and a small museum is dedicated to his memory.

Where to stay
Speke Bay Lodge Tel: 028 262 1236; fax: 028 262 1237; email: spekebay@raha.com. Situated about 1km from the main Musoma road, 125km from Mwanza and 15km south of the Ndaraka Gate to Serengeti National Park, this attractive and moderately priced

lakeshore lodge consists of eight self-contained thatched bungalows and ten standing safari tents using common showers and toilets. Activities include birdwatching on the lake and game fishing by boat.

Serengeti Stop Over Tel: 027 253 7095; email: serengetiso@yahoo.com. This excellent new budget lodge lies along the eastern side of the main Mwanza–Musoma road, in an area where quite a bit of game can be present, about 1km south of the Ndaraka Entrance Gate to Serengeti National Park and 18km south of Bunda. The lodge consists of three *bandas* and a campsite with hot showers and cooking shades. Camping costs US$7 per person and *banda* accommodation US$30 per person B&B. A great advantage of staying here for motorised travellers coming from Kenya or Mwanza is that park fees are only payable once you enter the park. The lodge can arrange safaris to Serengeti National Park, which will work out more cheaply than a safari out of Arusha, if only because the lodge is a mere 1km from the entrance gate and 135km from Seronera, so that an overnight or day trip is a realistic possibility. The cost of a vehicle to carry up to five people for a day trip into the park is US$130. Other activities on offer include a walking safari to Lake Victoria at US$18 per trip, traditional and game fishing trips, a visit to the Nyerere Museum, and dancing and other cultural activities.

Bunda

Bunda is the largest town on the Mwanza–Musoma road, more substantial than maps suggest, but otherwise only moderately intriguing. It has a scenic position at the foot of a range of steep granite hills, which – should you have the inclination to climb – would doubtless offer a superb vantage point over Lake Victoria and the Serengeti plains. Bunda is also a route focus of sorts, where Arusha-based safari companies generally drop off passengers heading to Mwanza, and a good place to pick up road transport to Ukerewe Island. There are several guesthouses in Bunda, none of which is very special or costs more than Tsh3,000.

Butiama

This otherwise undistinguished small town is of note as the birthplace of former President Julius Nyerere, and it is also where he is buried. The Mwalimu Julius K Nyerere Memorial Museum was officially opened here in July 1999, and contains a variety of exhibits relating to Tanzania's first president, including various personal possessions and gifts presented to him on his inauguration and retirement, as well as to the local Zanaki culture. Nyerere's grave and family home can also be visited. Entrance costs US$1 per person. Butiama lies off the main road along a 30–40km side road branching from Bunda. The drive from Bunda takes less than an hour in a private vehicle, and there is some public transport.

Tarime

Tarime is the second largest town in Mara region, with a population of around 25,000. It actually lies to the north of Musoma, about 20km before reaching the border with Kenya. There are several guesthouses and basic hotels in Tarime, though the only circumstance in which you'd be likely to prevail upon them is if you arrived from Kenya late in the day, or wanted somewhere to crash before crossing into Kenya from Tanzania. In all other respects Musoma is a far more attractive place to spend a night or two.

MUSOMA

Situated on the eastern shores of Lake Victoria, Musoma is the administrative centre of Mara District, and a reasonably substantial town, with a population estimated at around 150,000 in 2001. Musoma's compact town centre shares with Mwanza and Bukoba a likeable combination of rundown colonial architecture – the Old Boma on Mkendo Hill dates to the German period – and friendly African bustle. And its setting, on a narrow, rocky peninsula that bounds the all but disused harbour, is the equal of any port on Lake Victoria, terminating in an impressive granite outcrop covered in clucking cormorants and offering an almost 360° vantage point for sunsets over the lake. Unfortunately, however, because it is tucked up so close to the Kenyan border, Musoma is something of a dead end in terms of travel within Tanzania, and it would be difficult to justify a special diversion there. For travellers headed between Mwanza and the Kenyan port of Kisumu, however, this remote but hospitable port is likely to prove a more than agreeable place to break up the trip. Two possible water excursions from Musoma are to Lukuba Island, known for its impressive breeding bird colonies, and to the crocodile-infested Mara River mouth – the Peninsula Hotel can arrange these trips in its 13-seater boat for Tsh40,000 per hour. The Nyerere Museum in Butiama also makes for an easy day trip out of Musoma.

Getting there and away

Musoma lies about 180km from Mwanza along an 18km-long side road branching west from the main road towards the Kenyan border. The road between Mwanza and Musoma is surfaced and in pretty good nick for most of its length, the major exception being the very bumpy 30km stretch immediately outside of Mwanza. The drive takes the best part of three hours in a private vehicle. Regular buses run along the road, taking about four to five hours one-way, but since they leave when full rather than to any schedule, it's normal to wait two to three hours to get going. Small and very regular minibuses cover the stretch between Musoma and Bunda, but don't seem to operate any further south towards Mwanza. Coming from the Kenyan side, direct buses between Kisumu and Mwanza run past the junction to Musoma, but generally bypass the town itself. If you need to get out at the junction, you'll have no difficulty finding transport on to Musoma.

For details of stopovers along the road north and south of Musoma, see the preceding heading *Between Mwanza and the Kenyan Border*.

An airstrip lies on the outskirts of central Musoma between the Catholic Hostel and the Peninsula Hotel. Eagle Air and Precision Air run regular flights to and from Mwanza.

However you arrive in Musoma, should you want to stay at one of the beach hotels, the standard fare for a taxi is Tsh1,000.

Where to stay
Moderate
Peninsula Hotel Tel: 028 264 2546. The former government Lake Hotel, recently privatised, revamped and renamed, is a well-maintained and atmospheric wood and whitewash set-up situated on a somewhat sterile stretch of lakeshore about 500m west of the town centre. Coming from elsewhere in Tanzania, it's very good value, charging Tsh25,000/35,000 for standard self-contained single/double with satellite television, AC, fridge and hot bath, or Tsh45,000–60,000 for various suites. The open-sided restaurant on the ground floor serves a variety of Western and Indian dishes for around Tsh3,000.

Afrilux Hotel Tel: 028 262 0031. This smart and perhaps slightly self-consciously modern four-storey hotel is situated right in the town centre, 500m from the bus station. The clean self-contained rooms are all you could possibly ask for at Tsh10,000/15,000 single/double with satellite television, fan and running hot water. The restaurant and garden bar serve decent Continental and Indian meals for around Tsh3,000.

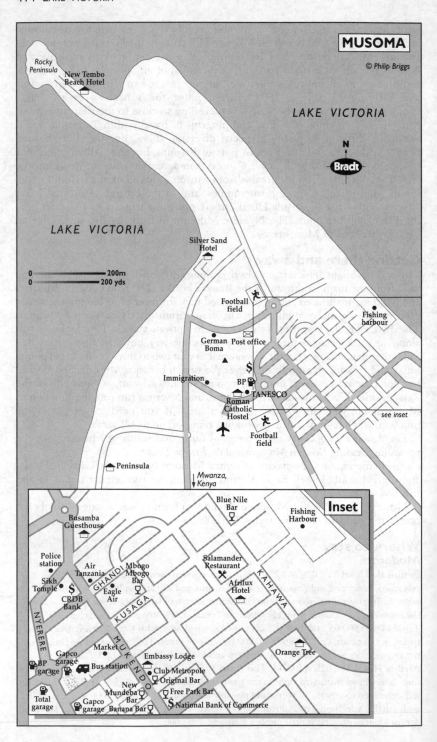

Budget

New Tembo Beach Hotel Tel: 028 262 2887. Difficult to fault the location, which is easily the best of any hotel in Musoma, on a sandy private beach a few hundred metres from the rocky outcrop at the end of Musoma Peninsula. But the rooms, though adequate – fresh paint, fan – seem optimistically priced at non-resident rates of Tsh12,000 double using common shower, Tsh14,000 self-contained single, or Tsh16,000 self-contained double. The resident rates – about half-price – are far more realistic, but negotiation doesn't seem to be the done thing. Camping costs a flat US$5 per person.

Orange Tree Hotel Tel: 028 262 2353. This established budget hotel has possibly seen better days, but it remains a friendly, sensibly priced option at Tsh6,000/8,400 for a self-contained single/double for residents. Although higher and rather unrealistic non-resident rates (US$10/14) are posted up at reception, they seem to be for show only – you should be allowed to pay resident rates.

Shoestring

Roman Catholic Conference Centre & Hostel Tel: 028 262 0168. This is the best budget option in town, situated about 200m from the bus station along the road towards the airport, and consisting of 30 clean double rooms with netting (but no fan) for Tsh4,000. A canteen serves inexpensive local meals.

Silver Sand Hotel Tel: 028 262 2740. Situated about 1km out of town, within a wooded compound that would overlook the beach were it not enclosed by tall stone walls, the Silver Sand Hotel has definitely seen better days, but it's a friendly and affordable set-up all the same. Faintly musty self-contained single rooms with netting but no fan, and a functional shower, cost Tsh3,500. Meals are by prior arrangement only.

WEST FROM MWANZA BY ROAD

The roads heading west from Mwanza to Geita and Biharamulo, then branching northward to Bukoba or westward to the Rwanda border, are generally in poor condition, as are the buses that traverse them. For travellers who are using public transport, and who simply want to get between Mwanza and Bukoba as efficiently as possible, a far better option than bussing it would be to use the overnight ferry service that runs between the two ports four times weekly. You would need to use these roads, however, should you be planning on crossing overland into Rwanda, or on travelling by road to one of the mainland ports from which you can reach Rubondo Island National Park. Overlanders driving between Tanzania and Rwanda or Uganda will also use these roads.

The most significant towns along the road running west from Mwanza are Geita and Biharamulo. Buses do run directly between Mwanza and Biharamulo, a 300km journey that entails a full day on the road, and it would certainly be possible to cover this stretch in a day in a private vehicle. There is, however, much to be said for breaking the journey into 125km and 175km stretches by staying over in Geita. If you're heading on to Rubondo, the best options are either to fly there from Geita or else to bus on from Geita to Muganza, as covered in greater detail under the section on *Rubondo Island National Park* on pages 420–7. Details of travelling between Biharamulo and Bukoba or the Rwandan border are included below. An alternative to bussing along the southern lakeshore would be to catch a ferry from Mwanza to Maisome Island or Nyamirembe, and proceed overland from there.

Geita

The booming town of Geita, which lies about 120km west of Mwanza, has emerged as the lynchpin of Tanzania's recently revitalised gold mining industry. Tanzania was a minor gold producer in the colonial era, but production ground to

A DYING LAKE

The risk of sodium cyanide from the gold mines finding its way into Lake Victoria (see *Geita*, pages 415 and 418–19) is potentially the latest in a series of manmade ecological disasters to have afflicted the lake over the last century. The degradation started in the early colonial era, with the clearing of large tracts of indigenous vegetation and drainage of natural swamps to make way for plantations of tea, coffee and sugar. One result of this was an increase in the amount of topsoil washed into the lake, so that the water became progressively muddier and murkier during the 20th century. More serious was the wash off of toxic pesticides and other agricultural chemicals, which in addition to polluting the water contain nutrients that promote algae growth, in turn tending to decrease oxygenation levels. The foundation of several large lakeshore cities and plantations attracted migrant labourers from around the region, many of whom settled at the lake, leading to a disproportionate population increase and – exacerbated by more sophisticated trapping tools introduced by the colonials – heavy overfishing.

By the early 1950s, the above factors had conspired to create a noticeable drop in yields of popular indigenous fish, in particular the Lake Victoria tilapia (*ngege*), which had been fished close to extinction. The colonial authorities introduced the similar Nile tilapia, which restored the diminishing yield without seriously affecting the ecological balance of the lake. More disastrous, however, was the gradual infiltration of the Nile perch, a voracious predator that feeds almost exclusively on smaller fish, and frequently reaches a length of 2m and a weight exceeding 100kg. How the perch initially ended up in Lake Victoria is a matter of conjecture – game fishermen might have introduced some perch, while others possibly swam downriver from Uganda's Lake Kyoga, where they had been introduced in the mid-1950s. But, however they first arrived in Lake Victoria, Nile perch regularly turned up in fishermen's nets from the late 1950s. The authorities, who favoured large eating fish over the smaller tilapia and cichlids, decided to ensure the survival of the alien predators with an active programme of introductions in the early 1960s.

It would be 20 years before the full impact of this misguided policy hit home. In a UN survey undertaken in 1971, the indigenous haplochromine cichlids still constituted their traditional 80% of the lake's fish biomass, while the introduced perch and tilapia had effectively displaced the indigenous tilapia without otherwise altering the ecology of the lake. A similar survey undertaken ten years later revealed that the perch population had exploded to constitute 80% of the lake's fish biomass, while the haplochromine cichlids – the favoured prey of the perch – now accounted for a mere 1%. Lake Victoria's estimated 150–300 endemic cichlid species, all of which have evolved from a mere five ancestral species since the lake dried out 10–15,000 years ago, are regarded to represent the most recent comparable explosion of vertebrate adaptive radiation in the world. Ironically, these fish also are currently undergoing what Boston University's Les Kauffman has described as 'the greatest vertebrate mass extinction in recorded history',

For all this, the introduction of perch could be considered a superficial success within its own terms. The perch now form the basis of the lake's thriving fishing industry, with up to 500 metric tonnes of fish meat being exported from the lake annually, at a value of more than US$300 million, by commercial fishing concerns in the three lakeshore countries. The tanned perch hide is used as a substitute for leather to make shoes, belts, and purses, and the dried swim bladders, used to filter beer and make fish stock, are exported at a rate of around US$10 per kg. The flip side of this is that as fish exports increase, local fishing communities are forced to compete against large commercial companies with better equipment and more economic clout. Furthermore, since the perch is too large to roast on a fire and too fatty to dry in the sun, it does not really meet local needs.

The introduction of perch is not the only damaging factor to have affected Lake Victoria's ecology. It is estimated that the amount of agricultural chemicals being washed into the lake has more than doubled since the 1950s. Tanzania alone is currently pumping two million litres of untreated sewage and industrial waste into the lake daily, and while legal controls on industrial dumping are tighter in Kenya and Uganda, they are not effectively enforced. The agricultural wash off and industrial dumping has led to a further increase in the volume of chemical nutrients in the lake, promoting the growth of plankton and algae. At the same time, the cichlids that once fed on these microscopic organisms have been severely depleted in number by the predatorial perch.

The lake's algae levels have increased fivefold in the last four decades, with a corresponding decrease in oxygen levels. The lower level of the lake now consists of dead water – lacking any oxygenation or fish activity below about 30m – and the quality of the water closer to the surface has deteriorated markedly since the 1960s. Long-term residents of the Mwanza area say that the water was once so clear that you could see the lake floor from the surface to depths of 6m or more; today visibility near the surface is more like one metre.

A clear indicator of this deterioration has been the rapid spread of water hyacinth, which thrives in polluted conditions leading to high phosphate and nitrogen levels, and then tends to further deplete oxygen levels by forming an impenetrable mat over the water's surface. An exotic South American species, the water hyacinth was introduced to East Africa by expatriates in Rwanda, and made its way down to Lake Victoria via the Kagera River. Unknown on the lake prior to 1989, it has subsequently colonised vast tracts of the lake surface, and clogged up several harbours, where it is barely kept under control by constant harvesting. To complete this grim vicious circle, Nile perch, arguably the main cause of the problem, are known to be vulnerable to the conditions created by hyacinth matting, high algae levels and decreased oxygenation in the water.

As is so often the case with ecological issues, what might at first be dismissed by some as an esoteric concern of bunny-huggers in fact has wider implications for the estimated 20–30 million people resident in the Lake Victoria basin. The infestation of hyacinth and rapid decrease in indigenous snail-eating fish has led to a rapid growth in the number of bilharzia-carrying snails. The deterioration in water quality, exacerbated by the pumping of sewage, has increased the risk of sanitary-related diseases such as cholera spreading around the lake. The change in the fish biomass has encouraged commercial fishing for export outside of the region, in the process depressing the local semi-subsistence fishing economy, leading to an increase in unemployment and protein deficiency. And there is an ever growing risk that Africa's largest lake will eventually be reduced to a vast expanse of dead water, with no fish in it at all – and ecological, economic and humanitarian ramifications that scarcely bear thinking about.

a halt in the post-colonial era, to be resuscitated in the 1990s following the discovery of several new seams in the Lake Victoria region. In the late 1990s, Tanzania attracted an international gold rush with few modern peers. Exports rocketed from less than US$10 million in 1998 to more than US$100 million in 2001, and the country is now ranked as the continent's third-largest gold producer after the established giants South Africa and Ghana.

Jointly owned by Ghana's Ashanti Goldfields and the South African AngloGold Company, the Geita Gold Mine cost US$165 million to construct, and it is reputedly the second largest on the continent outside of South Africa. It was formally opened in August 2000 by President Mkapa, and during the first 18 months of activity, more than 150,000 ounces of gold were extracted. The mine's reserves are estimated to stand at around 15 million ounces, which at present rates of production should keep it ticking along nicely for at least another decade. The town of Geita, meanwhile, has grown from being a rather insignificant settlement to probably the twelfth most populous in the country, with a population approaching 150,000 in 2001.

Geita Gold Mine has attracted its far share of controversy during its short existence. Even before the mine was operational, several respected conservation bodies expressed concerns about the potential consequences of toxic sodium cyanide used in the gold extraction process leaking into the Nyamalembo River, which flows through Geita into nearby Lake Victoria. Tundu Lissu, of the US-based World Resource Institute described the project as 'a disaster in the making', going on to say that 'should any of this cyanide find its way into the lake, then Tanzania will not suffer alone but so will her neighbours and millions of other people.'

These concerns were stoked within months of the mine opening, when villagers in nearby Nyakabale reported several human fatalities and loss of livestock, apparently caused by a toxic substance infiltrating the village's main water source following heavy rains. The mine has refuted widespread allegations of culpability, and the results of subsequent tests of samples taken from the dead livestock and affected water source have yet to be made public – some sources suggest agricultural pesticide rather than cyanide might have been responsible for the deaths. Whatever the truth of the matter, this much is irrefutable: mistakes happen, sodium cyanide is toxic, and Geita lies a mere 20km from an inland sea whose waters support an estimated 30 million people across three countries.

Another unrelated scandal erupted in 2001, when it emerged that hundreds of people who had been displaced by the construction of the gold mine never received the full agreed compensation payment. It appears that the mining company made the full payment of slightly more than US$5 million to the government officials responsible for co-ordinating individual compensations in 1999. But it has been alleged that somewhere along the line the official books were cooked and an undisclosed proportion of this amount was diverted away from the local people for whom it was intended. A task force appointed by the government's Prevention of Corruption Bureau is currently investigating the allegations.

Geita might be two-thirds of the way to fulfilling the 'sex, money and scandal' criteria that make for a good soap opera, but the town could hardly have less to offer travellers, especially as the substantial expatriate community is based in a discrete mine compound. Still, for travellers heading from Mwanza to Rubondo Island, Rwanda or Bukoba, Geita forms a convenient stopover, linked by regular buses to Mwanza (four to five hours) and plenty of (generally very slow) transport heading further west. There's no shortage of budget accommodation in Geita. The **Africa Inland Church Hostel** (tel: 028 252 0029) has been recommended as a clean, basic and peaceful place to sleep over. The **Lake View Hotel**, under French management, has slightly better rooms but is potentially rowdier, since it's a favoured drinking hole with miners, with an atmosphere that completes the soap opera trio referred to above. Cheaper guesthouses abound.

Maisome Island
This inhabited island lies in the southwest of Lake Victoria, where it is separated from the slightly larger Rubondo Island by about 10km of open water. The lushly forested western half of Maisome is currently protected within a forest reserve and may at some point be incorporated into Rubondo Island National Park. At present, however, the forest can be explored without paying fees, and it harbours a similar range of birds to the national park, though not the large mammals. Ferries between Mwanza and Nyamirembe (see box *Lake Victoria Ferries*, page 405) stop at Maisome in both directions. It is also possible to arrange for local fishermen to take you from Maisome to Rubondo Island or to Nyamirembe on the mainland. I'm told that basic guesthouses are available on Maisome, and it should be no problem pitching a tent. The staff at the ferry office in Mwanza can be very helpful with information about places where ferries stop.

Biharamulo
In direct contrast to Geita, Biharamulo, roughly 175km to its west, is a former German administrative centre boasting an attractively laid-out, albeit rather rundown, old town centre of shady avenues lined with a few German buildings. In addition to the usual motley collection of central guesthouses, of which the **Sunset Inn** is about the best, accommodation is available at the **Old Boma**, on a hilltop about 1km from the town centre. Built in 1890 and recently restored as a guesthouse by a Dutch couple, the Old Boma is a lovely atmospheric retreat, charging around Tsh8,000 for a double room.

Biharamulo is the nearest town to the obscure **Biharamulo Game Reserve**, a 950km² sanctuary dominated by *miombo* woodland and situated on the mainland roughly opposite Rubondo Island National Park. The reserve is known for its substantial population of roan antelope, and also supports other large mammals such as elephant, impala and topi, but visitors are thin on the ground and facilities non-existent. The rough road between Biharamulo town and the small lake port of Nyamirembe – the latter accessible by ferry from Mwanza – skirts the southern boundary of the reserve. For permission to visit the game reserve, and any other information, you must first visit the reserve headquarters in Biharamulo town.

To Rwanda
The Rusumo Falls border post between Tanzania and Rwanda is reached from Biharamulo by following the main road south for 50km to the junction town of Lusahanga, where basic guesthouse accommodation can be found should you want to break up the trip. A right turn at Lusahanga leads to the border after 90km. The substantial town of **Ngala** has several basic guesthouses and is situated about 10km from the border. Buses run directly from Biharamulo to Ngala, typically taking about 5–6 hours. Once at Ngala, there is local transport to the border post.

About 20km before the Rusumo border, the road crosses into the southwest extreme of the 1,900 km² **Burigi Game Reserve**, which was gazetted in 1972 and has subsequently been proposed as a national park. Jointly managed with the almost contiguous Biharamulo Game Reserve, Burigi harbours significant numbers of lion, elephant, buffalo, giraffe and various antelopes. Although the animal populations of the two reserves were greatly reduced by subsistence poaching during the Rwanda refugee crisis, an aerial survey undertaken in 1998 indicated a fair level of recovery. Estimated combined figures for the reserves based on the survey include 240 eland, 300 giraffe, 2,800 impala, 98 roan antelope, 32 sable antelope, 160 topi, 600 zebra and 94 waterbuck (elephant and buffalo were counted but the figures were not considered sufficiently reliable for an estimate to be made). Arguably of greater ecological importance than the actual game reserve are the permanent and seasonal papyrus swamps connecting **Lake Burigi** and the **Kagera River** immediately to the north. One of the largest swamp systems in East Africa, this area forms an important refuge for the sitatunga antelope and localised swamp-related birds such as the impressive shoebill and lovely papyrus gonolek. With a private 4WD vehicle, and permission from the game department office in Biharamulo, it should be possible to explore the reserve and surrounding areas along a rough road running north from the Rusumo road towards Karagwe.

The bridge at the border between Tanzania and Rwanda overlooks the **Rusumo Falls**, a voluminous and impressive rush of white water on the Kagera River. It is here that the first German administrator entered modern-day Rwanda in 1894, and also where Belgian troops recorded their first decisive victory over the German colonists in 1916. More recently, in 1994, Rusumo Bridge served as the funnel through which an estimated 500,000 Rwandans – half of them within one 24-hour period – fled from their home country to refugee camps around Ngala and elsewhere in northwest Tanzania. Journalists reporting on the exodus described standing on the bridge and counting the bloated bodies of genocide victims tumbling over the waterfall at a rate of one or two per minute.

The 160km road between Rusumo and Kigali (the capital of Rwanda) is in very good condition, and minibus taxies take no more than four hours to cover it. If you prefer to stop along the way, the first accommodation you'll come across is the **Fine Corner Guesthouse** in Nyakarimbi village, about 20km past the border, while better rooms can be found at the **Umbrella Pine Guesthouse** in Kibungo, 60km past the border.

Muleba and the Bukoba Road

Regular buses run along the 165km road between Biharamulo and Bukoba, taking about six hours or longer, depending on road conditions. One potential stopover is the port of Muleba, which lies about 60km south of Bukoba and is an important depot for coffee grown in the hilly vicinity. Ferries between Mwanza and Bukoba stop at Muleba, and regular *dalla-dallas* between Bukoba and Muleba take about two hours. A scattering of cheap local lodgings includes the **Nshamba**, **Size** and **Victor Guesthouses**.

RUBONDO ISLAND NATIONAL PARK

The only bona fide tourist attraction on Lake Victoria is the underrated Rubondo Island National Park, which lies in the southwest corner of the lake, some 200km west of the Serengeti as the crow flies, where it forms a potentially very different extension to a standard northern Tanzania safari package. That so few tourists do actually make it to Rubondo – a grand total of 60 non-residents over the year 2000 – is in some part because the island's attractions are more low-key and esoteric than those of Tanzania's high profile savannah reserves. But a greater factor in Rubondo's obscurity is quite simply that the park long lacked for the sort of tourist infrastructure and ease of access that would have made it realistic goal for any but the most intrepid or wealthy of travellers.

All that has changed, at least in theory, following the construction of Flycatcher Safaris' indisputably lovely Rubondo Island Camp, and the more recent

BIRDING IN RUBONDO

With its combination of aquatic and forested habitats, Rubondo Island makes for an alluring destination for birdwatchers, especially as it can so easily be explored on foot. Oddly, the park's avifauna has never been properly studied, with the result that the only checklist, compiled from reported sightings by the Frankfurt Zoological Society and available at the Rubondo Island Camp, tallies up at a relatively low 225 species. It is likely that a substantial number of forest species that are resident on the island, or regular visitors, have thus far gone unrecorded.

The main avian attraction for casual visitors will be the concentrations of large waterbirds that occur along the island's swampy shores. Rubondo hosts Lake Victoria's densest fish eagle population – 638 individuals were recorded in a 1995 census – as well as large numbers of open-billed and yellow-billed storks. An excellent spot for varied waterbirds (as well as aquatic mammals and reptiles) is Mlaga Bay on the western side of the island, where some of the more prominent species are Goliath, purple and squacco heron, long-toed plover, blue-headed coucal, swamp flycatcher and various weavers. Of interest less for their variety than for their volume of birds are the so-called Bird Islands, a pair of tiny rocky islets that lie about 1km off the southeast shore of Rubondo, and support breeding colonies of various cormorants, egrets and ibises.

Dedicated birders are likely to be more interested in the forest and other terrestrial species. Two common birds on the island – Viellot's black weaver and black-and-white casqued hornbill – are Guinea-Congo biome species with a very limited range in Tanzania. The lodge grounds and adjacent road and forest loop – where it is permitted to walk unguided – is as good a place as any to seek out other forest birds. Among the more interesting species recorded in this area are the blue-breasted kingfisher, grey-winged akalat, snowy-headed robin-chat, paradise flycatcher, common wattle-eye and green twinspot. The area around the lodge is also the main stomping – and screeching – ground for the recently introduced flock of African grey parrots.

introduction of scheduled flights to Rubondo from the Serengeti and Mwanza. In practice, however, Rubondo remains probably the most underpublicised and least visited of all Tanzania's national parks. This is a real shame, because it is a lovely retreat, offering the combination of a near perfect climate, atmospheric jungle-fringed beaches, some unusual wildlife viewing, and the opportunity to explore it all on foot or by boat. Rubondo may not be to everybody's taste, but the island can be recommended without reservation to anybody with a strong interest in birds, walking or game fishing – or simply a yen to escape to an uncrowded and blissfully peaceful tropical paradise!

Gazetted in 1977, the 457km² national park is dominated by the green and undulating 240km² island for which it is named, but it does protect another 11 islets, none much larger than 2km², and there is talk of extending the boundary eastward to incorporate the forested west of Maisome Island. Rubondo Island itself essentially consists of a partially submerged rift of four volcanically formed hills, linked by three flatter isthmuses, and it measures 28km from north to south but is nowhere more than 10km wide. The highest point on Rubondo is the Msasa Hills in the far south, which reaches an elevation of 1,486m (350m above the level of the

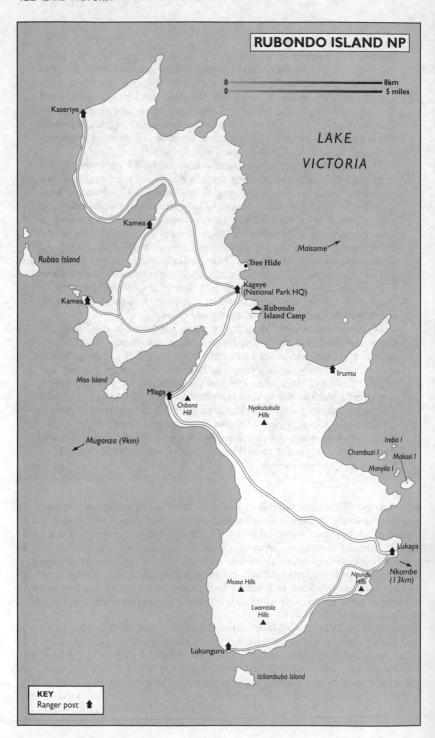

RUBONDO ISLAND NP

0   8km
0   5 miles

Kaseriye

LAKE

VICTORIA

Kamea

Rubiso Island

Maisome

Tree Hide

Kamea

Kageye
(National Park HQ)

Rubondo
Island Camp

Miso Island

Irumu

Mlaga

Chibona
Hill

Nyakutukula
Hills

Muganza (9km)

Iroba I

Chambuzi I

Makosi I

Manyila I

Lukaya

Nkombe
(13km)

Msasa Hills

Ngundu
Hills

Lwamtola
Hills

Lukunguru

Izilambuba Island

KEY
Ranger post

lake). The park headquarters, airstrip and various accommodation facilities lie within 2km of each other at Kageye, on the central isthmus, about 10km from the northern tip at the narrowest part of the island.

The dominant vegetation type is closed canopy lowland forest, which covers about 80% of the island's surface area. This is interspersed with patches of open grassland and, all but restricted to the Lukaya area, acacia woodland. The eastern lakeshore is characterised by rocky areas and sandy beaches (such as those in front of the lodge and camp), while the western shore supports extensive papyrus swamps, often lined with wild date palms. Between December and March, an estimated 40 terrestrial and epiphytic orchid species come into bloom, as do gloriosa and fireball lilies. The red coral tree, which flowers almost all year round, is also a spectacular sight. The fauna of Rubondo doesn't offer the easy thrills of many savannah reserves, but an unusual range of large mammals is present, notably chimpanzee, elephant and sitatunga, as well as a profusion of birds and butterflies (see boxes *Rubondo's Wildlife* on page 424 and *Birding in Rubondo* on page 421).

A wide variety of activities can be arranged either through Rubondo Island Camp or through the National Park headquarters. A good, inexpensive introduction to the park, taking two to four hours depending on how often you stop, is the guided trail to Pongo Viewpoint and Nhoze Hide, the latter a good place to see sitatunga, a variety of birds and – very occasionally – elephant. Another popular activity is chimpanzee tracking from either Kamea or Irumu ranger posts (ask at headquarters which of the two currently offers the better chance). This generally takes about six hours, with a 50–60% chance of encountering chimps at present, and it costs US$25 per person inclusive of a guide and transport to the ranger post. Other options include boat trips to the swampy Mlaga Bay or Bird Island, fishing expeditions (the record catch is a 108kg Nile perch), and walks on more remote parts of the island to look for colobus monkeys or giraffes.

As for unguided activities, quite a bit of wildlife and lots of birds can be seen in the grounds of Rubondo Island Camp and the national park campsite, while the roughly 1km footpath and road between the two can be walked unaccompanied as a loop. Swimming is reputedly safe, at least at the beaches in front of the lodge and camp. The lake water is regularly tested for bilharzia, thus far always with a negative result, and – bearing in mind that human beings form an integral part of the bacteria's life cycle – all residents of the island take the bilharzia cure as a precautionary routine every six months. Do be aware that crocs occasionally swim past the beaches, so far without incident – still, you might want to look before you leap in!

Rubondo has a remarkably pleasant climate all year through, with temperatures rarely falling outside a range of 20–25°C by day or by night. The average annual rainfall is around 1,200m, with the driest months being June to September and January and February. These dry months are the perfect time to visit Rubondo, but the park and lodge are open all year round, and there is no serious obstacle to visiting during the rains. The entrance fee of US$15 per 24 hours must be paid in hard currency. A national park fishing licence valid for three days costs US$50.

Getting there and away

The simplest way to get to Rubondo is by air. Coastal Travel has recently implemented a daily scheduled service connecting Rubondo to Geita (US$40 one-way), Mwanza (US$70) and Grumeti in the Western Corridor of Serengeti National Park (US$110). For travellers appending a visit to Rubondo to a standard northern circuit safari, the easiest option would be to fly direct from Grumeti. For

RUBONDO'S WILDLIFE

Rubondo Island is unique among Tanzania's national parks not only in its aquatic location, but also in that it was conceived less as a game reserve than as a sort of 'floating zoo'. Proclaimed a forest reserve in German times, the island was upgraded to a game reserve in 1966, at the behest of Professor Bernhard Grzimek of the Frankfurt Zoological Society. Grzimek, best known for his tireless efforts to protect the Serengeti, believed that the forested island would make an ideal sanctuary for the breeding and protection of introduced populations of endangered Congolese rainforest species such as golden cat, okapi, bongo and lowland gorilla. This plan never quite attained fruition, even though several chimpanzees were introduced to the island along with small numbers of elephant, giraffe, roan antelope, suni, black-and-white colobus monkey and black rhinoceros – most of which would not normally be regarded as forest-specific species. This arbitrary introduction programme was abandoned in 1973, only to be resurrected briefly in July 2000, when a flock of 37 grey parrots – captured in Cameroon for sale in Asia and confiscated in transit at Nairobi – were released on to the island.

Not all of the mammal re-introductions were a success. The 16 **black rhinoceros** that were relocated from the Serengeti in 1965 were poached in the 1970s, while the five **roan antelope** introduced in 1967 evidently died of natural causes before producing any offspring. By contrast, the six sub-adult **elephants** that were released on to the island over 1972–73 have bred up to a population of 30–40, with the larger herds concentrated in the south, and the lone bulls ranging all over the island – they are quite regularly seen around the park headquarters and lodge. Some concern has been expressed that an overpopulation of elephants could lead to the destruction of the natural forest, but the herd would probably need to grow to 200 before this became a real threat, and contraception can be used to keep numbers in check.

The introduced **black-and-white colobus** also occasionally roam close to the lodge, but the main population of about 30 is concentrated in the far south of the island, and their normal territory can be reached by boat or car, followed by a 10-minute walk. The **giraffe** herd is most likely to be encountered in the restricted area of acacia woodland around Lukaya, some distance south of the lodge and park headquarters. The **suni** are the most elusive of the introduced species, because they are so small, and secretive by nature.

Between 1966 and 1969, eight male and nine female **chimpanzees** were released on to the island, all of them born wild in the Guinean rainforest belt but captured when young to be taken to European zoos and circuses. Some had been held in good zoos where they had the company of other chimpanzees, while others were caged inadequately or in solitary confinement. Several individuals were regarded to be troublesome and had regularly attacked or bitten their keepers, and two of the males were shot after their release because they had attacked people living on the island. The others appeared to settle down quickly. Two newborn chimps were observed in 1968, and it is now estimated that the total community numbers at least 30, most of them second or third generation, but it is possible that a couple of the original individuals survive. The chimps are normally resident in the central and northern parts of the island, near the Kamea

those trying to keep costs to a minimum, the best bet would be to bus from Mwanza to Geita and pick up the flight in Geita. For travellers coming from elsewhere in the country, it is easiest to fly to Mwanza (direct flights from Dar es

and Irumu Ranger Posts, which respectively lie about 5km northwest and a similar distance southeast of the park headquarters at Kageye.

In 1996, the Frankfurt Zoological Society and Tanzania National Park initiated a joint project with the dual purpose of monitoring chimpanzee numbers and behaviour, and habituating a community for tourist visits. **Chimpanzee tracking** is now offered to visitors, but with so few chimps ranging over such a large area, the odds of an encounter are far smaller than in the parks of Lake Tanganyika. At this stage, it is most sensible to view the excursion as a forest walk with a chance of seeing chimpanzees. However, a new research project scheduled for implementation over the course of 2002/3 may hasten the habituation process as well as improving the day-to-day information regarding the exact whereabouts of the chimps.

The presence of glamorous introduced animals such as elephant and chimpanzee should not shift focus away from an interesting assemblage of naturally occurring residents, including the aquatic **hippopotamus**, **crocodile** and **water monitor**. There is no better place anywhere in Africa to observe the **spot-necked otter**, a widespread but elusive diurnal predator that feeds mainly on fish and frogs. A few pairs of otter are resident in the rocky bay around the lodge and camp – we regularly saw them swimming past on our recent visit, and were told that during the breeding season the den can sometimes be seen through binoculars. The only terrestrial predators that occur on the island are the **marsh mongoose** and **large-spotted genet**, the latter regularly coming to feed around the lodge at dinnertime. **Vervet monkeys** are numerous and easily seen all over Rubondo, but no other primate species occurs there naturally. This is difficult to explain given the variety of primates that are present in similar island habitats on the Ugandan part of the lake, and that the lake dried up fully in the biologically recent past, which would have allowed a free flow of species between the island and mainland forests.

Two closely related antelope species occur naturally on the island, the swamp-dwelling **sitatunga** and forest-dwelling **bushbuck**. The sitatunga is a widespread but localised species, with uniquely splayed hooves that allow it to manoeuvre through swampy habitats, and Rubondo is one of only two East African parks where it is easily observed. The males of both these antelopes are very handsome, with large spiralled horns, but the sitatunga is larger, shaggier in appearance, and grey where the bushbuck is chestnut-brown. The females of both species are smaller and less striking, but easily distinguished from each other, since the bushbuck is striped on its sides, whereas the sitatunga is unmarked. Rubondo's sitatunga population probably exceeds 10 individuals per square kilometre, and is not so habitat specific as elsewhere, apparently – and unexpectedly – outnumbering bushbuck even in the forest. Researchers have noted that the sitatunga of Rubondo's forests are more diurnal than is normally the case, and have less splayed feet and darker coats than those resident in the swamps – whether this is genetically influenced, or a function of wear and sun bleaching, is difficult to say. A possible explanation for this anomalous situation is that sitatunga colonised the island and expanded into forested habitats before there were any bushbuck around.

Salaam and Kilimanjaro International Airport, connecting to Zanzibar) and hop on a Rubondo-bound flight there. At the time of writing, daily departures are guaranteed, with the provision that a minimum of three passengers is booked on to the flight. For this reason, it would make sense for independent travellers to make advance contact with Coastal Travel in Dar es Salaam (see page 301) or Flycatcher Safaris in Arusha (see under *Where to stay* below) to fit their timing around flights that are already booked.

Rubondo can also be reached by driving or bussing to one of the nearby mainland ports, though it should be noted that this will involve far more hassle than simply flying from Geita, and will probably not work out any more cheaply. The closest port is Muganza, which lies only 9km from the Mlaga ranger post. Muganza is connected to Mwanza by one daily bus, but this is a long, cramped ride, so you might want to break it up with a night in Geita. Alternatively, you can reach Muganza by catching a ferry from Mwanza to Nyamirembe (see box *Lake Victoria Ferries*, page 405, for details) then catching a lift – or, if traffic is light, walking – the last 20km stretch of road to Muganza. Once in Muganza, there are a few basic guesthouses, and the Lutheran Mission Hospital can radio through to the park rangers to arrange for a boat to collect you. This will cost US$30 per party in either direction, to which must be added a fee of US$15 per party each way for the road transfer from Mlaga to the park headquarters. You could cut this cost by arranging a private boat charter from Muganza to Mlaga – around US$20 – where they can radio through to the headquarters for a vehicle to collect you. It's possible to walk the roughly 10km between Mlaga and the park headquarters, but you'll need to wait for a ranger to collect you and will still need to pay a guide fee, so it's hardly worth it.

It is possible to charter a boat to Rubondo directly from Nyamirembe, but this can cost as much as US$120 each way. Another potential mainland springboard is Nkome Port, which can be reached from Mwanza by road via Geita, or by any ferry heading to Nyamirembe or Maisome. The stretch of road between Geita and Nkome may be impassable in the rainy season and it requires a good 4WD at the best of times, and the boat transfer will cost about US$80.

A final option – untested to the best of my knowledge, but with some theoretical advantages – would be to catch the ferry from Mwanza to Maisome Island and there arrange a private boat charter to Rubondo. The biggest advantage of this is that boats from Maisome (unlike those from Muganza) approach the island from the east, so they can drop you right at the park headquarters. And if things don't work out, the extensive forest on the western side of Maisome should provide some compensation for not reaching Rubondo!

Where to stay
Upmarket
Rubondo Island Camp Tel: 027 6983 or 027 254 4109; fax: 027 254 8261; email: flycat@habari.co.tz; web: www.flycat.com. This attractive and immensely tranquil tented lodge, owned and managed by Flycatcher Safaris, consists of ten luxury self-contained *banda*s, each with a private veranda. It has a truly fabulous location, with tall forest gallery rising high behind the tents, and a sandy palm-lined beach fringed by rocky outcrops directly in front of them. The open-sided communal areas stand on one of the rocky outcrops, offering a pretty view over the lake. This leads down to a secluded beachfront platform where a variety of large waterbirds have taken up more-or-less permanent residence. Pied and malachite kingfishers hawk for food, paradise flycatchers flutter in the trees – and the occasional pair of otters swims past. The swimming pool is built in a natural rock outcrop. A good selection of boat and foot excursions can be arranged at the camp, ranging in price from US$15 to US$35 per person, as can fishing trips for US$50 per boat plus US$20 rod hire. Full board rates are US$160/280 single/double, while all-inclusive rates (including park fees, drinks,

laundry, and all activities except for fishing,) are US$250/460. A stay of at least three nights' duration is recommended to make the most of Rubondo, and Flycatcher offers a variety of attractively priced fly-in packages ranging from three to seven nights long. In addition to the Arusha contact details supplied above, Flycatcher's Swiss head office can be contracted at tel: 0041 32 392 54 50; fax: 0041 32 392 54 51 email: flycat@swissonline.ch. Small emails without attachments can be sent directly to Rubondo Island Camp at rubondo@hf.habari.co.tz.

Budget
National Park Campsite and *Bandas* The national park *banda* and camping site lies on a lovely forest-fringed beach about 1km north of Rubondo Island Camp and a similar distance from the park headquarters. Camping or accommodation in rather grotty chalets using common showers costs US$20 per person, while the much smarter new self-contained chalets cost US$50 per person. No meals are available, and it's advisable to bring most of what you will need with you, but a shop in the park headquarters does sell a few basic foodstuffs (essentially what the national park staff would eat), as well as warm beers and sodas. A cook can be arranged on request. Travellers staying at the *bandas* are welcome to visit Rubondo Island Camp for a chilled drink or a meal – it's fine to walk along the footpath or road between the *banda* site and camp unaccompanied, but the camp would need a bit of advance warning to prepare meals. They charge US$8 for breakfast, US$12 for lunch and US$15 for dinner.

BUKOBA
Updated with permission from the excellent website www.gvogl.tripod.com, which contains detailed travel information about Bukoba compiled by VSO volunteers Tony Pike and Greg Vogl.
Founded as a German administrative centre by the Emin Pasha in 1890, Bukoba is today the regional headquarters of Kagera, and the second most important port on the Tanzanian part of Lake Victoria, though its population of around 50,000 is far smaller than that of Musoma. Bukoba is situated about 50km south of the Ugandan border on a lush, moist and hilly stretch of lakeshore that supports a thriving coffee industry as well as recently discovered deposits of nickel and cobalt that are likely to be exploited in the near future. The main food crop and dietary staple of the Bukoba area, as in Uganda, is *batoke* (or *matoke*), a large green banana that is roasted or steamed, and eaten in much the same manner as *ugali* elsewhere in Tanzania.

Bukoba's flat, compact town centre is dominated by several mid-20th-century Asian buildings – most in a poor state of repair – and lies about 1km inland of the lakeshore, to which it is connected by the leafy Jamhuri Road. At the lake end of Jamhuri Road, near the Lake View Hotel, stands a cluster of old German buildings, including the Old Boma and Magistrate's Court, the original post office, the German cemetery, and the first general store, known locally as *duka kubwa* (big shop). The main port and ferry terminal is situated on a separate part of the lakeshore, about 3km from the town centre along Government Road. There is little in the way of sightseeing in Bukoba, but it is an agreeable place. Points of interest include the impressive Catholic Cathedral built by Bishop Hirth between 1893 and 1904 and currently being renovated, and the marshy area between the town and the lake, which supports a surprisingly large variety of waterbirds. Further afield, Musira Island, which lies a short distance from the shore and is accessible by boat, has a small fishing village and is enjoyable to visit. Nyamukazi is a picturesque fishing village about 20 minutes' walk from town, on the other side of the airport.

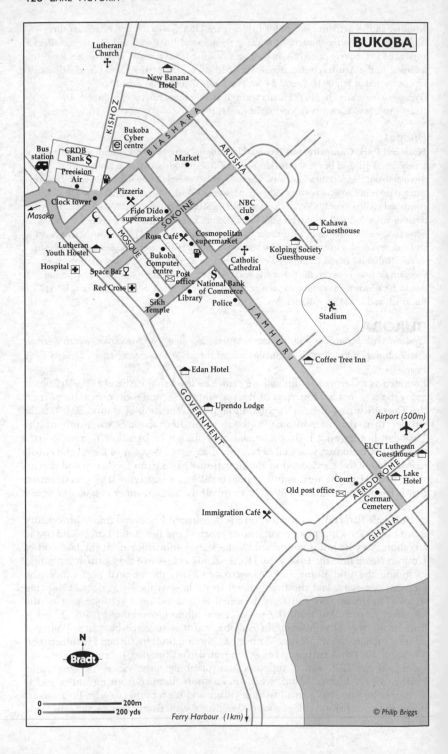

BUKOBA

Lutheran Church

New Banana Hotel

KISHOZ

BIASHARA

ARUSHA

Bukoba Cyber centre

Market

Bus station

CRDB Bank $

Precision Air

Pizzeria

Clock tower

Masaka

Fido Dido supermarket

SOKOINE

NBC club

Kahawa Guesthouse

Rosa Café

Cosmopolitan supermarket

Kolping Society Guesthouse

MOSQUE

Lutheran Youth Hostel

Hospital

Space Bar

Bukoba Computer centre

Post office

Catholic Cathedral

Red Cross

National Bank of Commerce

Library

Sikh Temple

Police

JAMHURI

Stadium

Edan Hotel

Coffee Tree Inn

Upendo Lodge

GOVERNMENT

Airport (500m)

ELCT Lutheran Guesthouse

Court

Lake Hotel

AERODROME

Old post office

German Cemetery

Immigration Café

GHANA

N

Bradt

0   200m
0   200 yds

Ferry Harbour (1km)

© Philip Briggs

Getting there and away

The airport is on Aerodrome Road along the lake. Precision Air (travel agent near the bus stand) and Eagle Air (travel agent in the Cyber Centre) run daily flights to Mwanza, where you can get a connection to Dar es Salaam, Arusha, Kampala, Nairobi, etc. You can also book a ticket from Fourways Travel in Mwanza (tel: 250 2273 or 250 2630, email: fourways.mza@raha.com). The main bus stand is in the centre of town. The best company for long hauls is Tawfiq, which runs to Kampala (5–6 hours, Tsh10,000), Dar es Salaam (Tsh38,000) and Nairobi (Tsh25,000). Tickets can be booked in advance at the nearby Tawfiq office. Other buses go to Kigoma, Kasulu and Kibondo. *Dalla-dallas* run to smaller towns such as Muleba (Tsh2000), Nshamba (Tsh2000), Rubya (Tsh2500) and Karagwe (Tsh3000). They leave when full, which can often involve a very long wait, and are very crowded. Taxis can be found at the market, near the bus stand and at the port, and charge at least Tsh1,000 for a charter trip in town.

Travellers who visit Bukoba by land generally do so on their way to or from Uganda. Details of this route are included in the *Getting to Tanzania* section on pages 55–63. Details of the overnight ferries that run three times weekly between Bukoba and Mwanza are in the box about *Lake Victoria Ferries* on page 405). Details of land travel between Bukoba and Mwanza are under the heading *West from Mwanza by Road* on page 415.

Where to stay
Moderate
The established option in this category is the recently renovated **Lake Hotel**, which has a scenic location at the lakeshore end of Jamhuri Road, and is overhung with an aura of fading colonial charm. Double rooms cost about Tsh20,000 with fans and mosquito nets, and camping costs US$3 per person. A newer recommendation in this range is the **Eden Hotel**, which is near to the Red Cross and has rooms with air conditioning. **Upendo Lodge**, close to the police station, charges around Tsh12,000 for a double room, and has a television lounge and bar.

Budget
The **Evangelical Lutheran Church of Tanzania (ELCT) Guesthouse** near the Lake Hotel has comfortable, clean, safe self-contained rooms with hot water, air conditioning and a communal television room for around Tsh5,000 per person. The **Catholic Youth Centre** has self-contained rooms for Tsh5,000/6,000 single/double, and good business facilities including a fax machine, computer and secretarial services. If you prefer not to stay in an institution, the central **New Banana Hotel** is reasonable value at similar prices.

Shoestring
The popular **Lutheran Youth Hostel (Nyumba ya Vijana)** charges Tsh2000 per person for clean, secure four-bed dormitories and double rooms. The **Kahawa Guest House** is the best of the more central places, while the **Spice Beach Hotel** (between the Lake Hotel and the port) is recommended as a lakeshore alternative.

Where to eat
Recommended for cheap lunches and snacks is the **Rose Café**, which serves *matoke*, beans, samosas, fruit juice, etc, and is popular with volunteers working in and around Bukoba. The **Pizzeria** near the market serves chicken, vegetarian and meat pizzas, as well as sausages and chips, but is open in the mornings only. The **Kolping Café** opposite the Kahawa Guesthouse near the cathedral dishes up

IN THE COURT OF KING RUMANIKA

In December 1861, Speke and Grant arrived at King Rumanika's capital near Lake Lweru Ruabishonga, a marshy expanse fed by the Kagera, 120km inland of Bukoba. Rumanika was the 20th ruler of Karagwe, a centralised political state probably founded in the 16th century, alongside the states of Buganda and Bunyoro (in Uganda) and Rwanda, with which Karagwe shared strong historical and cultural affiliations. Rumanyika extended a warm reception to the first Europeans he had ever encountered, and Speke's account of his month in Karagwe is a fascinating depiction of an African society untouched by European influences:

> As we entered, we saw sitting cross-legged on the ground Rumanika the king, and his brother Nnanaji, both of them men of noble appearance and size. The king was plainly dressed in an Arab's black choga, and wore, for ornament, dress-stockings of rich-coloured beads, and neatly-worked wristlets of copper. Nnanaji, being a doctor of very high pretensions, in addition to a check cloth wrapped round him, was covered with charms. At their sides lay huge pipes of black clay. The first greetings of the king, delivered in good KiSwahili, were warm and affecting... Having shaken hands in true English style... the ever-smiling Rumanika begged us to be seated on the ground... and [asked] what we thought of Karagwe, for it had struck him his mountains were the finest in the world; and the lake, too, did we not admire it?
>
> One of the young princes... happening to see me sit on an iron chair, rushed back to his father... This... ended by my getting a summons to show off the white man sitting on his throne; for of course I could only be... a king of great dignity, to indulge in such state... I did as I was bid, and... Rumanika, as gentle as ever, then burst into a fresh fit of merriment, and... finished off by saying, with a very expressive shake of the head, 'Oh, these *Wazungu*, these *Wazungu*! They know and do everything.'
>
> We adjourned to [Rumanika's] private hut, which rather surprised me by the neatness with which it was kept. The roof was supported by numerous clean poles, to which he had fastened a large assortment of spears – brass-headed with iron handles, and iron-headed with wooden ones – of excellent workmanship. A large standing-screen, of fine straw-plait work, in elegant devices, partitioned off one part of the room; and on the opposite side, as mere ornaments, were placed a number of brass grapnels and small models of cows, made in iron for his amusement by the Arabs at Kufro.
>
> The wives of the king and princes were fattened to such an extent that they could not stand upright... I was struck with... the extraordinary dimensions, yet pleasing beauty, of [an old prince's] wife. She could not rise; and so large were her arms that, between the joints, the flesh hung down like large, loose-stuffed puddings... [I enquired] what they did with so many milk-pots, [and the man] pointing to his wife said 'This is all the product of those pots: from early youth upwards we keep those pots to their mouths, as it is the fashion at court to have very fat wives... [On another day] I called on one of [Rumanika's] sisters-in-law... another of those wonders of obesity, unable to stand excepting on all fours... After getting her to sidle and wriggle into the middle of the hut, I... took her dimensions [58cm

around the arm, 132cm around the chest, 79cm around the thigh, 61cm around the calf]... The daughter, a lass of sixteen, sat stark-naked before us, sucking at a milk-pot, on which the father kept her at work by holding a rod in his hand, for as fattening is the first duty of fashionable female life, it must be duly enforced by the rod if necessary.

Dr K'yengo, who was now living with Rumanika as his head magician, added that, whilst he was living in Utambara, the Watuta invested his *boma* six months; and finally, when all their cows and stores were exhausted, they killed all the inhabitants but himself, and he only escaped by the power of the charms which he carried about him. These were so powerful, that although he lay on the ground, and the Watuta struck at him with their spears, not one could penetrate his body."

Rumanika spent the night doing homage and sacrificing a bullock at the tomb of his father Dagara... It transpired that the old king's body, after the fashion of his predecessors, was sewn up in a cow-skin, and placed in a boat floating on the lake, where it remained for three days, until decomposition set in and maggots were engendered, of which three were taken into the palace and given in charge to the heir-elect; but instead of remaining as they were, one worm was transformed into a lion, another into a leopard, and the third into a stick. After this the body of the king was taken up and deposited on the hill... where... the people erected a hut over him, and, thrusting in five maidens and fifty cows, enclosed the doorway in such a manner that the whole of them subsequently died from starvation.

Rumanika could not understand how it was I spent so much and travelled so far, or how it happened such a great country as ours could be ruled by a woman. He asked the Queen's name, how many children she had, and the mode of succession; then, when fully satisfied, led the way to show me what his father Dagara had done when wishing to know of what the centre of the earth was composed. At the back of the palace a deep ditch was cut, several yards long, the end of which was carried by a subterranean passage into the palace, where it was ended off with a cavern led into by a very small aperture. It then appeared that Dagara, having failed, in his own opinion, to arrive any nearer to the object in view, gave the excavating up as a bad job, and turned the cave into a mysterious abode, where it was confidently asserted he spent many days without eating or drinking, and turned sometimes into a young man, and then an old one, alternately, as the humour seized him.

Rumanika... said... marriage in Karagwe was a mere matter of money. Cows, sheep, and slaves have to be given to the father for the value of his daughter; but if she finds she has made a mistake, she can return the dowry-money, and gain her release. The Wahuma, although they keep slaves and marry with pure negroes, do not allow their daughters to taint their blood by marrying out of their clan. In warfare it is the rule that the Wahinda, or princes, head their own soldiers, and set them the example of courage, when, after firing a few arrows, they throw their bows away, and close at once with their spears... Life is never taken in Karagwe, either for murder or cowardice, as they value so much their Wahuma breed; but, for all offences, fines of cows are exacted according to the extent of the crime.

inexpensive fish, meat, rice and *matoke* and has a television. Similar are the **Bona Bana Café** and **Space Bar** near the Red Cross.

For evening meals, the **Lake Hotel** is recommended for its view of the lake and good variety of food and drink, but it's relatively expensive and service is slow. The satellite television and outdoor beer garden make it a popular *wazungu* hangout, particularly on Friday nights. Also recommended is the restaurant at the **Eden Hotel**, which has a varied menu – again expensive and generally slow service – as well as satellite television and a pool table. Cheaper options include the lakeshore **Bukoba Club** (opposite the Lake Hotel) and **Spice Beach Hotel**, and the more central **West End Restaurant** near the bus stand and **NBC Club** near the National Bank of Commerce.

If you're self-catering, or want to stock up on packaged goods before visiting Minziro Forest or catching the ferry, the **Fido Dido Supermarket** and **Cosmopolitan Provision Store** stock packaged and refrigerated imported goods, including bread and many types of biscuits and drinks.

Discos often take place on Friday, Saturday and Sunday nights at **Red Cross** (near the government hospital), the **Coffee Tree Inn** (near the stadium) and **NBC Club** (near the NBC bank).

General information

Tourist information There is no tourist information office in Bukoba.

Foreign exchange The National Bank of Commerce (NBC) near the Catholic Cathedral has foreign exchange facilities, but travellers coming from Uganda should note that it doesn't exchange Ugandan shillings – you're best off trading any excess Ugandan money for Tanzanian currency at the border post.

Internet The best option is the Bukoba Cyber Centre (bcc@bukobaonline.com or bcyberc@yahoo.com) near Danico and the CRDB, since it is the only internet provider in Bukoba; everyone else gets their internet access from BCC or Dar es Salaam. Internet access costs Tsh2,000 per hour, Tsh8,000 for a five-hour pass valid for one month.

Swimming There is no swimming pool in town, but a number of nearby beaches are worth a visit, including Bunena beach, within easy walking distance of town. The lake is infested with bilharzia, so swimming anywhere carries an element of risk.

Sporting facilities The Bukoba Club has tennis, snooker, table tennis and darts. The Kaitaba Stadium hosts football matches and other events including concerts and the annual celebrations of Farmers' Day on August 8. The Red Cross has a basketball court and volleyball net.

Excursions from Bukoba
Bwanjai rock art
Half a dozen ancient rock art sites are dotted around northern Kagera, of which the most impressive is a large rock shelter at the village of Bwanjai, about 25km northwest of Bukoba, and linked to it by erratic *dalla-dallas*. Unlike the better-known Kondoa rock art sites, there are no naturalistic efforts on the Bwanjai panel, nor any animal portraits, although a few heavily stylised human figures are present. The panel is otherwise dominated by blocks of red dots, and a cluster of strange symbols that look a bit like a tripod with antennae at the top. What these symbols might signify is anybody's guess, since local people have no tradition relating to the paintings except that they have always been there. It has been suggested the

Bwanjai paintings are relatively recent, possibly the work of Bantu-speakers living in the area prior to the 16th-century formation of the Karagwe Empire.

Minziro Forest Reserve

Dr Terry Oatley, with additional information by Philip Briggs

The 250km² Minziro Forest Reserve abuts the Ugandan border some 20km inland of Lake Victoria, where it is bounded to the east by the Kagera River. One of the largest forest reserves anywhere in Tanzania, Minziro is essentially a southern extension of Uganda's Malabigambo Forest, which runs northwards to Sango Bay. The topography of the reserve is generally flat, but dotted with small rocky hills, and most areas below 1,150m are subject to seasonal flooding from the Kagera between October and May. Roughly three-quarters of the reserve is comprised of groundwater forest, with a tree composition divided about equally between western lowland and eastern montane species, while the remainder is predominantly open grassland, with extensive papyrus beds running along the riverbanks.

Minziro is unique within Tanzania for the predominantly West African affinities of its fauna. This is perhaps most evident in the birdlife, which had received little attention prior to a pioneering ornithological trip undertaken by Neil and Liz Baker in 1984. This and subsequent expeditions have produced a formative bird checklist of approximately 250 species, of which 56 are restricted to the Guinea-Congo biome and unknown elsewhere in Tanzania – representing about 5% of the national checklist! It should be noted that this is essentially a political rather than a biological phenomenon – had the boundaries drawn up by the European colonists been slightly different, Minziro might lie within Uganda, where most of its Guinea-Congo biome species are common.

Nevertheless, Minziro is an extremely alluring birding destination. A long list of birds recorded nowhere else in Tanzania includes forest francolin, great blue turaco, white-bellied kingfisher, shining blue kingfisher yellow-crested woodpecker, orange-throated forest robin, lowland akalat, blue-shouldered robin-chat, fire-crested alethe, white-tailed ant thrush, chestnut wattle-eye, red-headed bluebill, and at least half a dozen greenbuls. In addition to this, the grasslands of the Minziro-Sango Bay area have been recently confirmed as an important wintering ground for the endangered blue swallow, a migrant from further south, and the papyrus swamps along the Kagera River harbour the globally threatened (and very beautiful) papyrus gonolek.

Another indication of Minziro's biodiversity is a tally of at least 500 butterfly species. Large mammals are more poorly represented, probably partially the result of local subsistence poaching, but the forest's western affiliations are manifested in three monkey species (Angola colobus, grey-cheeked mangabey and red-tailed monkey), as well as red-legged sun squirrel, western tree hyrax (vociferous at night) and Peter's duiker. Buffalo and elephant visit the reserve seasonally, the bushbuck is common in the forest, and hippopotami are present but rare along the river, which also supports a substantial population of crocodiles and monitor lizards.

In 1998, the Minziro-Sango Bay area had been one of several East African cross-border sites focused on by the UNDP-GTZ Cross-Borders Biodiversity Project. If you are thinking of visiting the forest, it's well worth exploring their excellent and very detailed website (www.x-borderbiodiversity.tripod.com). Also recommended is Terry Oatley's article about Minziro in the February/March 2001 issue of *Africa Birds & Birding*, which can be ordered through www.africa-geographic.com.

LAKE VICTORIA AND THE RIDDLE OF THE NILE

The first European to see Lake Victoria was John Hanning Speke, who marched from Tabora to the site of present-day Mwanza in 1858 following his joint 'discovery' of Lake Tanganyika with Richard Burton the previous year. Speke named the lake for Queen Victoria, but prior to that Arab slave traders called it Ukerewe (still the name of its largest island). It is unclear what name was in local use, since the only one used by Speke is Nyanza, which simply means lake.

A major goal of the Burton-Speke expedition had been to solve the great geographical enigma of the age, the source of the White Nile. Speke, based on his brief glimpse of the southeast corner of Lake Victoria, somewhat whimsically proclaimed his 'discovery' to be the answer to that riddle. Burton, with a comparable lack of compelling evidence, was convinced that the great river flowed out of Lake Tanganyika. The dispute between the former travelling companions erupted bitterly on their return to Britain, where Burton – the more persuasive writer and respected traveller – gained the backing of the scientific establishment.

Over 1862–63, Speke and Captain James Grant returned to Lake Victoria, hoping to prove Speke's theory correct. They looped inland around the western shore of the lake, arriving at the court of King Mutesa of Buganda, then continued east to the site of present-day Jinja, where a substantial river flowed out of the lake after tumbling over the cataract that Speke named Ripon Falls. From here, the two explorers headed north, sporadically crossing paths with the river throughout what is today Uganda, before following the Nile to Khartoum and Cairo.

Speke's declaration that 'The Nile is settled' met with mixed support back home. Burton and other sceptics pointed out that Speke had bypassed the entire western shore of his purported great lake, had visited only a couple of points on the northern shore, and had not attempted to explore the east. Nor, for that matter, had he followed the course of the Nile in its entirety. Speke, claimed his detractors, had seen several different lakes and different stretches of river, connected only in Speke's deluded mind. The sceptics had a point, but Speke had nevertheless gathered sufficient geographical evidence to render his claim highly plausible, and his notion of one great lake, far from being mere whimsy, was backed by anecdotal information gathered from local sources along the way.

Matters were scheduled to reach a head on September 16 1864, when an eagerly awaited debate between Burton and Speke – in the words of the former 'what silly tongues called the "Nile Duel"' – was due to take place at the Royal Geographical Society (RGS). And reach a head they did, but in circumstances more tragic than anybody could have anticipated. On the afternoon of the debate, Speke went out shooting with a cousin, only to stumble while crossing a wall, in the process discharging a barrel of his shotgun into his heart. The subsequent inquest recorded a verdict of accidental death, but it has often been suggested – purely on the basis of the curious timing – that Speke deliberately took his life rather than face up to Burton in public. Burton, who had seen Speke less than three hours earlier, was by all accounts deeply troubled by Speke's death, and years later he was quoted as stating 'the uncharitable [say] that I shot him' – an accusation that seems to have been aired only in Burton's imagination.

Speke was dead, but the 'Nile debate' would keep kicking for several years. In 1864, Sir Stanley and Lady Baker were the first Europeans to reach Lake Albert and nearby Murchison Falls in present-day Uganda. The Bakers, much to the delight of the anti-Speke lobby, were convinced that this newly named lake was a source of the Nile, though they openly admitted it might not be the only one. Following the Bakers' announcement, Burton put forward a revised theory, namely that the most remote source of the Nile was the Rusizi River, which he believed flowed out of the northern head of Lake Tanganyika and emptied into Lake Albert.

In 1865, the RGS followed up on Burton's theory by sending Dr David Livingstone to Lake Tanganyika. Livingstone, however, was of the opinion that the Nile's source lay further south than Burton supposed, and so he struck out towards the lake along a previously unexplored route. Leaving from Mikindani in the far south of present-day Tanzania, Livingstone followed the Rovuma River inland, continuing westward to the southern tip of Lake Tanganyika. From there, he ranged southward into present-day Zambia, where he came across a new candidate for the source of the Nile, the swampy Lake Bangweulu and its major outlet the Lualaba River. It was only after his famous meeting with Henry Stanley at Ujiji, in November 1871, that Livingstone (in the company of Stanley) visited the north of Lake Tanganyika and Burton's cherished Rusizi River, which, it transpired, flowed *into* the lake. Burton, nevertheless, still regarded Lake Tanganyika to be the most likely source of the Nile, while Livingstone was convinced that the answer lay with the Lualaba River. In August 1872, Livingstone headed back to the Lake Bangweulu region, where he fell ill and died six months later, the great question still unanswered.

In August 1874, ten years after Speke's death, Stanley embarked on a three-year expedition every bit as remarkable and arduous as those undertaken by his predecessors, yet one whose significance is often overlooked. Partly, this is because Stanley cuts such an unsympathetic figure, the grim caricature of the murderous pre-colonial White Man blasting and blustering his way through territories where Burton, Speke and Livingstone had relied largely on diplomacy. It is also the case, however, that Stanley set out with no intention of seeking out headline-making fresh discoveries. Instead, he determined to test out the various theories that had been advocated by Speke, Burton and Livingstone about the Nile's source. First, Stanley sailed around the circumference of Lake Victoria, establishing that it was indeed as vast as Speke had claimed. Stanley's next step was to circumnavigate Lake Tanganyika, which, contrary to Burton's long-held theories, clearly boasted no outlet sufficiently large to be the source of the Nile. Finally, and most remarkably, Stanley took a boat along Livingstone's Lualaba River to its confluence with an even larger river, which he followed for months with no idea as to where he might end up.

When, exactly 999 days after he left Zanzibar, Stanley emerged at the Congo mouth, the shortlist of plausible theories relating to the source of the Nile had been reduced to one. Clearly, the Nile did flow out of Lake Victoria at Ripon Falls, before entering and exiting Lake Albert at its northern tip to start its long course through the sands of the Sahara. Stanley's achievement in putting to rest decades of speculation about how the main rivers and lakes of East Africa linked together is estimable indeed. He was nevertheless generous enough to concede that: 'Speke now has the full glory of having discovered the largest inland sea on the continent of Africa, also its principal affluent as well as its outlet. I must also give him credit for having understood the geography of the countries we travelled through far better than any of us who so persistently opposed his hypothesis.'

Getting there and away

The village of Minziro, within the forest reserve, lies approximately 90km from Bukoba, a drive of about two hours in dry conditions. To get there, first follow the road towards the Ugandan border inland for 55km to the small town of Kyaka, crossing a bridge over the Kagera River, then passing through the Kyaka checkpoint, where you must turn right on to the district road to Minziro. This recently upgraded road passes through some eucalyptus plantations and then through banana plots of the local Haya people, approaching a small hill known locally as Kele, which is a dominant topographical feature. From there on the road traverses the forest reserve, passing through the grassland and a block of the forest proper, emerging again into grassland before eventually climbing rising ground into Minziro village. From the track up to the church on top of the hill above the village one can obtain a good view of the extent of the forest on both sides of the cleared strip marking the Ugandan border.

The road to Minziro is in good condition and accessible to normal two-wheel drive vehicles, but 4WD and good ground clearance is necessary for off-road excursions, which are advisable only from July to September when the swampy ground has dried out.

Using public transport, it is straightforward enough to catch any public transport towards the Ugandan border as far as Kyaka. A few minibus *dalla-dallas* run daily along the road between Kyaka and Minziro; it is not clear whether these leave direct from Kyaka or from Bukoba. There is no accommodation in Kyaka, so an early start is recommended.

Where to stay

There are no local guesthouses at Minziro, so visitors wishing to overnight in the forest reserve must camp out, after first obtaining the necessary permit from the Forestry Office in Bukoba.

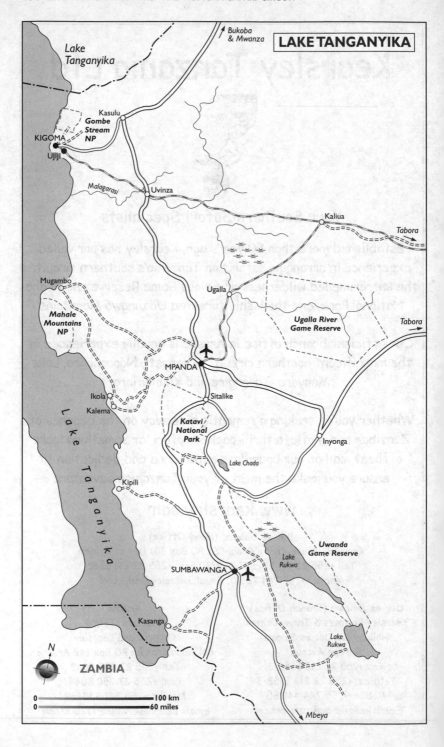

Lake Tanganyika and the Western Safari Circuit

Following the contours of the Rift Valley along the border between Tanzania and the Congo, Lake Tanganyika is something of a statistician's dream, measuring 675km from north to south, an average of 50km wide, and reaching a depth of up to 1,435m. Tanganyika holds a volume of water seven times greater than that of Lake Victoria (the largest lake on the continent), and it is the longest freshwater body in the world, as well as the second deepest after Lake Baikal in Russia. It is also a very beautiful lake, hemmed in by the verdant hills on either side of the Rift Valley, and boasting crystal clear water that adds credibility to its reputation for having the lowest pollution levels of any lake in the world. Lying at a relatively low altitude of 730m, the lake and its hinterland can be quite hot and sticky, but the climate is generally drier and cooler than anywhere along the coast.

Lake Tanganyika is at least three million years old, and although it is fed by more than 50 rivers and streams, its sole outlet is the Lukuga River, into which it overflows only in years of exceptionally high rainfall. Due to its great age and isolation from any similar habitat, Lake Tanganyika forms one of the most biologically rich aquatic habitats in the world, supporting more than 500 fish species of which the vast majority is comprised of endemic cichlids (see box *Cichlids of the Great Lakes*, pages 476–7). The most important fish economically is the dagaa, a tiny plankton-eater that lives in large shoals and is sun-dried on the lakeshore for sale throughout western Tanzania. One of the most characteristic sights along any inhabited part of the lakeshore is the nocturnal spectacle of hundreds of small fishing boats lit by small lamps and bobbing in the waves like a low-lying swarm of fireflies.

The only substantial town on the Tanzanian lakeshore, and normal entry point to the region, is Kigoma. This attractively sleepy port was founded under German rule 6km away from Ujiji, the 19th-century Arab trading post where Burton and Speke first reached the lakeshore in 1858, and the historic meeting between Livingstone and Stanley took place in 1872. The main tourist attractions of the region are the two national parks that fringe the lakeshore, Gombe Stream and Mahale Mountains, which are best known for their habituated chimp communities, the most approachable wild chimp populations anywhere in Africa. Some distance east of the lake, the little-known and underrated Katavi National Park protects a similar range of plains animals to more accessible southern reserves such as Ruaha and Selous. Very few fly-in tourists ever get close to Lake Tanganyika, but the area does attract an erratic trickle of backpackers, for whom the weekly lake ferry service ranks as one of East Africa's most compelling public transport rides.

TABORA

All roads – and, perhaps more to the point, all railway lines – through central Tanzania lead to Tabora, a substantial town of around 150,000 people, and the administrative centre of the synonymous region. Travellers chugging directly between the coast and Lake Tanganyika or Victoria will see little of Tabora other than the rather chaotic railway station to the northeast of the town centre, and it would take some imagination to portray this as any great loss.

Located in the heart of Tanzania's hot dusty central plateau, Tabora is a friendly and relaxed place, and its spacious layout of shady avenues lined with mango and flame trees goes some way to blunting the seasonally torrid climate. What's more, Tabora can stake a reasonable claim to be the oldest urban settlement in the Tanzanian interior, having been an important centre of trade since the early 19th century (see *The Land of the Moon*, pages 444–5). For all that, the modern town is fairly unmemorable, and – with the exception of Livingstone's *Tembe* at nearby Kwihara – there really isn't much to do or see in the immediate vicinity. Nevertheless, anybody who travels extensively around western Tanzania is a likely to end up in Tabora at some point, be it to overnight between long drives, to change buses, or to switch between trains heading to or from Kigoma, Mwanza or Mpanda.

Getting there and away

Tabora is where the railway line from Dar es Salaam splits into a northern branch heading to Mwanza and a western branch heading to Kigoma. It is also the terminal of the railway line south to Mpanda. The trains that run from between Dar es Salaam and Kigoma or Mwanza generally stop in Tabora for at least two hours for shunting, but there is no need for passengers to disembark. Travellers who are heading between Mwanza and Kigoma, however, will need to change trains at Tabora, as will travellers heading to or from either of these towns, or Dar es Salaam, to Mpanda. Under normal circumstances, changing trains will involve spending a full day in Tabora, and possibly an overnight stay. Frustratingly, it is not possible to book a train ticket out of Tabora from anywhere else, which means that travellers intending to change trains will have to pitch up and hope for the best. Fortunately, the first- and second-class carriages between Tabora and Mpanda are seldom fully booked, while on the main Central Railway line at least one carriage in each class is normally set aside for passengers embarking at Tabora, so obtaining a ticket on the day is normally straightforward. If you have to spend a full day in Tabora between trains, and want somewhere to leave luggage and have a shower, your best bet is to take one of the cheaper (Tsh3,000) rooms at the nearby Aposele Inn & Guesthouse.

Details of the train schedules out of Dar es Salaam, Kigoma and Mwanza are included in the box *The Central Railway* on pages 374–5. Travellers crossing between Kigoma and Mwanza via Tabora can expect trains from either port to arrive in Tabora about 12–14 hours after departure, in other words at around breakfast time on Wednesday, Friday, Saturday and Monday. Trains to Kigoma or Mwanza typically pass through Tabora around 26 hours after they leave Dar es Salaam, in other words shortly after sunset on Wednesday, Thursday, Saturday and Monday. On the Mpanda sideline, trains leave from Tabora on Monday, Wednesday and Friday at 21.00 and from Mpanda on Tuesday, Thursday and Saturday at 13.00, with the trip taking anything from 10 to 15 hours. Delays are increasingly frequent on the main Central Railway, which can be frustrating when waiting for trains heading to Kigoma or Mwanza, as a long delay en route from Dar es Salaam will leave you hanging around the station into the wee hours of the morning. The

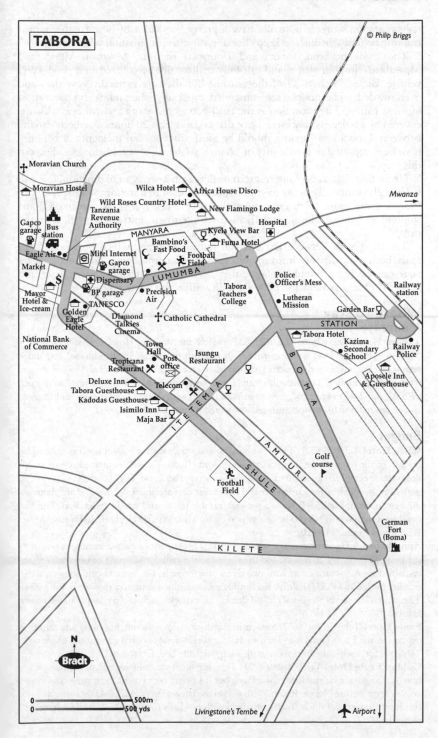

TABORA

© Philip Briggs

✝ Moravian Church

🏠 Moravian Hostel

Wilca Hotel 🏠 🏠 Africa House Disco

Wild Roses Country Hotel 🏠 New Flamingo Lodge
Tanzania
Revenue
Authority

Gapco 🏭
garage Bus
station

MANYARA

Kyela View Bar 🍺 Hospital ✚
🏠 Fuma Hotel

Mwanza

Eagle Air ●

Market ●

e Mitel Internet
Gapco
garage

Bambino's
Fast Food

Football
Field

Police
Officer's Mess ●

Railway
station

$ 💲

✚ Dispensary

LUMUMBA

Tabora
Teachers
College ●

● Lutheran
Mission

Garden Bar 🍺

Mayor
Hotel &
Ice-cream

🏠 BP garage
🏠 TANESCO

● Precision
Air

✝ Catholic Cathedral

STATION

Golden
Eagle
Hotel

Diamond
Talkies
Cinema

🏠 Tabora Hotel

Kazima
Secondary
School

Railway
Police

National Bank
of Commerce

Town
Hall

Post
office ✉

Isungu
Restaurant

Aposele Inn
& Guesthouse

Tropicana
Restaurant

BOMA

Deluxe Inn 🏠
Tabora Guesthouse 🏠

Telecom ●

Kadodas Guesthouse 🏠

ITETEMIA

Isimilo Inn 🏠
Maja Bar 🍺

JAMHURI

Golf
course ▶

SHULE

🏃
Football
Field

N

Bradt

0   500m
0   500 yds

KILETE

German
Fort
(Boma) 🏰

Livingstone's Tembe ↙   ✈ Airport ↓

railway station workers normally have a pretty good idea of how far the train is running behind schedule, so keep checking the current situation with them.

The roads between Tabora and Dodoma, Kigoma, Mwanza, Mbeya and Mpanda are in poor shape, and can only realistically be covered in a good 4WD vehicle. Buses do cover all of these roads, but they are generally very slow and overcrowded, and cannot be recommended, especially when trains also cover most of these routes. The exception is the road between Tabora and Mbeya, which is covered by a twice-weekly bus service that takes at least 20 hours. Anybody driving between Tabora and Kigoma should be aware that several incidents of banditry have been reported in the vicinity of Uvinza, so do ask around before heading out this way.

Given that Tabora is of interest to travellers primarily as a rail junction, few will specifically want to fly to the town. Should you be in that minority, however, both Precision and Eagle Air run scheduled flights between Dar es Salaam and Kigoma stopping at Tabora. The airline offices are in the town centre, and marked on the map.

Tabora sprawls between the bus and railway stations, which lie a good 2km apart, both some distance from all but a couple of accommodation options. Charter taxis can easily be found outside either of the public transport terminals, and generally charge around Tsh1,000 for a lift within the town centre.

Where to stay
Moderate
Tabora Hotel Tel: 026 6670 ext 2378. Formerly the Railway Hotel, and still owned by TRC, the Tabora Hotel was originally built as a hunting lodge in the colonial era, and it retains a convincing and attractive period character with its wide shady balconies and whitewashed exterior. Temporarily closed for renovations in 2001, but scheduled to re-open in 2002, the Tabora Hotel is conveniently located close to the railway station, and likely to charge around Tsh10,000 for clean self-contained double rooms with nets.

Budget
Wilca Hotel Tel: 026 5397. This long-serving and very pleasant budget hotel is situated to the east of the town centre about 500m along Boma Road. The self-contained rooms with hot water, net and fan are centred on a green courtyard and cost Tsh7,000/8,000 double/twin. Meals at the garden bar and restaurant cost around Tsh2,500 and are about the best in town. Facilities include a pool table, table tennis and satellite television. The hotel isn't signposted, but can be recognised by its white outer wall about 100m past the Wild Roses Country Hotel.

Aposele Inn & Guesthouse Tel: 026 260 4510. This superior new guesthouse is one of the best places to stay in Tabora, and the closest to the railway station. The large self-contained rooms, which come with two three-quarter beds, fan, net and cold shower, are excellent value at Tsh5,000, as are the double rooms using a common shower at Tsh3,000. The garden bar serves the usual chilled drinks, plus snacks such as *chipsi mayai* and *mishkaki* kebabs.

Fama Hotel Tel: 026 260 4657. Similar in standard to Aposele Inn, but older and more expensive, the Fama Hotel is a clean, friendly and reasonably central guesthouse charging Tsh6,000 for a self-contained room with a large double bed, fan and net.

Golden Eagle Hotel Tel: 026 260 4851. This, the most centrally located of the budget hotels, is looking a bit rundown these days, but it's pretty convenient for travellers who arrive or are leaving by bus. Rooms with two beds, fan and net cost Tsh4,000 using a common shower or Tsh6,800 self-contained with hot bath (but no plug). A fair restaurant is attached.

Shoestring

Moravian Hostel Tel: 026 260 4710. This long serving hostel is easily the best shoestring option in Tabora, charging Tsh2,000 for a room with two beds, netting but no fan and use of clean common showers and toilets. The one drawback is that, situated behind the bus station, it's not madly convenient for travellers arriving and leaving by train.

Wild Roses Country Hotel This is about the best of a cluster of cheap guesthouses situated along Boma Road towards the Wilca Hotel, most of which charge around Tsh2,000–2,500 for a room. It's worth noting that the cheaper rooms at the Aposele Inn are far nicer than any of the guesthouses in this cluster – and also closer to the railway station – without being significantly pricier.

Where to eat

For full meals, the best bet is currently the **Wilca Hotel**, which serves various stews and curries for around Tsh2,500, though the **Tabora Hotel** will probably supersede it when open again. In the town centre, **Bambino's Fast Food** serves reasonable curries and other main dishes for around Tsh1,500, as well as snacks, juice, tea and coffee. Far better, however, is **Mayor Hotel & Ice Cream** near the bus station, which serves a wide range of Indian snacks, light meals such as grilled chicken and chips, and excellent ice cream and pineapple juice. The **Hotel Tropicana** is similar but seedier.

General information

Foreign exchange The central National Bank of Commerce, open from 08.30 to 15.00 Monday to Friday and 08.30 to 12.30 Saturday, exchanges cash and travellers' cheques at the usual rates. There is no private foreign exchange bureau.

Internet At present, there is no local server in Tabora, which means that the only internet café, Mitel Internet on Lumumba Road, is very slow and expensive at Tsh2,500 per 15 minutes.

Taxis Plenty of charter taxis can be found around the bus station, and also at the railway station whenever trains arrive. Expect to pay around Tsh1,000 for a charter within the town centre, or Tsh6,000–10,000 for a charter to Livingstone's *Tembe* at Kwihara.

Excursions from Tabora
Livingstone's Tembe

Preserved as a museum by the Department of Antiquities, the *tembe* – Arab house – where Livingstone resided during his sojourn in Tabora in 1872 is situated about 6km from the town centre at the otherwise defunct settlement of Kwihara. Despite the Livingstone association, the house was in fact the residence of one of the Arabs resident at Tabora in the mid- to late-19th century. An information sheet at the museum indicates that the *tembe* belonged to the notorious slave trader Tibbu Tip. The contemporary journals of Stanley and Livingstone, as well as other external sources, state that it actually belonged to Said bin Salim, the local governor appointed by the Sultan of Zanzibar. Originally, the *tembe* at Kwihara – which means 'in the open' in the Nyamwezi tongue – must have served as an out-of town governor's residence, but after Mirambo captured Tabora in 1871 Kwihara became the main local Arab settlement in the area for a brief period.

Livingstone's *Tembe* is a typical Arab merchant's house of the period, an attractive red clay quadrangle of large rooms built around a central courtyard and set beneath tall shady mango trees, said to date to before Livingstone's time. In 1871, Henry Stanley resided for a full three months in the house – which he

THE LAND OF THE MOON

Beyond Ugogo undulated the Land of the Moon, or Unyamwezi, inhabited by a turbulent and combative race, who are as ready to work for those who can afford to pay as they are ready to fight those they consider unduly aggressive. Towards the middle of this land, we came to a colony of Arab settlers and traders. Some of these had built excellent and spacious houses of sun-dried brick, and cultivated extensive gardens. The Arabs located here were great travellers. Every region round about the colony had been diligently searched by them for ivory. If Livingstone was anywhere within reach, some of these people ought surely to have known.

From the autobiography of Henry Stanley, describing his arrival in Tabora, where he would be stalled for three months in 1871 before continuing to Ujiji and his legendary meeting with Livingstone

The Nyamwezi are Tanzania's second most numerous tribe after the Sukuma, whose territory borders theirs to the north. Prior to the early 19th century, however, Nyamwezi-Sukuma was a more-or-less homogenous cultural entity, comprised of at least 200 autonomous *ntemi* chieftaincies. This decentralised society would later polarise into two distinct (and occasionally antagonistic) political units, which evidently referred to each other as Usukuma and Utakama – simply meaning the lands to the north and the south. When and how Utakama became Unyamwezi – and its Nyamwezi inhabitants acquired the lunar association – goes unrecorded. But, since these names stem from the Swahili word *mwezi* (moon), an external origin seems likely. Coincidence or not, the Arab colony in Unyamwezi was, at least in the eyes of a succession of Victorian explorers, the last 'civilised' port of call en route to the terra incognito in which it was assumed lay the fabled Source of the Nile: Ptolemy's mysterious Mountains of the Moon.

The foundation of the Arab colony referred to by Stanley, on the site of present-day Tabora circa 1800, was almost certainly the catalyst for the rift between Usukuma and Unyamwezi. Described by Speke as 'the great central slave and ivory merchants' depot', this settlement lay where the three most important caravan routes out of Bagamoyo diverged, one leading to Ujiji on Lake Tanganyika, another to Lake Victoria, and the third to the south of Lake Tanganyika. The Arabs, and the European explorers, generally referred to the Arab colony as Kazeh, and most modern sources follow suit, implying that Tabora is a newer name, but as early as 1861 Speke unambiguously wrote of Kazeh as 'the name of a well in the village of Tbora'.

The local *ntemi* chiefs became increasingly involved in the ivory and slave trade at Tabora. Initially, their role was peripheral, providing porters and fresh produce to the caravans that rolled in from the coast, but eventually they would come to control the trade at its source, launching slave raids into neighbouring territories and exchanging the captives for imported goods, most significantly guns and ammunition. The ensuing local power struggle led to the collapse of the *ntemi* chiefdoms and formation of a more centralised local polity – essentially Unyamwezi – under chief Fundi Kira, who ensured Arab support by allowing free trade within his territory. By contrast, Usukuma, which was further removed from the main caravan routes, still adhered to the *ntemi* system of old, and its villages became one of the prime targets of Nyamwezi slave raids.

In 1858, when Burton and Speke rested up at Tabora before marching westward to Lake Tanganyika, the town supported about 25 Arab merchants, including a governor appointed by the Sultan of Zanzibar. Every merchant had his own *tembe*, a house built with local material but to palatial proportions, centred on a large courtyard, with separate quarters for his slaves and his harem. Speke returned to Tabora in 1861, and wrote that: 'Instead of the Arabs appearing merchants, as they did formerly, they looked more like great farmers, with huge stalls of cattle attached to their houses.' Speke's arrival at Tabora in 1861 coincided with a period of great instability. King Manua Sera, the successor of Fundi Kira, had imposed a tax on all goods entering his territory, and the Arabs responded by driving him from Tabora and installing a puppet king on his throne. Manua Sera blockaded the main caravan routes and launched a series of successful attacks on pursuant Arab troops, and although he never regained the throne, he was still leading the Arabs a merry dance when Speke left Tabora.

This civil war paved the way for the emergence of King Mirambo, a Nyamwezi of noble birth who grew up among Ngoni refugees from Zululand, and adopted their brutally effective military tactics to capture the Uyowa chiefdom in 1860. Over the next decade, Mirambo's army conquered one chiefdom after the next, installing a puppet leader of local nobility, to build an empire extending to Sumbwa in the north, Sukuma in the east, Nyaturu in the south and Tongwe in the west. Mirambo was able to demand large taxes – preferably exacted in the form of firearms – from caravans passing through to Tabora. The Arab merchants were less than enthralled by the growing power wielded by this hostile local leader. By 1871 the rival forces were engaged in what would today be described as guerrilla warfare.

It was the inevitable showdown between the Arabs and Mirambo that caused Stanley's search for Livingstone to be stalled by three months at Kwihara, 6km from Tabora. In August 1871, according to Stanley, a 2,000-strong Arab force 'waving banners denoting the various commanders, with booming horns, and the roar of fifty brass drums' left to hunt down Mirambo. When the attack was launched, Mirambo's army appeared to retreat, but in fact they circled behind the Arab forces and ambushed them on their way home. Mirambo followed up this victory by capturing and razing Tabora itself. Having established a stronghold at Tabora, Mirambo became the main supplier of slaves to the Arab traders, and his superior military strength convinced the Arabs it was worth paying him taxes to maintain the peace.

The former warmonger clearly recognised that diplomacy had its place. Aware of the growing British influence at Zanzibar, Mirambo attempted to woo the British Consul John Kirk by inviting the British to establish missions and trade outposts within Unyamwezi. In his letter to Kirk, Mirambo stated that 'the country is a hundred times more prosperous, tenfold more peaceful and a thousandfold safer than it was before I became chief. I wish to open it up, to learn about Europeans, to trade honestly with all, and to cultivate peaceful friendships.' Mirambo died in 1884, but his defiant pride lived on in his successor Isike, who resisted German colonisation by blockading the caravan routes and successfully ambushing any German troops sent to the region. In January 1893, the Germans led a large surprise attack on Tabora. Isike, realising he didn't stand a chance and unwilling to be captured, blew up his fort, in the process taking his own life.

described as a 'most comfortable place' – while waiting for the war between the Arabs and King Mirambo to subside, so that he could head towards Lake Tanganyika to seek the lost Doctor Livingstone. Stanley's travel companion John William Shaw stayed with him at Kwihara, and set off alongside him towards Lake Tanganyika, but was forced to turn back through illness. Shaw died at Kwihara and is buried in a marked grave in a field next to the *tembe*.

Following their famous meeting at Ujiji in November 1871, Stanley and Livingstone returned to Kwihara and the *tembe* on February 18 1872. A month later, Stanley set back off to the coast, promising to send Livingstone a caravan of fresh supplies as soon as he arrived. Livingstone spent 189 days 'wearily waiting' at Said bin Salim's residence before the provisions finally arrived, and he was free to embark upon what would prove to be his final, fatal expedition south to Lake Bangweulu. In August 1873, Cameron, Dillon and Murphy, members of a Royal Geographical Society expedition sent out to assist Livingstone, arrived at Kwihara in poor health and spent several months recuperating at the *tembe*. Before the ailing trio was fully recovered, however, Livingstone's porters Chuma and Sisi arrived at Kwihara carrying their leader's sun-dried remains. Today, the main rooms in the front of the house exhibit several old documents (including contemporary newspaper reports) and fading photographs relating to Livingstone and his discovery by Stanley.

To get to the restored *tembe* from Tabora, follow Boma Road out of town past the traffic circle in front of the Old Boma. About 50m past this traffic circle, follow the right fork, signposted for the Huima Training and Conference Centre. After about 1km, you pass the Wasichama Secondary School, then after another 2km, you must turn right along a side road marked with a fading blue signpost reading 'Livingstone's *Tembe*'. The *tembe* lies about 2km along this road in a grove of mango trees. The road is flat enough that you could easily walk out over about an hour, bearing in mind that the area gets very hot in the middle of the day. A taxi from the town centre will charge Tsh6,000–10,000 for the round trip. Alternatively, occasional *dalla-dallas* to the small village of Kipalapala can drop you at the turn-off 2km from the *tembe*.

Rungwa Game Reserve
The Rungwa Game Reserve is an extension of the Ruaha ecosystem and protects similar animals to Ruaha National Park. It is ten hours from Tabora by bus, and there is no guarantee you will be allowed in. To get there, ask a bus to Mbeya to drop you at Rungwa village on the park boundary. At the village, speak to the head ranger for permission to walk in the park and to organise a guide. Bring a tent and food with you.

Uvinza
Situated along the Central Railway line between Tabora and Kigoma, Uvinza – which means 'Place of Salt' – is the site of a vast salt mine, which has been worked for at least 1,500 years. Mining activity peaked in the days of the 19th-century caravans, which often stopped at Uvinza to transport salt to Ujiji for export across Lake Tanganyika, as well as to other trading centres en route to the coast. Whether anybody would want to break up the train trip for a couple of nights to see a salt mine is an open question, but it is certainly possible to visit it, and there are a few basic guesthouses dotted around the small town.

KIGOMA
The largest port and most important transport hub on the eastern shores of Lake Tanganyika, Kigoma sprawls attractively across hilly, green slopes rising from Kigoma Bay, a deep natural harbour protected to the south by the narrow Bangwe

Peninsula. Although this superb bay has presumably been inhabited for millennia, Kigoma owes its modern significance to the German colonials, who favoured it as a regional administration centre over the more established 19th-century Arab slave trading centre at Ujiji, only 6km to the southeast. The ascendancy of Kigoma over Ujiji was sealed in February 1914, when the railway line from the coast finally reached the nascent German port, almost 10 years after the first tracks had been laid at the coast, and mere months before the outbreak of World War I.

Kigoma is definitely one of the more characterful towns in the East African interior: an almost archetypal tropical African port whose cinematic sense of place is enhanced by a conspicuously easygoing mood and captivating setting alongside the crystal clear waters of Lake Tanganyika. Given its relatively remote location, Kigoma also has a surprisingly cosmopolitan flavour, at times positively crawling with independent travellers waiting for various transport connections, not to mention African cross-border businessmen taking advantage of Lake Tanganyika's status as an international free trade zone. In recent years, Kigoma has also become a focal point for UN and other international aid organisations involved with a number of refugee camps associated with the ongoing instability in the neighbouring states of Burundi and the DRC.

Kigoma's compact town centre is dominated by a long mango-lined avenue, which snakes uphill from the lakeshore railway station and harbour to the market and bus station. Sightseeing in the town centre is pretty much restricted to the railway station itself – a fine example of German colonial architecture – and the so-called Kaiser House, which is reputedly linked to the railway station by a subterranean escape tunnel excavated during World War I. There is, however, plenty to see in the immediate vicinity. The main mango-lined avenue described above continues running southeast out of town, passing after about 2km through the small but bustling suburb of Mwanga, before arriving after another 4km at the historic port of Ujiji. To the south of the town centre, a dirt road runs out of town, past the prison and upmarket Kigoma Hilltop Hotel, to the fishing village of Katonga, Zungu Beach and the (currently closed) Kitwe Point Chimpanzee Sanctuary. Another road running north from the town centre leads past a series of tall fuel-storage towers – the contents of which are mostly exported to neighbouring countries – to the fishing village of Kibirizi, where local boats leave daily for Gombe Stream National Park.

In addition to some worthwhile local sightseeing, Kigoma is the obvious springboard from which to undertake a tourist activity which, given Tanzania's high profile as a safari destination, has to rank as the most inexplicably under-subscribed in the country. In a 1943 *Tanganyika Notes and Records* article about the distribution of chimpanzees in mainland Tanzania, the former District Officer of Kigoma, Captain Grant, recalled that 'it was a rare but occasional sight to see a family party on the lakeshore inside Kigoma Bay opposite the township.' You'd have to imbibe some seriously heavy stuff to be treated to such an apparition from Kigoma today, but the nearby Gombe Stream and Mahale Mountains National Parks vie with each other as *the* best place in Africa to see habituated wild chimps in their natural habitat. If you're in the area, and can afford the time and expense, the chimpanzee tracking at Gombe or Mahale is simply not to be missed.

Getting there and away

The only realistic ways to get to Kigoma are by air, rail or water. Flights to Kigoma used to be subject to regular cancellations, but the situation has improved greatly over the past couple of years, with Precision Air and Air Tanzania between them now operating five regular and reliable scheduled flights to Kigoma weekly. The Air Tanzania flights run on Tuesdays and Fridays, leaving Dar es Salaam at 07.00,

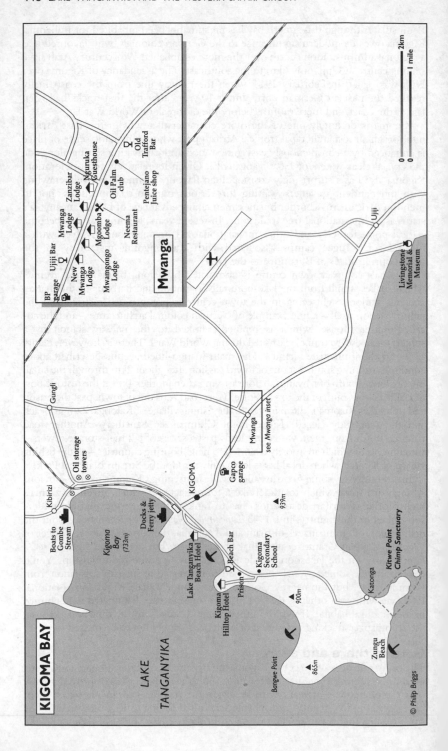

Mwanga

- BP garage
- Ujiji Bar
- New Mwanga Lodge
- Mwanga Lodge
- Mwangongo Lodge
- Zanzibar Lodge
- Nguruka Guesthouse
- Old Trafford Bar
- Oil Palm club
- Pentejano Juice shop
- Mgoomba Lodge
- Neema Restaurant

KIGOMA BAY

- Ujiji
- Livingstone Memorial & Museum
- Gungli
- Oil storage towers
- Kibirizi
- Boats to Gombe Stream
- Docks & Ferry jetty
- Kigoma Bay (733m)
- KIGOMA
- Gapco garage
- Mwanga see Mwanga inset
- 939m
- Lake Tanganyika Beach Hotel
- Beach Bar
- Kigoma Secondary School
- Kigoma Hilltop Hotel
- Prison
- 900m
- Katonga
- Kitwe Point Chimp Sanctuary
- Bangwe Point
- 865m
- Zungu Beach
- LAKE TANGANYIKA

2km
1 mile

© Philip Briggs

then stopping at Kilimanjaro International Airport (for Arusha and Moshi) and Mwanza before arriving at Kigoma at 11.35. The return flight leaves Kigoma at 14.05 and once again stops at Mwanza and Kilimanjaro before arriving in Dar es Salaam at 19.35. The one-way fare from Dar es Salaam is Tsh149,000, from Kilimanjaro it is Tsh159,000, and from Mwanza it is Tsh54,000. Precision Air flies from Dar es Salaam to Kigoma via Tabora on Wednesdays and Sundays, leaving Dar es Salaam at 07.30 and Kigoma at 10.35. It also has a Sunday flight linking Mombasa, Zanzibar and Dar es Salaam directly to Kigoma.

The railway is covered in the box *The Central Railway* on pages 374–5 and the ferry in the box *The MV Liemba* on pages 462–3. You could come to Kigoma by road from Mwanza, but you would be measuring the journey in days.

Where to stay
Upmarket
Kigoma Hilltop Hotel Tel: 028 280 4435/6/7; fax: 028 280 4434; email: kht@raha.com or info@kigoma.com; web: www.kigoma.com. Perched dramatically on a cliff overlooking Kigoma Bay roughly 2km south of the town centre, this excellent hotel is easily the best in Kigoma. Facilities include a large swimming pool, watersports equipment, fishing, snorkelling, various indoor games, a gymnasium, secretarial services, a generator and a private beach. Accommodation is in self-contained, air-conditioned chalets with satellite television, hot water and fridge. Standard rooms cost US$45/60 single/double B&B for residents and US$60/75 for non-residents, while double suites range in price from US$100 to US$150. The attached restaurant serves good Indian and Western dishes in the Tsh4,000-plus range. Alcohol is not sold on the premises, but guests are permitted to bring their own with them. The Kigoma Hilltop is a good contact for tours to the western national parks, since the management owns a private motorboat, has constructed a tented camp at Mahale in 2001, and intends to build similar camps at Gombe and Katavi over the next year or so.

Moderate
Lake Tanganyika Beach Hotel Tel: 028 280 2694. Formerly the Railway Hotel, this recently privatised hotel has a perfect location, right on the lakeshore, and only a short walk from the town centre. The self-contained rooms are a bit rundown, but reasonable value at Tsh9,000/12,000 single/double with net, fan and an erratic hot water supply. The food is pretty good, various stews and curries at around Tsh3,500, and the spacious gardens running down to the lakeshore are perfect for a chilled drink at sunset, or afterwards – assuming, that is, the bar staff remembered to put the beers in the fridge!
Aqua Hotel Tel: 028 280 2586 This small, comfortable hotel is effectively closed for a few years, while all rooms have been leased to an aid organisation. When it will re-open, and at what rate, are unknown.

Budget
Lake View Hotel Tel: 028 280 2349. Formerly a popular shoestring option, the Lake View Hotel is situated on the main road between the railway station and the market – a convenient location, though well out of sight of the lake. Currently closed for major renovations, it is scheduled to re-open, with all rooms self-contained, in late 2002. Expect rates to be around Tsh5,000 for a double.
Zanzibar Lodge Tel: 028 280 3306. Situated in Mwanga, on the Ujiji road about 2km from Kigoma town centre, this is a very clean, smart double-storey lodge built around a central courtyard and with a decent restaurant attached. The self-contained double or twin rooms with net and fan are excellent value at Tsh5,000, as are similar rooms using common showers at Tsh3,500. The one drawback is the significant distance from the town centre, though the regular *dalla-dallas* between Kigoma and Ujiji run right past the entrance.

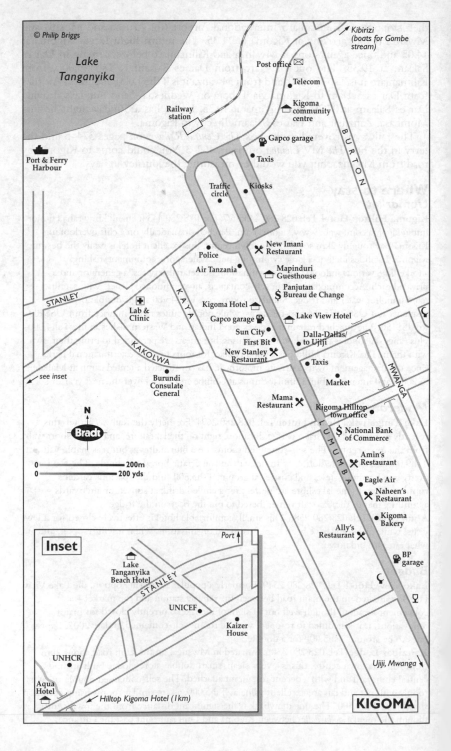

© Philip Briggs

Lake Tanganyika

Kibirizi
(boats for Gombe
stream)

Post office ✉

Telecom

Kigoma
community
centre

Railway
station

Gapco garage

Port & Ferry
Harbour

Taxis

Traffic
circle

Kiosks

New Imani
Restaurant

Police

Mapinduri
Guesthouse

Air Tanzania

Panjutan
Bureau de Change

STANLEY

$

KAYA

Kigoma Hotel

Lake View Hotel

Lab &
Clinic

Gapco garage

KAKOLWA

Sun City

Dalla-Dallas/
to Ujiji

First Bit

New Stanley
Restaurant

Taxis

see inset

Market

Burundi
Consulate
General

Mama
Restaurant

Kigoma Hilltop
town office

N

National Bank
of Commerce

Bradt

Amin's
Restaurant

0   200m
0   200 yds

Eagle Air

Naheen's
Restaurant

Kigoma
Bakery

Ally's
Restaurant

BP
garage

BURTON

MWANGA

LUMUMBA

Inset

Port ↑

Lake
Tanganyika
Beach Hotel

STANLEY

UNICEF

Kaizer
House

UNHCR

Aqua
Hotel

Ujiji, Mwanga

Hilltop Kigoma Hotel (1km)

KIGOMA

New Mwanga Hotel Tel: 028 280 4645. Also situated right on the Ujiji road as it passes through Mwanga, this hotel is identical in price to the Zanzibar Lodge, and offers about the same facilities. It does feel a lot scruffier, however, and is a definite second choice in this part of town. Same thing goes for the affiliated and identically priced Mwanga Hotel a block away.

Shoestring

Kigoma Community Centre Conveniently located along the short road between the railway station and the post office, this church-run hostel is rather rundown but not unreasonably priced at Tsh1,500/2,000 single/double.

Kigoma Hotel Situated opposite the Lake View Hotel, this place used to be popular with budget travellers, but it's gone seriously downhill of late. On the plus side, it is very central, and the asking rate of Tsh1,400/2,000 for a single/double is a pretty fair reflection of what you get.

Mapinduzi Guesthouse Another centrally located dump charging Tsh2,000 for a basic double.

Where to eat and drink

The restaurants at the **Kigoma Hilltop** and **Lake Tanganyika Beach Hotels** can both be recommended for Western and Indian meals, with the Lake Tanganyika hotel marginally cheaper and considerably more convenient should you be walking from the town centre. Otherwise, the pick of the eateries in the town centre is the smart **New Stanley Restaurant**, which serves a variety of grills and other dishes for around Tsh2,500. You can eat inside (there are fans) or in an open area adjacent to the main restaurant.

Of the places catering more to local palates, **Ally's Restaurant** serves a wide variety of inexpensive meals and snacks, as do the nearby **Naheen's** and **Amin's Restaurants**. On the road between the railway station and market, **First Bits** serves a variety of light snacks and juices, while **Sun City** – in addition to various game machines and a pool table – has ice-cream and popcorn.

If you're stocking up on food before heading to Gombe Stream or Mahale Mountain, the central **market** and the shops immediately around it are very well stocked with fresh fruits and vegetables and imported tinned and other packaged goods. The **Kigoma Bakery** roughly opposite Ally's Restaurant bakes fresh bread every morning.

There's sometimes a **disco** at night behind the **New Stanley Restaurant**, while the most convenient spot for a few drinks on the lakeshore is the **Lake Tanganyika Beach Hotel**. Better still is the anonymous **beach bar** that lies a few hundred metres further from the town centre, between a football field and the prison. Located on a sandy palm-lined beach where local people swim, this earthy but welcoming bar serves the coldest beers in Kigoma, at very cheap prices – and our evening was made complete by the bizarre sight of a pennant-winged nightjar fluttering and hawking over the lake.

General information

Foreign exchange The National Bank of Commerce opposite the market exchanges travellers' cheques and cash at the usual rates. The private Panjutan bureau de change on the main road between the railway station might well do the same, but we never saw it open once over a week travelling in and out of Kigoma.

Internet There is no internet café in Kigoma at the time of writing, though this is bound to change.

Swimming The swimming pool at the Kigoma Hilltop Hotel is open to non-hotel residents for a small fee. Local people swim with apparent impunity at the sandy beach bar next to the prison, but that doesn't necessarily mean it is free of bilharzia. Zungu Beach near Katonga (see *Excursions from Kigoma* below) reputedly is.

Excursions from Kigoma
Ujiji
The small but sprawling lakeshore port of Ujiji, dwarfed today by the nearby and more modern town of Kigoma, is best known as the place where the immortal enquiry 'Doctor Livingstone, I presume?' was made by Stanley on November 10 1871 (see box, *Ujiji, November 10 1871*, pages 454–5). Ujiji's historical significance does, however, extend beyond the utterance of one Victorian banality. For centuries, it was the main port from which the salt mined at nearby Uvinza was transported across the lake to the present-day eastern Congo. In about 1800, Ujiji was settled by Arab traders from the coast, and began its rise to prominence as the lakeshore terminal of the most important ivory and slave caravan route to Bagamoyo, eventually to be governed by an agent of the Sultan of Zanzibar. Ujiji is also where, in 1858, the exhausted Burton and Speke – the former with an ulcerated jaw and practically paralysed below the waist, the latter partially blind and driven close to dementia by an insect that burrowed into his ear canal – arrived on the shore of the 'Sea of Ujiji'.

For all its historical associations, Ujiji today is something of a backwater, and although it displays some Swahili influences one wouldn't normally associate with this part of the country, anybody who visits the small port expecting to find a thriving market town will be disappointed. Most travellers passing through Kigoma do nevertheless make the short trip to Ujiji, primarily for the monument and museum dedicated to Livingstone and Stanley's meeting at the port in 1871 (see box *History of a Monument*, page 456). Decorated with an engraved outline of Africa, the stone monument stands under a shady mango tree, and bears a brass plaque reading 'Under the mango tree which then stood here Stanley met Livingstone 10th November 1871'. A smaller monument dedicated to Burton and Speke stands alongside it.

The **Livingstone Museum**, adjacent to the monument, consists of several large and virtually empty rooms, one of which contains a few ineptly executed and comically captioned paintings of the great explorer, as well as life-size papier mâché statues of Stanley and Livingstone doffing their caps in greeting. Attempts to maintain a straight face in this mildly surreal scenario will be further subverted by the caretaker, who treats visitors to an informative lecture about Livingstone, delivered in a rising monotone suggestive of a church sermon. Entrance to both the monument and museum is free, though the caretaker will expect a donation of Tsh2,000.

The Livingstone Museum is also a good place to see traditional Ha dancing, since the Washirika Dance Troupe – complete with traditional dresses made from the bark of the Marimba tree – practices in its grounds from 17.00 to 18.00 every Wednesday, Friday and Sunday. Watching the rehearsals is free – though a small donation will almost certainly be asked for – but you'll need to negotiate with the caretaker if you want to take photographs or arrange a special performance beyond practice time. Outside of dancing hours, having dutifully snapped a picture of yourself and a pal shaking hands in front of the Livingstone Monument, the most interesting aspect of Ujiji is the traditional harbour, where you can to watch local fishermen and boat builders ply their respective trades.

A good surfaced road covers the 6km between Ujiji and Kigoma. A regular *dalla-dalla* service runs back and forth between the two ports, charging Tsh100 per person, and leaving Kigoma from next to the market every five minutes or so. Assuming you're mainly interested in the Livingstone Museum and Monument, the signposted junction lies on the outskirts of central Ujiji – the conductor will drop you off there if you ask for 'Livingstone'. From the junction, it's a walk of about five minutes to the monument and museum, along a straight road populated by some of the most vociferous children in Tanzania (Stanley's description of arriving in Ujiji to a mob that 'bawled a jangling chorus of "Jambo"' still rings true today!). When you're ready to return to Kigoma, walk back to the junction, and any passing *dalla-dalla* will pick you up.

Katonga and Kitwe Point Sanctuary

The small fishing village of Katonga, which lies on a pretty, sheltered bay some 5km south of Kigoma, is a good place to observe traditional fishing activities such as sun-drying the small dagaa fish or smoking larger fish such as tilapia. The roughly 2km turn-off to Zungu Beach – the best bathing spot in the Kigoma area – lies about 500m before Katonga on the road back towards Kigoma.

Separated from Katonga by a fence, the 300-acre Kitwe Point Sanctuary stands on a hilly wooded peninsula that was deeded to the Jane Goodall Institute after plans to develop it as an educational wildlife zoo faltered. In addition to a few zebra, wildebeest and vervet monkey, the sanctuary is home to three orphaned chimpanzees that were confiscated by the Tanzanian authorities in 1994. It lies in an area of regenerating forest, next to the lake, and would be of some interest to birders. Until recently, visitors were welcome to visit the sanctuary at feeding time (16.00) daily except for on Wednesdays, Sundays and the first Monday of any given month. Unfortunately, the apes started to display increasingly aggressive behaviour towards visitors, forcing the sanctuary to close 'for renovations'. It is likely that the chimps will be transferred to a more suitable location in the near future, after which the sanctuary may re-open.

The dirt road from Kigoma to Katonga is plied by regular *dalla-dallas*, terminating at the market about 200m from the sanctuary entrance.

German Fortifications

On the hill near the Hilltop Hotel stand some German fortifications constructed at the start of World War I. The most interesting of these is an emplacement for the 105mm naval gun that was taken from the *Von Goetzen* (*Liemba*) and was carried away by the Germans when they retreated from Kigoma – it's final destination is a mystery! There are also some interconnecting trenches, ammunition stores, and large stone and cement bunkers on the hill. Note that the hills on the other side of the bay (north) are in a military area, and people will hop out of the bushes to tick you off if you try to climb them.

GOMBE STREAM NATIONAL PARK

Renowned for its chimpanzees, or more accurately perhaps the research into their behaviour undertaken by the groundbreaking primatologist Jane Goodall, Gombe Stream is one of a handful of African national parks that could reasonably claim to be a household name in the west. Yet, surprisingly, Gombe Stream remains a surprisingly low-key and little-visited reserve, moreover one whose profile has shrunk – along with its annual tally of tourist visits – over a 15-year period during which Tanzania as a whole attracted a consistent growth in tourist numbers. The reasons for this decline are manifold. Gombe Stream's relatively remote location has always been, and remains, a dissuasive factor for short-stay visitors to Tanzania. Meanwhile, backpacker traffic, once the mainstay of the park, has abated due to the

UJIJI, NOVEMBER 10 1871

In March 1866, Dr David Livingstone, the most famous and arguably the greatest explorer of his – or perhaps any – era, set off from the coastal port of Mikindani with the aim of resolving the whereabouts of the source of the Nile. Almost nothing concrete was heard of Livingstone over the next few years, and rumours of his death vied with equally difficult to substantiate rumours of his imminent return to the coast. So it was that, in 1869, the American journalist Henry Morton Stanley, then on assignment in Spain, received a telegram from his editor at the *New York Herald* bearing a simple command that would take him two wearisome years to fulfil: 'Find Livingstone!' The rest, as they say, is history.

In his autobiography, published in 1909, Stanley recalled the momentous day:

> We slept at a chief's village in Ukaranga, with only one more march of six hours, it was said, intervening between us and the Arab settlement of Ujiji, in which native rumour located an old, grey-bearded, white man, who had but newly arrived from a distant western country. It was now 235 days since I had left the Indian Ocean and 50 days since I had departed from [Tabora]... At cockcrow...we strengthened ourselves with a substantial meal, and, as the sun rose in the east, we turned our backs to it, and the caravan was soon in full swing on the march... About eight o'clock we were climbing the side of a steep and wooded hill, and [from] the very crest... I saw, as in a painted picture, a vast lake in the distance below, with its face luminous as a mirror, set in a frame of dimly blue mountains... For hours I strode nervously on... brushing past the bush on the hill-slopes and crests, flinging gay remarks to the wondering villagers who looked on... in mute surprise, until near noon, when, having crossed the last valley and climbed up to the summit of the last hill: Lo! Lake Tanganyika was distant from us but half a mile...
>
> Hard by the lake shore, embowered in palms, on this hot noon, the village of Ujiji broods drowsily. No living thing can be seen moving to break the still aspect of the outer lines of the town and its deep shades... I rested awhile, breathless from my exertions; and, as the stragglers were many, I halted to reunite and reform for an imposing entry. Meantime, my people improved their personal appearance; they clothed themselves in clean dresses, and snowy cloths were folded round their heads. When the laggards had all been gathered, the guns were loaded to rouse up the sleeping town. It is an immemorial custom, for a caravan creeps not up into a friendly town like a thief. Our braves knew the custom well; they therefore volleyed and thundered their salutes as they went marching down the hill slowly, and with much self-contained dignity. Presently, there is a tumultuous stir visible on the outer edge of the town. Groups of men in white dresses, with arms in their hands, burst from the shades, and seem to hesitate a moment, as if in doubt; they then come rushing up to meet us, pursued by hundreds of people, who shout joyfully, while yet afar, their noisy welcomes.
>
> The foremost... cried out: 'why, we took you for Mirambo and his bandits, when we heard the booming of the guns. It is an age since a

caravan has come to Ujiji. Which way did you come? Ah! You have got a white man with you! Is this his caravan?' Being told it was a white man's caravan by the guides in front, the boisterous multitude pressed up to me, greeted me with salaams, and bowed their salutes. Hundreds of them jostled and trod upon one another's heels... when a tall black man, in long white shirt, burst impulsively through the crowd on my right, and bending low, said 'Good morning, sir,' in clear, intelligent English.

'Hello!' I said, 'Who in the mischief are you?'

'I am Susi, sir, the servant of Dr. Livingstone.'

'What! Is Dr. Livingstone here in this town?'

'Yes, sir.'

'But, are you sure; sure that it is Dr. Livingstone?'

'Why, I leave him just now, sir.'

'Well, now that we have met, one of you had better run ahead, and tell the Doctor of my coming.'

The same idea striking Susi's mind, he undertook in his impulsive manner to inform the Doctor, and I saw him racing headlong, with his white dress streaming behind him like a wind-whipped pennant. The column continued on its way, beset on either flank by a vehemently enthusiastic and noisily rejoicing mob, which bawled a jangling chorus of 'Jambo' to every mother's son of us, and maintained an inharmonious orchestral music of drums and horns. I was indebted for this loud ovation to the cheerful relief the people felt that we were not Mirambo's bandits, and to their joy at the happy rupture of the long silence that had perforce existed between the two trading colonies of [Tabora] and Ujiji.

After a few minutes we came to a halt. The guides in the van had reached the marketplace, which was the central point of interest. For there the great Arabs, chiefs and respectabilities of Ujiji had gathered in a group to await events; thither also they had brought with them the venerable European traveller who was at that time resting among them. The caravan pressed up to them, divided itself into two lines on either side of the road, and, as it did so, disclosed to me the prominent figure of an elderly white man clad in a red flannel blouse, grey trousers, and a blue cloth, gold-banded cap.

Up to this moment my mind had verged upon non-belief in his existence, and now a nagging doubt intruded itself into my mind that this white man could not be the object of my quest, or if he were, he would somehow contrive to disappear before my eyes... 'It may not be Livingstone after all,' doubt suggested. If this is he, what shall I say to him? My imagination had not taken this question into consideration before. All around me was the immense crowd, hushed and expectant, and wondering how the scene would develop itself.

Under all these circumstances I could do no more than exercise some restraint and reserve, so I walked up to him, and, doffing my helmet, bowed and said in an inquiring tone:

'Dr. Livingstone, I presume?'

'Smiling cordially, he lifted his cap, and answered briefly:

'Yes.'

THE HISTORY OF A MONUMENT

The earliest monument to Livingstone and Stanley, erected by Belgium after the end of World War I, consisted of a bland, whitewashed concrete slab placed over the base of the mango tree under which their famous meeting is said to have taken place. Unfortunately, this concrete eyesore caused the roots of the original tree to decay: photographs taken in 1921 and 1930 show that over the course of a decade a flourishing and thickly foliated tree had been reduced to a bare stump with only a few scraggly branches remaining.

In August 1930, the dying tree was felled, but not before the District Officer of Kigoma, Captain Grant, had the foresight to graft a new tree from the original. A new, obelisk-like monument bearing a brass plaque donated by the Royal Geographical Society was constructed next to the grafted shrub. Shortly after World War II, the obelisk was removed and its plaque was transferred to a newly built stone structure, the one that still stands at the site today, in the shadow of the mango tree grafted from the original by Captain Grant.

Poignant stuff, at least until you discover that Stanley's journal suggests the meeting took place near the old marketplace, several hundred metres from the modern monument, and that the tree shown in the 1921 photograph was too young to have offered any significant cover 50 years earlier. The probability is that when the German colonisers quizzed local residents about where the famous meeting took place, they simply invented a plausible site – a scenario that will be familiar to anybody who has regularly asked for directions in Africa!

unusually high fee structure, the introduction of cheap chimp tracking in several Ugandan reserves, and the eastward shift of popular overland routes following the succession of civil wars in Rwanda, Burundi and the DRC.

Travel patterns may change, but Gombe Stream remains a thoroughly worthwhile destination. True, the more southerly Mahale Mountain National Park, the other 'chimp reserve' on Lake Tanganyika, is much larger, and correspondingly wilder in atmosphere, but then Gombe Stream is the more accessible goal for independent travellers. Furthermore, and disregarding financial considerations, you could go chimp tracking a dozen times practically anywhere else in Africa, and still not be adequately prepared for the in-your-face encounters with wild chimpanzees that characterise either of the two national parks on Lake Tanganyika. Whether you visit Gombe or Mahale, you will, with a modicum of luck, be treated to one of most extraordinary and memorable wildlife experiences our planet has to offer!

Gazetted as a game reserve in 1943 and accorded its current conservation status in 1965, Gombe Stream is Tanzania's smallest national park, extending over some 52km² of hilly terrain climbing from the lakeshore, at an altitude of 773m, to above 1,500m at the top of the rift escarpment. At no point measuring more than 3.5km from east to west, the narrow national park is transected by a series of 13 streams which carve steep valleys into the rift escarpment before flowing into the lake. This rugged topography is covered not in the rainforest one might expect of a reserve whose best-known inhabitants are chimpanzees, but rather in thick *brachystegia* woodland that gives way to narrow belts of lush riparian forest along the river courses.

Gombe's chimpanzee research project, the longest-running study of an individual wild animal population in the world, was initiated by Jane Goodall in 1960 and sponsored by Louis Leakey, who felt that his protégé's lack of scientific training would allow her to observe chimpanzee behaviour without preconceptions. After initial difficulties trying to locate her subjects, Goodall overcame the chimps' shyness through the combination of a banana-feeding machine and sheer persistence. Since the late 1960s Goodall's work has achieved both popular and scientific recognition. Her painstaking studies of individual chimps and the day-to-day social behaviour of troops have been supplemented by a series of observations confronting conventional scientific wisdom. Observations that initially caused controversy – tool-making, inter-troop warfare and even cannibalism – have since been widely accepted. Much of Goodall's work is described in her books *In the Shadow of Man* and *Through a Window*, which are highly recommended to interested readers. Those who have read her books will be interested to know that Fifi, a three-year old when Goodall first arrived at Gombe Stream in 1960, was alive and well and regularly seen by tourists in 2001!

The park's population of roughly 100 chimpanzees is divided across three communities. The habituated Kasekela community studied by Jane Goodall is the largest of the three, numbering about 45 individuals in 2001, and its territory lies in the central part of the park, around the Kasekela research centre, rest camp and river. To see the chimpanzees, however, you will need to go on a guided walk from the research centre, which costs US$20 per party. A few years ago, it was normally very easy to locate chimps, because they still made routine visits to the feeding station established by Goodall above the research centre. The practice of feeding chimps was discontinued in 1995, however, so chimp tracking now normally involves some fairly strenuous walking on steep slopes. The best time to track the chimps is shortly after sunrise, because the guides normally know where they nested the previous night, and are thus likely to find them quite easily. During the dry season, when the chimps tend to forage on the lower slopes of the escarpment, it often takes less than an hour to locate a group. In the wet season, when the chimps forage higher and walking conditions are tougher, it could take three or four hours.

Although it is the chimpanzees that hog the limelight, Gombe Stream harbours a surprisingly varied fauna for a park of its small size. Fascinating in their own right are the olive baboons that beachcomb in front of the rest camp. These have been the subject of ongoing research since 1967, and – like their larger and more celebrated cousins – they are apparently oblivious to the presence of humans, without showing any of the aggression one normally associates with baboons that forage close to habitations. Other common primates in Gombe are vervet, blue, red-tailed and red colobus monkeys, the latter frequently seen while searching for chimps. Most of the other mammals found there are secretive or nocturnal, and are seldom seen by visitors. The only part of the park where you may walk unguided is along the lakeshore and in the immediate vicinity of the rest camp, which is a good place to seek out some of the 200 bird species recorded in the park. Of particular note are the palmnut vultures and fish eagles that perch on palms and other trees along the lakeshore, and the gem-like Peter's twinspot, a normally elusive forest bird that is tame and easily seen within the rest camp.

Because they are genetically so similar to humans, chimpanzees are susceptible to most diseases borne by humans. If you are unwell, do not visit the park. Even a common cold has the potential to kill a chimpanzee, which may not share your immunity.

CHIMPANZEES

Almost certainly, you'll hear them before you see them: from somewhere deep in the forest, an excited hooting, just one voice at first, then several, rising in volume and tempo and pitch to a frenzied unified crescendo, before stopping abruptly or fading away. Jane Goodall called it the 'pant-hoot' call, a kind of bonding ritual that allows any chimpanzees within earshot of each other to identify exactly who is around through the individual's unique vocal stylisation. To the human listener, this eruptive crescendo is one of the most spine chilling and exciting sounds of the rainforest, and an almost certain indicator that visual contact with man's closest genetic relative is imminent.

It is, in large part, our close evolutionary kinship with chimpanzees that makes these sociable black-coated apes of the forest so enduringly fascinating. Humans, chimpanzees and bonobos (also known as pygmy chimpanzees) share more than 98% of their genetic code, and the three species are far more closely related to each other than they are to any other living creature, even gorillas. Superficial differences notwithstanding, the similarities between humans and chimps are consistently striking, not only in the skeletal structure and skull, but also in the nervous system, the immune system, and in many behavioural aspects – bonobos, for instance, are the only animals other than humans to copulate in the missionary position.

Unlike most other primates, chimpanzees don't live in troops, but instead form extended communities of up to 100 individuals, which roam the forest in small socially mobile subgroups that often revolve around a few close family members such as brothers or a mother and daughter. Male chimps normally spend their entire life within the community into which they were born, whereas females are likely to migrate into a neighbouring community at some point after reaching adolescence. A highly ranking male will occasionally attempt to monopolise a female in oestrus, but the more normal state of sexual affairs in chimp society is non-hierarchical promiscuity. A young female in oestrus will generally mate with any male that takes her fancy, while older females tend to form close bonds with a few specific males, sometimes allowing themselves to be monopolised by a favoured suitor for a period, but never pairing off exclusively in the long term.

Within each community, one alpha male is normally recognised – though coalitions between two males, often a dominant and a submissive sibling – have often been recorded. The role of the alpha male, not fully understood, is evidently quite benevolent – chairman of the board rather than crusty tyrant. This is probably influenced by the alpha male's relatively limited reproductive advantages over his potential rivals, most of whom he will have known for his entire life. Other males in the community are generally supportive rather than competitive towards the alpha male, except for when a rival consciously contests the alpha position, which is far from being an everyday occurrence. In Mahale's Mimikere Community, for instance, an alpha male called Ntologi retained his status from 1979 to 1995, interrupted for about a year towards the end of that period.

Prior to the 1960s, it was always assumed that chimps were strict vegetarians. This notion was rocked when Jane Goodall witnessed a group of chimps hunting down a red colobus monkey, something that has since been discovered to be common behaviour, particularly during the dry season when other food sources are depleted. Over subsequent years, an average of 20 kills has been recorded in Gombe annually, with red colobus being the prey on more than half of these occasions, though young bushbuck, young bushpig and even infant chimps have also been victimised and eaten. In the dry season, visitors are quite likely to see an attempted hunt at Gombe, though a successful kill is less commonplace. The normal modus operandi is for four or five adult chimps to slowly encircle a colobus troop, then for another chimp to act as a decoy, creating deliberate confusion in the hope that it will drive the monkeys into the trap, or cause a mother to drop her baby.

Although chimp communities appear by-and-large to be stable and peaceful entities, intensive warfare has been known to erupt once each within the habituated communities of Mahale and Gombe. In Mahale, one of the two communities originally habituated by researchers in 1967 had exterminated the other by 1982. A similar thing happened in Gombe Stream in the 1970s, when the Kasekela community as originally habituated by Goodall divided into two discrete communities. The Kasekela and breakaway Kahama community co-existed alongside each other for some years. Then in 1974, Goodall returned to Gombe Stream after a break to discover that the Kasekela males were methodically persecuting their former community mates, isolating the Kahama males one by one, and tearing into them until they were dead or terminally wounded. By 1977, the Kahama community had vanished entirely.

Chimpanzees are essentially inhabitants of the west and central African rainforests, and the Tanzanian population of perhaps 2,000 individuals represents less than 1% of the continental total. Somewhat paradoxically, however, much of what is known about wild chimpanzee society and behaviour stems from the ongoing research projects that were initiated in Gombe Stream and Mahale Mountain National Parks back in the 1960s. One of the most interesting patterns to emerge from the parallel research projects in these nearby reserves is a large number of social and behavioural differences in the two populations that can only be described as cultural.

One striking difference between the two populations is their apparently inexplicable food preferences. Of the various plants that occur in both national parks, as many as 40% that are utilised as a food source by one community are left untouched by the other. In Gombe Stream, for instance, you'll often see chimps in the vicinity of palm trees, and the palmnut seems to be considered to be something of a delicacy. Exactly the same palms are found at Mahale, but the chimps have yet to be recorded eating from them. Likewise, the 'termite-fishing' behaviour that was first recorded by Jane Goodall at Gombe Stream in the 1960s has a parallel in Mahale, where the chimps are often seen 'fishing' for carpenter ants in the trees. But the Mahale chimps have never been recorded fishing for termites, while the Gombe chimps are not known to fish for carpenter ants. At Mahale, you're bound to come across chimps grooming each other with one hand while holding each other's other hand above their heads – once again, behaviour that has never been noted at Gombe. More than any structural similarity, more even than any single quirk of chimpanzee behaviour, it is such striking cultural differences – the influence of nurture over nature if you like – that brings home our close genetic kinship with chimpanzees.

National Park fees

Gombe Stream's entrance fee of US$100 per 24 hours is the highest for any Tanzanian National Park. Since 1997, however, the US$100 entrance fee per 24 hours has been applicable only to time spent in the forest, not to time spent in the rest camp. The significance of this to independent travellers, for whom a two-night stay is enforced by the lake-taxi schedules, is that (assuming all forest walks take place within 24 hours) they now need only pay US$100 in entrance fees, as opposed to the US$200 they would have paid before.

In addition to the park entrance fees, visitors will need to pay US$10 per person per night for the most basic accommodation, as well as a daily guide fee of US$20 per group. Add on transport, food and drink costs, and a two-night stay for two people will work out at around US$150 per person. Expensive as this sounds, it's no more than you would pay for a similar period on a camping safari elsewhere in Tanzania. And, given that tracking wild chimpanzees has to rank as one of the most fulfilling wildlife experiences in the world, it's an absolute bargain compared to the US$100 many backpackers are willing to spend on a bungee jump at Victoria Falls!

Do note that fees must be paid in hard currency, ideally US dollars. Travellers' cheques are accepted, but change – whether in local or hard currency – may not be available, so make sure you have the right denomination cheques or banknotes.

Further information

The 72-page booklet *Gombe Stream National Park*, written and illustrated by David Bygott and published by Tanzania National Parks in 1992, was the last of the old US$5 series of booklets to be compiled, and is probably the most comprehensive. It's an essential purchase, with full checklists, detailed coverage of chimpanzee behaviour, and much other excellent background information. The practical information is inevitably rather dated, and best ignored where it clashes with information included in this Bradt guide.

A Gombe Stream National Park title in the newer and glossier series of booklets co-published by Tanzania National Parks and the Africa Publishing Group is scheduled and likely to be available in the next year or two.

Getting there and away

Organised tours

Most safari operators based outside of Kigoma can arrange Gombe safaris, but they will generally be working with a local operator. The best place locally to arrange organised trips to Gombe Stream is the Kigoma Hilltop Hotel which offers a variety of package excursions for between one and twelve people using their own motorboat, a trip of 25 minutes in either direction. The packages range from three to eight days in duration (with the first and/or last night being spent at their hotel in Kigoma) and vary greatly in price depending on duration and number of passengers. To give an idea, a three-day, two-night trip (which includes one night in the park) would cost US$776 for one person, US$504 per person for two people, US$393 per person for four people, or US$322 per person for 12 people. A five-day, four-night package (including two nights in the park) will cost US$1,336, US$965, US$835 or US$756 per person for one, two, four or 12 people respectively. These rates include national park fees, guide fees, all meals, boat transfers, collection from the airport, and accommodation in Kigoma and in the national park *banda*s. The rates do not include flights (or other transport) to Kigoma from elsewhere in the country.

The Kigoma Hilltop Hotel also organises combined packages to Gombe Stream and Mahale Mountains, lasting from six to ten days in total. Sample prices are US$2,594, US$1,677, US$1,293 or US$1,047 per person for a six-day package, and US$3,185, US$2,198, US$1,969 or US$1,517 per person for an eight-day package, for one, two, four or twelve people. The contact details and website for the Kigoma Hilltop Hotel are listed under Kigoma in the *Where to stay* section.

Independent visits

The southern boundary of Gombe Stream National Park lies only 16km north of Kigoma, and the Kasekela Research Station and Tourist Camp is situated on the lakeshore about 8km further north. Although there is no road into Gombe Stream, this is one of the few national parks in East Africa that is easily accessed on public transport and can only be explored on foot, making it an excellent goal for independent travellers.

The cheapest way to get to Kasekela is with one of the lake-taxis that run between the beach at Kibirizi village, 3km north of Kigoma, and a village called Mwamgongo on the northern boundary of the national park. These lake-taxis stop by request at all lakeshore settlements on the way, Kasekela Rest Camp included. At least two boats ply the route daily, generally leaving from Kibirizi between 13.00 and 14.00 and taking from two to four hours to get to Kasekela, depending on the number and duration of stops. On the return trip, the lake-taxis generally pass Kasekela between 07.00 and 08.00 and arrive at Kibirizi two to three hours later. The fare in either direction is Tsh1,000 per person.

Several random practical issues regarding the lake-taxis should be raised. Firstly, there is no public transport along the 3km road between Kigoma and Kibirizi, which means that you must either walk or use a charter taxi. If you opt for the latter, plenty of taxis can be found around the railway station or the market, and the fare to Kibirizi should be around Tsh3,000. Secondly, the lake-taxis are not covered, and they can become uncomfortably hot in the sun, so if you have an umbrella take it along, otherwise bring a hat and sunscreen – as well as a bottle of water to drink on the way.

Finally, the timing of the lake-taxis effectively forces travellers using public transport to spend at least two nights at Gombe Stream. Should you want to visit the park as a day excursion from Kigoma or a one-night trip, for instance because you need to catch a ferry or train elsewhere, you can arrange a private boat charter at Kibirizi (we were quoted Tsh55,000 for an overnight trip). More efficiently – 30 minutes each way – the Kigoma Hilltop Hotel will rent out its motorboat, which seats up to 12 people, at a flat fee of US$250 per party for the round trip, plus US$50 for every night spent in the park.

Where to stay and eat

The only accommodation at present is situated at the **Kasekela Research Station and Rest Camp**. The smarter accommodation is in the resthouse, which contains two twin rooms with nets but no fan, as well as a screened porch, and costs US$20 per person. There is also a hostel with smaller, scruffier rooms that lack for nets, but cost US$10 per person only. Camping is permitted, too, but since it costs US$20 per person, there's no advantage in pitching a tent.

In theory, the accommodation is self-catering, but in practice there aren't formal facilities available for cooking, and you'll end up spending hours arranging to have pots, crockery, cutlery, charcoal, etc brought to you. If you do bring food, a local cook is available to put a meal together, but you should be prepared to give him a reasonable tip. Alternatively, rather than weigh yourself down with groceries from Kigoma, one of the ladies in the staff village will gladly prepare a simple meal – fish, beans, rice, chapatis and tea – at a very reasonable price. A staff shop sells biscuits and a few other basic foodstuffs, and visitors are welcome to visit the staff bar, which is stocked with beer and sodas. It might nevertheless be a good idea to bring mineral water and some fruit with you – though do be warned that the baboons are likely to attack anybody who carries food outdoors. If you do camp, don't leave any food in your tent, or the baboons are likely to knock it down.

MAHALE MOUNTAINS NATIONAL PARK

A reasonable, albeit somewhat glib, potted description of Mahale Mountains National Park is that it is basically a grand scale version of Gombe Stream. Another might be that it is quite simply one of the most beautiful national parks anywhere in Africa. The crystal clear waters and deserted sandy beaches that characterise this part of Lake Tanganyika would be pretty damn alluring even without the forested peaks that rise high above them. As it is, the setting is scenically reminiscent of a volcanic island beach resort somewhere deep in the Indian Ocean. And with the added bonus that these forests are inhabited by the greatest number of primate species of any Tanzanian national park, including an estimated 700 to 1,000 chimpanzees divided across a dozen communities.

Gazetted in 1985, Mahale Mountains National Park extends over 1,613km², making it 30 times larger than Gombe Stream. Set on a mountainous knuckle that juts into Lake Tanganyika some 150km south of Kigoma, the park is dominated topographically by the Mahale Range. This is a part of the Rift Valley escarpment

THE MV LIEMBA

The MV *Liemba* is the 800-ton steamer that operates as the main ferry service on Lake Tanganyika, doing a weekly circuit of the eastern side of the lake from Kigoma south to Mpulungu in Zambia, and (prior to the recent civil war) north to Bujumbura in Burundi. Originally called the *Graf von Goetzen,* this historic ship arrived at Kigoma in pieces shortly before the outbreak of World War I, having been transported by rail from Dar es Salaam by the German colonists. The ship was assembled at Kigoma, before embarking on an aborted maiden voyage to Kasanga carrying 700 soldiers during the early months of the war. Shortly after this, the Germans decided to scupper the boat in the Malagarasi River mouth rather than let it fall into enemy hands. In 1927, the British and Belgians, who between them ruled the various lakeshore territories after World War I, undertook the costly task of rescuing the boat from its watery grave. The *Graf von Goetzen* was renamed the *Liemba* (according to Livingstone, the local name for Lake Tanganyika), and it has subsequently steamed up and down the lake almost continually. The oft-repeated story that *Liemba* was used in the filming of *The African Queen* is, to the best of my knowledge, a myth.

In theory, the *Liemba* does a round trip every week between Kigoma, Bujumbura and Mpulungu, stopping at several small ports on the lakeshore south of Kigoma. It departs from Kigoma at 16.00 Wednesday and arrives in Mpulungu at 10.00 Friday. It then turns back at 16.00 Friday and arrives in Kigoma at 10.00 Sunday. It leaves Kigoma at 16.00 Sunday and arrives in Bujumbura at 10.00 Monday. The return trip from Bujumbura departs at 16.00 Monday and arrives back in Kigoma at 10.00 Tuesday. Due to sanctions against Burundi, the Bujumbura leg of this voyage hasn't been running for some time, but rumour is that it will resume with the lifting of these sanctions. Although the departures are reasonably punctual,

that rises sharply from the lakeshore to the 2,462m Nkungwe Peak – which can be climbed as a very long and tiring day's hike from the lakeshore camps – and six other peaks that exceed 2,000m in elevation. It is awe-inspiring to swim off one of the (reputedly bilharzia-free) beaches of Mahale, look up at the mountains, and recognise that you are roughly midway in altitude between the highest peak in the range and the deepest point on the floor of the lake that surrounds you!

The Mahale Mountains were one of the last parts of East Africa to be explored by outsiders. The British naval officer Verney Lovett Cameron passed below the mountains in 1873 on his way to becoming the first European to cross equatorial Africa from the Indian to the Atlantic coastline, and gave brief mention to them in *Across Africa*, the book he published in 1877. Aside from sporadic visits to the lower slopes by the White Fathers based at Kalema between 1911 and 1916, however, the area was ignored until 1935, when Dollman exhibited a chimpanzee skull found at Mahale to the Linnaean Society of London. No European is known to have ascended the highest peak in the range before 1940, and it was only in 1958 that a team of Oxford scientists started serious scientific exploration of the area.

The altitude range of Mahale is reflected in its wide variety of habitats, with a floral composition that reflects a unique combination of influences associated with the eastern savannah, western rainforest and southern *miombo* woodland biomes. Altogether, some 15 different plant communities are recognised, but in simplistic terms there are four main vegetation zones. The foothills of the western slopes and most of the eastern slopes support a cover of open canopied woodland of various

protracted delays for loading at the smaller ports can cause it to gradually fall behind schedule by up to ten hours

Ticket prices for the *Liemba* have risen greatly in recent years, and non-residents *must* now pay for them in US dollars cash – local currency and travellers' cheques are not accepted. The full one-way trip from Kigoma to Mpulungu costs US$55 first class, US$45 second class and US$30 for third class. Tickets from Kigoma to Lugosa and Kasanga respectively cost US$50/50/28 or US$25/20/15 for first/second/third class. All fares include the US$5 port tax. First-class berths consist of clean, comfortable and lockable two-berth cabins, while second class consists of scruffier but perfectly adequate lockable four-bed cabins. Third class is deck only, which – since the deck is far from being crowded – is fine for shorter hops, but risky for luggage on overnight trips. A restaurant and bar serves decent meals for Tsh1,700, as well as cold beers, sodas and imported wines and spirits.

The ferry stops at numerous lakeshore villages, of which the most significant to travellers are Lugosa (for Mahale Mountains National Park) and Kasanga (the last port before the Zambian border, with a few basic guesthouses and road transport to Sumbawanga and on to Mbeya). There is nowhere for ships to dock at most of these villages, so the ferry is greeted by a floating market selling dried fish and other foodstuffs, while passengers are ferried to and from the shore on rickety fishing boats. Viewed from the upper decks this is a richly comic sight. If you are disembarking, however, it is a rather nightmarish experience, the hold seething with passengers climbing over each other, the ticket officer frantically trying to identify and extract fares from the newcomers, and small boats at the exit gate ramming each other trying to get the best position. For more information about minor ports, read the section *The Southeastern Lakeshore*, page 470.

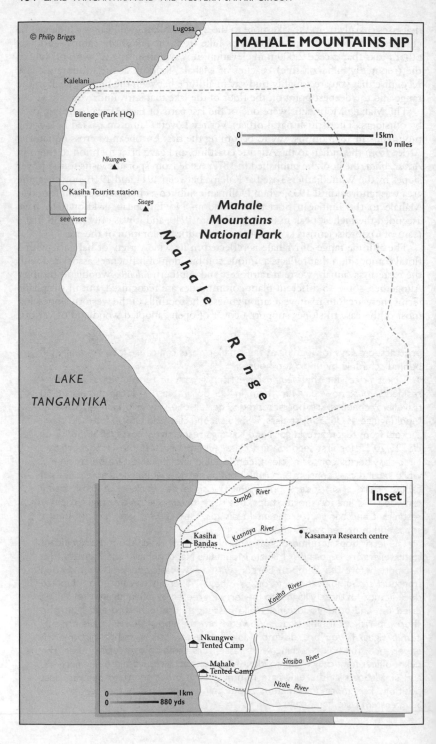

© Philip Briggs

MAHALE MOUNTAINS NP

Lugosa

Kalelani

Bilenge (Park HQ)

0   15km
0   10 miles

Nkungwe ▲

Kasiha Tourist station

see inset

Sisaga ▲

Mahale
Mountains
National Park

Mahale Range

LAKE
TANGANYIKA

Inset

Sumba River

Kasnaya River

Kasiha
Bandas

● Kasanaya Research centre

Kasiha River

Nkungwe
Tented Camp

Mahale
Tented Camp

Sinsiba River

Ntale River

0   1km
0   880 yds

types, dominated by *brachystegia* woodland, which probably accounts for about 60–70% of the park's area. Although small in area, the closed canopy riparian woodlands that follow watercourses through the western foothills are of great ecological significance, as they provide refuge to species more normally associated with rainforest habitats. At higher elevations, particularly on the moister western slopes, which receive an average annual rainfall of 2,000mm, Afro-montane forest predominates, interspersed with patches of bamboo forest, and containing some species more typical of the western lowland forests. Towards the peaks, the forest gives way to montane grassland and patches of heather studded with proteas and other flowering plants.

The main tourist attraction of Mahale Mountains is the opportunity to track a wild chimpanzee community that has been habituated for almost as long as its counterpart at Gombe Stream. In 1961, the future national park was one of several areas visited by a team of primatologists from the University of Kyoto in Japan looking for a suitable site to study chimpanzees. The expedition agreed that Mahale was the most promising site, and in 1965 a permanent research centre was established at Kasoge, about 1km inland of the lakeshore, close to the present-day tourist camp at Kasiha. Over the course of the next five years, the two communities whose territories lay closest to the camp were habituated, using a feeding system similar to that pioneered by Jane Goodall further north along the lake.

Over the next 15 years, the Japanese scientists documented a fascinating series of developments in the local chimpanzee population. In 1967, the habituated Mimikere and Kajabala communities were comprised of about 100 and 27 individuals respectively, with territories that bordered each other. During the early years of the study, however, the smaller community gradually shrank in number, partially through the migration of females to the neighbouring territory, and partially due to a protracted inter-community war that resulted in several fatalities, including the killing of two successive alpha males in the Kajabala Community. By 1982, no adult males were left in the Kajabala Community, and the surviving females and youngsters were integrated into the Mimikere community, which was free to occupy its former rival's territory. As with the chimp research project at Gombe Stream, the Kyoto University project at Mahale Mountains continues to this day, with the Mimikere community – now numbering about 80 individuals – being the main subject of study, as well as of tourist visits.

A common misconception about Mahale is that the habituated chimps are less approachable than their counterparts at Gombe. This is far from being the case – indeed, it is quite remarkable to find oneself in the midst of a group as it moves along a forest trail, and have a full-grown male chimpanzee brush past you casually as if you were just another tree in his way. What is true, however, is that the habituated community at Mahale occupies a far larger territory, which means that locating chimps can entail far more walking, with a higher risk than at Gombe of missing out altogether. As a rule, the odds of finding the chimps easily improves towards the end of the dry season, from July to October, when they tend to stick to the lower slopes of the mountain, sometimes even walking through the various tourist lodgings on the lakeshore. During the rainy season of November to April, the forest trails are tougher underfoot, and the chimps are often more difficult to locate, so a flying visit might well result in disappointment. But at any time of year, you'd be extremely unfortunate to spend two or three days in the park and not encounter any chimps at all.

Of the eight other primate species recorded in Mahale Mountains, at least five are likely to be encountered on the lakeshore and in nearby *brachystegia* woodland. These are yellow baboon, red colobus, blue monkey, red-tailed monkey and vervet monkey. An endemic race of Angola black-and-white colobus is more-or-less confined to the montane forest of the higher slopes, while the lesser galago and thick-tailed greater galago are nocturnal and more likely to be heard than seen. Other lowland forest species are similar to those found at Gombe, but supplemented by isolated populations of West African species such as brush-tailed porcupine and giant forest squirrel. The eastern slopes of Mahale support savannah and woodland species such as elephant, lion, African hunting dog, roan antelope, buffalo and giraffe, but the only such creature that is frequently seen by tourists is the warthog. Lions, however, have killed several chimps in the forest, and African hunting dogs were once recorded on the beach!

No proper study of Mahale's birdlife has yet been undertaken, but at least 230 species have been recorded. Among the more colourful and interesting species likely to be seen close to the tourist lodges are crowned eagle, scaly francolin, crested guinea-fowl, Ross's turaco, giant kingfisher, blue-cheeked bee-eater, trumpeter hornbill, crested malimbe and Viellot's black weaver. The forests of Mahale are the only place in Tanzania where the rare bamboo warbler and Stuhlman's starling have been recorded, and they support an endemic race of the globally threatened Kungwe apalis.

National Park fees

The entrance fee to Mahale Mountains is US$50 per 24 hours. In addition to the park entrance fee, a guide fee of US$20 per party must be paid for all chimp walks, and the cheapest accommodation within the park costs US$20 per person. Even if you walk to the park, a charge of US$20 is likely to be asked to cover fuel costs for the boat transfer to Kasiha, where chimp walks start.

The relatively high entrance fee often scares off budget conscious travellers who assume the ferry schedule will enforce a stay of several days' duration within the national park. It is, however, possible – and totally legitimate – to restrict yourself to one 24-hour period within the park, by camping at the village outside the northern boundary. Do this, and the total cost of a day's chimp tracking will be US$50 per person, plus US$40 divided by the number of people in the party. Assuming that you walk to the park headquarters from Lugosa and camp at villages outside the park, the costs attached to the days you'd spend outside the park would be negligible. For more details see *Getting there and away* below.

Further information

Mahale National Park is the subject of a beautifully produced coffee-table book entitled *Mahale: A Photographic Encounter with Chimpanzees*, by Angelika Hofer, Michael Huffman and Gunter Ziesler (Sterling Publishing, New York, 2000). The Tanzania National Park booklet *Gombe Stream National Park* has a short section about Mahale, and much of the background material for Gombe is pertinent to both national parks. It is likely to be superseded in the next year or two by a scheduled *Mahale Mountains National Park* title in the newer and glossier series of booklets co-published by Tanzania National Parks and the Africa Publishing Group.

Getting there and away
Organised tours
The main local specialists in trips to Mahale are the two companies that have permanent tented camps in the park, ie: Future Primitive in Arusha and the Kigoma Hilltop Hotel in Kigoma (for contact details see *Where to stay* below). As with their respective tented camps, Future Primitive arranges very exclusive visits

at the top end of the safari price bracket, generally involving charter flights and tied in with a stay at their tented camp in Katavi National Park. One-week charter packages taking in Katavi and Mahale and leaving from Dar es Salaam, Kilimanjaro Airport or any of the northern reserves cost between US$3,350 and US$3,750 per person all-inclusive depending on the departure point. Four-day visits to Mahale cost from US$1,595 to US$1,995 per person all-inclusive, again depending on the departure point.

As with Gombe, the Kigoma Hilltop Hotel can arrange a wide variety of all-inclusive packages for between one and 12 people, using their private motorboat to transfer between Kigoma and the national park, a four- to five-hour trip. To give some idea, the shortest itinerary, two nights in the park with a night in Kigoma on either side, costs US$2,049 for one person, US$1,317 per person for two people, US$1,001 per person for four people and US$797 per person for 12 people. The longest itinerary, five nights in the park with one night in Kigoma on either side, costs US$3,027 for one person, US$2,190 per person for two people, US$1,821 per person for four people and US$1,592 per person for 12 people. The hotel also arranges combined Mahale and Gombe packages using their motorboat, as covered under the Gombe Stream section earlier in this chapter. Charter trips from Arusha can be arranged too, but obviously at a significantly higher cost.

The Kigoma Hilltop Hotel also offers a cheaper seven-day, six-night package using the MV *Liemba* rather than a private motorboat, which includes three nights at Mahale National Park, two nights at the Kigoma Hilltop Hotel and a night on the boat. This costs US$1,525 for one person, US$1,208 per person for two people, US$1,099 per person for four people and US$1,037 per person for 12 people. For independent travellers, this cost could be shaved further by arranging your own accommodation in Kigoma and your own ferry ticket, and arranging the local boat transfer and accommodation through the Kigoma Hilltop Hotel.

Independent visits

Reaching Mahale Mountains on public transport is neither as quick nor as straightforward as getting to Gombe Stream, but it is nevertheless eminently do-able, and if you are prepared to put in a bit of legwork, the trip can work out more cheaply than a visit to Gombe Stream. Mahale is also, all things considered, probably the more exciting trip, not only in terms of the wildlife and the scenery, but also as an overall adventure. There are several options and variations, so it is worth reading the section below carefully to decide which best suits your comfort levels and budget.

Four local landmarks are of significance in the information included below. Two are villages outside of the park boundaries: Lugosa (also known as Magambo or Buhingu), 15km north of the park and the closest port used by the MV *Liemba*, and Kalelani almost immediately outside the northern boundary. Within the park, the headquarters at Bilenge, only 1km south of Kalelani, are where all park fees must be paid. The tourist camp at Kasiha about 10km further south is the site of the national park's Mango Tree Rest Camp and the starting point for chimp tracking and other forest walks.

The most reliable and comfortable way to get within striking distance of Mahale Mountains is to board the lake ferry MV *Liemba* to Lugosa. If you are visiting the park as a round trip from Kigoma, the MV *Liemba* is scheduled to depart on its southern leg on Wednesdays at 16.00, and it generally arrives at Lugosa between midnight and 02.00 on Thursdays. For the return trip, the *Liemba* passes Lugosa at any time between 21.00 on Saturday and 06.00 on Sunday, arriving in Kigoma about 10–12 hours later. It is possible to visit the park by ferry en route between

Kigoma and a more southerly port such as Ikola, Kasanga or Mpulungu, but since the ferry only runs once a week in either direction, this would enforce a stay of a full week in the vicinity of Mahale. Tickets between Kigoma and Lugosa cost US$25/20/15 for first/second/third class, inclusive of port tax. If you're looking to cut costs, third class is fine for this relatively short hop.

Travellers who want to spend the full three days in the park can arrange in advance for the national park's motorised boat to meet the ferry at Lugosa and transport them directly to the park headquarters (to sort out fees) and then on to the rest camp at Kasiha. The transfer costs US$50 per party one-way and the boat should easily accommodate up to a dozen people. Advance arrangements can be made with the captain of the *Liemba*, who maintains radio contact with the park headquarters before arriving there, or through the Kigoma Hilltop Hotel in Kigoma.

The cheaper but more adventurous option is to disembark from the *Liemba* at Lugosa, where several local boats meet the ferry to transport passengers to the shore for Tsh200. There is no accommodation at Lugosa, but a local guesthouse is under construction, and until such time as it opens, camping – or kipping out on the beach – is regarded to be perfectly safe. From Lugosa, you can easily arrange a boat transfer on to Kalelani or Bilenge with a local fisherman, for which you should expect to pay up to Tsh10,000 per party. Another possibility would be to wait for the daily lake-taxi between Kigoma and Kalelani (see next paragraph), which charges Tsh1,000 per person for the stretch between Lugosa and Kalelani. Cheaper still – and less dependent on the vagaries of local transport – would be to walk along a flat 15km footpath that more-or-less follows the lakeshore from Lugosa to Bilenge via Kalelani. If you want to tie this in with the ferry timetable, you'd need to walk south on Thursday, spend Friday tracking chimps, and then walk back north to Lugosa on Saturday to meet the ferry which heads to Kigoma on Saturday night.

Two boat services other than the MV *Liemba* connect Kigoma and Kalelani, and while neither is as comfortable or as reliable as the venerable lake ferry, they do have the advantage of cutting out the hassle of getting between Lugosa and Kalelani, as well as offering greater flexibility over timing. The first possibility is the reasonably comfortable MV *Bulombola*, which does the trip twice a week, charging Tsh2,500 (third class only) in either direction. This boat currently leaves from Kigoma port on Friday and Monday at 18.00, and leaves from Kalelani on Sunday and Wednesday at 06.00, taking up to 18 hours in either direction depending on the duration of stops at intermediate ports. If the timing worked out, it might be possible to squeeze in a chimp-tracking excursion after the boat arrives, and to return to Kigoma with the same vessel the next morning, but I wouldn't rely on this coming together.

Suitable only for the truly intrepid or masochistic, a local lake-taxi service runs between Ujiji and Kalelani daily except Sundays, in theory leaving from Ujiji at 18.00 and from Kalelani at 06.00. Be warned, however, that the lake-taxis are crowded, unsafe, uncovered, and can take up to 24 hours to cover the distance. It is also worth noting that, while no scheduled transport other than the MV *Liemba* heads south from Lugosa or Kalelani, you can usually expect one or two lake-taxis per week to run between one of the ports and Kalema or Ikola to the south.

However you get to Kalelani, there is no accommodation, but camping on the beach is regarded as safe, and will allow you to visit the park as a day trip, thus paying only one day's park entrance fees. Alternatively, you could sleep at the national park resthouse at Bilenge or the tourist camp at Kasiha (see *Where to stay* below), bearing in mind that spending the nights either side of your chimp walk at the resthouse would mean paying two day's park entrance fees. All fees must be paid and chimp walks arranged at Bilenge, from where you will be transferred by boat to Kasiha. No formal charge is levied for the transfer from Bilenge to Kasiha (at least not for visitors who are going on a chimp walk or staying at Mango Tree Rest Camp), but you may be asked to cover fuel (around US$20 per party for the round trip).

Where to stay
Exclusive
The Original Mahale Camp Tel: 027 255 3819/20; email: BOOKINGSFP@FPRIM.COM. Established in 1990 on a sandy private beach about 3km south of Kasiha tourist camp, Future Primitive's camp is in the classic old-style safari camp mould. The six double tents, which are spaced out along the patch of woodland that verges the beach, combine a high level of comfort with a winning rusticity epitomised by the open-air long-drop toilet and shower attached to each tent. The common dining and reception area is a stylish two-storey wood, thatch and canvas construction with a good library of reference books. In addition to chimp tracking and other walks, visitors can snorkel in the lake from a large sailing dhow, the only one of its sort in this part of Tanzania. The understated bush chic does, however, come at a price – US$630/1,070 single/double inclusive of meals, drinks, national park fees and all activities – though most people will visit as part of a fly-in package arranged by Future Primitive. Open May to November only.

Upmarket
Nkungwe Camp Tel: 028 280 4435/6/7; fax: 028 280 4434; email: kht@raha.com; web: www.kigoma.com. Built in 2001 by the owners of the Kigoma Hilltop Hotel, this excellent and reasonably priced lodge stands on a secluded sandy beach (reputedly safe for swimming) near the Sisimba River mouth about halfway between the Original Mahale Camp and the tourist camp at Kasiha. The accommodation is in about half a dozen furnished standing tents, each with a large double bed and an en-suite flush toilet and shower, and lit by generator at night, while the dining and lounge area consists of a large raised wooden construction on the beach. Accommodation costs US$176 per person FB, though most people will be likely to visit on a package arranged by the Kigoma Hilltop. No alcohol is sold, but you can bring your own from Kigoma, and the staff can arrange beers from the park headquarters. Open March to November only.

Budget
Mango Tree Rest Camp The main national park rest camp at Kasiha is situated in a glade of mango trees about 100m inland of the lakeshore, some 10km south of the park headquarters. Formerly very rundown, the four old rooms in a block using common showers have recently been refurbished, and another six semi-detached self-contained rooms were constructed in 2001. All rooms are clean and brightly painted, have two beds with netting, and so far as we could ascertain cost US$20 per person irrespective of whether they are self-contained or use common showers. There is no electricity or running water, but kerosene lamps and bucket showers are available, or you can swim in the lake. No food is available, so you'll need to bring everything with you from Kigoma, whether you want to self-cater or arrange a local cook. Beers and other drinks can be bought at the park headquarters, which you will need to visit in order to pay park fees before coming to the rest camp. Camping is not permitted.

Bilenge Welfare Club and Resthouse Two types of accommodation are available at the park headquarters at Bilenge, both primarily aimed towards visiting park officials but also open to tourists. The improbably named Welfare Club is essentially a staff bar, complete with satellite television, and with three small twin rooms attached. The resthouse, which has a pretty, isolated location above the lakeshore about 300m from the main headquarters buildings, consists of two twin bedrooms, a lounge, and an equipped kitchen. Either way, accommodation costs US$20 per person, so the choice rests mainly on whether you want to socialise with the rangers or to chill out in the bush. Drinks are available at the bar, and basic local meals can easily be arranged with the staff at the headquarters, though it might still be a good idea to bring a supply of tinned and packaged food. Note that although all park fees must be paid at Bilenge, all chimp-tracking excursions leave from Kasiha, for the simple reason that it lies within the territory of the habituated chimp communities.

THE SOUTHEASTERN LAKESHORE

The lakeshore ports that lie to the south of Mahale Mountains National Park are most likely to be visited by travellers who want to travel on the MV *Liemba*, but do not want to visit Mahale or to cross into Zambia. The four main ports on the southern lakeshore, starting in the north, are Ikola, Kalema, Kipili and Kasanga. Which one of these ports you decide to disembark at will depend largely on your onward travel plans. Ikola and Kalema, which lie only 15km apart, are linked by road to Mpanda, railhead of a southern branch line to Tabora, with onward rail links to Dar es Salaam, Kigoma and Mwanza. Kipili lies about 80km south of these two ports, close to the substantial town of Namanyere. Kasanga is the most southerly port on the Tanzanian part of the lake, situated within striking distance of the spectacular Kalambo Falls and linked by road to Sumbawanga, from where

KALAMBO FALLS

Adapted from the corresponding section in Chris McIntyre's 'Zambia: The Bradt Travel Guide'

The Kalambo River, which for a short distance marks the boundary between Zambia and Tanzania, is one of the three main feeders of Lake Tanganyika. At the Kalambo Falls, the river plunges over the Rift Escarpment in a single vertical drop of 211m, the second highest waterfall in Africa (about double the height of the Victoria Falls) and the twelfth highest in the world. The width of the waterfall varies seasonally from 3m to 15m, and is at its most spectacular towards the end of the wet season, during February and March, but it is worth visiting at any time of year. During the dry season, a large colony of marabou storks breed in the sheer cliffs next to the waterfall.

Just above the waterfall, by the side of the river, the Kalambo Falls archaeological site is one of the most important in southern Africa, having seen almost continuous human occupation for at least 60,000 years. The earliest tools discovered at the site may be over 100,000 years old, a semi-circle of stones suggests some form of wind-break, and three hollows lined with grass were probably where the inhabitants slept. The earlier sites of occupation were regularly flooded by the river, which deposited a fine layer of sand, preserving the tools and artefacts in a neat chronological sequence of layers that have been exposed by subsequent erosion by the river. The site is unique in that, in addition to the wealth of tools and other cultural artefacts, it has yielded contemporary organic remains such as wood, charcoal and pollens, often in association with undisturbed, prehistoric camping places. Kalambo is also thought to contain the earliest evidence of fire in sub-Saharan Africa, a tremendously important step for Stone Age man, since it enabled him to keep warm and cook food, as well as scare off aggressive animals. Burning areas of grass may even have helped him to hunt. The site is also noted for evidence of

regular buses continue southeast to the Tanzam highway and Mbeya, the principal town of the Southern Highlands.

The MV *Liemba* stops at all four of the ports mentioned on both the southward and the northward leg of its return trip between Kigoma and Mpulungu. With the exception of Kasanga, there are no proper jetties at any of these ports, so the ferry is met by a flotilla of small boats that take disembarking passengers to the shore. On the southward leg from Kigoma, the ferry typically arrives at Ikola an hour or two before noon on Thursday, at Kalema about one hour later, at Kipili in the late afternoon or early evening of the same day, and at Kasanga early on Friday morning. On the northbound leg, the ferry typically arrives at Kasanga early on Friday evening, at Kipili early on Saturday morning, and at Kalema then Ikola at around noon on the same day. Timings will depend greatly on the duration of various loading stops, and it isn't unusual for the ferry to fall progressively further behind schedule over the course of its voyage, so that it might be six to eight hours behind schedule towards the end of the northern leg. For further details, see the box MV *Liemba* on pages 462–3. In addition to the ferry, occasional lake-taxis run between the various ports listed, as well as to Lugosa (near Mahale Mountains), but there is no fixed schedule.

Ikola

This pretty, traditional port has a remote and welcoming atmosphere, as well as strong trade links with several ports on the Congolese part of the lake. Although of

much later settlement, from the early Iron Age. Archaeologists even speak of a Kalambo tradition of pottery, for which they can find evidence in other sites in northern Zambia. In the 8th century BC, early Iron Age farmers displaced the original Stone Age inhabitants, and there is evidence of at least four different Iron Age settlements at the site between the 5th and 11th centuries AD.

The Kalambo River mouth is about 15km south of Kasanga, and adventurous backpackers could use the lake-taxis that ply between Kasanga and Mpulungu in Zambia to drop you off at the river mouth and pick you up the next day. You could also hire a private boat in Kasanga to take you further upstream near to the base of the falls, and ask to be collected the following day. From the pool at the base of the waterfall, it is a strenuous two-hour climb to the top. A simpler alternative route, omitting this steep ascent, involves a short ride in a pick-up truck out of Kasanga, then a roughly eight-hour round trek to the top of the waterfall and back. Either way, the trails are not clearly marked so you will need a local guide. Readers have recommended a local guide called Peter, who usually meets the lake ferry at the jetty in Kasanga, and Mr Mapata, who speaks good English and lives in Kasanga-Muzi about 45 minutes' walk from the ferry jetty.

The waterfall can be reached along a rough road – often almost impassable in the rains – that runs east and is signposted from the road between Kasanga and Mpala in Zambia. The turn-off might theoretically lie in Zambia, nobody seems to know for sure, but in practice the border area above the waterfall is something of a no-man's land, and there's unlikely to be any problem with immigration provided that you arrive and return from the same country. Vehicles left unattended near the waterfall are likely targets for theft, so consider taking extra safety precautions, like having someone with you to look after the vehicle. Camping is permitted at the top of the waterfall, but you will need to bring all your own food and equipment.

less inherent interest than Kalema to its south, Ikola does boast accommodation, as well as better transport links on to Mpanda. The best – in fact only – place to stay is the **Zanzibar Guesthouse**, which is located two doors away from the police station. Owned and managed by a friendly and helpful Zanzibari-Zambian couple, both of whom speak good English, the guesthouse has several basic but clean and inexpensive rooms, and although no food is served, the owners will happily show you a local restaurant, or cook you fish by special arrangement. Trucks to Mpanda generally leave a few times a week, and will take paying passengers, but realistically you should expect to spend one to three nights in Ikola before anything heads off to Mpanda.

Kalema

Kalema is perhaps the most inherently interesting of the ports south of Mahale Mountains. It started life as a staging post between Tabora and the Congolese port of Mpala during the slave-trading era, and was settled in 1879 by Belgians with slaving interests. In 1885, the White Fathers established one of the first missions in the Tanzanian interior at Kalema. The main mission building, built in 1893 and still in good condition, has a whitewashed, rather Mediterranean exterior, and is fortified with ramparts and gun slits that helped to ward off frequent attacks by Wabende slave raiders in its early years. The White Fathers' church, built in 1890, is also still standing today. Surprisingly, the Kalema Mission is the best part of 1km inland from the jetty. The story is that when the White Fathers landed in Kalema, the level of Lake Tanganyika was marginally higher than it is today and so the hill under which the mission was built would then have been right on the shore. The high water level of the 1880s is probably attributable to the rocks and silt that blocked the Lukaga River, the lake's main outlet, as noted by Stanley a decade earlier. There is no accommodation in Kalema, but it is fine to camp in the police compound, and there is a guesthouse in Ikola only 15km to the north.

Kipili

This attractive lakeshore port, which lies about 40km east of Namanyere town, has recently been recommended as a worthwhile stop not only for ferry travellers, but also for overlanders who want to break up the drive between Sumbawanga and Mpanda with a few nights at the lake. The best place to stay is the guesthouse at the **Saint Benedict Catholic Mission**, which charges around Tsh6,000 for a double room. Camping is permitted in the mission grounds at no charge, but if you take advantage of this generosity, please leave a realistic donation. For travellers using public transport, there are occasional *dalla-dallas* between Kipili and **Namanyere**, where the pick of a few local hotels is the **Matunda Garden Inn & Annex Hotel**. More regular public transport links Namanyere to Sumbawanga and Mpanda.

Kasanga

Founded in the German colonial era under the name Bismarckburg, Kasanga is the most southerly port on this stretch of the lakeshore, and the largest – which isn't saying a great deal, though it evidently recently inspired the ferry authorities to construct a proper jetty. In 1998, a dog called Immigration, resident in Kasanga, made local headlines when it was sentenced to death by a judge for lowering the name of 'a highly respected and law-abiding government department'. There are a couple of very basic guesthouses in Kasanga, and at least two buses weekly run to and from Sumbawanga, normally timed to coincide with the ferry arrivals, as well as more regular *dalla-dallas*. The 211m-high Kalambo Falls lie on the border with

Zambia about 20km south of town, and can be visited as a day or overnight trip from Kasanga (see box *Kalambo Falls*, pages 470–1).

MPANDA

The small and rather nondescript town of Mpanda is, despite its remote location, a significant route focus for travellers exploring the infrequently visited southwest of Tanzania, as well as being the northern springboard for visits to the nearby Katavi National Park. Straddling the rough dirt road that connects Kigoma to Mbeya via Sumbawanga, Mpanda is also the southern terminal of a branch line of the Central Railway that runs southwest from Tabora. Mpanda is linked by road to the Lake Tanganyika ferry ports of Ikola and Kalema.

Getting there and away

The most likely reasons why travellers would pass through Mpanda are to visit Katavi National Park, to travel by road between Kigoma and the Zambia border area, or to see part of Lake Tanganyika from the ferry before looping back north by rail between Mpanda and Tabora.

For those coming to or from Mpanda by lake ferry, the closest ports are Ikola and Kalema. There is no regular road transport from either port to Mpanda, but a few passenger-carrying trucks run up and down the road every week, taking up to five hours in dry weather and much longer – or possibly not running at all – after heavy rain. Based on our experience, and that of other travellers, a two- to three-day wait for transport is par for the course.

The best option travelling northward from Mpanda is the thrice-weekly train service to and from Tabora. These trains leave from Tabora on Monday, Wednesday and Friday at 21.00 and from Mpanda on Tuesday, Thursday and Saturday at 13.00. Departures are generally quite punctual, but the actual trip typically takes anything from 10 to 15 hours. There is no restaurant car or bar on the train, and although some food and drink can be bought at stations, you'd best stock up for the trip. For more details of fares and bookings, as well as onward rail connections from Tabora to Kigoma, Mwanza and Dar es Salaam, see the box *The Central Railway* on pages 374–5. Note that although there is no formal public transport along the road between Mpanda and Kigoma via Uvinza, a few trucks usually run this way most days, taking at least 12 hours.

The road south from Mpanda to Sumbawanga via Sitalike and Katavi National Park used to be very lightly trafficked, but there now appears to be at least one bus daily, as well as several *dalla-dallas* that meet all trains arriving in Mpanda. The Super City Hotel complex is the hub of all public transport out of Mpanda, and we've always found people here to be very helpful with advice and information about transport.

Where to stay and eat

Super City Hotel Three different guesthouses, as well as a restaurant and a couple of bars, are confined within this fenced compound on the Sumbawanga road about 1km out of the town centre. The best lodging, to your far left as you enter the compound, is the multi-storey Super City Hotel, which charges a very reasonable Tsh2,500/3,000 for clean and airy self-contained single/twin rooms with running water. The other guesthouses are more basic and cheaper. The restaurant, which serves grilled chicken or fish and chips, is very variable in standard. Most truck drivers stay here, and all southbound public transport leaves from the compound entrance, so it's a good place for lifts to Katavi and Sumbawanga. If you arrive at Mpanda by train, walk uphill from the railway station for about 200m to a traffic circle, where you need to turn right and follow the Sumbawanga road for a few hundred metres to reach the Super City complex.

KATAVI NATIONAL PARK

In the 1980s, when Tanzania's elephant and rhino poaching crisis had reached its calamitous peak, Nicholas Gordon, author of *Ivory Knights*, described Katavi National Park as 'isolated and unloved, and in need of support'. He did not exaggerate. When I researched the first edition of this guide in 1992, my advance enquiries about the park drew a consistent blank from numerous safari operators in Arusha and Dar es Salaam. And, when I visited Katavi, with little idea of what to expect, a squint at the visitors' book revealed why information had been so difficult to obtain: incredibly, fewer than 20 parties of tourists had passed through the park's entrance gate over the previous two years. Katavi, in 1992, was Tanzania's great forgotten reserve, one that seemed likely to join the ranks of those under-policed and neglected national parks – so common in West Africa – whose existence has increasingly little meaning outside of the statute books.

Today, while Katavi remains probably the most obscure and least visited of Tanzania's major savannah reserves, its stock has risen immeasurably over the last decade. In 1995, the solitary concrete bunker that had formerly been the park's only nominal tourist accommodation was supplemented by the opening of a top-notch seasonal tented camp overlooking Lake Chada. Two years later, the 2,250km² park as originally gazetted in 1974 was extended to the southeast to cover an area greater than 4,500km², making Katavi the country's third biggest national park, while a similarly extensive area to the southwest of the park was gazetted as the Rukwa Game Reserve. Furthermore, far from drawing blanks from safari operators elsewhere in the country, mention of Katavi now tends to draw a flurry of animated discussion. During the period we spent researching this fourth edition, we heard unsubstantiated rumours that at least five different safari operators or lodge owners intend to build a lodge in the park over the next few years.

Katavi lies within the so-called Rukwa Rift, a shallow easterly extension of the main Western Rift Valley that culminates in the extensive Lake Rukwa basin to the east of the national park. The dense cover of dry *brachystegia* woodland that characterises Katavi is transected by the Katuma and Kapapa Rivers, which converge to become the Kavu River, a major effluent of Lake Rukwa. Because they are highly seasonal in the volume of water they carry, all the rivers are flanked by open floodplains throughout their course. In three places, however, the rivers run through large, shallow depressions, depicted in bright blue on most maps, but actually open expanses of tall, yellow grass and fine alluvial dust which are transformed into lush marshes or shallow lakes during the height of the rainy season. These are Lake Katavi on the Katuma River about 2km west of the main Mpanda–Sumbawanga road, the Chemchem Springs to the west of the Usevia road, and Lake Chada at the confluence of the Katuma and Kapapa Rivers about 3km east of the Usevia road. The name Katavi, incidentally, is said locally to derive from Katabi, a deified traditional healer who lived close to the synonymous lake.

Katavi is a classic dry season reserve. During the rains, from late November to April, the wildlife disperses far and wide into the woodland, game viewing is by all accounts erratic, and the sweltering heat and humidity, combined with hordes of mosquitoes and other insects, make for a highly uncomfortable safari prospect. After the last rains fall, however, the Katuma is reduced to a sluggish, muddy stream, in parts little more than a metre wide, yet the only source of fresh water for miles in any direction. It is then that the park comes into its own, with the three main floodplains attracting copious concentrations of wildlife, particularly between August and early November.

If ever a national park warranted that well-worn accolade of Africa's best-kept game viewing secret, it is surely Katavi in the dry season. Among the more

KATAVI NATIONAL PARK 475

prominent large mammals on the floodplains are elephant (over 4,000 are resident in the area), zebra, giraffe, hartebeest, topi, impala, reedbuck and Defassa waterbuck. Lions are abundant, with several different prides' territories converging on each of the so-called lakes. Spotted hyenas are regularly sighted in the early morning, while leopards are common but elusive in the fringing woodland. A notable feature of the park is its thousand-strong buffalo herds – at least three or four such herds roam along the river and associated floodplains. The woodland is less rewarding for game, at least in terms of volume, but it is where you are most likely to encounter eland, sable and roan antelope, which are drawn to the open grassland only at the very end of the dry season.

Most remarkable of all, perhaps, are the spectacular numbers of hippos that converge on any stretch of the river sufficiently deep to wallow in during the dry season. There are several pools where hundreds of hippo can reliably be seen, flopped all over each other like seals at a breeding colony. These huddled concentrations consist of several different pods that would not normally associate with each other during the rains (when they are able to disperse more widely into the seasonal marshes and lakes) and as a result the territorial competition between rival males is fierce. Bloody fights are an everyday occurrence, with dominance over any given hippo pool often passing from one bull to another several times in the course of a season, and the rejected behemoths being forced to spend their days foraging on the plains alongside the buffalo and zebra. I've not encountered anything like this anywhere else in Africa – the hippo density per kilometre of riverfront must be comparable to that of the Rufiji River or the Victoria Nile, except that instead of occupying a wide, deep river the hippos are squeezed into a shallow, muddy stream!

The rivers also harbour some impressively proportioned crocodiles, as well as concentrations of water-associated birds such as yellow-billed, open-billed and saddle-billed stork, pink-backed pelican, Africa spoonbill, and numerous herons, egrets and plovers. Raptors are well represented, with fish eagle, bateleur and white-backed vulture prominent. The acacia grove around Katavi Tented Camp is a particularly rewarding spot for woodland birds such as little bee-eater, red-billed hornbill, lilac-breasted roller, sulphur-breasted bush shrike, black cuckoo-shrike, African golden oriole, paradise flycatcher and crested barbet. A characteristic sound of the floodplain is the gurgling chuckle of yellow-throated sandgrouse, which flock along the river to drink about two hours after sunrise and shortly before sunset.

Less endearing altogether are Katavi's notorious tsetse flies, whose unusually vicious bites – uniquely in my experience and commented on by several other people who've visited the park – often result in painful swelling. Fortunately, the tsetse flies are more-or-less restricted to thickets and woodland away from the main game viewing circuits on the floodplains. Self-drive visitors should be alert to the elephants, which (presumably an aftermath of the poaching that subsided a decade back) are among the most aggressive in Africa and should definitely be given the right of way. It is also worth noting that the roads in the park are mostly in poor condition, and signposts are non-existent, which given that the game tends to be concentrated in a few specific areas – makes it well worth hiring a guide from the park headquarters. Finally, you should take local advice before exploring the park beyond the main roads during the rainy season (November to March) – game viewing is poor at this time of year, and if the mosquitoes don't get you, the inundated black cotton soil along the seasonal tracks almost certainly will.

Such minor inconveniences are part and parcel of experiencing a tract of practically untrammelled bush that offers the alluring combination of tiny tourist

CICHLIDS OF THE GREAT LAKES

The staggering diversity of Tanzania's terrestrial fauna is old news, but few people are aware that Tanzania also probably harbours the greatest freshwater fish diversity of any country in the world. Significant portions of all of Africa's three great freshwater bodies – Lakes Victoria, Tanganyika and Nyasa-Malawi – lie within the borders of Tanzania, and each one of them harbours a greater number of fish species than any other lake in the world bar the other two. Which of the three lakes supports the greatest fish diversity is an open question, since new species are regularly discovered and large parts of the lakes remain practically unexplored by ichthyologists. Lake Victoria almost certainly takes the wooden spoon, because it is relatively young, but the most conservative estimates for Lakes Nyasa-Malawi and Tanganyika are around 500 species apiece – a greater number of freshwater species than are found in Europe and North America combined. The actual tally may well be closer to 1,000 species in each lake, of which more than 90% are endemic to that particular lake.

All well and good to trot out the boring statistics, but the greater significance of the great lakes' fish diversity is that it is the product of the most dramatic incidence of explosive speciation known to evolutionists. The majority of these fish species are cichlids – pronounced 'sicklids' – members of a perch-like family of freshwater fishes called cichlidae that ranges through the Middle East, Madagascar, Asia and South and Central America. It is in Africa's three largest lakes, however, that this widespread family has undergone an unprecedented explosion of evolutionarily recent speciation that has resulted in it constituting an estimated 5% of the world's vertebrate species!

The cichlids of Africa's great lakes are generally divided into a few major groupings, often referred to by scientists by their local Malawian names, such as the small plankton-eating *utaka*, the large, pike-like and generally predatory *ncheni*, the bottom-feeding *chisawasawa*, and the algae-eating *mbuna*. People who have travelled in any part of Africa close to a lake will almost certainly have dined on one or other of the *tilapia* (or closely related *oreochromis*) cichlids, large *ncheni* that make excellent eating and are known in Malawi as *chambo*. To aquarium keepers, snorkellers and scuba divers, however, the most noteworthy African cichlids are the *mbuna*, a spectacularly colourful group of small fish of which some 300 species are known from Lake Nyasa-Malawi alone.

The *mbuna* of Lake Nyasa-Malawi first attracted scientific interest in the 1950s, when they formed the subject of Dr Geoffrey Fryer's classic study of adaptive radiation. This term is used to describe the explosion of a single stock species into a variety of closely related forms, each of which evolves specialised modifications that allow it to exploit an ecological niche quite different to that exploited by the common ancestral stock. This phenomenon is most likely to occur when an adaptable species colonises an environment where several food sources are going unused, for instance on a newly formed volcanic island or lake. The most celebrated incidence of adaptive radiation – the one that led Charles Darwin to propose the theory of evolution through natural selection – occurred on the Galápagos Islands, where a variety of finch species evolved from one common seed-eating ancestor to fill several very different ecological niches.

volumes and superlative game viewing – put it this way, in which other African national park are you likely to see more lions that you are other people? This impression is reinforced by several comments in the tented camp's visitors' book,

The explosive speciation that has occurred among Africa's cichlids is like Darwin's finches amplified a hundredfold. The 500 or more cichlid species present in each of Lake Tanganyika and Lake Nyasa-Malawi are evolved from a handful of river cichlids that entered the lakes when they formed about two to three million years ago. More remarkable still is that the 200 or so cichlids in Lake Victoria – many of which are now extinct or heading that way (see box *A Dying Lake* on pages 416–17) – have all evolved from a few common ancestors over the 10,000–15,000 years since the lake last dried up. In all three lakes, specialised cichlid species have evolved to exploit practically every conceivable food source: algae, plankton, insects, fish, molluscs and other fishes. Somewhat macabrely, the so-called kiss-of-death cichlids feed by sucking eggs and hatchlings from the mouths of mouth-brooding cichlids! No less striking is the diverse array in size, coloration and mating behaviour displayed across different species. In addition to being a case study in adaptive radiation, the cichlids of the great lakes are routinely cited as a classic example of parallel evolution – in other words, many similar adaptations appear to have occurred independently in all three lakes.

Not only have cichlids undergone several independent radial explosions in all three of Africa's great lakes, but the same thing has happened in microcosm in many smaller lakes throughout the continent. Uganda's Lake Nabugabo, for instance, harbours five endemic cichlid species, all of which must have evolved since the lake was separated from Lake Victoria by a sandbar less than 4,000 years ago. Why cichlids and not any of several other fish families is a question that is likely to keep ichthyologists occupied for decades to come. One factor is that cichlids are exceptionally quick to mature, and are thus characterised by a very rapid turnover of generations. They also appear to have an unusually genetically malleable anatomy, with skull, body, tooth and gut structures readily modifying over a relatively small number of generations. Their capacity to colonise new freshwater habitats is boosted by a degree of parental care rare in other fish – the mouth-brooders, which include all but one of the cichlid species of Lake Nyasa-Malawi, hold their eggs and fry in their mouth until they are large enough to fend for themselves. Most fascinating, bearing in mind that the separation of breeding populations lies at the core of speciation, there is mounting evidence to suggest that cichlids have a unique capacity to erect non-physical barriers between emergent species – possibly linked to a correlation between colour morphs and food preferences in diverging populations.

Tanzania's lake cichlids are never likely to rival the country's terrestrial wildlife as a tourist attraction. All the same, it is mildly astonishing that, at the time of writing, virtually no snorkelling or diving facilities exist for tourists visiting the Tanzanian shores of any of the three great lakes. Lake Tanganyika, in particular, already lies at the core of a nascent tourist circuit incorporating the game-rich plains of Katavi National Park and chimp-tracking in the lakeshore forests of Gombe Stream and Mahale Mountains. What more logical extension to this circuit than snorkelling and diving excursions – already offered by lodges on the small Zambian stretch of lake frontage – in a lake that has justifiably been described as a 'unique evolutionary showcase'?

many written by East African residents: 'Africa as it must have been 200 years ago', 'the best park in East Africa', 'safaris like they were 30 years ago'… Katavi does, however, seem to be generating a high degree of interest among safari operators elsewhere in Tanzania and, while the remote location alone makes package tourism somewhat improbable in the foreseeable future, a gradual increase in visitors seems inevitable over the next few years. For the sake of the future conservation of this underrated park, an increase in tourist revenue can only be a good thing. Nevertheless, adventurous readers – whether they take an upmarket safari or travel independently – are unlikely to regret visiting Katavi before its remarkable wilderness character is diluted by the greater recognition it undoubtedly warrants.

National park fees

The entrance fee has recently increased to US$20 per 24 hours. For travellers who are simply passing through, no entrance fee is charged for driving or using public transport along the two public roads that pass through the park, ie: the road between Mpanda and Sumbawanga, and the road that branches southeast from Sitalike to Usevia. It is, however, illegal to deviate from these roads on to side roads, or into the bush, without having paid park fees. Park fees can only be paid at the headquarters near Sitalike, so people who are driving up from Sumbawanga and want to explore beyond the main roads must first report to the park headquarters.

Getting there and away
Organised tours

The only established specialist in Katavi is Future Primitive, which operates the Original Katavi Camp. One-week charter packages taking in Katavi and Mahale and leaving from Dar es Salaam, Kilimanjaro Airport or any of the northern reserves cost between US$3,350 and US$3,750 per person all inclusive depending on the departure point. Stand-alone visits to Katavi National Park can also be arranged.

Independent visits

Remote and seldom visited it may be, but paradoxically Katavi is actually one of the more accessible national parks to independent travellers, since the main road between Mpanda and Sumbawanga runs right through it. The main entrance gate and park headquarters are situated alongside this road at the northern extreme of the park, about 1km south of the village of Sitalike, 200km north of Sumbawanga and 35km south of Mpanda. The main road between these towns is not in the greatest nick, and can be particularly bad after rain, so in a private vehicle you should probably expect the drive from Mpanda to take 45 minutes to one hour, and from Sumbawanga about 4–5 hours. Make sure you carry enough fuel, since there is nowhere to fill up between Mpanda and Sumbawanga.

Using public transport, several trucks and *dalla-dallas* run between Mpanda and Sitalike daily, leaving Mpanda from in front of the Super City Hotel complex, taking about an hour in either direction, and charging Tsh1,000 per person. From Sitalike you can walk to the park headquarters in about 15 minutes, crossing a river en route where a pod of hippos are resident. Accommodation is available at the park headquarters, and 4WD vehicles can be hired for US$100 per day per party inclusive of fuel, which is cheaper than a day on safari in the northern circuit for two or more people. Alternatively, you could try setting up a day or overnight safari out of Mpanda with one of the 4WDs that serve as *dalla-dallas* along the local roads. I have no idea what this would cost, but we were asked a flat fee of Tsh10,000 for a private transfer between Mpanda and Sitalike, and its bound to be cheaper than hiring a national park vehicle.

For people driving themselves, the excellent game viewing circuit around the Chada floodplain is most easily reached by following the public road that branches to the southeast at Sitalike, heading towards the small town of Usevia outside the southern boundary of the park. Initially, this road isn't very promising, passing through dense *brachystegia* woodland that is sparsely populated with game. After about 40–50km, however, you reach a bridge across the Katuma River – look out for the concentrations of hippo below it – and about 1km further a track to the left runs towards the Chada floodplain. A few *dalla-dallas* daily run from Mpanda to Usevia, where there are a couple of basic guesthouses.

Where to stay
Exclusive
The Original Katavi Camp Tel: 027 255 3819/20; email: BOOKINGSFP@FPRIM.COM. This superbly singular wilderness lodge, the only upmarket accommodation anywhere in Katavi National Park, is set in a glade of tall acacia trees overlooking the seasonal Lake Chada floodplain. The set-up is rather basic by comparison to the package lodges of the northern circuit, consisting of half a dozen standing double tents, comfortable but not luxurious, each with a private open-air hot shower and long-drop toilet. And, because the camp is broken down entirely every November and reconstructed in May the following year, there are no concrete or stone structures, no neat footpaths, no lawns, no fences – just a few tents in a patch of pristine woodland regularly traversed by elephants, lions and other large mammals. It is precisely this air of uncluttered rusticity that lends Katavi Camp its exclusivity – more perhaps than any other lodge I've visited in Africa, it offers a raw bush experience harking back to safaris as they must have been in the days of Karen Blixen and Denis Finch-Hatton. And this compelling wilderness atmosphere takes on a heightened immediacy at night, when it's not unusual to hear several prides of lion and numerous hyenas calling at the same time, while elephants and hippos crash through the surrounding bush. Not for the faint of heart, perhaps, but in its own understated way arguably the finest and most exciting upmarket camp in Tanzania. Accommodation costs US$590/990 single/double inclusive of all meals, drinks, park fees and activities. The management also arranges fly-camp safaris and game drives into the new park extension towards Lake Rukwa and the Rungwa River, as well as game walks on to the game-rich floodplain and drives in open-topped Land Rovers. The lodge is most often visited as part of a fly-in charter package together with the Original Mahale Camp in Mahale Mountain National Park, which is owned by the same company.

Moderate
Park Headquarters Resthouse A well-equipped resthouse (with satellite television!) aimed primarily at visiting TANAPA officials but also open to tourists can be found at the park headquarters about 500m from the main road to Sumbawanga and 1km south of Sitalike. Accommodation costs US$30 per person per night. Basic meals are available, and beers and sodas are served at the staff bar.

Budget
Lake Katavi Resthouse The unfurnished two-room concrete bunker that overlooks the Katavi floodplain, 15km south of the entrance gate and about 1km west of the main Sumbawanga road, is extortionately poor value at US$20 per person per night. It does, however, boast a stunning situation, and there is excellent game viewing from the balcony. No mattresses or bedding are available, so you will need your own sleeping bag. Firewood is available, but drinking water must be brought from a spring near the entrance gate. The rangers will fill up a jerry can on request. Bring all provisions from Mpanda or Sumbawanga.

LAKE RUKWA

One of the most alluring and remote wilderness destinations in East Africa, Rukwa is a shallow alkaline lake with an average depth of about 4m, which fills a sump in a truncated branch of the western Rift Valley and has no known outflows. The first European to visit the lake was John Speke, but it was not explored further until the 1880s, when the Scots geologist Joseph Thomson (he of gazelle fame) followed much of its shore. With a surface area of roughly 2,500km², Rukwa is by far the largest lake to lie entirely within Tanzania, but seasonal fluctuations in water level often split it into two discrete expanses of open water separated by a vast marshy plain. The lake's extensive floodplain attracts large ungulate herds after the November rains, and in 1997 the northern part of the lake and its hinterland were gazetted as the Rukwa Game Reserve, part of a contiguous protected area of greater than 10,000km² centred on the adjacent Katavi National Park.

Rukwa supports a mammalian fauna similar to that of Katavi, but is also an important stronghold for the localised puku. According to scientists who know it well, oft-repeated stories of albino giraffes and unusually striped zebra in the Rukwa area are legend bordering on myth. The lake is, however, notable for its high densities of crocodiles and hippos. The lake's avifauna was last studied in the 1950s, when a checklist of 363 species was compiled, but it is known to support innumerable flocks of various water-associated birds, notably white pelican, lesser flamingo, glossy ibis, spur-winged goose and African skimmer. The rare and magnificent shoebill stork is resident in papyrus swamps, as is the localised Tanzania masked weaver. At least one fish species is endemic to the lake.

No settlements of any substance lie on the lakeshore, which means it is only feasible to visit Rukwa in a private 4WD vehicle. Any such trip should be treated as a full-scale expedition, carrying an adequate supply of spares, fuel, food, drinking water and camping equipment. The approach roads are rough and may become impassable after rain. The safest time to visit is between March and October, but there is more game in the wet months. Rukwa can be approached from Mbeya (via Chunya), from Sumbawanga (via the Ufipa Plateau) or from Katavi National Park. The management of the Original Katavi Camp can arrange fly-camping excursions to Lake Rukwa.

Shoestring

Unfortunately for budget travellers, no lodging apart from the resthouse at the park headquarters is available at Sitalike, though judging by the amount Sitalike has grown in recent years, it is probably only a matter of time before something opens. There are, however, a couple of basic local guesthouses in **Usevia**, which is reachable by public transport (see *Getting there and away* above) and would make a workable base from which travellers with their own vehicle could explore the park on day trips.

Camping

Self-sufficient travellers with private transport may camp at a number of places in the park, including outside the hut at the Katavi floodplain. The best site is at Lake Chada. Campsites are basic, with firewood but no drinking water.

SUMBAWANGA

The name of this town of some 75,000 souls might sound like the chorus of a Hollywood musical about Africa. The reality is somewhat more mundane – Sumbawanga, administrative capital of the vast but thinly populated Rukwa region, is a reasonably substantial and equable mid-altitude town, but wholly unmemorable. It is, however, the largest settlement along the 500km road between Mpanda and Tunduma (on the Tanzam Highway), and it also lies at the junction for a road southwest to Kasanga, the most southerly port on the Tanzanian part of Lake Tanganyika. Most travellers heading through this part of the country will overnight there at some point, but they are unlikely to be inspired to stay any longer than they need to.

The Ufipa Plateau between Sumbawanga and Lake Rukwa consists of a roughly 1,000km² block of land above the 2,000m contour, and is of interest for its extensive cover of montane grassland and forest habitats. In addition to several endemic flowering and other plant species and a varied selection of localised forest and grassland birds, the plateau harbours an isolated population of red colobus monkey. In a private vehicle, the plateau can be explored by driving out of Sumbawanga for an hour or so along the road towards Lake Rukwa. On public transport, according to a ranger at Katavi, you can get from Sumbawanga to the village of Kijiji on the back of a pick-up truck, and from there walk to another village called Mpondo, where there are spectacular views over Lake Rukwa.

Getting there and away

There is now normally one bus daily between Mpanda and Sumbawanga, as well as a steady stream of trucks, typically taking from six to ten hours in either direction depending on road conditions. Several buses daily run between Sumbawanga and Mbeya via Tunduma, leaving in either direction at 07.00 (book a seat in advance) and taking about eight hours either way. Heading to or from Kasanga on Lake Tanganyika, there are a couple of buses a week and a few pick-up trucks daily generally leaving before noon – ask around at the market.

Where to stay and eat

Moravian Conference Centre Tel: 025 280 2853; email: confcen@twinga.com. Situated on Nyerere Road in the town centre, this recent three-storey construction offers the most comfortable accommodation in Sumbawanga. Facilities include an affordable cafeteria and dining hall, a business centre with fax and email services, and satellite television. First-floor rooms using common showers cost Tsh8,000/16,000/19,000 single/double/triple B&B, while self-contained rooms cost Tsh10,000/20,000 single/double. Smaller, cheaper self-contained rooms on the second floor cost Tsh5,000/10,000 single/double.

Forest Way Country Club Tel: 025 280 2117. This pleasant hotel, built in 1998, is situated about 1km up Nyerere Road on the left, and well signposted. Self-contained rooms cost Tsh10,000/15,000 single/double. It's very clean, the food is good, and the staff have been described as 'probably the friendliest staff I have come across in any hotel in Tanzania'.

Upenda View Inn Tel: 025 280 2242. Situated about two blocks from the bus station, this is a reasonably comfortable hotel, perhaps beginning to show its age slightly, but very good value nonetheless at Tsh5,000 for a clean self-contained double room. A garden bar and good restaurant with a varied menu and delicious home-made soup are attached.

Zanzibar and **Equator Guesthouses** About the best of several cheap guesthouses dotted around the bus station, with acceptable rooms for Tsh1,500/2,000 single/double.

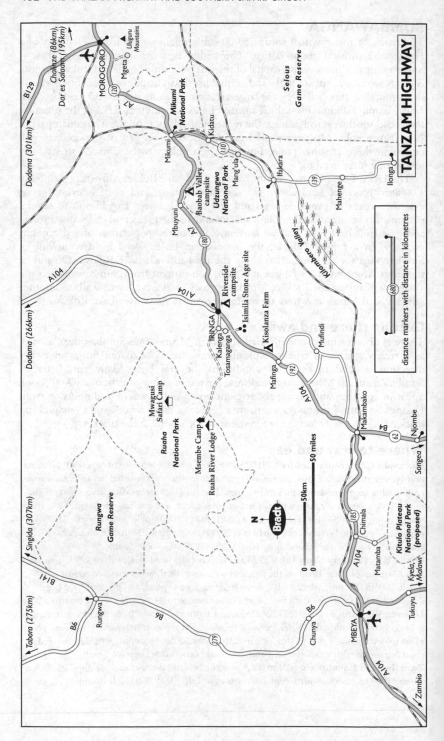

The Tanzam Highway and Southern Safari Circuit

The Tanzam Highway, so-named because it links
Tanzania to Zambia, is the main road through southern
Tanzania. It forks southwest from the main Arusha road
at Chalinze, some 100km west of Dar es Salaam, before
passing through (or by) Morogoro, Mikumi, Iringa and
Mbeya, reaching the Zambian border at Tunduma. The
road distance between Dar and Tunduma is roughly
1,000km. This chapter picks the road up at Chalinze and
follows it southwards to Iringa.

The region's most significant physical features are the Uluguru
Mountains near Morogoro and the Udzungwa Mountains near
Mikumi. The Rufiji River, the largest in Tanzania, passes through the region, as
does its major tributaries the Great Ruaha and Kilombero Rivers. The stretch of
road from Morogoro to Iringa is very scenic, passing through Mikumi National
Park, where quite a bit of game can be seen from the road. It then follows the
Ruaha River through the baobab-clad western foothills of the Udzungwa
Mountains, now the site of the promising Baobab Valley private conservancy and
campsite.

The Tanzam Highway offers access to southern Tanzania's most alluring
conservation areas: the Selous Game Reserve and Ruaha and Mikumi National
Parks. This southern safari circuit is less developed for tourism than its northern
equivalent, but the facilities and safari packages that do exist are generally tailored
more toward the upper end of the market. By comparison with the northern
reserves, only a tiny proportion of visitors to Tanzania explore any of the southern
reserves, and those who do tend to visit one specific reserve rather than following
a circuit through several. In terms of game viewing, these southern reserves don't
really compare to the Serengeti and Ngorongoro – what could? – but they are still
very well stocked, and have a distinctly more untrammelled character that arguably
makes for a more memorable and holistic experience. Were this cluster of reserves
not in the same country as the Serengeti et al, then it would be more widely
recognised as one of the finest in Africa.

The most popular safari destination in southern Tanzania is probably the
Selous, the largest game reserve in Africa (and possibly in the world), covering
a vast area of *miombo* woodland lying between the Tanzam Highway and the
south coast. Of the others, many people with long experience in Africa rate the
Ruaha National Park, which lies to the west of the highway near Iringa, as one
of their favourite reserves anywhere on the continent. Also very rich in big
game, Mikumi National Park is bisected by the Tanzam Highway, which makes
it of great interest to those travellers who bus or drive between Iringa and
Morogoro. The more recently proclaimed Udzungwa Mountains National
Park, which lies south of Mikumi towards Ifakara, doesn't offer a conventional

safari experience, but it is of great interest to hikers and birders, and harbours three endemic forms of primate.

While the region covered in this chapter boasts some excellent game viewing for those who are in a position to set up organised safaris, it has relatively little to offer independent budget travellers. The only glaring exception to this generalisation is the Mikumi, Udzungwa and Ifakara area, which offers much to backpackers with an energetic, explorative temperament. Both Iringa and Morogoro are lively and substantial towns with inherently attractive settings, making them good stopovers

THE TAZARA RAILWAY

Built in the 1970s with Chinese assistance, the Tazara Railway connects Dar es Salaam to Kapiri Mposhi in Zambia, via the Selous Game Reserve, Ifakara, Mbeya and Tunduma. Recent improvements to the roads in southern Tanzania mean that the train can no longer be emphatically recommended over the equivalent bus services, but it does remain a more relaxed and probably safer way to travel. Overnight trains, while technically slower than buses, allow you to cover distance in your sleep rather than to waste daylight hours in buses.

At the time of writing, three passenger trains in either direction run along the railway weekly, though only two continue past Mbeya to Kapiri Mposhi. The two express trains leave from Dar es Salaam on Tuesday and Friday at 17.30, and from Kapiri Mposhi on the same days at 14.00, taking around 36 hours each way and stopping at Ifakara, Makambako, Mbeya and Tunduma. One additional slow train runs every week from Dar es Salaam to Mbeya, leaving Dar es Salaam on Monday at 09.30 and Mbeya at 15.00 Tuesday. One advantage of the slow trains is that they are scheduled to pass through the Selous Game Reserve during daylight hours, and there is usually plenty of game to be seen. All trains have dining cars. Meals are decent enough as these things go, and reasonably priced. Beers and sodas are normally available.

There are three classes on all trains. First class consists of two-berth compartments and second class consists of six-berth compartments. Men and women may not share a first or second class compartment unless they book the whole compartment. Third class consists of seated carriages, but there are always more passengers than seats; it's only worth thinking about if you value neither your comfort nor your possessions.

Theft from train windows at night is not unusual, so close the windows securely when you turn the light off. A block of wood is provided for this purpose; if you cannot find one in your compartment speak to the steward. Don't leave loose objects lying around the compartment; keep your luggage under the bunks. If you leave the compartment, take all valuables with you.

It is advisable to book train tickets three days to a week in advance. Fares are around US$25/20 first/second class between Dar es Salaam and Mbeya, and can be paid for in local currency. In Dar es Salaam, a 50% discount on the Tazara line is given to anyone with a student card. Sorting this out will take a couple of hours. You must first collect an application form from the Tazara station, then go to the Department of Education on Kivukoni Front where the form will be stamped, and finally return to the station to buy a ticket.

along the long road between Dar and Mbeya, but neither could be described as a compelling travel destination. Morogoro, meanwhile, is gradually being developed as a base for hikes into the Uluguru Mountains, which rank with the Udzungwa and Usambara as the most ecologically important in the Eastern Arc formation. Iringa, by contrast, is a good base for day trips to two spots that are as fascinating and accessible as they are underpublicised, the Isimila Stone-Age Site and Kalenga Museum.

CLIMATE

Much of the area covered in this chapter is low-lying, hot and dry. The towns running along the eastern base of the Udzungwa Mountains have a relatively moist climate, and can be swelteringly hot and humid during the rains. The higher slopes of the Udzungwa and Uluguru Mountains are more temperate, as is the town of Iringa, where you might even find yourself putting on a light jumper in the evening. The rainfall pattern is typical of Tanzania, with the bulk of the rain falling between November and March. Aside from the main mountain ranges, this part of Tanzania is characterised by low rainfall figures.

GETTING AROUND

There is plenty of transport along the Tanzam Highway. The road is tarred and reasonably maintained, with far fewer pot-holes these days than was the case a few years ago. In addition to direct buses between Dar es Salaam and Mbeya, which take 10–15 hours, there are also local bus services connecting the various towns along the way. Hitching is a possibility along this road, though the only time I have tried it, outside Iringa, I waited two hours without any luck before being picked up by a bus!

The Tazara Railway runs roughly parallel to the Tanzam Highway for most of its length. Coming from the south, the railway and road run alongside each other between Mbeya and the junction town of Makambako, before the railway line forks to the east, passing through Ifakara and the northwestern corner of the Selous Game Reserve en route to Dar es Salaam.

There is not a great deal of transport running along the side roads off the Tanzam Highway, though several buses daily connect Morogoro and Mikumi to Mang'ula, the springboard for visits to Udzungwa National Park, and Ifakara to its south. The latter town is something of a minor route focus, since the Tazara Railway also connects it to Dar es Salaam and Mbeya.

The only realistic way to visit the main game reserves on the southern circuit is on an organised safari. In contrast to the northern safari circuit, the reserves in southern Tanzania are most normally visited as part of a fly-in package, though it is equally possible to arrange a road safari to any of them. Several companies in Dar es Salaam arrange safaris along the southern circuit, as do most of the Arusha-based safari companies listed on pages 127–9.

CHALINZE

Just over 100km west of Dar es Salaam, Chalinze is an untidy and unmemorable semi-urban sprawl located at one of the most important road junctions in Tanzania, where the Tanzam Highway south to Mbeya and main surfaced road north to Arusha and Moshi converge. The only reason you'd be likely to stop in Chalinze, however, is if you were travelling between north and south on public transport and wanted to bypass Dar es Salaam. You shouldn't have to wait long for a vehicle in any direction out of Chalinze, but there are a couple of basic guesthouses should you need to spend the night. Its strategic position aside,

Chalinze is enlivened only by the numerous vendors and stalls which sell food and curios to passing bus passengers.

MOROGORO

Situated at an altitude of around 500m, roughly 200km inland of Dar es Salaam by road, Morogoro is an unusually attractive town, as much for its orderly layout and open green feel as for the magnificent backdrop provided by the Uluguru Mountains towering to 2,635m on the southern horizon. Morogoro lies at the centre of a rich agricultural region, and its bustling fruit and vegetable market is an important supplier of fresh produce for Dar es Salaam. It is also one of the country's fastest-growing towns, with an estimated population of 250,000 in 2002, making it the third-largest settlement (after Dar es Salaam and Mwanza) on the Tanzanian mainland.

Aside from the Uluguru Mountains, covered under a separate heading below, there are few tourist attractions in the immediate vicinity of Morogoro, but the town has a healthy, lively atmosphere and it forms an agreeable first stop for travellers bussing south along the Tanzam Highway. A worthwhile short walk from the town centre, particularly if you are interested in birds or plants, leads to the Rock Garden Resort, a small botanical garden dominated by indigenous plants situated on the lower slopes of the Uluguru Mountain, about 1km past the Morogoro Hotel. The only noteworthy architectural landmarks are the Old German Boma, which lies about 1km from the town centre along Boma Road, and the German-era railway station in the town centre.

Getting there and away

Buses between Dar es Salaam and Morogoro leave every hour or so and take about three hours. There is also regular public transport along the surfaced roads from Morogoro to Iringa and Ifakara to the south and to Dodoma to the west. Morogoro lies on the Central Railway line, about halfway between Dar es Salaam and Dodoma, but it's far easier and quicker to travel between these towns by road.

Where to stay
Upmarket
New Acropol Hotel Tel: 023 260 3403; fax: 023 260 3952. This small Canadian-owned hotel with its bright airy rooms and stylish décor is an unexpected gem, and thoroughly recommended as a refreshing alternative to the blandly functional hotels that otherwise characterise Morogoro. Self-contained rooms with a large double bed, sofa, fridge, satellite television and AC cost Tsh42,000 single or double B&B. The attached restaurant, also very atmospheric, serves pizzas for around Tsh3,000 and steak and seafood grills for around Tsh5,000.

Hotel Oasis Tel: 023 260 4178/3135; mobile: 0744 377601/2; fax: 023 260 4830; email: hoteloasis@morogoro.net. Opened in 1998, the Hotel Oasis is a smart, central, well-managed and very reasonably priced multi-storey hotel centred on a neat green courtyard and catering primarily to business travellers. Self-contained rooms with AC, nets, satellite television and fridge cost Tsh25,000/35,000 single/double B&B. Larger suites are available ranging in price from Tsh45,000 to 75,000. An attached business centre charges Tsh1,000 per hour for internet use, and there's a good Indian restaurant on the ground floor asking around Tsh3,000 for vegetarian dishes and Tsh4,000 for meat dishes.

Moderate
Kola Hill Hotel Tel: 023 260 3707; fax: 023 260 4394. Set in a rather barren garden in the Uluguru foothills about 3km from the town centre along the old Dar es Salaam road, the

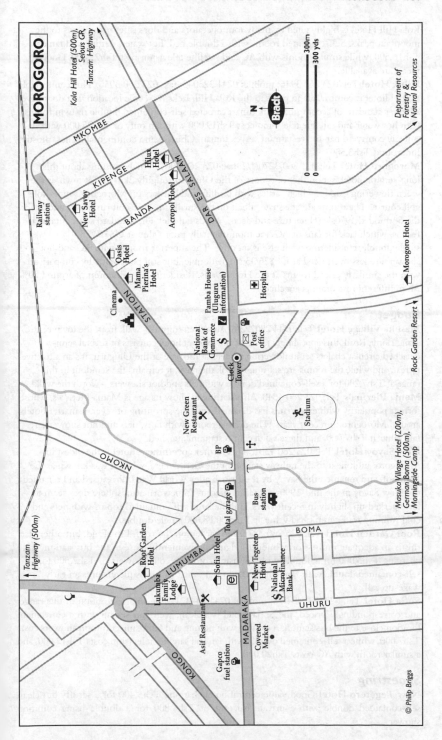

MOROGORO

Kola Hill Hotel (500m), Selous GR, Tanzar Highway

MKOMBE

KIPENGE

BANDA

Hilux Hotel

Acropol Hotel

DAR ES SALAAM

New Savoy Hotel

Railway station

Oasis Hotel

Mama Pierina's Hotel

STATION

Cinema

Pamba House (Uluguru information)

Hospital

Morogoro Hotel

National Bank of Commerce

Post office

Clock Tower

Rock Garden Resort

Department of Forestry & Natural Resources

N

Bradt

300m
300 yds

NKOMO

New Green Restaurant

BP

Stadium

Tanzam Highway (500m)

Roof Garden Hotel

LUMUMBA

Total garage

Bus station

Masuka Village Hotel (200m), German Boma (500m), Morningside Camp

Lukumba Family Lodge

Sofia Hotel

BOMA

Asif Restaurant

MADARAKA

New Tegetero Hotel

National Microfinance Bank

UHURU

KONGO

Gapco fuel station

Covered Market

© Philip Briggs

Kola Hill Hotel is highly rated by many tour operators and does offer great views to the mountain peaks. Self-contained rooms with a double bed, hot water, netting and fan cost Tsh16,500, while similar rooms with AC and satellite television cost Tsh22,800. Good meals are available.

Hilux Hotel Tel: 023 260 3946; mobile: 0741 323048; fax: 023 260 3956. This comfortable central hotel is comparable in price to the Kola Hill, lacks its scenic location, but does have a higher standard of accommodation. Smart carpeted self-contained double or twin rooms with hot water and satellite television cost Tsh19,000 with fan only or Tsh25,000 with AC. A lively courtyard bar and restaurant serves Indian, Chinese and continental dishes, mostly for around Tsh3,500.

Morogoro Hotel Tel: 023 260 3270/1/2; fax: 023 260 4001. The best thing about this long-serving hotel, set on the footslopes of the Uluguru roughly 2km out of town, is the green flowering garden, which rattles with birdlife and borders on Morogoro's nine-hole golf course. The rooms are adequate, albeit on the small side and a bit rundown, and as for the outmoded 1970s' architecture and décor, words fail me! The standard self-contained rooms, which lack for fans or AC, are monumentally poor value at US$20/25 single/double, considering what else is on offer. The superior rooms, with AC and hot shower, are less overpriced at US$25/35 single/double, but still poor value by comparison with the similarly priced rooms at the Hotel Oasis. Residents get a discount of around 20%. An indifferent restaurant is attached.

Budget

Masuka Village Hotel Tel: 0744 280223/6. About ten minutes' walk from the town centre along Boma Road, this appealingly idiosyncratic budget hotel consists of several semi-detached circular chalets set in flowering gardens at the base of the Uluguru. It's an attractive retreat, and while the rooms are starting to look their age, it remains the standout in this range at Tsh7,200 for a self-contained double with nets and hot showers – worth the walk!

Mama Pierina's Tel: 023 260 4640. Also starting to show its age is Mama Pierina's, whose former popularity with expatriates has declined with the sprouting of several smarter hotels around Morogoro in recent years. The double rooms with fans, nets and hot showers are fair value at Tsh7,000, and there's a decent restaurant attached.

New Savoy Hotel Tel: 023 260 1301. This former government hotel is the oldest in Morogoro, built next to the railway station in the German era, when it was known as the Bahnhof, and renamed the Savoy by the British after World War I. Privatised and renamed the New Savoy in the mid-1990s, its rather gloomy, timeworn atmosphere does seem to have perked up slightly in recent years, and the large self-contained rooms with nets and cold running water aren't bad value at Tsh5,000/8,000 single/double.

Roof Garden Hotel Tel: 023 260 3875. No garden on the roof, I'm afraid, but otherwise this is an adequate multi-storey budget lodging, conveniently close to the bus station, and charging Tsh5,000 for a double with fan using common cold showers or Tsh7,500 for a self-contained double with fan. The location right next to a mosque ensures an early wake-up call.

Sofia Hotel Tel: 023 260 4847/8; mobile: 0741 334421. The smartest option in this range, and correspondingly priced, the Sofia Hotel is a clean, well-run set-up with a convenient location close to the bus station. A double with netting and fan using common showers costs Tsh7,000, while a self-contained double with fan and satellite television costs Tsh12,000, and a similar room with AC costs Tsh20,000.

Shoestring

New Tegetero Hotel Good value central hotel charging Tsh5,400 for a scruffy but clean self-contained double with a private balcony, or Tsh4,800 for a double using common showers.

Lukumba Family Lodging This friendly local guesthouse, close to the bus station, charges Tsh2,500 for a basic double using common showers.

Where to eat

Several of the hotels listed above have good restaurants. The pick of the bunch are probably the efficient Indian restaurant at the Hotel Oasis and the classy Continental restaurant at the New Acropol, but there's also good food available at the Hilux and Kola Hills Hotels. The best stand-alone eatery for some years has been the **New Green Restaurant**, which serves good Indian and Portuguese dishes in the Tsh3,000–4,000 range.

General information

Tourist information Details about hiking routes, camping and local guides for the Uluguru Mountains can be obtained from the Uluguru Mountains Biodiversity and Conservation Project in the Wildlife Conservation Society office on the top floor of Pamba House, next to the National Bank of Commerce and opposite the post office. The Morogoro Cultural Program is also based out of this office. Tel: 023 260 3122; fax: 023 260 3766; email: uluguru@morogoro.net; web: www.africaconservation.com/uluguru.

Foreign exchange The National Bank of Commerce on the old Dar es Salaam road exchanges foreign currency, travellers' cheques and cash during normal banking hours. There is no private bureau de change in Morogoro.

Internet There's a good internet café opposite the New Tegetero Hotel, charging Tsh500 per 30 minutes' access. Internet access is also available at the Hotel Oasis at Tsh1,000 per hour.

THE ULUGURUS

The Uluguru Mountains consist of two linked massifs that rise sharply from the low-lying coastal plain south of Morogoro to form one of the country's most important catchment areas, the main source of water for the combined four million residents of Dar es Salaam and Morogoro. The Northern Uluguru – the dramatic backdrop to Morogoro – includes several peaks reaching an elevation of around 2,200m, while the higher Southern Uluguru is dominated by the 2,500m Lukwagule Plateau, rising to the 2,635m Kimhandu Hill in the far south. The northern and southern massifs are separated by the Bunduki Depression, which drops to an altitude of around 1,700m but is still far higher than the surrounding plains. An estimated 100,000 people of the Luguru tribe live in the mountains, taking advantage of the moist climate and fertile soil to cultivate a variety of fruits, vegetables and other crops throughout the year.

Like the more accessible and publicised Usambara and Udzungwa Mountains, the Ulugurus form part of the ancient and biologically diverse Eastern Arc formation. Despite extensive deforestation over the last century, particularly on the lower slopes, the Ulugurus support a combined total of at least 500km^2 of natural forest across five separate core blocks, all of which are gazetted as forest reserves. These forests harbour a wealth of Eastern Arc endemics, including at least 40 vascular plant species, ten reptile and amphibian species, and perhaps 150 invertebrate species that are totally unique to the Ulugurus. For ornithologists, the forests of the Uluguru provide an important refuge for numerous Eastern Arc specials and other localised species, including Usambara eagle owl, Chapin's apalis, white-winged apalis, Kretschmer's longbill and Uluguru violet-backed sunbird. The undoubted avian star, however, is the beautifully marked and very vociferous

– but equally elusive – Uluguru bush shrike, a species that is unique to the Ulugurus, as are Loveridge's sunbird and the Uluguru grey-throated greenbul. Mammals present in the forests include suni antelope, blue, red and Abbott's duikers, black-and-white colobus, blue monkey, Zanzibar and mountain galago, leopard and chequered elephant shrew.

For those whose main interest in the Ulugurus is their natural history, the best reasonably accessible starting base from which to explore the forest is the village of Nyandira on the northwest slopes of the Southern Uluguru. To get here, you need to follow the Tanzam Highway south from Morogoro for about 20km until you reach Masomba College, where a rough road to the left (4WD only and often impassable during the rains) leads after 20km to Mgeta and then after another 5km to Nyandira. In Nyandira, decent accommodation is available at around Tsh10,000 bed and breakfast at the **UMADEP Guesthouse**. If you're dependent on public transport, at least one bus per day runs between Morogoro and Mgeta, but you'll most likely have to walk the final stretch to Nyandira. From Nyandira, it's about 3km by foot to the village of Chenzema and the forested slopes below the Lukwagule Plateau. It is strongly recommended that prospective visitors first visit the Uluguru Mountains Biodiversity and Conservation Project office in Morogoro for current information and advice, possibly arrange a guide and forestry permits, and confirm availability of accommodation at the affiliated guesthouse in Nyandira.

The Uluguru Mountains Biodiversity and Conservation Project office is also the base for arranging local day trips into the Northern Uluguru with the recently instituted Morogoro Cultural Tourism Program, which currently offers two types of tour. The first is a round day walk to Morningside Camp, a disused German-era research station set near a patch of natural forest halfway up the mountain, passing a waterfall on the way and offering great views back across the town. The second is a half-day cultural tour to Nugutu, a small Luguru village one hours' walk or a Tsh3,000 taxi ride away from Morogoro. Here you will be shown various local craftspeople at work, see a traditional dance performance, and can also arrange to visit a traditional healer or to be given a local cooking lesson. The costs of the activities depend on group size, but are very reasonable. The Morningside hike ranges from Tsh5,500 for one person to Tsh1,500 per person for six or more people, while the Nugutu cultural tour ranges from Tsh9,750 for one person to Tsh5,000 per person for six or more people.

SELOUS GAME RESERVE

Extending over more than 45,000km², the Selous is Africa's single largest game reserve, three times larger than the Serengeti, more than twice the size of South Africa's Kruger National Park, and roughly 50% bigger than either Belgium or Swaziland. It is, furthermore, the core sanctuary within the greater Selous-Niassa ecosystem, which extends over 155,000km² of practically uninhabited *miombo* woodland in southern Tanzania and northern Mozambique. Three-quarters of this vast area – the largest chunk of comparably untrammelled bush left in Africa – is accorded some form of official protection. Within Tanzania, the Mikumi and Udzungwa Mountains National Parks border the western Selous, as does the vast and swampy Kilombero Game Protected Area. To the south of the Selous, and linked to it by a well-established game corridor, lies Mozambique's 23,400km² Niassa Game Reserve.

The Selous' claim to lie at the core of what is arguably the greatest surviving African wilderness is supported by the prodigious large mammal populations protected within the reserve and the greater ecosystem. The elephant herd of 65,000

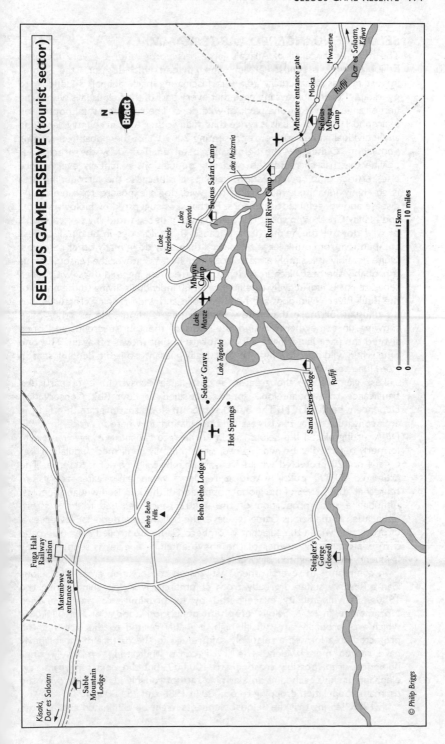

SELOUS GAME RESERVE (tourist sector)

N

Bradt

Mtemere entrance gate
Mwasene
Mloka
Rufiji
Dar es Salaam, Kilwa
Selous Mbega Camp
Lake Mzizima
Selous Safari Camp
Rufiji River Camp
Lake Siwandu
Lake Nzelakela
Mbuyu Camp
Lake Manze
Lake Tagalala
Selous' Grave
Hot Springs
Rufiji
Sand Rivers Lodge
Beho Beho Lodge
Beho Beho Hills
Steigler's Gorge (closed)
Fuga Halt Railway station
Matembwe entrance gate
Kisaki, Dar es Salaam
Sable Mountain Lodge

0   15km
0   10 miles

© Philip Briggs

SELOUS' ENDANGERED LARGE MAMMALS

The most endangered of Africa's large carnivores, after the very localised Ethiopian wolf, is almost certainly the **African wild dog**, and the Selous' importance as a sanctuary for this fascinating pack animal is difficult to overstate. Recent surveys indicate that every part of the Selous falls within the home range of at least one pack of wild dogs. The reserve's total population of around 1,300 individuals is twice that of any other African country, let alone any individual game reserve, representing 20–30% of the global free-ranging population. Quite why the Selous has been unaffected by the precipitous decline that has characterised wild dog populations practically everywhere else in Africa is an open question. Perhaps it is because the surrounding area is so thinly inhabited, minimising the wild dog's exposure to canid-borne disease and vengeful stock farmers. Perhaps, as suggested by biologists Scott and Nancy Creel, who spent the best part of a decade studying several packs of wild dogs in the Selous, it is because the wild dogs in Selous face less competition from other large predators than they do in many other reserves. Quite possibly, it is simply a matter of good luck. Whatever the reason, Selous is probably the best place in Africa to see free-ranging wild dogs, with three separate packs, collectively totalling about 60 individuals, living to the north of the Rufiji River. Wild dogs are highly mobile and wide-ranging creatures, but it's unusual for more than a few days to pass without one or other pack showing up somewhere around the lakes of the tourist circuit, and once sighted the pack is normally easy to locate until it moves off again. The one time when wild dog sightings are practically guaranteed is the denning season from June to August.

Less glamorously, the greater Selous-Niassa ecosystem is of particular significance to two antelope species classified as Low Risk Conservation Dependent by the IUCN. The 8,000 **sable antelope** that migrate through the area constitute by far the largest wild population anywhere in Africa. In 1998, DNA testing placed the Selous' sable in the race *Hippotragus niger roosevelti*, formerly regarded to be endangered, since the only confirmed population was a herd of 120 protected within Kenya's Shimba Hills National Reserve. The estimated 50,000 **puku antelope** resident within the greater ecosystem represent about 75% of the global population of this localised wetland species. Although a small proportion of the puku's range lies within the western boundaries of the Selous Game Reserve, the bulk is accorded a far lower level of protection within the adjacent Kilombero Game Controlled Area (see page 515). Unfortunately, neither of the above antelope species is seen with any frequency in the main tourist circuit.

In common with several other East African conservation areas, the Selous Game Reserve suffered greatly from commercial ivory poaching during the 1980s, its vulnerability exacerbated by its proximity to then war-torn Mozambique. In 1976, Selous' **elephant** population stood at around 110,000, which was probably an artificial high, arguably related to the fact that the protected area formed a relatively safe refuge for herds that might formerly have ranged more widely. The 1981 census indicated a relatively small numerical drop, possibly seasonal, to 100,000, but the next ten years saw elephants being poached at an alarming rate of roughly 20 per day, with the estimated population dropping to 55,000 in 1986 and 25,000 in 1989.

In 1988, fearing that the Selous' elephants might be eliminated entirely, the

Tanzanian government launched the Selous Conservation Programme with support from several international conservation agencies such as the Frankfurt Zoological Society, the African Wildlife Foundation and the World Wide Fund for Nature. This programme aimed to involve bordering communities in conservation activities, as well as raising funds for better policing of the reserve. Aided by the controversial CITES ban on ivory in the early 1990s, poaching was brought under control. By 1994, the Selous' elephant population had climbed back above 30,000. The most recent aerial survey in 1998 placed the population at 55,000–60,000, and today the population of the greater ecosystem probably stands at a healthy 65,000.

In 1980, Selous's estimated herd of 3,000 **black rhinoceros** was the largest to be confined within any one East African conservation area. It still is, come to think of it, but with the critical difference that the most optimistic estimates place the current population at fewer than 150. The only viable rhino herd that is resident to the north of the Rufiji consists of about ten individuals resident in the Kidai sector and Beho Beho Hills of the northwest. The Sand Rivers Selous Rhino Project – established by the lodge of the same name in 1995 – has been largely responsible for funding a 12-ranger anti-poaching unit that closely monitors this group of rhinos, and has recently extended its attention to elsewhere in the reserve with a patrol plane. Given the limited gene pool from which southern Africa's large black rhino population derives, the survival of the genetically distinct Selous population, together with that of the so-called desert rhinos of Namibia, is not merely of local significance.

Paradoxically, a significant factor in stemming the poaching within Selous has been the utilisation of almost 90% of the reserve for low-volume trophy hunting. Whatever one might feel about the sort of individual who is prepared to pay vast sums of money to blow the brains out of a lion or elephant or kudu in the prime of its life, the hunting concessions are by all accounts well monitored, and their benefits are clear. Firstly, the lessors have a strong interest in driving poachers off their concessions, and thus play an important role in policing remote parts of the reserve. Secondly, the revenue derived from the hunting concessions and their patrons – four times the sum raised by less pugnacious forms of tourism – form an important source of funding for anti-poaching patrols and reserve management.

Setting aside ethical issues, the low-volume hunting does have several negative effects. The large tuskers that once characterised the region are today conspicuously absent, and although the commercial poaching of the 1980s is primarily to blame for this, trophy hunting – which targets the most physically impressive specimens of most species – does not help the situation. It is also noticeable how skittish much of the Selous' wildlife is – proof, say those who subscribe to the Selous myth machine, that the animals here are 'wilder' than in other reserves. A far more plausible explanation, given that the Selous is not *that* lightly trafficked, is that many of its animals regularly cross between the sanctuary of the tourist sector and neighbouring hunting concessions. For the time being, the hunting concessions form an integral part of the management strategy for Africa's largest game reserve, but it is to be hoped that the day will come when a greater volume of non-hunting tourists will justify allocating a larger portion of the Selous to conventional safaris.

is the largest of any modern African ecosystem, representing more than half of the Tanzanian population, and 5–10% of the African total. The buffalo population, estimated at 120–150,000, is probably the largest on the continent, and the reserve's 40,000 hippo and 4,000 lion must also be there or thereabouts. The Selous also harbours an estimated 100,000 wildebeest, 35,000 zebra, 25,000 impala and significant herds of greater kudu, hartebeest and eland. It is also one of the most important sanctuaries in Africa for the black rhinoceros, African wild dog, and sable and puku antelope (see box *Selous' Endangered Large Mammals*, pages 492–3).

That the Selous ranks as one of East Africa's most alluring and satisfying safari destinations is not in dispute. However, given that much of the publicity surrounding the Selous bangs on and on about its vast area, prospective visitors should be aware that the extent of the reserve is in practice something of a red herring. The Selous is divided into two disproportionate parts by the Rufiji, Tanzania's largest river, which together with the Great Ruaha, a major tributary, runs through the reserve from west to east. The roughly 90% of the Selous that lies to the south of the river has been divided into a number of privately leased hunting concessions, all of which are off-limits to casual tourism. A proportion of the northern sector has also been set aside for hunting concessions, with the remainder – no more than 5% of the reserve's total area – forming what to all intents and purposes is the Selous Tourist Reserve. The five main lodges (and most tourist activities) are actually concentrated within an area of 1,000km² immediately north of the Rufiji.

Fortunately, the public part of the Selous is wonderfully atmospheric, a dense tract of *miombo* wilderness abutting the meandering Rufiji River, and an associated labyrinth of five pretty lakes connected to each other and the river by numerous narrow streams. Arriving by light aircraft, as most visitors do, it is exhilarating to sweep above the palm-fringed channels teeming with hippos and waterfowl, the swampy islets where immense herds of elephant and giraffe graze alongside each other, and exposed sandbanks where antelope drink and all manner of shorebirds scurry about. No less exciting are the boat excursions along the Rufiji, which generally culminate with a brilliant red sun setting behind the tall borassus palms and baobabs that line the wide sandy watercourse. Gulp-inducing dentist-eye views of the Selous' trademark gigantic crocs can pretty much be guaranteed from the boat, as can conferences of grunting, harrumphing hippos – and you'd be unlucky not to be entertained by herds of elephant, buffalo or giraffe shuffling down to drink.

The most memorable aspect of the boat trips, however, is the profuse birdlife. Characteristic waterbirds along this stretch of the Rufiji include yellow-billed stork, white-crowned and spur-winged plovers, various small waders, pied and malachite kingfishers, and African skimmer. Pairs of fish eagle and palmnut vulture perch high on the borassus palms, seasonal breeding colonies of carmine and white-throated bee-eater swirl around the mud cliffs that hem in some stretches of the river, and pairs of trumpeter hornbill and purple-crested turaco flap between the riparian trees. Worth looking out for among a catalogue of egrets and herons is the Malagasy squacco heron, a regular winter visitor, while the elusive Pel's fishing owl often emerges at dusk to hawk above the water.

Game drives along the network of rough roads to the north of the Rufiji are reliably rewarding, especially towards the end of the dry season, when large mammals concentrate around the five lakes. More frequently seen ungulates include impala, common waterbuck, bushbuck, white-bearded wildebeest, eland, greater kudu, buffalo and common zebra. The northern sector of the park has been dubbed Giraffic Park, with some justification, as herds exceeding 50 individuals come down to drink in the heat of the afternoon. Oddly, the giraffe are entirely absent south of the Rufiji, which also forms a natural barrier between the ranges of the distinctive white-bearded and Niassa races of wildebeest. The endangered African wild dog is commonly observed, as is the spotted hyena, while leopards are common but elusive, but cheetah have not been recorded in this part of the reserve for about 20 years.

Much in evidence, with two or three different prides' territories converging on each of the five large lakes, are Selous' lions, which typically have darker coats and less hirsute manes than their counterparts elsewhere in East Africa. During the dry season, the lions of Selous evidently rely on an unusual opportunistic diurnal hunting strategy, rarely straying far from the lakes, where they rest up in the shade to wait for whatever ungulate happens to venture within pouncing distance on its way to drink. On our most recent visit to Selous, we witnessed or came across the aftermath of half-a-dozen diurnal hunts, but – despite seeing lions in most morning drives – we saw no evidence of a single nocturnal lion kill. Based on our experience, the Selous probably offers a better chance of seeing a lion kill than almost any reserve in Africa.

While the marketing line of 'only five small camps in a 50,000km² wilderness' does rather overstate the exclusivity of the Selous experience, it is true that a mere 5,000 foreigners annually – about 1% of tourist arrivals to Tanzania – ever make it to this excellent reserve. Particularly if one is based at one of the western lodges – Beho Beho, Sand Rivers and Sable Mountain – it is still possible to undertake a game drive in the Selous without coming across another vehicle. Whereas the northern circuit is dominated by large impersonal hotels that evidently aim to shut out the bush the moment you enter them, the Selous boasts a select handful of low-key, eco-friendly, thatch-and-canvas lodges whose combined bed capacity amounts to little more than 100 clients. Furthermore, because the Selous is not subject to the regulations that govern Tanzania's national parks, visitors are offered a more primal and integrated bush experience than the usual repetitive regime of one game drive after another. In addition to boat trips, all lodges offer guided game walks, which come with a real likelihood of encountering elephant or buffalo – even lion – on foot. Better still are the overnight fly-camping excursions offered by most camps, which entail sleeping beneath a glorified mosquito net on the shore of a lake teeming with hippos and crocs – thrilling stuff!

Roads within the Selous become impassable after heavy rain. As a consequence the camps close towards the end of the wet season, in April, and re-open in July. An entrance fee of US$25 per person per day is charged.

Further information
Two useful booklets, similar to the old-style TANAPA booklets, have been published about Selous in collaboration with the GTZ. These are *Selous Game Reserve: A Guide to the Northern Section* and the glossier *Selous: Africa's Largest & Wildest Game Reserve*. Most of the lodges will stock one or other booklet, and there's not a lot to choose between them textually.

Getting there and away
Package safaris
Most safari companies in Dar es Salaam or Zanzibar, as well as all the camps listed under *Where to stay* below, offer a variety of fly-in packages to the Selous, optionally combined with Ruaha National Park, and typically running from two to seven nights in duration. Almost all fly-in packages use the scheduled daily flight from Dar es Salaam and Zanzibar to Selous and Ruaha, which is operated by Coastal Travel, and can stop at any of the camp airstrips by prior arrangement.

SELOUS AND THE SELOUS: SOME HISTORY

In 1859, Burton and Speke passed through a part of what would later become the Selous Game Reserve, and noted that the area lacked for any significant human settlements. This absence can largely be explained by the local abundance of tsetse flies, which carry livestock diseases, as well as the limited amount of permanent water to be found south of the Rufiji River. Another factor, doubtless, would have been regular slave raids associated with the Arab trading post of Kisaki, today an overgrown village set on the northern boundary of game reserve, but in the 19th century the junction of two main caravan routes into the interior. In 1905, the region was further depopulated, particularly around the fertile Mutumbi Hills, when the German colonial authorities undertook a brutal series of raids in retaliation to the Maji-Maji uprising. The section of the present-day Selous Game Reserve lying to the north of the Rufiji River was gazetted in the same year as a gift from Kaiser Wilhelm to his wife, earning it the local nickname Shamba la Bibi (The Woman's Field).

Selous (pronounced 'Seloo') is named in honour of Frederick Courtney Selous, who left England for Africa in 1871 as an athletic 18-year-old – his school pals called him The Mighty Nimrod – and spent the next four decades acquiring a reputation as perhaps the most accomplished hunter of his age. Selous served as Great White Hunter to the likes of Theodore Roosevelt, and was contemporaneously renowned as a writer of several rollicking African hunting yarns, most notably A Hunter's Wanderings in Africa. A staunch patriot, Selous served as right-hand man to Cecil John Rhodes in his campaign to annexe present-day Zimbabwe to the British Empire, though he also achieved brief notoriety in 1899 for speaking out against England's war on the Boer Republics of South Africa.

In 1914, when war broke out between Britain and Germany, Selous was more than 60 years old, yet he unhesitatingly volunteered, to be appointed Captain of the 25th Royal Fusiliers, and won a DSO in 1916. With his intimate

Drive-in safaris to the Selous might be marginally cheaper than fly-in safaris, but the actual drive takes the best part of a full day in either direction and is not the most comfortable experience. The most common reason why some safaris drive rather than fly to Selous is to incorporate into the itinerary destinations that are not serviced by scheduled flights, such as Mikumi or Udzungwa National Parks. Whether you fly or drive, the price of the safari will vary greatly depending on which camp you stay at, your length of stay, how you travel to the reserve, and the size of your group.

No budget camping safari industry is dedicated to the Selous, and the daily cost of most itineraries will be at least as expensive as that of a top-of-the-range lodge safari in northern Tanzania. The closest thing to a budget Selous safari is a package offered by Sable Mountain Lodge, the most westerly and cheapest of the park's lodges, which involves catching the Tazara Railway to Kisaki, where the lodge vehicle will meet you.

Self-drive

The Selous can be visited only in a 4WD vehicle. The drive from Dar es Salaam takes at least eight and often 10 or 12 hours, and the roads are often impassable during the height of the rainy season (March to May). Self-drive visitors normally approach the Selous from one of two directions, with the less popular but shorter

knowledge of the bush, Selous was the automatic choice to head up the chase after the ragtag German guerrilla army that Colonel von Lettow led through southern Tanzania for longer than a year, consistently evading or defeating the British troops. On New Year's Day 1917, the opposing troops converged on each other close to the banks of the Beho Beho River, and Selous was shot dead by a sniper. The most famous casualty of East Africa's so-called 'Battle of the Bundu', Selous was held in such universal esteem that Colonel von Lettow, upon hearing of his death, described the old hunter as having been 'well known among the Germans, on account of his charming manner and exciting stories'.

Less than two years later, the writer P H Lamb trekked to the site of the simple wooden cross that marked the spot where the septuagenarian Selous had fallen and was buried. 'It is,' Lamb reported, 'a wild inhospitable district, the haunt of a great variety of big game, including elephants, giraffes and rhinos. Not more than four miles away is a warm salt spring running down into a salt lake, where hippos, wild ducks, egrets and numerous other wild fowls abound. But despite these alleviations it can hardly be called a fascinating part of the world, and the object of most people who have seen it will be to avoid it carefully in the future.'

While the opening sentences of Lamb's report could have been written yesterday, hindsight does lend a certain irony to his final prediction. Five years after Selous' death, the plains of the Shamba la Bibi were greatly extended by the British colonists to incorporate a number of existing game reserves south of the river, and the whole was named in honour of the hero buried within the reserve. The Selous Game Reserve reached its present size and shape in the 1940s, when the colonial government moved the remaining tribes out of the area to combat a sleeping sickness epidemic. It has been declared a World Heritage Site, one of three in Tanzania, and far from being carefully avoided, the site of Selous' Grave lies within 15km of two of the most exclusive and costly safari lodges in Tanzania!

(240km) route involving following the unsurfaced south coast road to Kibiti, then travelling through Mkongo and Mloka to the Mtemere Gate.

The more scenic and longer (330km) but not necessarily slower route involves following the surfaced Tanzam Highway to Morogoro, from where the 140km-long Matombo road leads southwards via Kisaki to Matembwe Gate on the northwest border of Selous. This route is named after the twin peaks called Matombo (which means 'breasts' in the local Luguru language) that lie alongside the road. If you use this road, look out for the interesting roadside quartzite formations about 50–60km south out of Morogoro just after the small town of Mkuyuni, and for the forest-fringed Ruvu River (plenty of monkeys) between Mgazi and Kisaki. A third route, directly connecting Mikumi National Park to Selous via Kisaki, has been under construction for some time now, but it is unlikely to open for a few years yet. Before travelling down, do seek the advice of whichever camp you are heading to, as the better route will vary according to the location of your camp and the current state of the different roads, and you will need precise directions.

For backpackers using public transport, it is possible to travel from Morogoro as far as Mgazi, a small town 15km before Kisaki that has at least one small guesthouse. Having done that, exactly how you would get into the reserve from Mgazi – or indeed get around the reserve – beats me!

Where to stay
Exclusive
Sand Rivers Selous Tel: 022 286 5156; fax: 022 286 5731; email: sand-rivers@twiga.com; web: www.sandrivers.com. Set above a wide, sandy bend in the Rufiji River, this is probably the most luxurious lodge in the Selous, and the most isolated, situated in the wild southwest of the public part of the reserve, an area that is infrequently visited by vehicles from the other lodges. The lodge consists of 16 airy and elegant stone and *makuti* units, each with a large double bed, en-suite shower and toilet, and private balcony overlooking the river. There is a swimming pool. The emphasis at Sand Rivers is very much on walking safaris, and the standard of guiding is exceptionally high. Game drives are also offered, with nearby Lake Tagalala being one obvious goal, and it is the only lodge that offers boat trips through the stunning Stiegler's Gorge, the most reliable place in the reserve for sightings of leopard and black-and-white colobus monkey. Plenty of animals come down to the river to drink, and black rhino are resident in the surrounding dense bush, though seldom seen by tourists. Full board rates inclusive of all activities are US$730 double.

Beho Beho Camp Tel: 022 260 0352/3/4; fax: 022 260 0347; email: oysterbay-hotel@twiga.com. This recently renovated and refurbished lodge, which formally re-opened in October 2002, consists of 12 large and attractively decorated en-suite stone cottages set on the footslopes of the Beho Beho Hills in the west of the public part of the reserve. A particularly attractive feature of this lodge is the tall *makuti*-roofed lounge and dining area, which offers a fabulous view over the plains to Lake Tagalala. Although Beho Beho is the only lodge within Selous set away from the river, a permanent pool below supports a resident pod of hippos and attracts a surprising amount of game and birdlife. As with Sand Rivers, the relatively remote location means that far fewer tourist vehicles are found in the vicinity, and excellent game viewing can be had at nearby Lakes Tagalala and Manze. Game walks are offered, as are boat trips on Lake Tagalala, which reputedly – and credibly – has one of the highest crocodile populations in Africa. Nearby sites of interest include Selous' Grave and a group of hot springs set in a patch of riparian woodland. Full board rates inclusive of all activities are US$350 single, US$500 double, plus national park fees.

Selous Safari Camp Tel: 022 213 4802; fax: 022 211 2794; email: info@selous.com; web: www.selous.com. Almost entirely rebuilt after the El Niño floods a few years back, this plush camp on the shores of Lake Siwando consists of 12 spacious double standing tents, set far apart from each other, and with fans, attached open-air showers, and a good view. The common lounge and dining area is a fabulous stilted treehouse lit at night by dozens of gas lamps. Game drives, boat trips, guided walks and fly-camping are all offered.

Upmarket
Rufiji River Camp Tel: 22 277 5164; fax: 22 277 5165; email: info@hippotours.com; web: www.hippotours.com. The first lodge to be established in the Selous, the ever popular and reasonably priced Rufiji River Camp is situated at the eastern extremity of the tourist sector overlooking an atmospheric stretch of the Rufiji River alive with hippos and crocs and regularly visited by elephants. The camp consists of 20 standing tents with en-suite facilities and fans, spaced along the river in a lush stretch of woodland populated by monkeys and numerous birds – and occasionally visited by more exciting large mammals. The lodge has a refreshingly informal and unpretentious atmosphere and delicious home-cooked food reflecting the nationality of the laidback Italian owner-manager. Rufiji River Camp offers an excellent range of boat and foot activities, as well as half-day game drives encompassing the three nearby lakes, full-day excursions further afield and overnight fly-camping. Full board accommodation exclusive of activities but inclusive of park fees costs US$175 per person, with any activities charged at US$30 per person, while FB accommodation inclusive of activities and park fees costs US$235 per person.

499

Coastal Aviation
The flying safari company

Flies to all National Parks...
and Tourist Destinations

Dar es Salaam Head Office:
Tel: +255-22-2117 959 or 960, Fax: +255-22-2118 647
Toll free: +255-741-800 285
Zanzibar Internation Airport:
Tel/Fax: +255-24-2233 112,
Cell: +255-741-670 815 or +255-747-414 201
Arusha Representative:
Fax: +255-27-2505446
Cell: +255-741-239 433 or +255-744-317 808,

Email: aviation@coastal.cc
www.coastal.cc

Mbuyu Tented Camp Tel: 0742 781971; fax: 022 211 1139; email: stgs@twiga.com; web: tanzania-safari.com. This attractively located camp lies on the shore of Lake Nzerakera, and its lounge and dining area are built around a large baobab tree. Accommodation is in 20 self-contained tents with en-suite toilet and shower, and attractive ethnic décor, but no fan. The tents are arranged in two rows, one set in front of the lake, the other directly behind it, which makes it feel a bit more cramped than the other Selous lodges. An attractive feature is the stilted hide at the far end of the camp, overlooking the lake, which is visited by numerous animals. The usual range of activities – game drives, guided walks, boat trips, fly-camping – are offered. Accommodation costs US$205/290 FB exclusive of activities or US$250/500 inclusive of activities.

Moderate
Sable Mountain Lodge Tel: 022 270 1497; mobile: 0741 323318; email: safariscene@intafrica.com. This relatively new lodge is situated 1km outside of the western park boundary near the Matembwe Gate, in a patch of small hills offering views into the surrounding dense *brachystegia* forest. It consists of eight double cottages, with en-suite hot shower and toilet and 24-hour electricity, set spaciously across the hillside. A treehouse on one of the slopes offers a grandstand view over a waterhole regularly visited by buffalo and elephant. The surrounding woodland is very thick, and guided walks offer the opportunity to see forest-associated species such as blue monkey, black-and-white colobus and the amazing chequered elephant shrew, as well as a host of forest birds including the exquisite Livingstone's turaco, a variety of hornbills and the vociferous forest weaver. Between December and May, sable antelope move into the area. Game drives concentrate on the plains north of the main cluster of lodges, which can be very worthwhile seasonally, with very few other vehicles around. Fly-camping is also available, as are river trips during the wet season on the lushly forested Mbega River. The base rate of US$95 per person makes this the most affordable established lodge in the Selous, especially if you arrange to go there by train rather than to fly.
Selous Mbega Camp Tel: 022 265 0250; fax: 022 265 0251; email: zapoco@afsat.com. This small and spanking new German-owned camp lies on the banks of the Rufiji immediately east of the park boundary close to the Mtemere Gate. Accommodation is in self-contained tents set in the riparian woodland fringing the river, and a tree house offers views over a small waterhole. Game drives, guided walks and boat trips can be arranged. Standard non-resident rates are US$95 per person sharing, but by prior arrangement substantial discounts are offered to backpackers who are prepared to bus from Dar es Salaam to the village of Mloka, about 4km from the camp (a free transfer is provided).

MIKUMI
The small town of Mikumi, which extends untidily along the Tanzam Highway immediately outside the southern border of the synonymous national park, was founded in 1914 by Chief Kikiwi of the Wavindunda tribe and is named for the borassus palms that used to flourish in the immediate vicinity. Mikumi was a rather ordinary small African village prior to the 1960s, when the present road between Morogoro and Iringa was constructed. Over subsequent years, however, it has expanded considerably, as the main service town to the adjacent national park, as well as an important stopover along the Tanzam Highway and the junction town for the B127 to Udzungwa National Park and Ifakara. Although the odd traveller might want to overnight in Mikumi between bus trips, the town is primarily of use as a budget base from which one could explore Mikumi National Park. Whatever else one might say about Mikumi, it's a pretty organised place, with a clutch of decent hotels and restaurants, and – unexpectedly – a couple of internet cafés!

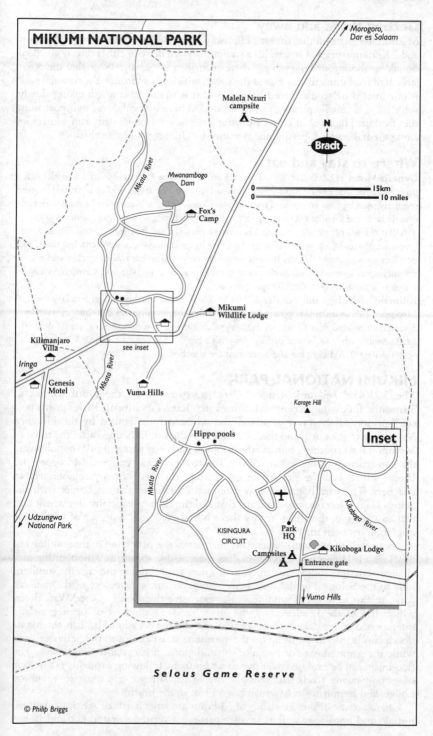

MIKUMI NATIONAL PARK

Morogoro,
Dar es Salaam

Malela Nzuri
campsite

Mkata River

Mwanambogo
Dam

N

Bradt

0   15km
0   10 miles

Fox's
Camp

Mikumi
Wildlife Lodge

Kilimanjaro
Villa

see inset

Iringa

Mkata River

Genesis
Motel

Vuma Hills

Karage Hill

Udzungwa
National Park

Inset

Hippo pools

Mkata River

Kikoboga River

KISINGURA
CIRCUIT

Park
HQ

Kikoboga Lodge

Campsites

Entrance gate

Vuma Hills

Selous Game Reserve

© Philip Briggs

Getting there and away

Mikumi lies right on the Tanzam Highway about 120km southwest of Morogoro and 200km northeast of Iringa. It's a straightforward drive in either direction – bank on taking about four hours to get there from Dar es Salaam. Note that the 50km stretch of road immediately east of the town, which runs through the national park, is punctuated by regular speed bumps, and it is in any case worth taking slowly, since there is usually plenty of game around. There is regular bus transport along the Tanzam Highway in either direction, and several buses daily run southward along the Ifakara road, passing the entrance to Udzungwa National Park.

Where to stay and eat

Genesis Motel Tel: 023 262 0466. Fax: 023 262 0443. The Genesis Motel is a moderately priced lodging that lies alongside the main road towards the Iringa end of town and is quite regularly used by tour groups and researchers. Comfortable self-contained *bandas* with two double beds and satellite television cost Tsh10,000 B&B per person, while suites cost Tsh30,000 B&B per person. The attached snake park is quite interesting, with Gabon viper, green mamba and rock python among the more intimidating species present, but the US$5 entrance fee seems mildly over the top for what you get. The bar is well stocked and the restaurant has a varied menu, with a four-course meal costing Tsh5,500. Camping, with access to a shower, costs Tsh2,000 per person.

Kilimanjaro Village Inn Tel: 023 262 0429. This very acceptable budget hotel on the Morogoro side of town is popular with tour drivers and recommended to budget travellers. A variety of rooms, all with fan, are available: those using common showers cost Tsh3,000 single/double while self-contained singles with a big double bed cost Tsh8,000 and suites cost Tsh10,000. A decent bar and restaurant are attached.

MIKUMI NATIONAL PARK

The 3,230km² Mikumi National Park, relegated to be the fourth largest in Tanzania following recent extensions to Katavi National Park, protects a combination of flat open grassland and wooded hills flanked by the Uluguru Mountains to the north and the Udzungwa to the south. Named after the town of Mikumi on its southern border, the national park was gazetted in 1964 following the construction of the section of the Tanzam Highway between Morogoro and Iringa, which had the side effect of opening up this formerly remote area to poachers. The park boundary was extended in 1975 to share a border with the Selous Game Reserve, which means that Mikumi is now officially an extension of that vast reserve, though in reality there has always been a degree of local game migration between the two.

About 80% of Mikumi – essentially the part of the park lying to the southeast of the Tanzam Highway – is more-or-less inaccessible to tourists, though this may change with the pending construction of a new road running through the southern hills to the Selous. For the time being, however, the centrepiece of the national park, at least in terms of wildlife, is the extensive floodplain of the Mkata River, which lies to the northwest of the main road. Comprised of open grassland interspersed with patches of acacia woodland and the occasional baobab, the Mkata floodplain is the closest thing on the southern safari circuit to the Serengeti, and while the game might not be quite so prodigious, it is certainly impressive. The floodplain can be explored over five to six hours by following a roughly 60km loop of game-viewing roads that starts at the main entrance gate near to Kikoboga Lodge, and terminates at Mwanambogo Dam in the north.

Characteristic of the grasslands of Mikumi are large herds of zebra, wildebeest, buffalo and impala, as well as smaller parties of warthog, waterbuck and Bohor reedbuck, and troops of vervet monkey and yellow baboon. Giraffe and elephant are common on the main road loop, especially in the vicinity of acacia trees. Lion and spotted hyena are also around in reasonable numbers, and if you don't see them by day you'll certainly hear them at night. Mikumi had a good reputation for African wild dog a few years back, but the resident pack is thought to have migrated to the Selous and sightings are unusual today. Of the rarer antelope, the Mkata Plain is probably the most reliable place in Tanzania for good sightings of the outsized eland, while the *brachystegia* woodland to the southeast of the main road harbours substantial populations of the impressive greater kudu and sable antelope. More than 400 bird species have been recorded in the park, though generally speaking the less visited woodland hosts a greater variety of birds than the grassland. Common birds on the floodplain include bateleur eagle, black-bellied bustard, lilac-breasted roller, ground hornbill, yellow-throated longclaw and long-tailed fiscal, while Mwanambogo Dam is a good place to see fish eagle and water-associated birds such as white-faced duck and African spoonbill.

Despite offering consistently good game viewing and being the most accessible of the country's national parks – transected by a surfaced trunk route only four hours' drive from Dar es Salaam – Mikumi has never featured prominently on safari itineraries through Tanzania. Probably the major reason for this is the somewhat demystifying presence of the main road, made doubly intrusive because until recently it also happened to lie within earshot of the park's only lodges. In my opinion, however, Mikumi – while perhaps the least atmospheric of the three main savannah reserves of the southern circuit – is emphatically worth a night or two on any road safari through southern Tanzania. It also makes for an excellent self-contained one- or two-night safari destination out of Dar es Salaam (the majority of visitors are in fact expatriate weekenders). It is worth noting, too, that the lodges at Mikumi remain extremely affordable by national standards and, ironically, once away from the main road, tourist traffic is very low by comparison with anywhere in northern Tanzania or even the main road loop through the Selous.

Two guided walking trails have recently been opened in Mikumi. The shorter trail passes through the Vuma Hills, and takes about five hours to complete, while the longer trail passes through the Ngotikwe Hills and takes about eight hours. The hikes cost US$20 per person and can be arranged at the main entrance gate

ROAD KILLS

The trunk road passing through Mikumi National Park has created an unusual hazard for the local wildlife. Road kills have accounted for a significant number of animal fatalities ever since the park's inception, but the problem was exacerbated in the 1990s following massive improvements to the road surface, as well as the steady increase in heavy traffic as Tanzania emerged from the economic trough of the 1980s. Between 1992 and 1997, more than 450 large mammal road kills were reported from Mikumi. The most affected species were civet (110), impala (85), hare (50), buffalo (42), black-backed jackal (32) and baboon (23) – but speeding trucks also accounted for a leopard and ten lions, and somewhat incredibly contrived to kill seven elephants. In order to slow down the trucks and stem the carnage, the 50km stretch of public road running through Mikumi has recently been studded with speed bumps (sleeping policemen). No figures are available as yet to show how effective this measure has been.

close to Kikoboga Lodge. An early start is recommended to avoid the heat of the afternoon.

Fees and further information

A park entrance fee of US$15 per person per 24 hours must be paid in hard currency. An excellent colour booklet called *Mikumi*, published by the African Publishing Group in collaboration with TANAPA, is sold at the entrance gate for US$8.

Getting there and away

Safaris to Mikumi generally run from Dar es Salaam, which is four hours away by road. It would be possible to visit the park for one or two nights as a stand-alone trip, but normally Mikumi is combined with a longer road safari to Selous, Ruaha and/or Udzungwa. Mikumi can be reached in an ordinary saloon car, but a 4WD is needed to drive within the park.

Travellers using public transport through the south should see plenty of game from the main road (I once counted ten mammal species including a herd of 20 eland and four herds of elephant), but this isn't quite the same as spending time in the park itself. I have never heard of a traveller doing so, but it should be relatively cheap (and quite straightforward) to organise a day trip into the national park out of Mikumi town. The Genesis Motel should be able to put you in touch with the owner of a suitable vehicle. Mikumi may not be the most fashionable reserve in Tanzania, but it is perhaps the only one that offers the combination of large numbers of plains animals and easy access from a reasonably substantial town located on a major thoroughfare.

Although Mikumi is accessible all year through, the black cotton soil of the Mkata floodplain routinely becomes waterlogged during the rainy season, and when this occurs the main game-viewing circuit is effectively out of bounds. It is therefore advisable to check current road conditions in advance should you intend to visit the park between November and April.

Where to stay
Upmarket

Vuma Hills Tented Camp Tel: 000 871 76 203 1650; email: 4vuma@bushmail.net; web: www.vuma.org. This small and intimate owner-managed tented camp, set amongst the thick *brachystegia* woodland of the Vuma Hills to the southeast of the Tanzam Highway, has deservedly acquired a reputation as a first-class weekend retreat among expatriates working in Dar es Salaam. Classic safari accommodation is provided in large standing tents perched on stilted wooden platforms that offer a fabulous view over the wooded plains below. The food is excellent, too, made largely with imported ingredients and with a strong Italian influence, and there is a small swimming pool. Vuma Hills is probably the most atmospheric and aesthetically pleasing lodge in Mikumi, with traffic from the main road only faintly audible, but its one drawback is that there isn't a great deal of game visible from the camp or on the roads immediately around it. Full-board rates exclusive of park entrance fees are US$130/220 single/double from July to September, US$115/190 October to February and US$100/170 from March to June. Half-board rates are US$15 per person per day less. Game drives are available at US$25–40 per person, while guided walks cost US$25 per person.

Fox's Safari Camp Tel/fax: (UK) 1452 862288; tel: 0744 237422, 0741 237422; fax 0741 327706; email: fox@tanzaniasafaris.info or fox@bushlink.co.tz; web: www.ruahariverlodge.com. This brand new lodge, under the same ownership as Ruaha River Lodge and Lazy Lagoon in Bagamoyo, is the only one in Mikumi to lie far enough from the Tanzam Highway that the tranquillity of the bush isn't interrupted by the rumble of passing trucks. Situated on a rocky hillside offering wide views in all directions, the camp consists of eight luxurious self-contained tents raised on wooden platforms, and it lies in the middle of the excellent game-viewing circuit through the Mkata Plains. Day trips to Udzungwa National Park are arranged by request. Full board accommodation exclusive of game drives costs US$162/240 single/double, while the same inclusive of game drives and park fees is US$267/450 single/double.

Moderate

Kikoboga Lodge Tel: 022 260 0352/3/4; fax: 022 260 0347; email: oysterbay-hotel@twiga.com. This underrated and very reasonably priced lodge (formerly called Mikumi Wildlife Camp) is situated about 1km from the Tanzam Highway through the main park entrance gate, in the thick of the animal action at the start of what is indubitably the park's best game-viewing circuit. Accommodation consists of 12 large and well appointed self-contained stone cottages, each with a large double bed, mosquito netting and a private patio. The best feature of Kikoboga, certainly if close-up wildlife encounters are your top priority, is the pair of waterholes situated right in front of the dining area and cottages. Particularly during the dry season, these waterholes attract a steady stream of zebras, giraffes and elephants, sometimes a passing lion or hyena, as well as a resident flock of very habituated marabou storks. Be warned, too, that the elephants are also rather partial to sipping the water in the small swimming pool! The one drawback of this lodge is its proximity to the main road, which means that the rumble of passing trucks vies with the nocturnal howling of the hyenas. Casual visitors are welcome to drop in for snacks, which are mostly in the Tsh3,000–5,000 range.

New Mikumi Wildlife Lodge Tel: 022 277 3486; mobile: 0744 290229; email: pielinalamba@hotmail.com. Only two things about this recently privatised former government hotel could reasonably be described as new, and those are the satellite televisions in the rooms, and the recent addition of the word 'New' to the lodge's name! The New Mikumi Wildlife Lodge, without putting too fine a point on it, is a vast ugly monolith with architecture and fittings that are evidently biding their time for the next 1970s revival, and a cavernous interior rendered vaguely surreal by the reliable absence of any custom. On the plus side, the lodge does have a superb location, on a hillside overlooking a large waterhole where hippos grunt merrily and plenty of other wildlife comes past to drink. The large rooms aren't bad either, come to think of it, dominated as they are by large-screen windows facing the waterhole, and with large double bed, fan, hot shower and bath and satellite television. Aesthetics aside, it's really not bad value at US$66/77 single/double B&B for non-residents, and a real bargain if you can persuade them to offer you the residents rate of Tsh33,000/44,000 single/double.

Budget

Travellers on a tight budget have the option of staying overnight at one of the hotels or guesthouses in Mikumi town, which lies only 20km from the main entrance gate along the surfaced Tanzam Highway.

Camping

Malela Nzuri Campsite This underpublicised private campsite lies 4km along a clearly signposted side road that leads northwest from the Tanzam Highway about 5km from the national park boundary on the Morogoro side. Set in a patch of thick *brachystegia* woodland bordering the national park, the campsite is pleasantly rustic in atmosphere and quite a bit of game passes through during the rains. About 6km further along the same side road, a small dam on the Mkata River harbours a resident pod of hippo and attracts plenty of game, particularly during the dry season. Visitors with their own transport can drive to the dam at night, and it's also permitted to camp on the shore – a watchman is posted there permanently. Either way, camping costs Tsh2,000 per person, and visitors need to be self sufficient in food and water. The Malela Nzuri Campsite should not be confused with the Malela Campsite and Quarry, which is signposted to the southeast of the Tanzam Highway perhaps 15km closer to Morogoro – we followed this road to its end and found the quarry but no sign of a campsite!

National Park Campsites There are also three campsites near the main gate, with long-drop toilets and firewood but no water, but they cannot be classed as great value for money at US$20 per person. Special campsites within the park cost US$40 per person.

UDZUNGWA MOUNTAINS NATIONAL PARK

Formally opened in October 1992 by Prince Bernhard of the Netherlands, Udzungwa is Tanzania's newest national park – a status it will relinquish once the proposed Saadani and Kitulo National Parks are gazetted – and the only part of the Eastern Arc mountains to be accorded an equivalent level of official protection. The 1,900km² national park protects a northeasterly block of the Udzungwa Range, less than one-fifth of the total area of what is the most extensive mountain range in Tanzania. In common with the other mountains of the Eastern Arc (see box *An African Galápagos?*, pages 222–4), Udzungwa is a metamorphic massif of some geological antiquity, comprised of ancient crystalline rock that rose above the surrounding plains at least 100 million years ago due to upward faulting in the earth's crust. Despite subsequent erosion, the modern massif has a wide altitude range, rising from an elevation of around 250m in the Kilombero Valley to the 2,576m Luhomero Peak. The name Udzungwa means Land of the Dzungwa, a subgroup of the Hehe who are said to have settled on the western slopes of the range after being driven away from the Iringa area during the internecine battles that accompanied the rise of Chiefs Munyigumba and Mkwawa.

The eastern escarpment of the Udzungwa supports sub-montane rainforest with a canopy reaching 50m in some areas. Central and southern parts of the plateau consist of rolling hilly country covered in grassland, *miombo* woodland and scattered patches of Afro-montane forest. Elevation decreases gradually to the west where there is arid woodland, and semi-desert conditions in the rain shadow of the mountains. Three-quarters of the forest cover has disappeared over the last 2,000 years, as a direct result of human activity, and at most 500km² of extant forest is protected within the national park, but this, together with a number of smaller forest reserves, is the most substantial tract found on any of the Eastern Arc ranges. Udzungwa is also unique within East Africa in that it boasts an unbroken cover of closed canopy forest spanning the full transition from lowland forest communities at 250m above sea level, through to montane forest communities at above 2,000m.

Because of this variety of habitats, Udzungwa is a strong contender for the accolade of Tanzania's single most important terrestrial biodiversity hotspot. More than 25% of the plant species recorded in Udzungwa are endemic, ranging from a recently described violet species of the genus *Saintpaulia* to a number of trees standing 30m tall or higher. The level of endemism among the Udzungwa fauna is the highest of any East African range, with several species of reptile, amphibian and particularly invertebrates being unique to the range. The most celebrated of the forest residents are a trio of endemic primate taxa, the Uhehe red colobus, Sanje crested mangabey and Matunda galago, all likely to be proved to be full species with time. What is remarkable about the first two of these endemics is their geographical isolation from other closely allied species. Aside from one population on the Tana River in Kenya, the mangabey group of monkeys is essentially restricted to the Congolese and Guinean rainforests thousands of kilometres to the

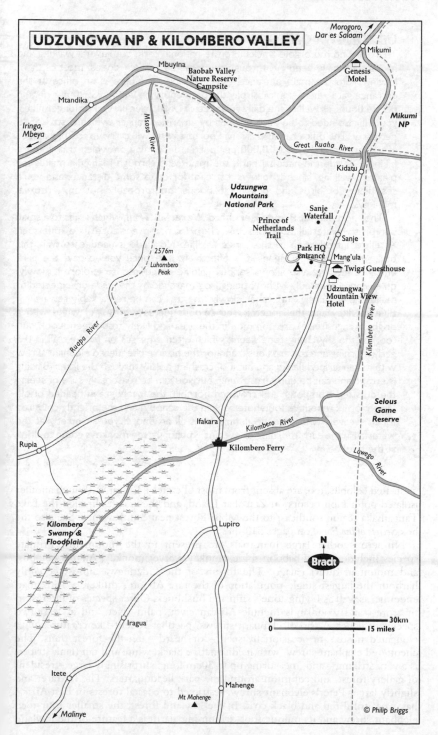

UDZUNGWA NP & KILOMBERO VALLEY

Morogoro, Dar es Salaam
Mikumi
Genesis Motel
Mikumi NP

Mbuyina
Baobab Valley Nature Reserve Campsite

Mtandika

Iringa, Mbeya

Msoso River

Great Ruaha River

Kidatu

Udzungwa Mountains National Park

Sanje Waterfall

Prince of Netherlands Trail

Park HQ entrance

Sanje

Mang'ula

Twiga Guesthouse

2576m
Luhombero Peak

Udzungwa Mountain View Hotel

Kilombero River

Ruapa River

Selous Game Reserve

Ifakara

Kilombero River

Kilombero Ferry

Luwego River

Rupia

Kilombero Swamp & Floodplain

Lupiro

N

Bradt

0   30km
0   15 miles

Iragua

Itete

Mahenge

Malinye

Mt Mahenge

© Philip Briggs

UDZUNGWA ON FOOT

There are no motorable tracks into the national park, but several walking and hiking trails have been cut through the forested eastern slopes, most of them leaving from the main entrance gate at Mang'ula. There is an office at the entrance gate where you must pay the park entrance fee of US$20 per person per 24 hours, as well as the daily guide fee of US$10 per party. For longer hikes, you will also need to be accompanied by an armed ranger, which costs US$25 per party. The office can also arrange porters, who will carry up to 20kg apiece at a charge of Tsh5,000–10,000 per porter depending on which trail you are hiking. Outside the national park, the main road through Mang'ula makes for pleasant walking, since it follows a stream for quite some distance, and you'll see plenty of birds and possibly baboons, but probably not any arboreal monkeys.

The short and flat **Prince Bernhard Waterfall Trail**, which leads to a small but pretty waterfall no more than 1km from the entrance gate, offers an excellent introduction to the park's wildlife. No guide is needed to walk this trail, which not only means it is effectively free once you've paid the park entrance fee, but also allows serious wildlife enthusiasts to explore it slowly, quietly and repeatedly without being frog-marched by the guide or expected to make idle chit-chat. And, taken slowly, the trail can be remarkably rewarding. Blue monkey and the endemic red colobus (actually grey and white with a bright orange fringe) are common in the area and likely to be seen. Look out, too, for the shy Livingstone's suni, which often emerges on to the trail in the early morning and towards dusk, and for the bizarre chequered elephant shrew with its tan striped flanks and habit of crashing noisily through the litter. Birding is erratic and can be quite frustrating, but you can be reasonably sure of seeing the outsized trumpeter and crowned hornbill, the lovely green-headed oriole (listen for its repetitive four-note song in the canopy) and the brightly coloured forest weaver, whose gentle fluting call is all around. If you sit quietly at the waterfall in the early morning or evening, you might see monkeys come to drink at the pool below it.

west. Red colobus, too, are absent from most of eastern Tanzania, though another isolated population occurs on Zanzibar Island, and they range through the Lake Tanganyika region southeast to the Mbisi Forest near Sumbawanga. See also the box *Secrets of the Forest* on pages 510–11.

Numerous other large mammals are present in the mountains. Primate species include yellow baboon, blue monkey, vervet monkey, Angola colobus, and mountain dwarf galago. The forests of the Udzungwa almost certainly harbour the largest single population of the rare Abbott's duiker, a Tanzanian endemic, as well as Livingstone's suni and bushbuck. Other species of interest in the forest and woodlands include African civet, palm civet, and at least two species of genet. A trio of elephant shrews, peculiar rodent-like creatures with elongated noses, are occasionally seen – or heard – on the forest trails. The chequered elephant shrew, with its distinctive black, white and tan flank stripes, is a very striking – and, measuring up to 30cm long, surprisingly large – resident of gallery forest, and common around the park headquarters. The far rarer and slightly larger Peter's elephant shrew, restricted to coastal forests in East Africa, has a beautiful red and black coat. In the lowland forest, the smaller four-toed elephant shrew and its unique foot-drumming alarm is a feature of the lowland

The most popular guided hike is the **Sanje Waterfall Trail**, a round trip of at least four hours' duration leading to the Sanje Waterfall, in fact a series of falls that plunge more than 300m down over three separate stages, with a pool at the base where swimming is permitted. This trail offers excellent forest birding, and you can be practically sure of seeing the endemic red colobus as well as black-and-white colobus. The Sanje crested mangabey was first heard by researchers in the vicinity of the waterfall, but it is not normally resident in the area, and is unlikely to be seen by casual visitors. The area around the waterfall is legendarily rich in butterflies, including several endemic taxa, with activity typically peaking from mid-morning to mid-afternoon. Visitors with a vehicle have the option of using a shorter trail, by driving back along the Mikumi road towards the Sanje Ranger Post, which lies a couple of hundred metres below the base of the waterfall. Alternatively, if the above trail seems too daunting, the shorter **Sonjo Trail** is about half the length, usually takes around three hours to cover, and passes two smaller waterfalls.

The longest existing hike is the **Mwanihana Trail**, a 38km circuit to Mwanihana Peak, at 2,150m the second-highest point in the range, that normally takes three days to complete with two nights spent camping on the mountain. This is the only trail that exposes visitors to the closed canopy montane forest and grassland habitats of the range's higher slopes. As such, it provides the best chance within the national park of encountering the endemic mangabey, the rare Abbott's duiker, larger mammals such as buffalo and elephant, as well as some of the more interesting birds. Prospective hikers will need to have their own camping gear, and to carry all the food they will need. An armed ranger is mandatory, due to the presence of potentially dangerous animals, and a porter is recommended if you want to make the most of the hike.

The park headquarters can also arrange visits to a traditional healer for Tsh5,000 per party, and are in the process of opening up several new trails to various traditional shrines, caves and other sites of interest in the national park.

forest after dark, especially on dry nights when the leaf litter makes more noise. Udzungwa fringes the Mikumi-Selous ecosystem, and a number of typical savannah and woodland species are resident – or regularly pass through – the dry corridor in its rain shadow: lion, elephant, leopard, buffalo, sable antelope, lesser kudu, aardwolf, white-tailed mongoose and Senegal galago.

The Udzungwa Mountains are particularly alluring to birdwatchers, with more than 400 species recorded in the national park and/or the various forest reserves, including at least 25 of the 32 species unique to the Tanzania-Malawi Endemic Bird Area. Tanzanian endemics and species that generate a high degree of interest among visiting birdwatchers are the Nduk eagle-owl, dappled mountain robin, spot-throat, Swynnerton's robin, white-chested alethe, white-winged apalis, Chapin's apalis, banded green sunbird, Usambara weaver and Kipengere seedeater. Three bird species, the Iringa akalat, rufous-winged sunbird and Udzungwa forest partridge, are often cited as endemic to the Udzungwa Mountains. The akalat has in fact been recorded in a handful of other forests and the partridge was recently discovered in the remote Rubeho Mountains, but Udzungwa is certainly the main stronghold for all three species. It should be noted that several of the more interesting birds of Udzungwa are more-or-less absent from the eastern footslopes as passed through by the day trails out of the park headquarters. Dedicated birdwatchers are advised to skip the national park in favour of the forest reserve on the western side of the mountains – accessible from Iringa (see pages 517–25) – for a realistic chance of seeing the Udzungwa specials.

Despite its ecological significance, Udzungwa Mountains National Park remains a somewhat esoteric destination, though interest has definitely picked up over the last few years, and we saw a couple of tour groups hanging around when we last visited the park. For tourists exploring the southern safari circuit by road, the park makes for a straightforward day trip or overnight excursion from Mikumi, and there are now a couple of low-key but affordable hotels situated

SECRETS OF THE FOREST

Until recently, the Udzungwa Mountains and environs were poorly known to scientists, certainly by comparison with the more accessible Usambara or Uluguru ranges. The main reason for this is that early biological exploration in the Udzungwa concentrated on more developed and easily accessible parts of the central and southern plateau. Forests visited were mostly secondary with widespread Afro-montane species. Only in more recent times have researchers visited the primary forests along the eastern escarpment, resulting in a flurry of recent new discoveries.

The endemic **rufous-winged sunbird**, for instance, was first described in 1984, while the **Udzungwa forest partridge** was discovered as recently as 1991. The story behind the discovery of the partridge is that two Danish biologists working in the mountains noticed an unusual pair of feet swimming in a chicken stew that had been prepared for them by a local cook. The next day, a local guide snared them another 'wild chicken', and it turned out to be an unknown fowl more closely related to the forest partridges of Asia than to any African bird. Placed in its own genus, the Udzungwa forest partridge is now recognised to be the sole representative of a otherwise extinct lineage that dates back more than 15 million years, when the forests of East Africa and Asia were probably linked to each other via the Middle Eastern coast.

The endemic **Sanje crested mangabey** was unknown to Western science until 1979, and the circumstance of its discovery by the ecologists Katherine Homewood and Alan Rodgers illustrates just how little attention the area had previously received from biologists. Homewood, studying the red colobus at Sanje waterfall while suffering from a fever, heard a distinctly mangabey-like whooping call. At first she thought she was hallucinating with fever or that Rodgers was somewhere nearby playing a recording of a mangabey call as a joke. But Homewood's guide Langson recognised the call as that of a monkey and known locally as n'golaga, and different to a baboon or red colobus. The next day, Langson led the researchers to a troop of monkeys sitting high in the canopy, and their suspicion was confirmed: these were definitely a type of mangabey, furthermore one significantly different in appearance to the closest population, which lives about 1,000km further north on Kenya's Tana River. Langson, incredulous that this large monkey, with its loud and distinctive call, could have been overlooked by other wazungu, casually mentioned that an orphaned n'golaga was resident in Sanje village on the main Ifakara–Mikumi road. The excited researchers rushed to the village, and there they were able to photograph the tame young

close to the park entrance. The eastern footslopes can easily be explored using a limited network of guided and unguided day trails (see box *Udzungwa on Foot*, pages 508–9), with a good chance of encountering the endemic red colobus. Disappointingly, however, the higher slopes can only be reached along more arduous overnight trails, and there is no accommodation set within the forest (aside from the national park campsites). For these logistical reasons, I would have to recommend Amani Nature Reserve (which has accommodation in the thick of the Eastern Usambara forest and boasts a far superior network of trails) over Udzungwa to first-time visitors to Tanzania seeking an introduction to the Eastern Arc forests.

mangabey, which clearly belonged to an undescribed race or species. Twenty years after it was discovered, the Sanje crested mangabey had the dubious distinction of being the solitary East African species included on a list of the world's 25 most threatened primate taxa compiled by the IUCN Primate Specialist Group.

While the endemic birds and mammals tend to receive the greatest attention, the abrupt recent decline in the population of an amphibian endemic to the Udzungwa illustrates how precarious the situation of a range-restricted species can be. One of seven species in a genus of toads endemic to Tanzania, the yellow-streaked **Kihansi spray toad**, is so tiny that an adult can fit on a human fingernail, and unusual among amphibians in that it does not lay eggs, but rather gives birth to a brood of live miniatures. The extremely localised range of the Kihansi spray toad is a unique 20,000m^2 ferny habitat – which also contains three plant species found nowhere else – sustained by the spray from a single series of waterfalls on the Kihansi River. When the toad was first discovered in 1996, the population was estimated to stand at more than 10,000. Subsequently, something like 90% of the river's water has been diverted to feed a government hydroelectric dam that generates a third of the nation's electricity supply, and the formerly substantial waterfall has been reduced to a quiet trickle. As a result, the toad's unique habitat was temporarily reduced to about 5,000m^2, and by March 2001 the toad population had declined to perhaps 6,000 individuals. In the *East African* of August 20–26 2001, environmental writer Ann Outwater reported that the Tanzanian government responded to the toad's decline by supplementing the spray with piped sprinklers. It has also instituted a study to determine the toad's breeding and feeding requirements, with a long-term view to regulating the water flow into the hydro-electric scheme accordingly or to provide irrigation to the wetland habitat. Failing that, the only chance for the Kihansi spray toad would be to close the dam, a solution that can scarcely be considered viable given the importance of the hydro-electric scheme and the huge investment made into it.

On a more positive note, the list of Udzungwa endemics grows with practically every passing year, a prominent recent discovery being the **Matundu dwarf galago** *Galagoides udzungwensis* in 1996. Furthermore, three endemic species of bird have been discovered in the Kilombero Valley immediately southwest of Udzungwa in the last few years, and it has been noted that several Eastern Arc specials likely to occur within the Udzungwa Mountain National Park have yet to be actually recorded there. One can only guess at how many birds and other creatures endemic to the Udzungwa still await scientific discovery.

Fees and further information

The entrance fee of US$15 per person per 24 hours must be paid in hard currency. All but one of the walking trails attracts a mandatory guide fee of US$10 per party. An excellent source of background information about the park is the booklet *Udzungwa Mountains*, published in 1999 by the African Publishing Group in collaboration with TANAPA. In common with most other popular literature, this booklet is occasionally misleading, failing to distinguish clearly between the mountain range and the national park (the latter protecting only one-fifth of the former) or to stress the logistical limitations of exploring Udzungwa beyond a small part of the eastern foothills.

Getting there and away

The access road to Udzungwa National Park is the B127, which connects the town of Mikumi on the Tanzam Highway to Ifakara on the Tazara Railway over a distance of roughly 100km. The park can be approached either by road or by rail. Backpackers who are visiting the park as a round trip out of Dar es Salaam might think about arriving by rail and returning by road. The slow train from Dar to Ifakara passes through the Selous Game Reserve in daylight, and returning by road you will pass through Mikumi National Park.

In a private vehicle, the drive from Mikumi town to the park entrance gate at Mang'ula shouldn't take much longer than an hour (which means visitors seeking more comfortable accommodation than is available locally could visit Udzungwa as a day trip from one of the lodges in Mikumi National Park). The road to Udzungwa is clearly signposted out of Mikumi town, and it is surfaced as far as Kidatu (sometimes also referred to as Kilombero, the name of the adjacent sugar estate), which lies 37km south of Mikumi. South of Kidatu, the road passes through the village of Sanje after about 13km, then about 2km further on it passes the Sanje Ranger Post, the starting point for the short route to Sanje Waterfall. After another 10km or so, the road reaches Mang'ula, site of the main entrance gate and the park headquarters (signposted to the right) as well as two of the hotels listed below.

Getting to Udzungwa by bus used to be a rather hit-and-miss procedure involving long waits and a high probability of having to overnight in Kidatu. This is no longer the case; following recent improvements to the road as many as a dozen buses run between Mikumi and Ifakara daily, all of them passing the park entrance gate and lodges at Mang'ula. Many of these buses continue to (or come from) Morogoro or Dar es Salaam, but if you don't use a direct bus from one of these towns, the best place to pick up Ifakara-bound transport is at the junction in Mikumi town. The Zanil and Baraka buses are recommended.

All trains on the Tazara line stop at Ifakara, usually in the evening, which means you should plan on spending a night in Ifakara (covered later in the chapter).

Where to stay
Moderate
Udzungwa Mountain View Hotel Tel: 023 262 0466; fax: 023 262 0443. Affiliated to the Genesis Hotel in Mikumi, and very similar in standard, this comfortable small hotel lies on the Ifakara road only ten minutes' walk from Mang'ula and the Udzungwa park headquarters. Self-contained doubles cost Tsh10,000 per person including a full English breakfast. The restaurant has a varied menu, with most dishes costing Tsh5,500. The management can organise day trips and hikes into the adjacent national park.
Sanje Waterfall Hotel Tel: 023 262 0466; fax: 023 262 0443. Situated close to Sanje village about halfway between Mang'ula and Kidatu, this is a new place run by the same

people who own the Udzungwa Mountain View. It was functioning as a bar and restaurant only in late 2001, but rooms are under construction and should be operating by the time you read this.

Budget

Twiga Hotel Situated in Mang'ula about 500m from the park entrance gate, this excellent budget hotel was reputedly constructed in the 1970s to house Chinese contractors involved in the construction of the Tazara Railway. Now privately owned, it has taken on a new lease of life in recent years thanks to its proximity to the national park. Clean self-contained double rooms, with two beds, netting, a fan, and an erratic water supply, cost Tsh5,000. There is a satellite television in the bar, and the large garden area is dotted with summerhouses and offers a view of the mountains. The restaurant serves decent meals such as chicken casserole or pepper steak for around Tsh2,000, and it will also prepare sandwiches for hikers needing some lunchtime sustenance.

Shoestring

There is no shoestring accommodation in the immediate vicinity of the park entrance gate, but numerous cheap local lodges can be found in Kidatu. The best of these is the **Lobore Guesthouse**, which charges Tsh4,000 for a self-contained double and Tsh2,500/3,000 for a single/double using common showers. Similarly priced alternatives include **Mkanga Guesthouse**, **Stop Over Lodge** and **Maryland Lodge**.

Camping

A series of campsites has been cut into the forest along the stream immediately uphill of the park headquarters at Mang'ula. The campsites are very atmospheric, but as usual they lack any facilities other than a dirty long-drop toilet, and, given the affordability of hotel rooms in Mang'ula, are unlikely to attract any but the most dedicated of campers at US$20 per person.

SOUTH OF UDZUNGWA

Few travellers ever make it to Udzungwa National Park, and fewer still follow the B127 further south to Ifakara, the springboard for an adventurous foray into the little-known Kilombero Valley and remote town of Mahenge on the mountain of the same name. With three recently discovered bird species endemic to the Kilombero Valley, this untrammelled area is of particular interest to birdwatchers, but – bordering the Selous Game Reserve – it also supports a diverse mammal fauna. Although Ifakara, Mahenge and the section of the Kilombero River along the road between them are all perfectly accessible on public transport, the area is best explored in a private vehicle or on one of the organised safaris recently initiated by Tembowengi (more details below).

Ifakara

The substantial but somewhat unfocused town of Ifakara sprawls from the banks of the Umena River, a tributary of the Kilombero, roughly 100km south of Mikumi by road and about 40km south of the entrance to the Udzungwa National Park. The main local point of interest, about 5km south of the town centre, is the ferry crossing of the Kilombero River, discussed in further detail under the heading *Kilombero Valley* below. The town is also the site of an important station on the Tazara Railway, which stands isolated in an unconvincing patch of semi-suburbia about 5km from the town centre and 1.5km off the road back towards Udzungwa and Mikumi.

Getting there and away

To reach Ifakara in a private vehicle, follow the main road from Mikumi south past the Udzungwa entrance gate and Udzungwa Mountain View Hotel for about 40km. This stretch of road is not in the greatest condition, so you should allow about an hour for the drive. Regular buses run between Ifakara and Mikumi, passing through Mang'ula (the site of the Udzungwa entrance gate) and generally continuing to Morogoro and Dar es Salaam.

All trains along the Tazara line stop at Ifakara, but the slow trains are recommended for wildlife viewing, since they are scheduled to pass through the Selous Game Reserve during daylight. The Ifakara railway station, 5km from the town centre, looked pretty desolate when we passed by recently, but I'd assume that plenty of public transport and possibly taxis arrive there to meet any coming train. If not, the closest accommodation is at the New Sumi Guesthouse about 1km from the railway station along the feeder road to the main Ifakara–Mikumi road.

Where to stay
Budget and shoestring

Mack Guesthouse Tel: 023 202 5244. Probably the pick of a fairly indifferent bunch of local guesthouses, the Mack Guesthouse charges Tsh5,000 for a clean self-contained room with a large double bed, fan, and cold running water. The guesthouse lies on Sokoni Road, a block from the main Mikumi road about 1km back from the bus station, so if you're arriving by bus from Mikumi ask the conductor to drop you off at the junction (signposted for the Muyamba Guesthouse) before you arrive in the town centre.

Muyumba Guesthouse Tel: 023 261 0159. This clean but potentially noisy guesthouse charges Tsh2,000/3,000 for an adequate single/double using common showers, or Tsh3,000 for a self-contained room with a three-quarter bed, all with a fan. It is situated around the corner from the Mack, and the same advice applies for travellers arriving by bus.

Vunjo Guesthouse Spotless self-contained rooms with fan and net, good value at Tsh4,000 double. Also situated close to the Mack, if arriving by bus.

Goa II Guesthouse The only decent guesthouse in the town centre, this charges Tsh4,000 for a self-contained room with a double bed and fan. To get there from the main traffic circle and CCM Monument, follow the Mikumi road for about 200m, turn right into a side road opposite the main market, and then after another 100m turn right into Uhuru Road.

New Sumi Guesthouse This good value guesthouse lies about 4km from the town centre and 500m from the Mikumi road along the side road to the railway station. All rooms have a double bed, a fan and netting, and they cost Tsh3,000 using a common shower or Tsh4,000 self-contained.

Kilombero Valley

Flanked by the Udzungwa Mountains to the northwest and the Mahenge Massif to the southeast, the 4,000km^2 Kilombero Valley is a low-lying floodplain following the course of the Kilombero River (and various tributaries) before it flows into the Great Ruaha at Kidatu on the western boundary of Selous Game Reserve. Despite being accorded the relatively lowly conservation status of a Game Protected Area, the Kilombero Valley is the largest low-altitude wetland in East Africa, a significance that has recently been acknowledged with a proposal to designate it as Tanzania's second RAMSAR wetland site. Much of the wetland is seasonal, with the river being reduced to a 100m-wide flow for most of the year, but spilling over to become an extensive marsh during the wet season. During years of exceptional rain, this flooding might in places extend for up to 15–20km on either side of the main watercourse. There are also two extensive permanent swamps in the valley, one at Kibasira near the village of Mofu and the other in the far southwest on the Kihansi River.

Until recently accorded scant attention by biologists, and still today practically unknown within the safari industry, the Kilombero Valley is proof positive – should any be needed – of the quite extraordinary natural wealth and biodiversity contained within Tanzania. As a western extension of the greater Selous-Niassa ecosystem, it forms an important dry season feeding ground for local migrants such as elephant, of which up to 5,000 are estimated to congregate in the area at times. Large numbers of hippo, crocodile and buffalo are resident, and local researchers claim that the density of lions exceeds that of the Selous itself. Waterbuck and reedbuck are common on the floodplain, while areas of *brachystegia* woodland harbour herds of sable antelope and small parties of greater kudu. Most remarkable of all is the high density of the kob-like puku antelope, estimated to stand at around 50,000, about 70% of the total global population.

Kilombero made ornithological headlines in 1986 when a previously undescribed species of weaver was observed in the swamp. This was subsequently named the Kilombero weaver, and is illustrated in all recent East African field guides. Two further new species of bird in the genus *cisticola* have also been identified, though both await formal description and are as yet not illustrated in any field guide. (For identification purposes, the white-tailed or melodious cisticola is reputedly rather similar to the winding cisticola, while the Kilombero cisticola is allied to the black-lored cisticola and performs a similar duet during the breeding season). All three of these birds are thought to be endemic to the valley, and can be seen with relative ease if you know where to look. Aside from these endemics, the wetland supports an impressive variety of water-associated birds, notably open-billed stork, African skimmer, Madagascar squacco heron, Pel's fishing owl, half-collared kingfisher and coppery-tailed coucal. Nine species of plant, one amphibian and three reptiles are endemic to the area.

For backpackers, it would be difficult to get deep into the Kilombero Valley, but it's straightforward enough to take public transport or hire a bicycle out of Ifakara to the ferry jetty on the river 5km south of town. Hippos and crocs are likely to be seen here, as is a variety of birds, possibly even an endemic or two. There are also several boatmen around who will gladly take you out on the river, in the direction of Selous Game Reserve, where you stand a better chance of seeing big game – notably elephant – and a wider selection of birds. There's no fixed rate, but Tsh15,000 for a four-hour canoe trip seems to be the starting price. With a private 4WD vehicle, you could take the vehicle ferry across the river, carry on towards Mahenge for about 20km, and then turn right, arriving after 60km at Mtimbira, where there is an old Lutheran Mission with a guesthouse close to the widest part of the floodplain. Note that the status of the ferry is uncertain at the time of going to print, after it sank in April 2002, tragically killing 100 passengers.

Organised visits to Kilombero can be arranged with a recently established eco-tourism venture called Tembowengi – Swahili for 'Many Elephants' – which is based in Dar es Salaam and owned by a former volunteer who worked in the area for several years. The project is run in collaboration with local communities and will help to provide them with clean drinking water, education and medical assistance, thereby creating a local incentive to protect an environment that is starting to be affected adversely by subsistence poaching and the demands of an ever growing population. Safaris will include a night or two at the fishing village of Mikeregembe on the border of the Selous Game Reserve, where elephants are regularly seen from a specially constructed tree platform. They also involve camping at Mofu, on an animal rich part of the floodplain close to the permanent Kibasira Swamp. Activities include game drives, guided walks, canoe trips, and visits to traditional healers and modern dispensaries. A minimum of five days in recommended. Tel: 0744 481483; email: roy@tembowengi.com; web: www.tembowengi.com.

Mahenge

This remote small town lies about 80km south of Ifakara on the edge of an escarpment on Mount Mahenge, one of the smaller and less explored parts of the Eastern Arc formation. Surrounded by flowering green meadows, Mahenge comes as something of a relief climatically after the muggy lowlands, its breezy highland atmosphere underscored by the large gleaming white Swiss-style mission church and attached technical training college. The surrounding countryside could offer some interesting walking possibilities, with an estimated 300km^2 of natural forest still surviving on the slopes of the mountain, though nothing has been developed for tourism at the time of writing.

In 1905, the German fort at Mahenge was the site of what is regarded to have been the pivotal battle of the Maji-Maji rebellion. Led by a spirit medium, several thousand followers of the movement marched on to the fort, practically unarmed, since they believed that the magic water would render them immune to bullet fire. The German soldiers waited until the rebels were within firing range, and then launched a twin machine-gun attack on the marching masses, cutting down the deluded warriors row by row until eventually the survivors fled in retreat. Hundreds of rebels were killed or wounded in the attack, and as word of the calamitous engagement spread around the colony, the rebellion gradually subsided.

The road between Ifakara and Mahenge is not in the greatest condition, and it involves a ferry-crossing at the Kilombero River 5km south of Ifakara, so the drive in a private 4WD will take at least two hours in total. Buses leave regularly between the two towns, sometimes taking some time to fill up with passengers, and the actual journey is three to four hours in duration. There is at least one place to stay in Mahenge, the **Original Pogoro Guesthouse** (tel: 023 262 0386). The **McDonald Bar** has been recommended for snacks, drinks and local travel advice.

BAOBAB VALLEY RUAHA RIVER CAMPSITE

This recently established 700km^2 private conservancy, transected by the Tanzam Highway about 50km west of Mikumi town, already provides an alluringly affordable alternative to the nearby national parks, and it seems destined to become a very popular fixture on the backpacker and overlander circuit when fully developed. Abutting the western border of Udzungwa National Park, Baobab Valley protects a dry woodland habitat reminiscent more of Ruaha or Tarangire National Parks than the forests associated with the Eastern Arc mountains. The conservancy is set in a magnificent stretch of the valley carved by the Great Ruaha River, with steep slopes studded with an astonishingly dense concentration of eerie, ancient baobab trees. Plenty of wildlife is found in the area – notably greater and lesser kudu, a significant but seasonal elephant population, and even the odd large predator – and the birdlife is fantastic.

The campsite, open at the time of writing but still under development, is set about 2km from the main road in the lush riparian woodland fringing the Great Ruaha. Facilities currently consist of a swimming pool, a bar and restaurant, and a spacious camping area amongst the baobabs, but rooms should be available by 2003. A day walking trail through the surrounding bush has already been cut, and long-term plans include overnight hikes, visits to a waterfall on the Udzungwa side of the river, and canoeing excursions. Camping costs US$3 per person and the rooms should be in the US$15–30 price range. Baobab Valley is clearly signposted from the main road and any bus heading between Mikumi and Iringa can drop you at the junction, from where it's 20 minutes' walk to the campsite. For further information, you can email the owners at baobab_valley@hotmail.com.

IRINGA

Perched at an elevation of around 1,500m on a small plateau above a steep escarpment rising to the north of the Tanzam Highway, Iringa is an important regional administrative centre with a population of around 145,000, making it the third-largest town in southern Tanzania after Morogoro and Mbeya. While it could scarcely be described as exciting, Iringa is an agreeable and interesting place to spend a couple of days in transit between Dar es Salaam and Mbeya. In addition to offering great views over the Ruaha Valley, the compact town centre is studded with old German and Asian buildings centred around the old market, an excellent place to buy the rugs and baskets for which the region is famed. Majumba Street, the main trading road, is also very colourful and lively. Rather more sombre is the German War Cemetery down the road from the Iringa Hotel.

Iringa is the principal town of the Hehe people, who provided perhaps the most sustained resistance of any local tribe to the German colonisation of the Tanzania interior (see box *Chief Mkwawa ahd Uhehe*, pages 522–3). The town's name is a corruption of the Hehe word *lilinga*, a reference to the large fort built by the Hehe Chief Mkwawa at Kalenga to the southwest of the modern town. Several interesting sites related to Mkwawa can be visited from Iringa, of which the closest, about 2km from the town centre past the Lutheran Guesthouse, is Gangilonga – 'Talking Rock' – where the chief used to meditate and hold conferences. Further afield, the Isimila Stone Age Site is not only of archaeological interest, but also lies close to some bizarre sandstone formations. Iringa is best known to tourists as the springboard for road safaris into the Ruaha National Park.

Getting there and away

Iringa town centre lies about 2km north of the Tanzam Highway along a steep ascent road 310km southwest of Morogoro and 390km northeast of Mbeya – in a private vehicle allow four to five hours for either drive. On public transport, you can get to Iringa very easily from anywhere on the Tanzam Highway, but getting away is not quite so straightforward, as relatively few buses along the Tanzam Highway actually start their journey in Iringa. For this reason, and despite the apparent plethora of traffic in Iringa's busy bus station, it is advisable to book a seat on a bus departing from Iringa on the day before you want to travel. Iringa is about nine hours from Dar es Salaam by bus.

Seats for Dodoma-bound buses should also be booked in advance. The road is terrible and the trip takes up to 12 hours.

Where to stay
Moderate
MR Hotel Tel: 026 270 2006; fax: 026 170 2661; email: mrhotel@costech.gm. The MR Hotel is the smartest hotel in Iringa, and while is doesn't conform to international standards, it is very clean and well run and has a good reputation. It is centrally located on Mkwawa Road, around the corner from the bus station, and has a decent restaurant serving international cuisine. Self-contained rooms with satellite television and a fan cost Tsh25,000/35,000.

Budget

Huruma Baptist Mission Guesthouse & Conference Centre Tel: 026 270 0184; fax: 027 270 0172; email: hbcc@maf.org.tz. Set in large green grounds studded with euphorbia trees about 2.5km from the town centre along Togwa Road, this mission guesthouse is popular with self-drive visitors to Iringa, but its location is rather inconvenient for those using public transport. The large self-contained rooms have hot running water, and despite smelling a tad musty, they are reasonable value at Tsh8,000/12,000 single/double B&B. Rooms with three, four or five beds are also available at Tsh15,500, 18,000 and 20,500 B&B respectively, while rooms with one double bed and a television cost Tsh12,500. Decent local meals are available from the canteen at Tsh12,500. Alcohol and smoking are forbidden on the premises; hard drugs presumably get a firm thumbs down too.

Isimila Hotel Tel: 026 270 2605; fax: 026 270 2868. This clean and reasonably comfortable multi-storey hotel lies about ten minutes' walk from the bus station along the Dodoma road. The self-contained rooms with hot water are good value at Tsh7,500 for a single (with a double bed) or Tsh9,600 for a double (two beds). The one drawback is that there is no netting in most of the rooms, and the mosquitoes can be vicious. The ground-floor restaurant serves good food, mostly Indian dishes, for around Tsh2,500.

Iringa Hotel Formerly the government Railway Hotel (not that there's a railway station anywhere in Iringa), the Iringa Hotel has had a topsy-turvy time of it since being privatised a few years ago. It had literally just re-opened in late 2001, and was charging an eminently negotiable Tsh8,000 for a large and clean but rather dingy self-contained double with cold running water (hot water supplied by the bucket).

Embalasasa Motel This fairly smart new hotel, which lies on the main road around the corner from the bus station, feels a touch overpriced at Tsh8,000/12,000 for a self-contained single/double with a fan and net, but it is probably the most comfortable central option in this range.

Shoestring

Lutheran Centre Guesthouse Tel: 026 270 2286. This quiet church hostel, situated about ten minutes' walk from the bus station, may not have a madly convenient location, but it is nevertheless a long-standing favourite with backpackers, and is certainly the best value in its range. Small but reasonably clean rooms with nets cost Tsh1,700/2,500/3,000 single/double/triple using common showers, while a self-contained single (with a double bed) costs Tsh3,000. Dormitory beds are available at Tsh1,000 per head.

Staff Inn White House Lodge The best of several cheapies dotted around the bus station, this lodge charges Tsh4,000/5,000 for a clean single/double room using a common shower.

Ruaha International Hotel Another good local guesthouse, situated off the Dodoma Road about ten minutes' walk from the bus station, this place charges Tsh2,500/4,000 for a single/double using common showers or Tsh4,000/4,500 for a self-contained single/double. The location is very quiet, and so too is the hotel, except over weekends when the central courtyard is sometimes transformed into a loud disco – it's probably worth checking out whether it's a party night before you commit to taking a room.

Countryside Hotel Situated in a green compound 500m from the Tanzam Highway, along a signposted turn-off about 1km towards Mbeya from the main junction to Iringa town centre, this small hotel is only really convenient for travellers with their own transport. It is probably better value that anything in town, however, charging Tsh6,000 for a large self-contained room with a double bed, or Tsh5,000 for a smaller room with a three-quarter bed. Contrary to what the signpost reads, camping is not available.

Camping

Riverside Campsite Tel: 026 272 5280; email: masumba@twiga.com. This attractively rustic campsite lies along a pretty stretch of the Little Ruaha River, some 13km from Iringa and

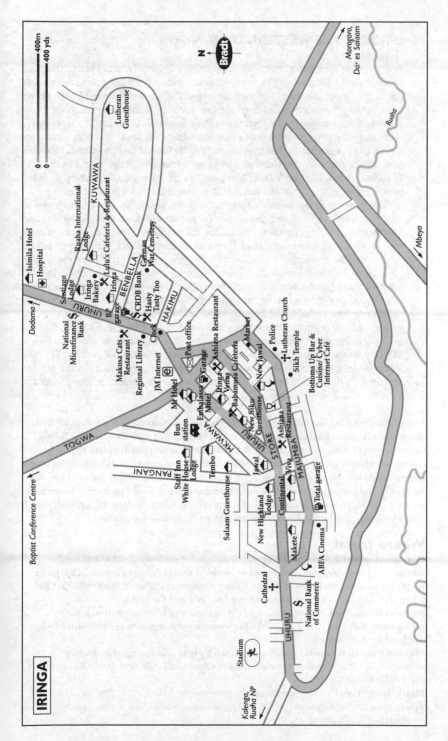

IRINGA

N

Bradt

0 400m
0 400yds

Baptist Conference Centre

Dodoma

TOGWA

Staff Inn
White House
Lodge

Tembo

PANGANI

Salaam Guesthouse

New Highland
Lodge

Continental

Makete

Cathedral

National Bank
of Commerce

Stadium

UHURU

Kalenga,
Ruaha NP

Bus
station

Mr Hotel

Embalasasa
Motel

Jawal

Viva

Total garage

ABFA Cinema

MKWAWA

UHURU

STORE

MAJUMBA

Ashiana
Restaurant

Baibamusa Cafeteria

Iringa
Venus

New Siku
Guesthouse

New Jawal

Market

Ashiana Restaurant

JM Internet

Regional Library

Makosa Cats
Restaurant

Clock

Post office

Garage

National
Microfinance
Bank

UHURU

BP
garage

Santiago
Lodge

Isimila Hotel
Hospital

Iringa
Bakery

CRDB Bank

HAKIMU

BENBELLA

Lulu's Cafeteria & Restaurant

Ruaha International
Lodge

KUWAWA

Lutheran
Guesthouse

Hasty
Tasty Too

German
War Cemetery

Police

Lutheran Church

Sikh Temple

Bottoms Up Bar &
Cuisine/ Cyber
Internet Café

Morogoro,
Dar es Salaam

Ruaha

Mbeya

Ruaha

BIRDING THE WESTERN UDZUNGWA
David Moyer

A reasonable assumption made by many birders visiting Tanzania is that the place to seek out the Udzungwa Mountain endemics and near endemics is in the national park. This is not the case. Although birding in the eastern forests of the national park is very rewarding, and key species such as rufous-winged sunbird and Swynnerton's robin might be seen above Sanje waterfall, the most alluring endemic – Udzungwa partridge – has yet to be recorded in this area. The best chance for seeing that species, and other specialities, is in the forests on Luhombero Mountain (the tallest point in the national park) and Ndundulu Ridge and Nyumbanitu Mountain in the adjacent West Kilombero Forest Reserve, all of which lie in the western part of the range and not realistically approached from Mang'ula.

The gateway to the western forests, Udekwa, lies three hours from Iringa by road – much longer during the rains. To get to Udekwa, follow the Tanzam Highway out of Iringa towards Mikumi for 45km to Ilulu, then ask for the turning to Udekwa and follow this road for two to three hours. Ask for directions whenever you encounter a junction as there are no signposts. The best time to go looking for the forest birds is from September to early December; I would advise against going there from mid-December to April. Before visiting, a permit (Tsh 5,000 per day) must be obtained from the Regional Catchment Forestry Office in Iringa; tel: 026 270 2246/0175; email: memairinga@twiga.com.

In Udekwa, report to the village government office near the school. Ask the village chairman or secretary to assist with the selection of porters. Never select porters on your own! If anything goes wrong, you will not receive help from the village government. I usually then make an agreement for the porters to come to the Chui Campsite (7km into the forest reserve at the end of the

about 1.5km from the Tanzam Highway in the direction of Morogoro. More than 300 bird species have been recorded in the vicinity, with the elusive African finfoot and Pel's fishing owl both present along the river, and guided bird walks (the property is owned by one of the country's leading ornithologists) are offered for Tsh8,000 per person. Horse-riding excursions and mountain bike hire can also be arranged. Camping costs Tsh2,500 per person. There is a bar on site, and firewood is available, but visitors must bring all food with them. The campsite is clearly signposted from the main road. If you're driving, take care along the approach road. If you're walking, expect it to take 15–20 minutes to get there from the junction.

Where to eat

Bottoms-Up Bar & Cuisine This lively first-floor bar on Store Road boasts satellite television, a pool table, and a good stock of alcoholic drinks. The restaurant, in a separate room, has an extensive menu of Indian, Chinese and other dishes in the Tsh2,500–3,500 range. The service isn't the quickest, but the food is about the best in town.

Ashiana Restaurant Two restaurants of this name are to be found in Iringa, both presumably under the same ownership. Both serve a good selection of inexpensive Indian and local meals and snacks.

Makosa Cats Restaurant Formerly the Hoteli Ya Kati, this rather seedy-looking restaurant on Uhuru Road serves a selection of Continental, Chinese and Indian dishes in the Tsh2,500–3,000 range.

Hasty Tasty Too This long-serving eatery opposite the Makosa Cats Restaurant serves a variety of tasty and inexpensive stews, juices and Indian snacks, but is closed in the evenings and on Sundays.

motorable track) very early the next morning and I start the expedition from there. This may no longer be necessary once a planned village campsite – which will ensure that the villagers get some revenue from tourist visits – is built near the ranger post 4km from Udekwa.

From Udekwa or Chui, you can go to one of two campsites. The most accessible is in Luala Valley, a grassy glade in the forested Ndundulu ridge. Luala is at an altitude of 1,900m and it can be very cold at night, down to 2°C, especially from June to August. Take good rain-gear as it can rain during any month up there. Luala is a five- to six-hour walk from Chui Campsite, very steep and tiring in places. After about one-and-a-half hours, you enter the forest and head up the ridge along a path that offers good birding. From Luala, the forest trails to the northeast toward Luhombero Mountain are a good place to find Udzungwa partridge and rufous-winged sunbird.

Alternatively, you can also go to Mufu Camp, where the partridge was originally discovered. This is about a six-hour walk from Chui, also quite steep. The Mufu camp is right in the middle of the forest and dappled mountain robin, Iringa akalat, Swynnerton's robin, Nduk eagle owl and Udzungwa partridge can be seen around the camp.

Organised birding safaris to the Western Udzungwa can be arranged through Masumbo. The cost will depend on what the visitors require. Masumbo can simply supply a bird guide and arrange permits and porters. Or they can deal with the whole safari from arrival in Dar es Salaam to departure, including all logistical arrangements, tents, food, etc – and visits to other key birding sites in Tanzania as specified. On tours led by Masumbo most of the species that birders will want to see are virtually guaranteed. For more details, contact Masumbo directly; tel: 026 272 5280; email: masumbo@masumbo.co.tz.

Lulu's Café & Restaurant This pleasant café in the back streets off Uhuru Road is recommended for snacks, light meals and ice-cream, eaten indoors or on the garden patio. Opening hours are 09.00 to 15.30 and 08.30 to 21.00 Monday to Saturday.

General information
Foreign exchange Cash and travellers' cheques can be converted to local currency at the National Bank of Commerce on Uhuru Road during normal banking hours. No private foreign exchange facilities exist in Iringa.

Internet The excellent Cyber Internet Centre on Store Road below the Bottoms-Up Bar, which charges Tsh1,500 for an hour online, has about a dozen computers and works on a quick server, and it stays open until 21.00.

Excursions from Iringa
Kalenga
This small village on the banks of the Ruaha was the site of Mkwawa's fortified capital before it was destroyed by German cannon fire in 1894. A small site museum in the village houses Mkwawa's bullet-shattered skull and several of his personal effects, including some of his clubs, spears and guns. Outside the museum stand the tombs of Mkwawa's son and grandson, Chief Sapi Mkwawa and Adam Sapi Mkwawa, the latter famous in his own right as the first Speaker of Parliament in independent Tanzania. About 500m from the museum is another tomb, that of the German Commander Erich Maas who died in the battle for Kalenga.

CHIEF MKWAWA AND UHEHE

The area around Iringa is known as Uhehe: homeland of the Hehe, the dominant regional military force during the late 19th century (the name Hehe derives from the warriors' feared *hee-hee* battle cry) and the most successful in initially resisting German colonisation. The Hehe Empire probably started to take shape in 1850 under Chief Munyigumba, who gradually asserted his control over about 100 *ntemi* chieftaincies to forge a centralised polity ruled from his capital at Lungemba, 10–15km south of modern-day Iringa. The formation of Uhehe coincided with a widespread trend towards centralisation in the Tanzanian interior, a phenomenon that is widely attributed to the new threat posed by militant Ngoni warriors coming from the south, and the economic opportunities created by the arrival of the slave caravans from the coast.

Chief Munyigumba died in 1879 (the tree under which he was reputedly buried can still be seen at Lungemba), prompting a violent secession dispute. Local tradition has it that Munyigumba appointed his younger brother Muhalwike as his chosen successor, or failing that asked that the empire be divided between his two eldest sons. Instead, Munyigumba's son-in-law Mwamubambe seized the throne by force, and had Muhalwike and one of the chosen royal sons killed for good measure. The other son, only 21 years old at the time, was forced into exile. Unfortunately for Mwamubambe, he had little popular support, and the Hehe elders conspired with the exiled heir to overthrow him. Mwamubambe and 1,000 of his warriors were killed in battle at a place now known as Lundamatwe – 'where skulls are heaped'.

Munyigumba's only surviving heir was appointed Chief of the Hehe, and he took on (or subsequently acquired) the throne name Mkwawa, reputedly a diminutive form of Mukwavinyika – 'the conqueror of lands'. Mkwawa made his capital at Kalenga, 15km west of present-day Iringa, from where he embarked on a series of military campaigns to expand the empire he had inherited into territories traversed by the trade caravans from the coast. By doing so, Mkwawa was able to extract substantial levies from the passing caravans, as well as selling enemies captured in battle to the slave traders. Within a decade of Mkwawa assuming power, the military prowess of the Hehe and tactical skills of their young chief had acquired legendary status among follower and foe alike.

In 1888, as Mkwawa continued to expand his territory ever coastward, Germany was securing its first permanent foothold on the East African mainland at Bagamoyo. Initially, the Germans had little interest in the interior, preoccupied as they were with asserting their legitimacy at the coast. By 1891, however, Germany had not only quelled a series of coastal rebellions, but it had also gained nominal custody over the interior of modern-day Tanzania by treaty with Britain. Mkwawa, aware of these ominous developments, mobilised his army, at the same time announcing that Uhehe would remain an independent state irrespective of the lines drawn on maps in Europe. Germany, meanwhile, recognised that Mkwawa, more even than Chief Mirambo of Nyamwezi, was likely to prove the most formidable obstacle to actualising its nominal rule over the interior.

In July 1891, the German Commissioner Emil von Zelewski led a formidably armed expedition of 13 German officers and 570 Africans troops and porters into Uhehe. The German troops burned down several Hehe villages as they entered the territory, and shot dead the three envoys that Mkwawa had sent to open negotiations. Mkwawa took this second act to be an open declaration of war, and – quietly keeping tabs on the German progress – he set a trap for the invaders at a rocky gorge on the Little Ruaha River near Lugalo, 15km east of Iringa. On August 17, as Zelewski and his troops set up camp, some 3,000 Hehe warriors armed with spears and a few guns suddenly surged across the shallow river, closing in on the German troops to enforce hand-to-hand combat. Within 15 minutes, Zelewski and all but three of the German officers and 140 of the Africans under his command lay dead. Mkwawa was able to boost his armoury by making off with hundreds of rifles and many rounds of ammunition. A monument to Zelewski and the other slain officers still stands at Lugalo today.

Following this victory, Mkwawa set about fortifying Kalenga, by raising a 4m-high stone enclosure around the royal village, and surrounding that with a deep trench. He also tormented the Germans by launching the odd surprise attack on their positions, on one occasion wiping out an entire garrison at Kondoa. The Germans lusted for revenge but bided their time, seeking to isolate Uhehe by forging alliances with neighbouring chiefs who were unsympathetic to Mkwawa. By doing this, they were able to approach Kalenga from an unexpected angle and to take Mkwawa by surprise. On October 28 1894, the Germans set a row of cannons high on a hill above Kalenga, and bombarded the fortified capital for two days, before descending to the fort to engage in hand-to-hand combat pitting their bayonets against the Hehe spears. The Germans easily took possession of the fort, then destroyed the ammunition store, and confiscated the chief's stockpiles of ivory and guns.

Mkwawa proved to be more elusive. Having fled Kalenga when defeat became inevitable, Mkwawa spent the next four years roaming through Uhehe, inflicting occasional guerrilla attacks on various German garrisons. His success in evading the Germans can be attributed to the loyalty of his subjects, who refused to give away his position. No German knew what Mkwawa looked like, and even when the German Governor offered a reward of 5,000 rupees for Mkwawa's head, it was to no avail. The chief's luck eventually ran out on June 19 1898, while encamped at Mlambalasi, 50km west of Iringa. A German garrison surrounded the camp, and Mkwawa, facing certain defeat, opted to shoot himself rather than be taken captive.

The German sergeant who arrived at the fatal scene unceremoniously cut off Mkwawa's head and took it to Iringa. Mkwawa's decapitated corpse was buried at Mlambalasi, but his skull was taken to the Bremen Anthropological Museum in Germany. There it would remain until 1954, when – 56 years to the day after Mkwawa's death – Sir Edward Twining handed it over to Mkwawa's grandson, Chief Adam Sapi Mkwawa. Until 1998, the skull was displayed rather unceremoniously at the Mkwawa Museum in Kalenga. On the centenary of Mkwawa's death, the skull was finally returned to Mlambalasi to be interred alongside the chief's body, and a memorial to the chief – still widely revered in Tanzania for his role in resisting colonisation – was unveiled. Travellers who wish to see the memorial can reach it along an 11km road signposted to the right 40km out of Iringa en route to Ruaha National Park.

For further information, check out the website www.mkwawa.com, which describes several sites associated with Chief Mkwawa and includes several photos.

The museum caretaker will happily take you around the village, which seems pretty unremarkable to the untrained eye, but is in fact dotted with remnants of Mkwawa's capital: the remains of fortified walls, the mound used by the chief to address his people, and the foundations of his home. The caretaker will also point out the ridge from where the Germans unleashed the barrage of cannon fire that destroyed the capital. This hill has since become known as Tosamaganga (throwing stones), and is now the site of a quaint 1930s' Italian mission.

Pick-up trucks to Tosamaganga and Kalenga leave Iringa every hour or so. They wait for passengers at the end of the surfaced road 200m past Samora Stadium. At Kalenga you will be dropped off next to the market; it is a five-minute meander through the village from there to the museum. Keep asking for directions. If your Swahili is limited, asking for Mkwawa will get you further than asking for a museum.

Isimila Stone Age Site

Situated some 22km south of Iringa off the Tanzam Highway, the seasonal Isimila watercourse, which generally only flows after very heavy rain, has yielded one of the richest assemblages of Stone Age tools known anywhere in the world. The significance of the site was first recognised by a local schoolboy who collected two rucksacks full of stone implements, amongst them a 40cm-long axe weighing 4kg, in 1951. The site was first excavated in 1957–58 by Dr Howell and Mr Cole of the Chicago University, and again over 1969–70 by Drs Keller and Hansen of the University of Illinois.

The reason why the watercourse at Isimila has yielded such a wealth of ancient tools is that it cuts through a series of sediment layers deposited on the bed of a shallow lake or marsh that flourished for a few thousand years before drying out perhaps 60,000 years ago. The majority of the tools unearthed at the site date from when the lake was active and its shore was inhabited by Stone Age hunter-gatherer settlements. The tools are not the oldest known from East Africa – similar implements of half a million years old have been found at Olduvai Gorge and other sites – but they do form an unusually varied and numerous showcase of late Acheulean-culture workmanship. The site museum houses a selection of these tools, including several pear-shaped hand-axes, as well as picks, cleavers, hammers and cutting stones.

The site has also thrown up the fossilised bones of several large mammals, giving a good impression of what the area's large fauna must have looked like at the time. These include several extinct swine species, including a giant variety of pig far larger than any that survives today, one extinct antelope, and an ungulate closely related to the giraffe, but with large antlers and a relatively short neck. The fossilised bones and teeth of the extinct *Hippopotamus gorgops* – another extinct species with telescopic projecting eyes – are protected in a shelter on site.

Even if you have no interest in archaeology, Isimila is worth visiting for the scenic gully that lies ten minutes' walk away from the Stone Age Site. Within this gully are a number of striking sandstone pillars that were carved by an extinct river and stand up to 10m high, a scene that looks for all the world like the set of a Lilliputian cowboy movie.

Isimila lies about 2km from the Tanzam Highway along a turn-off signposted about 20km from Iringa in the direction of Mbeya. If you don't have private transport, you could hire a taxi from Iringa (expect to pay around Tsh12,000 for the round trip), or ask any bus heading south to drop you at the junction, from where it's a 20-minute walk to the archaeological site. Entrance to the site costs Tsh1,000, and an informative booklet written by Neville Chittick in 1972 is available for Tsh500. Drinks are available at the site. A campsite (with toilet and showers) and restaurant, under construction at the time of writing, are scheduled to open before the end of 2002.

Kisolanza Farm

This 1,000ha farm, which lies alongside the Tanzam Highway some 50km southwest of Iringa and 20km before Mafinga, is one of the most attractive places to break up the long road trip between Morogoro and Mbeya. Kisolanza Farm, owned by the same family for longer than 60 years, is divided more-or-less evenly between cultivation and natural vegetation, and its atmosphere and climate fall midway between the English countryside and the African bush. Guests can walk freely around the farm roads, from where an impressive checklist of 250 bird species has been recorded.

The smartest accommodation at Kisolanza consists of three self-contained cottages, set in the lushly flowering lawns of the Old Farm House, the original family residence. The cottages cost US$50 per person, inclusive of a home-cooked dinner and large breakfast in the main house. There are two campsites set about 1km from the main house, one aimed at overland trucks, the other at private campers, and both cost Tsh2,000 per person. Also available are a few self-catering wood-and-thatch chalets, which cost Tsh12,000 double. Campers and self-caterers can buy a variety of fresh farm produce – meat, eggs, vegetables but no dairy products – at the kiosk at the main gate. A picnic site has been set up for passing day visitors.

Kisolanza Farm and The Old Farm House are clearly signposted along the Tanzam Highway, to the left coming from Iringa. The Scandinavia Coaches between Dar es Salaam and Mbeya will drop and collect visitors at the gate. The email is kisolanza@cats-net.com.

Mufindi

This highland area to the south of Iringa, known for its tea production, has recently become accessible to tourists with the opening of the **Fox's Southern Highlands Lodge**. Lying at an altitude of greater than 2,000m, this homely lodge consists of eight log cabins and a two-storey stone-and-wood fishing lodge with a ground floor restaurant and upstairs bar and snooker room. The walls are covered with carved replicas of record rainbow trout, caught in the area through most of the last century, surrounding an enormous stone fireplace with a roaring fire that is lit all year round. There is excellent walking in the surrounding montane forest, which harbours similar species to those found in Udzungwa National Park minus the endemics, as well as some good drives and mountain biking opportunities. The lodge lies some 45km to the east of the Tanzam Highway, and can be reached from Iringa by following the Tanzam Highway towards Mbeya for 70km, then turning left at Mafinga. Transport can be arranged from Iringa or Mafinga for people without vehicles. The rate of US$65 per person sharing includes full board and all activities (guided forest walks, mountain biking, boating and swimming in lakes, horse riding and fishing for rainbow trout).

RUAHA NATIONAL PARK

Tanzania's second-largest national park extends over 10,300km² of wooded hills and open plains to the west of Iringa, and it lies at the core of a greater ecosystem, embracing six other protected areas including the contiguous Rungwa and Kizigo Game Reserves, that is five times larger. Ruaha is widely regarded by Tanzania's safari cognoscenti to be the country's best-kept game viewing secret (personally, I'd bestow this accolade on Katavi, which, if not the better reserve, is certainly the bigger secret), and it has unquestionably retained a compelling wilderness

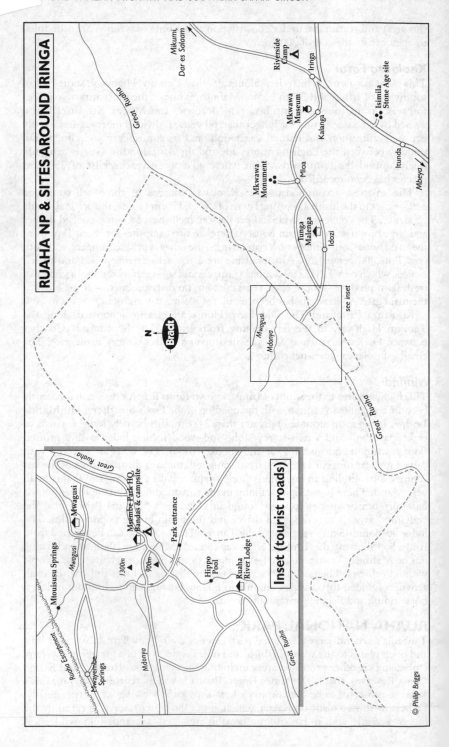

RUAHA NP & SITES AROUND IRINGA

Mikumi, Dar es Salaam

Great Ruaha

Riverside Camp

Iringa

Mkwawa Museum

Kalanga

Isimila Stone Age site

Itunda

Mbeya

Mkwawa Monument

Mloa

Tunga Malenga

Idozi

see inset

N

Bradt

Mwagusi

Mdonya

Great Ruaha

© Philip Briggs

Inset (tourist roads)

Great Ruaha

Mwagusi

Mwagusi

Mtouisusu Springs

Rudha Escarpment

Mwayembe Springs

Mwagusi

130m

900m

Msembe Park HQ, Bandas & campsite

Park entrance

Hippo Pool

Ruaha River Lodge

Mdonya

Great Ruaha

character that is increasingly savoury in this day of package safaris and hundred-room game lodges. The dominant geographical feature of the park is the Great Ruaha River, which follows the southeast boundary for 160km, and is known to the local Hehe people as the Lyambangori (Ruaha being a corruption of the Hehe word *luhava*, which simply means river). Only the small part of the park around the river is developed for tourism, but with just two small lodges currently operating – though more are likely to open over the next couple of years – even this limited 400km road circuit sees relatively few visitors, and has a reassuringly untrammelled mood.

Ruaha has a hot and rather dry climate, with an average annual rainfall of around 500mm falling almost exclusively between October and May, and peaking in February and March. Daytime temperatures in excess of 40°C are regularly recorded, particularly over October and November before the rains break, but a very low humidity level makes this less noticeable than might be expected, and it cools down reliably at night. The best game viewing is generally from May to November, but the bush is greener and prettier from January to June, and birding peaks during the European winter months of December to April. The vegetation of Ruaha is transitional to southern *miombo* and eastern savannah biomes, and a wide variety of habitats are protected within the park, including riparian forest along the watercourses, swamps, grassland, and acacia woodland. The dominant vegetation type is *brachystegia* woodland. Several areas of the park support an impressive number of large baobab trees, and much of the scenery is strongly reminiscent of Tarangire National Park on the northern circuit.

The floral variety of Ruaha is mirrored by the variety of wildlife likely to be seen over the course of a few days on safari. The most common ungulates, not unusually, are the widespread impala, waterbuck, bushbuck, buffalo, zebra and giraffe, all of which are likely to be encountered several times on any given game drive. The park lies at the most southerly extent of the range of several East African ungulate species, including lesser kudu and Grant's gazelle. Yet it also harbours a number of antelope that are rare or absent in northern Tanzania, most visibly the splendid greater kudu – some of the most handsomely horned males you'll come across anywhere in Africa – but also the more elusive roan and sable antelope. The elephant population is the largest of any Tanzanian national park, despite heavy losses due to poaching in the 1980s, with some 12,000 elephants migrating through the greater Ruaha ecosystem. The most impressive pair of tusks weighed in the 20th century – combined weight 201kg – were from an individual shot in Ruaha in the 1970s, but the poaching of the recent past means you're unlikely to see anything comparable these days.

Ruaha is an excellent park for predators. Lions are not only numerous and very habituated to vehicles, but the prides tend to be unusually large, often numbering more than 20 individuals. The park also boasts a justified reputation for good leopard sightings, and while it's not as reliable as the Seronera Valley in the Serengeti, leopard are usually seen every few days and they are less skittish than in many game reserves. Cheetah, resident on the open plains, are quite often encountered in the Lundu area – known locally as the mini Serengeti – northeast of the Mwagusi River. More than 100 African wild dogs are thought to be resident in the greater Ruaha ecosystem. Wild dogs are known to have very wide ranges, and their movements are often difficult to predict, but one pack of about 40 individuals regularly moves into the Mwagusi area, generally hanging around for a few days before wandering elsewhere for a couple of weeks. Visitors who particularly want to see wild dogs should try to visit in June or July, when they are normally denning, and are thus more easy to locate than at other times of year. Black-backed jackal and spotted hyena are both very common and easily seen, and the rarer striped hyena, though seldom observed, is found here at the southern limit of its range.

With 450 species recorded, Ruaha also offers some excellent birding, once again with an interesting mix of southern and northern species. Of particular note are substantial and visible populations of black-collared lovebird and ashy starlings, Tanzanian endemics associated with the Maasai Steppes found here at the southern extreme of their distribution. By contrast, this is perhaps the only savannah reserve in East Africa where the crested barbet – a colourful yellow and black bird whose loud sustained trilling is a characteristic sound of the southern African bush – replaces the red-and-yellow barbet. Raptors are well represented, with bateleur and fish eagle probably the most visible large birds of prey, and the localised Eleanora's falcon quite common in December and January. The watercourses support the usual water birds.

Fees and further information

An entrance fee of US$20 per 24 hours must be paid in hard currency. The *Ruaha* booklet published in 2000 by the African Publishing Group in association with TANAPA, is normally available at the lodges, and contains useful maps, animal descriptions and checklists, and details of where to look for localised species. The older 64-page booklet *Ruaha National Park* is just as useful, and cheaper, assuming that you can locate a copy!

Getting there and away

The most straightforward way to reach Ruaha is by air, using Coastal Travel's daily scheduled flight from Dar es Salaam and the Selous Game Reserve. Fly-in packages, most often combined with a visit to Selous, can be arranged directly through the lodges listed below, or through any safari operator in Dar es Salaam or Arusha. A minimum stay of three nights is recommended. Stand-alone drive-down packages to Ruaha are less attractive, because of the driving distance involved, but Ruaha can easily be visited by road as part of a safari taking in some of the other southern national parks and reserves.

For self-drive visitors, the main park entrance gate lies about 100km west of Iringa along a reasonably maintained dirt road that takes about three hours to cover. The approach road is probably only suitable for 4WD vehicles, and the roads within the park definitely are. The road to Ruaha out of Iringa is essentially a western extension of the main Uhuru road. It passes through Kalenga, former capital of Chief Mkwawa, after about 15km, and after another 25km it passes the signposted 11km side road north to Mlambalasi, where Mkwawa took his life and was buried, and the site of a centenary memorial erected in 1998. Another 20km or so closer to Ruaha, the road branches into two forks, which converge shortly before the entrance gate. I'm not aware of any substantial difference between the two forks in terms of distance or quality, but you should take the left fork if you intend to stay at Tungamalenga Campsite.

Ruaha is not a realistic goal for budget-conscious independent travellers. It used to be possible to arrange a relatively affordable camping safari out of Iringa through Iringa Safari Tours, but their office on the corner of Uhuru Avenue between Benbella Street and Karume Road looked definitively closed in late 2001. It is possible to get to the Tungamalenga Campsite using a daily bus that leaves Iringa at 13.00 and passes the campsite at 18.00, coming past again on the return trip at around 04.00 the next morning. The campsite can arrange transport to the entrance gate for Tsh25,000 per vehicle one-way, but they are not permitted to take game drives into the park, so you'd practically be forced to be collected by one of the lodges and stay there.

Ruaha is best visited between July and November, when animals concentrate around the river. Internal roads may be impassable during the rainy season (December to May).

Where to stay
Exclusive
Mwagusi Safari Camp Tel/fax: (UK) 20 8846 9363; email: tropicafrica.uk.@virgin.net. This small and exclusive tented camp, situated on the north bank of the seasonal Mwagusi River, is to my taste one of the most alluring lodges anywhere in East Africa, immensely comfortable, yet with a real bush atmosphere. The accommodation, strung along the riparian woodland fringing the river, consists of about a dozen spacious walk-in tents, enclosed in a wood, thatch and reed shelter, each of which has a vast shower and toilet area, and a private balcony. Because the lodge is owner-managed, the service is top-notch, and includes some great touches – most memorably, starlit bush dinners around a campfire in a clearing above the camp or in the riverbed. Game viewing from the camp is superb, with elephant and greater kudu regularly putting in an appearance, and plenty of birds hopping around the trees. Wild dog are regularly sighted in the area, several lion prides are resident, and the closest game-viewing circuits are situated far enough from the larger Ruaha River Lodge and park headquarters that you feel you have the whole park to yourself. Game walks with an armed ranger are also offered, with a good chance of encountering elephants and other large animals on foot. All-inclusive fly-in rates are slightly higher than at Ruaha River Lodge, but drive-in rates exclusive of activities are about the same.

Upmarket
Ruaha River Lodge Tel/fax: (UK) 1452 862288; tel: 0744 237422, 0741 237422; fax: 0741 327706; email: fox@tanzaniasafaris.info or fox@bushlink.co.tz; web: www.ruahariverlodge.com. This highly regarded and comfortable private camp is situated on a rocky hillside above a set of rapids on the Ruaha River 10km from the entrance gate. Game viewing is excellent from the camp, with rock hyrax scuttling around everywhere, hippos resident on the river and many other animals coming down to drink. Accommodation is in unpretentious stone cottages or fixed tents. There is a restaurant and bar. Full-board accommodation for drive-in customers costs US$140/200 single/double for non-residents or US$55 per person for residents, in addition to which US$35 per person must be paid per game drive. A full fly-in package costs US$240/400 single/double, inclusive of all meals, game drives, park fees and airport transfer, but exclusive of the cost of the flight.

Budget and camping
Msembe Camp This national park camp near the headquarters lies close to the river and some extensive open plains teeming with game. The accommodation isn't up to much – nine prefabricated self-contained double *banda*s and two family *banda*s that look like they must get seriously hot during the middle of the day – but it's the cheapest on offer within the park at US$20 per person. Bedding, firewood and water are provided, and drinks can be bought at the nearby staff bar, but all food must be brought with you.
Tungamalenga Camp Tel: 0741 414416 or 409270; email: tungacamp@yahoo.com. This new camp and curio shop is situated about 27km before the park entrance gate on the left fork coming from Iringa. The small self-contained *banda*s have two beds each and netting, and are reasonable value for residents at Tsh5,000 per person, but seem insanely overpriced for non-residents at US$25 per person. Camping, with access to a clean shower and toilet and a self-catering area, costs US$10 per person. Meals are available by arrangement at US$2–3.

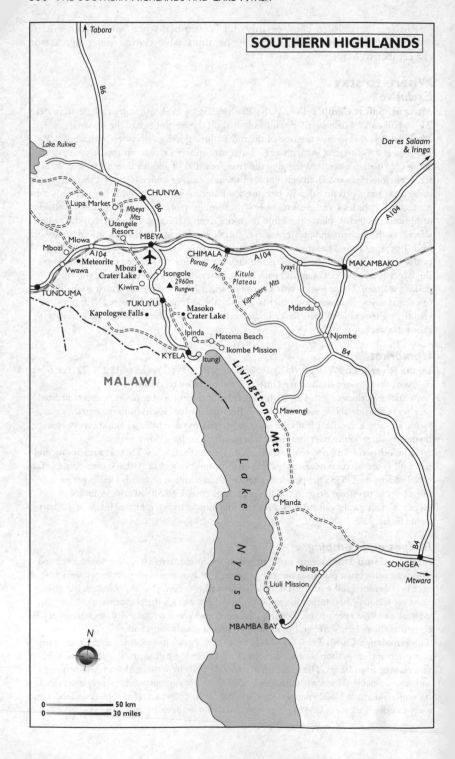

The Southern Highlands and Lake Nyasa

Roughly bounded by the Tanzam Highway to the west, Songea to the east, Makambako to the north, and Zambia and Malawi to the south, the Southern Highlands of Tanzania, though exceptionally pretty and reasonably cheap and easy to get around, are seldom explored by travellers. The principal town of the Southern Highlands is Mbeya, an important overland route focus, since it is where travellers heading to Malawi will disembark from their bus or train to divert eastwards off the Tanzam Highway. Other major towns in the region include Tukuyu, Songea, Njombe and Kyela.

The most significant physical feature in this part of Tanzania is Lake Nyasa (the name used locally for the Tanzanian portion of Lake Malawi), where Matema Beach provides an alluring goal for those looking for a cheap and scenic place to chill out. A number of mountain ranges form the Rift Valley escarpment on either side of the lake: the Poroto and Kipengere lie to the north of Lake Nyasa, while the Livingstone Mountains rise dramatically to the immediate north east. The opportunities for hikes and day walks in these mountains are practically limitless, with Ngosi Crater Lake, Mount Rungwe and Kitulo Plateau perhaps the pick of a number of local beauty spots.

CLIMATE

With altitudes ranging from below 500m to over 2,900m this region has a varied climate. Lake Nyasa (478m) is hot and humid, but the rest of the region is temperate, and in the highlands you'll need some reasonably warm clothing at night. The area south of Tukuyu has the highest rainfall of anywhere in Tanzania. For hikers, the dry season between May and October might superficially seem the best time of year, but the scenery is far less attractive than in the wet season, it is often very cold at night, and you'll miss out on the flower displays that form one of the regional highlights.

GETTING AROUND

Mbeya, the main gateway to the region, can be approached by rail or road from Dar es Salaam or by road from western Tanzania. See *Mbeya* for details. Songea, the main route focus on the eastern side of the lake, can be approached from Makambako on the Tanzam Highway, from Mbamba Bay on the lakeshore, or from Mtwara on the south coast.

Within the region there is plenty of transport along the Mbeya–Kyela road, the Songea–Makambako road and the Tanzam Highway. Two ferries a week run between Itungi and Mbamba Bay on Lake Nyasa. Transport on side roads is less erratic than in most parts of the country, but it can still be pretty rough going.

THE SOUTHERN HIGHLANDS

Tanzania's Southern Highlands, centred around Mbeya, are often perceived to form a practically contiguous extension of the Eastern Arc mountains to their north, and the two biomes do indeed share some strong biological affinities. The geology of the Southern Highlands and affiliated ranges in bordering parts of Mozambique, Malawi and Zambia, which together form the Southern Rift Montane Eco-region, is, however, quite unique, representing some of the most ancient and the most modern rock formations on the African continent.

Underlying most of the Southern Highlands are the Pre-Cambrian Ubendian sediments, named after a locale close to Lake Tanganyika, and comprised of quartzite and other crystalline rocks that formed at least two billion years ago when two tectonic plates drifted into each other. The vast, high mountain range created by this collision, comparable perhaps to the modern Himalayas, has subsequently been eroded to comparative insignificance, while in lower-lying areas the original crystalline rocks have been overlaid by other sediments during periods when they lay underwater. The Mbeya Range, which rises above Mbeya, is probably the most substantial single relic of this ancient geological activity.

A more recent factor in shaping the topography around Mbeya has been the tectonic drift responsible for the formation of the Great Rift Valley. The Southern Highlands lie at the juncture of two separate rifts – the main eastern rift and smaller Rukwa branch – resulting in a high level of volcanic activity, particularly over the last four million years. The volcanic landscape east of Mbeya is dominated by Mount Rungwe, which last erupted about 200 years ago, as well as several extinct or dormant volcanoes and crater lakes, most notably Ngosi. Solidified lava flows are in strong evidence throughout this region, most strikingly at Daraja la Mungu, a natural bridge of basaltic lava rock that spans a gorge comprised of almost two-million-year-old crystalline rock. Then, of course, there is the 585km-long, 700m-deep Lake Nyasa, set at an altitude of around 500m on the Rift Valley floor below an escarpment rising to almost 2,500m.

The indigenous vegetation of the Southern Rift Montane Eco-region shares several superficial similarities with that of the Eastern Arc mountains, largely due to the two regions' geographical proximity, but in other respects they are very different. The main reason for these differences is that, over the last 30 million years, the forested Eastern Arc mountains have experienced an ecological continuity unparalleled in East Africa, partly because their precipitation patterns are most strongly influenced by the Indian Ocean, and partly because of their geological stability. The modern rainfall patterns of the Southern Highlands are, by contrast, linked primarily to Lake Nyasa, and the area has undergone large-scale topographic transformations in the relatively recent geological past.

The varied vegetation of the Southern Highlands is shaped locally by the region's wide contrasts in altitude and climate, with the average annual rainfall ranging from around 800mm on the Ufipa Plateau to almost 3,000mm in parts of the Livingstone and Poroto Mountains. Broadly speaking, the predominant vegetation type below about 1,800m is savannah or thick *miombo* woodland comprised primarily of trees in the genera *Brachystegia, Isoberlinia* and *Julbernardia*. Closed canopy montane rainforest generally blankets the slopes between 1,800m and 2,300m, often interspersed with stands of tall bamboo (*Sinarundinaria alpina*) forest. Higher altitudes are dominated by open montane grassland, dotted with seasonal marshes, and in some areas divided from the forest zone by a belt of heather and moorland.

The woodland and forest zones of the Southern Rift Montane Eco-region are characterised by a significantly lower floral and faunal diversity than the more ancient forests of the Eastern Arc, and also harbour far fewer endemic species. Not so, however, the grassland and heath communities, which support possibly the richest variety of flowering plants of any East African eco-region, particularly on Malawi's Nyika Plateau and the Kitulo Plateau east of Mbeya. Orchids are particularly well represented – some 300 species, the highest total anywhere in the world, have been identified on the Nyika plateau alone – as are proteas, aloes, fireball lilies and various smaller and less distinctive colourful flowers. The wet season floral displays on the Kitulo Plateau are arguably the most under-rated natural spectacle anywhere in Tanzania.

The Southern Highlands are of great interest to ornithologists. Three Tanzanian endemics are represented in the area, namely Uhehe fiscal, Iringa akalat and Kipengere seedeater. Grassland species whose range is centred on the Southern Rift Montane Eco-region include the spectacular buff-shouldered widowbird and somewhat duller yellow-browed seedeater and churring cisticola. The montane forests are especially rewarding, with widespread gems such as bar-tailed trogon, starred robin-chat and paradise flycatcher occurring alongside several skulkers endemic to the Eastern Arc and Southern Rift Mountains, notably Fuelleborn's black boubou, Sharpe's akalat, spot-throat and long-billed tailorbird. By comparison, large mammals are poorly represented, though most forests harbour populations of Angola black-and-white colobus (an endemic Southern Highlands race *Colobus angolensis sharpei*), vervet and blue monkey. Also present are the elusive bushpig, bushbuck, suni, Harvey's duiker, bush duiker and (on Rungwe only) the rare Abbott's duiker, a Tanzanian endemic. Smaller mammals include endemic semi-melanistic races of Tanganyika mountain squirrel and chequered elephant shrew, while endemic reptiles include three species each of chameleon, snake and amphibian.

With the notable exception of Malawi's Nyika National Park, the Southern Rift Mountains are accorded a relatively low conservation status, and not protected at all within Zambia or Mozambique. Tanzania has 28 demarcated forest reserves within the region, only a handful of which cover more than 100km^2, and another 20 or so are possibly to be gazetted in the foreseeable future. The most important of these reserves in terms of area and environmental integrity are on the Chimala Scarp (below the Kitulo Plateau), the Livingstone Mountains, the Mbeya Range, the Poroto Ridge (around Mount Ngosi) and Mount Rungwe. While most of these large reserves still contain substantial tracts of indigenous forest, grassland and heath, several smaller reserves have been seriously compromised through a combination of subsistence wood collection, charcoal making, grazing, bush fires, clearing for cultivation, and pit sawing.

The conservation profile of the region is likely to be raised following the recent establishment of the Southern Highlands Conservation Programme (SHCP), a Wildlife Conservation Society (WCS)-funded project dedicated to the study and conservation of the highland habitats and species of southern Tanzania. It is based in Mbeya and can be contacted at enquiries@southernhighlandstz.org. It also has a new website: www.southernhighlandstz.org. A significant recent conservation development in the Southern Highlands is the proposed upgrading of the Kitulo Plateau, the most important grassland in the south, and currently unprotected, to become a national park in 2002/3.

MBEYA

Perched at an altitude of 1,737m in a valley below the extensive Mbeya Range, the town of Mbeya was established as recently as 1927 to service the Lupa gold fields near Chunya. Although the mining ceased in the 1950s, Mbeya has continued to prosper thanks to the rich agricultural land that surrounds it, and its strategic position along the Tanzam Highway and Tazara Railway. With a population exceeding 200,000, it is today the fifth-largest town in Tanzania. Mbeya is an appealing town, with a skyline dominated by the impressive – and climbable – Mbeya and Loleza Peaks. It also has an unusually Westernised, bustling feel and shows few of the signs of neglect that characterise many other Tanzanian towns. Mbeya is mainly visited by travellers as a stop-off point on the way to Zambia or Malawi, but it is a good base for exploring the Southern Highlands.

Getting there and away

Most people travel between Mbeya and Dar es Salaam by the Tazara Railway (details of which are included under the heading *By rail* in *Chapter 4*). There are also regular buses between Dar es Salaam and Mbeya, an 893km trip which takes up to 20 hours in local buses and about 12 hours on the excellent Scandinavia Coach service, which operates two buses daily. Overnight buses on this route have a bad reputation for theft, so if you stick to local buses, it is advisable to split the trip at Iringa.

From western Tanzania, the most comfortable option would be to get to Dar es Salaam by train and proceed to Mbeya from there. A more adventurous route goes via Mpanda and Sumbawanga; see *Chapter 16*. At least two buses every week run along the little-used road connecting Tabora to Mbeya, passing through one of the most remote parts of Tanzania. This trip will take at least 20 hours.

Buses to local destinations such as Kyela, Tukuyu, Njombe and Tunduma leave regularly from the central bus station on a fill-up-and-go basis. There are also several buses daily to Iringa, Songea and Sumbawanga, but these should be booked in advance.

Where to stay
Upmarket

Utengule Country Hotel Tel: 025 256 0100; fax: 025 256 0089; email: utengule@twiga.com; web: www.utengule.com. Far more attractive than any of the accommodation options within Mbeya, the Utengule Country Hotel is situated on a 500-acre coffee estate near Luiji, less than 30 minutes' drive from the town centre on the foothills of the 2,834m Mbeya Peak. The forested slopes around the lodge harbour a wide variety of birds, as well as monkeys and other small mammals, and also form a useful base for hikes in the Mbeya Range. Facilities include a large swimming pool, tennis and squash courts, mini-golf, a pool table, and mountain bike and motorbike hire. The lodge manager is very knowledgeable about excursions further afield in the Southern Highlands. The restaurant is widely regarded to be the best in the region. Accommodation rates range from US$45/80 for a standard single/double B&B to US$100 for a double bungalow. To get there from Mbeya, take the Tanzam Highway south for about 12km until you reach Mbalizi junction, then follow the side road to the right, which is signposted for the lodge, after another 8km. About halfway between the junction and the hotel, on the left side of the road, lie the remains of a derelict walled village, built by a local chief in 1879 as defence against the expansionist Hehe Empire of Iringa Region.

Mount Livingstone Hotel Tel: 025 250 3331/4; fax: 025 250 4190; email: mtlivingstone@hotmail.com. The comfortable but unremarkable Mount Livingstone Hotel narrowly slips into the upmarket range, more than anything due to the absence of anything better in the town centre. Self-contained rooms with hot water and satellite television cost

US$40/60 single/double for non-residents or Tsh20,000/30,000 for residents. You'll probably be permitted to pay resident rates if you politely insist, in which case it's pretty good value.

Moderate

Mbeya Peak Hotel Tel: 025 250 3473. Central and popular with local business travellers, the Mbeya Peak Hotel charges a very reasonable Tsh12,500 for a clean and neatly furnished self-contained double with hot water. A good restaurant and garden bar are attached, and the latter often hosts live music over weekends.

Rift Valley Hotel Tel: 025 250 4429. Less central and quieter than the above, but otherwise similar in standard, the Rift Valley Hotel charges Tsh12,000/14,000 for a self-contained double with hot water. The ground floor restaurant is pretty good value, too, serving a variety of curries and grills for around Tsh3,000.

Sombrero Hotel Adjacent to the synonymous restaurant, this hotel is scheduled to open in 2002 and will charge around Tsh10,000 for a self-contained double with satellite television and telephone in all rooms.

Budget

Holiday Lodge Tel: 025 250 2821/3375. The Holiday Lodge has been one of Mbeya's best budget lodges for some years now, with the one drawback for budget travellers that it's a solid 1km walk from the bus station. Clean, spacious rooms with large beds, a writing desk and piping-hot showers in the evening cost Tsh5,000/7,000 single/double. The friendly management speaks good English, and there's a decent bar and restaurant around the corner at the Rift Valley Hotel.

New Millennium Hotel Tel: 025 250 0599. This new, clean lodge opposite the bus station is also excellent value, charging Tsh4,000 for a room using common shower, Tsh5,000 for a self-contained room, or Tsh6,000 for a self-contained room with satellite television. All rooms are 'singles' with one double bed.

Karibuni Centre Tel: 025 250 3035; fax: 025 250 4178; email: mec@maf.org. Situated 500m from the Tanzam Highway in the grounds of the Mbalizi Evangelical Church, this hostel offers very clean and comfortable rooms for Tsh6,000/8,000 single/double. The out-of-town location counts against it for travellers without private transport.

Mbeya Green View Inn & Campsite Tel: 025 250 0287. This pleasant new lodge lies along the Chunya road, not far from the Rift Valley Hotel, but some distance from the bus station. The rooms are very clean and comfortable, but they are nothing out of the ordinary and seem relatively steeply priced at Tsh8,000 for a double using common shower or Tsh15,000 for a self-contained double with hot water. Camping in the grassy walled enclosure adjacent to the main lodge costs Tsh3,000 per person. Meals are available at Tsh1,800.

Shoestring

Moravian Youth Hostel This long-established backpackers' haunt lies a few minutes' walk out of town along Jacaranda Road, and offers clean, secure accommodation for Tsh3,500 double. Aside from the somewhat institutional character of the set-up, the main disadvantage of staying here, assuming that you intend to eat or drink in the town centre, is that the road out to the hostel has a reputation for nocturnal muggings.

Warsame Guesthouse Basic but adequately clean local guesthouse that seems far more inviting than anything in the cluster of cheapies scattered around the bus station. Rooms using a common shower cost Tsh2,000/3,000 single/double.

Where to eat

The upmarket and moderate hotels listed above all boast adequate to good restaurants, with the one at **Utengule Country Hotel** – open daily except for

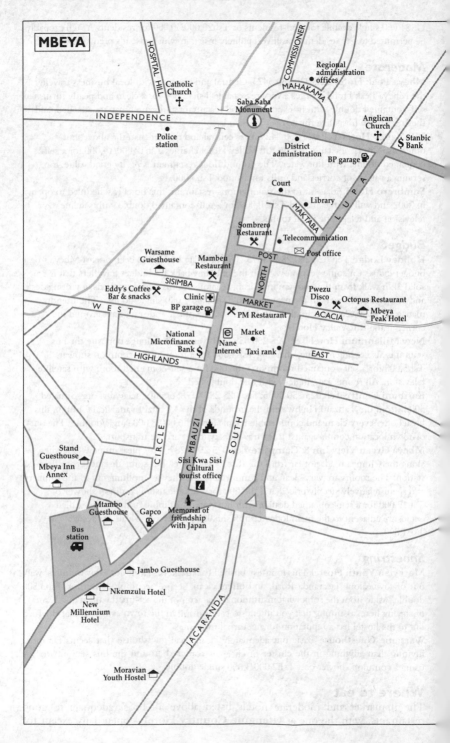

MBEYA

HOSPITAL HILL

Catholic Church

Saba Saba Monument

COMMISSIONER

Regional administration offices

MAHAKAMA

INDEPENDENCE

Police station

District administration

Anglican Church

Stanbic Bank

BP garage

Court

Library

LUPA

MAKTABA

Sombrero Restaurant

Telecommunication

Post office

Warsame Guesthouse

Mambeu Restaurant

POST

SISIMBA

Eddy's Coffee Bar & snacks

Clinic

NORTH

Pwezu Disco

Octopus Restaurant

BP garage

MARKET

Mbeya Peak Hotel

WEST

PM Restaurant

ACACIA

National Microfinance Bank

Nane Internet

Market

Taxi rank

EAST

HIGHLANDS

CIRCLE

MBAUZI

SOUTH

Stand Guesthouse

Mbeya Inn Annex

Sisi Kwa Sisi Cultural tourist office

Mtambo Guesthouse

Gapco

Memorial of friendship with Japan

Bus station

Jambo Guesthouse

Nkemzulu Hotel

New Millennium Hotel

JACARANDA

Moravian Youth Hostel

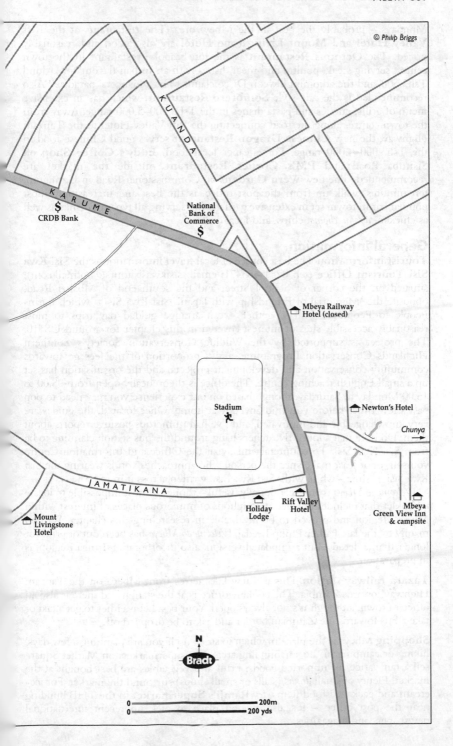

© Philip Briggs

KUANDA

KARUME

$
CRDB Bank

National
Bank of
Commerce
$

Mbeya Railway
Hotel (closed)

Stadium

Newton's Hotel

Chunya →

JAMATIKANA

Holiday
Lodge

Rift Valley
Hotel

Mount
Livingstone
Hotel

Mbeya
Green View Inn
& campsite

N

Bradt

0   200m
0   200 yds

Mondays – probably the best in the Mbeya area. The restaurants at the **Rift Valley Hotel** and **Mount Livingstone Hotel** are also good and reasonably priced. The **Octopus Restaurant** is the top bespoke restaurant in the town centre, serving steak, poultry and meat dishes with an Indian flavour for around Tsh3,500, and the adjoining Pwezu Disco claims to be a 'dancers' paradise'! Also recommended is the café-style **Sombrero Restaurant**, which has an extensive menu of grills, curries and pasta dishes in the Tsh2,500–3,000 range. Away from the town centre, along the road connecting the Rift Valley Hotel to the Tanzam Highway, the new **Chinese Dragon Restaurant** serves good Chinese food in the Tsh3,000–4,000 range. For cheaper local food, **Eddy's Coffee Shop** on Sisimba Road and **PM's Corner Restaurant** outside the market are recommended. The new **Weru Gardens** on Commissioner Road in Uzunguni, ten minutes' walk up from the post office, is the best and increasingly most popular bar in town, set in extensive gardens and serving all types of drinks as well as chicken, *nyama choma*, chips, and local dishes.

General information

Tourist information The best source of local travel information is the **Sisi Kwa Sisi Tourism Office** (tel: 0741 463471; email: sisikwasisitours@hotmail.com), situated on the corner of School Street and the south end of Mbalizi Road, opposite the 'Memorial of Friendship with Japan'. Sisi Kwa Sisi – which means People to People or Pull Together – can arrange guided day trips to most reasonably accessible sites of interest covered in this chapter for around US$10. The project is supported by the Wildlife Conservation Society's Southern Highlands Conservation Programme, and a proportion of the fees go towards community conservation and development projects, and the organisation has set up a small English teaching centre. The office is theoretically open from 08.00 to 15.00 Monday to Saturday, though based on our experience you may need to pop past a few times before you find anybody at home! Once located, the guides are very knowledgeable and motivated, and I've had numerous positive reports about them. Do note that a lot of flycatchers hang around the bus station claiming to be from Sisi Kwa Sisi. To counteract this, visit the Office and Information Centre yourself, or at least make sure the person who approaches you is wearing the Sisi Kwa Sisi T-shirt – white with 'Sisi Kwa Sisi' written across it in red.

Welcome to Mbeya is an exceptionally useful – though almost impossible to locate – booklet that includes detailed descriptions of numerous places of interest within Mbeya Region and proved to be invaluable in researching this chapter. Written mainly by the late Father Philip Leedal, *Welcome to Mbeya* has been out of print for longer than a decade, but an updated version, also incorporating Iringa Region, is in preparation.

Tazara railway station This is a few kilometres from Mbeya on the Tanzam Highway towards Zambia. The booking office is at the station and there is also an office in town, although it's not always open. Your best bet is either to get a taxi or take a bus towards the Zambian border and ask to be dropped off.

Shopping Mbeya is the place in which to stock up if you are planning a few days' hiking or camping in the surrounding area. The supermarkets on Market Square sell a fair variety of imported goods. Fruit and vegetables are best bought at the market. Plenty of small *dukas* (stalls or small shops) surround the market. For ice-cream and packaged food items, try **Ramji's Supermarket** in the THB building near the post office – it's also a good place to pick up recent international newspapers and magazines.

Internet The best internet café is **Nane Internet**, on Mbalizi Road outside the central market, which charges Tsh500 per 30 minutes.

Foreign exchange The National Bank of Commerce on Karume Avenue offers foreign exchange facilities for travellers' cheques and cash. There don't seem to be any private bureaux de change in Mbeya, which could be problematic for travellers arriving from Malawi or Zambia outside of normal banking hours. If you are likely to be in this position, try to change enough cash at the border to see you through the next working day. The recently opened Stanbic Bank at the top of the town also changes cash at reasonable rates.

Excursions from Mbeya

This section covers places of interest that lie along, or are most easily accessed from, the Tanzam Highway, as well as those to the west of Mbeya town. The numerous scenic sites around Tukuyu (on the road towards Lake Nyasa and the Malawi border) are covered separately later in the chapter, under the heading *Excursions from Tukuyu*. Most of the places of interest around Tukuyu could be visited as a day trip out of Mbeya, whether independently or with a guide from the Sisi Kwa Sisi tourism office in Mbeya.

The Mbeya Range

The mountain range for which the town of Mbeya is named consists of a roughly 25km-long southwest facing gneiss escarpment that forms an important watershed for both the Lake Nyasa and Lake Rukwa drainage systems. The range contains three major peaks, of which the central 2,835m Mbeya peak is the tallest, flanked by the 2,273m Pungulumo Peak to the southwest, and the 2,656m Loleza or Kaluwe peak to the northwest above Mbeya town centre. In 1957, the upper slopes of the mountains were gazetted as the roughly 160km^2 Mbeya Range Forest Reserve.

Although 5% of the forest reserve has been used for exotic pine and eucalyptus plantations, the remainder supports a fundamentally indigenous vegetation cover, compromised in recent years by dry season bush fires, and cultivation at lower elevations. Below the 2,000m contour, the natural vegetation is mainly open canopy *miombo* woodland, dominated by various *brachystegia* species. At higher altitudes, open grassland and heath predominate, interspersed with strips of riparian closed canopy *Hagenia* forest. The grassland, which receives a mean annual rainfall of 1,750mm, hosts impressive wildflower displays during the rainy season, with proteas and terrestrial orchids well represented. Blue and vervet monkeys are thinly distributed in forest patches, along with dik-dik, bushpig and a wide variety of birds.

From Mbeya town, Loleza Peak can be ascended in about two hours, by following Hospital Hill Road from the town centre to the hospital, then climbing a footpath through the forest behind the hospital immediately before the electricity lines. The higher Mbeya peak is most easily climbed from the Utengule Country Hotel in Luiji, about 25km from Mbeya town by road. Several routes can be used, and the staff at Utengule can advise you about current conditions. The round hike takes about six hours and is steep in parts, so it should only be attempted if you are reasonably fit. If you want to do a longer hike in the area, you can cross from Mbeya Peak to Pungulumo Peak at the western extreme of the range. The footpaths to all three peaks are indistinct in places, and mist is a real risk at higher altitudes, so it is advisable to arrange a guide either from the Sisi Kwa Sisi tourist office in Mbeya or else from Utengule Country Hotel.

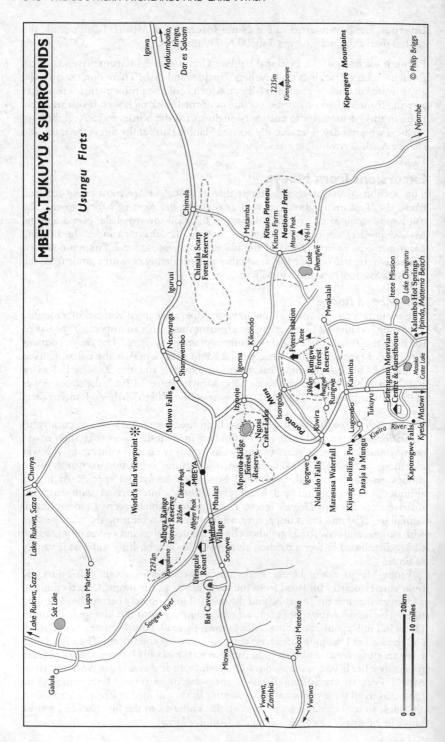

MBEYA, TUKUYU & SURROUNDS

© Philip Briggs

Songwe Valley Caves and Hot Springs

The small town of Songwe, which straddles the Tanzam Highway about 25km south of Mbeya, is the site of a large factory that produces cement from the surrounding limestone sediments. Of greater interest to tourists, however, are the nearby caves and hot springs in the Songwe River Valley. These can be reached by following the Tanzam Highway for about 3km south of Songwe town, crossing a small bridge, almost immediately after which you need to turn right on to an unsignposted dirt road. After following this rough track for about 2km, you'll reach a quarry and a group of limestone kilns, where you need to turn left on to a smaller track and follow this for about 8km to an Italian construction camp in a pink marble quarry.

From the marble quarry, anybody will be able to direct you the caves, which lie a few minutes' walk away. The caves are eroded into a limestone cliff and have at least two entrances, which you can walk between with a decent torch, though it would be dangerous to go too far in. They also offer an attractive view over the river, and host large seasonal bat colonies, comprised of at least six different species, which stream out of the entrances at dusk to spectacular effect. Some small hot springs lie at the base of the cliff below the caves. Larger and more beautiful are the springs and geysers that erupt from the ground one to two hours' walk away at Malonde.

If you want to stay overnight in Songwe, the **Songwe Hotel** has affordable self-contained rooms, and there are a few local guesthouses. Worth noting perhaps that the village at the Malawi border post near Kyela is also called Songwe, because it also lies on the Songwe River.

Mbozi Meteorite

This substantial meteorite lies on the slopes of Merengi Hill near Mbozi Mission, about 70km southwest of Mbeya. The meteorite was first reported to Western science in 1930, by a South African land surveyor W H Nott, whose attention was drawn to the rock by a local assistant who refused to go anywhere near it, on account of its purported supernatural powers. Nott's initial measurements of the rock created a stir among mineralogists by indicating it to be the largest meteorite on the earth's surface, weighing more than 70 tonnes. It actually weighs 12 tonnes, making it the eighth-largest in the world.

The Mbozi meteorite is classified as a siderite, which is a meteorite comprised almost entirely of nickel-iron alloy (an extremely rare alloy on the earth's surface) as opposed to igneous rock, and it is the only such one known in Africa. The rock is smaller than a Land Rover, and is composed of 90.45% iron and 8.69% nickel, with traces of copper, sulphur and phosphorus. The outer crust of the meteorite is darkened by metal fusion caused by the scorching heat that was generated when it fell through the earth's atmosphere – essentially a shooting star so large that it was able to reach the planetary surface before it burned out.

With a private vehicle, Mbozi can easily be visited from Mbeya in conjunction with the bat caves at Songwe. To get there, follow the Tanzam Highway for about 30km south of Songwe until you see the dirt road to Mbozi signposted to your left. The meteorite lies 13km along this road, just past the village of Ndolezi. No entrance fee is charged, but a caretaker is present at the site. There is no formal accommodation in the immediate vicinity of the meteorite, but the Sisi Kwa Sisi tourist office in Mbeya can arrange a village stay on a nearby agricultural plot. There is no public transport between the Tanzam Highway and the meteorite.

Chunya, Lake Rukwa and surrounds

The intriguing small town of Chunya, which lies about 50km northwest of Mbeya as the crow flies, was the site of a local gold rush in the 1920s and 1930s. Mining

HIKING FROM IZYONJE TO MATEMA BEACH

Gerhard Buttner is the first person I've heard from who has hiked across the Kitulo Plateau, and he sent me a letter describing the trip in February 1998. The following is an edited extract:

We settled on a north-to-south route connecting some spots described in *Welcome to Mbeya*. Starting at Izyonje near Lake Ngosi, we hiked via the Kitulo Plateau (where the Kitulo Government Farm rents out an entire three-bed guesthouse for US$3) through Mtorwi, Makete and Bulongwa to Matema Beach on the shores of Lake Nyasa. It took us six days of stiff walking with our packs to do this route, but we detoured a fair bit to climb Mtorwi and to the Kitulo Plateau. The straight crossing north–south could be done in four to five days, but the detouring can be recommended.

Hardly any English is spoken in these mountains. The area has some scenic spots, but many are highly populated farming settlements and finding isolated camping spots was not easy. People couldn't quite understand what we wanted in this area, but they were never unfriendly in spite of a rumour that we had come to plant bombs in the forest! Local people walk across parts of these mountains, but the last people before us to attempt crossing the whole area were two Germans who never completed their journey in the 1980s because

activity ceased in the 1950s, because it was no longer profitable, but Chunya did subsequently enjoy a short-lived tobacco boom before degenerating into something approaching a ghost town. Many of the grander buildings in Chunya are now boarded up, and there is a general air of faded prosperity about the town centre. Local gold prospectors still pan the river that runs through town, and there is talk of reworking the gold using modern methods.

The most direct route to Chunya leaves from central Mbeya roughly opposite the Rift Valley Hotel. This scenic 72km road takes two to three hours to drive by 4WD in dry weather, but it might take longer – or be practically impassable – after rain. A worthwhile diversion, assuming you are driving yourself, is the World's End Viewpoint, which lies a short distance from the Chunya road 22km from Mbeya, and offers excellent views across the Rift Valley escarpment to the Usunga Flats. Using public transport, a few pick-up trucks ply the road from Mbeya to Chunya daily, and you should be able to get to Chunya and back within a day. There are, however, a couple of guesthouses in Chunya should you opt – or be forced – to stay the night.

In a private 4WD vehicle, it would be possible to return from Chunya using a second, longer and more southerly route through Makongolosi, Saza, Kanga, Utengule Country Hotel and Mbalizi. A couple of points of interest lie within striking distance of this route. The first is a small soda lake called **Magadi**, which often supports flocks of flamingo between July and October, and is situated about 5km east of the road at Kanga. Second is the century-old **White Fathers Mission** at Galula, which is notable for its large wooden church built in the 1920s, and lies 4km from the road along a westerly turn-off situated about 8km past Kanga in the direction of Mbeya.

Following the above loop, you'll have regular views over Lake Rukwa, but it is also possible to drive down to the lakeshore, either heading west from Chunya via Saza to Mbangala, a roughly two-hour drive, or heading west from the Galula Mission to

they nearly landed in jail as suspected South African spies. A few times, villagers joined us for a few hours to show us the way, without ever asking for a guiding fee. We communicated with their few words of English and our limited Swahili. You will need your own food, but *ugali*, potatoes and some tomatoes and onions can occasionally be traded.

The most spectacular part of the walk was the endless drop down to Matema Beach. Villagers walk this path once a week on market day, as a greater variety of products is available on the plains around Matema.

Gerhard adds that knowing the Swahili words listed in the language section of this guide without having to look them up is the minimum you'll need to get by. He also notes that what several maps show as the 'Kipengere Mountains' are referred to by locals as the Livingstone Mountains, and that the name Kipengere is used locally to refer to the inhabited plains.

As something of an aside to the above, when I researched the first edition of this guide, Hilary Bradt passed me a letter written by a couple of hikers who aborted their trip after having spent a day or two convincing the police not to lock them up as spies. This was almost certainly the German couple Gerhard heard about, so it really does sound as if Gerhard might have been the first *mzungu* to cross this way in a decade! If you decide to follow in his footsteps, do write and let me know how it went.

Totoe. There is no accommodation in the vicinity of Rukwa, nor any public transport beyond Chunya, and even in a private vehicle it's not an area where you'd want the vehicle to break down. For more coverage of Lake Rukwa, see page 480.

Mlowo Falls

This waterfall lies alongside the Tanzam Highway towards Iringa, some 33km from Mbeya town. It is a very scenic spot, with the Mlowo River tumbling over a 15m-high basaltic cliff into a large pool, before flowing through a steep narrow gorge lined with euphorbia shrubs. The waterfall itself faces away from the main road, and is therefore not visible from it. If, however, you park (or disembark from a bus) next to the bridge across the Mlowo River (no more than 1km before Shamwembo village), a short footpath leads to a good viewpoint over the waterfall, and a bridge over the gorge.

Kitulo Plateau Proposed National Park

Based primarily on information supplied by Tim Davenport of the Southern Highlands Conservation Programme (see box 'The Southern Highlands', pages 532–3 for further details of this organisation).

Known locally as *Bustani ya Mungu* (God's Garden) and elsewhere as the Serengeti of Flowers, the unique Kitulo Plateau – formerly known as the Elton Plateau after the British explorer who first traversed it in 1873 – is one of Tanzania's most neglected biological gems. Perched at an altitude of above 2,600m, between the Kipengere Range and the Poroto and Livingstone Mountains, the plateau is comprised of 273km² of Afro-montane and Afro-Alpine grassland, representing the largest and most important plateau grassland community in Tanzania. The profile of the Kitulo Plateau will be boosted following a government announcement in February 2002 that 13,500ha will be gazetted as a national park – the first in tropical Africa to be gazetted primarily for its floristic significance.

Kitulo has long been heralded as a botanists' paradise, boasting a rich floral diversity influenced by its fertile volcanic soils and an average annual rainfall of 1,400mm. The 350 species of vascular plants documented to date include 45 species of terrestrial orchid, as well as the yellow and orange red-hot poker *Kniphofia kirkii* (a Southern Highland endemic), aloes, proteas, geraniums, giant lobelias, lilies and aster daisies. Many of the species are of restricted distribution: 31 are Tanzanian endemics, 16 are endemic to Kitulo/Kipengere, ten are restricted to Kitulo/Poroto, and at least three are endemic to the plateau itself and two more known only from the plateau and adjoining forests. Trees are relatively sparse on the plateau, except along the streams, though the Ndumbi Gap below Mount Mtorwi supports a patch of juniper trees some of which stand 50m high – reputedly the tallest junipers in the world. It is, however, the abundance of flowering plants in the wet season, starting in November and running through to April, that immediately impresses, and the phenomenon has been described as 'one of the great floral spectacles of the world'.

The plateau is also home to important animal species including some national and regional endemics. Breeding colonies of blue swallow and Denham's bustard, as well as species such as lesser kestrel, pallid harrier, mountain marsh widow, Njombe cisticola and Kipengere seedeater, contribute to the plateau being listed as an Important Bird Area. The satyrid butterfly *Neocoenyra petersi* is endemic to Kitulo, and Southern Highland endemic chameleons, lizards and frogs are also found. Two of the highest peaks in the Southern Highlands rise from the plateau: the 2,961m Mount Mtorwi and the 2,929m Chaluhangi Dome.

The best road to the Kitulo Plateau leads from Chimala on the Tanzam Highway 78km east of Mbeya. Chimala is readily accessible on public transport from Iringa or Mbeya, and it boasts the usual motley collection of local guesthouses, of which the **Sun Valley**, **Miami** and **Lutheran Guesthouses** are relatively good. From Chimala, a spectacular road called Hamsini na Saba (57 – a reference to the number of hairpin bends along its length) leads to the small town of Matamba. This drive takes up to two hours in a private vehicle, and it is covered by a couple of 4WD *dalla-dallas* daily. There are a couple of quite decent local guesthouses in Matamba. From Matamba, it's a one-hour drive or three-hour walk – no public transport – to the edge of the plateau. The only accommodation on the plateau is the very inexpensive and reasonably comfortable resthouse at the state-owned **Kitulo Farm** (likely to become the new park headquarters), which would take the best part of day to reach on foot from Matamba, but is only a couple of hours away by road. The easiest way to set up a trip to the plateau is with Sisi Kwa Sisi in Mbeya. You should certainly pop into their office for current information before heading to Kitulo, since it is not yet clear what fees and other regulations will come into play after the national park is formally gazetted.

Another road leads from the Uyole–Tukuyu road up to Kitulo. It is currently being mended (in theory).

TUKUYU

This amorphous small town, set at an altitude of 1,650m in the Poroto Mountains 70km south of Mbeya by road, is salvaged from anonymity by its setting at the base of Mount Rungwe, the second-highest peak in the Southern Highlands (Mtorwi on the Kitulo Plateau pips it by a metre). Originally called Neu Langenburg, the town was founded as a German administrative centre in the late 19th century after its namesake near Ikombe Mission on Lake Nyasa was abandoned due to the high incidence of malaria. The modern name of Tukuyu derives from the extinct volcanic hill called Ntukuyu across which the town sprawls. Pretty setting aside, Tukuyu is of interest primarily as a base from which to explore the surrounding mountains, which are studded with waterfalls, crater lakes and forest patches – all capped by stirring views to Lake Nyasa more than 1,000m below.

Getting there and away
Tukuyu lies along the surfaced road between Mbeya and Kyela, about 70km or an hour's drive from either town. Regular buses run in both directions on a fill-up-and-go basis, taking about two hours to either Mbeya or Kyela. Public transport is more

UNYAKYUSA
The fertile slopes between Mbeya and Lake Nyasa are referred to as Unyakyusa – the home of the Nyakyusa, a group of around one million people whose territory crosses over into neighbouring Malawi, where they are known as the Ngonde. Blessed with rich volcanic soil and an annual rainfall exceeding 1,500mm, the verdant mountains of Unyakyusa are dotted with small subsistence farms growing bananas, mangoes, grains, tea and coffee, set around the neatly painted Nyakyusa homesteads that led the explorer Joseph Thomson to describe Unyakyusa as 'perfect Arcadia'. The origin of the Nyakyusa has been a source of some speculation, for their Bantu language has a vocabulary significantly different to that of any neighbouring tongue, and it is one of the few Bantu languages that does not make significant use of tones.

Nyakyusa society, before it was undermined by the Ngoni wars, and the missionary and colonial influence, had a uniquely egalitarian structure based around so-called 'age villages'. When a set of adolescents reached puberty, they would all leave their villages of birth to found a new community at an uninhabited site. This new village would function rather like a commune, as an economically self-sufficient unit in which work was divided equally between men and women, crop and land rotation were practised, and cattle were distributed between the wealthier members of the community and their poorer age peers. The village would be abandoned once the last of the founding age-set had died, possibly to be re-inhabited a couple of generations later.

Traditional Nyakyusa society has several unusual customs relating to death. At a funeral, the mourners indulge in an elaborate ritual dance which, as might be expected, expresses their anger and loss, but also involves the ritualised mocking of the dead, often resulting in violent quarrels and sometimes murder. Corpses, instead of being buried, were left out in the open at a sacred grove called *Itago*, which literally means a place of casting away, and is the derivative of local place names such as Itaga and Itagata. The geographer Kerr-Cross, who visited Unyakyusa in 1893, documented how 'on the crests of rounded mounds of considerable size are to be seen clumps of thick forest ... the burial-places of their ancestors.' In 1925, McKenzie described how: 'In the long past, when a man was dying, and all hope of recovery had been abandoned, he was carried to the *Itago*, placed in a sitting position, and left to die. After death, the flesh was devoured by birds or beasts.' McKenzie noted that 'nowhere, as far as I have discovered, is this repulsive practice now followed.'

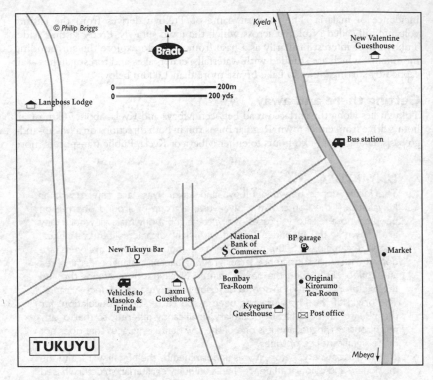

erratic on by-roads leading east and west from the main surfaced road, but there is a fair amount of private traffic along most roads, and vehicles will generally take passengers for a fee, so exploring the area over a few days from one base is possible.

Where to stay and eat

The **Langboss Hotel**, though hardly luxurious, is an above par local guesthouse situated 1km out of town along the Masoko road with a marvellous view of Mount Rungwe. The rooms are clean and comfortable, and cost Tsh2,000/3,000 single/double using a common (and generally hot) shower, or Tsh4,000 for a self-contained double. There is a bar and restaurant (meals must be ordered in advance). If you are hiking, you can leave excess gear at the hotel.

Best of the rest is the more central and very pleasant **Laxmi Guesthouse**, which charges Tsh1,500 for a single using common shower, or Tsh3,000 for a self-contained double with hot water.

Further afield, an excellent base, particularly for motorised travellers, is the resthouse at the **Lutengano Moravian Centre**, which lies 12km from Tukuyu and 7km from the main Kyela road, along the side road to the Kaporogwe Waterfall (see *Kaporogwe Waterfall* later in the chapter). Set in large, green grounds, the resthouse charges Tsh1,500/2,500/3,000 for clean single/double triple rooms sharing a common shower. Camping is permitted at Tsh1,000 per person, and meals are available by advance order.

There are two places to stay between Tukuyu and Mbeya. The basic **New Nsungwa Guesthouse** is a standard local lodge in the small town of Kiwira, about 10–15km north of Tukuyu, close to the Marasusa and Ndulido Waterfalls. The **Isongole Fishing Camp** offers camping, accommodation and bar facilities about

3km north of Isongole, making it a useful base for ascents of Mount Rungwe and Ngosi Crater Lake.

On the Tukuyu–Ipinda road, the **GNG Guesthouse**, which lies 20km from Tukuyu, a kilometre or two past Masoko Crater Lake, has basic single rooms for Tsh2,000.

Excursions from Tukuyu

This area is ideal for casual rambling. Wander along any of its winding dirt roads and you will be rewarded with lovely views and scenery, varied birdlife and vegetation, and regular glimpses into rural African life. The following section runs more-or-less from north to south, describing some of the more accessible spots, most of which are easily visited as a day trip from Tukuyu. With time, initiative and 1:50,000 maps, you can explore further. The booklet *Welcome to Mbeya* has plenty of useful walking information, assuming that you can locate a copy.

Ngosi Crater Lake

The single most alluring natural attraction anywhere in the Southern Highlands, this beautiful body of emerald green water is nestled within the 300m-high walls of the collapsed caldera of Ngosi, an extinct volcano which last erupted at least two million years ago. The peak of Ngosi – 'Big One' in the local Safwa language – is at 2,620m the highest point within the 90km^2 Poroto Ridge Forest Reserve, and its upper slopes protect what is probably the largest extant patch of ecologically intact montane vegetation in the mountain range after those on Mount Rungwe. The eastern slopes of Ngosi support extensive stands of bamboo forest, standing up to 15m high. The other slopes are covered in montane forest, as is an area of 20km^2 within the caldera, and three small islands in the northern part of the lake.

The slightly brackish waters of the 4km^2, 75m-deep crater lake are too sulphurous to support any fish naturally – locals have tried to stock it but not surprisingly the fish keep dying. According to local legend, however, the lake does harbour a large snake-like monster with supernatural powers. The Lake Ngosi Monster reputedly has the power not only to change colour to blend with that of the lake, but also to change the lake's colour when it elects to reveal itself. Local people won't swim or fish in the lake, and tend to blame local disasters on the monster's anger, which they appease by sacrificing a black goat, sheep or chicken. Lake Ngosi is also said to be the home of powerful ancestral spirits, which lend a special potency to any medicinal plants collected in the surrounding forest.

If the monster doesn't reveal itself, the dense forest along the footpath to the crater rim harbours readily observed troops of black-and-white colobus monkey, as well as a host of secretive forest birds characteristic of the Southern Highlands. The endemic Ngosi Volcano (or Poroto three-horned) chameleon *Chameleo fuelleborni*, a little-known species first described in 1900, is more-or-less restricted to the forested slopes of Ngosi. The male of this chameleon measures up to 20cm long, is mostly brown and green in colour (though it may go partially red, white and black) and has two small, lightly coloured pre-ocular horns and one rostral horn. The female is smaller and has less developed horns.

The turn-off to Ngosi Crater Lake is marked by a signpost on the surfaced road between Mbeya and Tukuyu, about 2km east of Isongole village and 35km from Mbeya. Follow this turn-off for about 3km though cultivated fields until you arrive at a sharp leftward fork, where you need to turn to the right, heading into the forest. After another 2km, a left turn takes you to a forest clearing where there is room to park a car. The footpath to the crater rim runs from close to the parking area, and the 5km ascent shouldn't take longer than two hours. Travellers without a vehicle will have no problem finding a *dalla-dalla* to drop them off at the junction, but will need to walk from there, adding another hour to the hike in each direction. Most visitors are content to enjoy the view from the rim, but there is a steep and rather treacherous footpath to the base of the caldera and the lakeshore. If you still have the energy on the way back from Ngosi, a 1km footpath to the left, about 1km after leaving the forest (2km before returning to the main Mbeya–Tukuyu road), leads to the 60m-deep Isungunia Explosion Crater, which hosts a rainy-season lake.

It is advisable to organise a guide to visit the lake, since the footpath is very indistinct in places. This is best done at the Sisi Kwa Sisi office in Mbeya, though informal guides can also be found around Isongole and the junction. During the rainy season, ask about the condition of the footpath in advance, as it is sometimes too muddy to be a realistic prospect.

Mount Rungwe

Dominating Tukuyu's northern skyline, the 2,960m Mount Rungwe is a dormant volcano studded with more than ten different calderas. The mountain formed about 2.5 million years ago and has experienced considerable activity in the last million years – ossified lava flows are clearly visible throughout the surrounding region. Several of the volcano's subsidiary calderas now harbour attractive crater lakes, while the explosion crater of the uppermost caldera is clearly visible from the peak – which also offers expansive views to Lake Nyasa, Lake Rukwa and the Kitulo Plateau. Rungwe is last thought to have erupted between 200 and 400 years ago, but a series of tremors over the cusp of 2000 and 2001 generated some concern locally that another eruption might be in store. The worst of these tremors measured 4.0 on the Richter scale, not cause for serious alarm to travellers, but sufficient to destroy 400 houses, leaving more than 5,000 people homeless.

The wild, uninhabited upper slopes of the mountain are protected within the 135km^2 Rungwe Forest Reserve, originally gazetted by the German colonial administration in 1902. Extensive indigenous montane forests are to be found within the forest reserve, particularly on the moister southern slopes, which receive up to 2,000mm of rainfall annually. Above the 2,500m contour, the dominating vegetation is montane grassland, separated from the forest in the southwest by a belt of heath moorland dotted with protea scrubs, terrestrial orchids and other wild flowers. The most visible forest mammals are black-and-white colobus and blue monkey, but the forest also forms an important refuge for the rare Abbot's duiker. The prolific birdlife is characteristic of Southern Highland forests.

The easiest and most popular ascent route of Rungwe starts at the Kagera Estate Timber Camp, which lies on the northeast footslopes of the mountain 18km from the surfaced Mbeya–Tukuyu road. To get there, follow a dirt side road that branches south from the main road at Isongole, turning sharply to the right at an intersection near the forestry office after 11km. The ascent to the rim from the timber camp takes about two hours, and it will take at least another hour to reach the peak. An alternative route, passing through the extensive montane forest on the western slopes and taking about six hours, leads from the Rungwe Moravian Mission, which lies about 7km from the main Mbeya–Kyela road along a turn-off close to Kiwira. It is possible to ascend the mountain using one route and to descend via the other.

Reasonably fit travellers should be able to ascend the mountain and return to the base within a day, at least during the dry months of June to November. Alternatively, with a tent and adequate preparation, one could spend a couple of days exploring the slopes. Either way, the combination of poorly marked, criss-crossing footpaths and occasional mist make it strongly advisable to climb with a local guide. This can be arranged locally, or at the Sisi Kwa Sisi office in Mbeya. The 1:50,000 map of Rungwe is sometimes available from the Department of Land and Surveys in Dar es Salaam.

Ndulido and Marasusa waterfalls

The Ndulido and Marasusa waterfalls lie within easy walking distance of the village of Kiwira on the main Mbeya–Tukuyu road, making them attractive goals to travellers dependent on public transport, especially as there is a guesthouse in Kiwira.

The Ndulido Falls lie on the Igogwe River about 5km northeast of Kiwira village. Although the waterfall is quite small, there's an interesting sinkhole alongside it, full of bats, but safe to walk through. To get there, follow the Igogwe road east out of Kiwira village for about 5km, with the river visible to your left most of the way, until you reach the Igogwe Hospital, from where it's ten minutes' walk to the waterfall.

The Marasusa Waterfall on the Kiwira River plunges over a large solidified lava flow, and there is a footpath to its base. To reach it, you also need to leave Kiwira along the Igogwe road, but after about 1km, having crossed the bridge across the Kiwira River, you need to turn left on to a side road that crosses the Igogwe River shortly before its confluence with the Kiwira River. The waterfall lies to the left about 4km along this side road.

Daraja la Mungu

One of the easier sites in the Poroto region to visit using public transport, Daraja la Mungu – The Bridge of God – is a spectacular natural rock bridge spanning the Kiwira River, which reputedly formed less than a thousand years ago by a water-cooled lava flow from Mount Rungwe. To get there from Tukuyu, follow the Mbeya road out of town for about 6km to Kyimo (also known as KK), and then take a left turn along a good dirt road signposted for the Prison Officers College. After 8km, this road passes through the village of Lugombo, connected to Kyimo by reasonably regular transport, especially on the busy market day of Monday.

Continuing through Lugombo, the road descends into the Kiwira Valley, reaching a large intersection after about 2km. Turn to the left here, along a road following the course of the Kiwira River, and after about 500m a large artificial bridge offers an excellent view over its natural counterpart. About 200m past the artificial bridge, you'll reach a complex of buildings – trainee prison officers' dwellings – where a clear footpath to the left leads across the natural bridge, and another one leads to the riverbank below the bridge. Note that photography of the natural bridge is forbidden without permission from the Prison Officers College, easy enough to obtain if you have sufficient time and patience.

Little more than 2km from the natural bridge, situated within the Prison Officers College compound, the Kijungu Boiling Pot consists of a small waterfall on the Kiwira River that tumbles into a circular pot-hole before flowing under a much smaller natural bridge. To reach Kijungu from Daraja la Mungu, walk back to the intersection 500m from the artificial bridge, and then turn left (in the opposite direction to Lugombo). After another 500m or so, you'll cross a bridge above a small waterfall (clearly visible from the intersection), immediately after which you need to turn right towards the college gates. The wardens will ask you to fill in the visitor's book and show your passport before guiding you to Kijungu, which lies about 1km past the gates.

Masoko Crater Lake

The main attraction along the 45km back road that connects Tukuyu to Ipinda (the closest town to Matema Beach on Lake Nyasa) is the attractive Masoko Crater Lake. As implied by its name – Masoko means Markets – a small market village lies adjacent to the lake which, although not as spectacular as Ngosi Crater Lake, is far easier to visit whether by public or private transport.

Masoko has some interesting historical associations. The solid stone building on the crater rim was constructed in 1912 to house the German Fifth Field Garrison, and it was the base from which Germany fought British troops in the neighbouring Nyasaland Protectorate. The stone building housed British troops between the wars, and it now serves as a courthouse. It is rumoured that towards the end of World War I, the Germans dumped a fortune in gold bars, money and military vehicles into the lake to avoid their falling into British hands – believable enough when you consider the same thing happened to the *Liemba* on Lake Tanganyika. Difficult to say whether there's anything to be read into the fact that the occasional German coin is washed up on the shore of the lake.

Masoko lies 19km from Tukuyu along the Ipinda–Matema road. A fair amount of traffic heads this way – predominantly overcrowded pick-up trucks. You may prefer to walk out: it's gently downhill most of the way, and very pretty with intimate, cultivated slopes occasionally giving way to magnificent vistas to Lake Nyasa. With an early start, you'll have no problem getting a lift back. There is no accommodation at the lake, but the GNG Guesthouse, a kilometre or two further along the Ipinda road, has basic single rooms for Tsh2,000.

If you are driving on south from Masoko towards Ipinda and Matema Beach, an easy and worthwhile diversion is to the old Itete Lutheran Mission and Hospital, which is built on an ancient volcanic plug overlooking the attractive Chungruru Crater Lake, home to the endemic Chungruru tilapia. To get there, follow the Ipinda road south from Masoko for about 5km, then, after crossing the bridge over the Mbaka River, turn left on to the Lwangwa road. About 10km along this road, a signposted right turn-off leads to the mission after 5km.

Kaporogwe Waterfall

The impressive Kaporogwe or Makete Waterfall plunges roughly 20m over a large basaltic ledge into the Kiwira Gorge about 15km downriver of Daraja la Mungu. An interesting feature of the waterfall is that it is possible to follow a footpath into a cave below the ledge, so that you can view it from behind. A second footpath leads to the base of the falls. A Tsh500 entrance fee is charged. According to the guides, a rope bridge across the Kiwira River lies about one hour's walk from the waterfall.

To reach Kaporogwe Waterfall, follow the Kyela road south from Tukuyu for about 5km, then turn right along a side road signposted for the Lutengano Moravian Centre. After 7km, you'll reach the Moravian Centre, which offers good value accommodation and camping (see *Where to stay* above). About 2km past the centre, turn left along a road signposted for Ilulwe School, passing the Katumba Dispensary after about 1km, then after another 500m you'll reach the school, where the road forks two ways. Take the right fork, then after another 1km a left fork, from where it's about 8km to the parking area above the waterfall. The footpath from the parking lot to the cave behind the waterfall takes about five minutes to walk.

LAKE NYASA

Split between Malawi, Mozambique and Tanzania, this 585km-long Rift Valley lake, enclosed by tall mountains, is arguably the most scenic body of water in

Africa. Although the Malawian part of the lake is more popular with travellers, the Tanzanian portion is perhaps more attractive, particularly Matema Beach on the northeast tip of the lake, where the combination of a stunning location and affordable accommodation more than justify the relatively minor effort required to get there. Unfortunately, the rest of the Tanzanian part of the lake – with the exception of the workmanlike Itungi Port – is relatively inaccessible. The only accessible place on the eastern lakeshore is Mbamba Bay, a lovely village that is linked to Songea by road and to Itungi Port on the western shore by ferry. Lake Nyasa boasts little in the way of terrestrial wildlife – vervet monkeys are common in some areas – but it does support a wide variety of birds, most conspicuously the vociferous fish eagle. The lake is also known for its great variety of fish and in particular its colourful cichlids (see box *Cichlids of the Great Lakes*, pages 476–7).

Lake Nyasa is most often referred to today as Lake Malawi, a name which, despite its widespread international usage, has no historical veracity. During the colonial era, and in recorded descriptions predating colonialism, the lake was universally referred to as Nyasa. The appellation Malawi came into use as recently as 1964, when the first post-independence government of the former Nyasaland Protectorate renamed both country and lake in order to nurture popular mystical associations between the new leadership and the legendary medieval Maravi Empire. Understandably, the neighbouring states were not particularly inclined to be influenced by this act of political expediency, and today the same body of water is known officially and colloquially as Lake Malawi in Malawi, Lake Nyasa in Tanzania and Lago Niassa in Mozambique.

Climatically, arriving at the lakeshore might take some adjustment coming from the cool highlands around Tukuyu. Less than 500m above sea level, Lake Nyasa can be swelteringly hot, though the breeze – sometimes a howling wind – that comes off the lake generally cools things down at night. Lake Nyasa has a bad reputation for cerebral malaria, so take your pills, continue to take them for four weeks after you leave the area, and get to a doctor quickly if you display malarial symptoms during that period.

Kyela

Kyela, the gateway town to the Tanzanian part of Lake Nyasa, comes as something of an anticlimax after the breathtaking 1,000m ascent from Tukuyu – with tantalising glimpses through the lush montane escarpment to the blue waters of the lake far below. Scruffy, sweaty and scenically unmemorable, Kyela is stranded some 10km inland of the lakeshore port of Itungi, and possesses all the oppressive attributes of the tropical lakeshore climate, bar the all-redeeming waterside breeze. It is also one of these irritating towns, so rare in Tanzania, whose more youthful residents are evidently unable to conquer the impulse to yell '*Mzungu!*' at any passing European. With Matema Beach beckoning to the north, you'd be unlikely to stay in Kyela out of choice, though you may need to should you intend to catch a ferry at Itungi Port. Fortunately, should you sleep over, Kyela's long-standing collection of tawdry shoestring guesthouses has of late been supplemented by a smattering of decent budget hotels.

Getting there and away

The normal approach route to Kyela is the 140km road from Mbeya, which passes through Tukuyu at the midway point and is surfaced except for the last 5km stretch between the junction to Songwe (on the Malawi border) and Kyela itself. In a private vehicle, this road can be covered in two and a bit hours without stops,

LAKE NYASA FERRIES

Due to the formidable natural obstacle formed by the Livingstone Mountains and associated ranges along the northeast of Lake Nyasa, no roads worth talking about connect the ports on the eastern and western shores. The best – indeed the only – way in which travellers can take a look at the more remote parts of Lake Nyasa, or get between the eastern and western shores, is by using the erratic ferry service that connects Itungi Port to Mbamba Bay. It's a wonderfully scenic trip, with the Livingstone Mountains rising sharply above the clear blue waters of the lake, and visits a number of ports that are otherwise practically cut off from the outside world. Luxurious, however, the boats are not. Facilities are very basic third-class only, and schedules somewhat whimsical, as the ferry stops interminably at one fishing village after the next, to be greeted by a flotilla of local dugouts whose occupants thrust fish, fruit and other goods to the passengers in the hope of a sale.

All going well, two Tanzanian ferries ply the Nyasa lakeshore, though it is often the case that one or other boat – very occasionally both – is in dry dock for repairs. The MV *Songea* leaves Itungi at around 07.00 on Monday and Thursday and arrives at Mbamba Bay at midnight the same day, after stopping at Lupingu, Manda, Lundu, Nindai and Liuli. After arriving at Mbamba Bay, the Monday ferry turns around more-or-less immediately, to arrive back at Itungi at 17.00 the next day. The Thursday ferry continues travelling on to Nkhata Bay in Malawi, arriving some time on Friday, before starting the return voyage to Itungi. The smaller MV *Iringa* leaves Itungi at 07.00 on Wednesday and arrives back on Thursday afternoon. This stops at most lakeside villages, including Matema, but doesn't go as far as Mbamba Bay. The above timings are *very* approximate. On both boats, there is only one seated class, and it is not normally overcrowded. Tickets cost US$4. Meals are available on board, as are sodas and beers.

More comfortable than either of the above boats is the Malawian MV *Ilala*, which normally crosses between Nkhata Bay and Mbamba Bay and back once weekly. In theory, it leaves Nkhata Bay at 01.00 on Tuesday morning, arrives at Mbamba Bay three to four hours later, and then starts the return trip at 07.30. In practice, the MV *Ilala* is just about always six to twelve hours behind schedule, and when it falls too far behind, the crossing to Mbamba Bay is omitted from its weekly voyage.

There is no accommodation in Itungi. You will have to spend the night in Kyela and get a vehicle to Itungi at around 05.30 on the morning of departure. Vehicles leave from in front of the TRC office, 1km out of town. There is a booking office at the TRC building, but as the ticket officer travels with the ferry it serves no practical function. You can buy a ticket at Itungi while you wait for the ferry to be loaded up.

while regular buses from Mbeya take about four hours, stopping at Tukuyu on the way. This is one of the most scenic roads in Tanzania, so be sure to get a window seat. Scandinavia Coaches and Zainab's buses offer direct bus services from Kyela to Dar es Salaam, passing through Mbeya, Iringa and Morogoro. The full fare to Dar es Salaam is Tsh13,000.

Buses from Mbeya all stop at the junction for the Songwe border post, 5km before the road from Mbeya enters Kyela, from where it is normally easy enough to catch a lift to the border post, though bicycle taxis are also available. Be warned that if you are intending to travel through to Kyela, local bus conductors are used to foreign travellers disembarking at this junction, and it may require some convincing before they accept that you know what you are doing! Arriving at the border in the late afternoon used to be unwise, because there was no accommodation and transport on to Karonga in northern Malawi was thin on the ground. These days, however, there is an excellent guesthouse at the border (see *Where to stay* below) and there is also plenty of onward transport.

In early 2002, the 5km stretch of dirt road between the junction and Kyela was temporarily closed for upgrading, which meant that all vehicles heading to Kyela had to veer south to the border and use a back route from there to Kyela township. Once the road re-opens, it should be surfaced all the way into Kyela.

All ferries on Lake Nyasa leave from Itungi Port 10km from Kyela. There is a ferry office about 1km out of town towards Itungi where departure times can be confirmed in advance. For further details, see the box *Lake Nyasa Ferries* opposite).

Where to stay
Moderate
Bujonde Beach Resort Tel/Fax: 025 250 0163; mobile: 0744 279095 or 420786. Located at the mouth of the Kiwira River, a short distance west of Itungi Port, this resort is currently under construction. It will offer camping and self-catering huts, as well as a bar and restaurant, boat hire, angling and snorkelling. Sixteen *bandas* are planned (standard, family and luxury).

Budget
MSM Lodge Arguably better than anything in town, this pleasant new lodge is situated in Songwe about 1km before the border post with Malawi. *Banda* accommodation costs Tsh2,500/3,500 single/double using common showers or Tsh4,500/5,000 self-contained. All rooms have fans, mosquito netting and running water. There is a beer garden and snack bar in the green grounds.

The Oberoi Park Tel: 025 254 0395. This smart new hotel, which lies 200m from the bus station, charges Tsh5,000 for a spotless self-contained room with a double bed, fan and running water. It's easily the best place in town, though the lack of mosquito netting in this climate is a serious oversight.

Pattaya Guesthouse Also quite close to the bus station, this is an above average guesthouse charging Tsh5,000 for a self-contained room with double bed or Tsh6,000 for one with two beds. The rooms are clean and have fans, but once again no mosquito netting!

Shoestring
Makete Half London Guesthouse Probably the best of the cheapies, and situated right opposite the bus station and market, this guesthouses charges Tsh3,500 for a reasonably clean self-contained room with double bed, fan and mosquito netting.

Where to eat
The **New Steak Inn Restaurant**, opposite the market, is clean and comfortable, and while the tantalisingly elaborate menu rather overstates the culinary options, it does serve a decent plate of chicken and chips for Tsh1,000. The **New Mummy Classic Restaurant** next to the Pattaya Guesthouse is a good, unpretentious local eatery.

Matema Beach

The long sandy tropical beach at Matema is perhaps the most beautiful anywhere on Lake Nyasa-Malawi. Situated on the lake's northern tip, Matema lies in the shadow of the Livingstone Mountains, which rise sharply to an altitude of nearly 2,500m within 4km of the lakeshore, with the Poroto Mountains set further back on the western horizon. Matema Beach is relatively undeveloped for tourism, certainly by comparison to such legendary Malawian backpacker hangouts as Nkhata Bay or Cape Maclear – which has its pros and cons. On the minus side are the facilities, which might politely be described as unexciting: a couple of decent if decidedly institutional church-run lodges that serve basic meals of the fish-and-*ugali* ilk, and operate a no alcohol policy. The flip side of the same coin is that Matema, unlike the more popular and buzzing Malawian beach hangouts, doesn't yet come across as a budding resort whose soul is gradually being eroded in order to accommodate the requirements of international travellers. Refreshingly rustic and uncompromisingly African, Matema is the kind of place that you could settle into for a while: swimming in the deliciously warm (and reputedly bilharzia-free) water, chatting to the local fishermen, undertaking local excursions, or just waiting for the sun to set behind the Poroto.

Getting there and away

The two main road routes to Matema converge at the small junction town of Ipinda, which lies about 10km inland of the lake as the crow flies and 27km from Matema by road. Coming from Mbeya or Kyela, the most normal route to Matema leads from the surfaced road between these two towns about 3km north of Kyela, from where it's a straightforward 14km run to Ipinda. Coming from Mbeya, a rougher but shorter 46km back route to Ipinda, via Masoko Crater Lake, runs from Tukuyu, where you need to turn left at the main intersection on the Kyela road, passing Langboss Lodge to your left after about 1km.

Direct public transport to Matema is restricted to a daily bus to and from Mbeya, passing through Tukuyu, Kyela and Ipinda, but since this bus arrives at Matema after dark and leaves again at 05.00, it's not all that convenient. It is easier to get to Matema using light vehicles. If you can't find a pick-up truck running directly between Kyela and Matema, you should find one from Kyela to Ipinda. There is also the odd pick-up truck running between Tukuyu and Ipinda via Masoko Crater Lake. The daily bus aside, there is normally some private transport between Ipinda and Matema, especially on Saturdays, and most vehicles will stop to pick up passengers for a small fee. Should you need to spend the night in Ipinda, there is a basic but adequate guesthouse behind the bank. It is also possible to walk between Ipinda and Matema in two to three hours, following the Lufirio River to its mouth 3km west of the mission. On the day before you plan to leave Matema, it's worth asking the mission whether any of their vehicles are heading to Ipinda the next morning.

The ferry that leaves Itungi at 07.00 Wednesday arrives at Matema an hour later. It also stops at Matema on Thursday afternoon on its way back to Itungi. Ferries to Mbamba Bay *do not* stop at Matema. The Lutheran Mission in Matema can arrange for a local canoe to take you to Itungi Port for Tsh2,000, and it should presumably be possible to make a similar arrangement privately for a transfer in the opposite direction.

Where to stay
Moderate

Matema Beach Evangelical Church Hostel This smart new church hostel, which lies on an attractive stretch of beach on the western fringe of Matema village, is popular with

KISI POTTERY

The small Kisi tribe, which lives in a series of small villages along the northwest shore of Lake Nyasa, is renowned throughout Tanzania and northern Malawi for the high quality and distinctively pale pottery it produces. The pots are made exclusively by women – Kisi men, like their peers elsewhere along the lake, are dedicated fishermen – and were originally made for home use and to trade with neighbouring tribes for agricultural produce. These days, however, Kisi pottery has been transformed into a lucrative cottage industry, the product of which is sold in bulk to traders at the Saturday market at Lyulilo near Matema, for distribution to larger markets in Kyela, Mbeya, Dar es Salaam, Karonga (in northern Malawi) and further afield.

About a dozen types of pot are made by Kisi women, each with a specific purpose. The largest pots, with a capacity of about 25 litres, are called *ngumbe* and used to store various grains. The smallest *tukalango* pots, by contrast, are about the size of a moderate saucepan and used exclusively for cooking. Younger women customarily learn their craft by making *tukalango*, graduating stage by stage to crafting *ngumbe* as they grow in age and skill.

The technique used by the potters is unique within Tanzania. First, a ball of unmoulded clay is placed on a circular plate and hollowed out with two hands to form a rudimentary bowl. The potter will then rotate the plate manually with one hand, while refining and evening the pot with the other. A white clay finish is then applied to the outside of the completed pot using a maize cob or a smooth pebble. The unfired pot will then be left out to sun-dry for a few days, before being decorated in geometric patterns using an ochre paste. Finally, once a sufficient number of pots are ready, they will be fired using a method similar to the one used by traditional brick-makers throughout rural Africa. A layer of banana leaves and firewood is placed in a depression, the pots are arranged on top of this, and then smothered with a thick cover of grass, to be left for about two hours in the smouldering fire.

Although the main Kisi pottery market is within easy walking distance of Matema, the bulk of the pottery sold there is produced at the village of Ikombe, which is situated close to a feldspar outcrop that gives the Kisi clay its attractive creamy white coloration. Ikombe lies only 30 minutes from Matema by local canoe, and visitors are welcome. If you are interested in a souvenir, the pots are very affordable, particularly if bought locally, where they sell for about a quarter of the price asked in Dar es Salaam.

expatriate families. Accommodation consists of a row of comfortable self-contained double-storey beachfront chalets with private verandas, costing Tsh15,000 for a three-bed unit and Tsh25,000 for a five-bed unit. A restaurant serves decent meals and chilled soft drinks, but no alcohol.

Budget and camping

Matema Lutheran Conference Centre and Retreat This well-established retreat, situated immediately below the main roundabout in the village, consists of numerous small *banda*s, with between one and four beds each, clustered above the beach. The rooms have comfortable beds and mosquito nets, but several are starting to look decidedly mildewed and scruffy. A beach kiosk sells cold sodas and coffee/tea, and a canteen serves substantial but uninteresting set meals, which must be ordered in advance, and cost Tsh2,000 per head. Self-contained rooms cost Tsh6,000 single and Tsh2,400 per person thereafter, while rooms using common showers cost Tsh4,800 single and Tsh1,800 per person thereafter. Camping is permitted for Tsh3,000 per tent. Although no alcohol is served, a small kiosk on the roundabout above the hostel sells lukewarm beers.

Excursions from Matema Beach

In the stifling heat of the lakeshore even the shortest stroll can feel like a major excursion, for which reason the best time to explore is the early morning. One pleasant 15-minute stroll leads along the beach east of Matema to the small fishing village of **Lyulilo**, renowned locally for its Saturday **pottery market** (see box *Kisi Pottery*, page 555). If you walk out there along the beach, you might want to return by a rough dirt road that runs a short distance inland, passing through lush tropical vegetation – plenty of birdlife – and neat traditional Nyakyusa homesteads.

Close to the lakeshore, about 500m past Lyulilo, **Pango Cave** (also known as Likyala Cave) was an important Nyakyusa sacrificial site in times of drought, before missionaries arrived in the area and forbade the practice. The cave harbours a significant bat colony, and a small waterfall close by tumbles into a cool, clear pool. The rocky lakeshore between Lyulilo and the cave hosts a large variety of colourful cichlids, and makes for excellent snorkelling, but you'll need your own gear to explore it. If you don't feel like walking, the Lutheran Mission can arrange a local boat to take you to the market or cave for Tsh1,000 per person.

Although the main regional pottery market is held at Lyulilo, the pots are mostly crafted at the village of **Ikombe**, which is the place to visit if you want to see the potters at work or to buy pottery on days other than Saturday. Ikombe can be reached on foot by following a rough footpath along the lakeshore past Lyulilo. Better, however, to travel there by canoe, which takes about 30 minutes in each direction, and costs Tsh1,500 for the round trip if organised through the Lutheran Mission in Matema.

In the opposite direction, heading along the beach for about 3km west of Matema, the extensive papyrus beds at the **Lufirio River Mouth** offer excellent birding as well as a chance of seeing crocodiles. Hippos are resident a short distance upriver. Once again, you have the option of walking from Matema, or of arranging a local canoe at the Lutheran Mission, which costs Tsh2,000 per person for the round trip.

A one-hour walk inland of the beach leads to the **Mwalalo Waterfall** – or more accurately the series of waterfalls formed by the Mwalalo River as it tumbles down the escarpment of the Livingstone Mountains. The Mwalalo River is the sole source of fresh water for the village and mission, who are concerned that travellers visiting the waterfall without a guide might pollute it. For this reason, you need permission from the village council and a local guide to visit the waterfall, all of which can easily be arranged through the mission for Tsh2,000 per person. More energetically, the mission can also arrange guided day walks up the **Livingstone Mountains**.

One warning: Crocodiles are not resident on Matema Beach, but they are common on rockier and shallower stretches of the lakeshore and at river outlets, where they kill villagers with a frequency that suggests you should definitely ask local advice before swimming, except on the main beach. Best, too, to avoid swimming after dark – crocs have been known to travel long distances at night.

Mbamba Bay

Mbamba Bay is the most southerly town on the Tanzanian part of Lake Nyasa. It is also the sole transport hub on the lake's eastern shore, connected by road to

THE BATTLE OF SPHINXHAFEN

The penultimate stop on the southbound ferry trip from Itungi to Mbamba Bay is Liuli, whose attractive natural harbour is overlooked by the sphinx-like rock formation referred to in the village's original German name of Sphinxhafen. Liuli is the site of the largest mission in this part of Tanzania, and the burial place of William Johnson, the Anglican missionary who co-founded the Likoma mission on an island in the Malawian part of the lake. Johnson is one of the most fondly remembered of all the missionaries who worked in the Lake Nyasa area; for 46 years he preached from a boat all around the lakeshore, despite being practically blind and well into his seventies when he died in 1928. Johnson's grave was for several decades a pilgrimage site for Malawian Christians.

Liuli's greatest claim to posterity is as the site of the first naval encounter of World War I, an incident trumpeted by a headline in *The Times* in London as 'Naval Victory on Lake Nyasa' and by a participant, Mr G M Sanderson, as 'pure comedy'. Shortly after war was declared, the British Commissioner of Nyasaland dispatched the protectorate's only ship, the *Gwendolyn*, to destroy its German counterpart, the *Hermann Von Wessman*. The *Gwendolyn*'s captain, Commander Rhoades, was informed at Nkhata Bay that the *Wessman* was docked for repairs at Sphinxhafen. He sailed into the harbour in the cover of dawn with a somewhat nervous crew. The only gunner was a Scots storeman who had trained several years previously as a seaman-gunner and who freely admitted that he remembered little of his training. After several misfires, caused by a combination of dud ammunition and rusty aiming, a shell finally connected with the German boat.

'Immediately afterwards,' wrote Sanderson several years later, 'a small white dinghy put off from shore, in which was a European clad in a singlet and a pair of shorts pulling furiously for the *Gwen*. Rhoades ordered 'Cease fire' and blessed silence fell. It was his drinking pal [Captain Berndt], the skipper of the *Wessman*, with whom every meeting was a drinking party. The dinghy came alongside and its furious occupant leaped to his feet and, shaking both fists above his head, exclaimed 'Gott for dam, Rrroades, vos you drunk?' It transpired that news of the war had not yet reached sleepy Sphinxhafen, and when Rhoades informed his old friend that he was now a prisoner of war, Sanderson wrote that 'one could see his anger turn to horror as he realised his fatal mistake.'

Good enough reason to pause when the boat stops at Liuli, though it's an open question whether you'd think about disembarking. Liuli lies on a lovely stretch of shore; the German mission and Johnson's grave are still there; and, who knows, with a bit of imagination you might even be able to conjure up the image of a semi-naked and infuriated Captain Berndt gesticulating from his dinghy.

More pragmatically, there's nowhere to stay, and when you want to move on you'll be reliant on the occasional mission vehicle heading to Mbamba Bay, or more likely the next ferry. Of course, if you have a tent and you don't mind a couple of days' wait for transport out, this might just add up to a most attractive off-the-beaten-track option – food, at least, shouldn't be a problem on the shore of this most fish-rich of lakes.

THE NGONI

The origin and history of most of Tanzania's ethnic groups is clouded by vagaries inherent in events recalled only through oral traditions and legends. Not so the Ngoni of Songea, who – as their name suggests – are an offshoot of the Nguni of what is today the coastal belt of the South African province of KwaZulu-Natal.

In the early 19th century, the iconic King Shaka forged the mighty Zulu Kingdom from hundreds of disparate small Nguni chiefdoms of KwaZulu-Natal. Most of the chiefdoms within the region were either obliterated or sublimated, but a handful – for instance the future Matebele of eastern Zimbabwe – managed to flee across the Limpopo River, beyond the reach of Shaka's ruthlessly efficient army. Another such group was the Ndandwe, led by Chief Zwangendaba, who crossed the Limpopo in the early 1820s, taking with them the innovative military tactics, lethal short-stabbing spear, and ruthless militancy that had been installed by Shaka.

After some years of roaming aggressively around present-day Zimbabwe, the Ndandwe, unable to hold out against the Matebele, were forced to head further north, crossing the Zambezi River in November 1835. In this virgin territory, Zwangendaba's well-drilled and ruthless war-band of about 2,000 warriors were able to ride roughshod over villagers who had never been exposed to their ruthless but effective style of warfare. The Ngoni carved a bloody swathe through what is today Tete Province of Mozambique and the Zambia–Malawi border area, raiding one community for cattle, crops and women, settling there until the plundered resources were depleted, before pushing on to find fresh quarry.

In 1845, Zwangendaba and his Ngoni reached Ufipa to the east of Lake Tanganyika, where they finally established a permanent settlement called Mapupo. Three year later, however, Zwangendaba died, resulting in a secession battle that splintered his army into at least half a dozen different factions. Some factions continued northwards, others retreated south. The precursors of the Songea Ngoni, however, were two allied groups led by former royal advisors called Zulugama and Mbonani, who marched in an easterly direction to the northern tip of Lake Nyasa.

The factions led by Zulugama and Mbonani defeated another Ngoni splinter group in a lakeshore clash a short distance southwest of present-day Matema Beach before settling at Mlangala about halfway between Matema and Mbamba Bay. Zulugama died at Mlangala in 1858, and Mbonani assumed temporary control of both factions. Two years later, Mbonani was invited to a feast by Chief Maseko, the leader of an unrelated group of Ngoni who had assumed control of a large area of neighbouring territory. Maseko tricked Mbonani and several of his advisors into falling into a large pit overlaid with mats, then speared them all to death.

Following this act of treachery, a punitive raid was led against the Maseko Ngoni, who were driven away to what is today southern Malawi. The power

Songea in the Southeast Highlands, by a thrice-weekly domestic ferry link to Itungi Port on the western shore, and by a weekly ferry to Nkhata Bay in Malawi. The small port of clay brick thatched houses lies on a pretty coconut-lined beach, with a western orientation offering several good vantage points to watch the sunset. I'm not aware of any specific sightseeing in the surrounding area, but it would be a pleasant place to chill out for a few days, and you can certainly arrange boat trips on to the lake with local fishermen.

vacuum created by this victory allowed the followers of Zulugama and Mbonani to take control of most of the northwest lake hinterland, after which they split into two discrete chieftaincies. Known respectively as Njelu and Mshope, the two chieftaincies remained firm allies throughout the remainder of the 19th century, though the Njelu were always the dominant military and political force. The Ngoni Empire was essentially forged between 1862 and the early 1870s, as the Njelu and Mshope expanded their territories coastward, launching characteristically merciless attacks on smaller tribes who were then co-opted into the kingdom under the local leadership of trusted generals. (The most famous of whom, incidentally, was Songea, whose camp lay about 2km from the modern town that bears his name.)

The Ngoni Empire peaked in influence during the 1880s, when they controlled practically the whole of the interior between the coast and Lake Nyasa. Its leadership had by this time also forged a strong trade relationship with the Arab merchants of Kilwa and Mikindani, and it was the brutal and frequent Ngoni slave raids that provided most of the human booty sold at the coastal ports. The indigenous tribes of the region – or at least those who had survived the slave raids – were fully integrated into the Ngoni Kingdom, and comprised the bulk of the royal army. Nevertheless, a rigid social distinction existed between the true Ngoni (ie: the descendants of the Ndandwe war-bands) and the new Ngoni, with all local and central leadership roles being reserved exclusively for the former.

In 1897, the Germans established a military base at Gumbiro, about 70km north of modern-day Songea. The Ngoni offered little initial resistance to the colonists, assuming that they would be able to forge with them a trade relationship similar to the one they had previously enjoyed with the Arab merchants. This was not to be, however, as the Germans rapidly demonstrated that they would only support Ngoni chiefs and generals who were unambiguously subordinate to the colonial authorities. In September 1905, spurred by news of the Maji-Maji rebellion elsewhere in the territory, King Chabruma of Mshope launched an unsuccessful attack on the garrison at Gumbiro and razed the Benedictine Mission at Maposeni. This was followed by a bloody battle in which the combined Mshope and Njelu armies were soundly defeated by the Germans.

Not content with this decisive victory, the Germans then launched a series of somewhat arbitrary punitive raids on local villages, razing crops, destroying homes, and executing villagers at whim. Chabruma of Mshope fled the country to die in exile in Mozambique. His less fortunate Njelu counterpart Mputa was hanged by the Germans, together with all his sub-chiefs and generals, robbing the Ngoni of legitimate leadership from grassroots up. The Germans would later install puppet kings over Mshope and Njelu, but the Ngoni Kingdom, born of violence only 40 years earlier, was essentially an entity of the past – destroyed by a similarly ruthless but better armed conquering power.

Getting there and away

The only road route in or out is the 170km dirt road that leads east to Songea in the southeast highlands, passing through the small but well-equipped town of Mbinga about 65km from Mbamba Bay. The stretch of road between Mbamba Bay and Songea is thrilling, clinging to the mountainside and offering dramatic views back to the lake as it winds up the Rift Valley escarpment wall through well-developed *miombo* woodland. It is also very slow, and potentially treacherous after rain!

There used to be an erratic bus service between Mbamba Bay and Mbinga, but this doesn't seem to operate anymore. A few 4WD vehicles do cover the road daily, leaving when they are full and taking about three hours in good weather. In wet weather, the trip can take twice as long, divided between trudging up muddy slopes while the driver tries to free his vehicle, and clinging terrified and dripping to the sides of the overloaded vehicle while it skids uncertainly around the precipitous road. I imagine the road would be impassable after heavy rain.

Depending on how well the trip from Mbamba Bay goes, Mbinga might come across as a veritable oasis, or as just another dull small African town. Whatever else, once you hit Mbinga there is plenty of decent accommodation (see *Where to Stay* below), regular transport along a well-maintained dirt road to Songea, and even a 'Special Video Bus' to Dar es Salaam three days a week.

For details of ferries to Itungi Port and Nkhata Bay, see the box *Lake Nyasa Ferries*, page 552.

Where to stay and eat

A few years back, accommodation in Mbamba Bay was limited to one very basic guesthouse, but there are now several possibilities, partly as a result of the recent resumption of international ferry services to Nkhata Bay in Malawi. The pick of the hotels are the laboriously named **Neema Beach Guest Garden Hotel Bar and Pharmacy** and more succinct **Nyasa View Lodge**, both of which charge around Tsh6,000 for self-contained double and have a bar and restaurant.

The lovely **Chinula Paradise and Lundu Island** (Tel/fax: 025 250 0163 or 0744 279095/420786), located on a pristine beach 10km north of Mbamba Bay along the Liuli road, is currently being renovated. It will soon re-open with eight double chalets, a bar and restaurant, boat hire, diving and snorkelling (all equipment for hire). An affiliated honeymoon camp will be situated on Lundu Island, just 1.5km offshore. Prices are not yet available.

If you want to overnight in Mbinga, there are a few basic guesthouses dotted around the bus station, while the unexpectedly smart **Mbicu Hotel** offers self-contained rooms with satellite television and air conditioning for around Tsh6,000, as well as a restaurant and coffee bar.

THE SOUTHEAST HIGHLANDS

The seldom visited highlands to the east of Lake Nyasa hold little of compelling interest, and few travellers would explore the area for its own sake. The region is most likely to be passed through by the few travellers who cross between Mtwara on the south coast and the Tanzam Highway or Lake Nyasa. Songea is the main regional transport hub, connected to Makambako on the Tanzam Highway via a good surfaced 300km road through Njombe, to Mbamba Bay on Lake Nyasa by a rougher 170km road, and to Masasi in the east by one of the most appalling roads in the country.

Songea

Situated at the junction of the road to Mbamba Bay and the road connecting the Tanzam Highway to the south coast, Songea is the administrative centre of the remote Ruvuma Region. Arriving in Songea from the south coast or Lake Nyasa, its busy market, well-stocked supermarkets and general state of good repair are a welcome re-connection with the modern world. Until the ivory moratorium in 1989, Songea was a major centre for poachers smuggling ivory out of the Selous, and it has subsequently become an important centre for the

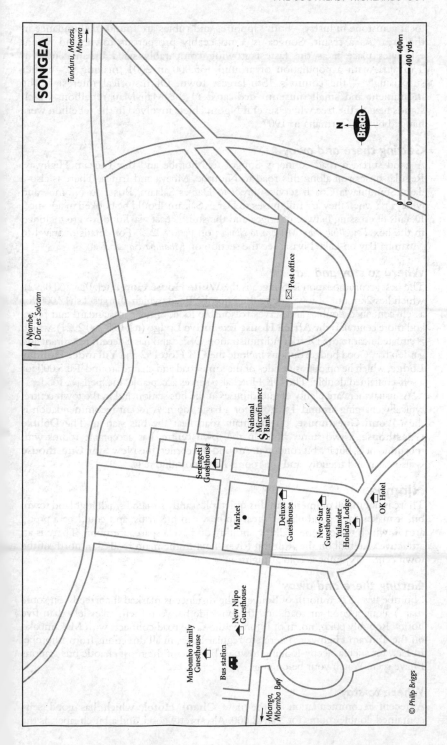

SONGEA

Njombe,
Dar es Salaam

Tunduru, Masasi,
Mtwara

Bradt

N

Post office

National
Microfinance
Bank

Serengeti
Guesthouse

Market

Deluxe
Guesthouse

New Star
Guesthouse

Yulander
Holiday Lodge

OK Hotel

New Nipo
Guesthouse

Mubombo Family
Guesthouse

Bus station

Mbanga,
Mbamba Bay

© Philip Briggs

400m
400 yds

local gemstone industry – both sapphires and rubies are found in abundance in the area. As a result, Songea is a noticeably prosperous town, and recent estimates place it as the fastest-growing comparably sized urban centre in Tanzania, with a population of around 135,000 in 2001, making it – rather surprisingly – the county's 15th-largest town. Of historical interest is the monument and small museum dedicated to the Maji-Maji rebellion, which stands next to the tree where several Ngoni chiefs involved in the rebellion were hanged by the Germans in 1907.

Getting there and away
A good surfaced road connects Songea to Njombe and the Tanzam Highway. Regular buses run along this road to Njombe, Mbeya and Iringa. There is also a daily Scandinavia Coach service direct to Dar es Salaam. Buses to Njombe and Mbeya go when they are full; buses to Dar es Salaam should be booked in advance. Details of crossing between Songea and the south coast via Tunduru are included in the box *Travelling from Mtwara to Songea* on page 602–3. For details of travel to Mbamba Bay on Lake Nyasa, see the section on *Mbamba Bay* above.

Where to stay and eat
The best accommodation in Songea is the **White House Hotel** (tel: 025 260 0892), which lies 2km out of town along the Njombe Road, which charges Tsh12,000 for a self-contained double, and serves reasonable food. Similar in standard and price, and more central, is the **Africa House Executive Lodge** (tel: 025 260 2921), which is situated near to the District Administration Office and has a decent restaurant and garden bar. Good budget options include the **OK Hotel 92** and **Yulander Holiday Lodge**, which lie on opposite sides of the same road and charge around Tsh5,000 for a self-contained double. The OK Hotel also serves acceptable, inexpensive food.

As usual there are plenty of guesthouses at the bus station and in the town centre, typically charging around Tsh2,000 for a basic room. A recent recommendation is the **Mkomi Guesthouse**, on the main road near the bus station. The **Deluxe Guesthouse**, a two-storey hotel in the town centre, has acceptable rooms with mosquito nets, but it's bit rundown. Around the corner, the **New Star Guesthouse** is also clean and friendly, and the rooms have mosquito nets.

Njombe
There is not much of interest in this quiet, pleasantly situated small highland town, but it makes for a good place to rest up between bus trips, and could be a pretty area in which to do some walking should you have a spare afternoon. There is an attractive waterfall on the Ruhudji River, next to the main road 2km north of the town centre. Njombe is cold at night.

Getting there and away
Njombe lies 237km north of Songea (the distance is marked incorrectly on some maps) along a good tar road, and the bus ride between them takes less than five hours. Roughly 60km north of Njombe the same road connects with Makambako on the Tanzam Highway. There are regular buses in all directions from Njombe. In fact, for such a sleepy-looking town, it has one of the most chaotic bus stations I have seen. Watch your belongings.

Where to stay
A recent recommendation is the new **Chani Hotel**, which has good self-contained double rooms for Tsh12,000. Also pretty good, and a bit cheaper, is the

two-storey **Milimani Motel** 250m from the bus station towards Songea, which has a good bar and restaurant, and clean rooms with hot showers. The **Lutheran Centre Hostel**, 50m and signposted from the main road, offers beds in clean, recently furnished dormitories for Tsh2,000 per person, and it has a fair canteen. Several basic guesthouses are studded around the bus station.

Makambako

Makambako lies at the junction of the Tanzam Highway and the road southeast towards Njombe and Songea. The most likely reason why you'd stop off here for the night is between bus trips, though it's also worth noting that it contains just about the only decent accommodation along the 390km stretch of the Tanzam Highway between Mbeya and Iringa. The accommodation in question is the unexpectedly good **Uplands Hotel**, which charges Tsh4,000/8,000 for a self-contained single/double with hot water, and serves good food for Tsh2,000. For cheaper accommodation, the **Lutheran Hostel** on the Iringa side of the main junction is the best bet.

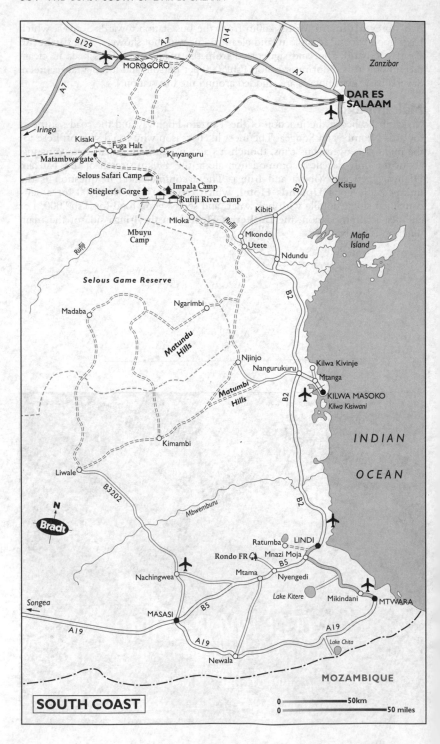

SOUTH COAST

The Coast South of Dar es Salaam

The 600km coastline stretching from Dar es Salaam south to the Rovuma River on the Mozambique border is remote in character and seldom visited by outsiders. There are few towns of real substance – only Mtwara and arguably Lindi qualify – and the region's poor road infrastructure has rendered them to be among the most isolated settlements of comparable size in East Africa. Certainly, the south coast will offer little to travellers who value their creature comforts: perhaps three or four hotels throughout the region could conceivably be described as tourist class; few people speak more than the most rudimentary English; bona fide tourist attractions are thin on the ground – and public transport is crowded and painfully slow.

Despite all this, the south coast is a fascinating, thought-proyoking and often enchanting area, endlessly rewarding to those with a sense of adventure and curiosity. The older towns are profoundly Swahili in character, their roads lined with crumbling German and Arab buildings that generate a time-warped atmosphere like something out of a Graham Greene novel. The people, too, retain a gracious, slow pace of life, one into which it is easy to slip, provided that you dress and behave in accordance with the conservative Muslim culture that dominates the region. Scenically, the south coast is all you might expect: stunning palm-lined beaches, thick mangrove swamps, and (as you head away from the beaches) baobab-studded acacia scrub. And, while there is an element of travel for its own sake attached to exploring this region, it does boast one genuine travel highlight in the form of Kilwa Kisiwani, far and away the most impressive and historically significant of the medieval Swahili ruins that line Africa's Indian Ocean coast.

The south coast's atmospheric aura of isolation can easily be romanticised, but there is a depressing reality behind the picturesque backwater images. I was struck by the number of beggars and cripples in the towns, by the malnourished children in roadside villages, and by the total lack of industry. This situation should be partly remedied when – or should that be if – long-standing plans to extend the surfaced road between Mtwara and Lindi north as far as Dar es Salaam, and to bridge the Rovuma on the Mozambican border, ever come to fruition.

The most important stopovers along the south coast, starting in the north, are Kilwa Masoko (the modern mainland town opposite the island of Kilwa Kisiwani), Lindi, Mikindani and Mtwara. This chapter also includes coverage of the Makonde Plateau, the area immediately inland of Lindi and Mtwara, renowned for its carving and painting traditions. The major towns on the plateau are Masasi and Newala.

CLIMATE
Like the rest of the Tanzanian coast, this region is hot and humid at all times. The ideal time to visit is in the drier, cooler months between April and October.

GETTING AROUND
At present, Air Tanzania flies twice weekly between Dar es Salaam and Mtwara, and Eagle Air operates flights between the above two towns, stopping at Lindi and Kilwa Masoko, four times a week. The only day on which there is no flight at all is Wednesday. Schedules do change regularly, but current flight details are posted under the 'how to get there' page of the Old Boma's website www.mikindani.com. Fares range from about US$90 one-way between Dar es Salaam and Mtwara with Air Tanzania to Tsh45,000 between Dar es Salaam and Kilwa Masoko.

The 590km road between Dar es Salaam and Mtwara near the Mozambican border can be divided into three main stretches. The first 150km or so between Dar es Salaam and the Rufiji River is sporadically paved, but in fairly poor condition throughout and frequently impassable after rain. The roughly 320km stretch between the Rufiji and Lindi is unsurfaced the whole way, and again often impassable during the wet season. The final 110km road between Lindi and Mtwara is surfaced the whole way, and in a good state of repair. A bridge currently being constructed over the Rufiji River should become operational during the lifespan of this fourth edition, but as things stand there is only a motor ferry, which generally entails a delay of about 30 minutes. In a private 4WD it would be just about possible to drive between Dar es Salaam and Mtwara with a very early start, but more realistic to stretch the journey over two days. Kilwa lies at about the halfway point, and is probably the most interesting accessible stopover.

During the dry season, daily buses run between Dar es Salaam and all the large towns covered in this chapter, but the road is often impassable during the rains. Buses running from Dar es Salaam all the way to Mtwara can take up to 24 hours, so again it makes sense to break up the journey at Kilwa and Lindi. Further south, good local bus services run along on the surfaced roads connecting Lindi, Mtwara and Masasi. The south coast can also be reached by road from the Southern Highlands; see box *Travelling from Mtwara to Songea* on pages 602–3.

The ideal way to explore the south coast on public transport would be to take a boat from Dar es Salaam to Mtwara and then work your way back overland. For details of boats, see the *Getting there and away* section under Mtwara.

KILWA AND SURROUNDS
Situated halfway between Dar es Salaam and the Mozambican border, the roughly 20km² island of Kilwa – which translates as 'Place of Fish' – is separated from the mainland by a palm-fringed channel no more than 2km wide. The small island supports a modest fishing community estimated at 300 people in 1974. In medieval times, by contrast, it housed the most important and opulent settlement anywhere on the eastern coast of Africa, for 300 years the hub of a thriving international trade dominated by gold that was mined in the distant highlands of present-day Zimbabwe. Kilwa never fully recovered from a sacking by the Portuguese in 1505, and following a brief, late-18th-century revival, the island was forsaken in favour of a newer settlement on the nearby mainland. By 1820, the great medieval city immortalised as Quiloa in Milton's *Paradise Lost*, and once thought to be the site of King Solomon's mythical mines, had been reduced to little more than a fishing village. And yet what does survive of the abandoned city – the haunted mosques, derelict palaces and lonely tombs – stands today as the most architecturally impressive and expansive testament to the so-called Golden Age of the Swahili

Coast. If you are thinking of heading this way, do first pop into the National Museum in Dar es Salaam, where an extensive display about Kilwa serves as a good historical primer for a visit to the actual site.

The ruined city of Kilwa (and adjacent fishing village) is today known as Kilwa Kisiwani (Kilwa on the Island), in order to distinguish it from two larger and more modern mainland towns that also bear the name Kilwa. The elder of these is Kilwa Kivinje (Kilwa of the Casuarina Trees), which was established circa 1800 by the Omani Arabs who abandoned Kilwa Kisiwani, and – as the coastal terminus of the 19th-century caravan route to Lake Nyasa – it had a status equivalent to Bagamoyo, effectively its northern counterpart. By contrast, Kilwa Masoko (Kilwa of the Market) is a far more modern entity, established during the colonial era, and now the main transport and commercial hub of the region, as well as the site of its administrative headquarters and most of its guesthouses.

The main interest of the Kilwa area is undoubtedly its history and architecture. Viewed in tandem, Kilwa Kisiwani and Kilwa Kivinje are possibly unique in containing well preserved buildings that represent virtually every stage in a millennium of coastal history, from the Golden Era of the Shirazi, through Portuguese domination and the Omani slave trade, to the early German colonial era. History aside, the Kilwa area – and Kilwa Kivinje in particular – is a good place to immerse oneself in a traditional Swahili port-cum-fishing-village culture. The surrounding coast is also very attractive, and a good swimming beach lies on the outskirts of Kilwa Masoko.

Kilwa Kisiwani lies towards the southern end of the Songo Songo Archipelago, a 50km-long conglomeration of islands and atolls formed many thousands of years ago when an estuary system flooded. Several other islands in the archipelago – most notably Songo Mnara – were settled in medieval times and today host extensive stone ruins. The archipelago also incorporates perhaps the most extensive of Tanzania's unprotected reef systems, comprising roughly 80km of coastal reef and 40 smaller patch reefs, though at present few local facilities exist for snorkelling or diving. In common with other offshore reefs in Tanzania, those around Kilwa have suffered some damage as a result of coral mining and dynamite fishing, but the deeper reefs are regarded to be in pristine condition, and there is some talk of gazetting the entire archipelago as a marine park. The surrounding seas reputedly harbour the world's densest population of dugong – a large and peculiar marine mammal, believed to have been the origin of the mermaid myth – but you would be extraordinarily fortunate to encounter one.

History
Almost wholly ignored by Tanzania's safari-based tourist industry and equally neglected in Western school curricula, Kilwa is – or was, in its medieval pomp – one of the most historically important settlements anywhere in Africa. For longer than three centuries, it formed the pivot of a gold trading network that linked the interior of what is today Zimbabwe with the Sultanates of Arabia, as well as medieval China and India. It was described contemporarily, by the most widely travelled man of his age, as 'one of the most beautiful and well-constructed cities in the world'. Its finest buildings – the Great Mosque and the Sultan's Palace or Husuni Kubwa – formed the undisputed apex of Swahili architectural aspirations. And yet, symptomatic of Kilwa's unenviable status as a forgotten town, locals today credit the latter building to the Portuguese settlers, whose presence in the Indian Ocean from 1498 onwards was the instrument of Kilwa's decline.

Many details of Kilwa's past are open to conjecture, but a combination of extensive archaeological excavations, contemporary descriptions and two surviving versions of the *Kilwa Chronicle* (written in 1520 under the supervision of the then-exiled Sultan) mean it's far better understood than that of many other medieval Swahili settlements.

Kilwa Kisiwani was occupied by the Shirazi precursors of the Swahili in about 800AD, though little is known about this early period. In 1150, the island was settled by Ali bin Al-Hasan, whose father, according to the *Kilwa Chronicle*, had a dream in Shiraz in which 'he saw a rat with an iron snout gnawing holes in the town wall... a prophecy of the ruin of their country'. The father and his six sons set sail for East Africa, where they disembarked at seven different ports. According to this tradition, Ali was known locally as Nguo Myingi (many clothes) after having traded Kilwa Kisiwani with the 'infidel king' of the facing mainland, in exchange for a quantity of cloth, 'some white, some black, and every other colour besides' sufficient to 'encircle the island'.

Tradition has it that Ali bin Al-Hasan ruled over Kilwa for 40 years, and his importance can be gauged by the fact that coins bearing his name – probably minted long after his death – have been found as far afield as Pemba and Mafia Islands. The dynasty he founded endured for 150 years, and is widely credited with having established Kilwa as a significant trade centre, whose sphere of influence stretched at least as far as Mafia and quite possibly beyond it. The earliest surviving reference to Kilwa is in an Arabic document written in 1222, and while it is less than illuminating ('a town in the country of the Zanj' if you really want to know), it does confirm that Kilwa had already become a rather important trading centre.

Another Arabic document, written a few years later, goes further in describing Kilwa as the principal port between Mogadishu and Madagascar, confirming that the island port flourished under Ali bin Al-Hasan and his successors. Kilwa does, however, seem to have entered a period of political (though perhaps not economic) turmoil in the late 13th century, initiated by repeated conflicts with the indigenous Shanga kingdom of the nearby island of Sanje ya Kati. According to the *Kilwa Chronicle*, the Sultan of Kilwa was, during this period, twice overthrown by the Shanga, who installed their leader in his place, but in both instances the upstart ruler was soon deposed by the islanders and a sultan of the Al Hasan dynasty reinstalled. This instability in turn seems to have prompted a series of internal coups, culminating in 1300 with the ascent of Sultan Al-Hasan Mahdali and the foundation of the Mahdali dymasty.

Al-Hasan Mahdali's was a short reign, as was that of his son and successor Sulaiman, who was killed by followers of the old Sultan. Stability was finally restored during the reign of Sultan Al-Hasan bin Sulaiman (1310–32), a highly respected scholar who had studied in Aden and made the pilgrimage to Mecca, and it was maintained during that of his brother Daud bin Sulaiman (1332–56). These two brothers presided over what was almost certainly Kilwa's peak in international prominence and commercial prosperity. Al-Hasan is generally accredited with the reconstruction of the Great Mosque and the domed extension to that building, and it was also he who built the splendid out-of-town palace now known as the Husuni Kubwa.

To explain Kilwa pre-eminence during the early 14th century, one needs to look at the broader pattern of the medieval gold trade out of Africa. The inland source of this gold, long shrouded in mystery, gave rise to such myths as King Solomon's Mines. It is known today that the gold was mined in the vicinity of Great Zimbabwe, the fabulous stone ruin for which the country Zimbabwe is named. The mechanism of trade between Great Zimbabwe and the coast remains a matter of conjecture. A coin minted at Kilwa has been unearthed at Great Zimbabwe, but cultural and architectural parallels between the two cities are non-existent, nor is there any evidence to suggest that the coastal traders ever visited – or indeed knew of – Great Zimbabwe.

What is certain is that the gold arrived at the coast at the port of Sofala (south of Beira in modern-day Mozambique), from where, prior to the mid-13th century, local middlemen must have transported it north along the coast to the Somali port of Mogadishu. This trade pattern probably reflects the inability of contemporary Arab vessels to sail much further south than Mogadishu within the annual monsoon cycle. As the volume of coastal trade increased, however, improvements in Arab navigation and ship design allowed them to penetrate steadily further south. But Sofala would have been beyond their reach whatever they did, since the winds south of Kilwa are notoriously fickle. Nevertheless, it would have suited the merchants of Sofala to bring the centre of trade closer to home. Kilwa was the ideal compromise, since it was the closest port to Sofala within easy reach of Arab vessels. It is often suggested, too, that the Mahdali dynasty had its roots in Sofala, but even if this is untrue, Sofala and Kilwa were clearly able to assume full control of the gold trade by the early 14th century.

Kilwa at this time was the dominant town on the coast, with a population exceeding 10,000, the first coin mint in sub-Saharan Africa, and an extensive system of wells (the latter still in use today). The Friday Mosque and Husuni Kubwa, the most impressive buildings on the island, if not the entire coast, date to this period. In addition to gold, Kilwa exported ivory and ebony, and it imported such fineries as eastern cloth and Chinese porcelain. The wealthy traders lived in houses of coral and some had small private mosques. Ordinary townsmen lived in mud-and-wattle huts. Even though some Arab traders settled on Kilwa, the vast majority of its occupants were local Swahili. The island was too small to be self-sufficient in food, so had extensive agricultural interests on the mainland. The only surviving description of Kilwa in this era, penned by Ibn Buttata, the greatest globetrotter of his era, is reproduced in the box *Contemporary Impressions of Kilwa Kisiwani*, pages 574–5.

Towards the end of Sultan Duad's rule, the maritime gold trade through Kilwa slowed almost to a standstill. The cause of this unexpected slump must have baffled the islanders, but almost certainly it was linked to the King of Timbuktu's trans-Saharan trek to the Mediterranean a few years earlier. Timbuktu, at this time, was the Sahelian equivalent to Kilwa, the trade funnel for gold mined in the rainforests of West Africa, and when its king arrived in Cairo, he carried such an abundance of golden gifts that the gold market temporarily collapsed. The long voyage south to Kilwa must suddenly have looked financially unattractive to Arabian merchants who could as easily pick up other popular trade items, such as ivory and tortoiseshell, further north. The loss of trade, possibly exacerbated by the Black Death that struck much of Europe and Arabia over 1346–49, caused a serious economic slump in Kilwa, presumably the reason why the Husuni Kubwa was abandoned after the death of Sultan Daud. For the next 50 years, Kilwa was almost forgotten by the outside world.

In the early 15th century, a sudden increase in the demand for gold across Europe and Arabia sparked a reversal in Kilwa's fortunes. The Arabian ships started to arrive as regularly as they had in the commercial heyday of the 1330s, and although the Husuni Kubwa remained in disuse, the town centre experienced a huge influx of wealth and corresponding construction boom. The Great Mosque was fully renovated, several ornate smaller mosques were built, and Makutani Palace was erected to house the incumbent Sultan Mohammed bin Sulaiman (1412–21) and his son and successor Al Malik bin Mohammed (1421–41), the latter regarded to be one of the islands greatest leaders. For reasons that are unclear, however, Kilwa seems to have slid backwards economically after Al Malik's death – a protracted secession dispute described in somewhat confusing terms in the *Kilwa Chronicle* might have been a factor in this. Kilwa remained an important trade centre, but Mombasa was steadily in the ascendant from 1450 onwards, and it had probably become the dominant coastal trade centre well before the end of the 15th century.

In 1498, the Portuguese explorer, Vasco da Gama, rounded the Cape and sailed up the east coast on his way to establishing trade links with India. He described Kilwa in detail, but as he was not allowed to go near the island, his report is probably pure fabrication. Da Gama received an equally hostile reception in Mombasa, but did meet with the Sultan there, who may have exaggerated the declining Kilwa's strength to frighten the Portuguese away from the coast. Da Gama's description of Kilwa might explain why the island was so heavily targeted when the Portuguese took over the coast in 1505. Three-quarters of Kilwa's residents were killed or forced to flee. A Portuguese fort was built, the gold trade moved to Mozambique and the Sultan exiled to the mainland.

Little is known of events on and around Kilwa over the next 250 years. The Portuguese fort that would later form the foundation of the Omani Gereza was abandoned in 1512, when most of the garrison succumbed to malaria. In 1587, the island's 3,000 remaining residents were rounded up and imprisoned, to become rations for the cannibalistic Zimba. An Omani settlement reported on the island in 1712 had vanished by 1719. But the first real indication of Kilwa's re-emergence as a trade centre, and the nature of this future trade, came in 1776, when the Sultan of Kilwa – presumably of Shirazi or indigenous descent – signed a contract to provide a French merchant from Mauritius with 1,000 slaves annually.

This treaty fell through in 1784 when Kilwa was attacked by, and made subject to, the Sultan of Oman. The island was re-occupied by Omani agents, who left their mark in the form of the large fort (Gereza) on the waterfront, and minor restoration work to the Great Mosque and Makutani Palace. In 1812, when HMS *Nisus* anchored off Kilwa, James Prior noted that the Gereza was still in use as the Omani governor's residence, but was unimpressed by the scattering of thatch huts that comprised the town 'if town it should be called'. Within a few years of this, the Omani settlers evacuated the island to establish the mainland town of Kilwa Kivinje. Kilwa Kisiwani went into terminal decline thereafter – the last Sultan of Kilwa, interviewed by Lieutenant Christopher of the *Tigris* in 1846, was captured by the Sultan of Zanzibar and sent into exile before 1856.

Within years of its establishment, Kilwa Kivinje had become the centre of the southern slave trade. By the mid-19th century it was a very wealthy town, with up to 20,000 slaves passing through annually. Although the Sultan of Zanzibar outlawed the slave trade in 1873, it persisted out of Kilwa for longer than anywhere else, but had been stopped almost entirely by 1880. Many of Kilwa's slave traders established rubber plantations and business continued to prosper. In 1886, Kilwa Kivinje became a German administrative centre, and it remained a town of regional importance during the first half of the 20th century. Since the end of World War II it has gradually been reduced to backwater status, with the more modern town of Kilwa Masoko serving as the regional headquarters.

Getting there and away

The quickest way to get to Kilwa is by air. Eagle Air flies between Dar es Salaam, Kilwa and Mtwara on Tuesdays and Fridays. The fare between Dar es Salaam and Kilwa is a relatively reasonable Tsh45,000 one-way. Air charters, by contrast, are likely to cost well in excess of US$500.

Kilwa Masoko and Kilwa Kivinje both lie about 12km east of the junction town of Nangurukuru, which straddles the main road towards Mtwara, some 300km south of Dar es Salaam. Nangurukuru is connected to Kilwa Masoko by a good surfaced road, plied by a steady stream of pick-up trucks and minibuses that take about 20 minutes to travel in either direction. Kilwa Kivinje, which lies at the end of a 3km-long side road branching north from the surfaced road between Nangurukuru and Kilwa Masoko, is serviced by plenty of transport from both of these towns. Nangurukuru itself is a bit of a dump, and the last place you'd probably choose to spend a night, but if necessity dictates it does have a basic guesthouse.

In a private 4WD, the drive from Dar es Salaam to Kilwa should take six to eight hours. Using public transport, a few bus services run daily between Kilwa Masoko and Dar es Salaam, an eight- to twelve-hour journey depending on the current condition of the road – and that of the bus! The best service at present is the Burudani Bus, which usually makes it through in about eight hours. This bus leaves Dar es Salaam at 06.00 from the rather obscurely located Ubungo terminal. It is strongly advised that you make enquiries and book a ticket a day or two before you want to travel, and realistically you'll need to arrange for a taxi to collect you at your hotel on the morning of departure. The return service leaves Kilwa Masoko at 05.30 and passes through Kilwa Kivinje 30 minutes later to pick up passengers departing from there. (The agent for tickets out of Kilwa Kivinje is the cloth shop next to the *hoteli* opposite the main covered market.) Buses sometimes stop running during the main rainy season, which runs from January to March. If for some reason you need to overnight en route between Dar es Salaam and Kilwa, reputedly the last village with any accommodation is Ikwiriri, some distance before the Rufiji ferry.

The alternative to catching a direct bus from Dar es Salaam would be to catch a bus to Mtwara or Lindi (with the advantage that they leave from the main bus station in Dar es Salaam), get off at Nangurukuru, and make your way to Kilwa from there. Be aware, however, that as things stand any bus leaving Dar es Salaam after midday is likely to spend the night at Ndundu on the Rufiji River – ghastly, according to those who've had the experience.

There has never, that I'm aware of, been any direct bus service from Kilwa south towards Lindi or Mtwara. If you're heading south from Kilwa, the best option is to hop on a pick-up truck to Nangurukuru, and wait there for a seat on a southbound bus coming from Dar es Salaam. Rather more straightforward to travel to Kilwa from the south, as any bus heading to Dar es Salaam from Lindi, Mtwara or Masasi can drop you at Nangurukuru.

Occasional dhows run from Kilwa Kivinje to Mafia Island and other points along the coast. Dhows also run north to Dar es Salaam and south to Mtwara when the roads are flooded after heavy rain. Fares are negotiable, assuming that the captain is willing to ignore a ruling that prevents foreigners from boarding long-haul passenger dhows.

UTETE FERRY

Most travellers will cross the Rufiji on the main Kilwa road south of Kibiti, but there is a second ferry towed by an antiquated diesel tugboat, lying 30km further east at Utete, en route to the major eastern entrance gate to the Selous Game Reserve. Situated on the south bank of a wide bend in the river, Utute today is a patented backwater, but it was an important administrative centre in the German colonial era. Numerous colonial buildings still stand in various states of disrepair, notably the impressive Old Boma, built in 1893 and now the District Commissioner's office.

Kilwa Masoko

Kilwa Masoko is the best-equipped base for exploring the Kilwa area, though it is of less inherent interest than its two more antiquated namesakes. Few tourists make it to Kilwa, but the atmosphere is very welcoming, and anybody who speaks English is likely to accost you for a chat. The nominal town centre consists of a small grid of dirt roads emanating from a central market, and it lies about 1km inland of the harbour, to which it is connected by a tar road. All the accommodation is in the town centre near the market, while most government buildings and banks are found along the main tar road towards the harbour.

Aside from being a useful base, Kilwa Masoko does boast an attractively sandy baobab-lined beach, a short distance east of the harbour. To get there from the town centre, walk down the main tar road for about 300m, then turn left at the CCM buildings (just past the bank near a statue of a running man), from where it's about 100m to the beach.

Where to stay and eat
Moderate
Kilwa Ruins Beach Hotel Tel: Kilwa Masoko 137 or 023 220 2876; fax: 0744 794110. This new beachfront development, set on the fringe of Kilwa Masoko facing Kilwa Kisiwani, provides a long overdue alternative to the plethora of low-key guesthouses that characterise the Kilwa area. It currently consists of five standing tents with en-suite facilities set in the middle of a rather barren plot overlooking the beach, but there are plans to develop it into a proper beach resort with swimming pool et al over the next couple of years. The lodge can arrange excursions to the ruins on Kilwa Kisiwani and Songo Mnara, as well as game fishing, snorkelling and other watersports. Accommodation costs US$60/90 single/double B&B. The restaurant is far and away the best place to eat in the Kilwa area, with meals costing around Tsh5,000.

Budget
Mjaka Family Village Situated on the main road close to the bus terminal and market, this is a comfortable new locally run lodge consisting of about a dozen self-contained single chalets with a small lounge and cold running water. Good value at Tsh5,000 per unit.

Shoestring
New Mjaka Guesthouse This dependable guesthouse, situated alongside the Mjaka Family Village, was until recently the best place to stay in the Kilwa area, and it remains the clear pick among the lower cost lodgings. Clean self-contained single rooms with a three-quarter bed, fan and net cost Tsh3,000, while rooms using the communal shower cost Tsh2,000/3,000 single/double. There's usually running water (though you may need to ask the staff to switch it on!), and acceptable, inexpensive local food is served in the attached restaurant.

Masoko Hilton Hotel Of a standard with the above, though a bit scruffier, the Hilton stands opposite the bus station and charges Tsh2,000 for a single with three-quarter bed using common shower or Tsh3,000 for a self-contained single. No doubles are available.

Salama Guesthouse About the best of the other half-dozen basic guesthouses dotted around town, this charges Tsh2,500 for an adequate but basic double room.

Kilwa Kisiwani

The modern village of Kilwa Kisiwani is a sleepy mud-and-thatch settlement with little to distinguish it from hundreds of similar fishing villages all along the Tanzanian coast. It is, however, surrounded by perhaps the most compelling ruins anywhere in East Africa, and few people would visit Kilwa without dedicating at

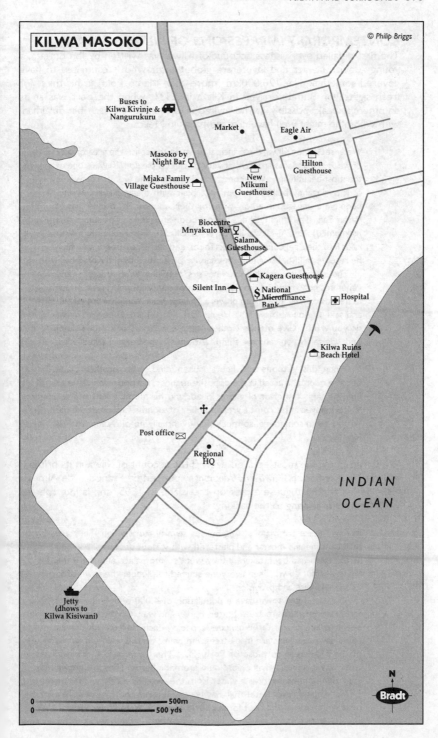

KILWA MASOKO

© Philip Briggs

Buses to
Kilwa Kivinje &
Nangurukuru

Market

Eagle Air

Masoko by
Night Bar

Hilton
Guesthouse

Mjaka Family
Village Guesthouse

New
Mikumi
Guesthouse

Biocentre
Mnyakulo Bar

Salama
Guesthouse

Kagera Guesthouse

Silent Inn

National
Microfinance
Bank

Hospital

Kilwa Ruins
Beach Hotel

Post office

Regional
HQ

INDIAN
OCEAN

Jetty
(dhows to
Kilwa Kisiwani)

0   500m
0   500 yds

N

Bradt

CONTEMPORARY IMPRESSIONS OF KILWA KISIWANI

The first detailed eye-witness account of Kilwa was written by Ibn Buttata, a young Arabian lawyer and inveterate globetrotter who is estimated to have covered something like 120,000km (more than Marco Polo) in his thirst for fresh sights. Ibn Buttata arrived in Kilwa in 1331, when the port was at its commercial peak, possibly at the invitation of Sultan Al-Hasan bin Sulaiman, with whom he might well have crossed paths in Mecca.

> We... set sail for Kilwa, the principal town on the coast, the greater part of whose inhabitants are Zanj of very black complexion. Kilwa is one of the most beautiful and well-constructed towns in the world. The whole of it is elegantly built. The roofs are built with mangrove poles. The people are engaged in a holy war, for their country lies beside that of Pagan Zanj. The chief qualities are devotion and piety...The sultan...[is nicknamed] Abu Al-Mawahib (Giver of Gifts)... He frequently makes raids into the Zanj country, attacks them, and carries off booty, of which he reserves a fifth, using it in the manner prescribed by the Koran...
>
> The sultan is very humble: he sits and eats with beggars, and venerates holy men and the descendants of the prophets... One Friday as he was coming away from prayer... a faqir from Yemen stopped him and said 'O Abu Al-Mawahib'. He replied: 'Here I am, O beggar! What do you want?' 'Give me the clothes you are wearing!' And [the sultan] said: 'Certainly you can have them.' 'At once?' [the beggar] asked. 'Yes, immediately!'
>
> When this virtuous and liberal sultan died... his brother Daud became ruler, and acted in the opposite manner. If a poor man came to him, he said: 'the giver of gifts is dead, and has nothing left to give.' Visitors stayed at his court a great number of months, and only then did he give them something, so much that eventually no-one came to visit him.

With grim irony, the most detailed eyewitness account of Kilwa in its prime is included in *The Sack of Kilwa and Mombasa*, penned by Francisco de Almeida after he led the Portuguese attack on the island in 1505, and is interspersed with comments relating to the sacking:

> In Kilwa there are many strong houses several stories high. They are built of stone and mortar and plastered with various designs... As soon as the town had been taken... they went to the palace and there the cross was put down. Then everyone started to plunder the town of all its merchandise and provisions.
>
> The island and town have a population of 4,000 people. It is very fertile and produces maize... butter, honey and wax. On the trees hang beehives like jars of three *almudes* capacity, each closed with woven palm leaves... There are many trees and palms on the mainland, some of them different to those of Portugal... There are sweet oranges, lemons, vegetables, small onions, and aromatic herbs. They are grown in gardens and watered with water from the wells.
>
> Here also grows betel that has leaves like ivy and is grown like peas with sticks at the root for support. Wealthy Arabs chew the leaf,

together with specially prepared limes that look like an ointment. They keep the leaves as if they were to be put on wounds. These leaves make the mouth and teeth very red, but are said to be most refreshing.

There are more black slaves than white moors here: they are engaged on farms growing maize and other things... The soil is red, the top layer being sandy; the grass is always green. There are many fat beasts, oxen, cows, sheep and goats and also plenty of fish; there are also whales which swim around the ships. There is no running drinking water on this island. Near the island there are other small inhabited islands. There are many boats as large as a caravel of 50 ton and other smaller ones... They sail from here to Sofala, 255 leagues away.

People here sleep raised above the ground in hammocks made of palm leaves, in which only one person can lie. Flasks of very good perfume are exported from here and a large quantity of glass of all types and all kinds of cotton piece goods, incense, resin, gold, silver and pearls. The Grand Captain ordered the loot to be deposited under seal in a house. The fortress of Kilwa was built out of the best house there was. All the other houses were pulled down. It was fortified and guns were set in place.

Cotton is found in abundance. It is of good quality... The slaves wear a cotton cloth around the waist and down to the knees; the rest of the body is naked. The white Arabs and slave owners wear two pieces of cotton cloth, one around the waist down to the feet, and the other over the shoulders and reaching down to the first cloth. There are copper coins [but] no gold coin. The Grand Captain... saw 25 gazelle which had been let loose on the island... There are many vaulted mosques, one of which is like that of Cordova. All the upper-class Moors carry a rosary.

The contrast between the above and James Prior's 1812 description of the island during the brief Omani re-occupation is striking:

The present town, if town is should be called, consists merely of a number of huts, scattered from the margin of the sea to a mile from its shore; the glittering white of only two stone houses enlivens and embellishes the cocoa-thatched metropolic... Quiloa seems to offer only ivory and tortoiseshell for commerce... The number of slaves formerly exported used to be many thousands, but at present the demand is confined to the Arabs, who do not take many. The articles principally in request here are arms, ammunition, dollars, tobacco, coarse cloths, and hardware. Refreshments... seem scarce, and the natives poor... The [Arab] people are generally good figures... they domineer over the Negro nations within their reach [and] sometimes make war to get more slaves, but more generally get them in traffic with people that come from a considerable distance in the interior. The common dress is a piece of cotton cloth wrapped around the middle, and extending to the knee, and another thrown loosely over the shoulders... They profess Mohammedism, but do not very strictly adhere to it.

EXPLORING KILWA KISIWANI

The **Gereza** is the partially collapsed quadrangular building that first draws the eye when you sail across to the island. Gereza is a Swahili word meaning prison; it in turn is derived from a Portuguese word meaning church. The Gereza on Kilwa, however, is a fort. It was built by Omani Arabs in about 1800 and incorporates the walls of a smaller Portuguese fort built in 1505. It has thick coral walls and an impressive arched door.

Walking uphill from the Gereza, you pass first through the small modern village before arriving in the medieval **city centre**. It is difficult to gain much of a feel for the layout of the original town, since many of the smaller stone buildings have vanished without trace, largely through the removal of rubble as building material. The most important structures – the mosques and palaces – have been left untouched, however, because they are still regarded as sanctified.

The first building you'll pass through is the **Great Mosque**, also known as the Friday Mosque, which would have been the focal point of spiritual life in medieval Kilwa. This is the largest mosque of its period anywhere on the coast, with 30 bays covering an extent of about 100m², and it is also the best preserved and most aesthetically satisfying of all extant Shirazi buildings. The original mosque, as erected in around 1050 by the first Sultan of Kilwa, Ali bin Al Hasan, was more modest in ambition than the present structure and reputedly collapsed in the late 13th century. It was rebuilt in about 1320 under Sultan Al-Hasan bin Sulaiman, who elaborated on the original design by adding an imposing new wing of 16 domed ceiling cupolas supported by rows of tall arches – unquestionably the mosque's distinguishing architectural features. These ostentatious flourishes, intended to show off the contemporary wealth and sophistication of Kilwa, may also reflect architectural influences absorbed during the sultan's pilgrimage to Mecca as a teenager. Renovations in the 15th and 18th centuries notwithstanding, it is to the immense credit of the masons involved that their handiwork remains in such fine shape almost 700 years later.

Several **other mosques** are dotted around the old town. Close to the Great Mosque is the so-called Small Domed Mosque, which dates to the 15th century, and is again built over an older structure. This mosque has three bays, three aisles and seven ceiling domes, some still intact, but its fine decorations have been removed by modern visitors. Close to the Gereza stands the Malindi Mosque – associated with a family of settlers from Malindi in modern-day Kenya – a 15th-century construction that was extensively renovated during the late 18th-century Omani re-occupation of the island. The Jangwani Mosque was a similar structure to the Small Domed Mosque, but is now almost entirely collapsed.

least half a day to looking around this fabulous complex, detailed more fully in the box *Exploring Kilwa Kisiwani*, above.

Getting there and away

Setting up a visit to the island, which is separated from the mainland by a 2km channel, is straightforward enough. The first step is for you and your passport to pay a visit – and an entrance fee of Tsh1,500 – to the cultural officer in the regional administrative headquarters that lie opposite the post office along the main road between the town centre and the port. This is technically only open during normal

West of the mosques, the tall, triangular **Makutani Palace** is still very well preserved. The palace was built and fortified in the 15th century after the Husuni Kubwa fell into disuse (see below), and it is enclosed by a low, crumbling 18th-century wall built by the Omani. Also of interest, a few hundred metres south of the Great Mosque, the **Sultan's Mausoleum** houses the tombs of many of Kilwa's most important sultans. All around town you'll see traces of the **ancient well system**, which is still used by the villagers today.

The eminent archaeologist Neville Chittick, who carried out excavations on the island from 1958 onwards, described the **Husuni Kubwa**, which lies about 1km east of the main ruins on a low cliff overlooking the sea, as 'the only attempt to go beyond the merely practical and approach the grand'. It is thought that this vast building was constructed in about 1320 by Al-Hasan bin Sulaiman, the second ruler of the Abu-al-Mawahib dynasty, to serve as both a palace and a storehouse. It was probably lived in for only two generations, before being abandoned as too costly to maintain during the late-14th-century slump in the gold trade. In some aspects – its geometrical design, for instance – Sulaiman's clifftop palace is a typical Swahili building, but its scale and complexity are unprecedented, and many of its features are unique. The building incorporates extensive domestic quarters, an audience court, several large ornamental balconies, a stairwell to the beach, and even a swimming pool. Few walls are still left standing after six centuries of disuse, but the ground plan and main features of the Husuni Kubwa are clearly discernible.

Oddly, locals often refer the Husuni Kubwa as São Jago, reflecting a widespread local belief that it is of Portuguese origin (even the Department of Antiquities guides, who really should know better, call it the Portuguese House). Persistent as this Portuguese association might be locally, it lacks for any historical foundation. Archaeologists are unanimous in asserting that the construction is entirely consistent with medieval Swahili architecture, and lacks for any features that would suggest a Portuguese influence. Furthermore, a large number of coins, pottery shards and other 14th-century artefacts have been unearthed in the ruins.

Husuni derives from an Arab word meaning fort, but there is no evidence to suggest the building ever had a defensive purpose. This name Husuni Kubwa has been attached to the former palace by virtue of its proximity to a smaller, square building known as **Husuni Ndogo**, which does superficially resemble a fort (*kubwa* and *ndogo* are KiSwahili for large and small). The purpose of the Husuni Ndogo is a mystery – there is no comparable building elsewhere in East Africa – but it has been variously and inconclusively cited as a mosque, a storehouse, a minor residence, and a fortified market place.

office hours from Monday to Friday, but you should be able to locate the cultural officer – or find somebody else to help you – over weekends. If at all possible, there's some sense in trying to deal with these formalities the day before you want to visit the island.

The cultural officer can help to organise a fishing dhow charter to the island, which will probably cost around Tsh10,000 per party for the round trip, depending on your negotiating skills and how long you want to spend on the island. Alternatively, you can just head down to the dhow harbour yourself, pay the statutory Tsh200 harbour tax, and chat to the dhow captains who hang around

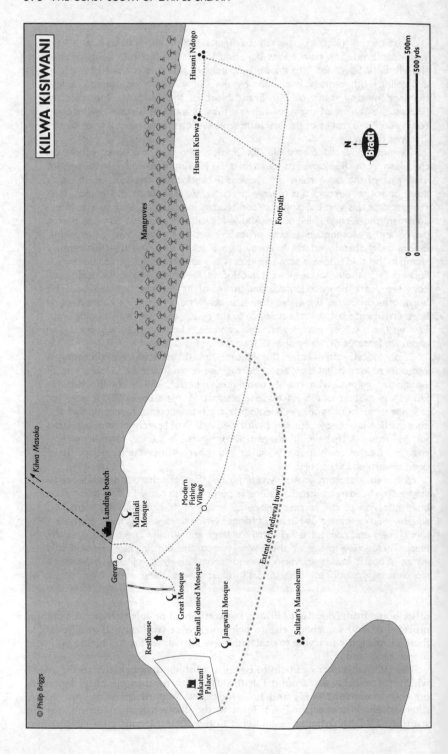

KILWA KISIWANI

© Philip Briggs

there. Local people use these dhows as public transport between the mainland and the island; you should only pay Tsh1,000 one-way per person (perhaps less) if you don't take a private charter. The trip usually takes 15–30 minutes each way, though in becalmed conditions it's been known to take an hour. Upon reaching the island, you'll be met by one of the two caretaker/guides, who speak little English and are less than fully conversant with the island's history, but are otherwise very helpful. Should you elect to be guided around the ruins (you are unlikely to find the Husuni complex unguided), the caretaker will expect a tip.

Where to stay
Although most travellers visit Kilwa Kisiwani as a day trip, the Department of Antiquities has, um, restored a small cottage next to the ruined palace to serve as a resthouse for the use of tourists. One dreads to think what the cottage looked like prior to restoration, but as things stand it consists of four large but bare rooms, each with one double bed and a resident bat colony. The building has no electricity, and thus no fan, but the rooms are unexpectedly cool. The caretakers will bring you bedding, mosquito (bat?) nets and a paraffin lamp on request. Minor discomforts aside, the resthouse does offer the rather wonderful opportunity to be among these atmospheric ruins after dark, and to explore them in the gorgeous post-dawn and pre-dusk light. Accommodation costs Tsh3,000 per room. All food, drinks and water should be brought across from the mainland.

Kilwa Kivinje
The small, rundown town of Kilwa Kivinje, though less frequently visited than Kilwa Kisiwani, is no less absorbing in its own way. A living memorial to a more prosperous past, Kilwa Kivinje gives the overall impression of a once-important town gradually returning to its fishing village roots – much of the main street consists of boarded-up shops, while mud huts have been built using the walls of old Omani fortifications.

You don't have to know much about the history of Kilwa Kivinje to pick up the broad thread just by walking around the old town, which came to prominence as an Omani slave-trading centre in the early 19th century. The crumbling remains of Omani dwellings and fortifications are dotted all around, and while none is habitable, many are in good enough condition to allow you to imagine what they must have looked like 150 years ago. There is an interesting mosque and, to the east of the town, an old Muslim graveyard.

In February 1859, on their return trip from 'discovering' Lake Tanganyika, Burton and Speke diverted to Kilwa Kivinje to fulfil a promise made by Burton prior to starting the expedition. The town was, at the time, in the grip of a terrible cholera epidemic, and Burton wrote of how 'corpses lay in the ravines and dead Negroes rested against the walls of the Customs House. The poorer victims were dragged by the leg along the sand to be thrown into the ebbing water of the bay; those better off were sewn up in matting. Limbs were scattered in all directions and heads lay like pebbles on the beach.' They did not stay in Kilwa Kivinje long.

The whitewashed German Boma, overlooking the waterfront, is still the town's largest building, used as an administrative centre into the 1950s, but serving no apparent purpose today. A cannon, presumably dating to World War I, stands on the common (complete with park benches) between the Boma and a stone seawall. Behind the Boma a small monument commemorates two Germans who died in 1888. Another relic of the German era is the covered central market. The

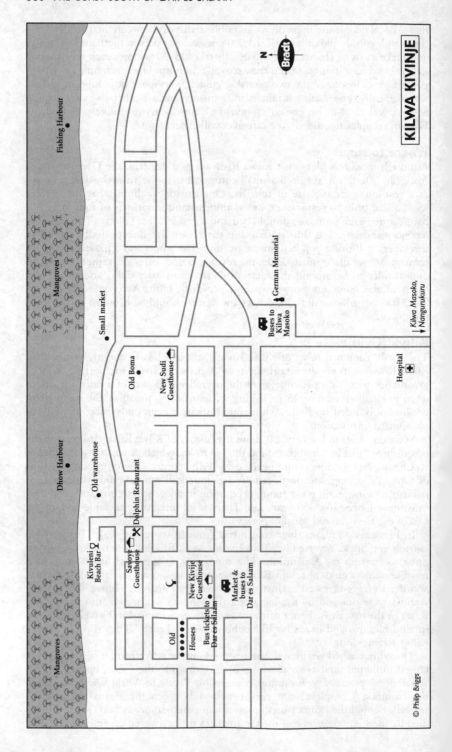

KILWA KIVINJE

© Philip Briggs

roads radiating out from the market offer glimpses of Kilwa Kivinje in the 1940s and 1950s: double-storey buildings with ornate balconies, small homes with Zanzibar-style doors, and shops still carrying steel advertising boards which must date to the 1950s.

Historical interest aside, Kilwa Kivinje lies on an attractive beach surrounded by an extensive mangrove swamp, where odd little mud-skippers scuttle across the sand, and pairs of the beautiful mangrove kingfisher emit their high descending call from bare branches. It's also a very traditional Muslim town, marked by the characteristic Swahili reserve – though tourists remain a rare enough site that you'll find no shortage of people wanting to practice their English on you. It's fascinating to watch the local fishermen at work along the beach to the south of the Boma, or youngsters preparing to smoke the day's catch in the back streets. In the right frame of mind, there would be worse places to settle into for a few days.

Where to stay and eat
Accommodation options in Kilwa Kivinje are limited to four basic local lodgings, of which the **New Sudi Guesthouse** is narrowly the best, charging Tsh1,000/1,400 for a single/double with nets but no fans, and communal bucket showers. The scruffier **New Kivinje Hotel** opposite the covered market has fans in the rooms. Only a few years ago, alcohol was unavailable in Kilwa Kivinje, but there are now two bars serving lukewarm beer to a rather limited clientele. The nicest of these is the waterfront **Kivuleni Beach Bar**, run by a friendly Makonde woman who intends to build an adjoining guesthouse before the end of 2002. The **Kivuleni Beach Bar** serves chips *mayai*, and with advance notice you could arrange for them to prepare fresh fried or grilled fish. It also hosts live *taarab* music on occasion. Otherwise, the options for eating out in Kilwa Kivinje are limited to a couple of *hotelis* near the market serving cheap, basic meals.

Songo Mnara Island
Songo Mnara, situated about 10km south of Kilwa Kisiwani, is the site of a second ruined city contemporaneous with, but politically subservient to, medieval Kilwa. Little is known about the origin and history of this city, which is rather odd when you consider its proximity to Kilwa, probably the most thoroughly documented of all the Shirazi city-states. Referred to as Songo in a handful of old documents, the town was allegedly built by Ali Hussein, the founder of Kilwa, and the general layout indicates that it started life as a fortified outpost to defend the main sea route into the harbour against naval attacks. Most of the constructions on Songo Mnara date from the 15th century or earlier, but – like Kilwa Kisiwani – the old town was re-occupied by the Omani in the late 18th century, and some renovation and new building occurred during this period. In 1812, Captain Philip Beaver of HMS *Nisus*, the first British ship to enter Kilwa harbour, explored the ruins at Songo Mnara with the ship's surgeon James Prior. The notes made by Prior indicate that the Omani had recently abandoned the city they briefly re-occupied.

Some extracts from Prior's notes follow, with original imperial measurements converted to metric:

> We discovered a large well… about 6m in depth [and] hollowed out of calcareous rock… formerly enclosed by a wall, part of which is still standing. Further on, towards Pagoda Point, appeared several decayed huts, tenanted by bats and reptiles… The first object [after this] was a small cemetery, about 12m square, enclosed with stone and raised less than 1m above the ground; the graves were convexly raised… with stones at the head

and feet... but no trace could we find of inscriptions... Attached [were] the remains of... a place of worship, above 7x4m. The walls remaining seemed about 5m high, built of stone, cemented by mortar formed by the bastard coral... in which were wedged many pieces of coconut shell, that seemed of no other use than of emblems... An arched door in front, and two in rear, formed the entrances, and a circular white stone raised above the ground may, perhaps, have received the inclined knee of many a humble supplicant for divine mercy... Two or three hundred metres from this spot lie the ruins of a stone building, larger than any at present possessed by the Quiloans, except the residence of the Sultan. Its apartments have been numerous... the walls are broad... and their height must have been considerable. Captain Beaver thought he could distinguish the remains of Saxon arches; but this resemblance is probably accidental.

Although the name Songo is an ancient one, Mnara is a relatively modern appellation meaning 'tower', and it refers to the tall but collapsed minaret of the 15th-century mosque visited by Prior – one of four ruined mosques in the complex. The large labyrinthine building with the beautiful arched doors that drew the interest of Captain Beaver is generally referred to as the Sultan's Palace, but since the island had no sultan, it probably served as a secondary residence for the Sultan of Kilwa, or housed his local representative. In terms of impact, the ruins on Songo Mnara don't match those on Kilwa Kisiwani, but some archaeologists regard then to be of greater architectural merit. They have also suffered less damage through the removal of building material over the centuries, so that one can gain a far clearer idea of the layout of the ordinary houses and the town as a whole.

If nothing else, Songo Mnara makes for an enjoyable day out, and it provides a good pretext for staying on an extra day at Kilwa before braving the public transport again. A daily passenger boat runs between Kilwa Masoko and Songo Mnara via Pande, but this service is sometimes cancelled. You can also arrange private transport in a local fishing dhow. The snorkelling in the surrounding reefs is reputedly very good, and the Kilwa Ruins Lodge in Kilwa Masoko can arrange combined sightseeing and snorkelling day trips to the island. For those with a serious interest in coastal archaeology, it would be possible, over the course of a day, to combine a visit to Songo Mnara with two other islands that contain substantial ruins. The first of these is the ruined town on **Sanje Mjoma**, which lies about 3km from Songo Mnara, and is noted for several large coral houses enclosed in courtyards with tall arched entrances. The second is **Sanje Ya Kati**, the capital of the Shanga people, a local tribe who resisted the rule of the Shirazi at Kilwa into the 13th century.

Songo Songo Island

The 3km^2 coral island of Songo Songo is the most northerly in the Kilwa archipelago, lying about 40km north of Kilwa itself. It has recently grabbed a few headlines as the site of the long-mooted Songas Project, which received full funding in late 2001 and is likely to be operational in 2003. The natural gas from two onshore and three offshore gas wells, discovered in 1974, will be extracted and processed on site, then piped to Dar es Salaam to fuel Ebbing Electric Generator, which has a capacity of greater than 100MW but is currently fuelled by expensive imported oil. Of greater interest to travellers, perhaps, is Songo Songo's attractive sandy beach, and a vast coral cave haunted by a profusion of bats and reached via a concrete staircase that was built during World War I when the cave served as a German ammunition dump.

Songo Songo makes for an easy day trip from Kilwa Kivinje. Passenger dhows do the return trip most days, taking about three hours in either direction, and charging a fare of Tsh1,000 per person. Whether or not travellers will be welcomed on the island once the gas project hits the go button is an open question. For current details of dhow departures, chat to the owner of the New Sudi Hotel or the Eagle Air agent in Kilwa Kivinje.

Matumbi Caves

The Matumbi Hills to the west of Kilwa are, according to the findings of a German-Turkish expedition in 1994 and German-Italian one in 1995, the site of a limestone cave network far more extensive than the more famous and regularly visited caves at Amboni near Tanga. The caves were first brought to the attention of scientists in 1910 by a local Catholic missionary Ambros Mayer and were further explored in 1911 by a police sergeant called Thurmann. Prior to that, the Mutumbi Caves had formed an important hideaway for local rebel troops during the Maji-Maji revolution. The most impressive cave, Nangoma, is revered locally for housing an important deity, and its name probably derives from the Swahili *ngoma* – dance – suggesting a history of use for ritual celebrations. The 1995 expedition determined that it opens into a passage stretching for 7.5km into the hills, making it the longest measured cave in Tanzania and the 13th-longest in Africa. Within it lie several potentially interesting fossil beds as well as a few small waterfalls. Also of interest is the 1km-deep Mpatawa Cave, the main entrance gallery of which contains lots of boulders and corroded calcite formations. The Namaingo Caves have a total length of 2.4km.

Remote, undeveloped for tourism, and impossible to explore without private transport, the Matumbi Caves have recently been the subject of a low-key campaign for greater recognition and publicity, led by a local elder Abdullah Botori Mweyo, who helped the 1995 expedition locate several previously undocumented caverns. At the time of writing, the best place from which to explore the caves is the remote Kipatimu Mission, some four hours drive from Kilwa in the Matumbi Hills. Although rooms and meals might be available here, it would be advisable to carry a tent and a supply of food. Abdullah Botori Mweyo can usually be contacted through the mission. It would be extremely foolhardy to attempt exploring the area without local guidance or to venture deep into the caves unless you are an experienced caver with good equipment. Matumbi is mentioned in this guide primarily in the hope it might generate greater interest in bodies able to develop and promote it for eco-tourism. For a full report of the 1995 expedition with good maps, check out www.uni-geophys.gwdg.de/~gkaufman/caving/tansania/tansania_frames_main.html.

LINDI

This compact, somewhat decrepit port on the western bank of the Lukuledi Estuary is the most substantial town along the 600km stretch of coast between Dar es Salaam and Mtwara. It is also the administrative capital of the vast but thinly populated Lindi region, which at 66,000km² is about the same size as the Republic of Ireland. It seems more than probable that Lindi's fine location has long been the site of a fishing village, possibly even a trading centre, but historical references to Lindi are few indeed. Nor, so far as I'm aware, has any trace ever been found of a Shirazi or Portuguese settlement on the estuary. Lindi in its present incarnation most probably started life as an Omani port in the late 18th century, though oral traditions suggest it may have existed for a century or so before the Omani entered the picture locally (see box '*The Ancient History of Lindi*', pages 584–5).

'THE ANCIENT HISTORY OF LINDI'

The above is the title of the intriguing if somewhat effusive history of Lindi that was transcribed by the German scholar Velton in the 1890s based on local oral sources. Lindi, according to this document, was established by a Makonde leader called Kitenga, and its name refers to a large pit latrine on the town's outskirts. The date of foundation is not specified, but subsequent events related by the document, which can be dated in conjunction with references to three different Sultans of Zanzibar, indicate that it must surely have been before 1750.

After some years in power, Kitenga agreed to 'sell' his town to a Makua leader called Mtukura. In exchange, Kitenga was given all of Mturuka's worldly goods: 'a female slave, a powder mortar for grinding snuff a cubit long, lengths of American cloth, and the head and liver of a wild pig'! Mturuka evidently assumed the title of Sultan and founded a dynasty that appears to have ruled for three or four generations, all the time producing copious numbers of children. Many of the children were apparently married into wealthy Arabic families, a common brand of upward mobility along the coast, where a Shirazi or Omani pedigree stood one in high social and commercial stead. Unfortunately, it was such a liaison – the marriage of two of the sultan's daughters to a pair of prominent merchant brothers from Zanzibar in 1830 or thereabouts – that led directly to Lindi being co-opted into the Omani Sultanate of Zanzibar.

The newlywed brothers evidently went behind the back of their father-in-law to usurp control of Lindi. They sailed to Zanzibar to make Sultan Seyyid Said an offer no acquisitive megalomaniac could refuse: 'We have built a fort at Lindi: now give us your authority to judge the [local people], and all taxes we collect will be for you'. So it was that Nasoro bin Isa, the elder brother, became *ipso facto* Sultan of Lindi, instituting a regime characterised by the oral traditions as

Lindi lay within the Sultanate of Zanzibar throughout the 19th century, serving as a stop on the slave caravan route from Lake Nyasa. It was never as well known – nor, presumably, as prosperous – as Kilwa Kivinje to the north. Captain Foot, who explored the south coast extensively in 1881, when commenting on the relative status of Mikindani implied clearly that he regarded Lindi, among ports 'south of Bagamoyo', to be second only to Kilwa. Nevertheless, modern Lindi boasts few relics of the Omani era. A chimney-like stone tower opposite the NBC Club is said to have been an Omani gaol, and the clock tower on the roundabout at the town centre was built under the rule of the Sultan of Zanzibar. Otherwise, unlike Zanzibar or even Kilwa Kivinje, Lindi has a modern layout of interlocking gridiron streets, and few buildings that exceed two storeys in height.

There is, by contrast, every indication that Lindi prospered in the colonial era. With one eye closed, you can even imagine that the main beach served as a resort of sorts, possibly used by farmers living up-country. Today, however, the beachfront benches are all broken, and they probably go months at a stretch without being perched on by a tourist. In the town centre, numerous posh colonial era buildings are ruined or heading that way, while the derelict German Boma (marked on a 1970 map as the Area Commissioner's Residence) houses nothing but trees. A cyclone that hit the town in the 1950s may go some way to explaining this general state of disrepair, but the deeper cause of Lindi's decline has been the development of Mtwara as the main port and city for this part of Tanzania.

Whatever its history – and even that seems to have been lost or forgotten – Lindi is now something of a backwater. It is a pleasant and interesting place to visit, but

'evil'. Nasoro and his brother Mohammed 'killed their relatives and sold them into slavery', whilst Sultan Said 'knew nothing of how for five years his subjects suffered oppression'. The situation deteriorated when 'the Almighty God sent... a very great famine that lasted seven years... caused by locusts [that] did not leave a single [crop] living, but ate everything'.

Nasoro, who did not survive the famine, was succeeded first by his brother Mohammed 'who remained in power for a long time', and then by his son Hemedi bin Nasoro. After the death of Sultan Said of Zanzibar in 1854 (at around the same time Hemedi assumed power), his successor Majid sent a military expedition to Lindi to capture the fort and install direct Zanzibari rule. This event precipitated decades of hostility and sporadic wars between the coastal people of Lindi, who accepted the new order, and their up-country neighbours and kin, who did not. This tradition is largely substantiated by references in Vice Consul Elton's 1874 report on visiting Mikindani (see box *Mikindani Bay: Past & Present*, pages 594–5). The squabbling factions 'never agreed until the Germans came', one reason perhaps why Lindi never acquired the political or commercial status of Kilwa Kivinje.

A report from the Deputy Commissioner of German East Africa, dated September 1890, states that 'In Lindi also, lately, caravan trade has considerably increased. A caravan that arrived not long ago counted 1,200 heads and brought 340 tusks; the entire arrival of the last six weeks is estimated to be at least 700 tusks.' The so-called Ancient History, too, suggests that the arrival of the Germans fostered renewed trade activity and harmony in Lindi. This is probably because the withdrawal of Zanzibar allowed Rashid bin Shabawa, the leading light of the popular dynasty that had been displaced in the 1830s, to regain his rightful position as Sultan of Lindi – albeit within the constraints of colonial rule.

also a depressing reminder of what much of Tanzania was like in the mid-1980s. The only part of town which seems to escape the general air of torpor is the busy bus station, which – when the electricity is working – rings late into the night with the chimes of Congolese guitars and the pumping bass of reggae. Here the town's unemployed youth and orphaned children hang around all day, breaking into unselfconscious dances, while vendors scrape a living selling fried chicken and dried fish, melting sweets and single cigarettes to passing bus passengers. Another modern landmark, and a sporadic host to large crowds, is the football stadium on Makongoro Street – somewhat improbably, Lindi's football team is regularly battling it out in Tanzania's First Division.

From Lindi, regular motorised ferries cross the Lukuledi estuary, taking about five minutes, and leaving from the jetty next to the defunct Beach Hotel. The ferries land at Kitunda, a small village where the people spend their time drinking local beer and farming their *shambas*. There is little to do in Kitunda, but there is a fantastic view if you walk a little way up the hill. A 90-minute walk, starting by heading uphill from Kitunda takes you to a quiet, thickly vegetated and very beautiful beach. The Lukuledi estuary can be explored more thoroughly by hiring a local boat at a negotiable price – crocodiles can reportedly be seen 10–12km upstream. It is also possible to hire a boat in the bay, to do some snorkelling or to visit the large colony of fruit bats resident on Kisiwa Cha Popo (Island of Bats).

A number of excellent beaches are scattered around Lindi Bay. The largest, on the northern edge of town, is white and sandy with hardly any rocks; a few small wooden fishing boats lie on the shore and children play football throughout the

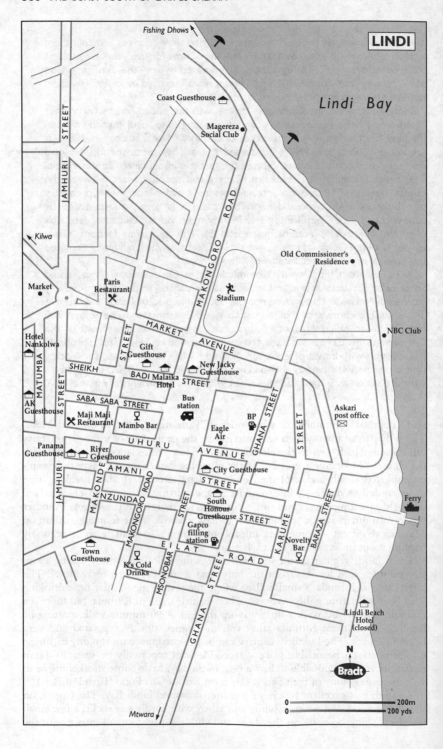

day. On the western side of the bay are several more secluded beaches – including Ras Bora, Mitema (the biggest and best) and Mitwero.

Getting there and away

Lindi lies about 470km south of Dar es Salaam along a road that is mostly in poor condition, and often becomes impassable after rain. With a very early start, it would be possible to cover this route in a private 4WD over a full day, assuming the road isn't in particularly poor shape. Three or four buses run between Dar es Salaam and Lindi daily. All of them leave Lindi in the early morning, which makes it advisable to book your seat a day ahead. The best service at the time of writing is operated by Born Coast, and leaves Lindi at around 07.30, passing through Nangurukuru for Kilwa at around 11.00, and reaching Dar es Salaam towards dusk. Buses heading in the opposite direction leave Dar es Salaam from the main bus terminal between 07.00 and 08.00; again, advance booking is strongly recommended. In practise, few travellers would want to bus directly between Lindi and Dar es Salaam, thereby omitting Kilwa from their itinerary.

If you've come to Lindi from Dar es Salaam, the 110km surfaced road south to Mtwara via Mikindani comes as a thoroughly pleasant surprise, as does the 165km road to Masasi, which branches west at Mnazi Moja (aka Mingoyo), about 20km from Lindi on the Mtwara road. Regular public transport runs between Lindi and Mikindani or Mtwara throughout the day, with vehicles generally leaving when they are full, but best to travel with the express minibuses that leave in either direction at 10.00 and 13.00. Tickets cost around Tsh1,500.

There are no direct buses between Lindi and Masasi, so you'll need to change vehicles at Mnazi Moja, which is shown by the name Mingoyo on most maps, and straddles the junction of the roads southeast towards Mtwara and southwest towards Masasi about 30km south of Lindi. Mnazi Moja evidently thrives on its strategic location, with the street vendors offering a smorgasbord of roadside snacks second to none: fried and stewed chicken, fish, prawns, meat kebabs, cakes and fruit. If you are travelling from Lindi to Masasi, you must first head to Mnazi Moja to pick up a westbound vehicle. You're very unlikely to get stuck overnight, but there are a few basic guesthouses in Mnazi Moja if you do.

A small, very crowded bus does a daily run between Lindi and Newala. It leaves Newala at 05.00, gets to Lindi at midday, and then turns back.

THE BRITISH CLUB

Brian Currie

The NBC Club in Lindi was formerly The British Club – a base for the expatriate community in the 1950s. I have a large amount of memorabilia from this Club because one of my neighbours managed the sisal estate in Lindi and was a member. Current and old photos show the building as remarkably unchanged. I showed a photo of the Greek Section of the Club to the Greek owner of the Palm Beach Hotel in Dar es Salaam. He recognised some of the people and said he thought at one time there was a Greek Orthodox Church in Lindi. He said, 'Of course, those people in Lindi were rather liberal'. I asked him to explain, since liberal is not the first thing one thinks of with these clubs. He told me that the clubs in Dar es Salaam and Zanzibar only allowed European members. Of course, Italians and Greeks were not counted as Europeans – meaning the Lindi Club was rather left wing. How times have changed!

THE KILLER CAT OF LINDI

The coastal forests of Lindi have only recently attracted the attention of biologists. But locals have long known them to be the favoured stalking ground of the most fearsome of African predators: a terrifying striped feline, larger than a donkey, more ferocious than a lion, and known as the *mngwa*!

In 1937, Captain W Hichens, an experienced hunter, wrote a sympathetic account of the *mngwa* legend as part of an article entitled *African Mystery Beasts*. Hichens asserts that vast tracts of coastal forest have never been trodden by a European – a fair point in 1937, given that the extensive jungle-bound Gedi Ruins in Kenya had gone undiscovered until four years earlier. He also points to the antiquity of the legend, which stretches back to a 13th-century Swahili hunting song that goes: 'I... press into the forest, to be devoured by the *mngwa*; and if the *mngwa* seizes me, devouring my flesh, that is the fortune of the hunt.'

Hichens recounts his own vicarious experiences of this mysterious creature:

> A man was brought in to me at Mchinga on a litter, terribly mauled by some great beast. He said it was a *mngwa*. As he himself was a brave and skilful hunter, who had often tracked down lions, leopards and other 'killers' with me and other white men, why should we suppose that in this case he mistook a lion or a leopard for some other beast? On another occasion, at Lindi, a *mngwa* took to prowling the village at night, killed several villagers and, finally, a policeman on point at the market. For nights the whole town lived in fear, and although we doubled the police guards we had difficulty in getting the men to go on duty. But I have seen those same men rout a lion out of a bush-patch with sticks! They swore that this beast was not a lion, nor a leopard, but a *mngwa*. We made every effort to waylay it, but, unfortunately, were not successful; nor did we get a lion, as we might reasonably have done had it been one.

Many of the coastal forests around Lindi still await formal scientific study, and it seems highly likely that they harbour several as yet undescribed small vertebrate species. Rather more difficult is to accept that a ferocious donkey-sized feline still prowls undetected within the tangled undergrowth. And yet the very persistence of the *mngwa* legend makes it tempting to think it has a basis in fact, perhaps some long extinct predator that has survived in the folk memory.

The full text of 'African Mystery Beasts' is reprinted online at www.herper.com/AFmystery.html.

Where to stay
Budget
Malaika Hotel Tel: 023 220 2880. Far and away the best lodging in Lindi at the time of writing (not, it must be said, a major commendation), the Malaika Hotel is situated on Market Street, a couple of blocks from the bus station. Clean, spacious self-contained rooms with a double bed, fan and netting cost Tsh7,000. The attached restaurant is also one of the best in town.

Nankolwa Guesthouse This popular guesthouse seems poor value by comparison to the Malaika, charging Tsh6,000 for a double room with a fan (but no nets) using communal showers, or Tsh8,000 for a similar self-contained room. I've received positive reports about the excellent menu and friendly staff, but neither was in evidence on our recent stay.

Shoestring

South Honour Guesthouse Situated around the corner from the bus station, this friendly guesthouse has been about the best of Lindi's cheapies for nigh on a decade. The rooms are looking a bit frayed at the seams, but they are adequately clean, and it's difficult to argue with an asking price of Tsh2,000/3,000 single/double with net, fan and use of common bucket shower. Several other guesthouses of a similar price and standard lie in the roads around the bus station.

Coast Guesthouse The main asset of this otherwise ordinary guesthouse, assuming that you don't mind the 10–15-minute walk from the bus station, is its fabulous location on the palm-lined beach immediately north of the town centre. The rooms are a bit dingy, but clean enough, and as good value as anything in town at Tsh2,000 for a single with three-quarter bed, fan and netting.

Lindi Beach Hotel Still marked on most maps of Lindi, this colonial era hotel – nicknamed the Dysentery Arms in its distant prime – finally did the decent thing and collapsed entirely in about 1997. Prime location notwithstanding, we saw no indication in 2001 that it might one day be renovated or re-opened.

Where to eat

The food at the **Nankolowa Guesthouse** is recommended, but you must place an order over breakfast. The **Malaika Hotel** serves decent local food in the Tsh1,500–2,000 range, but the portions tend to amount to a starch mountain of rice or *ugali* accompanied by a token lump of meat. A better option in my experience, the **NBC Club** is a great place for a beer on the waterfront, and – with a couple of hours' warning – the staff will fry up a filling half-chicken and chips for Tsh1,200. There are also a few *hotelis* around the market, and vendors sell snacks all day at the bus station.

Len Coleman writes: 'A local speciality is large prawns (up to 20cm long excluding antennae), which are caught mainly in the rainy season. Prawns aren't generally consumed locally or served at restaurants in Lindi, but you can order direct from the fish market near the defunct Lindi Beach Hotel. They are of excellent quality, and the price is good (around US$2–3 per kg). The best time to buy is in the late afternoon before 16.30. It shouldn't be a problem to arrange for somebody to cook them for you.'

RUTAMBA AND SURROUNDS

The small town of Rutamba is situated about 30km east of Lindi as the crow flies, in a cashew-growing area studded with attractive lakes and offering easy access to two of the most significant of the 18 coastal forest reserves dotted around the vicinity of Lindi. Rutamba town is flanked to the south by the smallish Lake Nampawaru, and to the northeast by an oval lake covering some 3km² and also called Rutamba. The attractive 9km² Litopo Forest Reserve, which lies on the eastern shore of Lake Rutamba, is bounded to the south by the Lindi road starting 2km out of Rutamba town, and to the east by a long, narrow and apparently anonymous lake. The 7km² Chitoa Forest Reserve lies to the northwest of Rutamba, and is transected by a generally motorable track leading to Milola village.

The significance of the Litipo and Chitoa Forests is not so much the size of the protected areas, but that – unlike several larger forest reserves around Lindi – they

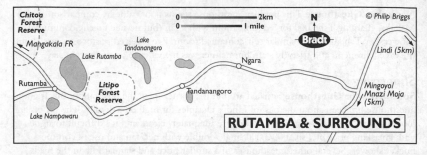

still contain a large component of closed canopy coastal forest. Both forest reserves are relatively poorly known in scientific terms, but a recent ornithological expedition to the area revealed them to be rich in coastal forest birds such as east coast akalat, Kretschmer's longbill, red-tailed ant thrush, Reichenow's batis, Livingstone's flycatcher and plain-backed sunbird. Litopo Forest also harbours a significant breeding population of the brilliantly coloured and highly sought after Angola pitta, while the very rare white-chested alethe has been recorded in Chitoa. The localised African finfoot and white-backed night heron are resident on the shady fringes of the lakes, along with a variety of more widespread water-associated birds. Mammals are more poorly represented – or perhaps just more elusive – but hippos live in some of the lakes, a small elephant population is known to inhabit the forest seasonally, and various small antelopes and primates are present.

Getting there and away

Rutamba lies about 45km from Lindi by road. To get there in a private vehicle, head south along the main surfaced road towards Mnazi Moja for about 20km, then turn right on to an unsurfaced road. This passes through Ngapa after about 10km, crossing a bridge over a river after another 8km or so, shortly before passing through Ngonja, after which it's another 5km to Rutamba. The trip should take about an hour in a private vehicle, and both forests are accessible by road, making this a perfectly feasible day trip out of Lindi.

The situation is not quite so straightforward for travellers without private transport. So far as I can ascertain, no formal pubic transport runs to Rutamba from Lindi. On most days, however, at least one truck will head out to the Rutamba area to collect cashew nuts, taking passengers for Tsh1,200 per person. These trucks normally stop to collect passengers at the junction on the edge of town, opposite the Shell garage, but it might be easier to ask around about suitable transport the day before you want to travel – the bus station is the best place to start making enquiries. Another option would be to catch public transport to Mnazi Moja as far as the Rutamba junction, and wait there for something to come along – you should get through with an early start, but if not then it will be easy enough to catch public transport back to Lindi. From Rutamba, the Litipo Forest Reserve can be reached on foot by following the main road back to Lindi for about 30 minutes, while the Chitoa Forest Reserve lies a similar distance along the road towards Milola.

Where to stay

Travellers who reach Rutamba using public transport or trucks, or who arrive in a private vehicle but want to seek out birds during the prime hours after dawn and before dusk, will need to spend the night. There are a few basic guesthouses to choose from. With permission, it should also be possible to pitch a tent on one of the lakes.

RONDO FOREST RESERVE

The scenic Rondo Plateau is among the most extensive and highest massifs in the southeast of Tanzania, rising to an altitude of 900m about 60km inland of Lindi and 15km north of the Masasi road. The upper slopes of the mountain support large areas of semi-deciduous hardwood forest, most of which is protected within the Rondo Forest Reserve. Like nearby Litipo, this forest received scant attention from biologists prior to the late 1980s, but initial surveys have revealed it to be an important biodiversity site. One reason for this is that while Rondo is essentially a typical coastal forest, it contains significant elements more characteristic of montane forest, and hosts more than 100 plant species found nowhere else, one of the densest concentrations of endemic plants in East Africa. A variety of monkeys and small mammals are present in the Rondo Forest Reserve, even perhaps the occasional elephant, and it is the type of locality for the Rondo dwarf galago, a primate species first discovered in the 1990s by Dr Simon Bearder.

The first serious ornithological study of Rondo, undertaken in 1988 by Holsten, Bräunlich and Huxham, demonstrated it to be of great interest to birdwatchers. The forest supports a similar but broader range of coastal forest birds to Litipo, of which the more conspicuous species include crested guineafowl, Livingstone's turaco, green coucal, Narina trogon, little spotted woodpecker, African broadbill, forest batis, crested flycatcher and forest weaver. Unlike any other forest in southeast Tanzania, however, these birds occur alongside forest species more normally associated with higher altitudes, for instance barred cuckoo, green-headed oriole, white-chested alethe, black-fronted bush shrike and Uluguru violet-backed sunbird. Rondo is the only known East African breeding site for the endangered spotted ground thrush, the most important breeding site in East Africa for the localised east coast akalat, and it harbours a significant breeding population of Angola Pitta. A form of green barbet that is apparently restricted to Rondo might well prove to be an endemic species once molecular analysis is complete. For a fuller account of Rondo's avifauna, the report of the 1988 expedition is posted online at www.ecology.uni-kiel.de/~bettinah/rondo.htm.

The extent of closed canopy forest on Rondo has been estimated variously at between 18km^2 and 50km^2, with the lower figure likely to be the more accurate, and it probably constitutes the third-largest remaining stand of primary coastal forest anywhere in Tanzania. Designated as a forest reserve since colonial times, much of the forest has been poorly protected in reality. The greatest damage occurred in the 1950s, when British contractors were permitted to fell an estimated 20km^2 of pristine forest to make way for exotic plantations. Commercial logging was suspended in the early 1990s, more as a result of the poor local infrastructure than of any conservation concerns, though some small-scale logging still occurs. Despite this, the damaged forest is regenerating in many areas, and the immediate threat to the established forest is probably negligible. All the same, the closed canopy forest covers a fraction of its extent in pre-colonial times, and it remains vulnerable to illegal burning and a possible resumption of misjudged forestry practices in the long term.

In 1960, Trevor Huddlestone, the renowned anti-apartheid activist and Bishop of Masasi – later to acquire the rather wonderful title of 'Archbishop of the Indian Ocean' – purchased the Steele Brothers logging company at Rondo. Huddlestone converted the logging concern into a mission, and was responsible for the construction of the octagonal church with magnificent stained glass windows that dominates it today. The resthouse lies within the mission grounds, and the older priests are a welcoming bunch. If you do visit Rondo, you might want to ask about a seldom visited rock art site that was discovered and described in the 1940s.

Writing in a 1950 edition of *Tanganyika Notes & Records*, rock art expert H A Fosbrooke noted that the roughly 3m² panel is 'on an overhanging rock' and includes two sets of pictures. The older ones 'depict hunting scenes, a mass *Ngoma* (dance), and an elephant with calf' while 'later date paintings are superimposed and show animals being killed by hunters'. The older paintings are reputedly badly faded, but the hunting scenes are well preserved.

Getting there and away

To get to Rondo from Lindi, first follow the surfaced Mtwara road south to Mnazi Moja (Mingoyo) junction, then turn right on to the surfaced road towards Masasi. The junction for Rondo is at the village of Nyengedi, which lies about 30km past Mnazi Moja, between the larger settlements of Narunyu and Mtama. If you turn right at the junction and follow a rougher unsurfaced road for another 17km you'll reach the mission after 45–60 minutes, depending on how recently it last rained. Travellers dependent on public transport should have no problem getting as far as Nyengedi – any vehicle travelling between Mnazi Moja and Masasi will drop you there – but there's no regular public transport from Nyengedi to Rondo, and hitching might entail a seriously long wait at the junction. The Old Boma in Mikindani offers overnight trips to the plateau at US$120 per person for two people or US$90 per person for three or four people, inclusive of 4WD transport, accommodation, guides, meals and hot beverages.

Where to stay

Although the Rondo Plateau sees very few tourists, a small resthouse can be found 20 minutes' walk from the edge of the forest reserve in the Rondo Anglican Mission and Theological College founded by Bishop Trevor Huddlestone. The resthouse was formerly the plantation manager's house, and although the décor is slightly faded, it's an unexpectedly comfortable set-up, with a great view over a steeply eroded canyon. Two bedrooms are available at Tsh5,000 per person. You should bring all food and drinks with you.

MIKINDANI

Sleepy Mikindani, which lies only 10km north of Mtwara, is of greater historical interest than its upstart neighbour, possessing a characteristic old Swahili town layout of narrow roads lined with balconied double-storey homesteads and carved Zanzibar doors. Little more than a fishing village today, Mikindani was at one time the most important port on the coast south of Kilwa Kivinje, and it is where Livingstone set off for his last expedition into the interior. A number of historical relics are dotted around the atmospheric old town; see box *Mikindani Bay: Past & Present* on pages 594–5. Although Mtwara overshadows Mikindani in most other respects today, Mikindani is probably the more appealing base for travellers – and worth visiting as a day trip even if you sleep in Mtwara.

For years neglected by travellers, Mikindani has recently been the focus of some exciting tourist developments. These were initiated and overseen by a British non-profit organisation called Trade Aid, which aims to install a sustainable eco-tourism structure to fund various community projects as well as providing local employment and educational opportunities. The pivot of this project was the restoration of the Old German Boma as a resthouse, which was completed in 1999, and now provides the best upmarket accommodation anywhere along the south coast. Other ventures include an organic market garden supplying the Boma, a tree nursery, and a small restaurant called Samaki to serve the local people. So far some

40 jobs have been created in the Boma, and a further 20 in the other ventures. The Old Boma is also an ideal base for relatively comfortable exploration of the region, since it arranges a variety of local excursions, from guided tours of old Mikindani, to overnight stays in the Rondo Forest Reserve and Lukwika Lumesule Game Reserve, to snorkelling trips to Mnazi Marine Reserve. Contact details are provided for the Old Boma under *Where to stay* below.

Getting there and away

Mikindani straddles the main surfaced road towards Lindi some 10km north of Mtwara, making it highly accessible whether by public transport or in a private vehicle. All buses heading between Lindi and Mtwara will stop at Mikindani on request. Regular light buses ply the road between Mtwara and Mikindani all day through.

There is no airstrip at Mikindani, but Mtwara Airport is only 15km distant. Road transfers from Mtwara Airport can be arranged in advance through the Old Boma, and taxis wait at the airport for all incoming flights. Air Tanzania flies to Mtwara thrice weekly at a fare of around US$90 one-way, and Eagle Air flies there twice weekly at a slightly higher cost.

Where to stay
Upmarket
The Old Boma Tel: 023 233 3875 or (UK) 01425 65 7774; fax: 01425 65 6684; email: tradeaid@netcomuk.co.uk or oldboma@mikindani.com; web: www.mikindani.com. The Old Boma, which dominates the skyline of Mikindani, is situated about 300m from the main road on the slopes of the 100m-high Bismarck Hill. Built under the Germans in 1895, the *boma* served as the regional administrative headquarters until they were relocated to Mtwara in 1947, then as a police station. It fell into disuse in the 1980s, and was in an advanced state of disrepair by the time it was taken over by Trade Aid in 1998. Now immaculately restored to its former whitewashed pomp, the *boma* doubles as the headquarters for Trade Aid and the smartest hotel anywhere on the south coast. Accommodation is in spacious, airy self-contained double rooms with netting, fan, hot bath and atmospheric Swahili furnishings. The wooded grounds contain a clean swimming pool and outdoor dining area, where a large evening buffet is served at Tsh5,000 per person. The upstairs rooms with a balcony cost US$109 double, while standard rooms cost US$89 double, inclusive of dinner and breakfast.

Budget
Ten Degrees South Tel: 023 233 4053; email: tendegreessouth@twiga.com. This friendly English-run lodge is aimed squarely at the few backpackers who pass through Mikindani, charging US$10 for a comfortable double room with a Zanzibar-style bed, netting and common shower. The outdoor restaurant, popular with locals and travellers alike, has a varied menu, with Thai, Indian and Portuguese dishes well represented, most in the Tsh3,000–4,000 range. There's a satellite television in the bar.
Mikindani Yacht Club Tel: 023 233 3875; email: myc@mikindani.com. This is a brand new beachfront lodge, locally owned, with a bar, a small seafood restaurant and a jetty. Stilted beach huts with netting cost Tsh12,000 per unit B&B. There are a couple of windsurfers for hire.

Information and day trips
The Old Boma acts as a tourist information centre and local tour operator. Several day excursions are on offer. These include guided walks through Mikindani (US$10 for two people; US$5 for each additional person), dhow trips (US$20–40

MIKINDANI BAY: PAST AND PRESENT

The present-day town of Mikindani – named for the palms (*mikinda*) that flourish in the vicinity – is not so antiquated as its timeworn façade might lead one to think. Essentially a late-19th-century settlement, Mikindani peaked commercially as an exporter of rubber and agricultural produce during the short period between the official abolition of the Omani slave trade and the advent of German colonialism, and it remained an important administrative centre until the end of World War II. The time-warped aura that envelops Mikindani today – much like that of Pangani or Kilwa Kivinje – is attributable to neglect and the lack of urban development following its abandonment as a regional centre, to Mtwara in 1947.

The human occupation of Mikindani Bay, the arc of small harbours and inlets on which both Mikindani and Mtwara are sited, presumably stretches back for millennia. The proto-Makonde had arrived in the area by the 9th century, and it has been postulated that Shirazi traders settled there at about the same time. No contemporary records or ruins survive to confirm that the bay ever hosted a Shirazi settlement, or, for that matter, a later Portuguese one. The first reference to Mikindani Bay (under a different name) is on Alexander Dalyrimple's 1796 map. Lieutenant Boteler of the HMS *Barracouta*, which anchored at the bay briefly in 1824, penned the earliest known first-hand account of the area. The major settlement at this time was Pemba, which ran along a peninsula at the northern entrance of the same harbour on which Mikindani stands today. Boteler describes Pemba as being dominated by a 'fine castellated building of the old Portuguese... on the side of a steep hill... neatly whitewashed [and] most likely garrisoned'. Boteler also noted that the bay was 'inhabited by Arabs, probably under the Sultan of Muscat'. Based on other British reports and French records, is it clear that during the late 18th and early 19th centuries Mikindani was a major supplier of slaves to Reunion, the Seychelles and the Comoros. The Arabic inhabitants referred to by Boteler can safely be assumed to have been Omani slave traders, and it was certainly they, rather than the Portuguese, who constructed the castellated fortifications on the hillside.

The most celebrated visitor to Mikindani was David Livingstone, who arrived on March 24 1866 and rented a house in Pemba, where he rested for two weeks before embarking on his final expedition into the African interior. Livingstone regarded Mikindani Bay to be 'the finest port on the coast', but he was unimpressed by its Arabic inhabitants, who he characterised as 'a wretched lot physically, thin, washed out creatures – many with bleary eyes'. Nor were they particularly devout: 'many of them came and begged brandy, and laughed when they remarked that they could drink it in secret, but not openly'. On enquiring about the history of the settlers, Livingstone was told they had 'not been here long' but noted that 'a ruin on the northern peninsula... built of stone and lime Arab fashion, and others on the northwest, show that the place has been known and used of old'. The fort described by Boteler was evidently disused by this time, perhaps as a result of a slump in the slave trade to the French Indian Ocean islands. This impression of economic decline is reinforced by Livingstone's reference to the 'agent of the Zanzibar customs house [who] presides over the customs, which are very small'. Trade had declined further by 1874, when Vice Consul Elton visited Mikindani Bay. According to Elton, the entire district had 'been subjected to attacks from the inland and neighbouring tribes, who have burnt the houses [and] lifted the cattle... It is proposed to desert Mikindani and make a stand at Lindi. Trade is at stand still'.

By 1880, when Vice Consul Holmwood visited Mikindani as part of an extensive tour of the south coast, the modern town was entrenched as the main urban centre, with a rapidly growing population 'both Arabs and natives... Banyans and Hindi'. Its fortunes, too, had undergone a dramatic upswing. Holmwood noted that 'Mikindani had prospered immensely since Livingstone had visited it', and felt that the recently established rubber plantations had resulted in 'a complete revolution [with] all classes deriving their income from it or through it'. He remarked on the 'large number of goats and cattle', and on how 'trade had increased exceedingly [with] almost all the produce of the Rovuma region finding its way there'. Holmwood ended his glowing appraisal by stating that 'South of Bagamoyo, Mikindani will now rank in importance next after Kilwa and Lindi. With its newly found prosperity, Mikindani formed the obvious choice for Germany's southeast regional headquarters, and it was settled as such in 1890. Mikindani remained the most important settlement on the bay, and the administrative centre for Rovuma region, until Mtwara harbour, 10km to the south, was developed to service the infamous post-war groundnut scheme (see *Good Intentions* pages 598–9).

The alleys of Mikindani are today possessed of an absorbing time-warped mood that makes the town more than the sum of its architectural landmarks. Nevertheless, a short stroll around reveals a wealth of buildings dating from the late Omani and German colonial periods. The most distinguished of these, built in 1895, the Old German Boma combines elements of German and Arabic architecture and was recently restored as a hotel (see *Where to stay*). Of a similar vintage, the ruined German Customs House, which stands on the waterfront next to the bus station and was possibly expanded from an Omani or Portuguese slave prison, was damaged during a British naval raid in 1916. The nearby Aga Kahn Building, also on the waterfront, is probably the oldest in town; built in the mid-19th century by a wealthy Arab trader and distinguished by its unusual staircase, it now serves as an Islamic pre-school. Several old Arab graves can been seen around town; it was customary in Mikindani to mark the tomb of a sultan with a baobab tree at each end, so the two would eventually intertwine.

A commemorative plaque celebrating 'the reputed dwelling place of David Livingstone' is posted with palpable disingenuity on the wall of a two-storey balconied building on the corner of the waterfront road. Livingstone almost certainly resided in Pemba rather than Mikindani (by all accounts an insignificant settlement in 1866), and his 'reputed dwelling place' is nothing more or less than one of several fading early- to mid-20th-century homesteads built by Arab or Indian merchants. Opposite to this house, the 'Old Slave Market' is a German building, post-dating the slave trade by two decades, but reputedly constructed over a former Omani slave market – which, some claim, previously served as a Portuguese ivory store. Whatever the truth of this story, the recent misconceived 'restoration' of the old market has forsaken much of its architectural integrity by bricking in the old arches and slapping lavish paint all over the stone exterior. Historical continuity, at least, is maintained by the clutch of – very good – local craft shops that now trade out of the restored market.

THE ROVUMA FERRY AND NORTHERN MOZAMBIQUE

Edited from a report of a trip in November 2001, by Ian Smith of the Old Boma in Mikindani.

From Mikindani, we drove down to the border post at Kilamba. We crossed the Rovuma River in a small punt for Tsh2,000 each. The river at this time of the year is low, although still hundreds of metres wide. It's a beautifully tranquil scene, boats and canoes quietly crossing, lots of birdlife and we saw three hippos, including a mother and calf. The purpose-built ferry was moored mid-stream, as it usually is at low tide. It is a relatively large ferry with a roll-on, roll-off design, and operates daily, year-round, at high tide. You should report one hour in advance and the cost for an ordinary 4WD is Tsh10,000. The paperwork involved to take a car across is minimal. On arrival at Mozambique customs a small fee is paid and insurance checked. Although the ferry runs all year round, the road from the Mozambique side of the river to Palma may be impassable from March to late May

When we arrived at the Mozambique side, there was only one pick-up, which would take us down to Moçimboa da Praia for around US$6 each. My travel companion squeezed into the front cabin, between driver, gear stick and passenger, and I sat up back with 12 others and countless luggage bags and sacks. Mozambique customs is about 3km inland and comprises a few basic daub-and-wattle huts. They issue a one-month tourist visa for US$55, as compared to US$35–40 in Dar es Salaam (depending on processing time).

We arrived in Palma after two hours. The old colonial buildings overlook a palm-fringed bay and by all accounts the view from the top of the hill was better than the reality of the village. We spent an hour in Palma, the point of interest being the local police 4WD, which had been rolled the night before,

per party), snorkelling and fishing motorboat trips (from US$120 per person) and a visit to Lake Chidya and the Rovuma River (US$35–45 per person). Overnight excursions include a snorkelling trip to Msimbati in the Mnazi Bay Marine Reserve (US$25–35 per person), a round excursion to the Rondo Plateau (US$90–120 per person) and a two-night safari to the wild Lukwika Lumesule Game Reserve (US$350–500 per person).

MTWARA

Mtwara is the administrative centre of Rovuma Region, and by far the largest town on the south coast, with a population rapidly approaching the 100,000 mark. In terms of Tanzanian travel, it is something of a dead end, but it does serve as the main springboard for travellers crossing over the Rovuma River into neighbouring Mozambique (see *Getting to Tanzania*, pages 55–63). Large it may be, but Mtwara is also a somewhat disjointed and unfocused settlement, reflecting ambitious but as yet unfulfilled development plans initiated by the colonial government after World War II. The nominal town centre, which lies about 1km inland, consists of a small, sleepy grid of roads that frame the tiny Aga Khan Park, and are surrounded by open fields. A more convincing hub of commercial activity is the Chiko Ngola area, around the main market and bus station, which lies about 1km south of the town centre. The modern harbour lies 1.5km northeast of the town centre, while the beach and smarter residential area of Shangani lie about 2km to the north. There appears to be a small industrial area to the east of the harbour.

killing one person. Tragic, but then again if the police driver is pissed, speeding and carrying passengers, perhaps hardly surprising. Mocimboa de Praia was, I believe, a bit of a holiday resort in colonial times, and it sports a faded club, gardens, children's playgrounds and wide avenues. Much smaller than Mtwara, it has an airstrip and a control tower. Accommodation was a basic pensão (US$4) and we had food at the faded Club de Moçimboa da Praia. Day two saw us go for a long walk around the bay. The north part of the bay has a large crane for loading produce on to boats and the old Rovuma ferry is also there. The primary exports are timber and cashew nuts. The south side of the bay has a long beach, plenty of dhow repairs and fishing and is very pleasant. A shallow, water entry along the beach, the incoming tide and offshore wind brought in dozens of dhows carrying a lot of fish.

The next morning we arose at 05.00 to get the pick-up to the border. This return journey could only be described as brutal with less space and more people squeezed on board. Add to that a driver whose main means of ironing out the bumps was to hit them at speed and you had the makings of a rather uncomfortable few hours. Transport to the Tanzania border post and Mtwara was in a packed, open Land Rover (Tsh3,000). It was so packed we had to divert through *shambas* on the outskirts of Mtwara to avoid the traffic police, eventually arriving with me hanging off the back, standing on the spare tyre. The *dalla-dalla* from Mtwara to Mikindani was positive luxury and an end to an exciting few days.

There are now two flights a week in each direction between Mtwara and Pemba (Mozambique), connecting with the Air Tanzania flights from Dar es Salaam to Mtwara. Pemba to Mtwara costs US$185, while Mtwara to Pemba costs US$205 (the difference being the tax).

Mtwara is a pleasant enough town without offering much in the way of scintillating sightseeing. The market itself is worth a look around, while the nominal town centre, lined with multi-storey Indian houses and shops that date almost exclusively to the 1950s, is gradually acquiring an endearingly time-warped atmosphere all its own. One worthwhile goal, depending to some extent on your interest in modern ecclesiastical art, is the Benedictine Church of Saint Paul, which lies in Majengo, ten minutes' walk southeast of the market, which is elaborately decorated with paintings executed over a two-year period by the German priest Polycarp Uehlien.

The Makonde carvers in Mtwara carve figures for export to Dar and Arusha, where they are sold for ten times the price to tourists. It is possible to buy them directly from the carvers, which is very cheap. To go to a representative workshop, head straight across the roundabout towards Mikindani, past the Lutheran Mission and turn-off for the airport, and the stalls are 300m further on the right side of the road.

At Shangani, to the north of the town centre, there is a good swimming beach surrounded by coral flats, the latter interesting for the rock pools that form on them and the wading birds that visit. Far better, however, is the fantastic beach on Msangamkuu, on the opposite side of the bay to Shangani. Regular dhows to Msangamkuu, charging Tsh50 per person, leave from Dhow Beach, past the Catholic Cathedral on the road to Shangani. The best reason for going to the beach is the brilliant snorkelling at low tide on the left side, but do be careful of jelly fish and the rather evil sea urchins with long black spikes and a shiny orange eye.

GOOD INTENTIONS

In the first edition of this guide, I commented that Mtwara sprawled in a manner suggesting that somebody once intended greater things for it. And indeed they did, as became clear recently when I came across P H Johnston's gushing article about Mtwara Bay in an issue of the *Tanganyika Notes and Records* dating to the late 1940s.

Prior to World War II, Mtwara was a village of little note when compared to the nearby, more historical settlement of Mikindani. Its one pre-war claim to posterity was that it was used as a location for the original silent version of *The Blue Lagoon*. (According to Johnston, another film crew arrived in 1928 – is there anybody out there who can elaborate on his assertion that 'strange but unfounded tales reached the home press as a result of this incursion into Mtwara'?)

In February 1947, Mtwara was chosen by the British administration as the port to be used by the infamous Groundnut Scheme of 1946–51. The idea behind this scheme was to turn southern Tanzania into a major groundnut producer. Britain pumped some 30 million pounds into creating the appropriate infrastructure before realising that the soil was unsuitable, and the area received insufficient rainfall to grow groundnuts. Not only was the scheme an expensive failure, but by coercing local farmers into replacing subsistence crops with groundnuts, its administrators caused more suffering than they ever alleviated. An entirely new port was built at Mtwara, 'to meet not only the needs of the groundnut project but also such further requirements as future development beyond the groundnut areas might call for'. If you've visited Mtwara, this isn't even funny, just grimly ironic.

In 1992, I met a Dutchman who was working for the fishery department at Mwanza on Lake Victoria. He had been baffled as to why so much of the fish exported from the lake was being sent to Mtwara. On a brief visit to this most remote of Tanzanian ports, situated on a stretch of coast abundantly rich in fish, he established that there was no deep-sea fishing equipment available to the residents of Mtwara. Only a large, modern and useless port!

Getting there and away

Mtwara Airport lies about 4km from the town centre. Air Tanzania flies from Dar es Salaam twice weekly at a fare of around US$90 one-way, and Eagle Air flies four times a week at a slightly higher cost, but stopping at Kilwa. Taxis are available to meet all incoming flights. Current flight details can be found on the website www.mikindani.com.

Buses between Dar es Salaam and Mtwara leave daily at around 05.30–06.30 from the main bus station and should be booked in advance. This trip should take about 12–15 hours in the dry season but can take a lot longer during the rains, and it's advisable to break it up with a stop at either Lindi or Kilwa – better still both! Recommended services include Sollo Senior and Born Coast, both of which charge around Tsh12,000 for a seat. Several buses daily run between Mtwara and Masasi, and Mtwara and Lindi. These leave when full, and take a few hours only. Express minibuses leave in either direction at 10.00 and 13.00. For details of crossing from Mtwara to Mozambique, see *To/from Mozambique,* on pages 62–3.

The MV *Safari* currently runs weekly between Dar es Salaam and Mtwara, leaving Dar es Salaam at 08.00 every Wednesday and from Mtwara at about the same time on Friday. The one-way fare is Tsh8,000 for residents or US$25 for non-residents, to which must be added a US$5 port tax payable in hard currency.

The surprising thing about Johnston's article, given that the colonials are generally portrayed as a bunch of exploitative taskmasters, is its genuine idealism. Paternalistic it might be, culture-bound it most definitely is, but the tone is more than anything one of giddy optimism. The groundnut project is 'a great decision ... one that will be, beyond doubt, the turning point in the history of at least one small part of Africa and its people... one that will advance the area and its people and provide opportunities of such progress in so short a time that none would ever have dreamed possible.' He even goes so far as to talk of Mtwara as a 'future Mombasa'.

It is easy enough to sneer with hindsight on our side. To give Johnston his due, his otherwise elegiac piece of prose ends soberly enough: 'Let it be hoped,' he asks, 'that our planners will really plan soundly', a prophetic plea that might as well have been written 20 years ago – or for that matter yesterday.

Fifty years after the Groundnut Scheme was first mooted, I spent an evening with a Danish aid worker who, after two months observing conditions in an African village, made the chilling observation that the West ought to implement a scheme which would 'teach African women how to bring up children properly'. She, and all the other culture-bound meddlers who would save Africa from itself, would do well to read Johnston's article, and then to visit Mtwara: a sprawling memorial to good intentions gone awry.

As something of a footnote, it appears that Mtwara's long under-utilised harbour might yet have its day as the lynchpin of the proposed Mtwara Corridor Project. This joint Tanzanian-Mozambican venture, initiated in 1997, is aimed to promote international trade and provide a much needed economic stimulus to the backwaters of southern Tanzania and northern Mozambique. The proposed bridge across the Rovuma River will be one step in this process, as will the resuscitation of Mtwara Harbour. It has recently been announced that the Tanzanian government will dedicate US$6 million to the dredging, widening and modernisation of the harbour, which will allow the world's largest seafaring vessels to dock there, and increase the port's cargo capacity from 150,000 to 400,000 tonnes.

It is not unknown for the schedule of the MV *Safari* to be changed or cancelled at short notice. However, the MV *Zahara* and MV *Mandeleo* also do this run upon occasion. Check at the harbour in Dar es Salaam for current details of southbound boats, or at the ferry offices at the fruit market in Mtwara for northbound departures. Book a first-class berth if you can (not all boats have classes), as the trip takes 18–24 hours and a bed (albeit cockroach infested) helps! Food is available, but you might want to bring along some supplies, particularly if you are vegetarian.

Where to stay
Upmarket
No truly upmarket accommodation is to be found in Mtwara at the time of writing, but the excellent Old Boma in Mikindani lies only 10km north of town.

Moderate
The Village Tel: 023 233 3670; mobile: 0744 691709; fax: 023 233 3879; email: village_tz@yahoo.com; web: www.geocities.com/village_tz. This beachfront hotel in Shangani, 2km from the town centre, opened at the end of 2001, and is currently the most attractive lodging around town. Accommodation in self-contained chalets costs Tsh25,000

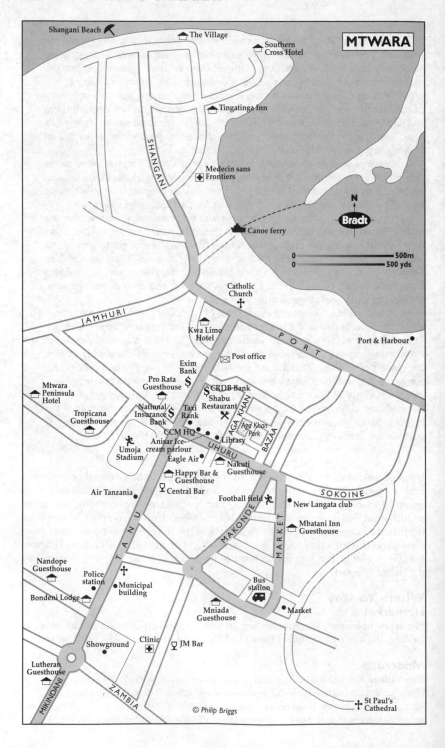

MTWARA

Shangani Beach

The Village

Southern Cross Hotel

SHANGANI

Tingatinga Inn

Medecin sans Frontiers

N

Bradt

Canoe ferry

0   500m
0   500 yds

Catholic Church

JAMHURI

PORT

Kwa Limo Hotel

Port & Harbour

Post office

Exim Bank

Pro Rata Guesthouse

Mtwara Peninsula Hotel

CRDB Bank

Shabu Restaurant

Tropicana Guesthouse

National Insurance Bank

Taxi Rank

Aga Khan Park

AGA KHAN

BAZAA

CCM HQ

Anisar Ice-cream parlour

Library

UHURU

Umoja Stadium

Eagle Air

Nakuti Guesthouse

Happy Bar & Guesthouse

Air Tanzania

Central Bar

Football field

SOKOINE

New Langata club

MAKONDE

Mbatani Inn Guesthouse

MARKET

TANU

Nandope Guesthouse

Police station

Municipal building

Bus station

Bondeni Lodge

Mniada Guesthouse

Market

Showground

Clinic

JM Bar

Lutheran Guesthouse

MIKINDANI

ZAMBIA

© Philip Briggs

St Paul's Cathedral

B&B per person. A good restaurant is attached, and the management can arrange game fishing cruises, diving trips and seasonal whale watching excursions.

Southern Cross Hotel Tel: 023 233 3206. The former Mtwara Beach Hotel closed about ten years ago and has been the subject of persistent rumours of renovation ever since. Rumour finally translated into reality in 2001, when the hotel was taken over by a Swedish company, and it should re-open in late 2002. No prices are available, but expect them to be comparable to The Village next door.

Mtwara Peninsula Hotel Tel: 023 233 3638. Despite the misleading name, this adequately comfortable business hotel isn't situated within smelling distance – let alone sight – of the ocean, but rather in the maze of back streets behind the football stadium. The layout of the hotel is essentially that of a jumped-up guesthouse, but the rooms are fine, and a pleasant beer garden and restaurant are attached. Prices range from US$20 for a small self-contained single with AC and satellite television to US$50 for a larger executive suite.

Makonde Beach Resort Tel: 023 233 3635. Also known as Litingi's, this small resort lies 2km off the Mikindani road, along a turn-off that is clearly signposted about 8km out of Mtwara. A self-contained double, with television and AC, costs Tsh18,000. The rocky beach is good for swimming at high tide and the view is attractive.

Budget

Tingatinga Inn Tel: 023 233 3146. This quiet, clean lodge, warmly recommended by several travellers, is set in an old suburban house on the wooded avenues of Shangani about five minutes' walk from the beach. Single/double rooms with fan and nets cost Tsh6,000/8,000 using common showers. There's no restaurant, but you can eat at The Village nearby.

Kwa Limo Hotel Tel: 023 233 3570/38. This small, reasonably central hotel lies a short distance from the main road towards Shangani, and offers adequate self-contained rooms with a double bed, fridge and fan for Tsh7,000. The open-air bar and restaurant is on the opposite side of the road.

Lutheran Guesthouse Tel: 023 233 3294. The guesthouse at the Lutheran Mission on the main circle on the Mikindani road is probably the best value in this range. Self-contained double rooms with satellite television cost Tsh7,000, while the four-bed dormitories (using common showers) cost Tsh2,000 per person. A garden restaurant is attached, but no alcohol is served.

Bondeni Lodge Self-contained rooms with net and fan, pleasant enough, but steeply priced at Tsh9,000. A good garden bar is attached.

Beach Villas One of the most pleasant places to stay in Mtwara if you are planning to hang around a while, is in one of the beach villas owned by the Benedictine Fathers. They are located on the lovely beach at Shangani, and have pretty gardens with gates leading to the sand. Arrangements must be made with the Benedictine Fathers at St Paul's Church in Majengo. You provide your own food.

Shoestring

Note that the cheapest option for single travellers is the dormitory accommodation at the Lutheran Guesthouse (listed under *Budget*).

Pro Rata Guesthouse Central and very clean, this small local hotel near the stadium is fair value at Tsh5,000 for a single (small bed) with net, fan and common shower. There's a lively garden bar and restaurant in front of the hotel.

Jajugu Holiday Lodge A bit rundown and scruffy, but fair value at Tsh4,000 for a double with net and fan using common shower or Tsh6,000 for a similar self-contained double.

Nandope Guesthouse The best of the real cheapies, and reasonably central, the Nandope Guesthouse charges Tsh3,500 for a clean room with a double bed, fan and netting, using common showers. Several similarly priced guesthouses are dotted around the market and bus station, but they are all pretty scruffy.

TRAVELLING FROM MTWARA TO SONGEA

This box was edited from notes made by Joe Williamson and Mike Wilks, who travelled from Mtwara to Mbamba Bay and back again in early 1999, but transport information has been updated with information from Suzanne Pegg, who travelled in December 2001.

The wild, scenic route between the south coast and Lake Nyasa is one of the most remote and least travelled in Tanzania. It is a trip that will take at least three days, longer if you want to break it up with a day's rest, and the road is mostly in poor condition. After the El Niño rains of 1997–98, the stretch between Songea and Tunduru was for some time covered by 4WD vehicles only, but there are now buses covering all legs of the route.

The journey is broken into three legs: Mtwara to Masasi (200km), Masasi to Tunduru (200km) and Tunduru to Songea (273km). The road degrades from Masasi onwards, but each leg can be done in a single day, though travel times depend greatly on the weather and availability of transport. Overall, 4WD vehicles are the fastest option on the roads west of Masasi, especially in the rainy season, but they may not be as comfortable as buses, are often double the price, and don't have fixed departure times. In this part of the country, you should try to establish the departure time and agree on a price as far in advance as possible, but even then you might wait for a few hours until there is a full load.

You may be able to do two legs in a day but this will mean leaving very early. It is best to get to the departure area between 04.30 and 06.00 to have guaranteed transport. It also helps to catch the first available vehicle while there are people waiting to go otherwise you may wait up to a day until there is a full vehicle ready to leave. The travelling times quoted are for dry season although it did start raining before our return trip so the return journey times were longer. Be prepared for travel times to double in the wet season.

Leg one: Mtwara/Mikindani to Masasi

Transport starts in Mtwara but we caught it in Mikindani and stopped in Ndanda instead of continuing to Masasi. The journey takes up to four hours by bus on mostly tarmac or good-quality roads with frequent stops and costs about US$3 between Mtwara and Masasi. The main stops en route are at Mnasi Moja (where the road forks to Lindi) and Ndanda. At most villages, the children offer a variety of fresh food and a selection of packaged food. In addition to food there are often odds and ends ranging from door locks to trainers on offer at the larger bus stands, such as Ndanda.

The first buses leave from the Indian section and then the main roundabout in Mtwara at about 05.30 and depart roughly every half-hour until mid-afternoon. In Mikindani the buses stop by the Old Prison. The Ndanda bus stop is a major lay-by near the hospital. A reasonable guesthouse can be found in Ndanda. For details of accommodation in Masasi, see *Masasi* page 609.

Where to eat

In Shangani, the **Finn Club** (daily membership US$1) has satellite television, table tennis and the best variety of food on offer in Mtwara. Otherwise, good eating-out options in Mtwara essentially boil down to the restaurants at **The Village** and **Mtwara Peninsula Hotel** (listed in the *Moderate* category), which

Leg two: Masasi to Tunduru

One bus daily runs in either direction along the 200km road between these two towns, and it should be booked as far in advance as possible. The bus departs at 09.00 (report at 08.00) and the journey takes about eight hours on a very rough sandy road through some fairly uninhabited areas. At most village stops there will be hawkers selling water, chicken, cashew nuts, etc. *Wazungu* are a true novelty, but few kids actually shout *mzungu*; they just stop, stare – and smile if you look friendly! If you can't get on the bus, a few lorries generally cover the route every day, taking about the same time, but are not very comfortable. I travelled in a lorry with no shade and 20–30 people for company. Make sure you have a padded bag to sit on or use a grain sack if they are carrying them.

Tunduru is an old mining town, but for travellers it serves as little more than a place to stop over for the night. Focused along one main street, the town is quite prosperous, but something of a backwater. Tunduru did enjoy a brief period of notoriety between 1985 and 1988 when, according to Nicholas Gordon's *Ivory Knights*, it was plagued by man-eating lions. Almost 50 people were killed, including the game warden sent to sort out the problem, and a further 28 were wounded. The offending cats have since been shot.

We stayed in the **Naweka Guesthouse**, which was adequate, with running water in the early morning and electricity in the evenings. The cost is about US$3 per night for a single room and US$4.50 for a self-contained room with a fan but no nets. The **Yakiti Guesthouse** is more basic, charging around US$2 for a single with a mosquito net. The **Sunrise Guesthouse** had self-contained rooms but no mosquito nets and cost US$4.50. Restaurants include the **Greenland Bar** and **Al Jazira Hotel**.

Leg three: Tunduru to Songea

One bus covers this route in either direction daily, leaving at 06.00, though you should report at 05.30. Tickets cost Tsh8,000 and it is normally necessary to book the afternoon before it travels. There are also Land Rovers for hire to Songea, which work out at the same price as the bus. The road is much worse than the stretch between Masasi and Tunduru and the trip takes at least seven hours, passing through many uninhabited areas, which become rather tedious scenically. Namtumbo is a good place on the way for refreshment.

Arriving in Songea, we were besieged by offers of trips to various places, and felt the bus stand reflected the bustling and prosperous feel of the town. Songea is possibly smaller than Mtwara but more centred and seems to have a better range of goods available, partly because the climate allows for a more regular and varied supply of fruit and vegetables. For changing money, there is the NBC (weekdays 08.30–15.00 and Saturday 08.30–12.00) as well as a CRDB bank. For accommodation, see *Songea*, page 562.

The obvious onward options from Songea are either to visit Mbamba Bay on the shore of Lake Nyasa, or else to head up to Njombe along the road to the Tanzam Highway.

typically charge Tsh3,000–4,000 for a main course. The Indian-run **Shabu Restaurant** in the old town centre serves simple Swahili and Indian dishes, while **Anisar Ice Cream** is the best place in town for ice-creams, milkshakes and the like. The cheaper local eateries are concentrated around the bus station; they are similar in price, and serve chip omelettes and goat kebabs. For a night out, the

Lucky Bar and Guesthouse has an above average garden bar, while the **Bandari Club** near the harbour usually has a live band.

General information

There is no private forex bureau in Mtwara, but several **banks** will change US dollars travellers' cheques and cash. A recently opened **internet** service is Winnie Secretarial Bureau, in the main street between the BP garage and post office. For **day tours and other information**, the best place to talk to is the Old Boma in Mikindani. The **White Cont** (a white shipping container) on the outside of the town centre sells luxury items such as baked beans, chocolate, shampoo and bug spray – it also serves very cold beers and sodas. Another good shop in the town centre is **Hen Flora's**, which sells most imported items, albeit at a price higher than any other shop in town. **IkoIko**, a booze warehouse at the top end of the straight road in this part of town, sells the cheapest spirits and wine in Mtwara and has a good choice.

EXCURSIONS FROM MTWARA AND MIKINDANI

The following excursions are equally open to travellers based at Mikindani or Mtwara. Organised trips to all the sites mentioned could be arranged through the Old Boma in Mikindani.

Msimbati Beach

Situated at the open-sea entrance to the maze of channels and harbours that constitutes Mikindani Bay, the idyllic beach at Msimbati stretches for kilometres between Ras Msimbati and Ras Ruwura peninsulas, 25km east of Mtwara as the crow flies, and a similar distance from the border with Mozambique. Msimbati was formerly known to travellers as the best place to pick up dhows to Mozambique – a role that has been made redundant by the recently installed ferry across the Rovuma River – but is a very beautiful spot in its own right, totally unspoilt and lined with broad palm trees. The white beach shelves steeply and the surrounding reef is not tidal, which means that swimming is good 24 hours a day. Because the beach is one of the few on the Tanzanian mainland to face west, the sunsets are generally spectacular.

Msimbati had its 15 minutes of fame when, on December 31 1959, the eccentric expatriate Leslie Latham Moore, a World War I veteran who retired to Msimbati, announced unilateral secession from Tanganyika. Latham Moore appointed himself the Sultan of Msimbati, and even went as far as designing a flag for the independent state – vertical green, blue and red stripes, with a Union Jack in the top left corner. The authorities tolerated this unusual but fairly harmless state of affairs for a time, but eventually Latham Moore was arrested and the sultanate disbanded. The sultan's modest palace still stands above the beach, now somewhat dilapidated and crawling with insects!

Msimbati Beach overlooks Mnazi Bay, which lies within the **Mnazi Bay-Rovuma Marine Park**, a multi-use conservancy running from Mtwara to the border with Mozambique. The boundaries of this extensive marine park, which is identical in status to Mafia Marine Park, were agreed to in 1999, and the park has subsequently been formally gazetted; conservation strategies will be developed and implemented under the IUCN over a period of five years. The park is an important breeding site for marine turtles, and it also harbours an extensive system of reefs and atolls. The superb reef that lies immediately off Msimbati Beach offers great snorkelling and the whole area has enormous potential for diving. The shallow bay is listed as an Important Bird Area, primarily for its large concentrations of crab plover and sand plover, but it also hosts a large number of other marine birds. A few trucks head from Mtwara to Msimbati daily, taking about an hour in either direction. Day or overnight snorkelling trips can also be arranged through the Old Boma in Mikindani. At present, there is no accommodation on the beach, though camping is permitted – and by all accounts safe. It's not normally a problem to buy fish and other seafood and coconuts from local fishermen. A new eco-friendly lodge is, however, under construction, and likely to open in early 2003. The lodge will consist of about 12 standing tents, fuelled by solar power, and it is likely to cost around US$90 per person. The lodge is being developed by the British owner of Ten Degrees South lodge in Mikindani, who can be contacted for further details (see the *Where to stay* entry under Mikindani for contact numbers).

Lake Kitere

This lake of roughly 3km² in extent lies on the Mambi River about 20km east of the main road between Lindi and Mikindani. It's a pretty spot, primarily of interest for its prolific birdlife, notably large numbers of pelicans and other water-associated birds. In the surrounding area, you'll still see traces of the Mtwara–Nachingwea Railway Line, yet another grand folly associated with the groundnut scheme: constructed in 1951, the railway was used for only three years before it was abandoned. To reach the lake, head northwest from Mikindani along the surfaced Lindi road for about 25km to Mpapura. Shortly after passing through Mpapura, take a turn-off to your left, and follow it for about 20km to Kitere village on the lakeshore. A limited amount of public transport runs to Kitere from Mpapura. There is no accommodation in Kitere, but if you can't find a room, it should be fine to pitch a tent.

Lake Chidya

This remote 10km² lake lies about 40km inland on the Mozambican border, where it feeds and is fed by the Rovuma River. It supports large numbers of crocodiles and hippos, as well as prodigious waterfowl and other birds. Access is from the small town of Kitaya, where a memorial is dedicated to the crew of a plane shot down during a conflict between Tanzanian and Mozambican guerrillas in the 1970s. Kitaya can be reached by following the Newala road out of Mtwara for about 35km to Nanguruwe, where you need to turn left at a major intersection and drive for another two hours or so towards the Mozambican border. Once at Kitaya, you need to hire a local boat to take you downstream for about 5km – elephants are quite frequently seen crossing this stretch of river – to enter the lake itself. Kitaya, while no metropolis, is quite a big town and an important border crossing: there should be some form of public transport there from Mtwara, and a basic guesthouse or two once you arrive.

THE MAKONDE PLATEAU

The Makonde Plateau, inland of Mtwara and Lindi, is home to East Africa's most renowned craftsmen, the Makonde carvers (see box *The Makonde*, pages 606–7). Tanzania's Makonde Plateau, which lies at an altitude of around 800m, is separated from the geologically similar but larger Mozambican Makonde Plateau by a steep valley, carved over millennia by the wide Rovuma River. It is thought that most of the plateau was originally covered in thick woodland and forest, but this is now reduced to relic forest patches and isolated trees. Today, the area is heavily cultivated, though the porous sandy soil is only capable of supporting low-scale agriculture. Subsistence crops include maize, sorghum and cassava, while cashew plantations yield the region's only widespread cash crop. For many Makonde smallholders, the peak cashew season, generally December, generates a sudden influx of cash, but little money comes in over the rest of the year.

The main towns of the Makonde area are Newala, high and breezy on the plateau, and the lower lying and hotter administrative centre of Masasi. The road to Newala probably provides the best easy overview of rural Makonde, climbing the plateau through dense *miombo* woodland and passing numerous Makonde villages. Immaculately neat and orderly, these villages apparently receive few visits from tourists – every time the bus stopped a crowd of curious children gathered around us and stared in open amazement. There is a strong missionary presence in

THE MAKONDE

The Makonde of southern Tanzania probably arrived on the plateau they currently inhabit many centuries ago, having migrated across the Rovuma from what is now northern Mozambique (a country that also still supports a large Makonde population). The Makonde are widely regarded to be the finest traditional sculptors in East Africa, and according to oral tradition they have been practising this craft for at least 300 years. Although the Makonde must have encountered Omani slave caravans heading between Lake Nyasa and the coast, they had restricted contact with Europeans until about 1910. As recently as 50 years ago, it was still commonplace for Makonde women to adorn themselves with gross lip plates similar to those worn by the Mursi in southern Ethiopia.

Makonde society has a decentralised political structure, with each village being overseen by a clan chief who is selected based on the matrilineal status of his family. The matrilineal system, unusual for this part of Africa, is a manifestation of the Makonde religion, which is centred on spirit worship of the first Makonde woman. Legend has it that a person, not yet a man, living alone in the foothills of the plateau, carved a piece of wood into the shape of a human figure. The carver left his creation outside his home before he retired for the night, and awoke to find it had been transformed into a living woman. Twice the woman conceived, but both times the child died after three days. Each time, the pair moved higher on to the plateau, believing this would bring them luck. The third child lived, and became the first true Makonde. The mother is regarded to be the spiritual ancestor of all the Makonde, and the legend is sometimes said to be a parable for the difficulty of creation and the necessity to discard unsatisfactory carvings.

In their purest form, the intricate, stylised carvings of the Makonde relate to this ancestral cult of womanhood, and are carried only by men, as a good luck charm. Traditional carvings almost always depict a female figure, sometimes surrounded by children. The large demonic masks that are also carved by the Makonde, more so perhaps in Mozambique than in Tanzania, are central to the traditional *sindimba* stilt dance, which is performed by men and women together. Makonde sculptures were practically unknown outside of Tanzania until a carving workshop was established at Mwenge in suburban Dar es Salaam during the 1950s. Subsequently, like any dynamic art form, Makonde sculpture has been responsive to external influences and subject to changes in fashion, with new styles of carvings becoming increasingly abstract and incorporating wider moral and social themes.

The most rustic of the new styles is the Binadamu sculpture, which depicts traditional scenes such as old men smoking pipes or women fetching water in a

the area with most schools and hospitals being run by missions. Some missions insist on importing Western luxury goods for local distribution. As a consequence, all sorts of unlikely items are offered for sale at the roadside, ranging from lace petticoats to brandname chocolates and toiletries.

Masasi

The principal town on the Makonde Plateau, Masasi is the end of the tar road for travellers heading cross-country towards Songea and Lake Nyasa, and despite a somewhat sweltering climate it will feel like something of a return to comfort for travellers coming from that part of Tanzania. Founded in 1875 by the University

relatively naturalistic manner. Altogether more eerie and evocative is the Shetani style, in which grotesquely stylised human forms, sometimes with animal-like features, represent the impish and sometimes evil spirits for which the style is named. Many Makonde and other East Africans leave offerings for Shetani sculptures, believing them to be possessed by ancestral spirits. Most elaborate of all are the naturalistic Ujamaa sculptures, which depict many interlocking figures and relate to the collective social policy of Ujamaa fostered by the late President Nyerere. Also known as People Poles or Trees of Life, these statues sometimes incorporate several generations of the carver's family, rising in circular tiers to be up to 2m high. A newer style called Mawingu – the Swahili word for clouds – combines human figures with abstract shapes to represent intellectual or philosophical themes. Today, the finest examples of the genre fetch prices in excess of US$5,000 from international collectors.

The Makonde traditionally shape their creations exclusively from *Dalbergia Melanoxylon*, a hardwood tree known locally as *mpingo* and in English as African blackwood or (misleadingly) African ebony. The carver – always male – will first saw a block of wood to the required size, then he creates a rough outline by hacking away excess wood with an instrument called an adze. The carving is all done freehand, with hammers, chisels and rasps used to carve the fine detail, before the final sculpture is sanded and brushed for smoothness. A large Ujamaa sculpture can take several months to complete, with some of the carving – appropriately – being undertaken communally. Traditionally, the craft was more or less hereditary, with sons being apprenticed to their fathers from a young age, and different families tending to work specific subjects related to their own traditions.

Many of the carvings you see elsewhere in Tanzania come from the Makonde Plateau (many, too, are carved by Makonde settled in Dar es Salaam). You will, however, need good local contacts to see any carvings locally, since most commercially produced ones are bought by dealers from elsewhere in the country. If you can buy directly from local carvers (most easily in Mtwara, which has a large Makonde population), you will get a better price than you would in Arusha or Dar es Salaam – and by cutting out the middleman the carver will also get a fair price. Defying popular misconception – and its name – the heartwood of the African blackwood is not jet black but dark brown, sometimes with a slightly red tone. Unfortunately, the above misconception has resulted in many carvers producing the desired affect by smearing on a layer of black shoe polish, which does little to enhance the natural grain of the wood. These days, many top Makonde sculptors use other media, such as soapstone, bone and verdite.

Missions to Central Africa as a refuge for freed slaves, Masasi has subsequently grown to be a modern and bustling small town, unexpectedly so considering its remote location. People on the coast joke that Masasi is *kama Ulaya* (like Europe), which might be stretching a point, but does reflect its sense of prosperity relative to somewhere like Lindi or Mikindani. A number of Tanzania's leading lights originate from Masasi, including the President Benjamin Mkapa, who still has a house in town.

Prosperous it might be, but from a traveller's perspective Masasi is pretty much just another small workaday African town and very hot. Makonde carvers might be seen at work along the back streets, and numerous food stalls and well-stocked shops line the main tar drag along which the town sprawls. The most distinguishing feature of Masasi is the surrounding Masasi Hills, a striking (and in the right light very beautiful) cluster of granite outcrops, strongly reminiscent of the famous *koppies* that punctuate rural Zimbabwe. Towering to an altitude of 951m above the roughly 400m-high plains, these hills have been accorded legal protection and are eminently climbable – there are worn tracks up most of them – and the views from the top are well worth the effort. Snakes and leopards still inhabit the hills, but troops of vervet monkey and a wide variety of *miombo*-associated birds are more commonly seen.

One of the few rock art sites in southern Tanzania lies in the vicinity of Masasi, within a sacred cave near Chiwata. Neville, the first European to see these paintings, described them in the 1940s as 'looking like the squiggles a small child might have made after dipping his fingers into a pot of thick dull-red paint'. Neville added that at the back of the cave were 'what looked like a decorative pattern of lines and loops and dots... and things that looked rather like a sort of Plimsoll mark or some astronomic symbols'. Should you be inspired to visit Chiwata, be warned that a recent expedition to the revered cave, undertaken by the Old Boma staff in Mikindani, found nothing more startling or ancient than graffiti dating to the 1980s!

If you want to explore the Masasi area, it's worth contacting a newly formed organisation called the Masasi Association of Geography and Antiquity (MAGA), which has an office called Efficiency Secretarial Services close to the Holiday Hotel (tel: 023 251 0267). MAGA is trying to promote tourism to the Masasi area, and have put together several hikes taking in sites such as Mount Mingongo, Mount Mtandi and Mkomaindo Rock combined with an overnight trek to see the Shimo la Mungu (Hole of God). MAGA can also arrange to see local dances and drumming in the villages on the Makonde Plateau, or to visit Makonde carving groups and cashew nut factories.

Getting there and away

A good surfaced 125km road connects Masasi to Mnazi Moja (Mingoyo) on the main road between Mtwara and Lindi. In a private vehicle, it should be possible to cover this distance in less than two hours. Most buses along this road leave from Mtwara, picking up passengers from Lindi at Mnazi Moja, and they generally depart every hour or so throughout the day, stopping at Mikindani. Despite being surfaced pretty much the whole way, the 200km-journey from Mtaara to Masasi takes from five to seven hours on public transport, due to the frequent stops.

There is a bus every other day in each direction between Masasi and Dar es Salaam. This leaves from in front of the Masasi Hotel, not from the regular bus station. Seats should be booked in advance at the Masasi Hotel.

A daily bus runs between Newala and Masasi, leaving Newala some time between 05.00 and 06.00 and arriving at Masasi at around 11.00. The bus then returns to Newala.

For details of the cross-country route between Masasi and the Lake Nyasa region, see box *Travelling from Mtwara to Songea*, pages 602–3.

Where to stay and eat

There are plenty of basic lodgings from which to choose: the **Mahenge Guesthouse** about five minutes' walk from the bus station is a recent recommendation. If nothing else, the attached bar serves cold beer and decent local food, and boasts a fantastic video collection including titles such as *The Return of the Drunken Mantis*, *Mafia v Ninja* and *Iron Fist Boxer*! A step up from these, the **Masasi Hotel**, **Holiday Lodge** and **Sayari Guesthouse** charge between Tsh5,000 and Tsh7,500 for clean and spacious rooms with fans and mosquito nets. Most of the guesthouses serve basic food, and there are many cheap eating places around the main squares. The **Top Spot Restaurant** near the Masasi Hotel serves cheap meals and cold beers and sodas in a garden.

Newala

This isolated, friendly town on the Makonde Plateau near the Mozambican border lacks for major landmarks or a tangible sense of history, but it is worth a visit just for the view across the Rovuma River to Mozambique. If you've spent a while on the coast, the bracing climate – Newala is one of the coldest places in southern Tanzania, prone to chilly breezes and damp mists – should also prove to be rather refreshing. The town itself is rather nondescript, with squat concrete houses in the centre of town changing to mud huts with thatch roofs as you head further out. Visitors should bring their passports and legal immigration documents, since the immigration officer is very keen and checks all the guesthouses daily.

There are some stunning viewpoints along the ridges around Newala, offering a panoramic view to the Rovuma River and Mozambique. The most accessible viewpoint is the legendary Shimu ya Mungu ('Hole of God'), near the old German *boma* on a hill outside town, which looks over a vast sheer escarpment to the Rovuma Valley and the mountains beyond – doubly fantastic at sunset! More ambitiously, you could cycle to the Rovuma River as a day trip (bikes can easily be hired so long as you leave a deposit) following the central road through town downhill. You could also arrange a vehicle to take you there (see box *Down to the Rovuma*, page 610).

The German *boma* is now a police station, and assuming that you speak some Swahili and are prepared to part with Tsh1,000 or so, it is possible to organise a short tour of the building with the head of police, whose office occupies the ground floor. Be warned, however, that this is bound to initiate a bout of checking passports and quizzing you about your reasons for being in Newala. At the cinema in the market, you can watch badly filmed videos with dodgy colours and a worse soundtrack for next to nothing. The large mission hospital next to the market would be useful in an emergency.

Getting there and away

Reaching Newala from Mtwara is simple. Direct buses leave twice an hour from the main bus stand in Mtwara throughout the day from around 06.00, using the poorly maintained dirt route, a six- to seven-hour journey which costs around US$3 per ticket. Another option is to go via Masasi, first catching a bus from Mtwara to Masasi, then changing bus for Newala. From Newala itself, four to five buses leave for Masasi every morning between 06.00 and midday. This trip is worth doing for the stretch immediately outside Newala, where the road follows a dramatic ridge. The road is very bumpy, however, and the ascent to the Makonde Plateau so poorly maintained that, coming from Masasi, it might be necessary to

DOWN TO THE ROVUMA

Extracted from notes by George Barrett, Matt Maddocks and Shaibu of the Old Boma in Mikindani, based on a trip in November 2001

After taking lunch in Newala, we headed off to the bus station to set up transport for a visit to Mchichira on the Rovuma River the next day. We sent Shaibu to handle the negotiations, knowing that the price would double the moment anyone saw a white face. He returned, having agreed with a Land Rover to pick us up at 06.00 and take us to the river and back for Tsh18,000. This sounded a good deal, as we had been warned that it might cost Tsh30,000. Another option would have been to catch a bus to Mahuta, 20km out of Newala on the Mtwara road, and hire a Land Rover there, but for the extra few shillings, the saved hassle was deemed worthwhile.

The next morning at 05.00, the Land Rover was outside and waiting, so we clambered out of bed, and were ready in minutes. However, in those few minutes, the Land Rover had sped away to pick up more people! Unconvinced by his promise to return at 06.00, we made our way down to the bus station anyway, but by 06.30 there was still no sign of the vehicle and another driver had turned up offering to take us for the same price. A complicated 30 minutes followed, with various people telling us which drivers were better, which would rip us off, which had cars that might make it as far as the river, and which had cars that might make it back as well! In the end, there was no sign of our original driver, so we gave the new one the money to buy fuel. No sooner had he started to fill up than the original driver arrived, and due to the considerably better quality of his car, we decided to go with him. After long arguments between the two drivers, we set off for the river, almost three hours after we had been woken up in a rush to get going!

Within 15 minutes, the Land Rover broke down for the first time. However, some tinkering under the bonnet had us off again, ever so slightly nervous as we descended the long steep hill into the valley floor. It took us two hours to get to the river; we picked up a local child en route, who guided us right to the banks, saving us the expected trek to the channel. The river was magnificent. We had heard about big rivers, but not seen anything wider than the Severn. The flood plain, which is swamped during the rainy season, was 3km across in places and extremely impressive. During the dry season, only a couple of deep and fast-flowing channels meander their way across the valley that divides Tanzania and Mozambique. Walking along the sandy, desert-like riverbed, we met a fisherman who offered us a trip in his canoe. However, beneath the surface we could see two of his other canoes (that had sunk), so we decided against it.

The trip back to Newala was uneventful except for breaking down a few times, spinning off the sandy road, and missing a tree by a whisker! We arrived back at the guesthouse, where the driver leapt out feeling quite cheated that he had taken *wazungu* down to the river for a price he would usually charge locals. He tried to add another Tsh5,000 to our bill, and asked for more petrol money, claiming he didn't know how far it was to the river! We refused to pay, but in the end we gave him an extra Tsh1,000 note to keep the peace.

disembark and hike to the top, which takes about 45 minutes. An overall journey time of three to four hours is typical.

Where to stay and eat

There are more than 15 guesthouses in Newala, most of which lie around the market and bus station and offer accommodation of a similar standard – a simple room with communal toilet facilities and bucket showers for around Tsh2,000. Two places stand out, **Plateau Lodge** and **Country Lodge**, both of which have ordinary and self-contained rooms in the Tsh10,000 range. The County Lodge can be found on the road to Masasi, and the Plateau Lodge is well signposted from the market, up towards 'Shimu ya Mungu', and the old German *boma* on the very top of the hill.

There are many places to eat, mostly in the market area. Meals on offer include the normal fish, rice and *ugali*, as well as the local favourite *chipsi mayai* (chip omelette), all for under US$2 each. Several notches above this is the food at the Country Lodge – a prawn salad, fresh fish and rice cooked to your preference for as little as US$5 – though a few hours' advance warning is required to eat here. The market sells speciality fruit such as *embe dodo* (large mangoes) and delicious custard apples.

Lukwika-Lumesule Game Reserve

This little-known 400km² game reserve, part of the greater Selous-Niassa ecosystem, lies on the Mozambican border roughly 100km south of Masasi where it effectively forms a northern extension to Mozambique's 23,400km² Niassa Game Reserve. Bounded by the Rovuma River to the south, and transected by the Lukwika River, it supports impressive numbers of hippo, crocodile and water-associated birds. Terrestrial species are similar to those in the Selous Game Reserve, including lion, leopard, African wild dog, elephant, sable antelope and greater kudu.

Basic *bandas* and camping facilities are available close to a freshwater stream. The Old Boma in Mikindani arranges safaris to the reserve, and is thinking of setting up a semi-permanent dry-season satellite camp there – check their website for current information. There is no network of game-viewing roads within the reserve, but you can drive directly to the Rovuma River from the camp, and explore the reserve on guided walks with an armed ranger.

At present, the reserve is leased as a hunting concession to a Portuguese operator, so casual visits are not permitted. Independent visitors will need written permission from the Officer for Natural Resources in Mtwara or Masasi, and must be self-sufficient in food, water and fuel. The route to the reserve is suitable only for well-maintained 4WD vehicles and experienced drivers. The roads become very slippery during the rainy season, and may be impassable between February and May, when visits cannot be recommended. The best game viewing is from June to December.

To reach Lukwika-Lumesule, follow the Tunduru road out of Masasi for about two hours to Michiga, where you need to follow a left turn-off to the Lukwika catchment area where the reserve is situated. The camp used by the Game Reserve project manager and his retinue is about one hour's drive along this road. In the dry season there is a useful shortcut, taking a left turn at the village of Mangaka, which takes only half an hour to get to the camp. Before entering the reserve, you will pass through Mpombe village, where you will need to fill in the visitors' book at the reserve office – a large warehouse behind a row of houses on the left as you leave the village. The first indication that you will have of being in the game reserve is an informal checkpoint just before the camp. Close to the camp, there is a grass airstrip suitable for light aircraft, usable in the dry season only.

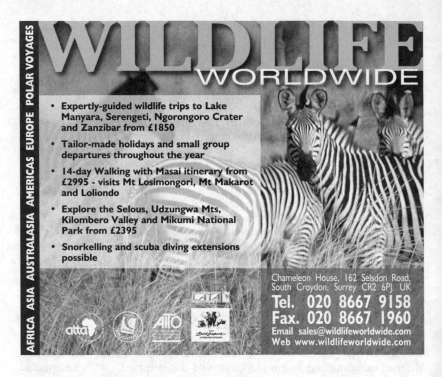

Appendix 1

LANGUAGE

Swahili, the official language of Tanzania, is a Bantu language which developed on the East African coast about 1,000 years ago and has since adopted several words from Arabic, Portuguese, Indian, German and English. It spread into the Tanzanian interior along with the 19th-century slave caravans and is now the *lingua franca* in Tanzania and Kenya, and is also spoken in parts of Uganda, Malawi, Rwanda, Burundi, Congo, Zambia and Mozambique.

Even if you are sticking to tourist areas, it is polite and can be useful to know a bit of Swahili. In Dar es Salaam, Zanzibar, Arusha, Moshi and the northern game reserves, you can get by with English well enough. If you travel in other parts of the country, you will need to understand some Swahili.

There are numerous Swahili–English dictionaries on the market, as well as phrasebooks and grammars. A useful dictionary for travellers is Baba Malaika's *Friendly Modern Swahili–English Dictionary* (MSO Training Centre for Development Co-operation, PO Box 254, Arusha, second edition, 1994), which costs around US$25. Better still, though probably too heavyweight for most travellers, is the *TUKI English–Swahili Dictionary* (University of Dar es Salaam, 1996; ISBN 9976 91129 7), which costs around US$16. Peter Wilson's *Simplified Swahili* (Longman) used to be regarded as the best book for teaching yourself Swahili, but it has probably been superseded by Joan Russell's *Teach Yourself Swahili* (Hodder and Stoughton, 1996; ISBN 0340 62094 3), which comes complete with a cassette and costs around US$15. Of the phrasebooks, the Lonely Planet's or Rough Guide's *Swahili* are both good. It is best to buy a Swahili book before you arrive in Tanzania as they are difficult to get hold of once you are there.

For short-stay visitors, all these books have practical limitations. Wading through a phrasebook to find the expression you want can take ages, while trying to piece together a sentence from a dictionary is virtually impossible. In addition, most books available are in Kenyan Swahili, which often differs greatly from the purer version spoken in Tanzania.

The following introduction is not a substitute for a dictionary or phrasebook. It is not so much an introduction to Swahili as an introduction to communicating with Swahili-speakers. Before researching this guide, my East African travels had mainly been in Kenya, Uganda and parts of Tanzania where English is relatively widely spoken. We learnt the hard way how little English is spoken in most of Tanzania. I hope this section will help anyone in a similar position to get around a great deal more easily than we did at first.

Pronunciation

Vowel sounds are pronounced as follows:

a	like the a in *father*
e	like the e in *wet*
i	like the ee in *free*, but less drawn-out
o	somewhere between the o in *no* and the word *awe*
u	similar to the oo in *food*

The double vowel in words like *choo* or *saa* is pronounced like the single vowel, but drawn out for longer. Consonants are in general pronounced as they are in English. *L* and *r* are often interchangeable, so that *Kalema* is just as often spelt or pronounced *Karema*. The same is true of *b* and *v*.

You will be better understood if you speak slowly and thus avoid the common English-speaking habit of clipping vowel sounds – listen to how Swahili-speakers pronounce their vowels. In most Swahili words there is a slight emphasis on the second last syllable.

Basic grammar

Swahili is a simple language in so far as most words are built from a root word using prefixes. To go into all of the prefixes here would probably confuse people new to Swahili – and it would certainly stretch my knowledge of the language. They are covered in depth in most Swahili grammars and dictionaries. The following are some of the most important:

Pronouns

ni	me	*wa*	they
u	you	*a*	he or she
tu	us		

Tenses   Tenses (negative)

na	present	*si*	present
ta	future	*sita*	future
li	past	*siku*	past
ku	infinitive	*haku*	negative, infinitive

From a root word such as *taka* (want) you might build the following phrases:

Unataka soda	You want a soda
Tutataka soda	We will want a soda
Alitaka soda	He/she wanted a soda

In practice, *ni* and *tu* are often dropped from simple statements. It would be more normal to say *nataka soda* than *ninataka soda*.

In many situations there is no interrogative mode in Swahili; the difference between a question and a statement lies in the intonation.

Greetings

There are several common greetings in Swahili. Although allowances are made for tourists, it is rude to start talking to someone without first using one or other formal greeting. The first greeting you will hear is *Jambo*. This is reserved for tourists, and a perfectly adequate greeting, but it is never used between Tanzanians (the more correct *Hujambo*, to which the reply is *Sijambo*, is used in some areas).

The most widely-used greeting is *Habari?*, which more-or-less means *What news?*. The normal reply is *Nzuri* (good). *Habari* is rarely used by Tanzanians on its own; you might well be asked *Habari ya safari?*, *Habari yako?* or *Habari gani?* (very loosely, *How is your journey?*, *How are you?* and *How are things?* respectively). *Nzuri* is the polite reply to any such request.

A more fashionable greeting among younger people is *Mambo*, especially on the coast and in large towns. Few tourists recognise this greeting; reply *Safi* or *Poa* and you've made a friend.

In Tanzanian society it is polite to greet elders with the expression *Shikamu*. To the best of my knowledge this means *I hold your feet*. In many parts of rural Tanzania, children will greet you in this way, often with their heads bowed and so quietly it sounds like *Sh..oo*. Don't misinterpret this by European standards (or other parts of Africa where *Mzungu give me shilling* is the phrase most likely to be offered up by children); most Tanzanian children are far too polite to swear at you. The polite answer is *Marahaba* (I'm delighted).

Another word often used in greeting is *Salama*, which means peace. When you enter a shop or hotel reception, you will often be greeted by a friendly *Karibu*, which means *Welcome*. *Asante sana* (thank you very much) seems an appropriate response.

If you want to enter someone's house, shout *Hodi!*. It basically means *Can I come in?* but would be used in the same situation as *Anyone home?* would in English. The normal response will be *Karibu* or *Hodi*.

It is respectful to address an old man as *Mzee*. *Bwana*, which means *Mister*, might be used as a polite form of address to a male who is equal or senior to you in age or rank, but who is not a *Mzee*. Older women can be addressed as *Mama*.

The following phrases will come in handy for small talk:

Where have you just come from?	*(U)natoka wapi?*
I have come from Moshi	*(Ni)natoka Moshi*
Where are you going?	*(U)nakwenda wapi?*
We are going to Arusha	*(Tu)nakwenda Arusha*
What is your name?	*Jina lako nani?*
My name is Philip	*Jina langu ni Philip*
Do you speak English?	*Unasema KiIngereze?*
I speak a little Swahili	*Ninasema KiSwahili kidigo*
Sleep peacefully	*Lala salama*
Bye for now	*Kwaheri sasa*
Have a safe journey	*Safari njema*
Come again (welcome again)	*Karibu tena*
I don't understand	*Sielewi*
Say that again	*Sema tena*

Numbers

1	*moja*	30	*thelathini*
2	*mbili*	40	*arobaini*
3	*tatu*	50	*hamsini*
4	*nne*	60	*sitini*
5	*tano*	70	*sabini*
6	*sita*	80	*themanini*
7	*saba*	90	*tisini*
8	*nane*	100	*mia (moja)*
9	*tisa*	150	*mia moja na hamsini*
10	*kumi*	155	*mia moja hamsini na tano*
11	*kumi na moja*	200	*mia mbili*
20	*ishirini*	1,000	*elfu (moja)* or *mia kumi*

Swahili time

Many travellers to Tanzania fail to come to grips with Swahili time. It is essential to be aware of it, especially if you are catching buses in remote areas. The Swahili clock starts at the equivalent of 06.00, so that *saa moja asubuhi* (hour one in the morning) is 07.00, *saa mbili jioni* (hour two in the evening) is 20.00, etc. To ask the time in Swahili, say *Saa ngapi?*.

Always check whether times are standard or Swahili. If you are told a bus leaves at nine, ask whether the person means *saa tatu* or *saa tisa*. Some English-speakers will convert to standard time, others won't. This does not apply so much where people are used to tourists, but it's advisable to get in the habit of checking.

Day-to-day queries

The following covers such activities as shopping, finding a room, etc. It's worth remembering most Swahili words for modern objects, or things for which there would not have been a pre-colonial word, are often similar to the English. Examples are *resiti* (receipt), *gari* (car), *polisi* (police), *posta* (post office) and – my favourite – *stesheni masta* (station master). In desperation, it's always worth trying the English word with an *ee* sound on the end.

Shopping

The normal way of asking for something is *Ipo* or *Zipo?*, which roughly means *Is there?*, so if you want a cold drink you would ask *Soda baridi zipo?* The response will normally be *Ipo* or *Kuna* (there is) or *Hamna* or *Hakuna* (there isn't). Once you've established the shop has what you want, you might say *Nataka koka mbili* (I want two cokes). To check the price, ask *Shillingi ngape?* It may be simpler to ask for a brand name: *Omo* (washing powder) or *Blue Band* (margarine), for instance.

Accommodation

The Swahili for guesthouse is *nyumba ya wageni*. In my experience *gesti* works as well, if not better. If you are looking for something a bit more upmarket, bear in mind *hoteli* means restaurant. We found self-contained (*self-contendi*) to be a good key-word in communicating this need. To find out whether there is a vacant room, ask *Nafasi zipo?*

Getting around

The following expressions are useful for getting around:

Where is there a guesthouse?	*Ipo wapi gesti?*
Is there a bus to Moshi?	*Ipo basi kwenda Moshi?*
When does the bus depart?	*Basi itaondoka saa ngapi?*
When will the vehicle arrive?	*Gari litafika saa ngapi?*
How far is it?	*Bale gani?*
I want to pay now	*Ninataka kulipa sasa*

Foodstuffs

avocado	*parachichi*	food	*chakula*
bananas	*ndizi*	fruit(s)	*(ma)tunda*
bananas (cooked)	*matoke/batoke*	goat	*(nyama ya) mbuzi*
beef	*(Nyama ya) ngombe*	mango(es)	*(ma)embe*
bread (loaf)	*mkate*	maize porridge	
bread (slice)	*tosti*	(thin, eaten at	
coconuts	*nazi*	breakfast)	*uji*
coffee	*kahawa*	maize porridge	
chicken	*kuku*	(thick, eaten as	
egg(s)	*(ma)yai*	staple with	
fish	*samaki*	relish)	*ugali*
meat	*nyama*	rice	*pilau*
milk	*maziwa*	salt	*chumvi*
onions	*vitungu*	sauce	*mchuzi/supu*
orange(s)	*(ma)chungwa*	sugar	*sukari*
pawpaw	*papai*	tea	*chai*
pineapple	*nanasi*	(black/milky)	*(ya rangi/maziwa)*
potatoes	*viazi*	vegetable	*mboga*
rice (cooked plain)	*wali*	water	*maji*
rice (uncooked)	*mchele*		

Days of the week

Monday	*Jumatatu*	Friday	*Ijumaa*
Tuesday	*Jumanne*	Saturday	*Jumamosi*
Wednesday	*Jumatano*	Sunday	*Jumapili*
Thursday	*Alhamisi*		

Useful words and phrases

afternoon	*alasiri*	no	*hapana*
again	*tena*	no problem	*hakuna matata*
and	*na*	now	*sasa*
ask (I am		only	*tu*
asking for...)	*omba (ninaomba...)*	OK or fine	*sawa*
big	*kubwa*	passenger	*abiria*
boat	*meli*	pay	*kulipa*
brother	*kaka*	please	*tafadhali*
bus	*basi*	person (people)	*mtu (watu)*
car (or any		road/street	*barabara/mtaa*
vehicle)	*gari*	shop	*duka*
child (children)	*mtoto (watoto)*	sister	*dada*
cold	*baridi*	sleep	*kulala*
come here	*njoo*	slowly	*polepole*
excuse me	*samahani*	small	*kidogo*
European(s)	*mzungu (wazungu)*	soon	*bado kidogo*
evening	*jioni*	sorry	*polepole*
far away	*mbale kubwa*	station	*stesheni*
friend	*rafiki*	stop	*simama*
good	*mzuri*	straight or direct	*moja kwa moja*
(very good)	*(mzuri sana)*	thank you	*asante*
goodbye	*kwaheri*	(very much)	*(sana)*
here	*hapa*	there is	*iko/kuna*
hot	*moto*	there is not	*hamna/hakuna*
later	*bado*	thief (thieves)	*mwizi (wawizi)*
like	*penda*	time	*saa*
(I would like...)	*(ninapenda...)*	today	*leo*
many	*sana*	toilet	*choo*
me	*mimi*	tomorrow	*kesho*
money	*pesa/shillingi*	want	*taka*
more	*ingine/tena*	(I want...)	*(ninataka...)*
morning	*asubuhi*	where	*(iko) wapi*
nearby	*karibu/mbale*	yes	*ndiyo*
	kidogo	yesterday	*jana*
night	*usiku*	you	*wewe*

Useful conjunctions include *ya* (of) and *kwa* (to or by). Many expressions are created using these; for instance *stesheni ya basi* is a bus station and *barabara kwa Mbale* is the road to Mbale.

African English

Although many Tanzanians speak a little English, not all speak it fluently. Africans who speak English tend to structure their sentences in a similar way to how they would in their own language: they speak English with Bantu grammar.

For a traveller, knowing how to communicate in African English is as important as speaking a bit of Swahili, if not more so. It is noticeable that travellers who speak English as a second language often communicate with Africans more easily than first language English-speakers.

The following ground rules should prove useful when you speak English to Africans:

- *Unasema KiEngereze?* (Do you speak English?). This small but important question may seem obvious. It isn't.
- Greet in Swahili then ask in English. It is advisable to go through the Swahili greetings (even *Jambo* will do) before you plough ahead and ask a question. Firstly, it is rude to do otherwise; secondly, most Westerners feel uncomfortable asking a stranger a straight question. If you have already greeted the person, you'll feel less need to preface a question with phrases like I'm terribly sorry and Would you mind telling me which will confuse someone who speaks limited English.
- Speak slowly and clearly. There is no need, as some travellers do, to speak as if you are talking to a three-year-old, just speak naturally.
- Phrase questions simply and with Swahili inflections. This bus goes to Dodoma? is better than Could you tell me whether this bus is going to Dodoma?; You have a room? is better than is there a vacant room?. If you are not understood, don't keep repeating the same question; find a different way of phrasing it.
- Listen to how people talk to you, and not only for their inflections. Some English words are in wide use; others are not. For instance lodging is more likely to be understood than accommodation.
- Make sure the person you are talking to understands you. Try to avoid asking questions that can be answered with a yes or no. People may well agree with you simply to be polite.
- Keep calm. No-one is at their best when they arrive at a crowded bus station after an all-day bus ride; it is easy to be short tempered when someone cannot understand you. Be patient and polite; it's you who doesn't speak the language.

GLOSSARY

Acacia woodland	type of woodland dominated by thorny, thin-leafed trees of the genus *Acacia*
banda	a hut, often used to refer to hutted accommodation at hotels and lodges
boma	traditional enclosure or homestead; administration building of the colonial era
bui-bui	black cloth worn veil-like by women, mainly in Islamic parts of the coast
Brachystegia woodland	type of woodland dominated by broad-leaved trees of the genus *Brachystegia*
Chama Cha Mapinduzi (CCM)	ruling party of Tanzania since independence
cichlid	family of colourful fish found in the Rift Valley lakes
closed canopy forest	true forest in which the trees have an interlocking canopy
dalla-dalla	light vehicle, especially minibus, serving as public transport
dhow	traditional wooden seafaring vessel
duka	kiosk
endemic	unique to a specific country or biome
exotic	not indigenous, for instance plantation trees such as pines and eucalyptus
forex bureau	bureau de change
fly-camping	temporary private camp set up remotely from a permanent lodge
guesthouse	cheap local hotel
hoteli	local restaurant
indigenous	naturally occurring
kanga	colourful printed cloth worn by most Tanzania women

kitenge (plural *vitenge*)	similar to *kanga*
koppie (or *kopje*)	Afrikaans word used to refer to a small hill such as those on the Serengeti
mandazi	deep-fried doughball, essentially the local variant on a doughnut
mishkaki	meat (usually beef) kebab
mzungu (pl *wazungu*)	white person
ngoma	Swahili dance
Omani era	period when the coast was ruled by the Sultan of Oman, especially 19th century
self-contained room	room with en-suite shower and toilet
savannah	grassland studded with trees
Shirazi era	medieval period during which settlers from Shiraz dominated coastal trade
taarab	Swahili music and dance form associated particularly with Zanzibar
TANAPA	Tanzania National Parks
ugali	stodgy porridge-like staple made with ground maize meal
woodland	area of trees lacking a closed canopy

Appendix

FURTHER READING
History and biography

A limited number of single-volume histories covering East Africa and/or Tanzania are in print, but most are rather textbook-like in tone, and I've yet to come across one that is likely to hold much appeal to the casual reader. About the best bet is Iliffe's *Modern History of Tanganyika* (Cambridge, 1979). For a more general perspective, Oliver and Fage's *Short History of Africa* (Penguin, sixth edition, 1988) is rated as providing the best concise overview of African history, but it's too curt, dry, wide-ranging and dated to make for a satisfying read.

If I were to recommend one historical volume to a visitor to Tanzania, it would have to be Richard Hall's *Empires of the Monsoon: A History of the Indian Ocean and its Invaders* (Harper Collins, 1996). This highly focused and reasonably concise book will convey a strong historical perspective to the general reader, as a result of the author's storytelling touch and his largely successful attempt to place the last 1,000 years of East and southern African history in an international framework.

Considerably more bulky, and working an even broader canvas, John Reader's *Africa: A Biography of the Continent* (Penguin, 1997) has met with universal praise as perhaps the most readable and accurate attempt yet to capture the sweep of African history for the general reader.

Several books document specific periods and/or regions in African history. Good coverage of the coastal Swahili, who facilitated the medieval trade between the gold fields of Zimbabwe and the Arab World, is provided in J de Vere Allen's *Swahili Origins* (James Currey, 1992). Among the better popular works on the early era of European exploration are Hibbert's *Africa Explored: Europeans in the Dark Continent* (Penguin, 1982) and Alan Moorehead's peerless classics of the genre history-as-adventure-yarn *The White Nile* and *The Blue Nile*, published in 1960 and 1962 respectively and available in Penguin paperback. An excellent biography pertaining to this era is Tim Jeal's *Livingstone* (Heinemann, 1973, recently reprinted). For an erudite, compelling and panoramic account of the decade that turned Africa on its head, Thomas Pakenham's gripping 600-page tome *The Scramble for Africa* was aptly described by one reviewer as '*Heart of Darkness* with the lights switched on'. For a glimpse into the colonial era itself, just about everybody who sets foot in East Africa ends up reading Karen Blixen's autobiographical *Out of Africa* (Penguin, 1937).

Field guides and natural history

If you have difficulty finding African natural history books at your local bookshop and you're not flying directly to South Africa (where you can pick them up easily) get hold of the Natural History Book Service, 2 Wills Road, Totnes, Devon TQ9 SXN; tel: 01803 865913 or Russel Friedman Books in South Africa; tel: 011 702-2300/1; fax: 011 702 1403.

Mammals

Dorst and Dandelot's *Field Guide to the Larger Mammals of Africa* (Collins) and Haltennorth's *Field Guide to the Mammals of Africa (including Madagascar)* (Collins), were the standard mammal field guides for years, but have been rendered obsolete by several newer and better books. The pick of these, especially if your interest extends to bats and other small mammals, is Jonathan Kingdon's *Field Guide to African Mammals* (Academic Press, 1997), which also contains a goldmine of information about the evolutionary relationships of modern species.

Chris and Tilde Stuart's *Field Guide to the Larger Mammals of Africa* (Struik Publishers, 1997) is better suited for space-conscious travellers who are serious about putting a name to all the large mammals they see. For backpackers, the same authors' *Southern, Eastern and Central African Mammals: A Photographic Guide* (Struik Publishers, 1993) is far lighter and still gives adequate detail for 152 mammal species. The Stuarts have also written the coffee-table format *Africa's Vanishing Wildlife* (Southern Book Publishers, 1996), an outstanding book of its sort and highly recommended as advance reading or as a souvenir.

Not a field guide in the conventional sense so much as a guide to mammalian behaviour, Richard Estes' superb *The Safari Companion* (Green Books UK, Chelsea Green USA, Russell Friedman Books South Africa, 1992) is well organised and informative but rather bulky for casual safari-goers.

Birds

Zimmerman, Turner, Pearson, Willet and Pratt's *Birds of Kenya and Northern Tanzania* (Russell Friedman Books, 1996) is a contender for the best single-volume field guide available to any African country or region. I would recommend it to any serious birder sticking to northern Tanzania, since it provides complete coverage for the northern safari circuit, the Usambara and Pare Mountains and Pemba Island, and although it stops short of Dar es Salaam and Zanzibar, this wouldn't be a major limitation. Unfortunately, it's too bulky, heavy and expensive to be of interest to any but the most bird-obsessed of backpackers, and the gaps in its coverage would limit its usefulness south of Dar es Salaam or in the Lake Victoria and Lake Tanganyika region.

Ber Van Perlo's *Illustrated Checklist to the Birds of Eastern Africa* (Collins, 1995) is a useful, relatively inexpensive and admirably compact identification manual describing and illustrating all 1,488 bird species recorded in Eritrea, Ethiopia, Kenya, Uganda and Tanzania. Unfortunately, however, the distribution maps and colour plates are often misleading, and the compact format means that descriptions are too terse and pictures too massed up to allow identification of more difficult genera. It is, however, far more useful than John Williams' pioneering but now obsolete *Field Guide to the Birds of East Africa*, also published by Collins and still referred to in many brochures and guides.

For any birding itinerary extending to parts of Tanzania west of the Serengeti or south of the Usambara, the best option is the brand new *Field Guide to the Birds of East Africa* by Williamson & Fanshawe. Published in early 2002, this field guide provides comprehensive coverage for the whole of Tanzania, as well as Kenya, Rwanda and Burundi, and based on limited field usage to date it seems excellent, with accurate plates, good distribution maps, and adequately detailed text descriptions.

Other field guides

Struik Publishers in South Africa produce top-quality field guides to everything from trees to fish, reptiles and amphibians, but it's probably the case that such books are too esoteric to find their way into even a tiny proportion of backpacks. Readers with specific interests should contact one of the addresses above for recommendations.

Wildlife studies

Those with an interest in ape behaviour would do well to read Jane Goodall's books about chimpanzee behaviour, *In the Shadow of Man* (Collins, 1971) and *Through a Window* (Weidenfield and Nicholson, 1990), based on her acclaimed research in Tanzania's Gombe Stream National Park. Also available is Nishida's *Chimpanzees of Mahale* (University of Tokyo, 1990), based on the similarly long-standing research project in Mahale Mountains

National Park. A more visually attractive alternative is the coffee-table book *Mahale: A Photographic Encounter with Chimpanzees*, by Angelika Hofer, Michael Huffman and Gunter Ziesler (Sterling Publishing, New York, 2000).

Bernhard Grzimek's renowned book *Serengeti Shall Not Die* (Collins, 1959) remains a classic evocation of the magic of the Serengeti, and its original publication was instrumental in making this reserve better known to the outside world. Iain Douglas-Hamilton's *Amongst the Elephants* (Penguin, 1978) did much the same for publicising Lake Manyara National Park, though the vast herds of elephants it describes have since been greatly reduced by poaching.

National parks

A series of excellent booklets was published in the early 1990s in association with TANAPA, covering most of the national parks in Tanzania. These are widely available in Arusha, and will cost US$5 at a reputable bookshop and considerably more when bought from a street vendor. The African Publishing House has recently published another similar series of glossier booklets, also in association with TANAPA and also widely available within Tanzania.

Travel literature
Travel guides

Bradt also publishes the dedicated *Zanzibar: The Bradt Travel Guide*, the most useful book for those who are travelling to the islands in isolation. For people combining a visit to Tanzania with one or other of its neighbours, a limited number of dedicated guides are available to most countries bordering Tanzania. For practical information, there are Bradt guides available to Uganda, Mozambique, Ethiopia, Malawi, Rwanda and Zambia, while of several travel guides to Kenya I can wholeheartedly recommend Richard Trillo's *Kenya: The Rough Guide*.

A number of compendium guides are available to various regions in eastern and southern Africa. Lonely Planet's *East Africa* is strong on Kenya and parts of northern Tanzania, somewhat weaker on Uganda and the rest of Tanzania, and provides the best coverage available on Burundi and eastern Congo. A Lonely Planet guide that will be useful to serious hikers is *Trekking in East Africa*, which covers most popular trekking areas between Ethiopia and Malawi. For backpackers planning an overland trip through eastern and southern Africa, the only single-volume guide dedicated to this region as a unit is Bradt's *East and Southern Africa: The Backpacker's Manual*, which covers practically every possible route and accessible attraction from northern Ethiopia south to Cape Town.

Two reasonably modern travelogues that touch on Tanzania are Dervla Murphy's *The Ukimwi Road* (John Murray, 1993) and Shiva Naipaul's *North of South* (Penguin).

Coffee-table books

The best book of this sort to cover Tanzania as a whole is Paul Joynson-Hicks' *Tanzania: Portrait of a Nation*, which contains some great down-to-earth cultural photography and lively anecdotal captions. Also recommended is *Journey through Tanzania*, photographed by the late Mohamid Amin and Duncan Willets and published by Camerapix in Kenya. Both of the above books are stronger on cultural, landmark and scenic photography than on wildlife photography, for which M Iwago's superb *Serengeti* (Thames and Hudson, 1987) has few peers. Also worth a look is John Reader's definitive *Kilimanjaro*. Javed Jafferji's atmospheric photographs are highlighted in *Images of Zanzibar*, while *Zanzibar – Romance of the Ages* makes extensive use of archive photographs dating to before the turn of the century. Both were published by HSP Publications in 1996, and are readily available on the island.

Travel magazines

The TTB produces a quarterly magazine called *Tantravel*, which normally includes a few gushing but interesting articles as well as plenty of ads, and can normally be picked up at Air Tanzania and tourist board offices. Far better is the quarterly magazine *Kakakuona: African*

Wildlife, which is produced by the Tanzania Wildlife Protection Fund, and frequently includes several good articles about conservation in Tanzania. Email: kakakuona@africaonline.co.tz.

For readers with a broad interest in Africa, an excellent magazine dedicated to tourism throughout Africa is *Travel Africa*, which can be visited online at www.travelafricamag.com. Recommended for their broad-ranging editorial content and the coffee-table standard photography and reproduction, the award-winning magazines *Africa Geographic* (formerly *Africa Environment and Wildlife*) and *Africa Birds & Birding* can be checked out at the website www.africa-geographic.co.za. Another South African magazine devoted to African travel is *Getaway,* though this tends to devote the bulk of its coverage to southern Africa.

Health

Self-prescribing has its hazards so if you are going anywhere very remote consider taking a health book. For adults there is *Bugs, Bites & Bowels: the Cadogan Guide to Healthy Travel* by Jane Wilson-Howarth (1999); if travelling with the family look at *Your Child's Health Abroad: A Manual for Travelling Parents* by Jane Wilson-Howarth and Matthew Ellis, published by Bradt in 1998.

Maps

A number of maps covering East Africa are available. The best is the Austrian-published Freytag-Berndt 1:2,000,000 map. The best current map of Tanzania is probably the 1:500,000 *Nelles Tanzania, Rwanda and Burundi,* 1:500.000. For most tourists, the map of Tanzania produced by the TTB and given away free at their offices in Arusha or Dar will be adequate.

A series of excellent maps by Giovanni Tombazzi covers most of the northern reserves, as well as Kilimanjaro, Mount Meru and Zanzibar. Colourful, lively and accurate, these maps are widely available throughout northern Tanzania, or they can be ordered directly from the co-publisher Hoopoe Adventure Tours (for contact details, see *Safari operators* page 128).

Town plans and 1:50,000 maps covering most parts of the country can be bought from the Department of Land and Surveys map sales office on Kivukoni Front in Dar es Salaam.

Fiction

Surprisingly few novels have been written by Tanzanians or about Tanzania (even a friend who has studied African literature failed to come up with one indigenous Tanzanian novelist). An excellent novel set in World War I Tanzania is William Boyd's *An Ice-cream War*, while the same author's *Brazzaville Beach*, though not overtly set in Tanzania, devotes attention to aspects of chimpanzee behaviour first noted at Gombe Stream.

A Tanzanian of Asian extraction now living in Canada, M G Vassanji, is the author of at least one novel set in Tanzania and the Kenyan border area, the prize-winning *Book of Secrets* (Macmillan, 1994). This is an atmospheric tale, with much interesting period detail, revolving around a diary written by a British administrator in pre-war Kenya and discovered in a flat in Dar es Salaam in the 1980s. Vassanji is also the author of *Uhuru Street*, a collection of short stories set in Dar es Salaam.

Novels set elsewhere in Africa, but which may be of interest to visitors to Tanzania, include the following:

Brink, A *An Act of Terror* or *A Dry White Season*
Cartwright, J *Maasai Dreaming*
Conrad, J *Heart of Darkness*
Dagarembga, T *Nervous Conditions*
Gordimer, N *July's People*
Kingsolver, B *The Poisonwood Bible*
Lambkin, David *The Hanging Tree*
Lessing, D *The Grass is Singing, Children of Violence* (5 volumes)
Mazrui, A *The Trial of Christopher Okigbo*
Mungoshi, C *Coming of the Dry Season*

Mwangi, M *Going down River Road*
Naipaul, V S *A Bend in the River*
Okri, B *The Famished Road*
Theroux, P *Jungle Lovers*
Thiong'o, N *Petals of Blood* or *A Grain of Wheat*
Slaughter, C *Antonia saw the Oryx First*
Van der Post, L *A Story like the Wind*

Websites
The following offer information on Tanzania and Zanzibar: www.intotanzania.com, www.allaboutzanzibar.com, www.africatravelresources.com.

KEY TO STANDARD SYMBOLS

—·—·—	International boundary	🏰	Historic building
------	District boundary	✝	Church or cathedral
------	National park boundary	♨	Buddhist temple
✈	Airport (international)	🏠	Buddhist monastery
✈	Airport (other)	🛕	Hindu temple
✛	Airstrip	☾	Mosque
🚁	Helicopter service	⚑	Golf course
▬▬	Railway	🎯	Stadium
----------	Footpath	▲	Summit
--🚗--	Car ferry	△	Boundary beacon
--⛴--	Passenger ferry	◉	Outpost
⛽	Petrol station or garage	✕—✕	Border post
🅿	Car park	⌂	Rock shelter
🚌	Bus station etc	⬚—⬚	Cable car, funicular
🚲	Cycle hire	═══	Mountain pass
Ⓜ	Underground station	○	Waterhole
⌂	Hotel, inn etc	✳	Scenic viewpoint
⛺	Campsite	❀	Botanical site
⬗	Hut	♧	Specific woodland feature
⚲	Wine bar	⚶	Lighthouse
✕	Restaurant, café etc	≂	Marsh
✉	Post office	⚘	Mangrove
✆	Telephone	🦅	Bird nesting site
ⓔ	Internet café	⚲	Turtle nesting site
✚	Hospital, clinic etc	⌣⌣	Coral reef
🏺	Museum	⟋	Beach
🐘	Zoo	🤿	Scuba diving
ℹ	Tourist information	🐟	Fishing sites
$	Bank		
⚱	Statue or monument		
∴	Archaeological or historic site		

Other map symbols are sometimes shown in separate key boxes with individual explanations for their meanings.

Index

Page numbers in bold indicate major entries; those in italics indicate maps.